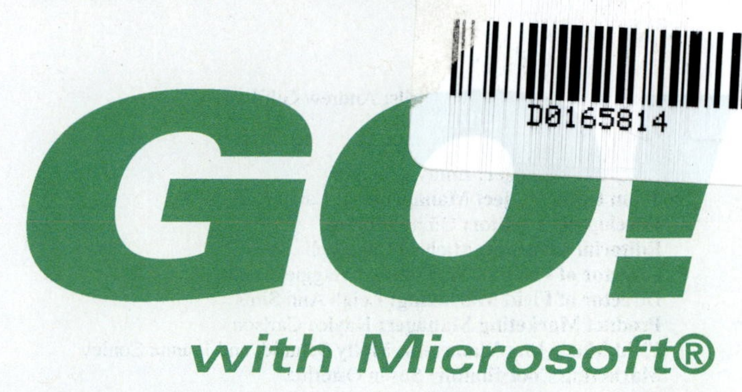

with Microsoft®

Word 2016

Comprehensive

Shelley Gaskin
and Alicia Vargas

PEARSON

Boston Columbus Indianapolis New York San Francisco
Amsterdam Cape Town Dubai London Madrid Milan Munich Paris Montréal Toronto
Delhi Mexico City São Paulo Sydney Hong Kong Seoul Singapore Taipei Tokyo

Vice President, Career Skills: Andrew Gilfillan
Executive Editor: Jenifer Niles
Project Manager: Holly Haydash
Program Manager: Emily Biberger
Team Lead, Project Management: Laura Burgess
Development Editor: Ginny Munroe
Editorial Assistant: Michael Campbell
Director of Product Marketing: Maggie Waples
Director of Field Marketing: Leigh Ann Sims
Product Marketing Manager: Kaylee Carlson
Field Marketing Managers: Molly Schmidt and Joanna Conley
Marketing Coordinator: Susan Osterlitz
Operations Specialist: Maura Zaldivar-Garcia
Senior Art Director: Diane Ernsberger
Interior and Cover Design: Carie Keller/Cenveo
Project Manager, Permissions: Karen Sanatar
Cover Credits: GaudiLab, Rawpixel.com, Pressmaster, Eugenio Marongiu, Boggy, Gajus, Rocketclips, Inc
Senior Art Director: Diane Ernsberger
Associate Director of Design: Blair Brown
Vice President, Product Strategy: Jason Fournier
Director of Media Development: Blaine Christine
Senior Product Strategy Manager: Eric Hakanson
Product Team Lead, IT: Zachary Alexander
Course Producer, IT: Amanda Losonsky
Digital Project Manager, MyITLab: Becca Lowe
Media Project Manager, Production: John Cassar
Full-Service Project Management: Lumina Datamatics, Inc.
Composition: Lumina Datamatics, Inc.
Printer/Binder: LSC Communications
Cover Printer: LSC Communications
Efficacy Curriculum Manager: Jessica Sieminski
Text Font: Times LT Pro

Library of Congress Cataloging-in-Publication Data

Library of Congress Control Number: 2016932299

5 17

ISBN 10: 0-13-444391-8
ISBN 13: 978-0-13-444391-1

Brief Contents

Table of Contents

Chapter 2 Creating Cover Letters and Using Tables to Create Resumes

Chapter 8 Creating Merged Documents 483

Chapter 9 Creating Forms, Customizing Word, and Preparing Documents for Review and Distribution 533

About the Authors

Shelley Gaskin, Series Editor, is a professor in the Business and Computer Technology Division at Pasadena City College in Pasadena, California. She holds a bachelor's degree in Business Administration from Robert Morris College (Pennsylvania), a master's degree in Business from Northern Illinois University, and a doctorate in Adult and Community Education from Ball State University (Indiana). Before joining Pasadena City College, she spent 12 years in the computer industry, where she was a systems analyst, sales representative, and director of Customer Education with Unisys Corporation. She also worked for Ernst & Young on the development of large systems applications for their clients. She has written and developed training materials for custom systems applications in both the public and private sector, and has also written and edited numerous computer application textbooks.

This book is dedicated to my students, who inspire me every day.

Alicia Vargas is a faculty member in Business Information Technology at Pasadena City College. She holds a master's and a bachelor's degree in business education from California State University, Los Angeles, and has authored several textbooks and training manuals on Microsoft Word, Microsoft Excel, and Microsoft PowerPoint.

This book is dedicated with all my love to my husband Vic, who makes everything possible; and to my children Victor, Phil, and Emmy, who are an unending source of inspiration and who make everything worthwhile.

GO! with Office 2016

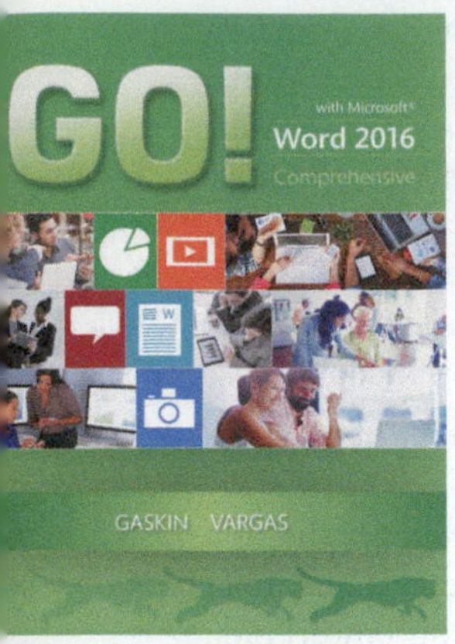

GO! with Office 2016 is the right approach to learning for today's fast-moving, mobile environment. The GO! Series focuses on the job and *success* skills students need to succeed in the workforce. Using job-related projects that put Microsoft Office into context, students learn the *how* and *why* at the moment they need to know, and because the GO! Series uses Microsoft procedural syntax, students never get lost in the instruction. For Office 2016, the hallmark GO! *guided practice-to-skill mastery pathway* is better than ever. Not only do students have multiple opportunities to work live in Microsoft Office to practice and apply the skills they have learned, but also, the *instructional* projects are now Grader projects, so students can work live in Office and receive auto-graded feedback as they learn!

By combining these new instructional Grader projects with the variety of existing Grader projects and the high-fidelity simulations that match the text, students have an effective pathway for learning, practicing, and assessing their abilities. After completing the instructional projects, students are ready to apply the skills with a wide variety of progressively challenging projects that require them to solve problems, think critically, and create projects on their own. The new *GO! with Google* projects also enable students to apply what they have learned in a different environment, and the integrated MOS objectives make this the one resource needed to learn Office, gain critical productivity skills, and prepare to get MOS certified!

What's New

Coverage of new features of Office 2016 ensures that students are learning the skills they need to work in today's job market.

NEW MyITLab 2016 Grader Projects In addition to the homework and assessment Graders already available, the A and B *instructional* projects are now Graders, enabling students to *learn by doing* live in the application *and* receive the instant feedback they need to ensure understanding.

MyITLab HTML 5 Training & Assessment Simulations for Office 2016 These simulations are rewritten by the authors to match the pedagogical approach of the textbook projects and to provide a direct one-to-one learning experience.

NEW Google Projects For each A and B instructional project in Chapters 1–3, students construct a parallel project using Google productivity tools. This gives students the opportunity to think critically and apply what they are learning about Microsoft Office to *other* productivity tools, which is an essential job skill.

NEW MOS Preparation MOS objectives are integrated into the text for easy review and reference for students who are preparing for a MOS certification exam. A MOS appendix is also included to provide a comprehensive list of the exam objectives.

NEW Lessons on the GO! How do you teach software that is constantly updated and getting new features all the time? This new project type will cover newer Microsoft apps such as Sway and MIX and things yet to come! These lessons are found in MyITLab and the Instructor Resource Center, and come with instructional content, student data files, solutions files, and rubrics for grading.

GO! To Work Page Here, students can review a summary of the chapter items focused on employability, including a MOS Objective summary, Build Your ePortfolio guidelines, and the GO! For Job Success soft skills videos or discussions.

Application Capstone Projects MyITLab grader Capstone projects for each application provide a variety of opportunities for students to ensure they have reached proficiency.

FOUR Types of Videos Students enjoy video learning, and these videos help students learn and gain skills and insight needed to succeed in the workforce.

- ***(NEW) GO! Walk Thru:*** Give students a quick 30-second preview of what they will do and create—from beginning to end—by completing each of the A and B Instructional Projects. These videos increase the student's confidence by letting the student see the entire project built quickly.
- ***GO! Learn How (formerly Student Training)*:** Students learn visually by viewing these instructor-led videos that are broken down by Objective for direct guidance. This is the personal instruction students need—especially outside of the classroom—to answer the *How do I?* questions.
- ***GO! to Work*:** These videos provide short interviews with real business information workers showing how they use Office in the workplace.
- ***GO! for Job Success:*** These videos or discussions relate to the projects in the chapter and cover important career topics such as *Dressing for Success*, *Time Management*, and *Making Ethical Choices*.

Expanded Project Summary chart This easy-to-use guide outlines all the instructional and end-of-chapter projects by category, including Instruction, Review, Mastery and Transfer of Learning, and Critical Thinking.

In-text boxed content for easy navigation *Another Way*, *Notes*, *More Knowledge*, *Alerts*, and *By Touch* instructions are included in line with the instruction—not in the margins—so students won't miss this important information and will learn it in context with what is on their screen.

MyITLab 2016 for GO! Let MyITLab do the work by giving students instantaneous feedback and saving hours of grading with GO!'s extensive Grader Project options. And the HTML5 Training and Assessment simulations provide a high-fidelity environment that provide step-by-step summary of student actions and include just-in-time learning aids to assist students: Read, Watch, Practice.

All other end-of-chapter projects, C, D, H, I, J, K, L, M, N, and O, have grading rubrics and solution files for easy hand grading. These are all Content-based, Outcomes-based, Problem-Solving, and Critical Thinking projects that enable you to add a variety of assessments—including authentic assessments—to evaluate a student's proficiency with the application.

IT Innovation Station Stay current with Office and Windows updates and important Microsoft and office productivity news and trends with help from your Pearson authors! Now that Microsoft Office is in the cloud, automatic updates occur regularly. These can affect how you to teach your course and the resources you are using. To keep you and your students completely up to date on the changes occurring in Office 2016 and Windows 10, we are launching the *IT Innovation Station*. This website will contain monthly updates from our product team and our author-instructors with tips for understanding updates, utilizing new capabilities, implementing new instructional techniques, and optimizing your Office use.

Why the GO! Approach Helps Students Succeed

GO! Provides Personalized Learning

MyITLab from Pearson is an online homework, training, and assessment system that will improve student results by helping students master skills and concepts through immediate feedback and a robust set of tools that allows instructors to easily gauge and address the performance of individuals and classrooms.

MyITLab learning experiences engage students using both realistic, high-fidelity simulations of Microsoft Office as well as auto-graded, live-in-the-application assignments, so they can understand concepts more thoroughly. With the ability to approach projects and problems as they would in real life—coupled with tutorials that adapt based on performance—students quickly complete skills they know and get help when and where they need it.

For educators, MyITLab establishes a reliable learning environment backed by the Pearson Education 24/7, 99.97 percent uptime service level agreement, and that includes the tools educators need to track and support both individual and class-wide student progress.

GO! Engages Students by Combining a Project-Based Approach with the Teachable Moment

GO!'s project-based approach clusters the learning objectives around the projects rather than around the software features. This tested pedagogical approach teaches students to solve real problems as they practice and learn the features.

GO! instruction is organized around student learning outcomes with numbered objectives and two instructional projects per chapter. Students can engage in a wide variety of end-of-chapter projects where they apply what they have learned in outcomes-based, problem-solving, and critical thinking projects—many of which require students to create the project from scratch.

GO! instruction is based on the teachable moment where students learn important concepts at the exact moment they are practicing the skill. The explanations and concepts are woven into the steps—not presented as paragraphs of text at the beginning of the project before students have even seen the software in action.

Each Project Opening Page clearly outlines Project Activities (what the student will do in this project), Project Files (what starting files are needed and how the student will save the files), and Project Results (what the student's finished project will look like). Additionally, to support this page, the GO! Walk Thru video gives students a 30-second overview of how the project will progress and what they will create.

GO! Demonstrates Excellence in Instructional Design

Student Learning Outcomes and Objectives are clearly defined so students understand what they will learn and what they will be able to do when they finish the chapter.

Clear Instruction provided through project steps written following Microsoft® Procedural Syntax to guide students where to go *and then* what to do, so they never get lost!

Teachable moment approach has students learn important concepts when they need to as they work through the instructional projects. No long paragraphs of text.

Clean Design presents textbook pages that are clean and uncluttered, with screenshots that validate the student's actions and that engage visual learners.

Sequential Pagination displays the pages sequentially numbered, like every other textbook a student uses, instead of using letters or abbreviations. Student don't spend time learning a new numbering approach.

Important information is boxed within the text so that students won't miss or skip the Another Way, By Touch, Note, Alert, or More Knowledge details so there are no distracting and "busy-looking" marginal notes.

Color-Coded Steps guide students through the projects with colors coded by project.

End-of-Project Icon helps students know when they have completed the project, which is especially useful in self-paced or online environments. These icons give students a clearly identifiable end point for each project.

GO! Learn How Videos provide step-by-step visual instruction for the A and B instructional projects—delivered by a real instructor! These videos provide the assistance and personal learning students may need when working on their own.

GO! Delivers Easy Course Implementation

The *GO!* series' one-of-a-kind instructional system provides you with everything you need to prepare for class, teach the material, and assess your students.

Prepare

- **Office 2013 to 2016 Transition Guide** provides an easy-to-use reference for updating your course for Office 2016 using GO!
- **Annotated Instructor Tabs** provide clear guidance on how to implement your course.
- **MyITLab Implementation Guide** is provided for course planning and learning outcome alignment.
- **Syllabus templates** outline various plans for covering the content in an 8-, 12-, or 16-week course.
- **List of Chapter Outcomes and Objectives** is provided for course planning and learning outcome alignment.
- **Student Assignment Tracker** for students to track their own work.
- **Assignment Planning Guide** Description of the *GO!* assignments with recommendations based on class size, delivery method, and student needs.
- **Solution Files** Examples of homework submissions to serve as examples for students.
- **Online Study Guide for Students** Interactive objective-style questions based on chapter content.

Teach

- **The Annotated Instructors Edition** includes the entire student text, spiral-bound and wrapped with teaching notes and suggestions for how to implement your course.
- **Scripted Lectures** present a detailed guide for delivering live in-class demonstrations of the A and B Instructional Projects.
- **PowerPoint Presentations** provide a visual walk-through of the chapter with suggested lecture notes included.
- **Audio PowerPoint Presentations** provide a visual walk-through of the chapter with the lecture notes read out loud.
- **Walk Thru Videos** provide a quick 30-second preview of what the student will do and create—from beginning to end—by completing each of the A and B Instructional projects. These videos increase the student's confidence by letting the student see the entire project built quickly.

Assess

- **A scoring checklist, task-specific rubric, or analytic rubric** accompanies every assignment.
- **Prepared Exams** provide cumulative exams for each project, chapter, and application that are easy to score using the provided scoring checklist and point suggestions for each task.
- **Solution Files** are provided in three formats: native file, PDF, and annotated PDF.
- **Rubrics** provide guidelines for grading open-ended projects.
- **Testbank questions** are available for you to create your own objective-based quizzes for review.

Grader Projects

- **Projects A & B** (Guided Instruction)
- **Project E Homework** (Formative) and Assesment (Summative) (Cover Objectives in Project A)
- **Project F Homework** (Formative) and Assesment (Summative) (Cover Objectives in Project B)
- **Project G Homework** (Formative) and Assesment (Summative) (Cover Objectives in Projects A and B)
- **Application Capstone Homework** (Formative review of core objectives covered in application)
- **Application Capstone Exam** (Summative review of core objectives covered in application—generates badge with 90 percent or higher)

GO! Series Hallmarks

Teach the Course You Want in Less Time

A Microsoft® Office textbook designed for student success!

- **Project-Based –** Students learn by creating projects that they will use in the real world.
- **Microsoft Procedural Syntax –** Steps are written to put students in the right place at the right time.
- **Teachable Moment –** Expository text is woven into the steps—at the moment students need to know it—not chunked together in a block of text that will go unread.
- **Sequential Pagination –** Students have actual page numbers instead of confusing letters and abbreviations.

Application Introductions – Provide an overview of the application to prepare students for the upcoming chapters.

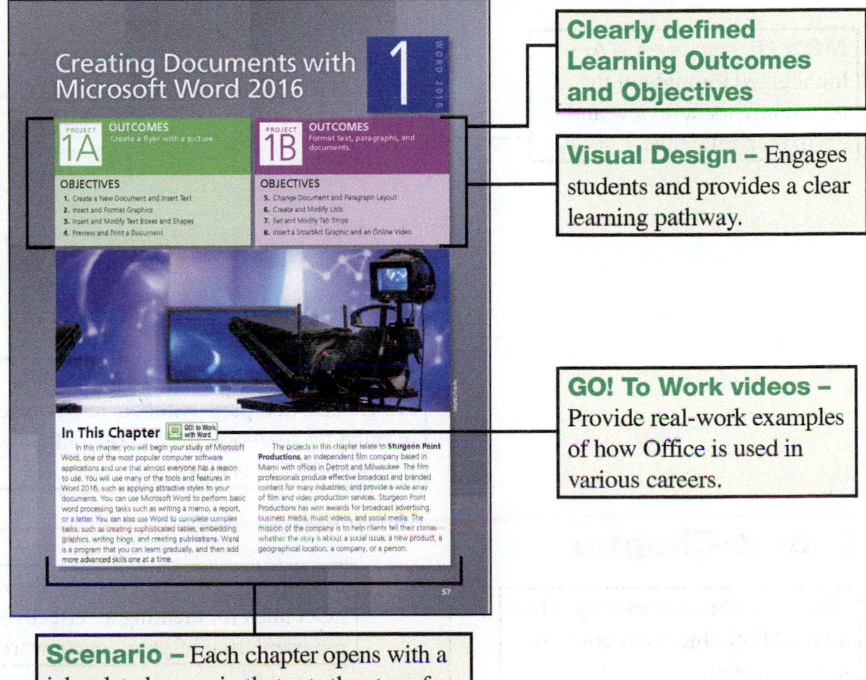

Creating Documents with Microsoft Word 2016
1
PROJECT 1A OUTCOMES Create a flyer with a picture.
PROJECT 1B OUTCOMES Format text, paragraphs, and documents.
OBJECTIVES
In This Chapter

Clearly defined Learning Outcomes and Objectives

Visual Design – Engages students and provides a clear learning pathway.

GO! To Work videos – Provide real-work examples of how Office is used in various careers.

Scenario – Each chapter opens with a job-related scenario that sets the stage for the projects the student will create.

Project Activities – A project summary stated clearly and quickly.

Project Files – Clearly shows students which files are needed for the project and the names they will use to save their documents.

Build from Scratch icons – Indicate which projects students build from scratch.

NEW GO! Walk Thru videos – Give students a 30-second overview of what they will create in the project.

1A Sales Report with Embedded Column Chart and Sparklines

PROJECT ACTIVITIES

In Activities 1.01 through 1.17, you will create an Excel worksheet for Michelle Barry, the President of Pro Fit Marietta. The worksheet displays the second quarter sales of cardio equipment for the current year and includes a chart to visually represent the data. Your completed worksheet will look similar to Figure 1.1.

PROJECT FILES

FIGURE 1.1 Project 1A Quarterly Sales

350 Excel | Chapter 1: CREATING A WORKSHEET AND CHARTING DATA

Simulation Training and Assessment – Give your students the most realistic Office 2016 experience with realistic, high-fidelity simulations.

NEW MyITLab Grader projects for Instructional A & B projects – Allow students to work live in the application to learn by doing.

Project Results – Shows students what successful completion looks like.

In-text Features

Another Way, Notes, More Knowledge, Alerts, and By Touch Instructions

Color Coding – Each chapter has two instructional projects, which is less overwhelming for students than one large chapter project. The projects are differentiated by different colored numbering and headings.

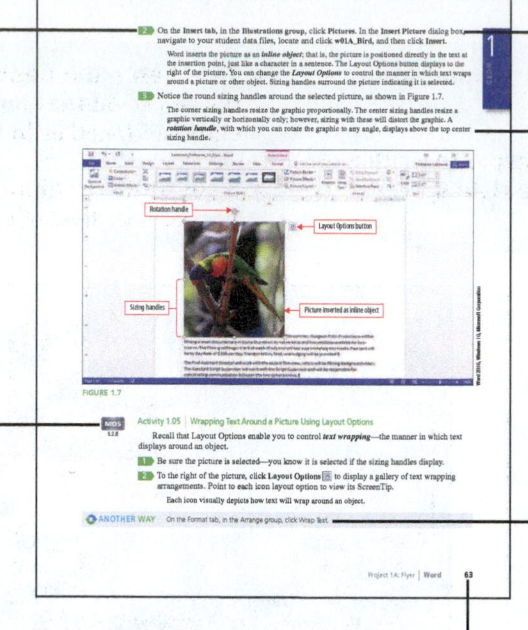
2 On the **Insert tab**, in the **Illustrations group**, click **Pictures**. In the **Insert Picture** dialog box, navigate to your student data files, locate and click **w01A_Bird**, and then click **Insert**.

Word inserts the picture as an ***inline object***; that is, the picture is positioned directly in the text at the insertion point, just like a character in a sentence. The Layout Options button displays to the right of the picture. You can change the ***Layout Options*** to control the manner in which text wraps around a picture or other object. Sizing handles surround the picture indicating it is selected.

3 Notice the round sizing handles around the selected picture, as shown in Figure 1.7.

The corner sizing handles resize the graphic proportionally. The center sizing handles resize a graphic vertically or horizontally only; however, sizing with these will distort the graphic. A ***rotation handle***, with which you can rotate the graphic to any angle, displays above the top center sizing handle.

FIGURE 1.7

MOS 5.2.6

Activity 1.05 | Wrapping Text Around a Picture Using Layout Options

Recall that Layout Options enable you to control ***text wrapping***—the manner in which text displays around an object.

1 Be sure the picture is selected—you know it is selected if the sizing handles display.

2 To the right of the picture, click **Layout Options** to display a gallery of text wrapping arrangements. Point to each icon layout option to view its ScreenTip.

Each icon visually depicts how text will wrap around an object.

ANOTHER WAY On the Format tab, in the Arrange group, click Wrap Text.

Project 1A: Flyer | Word 63

Microsoft Procedural Syntax – Steps are written to put the student at the right place at the right time.

Teachable Moment – Expository text is woven into the steps—at the moment students need to know it—not chunked together in a block of text that will go unread.

MOS Objectives – Are highlighted throughout the text to provide a review and exam prep reference.

Intext Callouts – Ensure that students will read this important material—Another Way, Notes, More Knowledge, Alerts, and By Touch instructions.

Sequential Pagination – Students are given actual page numbers to navigate through the textbook instead of confusing letters and abbreviations.

End-of-Chapter

MOS Skills Summary – List all the MOS objectives covered in the chapter.

Build Your ePortfolio – Provides guidelines for creating an effective representation of your course work.

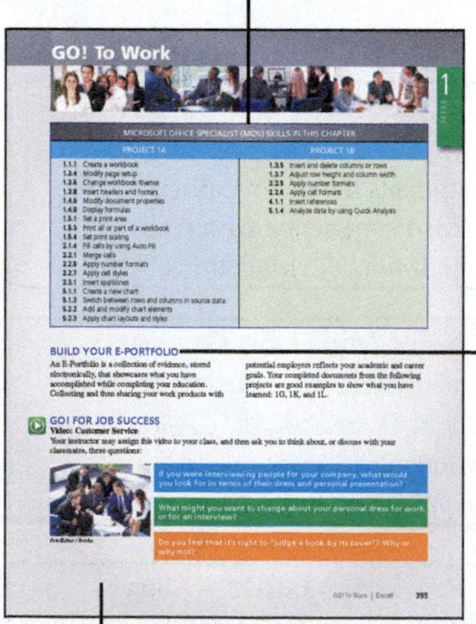
GO! To Work

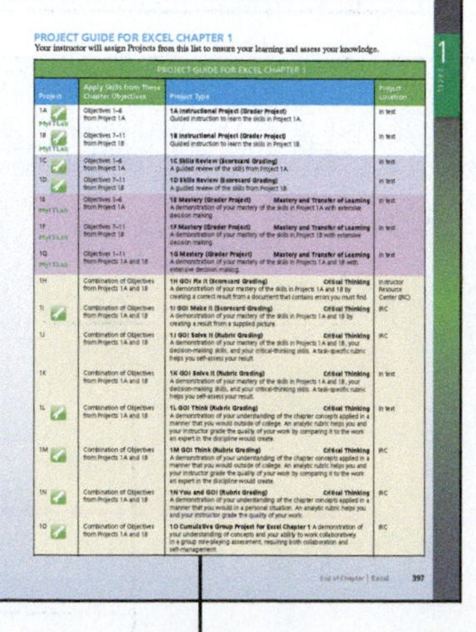
PROJECT GUIDE FOR EXCEL CHAPTER 1

GLOSSARY

GO! For Job Success – Soft skills, videos, and discussions to prepare students with the soft skills needed for today's work environment.

Review and Assessment Chart – Provides an easy-to-use guide to all the instructional and end-of-chapter projects by category from Mastery and Transfer of Knowledge to Critical Thinking.

End-of-Chapter Glossary – Gives students an easy way to review key terms.

End-of-Chapter

Objective List – Every end-of-chapter project includes a listing of covered Objectives from Projects A and B.

Grader Projects – In addition to the two Grader Projects for the instructional portion of the chapter (Projects A and B), each chapter has six MyITLab Grader projects within the end-of-chapter material—three homework and three assessment—clearly indicated by the MyITLab logo.

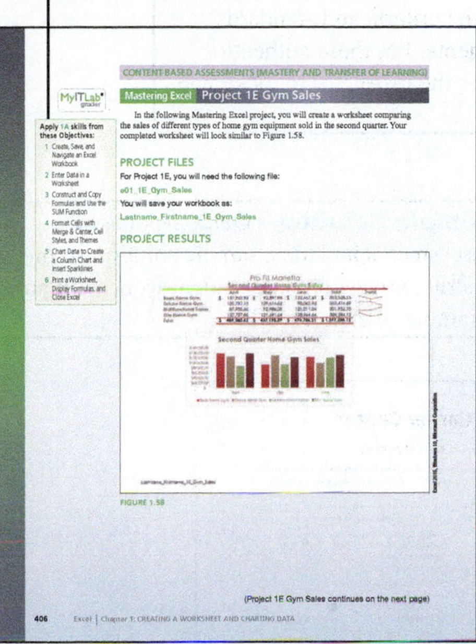

CONTENT-BASED ASSESSMENTS (MASTERY AND TRANSFER OF LEARNING)

Mastering Excel Project 1E Gym Sales

Apply 1A skills from these Objectives:

1 Create, Save, and Navigate an Excel Workbook
2 Enter Data in a Worksheet
3 Construct and Copy Formulas and Use the SUM Function
4 Format Cells with Merge & Center, Cell Styles, and Themes
5 Chart Data to Create a Column Chart and Insert Sparklines
6 Print a Worksheet, Display Formulas, and Close Excel

In the following Mastering Excel project, you will create a worksheet comparing the sales of different types of home gym equipment sold in the second quarter. Your completed worksheet will look similar to Figure 1.58.

PROJECT FILES

For Project 1E, you will need the following file:
e01_1E_Gym_Sales
You will save your workbook as:
Lastname_Firstname_1E_Gym_Sales

PROJECT RESULTS

FIGURE 1.58

(Project 1E Gym Sales continues on the next page)

406 Excel | Chapter 1: CREATING A WORKSHEET AND CHARTING DATA

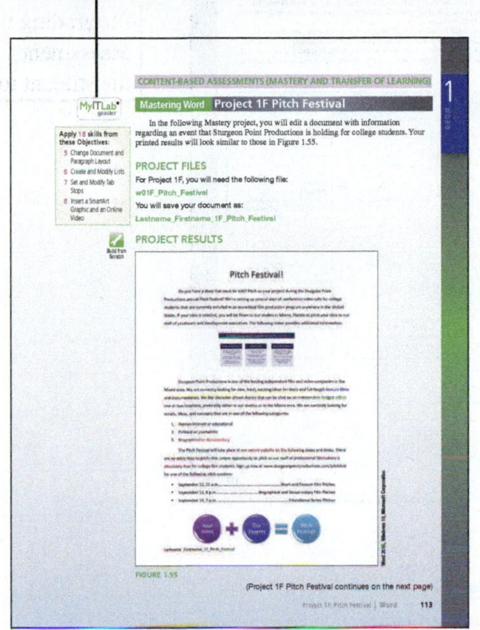

CONTENT-BASED ASSESSMENTS (MASTERY AND TRANSFER OF LEARNING)

Mastering Word Project 1F Pitch Festival

Apply 1B skills from these Objectives:

5 Change Document and Paragraph Layout
6 Create and Modify Lists
7 Set and Modify Tab Stops
8 Insert a SmartArt Graphic and an Online Video

In the following Mastery project, you will edit a document with information regarding an event that Sturgeon Point Productions is holding for college students. Your printed results will look similar to those in Figure 1.55.

PROJECT FILES

For Project 1F, you will need the following file:
w01F_Pitch_Festival
You will save your document as:
Lastname_Firstname_1F_Pitch_Festival

PROJECT RESULTS

Pitch Festival!

FIGURE 1.55

(Project 1F Pitch Festival continues on the next page)

Project 1F: Pitch Festival | Word 113

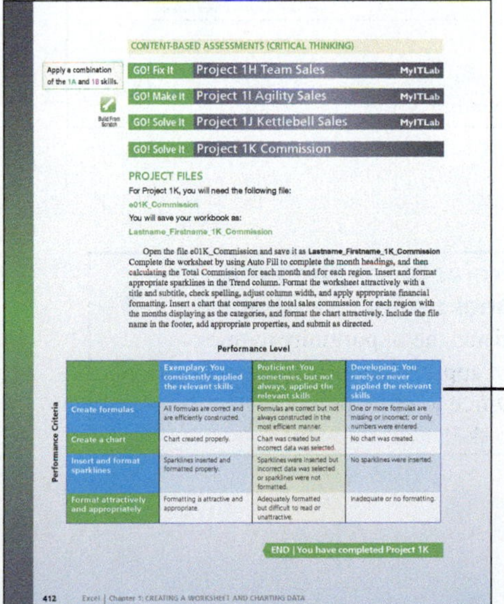

CONTENT-BASED ASSESSMENTS (CRITICAL THINKING)

Apply a combination of the 1A and 1B skills.

GO! Fix It Project 1H Team Sales MyITLab
GO! Make It Project 1I Agility Sales MyITLab
GO! Solve It Project 1J Kettlebell Sales MyITLab
GO! Solve It Project 1K Commission

PROJECT FILES

For Project 1K, you will need the following file:
e01K_Commission
You will save your workbook as:
Lastname_Firstname_1K_Commission

Open the file e01K_Commission and save it as Lastname_Firstname_1K_Commission. Complete the worksheet by using Auto Fill to complete the month headings, and then calculating the Total Commission for each month and for each region. Insert and format appropriate sparklines in the Trend column. Format the worksheet attractively with a title and subtitle, check spelling, adjust column width, and apply appropriate financial formatting. Insert a chart that compares the total sales commission for each region with the months displaying as the categories, and format the chart attractively. Include the file name in the footer, add appropriate properties, and submit as directed.

Performance Level

Performance Criteria	Exemplary: You consistently applied the relevant skills	Proficient: You sometimes, but not always, applied the relevant skills	Developing: You rarely or never applied the relevant skills
Create formulas	All formulas are correct and are efficiently constructed.	Formulas are correct but not always constructed in the most efficient manner.	One or more formulas are missing or incorrect; or only numbers were entered.
Create a chart	Chart created properly.	Chart was created but incorrect data was selected.	No chart was created.
Insert and format sparklines	Sparklines inserted and formatted properly.	Sparklines were inserted but incorrect data was selected or sparklines were not formatted.	No sparklines were inserted.
Format attractively and appropriately	Formatting is attractive and appropriate.	Adequately formatted but difficult to read or unattractive.	Inadequate or no formatting.

END | You have completed Project 1K

412 Excel | Chapter 1: CREATING A WORKSHEET AND CHARTING DATA

Task-Specific Rubric – A matrix specific to the GO! Solve It projects that states the criteria and standards for grading these defined-solution projects.

End-of-Chapter

Outcomes-Based Assessments – Assessments with open-ended solutions.

Outcomes-Based Assessments – Assessments with open-ended solutions.

Outcomes Rubric – A standards-based analytic rubric specific to the GO! Think projects that states the criteria and standards for grading these open-ended assessments. For these authentic assessments, an analytic rubric enables the instructor to judge and the student to self assess.

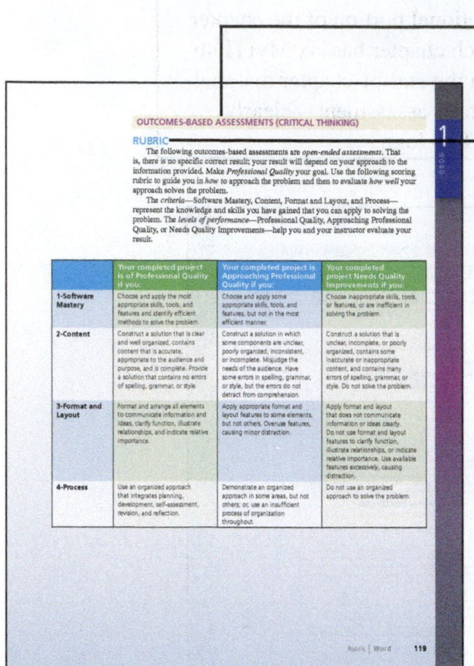

OUTCOMES-BASED ASSESSMENTS (CRITICAL THINKING)

RUBRIC

The following outcomes-based assessments are *open-ended assessments*. That is, there is no specific correct result; your result will depend on your approach to the information provided. Make *Professional Quality* your goal. Use the following scoring rubric to guide you in *how* to approach the problem and then to evaluate *how well* your approach solves the problem.

The *criteria*—Software Mastery, Content, Format and Layout, and Process—represent the knowledge and skills you have gained that you can apply to solving the problem. The *levels of performance*—Professional Quality, Approaching Professional Quality, or Needs Quality Improvements—help you and your instructor evaluate your result.

	Your completed project is of Professional Quality if you:	Your completed project is Approaching Professional Quality if you:	Your completed project Needs Quality Improvements if you:
1-Software Mastery	Choose and apply the most appropriate skills, tools, and features and identify efficient methods to solve the problem.	Choose and apply some appropriate skills, tools, and features, but not in the most efficient manner.	Choose inappropriate skills, tools, or features, or are inefficient in solving the problem.
2-Content	Construct a solution that is clear and well organized, contains content that is accurate, appropriate to the audience and purpose, and is complete. Provide a solution that contains no errors of spelling, grammar, or style.	Construct a solution in which some components are unclear, poorly organized, inconsistent, or incomplete. Misjudge the needs of the audience. Have some errors in spelling, grammar, or style, but the errors do not detract from comprehension.	Construct a solution that is unclear, incomplete, or poorly organized, contains some inaccurate or inappropriate content, and contains many errors of spelling, grammar, or style. Do not solve the problem.
3-Format and Layout	Format and arrange all elements to communicate information and ideas, clarify function, illustrate relationships, and indicate relative importance.	Apply appropriate format and layout features to some elements, but not others. Overuse features, causing minor distraction.	Apply format and layout that does not communicate information or ideas clearly. Do not use format and layout features to clarify function, illustrate relationships, or indicate relative importance. Use available features excessively, causing distraction.
4-Process	Use an organized approach that integrates planning, development, self-assessment, revision, and reflection.	Demonstrate an organized approach in some areas, but not others; or, use an insufficient process of organization throughout.	Do not use an organized approach to solve the problem.

Rubric | Word 119

Sample Solution – Outcomes-based assessments include a sample solution so the instructor can compare student work with an example of expert work.

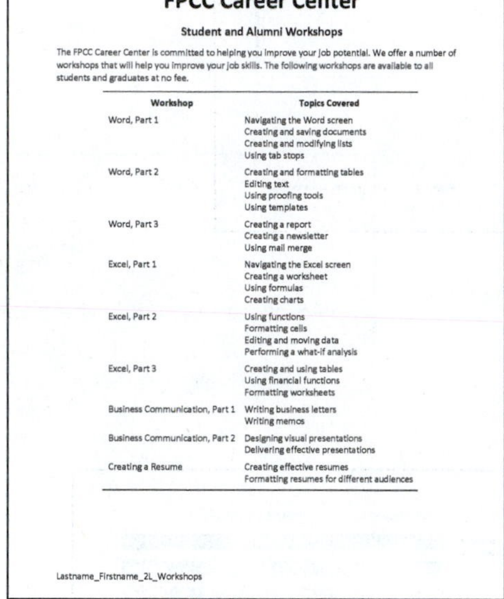

FPCC Career Center

Student and Alumni Workshops

The FPCC Career Center is committed to helping you improve your job potential. We offer a number of workshops that will help you improve your job skills. The following workshops are available to all students and graduates at no fee.

Workshop	Topics Covered
Word, Part 1	Navigating the Word screen Creating and saving documents Creating and modifying lists Using tab stops
Word, Part 2	Creating and formatting tables Editing text Using proofing tools Using templates
Word, Part 3	Creating a report Creating a newsletter Using mail merge
Excel, Part 1	Navigating the Excel screen Creating a worksheet Using formulas Creating charts
Excel, Part 2	Using functions Formatting cells Editing and moving data Performing a what-if analysis
Excel, Part 3	Creating and using tables Using financial functions Formatting worksheets
Business Communication, Part 1	Writing business letters Writing memos
Business Communication, Part 2	Designing visual presentations Delivering effective presentations
Creating a Resume	Creating effective resumes Formatting resumes for different audiences

Lastname_Firstname_2L_Workshops

GO! With Google — New Feature

Objective Creating an Inventory Valuation Report

ALERT! **Working with Web-Based Applications and Services**

Computer programs and services on the web receive continuous updates and improvements, so the steps to complete this web-based Activity may differ from the ones shown. You can often look at the screens and the information presented to determine how to complete the Activity.

If you do not already have a Google account, you will need to create one before you begin this activity. Go to http://google.com and in the upper right corner, click Sign In. On the Sign In screen, click Create Account. On the Create your Google Account page, complete the form, read and agree to the Terms of Service and Privacy Policy, and then click Next step. On the Welcome screen, click Get Started.

Activity | Creating an Inventory Valuation Report Using Google Sheets

In this Activity, you will use Google Sheets to create an inventory valuation report similar to the one you created in Project 1B.

1 From the desktop, open your browser (a browser other than Edge), navigate to **http://google.com** and then click the **Google Apps** menu. Click **Drive**, and then if necessary, sign in to your Google account.

2 Open your **GO! Web Projects** folder—or click New to create and then open this folder if necessary.

3 In the left pane, click **NEW**, and then click **Google Sheets**. From your Windows taskbar, open **File Explorer**, navigate to your Student Data Files for this chapter, and then in the **File List**, double-click the Word document **e01_1B_Web**; to complete this project quickly and eliminate extra typing, you will copy the data from a Word document.

4 In the displayed Word document, click anywhere in the text, and then in the upper left corner, click to select the **Table Select** to select the entire Word table. Right-click anywhere over the selection, and then click **Copy**. **Close Word. Close** the **File Explorer** window.

5 In your blank Google Sheet, with cell **A1** active, point to cell **A1**, right-click, and then click **Paste**. In the column heading area, point to the border between **column A** and **column B** to display the pointer, and then widen **column A** slightly so that all of the data in rows 4–10 displays.

6 Select the range **A1:E1**. On the toolbar, click **Merge cells**. On the toolbar, click the **Align arrow**, and then click **Center**. Repeat for the range **A2:E2**, and then apply **Bold** to cells **A1** and **A2**.

7 Select the range **B3:E3**, on the menu bar click **Format**, point to **Text wrapping**, and then click **Wrap**. **Center** these column titles and apply **Bold**.

8 Select the range **C4:C9**, on the menu bar click **Format**, point to **Number**, on the fly-out menu click **Number**, and then if necessary, on the toolbar, click **Decrease decimal places** two times.

9 Click cell **E4**, type = and then click cell **C4**. Type * and then click cell **D4**. Press Enter. Click cell **E4**, point to the fill handle in the lower right corner of the cell, and then drag down to cell **E9**.

10 Select the range **E4:E9**. On the toolbar, click **Functions**, click **SUM**, and then press Enter.

11 Select the range **D4:E4**, hold down Ctrl, and then select cell **E10**. On the menu bar, click **Format**, point to **Number**, and then in the fly-out menu click **Currency**.

12 Select cell **A10**, hold down Ctrl, and then click cell **E10**. Apply **Bold**.

13 Click cell **A1**, hold down Ctrl, and then click cell **A2**, cell **A10**, and cell **E10**. With the four cells selected, on the toolbar, click **Fill color**, and then in the fourth column, click the third color—**light yellow 3**.

14 At the top of the worksheet, click the text *Untitled spreadsheet*, and then using your own name, type **Lastname_Firstname_EX_1B_Web** and press ENTER.

(GO! With Google continues on the next page)

GO! With Google | Excel 393

Google Projects for each A & B instructional project in Chapters 1–3 – Provide students the opportunity to think critically and apply what they are learning about Microsoft Office to other productivity tools—an essential job skill.

Student Materials

Student Data Files – All student data files are available in MyITLab for Office 2016 or at www.pearsonhighered.com/go

FOUR Types of Videos help students learn and gain skills and insight needed to succeed in the workforce.

- ***(NEW) GO! Walk Thru*** is a brief overview of the A & B instructional projects to give students the context of what they will be doing in the projects
- ***GO! Learn How** (formerly Student Training)* instructor-led videos are broken down by Objective for direct guidance; this personal instruction answers the "how-do-I" questions students ask.
- ***GO! to Work*** videos provide short interviews with workers showing how they use Office in the workplace.
- ***GO! for Job Success*** videos or discussions relate to the projects in the chapter and cover important career topics such as *Dressing for Success, Time Management,* and *Making Ethical Choices*.

Matching and multiple choice questions provide a variety of review options for content in each chapter.

MOS Objective quiz provides a quick assessment of student understanding of the MOS objectives covered in the chapter. Helpful for courses focused on the pathway to MOS certification.

Available in MyITLab for Office 2016.

GO! with MyITLab

Gives you a completely integrated solution

Instruction ▪ Training ▪ Assessment

All of the content in the book and MyITLab is written by the authors, who are instructors, so the instruction works seamlessly with the simulation trainings and grader projects—true 1:1. eText, Training & Assessment Simulations, and Grader Projects.

Instructor Resources

All Instructor Resources found in MyITLab or at pearsonhighered.com/go

Annotated Instructor Edition – This instructor tool includes a full copy of the student textbook and a guide to implementing your course depending on the emphasis you want to place on digital engagement. Also included are teaching tips, discussion topics, and other useful pieces for teaching each chapter.

Assignment Sheets – Lists all the assignments for the chapter. Just add the course information, due dates, and points. Providing these to students ensures they will know what is due and when.

Scripted Lectures – A script to guide your classroom lecture of each instructional project.

Annotated Solution Files – Coupled with the scorecards, these create a grading and scoring system that makes grading easy and efficient.

PowerPoint Lectures – PowerPoint presentations for each chapter.

Audio PowerPoints – Audio versions of the PowerPoint presentations for each chapter.

Scoring Rubrics – Can be used either by students to check their work or by you as a quick check-off for the items that need to be corrected.

Syllabus Templates – For 8-week, 12-week, and 16-week courses.

Test Bank – Includes a variety of test questions for each chapter.

Instruction

Instruction: General

Syllabi templates demonstrate different approaches for covering the content in an 8-, 12-, or 16-week course.

Application Intro Videos provide a quick overview of what the application is and its primary function.

GO! to Work Videos put each chapter into context as related to how people use productivity software in their daily lives and work.

GO! For Success videos and discussions provide real-life scenarios exploring the essential soft skills needed to succeed in the workplace and professional settings.

Instruction: Hands-On *using one or more of the following:*

- **Interactive eText** allows students to read the narrative and instruction and also link directly to the various types of videos included.
- **(NEW) Walk Thru Videos** provide a quick 30-second overview of what students will do in the A & B instructional projects.
- **Scripted Lectures** are a detailed guide through the A & B projects from the book for you to use for in-class demonstration.
- **GO! Learn How** (previously Student Training) videos are instructor-led videos that provide guided instruction through each Objective and the related Activities.
- **PowerPoint Presentations** provide a visual walk-through of the chapter with suggested lecture notes included.
- **Audio PowerPoint Presentations** provide the visual walk-through of chapters with the lecture notes read aloud.
- **(NEW) A & B Instruction Projects** assigned to students. Students can complete the Instructional Projects 1A and 1B and submit for instructor review or manual grading. They can also submit as a MyITLab Grader project, which allows the students to work live in the application starting with files downloaded from MyITLab and then submitted for automatic grading and feedback.
- **(NEW) MOS Objectives** are covered throughout the chapter and are indicated with the MOS icon. Instructors use these to point students to content they would encounter on a MOS exam. If a course is focused on MOS preparation, this content would be emphasized in the instruction.

Practice

MyITLab Skill-based Training Simulation provides students with hands-on practice applying the skills they have learned in a simulated environment where they have access to Learning Aids to assist if needed (READ, WATCH, PRACTICE). All of the student's keystrokes are recorded so that instructors can review and provide support to the students. Instructor can set the number of times the students can complete the simulation.

MyITLab Homework Grader Projects (E, F, or G) provide students with live-in-the-application practice with the skills they learned in Projects A and B. These projects provide students with detailed reports showing them where they made errors and also provide "live comments" explaining the details.

Student Assignment Tracker for students to track their work.

Review

GO! Online activities (multiple choice and matching activities) provide objective-based quizzing to allow students to review how they are doing.

Testbank questions are available for instructors to create their own quizzes for review or assessment.

End-of-chapter online projects H–O provide Content-based, Outcome-based, and Critical Thinking projects that you can assign for additional review, practice, or assessments. These are graded manually by the instructor using the provided Solution Files and Grading Scorecards or Rubrics.

MOS Quizzes provide an objective-based quiz to review the MOS objective-related content covered in the chapter. Provides students with review to help if they plan to take a MOS Certification exam.

Assessment

MyITLab Skill-based Exam Simulation provides students with an assessment of their knowledge and ability to apply the skills they have learned. In the Simulated Exams, students do not have access to the Learning Aids. All of the student's keystrokes are recorded so that instructors can review and provide support to the students. Instructors can set the number of times the students can complete the simulation exam.

MyITLab Assessment Grader Projects (E, F, or G) provide students with live-in-the-application testing of the skills they learned in Projects A and B. These projects provide students with detailed reports showing the student where they made errors and also provides "live comments" explaining the details.

Prepared Exams are additional projects created specifically for use as exams that the instructor will grade manually. They are available by Project, Chapter, and Unit.

Pre-built Chapter quizzes provide objective-based quizzing to allow students to review how they are doing.

Testbank questions are available for instructors to create their own quizzes for review or assessment.

Reviewers Of The GO! Series

Abul Sheikh	Abraham Baldwin Agricultural College
John Percy	Atlantic Cape Community College
Janette Hicks	Binghamton University
Shannon Ogden	Black River Technical College
Karen May	Blinn College
Susan Fry	Boise State University
Chigurupati Rani	Borough of Manhattan Community College / CUNY
Ellen Glazer	Broward College
Kate LeGrand	Broward College
Mike Puopolo	Bunker Hill Community College
Nicole Lytle-Kosola	California State University, San Bernardino
Nisheeth Agrawal	Calhoun Community College
Pedro Diaz-Gomez	Cameron
Linda Friedel	Central Arizona College
Gregg Smith	Central Community College
Norm Cregger	Central Michigan University
Lisa LaCaria	Central Piedmont Community College
Steve Siedschlag	Chaffey College
Terri Helfand	Chaffey College
Susan Mills	Chambersburg
Mandy Reininger	Chemeketa Community College
Connie Crossley	Cincinnati State Technical and Community College
Marjorie Deutsch	City University of New York - Queensborough Community College
Mary Ann Zlotow	College of Dupage
Christine Bohnsak	College of Lake County
Gertrude Brier	College of Staten Island
Sharon Brown	College of The Albemarle
Terry Rigsby	Columbia College
Vicki Brooks	Columbia College
Donald Hames	Delgado Community College
Kristen King	Eastern Kentucky University
Kathie Richer	Edmonds Community College
Gary Smith	Elmhurst College
Wendi Kappersw	Embry-Riddle Aeronautical University
Nancy Woolridge	Fullerton College
Abigail Miller	Gateway Community & Technical College
Deep Ramanayake	Gateway Community & Technical College
Gwen White	Gateway Community & Technical College
Debbie Glinert	Gloria K School
Dana Smith	Golf Academy of America
Mary Locke	Greenville Technical College
Diane Marie Roselli	Harrisburg Area Community College
Linda Arnold	Harrisburg Area Community College - Lebanon
Daniel Schoedel	Harrisburg Area Community College - York Campus
Ken Mayer	Heald College
Xiaodong Qiao	Heald College
Donna Lamprecht	Hopkinsville Community College
Kristen Lancaster	Hopkinsville Community College
Johnny Hurley	Iowa Lakes Community College
Linda Halverson	Iowa Lakes Community College
Sarah Kilgo	Isothermal Community College
Chris DeGeare	Jefferson College
David McNair	Jefferson College
Diane Santurri	Johnson & Wales
Roland Sparks	Johnson & Wales University
Ram Raghuraman	Joliet Junior College
Eduardo Suniga	Lansing Community College
Kenneth A. Hyatt	Lonestar College - Kingwood
Glenn Gray	Lonestar College North Harris
Gene Carbonaro	Long Beach City College
Betty Pearman	Los Medanos College
Diane Kosharek	Madison College
Peter Meggison	Massasoit Community College
George Gabb	Miami Dade College
Lennie Alice Cooper	Miami Dade College
Richard Mabjish	Miami Dade College
Victor Giol	Miami Dade College
John Meir	Midlands Technical College
Greg Pauley	Moberly Area Community College
Catherine Glod	Mohawk Valley Community College
Robert Huyck	Mohawk Valley Community College
Kevin Engellant	Montana Western
Philip Lee	Nashville State Community College
Ruth Neal	Navarro College
Sharron Jordan	Navarro College
Richard Dale	New Mexico State University
Lori Townsend	Niagara County Community College
Judson Curry	North Park University
Mary Zegarski	Northampton Community College
Neal Stenlund	Northern Virginia Community Colege
Michael Goeken	Northwest Vista College
Mary Beth Tarver	Northwestern State University
Amy Rutledge	Oakland University
Marcia Braddock	Okefenokee Technical College
Richard Stocke	Oklahoma State University - OKC
Jane Stam	Onondaga Community College
Mike Michaelson	Palomar College
Kungwen (Dave) Chu	Purdue University Calumet
Wendy Ford	CUNY - Queensborough CC
Lewis Hall	Riverside City College
Karen Acree	San Juan College
Tim Ellis	Schoolcraft College
Dan Combellick	Scottsdale Community College
Pat Serrano	Scottsdale Community College
Rose Hendrickson	Sheridan College
Kit Carson	South Georgia College
Rebecca Futch	South Georgia State College
Brad Hagy	Southern Illinois University Carbondale
Mimi Spain	Southern Maine Community College
David Parker	Southern Oregon University
Madeline Baugher	Southwestern Oklahoma State University
Brian Holbert	St. Johns River State College
Bunny Howard	St. Johns River State College
Stephanie Cook	State College of Florida
Sharon Wavle	Tompkins Cortland Community College
George Fiori	Tri-County Technical College
Steve St. John	Tulsa Community College
Karen Thessing	University of Central Arkansas
Richard McMahon	University of Houston-Downtown
Shohreh Hashemi	University of Houston-Downtown
Donna Petty	Wallace Community College
Julia Bell	Walters State Community College
Ruby Kowaney	West Los Angeles College
Casey Thompson	Wiregrass Georgia Technical College
DeAnnia Clements	Wiregrass Georgia Technical College

Introduction to Microsoft Office 2016 Features

PROJECT 1A

OUTCOMES

Create, save, and print a Microsoft Office 2016 document.

OBJECTIVES

1. Explore Microsoft Office 2016
2. Enter, Edit, and Check the Spelling of Text in an Office 2016 Program
3. Perform Commands from a Dialog Box
4. Create a Folder and Name and Save a File
5. Insert a Footer, Add Document Properties, Print a File, and Close a Desktop App

PROJECT 1B

OUTCOMES

Perform commands, apply formatting, and install apps for Office in Microsoft Office 2016

OBJECTIVES

6. Open an Existing File and Save it with a New Name
7. Sign in to Office and Explore Options for a Microsoft Office Desktop App
8. Perform Commands from the Ribbon and Quick Access Toolbar
9. Apply Formatting in Office Programs and Inspect Documents
10. Compress Files and Get Help with Office
11. Install Apps for Office and Create a Microsoft Account

Imagewell10/Fotolia

In This Chapter

In this chapter, you will practice using features in Microsoft Office 2016 that work similarly across Word, Excel, Access, and PowerPoint. These features include managing files, performing commands, adding document properties, signing in to Office, applying formatting to text, and searching for Office commands quickly. You will also practice installing apps from the Office Store and setting up a free Microsoft account so that you can use OneDrive.

The projects in this chapter relate to **Skyline Metro Grill**, which is a chain of 25 casual, full-service restaurants based in Boston. The Skyline Metro Grill owners are planning an aggressive expansion program. To expand by 15 additional restaurants in Chicago, San Francisco, and Los Angeles by 2020, the company must attract new investors, develop new menus, develop new marketing strategies, and recruit new employees, all while adhering to the company's quality guidelines and maintaining its reputation for excellent service. To succeed, the company plans to build on its past success and maintain its quality elements.

PROJECT 1A Note Form

MyITLab
Project 1A Grader

PROJECT ACTIVITIES

In Activities 1.01 through 1.08, you will create a note form using Microsoft Word 2016, save it in a folder that you create by using File Explorer, and then print the note form or submit it electronically as directed by your instructor. Your completed note form will look similar to Figure 1.1.

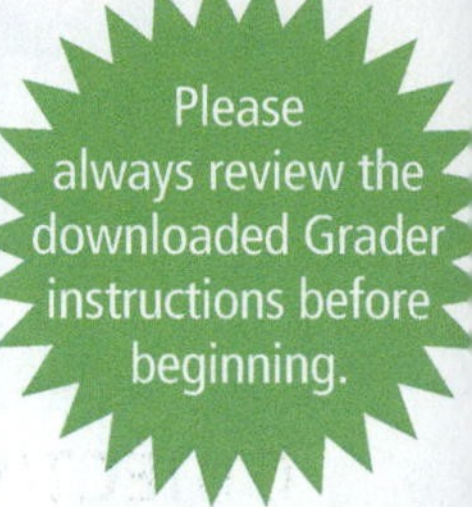
Please always review the downloaded Grader instructions before beginning.

PROJECT FILES

MyITLab
grader

If your instructor wants you to submit Project 1A in the MyITLab Grader system, log in to MyITLab, locate Grader Project1A, and then download the files for this project.

For Project 1A, you will need the following file:
New blank Word document

You will save your file as:
Lastname_Firstname_1A_Note_Form

PROJECT RESULTS

Build From Scratch

GO! Walk Thru Project 1A

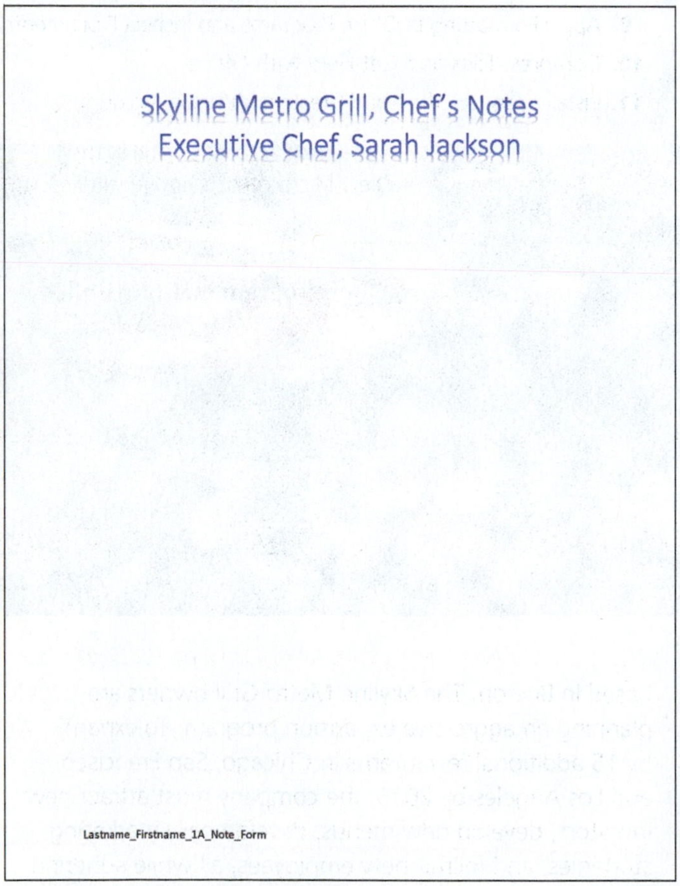

Skyline Metro Grill, Chef's Notes
Executive Chef, Sarah Jackson

Lastname_Firstname_1A_Note_Form

Word 2016, Windows 10, Microsoft Corporation

FIGURE 1.1 Project 1A Note Form

NOTE	If You Are Using a Touchscreen
	Tap an item to click it.
	Press and hold for a few seconds to right-click; release when the information or commands display.
	Touch the screen with two or more fingers and then pinch together to zoom out or stretch your fingers apart to zoom in.
	Slide your finger on the screen to scroll—slide left to scroll right and slide right to scroll left.
	Slide to rearrange—similar to dragging with a mouse.
	Swipe to select—slide an item a short distance with a quick movement—to select an item and bring up commands, if any.

Objective 1 Explore Microsoft Office 2016

NOTE Creating a Microsoft Account

Use a free Microsoft account to sign in to Office 2016 so that you can work on different PCs and use your OneDrive. If you already sign in to a Windows PC, tablet, or phone, or you sign in to Xbox Live, Outlook.com, or OneDrive, use that account to sign in to Office. To create a Microsoft account, you can use *any* email address as the user name for your new Microsoft account—including addresses from Outlook.com, Yahoo! or Gmail.

GO! Learn How Video OF1.1

The term ***desktop application*** or ***desktop app*** refers to a computer program that is installed on your PC and that requires a computer operating system such as Microsoft Windows. The programs in Microsoft Office 2016 are considered to be desktop apps. A desktop app typically has hundreds of features and takes time to learn.

An ***app*** refers to a self-contained program usually designed for a single purpose and that runs on smartphones and other mobile devices—for example, looking at sports scores or booking a flight on a particular airline. Microsoft's Windows 10 operating system supports both desktop apps that run only on PCs and ***Windows apps*** that run on all Windows device families—including PCs, Windows phones, Windows tablets, and the Xbox gaming system.

ALERT! **Is Your Screen More Colorful and a Different Size Than the Figures in This Textbook?**

Your installation of Microsoft Office 2016 may use the default Colorful theme, where the ribbon in each application is a vibrant color and the ribbon tabs display with white text. In this textbook, figures shown use the White theme, but you can be assured that all the commands are the same. You can keep your Colorful theme, or if you prefer, you can change your theme to White to match the figures here. To do so, open any application and display a new document. On the ribbon, click the File tab, and then on the left, click Options. With General selected on the left, under Personalize your copy of Microsoft Office, click the Office Theme arrow, and then click White.

Additionally, the figures in this book were captured using a screen resolution of 1280 x 768. If that is not your screen resolution, your screen will closely resemble, but not match, the figures shown. To view or change your screen's resolution on a Windows 10 PC, on the desktop, right-click in a blank area, click Display settings, and then on the right, click Advanced display settings. On a Windows 7 PC, right-click on the desktop, and then click Screen resolution.

MOS 1.1.1

Activity 1.01 | Exploring Microsoft Office 2016 and Creating a Blank Word Document

ALERT!

To submit as an autograded project, log into MyITLab, download the files for this project, and then begin with those files instead of a new blank document.

1 On the computer you are using, start Microsoft Word 2016, and then compare your screen with Figure 1.2.

Depending on which operating system you are using and how your computer is set up, you might start Word from the taskbar in Windows 7, Windows 8, or Windows 10, or from the Start screen in Windows 8, or from the Start menu in Windows 10. On an Apple Mac computer, the program will display in the dock.

Documents that you have recently opened, if any, display on the left. On the right, you can select either a blank document or a ***template***—a preformatted document that you can use as a starting point and then change to suit your needs.

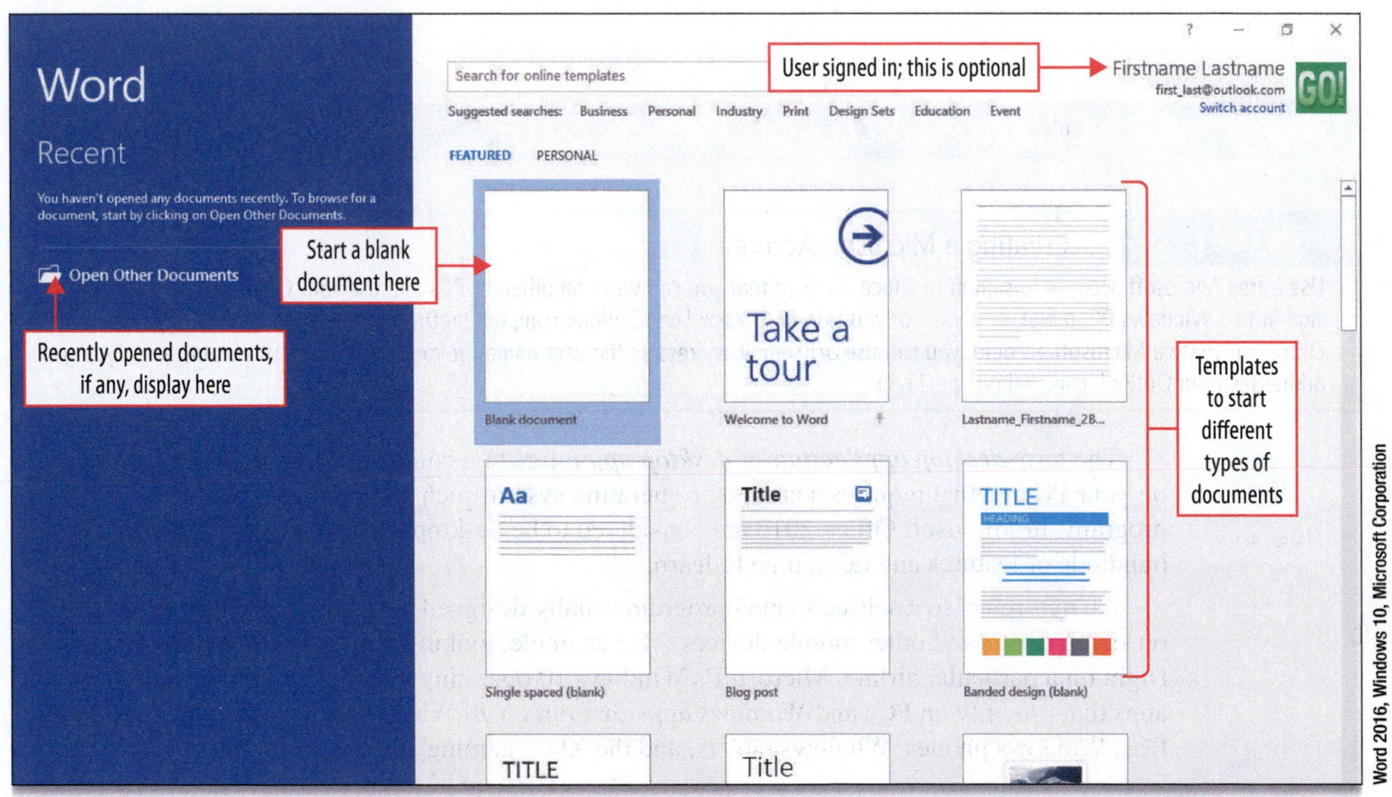

Word 2016, Windows 10, Microsoft Corporation

FIGURE 1.2

2 Click **Blank document**. Compare your screen with Figure 1.3, and then take a moment to study the description of these screen elements in the table in Figure 1.4.

NOTE Displaying the Full Ribbon

If your full ribbon does not display, click any tab, and then at the right end of the ribbon, click [pin icon] to pin the ribbon to keep it open while you work.

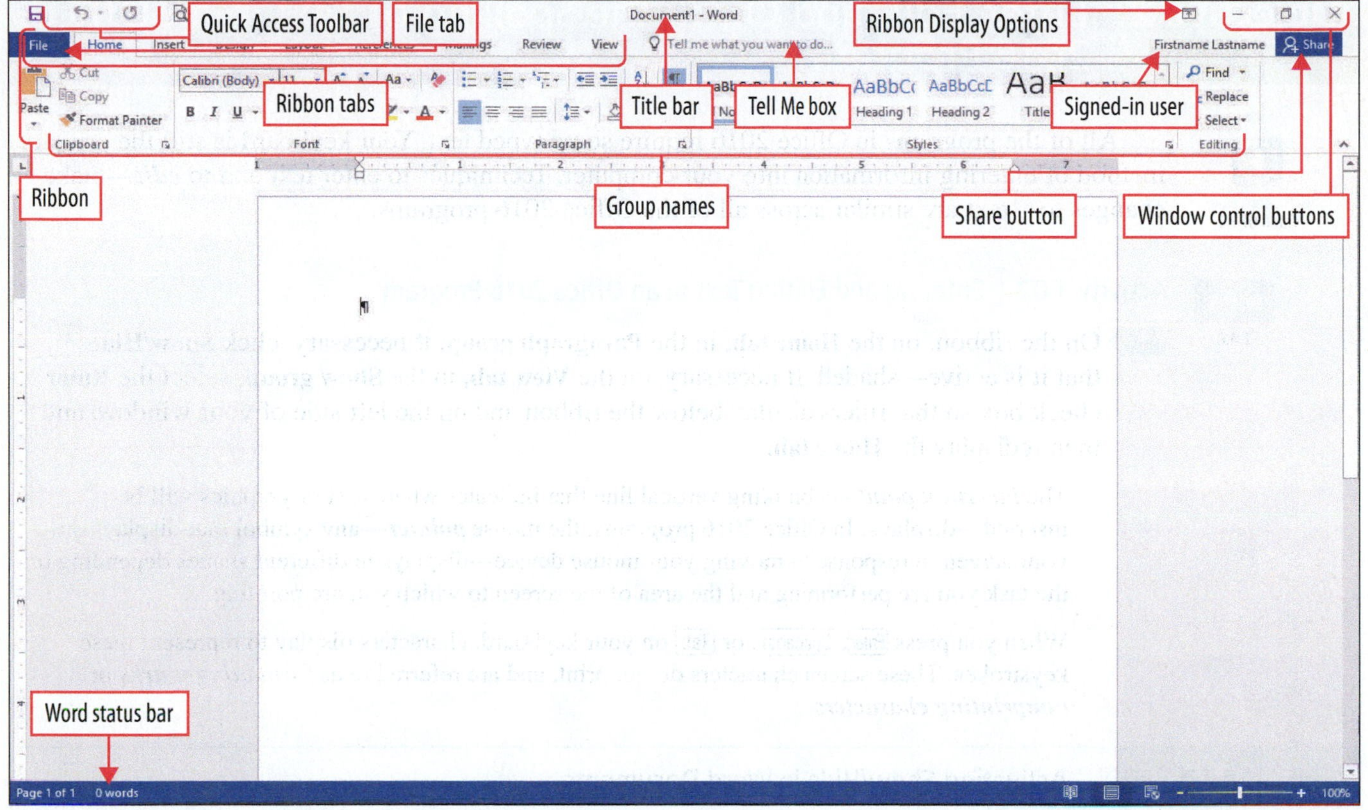

FIGURE 1.3 Word 2016, Windows 10, Microsoft Corporation

SCREEN ELEMENT	DESCRIPTION
File tab	Displays Microsoft Office Backstage view, which is a centralized space for all of your file management tasks such as opening, saving, printing, publishing, or sharing a file—all the things you can do *with* a file.
Group names	Indicate the name of the groups of related commands on the displayed tab.
Quick Access Toolbar	Displays buttons to perform frequently used commands and resources with a single click. The default commands include Save, Undo, and Redo. You can add and delete buttons to customize the Quick Access Toolbar for your convenience.
Ribbon	Displays a group of task-oriented tabs that contain the commands, styles, and resources you need to work in an Office 2016 desktop app. The look of your ribbon depends on your screen resolution. A high resolution will display more individual items and button names on the ribbon.
Ribbon Display Options	Displays three ways you can display the ribbon: Auto-hide Ribbon, Show Tabs, or Show Tabs and Commands.
Ribbon tabs	Display the names of the task-oriented tabs relevant to the open program.
Share button	Opens the Share pane from which you can save your file to the cloud—your OneDrive—and then share it with others so you can collaborate.
Signed-in user	Identifies the signed-in user.
Status bar	Displays file information on the left; on the right displays buttons for Read Mode, Print Layout, and Web Layout views; on the far right displays Zoom controls.
Tell Me box	Provides a search feature for Microsoft Office commands that you activate by typing what you are looking for in the Tell Me box; as you type, every keystroke refines the results so that you can click the command as soon as it displays.
Title bar	Displays the name of the file and the name of the program; the window control buttons are grouped on the right side of the title bar.
Window control buttons	Displays buttons for commands to change the Ribbon Display Options, Minimize, Restore Down, or Close the window.

Word 2016, Windows 10, Microsoft Corporation

FIGURE 1.4

Objective 2 Enter, Edit, and Check the Spelling of Text in an Office 2016 Program

GO! Learn How Video OF1.2

All of the programs in Office 2016 require some typed text. Your keyboard is still the primary method of entering information into your computer. Techniques to enter text and to ***edit***—make changes to—text are similar across all of the Office 2016 programs.

MOS 1.4.6

Activity 1.02 | Entering and Editing Text in an Office 2016 Program

1 On the ribbon, on the **Home tab**, in the **Paragraph group**, if necessary, click **Show/Hide** ¶ so that it is active—shaded. If necessary, on the **View tab**, in the **Show group**, select the **Ruler** check box so that rulers display below the ribbon and on the left side of your window, and then redisplay the **Home tab**.

The ***insertion point***—a blinking vertical line that indicates where text or graphics will be inserted—displays. In Office 2016 programs, the mouse ***pointer***—any symbol that displays on your screen in response to moving your mouse device—displays in different shapes depending on the task you are performing and the area of the screen to which you are pointing.

When you press Enter, Spacebar, or Tab on your keyboard, characters display to represent these keystrokes. These screen characters do not print, and are referred to as ***formatting marks*** or ***nonprinting characters***.

> **NOTE** Activating Show/Hide in Word Documents
>
> When Show/Hide is active—the button is shaded—formatting marks display. Because formatting marks guide your eye in a document—like a map and road signs guide you along a highway—these marks will display throughout this instruction. Many expert Word users keep these marks displayed while creating documents.

2 Type **Skyline Grille Info** and notice how the insertion point moves to the right as you type. Point slightly to the right of the letter *e* in *Grille* and click one time to place the insertion point there. Compare your screen with Figure 1.5.

A ***paragraph symbol*** (¶) indicates the end of a paragraph and displays each time you press Enter. This is a type of formatting mark and does not print.

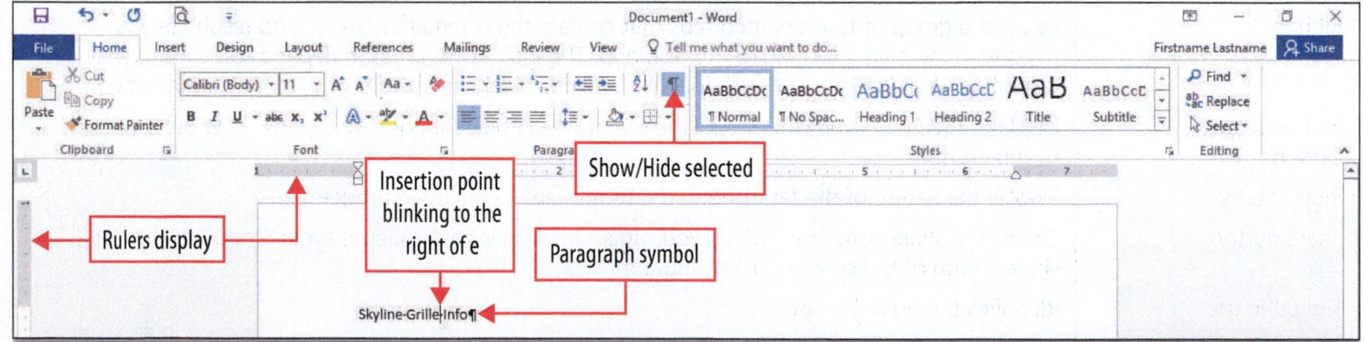

Word 2016, Windows 10, Microsoft Corporation

FIGURE 1.5

3 On your keyboard, locate and then press the Backspace key to delete the letter *e*.

Pressing Backspace removes a character to the left of the insertion point.

4 Press → one time to place the insertion point to the left of the *I* in *Info*. Type **Chef's** and then press Spacebar one time.

By ***default***, when you type text in an Office program, existing text moves to the right to make space for new typing. Default refers to the current selection or setting that is automatically used by a program unless you specify otherwise.

5 Press Del four times to delete *Info* and then type **Notes**

Pressing Del removes a character to the right of the insertion point.

6 With your insertion point blinking after the word *Notes*, on your keyboard, hold down the Ctrl key. While holding down Ctrl, press ← three times to move the insertion point to the beginning of the word *Grill*. Release Ctrl.

This is a ***keyboard shortcut***—a key or combination of keys that performs a task that would otherwise require a mouse. This keyboard shortcut moves the insertion point to the beginning of the previous word.

A keyboard shortcut is indicated as Ctrl + ← (or some other combination of keys) to indicate that you hold down the first key while pressing the second key. A keyboard shortcut can also include three keys, in which case you hold down the first two and then press the third. For example, Ctrl + Shift + ← selects one word to the left.

7 With the insertion point blinking at the beginning of the word *Grill*, type **Metro** and press Spacebar.

8 Press Ctrl + End to place the insertion point after the letter *s* in *Notes*, and then press Enter one time. With the insertion point blinking, type the following and include the spelling error: **Exective Chef, Madison Dunham**

9 With your mouse, point slightly to the left of the *M* in *Madison*, hold down the left mouse button, and then ***drag***—hold down the left mouse button while moving your mouse—to the right to select the text *Madison Dunham* but not the paragraph mark following it, and then release the mouse button. Compare your screen with Figure 1.6.

The ***mini toolbar*** displays commands that are commonly used with the selected object, which places common commands close to your pointer. When you move the pointer away from the mini toolbar, it fades from view.

Selecting refers to highlighting—by dragging or clicking with your mouse—areas of text or data or graphics so that the selection can be edited, formatted, copied, or moved. The action of dragging includes releasing the left mouse button at the end of the area you want to select.

The Office programs recognize a selected area as one unit to which you can make changes. Selecting text may require some practice. If you are not satisfied with your result, click anywhere outside of the selection, and then begin again.

BY TOUCH Double-tap on *Madison* to display the gripper—a small circle that acts as a handle—directly below the word. This establishes the start gripper. If necessary, with your finger, drag the gripper to the beginning of the word. Then drag the gripper to the end of *Dunham* to select the text and display the end gripper.

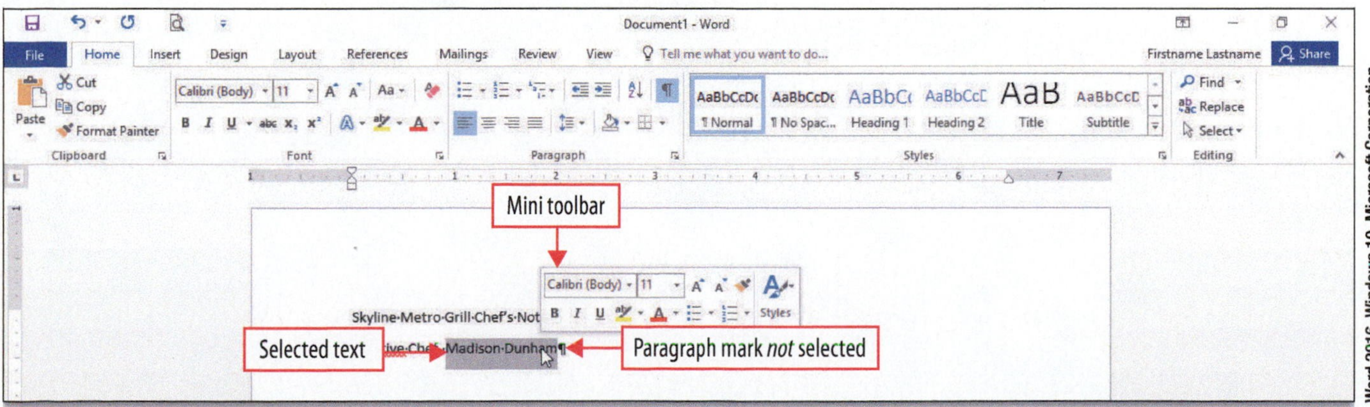

FIGURE 1.6

10 With the text *Madison Dunham* selected, type **Sarah Jackson**

In any Windows-based program, such as the Microsoft Office 2016 programs, selected text is deleted and then replaced when you begin to type new text. You will save time by developing good techniques for selecting and then editing or replacing selected text, which is easier than pressing the Del key numerous times to delete text.

Activity 1.03 | Checking Spelling

Office 2016 has a dictionary of words against which all entered text is checked. In Word and PowerPoint, words that are not in the dictionary display a wavy red line, indicating a possible misspelled word, a proper name, or an unusual word—none of which are in the Office 2016 dictionary.

In Excel and Access, you can initiate a check of the spelling, but red underlines do not display.

1 Notice that the misspelled word *Exective* displays with a wavy red underline.

2 Point to *Exective* and then ***right-click***—click your right mouse button one time.

A ***shortcut menu*** displays, which displays commands and options relevant to the selected text or object. These are ***context-sensitive commands*** because they relate to the item you right-clicked. These shortcut menus are also referred to as ***context menus***. Here, the shortcut menu displays commands related to the misspelled word.

Tap and hold a moment—when a square displays around the misspelled word, release your finger to display the shortcut menu.

3 Press Esc to cancel the shortcut menu, and then in the lower left corner of your screen, on the status bar, click the ***Proofing*** icon, which displays an *X* because some errors are detected. Compare your screen with Figure 1.7.

The Spelling pane displays on the right. Here you have many more options for checking spelling than you have on the shortcut menu. The suggested correct word, *Executive*, is highlighted.

You can click the speaker icon to hear the pronunciation of the selected word. If you have not already installed a dictionary, you can click *Get a Dictionary*—if you are signed in to Office with a Microsoft account—to find and install one from the online Office store; or if you have a dictionary app installed, it will display here and you can search it for more information.

In the Spelling pane, you can ignore the word one time or in all occurrences, change the word to the suggested word, select a different suggestion, or add a word to the dictionary against which Word checks.

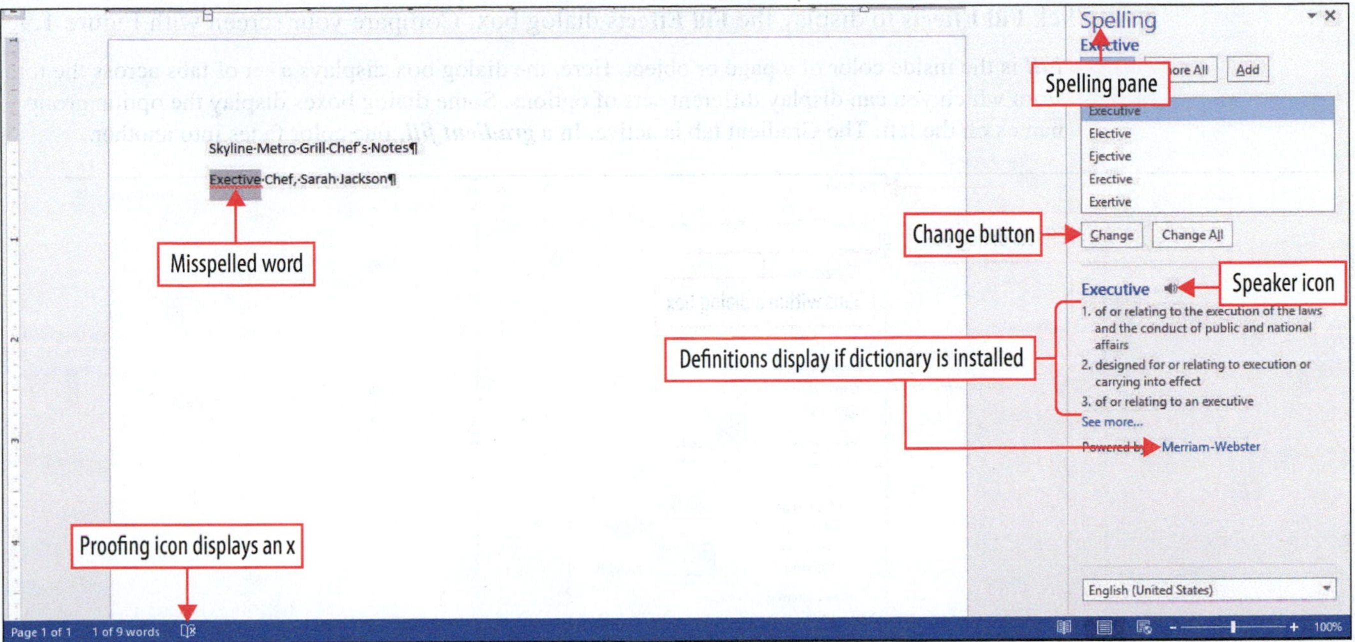

Word 2016, Windows 10, Microsoft Corporation

FIGURE 1.7

ANOTHER WAY Press F7 to display the Spelling pane; or, on the Review tab, in the Proofing group, click Spelling & Grammar.

4 In the ***Spelling*** pane, click **Change** to change the spelling to *Executive*. In the message box that displays, click **OK**.

Objective 3 Perform Commands from a Dialog Box

GO! Learn How Video OF1.3

In a dialog box, you make decisions about an individual object or topic. In some dialog boxes, you can make multiple decisions in one place.

Activity 1.04 | Performing Commands from a Dialog Box

1.3.6

1 On the ribbon, click the **Design tab**, and then in the **Page Background group**, click **Page Color**.

2 At the bottom of the menu, notice the command ***Fill Effects*** followed by an **ellipsis** (...). Compare your screen with Figure 1.8.

An ***ellipsis*** is a set of three dots indicating incompleteness. An ellipsis following a command name indicates that a dialog box will display when you click the command.

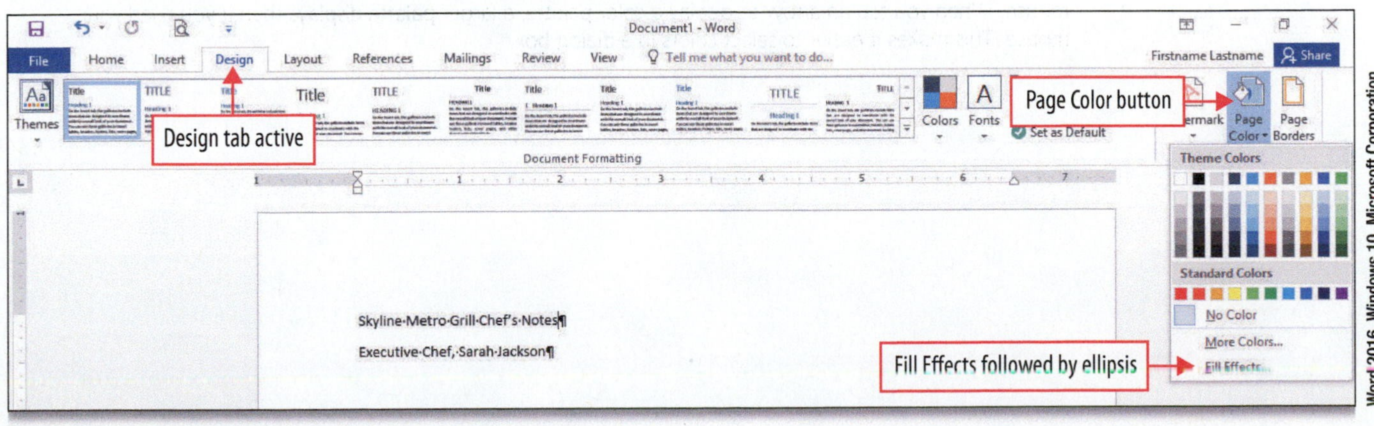

Word 2016, Windows 10, Microsoft Corporation

FIGURE 1.08

3 Click **Fill Effects** to display the **Fill Effects** dialog box. Compare your screen with Figure 1.9.

Fill is the inside color of a page or object. Here, the dialog box displays a set of tabs across the top from which you can display different sets of options. Some dialog boxes display the option group names on the left. The Gradient tab is active. In a ***gradient fill***, one color fades into another.

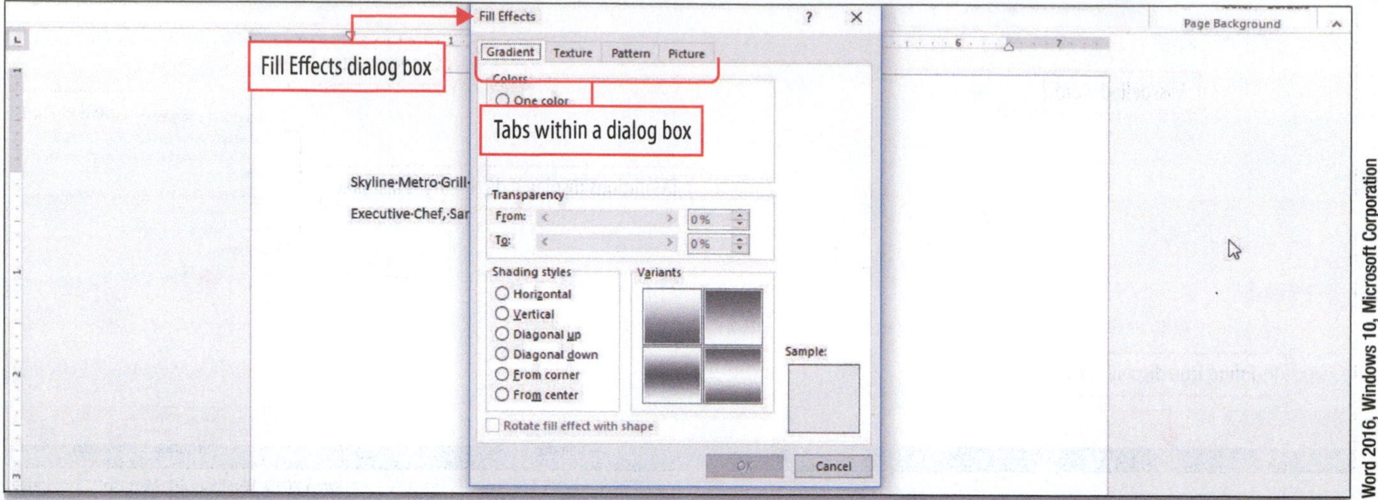

FIGURE 1.9

4 Under **Colors**, click the **One color** option button.

The dialog box displays settings related to the One color option. An ***option button*** is a round button that enables you to make one choice among two or more options.

5 Click the **Color 5 arrow**—the arrow under the text *Color 5*—and then in the third column, point to the second color to display the ScreenTip *Light Gray-25%, Background 2, Darker 10%*.

When you click an arrow in a dialog box, additional options display. A ***ScreenTip*** displays useful information about mouse actions, such as pointing to screen elements or dragging.

6 Click **Gray-25%, Background 2, Darker 10%**, and then notice that the fill color displays in the **Color 1** box. In the **Dark Light** bar, click the **Light arrow** as many times as necessary until the scroll box is all the way to the right. Under **Shading styles**, click the **Diagonal down** option button. Under **Variants**, click the **upper right variant**. Compare your screen with Figure 1.10.

This dialog box is a good example of the many different elements you may encounter in a dialog box. Here you have option buttons, an arrow that displays a menu, a slider bar, and graphic options that you can select.

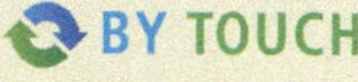

In a dialog box, you can tap option buttons and other commands just as you would click them with a mouse. When you tap an arrow to display a color palette, a larger palette displays than if you used your mouse. This makes it easier to select colors in a dialog box.

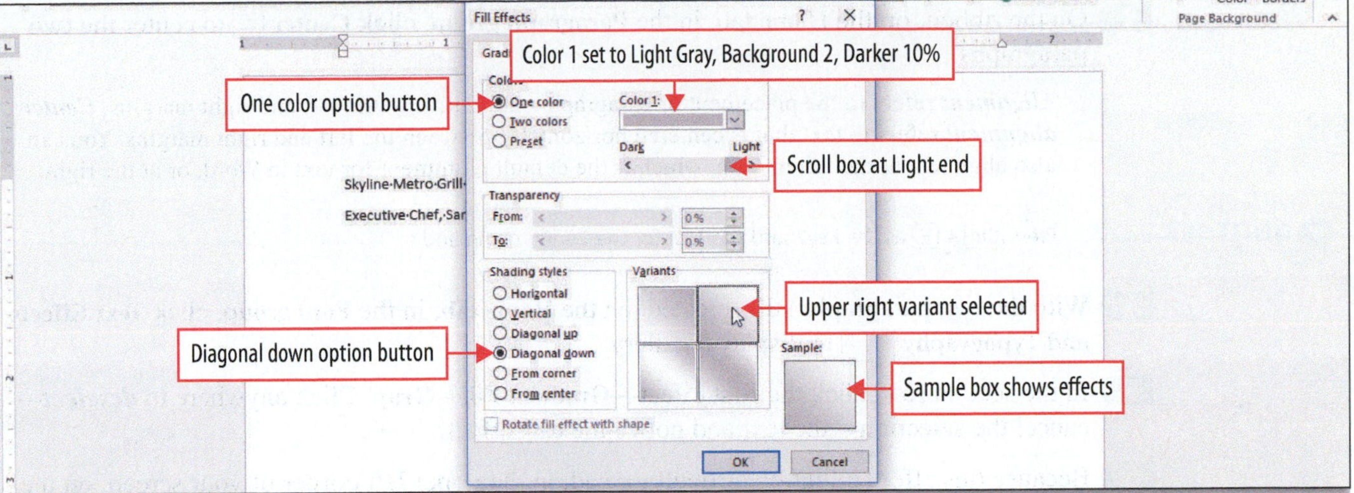

Word 2016, Windows 10, Microsoft Corporation

FIGURE 1.10

7 At the bottom of the dialog box, click **OK**, and notice the subtle page color.

In Word, the gray shading page color will not print—even on a color printer—unless you set specific options to do so. However, a subtle background page color is effective if people will be reading the document on a screen. Microsoft's research indicates that two-thirds of people who open Word documents on a screen never print them; they only read them.

Activity 1.05 | Using Undo and Applying a Built-In Style to Text

MOS 2.2.6

1 Point to the *S* in *Skyline*, and then drag down and to the right to select both paragraphs of text and include the paragraph marks. On the mini toolbar, click **Styles**, and then *point to* but do not click **Title**. Compare your screen with Figure 1.11.

A ***style*** is a group of ***formatting*** commands, such as font, font size, font color, paragraph alignment, and line spacing that can be applied to a paragraph with one command. Formatting is the process of establishing the overall appearance of text, graphics, and pages in an Office file—for example, in a Word document.

Live Preview is a technology that shows the result of applying an editing or formatting change as you point to possible results—before you actually apply it.

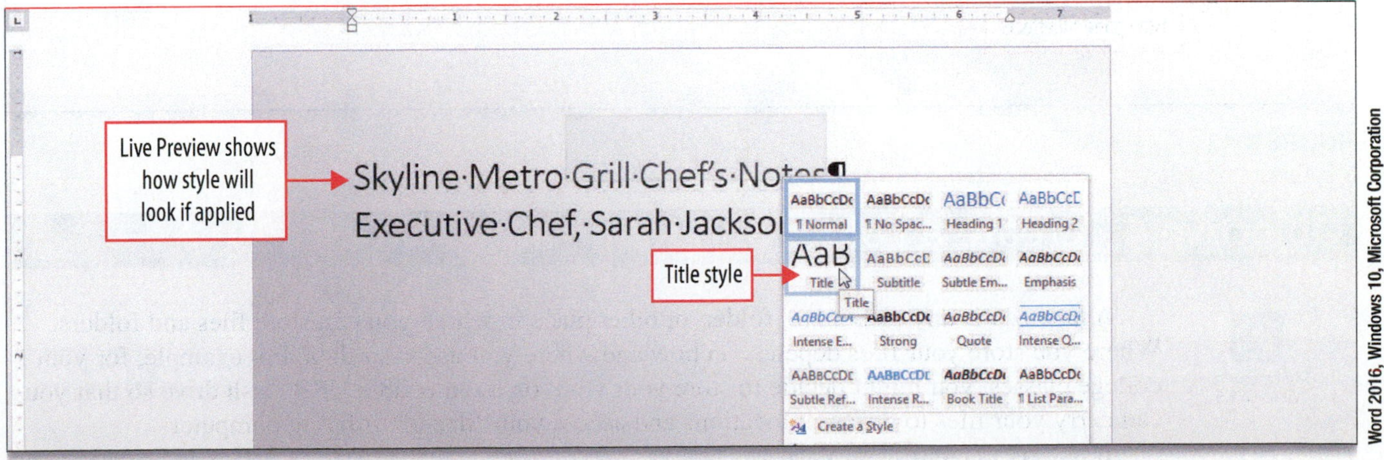

Word 2016, Windows 10, Microsoft Corporation

FIGURE 1.11

2 In the **Styles** gallery, click **Title**.

A ***gallery*** is an Office feature that displays a list of potential results.

3 On the ribbon, on the **Home tab**, in the **Paragraph group**, click **Center** [icon] to center the two paragraphs.

Alignment refers to the placement of paragraph text relative to the left and right margins. ***Center alignment*** refers to text that is centered horizontally between the left and right margins. You can also align text at the left margin, which is the default alignment for text in Word, or at the right.

ANOTHER WAY Press Ctrl + E as the keyboard shortcut for the Center command.

4 With the two paragraphs still selected, on the **Home tab**, in the **Font group**, click **Text Effects and Typography** [icon] to display a gallery.

5 In the second row, click the first effect—**Gradient Fill – Gray**. Click anywhere to ***deselect***—cancel the selection—the text and notice the text effect.

6 Because this effect might be difficult to read, in the upper left corner of your screen, on the ***Quick Access Toolbar***, click **Undo** [icon].

The *Undo* command reverses your last action.

ANOTHER WAY Press Ctrl + Z as the keyboard shortcut for the Undo command.

7 With all of the text still selected, display the **Text Effects and Typography** [icon] gallery again, and then in the second row, click the second effect—**Gradient Fill – Blue, Accent 1, Reflection**. Click anywhere to deselect the text and notice the text effect. Compare your screen with Figure 1.12.

As you progress in your study of Microsoft Office, you will practice using many dialog boxes and commands to apply interesting effects such as this to your Word documents, Excel worksheets, Access database objects, and PowerPoint slides.

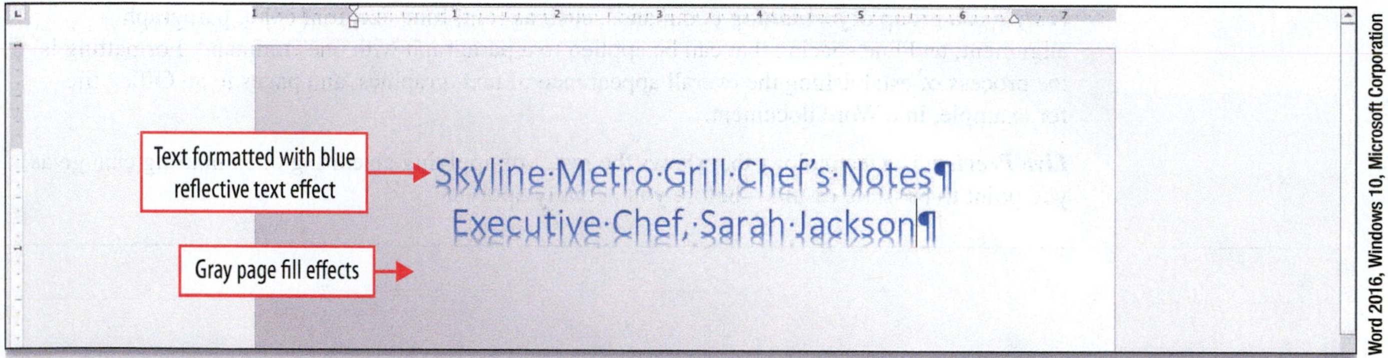

FIGURE 1.12

Objective 4 Create a Folder and Name and Save a File

GO! Learn How Video OF1.5

A ***location*** is any disk drive, folder, or other place in which you can store files and folders. Where you store your files depends on how and where you use your data. For example, for your college classes, you might decide to store your work on a removable USB flash drive so that you can carry your files to different locations and access your files on different computers.

If you do most of your work on a single computer, for example, your home desktop system or your laptop computer that you take with you to school or work, then you can store your files in one of the folders—Documents, Music, Pictures, or Videos—on your hard drive provided by your Windows operating system.

The best place to store files if you want them to be available anytime, anywhere, from almost any device is on your ***OneDrive***, which is Microsoft's free ***cloud storage*** for anyone with a free Microsoft account. Cloud storage refers to online storage of data so that you can access your data from different places and devices. ***Cloud computing*** refers to applications and services that are accessed over the Internet, rather than accessing applications installed on your local computer.

If you have an ***Office 365*** account—one of the versions of Microsoft Office to which you subscribe for an annual fee—your storage capacity on OneDrive is a terabyte or more, which is more than most individuals would ever require.

Because many people now have multiple computing devices—desktop, laptop, tablet, smartphone—it is common to store data *in the cloud* so that it is always available. ***Synchronization***, also called ***syncing***—pronounced SINK-ing—is the process of updating computer files that are in two or more locations according to specific rules. So if you create and save a Word document on your OneDrive using your laptop, you can open and edit that document on your tablet in OneDrive. When you close the document again, the file is properly updated to reflect your changes. Your OneDrive account will guide you in setting options for syncing files to your specifications.

You need not be connected to the Internet to access documents stored on OneDrive because an up-to-date version of your content is synched to your local system and available on OneDrive. You must, however, be connected to the Internet for the syncing to occur. Saving to OneDrive will keep the local copy on your computer and the copy in the cloud synchronized for as long as you need it. You can open and edit Office files by using Office apps available on a variety of device platforms, including iOS, Android, and Windows.

The Windows operating system helps you to create and maintain a logical folder structure, so always take the time to name your files and folders consistently.

Activity 1.06 | Creating a Folder and Naming and Saving a File

A Word document is an example of a file. In this Activity, you will create a folder in the storage location you have chosen to use for your files and then save your file. This example will use the Documents folder on the PC at which you are working. If you prefer to store on your OneDrive or on a USB flash drive, you can use similar steps.

1. Decide where you are going to store your files for this Project.

   As the first step in saving a file, determine where you want to save the file, and if necessary, insert a storage device.

2. At the top of your screen, in the title bar, notice that *Document1 – Word* displays.

   The Blank option on the opening screen of an Office 2016 program displays a new unsaved file with a default name— *Document1, Presentation1*, and so on. As you create your file, your work is temporarily stored in the computer's memory until you initiate a Save command, at which time you must choose a file name and a location in which to save your file.

3. In the upper left corner of your screen, click the **File tab** to display **Backstage** view. Compare your screen with Figure 1.13.

   Backstage view is a centralized space that groups commands related to *file* management; that is why the tab is labeled *File*. File management commands include opening, saving, printing, publishing, or sharing a file. The ***Backstage tabs***—*Info, New, Open, Save, Save As, Print, Share, Export*, and *Close*—display along the left side. The tabs group file-related tasks together.

   Here, the ***Info tab*** displays information—*info*—about the current file, and file management commands display under Info. For example, if you click the Protect Document button, a list of options that you can set for this file that relate to who can open or edit the document displays.

   On the right, you can also examine the ***document properties***. Document properties, also known as ***metadata***, are details about a file that describe or identify it, such as the title, author name, subject, and keywords that identify the document's topic or contents. To close Backstage view and return to the document, you can click ⊖ in the upper left corner or press Esc.

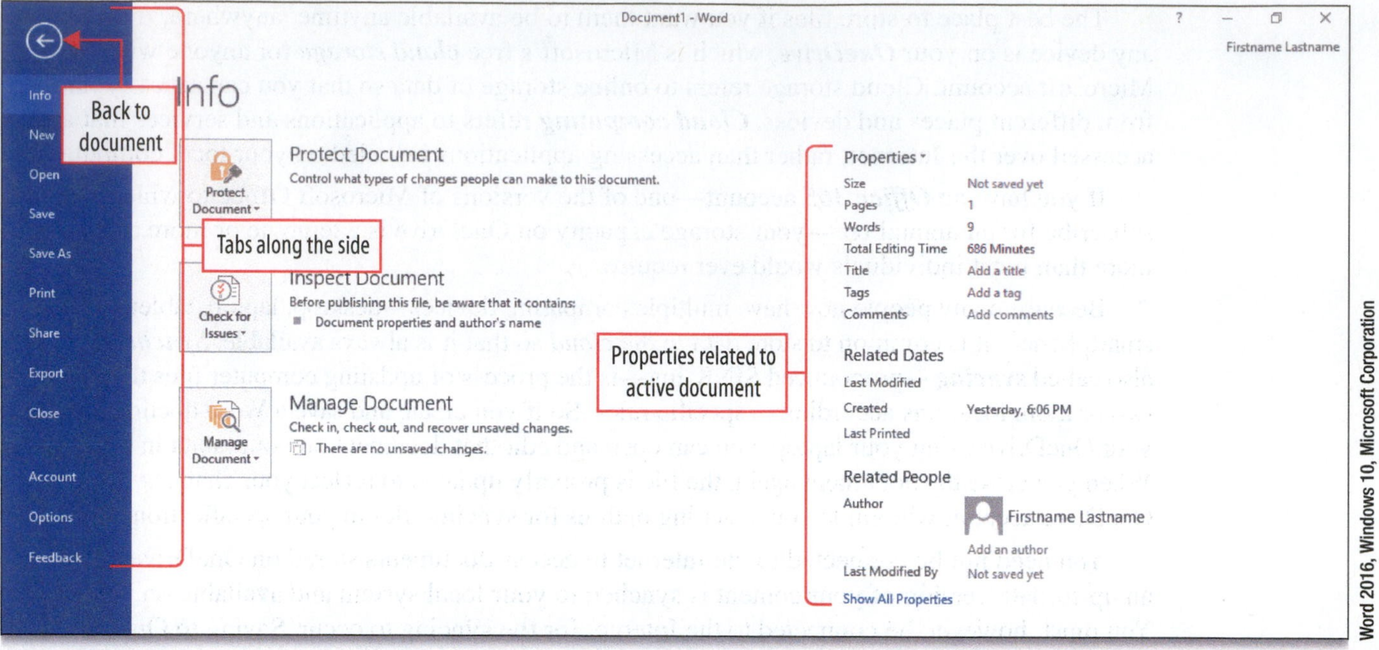

FIGURE 1.13

4 On the left, click **Save As**, and notice that the default location for storing Office files is your **OneDrive**—if you are signed in. Compare your screen with Figure 1.14.

When you are saving something for the first time, for example, a new Word document, the Save and Save As commands are identical. That is, the Save As commands will display if you click Save or if you click Save As.

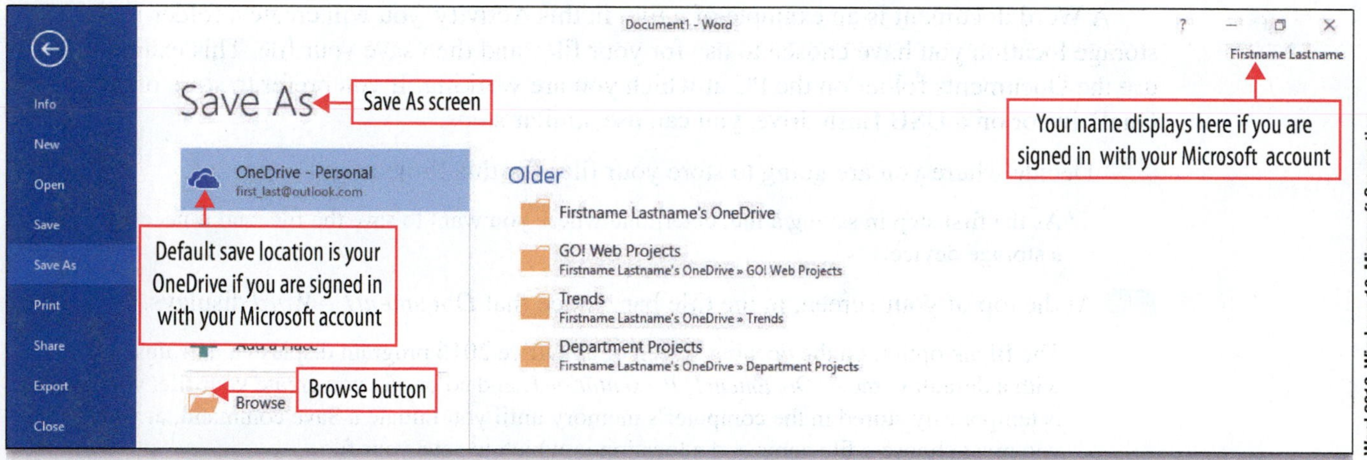

FIGURE 1.14

> **NOTE** Saving After Your File Is Named
>
> After you name and save a file, the Save command on the Quick Access Toolbar saves any changes you make to the file without displaying Backstage view. The Save As command enables you to name and save a *new* file based on the current one—in a location that you choose. After you name and save the new document, the original document closes, and the new document—based on the original one—displays.

5 To store your Word file in the **Documents** folder on your PC, click **Browse** to display the **Save As** dialog box. On the left, in the **navigation pane**, scroll down; if necessary click > to expand This PC, and then click **Documents**, or navigate to your USB flash drive or other location. In a college lab, your work may be lost if you store in the Documents folder. Compare your screen with Figure 1.15.

In the Save As dialog box, you must indicate the name you want for the file and the location where you want to save the file. When working with your own data, it is good practice to pause at this point and determine the logical name and location for your file.

In the Save As dialog box, a ***toolbar*** displays, which is a row, column, or block of buttons or icons, that displays across the top of a window and that contains commands for tasks you perform with a single click.

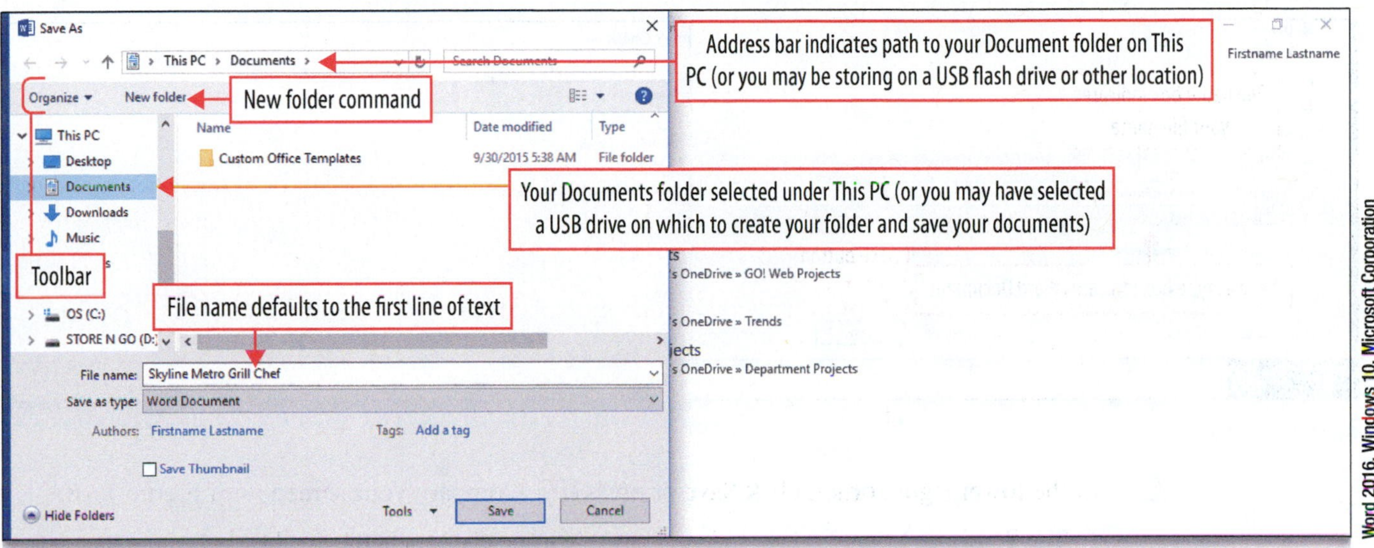

FIGURE 1.15

6 On the toolbar, click **New folder**.

In the file list, Windows creates a new folder, and the text *New folder* is selected.

7 Type **Office Features Chapter 1** and press Enter. Compare your screen with Figure 1.16.

In Windows-based programs, the Enter key confirms an action.

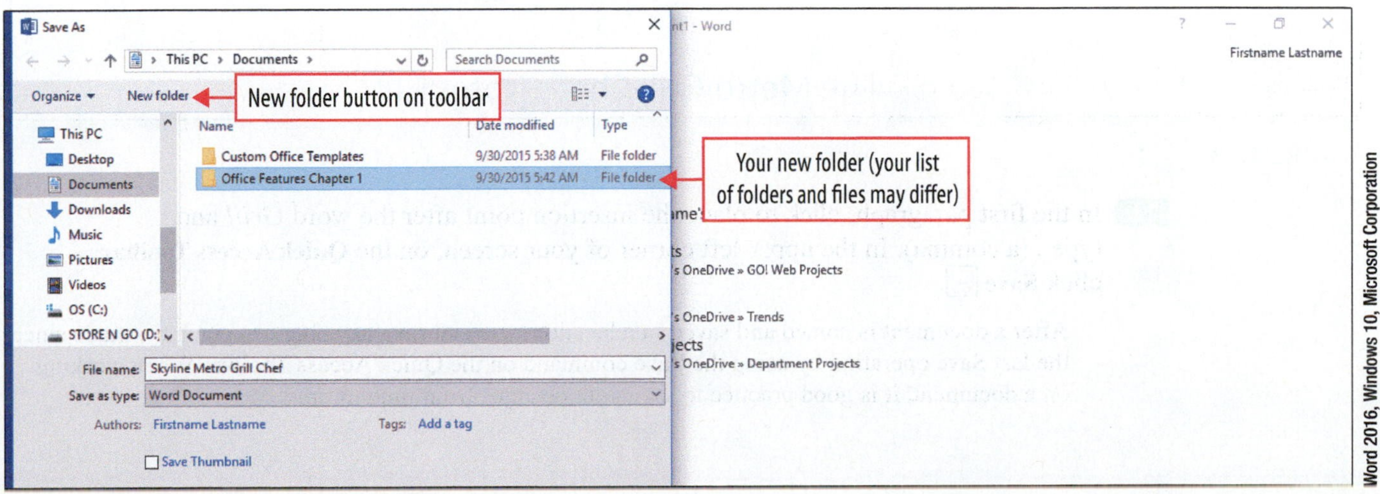

FIGURE 1.16

8 In the **file list**, double-click the name of your new folder to open it and display its name in the **address bar**.

9 In the lower portion of the dialog box, click in the **File name** box to select the existing text. Notice that as the suggested file name, Office inserts the text at the beginning of the document.

10 On your keyboard, locate the [-] key, to the right of zero on the number row. Notice that the [Shift] of this key produces the underscore character. With the text still selected and using your own name, type **Lastname_Firstname_1A_Note_Form** Compare your screen with Figure 1.17.

You can use spaces in file names, however, some people prefer not to use spaces. Some programs, especially when transferring files over the Internet, may insert the extra characters *%20* in place of a space. In general, however, unless you encounter a problem, it is OK to use spaces. In this instruction, underscores are used instead of spaces in file names.

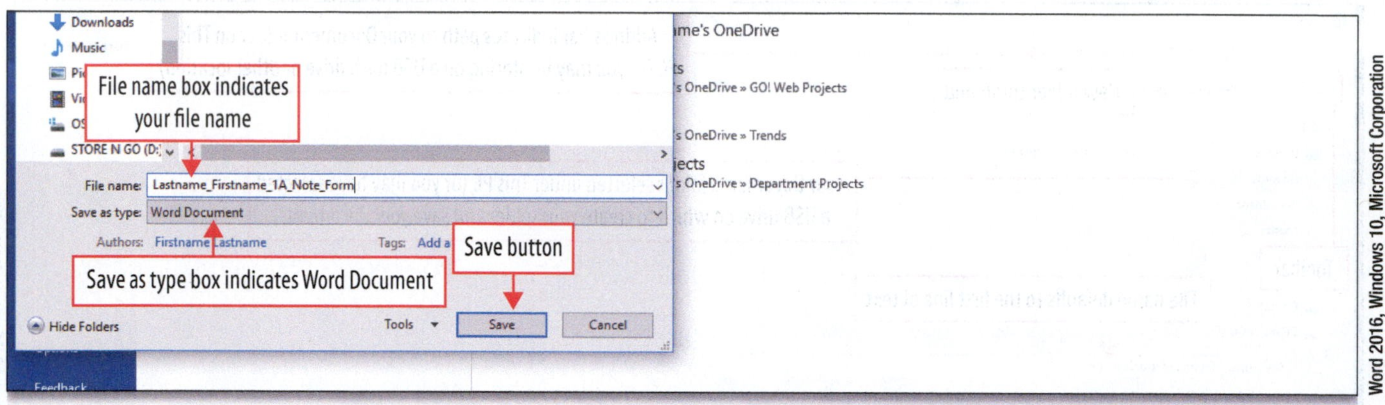

FIGURE 1.17

11 In the lower right corner, click **Save** or press [Enter]. Compare your screen with Figure 1.18.

The Word window redisplays and your new file name displays in the title bar, indicating that the file has been saved to the location that you have specified.

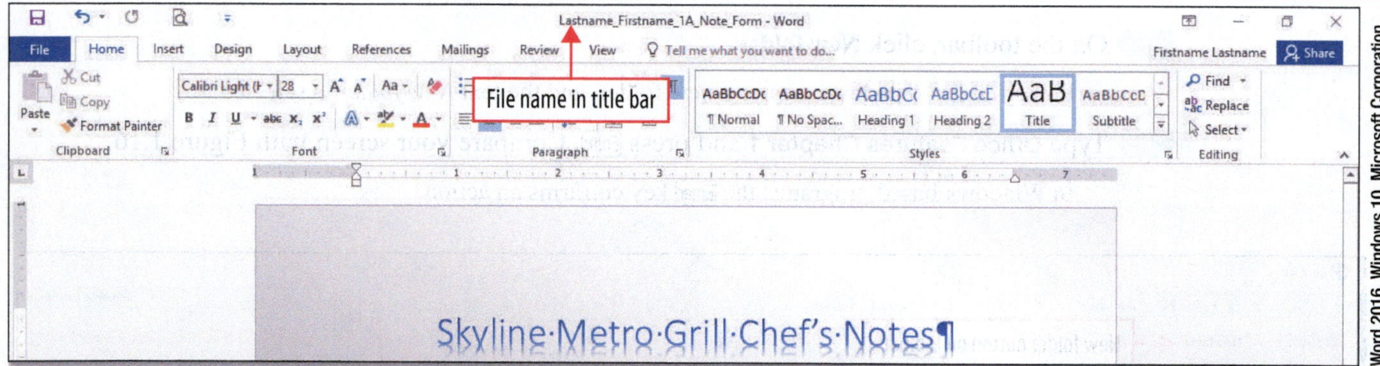

FIGURE 1.18

12 In the first paragraph, click to place the insertion point after the word *Grill* and type **,** (a comma). In the upper left corner of your screen, on the **Quick Access Toolbar**, click **Save** [Save icon].

After a document is named and saved in a location, you can save any changes you have made since the last Save operation by using the Save command on the Quick Access Toolbar. When working on a document, it is good practice to save your changes from time to time.

Objective 5 Insert a Footer, Add Document Properties, Print a File, and Close a Desktop App

GO! Learn How Video OF1.5

MOS 1.3.4, 1.4.5

For most of your files, especially in a workplace setting, it is useful to add identifying information to help in finding files later. You might also want to print your file on paper or create an electronic printout. The process of printing a file is similar in all of the Office applications.

Activity 1.07 | Inserting a Footer, Inserting Document Info, and Adding Document Properties

NOTE What Does Your Instructor Require for Submission? A Paper Printout, an Image That Looks Like a Printed Document, or Your Word File?

In this Activity, you can produce a paper printout or an electronic image of your document that looks like a printed document. Or, your instructor may want only your completed Word file.

1. On the ribbon, click the **Insert tab**, and then in the **Header & Footer group**, click **Footer**.

2. At the bottom of the list, click **Edit Footer**. On the ribbon, notice that the **Header & Footer Tools** display.

   The *Header & Footer Tools Design* tab displays on the ribbon. The ribbon adapts to your work and will display additional tabs like this one—referred to as ***contextual tabs***—when you need them.

   A ***footer*** is a reserved area for text or graphics that displays at the bottom of each page in a document. Likewise, a ***header*** is a reserved area for text or graphics that displays at the top of each page in a document. When the footer (or header) area is active, the document area is dimmed, indicating it is unavailable.

3. On the ribbon, under **Header & Footer Tools**, on the **Design tab**, in the **Insert group**, click **Document Info**, and then click **File Name** to insert the name of your file in the footer, which is a common business practice. Compare your screen with Figure 1.19.

   Ribbon commands that display ▾ will, when clicked, display a list of options for the command.

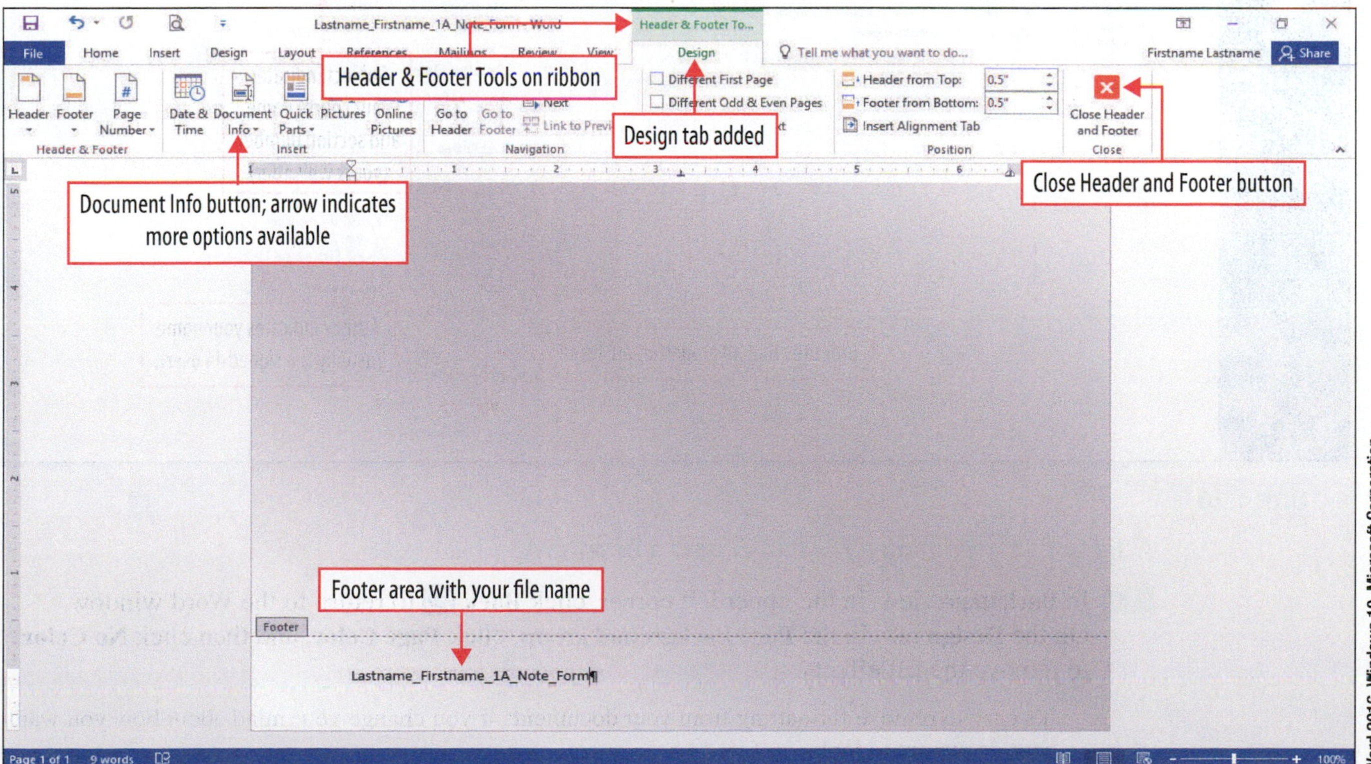

FIGURE 1.19

Word 2016, Windows 10, Microsoft Corporation

4 At the right end of the ribbon, click **Close Header and Footer**.

ANOTHER WAY Double-click anywhere in the dimmed document to close the footer.

5 Click the **File tab** to display **Backstage** view. On the right, at the bottom of the **Properties** list, click **Show All Properties**.

ANOTHER WAY Click the arrow to the right of Properties, and then click Advanced Properties to show and edit properties at the top of your document window.

6 On the list of **Properties**, click to the right of *Tags* to display an empty box, and then type **chef, notes, form**

Tags, also referred to as ***keywords***, are custom file properties in the form of words that you associate with a document to give an indication of the document's content. Adding tags to your documents makes it easier to search for and locate files in File Explorer, on your OneDrive, and in systems such as Microsoft ***SharePoint*** document libraries. SharePoint is collaboration software with which people in an organization can set up team sites to share information, manage documents, and publish reports for others to see.

BY TOUCH Tap to the right of Tags to display the Tags box and the onscreen keyboard.

7 Click to the right of *Subject* to display an empty box, and then type your course name and section #; for example, *CIS 10, #5543*.

8 Under **Related People**, be sure that your name displays as the author. If necessary, right-click the author name, click Edit Property, type your name, click outside of the Edit person dialog box, and then click OK. Compare your screen with Figure 1.20.

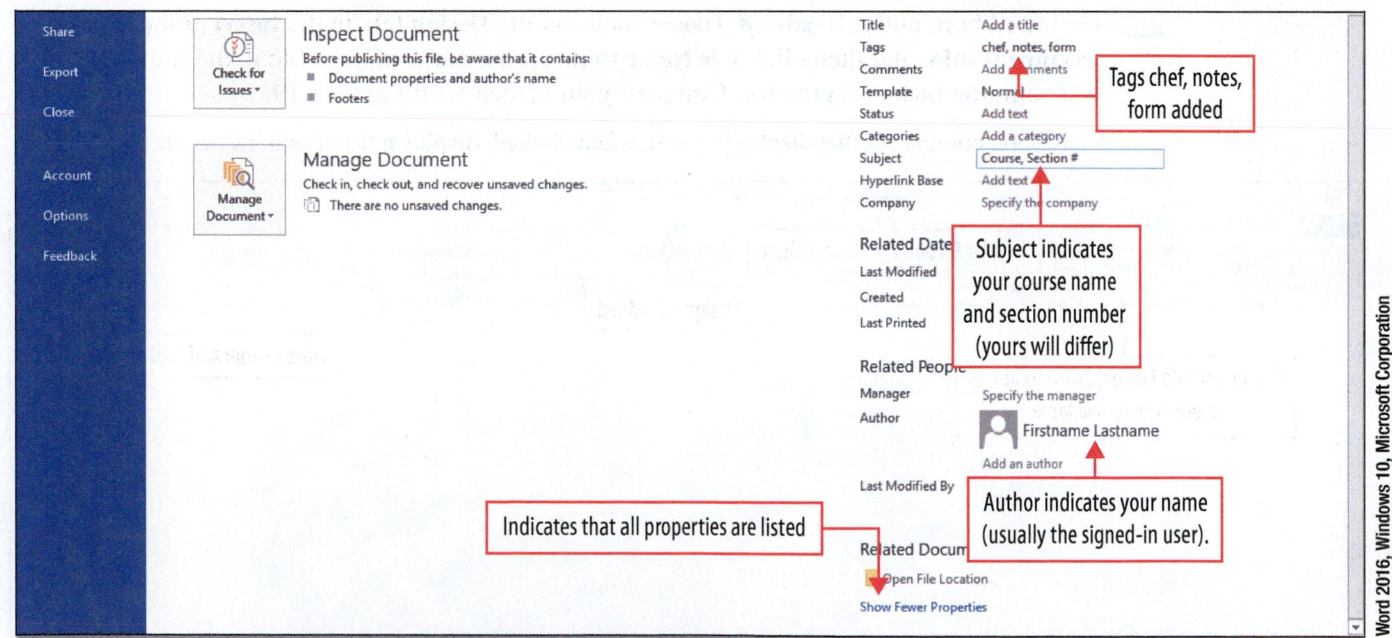

FIGURE 1.20

Activity 1.08 | Printing a File and Closing a Desktop App

1 In **Backstage** view, in the upper left corner, click **Back** to return to the Word window. On the **Design tab**, in the **Page Background group**, click **Page Color**, and then click **No Color** to remove the fill effects.

It's easy to remove formatting from your documents if you change your mind about how you want your document to look.

2 Click the **File tab** to return to **Backstage** view, on the left click **Print**, and then compare your screen with Figure 1.21.

Here you can select any printer connected to your system and adjust the settings related to how you want to print. On the right, the ***Print Preview*** displays, which is a view of a document as it will appear on paper when you print it.

At the bottom of the Print Preview area, in the center, the number of pages and page navigation arrows with which you can move among the pages in Print Preview display. On the right, the Zoom slider enables you to shrink or enlarge the Print Preview. ***Zoom*** is the action of increasing or decreasing the viewing area of the screen.

From the document screen, press Ctrl + P or Ctrl + F2 to display Print in Backstage view.

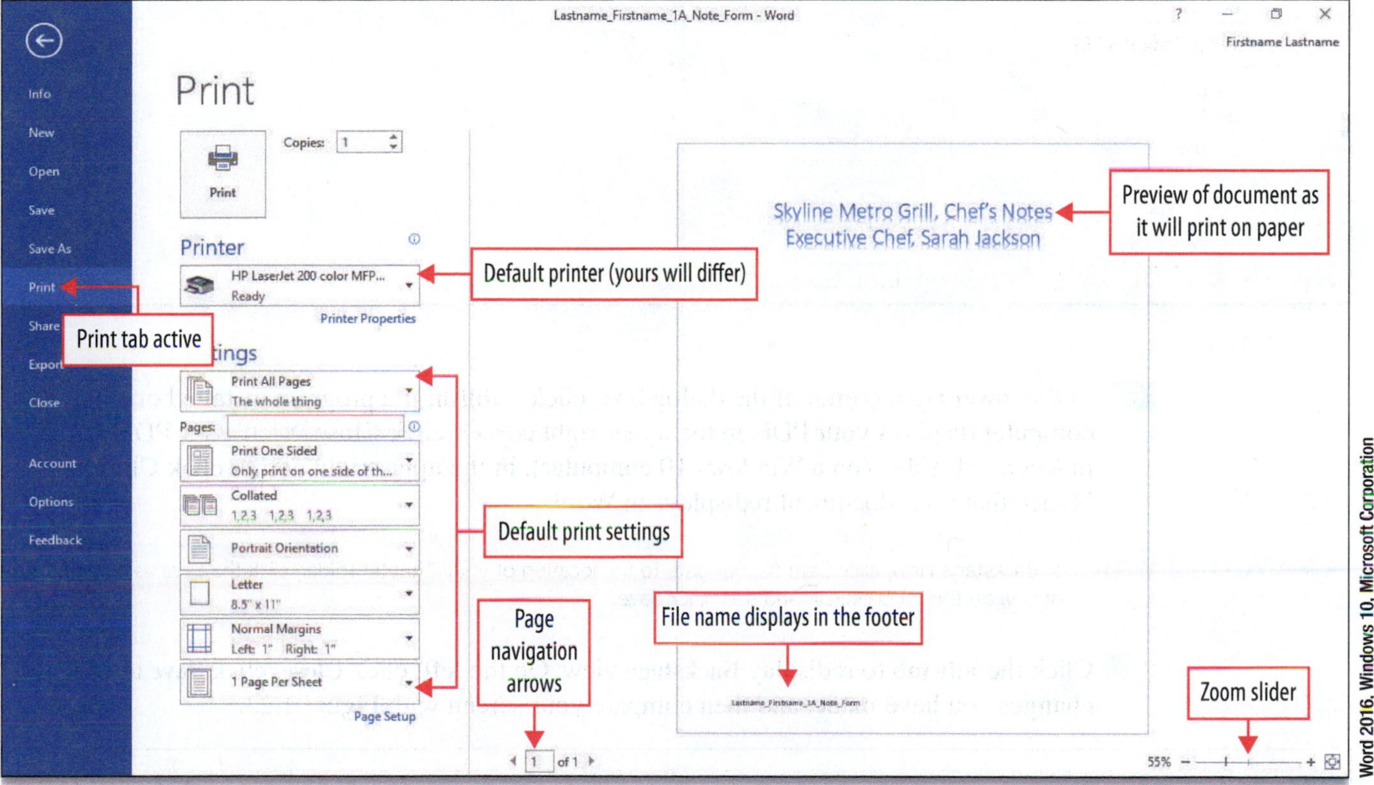

FIGURE 1.21

Word 2016, Windows 10, Microsoft Corporation

3 To create an electronic image of your document that looks like a printed document, skip this step and continue to Step 4. To print your document on paper using the default printer on your system, in the upper left portion of the screen, click **Print**.

The document will print on your default printer; if you do not have a color printer, the blue text will print in shades of gray. Backstage view closes and your file redisplays in the Word window.

4 To create an electronic image of your document that looks like a printed document, in **Backstage** view, on the left click **Export**. On the right, click the **Create PDF/XPS** button to display the **Publish as PDF or XPS** dialog box.

PDF stands for ***Portable Document Format***, which is a technology that creates an image that preserves the look of your file. This is a popular format for sending documents electronically, because the document will display on most computers.

XPS stands for ***XML Paper Specification***—a Microsoft file format that also creates an image of your document and that opens in the XPS viewer.

5 On the left in the **navigation pane**, if necessary expand > This PC, and then navigate to your **Office Features Chapter 1** folder in your **Documents** folder—or in whatever location you have created your Office Features Chapter 1 folder. Compare your screen with Figure 1.22.

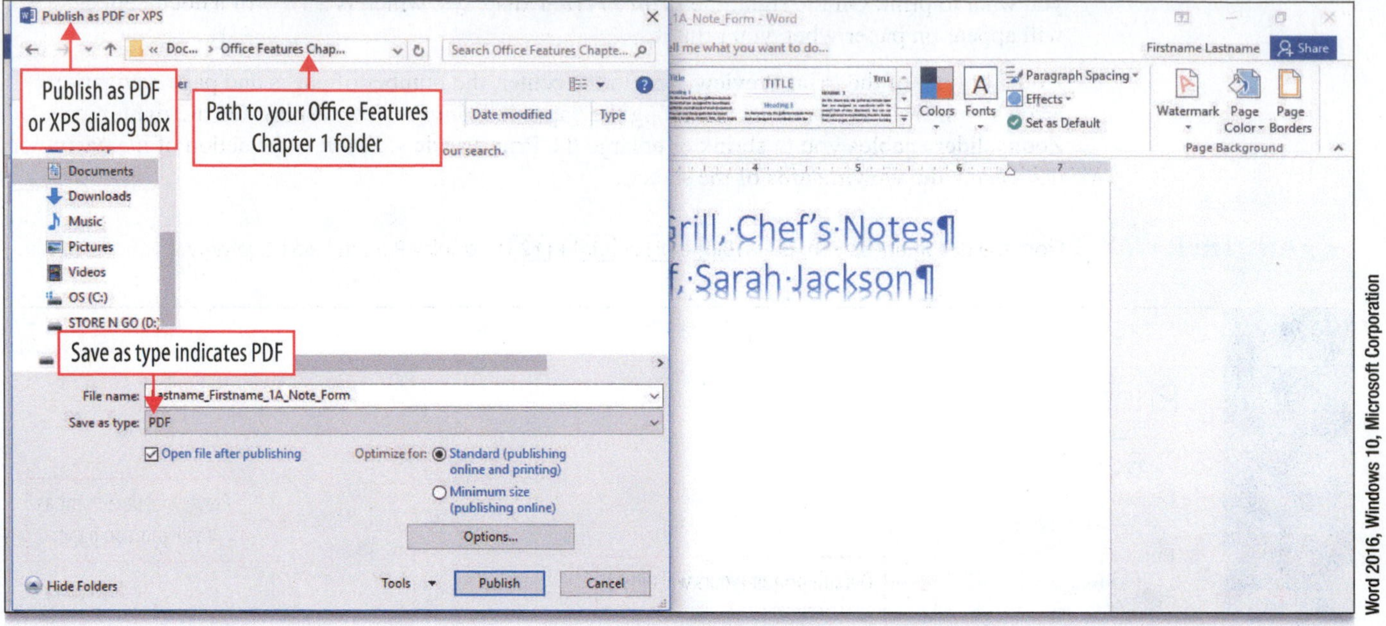

Word 2016, Windows 10, Microsoft Corporation

FIGURE 1.22

6 In the lower right corner of the dialog box, click **Publish**; if a program installed on your computer displays your PDF, in the upper right corner, click Close ☒. If your PDF displays in Microsoft Edge (on a Windows 10 computer), in the upper right corner click Close ☒. Notice that your document redisplays in Word.

In Backstage view, click Save As, navigate to the location of your Chapter folder, click the Save as type arrow, on the list click PDF, and then click Save.

7 Click the **File tab** to redisplay **Backstage** view. On the left, click **Close**, click **Save** to save the changes you have made, and then compare your screen with Figure 1.23.

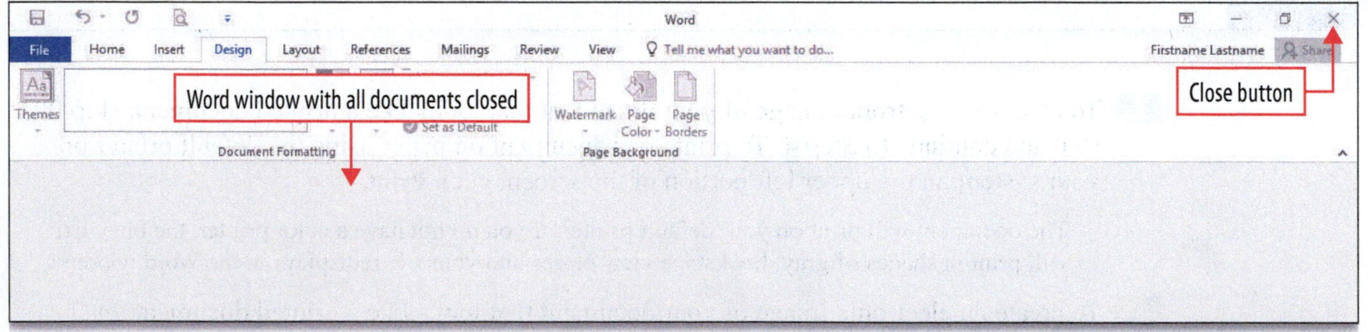

FIGURE 1.23

Word 2016, Windows 10, Microsoft Corporation

8 In the upper right corner of the Word window, click **Close** ☒. If directed by your instructor to do so, submit your paper printout, your electronic image of your document that looks like a printed document, or your original Word file.

END | You have completed Project 1A

PROJECT 1B

Memo

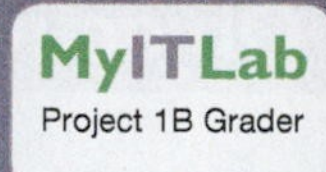

MyITLab
Project 1B Grader

PROJECT ACTIVITIES

In Activities 1.09 through 1.24, you will open, edit, and then compress a Word file. You will also use the Tell Me help feature and install an app for Office. Your completed document will look similar to Figure 1.24.

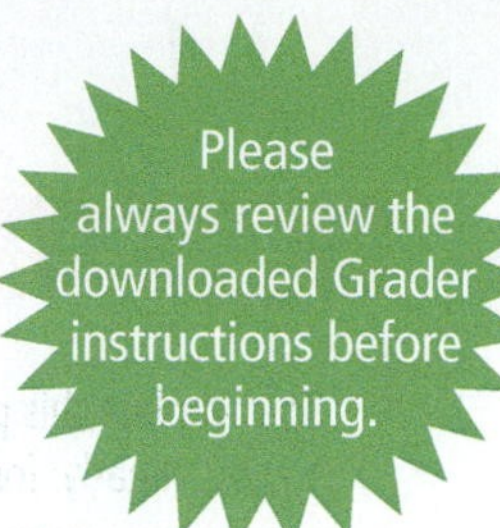

Please always review the downloaded Grader instructions before beginning.

PROJECT FILES

MyITLab
grader

If your instructor wants you to submit Project 1B in the MyITLab Grader system, log in to MyITLab, locate Grader Project1B, and then download the files for this project.

For Project 1B, you will need the following file:
of01B_Rehearsal_Dinner

You will save your file as:
Lastname_Firstname_1B_Rehearsal_Dinner

PROJECT RESULTS

GO!
…k Thru
…ect 1B

Skyline Metro Grill

TO: Sarah Jackson, Executive Chef
FROM: Laura Mabry Hernandez, General Manager
DATE: February 17, 2019
SUBJECT: Wedding Rehearsal Dinners

In the spring and summer months, wedding rehearsal dinners provide a new marketing opportunity for Skyline Metro Grill at all of our locations. A rehearsal dinner is an informal meal following a wedding rehearsal at which the bride and groom typically thank those that have helped them make their wedding a special event.

Our smaller private dining rooms with sweeping city views are an ideal location for a rehearsal dinner. At each of our locations, I have directed the Sales and Marketing Coordinator to partner with local wedding planners to promote Skyline Metro Grill as a relaxed yet sophisticated venue for rehearsal dinners. The typical rehearsal dinner includes the wedding party, the immediate family of the bride and groom, and out-of-town guests.

Please develop six menus—in varying price ranges—to present to local wedding planners so that they can easily promote Skyline Metro Grill to couples who are planning a rehearsal dinner. In addition to a traditional dinner, we should also include options for a buffet-style dinner and a family-style dinner.

This marketing effort will require extensive communication with our Sales and Marketing Coordinators and with local wedding planners. Let's meet to discuss the details and the marketing challenges, and to create a promotional piece that begins something like this:

Skyline Metro Grill for Your Rehearsal Dinner

Lastname_Firstname_1B_Rehearsal_Dinner

FIGURE 1.24 Project 1B Memo

Objective 6 Open an Existing File and Save It with a New Name

GO! Learn How
Video OF1.6

In any Office program, you can display the ***Open dialog box***, from which you can navigate to and then open an existing file that was created in that same program.

The Open dialog box, along with the Save and Save As dialog boxes, is a common dialog box. These dialog boxes, which are provided by the Windows programming interface, display in all Office programs in the same manner. So the Open, Save, and Save As dialog boxes will all look and perform the same regardless of the Office program in which you are working.

> **ALERT!** **To Complete This Project, You Will Need the Student Data Files That Accompany This Chapter**
>
> To complete this project, you will need the Student Data Files that accompany this chapter. Possibly your instructor has provided these to you already; for example, in the learning management system used by your college. Alternatively, to download the files, go to **www.pearsonhighered.com/go** On the left, narrow your choice by selecting the appropriate topic, and then on the right, locate and click the image of this book. In the window that displays, click Download Data Files, and then click the chapter name. Using the commands for your browser, store the zipped file in your storage location, and then use the Extract tools in File Explorer to extract the zipped folder. Instructions for extracting can be found in the Getting Started with Windows 10 chapter.

Activity 1.09 | Opening an Existing File and Saving It with a New Name

In this Activity, you will display the Open dialog box, open an existing Word document, and then save it in your storage location with a new name.

> **ALERT!** **To submit as an autograded project, log into MyITLab, download the files for this project, and begin with those files instead of the student data file.**

1. Be sure you have saved the folder **of01_student_data_files** for this chapter in your storage location; you can download this folder from **www.pearsonhighered.com/go** or it may have been provided to you by your instructor.

2. Start Word, and then on Word's opening screen, on the left, click **Open Other Documents**. Under **Open**, click **Browse**.

3. In the **Open** dialog box, on the left in the **navigation pane**, navigate to the location where you stored the **of01_student_data_files** folder for this chapter, and then in the **file list**, double-click the folder name **of01_student_data_files** to open the folder.

4. In the **file list**, double-click the file **of01B_Rehearsal_Dinner** to open it in Word. If **PROTECTED VIEW** displays at the top of your screen, in the center click **Enable Editing**.

   In Office 2016, a file will open in ***Protected View*** if the file appears to be from a potentially risky location, such as the Internet. Protected View is a security feature in Office 2016 that protects your computer from malicious files by opening them in a restricted environment until you enable them. ***Trusted Documents*** is another security feature that remembers which files you have already enabled.

   You might encounter these security features if you open a file from an email or download files from the Internet; for example, from your college's learning management system or from the Pearson website. So long as you trust the source of the file, click Enable Editing or Enable Content—depending on the type of file you receive—and then go ahead and work with the file.

5. With the document displayed in the Word window, be sure that **Show/Hide** is active; if necessary, on the Home tab, in the Paragraph group, click Show/Hide to activate it; on the View tab, be sure that Rulers are active. Compare your screen with Figure 1.25.

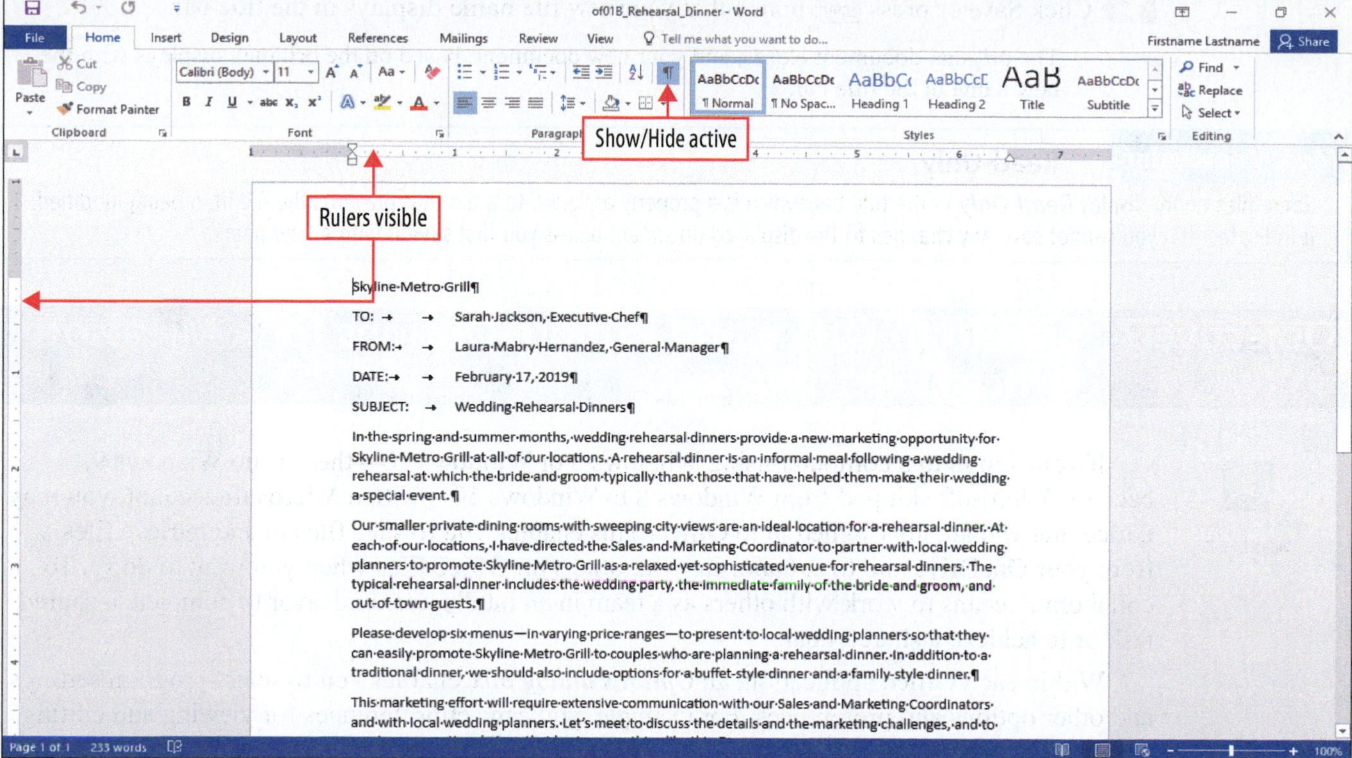

FIGURE 1.25

Word 2016, Windows 10, Microsoft Corporation

6 Click the **File tab** to display **Backstage** view, and then on the left, click **Save As**. Under **Save As**, click **Browse**.

7 In the **Save As** dialog box, use the **navigation pane** to navigate to and open the **Office Features Chapter 1** folder that you created to store your work from this chapter.

In Backstage view, on the right, you might also see your Office Features Chapter 1 folder listed, and if so, you can open it directly from there. The common dialog boxes Open, Save, and Save As remember your recently used locations and display them in Backstage view.

ANOTHER WAY From the Word window, press F12 to display the Save As dialog box.

8 Click in the **File name** box to select the existing text, and then, using your own name, type **Lastname_Firstname_1B_Rehearsal_Dinner** Compare your screen with Figure 1.26.

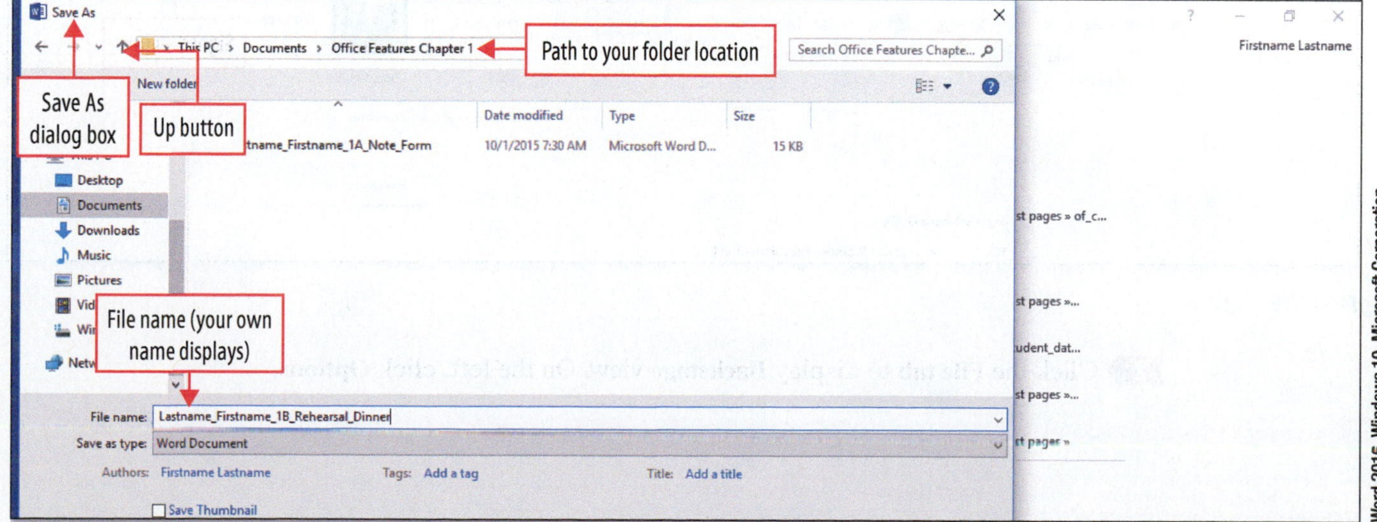

FIGURE 1.26

Word 2016, Windows 10, Microsoft Corporation

9 Click **Save** or press Enter; notice that your new file name displays in the title bar.

The original document closes, and your new document, based on the original, displays with the new name in the title bar.

More Knowledge **Read-Only**

Some files might display ***Read-Only*** in the title bar, which is a property assigned to a file that prevents the file from being modified; it indicates that you cannot save any changes to the displayed document unless you first save it with a new name.

Objective 7 Sign In to Office and Explore Options for a Microsoft Office Desktop App

GO! Learn How Video OF1.7

If you sign in to a computer using Windows 8 or Windows 10—there is no Windows 9, because Microsoft skipped from Windows 8 to Windows 10—with a Microsoft account, you may notice that you are also signed in to Office. This enables you to save files to and retrieve files from your OneDrive and to ***collaborate*** with others on Office files when you want to do so. To collaborate means to work with others as a team in an intellectual endeavor to complete a shared task or to achieve a shared goal.

Within each Office application, an ***Options dialog box*** enables you to select program settings and other options and preferences. For example, you can set preferences for viewing and editing files.

Activity 1.10 | Signing In to Office and Viewing Application Options

1 In the upper right corner of your screen, if you are signed in with a Microsoft account, click your name, and then compare your screen with Figure 1.27.

Here you can change your photo, go to About me to edit your profile, examine your Account settings, or switch accounts to sign in with a different Microsoft account.

ALERT! **Not Signed In to Office or Have Not Yet Created a Microsoft Account?**

In the upper right corner, click Sign in, and then enter your Microsoft account. If you have not created a free Microsoft account, click Sign in, type any email address that you currently use, click Next, and then click Sign up now. If you are working in a college lab, this process may vary.

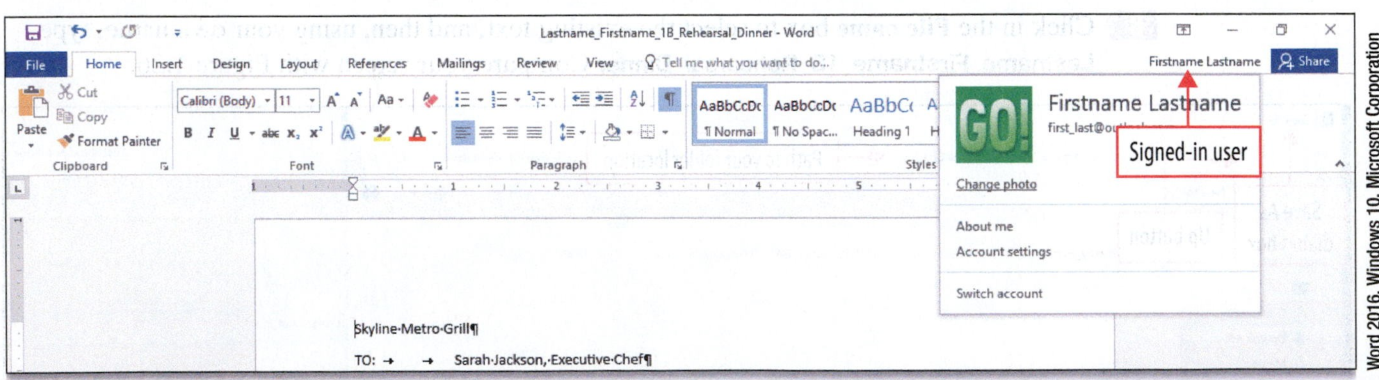

FIGURE 1.27

2 Click the **File tab** to display **Backstage** view. On the left, click **Options**.

3 In the **Word Options** dialog box, on the left, click **Display**, and then on the right, locate the information under **Always show these formatting marks on the screen**.

The Word Options dialog box—or the similar Options dialog box in any of the Office applications—controls nearly every aspect of the application. Next to many of the items, you will see small *i* icons, which when you point to them display a ScreenTip.

If you click each of the categories on the left side of the dialog box, you will see that the scope of each application is quite large and that you have a great deal of control over how the application behaves. For example, you can customize the tab names and group names in the ribbon.

If you are not sure what a setting or option does, in the upper right corner of the title bar, click the Help button—the question mark icon.

4 Under **Always show these formatting marks on the screen**, be sure the last check box, **Show all formatting marks**, is selected—select it if necessary. Compare your screen with Figure 1.28.

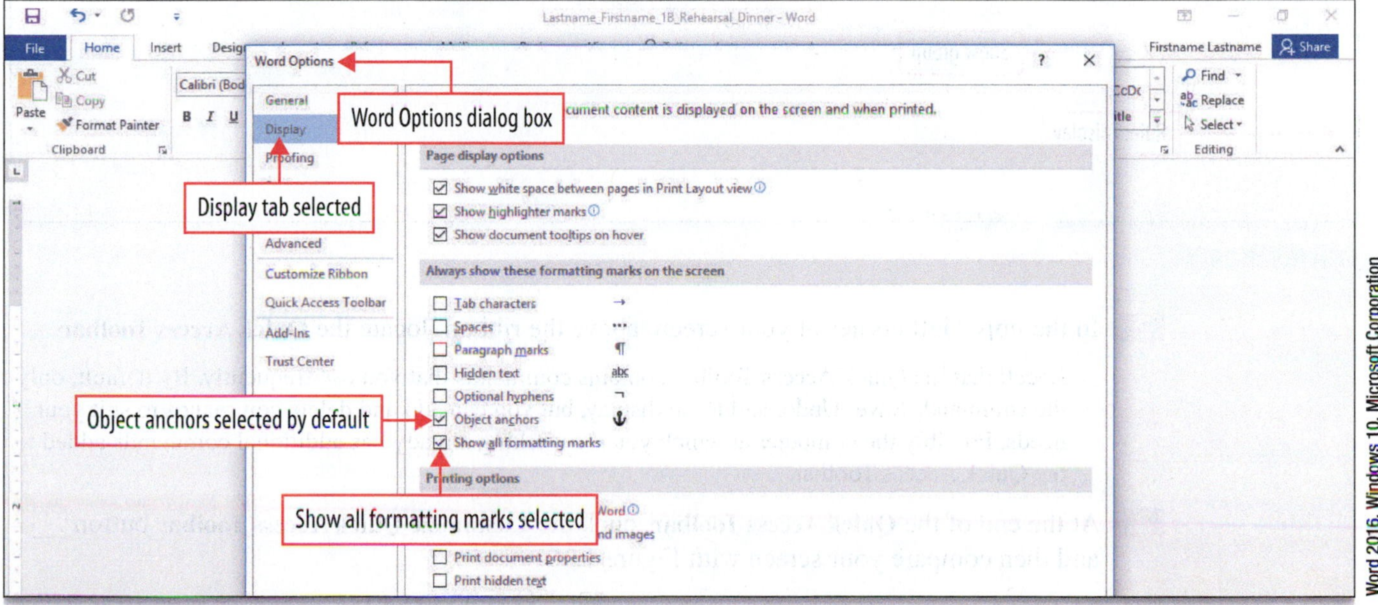

Word 2016, Windows 10, Microsoft Corporation

FIGURE 1.28

5 In the lower right corner of the dialog box, click **OK**.

Objective 8 Perform Commands from the Ribbon and Quick Access Toolbar

GO! Learn How Video OF1.8

The ribbon that displays across the top of the program window groups commands in the way that you would most logically use them. The ribbon in each Office program is slightly different, but all contain the same three elements: ***tabs***, ***groups***, and ***commands***.

Tabs display across the top of the ribbon, and each tab relates to a type of activity; for example, laying out a page. Groups are sets of related commands for specific tasks. Commands—instructions to computer programs—are arranged in groups and might display as a button, a menu, or a box in which you type information.

You can also minimize the ribbon so only the tab names display, which is useful when working on a smaller screen such as a tablet computer where you want to maximize your screen viewing area.

1.4.3

Activity 1.11 | Performing Commands from and Customizing the Quick Access Toolbar

1 Take a moment to examine the document on your screen. If necessary, on the ribbon, click the View tab, and then in the Show group, click to place a check mark in the Ruler check box. Compare your screen with Figure 1.29.

This document is a memo from the General Manager to the Executive Chef regarding a new restaurant promotion for wedding rehearsal dinners.

When working in Word, display the rulers so that you can see how margin settings affect your document and how text and objects align. Additionally, if you set a tab stop or an indent, its location is visible on the ruler.

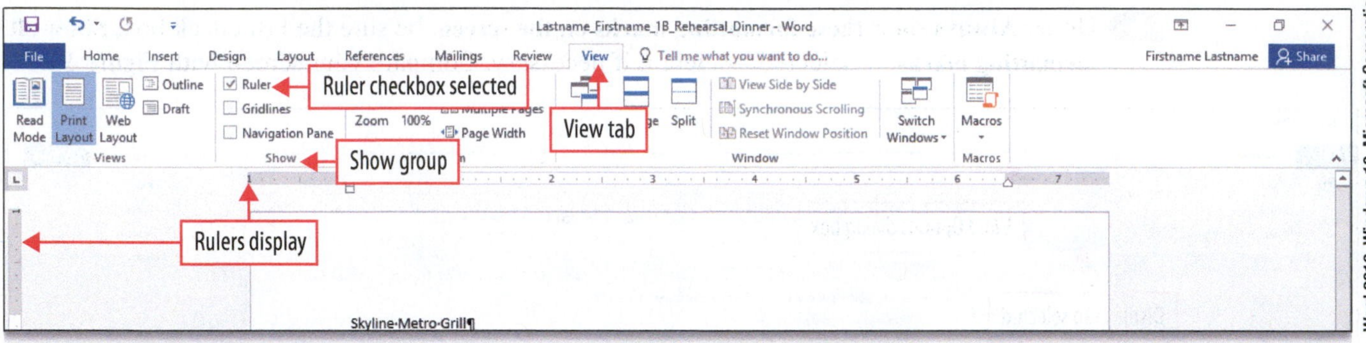

FIGURE 1.29

2 In the upper left corner of your screen, above the ribbon, locate the **Quick Access Toolbar**.

Recall that the Quick Access Toolbar contains commands that you use frequently. By default, only the commands Save, Undo, and Redo display, but you can add and delete commands to suit your needs. Possibly the computer at which you are working already has additional commands added to the Quick Access Toolbar.

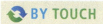

3 At the end of the **Quick Access Toolbar**, click the **Customize Quick Access Toolbar** button, and then compare your screen with Figure 1.30.

A list of commands that Office users commonly add to their Quick Access Toolbar displays, including New, Open, Email, Quick Print, and Print Preview and Print. Commands already on the Quick Access Toolbar display a check mark. Commands that you add to the Quick Access Toolbar are always just one click away.

Here you can also display the More Commands dialog box, from which you can select any command from any tab to add to the Quick Access Toolbar.

BY TOUCH Tap once on Quick Access Toolbar commands.

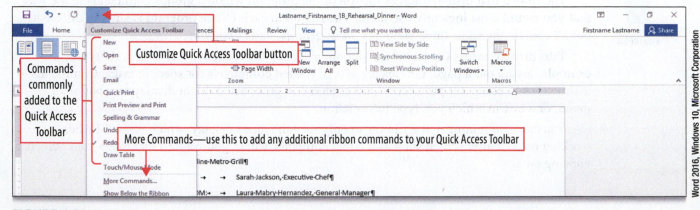

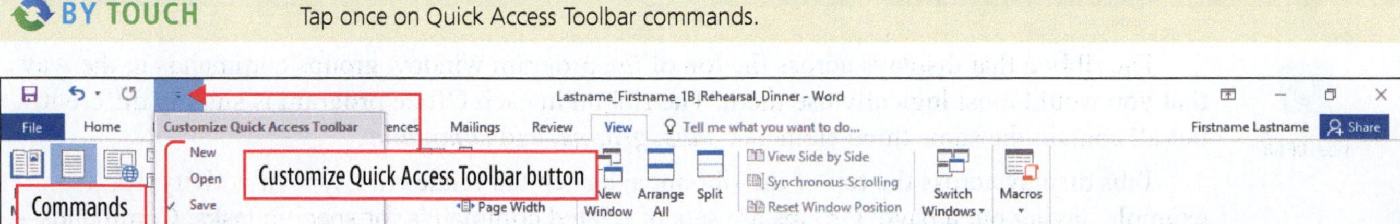

FIGURE 1.30

4 On the list, click **Print Preview and Print**, and then notice that the icon is added to the **Quick Access Toolbar**. Compare your screen with Figure 1.31.

The icon that represents the Print Preview command displays on the Quick Access Toolbar. Because this is a command that you will use frequently while building Office documents, you might decide to have this command remain on your Quick Access Toolbar.

Right-click any command on the ribbon, and then on the shortcut menu, click Add to Quick Access Toolbar.

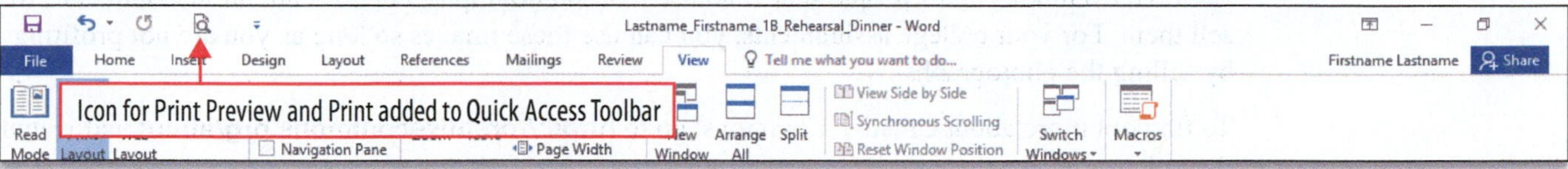

Word 2016, Windows 10, Microsoft Corporation

FIGURE 1.31

5.2.5

Activity 1.12 | Performing Commands from the Ribbon

1 In the first line of the document, if necessary, click to the left of the *S* in *Skyline* to position the insertion point there, and then press Enter one time to insert a blank paragraph. Press ↑ one time to position the insertion point in the new blank paragraph. Compare your screen with Figure 1.32.

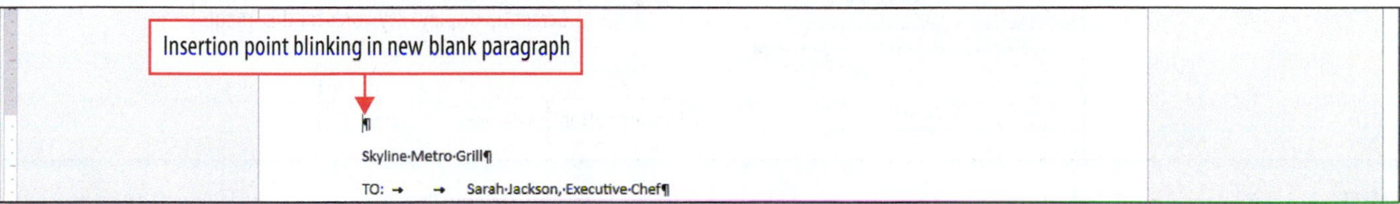

Word 2016, Windows 10, Microsoft Corporation

FIGURE 1.32

2 On the ribbon, click the **Insert tab**. In the **Illustrations group**, *point* to **Online Pictures** to display its ScreenTip.

Many buttons on the ribbon have this type of ***enhanced ScreenTip***, which displays useful descriptive information about the command.

3 Click **Online Pictures**, and then compare your screen with Figure 1.33.

In the Insert Pictures dialog box, you can search for online pictures using Bing Image Search, and, if you are signed in with your Microsoft account, you can also find images on your OneDrive by clicking Browse. At the bottom, you can click a logo to download pictures from your Facebook and other types of accounts if you have them.

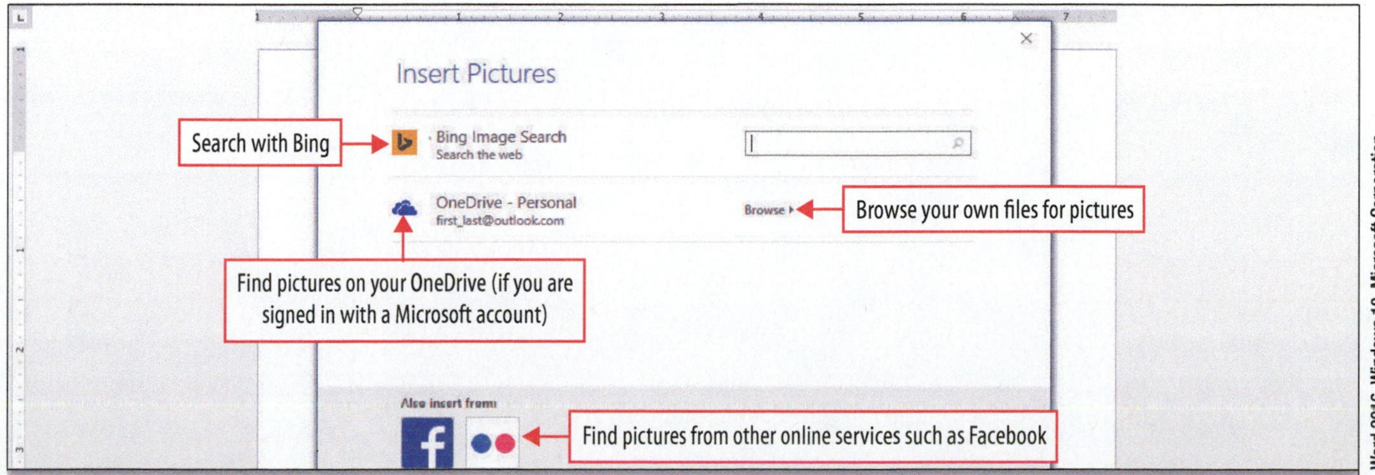

Word 2016, Windows 10, Microsoft Corporation

FIGURE 1.33

4 With the insertion point positioned in the **Bing Image Search** box, type **salad** and press Enter. Point to any of the results, and notice that keywords display. Compare your screen with Figure 1.34.

You can use various keywords to find images that are appropriate for your documents. The results shown indicate the images are licensed under ***Creative Commons***, which, according to **www.creativecommons.org** is "a nonprofit organization that enables the sharing and use of creativity and knowledge through free legal tools."

Creative Commons helps people share and use their photographs, but does not allow companies to sell them. For your college assignments, you can use these images so long as you are not profiting by selling the photographs.

To find out more about Creative Commons, go to **https://creativecommons.org/about** and watch the video.

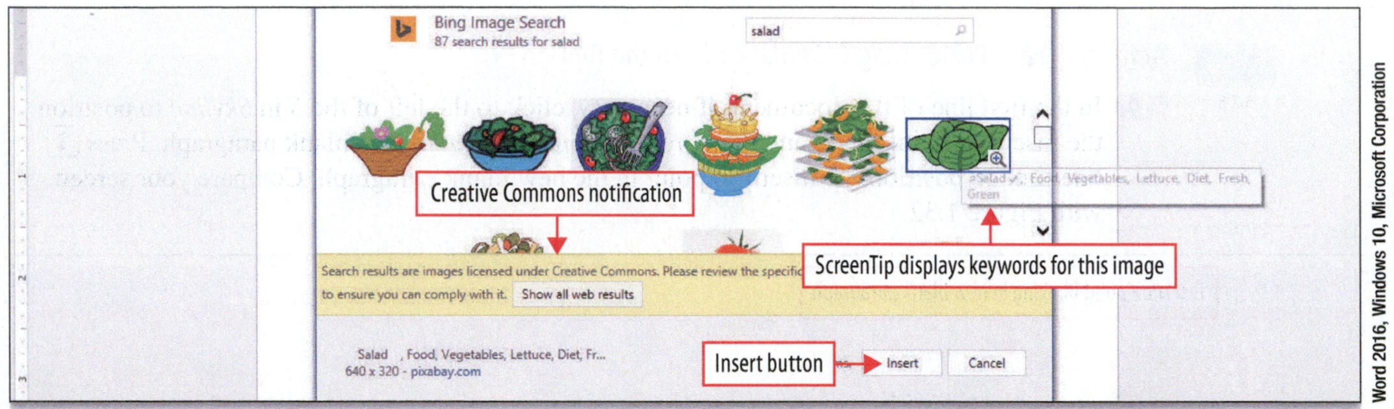

FIGURE 1.34

5 Locate an attractive picture of a salad on a plate or in a bowl that has a horizontal orientation—the picture is wider than it is tall—and then click that picture to select it. In the lower right corner, click **Insert**. In the upper right corner of the picture, point to the **Layout Options** button to display its ScreenTip, and then compare your screen with Figure 1.35.

Layout Options enable you to choose how the ***object***—in this instance an inserted picture—interacts with the surrounding text. An object is a picture or other graphic such as a chart or table that you can select and then move and resize.

When a picture is selected, the Picture Tools become available on the ribbon. Additionally, ***sizing handles***—small circles or squares that indicate an object is selected—surround the selected picture.

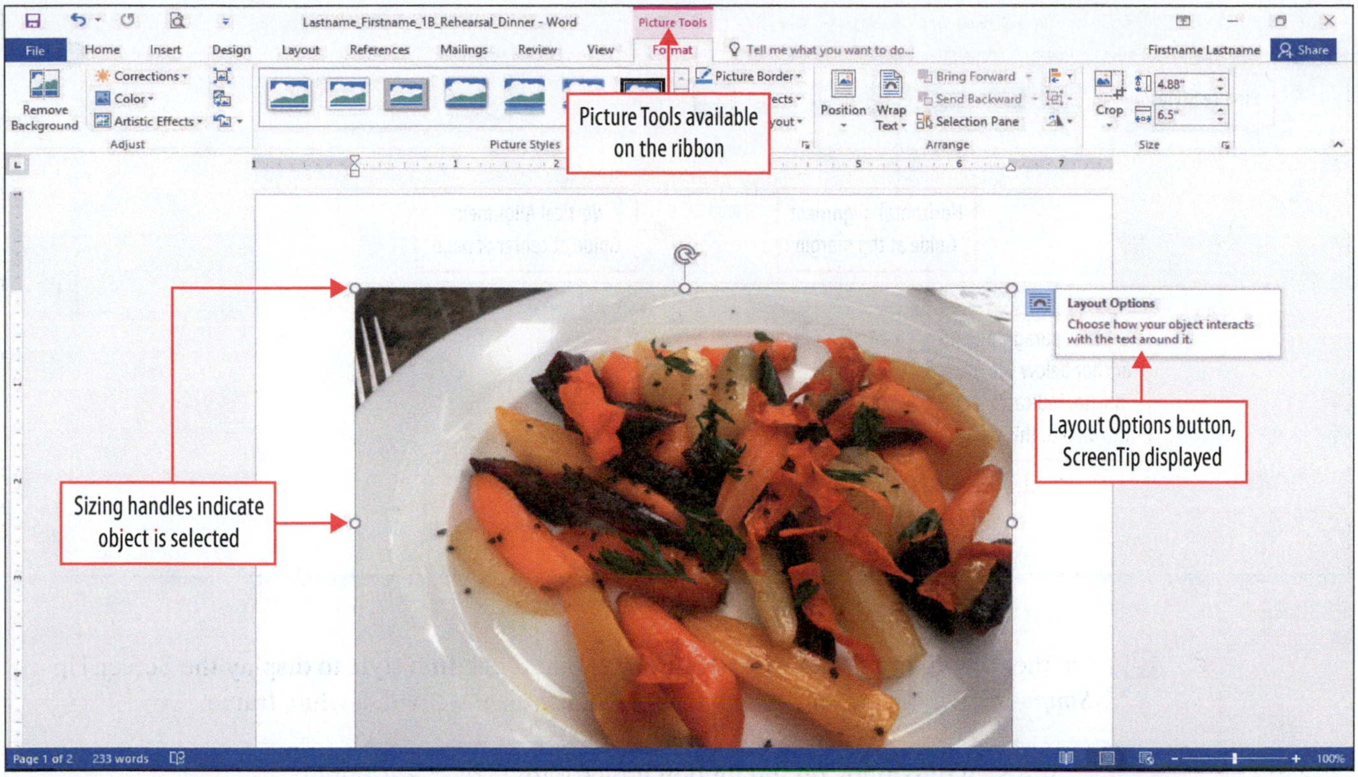

Word 2016, Windows 10, Microsoft Corporation

FIGURE 1.35

6 With the image selected, click **Layout Options**, and then under **With Text Wrapping**, in the second row, click the first layout—**Top and Bottom**.

7 On the ribbon, with the **Picture Tools Format tab** active, at the right, in the **Size group**, click in the **Shape Height** box to select the existing text. Type **2** and press Enter.

8 Point to the image to display the pointer, hold down the left mouse button to display a green line at the left margin, and then drag the image to the right and slightly upward until a green line displays in the center of the image and at the top of the image, as shown in Figure 1.36, and then release the left mouse button. If you are not satisfied with your result, on the Quick Access Toolbar, click Undo and begin again.

Alignment guides are green lines that display to help you align objects with margins or at the center of a page.

Inserted pictures anchor—attach to—the paragraph at the insertion point location—as indicated by an anchor symbol.

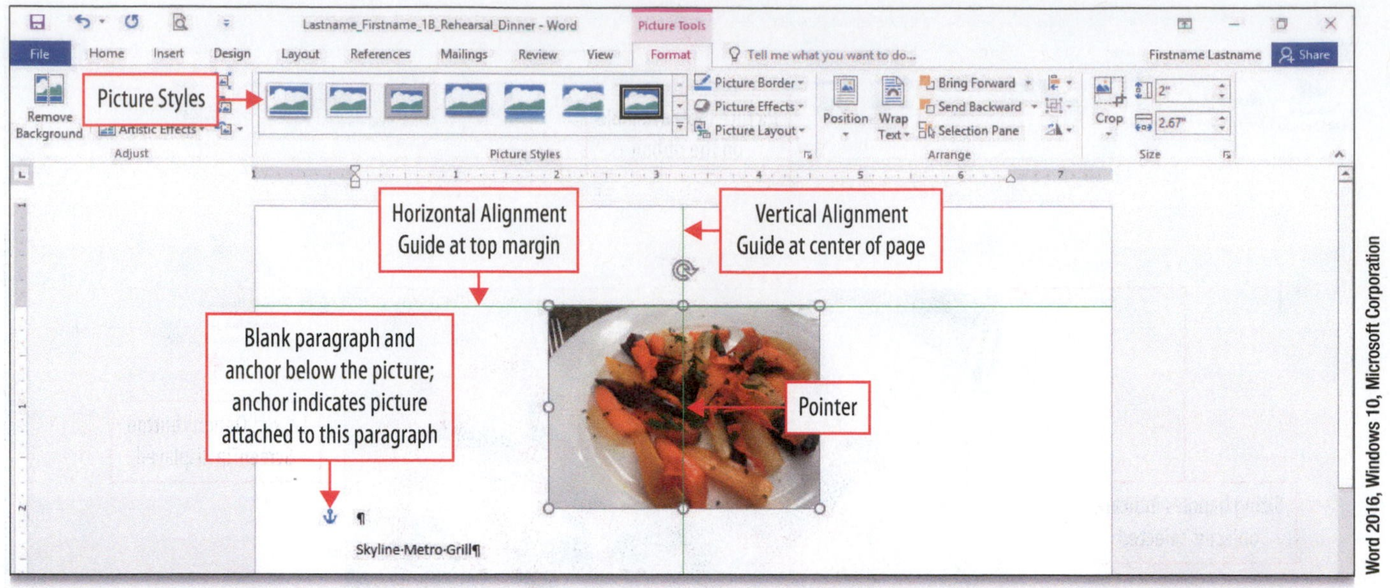

FIGURE 1.36

9 On the ribbon, in the **Picture Styles group**, point to the first style to display the ScreenTip *Simple Frame, White*, and notice that the image displays with a white frame.

NOTE The Size of Groups on the Ribbon Varies with Screen Resolution

Your monitor's screen resolution might be set higher than the resolution used to capture the figures shown here. At a higher resolution, the ribbon expands some groups to show more commands than are available with a single click, such as those in the Picture Styles group. Or, the group expands to add descriptive text to some buttons, such as those in the Arrange group. Regardless of your screen resolution, all Office commands are available to you. In higher resolutions, you will have a more robust view of the ribbon commands.

10 Watch the image as you point to the second picture style, and then to the third, and then to the fourth.

Recall that Live Preview shows the result of applying an editing or formatting change as you point to possible results—*before* you actually apply it.

11 In the **Picture Styles group**, click the second style—**Beveled Matte, White**—and then click anywhere outside of the image to deselect it. Notice that the Picture Tools no longer display on the ribbon. Compare your screen with Figure 1.37.

Contextual tabs on the ribbon display only when you need them.

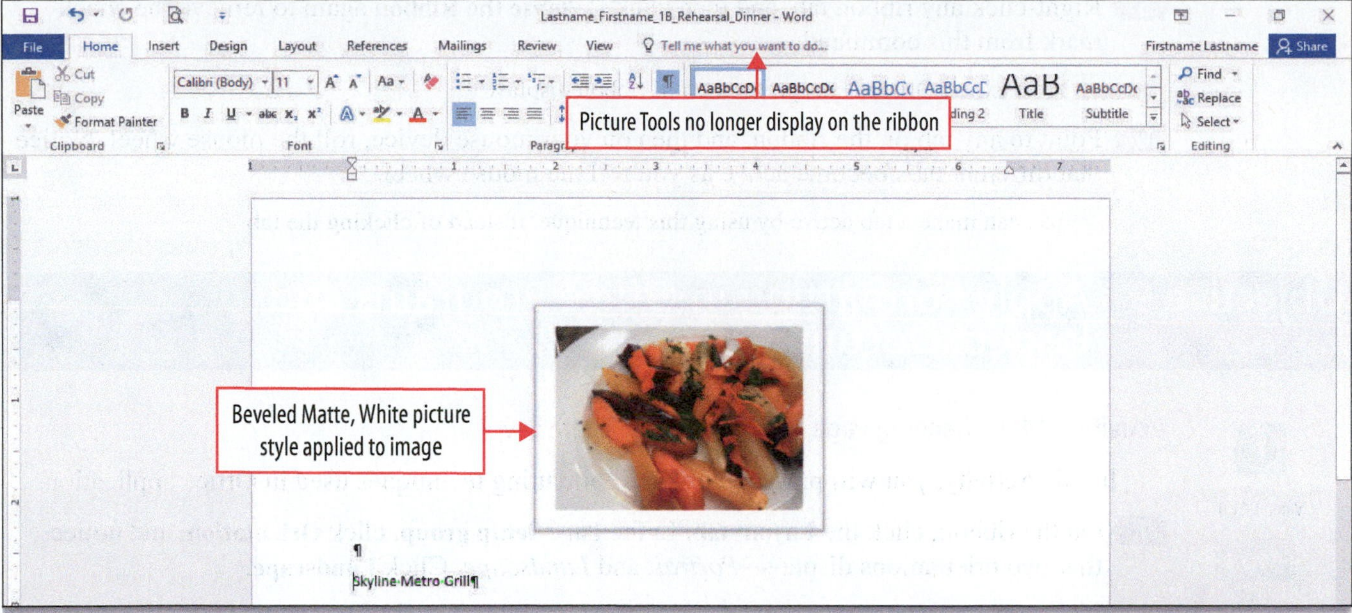

FIGURE 1.37

Word 2016, Windows 10, Microsoft Corporation

12 On the **Quick Access Toolbar**, click **Save** to save the changes you have made.

Activity 1.13 | Minimizing the Ribbon and Using the Keyboard to Control the Ribbon

Instead of a mouse, some individuals prefer to navigate the ribbon by using keys on the keyboard.

1 On your keyboard, press Alt, and then on the ribbon, notice that small labels display on the tabs. Press N to activate the commands on the **Insert tab**, and then compare your screen with Figure 1.38.

Each label represents a ***KeyTip***—an indication of the key that you can press to activate the command. For example, on the Insert tab, you can press F to open the Online Pictures dialog box.

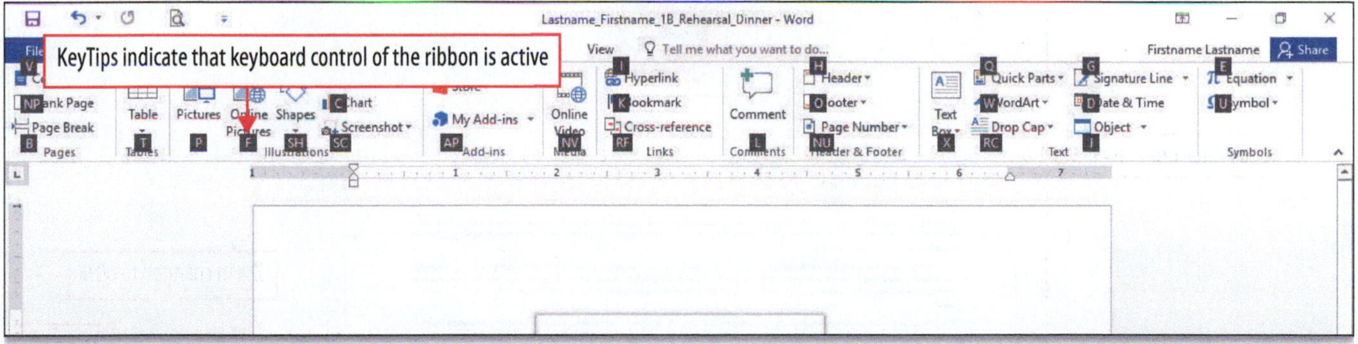

FIGURE 1.38

Word 2016, Windows 10, Microsoft Corporation

2 Press Esc to redisplay the KeyTips for the tabs. Then, press Alt or Esc again to turn off keyboard control of the ribbon.

3 Point to any tab on the ribbon and right-click to display a shortcut menu.

Here you can choose to display the Quick Access Toolbar below the ribbon or collapse the ribbon to maximize screen space. You can also customize the ribbon by adding, removing, renaming, or reordering tabs, groups, and commands, although this is not recommended until you become an expert Word user.

4 Click **Collapse the Ribbon**. Notice that only the ribbon tabs display. Click the **Home tab** to display the commands. Click anywhere in the document, and notice that the ribbon goes back to the collapsed display.

5 Right-click any ribbon tab, and then click **Collapse the Ribbon** again to remove the check mark from this command.

Most expert Office users prefer the full ribbon display.

6 Point to any tab on the ribbon, and then on your mouse device, roll the mouse wheel. Notice that different tabs become active as you roll the mouse wheel.

You can make a tab active by using this technique, instead of clicking the tab.

Objective 9 Apply Formatting in Office Programs and Inspect Documents

Activity 1.14 | Changing Page Orientation and Zoom Level

GO! Learn How Video OF1.9

MOS 1.4.2

In this Activity, you will practice common formatting techniques used in Office applications.

1 On the ribbon, click the **Layout tab**. In the **Page Setup group**, click **Orientation**, and notice that two orientations display—*Portrait* and *Landscape*. Click **Landscape**.

In ***portrait orientation***, the paper is taller than it is wide. In ***landscape orientation***, the paper is wider than it is tall.

2 In the lower right corner of the screen, locate the **Zoom slider**.

Recall that to zoom means to increase or decrease the viewing area. You can zoom in to look closely at a section of a document, and then zoom out to see an entire page on the screen. You can also zoom to view multiple pages on the screen.

3 Drag the **Zoom slider** to the left until you have zoomed to approximately *60%*. Compare your screen with Figure 1.39.

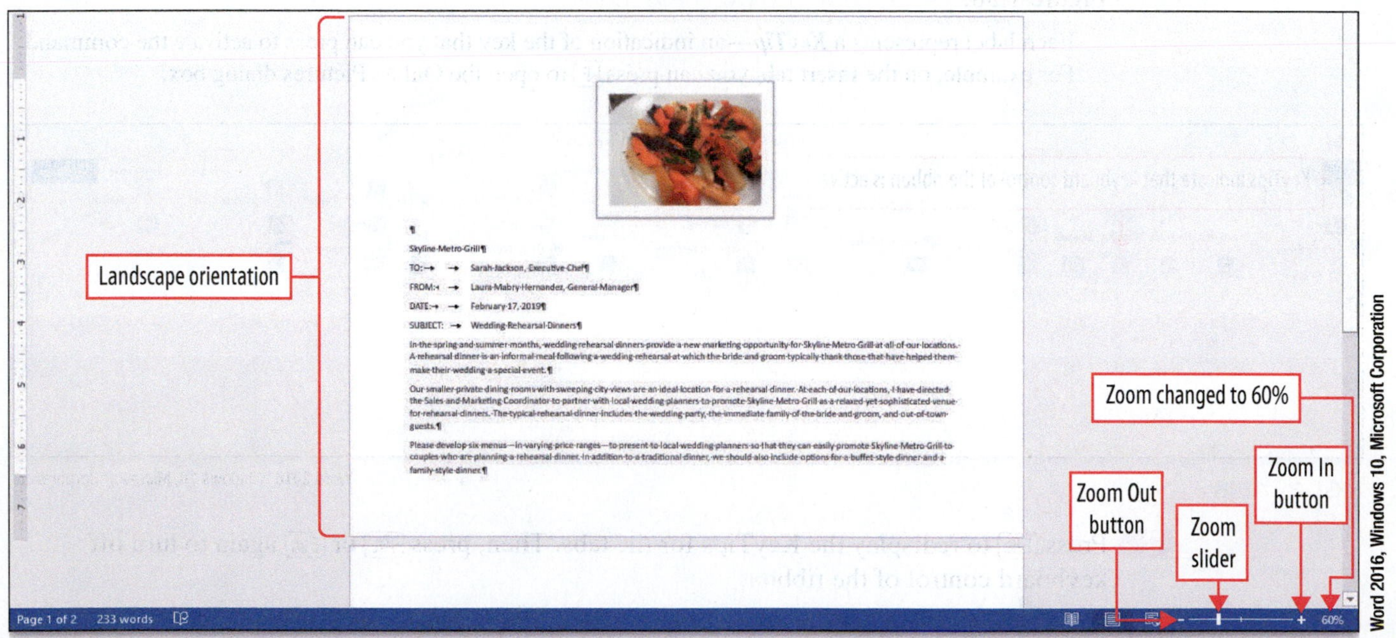

FIGURE 1.39

BY TOUCH Drag the Zoom slider with your finger.

4 Use the technique you just practiced to change the **Orientation** back to **Portrait**.

The default orientation in Word is Portrait, which is commonly used for business documents such as letters and memos.

5 In the lower right corner, click the **Zoom In** button as many times as necessary to return to the **100%** zoom setting.

Use the zoom feature to adjust the view of your document for editing and for your viewing comfort.

ANOTHER WAY You can also control Zoom from the ribbon. On the View tab, in the Zoom group, you can control the Zoom level and also zoom to view multiple pages.

6 On the **Quick Access Toolbar**, click **Save**.

More Knowledge **Zooming to Page Width**

Some Office users prefer ***Page Width***, which zooms the document so that the width of the page matches the width of the window. Find this command on the View tab, in the Zoom group.

Activity 1.15 | Formatting Text by Using Fonts, Alignment, Font Colors, and Font Styles

1 If necessary, on the right edge of your screen, drag the vertical scroll box to the top of the scroll bar. To the left of *Skyline Metro Grill*, point in the margin area to display the pointer and click one time to select the entire paragraph. Compare your screen with Figure 1.40.

Use this technique to select complete paragraphs from the margin area—drag downward to select multiple-line paragraphs—which is faster and more efficient than dragging through text.

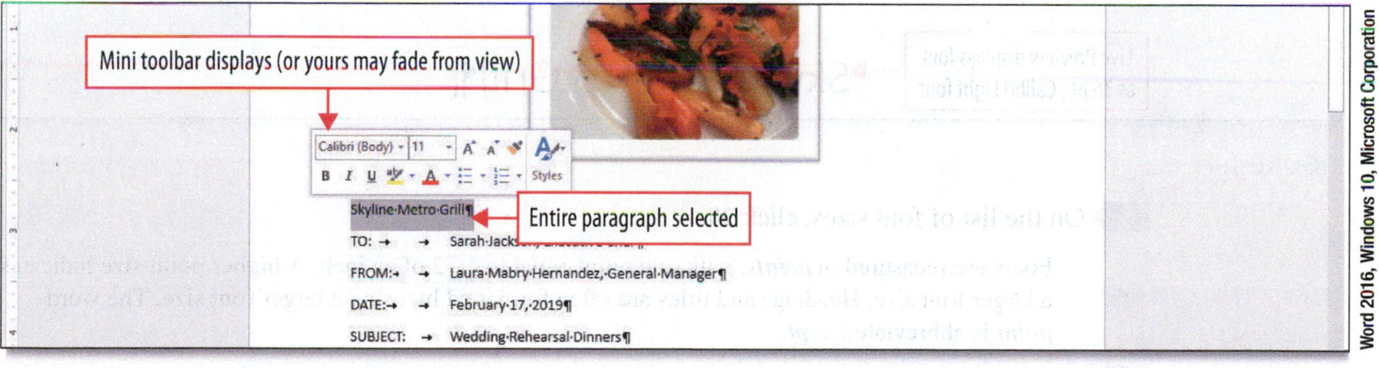

FIGURE 1.40

2 On the ribbon, click the **Home tab**, and then in the **Paragraph group**, click **Center** to center the paragraph.

3 On the **Home tab**, in the **Font group**, click the **Font button arrow** Calibri (Body). On the alphabetical list of font names, scroll down and then locate and *point to* **Cambria**.

A ***font*** is a set of characters with the same design and shape. The default font in a Word document is Calibri, which is a ***sans serif font***—a font design with no lines or extensions on the ends of characters.

The Cambria font is a ***serif font***—a font design that includes small line extensions on the ends of the letters to guide the eye in reading from left to right.

The list of fonts displays as a gallery showing potential results. For example, in the Font gallery, you can point to see the actual design and format of each font as it would look if applied to text.

4 Point to several other fonts and observe the effect on the selected text. Then, scroll back to the top of the **Font** gallery. Under **Theme Fonts**, click **Calibri Light**.

A ***theme*** is a predesigned combination of colors, fonts, line, and fill effects that look good together and is applied to an entire document by a single selection. A theme combines two sets of fonts—one for text and one for headings. In the default Office theme, Calibri Light is the suggested font for headings.

5 With the paragraph *Skyline Metro Grill* still selected, on the **Home tab**, in the **Font group**, click the **Font Size button arrow** [11], point to **36**, and then notice how Live Preview displays the text in the font size to which you are pointing. Compare your screen with Figure 1.41.

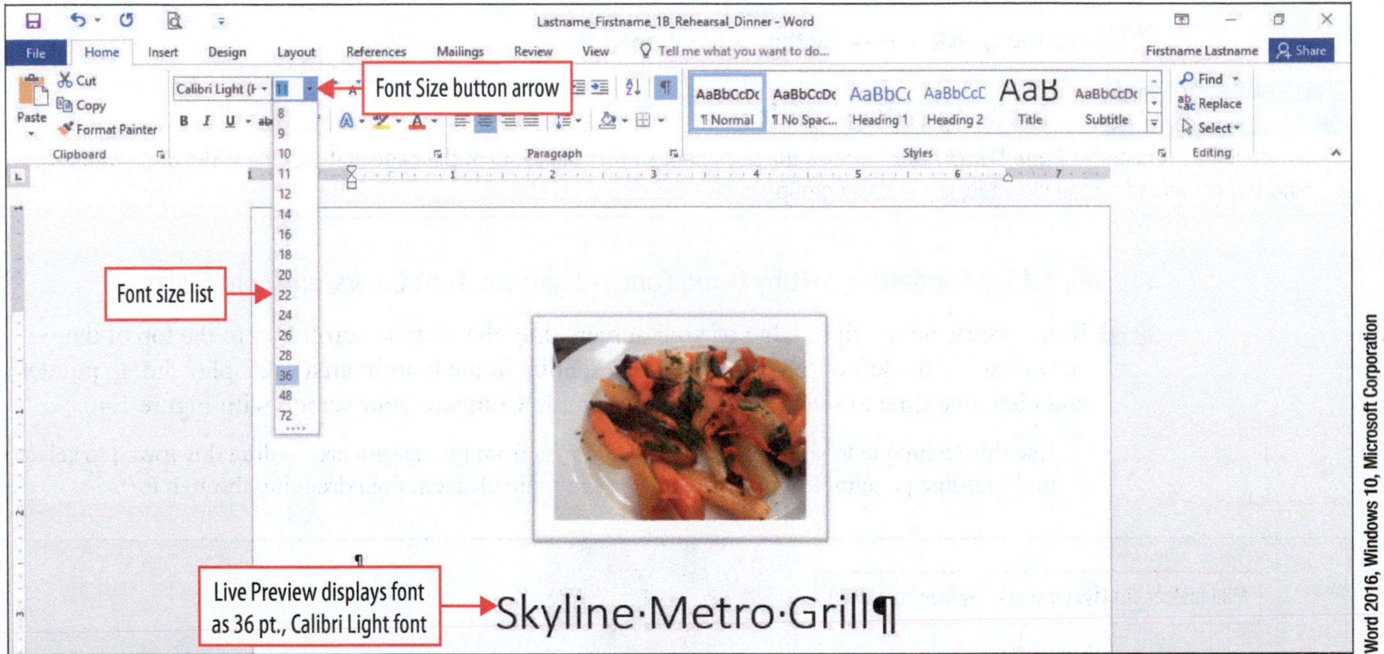

FIGURE 1.41

6 On the list of font sizes, click **20**.

Fonts are measured in ***points***, with one point equal to 1/72 of an inch. A higher point size indicates a larger font size. Headings and titles are often formatted by using a larger font size. The word *point* is abbreviated as ***pt***.

7 With *Skyline Metro Grill* still selected, on the **Home tab**, in the **Font group**, click the **Font Color button arrow** [A]. Under **Theme Colors**, in the last column, click the last color—**Green, Accent 6, Darker 50%**. Click anywhere to deselect the text.

8 To the left of *TO:*, point in the left margin area to display the [pointer] pointer, hold down the left mouse button, drag down to select the four memo headings, and then release your mouse button. Compare your screen with Figure 1.42.

Use this technique to select complete paragraphs from the margin area—drag downward to select multiple paragraphs—which is faster and more efficient than dragging through text.

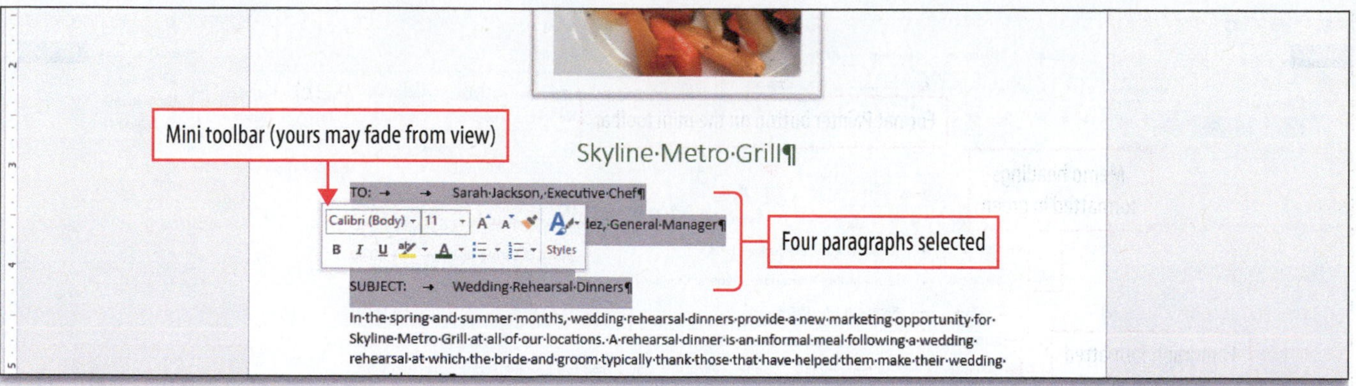

FIGURE 1.42

Word 2016, Windows 10, Microsoft Corporation

9 With the four paragraphs selected, on the mini toolbar, click the **Font Color** button, and notice that the text color of the four paragraphs changes.

The font color button retains its most recently used color—Green, Accent 6, Darker 50%. As you progress in your study of Microsoft Office, you will use other commands that behave in this manner; that is, they retain their most recently used format. This is commonly referred to as ***MRU***—most recently used.

Recall that the mini toolbar places commands that are commonly used for the selected text or object close by so that you reduce the distance that you must move your mouse to access a command. If you are using a touch screen device, most commands that you need are close and easy to touch.

10 On the right edge of your screen, if necessary drag the vertical scroll box down slightly to position more of the text on the screen. Click anywhere in the paragraph that begins *In the spring*, and then ***triple-click***—click the left mouse button three times—to select the entire paragraph. If the entire paragraph is not selected, click in the paragraph and begin again.

11 With the entire paragraph selected, on the mini toolbar, locate and then click the **Font Color button arrow**, and then under **Theme Colors**, in the sixth column, click the last color—**Orange, Accent 2, Darker 50%**.

12 In the memo headings, select the guide word **TO:** and then on the mini toolbar, click **Bold** and **Italic**.

Font styles include bold, italic, and underline. Font styles emphasize text and are a visual cue to draw the reader's eye to important text.

13 On the mini toolbar, click **Italic** again to turn off the Italic formatting.

A ***toggle button*** is a button that can be turned on by clicking it once, and then turned off by clicking it again.

2.2.2

Activity 1.16 | Using Format Painter

Use the Format Painter to copy the formatting of specific text or of a paragraph and then apply it in other locations in your document.

1 With TO: still selected, on the mini toolbar, click **Format Painter**. Then, move your mouse under the word *Sarah*, and notice the mouse pointer. Compare your screen with Figure 1.43.

The pointer takes the shape of a paintbrush, and contains the formatting information from the paragraph where the insertion point is positioned. Information about the Format Painter and how to turn it off displays in the status bar.

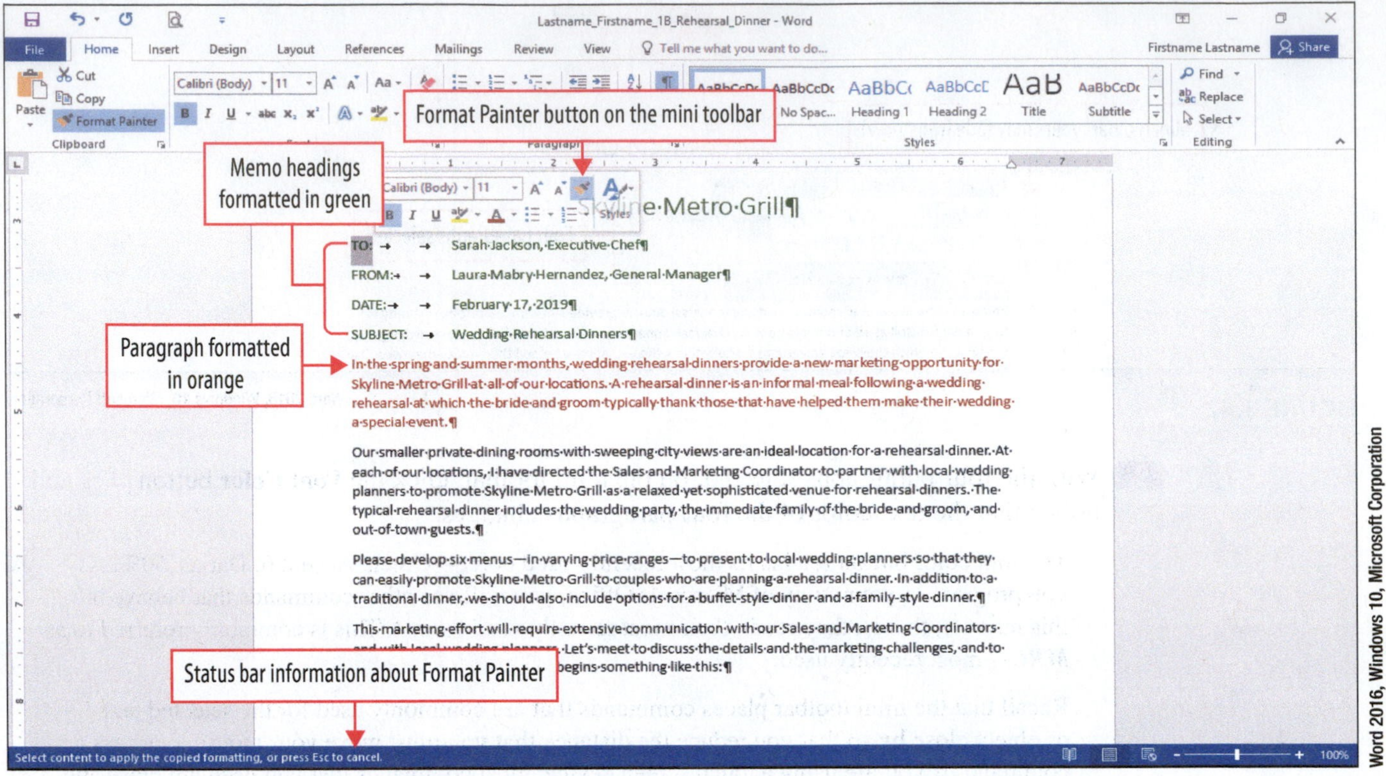

FIGURE 1.43

2 With the pointer, drag to select the guide word **FROM:** and notice that Bold formatting is applied. Then, point to the selected text *FROM:* and on the mini toolbar, *double-click* **Format Painter**.

3 Select the guide word **DATE:** to copy the Bold formatting, and notice that the pointer retains the shape.

When you *double-click* the Format Painter button, the Format Painter feature remains active until you either click the Format Painter button again, or press Esc to cancel it—as indicated on the status bar.

4 With **Format Painter** still active, select the guide word **SUBJECT:**, and then on the ribbon, on the **Home tab**, in the **Clipboard group**, notice that **Format Painter** is selected, indicating that it is active. Compare your screen with Figure 1.44.

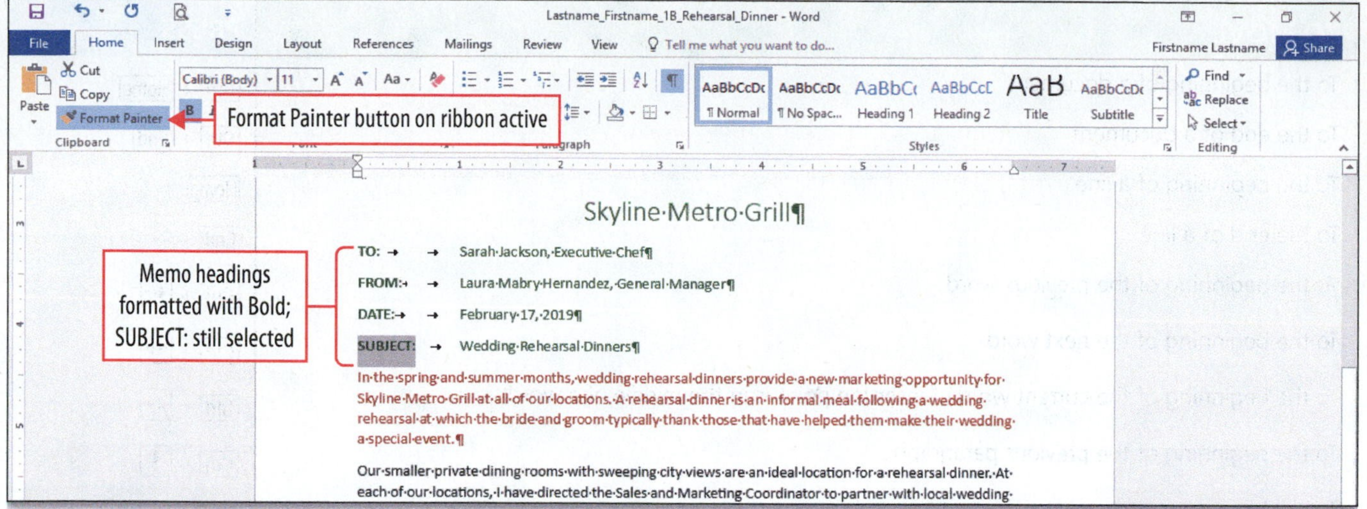

FIGURE 1.44

Word 2016, Windows 10, Microsoft Corporation

5 On the ribbon, click **Format Painter** to turn the command off.

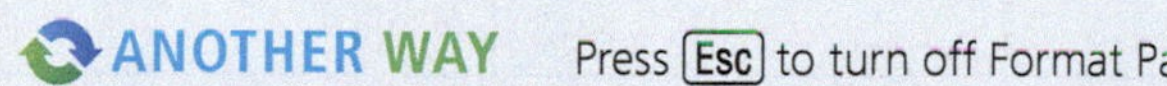

ANOTHER WAY Press Esc to turn off Format Painter.

6 In the paragraph that begins *In the spring*, triple-click again to select the entire paragraph. On the mini toolbar, click **Bold** and **Italic**. Click anywhere to deselect.

7 On the **Quick Access Toolbar**, click **Save** to save the changes you have made to your document.

MOS 2.1.2

Activity 1.17 | Using Keyboard Shortcuts and Using the Clipboard to Copy, Cut, and Paste

The ***Clipboard*** is a temporary storage area that holds text or graphics that you select and then cut or copy. When you ***copy*** text or graphics, a copy is placed on the Clipboard and the original text or graphic remains in place. When you ***cut*** text or graphics, a copy is placed on the Clipboard, and the original text or graphic is removed—cut—from the document.

After copying or cutting, the contents of the Clipboard are available for you to ***paste***—insert—in a new location in the current document, or into another Office file.

1 On your keyboard, hold down Ctrl and press Home to move to the beginning of your document, and then take a moment to study the table in Figure 1.45, which describes similar keyboard shortcuts with which you can navigate quickly in a document.

TO MOVE	PRESS
To the beginning of a document	Ctrl + Home
To the end of a document	Ctrl + End
To the beginning of a line	Home
To the end of a line	End
To the beginning of the previous word	Ctrl + ←
To the beginning of the next word	Ctrl + →
To the beginning of the current word (if insertion point is in the middle of a word)	Ctrl + ←
To the beginning of the previous paragraph	Ctrl + ↑
To the beginning of the next paragraph	Ctrl + ↓
To the beginning of the current paragraph (if insertion point is in the middle of a paragraph)	Ctrl + ↑
Up one screen	PgUp
Down one screen	PgDn

Word 2016, Windows 10, Microsoft Corporation

FIGURE 1.45

2 To the left of *Skyline Metro Grill*, point in the left margin area to display the pointer, and then click one time to select the entire paragraph. On the **Home tab**, in the **Clipboard group**, click **Copy**.

Because anything that you select and then copy—or cut—is placed on the Clipboard, the Copy command and the Cut command display in the Clipboard group of commands on the ribbon. There is no visible indication that your copied selection has been placed on the Clipboard.

ANOTHER WAY Right-click the selection, and then click Copy on the shortcut menu; or, use the keyboard shortcut Ctrl + C.

3 On the **Home tab**, in the **Clipboard group**, to the right of the group name *Clipboard*, click the **Dialog Box Launcher** button, and then compare your screen with Figure 1.46.

The Clipboard pane displays with your copied text. In any ribbon group, the ***Dialog Box Launcher*** displays either a dialog box or a pane related to the group of commands. It is not necessary to display the Clipboard in this manner, although sometimes it is useful to do so.

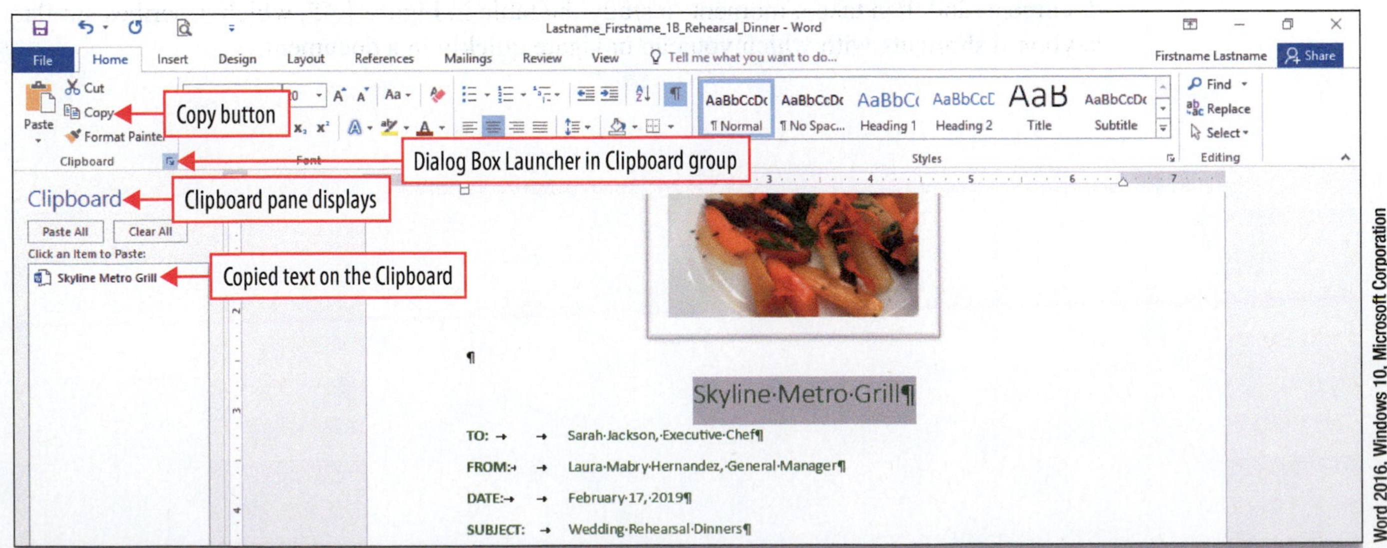

Word 2016, Windows 10, Microsoft Corporation

FIGURE 1.46

4 In the upper right corner of the **Clipboard** pane, click **Close** [X].

5 Press Ctrl + End to move to the end of your document. Press Enter one time to create a new blank paragraph. On the **Home tab**, in the **Clipboard group**, point to **Paste**, and then click the *upper* portion of this split button.

The Paste command pastes the most recently copied item on the Clipboard at the insertion point location. If you click the lower portion of the Paste button, a gallery of Paste Options displays. A ***split button*** is divided into two parts; clicking the main part of the button performs a command, and clicking the arrow displays a list or gallery with choices.

ANOTHER WAY Right-click, on the shortcut menu under Paste Options, click the desired option button; or, press Ctrl + V.

6 Below the pasted text, click **Paste Options** as shown in Figure 1.47.

Here you can view and apply various formatting options for pasting your copied or cut text. Typically you will click Paste on the ribbon and paste the item in its original format. If you want some other format for the pasted item, you can choose another format from the ***Paste Options gallery***.

The Paste Options gallery provides a Live Preview of the various options for changing the format of the pasted item with a single click. The Paste Options gallery is available in three places: on the ribbon by clicking the lower portion of the Paste button—the Paste button arrow; from the Paste Options button that displays below the pasted item following the paste operation; or on the shortcut menu if you right-click the pasted item.

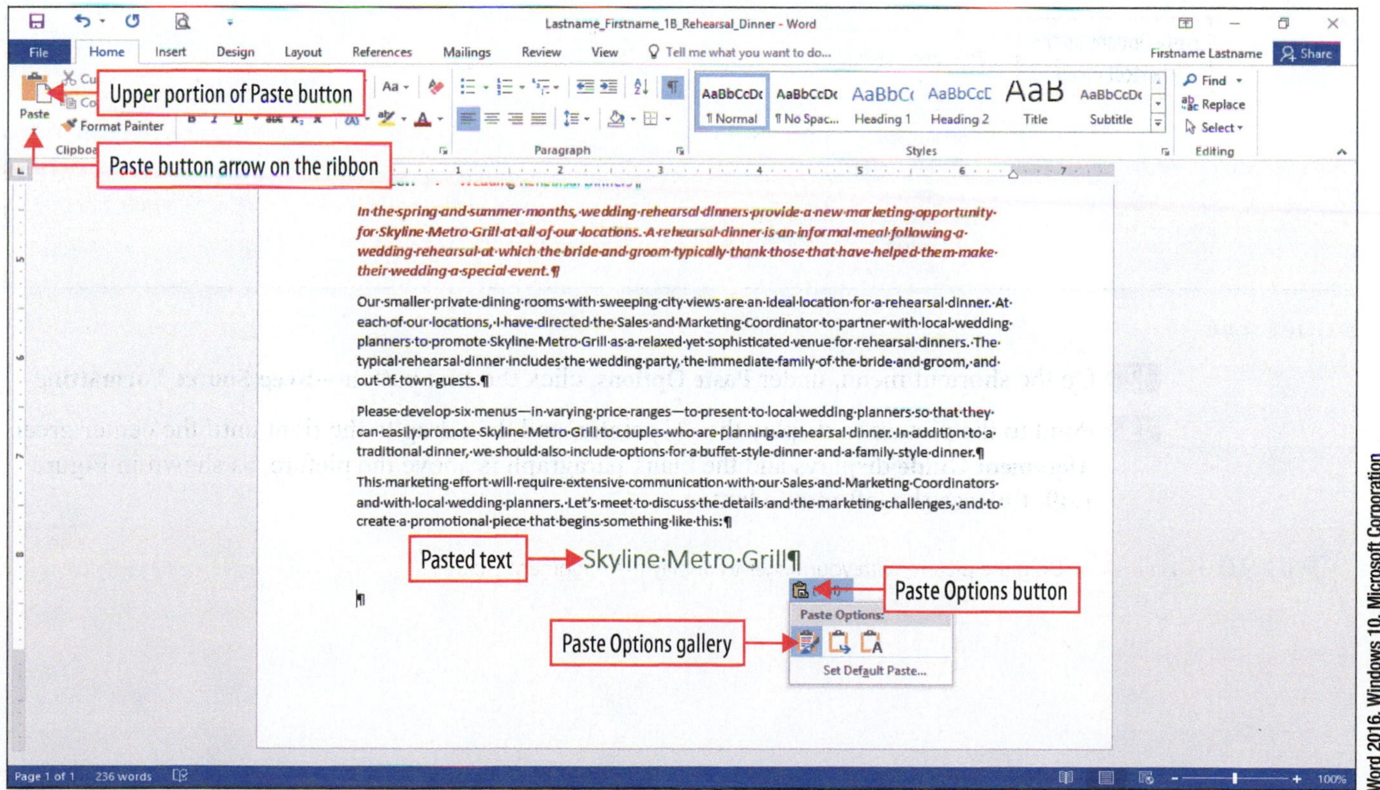

FIGURE 1.47

7 In the **Paste Options** gallery, *point* to each option to see the Live Preview of the format that would be applied if you clicked the button.

The contents of the Paste Options gallery are contextual; that is, they change based on what you copied and where you are pasting.

8 Press Esc to close the gallery; the button will remain displayed until you take some other screen action.

9 On your keyboard, press Ctrl + Home to move to the top of the document, and then click the **salad image** one time to select it. While pointing to the selected image, right-click, and then on the shortcut menu, click **Cut**.

Recall that the Cut command cuts—removes—the selection from the document and places it on the Clipboard.

ANOTHER WAY On the Home tab, in the Clipboard group, click the Cut button; or use the keyboard shortcut Ctrl + X.

10 Press Del one time to remove the blank paragraph from the top of the document, and then press Ctrl + End to move to the end of the document.

11 With the insertion point blinking in the blank paragraph at the end of the document, right-click, and notice that the **Paste Options** gallery displays on the shortcut menu. Compare your screen with Figure 1.48.

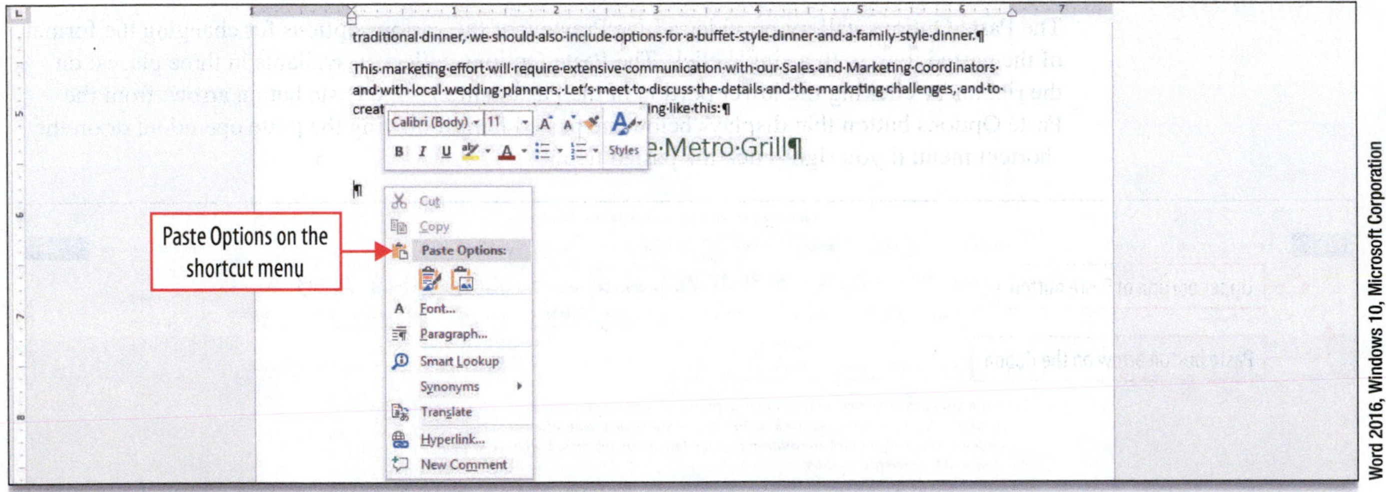

FIGURE 1.48

12 On the shortcut menu, under **Paste Options**, click the first button—**Keep Source Formatting**.

13 Point to the picture to display the pointer, and then drag to the right until the center green **Alignment Guide** displays and the blank paragraph is above the picture, as shown in Figure 1.49. Release the left mouse button.

BY TOUCH Drag the picture with your finger to display the Alignment Guide.

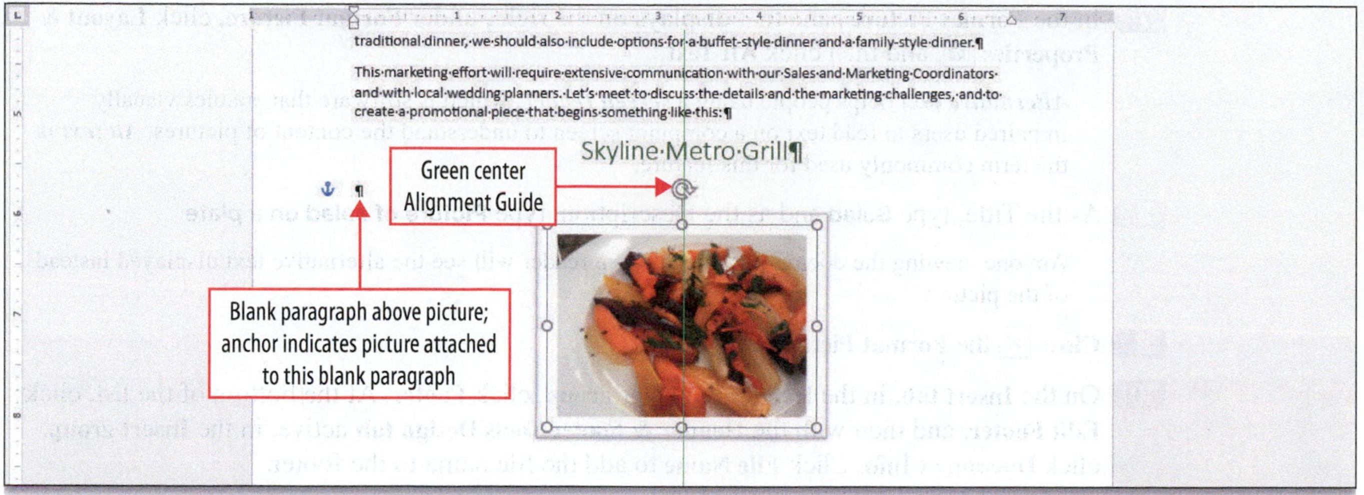

FIGURE 1.49

Word 2016, Windows 10, Microsoft Corporation

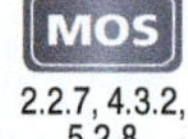
2.2.7, 4.3.2, 5.2.8

Activity 1.18 | Changing Text to WordArt and Adding Alternative Text for Accessibility

1 Above the picture, click to position the insertion point at the end of the word *Grill*, press Spacebar one time, and then type **for Your Rehearsal Dinner**

2 Select the text *Skyline Metro Grill for Your Rehearsal Dinner*, and then on the **Insert tab**, in the **Text group**, click **Insert WordArt** .

WordArt is an Office feature available in Word, Excel, and PowerPoint that enables you to change normal text into decorative stylized text.

3 In the displayed gallery, use the ScreenTips to locate and then click **Fill - Gold, Accent 4, Soft Bevel.**

4 With the WordArt surrounded with a solid line, on the **Home tab**, in the **Font group**, change the font size to **16**.

5 Point to the solid line surrounding the WordArt to display the pointer, and then drag the WordArt slightly to the right until the green center alignment guides display, as shown in Figure 1.50, and then release the mouse button to center the WordArt above your picture. Click outside of the WordArt to deselect.

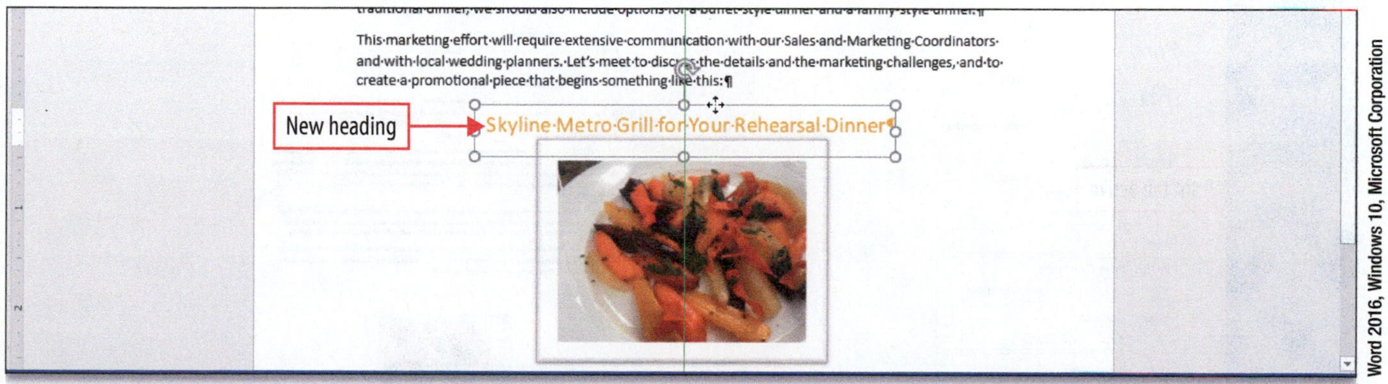

Word 2016, Windows 10, Microsoft Corporation

FIGURE 1.50

6 Point to the picture of the salad and right-click. On the shortcut menu, click **Format Picture**.

7 In the **Format Picture** pane that displays on the right, under **Format Picture**, click **Layout & Properties**, and then click **Alt Text**.

Alternative text helps people using a ***screen reader***, which is software that enables visually impaired users to read text on a computer screen to understand the content of pictures. ***Alt text*** is the term commonly used for this feature.

8 As the Title, type **Salad** and as the Description, type **Picture of salad on a plate**

Anyone viewing the document with a screen reader will see the alternative text displayed instead of the picture.

9 **Close** the **Format Picture** pane.

10 On the **Insert tab**, in the **Header & Footer group**, click **Footer**. At the bottom of the list, click **Edit Footer**, and then with the **Header & Footer Tools Design tab** active, in the **Insert group**, click **Document Info**. Click **File Name** to add the file name to the footer.

11 On the right end of the ribbon, click **Close Header and Footer**.

12 On the **Quick Access Toolbar**, point to the **Print Preview and Print icon** you placed there, right-click, and then click **Remove from Quick Access Toolbar**.

If you are working on your own computer and you want to do so, you can leave the icon on the toolbar; in a college lab, you should return the software to its original settings.

13 Click **Save** and then click the **File tab** to display **Backstage** view. With the **Info tab** active, in the lower right corner, click **Show All Properties**. As **Tags**, type **weddings, rehearsal dinners, marketing**

14 As the **Subject**, type your course name and number—for example, *CIS 10, #5543*. Under **Related People**, be sure your name displays as the author (edit it if necessary), and then on the left, click **Print** to display the Print Preview. Compare your screen with Figure 1.51.

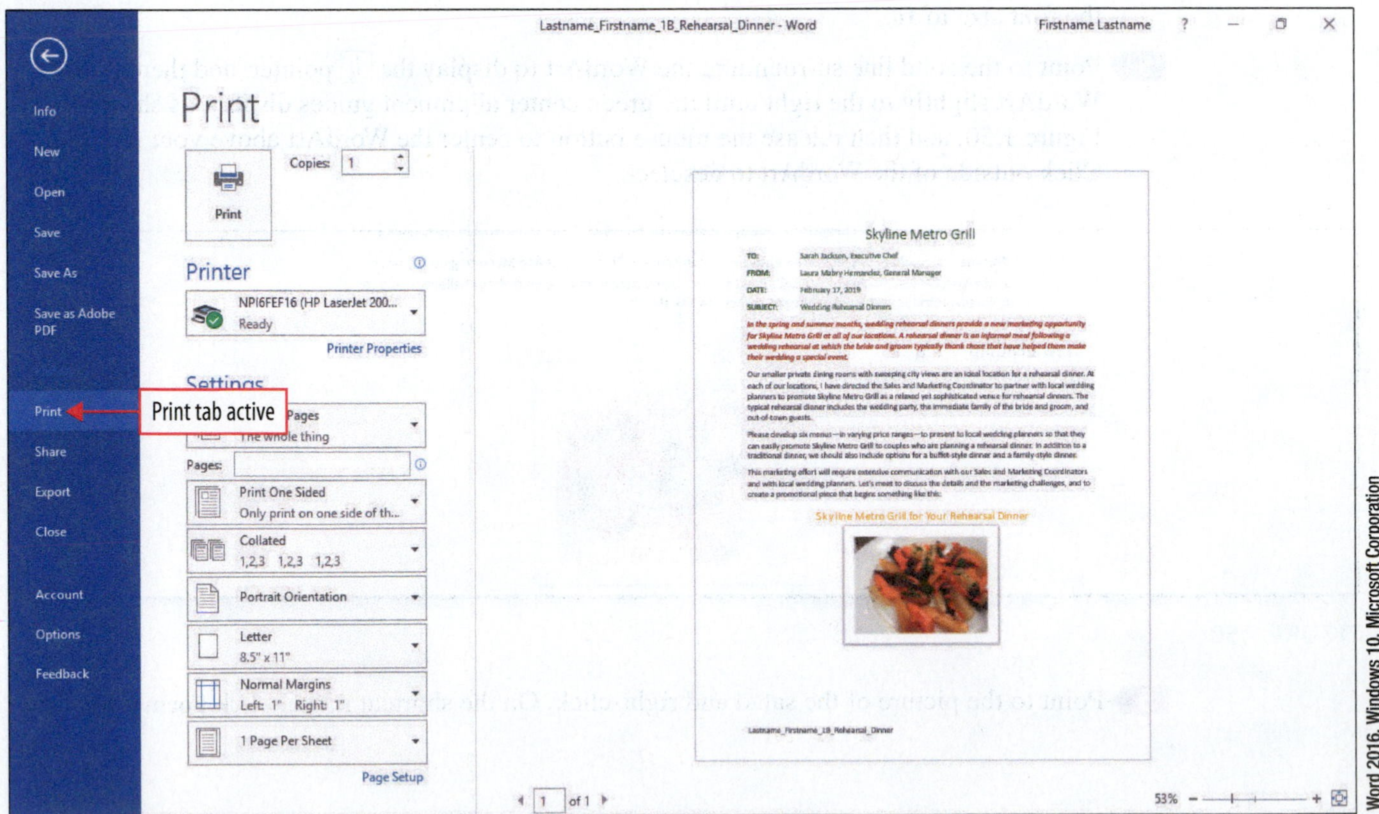

FIGURE 1.51

Word 2016, Windows 10, Microsoft Corporation

15 On the left side of **Backstage** view, click **Save**. In the upper right corner of the Word window, click **Close** [×]. If a message indicates *Do you want to keep the last item you copied?* click **No**.

This message displays if you have copied some type of image to the Clipboard. If you click Yes, the items on the Clipboard will remain for you to use in another program or document.

16 As directed by your instructor, create and submit a paper printout or an electronic image of your document that looks like a printed document; or, submit your completed Word file. If necessary, refer to Activity 1.08 in Project 1A.

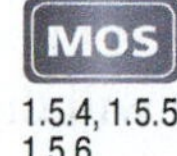
1.5.4, 1.5.5, 1.5.6

Activity 1.19 | Inspecting a Document

Word, Excel, and PowerPoint all have the same commands to inspect a file before sharing it.

1 If necessary, open your **Lastname_Firstname_1B_Rehearsal_Dinner** document.

2 Click the **File tab**, on the left, if necessary, click **Info**, and then on the right, click **Check for Issues**.

3 On the list, click **Inspect Document**.

The ***Inspect Document*** command searches your document for hidden data or personal information that you might not want to share publicly. This information could reveal company details that should not be shared.

4 In the lower right corner of the **Document Inspector** dialog box, click **Inspect**.

The Document Inspector runs and lists information that was found and that you could choose to remove.

5 Click **Close**, click **Check for Issues** again, and then click **Check Accessibility**.

The ***Check Accessibility*** command checks the document for content that people with disabilities might find difficult to read. The Accessibility Checker pane displays on the right and lists two objects that might require attention: a text box (your WordArt) and your picture.

6 **Close** [×] the **Accessibility Checker** pane, and then click the **File tab**.

7 Click **Check for Issues**, and then click **Check Compatibility**.

The ***Check Compatibility*** command checks for features in your document that may not be supported by earlier versions of the Office program. This is only a concern if you are sharing documents with individuals with older software.

8 Click **OK**. Leave your Word document displayed for the next Activity.

1.2.3

Activity 1.20 | Inserting a Bookmark

A ***bookmark*** identifies a word, section, or place in your document so that you can find it quickly without scrolling. This is especially useful in a long document.

1 In the paragraph that begins *Please develop*, select the text *six menus*.

2 On the **Insert tab**, in the **Links group**, click **Bookmark**.

3 In the Bookmark name box, type **menus** and then click **Add**.

4 Press Ctrl + Home to move to the top of your document.

5 Press Ctrl + G, which is the keyboard shortcut for the Go To command.

6 Under **Go to what**, click **Bookmark**, and then with menus selected, click **Go To**. **Close** the **Find and Replace** dialog box, and notice that your bookmarked text is selected for you.

7 **Close** [×] Word, and then click **Save**. Close any open windows.

Objective 10 Compress Files and Get Help with Office

GO! Learn How
Video OF1.10

A ***compressed file*** is a file that has been reduced in size. Compressed files take up less storage space and can be transferred to other computers faster than uncompressed files. You can also combine a group of files into one compressed folder, which makes it easier to share a group of files.

Within each Office program, you will see the ***Tell Me*** feature at the right end of the ribbon tabs, which is a search feature for Microsoft Office commands that you activate by typing what you are looking for in the Tell Me box.

Another method to get help with an Office command is to point to the command on the ribbon, and then at the bottom of the displayed ScreenTip, click Tell me more, which will display step-by-step assistance.

Activity 1.21 | Compressing Files

In this Activity, you will combine the two files you created in this chapter into one compressed file.

1 On the Windows taskbar, click **File Explorer**. On the left, in the **navigation pane**, navigate to your storage location, and then open your **Office Features Chapter 1** folder. If you have been using this folder, in might appear under Quick access. Compare your screen with Figure 1.52.

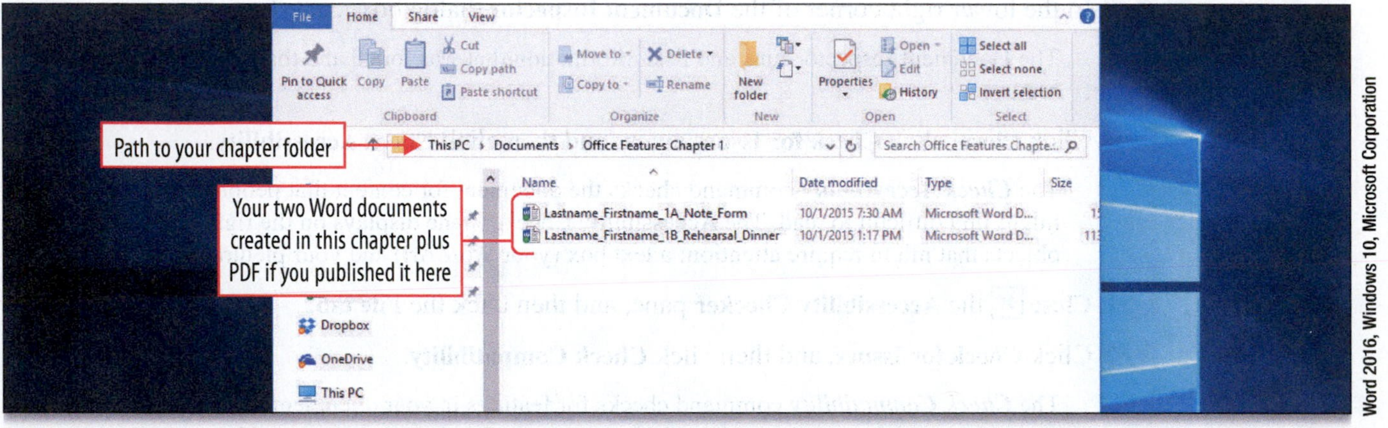

FIGURE 1.52

2 In the **file list**, click your **Lastname_Firstname_1A_Note_Form** Word file one time to select it. Then, hold down Ctrl, and click your **Lastname_Firstname_1B_Rehearsal_Dinner** file to select both files in the list.

In any Windows-based program, holding down Ctrl while selecting enables you to select multiple items.

3 On the **File Explorer** ribbon, click **Share**, and then in the **Send group**, click **Zip**. Compare your screen with Figure 1.53.

Windows creates a compressed folder containing a *copy* of each of the selected files. The folder name is selected—highlighted in blue—so that you can rename it. The default folder name is usually the name of the first file in the group that you select.

BY TOUCH Tap the ribbon commands.

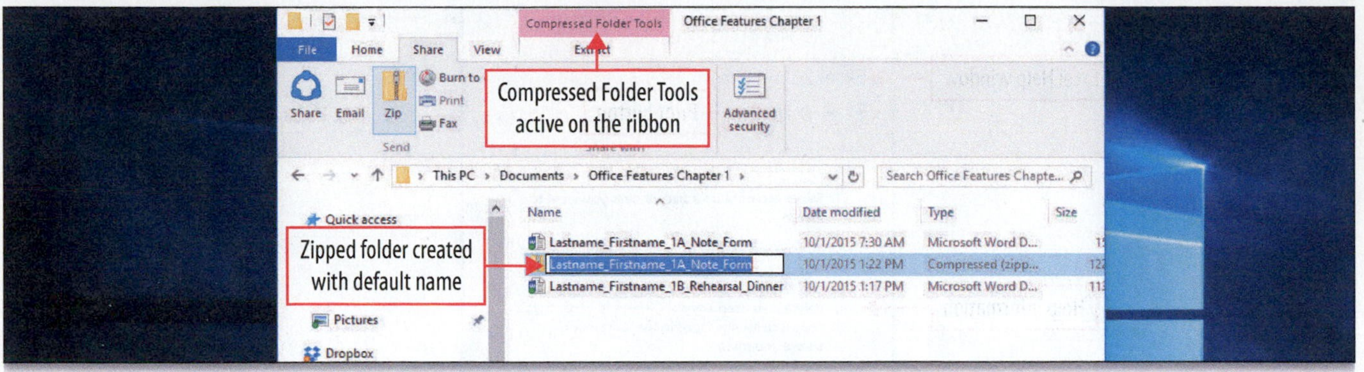

FIGURE 1.53

Word 2016, Windows 10, Microsoft Corporation

ANOTHER WAY Point to the selected files in the File List, right-click, point to Send to, and then click Compressed (zipped) folder.

4 With the folder name selected—highlighted in blue—using your own name, type **Lastname_Firstname_Office_Features_Chapter_1** and press Enter.

The compressed folder is ready to attach to an email or share in some other format.

5 In the upper right corner of the folder window, click **Close** ✕.

Activity 1.22 | Using Microsoft Office Tell Me and Tell Me More to Get Help

In this Activity, you will use Tell Me to find information about formatting currency in Excel.

1 Start Excel and open a **Blank workbook**. With cell **A1** active, type **456789** and press Enter. Click cell **A1** again to make it the active cell.

2 At the top of the screen, click in the **Tell me what you want to do** box, and then type **format as currency** In the displayed list, point to **Accounting Number Formats**, and then click **$ English (United States)**.

As you type, every keystroke refines the results so that you can click the command as soon as it displays. This feature helps you apply the command immediately; it does not explain how to locate the command.

3 On the **Home tab**, in the **Alignment group**, *point to* **Merge & Center**, and then at the bottom of the displayed ScreenTip, click **Tell me more**. At the right edge of the displayed **Excel 2016 Help** window, use the scroll bar to scroll about halfway down the window, and then compare your screen with Figure 1.54.

The ***Tell me more*** feature opens the Office online Help system with explanations about how to perform the task.

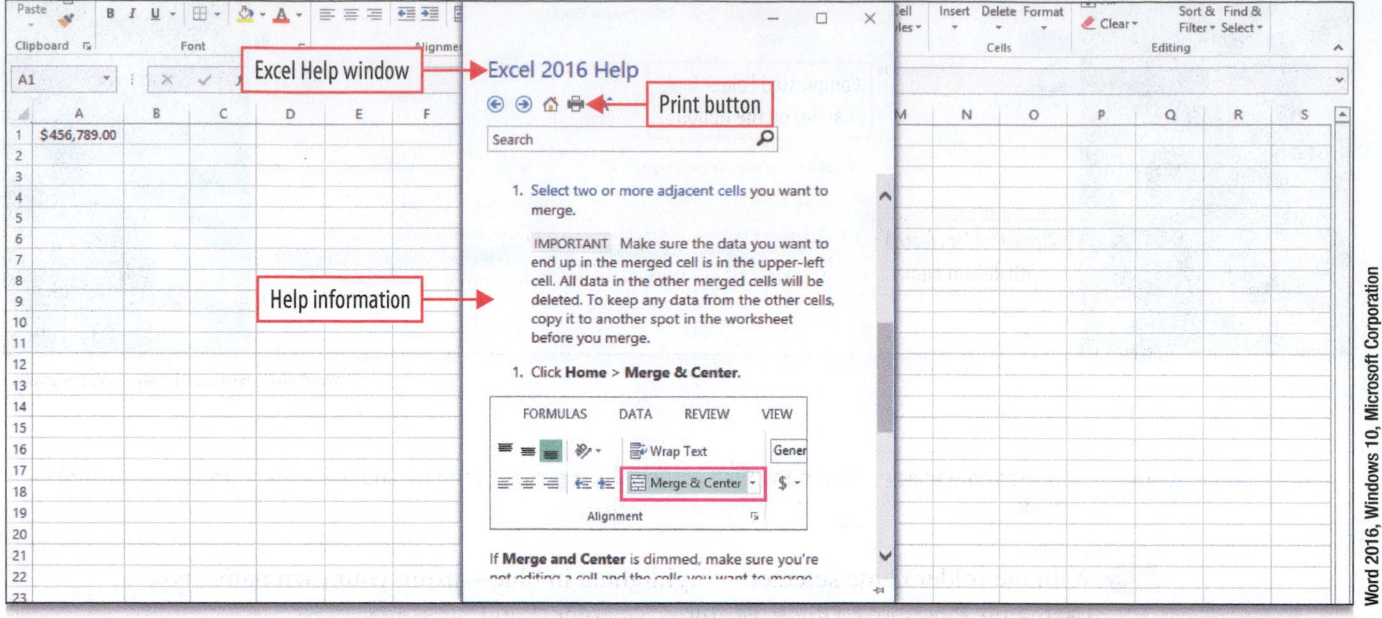

FIGURE 1.54

4. If you want to do so, at the top of the **Excel Help** window, click Print to print a copy of this information for your reference.
5. In the upper right corner of the Help window, click **Close**.
6. Leave Excel open for the next Activity.

Objective 11 Install Apps for Office and Create a Microsoft Account

ALERT!

Working with Web-Based Applications and Services

Computer programs and services on the web receive continuous updates and improvements. Thus, the steps to complete the following web-based activities may differ from the ones shown. You can often look at the screens and the information presented to determine how to complete the activity.

GO! Learn How
Video OF1.11

Apps for Office are a collection of downloadable apps that enable you to create and view information within your familiar Office programs. Apps for Office combine cloud services and web technologies within the user interface of Office. Some of these apps are developed by Microsoft, but many more are developed by specialists in different fields. As new apps are developed, they will be available from the online ***Office Store***—a public marketplace that Microsoft hosts and regulates on Office.com.

A ***task pane app*** works side-by-side with an Office document by displaying a separate pane on the right side of the window. For example, a task pane app can look up and retrieve product information from a web service based on the product name or part number selected in the document.

A ***content app*** integrates web-based features as content within the body of a document. For example, in Excel, you can use an app to look up and gather search results for a new apartment by placing the information in an Excel worksheet, and then use maps to determine the distance of each apartment to work and to family members. ***Mail apps*** display next to an Outlook item. For example, a mail app could detect a purchase order number in an email message and then display information about the order or the customer.

Activity 1.23 | Installing Apps for Office

1 With cell **A1** active, on your keyboard, press Delete to clear the cell. On the Excel ribbon, click the **Insert tab**. In the **Add-ins group**, click **Store**.

2 In the **Office Add-ins** dialog box, in the upper right, click in the **Search the Office Store** box, type **bing maps** and then press Enter.

3 Click the **Bing logo**, and then in the lower right corner, click **Trust It**.

4 If necessary, click Update. On the Welcome message, click **Insert Sample Data**.

Here, the Bing map displays information related to the sample data—this is a *content app*. Each city in the sample data displays a small pie chart that represents the two sets of data—revenue and expenses. Compare your screen with Figure 1.55.

This is just one example of many apps downloadable from the Office Store.

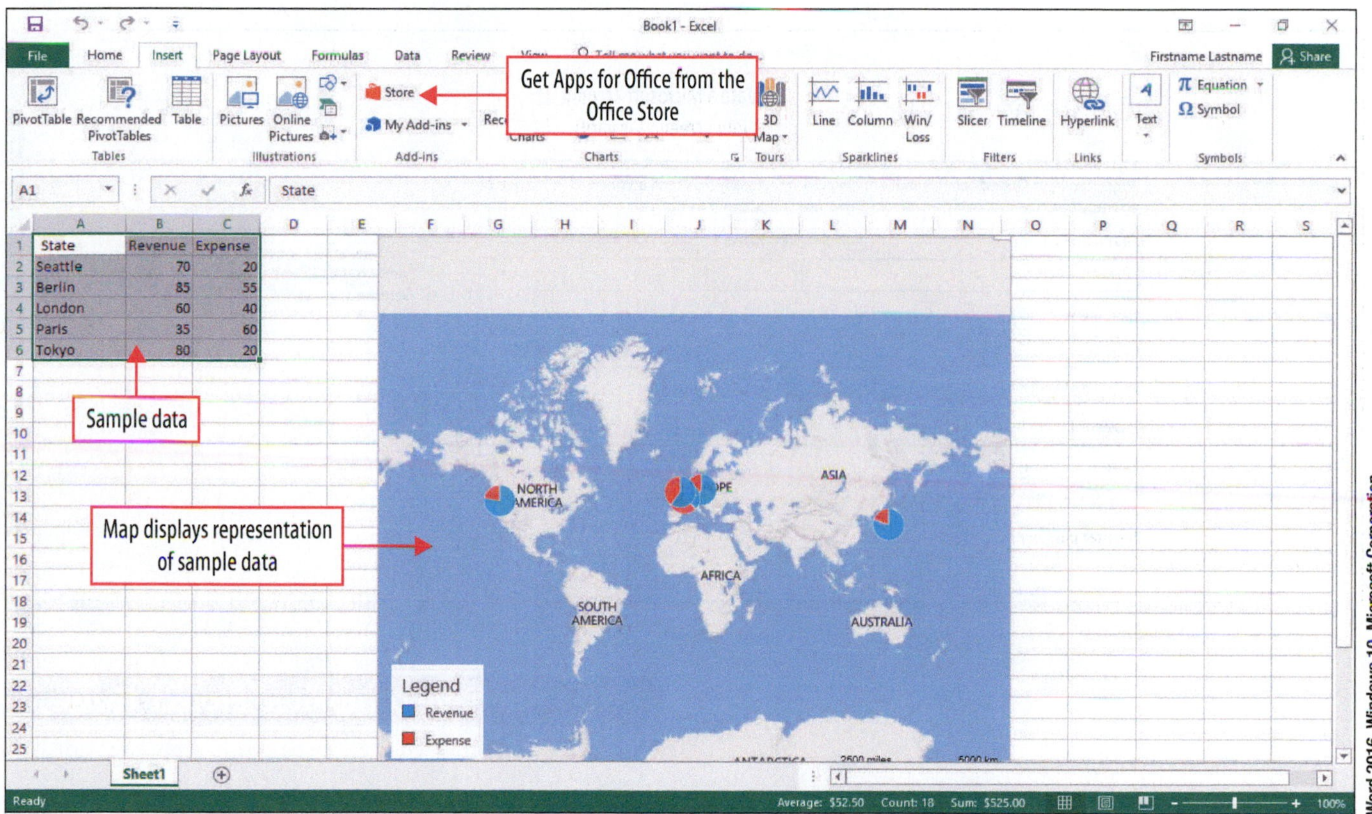

FIGURE 1.55

Word 2016, Windows 10, Microsoft Corporation

5 In the upper right corner of your screen, **Close** ✕ Excel without saving.

Activity 1.24 | Creating a Microsoft Account

ALERT! **This is an optional activity.**

You will find both Windows and Office to be much more useful if you sign in with a Microsoft account. If you already have an email account from **msn.com**, **hotmail.com**, **live.com**, or **outlook.com**, then you already have a Microsoft account. If you do not, you can create a free Microsoft account by following the steps in this activity.

In Windows 8 and Windows 10, you can use a Microsoft account to sign in to *any* Windows PC. Signing in with a Microsoft account is recommended because you can:

- Download Windows apps from the Windows Store.
- Get your online content—email, social network updates, updated news—automatically displayed in an app when you sign in.
- Synch settings online to make every Windows computer you use look and feel the same.
- Sign in to Office so that you can store documents on your OneDrive.

1 Use an Internet search engine to search for **create a microsoft account** or go to **signup.live.com** and at the bottom click **Sign up now**. You will see a screen similar to Figure 1.56. Complete the form to create your account.

You can use any email address that you currently have for your Microsoft account. Or, on this screen, you can create a new outlook.com account.

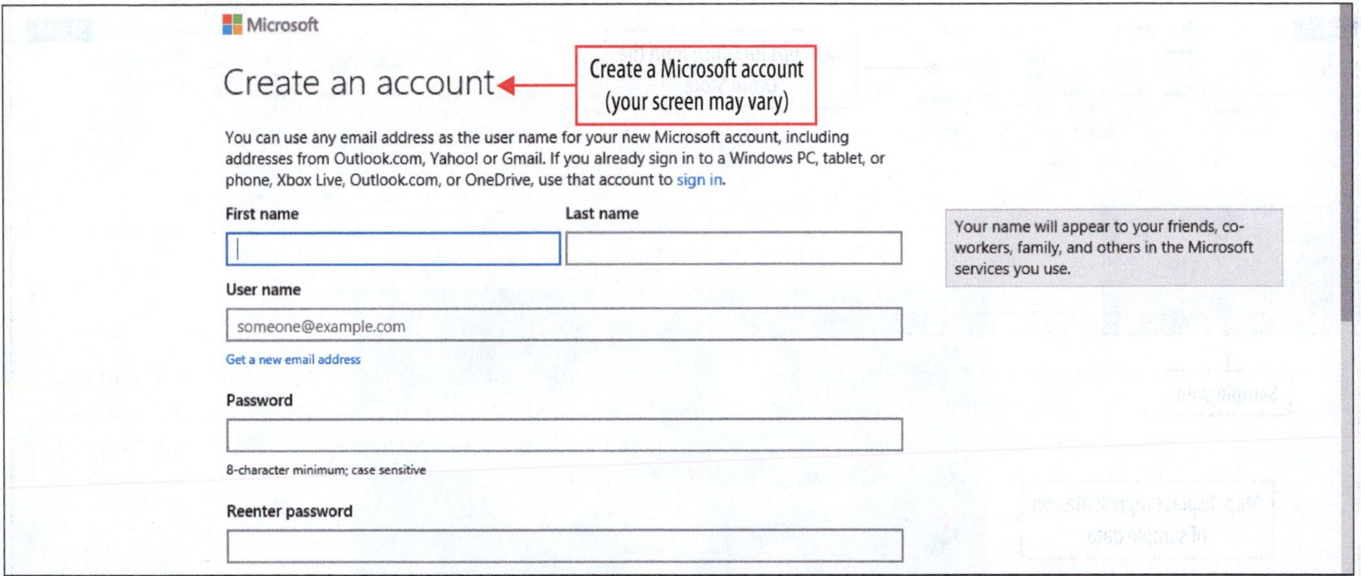

FIGURE 1.56

END | You have completed Project 1B

GO! To Work

Andrew Rodriguez / Fotolia; FotolEdhar/ Fotolia; apops/ Fotolia; Yuri Arcurs/ Fotolia

1 OFFICE 2016

MICROSOFT OFFICE SPECIALIST (MOS) SKILLS IN THIS CHAPTER	
PROJECT 1A	**PROJECT 1B**
1.1.1 Create a blank document **1.3.4** Insert headers and footers **1.3.6** Format page background elements **1.4.5** Add document properties **1.4.6** Show or hide formatting symbols **2.2.6** Apply built-in styles to text	**1.2.3** Create bookmarks **1.4.2** Customize views by using zoom settings **1.4.3** Customize the Quick Access toolbar **1.5.4** Inspect a document for hidden properties or personal information **1.5.5** Inspect a document for accessibility issues **1.5.6** Inspect a document for compatibility issues **2.1.2** Cut, copy, and paste text **2.2.2** Apply formatting by using Format Painter **2.2.7** Change text to WordArt **4.3.2** Add alt-text to document elements **5.2.5** Apply a picture style **5.2.8** Add alternative text to objects for accessibility

BUILD YOUR E-PORTFOLIO

An E-Portfolio is a collection of evidence, stored electronically, that showcases what you have accomplished while completing your education. Collecting and then sharing your work products with potential employers reflects your academic and career goals. Your completed documents from the following projects are good examples to show what you have learned: 1A and 1B.

END OF CHAPTER

SUMMARY

Many Office features and commands, such as accessing the Open and Save As dialog boxes, performing commands from the ribbon and from dialog boxes, and using the Clipboard are the same in all Office desktop apps.

A desktop app is installed on your computer and requires a computer operating system such as Microsoft Windows or Apple's Mac OS-X to run. The programs in Microsoft Office 2016 are considered to be desktop apps.

An app refers to a self-contained program usually designed for a single purpose and that runs on smartphones and other mobile devices—for example, looking at sports scores or booking a flight on a particular airline.

Within an Office app, you can add Apps for Office from the Office Store, which combine cloud services and web technologies within the Office user interface. Apps can be task pane apps, content apps, or mail apps.

GO! LEARN IT ONLINE

Review the concepts, key terms, and MOS skills in this chapter by completing these online challenges, which you can find at **MyITLab**.

Matching and Multiple Choice: Answer matching and multiple-choice questions to test what you learned in this chapter.

Lessons on the GO!: Learn how to use all the new apps and features as they are introduced by Microsoft.

MOS Prep Quiz: Answer questions to review the MOS skills that you practiced in this chapter.

GLOSSARY

GLOSSARY OF CHAPTER KEY TERMS

Alignment The placement of text or objects relative to the left and right margins.

Alignment guides Green lines that display when you move an object to assist in alignment.

Alt text Another name for alternative text.

Alternative text Text added to a picture or object that helps people using a screen reader understand what the object is.

App A self-contained program usually designed for a single purpose and that runs on smartphones and other mobile devices.

Apps for Office A collection of downloadable apps that enable you to create and view information within Office programs, and that combine cloud services and web technologies within the user interface of Office.

Backstage tabs The area along the left side of Backstage view with tabs to display screens with related groups of commands.

Backstage view A centralized space for file management tasks; for example, opening, saving, printing, publishing, or sharing a file. A navigation pane displays along the left side with tabs that group file-related tasks together.

Bookmark A command that identifies a word, section, or place in a document so that you can find it quickly without scrolling.

Center alignment The alignment of text or objects that is centered horizontally between the left and right margin.

Clipboard A temporary storage area that holds text or graphics that you select and then cut or copy.

Check Accessibility A command that checks the document for content that people with disabilities might find difficult to read.

Check Compatibility A command that searches your document for features that may not be supported by older versions of Office.

Cloud computing Applications and services that are accessed over the Internet, rather than accessing applications that are installed on your local computer.

Cloud storage Online storage of data so that you can access your data from different places and devices.

Collaborate To work with others as a team in an intellectual endeavor to complete a shared task or to achieve a shared goal.

Commands Instructions to a computer program that cause an action to be carried out.

Compressed file A file that has been reduced in size and thus takes up less storage space and can be transferred to other computers quickly.

Content app An app for Office that integrates web-based features as content within the body of a document.

Context menus Menus that display commands and options relevant to the selected text or object; also called *shortcut menus*.

Context-sensitive commands Commands that display on a shortcut menu that relate to the object or text that you right-clicked.

Contextual tabs Tabs that are added to the ribbon automatically when a specific object, such as a picture, is selected, and that contain commands relevant to the selected object.

Copy A command that duplicates a selection and places it on the Clipboard.

Creative Commons A nonprofit organization that enables sharing and use of images and knowledge through free legal tools.

Cut A command that removes a selection and places it on the Clipboard.

Default The term that refers to the current selection or setting that is automatically used by a computer program unless you specify otherwise.

Deselect The action of canceling the selection of an object or block of text by clicking outside of the selection.

Desktop app A computer program that is installed on your PC and requires a computer operating system such as Microsoft Windows; also known as a *desktop application*.

Desktop application A computer program that is installed on your PC and requires a computer operating system such as Microsoft Windows; also known as a *desktop app*.

Dialog Box Launcher A small icon that displays to the right of some group names on the ribbon and that opens a related dialog box or pane providing additional options and commands related to that group.

Document properties Details about a file that describe or identify it, including the title, author name, subject, and keywords that identify the document's topic or contents; also known as *metadata*.

Drag The action of holding down the left mouse button while moving your mouse.

Edit The process of making changes to text or graphics in an Office file.

Ellipsis A set of three dots indicating incompleteness; an ellipsis following a command name indicates that a dialog box will display if you click the command.

Enhanced ScreenTip A ScreenTip that displays more descriptive text than a normal ScreenTip.

Fill The inside color of an object.

Font A set of characters with the same design and shape.

Font styles Formatting emphasis such as bold, italic, and underline.

Footer A reserved area for text or graphics that displays at the bottom of each page in a document.

Formatting The process of establishing the overall appearance of text, graphics, and pages in an Office file—for example, in a Word document.

Formatting marks Characters that display on the screen, but do not print, indicating where the Enter key, the Spacebar, and the Tab key were pressed; also called *nonprinting characters*.

Gallery An Office feature that displays a list of potential results instead of just the command name.

Gradient fill A fill effect in which one color fades into another.

Groups On the Office ribbon, the sets of related commands that you might need for a specific type of task.

Header A reserved area for text or graphics that displays at the top of each page in a document.

Info tab The tab in Backstage view that displays information about the current file.

Inspect Document A command that searches your document for hidden data or personal information that you might not want to share publicly.

Insertion point A blinking vertical line that indicates where text or graphics will be inserted.

Keyboard shortcut A combination of two or more keyboard keys, used to perform a task that would otherwise require a mouse.

KeyTip The letter that displays on a command in the ribbon and that indicates the key you can press to activate the command when keyboard control of the Ribbon is activated.

Keywords Custom file properties in the form of words that you associate with a document to give an indication of the document's content; used to help find and organize files. Also called *tags*.

Landscape orientation A page orientation in which the paper is wider than it is tall.

Layout Options A button that displays when an object is selected and that has commands to choose how the object interacts with surrounding text.

Live Preview A technology that shows the result of applying an editing or formatting change as you point to possible results—*before* you actually apply it.

Location Any disk drive, folder, or other place in which you can store files and folders.

Mail app An app for Office that displays next to an Outlook item.

Metadata Details about a file that describe or identify it, including the title, author name, subject, and keywords that identify the document's topic or contents; also known as *document properties*.

Mini toolbar A small toolbar containing frequently used formatting commands that displays as a result of selecting text or objects.

MRU Acronym for *most recently used*, which refers to the state of some commands that retain the characteristic most recently applied; for example, the Font Color button retains the most recently used color until a new color is chosen.

Nonprinting characters Characters that display on the screen, but do not print, indicating where the Enter key, the Spacebar, and the Tab key were pressed; also called *formatting marks*.

Object A text box, picture, table, or shape that you can select and then move and resize.

Office 365 A version of Microsoft Office to which you subscribe for an annual fee.

Office Store A public marketplace that Microsoft hosts and regulates on Office.com.

OneDrive Microsoft's free cloud storage for anyone with a free Microsoft account.

Open dialog box A dialog box from which you can navigate to, and then open on your screen, an existing file that was created in that same program.

Option button In a dialog box, a round button that enables you to make one choice among two or more options.

Options dialog box A dialog box within each Office application where you can select program settings and other options and preferences.

Page Width A view that zooms the document so that the width of the page matches the width of the window. Find this command on the View tab, in the Zoom group.

Paragraph symbol The symbol ¶ that represents the end of a paragraph.

Paste The action of placing text or objects that have been copied or cut from one location to another location.

Paste Options gallery A gallery of buttons that provides a Live Preview of all the Paste options available in the current context.

PDF The acronym for *Portable Document Format*, which is a file format that creates an image that preserves the look of your file, but that cannot be easily changed; a popular format for sending documents electronically, because the document will display on most computers.

Pointer Any symbol that displays on your screen in response to moving your mouse.

Points A measurement of the size of a font; there are 72 points in an inch.

Portable Document Format A file format that creates an image that preserves the look of your file, but that cannot be easily changed; a popular format for sending documents electronically, because the document will display on most computers; also called a *PDF*.

Portrait orientation A page orientation in which the paper is taller than it is wide.

Print Preview A view of a document as it will appear when you print it.

Protected View A security feature in Office 2016 that protects your computer from malicious files by opening them in a restricted environment until you enable them; you might encounter this feature if you open a file from an e-mail or download files from the Internet.

pt The abbreviation for *point*; for example, when referring to a font size.

Quick Access Toolbar In an Office program window, the small row of buttons in the upper left corner of the screen from which you can perform frequently used commands.

Read-only A property assigned to a file that prevents the file from being modified or deleted; it indicates that you cannot save any changes to the displayed document unless you first save it with a new name.

Right-click The action of clicking the right mouse button one time.

Sans serif font A font design with no lines or extensions on the ends of characters.

Screen reader Software that enables visually impaired users to read text on a computer screen to understand the content of pictures.

ScreenTip A small box that that displays useful information when you perform various mouse actions such as pointing to screen elements or dragging.

Selecting Highlighting, by dragging with your mouse, areas of text or data or graphics, so that the selection can be edited, formatted, copied, or moved.

Serif font A font design that includes small line extensions on the ends of the letters to guide the eye in reading from left to right.

Share button Opens the Share pane from which you can save your file to the cloud—your OneDrive—and then share it with others so you can collaborate.

SharePoint Collaboration software with which people in an organization can set up team sites to share information, manage documents, and publish reports for others to see.

Shortcut menu A menu that displays commands and options relevant to the selected text or object; also called a *context menu*.

Sizing handles Small squares or circles that indicate a picture or object is selected.

Split button A button divided into two parts and in which clicking the main part of the button performs a command and clicking the arrow opens a menu with choices.

Status bar The area along the lower edge of an Office program window that displays file information on the left and buttons to control how the window looks on the right.

Style A group of formatting commands, such as font, font size, font color, paragraph alignment, and line spacing that can be applied to a paragraph with one command.

Synchronization The process of updating computer files that are in two or more locations according to specific rules—also called *syncing*.

Syncing The process of updating computer files that are in two or more locations according to specific rules—also called *synchronization*.

Tabs (ribbon) On the Office ribbon, the name of each task-oriented activity area.

Tags Custom file properties in the form of words that you associate with a document to give an indication of the document's content; used to help find and organize files. Also called *keywords*.

Task pane app An app for Office that works side-by-side with an Office document by displaying a separate pane on the right side of the window.

Tell Me A search feature for Microsoft Office commands that you activate by typing what you are looking for in the Tell Me box.

Tell me more A prompt within a ScreenTip that opens the Office online Help system with explanations about how to perform the command referenced in the ScreenTip.

Template A preformatted document that you can use as a starting point and then change to suit your needs.

Theme A predesigned combination of colors, fonts, and effects that looks good together and is applied to an entire document by a single selection.

Title bar The bar at the top edge of the program window that indicates the name of the current file and the program name.

Toggle button A button that can be turned on by clicking it once, and then turned off by clicking it again.

Toolbar In a folder window, a row of buttons with which you can perform common tasks, such as changing the view of your files and folders.

Triple-click The action of clicking the left mouse button three times in rapid succession.

Trusted Documents A security feature in Office that remembers which files you have already enabled; you might encounter this feature if you open a file from an e-mail or download files from the Internet.

Windows apps An app that runs on all Windows device families—including PCs, Windows phones, Windows tablets, and the Xbox gaming system.

WordArt An Office feature in Word, Excel, and PowerPoint that enables you to change normal text into decorative stylized text.

XML Paper Specification A Microsoft file format that creates an image of your document and that opens in the XPS viewer.

XPS The acronym for XML Paper Specification—a Microsoft file format that creates an image of your document and that opens in the XPS viewer.

Zoom The action of increasing or decreasing the size of the viewing area on the screen.

Introducing Microsoft Word 2016

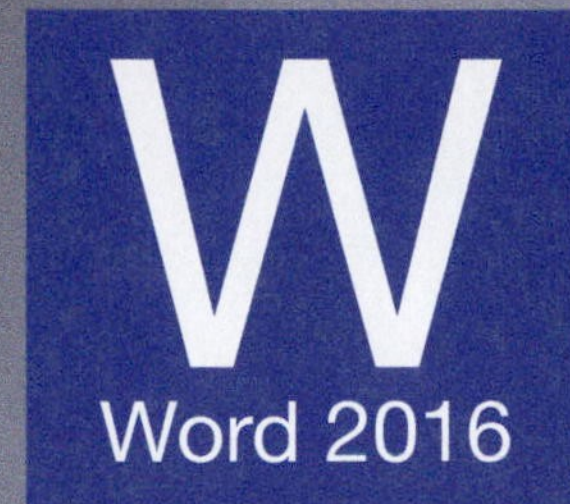

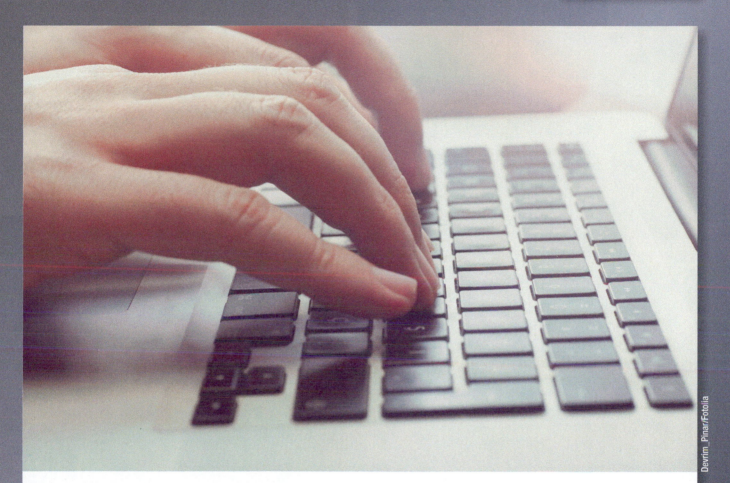

Devrim_Pinar/Fotolia

Word 2016: Introduction

Content! Defined by Merriam-Webster's online dictionary as "the topic or matter treated in a written work" and also as "the principal substance (as written matter, illustrations, or music) offered by a World Wide Web site," content is what you consume when you read on paper or online, when you watch video, or when you listen to any kind of music—live or recorded.

Content is what you *create* when your own words or performances are recorded in some form. For creating content in the form of words, Microsoft Office 2016 is a great choice. Rather than just a tool for word processing, Word is now a tool for you to communicate and collaborate with others. When you want to communicate with pictures or images in your Word document, Office 2016 has many features to help you do so. You can use Microsoft Word 2016 on a Windows desktop, laptop, or tablet. If your PC is touch-enabled, you will be able to use your fingers to work with Word. For example, the ribbon expands to make it easy to tap commands and you can resize images by moving your fingers on the screen.

Best of all, Microsoft Word 2016 is integrated into the cloud. If you save your documents to your cloud-based storage that comes with any free Microsoft account, you can retrieve them from any device and continue to work with and share your documents. Enjoy learning Word 2016!

Creating Documents with Microsoft Word 2016

PROJECT 1A

OUTCOMES
Create a flyer with a picture.

OBJECTIVES

1. Create a New Document and Insert Text
2. Insert and Format Graphics
3. Insert and Modify Text Boxes and Shapes
4. Preview and Print a Document

PROJECT 1B

OUTCOMES
Format text, paragraphs, and documents.

OBJECTIVES

5. Change Document and Paragraph Layout
6. Create and Modify Lists
7. Set and Modify Tab Stops
8. Insert a SmartArt Graphic and an Online Video

IvicaNS/Fotolia

In This Chapter

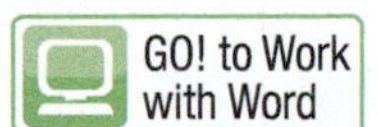

In this chapter, you will begin your study of Microsoft Word, one of the most popular computer software applications and one that almost everyone has a reason to use. You will use many of the tools and features in Word 2016, such as applying attractive styles to your documents. You can use Microsoft Word to perform basic word processing tasks such as writing a memo, a report, or a letter. You can also use Word to complete complex tasks, such as creating sophisticated tables, embedding graphics, writing blogs, and creating publications. Word is a program that you can learn gradually, and then add more advanced skills one at a time.

The projects in this chapter relate to **Sturgeon Point Productions**, an independent film company based in Miami with offices in Detroit and Milwaukee. The film professionals produce effective broadcast and branded content for many industries, and provide a wide array of film and video production services. Sturgeon Point Productions has won awards for broadcast advertising, business media, music videos, and social media. The mission of the company is to help clients tell their stories—whether the story is about a social issue, a new product, a geographical location, a company, or a person.

PROJECT 1A Flyer

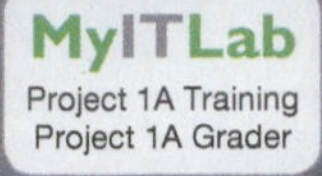

PROJECT ACTIVITIES

In Activities 1.01 through 1.16, you will create a flyer announcing two internships for a short documentary by Sturgeon Point Productions. Your completed document will look similar to Figure 1.1.

Please always review the downloaded Grader instructions before beginning.

PROJECT FILES

If your instructor wants you to submit Project 1A in the MyITLab Grader system, log in to MyITLab, locate Grader Project 1A, and then download the files for this project.

For Project 1A, you will need the following files:
New blank Word document
w01A_Text
w01A_Bird

You will save your document as:
Lastname_Firstname_1A_Flyer

PROJECT RESULTS

Build From Scratch

GO! Walk Thru Project 1A

Internships Available

Interviews will be held:
Friday and Saturday, January 14 and 15
In the Career Services Conference Room

This summer, Sturgeon Point Productions will be filming a short documentary in Costa Rica about its native birds and has positions available for two interns. The filming will begin the first week of July and will last approximately two weeks. Payment will be by Day Rate of $100 per day. Transportation, food, and lodging will be provided.

The First Assistant Director will work with the second film crew, which will be filming background video. The Assistant Script Supervisor will work with the Script Supervisor and will be responsible for coordinating communication between the two camera crews.

You must have a valid U. S. passport; no inoculations are necessary. Details are available on the company website.

To set up an interview, apply online at:
www.SturgeonPointProductions.com

Lastname_Firstname_1A_Flyer

Word 2016, Windows 10, Microsoft Corporation

FIGURE 1.1 Project 1A Internship Flyer

NOTE	If You Are Using a Touchscreen
	Tap an item to click it.
	Press and hold for a few seconds to right-click; release when the information or commands displays.
	Touch the screen with two or more fingers and then pinch together to zoom out or stretch your fingers apart to zoom in.
	Slide your finger on the screen to scroll—slide left to scroll right and slide right to scroll left.
	Slide to rearrange—similar to dragging with a mouse.
	Swipe to select—slide an item a short distance with a quick movement—to select an item and bring up commands, if any.

Objective 1 Create a New Document and Insert Text

GO! Learn How Video W1-1

When you start Word, documents you have recently opened, if any, display on the left. On the right, you can select a ***template***—a preformatted document that you can use as a starting point and then change to suit your needs. If you want to start a new, blank document, you can select the blank document template. When you create a new document, you can type all of the text, or you can type some of the text and then insert additional text from another source.

1.1.1, 1.4.6

Activity 1.01 | Starting a New Word Document

ALERT! **To submit as an autograded project, log into MyITLab and download the files for this project, and begin with those files instead of a new blank document.**

1 Start Word and then click **Blank document**. On the **Home tab**, in the **Paragraph group**, if necessary click **Show/Hide** ¶ so that it is active and the formatting marks display. If the rulers do not display, click the View tab, and then in the Show group, select the Ruler check box.

2 Type **Internships Available** and then press Enter two times. Then type the following text: **This summer, Sturgeon Point Productions will be filming a short documentary in Costa Rica about its native birds and has positions available for two interns.**

As you type, the insertion point moves to the right, and when it approaches the right margin, Word determines whether the next word in the line will fit within the established right margin. If the word does not fit, Word moves the entire word down to the next line. This is ***wordwrap*** and means that you press Enter *only* when you reach the end of a paragraph—it is not necessary to press Enter at the end of each line of text.

NOTE Spacing Between Sentences

Although you might have learned to add two spaces following end-of-sentence punctuation, the common practice now is to space only one time at the end of a sentence. Be sure to press Spacebar only one time following end-of-sentence punctuation.

3 Press Spacebar and then take a moment to study the table in Figure 1.2 to become familiar with the default document settings in Microsoft Word. Compare your screen with Figure 1.3.

When you press Enter, Spacebar, or Tab on your keyboard, characters display in your document to represent these keystrokes. These characters do not print and are referred to as ***formatting marks*** or ***nonprinting characters***. These marks will display throughout this instruction.

DEFAULT DOCUMENT SETTINGS IN A NEW WORD DOCUMENT	
SETTING	**DEFAULT FORMAT**
Font and font size	The default font is Calibri, and the default font size is 11 points.
Margins	The default left, right, top, and bottom page margins are 1 inch.
Line spacing	The default line spacing is 1.08, which provides slightly more space between lines than single spacing does.
Paragraph spacing	The default spacing after a paragraph is 8 points, which is slightly less than the height of one blank line of text.
View	The default view is Print Layout view, which displays the page borders and displays the document as it will appear when printed.

Word 2016, Windows 10, Microsoft Corporation

FIGURE 1.2

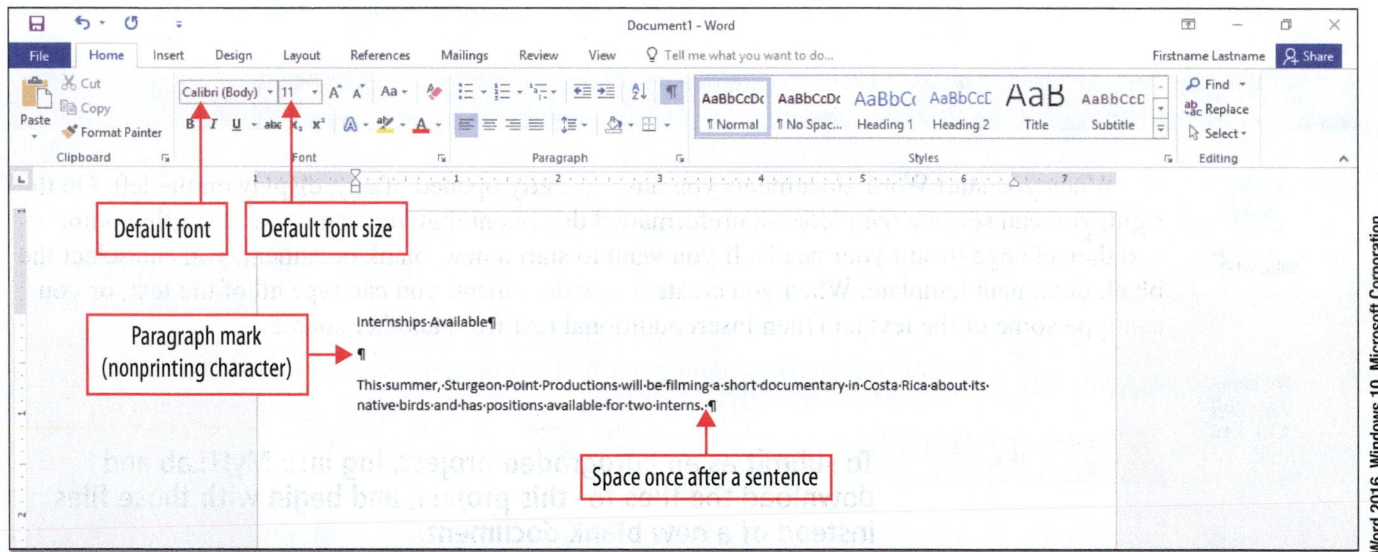

Word 2016, Windows 10, Microsoft Corporation

FIGURE 1.3

More Knowledge **Word's Default Settings Are Easier to Read Online**

Until just a few years ago, word processing programs used single spacing, an extra blank paragraph to separate paragraphs, and 12 pt Times New Roman as the default formats. Now, studies show that individuals find the Word default formats described in Figure 1.2 to be easier to read online, where many documents are now viewed and read.

1.1.4

Activity 1.02 | Inserting Text from Another Document

1 On the ribbon, click the **Insert tab**. In the **Text group**, click the **Object button arrow**, and then click **Text from File**.

ALERT! **Does the Object dialog box display?**

If the Object dialog box displays, you probably clicked the Object *button* instead of the Object *button arrow*. Close the Object dialog box, and then in the Text group, click the Object button arrow, as shown in Figure 1.4. Click *Text from File*, and then continue with Step 2.

2 In the **Insert File** dialog box, navigate to the student files that accompany this textbook, locate and select **w01A_Text**, and then click **Insert**. Compare your screen with Figure 1.4.

A *copy* of the text from the w01A_Text file displays at the insertion point location; the text is not removed from the original file.

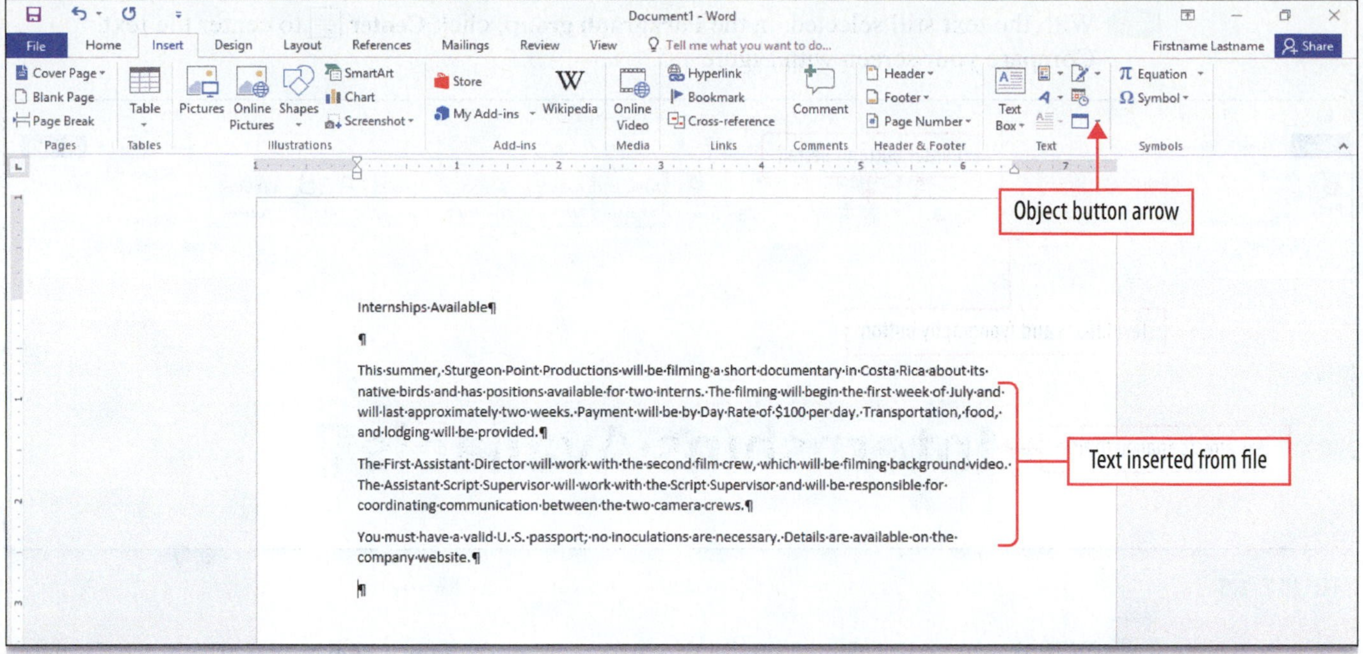

FIGURE 1.4

Word 2016, Windows 10, Microsoft Corporation

ANOTHER WAY Open the file, copy the required text, close the file, and then paste the text into the current document.

3. On the **Quick Access Toolbar**, click **Save**, and then under **Save As**, click **Browse**. Navigate to the location where you are saving your files for this chapter, and then create and open a new folder named **Word Chapter 1** In the **File name** box, using your own name, replace the existing text with **Lastname_Firstname_1A_Flyer** and then click **Save**.

Objective 2 Insert and Format Graphics

GO! Learn How Video W1-2

To add visual interest to a document, insert ***graphics***. Graphics include pictures, online pictures, charts, and ***drawing objects***—shapes, diagrams, lines, and so on. For additional visual interest, you can apply an attractive graphic format to text; add, resize, move, and format pictures; and add a page border.

2.2.6 and 2.2.10

Activity 1.03 | Formatting Text by Using Text Effects

Text effects are decorative formats, such as shadowed or mirrored text, text glow, 3-D effects, and colors that make text stand out.

1. Including the paragraph mark, select the first paragraph of text—*Internships Available*. On the **Home tab**, in the **Font group**, click **Text Effects and Typography**.
2. In the **Text Effects and Typography** gallery, in the third row, point to the first effect to display the ScreenTip *Fill – Black, Text 1, Outline – Background 1, Hard Shadow – Background 1*, and then click this effect.
3. With the text still selected, in the **Font group**, click in the **Font Size** box to select the existing font size. Type **52** and then press Enter.

   When you want to change the font size of selected text to a size that does not display in the Font Size list, type the number in the Font Size box and press Enter to confirm the new font size.

4 With the text still selected, in the **Paragraph group**, click **Center** to center the text. Compare your screen with Figure 1.5.

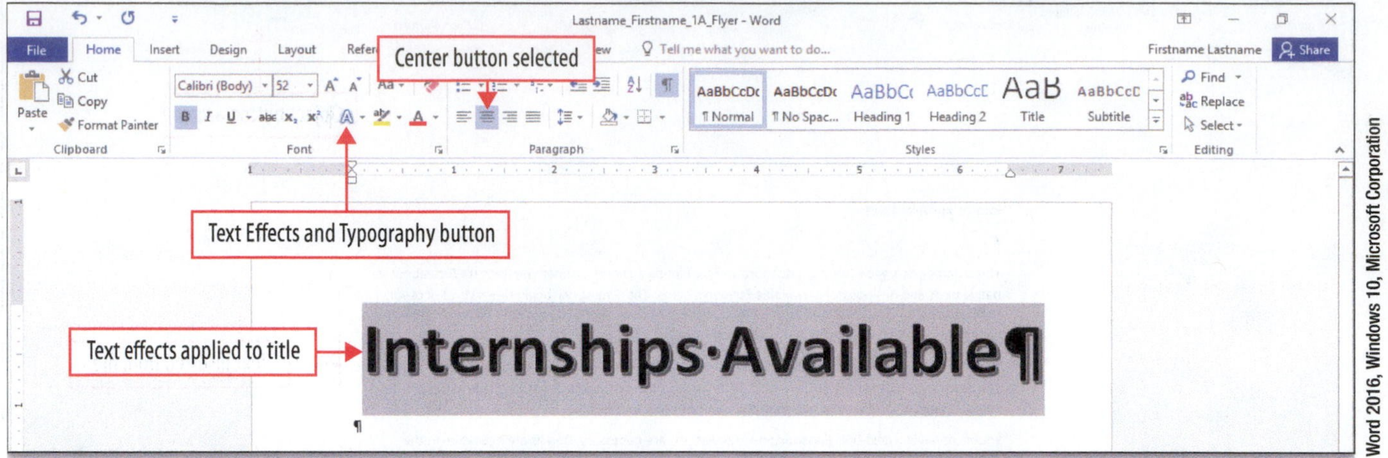

FIGURE 1.5

5 With the text still selected, in the **Font group**, click the **Font Color button arrow**. Under **Theme Colors**, in the sixth column, click the first color—**Orange, Accent 2**.

6 With the text still selected, in the **Font group**, click **Text Effects and Typography**. Point to **Shadow**, and then under **Outer**, in the second row, click the third style—**Offset Left**.

7 Click anywhere in the document to deselect the text, click **Save**, and then compare your screen with Figure 1.6.

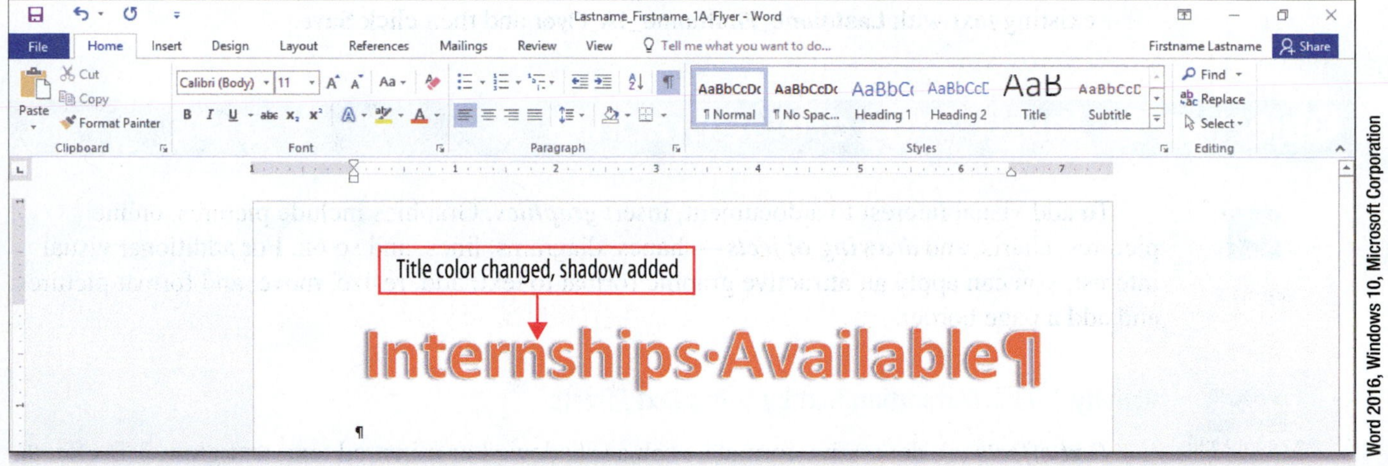

FIGURE 1.6

> **More Knowledge** **Clear Existing Formatting**
>
> If you do not like your text effect, you can remove all formatting from any selected text. To do so, on the Home tab, in the Font group, click Clear All Formatting.

5.1.2

Activity 1.04 | Inserting Pictures

1 In the paragraph that begins *This summer*, click to position the insertion point at the beginning of the paragraph.

2 On the **Insert tab**, in the **Illustrations group**, click **Pictures**. In the **Insert Picture** dialog box, navigate to your student data files, locate and click **w01A_Bird**, and then click **Insert**.

Word inserts the picture as an ***inline object***; that is, the picture is positioned directly in the text at the insertion point, just like a character in a sentence. The Layout Options button displays to the right of the picture. You can change the ***Layout Options*** to control the manner in which text wraps around a picture or other object. Sizing handles surround the picture indicating it is selected.

3 Notice the round sizing handles around the selected picture, as shown in Figure 1.7.

The corner sizing handles resize the graphic proportionally. The center sizing handles resize a graphic vertically or horizontally only; however, sizing with these will distort the graphic. A ***rotation handle***, with which you can rotate the graphic to any angle, displays above the top center sizing handle.

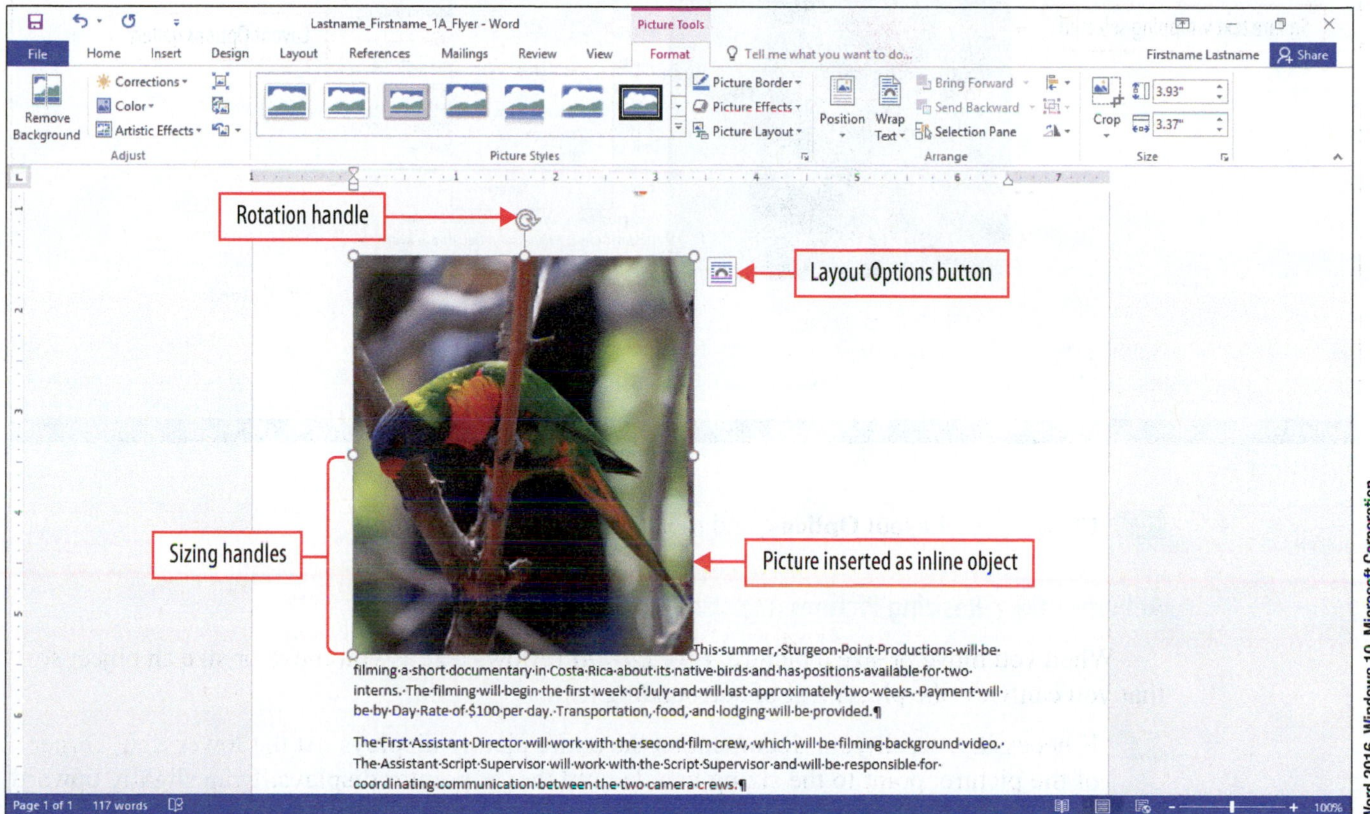

Lastname_Firstname_1A_Flyer - Word
Picture Tools
Rotation handle
Layout Options button
Sizing handles
Picture inserted as inline object
This·summer,·Sturgeon·Point·Productions·will·be· filming·a·short·documentary·in·Costa·Rica·about·its·native·birds·and·has·positions·available·for·two· interns.·The·filming·will·begin·the·first·week·of·July·and·will·last·approximately·two·weeks.·Payment·will· be·by·Day·Rate·of·$100·per·day.·Transportation,·food,·and·lodging·will·be·provided.¶
The·First·Assistant·Director·will·work·with·the·second·film·crew,·which·will·be·filming·background·video.· The·Assistant·Script·Supervisor·will·work·with·the·Script·Supervisor·and·will·be·responsible·for· coordinating·communication·between·the·two·camera·crews.¶

Word 2016, Windows 10, Microsoft Corporation

FIGURE 1.7

5.2.6

Activity 1.05 | Wrapping Text Around a Picture Using Layout Options

Recall that Layout Options enable you to control ***text wrapping***—the manner in which text displays around an object.

1 Be sure the picture is selected—you know it is selected if the sizing handles display.

2 To the right of the picture, click **Layout Options** to display a gallery of text wrapping arrangements. Point to each icon layout option to view its ScreenTip.

Each icon visually depicts how text will wrap around an object.

ANOTHER WAY On the Format tab, in the Arrange group, click Wrap Text.

3 From the gallery, under **With Text Wrapping**, click the first layout—**Square**. Compare your screen with Figure 1.8.

Select Square text wrapping when you want to wrap the text to the left or right of an image. To the left of the picture, an ***object anchor*** displays, indicating that the selected object is anchored to the text at this location in the document.

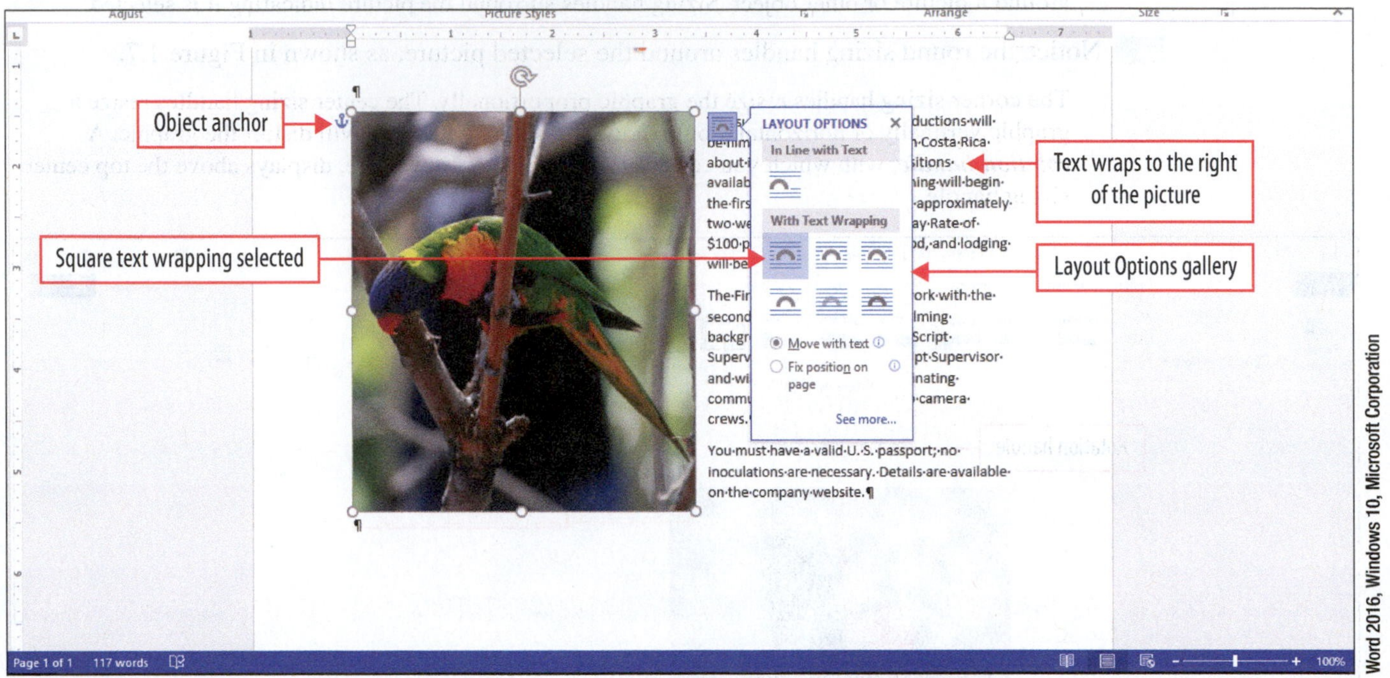

FIGURE 1.8

4 **Close** ☒ the **Layout Options**, and then **Save** 🖫 your document.

Activity 1.06 | Resizing Pictures and Using Live Layout

When you move or size a picture, ***Live Layout*** reflows text as you move or size an object so that you can view the placement of surrounding text.

1 If necessary, scroll your document so the entire picture displays. At the lower right corner of the picture, point to the sizing handle until the ⤡ pointer displays. Drag slightly upward and to the left. As you drag, a green alignment guide may display at the left margin. Compare your screen with Figure 1.9.

Alignment guides may display when you are moving or sizing a picture to help you with object placement, and Live Layout shows you how the document text will flow and display on the page.

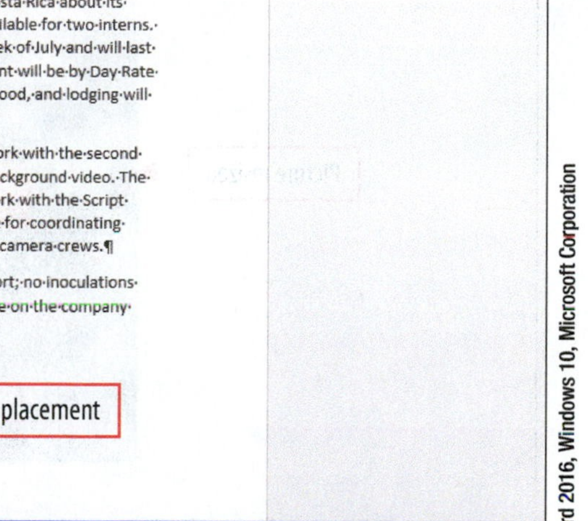

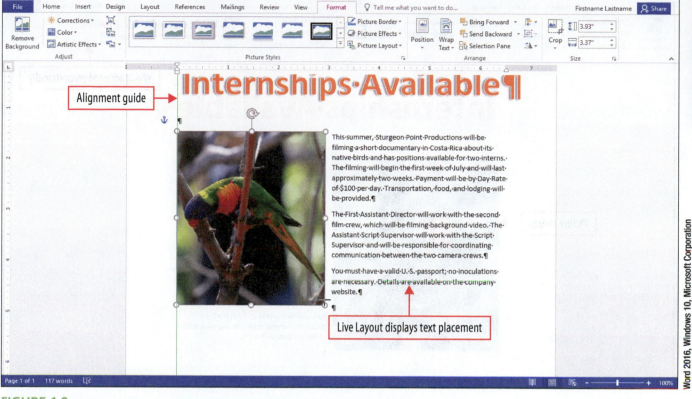

Word 2016, Windows 10, Microsoft Corporation

FIGURE 1.9

2 Continue to drag up and to the left until the bottom of the graphic is aligned at approximately **4 inches on the vertical ruler**. Notice that the graphic is proportionally resized.

3 On the **Quick Access Toolbar**, click **Undo** to restore the picture to its original size.

ANOTHER WAY On the Format tab, in the Adjust group, click Reset Picture.

4 On the ribbon, under **Picture Tools**, on the **Format tab**, in the **Size group**, click in the **Shape Height** box 0.29". Type **3.8** and then press Enter. If necessary, scroll down to view the entire picture on your screen, and then compare your screen with Figure 1.10.

When you use the Shape Height and Shape Width boxes to change the size of a graphic, the graphic will always resize proportionally; that is, the width adjusts as you change the height and vice versa.

ANOTHER WAY A ***spin box*** is a small box with an upward- and downward-pointing arrow that lets you move rapidly through a set of values by clicking. You can change the height or width of a picture object by clicking the Shape Height or Shape width spin box arrows.

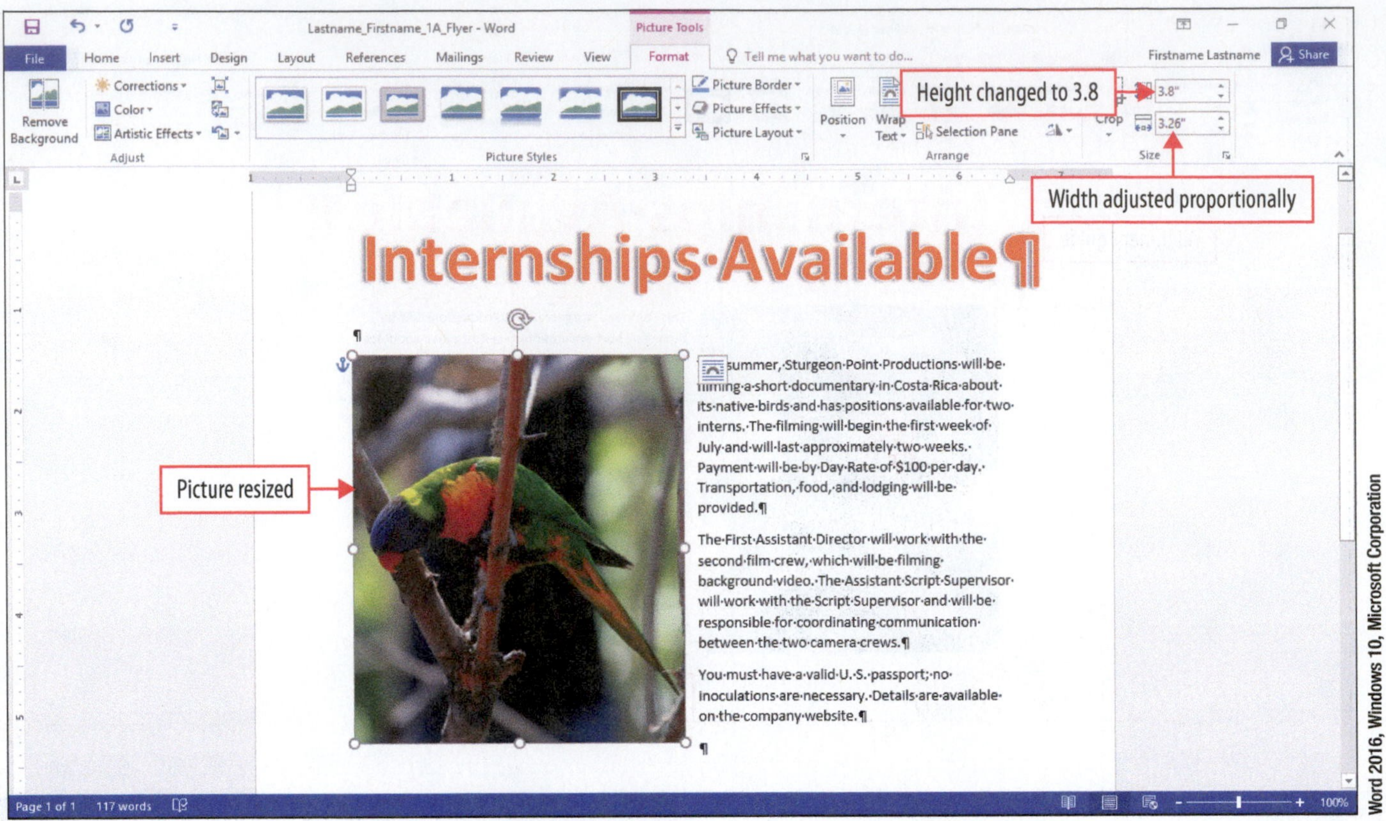

Word 2016, Windows 10, Microsoft Corporation

FIGURE 1.10

5 **Save** your document.

5.2.7

Activity 1.07 | Positioning a Picture

There are two ways to move a picture in a document. You can point to the picture and then drag it to a new position. You can also change the picture settings in a dialog box, which gives you more precise control over the picture location.

1 Be sure the picture is selected. On the ribbon, click the **Format tab**. In the **Arrange group**, click **Position**, and then click **More Layout Options**.

2 In the **Layout** dialog box, be sure the **Position tab** is selected. Under **Horizontal**, click the **Alignment** option button. To the right of **Alignment**, click the **arrow**, and then click **Right**. To the right of **relative to**, click the **arrow**, and then click **Margin**.

3 Under **Vertical**, click the **Alignment** option button. Change the **Alignment** options to **Top relative to Line**. Compare your screen with Figure 1.11.

With these alignment settings, the picture will move to the right margin of the page and the top edge will align with the top of the first line of the paragraph to which it is anchored.

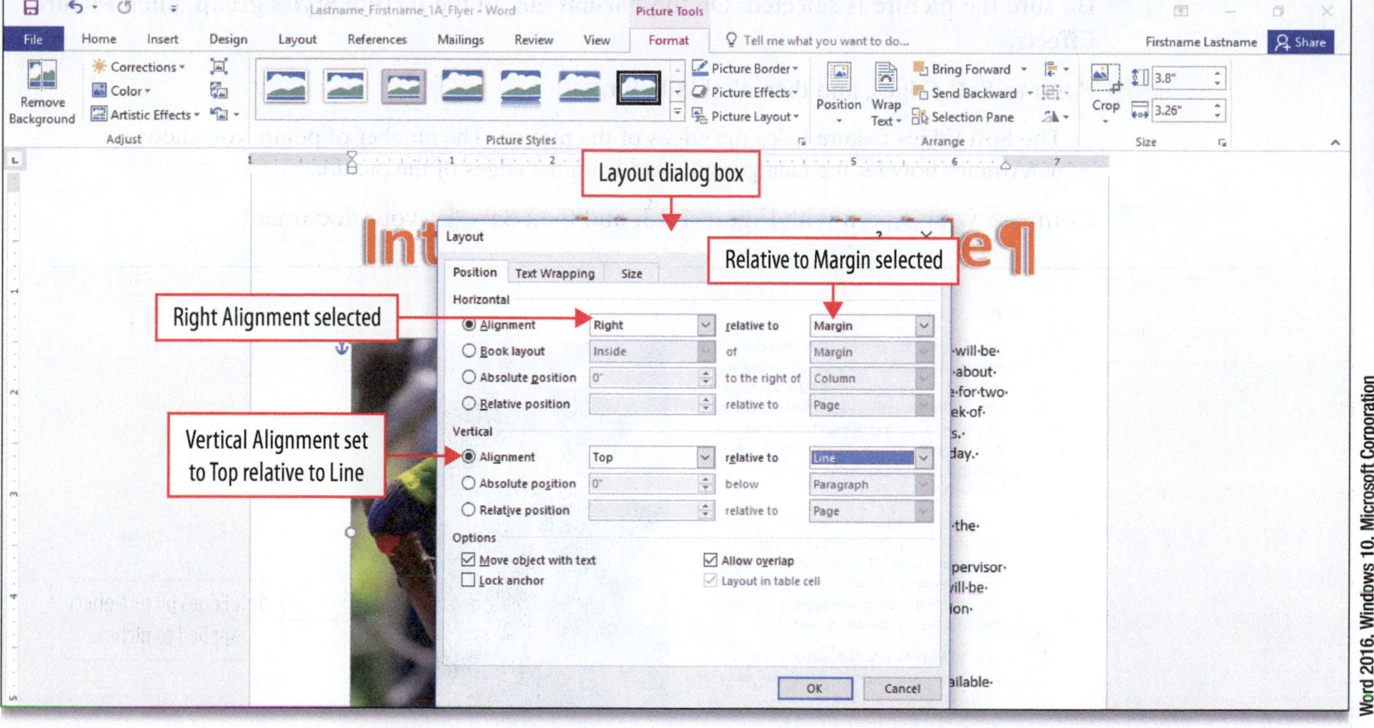

FIGURE 1.11

Word 2016, Windows 10, Microsoft Corporation

4 At the bottom of the **Layout** dialog box, click **OK**, and then on the **Quick Access Toolbar**, click **Save**. Notice that the picture moves to the right margin, and the text wraps on the left side of the picture. Compare your screen with Figure 1.12.

FIGURE 1.12

Word 2016, Windows 10, Microsoft Corporation

MOS 5.2.2

Activity 1.08 | Applying Picture Effects

Picture styles include shapes, shadows, frames, borders, and other special effects with which you can stylize an image. ***Picture Effects*** enhance a picture with effects such as a shadow, glow, reflection, or 3-D rotation.

1 Be sure the picture is selected. On the **Format tab**, in the **Picture Styles group**, click **Picture Effects**.

2 Point to **Soft Edges**, and then click **5 Point**.

The Soft Edges feature fades the edges of the picture. The number of points you choose determines how far the fade goes inward from the edges of the picture.

3 Compare your screen with Figure 1.13, and then **Save** your document.

¶
This·summer,·Sturgeon·Point·Productions·will·be·filming·a·short·documentary·in·Costa·Rica·about·its·native·birds·and·has·positions·available·for·two·interns.·The·filming·will·begin·the·first·week·of·July·and·will·last·approximately·two·weeks.·Payment·will·be·by·Day·Rate·of·$100·per·day.·Transportation,·food,·and·lodging·will·be·provided.¶
The·First·Assistant·Director·will·work·with·the·second·film·crew,·which·will·be·filming·background·video.·The·Assistant·Script·Supervisor·will·work·with·the·Script·Supervisor·and·will·be·responsible·for·coordinating·communication·between·the·two·camera·crews.¶
You·must·have·a·valid·U.S.·passport;·no·inoculations·are·necessary.·Details·are·available·on·the·company·website.¶
¶
Soft Edges picture effect applied to picture
Page 1 of 1 117 words
100%

FIGURE 1.13

> ***More* Knowledge** **Applying Picture Styles**
>
> To apply a picture style, select the picture. On the Picture Tools Format tab, in the Picture Styles group, click More, and then click the Picture Style that you want to apply.

5.2.1

Activity 1.09 | Applying Artistic Effects

Artistic effects are formats that make pictures look more like sketches or paintings.

1 Be sure the picture is selected. On the **Format tab**, in the **Adjust group**, click **Artistic Effects**.

2 In the first row of the gallery, point to, but do not click, the third effect—**Pencil Grayscale**.

Live Preview displays the picture with the *Pencil Grayscale* effect added.

3 In the second row of the gallery, click the third effect—**Paint Brush**. **Save** your document, and then notice that the picture looks more like a painting than a photograph. Compare your screen with Figure 1.14.

Internships·Available¶
This·summer,·Sturgeon·Point·Productions·will·be·filming·a·short·documentary·in·Costa·Rica·about·its·native·birds·and·has·positions·available·for·two·interns.·The·filming·will·begin·the·first·week·of·July·and·will·last·approximately·two·weeks.·Payment·will·be·by·Day·Rate·of·$100·per·day.·Transportation,·food,·and·lodging·will·be·provided.¶
The·First·Assistant·Director·will·work·with·the·second·film·crew,·which·will·be·filming·background·video.·The·Assistant·Script·Supervisor·will·work·with·the·Script·Supervisor·and·will·be·responsible·for·coordinating·communication·between·the·two·camera·crews.¶
You·must·have·a·valid·U.·S.·passport;·no·inoculations·are·necessary.·Details·are·available·on·the·company·website.¶
Paint Brush artistic effect applied to picture
Page 1 of 1 117 words
100%

FIGURE 1.14 Word 2016, Windows 10, Microsoft Corporation

Activity 1.10 | Adding a Page Border

Page borders frame a page and help to focus the information on the page.

1 Click anywhere outside the picture to deselect it. On the **Design tab**, in the **Page Background group**, click **Page Borders**.

2 In the **Borders and Shading** dialog box, on the **Page Border tab**, under **Setting**, click **Box**. Under **Style**, scroll the list and click the seventh style—double lines.

3 Click the **Color arrow**, and then in the sixth column, click the first color—**Orange, Accent 2**.

4 Under **Apply to**, be sure *Whole document* is selected, and then compare your screen with Figure 1.15.

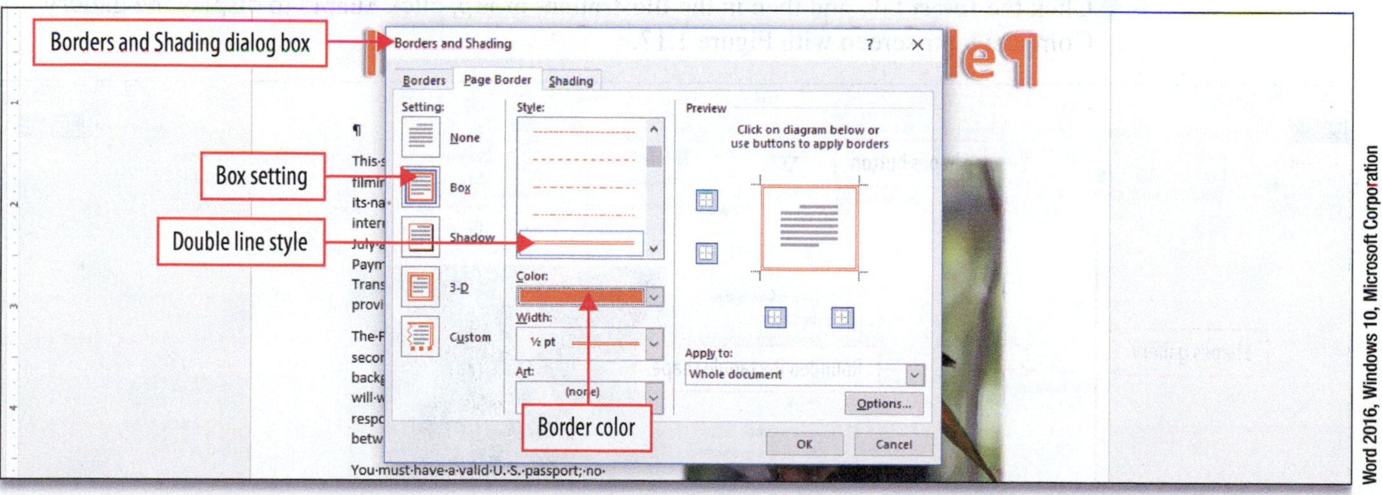
Borders and Shading dialog box
Borders and Shading
Borders
Page Border
Shading
Setting:
None
Box
Shadow
3-D
Custom
Style:
Color:
Width:
½ pt
Art:
(none)
Preview
Click on diagram below or use buttons to apply borders
Apply to:
Whole document
Options...
OK
Cancel
Box setting
Double line style
Border color

FIGURE 1.15 Word 2016, Windows 10, Microsoft Corporation

5 At the bottom of the **Borders and Shading** dialog box, click **OK**.

6 Press Ctrl + Home to move to the top of the document, click **Save**, and then compare your screen with Figure 1.16.

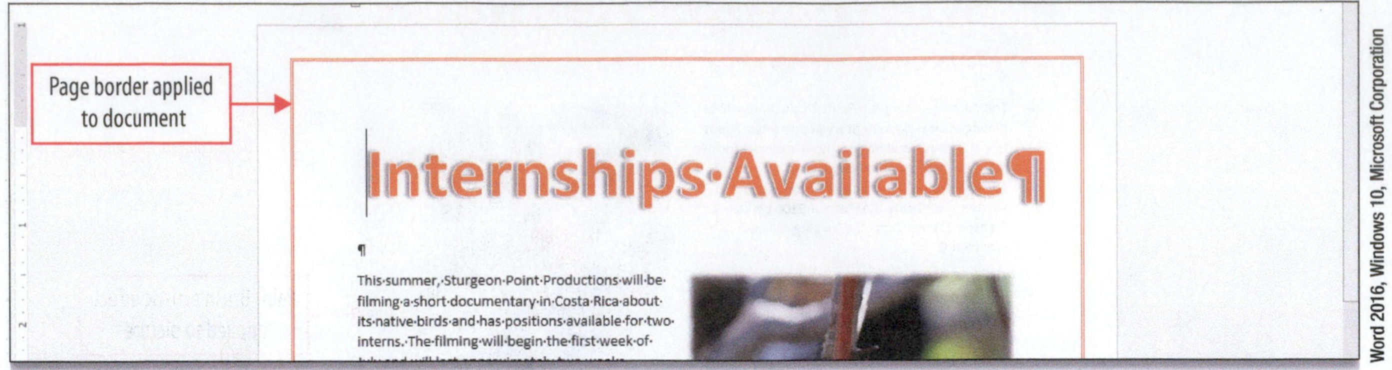

Word 2016, Windows 10, Microsoft Corporation

FIGURE 1.16

Objective 3 Insert and Modify Text Boxes and Shapes

GO! Learn How Video W1-3

Word has predefined ***shapes*** and ***text boxes*** that you can add to your documents. A shape is an object such as a line, arrow, box, callout, or banner. A text box is a movable, resizable container for text or graphics. Use these objects to add visual interest to your document.

5.1.1, 5.2.7

Activity 1.11 | Inserting, Sizing, and Positioning a Shape

1 Press ↓ one time to move to the blank paragraph below the title. Press Enter four times to create additional space for a text box, and notice that the picture anchored to the paragraph moves with the text.

2 Press Ctrl + End to move to the bottom of the document, and notice that your insertion point is positioned in the empty paragraph at the end of the document. Press Delete to remove the blank paragraph.

3 Click the **Insert tab**, and then in the **Illustrations group**, click **Shapes** to display the gallery. Compare your screen with Figure 1.17.

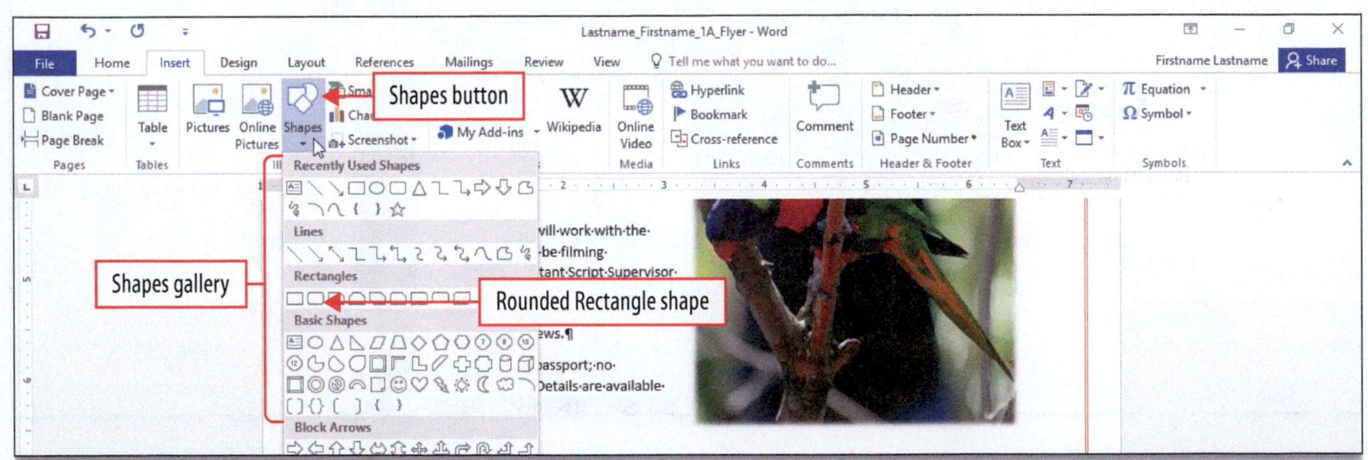

FIGURE 1.17

4 Under **Rectangles**, click the second shape—**Rounded Rectangle**, and then move your pointer. Notice that the ⊞ pointer displays.

5 Position the ⊞ pointer near the left margin at approximately **8 inches on the vertical ruler**. Click one time to insert a 1-inch by 1-inch rounded rectangle. The exact location is not important.

A blue rectangle with rounded edges displays.

6 To the right of the rectangle object, click **Layout Options**, and then at the bottom of the gallery, click **See more** to display the Layout dialog box.

ANOTHER WAY On the Format tab, in the Arrange group, click Position, and then click More Layout Options.

7 In the **Layout** dialog box, under **Horizontal**, click **Alignment**. To the right of **Alignment**, click the **arrow**, and then click **Centered**. To the right of **relative to**, click the **arrow**, and then click **Page**. Under **Vertical**, select the existing number in the **Absolute position** box, and then type **1** To the right of **below**, be sure that **Paragraph** displays. Click **OK**.

This action centers the rectangle on the page and positions the rectangle one inch below the last paragraph.

8 On the **Format tab**, click in the **Shape Height box** 0.29" to select the existing text. Type **1.5** and then click in the **Shape Width box** 1.07". Type **4.5** and then press Enter.

9 Compare your screen with Figure 1.18, and then **Save** your document.

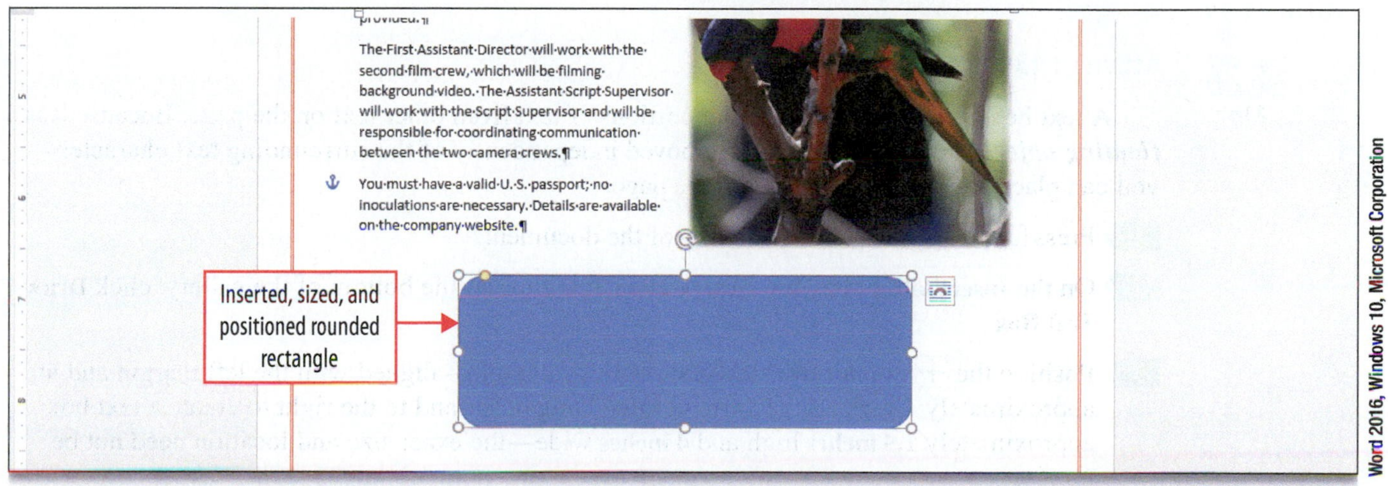

The·First·Assistant·Director·will·work·with·the·second·film·crew,·which·will·be·filming·background·video.·The·Assistant·Script·Supervisor·will·work·with·the·Script·Supervisor·and·will·be·responsible·for·coordinating·communication·between·the·two·camera·crews.¶
You·must·have·a·valid·U.S.·passport;·no·inoculations·are·necessary.·Details·are·available·on·the·company·website.¶
Inserted, sized, and positioned rounded rectangle
Word 2016, Windows 10, Microsoft Corporation

FIGURE 1.18

Activity 1.12 | Typing Text in a Shape and Formatting a Shape

MOS 5.2.4

1 If necessary, select the rectangle shape. Type **To set up an interview, apply online at:** and then press Enter. Type **www.SturgeonPointProductions.com**

2 Press Ctrl + A to select the text you just typed. Right-click over the selected text to display the mini toolbar, and then click **Bold** B. With the text still selected, click **Increase Font Size** three times to increase the font size to **16 pt**.

Use the keyboard shortcut Ctrl + A to select all of the text in a text box.

3 With the text still selected, on the mini toolbar, click the **Font Color button arrow**. Under **Theme Colors**, click **Black, Text 1**.

4 Click outside the shape to deselect the text. Click the border of the shape to select the shape but not the text. On the **Format tab**, in the **Shape Styles group**, click **Shape Fill**. In the sixth column, click the fourth color—**Orange, Accent 2, Lighter 40%**.

5 With the shape still selected, in the **Shape Styles group**, click **Shape Outline**. In the sixth column, click the first color—**Orange, Accent 2**. Compare your screen with Figure 1.19, and then **Save** your document.

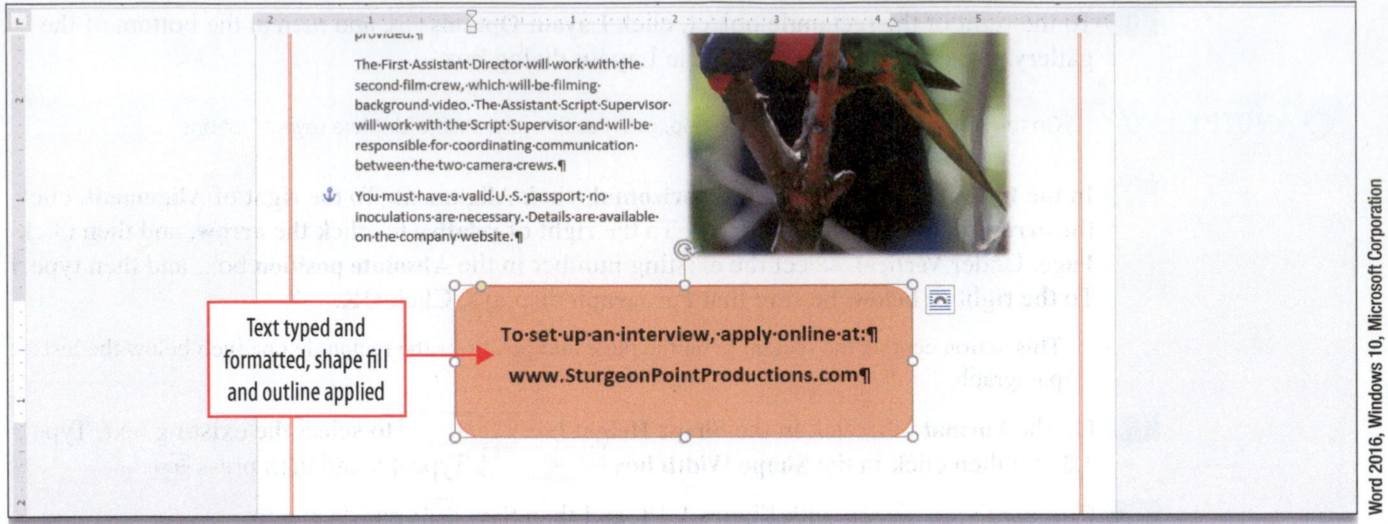

FIGURE 1.19

5.1.4

Activity 1.13 | Inserting a Text Box

A text box is useful to differentiate portions of text from other text on the page. Because it is a ***floating object***—a graphic that can be moved independently of the surrounding text characters—you can place a text box anywhere on the page.

1. Press Ctrl + Home to move to the top of the document.
2. On the **Insert tab**, in the **Text group**, click **Text Box**. At the bottom of the gallery, click **Draw Text Box.**
3. Position the ⊞ pointer over the first blank paragraph—aligned with the left margin and at approximately 1 inch on the vertical ruler. Drag down and to the right to create a text box approximately **1.5 inches** high and **4 inches** wide—the exact size and location need not be precise.
4. With the insertion point blinking in the text box, type the following, pressing Enter after each of the first *two* lines to create a new paragraph:

   Interviews will be held:
   Friday and Saturday, January 14 and 15
   In the Career Services Conference Room

5. Compare your screen with Figure 1.20, and then **Save** your document.

FIGURE 1.20

5.2.4

Activity 1.14 | Sizing and Positioning a Text Box and Formatting a Text Box Using Shape Styles

1. Point to the text box border to display the pointer. In the space below the *Internships Available* title, by dragging, move the text box until a horizontal green alignment guide displays above the first blank paragraph mark and a vertical green alignment guide displays in the center of the page, as shown in Figure 1.21. If the alignment guides do not display, drag the text box to position it approximately as shown in the Figure.

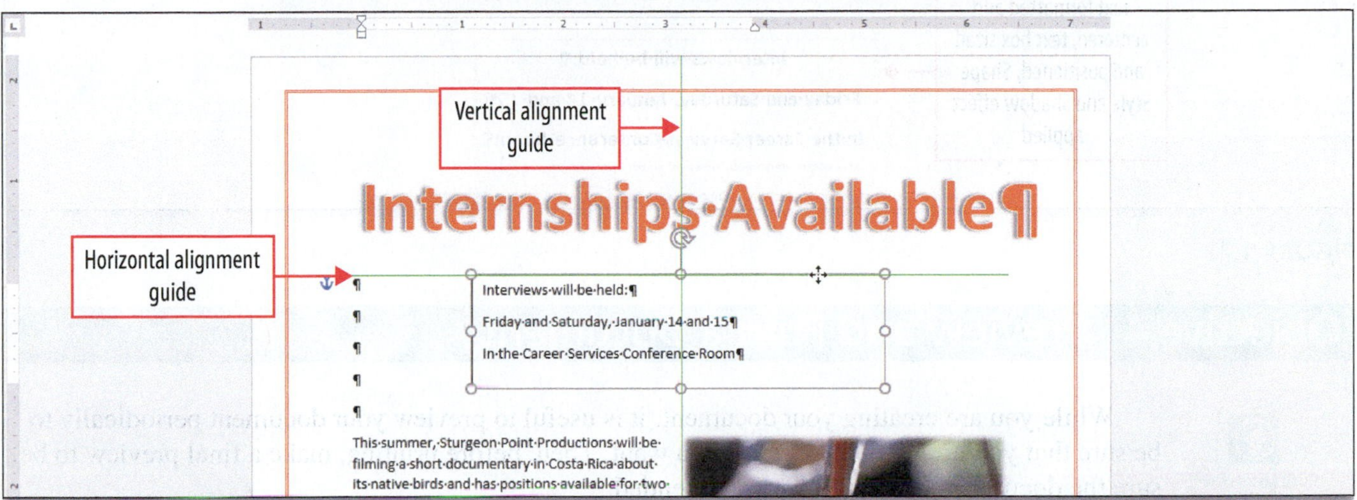

Vertical alignment guide
Internships·Available¶
Horizontal alignment guide
Interviews·will·be·held:¶
Friday·and·Saturday,·January·14·and·15¶
In·the·Career·Services·Conference·Room¶
This·summer,·Sturgeon·Point·Productions·will·be·
filming·a·short·documentary·in·Costa·Rica·about·
its·native·birds·and·has·positions·available·for·two·

Word 2016, Windows 10, Microsoft Corporation

FIGURE 1.21

2. To place the text box precisely, on the **Format tab**, in the **Arrange group**, click **Position**, and then click **More Layout Options**.
3. In the **Layout** dialog box, under **Horizontal**, click **Alignment**. To the right of **Alignment**, click the **arrow**, and then click **Centered**. To the right of **relative to**, click the **arrow**, and then click **Page**.
4. Under **Vertical**, click in the **Absolute position** box, select the existing number, and then type **1.25** To the right of **below**, click the **arrow**, and then click **Margin**.
5. In the **Layout** dialog box, click the **Size tab**. Under **Height**, select the number in the **Absolute** box. Type **1.25** and then under **Width**, select the number in the **Absolute** box. Type **4** and then click **OK**.

   The text box is sized correctly, centered horizontally, and the top edge is positioned 1.25 inches below the top margin of the document.
6. On the ribbon, under **Drawing Tools**, click the **Format tab**. In the **Shape Styles group**, click **More** , and then in the first row, click the third style—**Colored Outline – Orange, Accent 2**.
7. On the **Format tab**, in the **Shape Styles group**, click **Shape Effects**. Point to **Shadow**, and then under **Outer**, in the first row, click the first effect—**Offset Diagonal Bottom Right**.
8. Click in the text box, and then press Ctrl + A to select all of the text. Right-click over the selected text to display the mini toolbar, change the **Font Size** to **16** and apply **Bold** B. Press Ctrl + E to center the text.

   Ctrl + E is the keyboard shortcut to center text in a document or object.
9. Click anywhere in the document to deselect the text box. Compare your screen with Figure 1.22, and then **Save** your document.

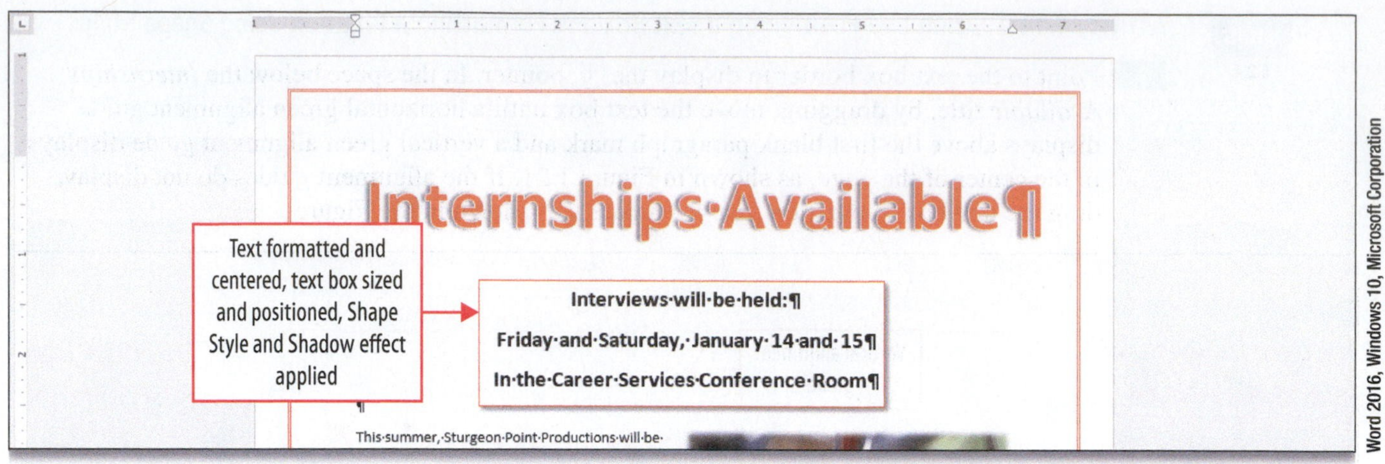
Internships·Available¶
Text formatted and centered, text box sized and positioned, Shape Style and Shadow effect applied
Interviews·will·be·held:¶
Friday·and·Saturday,·January·14·and·15¶
In·the·Career·Services·Conference·Room¶
This·summer,·Sturgeon·Point·Productions·will·be·
Word 2016, Windows 10, Microsoft Corporation

FIGURE 1.22

Objective 4 Preview and Print a Document

GO! Learn How Video W1-4

While you are creating your document, it is useful to preview your document periodically to be sure that you are getting the result you want. Then, before printing, make a final preview to be sure the document layout is what you intended.

1.3.4

Activity 1.15 | Adding a File Name to the Footer by Inserting a Field

Information in headers and footers helps to identify a document when it is printed or displayed electronically. Recall that a header is information that prints at the top of every page; a footer is information that prints at the bottom of every page. In this textbook, you will insert the file name in the footer of every Word document.

1. Click the **Insert tab**, and then in the **Header & Footer group**, click **Footer**.
2. At the bottom of the gallery, click **Edit Footer**.

   The footer area displays with the insertion point blinking at the left edge, and on the ribbon, the Header & Footer Tools display.

ANOTHER WAY At the bottom edge of the page, right-click; from the shortcut menu, click Edit Footer.

3. On the ribbon, under the **Header & Footer Tools**, on the **Design tab**, in the **Insert group**, click **Document Info**, and then click **File Name**. Compare your screen with Figure 1.23.

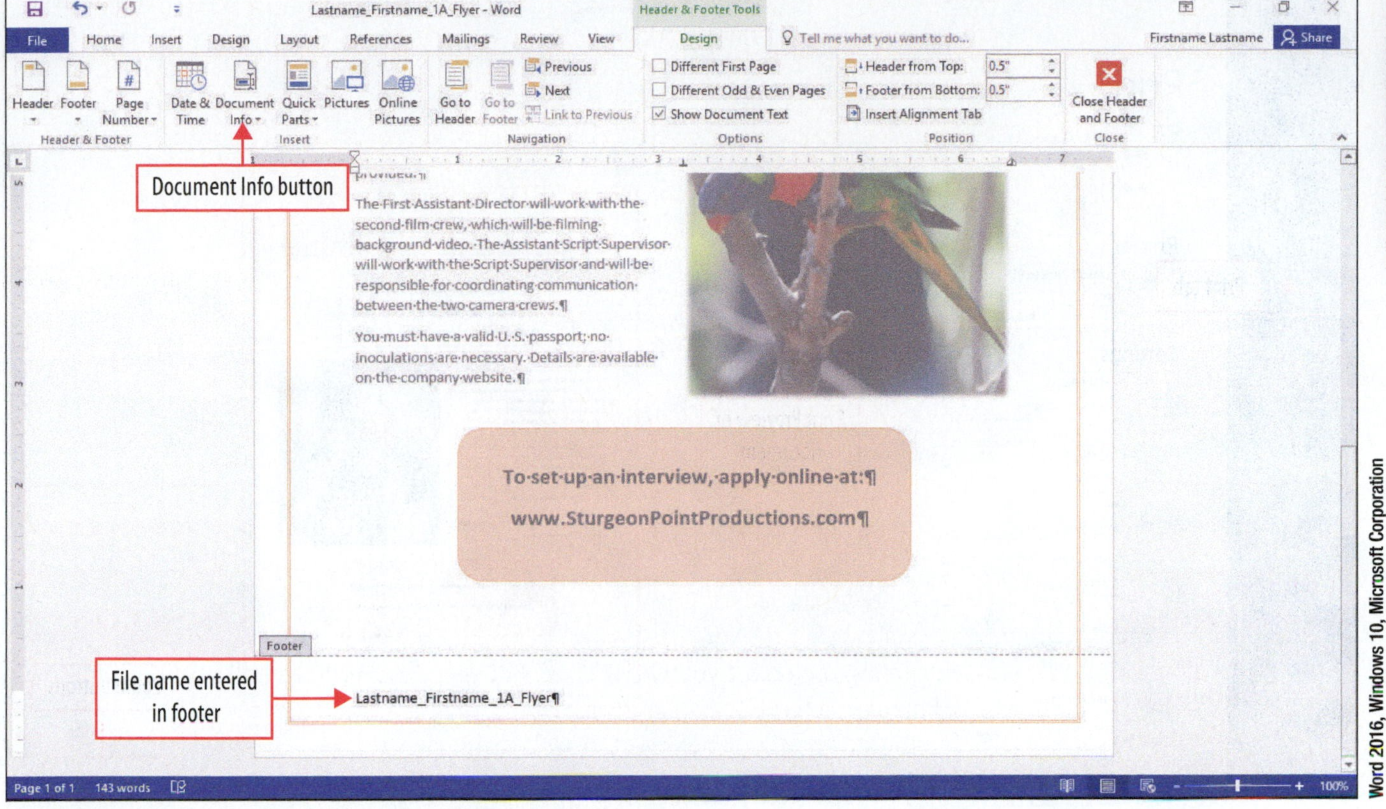

Word 2016, Windows 10, Microsoft Corporation

FIGURE 1.23

4 On the **Design tab**, click **Close Header and Footer**, and then **Save** your document.

When the body of the document is active, the footer text is dimmed—it displays in gray. Conversely, when the footer area is active, the footer text is not dimmed; instead, the document text is dimmed.

ANOTHER WAY Double-click in the document outside of the footer area to close the footer and return to the document.

1.4.5, 1.5.3

Activity 1.16 | Adding Document Properties and Previewing and Printing a Document

1 Press Ctrl + Home to move the insertion point to the top of the document. In the upper left corner of your screen, click the **File tab** to display **Backstage** view. On the right, at the bottom of the **Properties** list, click **Show All Properties**.

2 On the list of **Properties**, click to the right of **Tags** to display an empty box, and then type **internship, documentary**

3 Click to the right of **Subject** to display an empty box, and then type your course name and section number. Under **Related People**, be sure that your name displays as the author. If necessary, right-click the author name, click Edit Property, type your name, and click OK.

4 On the left, click **Print** to display the **Print Preview**. Compare your screen with Figure 1.24.

Here you can select any printer connected to your system and adjust the settings related to how you want to print. On the right, Print Preview displays your document exactly as it will print; the formatting marks do not display. At the bottom of the Print Preview area, in the center, the number of pages and arrows with which you can move among the pages in Print Preview displays. On the right, Zoom settings enable you to shrink or enlarge the Print Preview.

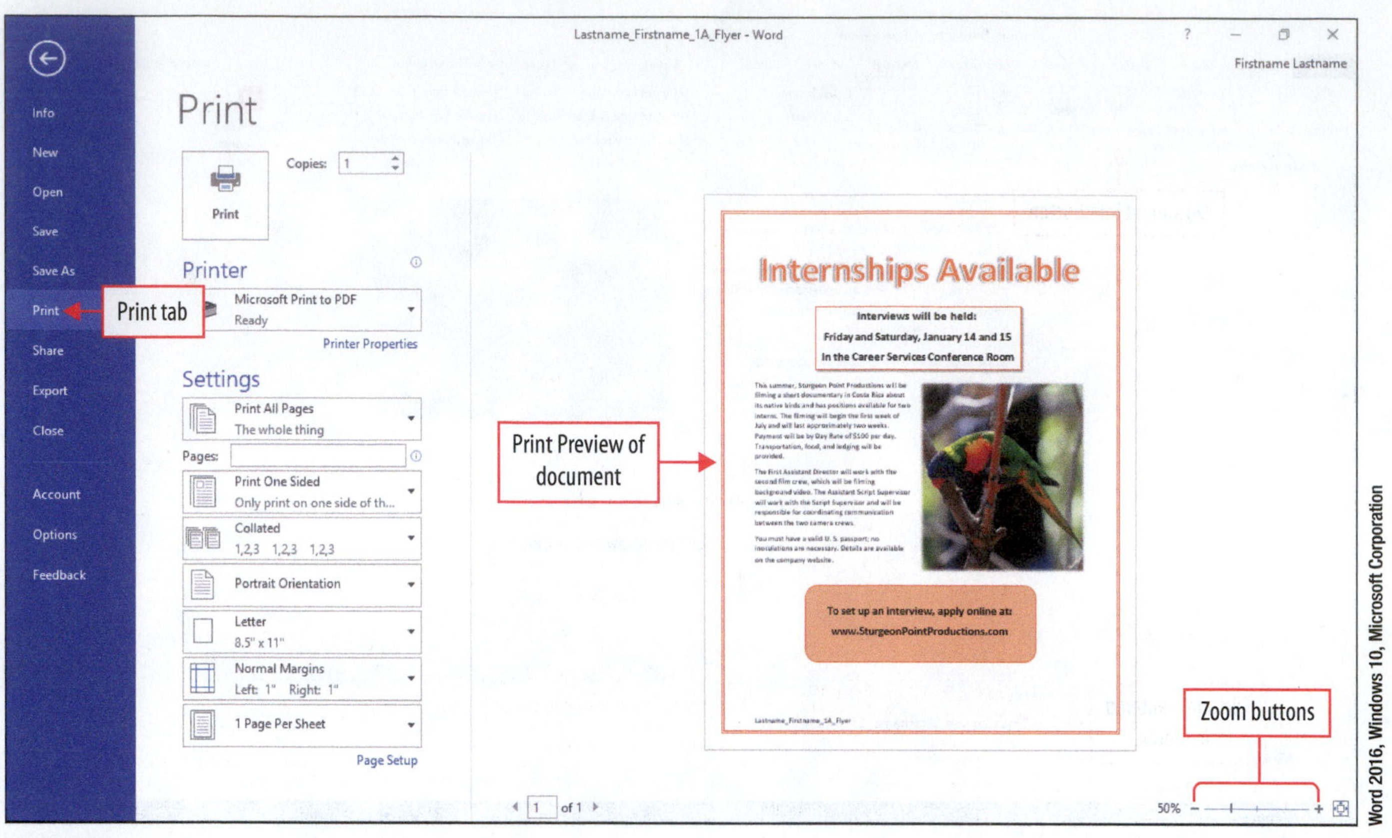

Word 2016, Windows 10, Microsoft Corporation

FIGURE 1.24

5 In the lower right corner of the window, click **Zoom In** several times to view the document at a larger size, and notice that a larger preview is easier to read. Click **Zoom to Page** to view the entire page.

6 If you want to print your document on paper using the default printer on your system, in the upper left portion of the screen, click **Print**.

The document will print on your default printer; if you do not have a color printer, colors will print in shades of gray. Backstage view closes and your file redisplays in the Word window.

7 **Save** your document. In the upper right corner of the Word window, click **Close** ✕. If directed by your instructor to do so, submit your paper printout, your electronic image of your document that looks like a printed document, or your completed Word file.

END | You have completed Project 1A

GO! With Google

Objective Create a Flyer Using Google Docs

uild from Scratch

ALERT! Working with Web-Based Applications and Services

Computer programs and services on the web receive continuous updates and improvements, so the steps to complete this web-based activity may differ from the ones shown. You can often look at the screens and the information presented to determine how to complete the activity.

If you do not already have a Google account, you will need to create one before you begin this activity. Go to http://google.com and, in the upper right corner, click Sign In. On the Sign In screen, click Create Account. On the Create your Google Account page, complete the form, read and agree to the Terms of Service and Privacy Policy, and then click Next step. On the Welcome screen, click Get Started.

Activity | Creating a Flyer

In this Activity, you will use Google Docs to create a flyer.

1 From the desktop, open your browser, navigate to http://google.com, and then sign in to your Google account. In the upper right corner of your screen, click **Google Apps** and then click **Drive**.

2 To create a folder in which to store your web projects, click **NEW**, and then click **Folder**. In the **New folder** box, type **GO! Web Projects** and then click **Create** to create a folder on your Google drive. Double-click your **GO! Web Projects** folder to open it.

3 In the left pane, click **NEW**, and then click **Google Docs** to open a new tab in your browser and to start an Untitled document. At the top of the window, click **Untitled document** and then, using your own name as the file name, type **Lastname_Firstname_1A_Google_Doc** and then press Enter to change the file name.

4 To the right of the file name, point to the small file folder to display the ScreenTip **Move to folder**. Click the file folder and notice that your file is saved in the GO! Web Projects folder. Compare your screen with Figure A.

5 Click in your document to close the Move to folder dialog box and to position the insertion point at the top of the document. Type **Internships Available** and then press Enter two times. Type **Interviews will be held Friday and Saturday, January 14 and 15 in the Career Services Conference Room.**

6 Press Ctrl + A to select all of the text. Click the **Font size arrow**, and then click **24**. With the text still selected, click **Center**.

7 Press Ctrl + End to move to the end of the document, and then press Enter. Click **Insert**, and then click **Image**. With **Upload** selected, click **Choose an image to upload**. Navigate to your student data files, click **w01A_Bird**, and then click **Open** to insert the picture.

8 Click the picture to select it, and then point to the square sizing handle at the upper left corner of the picture. Drag down and to the right until the sizing handle aligns with approximately **3 inches on the ruler**.

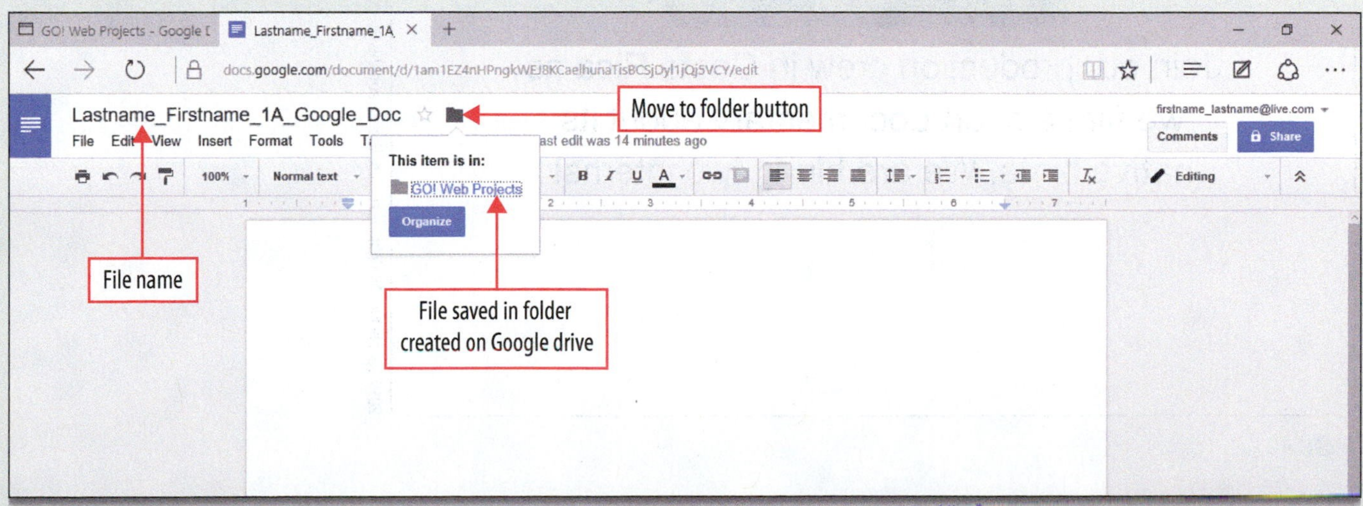

FIGURE A

(GO! With Google continues on the next page)

GO! With Google

9 Click to the right of the picture and then press Enter twice. Type **Join our production crew in Costa Rica as we film a short documentary about its native birds. We are hiring two interns!**

10 Select the title **Internships Available** and then click **Text color** [A]. In the third column, click the sixth color—**dark orange 1**, and then apply **Bold** [B]. Your document will look similar to Figure B.

11 Your document will be saved automatically. Sign out of your Google account. Submit as instructed by your instructor.

Internships Available

Interviews will be held Friday and Saturday, January 14 and 15 in the Career Services Conference Room.

Join our production crew in Costa Rica as we film a short documentary about its native birds. We are hiring two interns!

FIGURE B

PROJECT 1B

Information Handout

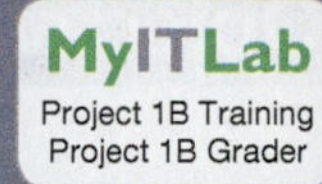

PROJECT ACTIVITIES

In Activities 1.17 through 1.29, you will format an information handout from Sturgeon Point Productions that describes internships available to students. Your completed document will look similar to Figure 1.25.

Please always review the downloaded Grader instructions before beginning.

PROJECT FILES

If your instructor wants you to submit Project 1B in the MyITLab Grader system, log in to MyITLab, locate Grader Project 1B, and then download the files for this project.

For Project 1B, you will need the following file:
w01B_Programs

You will save your document as:
Lastname_Firstname_1B_Programs

PROJECT RESULTS

GO! Walk Thru Project 1B

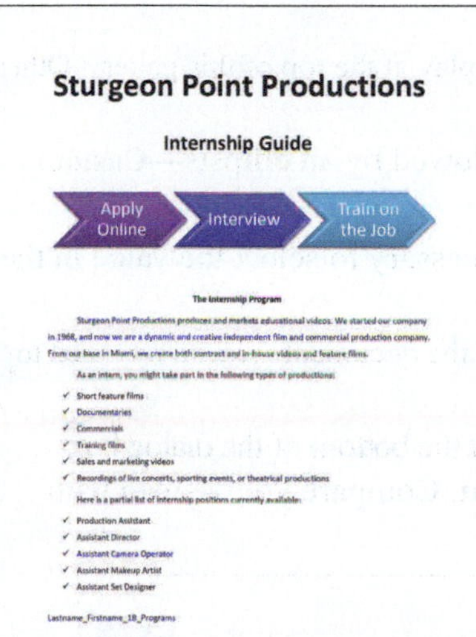

Sturgeon Point Productions

Internship Guide

Apply Online | Interview | Train on the Job

The Internship Program

Sturgeon Point Productions produces and markets educational videos. We started our company in 1968, and now we are a dynamic and creative independent film and commercial production company. From our base in Miami, we create both contract and in-house videos and feature films.

As an intern, you might take part in the following types of productions:

- ✓ Short feature films
- ✓ Documentaries
- ✓ Commercials
- ✓ Training films
- ✓ Sales and marketing videos
- ✓ Recordings of live concerts, sporting events, or theatrical productions

Here is a partial list of internship positions currently available:

- ✓ Production Assistant
- ✓ Assistant Director
- ✓ Assistant Camera Operator
- ✓ Assistant Makeup Artist
- ✓ Assistant Set Designer

Lastname_Firstname_1B_Programs

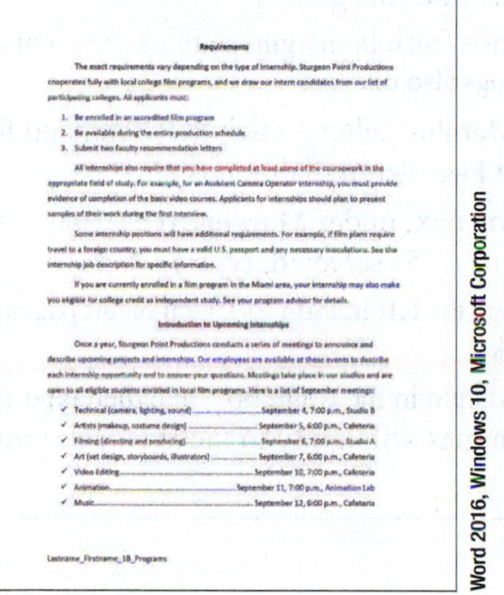

Requirements

The exact requirements vary depending on the type of internship. Sturgeon Point Productions cooperates fully with local college film programs, and we draw our intern candidates from our list of participating colleges. All applicants must:

1. Be enrolled in an accredited film program
2. Be available during the entire production schedule
3. Submit two faculty recommendation letters

All internships also require that you have completed at least some of the coursework in the appropriate field of study. For example, for an Assistent Camera Operator internship, you must provide evidence of completion of the basic video courses. Applicants for internships should plan to present samples of their work during the first interview.

Some internship positions will have additional requirements. For example, if film plans require travel to a foreign country, you must have a valid U.S. passport and any necessary inoculations. See the internship job description for specific information.

If you are currently enrolled in a film program in the Miami area, your internship may also make you eligible for college credit as independent study. See your program advisor for details.

Introduction to Upcoming Internships

Once a year, Sturgeon Point Productions conducts a series of meetings to announce and describe upcoming projects and internships. Our employees are available at these events to describe each internship opportunity and to answer your questions. Meetings take place in our studios and are open to all eligible students enrolled in local film programs. Here is a list of September meetings:

- ✓ Technical (camera, lighting, sound)..........September 4, 7:00 p.m., Studio B
- ✓ Artists (makeup, costume design)..........September 5, 6:00 p.m., Cafeteria
- ✓ Filming (directing and producing)..........September 6, 7:00 p.m., Studio A
- ✓ Art (set design, storyboards, illustrators)..........September 7, 6:00 p.m., Cafeteria
- ✓ Video Editing..........September 10, 7:00 p.m., Cafeteria
- ✓ Animation..........September 11, 7:00 p.m., Animation Lab
- ✓ Music..........September 12, 6:00 p.m., Cafeteria

Lastname_Firstname_1B_Programs

For more information and to sign up for our weekly newsletter, visit our website at www.sturgeonpointproductions.com. Be sure to view the following video to learn about some of the important skills you will develop as an intern with Sturgeon Point Productions.

Lastname_Firstname_1B_Programs

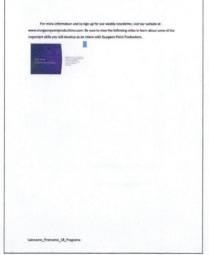

FIGURE 1.25 Project 1B Information Handout

Objective 5 Change Document and Paragraph Layout

Document layout includes ***margins***—the space between the text and the top, bottom, left, and right edges of the paper. Paragraph layout includes line spacing, indents, and tabs. In Word, the information about paragraph formats is stored in the paragraph mark at the end of a paragraph. When you press Enter, the new paragraph mark contains the formatting of the previous paragraph, unless you take steps to change it.

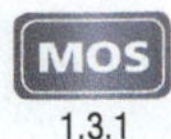

1.3.1

Activity 1.17 | Setting Margins

> **ALERT!**
> **To submit as an autograded project, log into MyITLab and download the files for this project, and begin with those files instead of w01B_Programs.**

1. Start Word, and then click **Open Other Documents**. Navigate to the student files that accompany this textbook, and then open the document **w01B_Programs**. On the **Home tab**, in the **Paragraph group**, be sure **Show/Hide** ¶ is active so that you can view the formatting marks.
2. Click the **File tab**, and then click **Save As**. Navigate to your **Word Chapter 1** folder, and then using your own name, **Save** the document as **Lastname_Firstname_1B_Programs**
3. Click the **Layout tab**. In the **Page Setup group**, click **Margins**, and then take a moment to study the settings in the Margins gallery.

   If you have recently used custom margins settings, they will display at the top of this gallery. Other commonly used settings also display.
4. At the bottom of the **Margins** gallery, click the command followed by an ellipsis—**Custom Margins** to display the **Page Setup** dialog box.
5. In the **Page Setup** dialog box, under **Margins**, press Tab as necessary to select the value in the **Left** box, and then, with *1.25*" selected, type **1**

   This action will change the left margin to 1 inch on all pages of the document. You do not need to type the inch (") mark.
6. Press Tab to select the margin in the **Right** box, and then type **1** At the bottom of the dialog box, notice that the new margins will apply to the **Whole document**. Compare your screen with Figure 1.26.

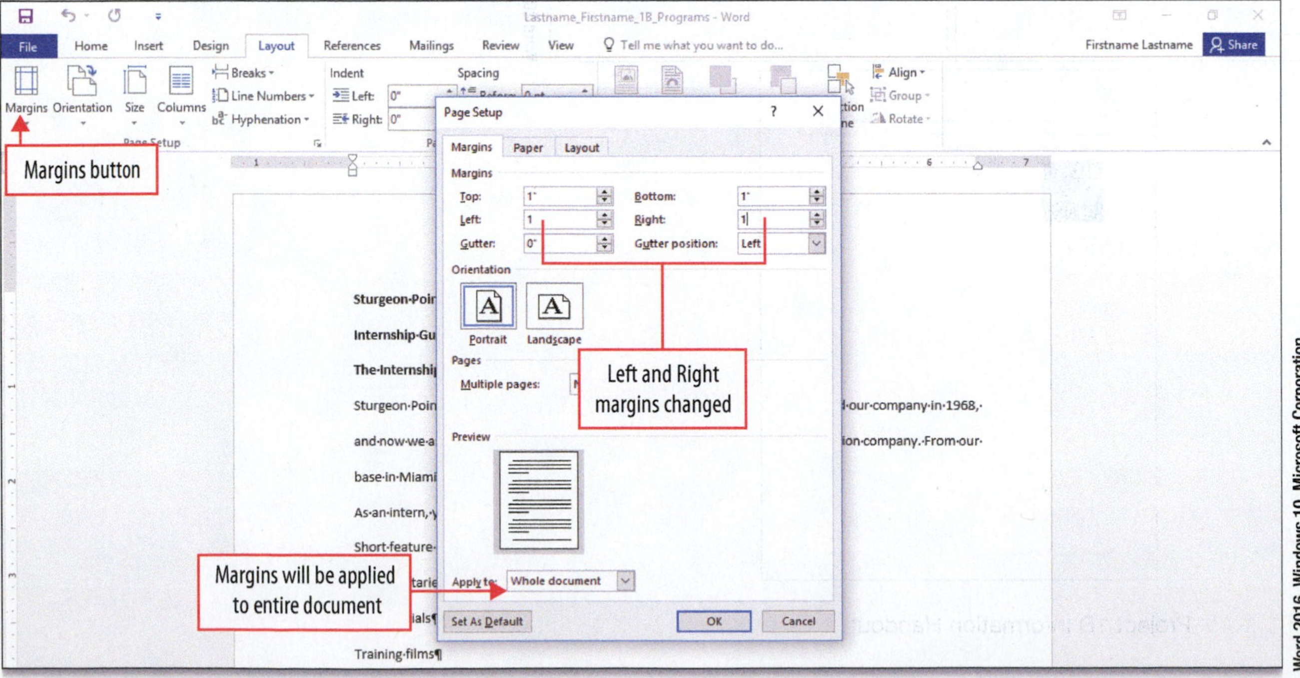

FIGURE 1.26

7 Click **OK** to apply the new margins and close the dialog box. If the ruler below the ribbon is not displayed, on the View tab, in the Show group, select the Ruler check box.

8 Scroll to position the bottom of **Page 1** and the top of **Page 2** on your screen. Notice that the page edges display, and the page number and total number of pages display on the left side of the status bar.

9 Near the bottom edge of **Page 1**, point anywhere in the bottom margin area, right-click, and then click **Edit Footer** to display the footer area.

10 On the ribbon, under the **Header & Footer Tools**, on the **Design tab**, in the **Insert group**, click **Document Info**, and then click **File Name**.

11 Double-click anywhere in the document to close the footer area, and then **Save** your document.

1 WORD

Activity 1.18 | Aligning Paragraphs

Alignment refers to the placement of paragraph text relative to the left and right margins. Most paragraph text uses ***left alignment***—aligned at the left margin, leaving the right margin uneven. Three other types of paragraph alignment are: ***center alignment***—centered between the left and right margins; ***right alignment***—aligned at the right margin with an uneven left margin; and ***justified alignment***—text aligned evenly at both the left and right margins. The table in Figure 1.27 shows examples of these alignment types.

TYPES OF PARAGRAPH ALIGNMENT		
ALIGNMENT	**BUTTON**	**DESCRIPTION AND EXAMPLE**
Align Left		Align Left is the default paragraph alignment in Word. Text in the paragraph aligns at the left margin, and the right margin is uneven.
Center		Center alignment aligns text in the paragraph so that it is centered between the left and right margins.
Align Right		Align Right aligns text at the right margin. Using Align Right, the left margin, which is normally even, is uneven.
Justify		The Justify alignment option adds additional space between words so that both the left and right margins are even. Justify is often used when formatting newspaper-style columns.

Word 2016, Windows 10, Microsoft Corporation

FIGURE 1.27

1 Scroll to position the middle of **Page 2** on your screen, look at the left and right margins, and notice that the text is justified—both the right and left margins of multiple-line paragraphs are aligned evenly at the margins. On the **Home tab**, in the **Paragraph group**, notice that **Justify** is active.

To achieve a justified right margin, Word adjusts the size of spaces between words, which can result in unattractive spacing in a document that spans the width of a page. Many individuals find such spacing difficult to read.

2 Press Ctrl + A to select all of the text in the document, and then on the **Home tab**, in the **Paragraph group**, click **Align Left**.

ANOTHER WAY On the Home tab, in the Editing group, click Select, and then click Select All.

3 Press Ctrl + Home to move to the beginning of the document. In the left margin area, point to the left of the first paragraph—*Sturgeon Point Productions*—until the pointer displays, and then click one time to select the paragraph.

Use this technique to select entire lines of text.

4 On the mini toolbar, in the **Font Size** box, select the existing number, type **40** and then press Enter.

Use this technique to change the font size to a size that is not available on the Font Size list.

5 Select the second paragraph—*Internship Guide*—and then on the mini toolbar, change the **Font Size** to **26 pt**. Point to the left of the first paragraph—*Sturgeon Point Productions*—to display the pointer again, and then drag down to select the first two paragraphs, which form the title and subtitle of the document.

6 On the **Home tab**, in the **Paragraph group**, click **Center** to center the title and subtitle between the left and right margins, and then compare your screen with Figure 1.28.

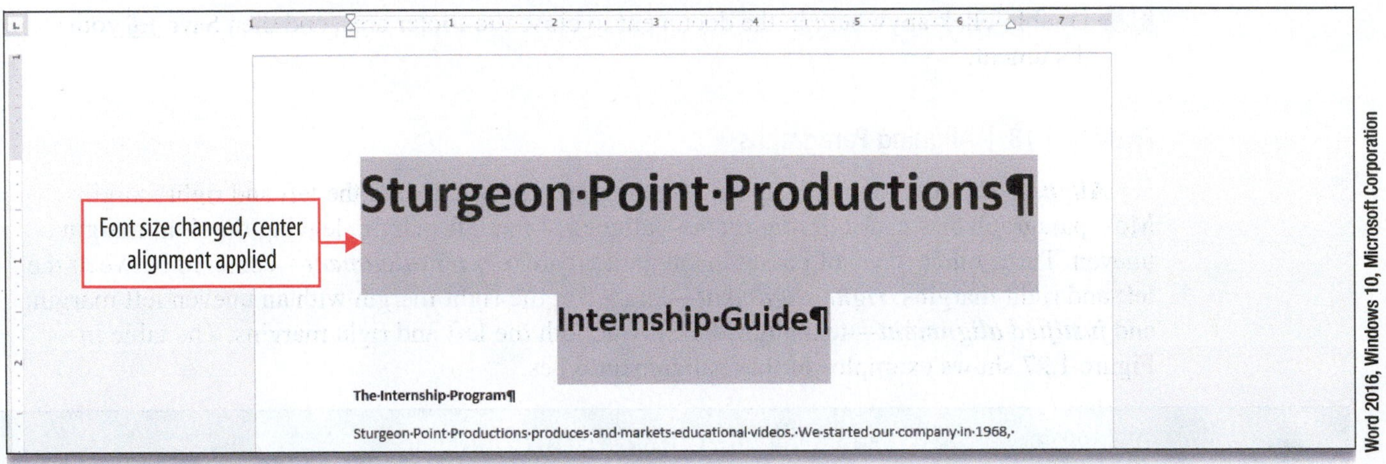

Sturgeon·Point·Productions¶
Font size changed, center alignment applied
Internship·Guide¶
The·Internship·Program¶
Sturgeon·Point·Productions·produces·and·markets·educational·videos.·We·started·our·company·in·1968,·
Word 2016, Windows 10, Microsoft Corporation

FIGURE 1.28

7 Near the top of **Page 1**, locate the first bold subheading—*The Internship Program*. Point to the left of the paragraph to display the pointer, and then click one time to select the text.

8 With *The Internship Program* selected, use your mouse wheel or the vertical scroll bar to bring the bottom portion of **Page 1** into view. Locate the subheading *Requirements*. Move the pointer to the left of the paragraph to display the pointer, hold down Ctrl, and then click one time. Release Ctrl, and then scroll to the middle of **Page 2**. Use the same technique to select the third subheading—*Introduction to Upcoming Internships*.

Three subheadings are selected; in Windows-based programs, you can hold down Ctrl to select multiple items.

9 Click **Center** to center all three subheadings, and then click **Save**.

2.2.3

Activity 1.19 | Setting Line Spacing

Line spacing is the distance between lines of text in a paragraph. Three of the most commonly used line spacing options are shown in the table in Figure 1.29.

LINE SPACING OPTIONS	
ALIGNMENT	**DESCRIPTION, EXAMPLE, AND INFORMATION**
Single spacing	**This text in this example uses single spacing**. Single spacing was once the most commonly used spacing in business documents. Now, because so many documents are read on a computer screen rather than on paper, single spacing is becoming less popular.
Multiple 1.08 spacing	**This text in this example uses multiple 1.08 spacing**. The default line spacing in Microsoft Word 2016 is 1.08, which is slightly more than single spacing to make the text easier to read on a computer screen. Many individuals now prefer this spacing, even on paper, because the lines of text appear less crowded.
Double spacing	**This text in this example uses double spacing**. College research papers and draft documents that need space for notes are commonly double-spaced; there is space for a full line of text between each document line.

FIGURE 1.29

Word 2016, Windows 10, Microsoft Corporation

1 Press Ctrl + Home to move to the beginning of the document. Press Ctrl + A to select all of the text in the document.

2 With all of the text in the document selected, on the **Home tab**, in the **Paragraph group**, click **Line and Paragraph Spacing**, and notice that the text in the document is double-spaced—**2.0** is checked. Compare your screen with Figure 1.30.

Tap the ribbon commands.

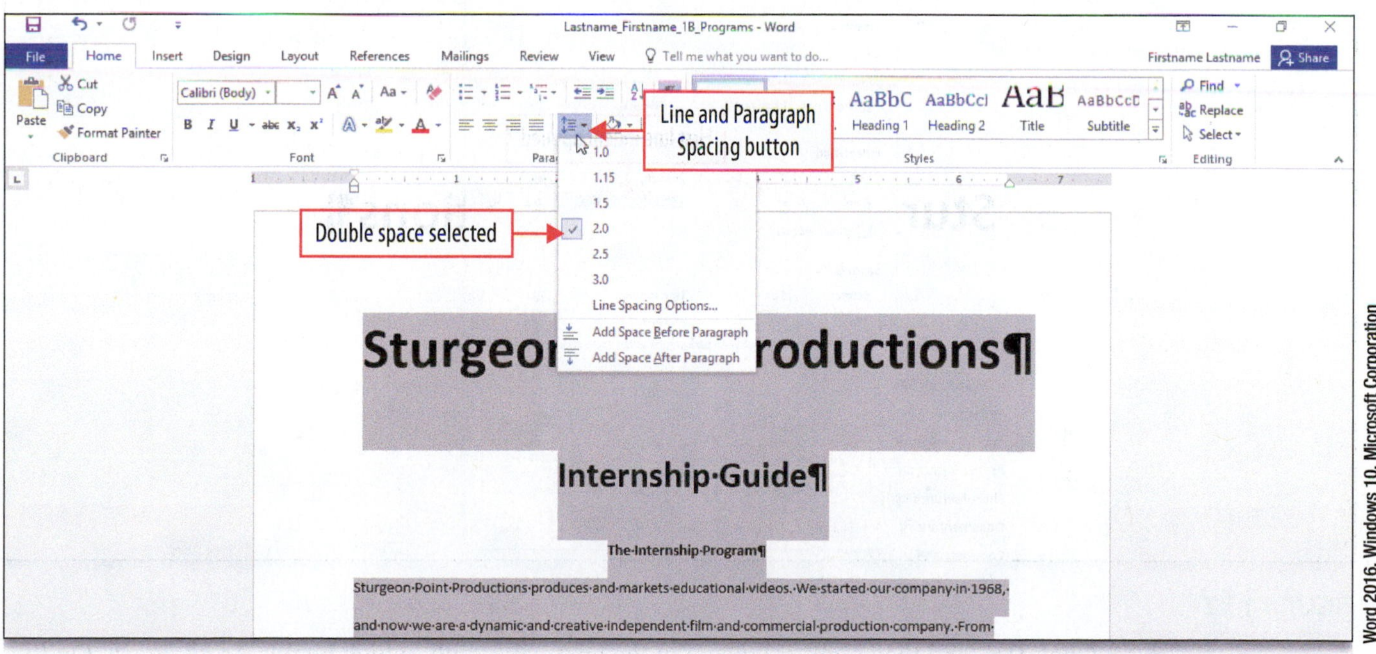

FIGURE 1.30

Word 2016, Windows 10, Microsoft Corporation

3 On the **Line Spacing** menu, click the *third* setting—**1.5**—and then click anywhere in the document to deselect the text. Compare your screen with Figure 1.31, and then **Save** your document.

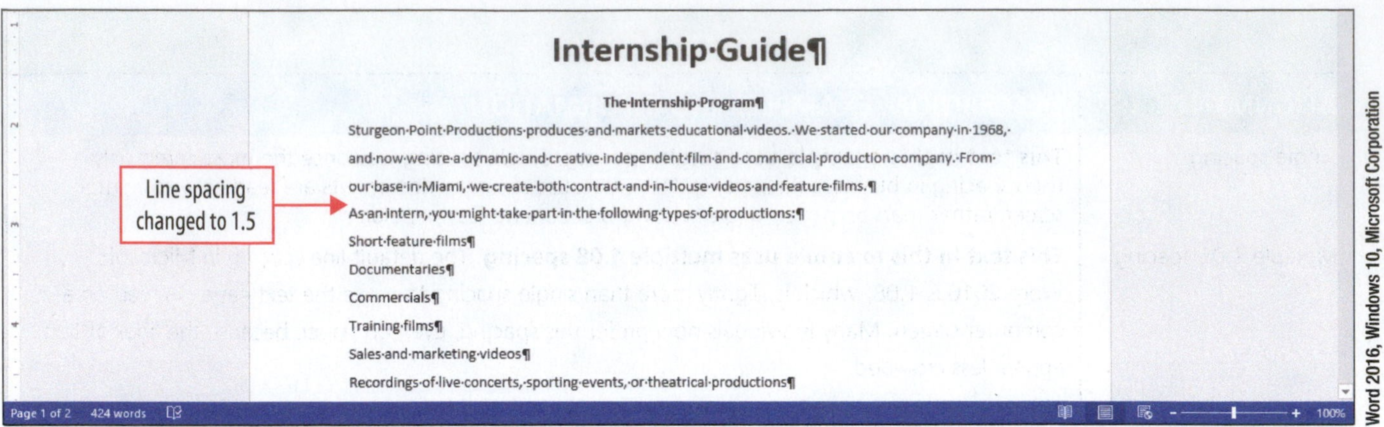

FIGURE 1.31

Activity 1.20 | Indenting Text

MOS 2.2.3

Indenting the first line of each paragraph is a common technique to distinguish paragraphs.

1 Below the title and subtitle of the document, click anywhere in the paragraph that begins *Sturgeon Point Productions produces*.

2 On the **Home tab**, in the **Paragraph group**, click the **Dialog Box Launcher**.

3 In the **Paragraph** dialog box, on the **Indents and Spacing tab**, under **Indentation**, click the **Special arrow**, and then click **First line** to indent the first line by 0.5", which is the default indent setting. Compare your screen with Figure 1.32.

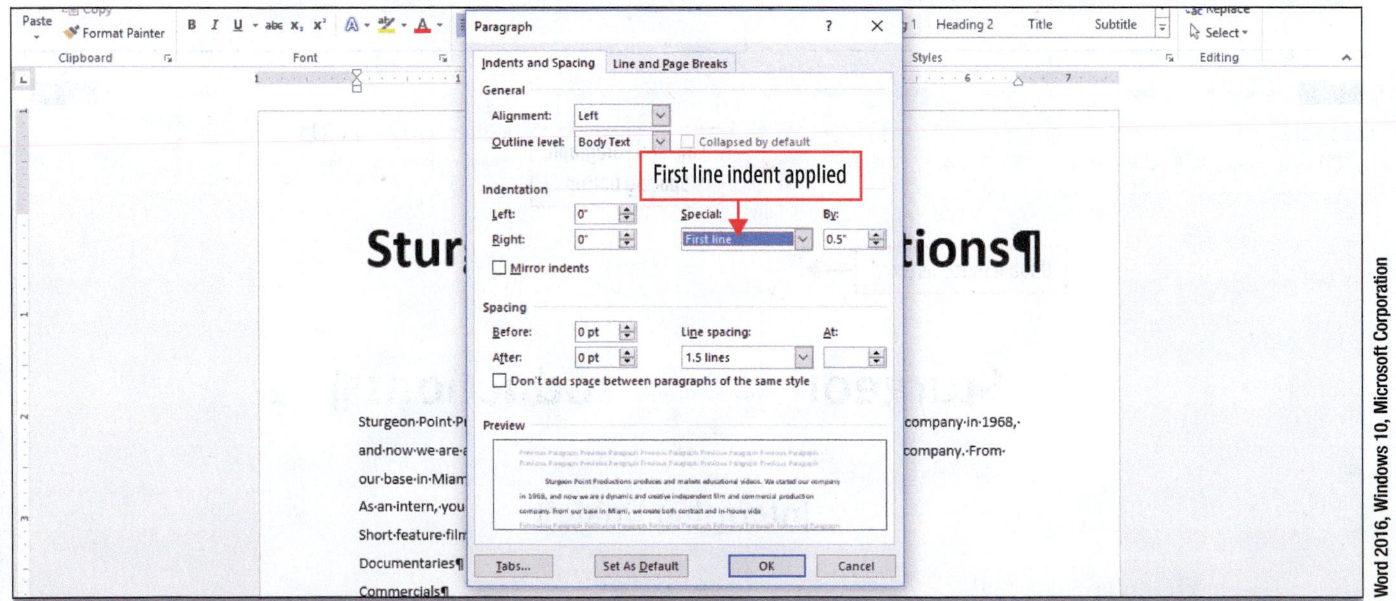

FIGURE 1.32

4 Click **OK**, and then click anywhere in the next paragraph, which begins *As an intern*. On the ruler under the ribbon, drag the **First Line Indent** marker to **0.5 inches on the horizontal ruler**, and then compare your screen with Figure 1.33.

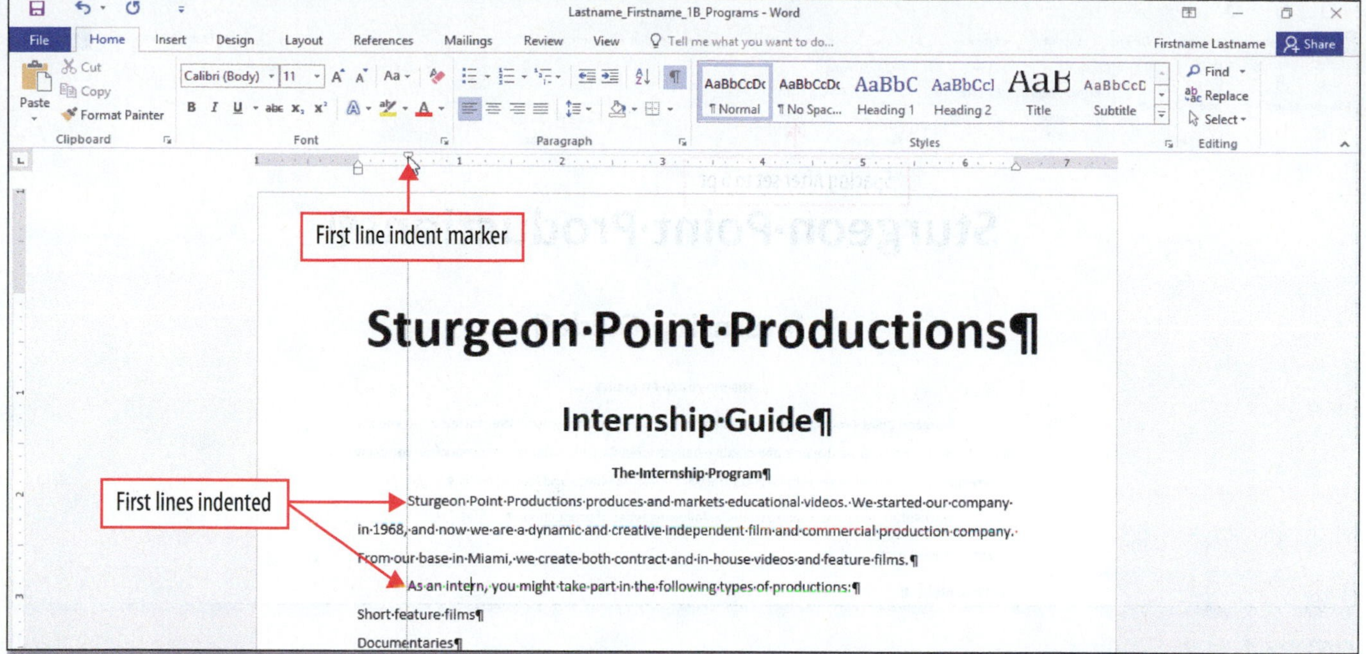

Word 2016, Windows 10, Microsoft Corporation

FIGURE 1.33

5 By using either of the techniques you just practiced, or by using the Format Painter, apply a first line indent of **0.5"** to the paragraph that begins *Here is a partial* to match the indent of the remaining paragraphs in the document.

6 **Save** your document.

1.2.3

Activity 1.21 | Setting Space Before and After Paragraphs

Adding space after each paragraph is another technique to differentiate paragraphs.

1 Press Ctrl + A to select all of the text in the document. Click the **Layout tab**, and then in the **Paragraph group**, under **Spacing**, click the **After spin box up arrow** one time to change the value to **6 pt**.

To change the value in the box, you can also select the existing number, type a new number, and then press Enter. This document will use 6 pt spacing after paragraphs to add space.

On either the Home tab or the Layout tab, display the Paragraph dialog box from the Paragraph group, and then under Spacing, click the spin box arrows as necessary.

2 Press Ctrl + Home, and then compare your screen with Figure 1.34.

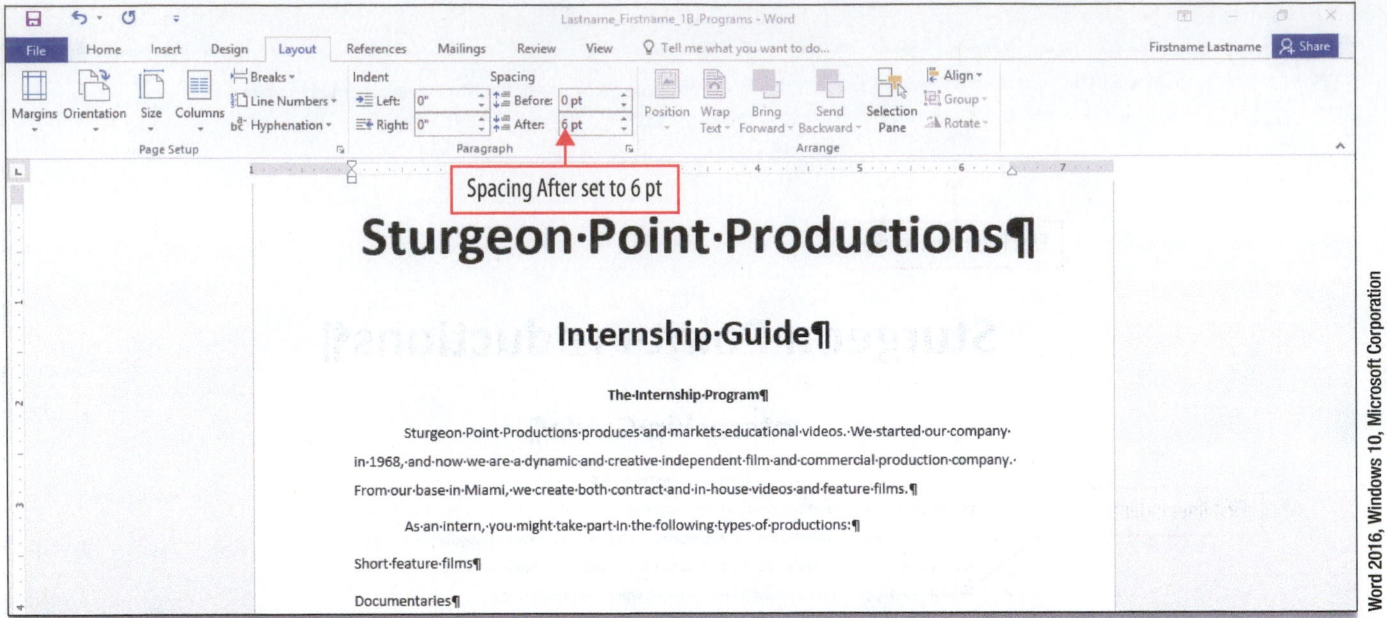

FIGURE 1.34

3 Near the top of **Page 1**, select the subheading **The Internship Program**, including the paragraph mark following it. Scroll down using the vertical scroll bar, hold down Ctrl, and then select the **Requirements** and **Introduction to Upcoming Internships** subheadings.

> **ALERT!**
> **Did your screen zoom when you were selecting?**
> Holding down Ctrl and using the mouse wheel at the same time will zoom your screen.

4 With all three subheadings selected, in the **Paragraph group**, under **Spacing**, click the **Before up spin box arrow** two times to set the **Spacing Before** to **12 pt**. Compare your screen with Figure 1.35, and then **Save** your document.

This action increases the amount of space above each of the subheadings, which will make them easy to distinguish in the document. The formatting is applied only to the selected paragraphs.

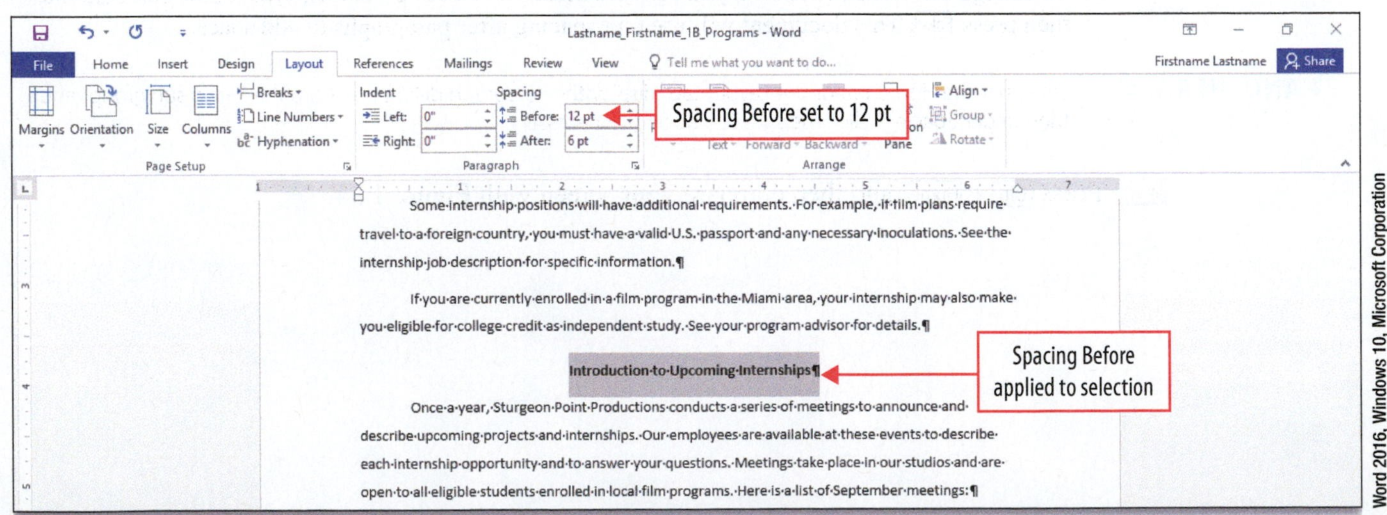

FIGURE 1.35

Objective 6 Create and Modify Lists

GO! Learn How Video W1-6

To display a list of information, you can choose a ***bulleted list***, which uses ***bullets***—text symbols such as small circles or check marks—to introduce each item in a list. You can also choose a ***numbered list***, which uses consecutive numbers or letters to introduce each item in a list.

Use a bulleted list if the items in the list can be introduced in any order; use a numbered list for items that have definite steps, a sequence of actions, or are in chronological order.

3.3.1

Activity 1.22 | Creating a Bulleted List

1 In the upper portion of **Page 1**, locate the paragraph *Short feature films*, and then point to this paragraph from the left margin area to display the pointer. Drag down to select this paragraph and the next five paragraphs—ending with the paragraph *Recordings of live concerts*.

2 On the **Home tab**, in the **Paragraph group**, click **Bullets** to change the selected text to a bulleted list.

The 6 pt spacing between each of the bulleted points is removed and each bulleted item is automatically indented.

3 On the ruler, point to **First Line Indent** and read the ScreenTip, and then point to **Hanging Indent**. Compare your screen with Figure 1.36.

By default, Word formats bulleted items with a first line indent of 0.25" and adds a Hanging Indent at 0.5". The hanging indent maintains the alignment of text when a bulleted item is more than one line.

You can modify the list indentation by using Decrease Indent or Increase Indent. Decrease Indent moves your paragraph closer to the margin. Increase Indent moves your paragraph farther away from the margin.

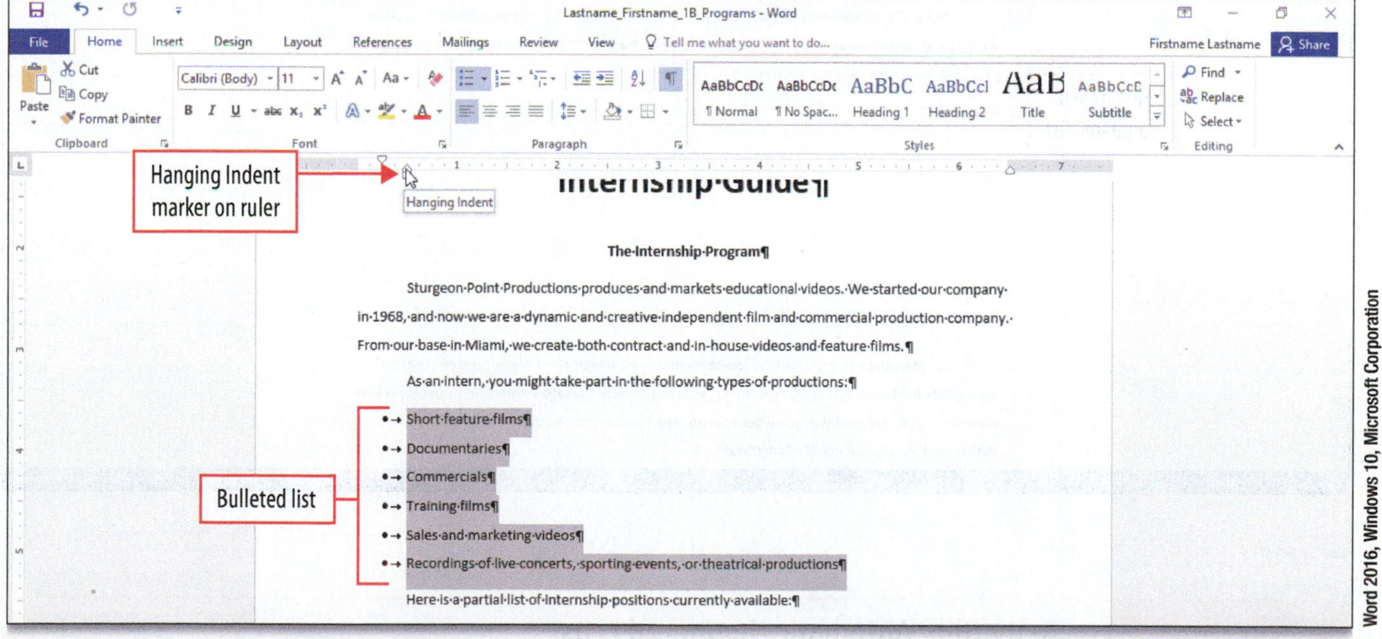

FIGURE 1.36

4 Scroll down slightly, and then by using the pointer from the left margin area, select the five internship positions, beginning with *Production Assistant* and ending with *Assistant Set Designer*. In the **Paragraph group**, click **Bullets**.

5 Scroll down to view **Page 2**. Apply bullets to all of the paragraphs that indicate the September meetings and meeting dates, beginning with *Technical* and ending with *Music*.

6 **Save** your document.

3.3.1

Activity 1.23 | Creating a Numbered List

1 Under the subheading *Requirements*, in the paragraph that begins *The exact requirements*, click to position the insertion point at the *end* of the paragraph, following the colon. Press Enter to create a blank paragraph. Notice that the paragraph is indented because the First Line Indent from the previous paragraph carried over to the new paragraph.

2 To change the indent formatting for this paragraph, on the ruler, drag the **First Line Indent** marker to the left so that it is positioned directly above the lower button.

3 Being sure to include the period, type **1.** and press Spacebar. Compare your screen with Figure 1.37.

Word determines that this paragraph is the first item in a numbered list and formats the new paragraph accordingly, indenting the list in the same manner as the bulleted list. The space after the number changes to a tab, and the AutoCorrect Options button displays to the left of the list item. The tab is indicated by a right arrow formatting mark.

Word 2016, Windows 10, Microsoft Corporation

FIGURE 1.37

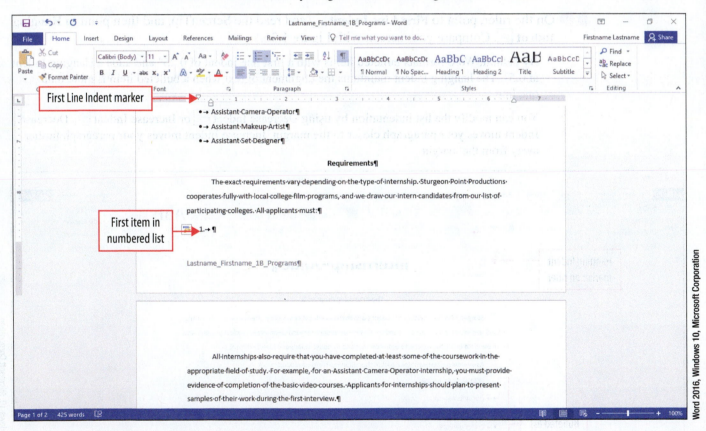

> **ALERT!**
>
> **Activating Automatic Numbered Lists**
>
> If a numbered list does not begin automatically, click the File tab, and then click the Options tab. On the left side of the Word Options dialog box, click Proofing. Under AutoCorrect options, click the AutoCorrect Options button. In the AutoCorrect dialog box, click the AutoFormat As You Type tab. Under *Apply as you type*, select the *Automatic numbered lists* check box, and then click OK two times to close both dialog boxes.

4 Click **AutoCorrect Options** , and then compare your screen with Figure 1.38.

From the displayed list, you can remove the automatic formatting here, or stop using the automatic numbered lists option in this document. You also have the option to open the AutoCorrect dialog box to *Control AutoFormat Options*.

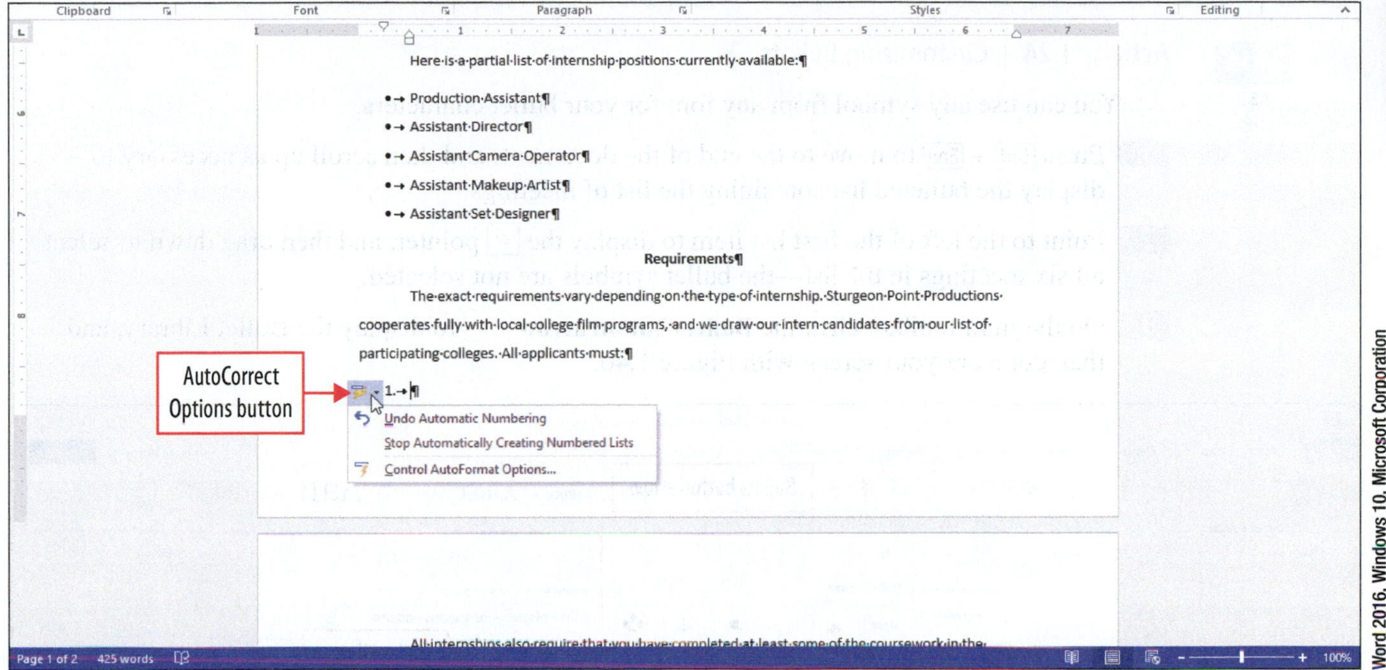

FIGURE 1.38

5 Click **AutoCorrect Options** again to close the menu without selecting any of the commands. Type **Be enrolled in an accredited film program** and press Enter. Notice that the second number and a tab are added to the next line.

6 Type **Be available during the entire production schedule** and press Enter. Type **Submit two faculty recommendation letters** and then compare your screen with Figure 1.39. **Save** your document.

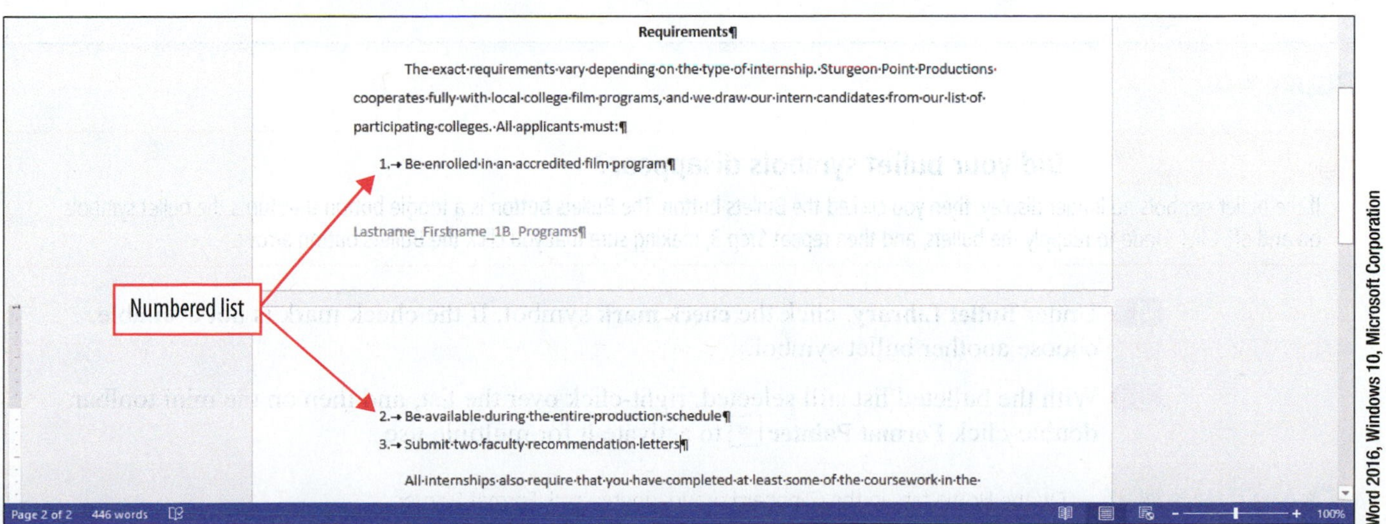

FIGURE 1.39

More Knowledge To End a List

To turn a list off, you can press Backspace, click the Numbering or Bullets button, or press Enter two times. Both list buttons—Numbering and Bullets—act as ***toggle buttons***; that is, clicking the button one time turns the feature on, and clicking the button again turns the feature off.

3.3.2

Activity 1.24 | Customizing Bullets

You can use any symbol from any font for your bullet characters.

1 Press Ctrl + End to move to the end of the document, and then scroll up as necessary to display the bulleted list containing the list of meetings.

2 Point to the left of the first list item to display the pointer, and then drag down to select all six meetings in the list—the bullet symbols are not selected.

3 On the mini toolbar, click the **Bullets button arrow** to display the Bullet Library, and then compare your screen with Figure 1.40.

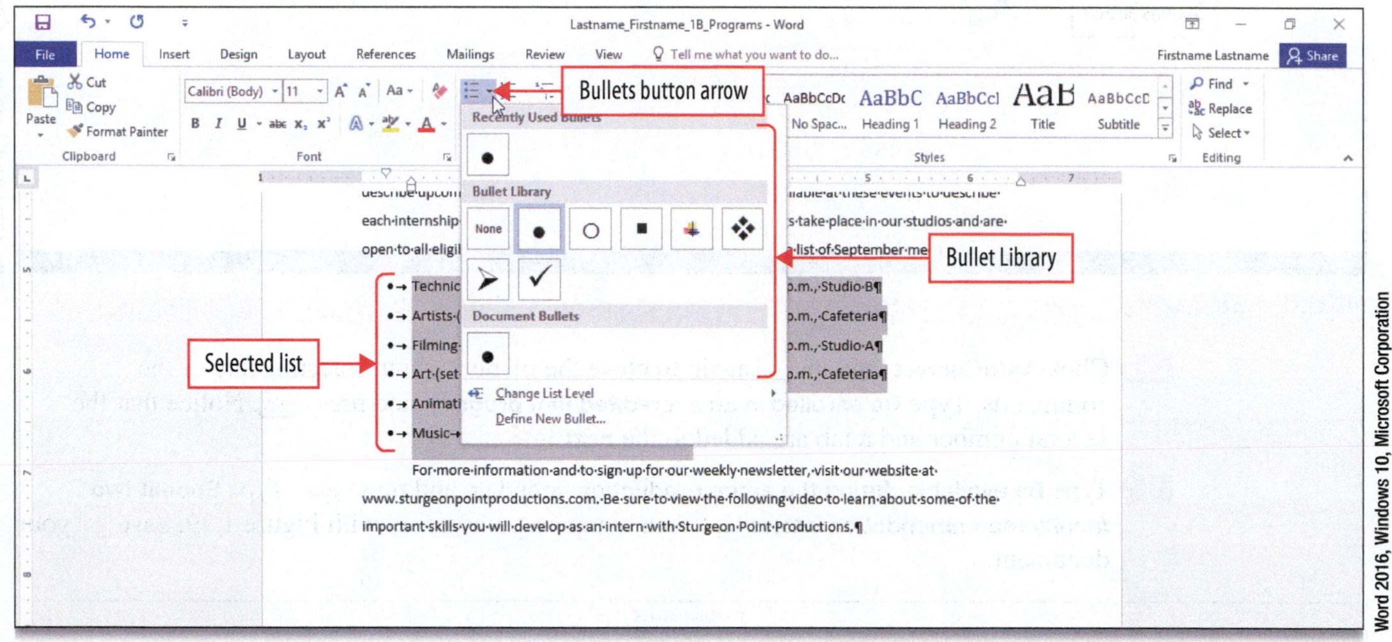

FIGURE 1.40

ALERT! Did your bullet symbols disappear?

If the bullet symbols no longer display, then you clicked the Bullets button. The Bullets button is a toggle button that turns the bullet symbols on and off. Click Undo to reapply the bullets, and then repeat Step 3, making sure that you click the Bullets button arrow.

4 Under **Bullet Library**, click the **check mark** symbol. If the check mark is not available, choose another bullet symbol.

5 With the bulleted list still selected, right-click over the list, and then on the mini toolbar, double-click **Format Painter** to activate it for multiple use.

ANOTHER WAY On the Home tab, in the Clipboard group, double-click Format Painter.

6 Use the vertical scroll bar or your mouse wheel to scroll to view **Page 1**. Move the pointer to the left of the first item in the first bulleted list to display the [pointer icon] pointer, and then drag down to select all six items in the list and to apply the format of the third bulleted list—the check mark bullets—to this list. Repeat this procedure to change the bullets in the second list to check marks. Press Esc to turn off **Format Painter**, and then **Save** your document. Compare your screen with Figure 1.41.

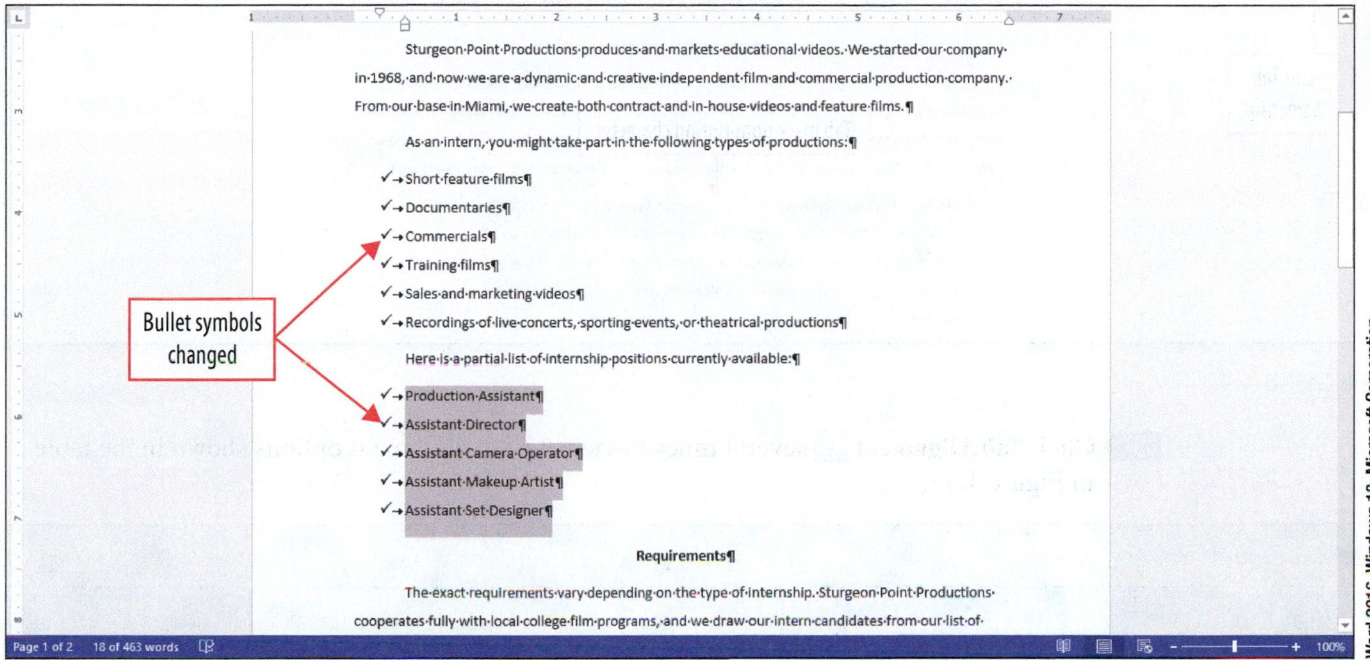

Sturgeon·Point·Productions·produces·and·markets·educational·videos.·We·started·our·company·in·1968,·and·now·we·are·a·dynamic·and·creative·independent·film·and·commercial·production·company.·From·our·base·in·Miami,·we·create·both·contract·and·in-house·videos·and·feature·films.¶
As·an·intern,·you·might·take·part·in·the·following·types·of·productions:¶
✓→Short·feature·films¶
✓→Documentaries¶
✓→Commercials¶
✓→Training·films¶
✓→Sales·and·marketing·videos¶
✓→Recordings·of·live·concerts,·sporting·events,·or·theatrical·productions¶
Here·is·a·partial·list·of·internship·positions·currently·available:¶
✓→Production·Assistant¶
✓→Assistant·Director¶
✓→Assistant·Camera·Operator¶
✓→Assistant·Makeup·Artist¶
✓→Assistant·Set·Designer¶
Requirements¶
The·exact·requirements·vary·depending·on·the·type·of·internship.·Sturgeon·Point·Productions·cooperates·fully·with·local·college·film·programs,·and·we·draw·our·intern·candidates·from·our·list·of·
Bullet symbols changed
Page 1 of 2
18 of 463 words
100%
Word 2016, Windows 10, Microsoft Corporation

FIGURE 1.41

Objective 7 Set and Modify Tab Stops

GO! Learn How Video W1-7

Tab stops mark specific locations on a line of text. Use tab stops to indent and align text, and use the Tab key to move to tab stops.

Activity 1.25 | Setting Tab Stops

1 Scroll to view the lower portion of **Page 2**, and then by using the [pointer icon] pointer at the left of the first item, select all of the items in the bulleted list. Notice that there is a tab mark between the name of the meeting and the date.

The arrow that indicates a tab is a nonprinting formatting mark.

2 To the left of the horizontal ruler, point to **Tab Alignment** to display the *Left Tab* ScreenTip, and then compare your screen with Figure 1.42.

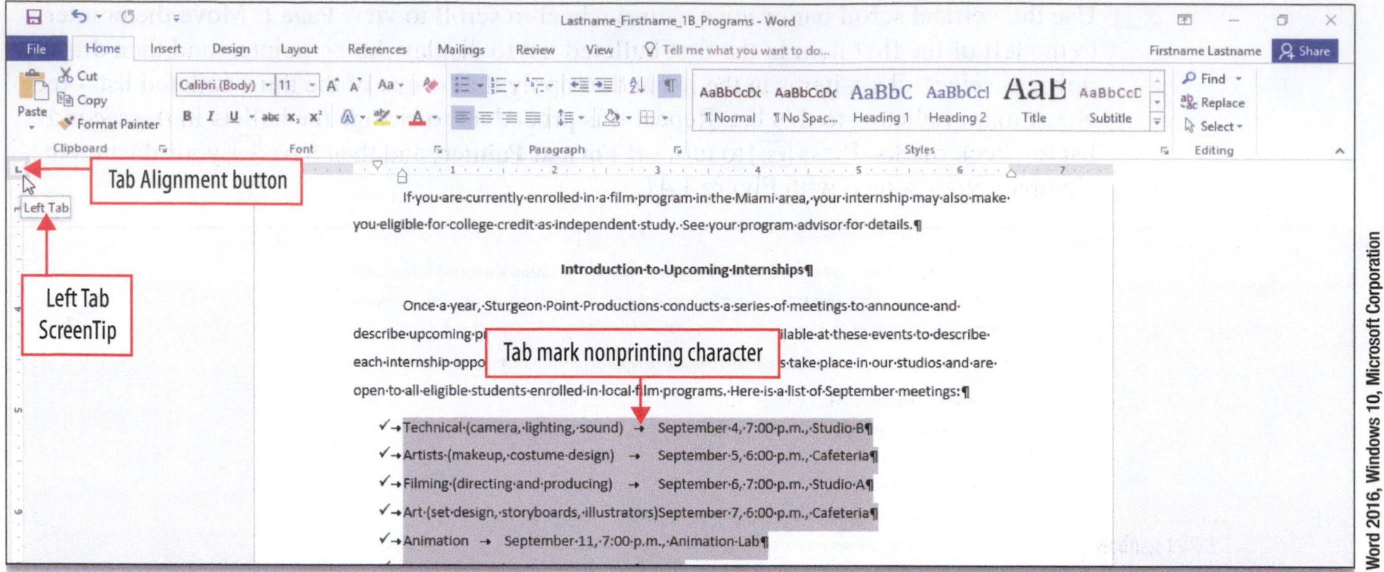

FIGURE 1.42

3 Click **Tab Alignment** several times to view the tab alignment options shown in the table in Figure 1.43.

TAB ALIGNMENT OPTIONS		
TYPE	TAB ALIGNMENT BUTTON DISPLAYS THIS MARKER	DESCRIPTION
Left		Text is left aligned at the tab stop and extends to the right.
Center		Text is centered around the tab stop.
Right		Text is right aligned at the tab stop and extends to the left.
Decimal		The decimal point aligns at the tab stop.
Bar		A vertical bar displays at the tab stop.
First Line Indent		Text in the first line of a paragraph indents.
Hanging Indent		Text in all lines except the first line in the paragraph indents.

Word 2016, Windows 10, Microsoft Corporation

FIGURE 1.43

4 Display **Left Tab**. Along the lower edge of the horizontal ruler, point to and then click at **3.5 inches on the horizontal ruler**. Notice that all of the dates left align at the new tab stop location, and the right edge of the column is uneven.

5 Compare your screen with Figure 1.44, and then **Save** your document.

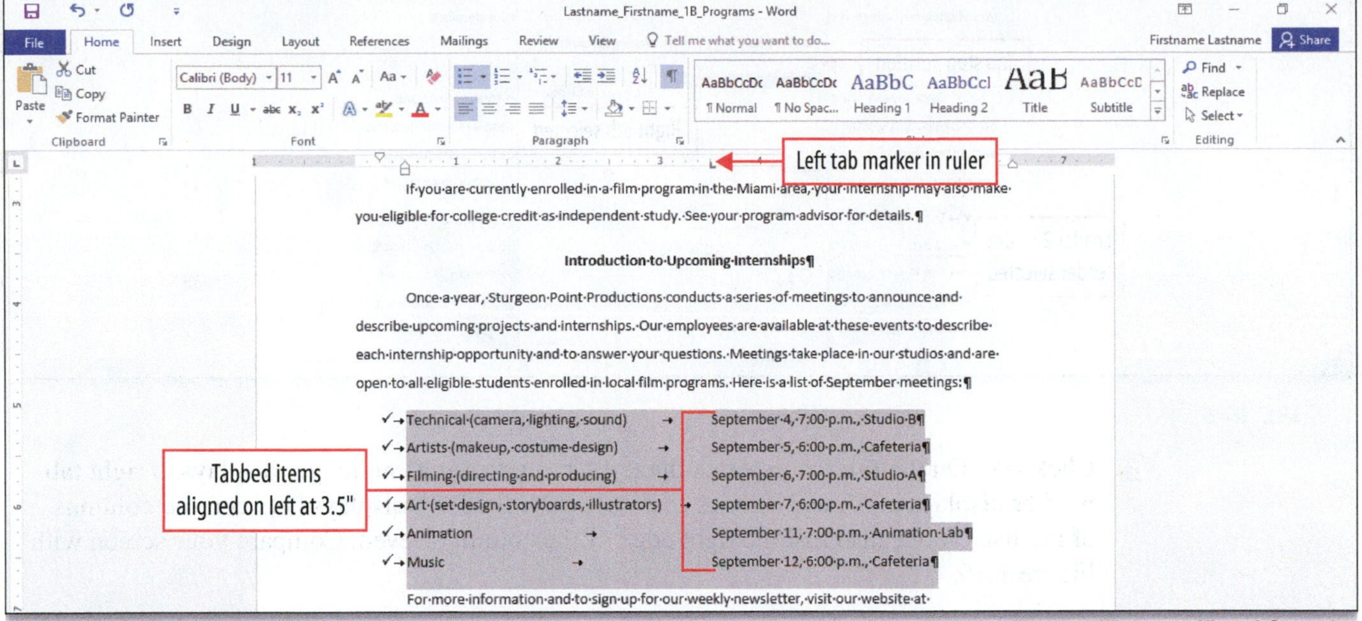

Word 2016, Windows 10, Microsoft Corporation

FIGURE 1.44

Activity 1.26 | Modifying Tab Stops

Tab stops are a form of paragraph formatting. Therefore, the information about tab stops is stored in the paragraph mark in the paragraphs to which they were applied.

1. With the bulleted list still selected, on the ruler, point to the new tab marker at *3.5 inches on the horizontal ruler*, and then when the *Left Tab* ScreenTip displays, drag the tab marker to **4 inches on the horizontal ruler.**

   In all of the selected lines, the text at the tab stop left aligns at 4 inches.

2. On the ruler, point to the tab marker that you moved to display the *Left Tab* ScreenTip, and then double-click to display the **Tabs** dialog box.

ANOTHER WAY On the Home tab, in the Paragraph group, click the Dialog Box Launcher. At the bottom of the Paragraph dialog box, click the Tabs button.

3. In the **Tabs** dialog box, under **Tab stop position**, if necessary select *4"* and then type **6**

4. Under **Alignment**, click the **Right** option button. Under **Leader**, click the **2** option button. Near the bottom of the **Tabs** dialog box, click **Set**.

   Because the Right tab will be used to align the items in the list, the tab stop at 4" is no longer necessary.

5. In the **Tabs** dialog box, in the **Tab stop position** box, click **4"** to select this tab stop, and then in the lower portion of the **Tabs** dialog box, click the **Clear** button to delete this tab stop, which is no longer necessary. Compare your screen with Figure 1.45.

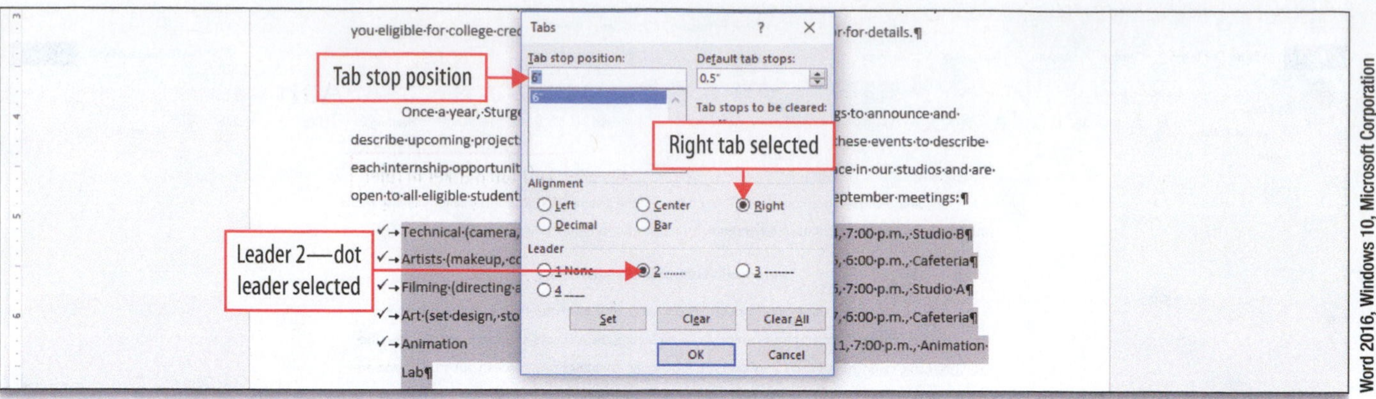

FIGURE 1.45

6 Click **OK**. On the ruler, notice that the left tab marker at *4″* no longer displays, a right tab marker displays at *6″*, and a series of dots—a ***dot leader***—displays between the columns of the list. Notice also that the right edge of the column is even. Compare your screen with Figure 1.46.

A ***leader character*** creates a solid, dotted, or dashed line that fills the space to the left of a tab character and draws the reader's eyes across the page from one item to the next. When the character used for the leader is a dot, it is commonly referred to as a dot leader.

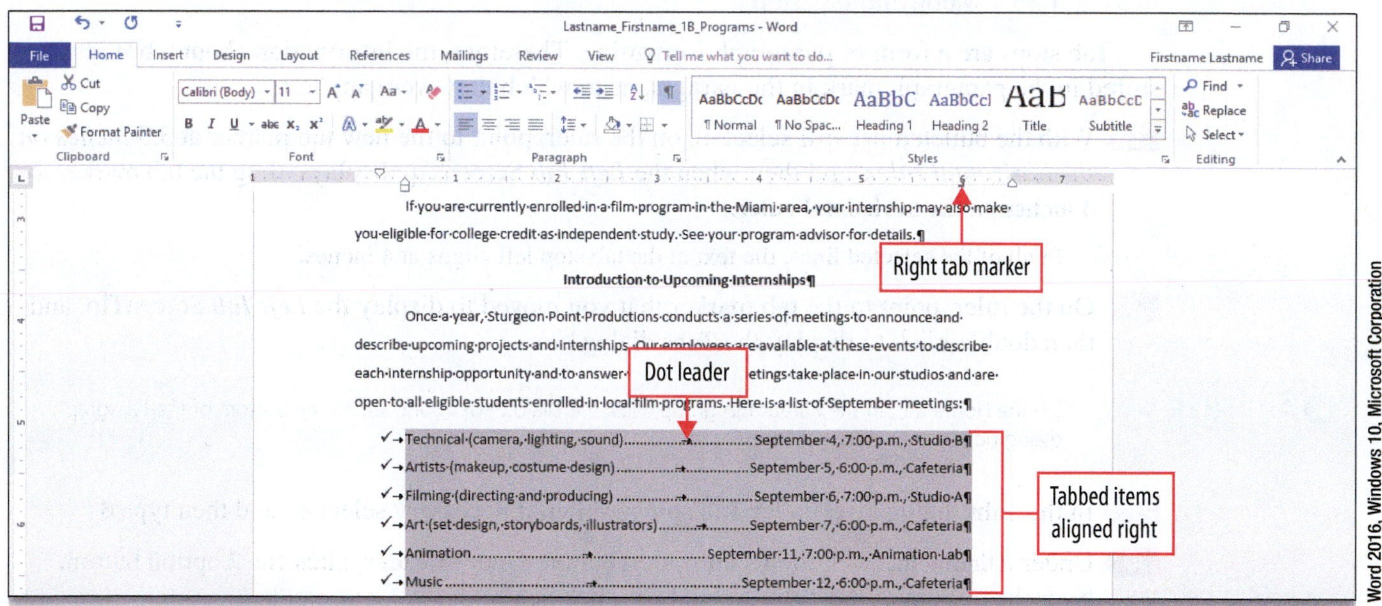

FIGURE 1.46

7 In the bulleted list that uses dot leaders, locate the *Art* meeting, and then click to position the insertion point at the end of that line, after the word *Cafeteria*. Press Enter to create a new blank bullet item.

8 Type **Video Editing** and press Tab. Notice that a dot leader fills the space to the tab marker location.

9 Type **September 10, 7:00 p.m., Cafeteria** and notice that the text moves to the left to maintain the right alignment of the tab stop.

10 **Save** your document.

Objective 8 Insert a SmartArt Graphic and an Online Video

GO! Learn How Video W1-8

SmartArt graphics are designer-quality visual representations of information, and Word provides many different layouts from which you can choose. You can also insert a link to an online video from a variety of online sources, thus enabling the reader to view the video when connected to the Internet. SmartArt graphics and videos can communicate your messages or ideas more effectively than plain text, and these objects add visual interest to a document or web page.

MOS 5.3.1

Activity 1.27 | Inserting a SmartArt Graphic

1. Press Ctrl + Home to move to the top of the document, and then click to the right of the subtitle *Internship Guide*.

2. Click the **Insert tab**, and then in the **Illustrations group**, point to **SmartArt** to display its ScreenTip. Read the ScreenTip, and then click **SmartArt**.

3. In the center portion of the **Choose a SmartArt Graphic** dialog box, scroll down and examine the numerous types of SmartArt graphics available.

4. On the left, click **Process**, and then by using the ScreenTips, locate and click **Basic Chevron Process**. Compare your screen with Figure 1.47.

   At the right of the dialog box, a preview and description of the SmartArt displays.

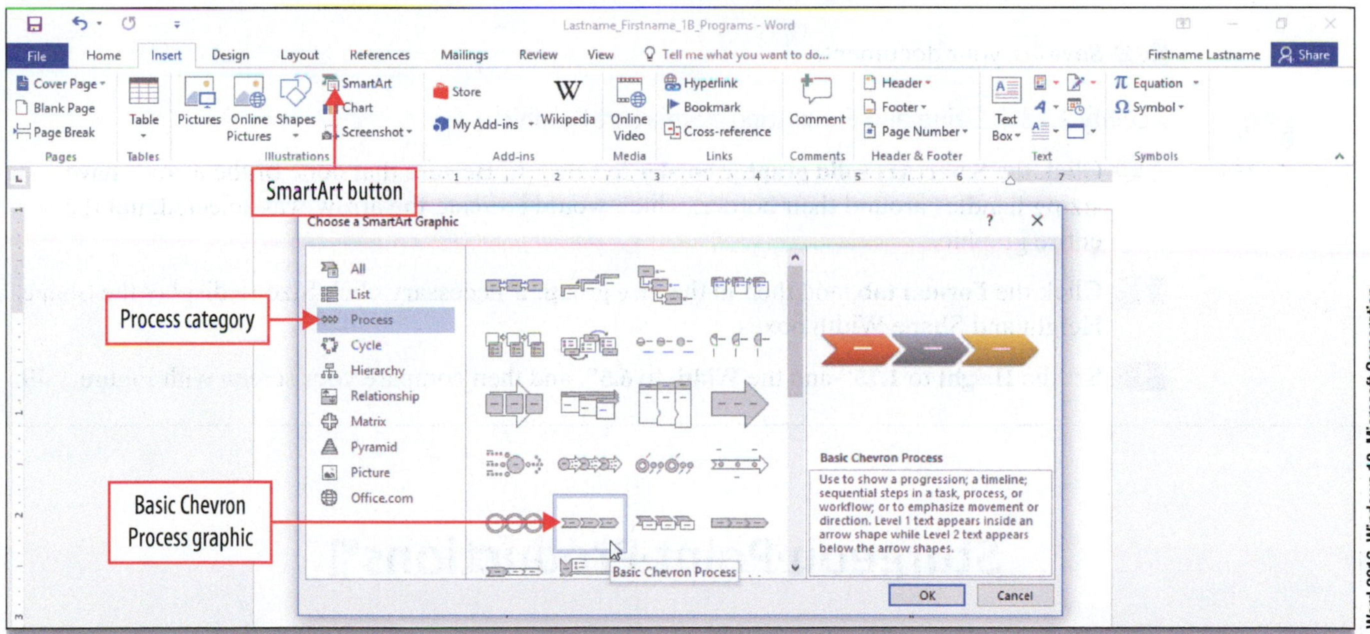

Word 2016, Windows 10, Microsoft Corporation

FIGURE 1.47

5. Click **OK** to insert the SmartArt graphic.

   To the left of the inserted SmartArt graphic, the text pane may display. The text pane provides one method for entering text into your SmartArt graphic. If you choose not to use the text pane to enter text, you can close it.

6. On the ribbon, under **SmartArt Tools**, on the **Design tab**, in the **Create Graphic group**, notice the **Text Pane** button. If the text pane button is selected, click Text Pane to close the pane.

7. In the SmartArt graphic, in the first blue arrow, click **[Text]**, and notice that *[Text]* is replaced by a blinking insertion point.

   The word *[Text]* is called ***placeholder text***, which is nonprinting text that indicates where you can type.

8 Type **Apply Online**

9 Click the placeholder text in the middle arrow. Type **Interview** and then click the placeholder text in the third arrow. Type **Train on the Job** and then compare your screen with Figure 1.48.

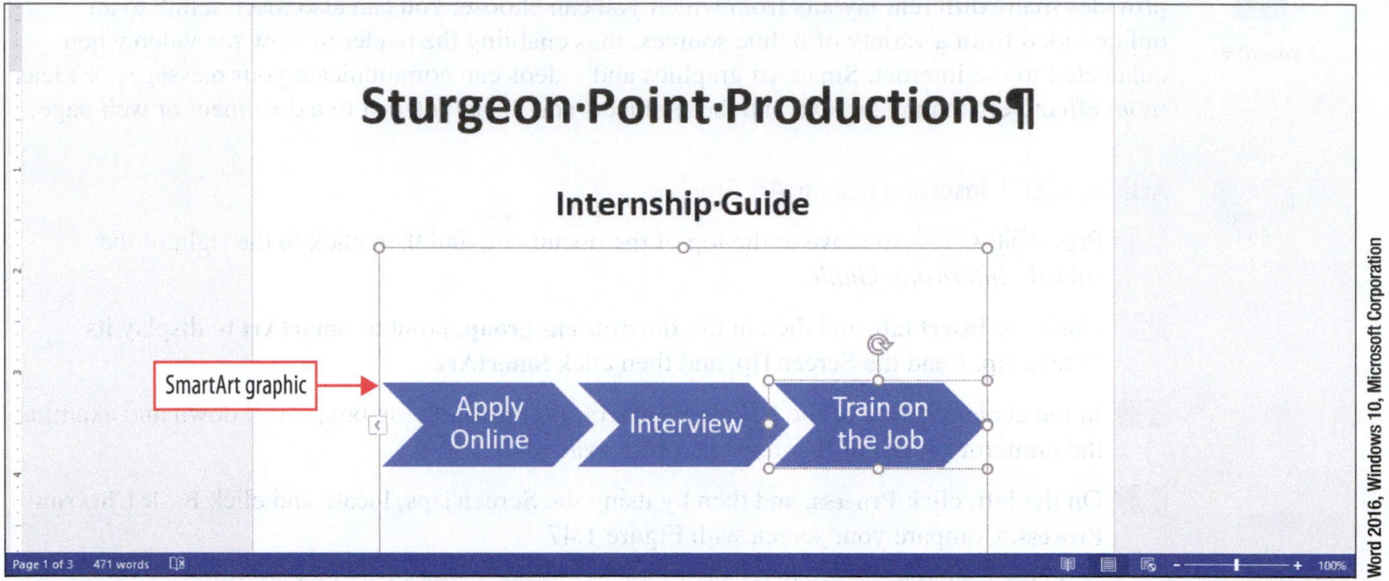

FIGURE 1.48

10 **Save** your document.

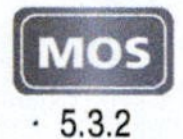

· 5.3.2

Activity 1.28 | Sizing and Formatting a SmartArt Graphic

1 Click the **SmartArt solid graphic border** to select it. Be sure that none of the arrows have sizing handles around their border, which would indicate the arrow was selected, not the entire graphic.

2 Click the **Format tab**, and then in the **Size group**, if necessary click Size to display the Shape Height and Shape Width boxes.

3 Set the **Height** to **1.75"** and the **Width** to **6.5"**, and then compare your screen with Figure 1.49.

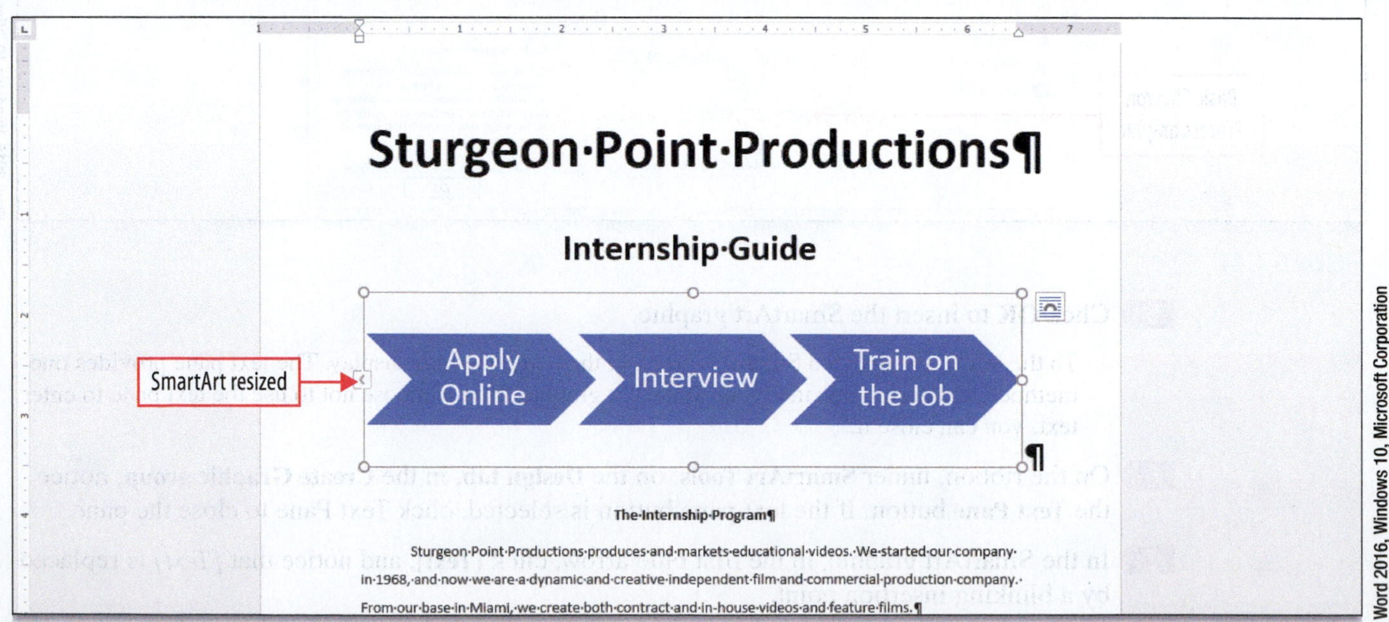

FIGURE 1.49

4 With the SmartArt graphic still selected, click the **SmartArt Tools Design tab**, and then in the **SmartArt Styles group**, click **Change Colors**. Under **Colorful**, click the fourth style—**Colorful Range - Accent Colors 4 to 5**.

5 On the **SmartArt Tools Design tab**, in the **SmartArt Styles group**, click **More**. Under **3-D**, click the second style—**Inset**. Click **Save**, and then compare your screen with Figure 1.50.

FIGURE 1.50

Activity 1.29 | Inserting an Online Video

Microsoft's research indicates that two-thirds of people who open Word documents never edit them; they only read them. So with more and more documents being read online—and not on paper—it makes sense that you may want to include videos in your Word documents.

1 Press Ctrl + End to move to the end of the document.

2 On the **Insert tab**, in the **Media group**, click **Online Video**.

Here you can search the web for an online video, search YouTube, or enter an ***embed code*** to insert a link to a video from a website. An embed code is a code that creates a link to a video, picture, or other type of ***rich media*** content. Rich media, also called ***interactive media***, refers to computer interaction that responds to your actions; for example, by presenting text, graphics, animation, video, audio, or games.

3 In the **Bing Video Search** box, type **Go 1B Video** and then press Enter.

Several videos display based on the search term that you typed.

4 Point to several of the videos and notice that a ScreenTip displays a description of the video. Click one of the videos that includes the words *Go 1B Video* in the ScreenTip, and then click **Insert**. Compare your screen with Figure 1.51.

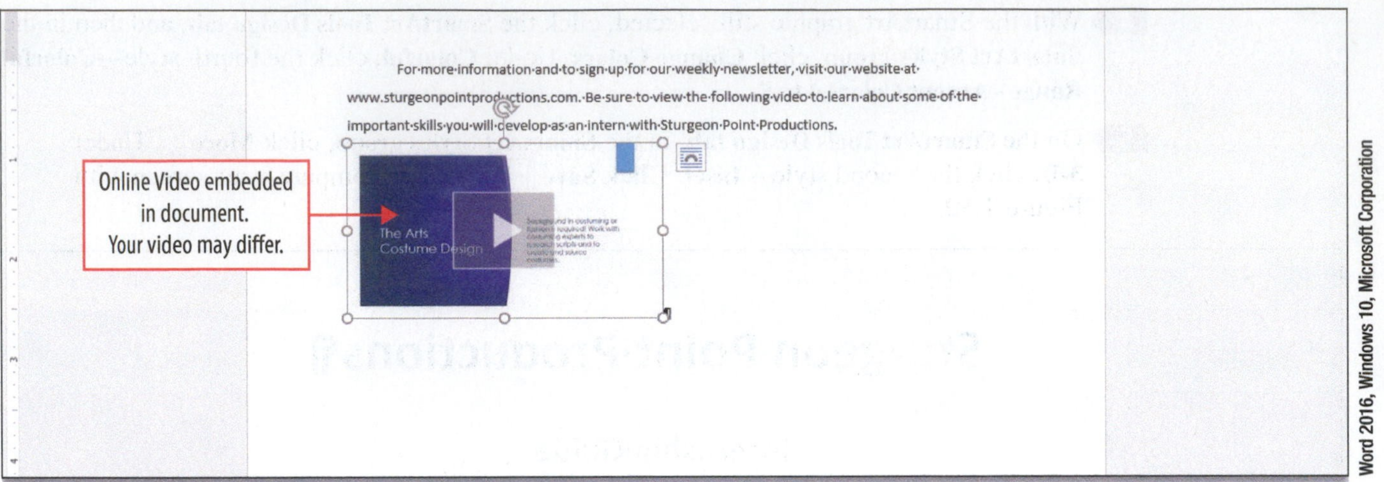

For more information and to sign up for our weekly newsletter, visit our website at www.sturgeonpointproductions.com. Be sure to view the following video to learn about some of the important skills you will develop as an intern with Sturgeon Point Productions.
Online Video embedded in document. Your video may differ.
The Arts Costume Design
Word 2016, Windows 10, Microsoft Corporation

FIGURE 1.51

ALERT! **Are you unable to locate or play the video?**

If you are unable to locate a video using the search words that you entered in Step 3, in the Bing Video Search box, type MyITLab and then insert the first video that displays. Depending upon your computer configuration, the video may not play.

5. On the **Picture Tools Format** tab, in the **Size** group, click in the **Height** box to select the value. Type **1.5** and then press Enter to change the size of the video.

6. Click **Save**, and then press Ctrl + Home to move to the top of your document.

7. Click the **File tab**, and then in the lower right portion of the screen, click **Show All Properties**. In the **Tags** box, type **internship** and in the **Subject** box, type your course name and section number. In the **Author** box, replace the existing text with your first and last name.

8. On the left, click **Print** to display **Print Preview**. At the bottom of the preview, click the **Next Page** and **Previous Page** buttons to move between pages. If necessary, return to the document and make any necessary changes.

9. **Save** your document. In the upper right corner of the Word window, click **Close**. If directed by your instructor to do so, submit your paper printout, your electronic image of your document that looks like a printed document, or your completed Word file.

END | You have completed Project 1B

GO! With Google

1 WORD

Objective Create an Information Handout

ALERT! Working with Web-Based Applications and Services

Computer programs and services on the web receive continuous updates and improvements, so the steps to complete this web-based activity may differ from the ones shown. You can often look at the screens and the information presented to determine how to complete the activity.

If you do not already have a Google account, you will need to create one before you begin this activity. Go to http://google.com and, in the upper right corner, click Sign In. On the Sign In screen, click Create Account. On the Create your Google Account page, complete the form, read and agree to the Terms of Service and Privacy Policy, and then click Next step. On the Welcome screen, click Get Started.

Activity | Creating a Handout with Bulleted and Numbered Lists

In this Activity, you will use Google Docs to create an information handout.

1 From the desktop, open your browser, navigate to **http://google.com**, and then sign in to your Google account. In the upper right corner of your screen, click **Google Apps**, and then click **Drive**. Double-click your **GO! Web Projects** folder to open it. If you have not created this folder, refer to the instructions in the first Google Docs project in this chapter.

2 In the left pane, click **NEW**, and then click **Google Docs**. Click **File**, and then click **Open**. Click **Upload**, and then click **Select a file from your computer**. From your student data files, click **w01_1B_Web** and then click **Open** to open the file and upload it to your GO! Web Projects folder.

3 In the upper left corner of the Google Docs window, select **w01_1B_Web** and then type **Lastname_Firstname_1B_Google_Doc** and then press Enter to rename the file.

4 Press Ctrl + A to select all of the text. Click **Line spacing**, and then click **1.5**. Click **Left align**.

5 Select the six lines of text beginning with *Short feature films* and ending with *Recording of live concerts*, and then click **Bulleted list** to apply bullets to the selected text. Select the list of internship positions beginning with *Production Assistant* and ending with *Assistant Set Designer*, and then click **Bulleted list**. Compare your screen with Figure A.

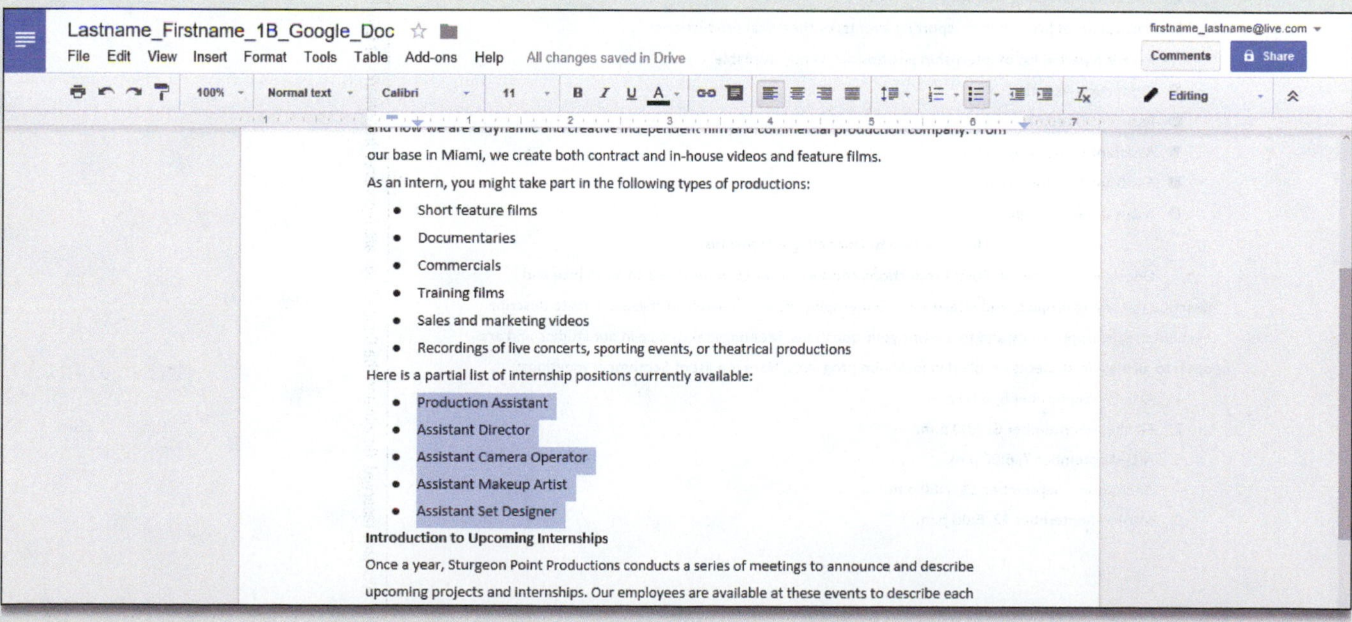

FIGURE A

(GO! With Google continues on the next page)

6 Select the last five lines of the document beginning with *Artists* and ending with *Music*. To create a numbered list from the selection, click **Numbered list** .

7 Select the first three lines of text in the document, and then click **Center** . Click in the *Introduction to Upcoming Internships* heading, and then click **Center** .

8 Click at the beginning of the paragraph that begins *Sturgeon Point Production produces and markets*, and then press Tab. Look at the ruler and notice that the first line indent is applied.

9 With the insertion point in the same paragraph, double-click **Paint format** . Then, click in the paragraphs that begin *As an intern*, *Here is a partial list*, and *Once a year* to apply the first line indent to each of the paragraphs. Click **Paint format** to turn it off. Compare your screen with Figure B.

10 Your document will be saved automatically. Sign out of your Google account, and then submit as instructed by your instructor.

Sturgeon Point Productions

Internship Guide

The Internship Program

Sturgeon Point Productions produces and markets educational videos. We started our company in 1968, and now we are a dynamic and creative independent film and commercial production company. From our base in Miami, we create both contract and in-house videos and feature films.

As an intern, you might take part in the following types of productions:

- Short feature films
- Documentaries
- Commercials
- Training films
- Sales and marketing videos
- Recordings of live concerts, sporting events, or theatrical productions

Here is a partial list of internship positions currently available:

- Production Assistant
- Assistant Director
- Assistant Camera Operator
- Assistant Makeup Artist
- Assistant Set Designer

Introduction to Upcoming Internships

Once a year, Sturgeon Point Productions conducts a series of meetings to announce and describe upcoming projects and internships. Our employees are available at these events to describe each internship opportunity and to answer your questions. Meetings take place in our studios and are open to all eligible students enrolled in local film programs. Here is a list of September meetings:

1. Artists—September 5, 6:00 p.m.
2. Filming—September 6, 7:00 p.m.
3. Art—September 7, 6:00 p.m.
4. Animation—September 11, 7:00 p.m.
5. Music—September 12, 6:00 p.m.

FIGURE B

GO! To Work

Andrew Rodriguez / Fotolia; FotolEdhar / Fotolia; apops / Fotolia; Yuri Arcurs / Fotolia

1 WORD

MICROSOFT OFFICE SPECIALIST (MOS) SKILLS IN THIS CHAPTER	
PROJECT 1A	**PROJECT 1B**
1.1.1 Create a blank document	**1.3.1** Modify page setup
1.1.4 Insert text from a file or external source	**2.2.3** Set line and paragraph spacing and indentation
1.3.4 Insert headers and footers	**3.3.1** Create a numbered or bulleted list
1.4.5 Add document properties	**3.3.2** Change bullet characters or number formats for a list level
1.4.6 Show or hide formatting symbols	**5.3.1** Create a SmartArt graphic
1.5.3 Print all or part of a document	**5.3.2** Format a SmartArt graphic
5.1.1 Insert shapes	**5.3.3** Modify SmartArt graphic content
5.1.2 Insert pictures	
5.1.4 Insert text boxes	
5.2.1 Apply artistic effects	
5.2.2 Apply picture effects	
5.2.4 Format objects	
5.2.6 Wrap text around objects	
5.2.7 Position objects	

BUILD YOUR E-PORTFOLIO

An E-Portfolio is a collection of evidence, stored electronically, that showcases what you have accomplished while completing your education. Collecting and then sharing your work products with potential employers reflects your academic and career goals. Your completed documents from the following projects are good examples to show what you have learned: 1G, 1K, and 1L.

GO! FOR JOB SUCCESS

Video: Personal Branding

Your instructor may assign this video to your class, and then ask you to think about, or discuss with your classmates, these questions:

FotolEdhar / Fotolia

How do you suggest job seekers communicate their unique value—their personal brand—to potential employers online?

What are the best ways to network online and offline?

What are some of the biggest pitfalls in using social media to communicate a personal brand?

END OF CHAPTER

SUMMARY

In this chapter, you started Word and practiced navigating the Word window, and you entered, edited, and formatted text. You also inserted text from another Word file.

Graphics include pictures, shapes, and text boxes. In this chapter, you formatted objects by applying styles, effects, and text-wrapping options, and you sized and positioned objects on the page.

SmartArt graphics visually represent your ideas, and there are many SmartArt graphics from which to choose. You can also use online videos in your documents to provide visual information to the reader.

Word documents can be formatted to display your information attractively. You can add a page border, add bulleted and numbered lists, change margins and tabs, and modify paragraph and line spacing.

GO! LEARN IT ONLINE

Review the concepts, key terms, and MOS skills in this chapter by completing these online challenges, which you can find at **MyITLab**.

Matching and Multiple Choice: Answer matching and multiple choice questions to test what you learned in this chapter.

Lessons on the GO!: Learn how to use all the new apps and features as they are introduced by Microsoft.

MOS Prep Quiz: Answer questions to review the MOS skills that you practiced in this chapter.

GO! COLLABORATIVE TEAM PROJECT (Available in MyITLab and Instructor Resource Center)

If your instructor assigns this project to your class, you can expect to work with one or more of your classmates—either in person or by using Internet tools—to create work products similar to those that you created in this chapter. A team is a group of workers who work together to solve a problem, make a decision, or create a work product. Collaboration is when you work together with others as a team in an intellectual endeavor to complete a shared task or achieve a shared goal.

PROJECT GUIDE FOR WORD CHAPTER 1

Your instructor will assign Projects from this list to ensure your learning and assess your knowledge.

Project Guide for Word Chapter 1			
Project	**Apply Skills from These Chapter Objectives**	**Project Type**	**Project Location**
1A MyITLab	Objectives 1-4 from Project 1A	**1A Instructional Project (Grader Project)** A guided review of the skills from Project.	In MyITLab and in text
1B MyITLab	Objectives 5-8 from Project 1B	**1B Instructional Project (Grader Project)** A guided review of the skills from Project.	In MyITLab and in text
1C	Objectives 1-4 from Project 1A	**1C Skills Review (Scorecard Grading)** A guided review of the skills from Project 2A.	In text
1D	Objectives 5-8 from Project 1B	**1D Skills Review (Scorecard Grading)** A guided review of the skills from Project 2B.	In text
1E MyITLab	Objectives 1-4 from Project 1A	**1E Mastery (Grader Project)** **Mastery and Transfer of Learning** A demonstration of your mastery of the skills in Project 2A with extensive decision making.	In MyITLab and in text
1F MyITLab	Objectives 5-8 from Project 1B	**1F Mastery (Grader Project)** **Mastery and Transfer of Learning** A demonstration of your mastery of the skills in Project 2B with extensive decision making.	In MyITLab and in text
1G MyITLab	Objectives 1-8 from Project 1A and 1B	**1G Mastery (Grader Project)** **Mastery and Transfer of Learning** A demonstration of your mastery of the skills in Projects 2A and 2B with extensive decision making.	In MyITLab and in text
1H	Combination of Objectives from Projects 1A and 1B	**1H GO! Fix It (Scorecard Grading)** **Critical Thinking** A demonstration of your mastery of the skills in Projects 1A and 1B by creating a correct result from a document that contains errors you must find.	Instructor Resource Center (IRC) and MyITLab
1I	Combination of Objectives from Projects 1A and 1B	**1I GO! Make It (Scorecard Grading)** **Critical Thinking** A demonstration of your mastery of the skills in Projects 1A and 1B by creating a result from a supplied picture.	IRC and MyITLab
1J	Combination of Objectives from Projects 1A and 1B	**1J GO! Solve It (Rubric Grading)** **Critical Thinking** A demonstration of your mastery of the skills in Projects 1A and 1B, your decision-making skills, and your critical thinking skills. A task-specific rubric helps you self-assess your result.	IRC and MyITLab
1K	Combination of Objectives from Projects 1A and 1B	**1K GO! Solve It (Rubric Grading)** **Critical Thinking** A demonstration of your mastery of the skills in Projects 1A and 1B, your decision-making skills, and your critical thinking skills. A task-specific rubric helps you self-assess your result.	In text
1L	Combination of Objectives from Projects 1A and 1B	**1L GO! Think (Rubric Grading)** **Critical Thinking** A demonstration of your understanding of the chapter concepts applied in a manner that you would outside of college. An analytic rubric helps you and your instructor grade the quality of your work by comparing it to the work an expert in the discipline would create.	In text
1M	Combination of Objectives from Projects 1A and 1B	**1M GO! Think (Rubric Grading)** **Critical Thinking** A demonstration of your understanding of the chapter concepts applied in a manner that you would outside of college. An analytic rubric helps you and your instructor grade the quality of your work by comparing it to the work an expert in the discipline would create.	IRC and MyITLab
1N	Combination of Objectives from Projects 1A and 1B	**1N You and GO! (Rubric Grading)** **Critical Thinking** A demonstration of your understanding of the chapter concepts applied in a manner that you would in a personal situation. An analytic rubric helps you and your instructor grade the quality of your work.	IRC and MyITLab
1O	Combination of Objectives from Projects 1A and 1B	**1O Collaborative Team Project for WORD Chapter 1** **Critical Thinking** A demonstration of your understanding of concepts and your ability to work collaboratively in a group role-playing assessment, requiring both collaboration and self-management.	IRC and MyITLab

GLOSSARY

GLOSSARY OF CHAPTER KEY TERMS

Alignment The placement of paragraph text relative to the left and right margins.

Alignment guide A green vertical or horizontal line that displays when you are moving or sizing an object to assist you with object placement.

Artistic effects Formats applied to images that make pictures resemble sketches or paintings.

Bulleted list A list of items with each item introduced by a symbol such as a small circle or check mark, and which is useful when the items in the list can be displayed in any order.

Bullets Text symbols such as small circles or check marks that precede each item in a bulleted list.

Center alignment The alignment of text or objects that is centered horizontally between the left and right margin.

Dot leader A series of dots preceding a tab that guides the eye across the line.

Drawing objects Graphic objects, such as shapes, diagrams, lines, or circles.

Embed code A code that creates a link to a video, picture, or other type of rich media content.

Floating object A graphic that can be moved independently of the surrounding text characters.

Formatting marks Characters that display on the screen, but do not print, indicating where the Enter key, the Spacebar, and the Tab key were pressed; also called nonprinting characters.

Graphics Pictures, charts, or drawing objects.

Inline object An object or graphic inserted in a document that acts like a character in a sentence.

Interactive media Computer interaction that responds to your actions; for example, by presenting text, graphics, animation, video, audio, or games. Also referred to as rich media.

Justified alignment An arrangement of text in which the text aligns evenly on both the left and right margins.

Layout Options Picture formatting options that control the manner in which text wraps around a picture or other object.

Leader character Characters that form a solid, dotted, or dashed line that fills the space preceding a tab stop.

Left alignment An arrangement of text in which the text aligns at the left margin, leaving the right margin uneven.

Line spacing The distance between lines of text in a paragraph.

Live Layout A feature that reflows text as you move or size an object so that you can view the placement of surrounding text.

Margins The space between the text and the top, bottom, left, and right edges of the paper.

Nonprinting characters Characters that display on the screen, but do not print; also called formatting marks.

Numbered list A list that uses consecutive numbers or letters to introduce each item in a list.

Object anchor The symbol that indicates to which paragraph an object is attached.

Picture effects Effects that enhance a picture, such as a shadow, glow, reflection, or 3-D rotation.

Picture styles Frames, shapes, shadows, borders, and other special effects that can be added to an image to create an overall visual style for the image.

Placeholder text Nonprinting text that holds a place in a document where you can type.

Rich media Computer interaction that responds to your actions; for example, by presenting text, graphics, animation, video, audio, or games. Also referred to as interactive media.

Right alignment An arrangement of text in which the text aligns at the right margin, leaving the left margin uneven.

Rotation handle A symbol with which you can rotate a graphic to any angle; displays above the top center sizing handle.

Shapes Lines, arrows, stars, banners, ovals, rectangles, and other basic shapes with which you can illustrate an idea, a process, or a workflow.

SmartArt A designer-quality visual representation of your information that you can create by choosing from among many different layouts to effectively communicate your message or ideas.

Spin box A small box with an upward- and downward-pointing arrow that lets you move rapidly through a set of values by clicking.

Tab stop A specific location on a line of text, marked on the Word ruler, to which you can move the insertion point by pressing the Tab key, and which is used to align and indent text.

Template A preformatted document that you can use as a starting point and then change to suit your needs.

Text box A movable resizable container for text or graphics.

Text effects Decorative formats, such as shadowed or mirrored text, text glow, 3-D effects, and colors that make text stand out.

Text wrapping The manner in which text displays around an object.

Toggle button A button that can be turned on by clicking it once, and then turned off by clicking it again.

Wordwrap The feature that moves text from the right edge of a paragraph to the beginning of the next line as necessary to fit within the margins.

CHAPTER REVIEW

Apply 1A skills from these objectives:

1. Create a New Document and Insert Text
2. Insert and Format Graphics
3. Insert and Modify Text Boxes and Shapes
4. Preview and Print a Document

Skills Review Project 1C Photography

In the following Skills Review, you will create a flyer advertising a photography internship with Sturgeon Point Productions. Your completed document will look similar to Figure 1.52.

PROJECT FILES

For Project 1C, you will need the following files:

New blank Word document
w01C_Building
w01C_Photographer

You will save your document as:

Lastname_Firstname_1C_Photography

PROJECT RESULTS

Build from Scratch

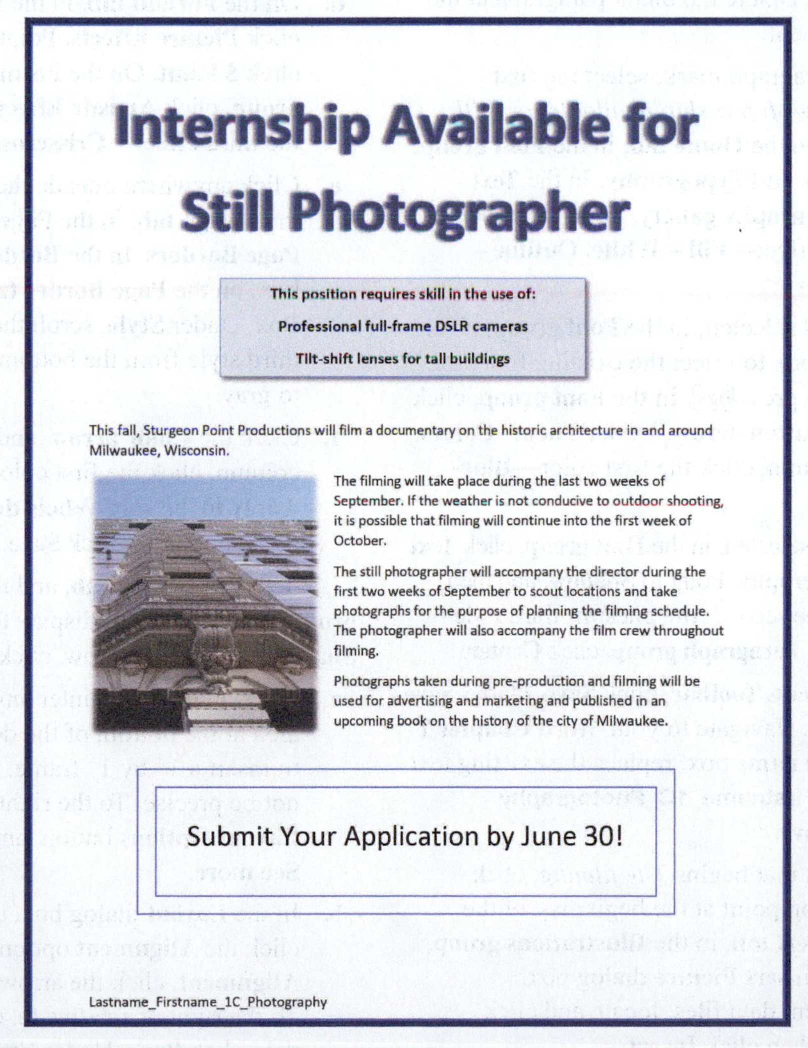

Internship Available for Still Photographer

This position requires skill in the use of:

Professional full-frame DSLR cameras

Tilt-shift lenses for tall buildings

This fall, Sturgeon Point Productions will film a documentary on the historic architecture in and around Milwaukee, Wisconsin.

The filming will take place during the last two weeks of September. If the weather is not conducive to outdoor shooting, it is possible that filming will continue into the first week of October.

The still photographer will accompany the director during the first two weeks of September to scout locations and take photographs for the purpose of planning the filming schedule. The photographer will also accompany the film crew throughout filming.

Photographs taken during pre-production and filming will be used for advertising and marketing and published in an upcoming book on the history of the city of Milwaukee.

Submit Your Application by June 30!

Lastname_Firstname_1C_Photography

Word 2016, Windows 10, Microsoft Corporation

FIGURE 1.52

(Project 1C Photography continues on the next page)

Skills Review Project 1C Photography (continued)

1 Start Word and then click **Blank document**. On the **Home tab**, in the **Paragraph group**, if necessary, click Show/Hide to display the formatting marks. If the rulers do not display, click the View tab, and then in the Show group, select the Ruler check box.

a. Type **Internship Available for Still Photographer** and then press Enter two times. Type the following text: **This fall, Sturgeon Point Productions will film a documentary on the historic architecture in and around Milwaukee, Wisconsin.** Press Enter.

b. On the ribbon, click the **Insert tab**. In the **Text group**, click the **Object button arrow**, and then click **Text from File**. In the **Insert File** dialog box, navigate to the student files that accompany this chapter, locate and select **w01C_Photographer**, and then click **Insert**. Delete the blank paragraph at the end of the document.

c. Including the paragraph mark, select the first paragraph of text—*Internship Available for Still Photographer*. On the **Home tab**, in the **Font group**, click **Text Effects and Typography**. In the **Text Effects and Typography** gallery, in the first row, click the fourth effect—**Fill – White, Outline – Accent 5, Shadow**.

d. With the text still selected, in the **Font group**, click in the **Font Size** box to select the existing font size. Type **44** and then press Enter. In the **Font group**, click the **Font Color button arrow**. Under **Theme Colors**, in the fourth column, click the first color—**Blue-Gray, Text 2**.

e. With the text still selected, in the **Font group**, click **Text Effects and Typography**. Point to **Shadow**, and then under **Outer**, in the second row, click the third style—**Offset Left**. In the **Paragraph group**, click **Center**.

f. On the **Quick Access Toolbar**, click **Save**. Under **Save As**, click **Browse**. Navigate to your **Word Chapter 1** folder. In the **File name** box, replace the existing text with **Lastname_Firstname_1C_Photography** and then click **Save**.

2 In the paragraph that begins *The filming*, click to position the insertion point at the beginning of the paragraph. On the **Insert tab**, in the **Illustrations group**, click **Pictures**. In the **Insert Picture** dialog box, navigate to your student data files, locate and click **w01C_Building**, and then click **Insert**.

a. To the right of the selected picture, click the **Layout Options** button, and then under **With Text Wrapping**, click the first option—**Square**. **Close** the Layout Options.

b. On the **Format tab**, in the **Size group**, click in the **Shape Height** box to select the value, type **2.7** and then press Enter.

c. With the picture selected, on the **Format tab**, in the **Arrange group**, click **Position**, and then click **More Layout Options**. In the **Layout** dialog box, on the **Position tab**, in the middle of the dialog box under **Vertical**, click the **Alignment** option button. To the right of **Alignment**, click the arrow, and then click **Top**. To the right of **relative to**, click the arrow, and then click **Line**. Click **OK**.

d. On the **Format tab**, in the **Picture Styles group**, click **Picture Effects**. Point to **Soft Edges**, and then click **5 Point**. On the **Format tab**, in the **Adjust group**, click **Artistic Effects**. In the fourth row, click the third effect—**Crisscross Etching**.

e. Click anywhere outside the picture to deselect it. On the **Design tab**, in the **Page Background group**, click **Page Borders**. In the **Borders and Shading** dialog box, on the **Page Border tab**, under **Setting**, click **Box**. Under **Style**, scroll the list and then click the third style from the bottom—a black line that fades to gray.

f. Click the **Color arrow**, and then in the next to last column, click the first color—**Blue, Accent 5**. Under **Apply to**, be sure **Whole document** is selected, and then click **OK**. Click **Save**.

3 Click the **Insert tab**, and then in the **Illustrations group**, click **Shapes** to display the gallery. Under **Basic Shapes**, in the second row, click the fifth shape—**Frame**.

a. Position the ⊞ pointer anywhere in the blank area at the bottom of the document. Click one time to insert a 1" by 1" frame. The exact location need not be precise. To the right of the shape, click the **Layout Options** button, and at the bottom click **See more**.

b. In the **Layout** dialog box, under **Horizontal**, click the **Alignment** option button. To the right of **Alignment**, click the arrow, and then click **Centered**. To the right of **relative to**, click the arrow, and then click **Page**. Under **Vertical**, click the **Absolute**

(Project 1C Photography continues on the next page)

Skills Review Project 1C Photography (continued)

position option button. In the **Absolute position** box, select the existing number, and then type **1** To the right of **below**, click the arrow, and then click **Paragraph**. Click **OK**.

c. On the **Format tab**, click in the **Shape Height** box. Type **1.5** and then click in the **Shape Width** box. Type **5.5** and then press Enter.

d. If necessary, select the frame shape. On the **Format tab**, in the **Shape Styles group**, click **More**. In the **Shape Styles** gallery, in the first row, click the sixth style—**Colored Outline - Blue, Accent 5**. Type **Submit Your Application by June 30!** Select the text you just typed, and then on the mini toolbar, change the **Font Size** to **22**.

4 Click outside of the frame to deselect it, and then press Ctrl + Home to move to the top of the document. Press ↓ two times to move to the blank paragraph below the title. Press Enter four times to make space for a text box.

a. On the **Insert tab**, in the **Text group**, click **Text Box**. At the bottom of the gallery, click **Draw Text Box**. Position the ┼ pointer over the first blank paragraph at the left margin. Drag down and to the right to create a text box approximately 1.5 inches high and 4 inches wide—the exact size and location need not be precise.

b. With the insertion point blinking in the text box, type the following, pressing Enter after the first two lines to create a new paragraph:

This position requires skill in the use of:
Professional full-frame DSLR cameras
Tilt-shift lenses for tall buildings

c. To precisely place the text box, on the **Format tab**, in the **Arrange group**, click **Position**, and then click **More Layout Options**. In the **Layout** dialog box, under **Horizontal**, click the **Alignment** button. To the right of **Alignment**, click the arrow, and then click **Centered**. To the right of **relative to**, click the arrow, and then click **Page**.

d. Under **Vertical**, click the **Absolute position** button. In the **Absolute position** box, select the existing number. Type **2** To the right of **below**, click the arrow, and then click **Margin**.

e. In the **Layout** dialog box, click the **Size tab**. Under **Height**, select the number in the **Absolute** box. Type **1** and then under **Width**, select the number in the **Absolute** box. Type **3.75** and then click **OK**.

f. In the text box, select all of the text. If necessary, right-click over the selected text to display the mini toolbar. Change the **Font Size** to **12**, apply **Bold**, and then press Ctrl + E to **Center** the text.

g. On the **Format tab**, in the **Shape Styles group**, click **Shape Effects**. Point to **Shadow**, and then under **Outer**, in the first row, click the first style—**Offset Diagonal Bottom Right**.

h. In the **Shape Styles group**, click **Shape Outline**. In the fifth column, click the first color—**Blue, Accent 1** to change the color of the text box border. Click **Shape Fill**, and then in the fifth column, click the second color—**Blue, Accent 1, Lighter 80%**. Click **Save**.

5 Click the **Insert tab**, and then in the **Header & Footer group**, click **Footer**. At the bottom of the menu, click **Edit Footer**. On the **Header & Footer Tools Design tab**, in the **Insert group**, click **Document Info**, and then click **File Name**. Double-click in the document outside of the footer area to close the footer and return to the document.

a. Press Ctrl + Home to move the insertion point to the top of the document. In the upper left corner of your screen, click the **File tab** to display **Backstage** view. On the right, at the bottom of the **Properties list**, click **Show All Properties**.

b. On the list of Properties, click to the right of **Tags** to display an empty box, and then type **internship, documentary** Click to the right of **Subject** to display an empty box, and then type your course name and section #. Under **Related People**, be sure that your name displays as the author. If necessary, right-click the author name, click Edit Property, type your name, and click OK.

c. **Save** your document. In the upper right corner of the Word window, click **Close**. If directed by your instructor to do so, submit your paper printout, your electronic image of your document that looks like a printed document, or your completed Word file.

END | You have completed Project 1C

CHAPTER REVIEW

Apply 1B skills from these Objectives:

5 Change Document and Paragraph Layout
6 Create and Modify Lists
7 Set and Modify Tab Stops
8 Insert a SmartArt Graphic and an Online Video

Skills Review Project 1D Internship

In the following Skills Review, you will edit an information handout regarding production and development internships with Sturgeon Point Productions. Your completed document will look similar to Figure 1.53.

PROJECT FILES

For Project 1D, you will need the following file:

w01D_Internship

You will save your document as:

Lastname_Firstname_1D_Internship

PROJECT RESULTS

STURGEON POINT PRODUCTIONS

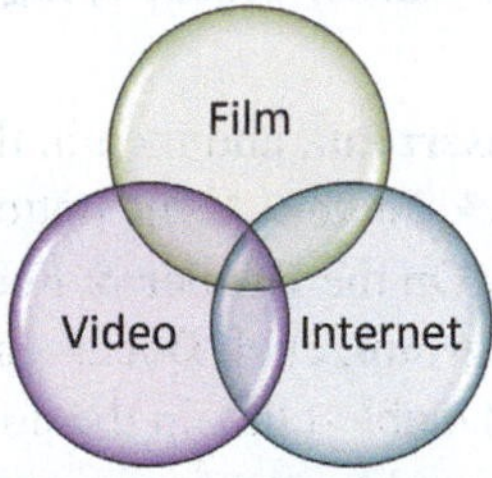

Sturgeon Point Productions is a full service film and video production facility located in Miami, Florida. Celebrating over 45 years of producing top quality commercial and independent film, our projects range from award winning documentaries and live action short features, to live concert and sporting events, to popular educational and training series of videos for schools, businesses, trade shows and multi-media presentations. We currently offer internships to film students in participating local colleges and universities, in both our development and production departments.

In-House Office Internships

Sturgeon Point Productions is looking for story analysts, research, post production and production assistants to work in our offices. We offer college credit as independent study at participating schools for one semester, which can be repeated for up to one year from the start date of the internship. To receive credit, interns must:

1. Be enrolled as a film major at a participating local college or university
2. Maintain a 3.0 GPA
3. Receive satisfactory monthly progress reports from their direct supervisor

Lastname_Firstname_1D_Internship

Following is a list of departments in our Miami office, currently seeking development and production interns:

- ✓ Development Department..Researcher
- ✓ Development Department..Asst. to Producer
- ✓ Development Department..Writer's Assistant
- ✓ Post Production..Asst. Editor
- ✓ Post Production..Asst. Sound Editor
- ✓ Production..Asst. Office Manager

Additional Information

For more information and to sign up for our weekly newsletter, visit our website at www.sturgeonpointproductions.com. Be sure to view the following video to learn about some of the important skills you will develop as an intern with Sturgeon Point Productions.

The Arts
Costume Design

Lastname_Firstname_1D_Internship

FIGURE 1.53

(Project 1D Internship continues on the next page)

Skills Review Project 1D Internship (continued)

1 Start Word, click **Open Other Documents**, and then click **Browse**. Navigate to your student files, and then open **w01D_Internship**. On the **Home tab**, in the **Paragraph group**, be sure **Show/Hide** is active. Click the **File tab**, and then click **Save As**. Navigate to your **Word Chapter 1** folder, and then **Save** the document as **Lastname_Firstname_1D_Internship**

a. Click the **Layout tab**. In the **Page Setup group**, click **Margins**, and then click **Custom Margins**. In the **Page Setup** dialog box, press Tab as necessary to select the value in the **Left** box. Type **1** and then press Tab to select the value in the **Right** box. Type **1** and then click **OK**.

b. Scroll down to view the bottom of **Page 1**, point anywhere in the bottom margin area, right-click, and then click **Edit Footer** to display the footer area. On the **Header & Footer Tools Design tab**, in the **Insert group**, click **Document Info**, and then click **File Name**. Double-click anywhere in the document to close the footer area.

c. Press Ctrl + A to select all of the text in the document, and then on the **Home tab**, in the **Paragraph group**, click **Align Left**.

d. Press Ctrl + Home. Select the document title, and then on the **Home tab**, in the **Paragraph group**, click **Center**.

e. Locate the first bold subheading—*In-House Office Internships*. Point to the left of the paragraph to display the [pointer] pointer, and then click one time to select the text. With *In-House Office Internships* selected, locate the subheading *Additional Information*. Move the pointer to the left of the paragraph to display the [pointer] pointer, hold down Ctrl, and then click one time to select both paragraphs. In the **Paragraph group**, click **Center**.

f. Press Ctrl + A to select all of the text in the document. On the **Home tab**, in the **Paragraph group**, click **Line and Paragraph Spacing**, and then click **1.5**.

2 Below the title of the document, click anywhere in the paragraph that begins *Sturgeon Point Productions is a full service*. On the **Home tab**, in the **Paragraph group**, click the **Dialog Box Launcher**.

a. In the **Paragraph** dialog box, on the **Indents and Spacing tab**, under **Indentation**, click the **Special arrow**, and then click **First line** to indent the first line by 0.5". Click **OK**, and then click anywhere in the paragraph that begins *Sturgeon Point Productions is looking for*. On the ruler under the ribbon, drag the **First Line Indent** marker to **0.5 inches on the horizontal ruler**.

b. Press Ctrl + A to select all of the text in the document. Click the **Layout tab**, and then in the **Paragraph group**, under **Spacing**, click the **After spin box up arrow** one time to change the value to **6 pt**.

c. Select the subheading **In-House Office Internships**, including the paragraph mark following it. Scroll down, hold down Ctrl, and then select the subheading **Additional Information**. With both subheadings selected, in the **Paragraph group**, under **Spacing**, click the **Before up spin box arrow** two times to set the **Spacing Before** to **12 pt**. **Save** your document.

3 Locate the first paragraph that begins *Development Department*, and then point to this paragraph from the left margin area to display the [pointer] pointer. Drag down to select this paragraph and the next five paragraphs so that six paragraphs are selected. On the **Home tab**, in the **Paragraph group**, click **Bullets** to change the selected text to a bulleted list.

a. Under the subheading *In-House Office Internships*, in the paragraph that begins *Sturgeon Point Productions is looking*, click to position the insertion point at the *end* of the paragraph, following the colon. Press Enter to create a blank paragraph. On the ruler, drag the **First Line Indent** marker to the left so that it is positioned directly above the lower button. Being sure to include the period, type **1.** and then press Spacebar to create the first item in a numbered list.

b. Type **Be enrolled as a film major at a participating local college or university** and then press Enter. Type **Maintain a 3.0 GPA** and then press Enter. Type **Receive satisfactory monthly progress reports from their direct supervisor**

c. Scroll down to view the bulleted list of departments, and then select all six bulleted items in the list. On the mini toolbar, click the **Bullets button arrow**, and then under **Bullet Library**, click the **check mark** symbol. If the check mark is not available, choose another bullet symbol.

(Project 1D Internship continues on the next page)

Skills Review Project 1D Internship (continued)

4 With the list selected, move the pointer to the horizontal ruler, and then point to and click at **3.5 inches on the horizontal ruler** to align the job titles at the tab mark.

a. With the bulleted list still selected, on the ruler, point to the new tab marker at **3.5 inches on the horizontal ruler**, and then when the *Left Tab* ScreenTip displays, drag the tab marker to **4 inches on the horizontal ruler**.

b. On the ruler, point to the tab marker that you moved to display the *Left Tab* ScreenTip, and then double-click to display the **Tabs** dialog box.

c. In the **Tabs** dialog box, under **Tab stop position**, if necessary select *4"*, and then type **6** Under **Alignment**, click the **Right** option button. Under **Leader**, click the **2** option button. Near the bottom of the **Tabs** dialog box, click **Set**.

d. Under **Tab stop position**, select **4"**, and then click **Clear** to delete the tab stop. Click **OK**. **Save** your document.

5 Press Ctrl + Home to move to the top of the document, and then in the title, click to the right of the *S* in *PRODUCTIONS*.

a. Click the **Insert tab**, and then in the **Illustrations group**, click **SmartArt**. On the left, click **Relationship**, and then scroll the list to the bottom. Locate and then click **Basic Venn**. Click **OK** to insert the SmartArt graphic. If necessary, close the Text Pane.

b. In the SmartArt graphic, click **[Text]** in the top circle shape. Type **Film** and then in the lower left shape, click the placeholder **[Text]**. Type **Video** and then in the third circle, type **Internet**

c. Click the SmartArt graphic border to select it. Click the **Format tab**, and then in the **Size group**, if necessary click **Size** to display the **Shape Height** and **Shape Width** boxes. Set the **Height** to **3"** and the **Width** to **6.5"**.

d. With the SmartArt graphic still selected, on the ribbon, under **SmartArt Tools**, click the **Design tab**, and then in the **SmartArt Styles group**, click **Change Colors**. Under **Colorful**, click the third style—**Colorful Range - Accent Colors 3 to 4**. On the **Design tab**, in the **SmartArt Styles group**, click **More** . Under **3-D**, in the first row, click the third style—**Cartoon**.

6 Hold down Ctrl and then press End to move to the end of the document. On the **Insert tab**, in the **Media group**, click **Online Video**. Click in the **Bing Video Search** box. Including the quotation marks, type **"Go 2013 1B video"** and then press Enter. In the first row, click the first video, and then click **Insert**.

a. On the **Format tab**, in the **Size group**, change the **Height** to **2.0**

b. Click the **File tab**, and then on the right, click **Show All Properties**. In the **Tags** box, type **internship** and in the **Subject** box type your course name and section number. If necessary, in the **Author** box, replace the existing text with your first and last name. Click **Save**.

c. Click the **File tab**, and then click **Print** to display **Print Preview**. At the bottom of the preview, click the **Next Page** and **Previous Page** buttons to move between pages. If necessary, return to the document and make any necessary changes.

d. **Save** your document. In the upper right corner of the Word window, click **Close**. If directed by your instructor to do so, submit your paper printout, your electronic image of your document that looks like a printed document, or your completed Word file.

END | You have completed Project 1D

CONTENT-BASED ASSESSMENTS (MASTERY AND TRANSFER OF LEARNING)

Mastering Word Project 1E Documentary

Apply 1A skills from these Objectives:

1. Create a New Document and Insert Text
2. Insert and Format Graphics
3. Insert and Modify Text Boxes and Shapes
4. Preview and Print a Document

In the following Mastery project, you will create a flyer announcing a special event being hosted by Sturgeon Point Productions. Your printed results will look similar to Figure 1.54.

PROJECT FILES

For Project 1E, you will need the following files:

New blank Word document
w01E_Antarctica
w01E_Filmmaker

You will save your document as:

Lastname_Firstname_1E_Documentary

PROJECT RESULTS

Build from Scratch

Sturgeon Point Productions Presents Aria Pacheco

Sturgeon Point Productions will be hosting its 5th ***Annual Script to Screen*** series, every Friday night this April in our Studio G screening room. All employees, interns, and film students with current school ID are welcome to share in this totally free, exciting evening, where our award-winning filmmakers from our Documentary and Short Feature Film Departments give a first-hand account of the filmmaking process and the challenges that went into their particular projects, from the script phase through production and finally, in distribution and marketing.

This year, we are proud to kick off the series with Aria Pacheco, who will discuss her multi-award winning documentary, **"Through the Cold."** This film documents the perils and triumphs of a team of scientists living in Antarctica. This compelling story, rich in visual complexity, follows the team as they prepare for the six months of darkness in the winter season. Celebrated film critic, Georges Harold, will be conducting an interview with Ms. Pacheco and select members of her crew following a screening of the film, which will take place on Friday, April 5th at 8 p.m. This event is guaranteed to fill up fast, so we suggest you get in line at least one hour prior to the screening.

"Through the Cold" has been heralded by critics across the country. Don't miss this chance to meet one of our greatest documentary filmmakers.

Date: April 5
Time: 8 p.m.
Place: Studio G Screening Room

Lastname_Firstname_1E_Documentary

FIGURE 1.54

(Project 1E Documentary continues on the next page)

CONTENT-BASED ASSESSMENTS (MASTERY AND TRANSFER OF LEARNING)

Mastering Word Project 1E Documentary (continued)

1 Start Word and display a **Blank document** with the ruler and formatting marks displayed.

2 Type **Sturgeon Point Productions Presents Aria Pacheco** and then press Enter. From your student data files, insert the text file **w01E_Filmmaker**. Using your own name, **Save** the document in your **Word Chapter 1** folder as **Lastname_Firstname_1E_Documentary**

3 To the document title, apply the **Fill – White, Outline – Accent 1, Glow – Accent 1** text effect, and then change the **Font Size** to **36**.

4 Change the title **Font Color** to **Blue-Gray, Text 2**—in the fourth column, the first color. Apply an **Outer Shadow** using **Offset Left**—in the second row, the third style. **Center** the title.

5 Position the insertion point at the beginning of the paragraph that begins with *This year*, and then from your student data files, insert the picture **w01E_Antarctica**.

6 Change the **Layout Options** to **Square** and then change the **Height** of the picture to **2.25** Using the **Position** command, display the **Layout** dialog box, and then change the **Horizontal Alignment** to **Right relative to** the **Margin**.

7 Apply a **10 Point Soft Edges** picture effect to the image, and then display the **Artistic Effects** gallery. In the third row, apply the fourth effect—**Mosaic Bubbles**.

8 Deselect the picture. Apply a **Page Border** to the document using the **Shadow** setting. Select the first style, and change the **Color** to **Blue-Gray, Text 2**. Change the **Width** to **3 pt**.

9 Below the last paragraph, draw a **Text Box** and then change the **Height** to **1.5** and the **Width** to **4.5**

10 To precisely place the text box, display the **Layout** dialog box. Change the **Horizontal Alignment** to **Centered, relative to** the **Page**, and then change the **Vertical Absolute position** to **0.5** below the **Paragraph**.

11 In the text box, type the following text:

Date: April 5
Time: 8 p.m.
Place: Studio G Screening Room

12 In the text box, change the font size of all the text to **18**. Apply **Bold** and **Center**. Apply a **Shape Style** to the text box—under **Theme Styles**, in the last row, select the second style—**Intense Effect – Blue, Accent 1**. Change the **Shape Outline** to **Black, Text 1**.

13 Insert the **File Name** in the footer, and then display the document properties. As the **Tags** type **documentary, interview** and as the **Subject** type your course and section number. Be sure your name is indicated as the **Author**. **Save** your file.

14 Display the **Print Preview** and, if necessary, return to the document and make any necessary changes. **Save** your document and **Close** Word. If directed by your instructor to do so, submit your paper printout, your electronic image of your document that looks like a printed document, or your completed Word file.

END | You have completed Project 1E

CONTENT-BASED ASSESSMENTS (MASTERY AND TRANSFER OF LEARNING)

Mastering Word Project 1F Pitch Festival

Apply 1B skills from these Objectives:

5 Change Document and Paragraph Layout
6 Create and Modify Lists
7 Set and Modify Tab Stops
8 Insert a SmartArt Graphic and an Online Video

In the following Mastery project, you will edit a document with information regarding an event that Sturgeon Point Productions is holding for college students. Your printed results will look similar to Figure 1.55.

PROJECT FILES

For Project 1F, you will need the following file:

w01F_Pitch_Festival

You will save your document as:

Lastname_Firstname_1F_Pitch_Festival

PROJECT RESULTS

Pitch Festival!

Do you have a story that must be told? Pitch us your project during the Sturgeon Point Productions annual Pitch Festival! We're setting up several days of conference video calls for college students that are currently enrolled in an accredited film production program anywhere in the United States. If your idea is selected, you will be flown to our studios in Miami, Florida to pitch your idea to our staff of producers and development executives. The following video provides additional information:

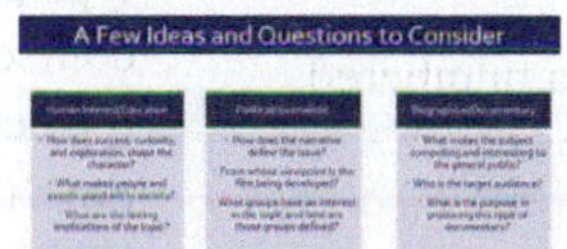

Sturgeon Point Productions is one of the leading independent film and video companies in the Miami area. We are currently looking for new, fresh, exciting ideas for short and full-length feature films and documentaries. We like character driven stories that can be shot on an independent budget within one or two locations, preferably either in our studios or in the Miami area. We are currently looking for scripts, ideas, and concepts that are in one of the following categories:

1. Human interest or educational
2. Political or journalistic
3. Biographical or documentary

The Pitch Festival will take place at our secure website on the following dates and times. There are no entry fees to pitch; this unique opportunity to pitch to our staff of professional filmmakers is absolutely free for college film students. Sign up now at www.sturgeonpointproductions.com/pitchfest for one of the following pitch sessions:

- September 12, 11 a.m...Short and Feature Film Pitches
- September 13, 8 p.m. ....Biographical and Documentary Film Pitches
- September 14, 7 p.m. ....Educational Series Pitches

Lastname_Firstname_1F_Pitch_Festival

FIGURE 1.55

(Project 1F Pitch Festival continues on the next page)

Mastering Word Project 1F Pitch Festival (continued)

1 Start Word, and then from your student files, open **w01F_Pitch_Festival**. Display formatting marks, and then **Save** the file in your **Word Chapter 1** folder as **Lastname_Firstname_1F_Pitch_Festival**

2 Insert the **File Name** in the footer, and then change the **Line Spacing** for the entire document to **1.5**. **Center** the document title, and then change the title font size to **24**. Change the **Top** and **Bottom** margins to **0.5**

3 Select the three paragraphs below the title, and then apply a **First line** indent of **0.5"**.

4 Select the entire document, and then change the **Spacing Before** to **6 pt** and the **Spacing After** to **6 pt**.

5 Select the last three paragraphs containing the dates, and then apply filled square bullets. If the bullets are not available, choose another bullet style. With the bulleted list selected, set a **Right** tab with **dot leaders** at **6"**.

6 Locate the paragraph that begins *Sturgeon Point Productions*, and then click at the end of the paragraph, after the colon. Press Enter and remove the first line indent from the new paragraph.

7 In the blank line you inserted, create a numbered list with the following three numbered items:

Human interest or educational
Political or journalistic
Biographical or documentary

8 Position the insertion point at the end of the document after the word *Pitches*. Do *not* insert a blank line. Insert a **SmartArt** graphic from the **Process** category. Toward the bottom of the gallery, select and insert the **Equation** SmartArt. Select the outside border of the SmartArt, and then change the **Height** of the SmartArt to **1** and the **Width** to **6.5**

9 With the SmartArt selected, change the layout to **Square**, and change the **Horizontal Alignment** to **Centered relative to** the **Page**. Change the **Vertical Alignment** to **Bottom relative to** the **Margin**.

10 In the first circle type **Your Ideas** and in the second circle type **Our Experts** In the third circle type **Pitch Festival!**

11 Change the SmartArt color to **Colorful Range – Accent Colors 4 to 5**. Apply the **3-D Polished** style.

12 Click at the end of the first paragraph below the title. Press Enter, remove the first line indent, and then center the blank line. Insert an **Online Video**. In the **Bing Video Search** box, type **Go 1F Video** and then insert the video that displays a blue SmartArt. Change the height of the video to **1.5** and then **Save**.

13 Display the document properties. In the **Tags** box, type **pitch festival** and in the **Subject** box, type your course name and section number. In the **Author** box, replace the existing text with your first and last name. **Save** the file.

14 Display the **Print Preview** and if necessary, return to the document and make any necessary changes. **Save** your document and **Close** Word. If directed by your instructor to do so, submit your paper printout, your electronic image of your document that looks like a printed document, or your completed Word file.

END | You have completed Project 1F

Mastering Word Project 1G Educational Website

Apply 1A and 1B skills from these Objectives:

1. Create a New Document and Insert Text
2. Insert and Format Graphics
3. Insert and Modify Text Boxes and Shapes
4. Preview and Print a Document
5. Change Document and Paragraph Layout
6. Create and Modify Lists
7. Set and Modify Tab Stops
8. Insert a SmartArt Graphic and an Online Video

Build from Scratch

In the following Mastery project, you will create a flyer that details a new educational website that Sturgeon Point Productions has developed for instructors. Your printed results will look similar to those in Figure 1.56.

PROJECT FILES

For Project 1G, you will need the following files:

New blank Word document
w01G_Education
w01G_Media

You will save your document as:

Lastname_Firstname_1G_Educational_Website

PROJECT RESULTS

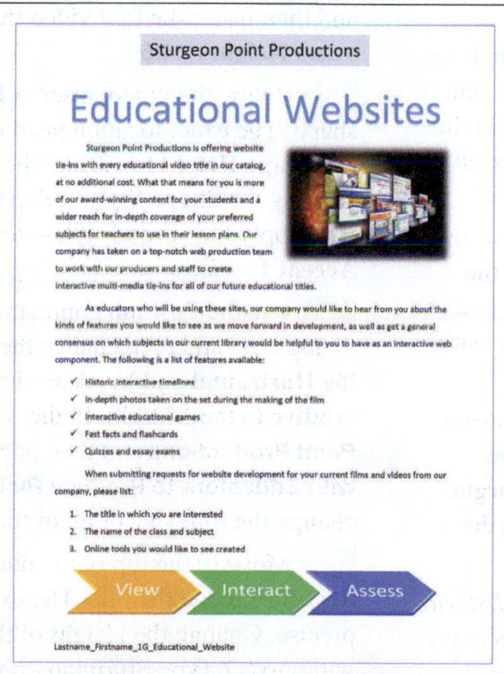

Sturgeon Point Productions

Educational Websites

Sturgeon Point Productions is offering website tie-ins with every educational video title in our catalog, at no additional cost. What that means for you is more of our award-winning content for your students and a wider reach for in-depth coverage of your preferred subjects for teachers to use in their lesson plans. Our company has taken on a top-notch web production team to work with our producers and staff to create interactive multi-media tie-ins for all of our future educational titles.

As educators who will be using these sites, our company would like to hear from you about the kinds of features you would like to see as we move forward in development, as well as get a general consensus on which subjects in our current library would be helpful to you to have as an interactive web component. The following is a list of features available:

- ✓ Historic interactive timelines
- ✓ In-depth photos taken on the set during the making of the film
- ✓ Interactive educational games
- ✓ Fast facts and flashcards
- ✓ Quizzes and essay exams

When submitting requests for website development for your current films and videos from our company, please list:

1. The title in which you are interested
2. The name of the class and subject
3. Online tools you would like to see created

Lastname_Firstname_1G_Educational_Website

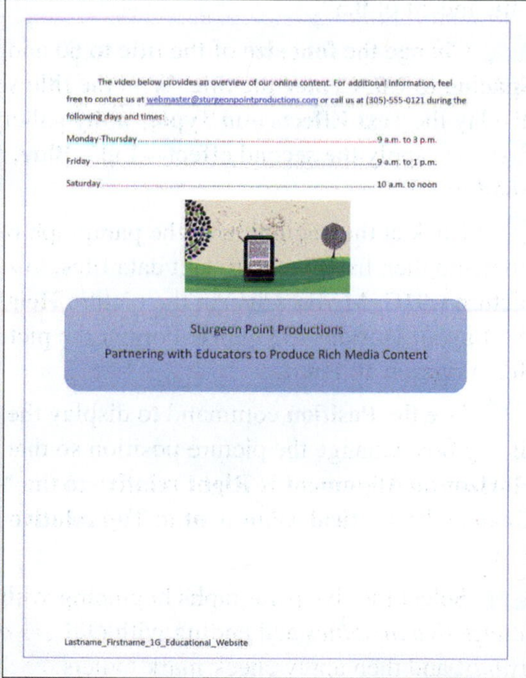

The video below provides an overview of our online content. For additional information, feel free to contact us at webmaster@sturgeonpointproductions.com or call us at (305)-555-0121 during the following days and times:

Monday-Thursday........9 a.m. to 3 p.m.
Friday........9 a.m. to 1 p.m.
Saturday........10 a.m. to noon

Sturgeon Point Productions
Partnering with Educators to Produce Rich Media Content

Lastname_Firstname_1G_Educational_Website

FIGURE 1.56

(Project 1G Educational Website continues on the next page)

CONTENT-BASED ASSESSMENTS (MASTERY AND TRANSFER OF LEARNING)

Mastering Word | Project 1G Educational Website (continued)

1 Start Word and display a blank document. Display formatting marks and the ruler. **Save** the document in your **Word Chapter 1** folder as **Lastname_Firstname_1G_Educational_Website**

2 Type **Educational Websites** and then press Enter. Type **Sturgeon Point Productions is offering website tie-ins with every educational video title in our catalog, at no additional cost.** Press Spacebar, and then with the insertion point positioned at the end of the sentence that you typed, insert the text from your student data file **w01G_Education**.

3 Change the **Line Spacing** for the entire document to **1.5** and the spacing **After** to **6 pt**. To each of the four paragraphs that begin *Sturgeon Point Productions*, *As educators*, *When submitting*, and *The video*, apply a **First Line** indent of **0.5"**.

4 Change the **font size** of the title to **50** and the **Line Spacing** to **1.0**. **Center** the title. With the title selected, display the **Text Effects and Typography** gallery. In the first row, apply the second effect—**Fill – Blue, Accent 1, Shadow**.

5 Click at the beginning of the paragraph below the title, and then from your student data files, insert the picture **w01G_Media**. Change the picture **Height** to **2** and the **Layout Options** to **Square**. Format the picture with **Soft Edges** in **10 Point**.

6 Use the **Position** command to display the **Layout** dialog box. Change the picture position so that the **Horizontal Alignment** is **Right relative to** the **Margin**. Change the **Vertical Alignment** to **Top relative to** the **Line**.

7 Select the five paragraphs beginning with *Historic interactive timelines* and ending with *Quizzes and essay exams*, and then apply check mark bullets.

8 In the paragraph below the bulleted list, click after the colon. Press Enter and remove the first line indent. Type a numbered list with the following three numbered items:

The title in which you are interested
The name of the class and subject
Online tools you would like to see created

9 With the insertion point located at the end of the numbered list, insert a **SmartArt** graphic. In the **Process** category, locate and select the **Basic Chevron Process**. In the first shape type **View** In the second shape type **Interact** and in the third shape type **Assess**

10 Change the SmartArt color to **Colorful Range – Accent Colors 4 to 5**, and then apply the **3-D Flat Scene** style. Change the **Height** of the SmartArt to **1** and the **Width** to **6.5** Change the **Layout Options** to **Square**, the **Horizontal Alignment** to **Centered relative to** the **Page**, and the **Vertical Alignment** to **Bottom relative to** the **Margin**.

11 Select the days and times at the end of the document, and then set a **Right** tab with **dot leaders** at **6"**.

12 Click in the blank line below the tabbed list, and **Center** the line. Insert an **Online Video**. In the **Bing Video Search** box, type **Pearson Higher Education Learning** and then insert the first video that displays. Change the video **Height** to **1.5**

13 Below the video, insert a **Rounded Rectangle** shape. The exact location need not be precise. Change the **Shape Height** to **1.5** and the **Shape Width** to **6.5** Display the **Shape Styles** gallery, and then in the fourth row, apply the second style—**Subtle Effect - Blue, Accent 1**.

14 Use the **Position** command to display the **Layout** dialog box, and then change the position so that both the **Horizontal** and **Vertical Alignment** are **Centered relative to** the **Margin**. In the rectangle, type **Sturgeon Point Productions** and then press Enter. Type **Partnering with Educators to Produce Rich Media Content** and then change the font size of all of the text in the text box to **16**.

15 Move to the top of the document and insert a **Text Box** above the title. The exact location need not be precise. Change the **Height** of the text box to **0.5** and the width to **3.7** Type **Sturgeon Point Productions** and then change the font size to **22 Center** the text.

16 Use the **Position** command to display the **Layout** dialog box, and then position the text box so that the **Horizontal Alignment** is **Centered relative to** the **Page** and the **Vertical Absolute position** is **0.5 below** the **Page**.

17 With the text box selected, display the **Shape Fill** gallery, and then in the next to last column, select the second color—**Blue, Accent 5, Lighter 80%**. Change

(Project 1G Educational Website continues on the next page)

Mastering Word Project 1G Educational Website (continued)

the **Shape Outline** to the same color—**Blue, Accent 5, Lighter 80%**.

18 Deselect the text box. Apply a **Page Border** to the document. Use the **Box** setting, and choose the first style. Change the **Color** to **Blue, Accent 5**.

19 Change the **Top** margin to **1.25** and insert the **File Name** in the footer.

20 Display the document properties. As the **Tags** type **website** and as the **Subject** type your course and section number. Be sure your name displays in the **Author** box. **Save** your document and **Close** Word. If directed by your instructor to do so, submit your paper printout, your electronic image of your document that looks like a printed document, or your completed Word file.

END | You have completed Project 1G

CONTENT-BASED ASSESSMENTS (CRITICAL THINKING)

Apply a combination of the 1A and 1B skills.

GO! Fix It | Project 1H Casting Call | MyITLab

GO! Make It | Project 1I Development Team | MyITLab

Build From Scratch

GO! Solve It | Project 1J Softball | MyITLab

GO! Solve It | Project 1K Production

PROJECT FILES

For Project 1K, you will need the following files:

w01K_Production
w01K_Studio

You will save your document as:

Lastname_Firstname_1K_Production

From the student files that accompany this textbook, locate and open the file w01K_Production. Format the document using techniques you learned in this chapter to create an appropriate flyer aimed at filmmakers. From your student data files, insert the picture w01K_Studio, and then format the picture with an artistic effect. Insert a SmartArt graphic that illustrates two or three important points about the company. Use text effects and text wrapping so that the flyer is easy to read and understand and has an attractive design. Save the file in your Word Chapter 1 folder as **Lastname_Firstname_1K_Production** and submit it as directed.

Performance Level

Performance Criteria	Exemplary: You consistently applied the relevant skills	Proficient: You sometimes, but not always, applied the relevant skills	Developing: You rarely or never applied the relevant skills
Use text effects	Text effects applied to text in an attractive and appropriate manner.	Text effects are applied but do not appropriately display text.	Text effects not used.
Insert and format a picture	The picture is inserted and text wrapping and an artistic effect are applied.	The picture is inserted but not formatted properly.	No picture is inserted in the document.
Insert and format SmartArt	The SmartArt is inserted and appropriately formatted.	The SmartArt is inserted but no formatting is applied.	No SmartArt is inserted in the document.

END | You have completed Project 1K

OUTCOMES-BASED ASSESSMENTS (CRITICAL THINKING)

RUBRIC

The following outcomes-based assessments are *open-ended assessments*. That is, there is no specific correct result; your result will depend on your approach to the information provided. Make *Professional Quality* your goal. Use the following scoring rubric to guide you in *how* to approach the problem and then to evaluate *how well* your approach solves the problem.

The *criteria*—Software Mastery, Content, Format and Layout, and Process—represent the knowledge and skills you have gained that you can apply to solving the problem. The *levels of performance*—Professional Quality, Approaching Professional Quality, or Needs Quality Improvements—help you and your instructor evaluate your result.

	Your completed project is of Professional Quality if you:	Your completed project is Approaching Professional Quality if you:	Your completed project Needs Quality Improvements if you:
1-Software Mastery	Choose and apply the most appropriate skills, tools, and features and identify efficient methods to solve the problem.	Choose and apply some appropriate skills, tools, and features, but not in the most efficient manner.	Choose inappropriate skills, tools, or features, or are inefficient in solving the problem.
2-Content	Construct a solution that is clear and well organized, contains content that is accurate, appropriate to the audience and purpose, and is complete. Provide a solution that contains no errors of spelling, grammar, or style.	Construct a solution in which some components are unclear, poorly organized, inconsistent, or incomplete. Misjudge the needs of the audience. Have some errors in spelling, grammar, or style, but the errors do not detract from comprehension.	Construct a solution that is unclear, incomplete, or poorly organized, contains some inaccurate or inappropriate content, and contains many errors of spelling, grammar, or style. Do not solve the problem.
3-Format and Layout	Format and arrange all elements to communicate information and ideas, clarify function, illustrate relationships, and indicate relative importance.	Apply appropriate format and layout features to some elements, but not others. Overuse features, causing minor distraction.	Apply format and layout that does not communicate information or ideas clearly. Do not use format and layout features to clarify function, illustrate relationships, or indicate relative importance. Use available features excessively, causing distraction.
4-Process	Use an organized approach that integrates planning, development, self-assessment, revision, and reflection.	Demonstrate an organized approach in some areas, but not others; or, use an insufficient process of organization throughout.	Do not use an organized approach to solve the problem.

OUTCOMES-BASED ASSESSMENTS (CRITICAL THINKING)

Apply a combination of the 1A and 1B skills.

GO! Think Project 1L Classes

PROJECT FILES

Build from Scratch

For Project 1L, you will need the following file:

New blank Word document

You will save your document as:

Lastname_Firstname_1L_Classes

The Human Resources director at Sturgeon Point Productions needs to create a flyer to inform full-time employees of educational opportunities beginning in September. The courses are taught each year by industry professionals and are designed to improve skills in motion picture and television development and production. Employees who have been with Sturgeon Point Productions for at least two years are eligible to take the courses free of cost. The classes provide employees with opportunities to advance their careers, gain valuable skills, and achieve technical certification. All courses take place in Studio G. Interested employees should contact Elana Springs in Human Resources to sign up. Information meetings are being held at 5:30 according to the following schedule: television development on June 15; motion picture production on June 17; and recording services on June 21.

Create a flyer with basic information about the courses and information meetings. Be sure the flyer is easy to read and understand and has an attractive design. Save the document as **Lastname_Firstname_1L_Classes** and submit it as directed.

END | You have completed Project 1L

Build from Scratch

GO! Think Project 1M Store MyITLab

Build from Scratch

You and GO! Project 1N Family Flyer MyITLab

Build from Scratch

GO! Collaborative Team Project Project 1O Bell Orchid Hotels MyITLab

Creating Cover Letters and Using Tables to Create Resumes

PROJECT 2A

OUTCOMES

Write a resume by using a Word table.

PROJECT 2B

OUTCOMES

Write a cover letter and print an envelope.

OBJECTIVES

1. Create a Table
2. Format a Table
3. Present a Word Document Online

OBJECTIVES

4. Create a Custom Word Template
5. Correct and Reorganize Text
6. Use the Proofing Options and Print an Envelope

Kaspars Grinvalds/Fotolia

In This Chapter

Tables are useful for organizing and presenting data. Because a table is so easy to use, many individuals prefer to arrange tabular information in a Word table rather than setting a series of tabs. For example, you can use a table when you want to present rows and columns of information or to create a format for a document such as a resume.

When using Word to write business or personal letters, use a commonly approved letter format, and always use a clear writing style. You will make a good impression on prospective employers if you use a standard business letter style when you are writing a cover letter for a resume.

The projects in this chapter relate to the **College Career Center at Florida Port Community College** in St. Petersburg, Florida, a coastal port city near the Florida High Tech Corridor. With 60 percent of Florida's high tech companies and a third of the state's manufacturing companies located in the St. Petersburg and Tampa Bay areas, the college partners with businesses to play a vital role in providing a skilled workforce. The College Career Center assists students in exploring careers, finding internships, and applying for jobs. The Center offers workshops for resume and cover letter writing and for practice interviews.

PROJECT
2A Resume

PROJECT ACTIVITIES

In Activities 2.01 through 2.11, you will create a table to use as the format for a resume. The director of the Career Center, Mary Walker-Huelsman, will use this model when assisting students with building their resumes. Your completed document will look similar to Figure 2.1.

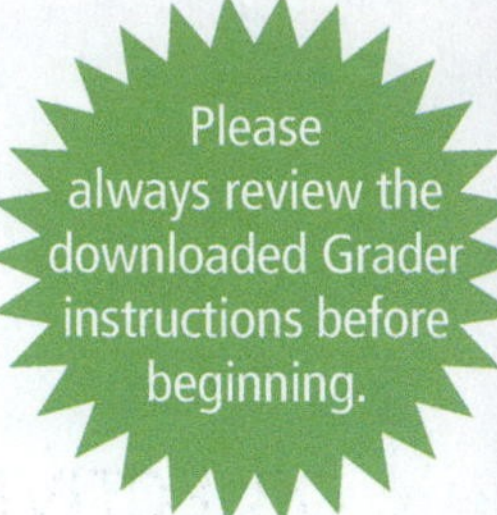

PROJECT FILES

MyITLab grader

If your instructor wants you to submit Project 2A in the MyITLab Grader system, log in to MyITLab, locate Grader Project 2A, and then download the files for this project.

For Project 2A, you will need the following file:
New blank Word document
w02A_Experience

You will save your document as:
Lastname_Firstname_2A_Resume

PROJECT RESULTS

Josh Hayes (727) 555-0313
1541 Dearborn Lane, St. Petersburg, FL 33713 jhayes@alcona.net

OBJECTIVE	Technology writing and editing position in the robotics industry, using research and advanced editing skills to communicate with customers.
SUMMARY OF QUALIFICATIONS	• Two years' experience in robotics lab for Aerospace Instruction Team • Excellent interpersonal and communication skills • Proficiency using Microsoft Word • Proficiency using page layout and design software • Fluency in spoken and written Spanish
EXPERIENCE	**Instructional Lab Assistant**, Florida Port Community College, St. Petersburg, FL July 2013 to June 2015 • Assist robotics professors with sophisticated experiments • Set up robotics practice sessions for Aerospace Instruction Team **Assistant Executive Editor**, Tech Today Newsletter, St. Petersburg, FL September 2012 to June 2013 • Wrote and edited articles for popular college technology newsletter • Responsible for photo editing, cropping, and resizing photos for newsletter • Received Top College Technology Publication Award **Teacher's Assistant**, Florida Port Community College, Aerospace Department, St. Petersburg, FL July 2013 to June 2015 • Helped students with homework, explained assignments, organized materials for professor • Set up robotics lab assignments for students
EDUCATION	**University of South Florida, Tampa, FL** Bachelor of Science, Mechanical Engineering, June 2015 **Florida Port Community College, St. Petersburg, FL** Associate of Arts, Journalism, June 2013
HONORS AND ACTIVITIES	• Elected to Pi Tau Sigma, honor society for mechanical engineers • Qualified for Dean's List, six semesters • Student Mentor, help other students in engineering programs

Lastname_Firstname_2A_Resume

Word 2016, Windows 10, Microsoft Corporation

FIGURE 2.1 Project 2A Resume

Objective 1 Create a Table

GO! Learn How Video W2-1

MOS 3.1.3

A ***table*** is an arrangement of information organized into rows and columns. The intersection of a row and a column in a table creates a box called a ***cell*** into which you can type. Tables are useful to present information in a logical and orderly format.

Activity 2.01 | Creating a Table by Specifying Rows and Columns

ALERT!

To submit as an autograded project, log into MyITLab, download the files for this project, and begin with those files instead of a new blank document.

1. Start Word and then click **Blank document**. On the **Home tab**, in the **Paragraph group**, if necessary click Show/Hide to display the formatting marks. If the rulers do not display, click the View tab, and then in the Show group, select the Ruler check box.

2. Click the **File tab** to display **Backstage** view, click **Save As**, and then click **Browse**. In the **Save As** dialog box, navigate to the location where you are storing your projects for this chapter. Create a new folder named **Word Chapter 2**

3. **Save** the file in the **Word Chapter 2** folder as **Lastname_Firstname_2A_Resume**

4. On the **Insert tab**, in the **Header & Footer group**, click **Footer**, and then at the bottom of the list, click **Edit Footer**. On the ribbon, in the **Insert group**, click **Document Info**, click **File Name**, and then at the right end of the ribbon, click **Close Header and Footer**.

5. On the **Insert tab**, in the **Tables group**, click **Table**. In the **Insert Table** grid, in the fourth row, point to the second square, and notice that the cells are bordered in orange and *2x4 Table* displays at the top of the grid. Compare your screen with Figure 2.2.

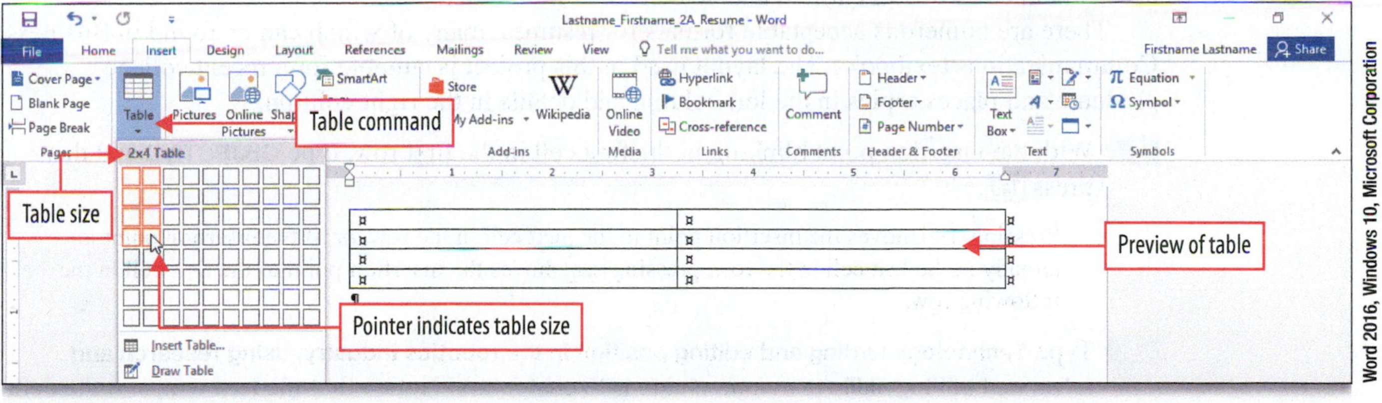

FIGURE 2.2

6. Click one time to create the table. Notice that formatting marks in each cell indicate the end of the contents of each cell; the mark to the right of each *row* indicates the row end. **Save** your document, and then compare your screen with Figure 2.3.

   A table with four rows and two columns displays at the insertion point location, and the insertion point displays in the upper left cell. The table fills the width of the page, from the left margin to the right margin. On the ribbon, Table Tools and two additional tabs—*Design* and *Layout*—display. Borders display around each cell in the table.

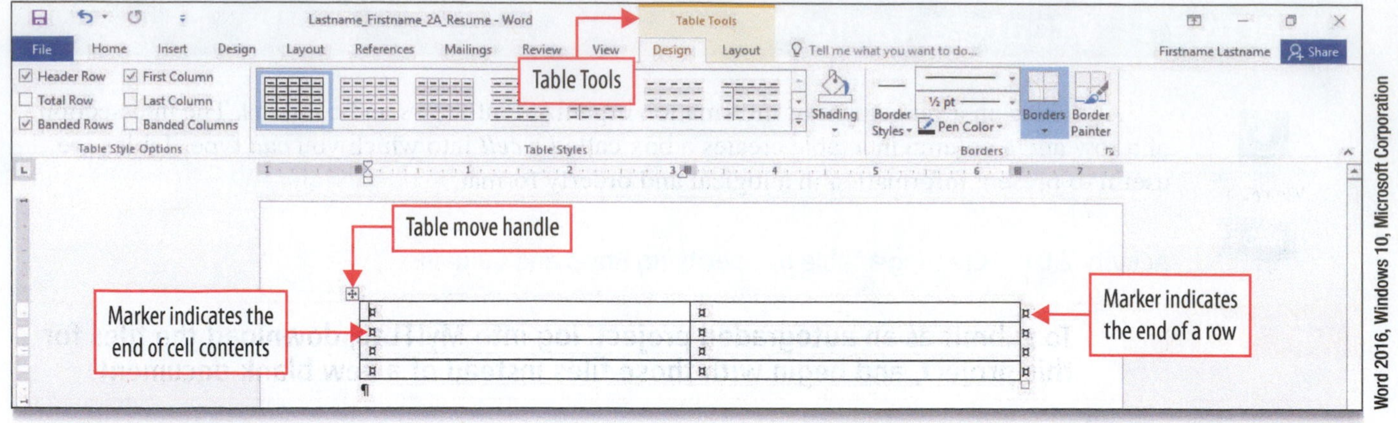

FIGURE 2.3

More Knowledge **Converting Text to a Table and Converting a Table to Text**

You can convert text you have already typed to a table. To do so, if necessary, first use commas or tabs within paragraphs to signal Word to create a column. Then, on the Insert tab, click Table, and click Convert Text to Table. In the Convert Text to Table dialog box, confirm the number of columns you want, indicate the delimiter character you used (e.g. Tab or Paragraph mark), and then click OK. You can convert a table to regular text and choose which text character to use to separate the columns. To do so, on the Table Tools Layout tab, in the Data group, click Convert to Text.

Activity 2.02 | Typing Text in a Table

In a Word table, each cell behaves similarly to a document. For example, as you type in a cell, when you reach the right border of the cell, wordwrap moves the text to the next line. When you press Enter, the insertion point moves down to a new paragraph in the same cell. You can also insert text from another document into a table cell.

There are numerous acceptable formats for resumes, many of which can be found in Business Communications textbooks. The layout used in this project is suitable for a recent college graduate and places topics in the left column and details in the right column.

1. With the insertion point blinking in the first cell in the first row, type **OBJECTIVE** and then press Tab.

   Pressing Tab moves the insertion point to the next cell in the row, or, if the insertion point is already in the last cell in the row, pressing Tab moves the insertion point to the first cell in the following row.

2. Type **Technology writing and editing position in the robotics industry, using research and advanced editing skills to communicate with customers.** Notice that the text wraps in the cell and the height of the row adjusts to fit the text.

3. Press Tab to move to the first cell in the second row. Type **SUMMARY OF QUALIFICATIONS** and then press Tab. Type the following, pressing Enter at the end of each line *except* the last line:

   Two years' experience in robotics lab for Aerospace Instruction Team
   Excellent interpersonal and communication skills
   Proficiency using Microsoft Word
   Proficiency using page layout and design software
   Fluency in spoken and written Spanish

The default font and font size in a table are the same as for a document—Calibri 11 pt. The default line spacing in a table is single spacing with no space before or after paragraphs, which differs from the defaults for a document.

4 **Save** your document, and then compare your screen with Figure 2.4.

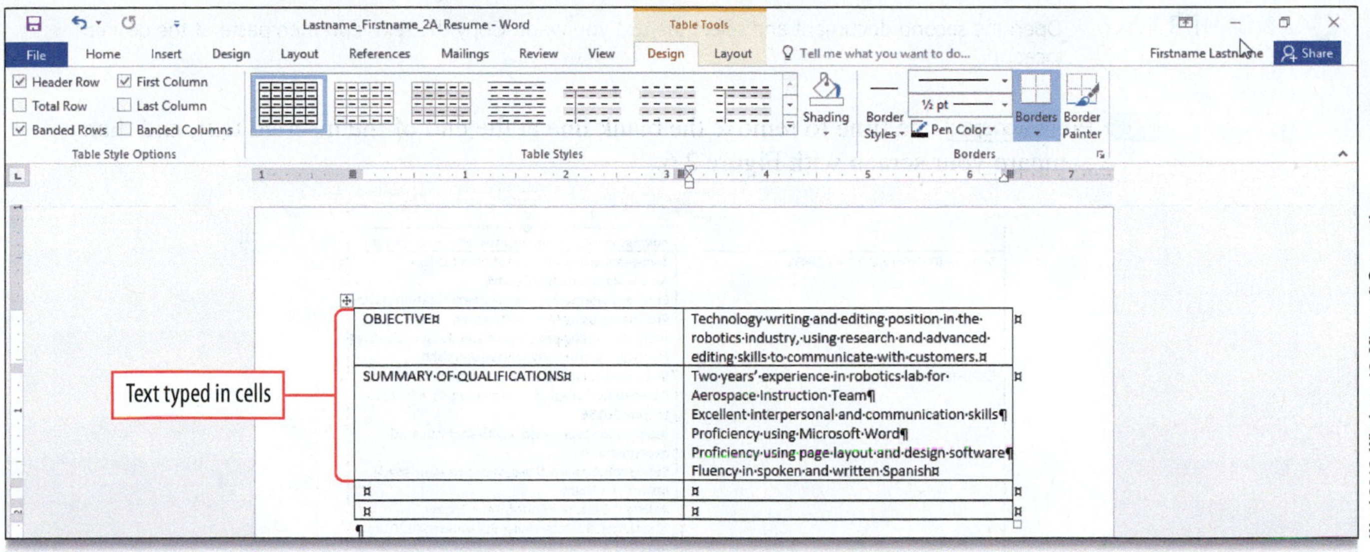

FIGURE 2.4

Activity 2.03 | Inserting Text from a File and Removing Blank Paragraphs

1.1.4

1 Press Tab to move to the first cell in the third row. Type **EXPERIENCE** and then press Tab.

2 Type the following, pressing Enter after each item, including the last item:

Instructional Lab Assistant, Florida Port Community College, St. Petersburg, FL July 2013 to June 2015
Assist robotics professors with sophisticated experiments
Set up robotics practice sessions for Aerospace Instruction Team

3 Be sure your insertion point is positioned in the second column to the left of the cell marker below *Instruction Team*. Compare your screen with Figure 2.5.

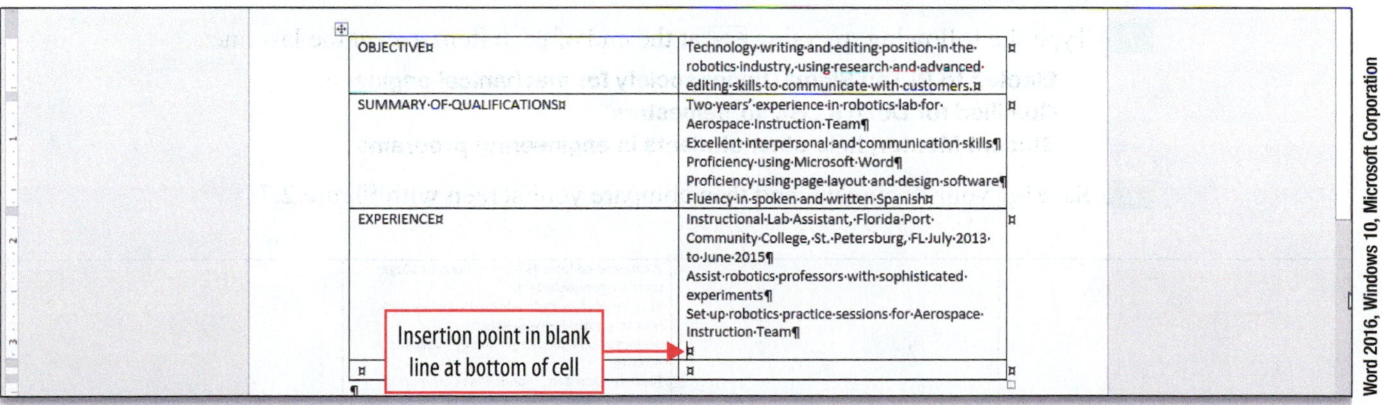

FIGURE 2.5

4 On the **Insert tab**, in the **Text group**, click the **Object button arrow**, and then click **Text from File**. Navigate to your student data files, select **w02A_Experience**, and then click **Insert**.

All of the text from the w02A_Experience document is added to the document at the insertion point.

ANOTHER WAY Open the second document and select the text you want. Copy the text, and then paste at the desired location.

5 Press Backspace one time to remove the blank line at the end of the inserted text, and then compare your screen with Figure 2.6.

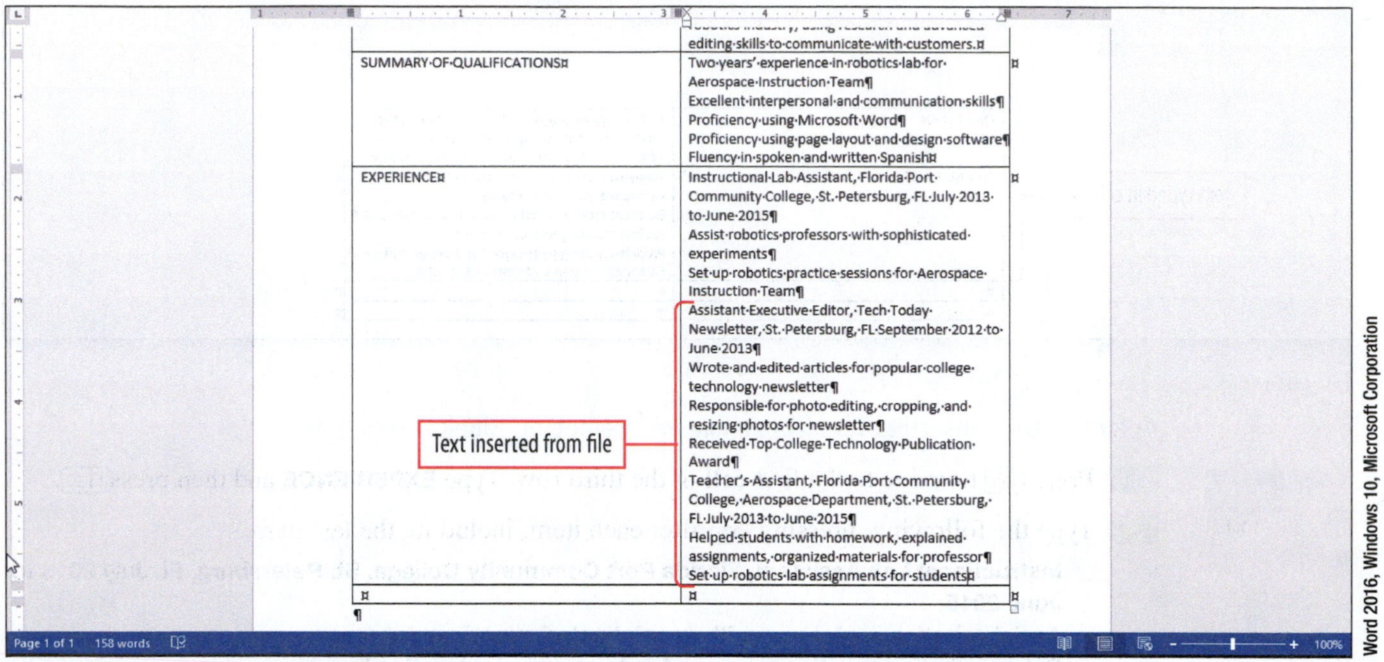

FIGURE 2.6

6 Press Tab to move to the first cell in the fourth row. Type **HONORS AND ACTIVITIES** and then press Tab.

7 Type the following, pressing Enter at the end of each item *except* the last one:

Elected to Pi Tau Sigma, honor society for mechanical engineers
Qualified for Dean's List, six semesters
Student Mentor, help other students in engineering programs

8 **Save** your document, and then compare your screen with Figure 2.7.

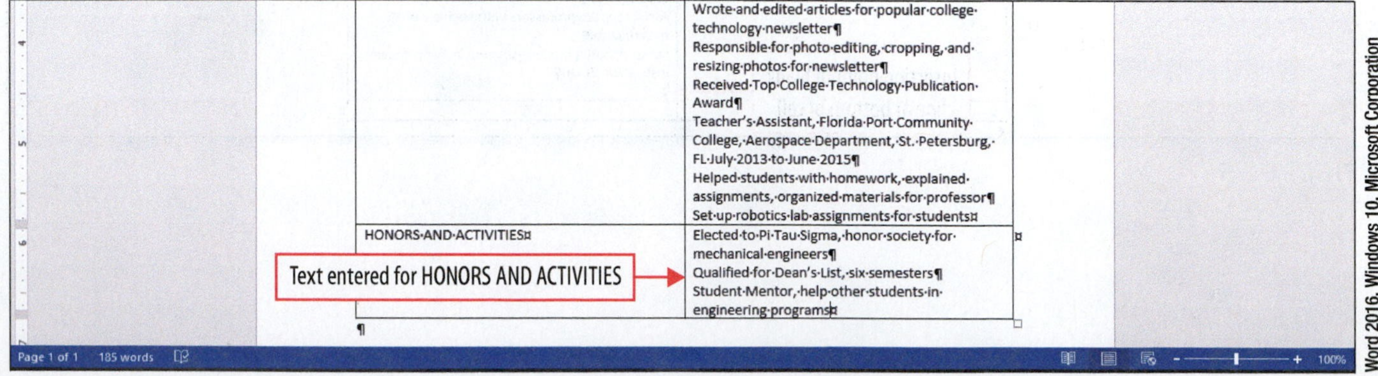

FIGURE 2.7

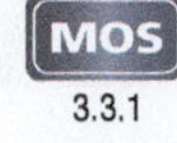

3.3.1

Activity 2.04 | Creating Bulleted Lists in a Table

1. Press Ctrl + Home to move to the top of your document, and then in the cell to the right of *SUMMARY OF QUALIFICATIONS*, select all of the text.

2. On the **Home tab**, in the **Paragraph group**, click **Bullets**.

   The selected text displays as a bulleted list to make each qualification more distinctive.

3. Click anywhere in the cell to deselect the bulleted text, and then drag to select all of the bulleted text again. In the **Paragraph group**, click **Decrease Indent** one time to align the bullets at the left edge of the cell.

4. Scroll as necessary so that you can view the entire *EXPERIENCE* and *HONORS AND ACTIVITIES* sections on your screen. With the bulleted text still selected, in the **Clipboard group**, double-click **Format Painter**.

5. In the cell to the right of *EXPERIENCE*, select the second and third paragraphs—beginning with *Assist* and *Set up*—to create the same style of bulleted list as you did in the previous step.

6. In the same cell, under *Assistant Executive Editor*, select the three paragraphs that begin *Wrote* and *Responsible* and *Received* to create another bulleted list aligned at the left edge of the cell.

7. In the same cell, select the paragraphs that begin *Helped* and *Set up* to create the same type of bulleted list.

8. In the cell below, select the paragraphs that begin *Elected*, *Qualified*, and *Student* to create a bulleted list.

9. Press Esc to turn off the **Format Painter**. Click anywhere in the table to deselect the text, **Save** your document, and then compare your screen with Figure 2.8.

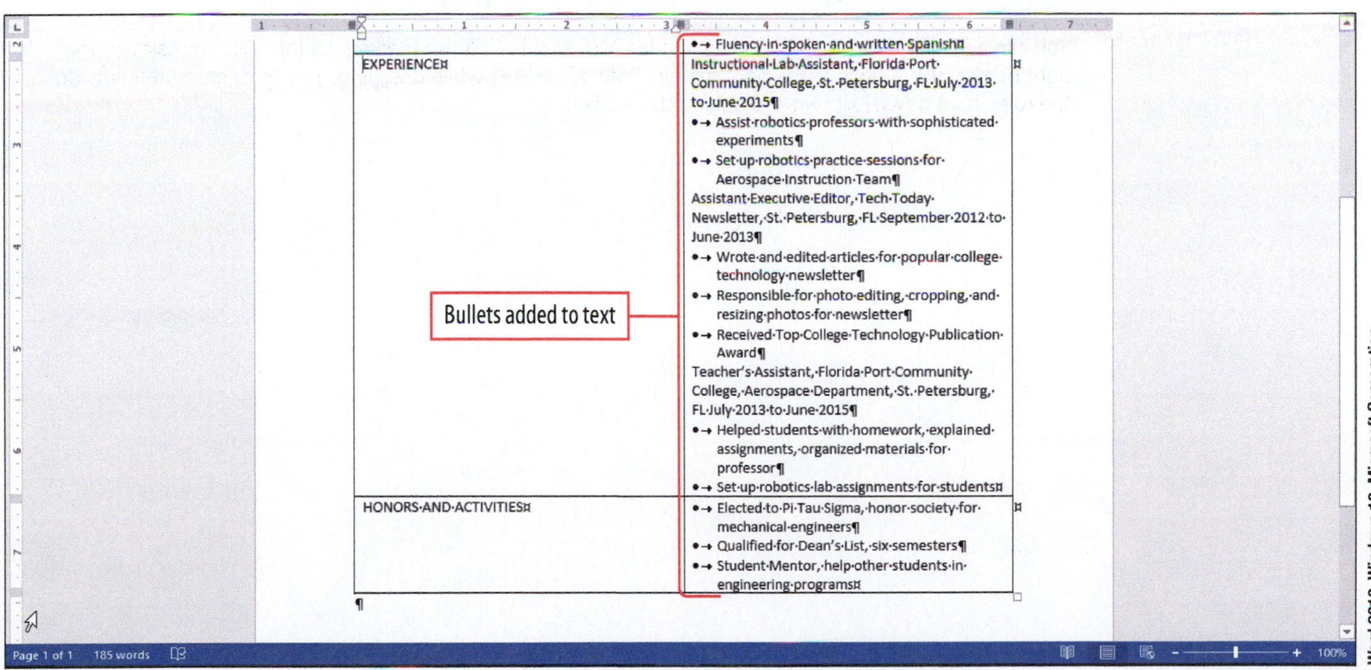

FIGURE 2.8

Objective 2 Format a Table

GO! Learn How Video W2-2

Use Word's formatting tools to make your tables attractive and easy to read. Types of formatting you can add to a table include changing the row height and the column width, removing or adding borders, increasing or decreasing the paragraph or line spacing, and enhancing the text.

3.2.4

Activity 2.05 | Changing the Width of Table Columns and Using AutoFit

When you create a table, all of the columns are of equal width. In this Activity, you will change the width of the columns.

1. Press Ctrl + Home. Click anywhere in the first column, and then on the ribbon, under **Table Tools**, click the **Layout tab**. In the **Cell Size group**, notice the **Width** box, which displays the width of the active column.
2. Look at the horizontal ruler and locate the **1.5-inch mark**. Then, in the table, in any row, point to the vertical border between the two columns to display the pointer.
3. Hold down the left mouse button and drag the column border to the left until the white arrow on the ruler is at approximately **1.5 inches on the horizontal ruler** and then release the left mouse button.
4. In the **Cell Size group**, click the **Width box down spin arrow** as necessary to set the column width to **1.4"** and notice that the right border of the table moves to the right.

   Adjusting column width by dragging a column border adjusts only the width of the column; adjusting column width with the Width box simultaneously adjusts the right border of the table.

5. In the **Cell Size group**, click **AutoFit**, and then click **AutoFit Window** to stretch the table across the page within the margins so that the right border of the table is at the right margin. **Save** and then compare your screen with Figure 2.9.

You can adjust column widths by dragging the Move Table Column markers on the ruler. To maintain the right border of the table at the right margin, hold down Shift while dragging. To display measurements on the ruler, hold down Alt while dragging the marker.

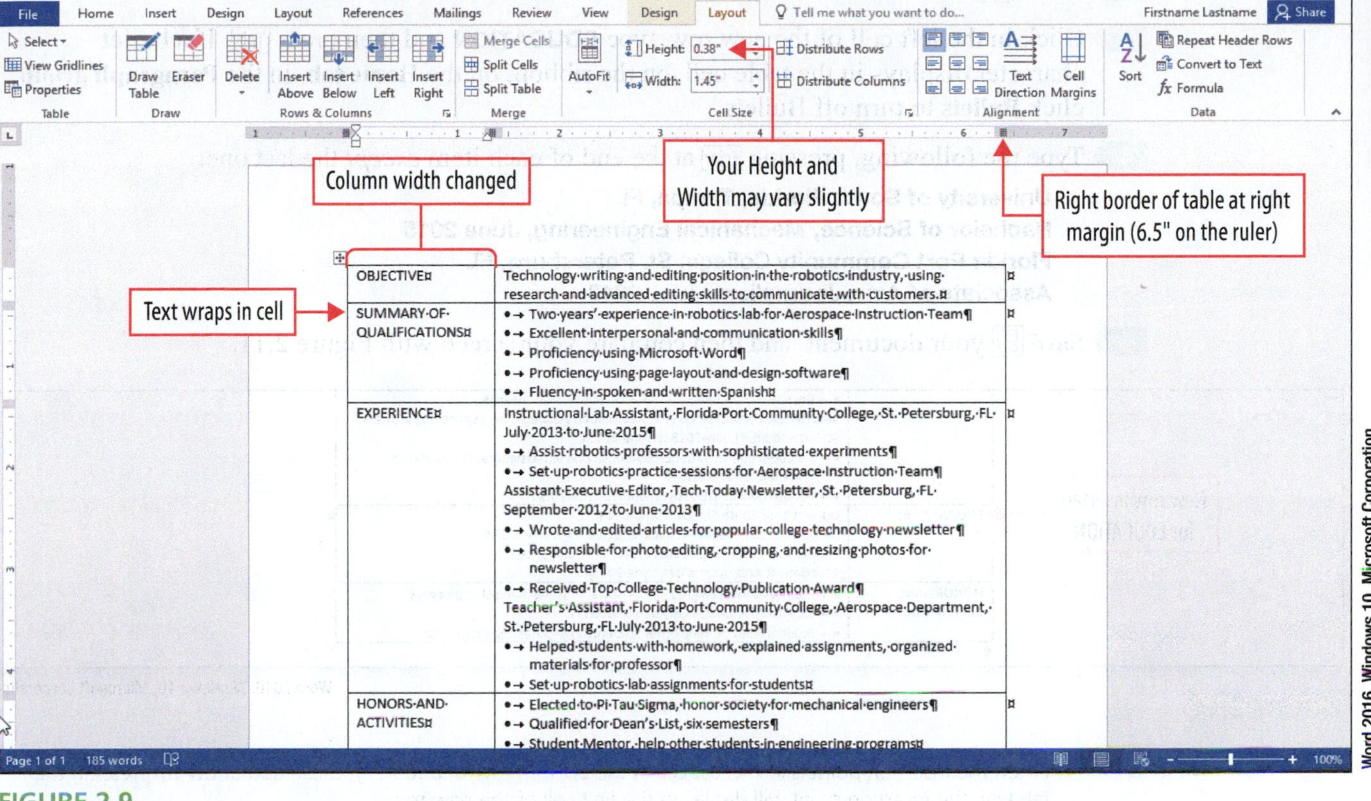

FIGURE 2.9

More Knowledge **Changing Column Widths**

You will typically get the best results if you change the column widths starting at the left side of the table, especially in tables with three or more columns. Word can also calculate the best column widths for you. To do this, select the table. Then, on the Layout tab, in the Cell Size group, click the AutoFit button and click AutoFit Contents.

Activity 2.06 | Using One-Click Row/Column Insertion to Modify Table Dimensions

One of the most common actions you will take in a table is adding another row or another column. By using ***One-click Row/Column Insertion*** you can do so in context by pointing to the left or top edge where you want the row or column to appear and then clicking the ⊕ button to add it.

1 Scroll to view the lower portion of the table. On the left border of the table, *point* to the upper left corner of the cell containing the text *HONORS AND ACTIVITIES* to display the **One-click Row/Column Insertion** button. Compare your screen with Figure 2.10.

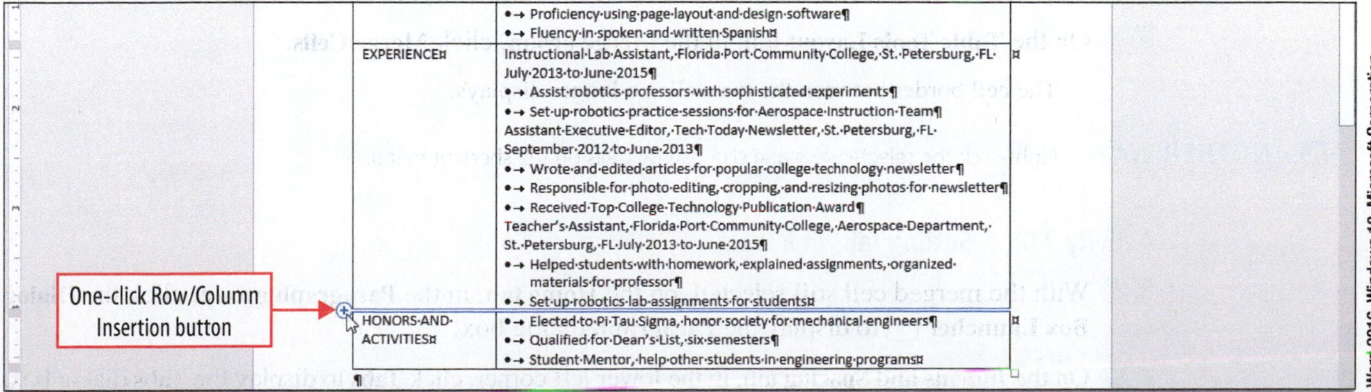

FIGURE 2.10

2 Click ⊕ one time to insert a new row above the *HONORS AND ACTIVITIES* row.

3 Click in the left cell of the new row, type **EDUCATION** and then press Tab. If a bullet character displays in the table cell, on the ribbon, on the **Home tab**, in the **Paragraph group**, click **Bullets** to turn off Bullets.

4 Type the following, pressing Enter at the end of each item *except* the last one:

University of South Florida, Tampa, FL
Bachelor of Science, Mechanical Engineering, June 2015
Florida Port Community College, St. Petersburg, FL
Associate of Arts, Journalism, June 2013

5 **Save** your document, and then compare your screen with Figure 2.11.

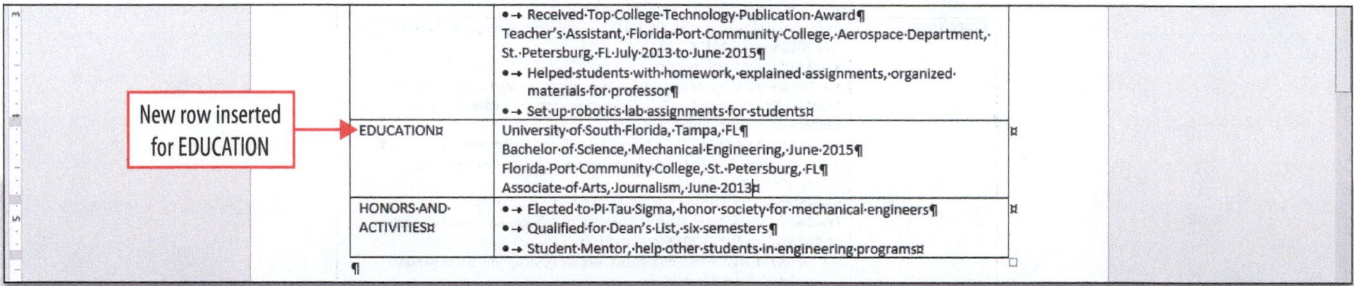

Word 2016, Windows 10, Microsoft Corporation

FIGURE 2.11

ANOTHER WAY When the insertion point is in the last cell in the bottom row of a table, you can add a row by pressing the Tab key; the insertion point will display in the first cell of the new row.

3.2.3

Activity 2.07 | Merging Table Cells

The title of a table typically spans all of the columns. In this Activity, you will merge cells so that you can position the personal information across both columns.

1 Press Ctrl + Home to move to the top of your document, and then click anywhere in the top row of the table.

2 On the **Table Tools Layout tab**, in the **Rows & Columns group**, click **Insert Above**.

A new row displays above the row that contained the insertion point, and the new row is selected. This is another method to insert rows and columns in a table; use this method to insert a new row at the top of a table.

ANOTHER WAY Right-click in the top row, point to Insert, and then click Insert Rows Above.

3 Be sure the two cells in the top row are selected; if necessary, drag across both cells to select them.

4 On the **Table Tools Layout tab**, in the **Merge group**, click **Merge Cells**.

The cell border between the two cells no longer displays.

ANOTHER WAY Right-click the selected row and click Merge Cells on the shortcut menu.

Activity 2.08 | Setting Tabs in a Table

1 With the merged cell still selected, on the **Home tab**, in the **Paragraph group**, click the **Dialog Box Launcher** to display the **Paragraph** dialog box.

2 On the **Indents and Spacing tab**, in the lower left corner, click **Tabs** to display the **Tabs** dialog box.

3 Under **Tab stop position**, type **6.5** and then under **Alignment**, click the **Right** option button. Click **Set**, and then click **OK** to close the dialog box.

4 Type **Josh Hayes** Hold down Ctrl and then press Tab. Notice that the insertion point moves to the right-aligned tab stop at 6.5".

In a Word table, you must use Ctrl + Tab to move to a tab stop, because pressing Tab is reserved for moving the insertion point from cell to cell.

5 Type **(727) 555-0313** and then press Enter.

6 Type **1541 Dearborn Lane, St. Petersburg, FL 33713** Hold down Ctrl and then press Tab.

7 Type **jhayes@alcona.net** **Save** your document, and then compare your screen with Figure 2.12.

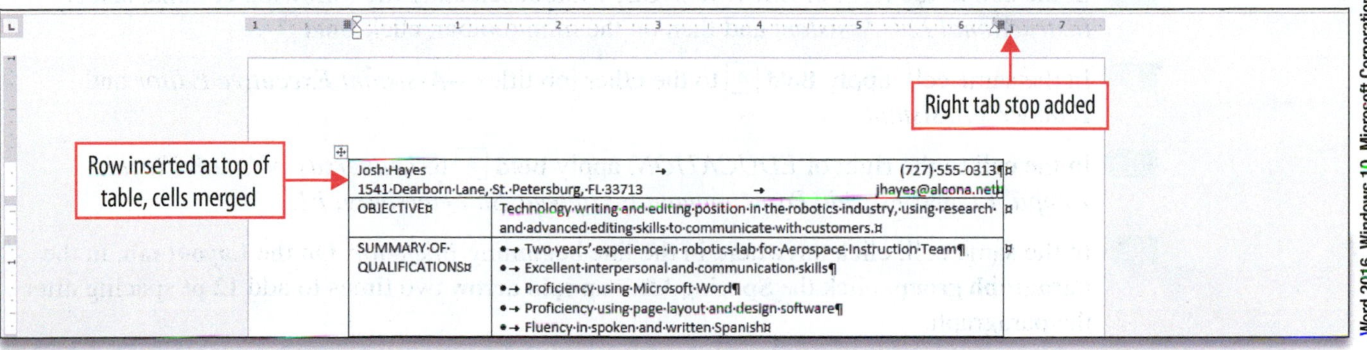

FIGURE 2.12

Activity 2.09 | Using Spacing After in a Table

1 In the first row of the table, select the name *Josh Hayes*, and then on the mini toolbar, apply **Bold** and change the **Font Size** to **16**.

2 Under *Josh Hayes*, click anywhere in the second line of text, which contains the address and email address.

3 On the **Layout tab**, in the **Paragraph group**, click the **Spacing After up spin arrow** three times to add **18 pt** spacing between the first row of the table and the second row. Compare your screen with Figure 2.13.

This action separates the personal information from the body of the resume and adds focus to the name.

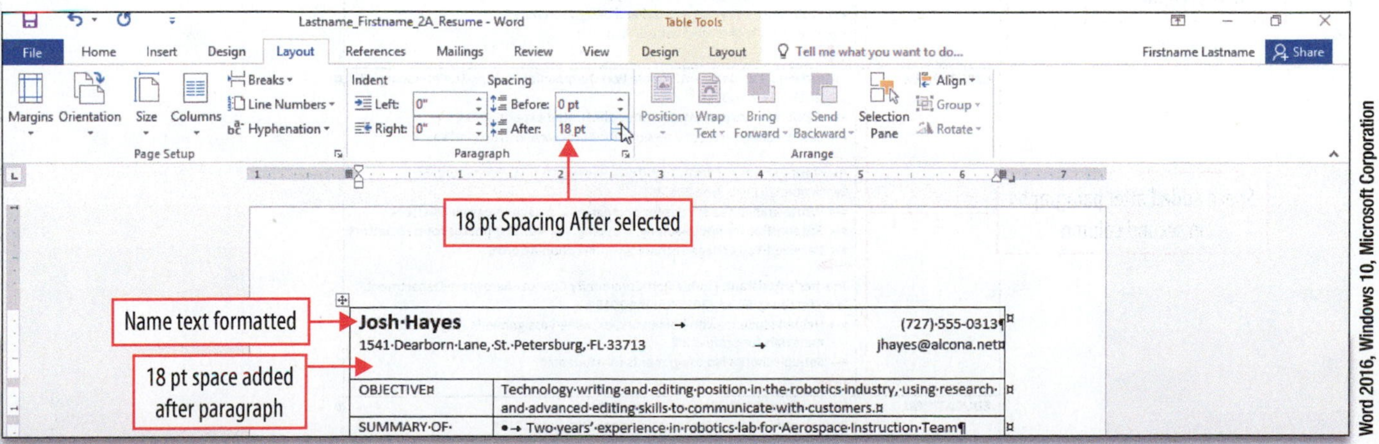

FIGURE 2.13

4 Using the technique you just practiced, in the second column, click in the last paragraph of *every cell* and add **18 pt Spacing After** including the last row; a border will be added to the bottom of the table, and spacing will be needed between the last row and the border.

5 In the second row, point to the word *OBJECTIVE*, hold down the left mouse button, and then drag downward in the first column only to select all the headings in uppercase letters. On the mini toolbar, click **Bold** [B].

NOTE Selecting Only One Column

When you drag downward to select the first column, a fast mouse might also begin to select the second column when you reach the bottom. If this happens, drag upward slightly to deselect the second column and select only the first column.

6 In the cell to the right of *EXPERIENCE*, without selecting the following comma, select *Instructional Lab Assistant* and then on the mini toolbar, click **Bold** [B].

7 In the same cell, apply **Bold** [B] to the other job titles—*Assistant Executive Editor* and *Teacher's Assistant*.

8 In the cell to the right of *EDUCATION*, apply **Bold** [B] to *University of South Florida, Tampa, FL* and *Florida Port Community College, St. Petersburg, FL*.

9 In the same cell, click anywhere in the line beginning *Bachelor*. On the **Layout tab**, in the **Paragraph group**, click the **Spacing After up spin arrow** two times to add **12 pt** spacing after the paragraph.

10 In the cell to the right of *EXPERIENCE*, under *Instructional Lab Assistant*, click anywhere in the second bulleted item, and then add **12 pt Spacing After** the item.

11 In the same cell, repeat this process for the last bulleted item under *Assistant Executive Editor*.

12 Scroll to view the top of your document, **Save** [save icon] your document, and then compare your screen with Figure 2.14.

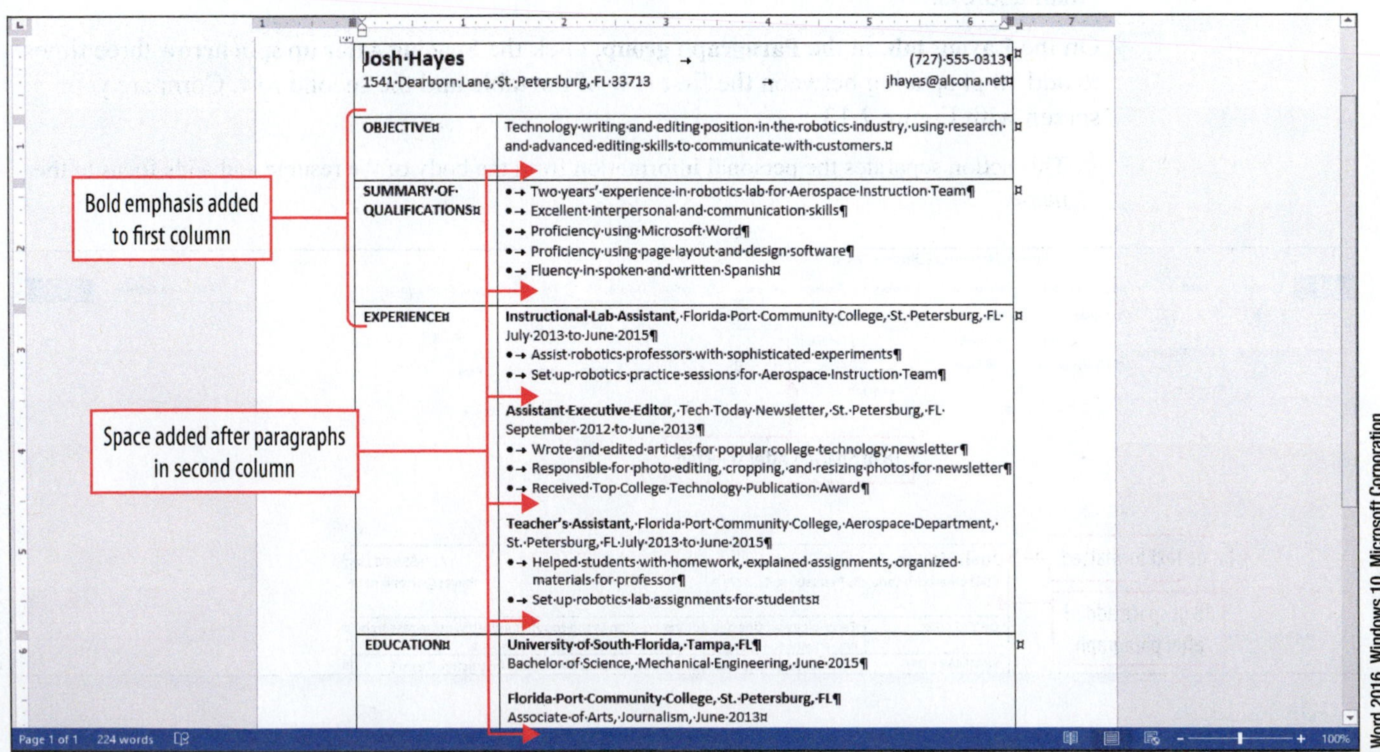

FIGURE 2.14

Activity 2.10 | Modifying Table Borders and Using Spacing Before

When you create a table, all of the cells have black 1/2-point, single-line, solid line borders that print unless you remove them. Most resumes do not display any cell borders. A border at the top and bottom of the resume, however, is attractive and adds a professional look to the document.

1 Scroll as necessary to view the top margin area above the table, and then point slightly outside of the upper left corner of the table to display the **table move handle** ⊞.

2 Click the ⊞ pointer one time to select the entire table, and notice that the row markers at the end of each row are also selected.

Shaded row markers indicate that the entire row is selected. Use this technique to select the entire table.

3 On the ribbon, under **Table Tools**, click the **Design tab**. In the **Borders group**, click the **Borders button arrow**, and then click **No Border**.

The black borders no longer display.

4 Press Ctrl + P, which is the keyboard shortcut to view the Print Preview, and notice that no borders display in the preview. Then, press **Back** to return to your document.

5 With the table still selected, on the **Design tab**, in the **Borders group**, click the **Borders button arrow**, and then at the bottom of the **Borders** gallery, click **Borders and Shading**.

6 In the **Borders and Shading** dialog box, on the **Borders tab**, under **Setting**, click **Custom**. Under **Style**, scroll down about one-third of the way, and then click the style with a **thick upper line and a thin lower line**.

7 In the **Preview** box at the right, point to the *top* border of the small preview and click one time.

ANOTHER WAY Click the top border button, which is one of the buttons that surround the Preview.

8 Under **Style**, scroll down if necessary, click the opposite style—with the **thin upper line and the thick lower line**, and then in the **Preview** box, click the *bottom* border of the preview. Compare your screen with Figure 2.15.

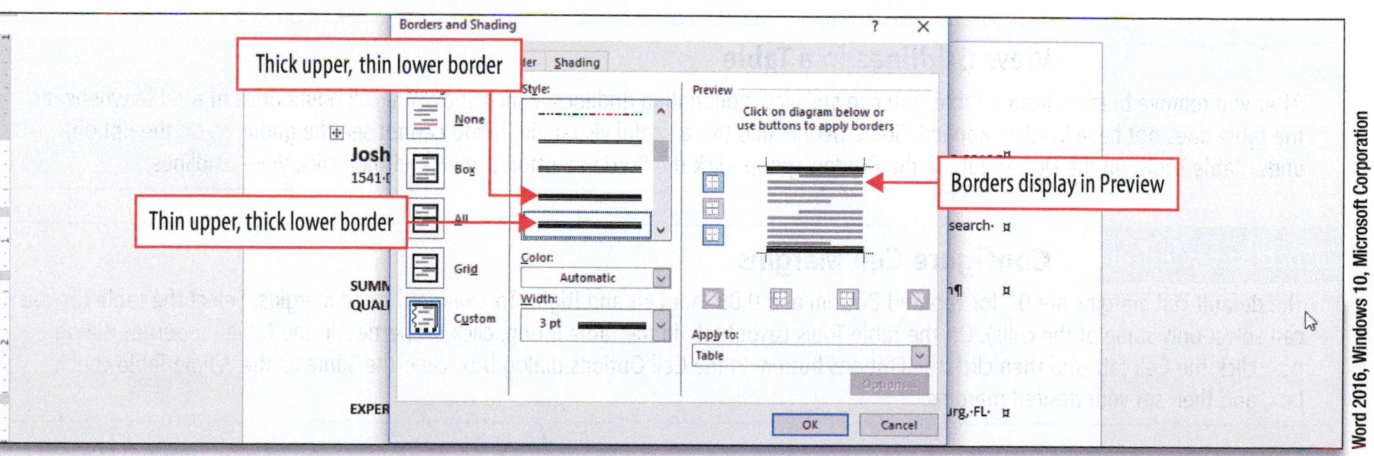

FIGURE 2.15

9 Click **OK**, click anywhere to cancel the selection, and then notice that there is only a small amount of space between the upper border and the first line of text.

10 Click anywhere in the text *Josh Hayes*, and then on the **Layout tab**, in the **Paragraph group**, click the **Spacing Before up spin arrow** as necessary to add **18 pt** spacing before the first paragraph.

11 Press Ctrl + P to display **Print Preview**. Compare your screen with Figure 2.16.

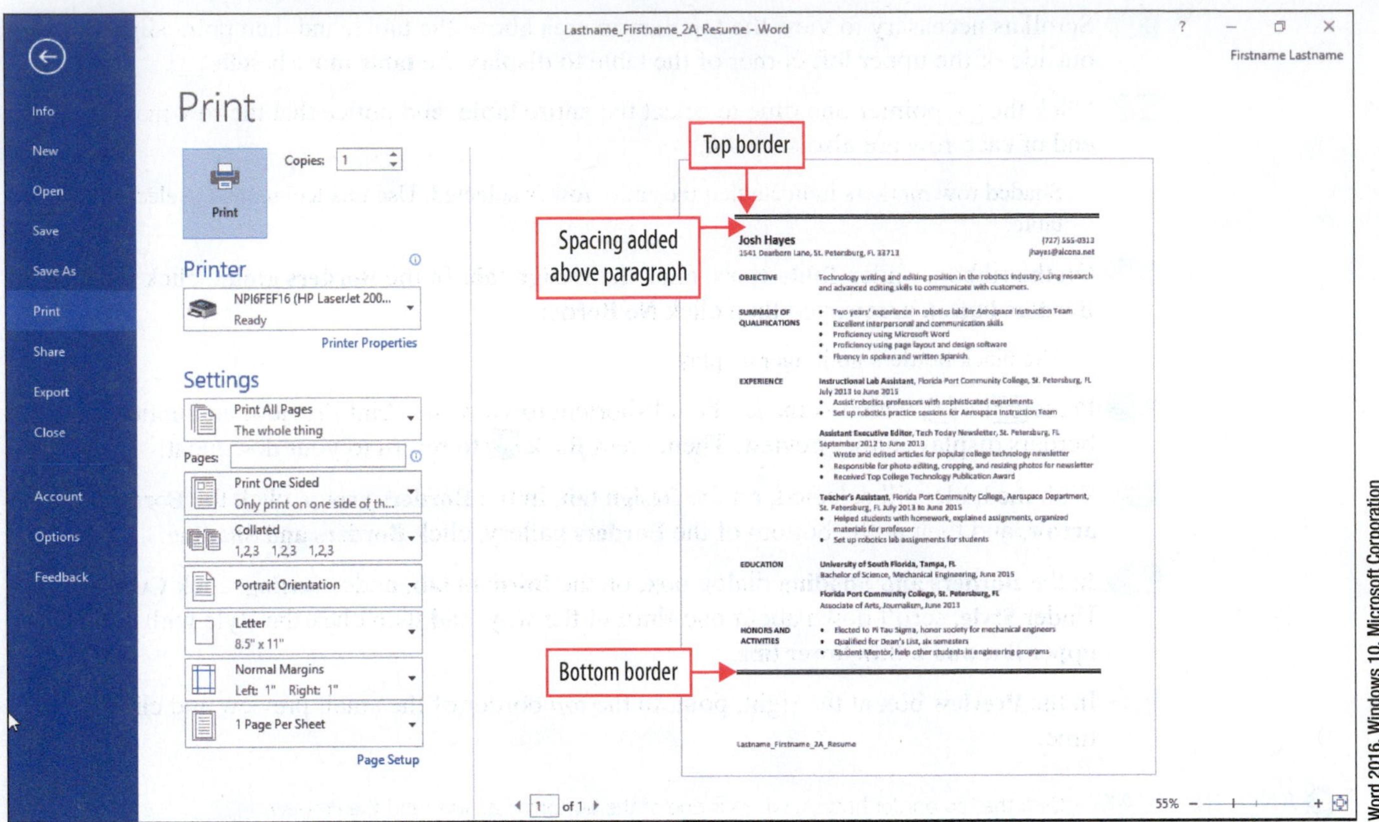

Word 2016, Windows 10, Microsoft Corporation

FIGURE 2.16

12 Press **Back** to return to your document, and then on the Quick Access Toolbar, click **Save**.

More Knowledge **View Gridlines in a Table**

After you remove borders from a table, you can still view nonprinting gridlines, which show the cell boundaries of a table whenever the table does not have borders applied. Some people find this a useful visual aid. If you cannot see the gridlines, on the ribbon, under Table Tools, on the Design tab, in the Borders group, click the Borders button arrow, and then click View Gridlines.

More Knowledge **Configure Cell Margins**

The default cell margins are 0" for Top and Bottom and 0.08" for Left and Right. To change the cell margins: Select the table (or you can select only some of the cells). On the Table Tools Layout tab, in the Table group, click Properties. In the Table Properties dialog box, click the Cell tab, and then click the Options button. In the Cell Options dialog box, clear the Same as the Whole Table check box, and then set your desired margins.

More Knowledge **Sorting Data in a Table**

You can sort information in a table. To do so, click anywhere in the table, and then on the Table Tools Layout tab, click Sort. In the Sort dialog box, if the first row contains header information, select the Header Row option button in the lower left corner of the dialog box. In the Sort By list, select the column on which you want to sort, select the Type if necessary, select Ascending or Descending, and then click OK.

Objective 3 Present a Word Document Online

GO! Learn How Video W2-3

Office Presentation Service enables you to present your Word document to others who can watch in a web browser. No preliminary setup is necessary; Word creates a link to your document that you can share with others via email or instant message. Anyone to whom you send the link can see your document while you are presenting online.

Individuals watching your presentation can navigate within the document independently of you or others in the presentation, so they can use a mouse, keyboard, or touch input to move around in the document while you are presenting it. If an individual is viewing a different portion of the document than the presenter, an alert displays on his or her screen. To return to the portion of the document that the presenter is showing, a Follow Presenter button displays.

While you are presenting, you can make minor edits to the document. If you want to share a copy of the document to the presentation attendees, you can select *Enable remote viewers to download the document* when you start the presentation. You can also share any meeting notes that you or others created in OneNote.

Activity 2.11 | Presenting a Word Document Online

If you are creating your own resume, it will be valuable to get feedback from your friends, instructors, or Career Center advisors before you submit your resume for a job application. In this Activity, you will present the resume document online for others to look at.

> **NOTE** You may be asked to sign in with your Microsoft account.
>
> You may be asked to sign in with your Microsoft account, even if you are already signed in, to present your document online.

1. With your resume document displayed, click **Save**.
2. Click the **File tab**, on the left click **Share**, and then under **Share**, click **Present Online**.
3. On the right, click **Present Online**. Wait a moment for the service to connect, and then compare your screen with Figure 2.17.

   There are several methods to send your meeting invitation to others. You can click Copy Link to copy and paste the hyperlink; for example, you could copy the link into a ***Skype*** window. Skype is a Microsoft product with which you can make voice calls, make video calls, transfer files, or send messages—including instant messages and text messages—over the Internet.

   You can also select Send in Email, which will open your Outlook email window if you use Outlook as your mail client.

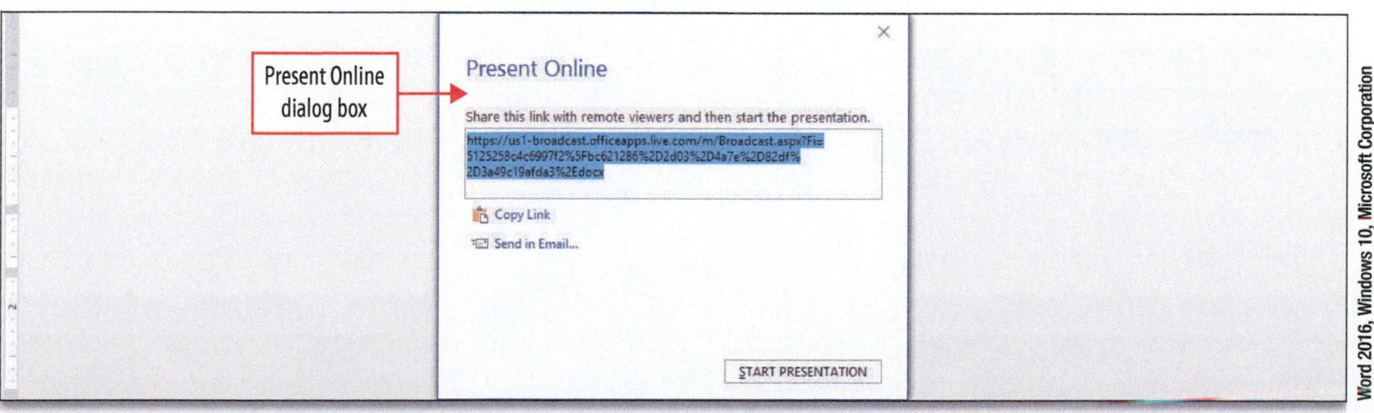

FIGURE 2.17

4. If you want to do so, identify a classmate or friend who is at a computer and available to view your presentation, select one of the methods to share, click **START PRESENTATION**, and when you are finished, on the ribbon, click **End Online Presentation**. If you are not ready to share your document right now, **Close** [X] the **Present Online** dialog box.

   If you present online, you will need to initiate voice communication using Skype or by simply phoning the other person.

5. Be sure you have closed the Present Online dialog box. On the ribbon, on the **Present Online tab**, click **End Online Presentation**, and then in the message, click **End Online Presentation**.

6. Press Ctrl + Home to move to the top of your document. In the lower right corner, click **Zoom In** [+] as necessary to set the Zoom level to **100%**. If necessary, on the **Home tab**, redisplay the formatting marks by clicking **Show/Hide**.

7. Click the **File tab**, and then in the lower right portion of the screen, click **Show All Properties**. In the **Tags** box, type **resume, Word table** and in the **Subject** box, type your course name and section number. In the **Author** box, be sure your name is indicated and edit if necessary.

8. On the left, click **Print** to display **Print Preview**. If necessary, return to the document and make any necessary changes.

9. **Save** your document. In the upper right corner of the Word window, click **Close** [X]. If directed by your instructor to do so, submit your paper printout, your electronic image of your document that looks like a printed document, or your original Word file.

END | You have completed Project 2A

GO! With Google

Objective Edit a Resume in Google Docs

ALERT! **Working with Web-Based Applications and Services**

Computer programs and services on the web receive continuous updates and improvements, so the steps to complete this web-based activity may differ from the ones shown. You can often look at the screens and the information presented to determine how to complete the activity.

If you do not already have a Google account, you will need to create one before you begin this activity. Go to http://google.com and, in the upper right corner, click Sign In. On the Sign In screen, click Create Account. On the Create your Google Account page, complete the form, read and agree to the Terms of Service and Privacy Policy, and then click Next step. On the Welcome screen, click Get Started.

Activity | Editing a Resume in Google Docs

In this Activity, you will use Google Docs to open and edit a Word table containing a resume similar to the resume you created in Project 2A.

1 From the desktop, open your browser, navigate to **http://google.com**, and then click the **Google Apps** menu ⋮⋮⋮. Click **Drive**, and then if necessary, sign in to your Google account.

2 Open your **GO! Web Projects** folder—or click New to create and then open this folder if necessary.

3 In the left pane, click **NEW**, and then click **File upload**. In the **Open** dialog box, navigate to your Student Data Files for this chapter, and then in the **File List**, double-click to open **w02_2A_Web**.

4 When the upload is complete, in the **Google Drive file list**, point to the file name, right-click, point to **Open with**, and then click **Google Docs** to open it in Google Docs.

5 Click anywhere in the word *OBJECTIVE*, right-click, and then click **Table properties**. Under **Table border**, click the **Table border width arrow**, and then click **0.5 pt**. Click **OK** to display the table and cell borders in the default black color.

6 On the menu bar, click **Table**, and then click **Insert row above**. In the first cell of the new row, type **Daniela Frank** Select the text you just typed, and then on the toolbar, click the **Font size arrow**, and then click **18**.

7 Press Tab to move to the second cell of the new row, and then type **1343 Siena Lane, Deerfield, WI 53531** Hold down Shift and press Enter. Type **(608) 555-0588** Hold down Shift and press Enter. Type **dfrank@alcona.net** Select all the text in the second cell that you just typed, and then on the toolbar, click **Right align**. In Google Docs, the phone number and possibly the email address may remain as hyperlinks. Compare your screen with Figure A.

(GO! With Google continues on the next page)

GO! With Google

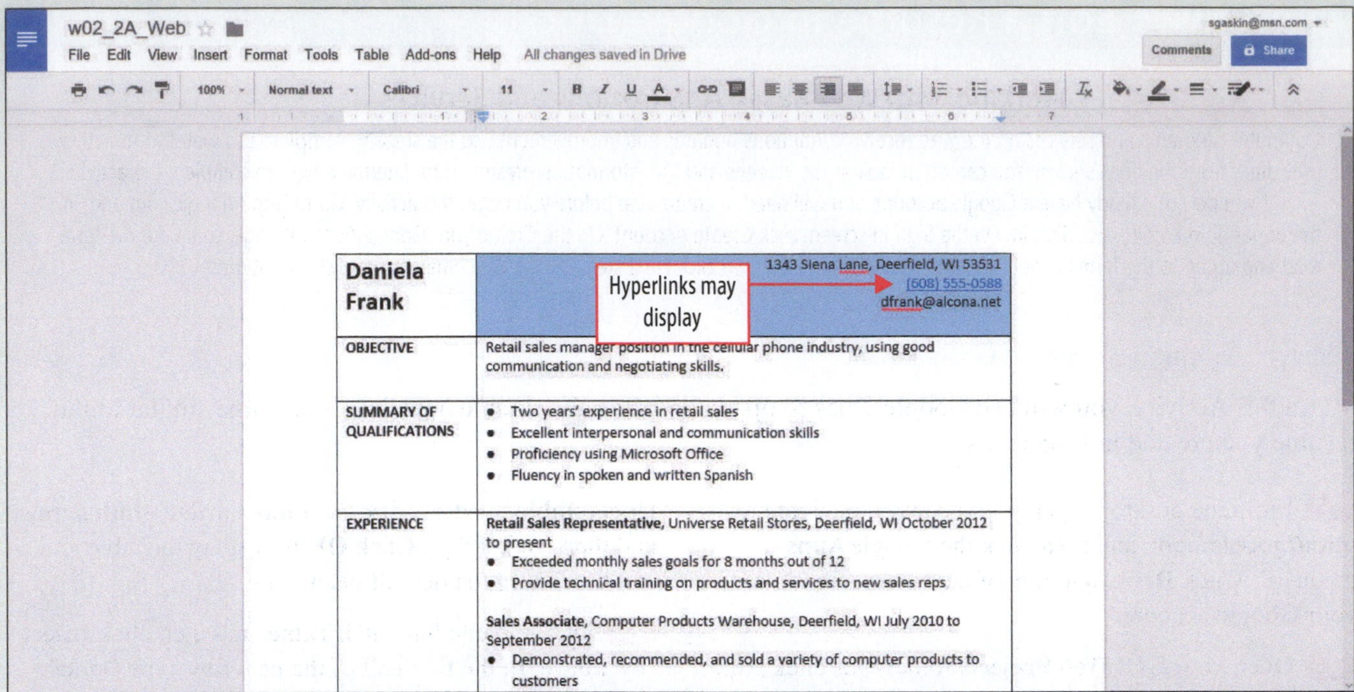

FIGURE A

8 Drag to select the two cells in the top row, right-click over the selection, and then click **Table properties**. Under **Cell background color**, click the arrow, and then in the top row, click the seventh color—**light gray 1**. Click **OK**.

9 Scroll down and click anywhere in the *EXPERIENCE* cell. Right-click, and then click **Insert row below**. In the first cell of the new row, type **EDUCATION**

10 Press Tab to move to the second cell in the new row, and then type **Madison Area Technical College, Madison, WI** Hold down Shift and press Enter.

11 On the toolbar, click **Bold** to turn off bold formatting, and then type **Associate of Arts in Information Systems, June 2014** and press Enter.

12 Right-click, click **Table properties**, and then change the **Table border width** to **0 pt** to remove the borders. Click **OK**.

13 Scroll as necessary to view the top of your document, and then compare your screen with Figure B.

(GO! With Google continues on the next page)

GO! With Google

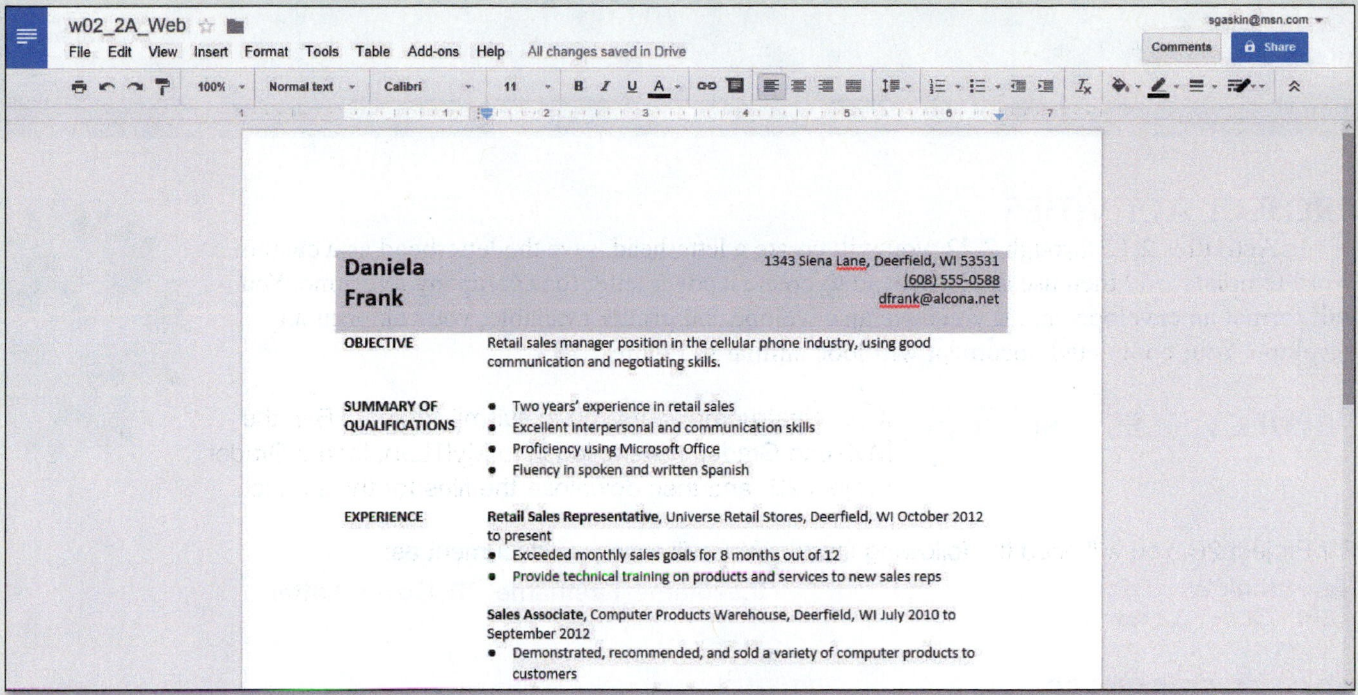

FIGURE B

14 Submit the file as directed by your instructor. In the upper right, click your user name, and then click **Sign out**. **Close** your browser window. Your file is automatically saved in your Google Drive.

PROJECT

2B Cover Letter and Envelope

MyITLab

Project 2B Training
Project 2B Grader

PROJECT ACTIVITIES

In Activities 2.12 through 2.22, you will create a letterhead, save the letterhead as a custom Word template, and then use the letterhead to create a cover letter to accompany a resume. You will format an envelope, and if you have an envelope and printer available, you can print an envelope. Your completed document will look similar to Figure 2.18.

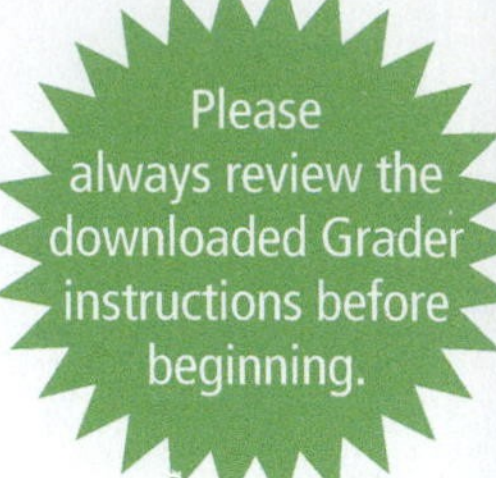
Please
always review the
downloaded Grader
instructions before
beginning.

PROJECT FILES

MyITLab
grader

If your instructor wants you to submit Project 2B in the MyITLab Grader system, log in to MyITLab, locate Grader Project 2B, and then download the files for this project.

For Project 2B, you will need the following files:
New blank Word document
w02B_Cover_Letter_Text

You will save your document as:
Lastname_Firstname_2B_Cover_Letter

Build From Scratch

GO! Walk Thru Project 2B

PROJECT RESULTS

Jennifer Garcia

1776 Bay Cliff Drive, Tampa, FL 33602
(727) 555-0347 jgarcia@alcona.net

October 8, 2015

Ms. Mary Walker-Huelsman, Director
Florida Port Community College Career Center
2745 Oakland Avenue
St. Petersburg, FL 33713

Dear Ms. Walker-Huelsman:

I am seeking a position in which I can use my computer and communication skills. My education and experience, outlined on the enclosed resume, includes a Business Software Applications Specialist certificate from Florida Port Community College.

With a permanent position as my ultimate goal, I hope to use the Florida Port Community College Career Center to secure a temporary job. I can be available for a flexible number of hours or days and am willing to work in a variety of businesses or organizations.

As my resume illustrates, I have excellent computer skills. I am an honor student at Florida Port Community College and have outstanding references. In addition, I have part-time work experience as a software tester, where I perform the following computer activities:

Microsoft Access	Test database queries
Microsoft Excel	Enter software test data
Microsoft Word	Create and mail form letters

You can contact me by email at jgarcia@alcona.net or by telephone at (727) 555-0347. I am available for an interview at your convenience.

Sincerely,

Jennifer Garcia

Enclosure

Lastname_Firstname_2B_Cover_Letter

Word 2016, Windows 10, Microsoft Corporation

FIGURE 2.18 Project 2B—Cover Letter and Envelope

Objective 4 Create a Custom Word Template

GO! Learn How Video W2-4

A ***template*** is a file you use as a starting point for a *new* document. A template has a predefined document structure and defined settings, such as font, margins, and available styles. On Word's opening screen, you can select from among many different templates—or you can create your own custom template.

When you open a template as the starting point for a new document, the template file opens a copy of itself, unnamed, and then you use the structure—and possibly some content, such as headings—as the starting point for a new document.

All documents are based on a template. When you create a new blank document, it is based on Word's ***Normal template***, which serves as the starting point for all blank Word documents.

1.3.3

Activity 2.12 | Changing the Document Style Set for Paragraph Spacing and Applying a Bottom Border to a Paragraph

ALERT! **To submit as an autograded project, log into MyITLab, download the files for this project and then begin with those files instead of a new blank document.**

A ***letterhead*** is the personal or company information that displays at the top of a letter, and which commonly includes a name, address, and contact information. The term also refers to a piece of paper imprinted with such information at the top. In this Activity, you will create a custom template for a personal letterhead.

1. Start Word and display a blank document; be sure that formatting marks and rulers display.

2. On the **Design tab**, in the **Document Formatting group**, click **Paragraph Spacing**.

   The Paragraph Spacing command offers various options for setting the line and paragraph spacing of your entire document. A gallery of predefined values displays; or you can create your own custom paragraph spacing.

3. On the list *point* to **Default** and notice the settings in the ScreenTip.

   Recall that the default spacing for a new Word document is 0 points of blank space before a paragraph, 8 points of blank space following a paragraph, and line spacing of 1.08.

4. Point to **No Paragraph Space** and notice the settings in the ScreenTip.

   The ***No Paragraph Space*** style inserts *no* extra space before or after a paragraph and uses line spacing of 1. This is the same format used for the line spacing commonly referred to as ***single spacing***. A ***style set*** is a collection of character and paragraph formatting that is stored and named.

5. Click **No Paragraph Space**.

   By using the No Paragraph Space style, you will be able to follow the prescribed format of a letter, which Business Communications texts commonly describe in terms of single spacing.

ANOTHER WAY On Word's opening screen, select the Single-spaced (blank) document; or, in a blank document, select the entire document, and then on the Home tab, in the Styles group, click No Spacing. Also, so long as you leave an appropriate amount of space between the elements of the letter, you can use Word's default spacing. Finally, you could use one of Word's predesigned templates for a cover letter and observe all spacing requirements for a letter.

6. Type **Jennifer Garcia** and then press Enter.

7. Type **1776 Bay Cliff Drive, Tampa, FL 33602** and then press Enter.

8 Type **(727) 555-0347 jgarcia@alcona.net** and then press Enter. If the web address changes to blue text, right-click the web address, and then click **Remove Hyperlink**.

9 Select the first paragraph—*Jennifer Garcia*—and then on the mini toolbar, apply **Bold** B and change the **Font Size** to **16**.

10 Select the second and third paragraphs. On the mini toolbar, apply **Bold** B and change the **Font Size** to **12**.

11 With the two paragraphs still selected, on the **Home tab**, in the **Paragraph group**, click **Align Right**.

ANOTHER WAY Press Ctrl + R to align text to the right.

12 Click anywhere in the first paragraph—*Jennifer Garcia*. In the **Paragraph group**, click the **Borders button arrow**, and then at the bottom, click **Borders and Shading**.

13 In the **Borders and Shading** dialog box, on the **Borders tab**, under **Style**, be sure the first style—a single solid line—is selected.

14 Click the **Width arrow**, and then click **3 pt**. To the right, under **Preview**, click the bottom border of the diagram. Under **Apply to**, be sure *Paragraph* displays. Compare your screen with Figure 2.19.

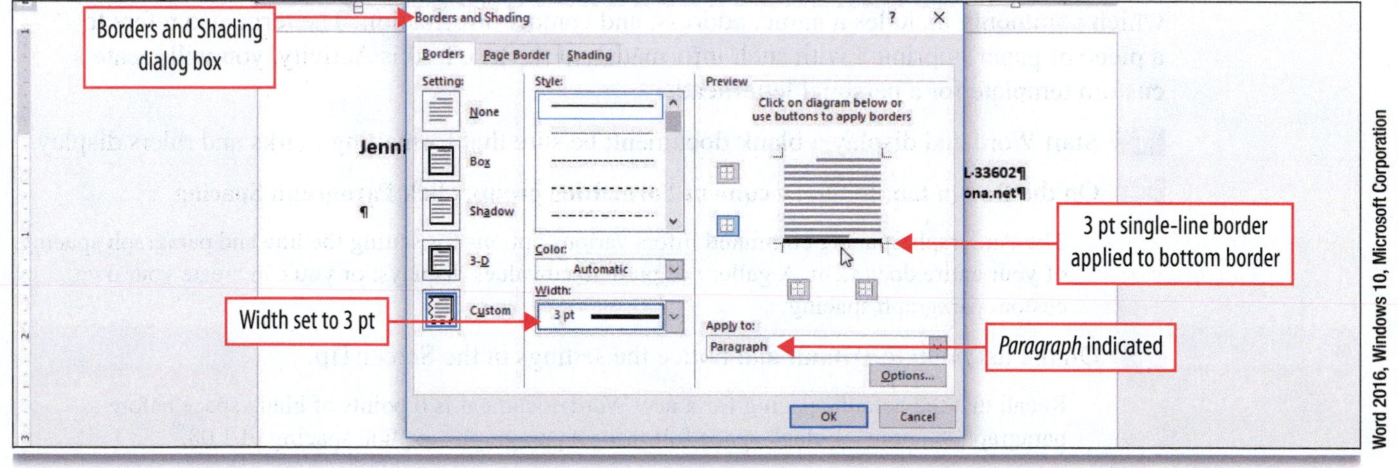

FIGURE 2.19

ANOTHER WAY Alternatively, under Preview, click the bottom border button.

15 Click **OK** to display a 3 pt line below *Jennifer Garcia*, which extends from the left margin to the right margin.

The border is a paragraph command and uses the same margins of the paragraph to which it is applied.

1.1.2

Activity 2.13 | Saving a Document as a Custom Word Template

After you create a document format that you like and will use again, for example, a letterhead for personal letters during a job search, you can save it as a template and then use it as the starting point for any letter.

1 Display the **Save As** dialog box. In the lower portion of the dialog box, in the **Save as type** box, at the right edge, click the **arrow**, and then click **Word Template**.

2 At the top of the **Save As** dialog box, notice the path, and then compare your screen with Figure 2.20.

By default, Word stores template files on your hard drive in your user folder, in a folder named Custom Office Templates. By doing so, the template is available to you from the Word opening screen.

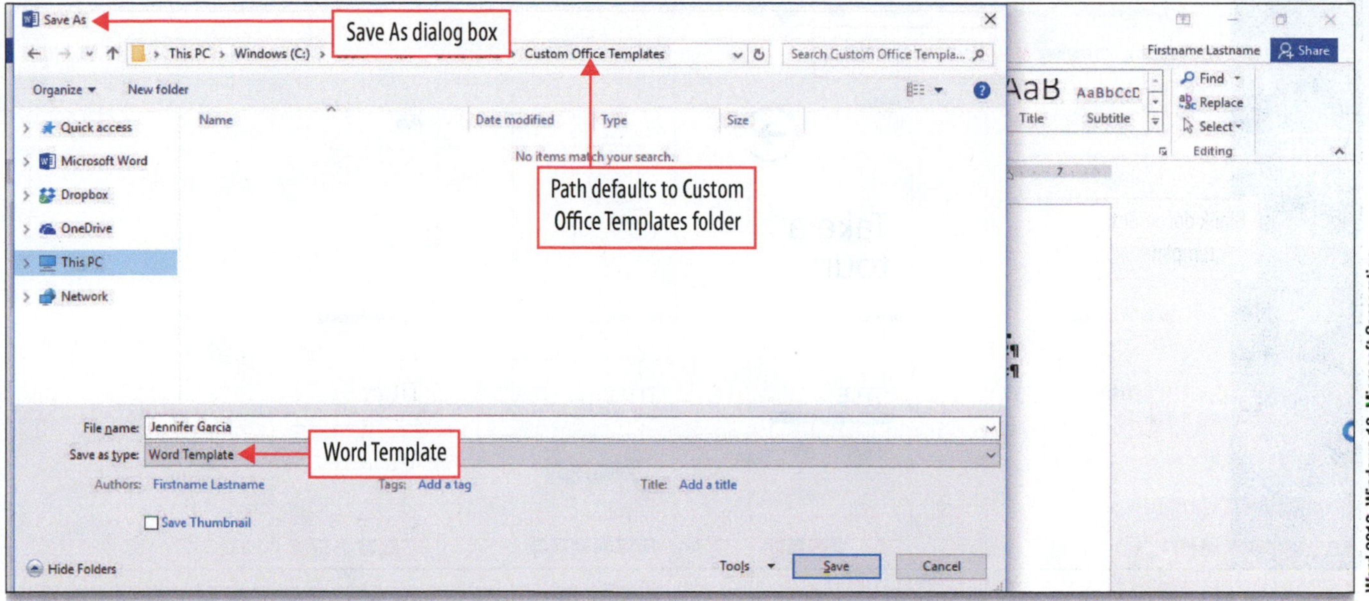

FIGURE 2.20

Word 2016, Windows 10, Microsoft Corporation

3 Click in the **File name** box, using your own name, type **Lastname_Firstname_2B_Letterhead_Template** and then click **Save**.

> **ALERT!** **Are you unable to save in the Custom Word Templates folder?**
>
> Some college computer labs block you from saving on the hard drive. If you are unable to save your template in the Custom Word Templates folder, navigate to your Word Chapter 2 folder in your storage location and save there. If you want to open a template that you stored in a location other than Word's default path, you must open the template directly from File Explorer—not from within Word—for it to open a new unnamed document based on the template.

4 Click the **File tab** to display **Backstage** view, and then click **Close** to close the file but leave Word open.

Activity 2.14 | Creating a Cover Letter from a Custom Word Template

A ***cover letter*** is a document that you send with your resume to provide additional information about your skills and experience. An effective cover letter includes specific information about why you are qualified for the job for which you are applying. Use the cover letter to explain your interest in the position and the organization.

> **ALERT!** **Were you unable to save in the Custom Word Templates folder?**
>
> If you saved your template file at your storage location because you were blocked from saving in the default folder on the hard drive, open your saved document, press F12 to display the Save As dialog box, and then in your storage location, save the document—using your own name—as Lastname_Firstname_2B_Cover_Letter. Then move to Activity 2.15.

1 With Word open but no documents displayed, click the **File tab** to display **Backstage** view, and then click **New** to display the new document options. Compare your screen with Figure 2.21.

Here you can create a new document from a blank document or from one of Word's many built-in or online templates.

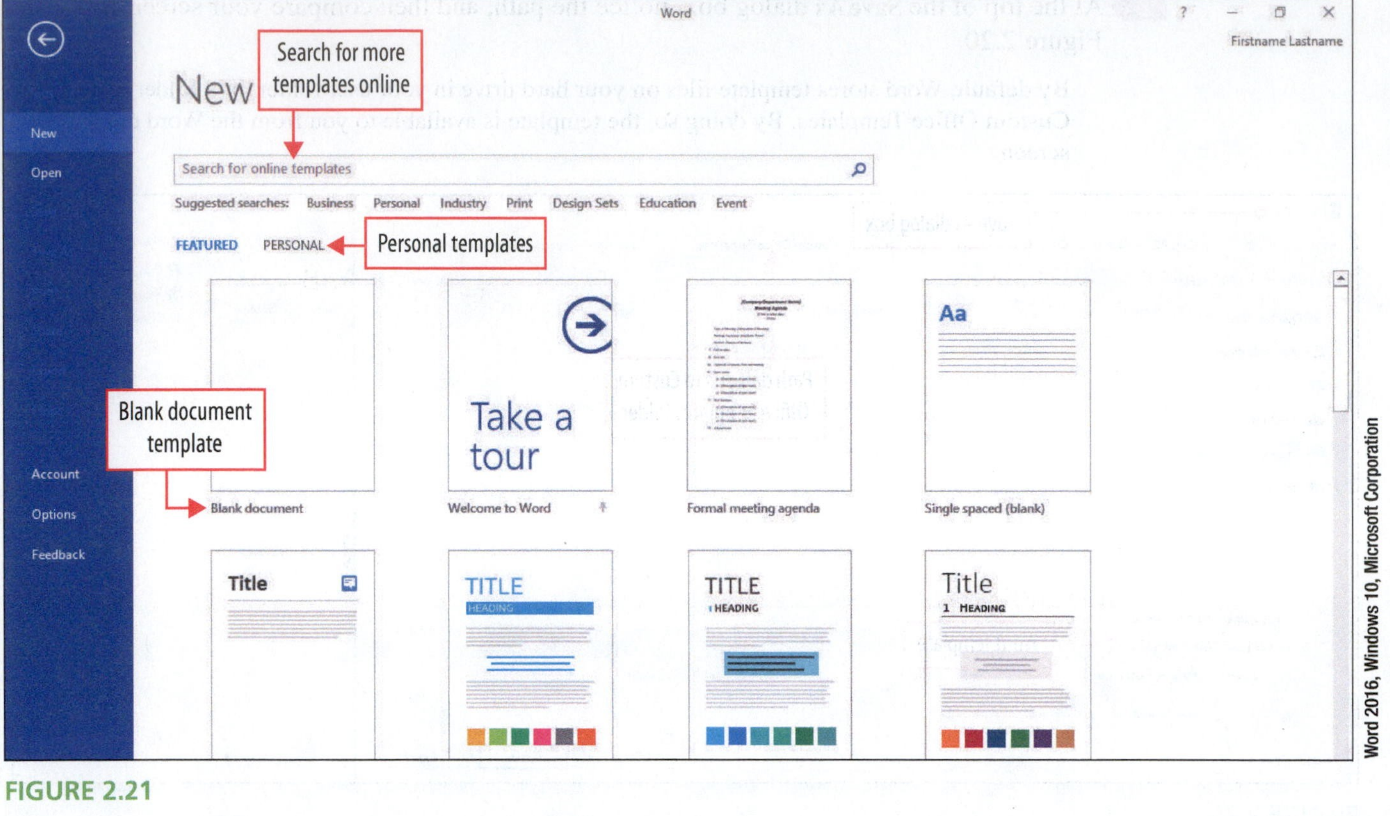

FIGURE 2.21

2 Under **Suggested searches**, click **Personal**, *point* to the name of your letterhead template, and then compare your screen with Figure 2.22.

Custom templates that you create and that are stored in the Custom Word Templates folder on your hard drive are accessible to you here whenever you want to create a new document from your stored template.

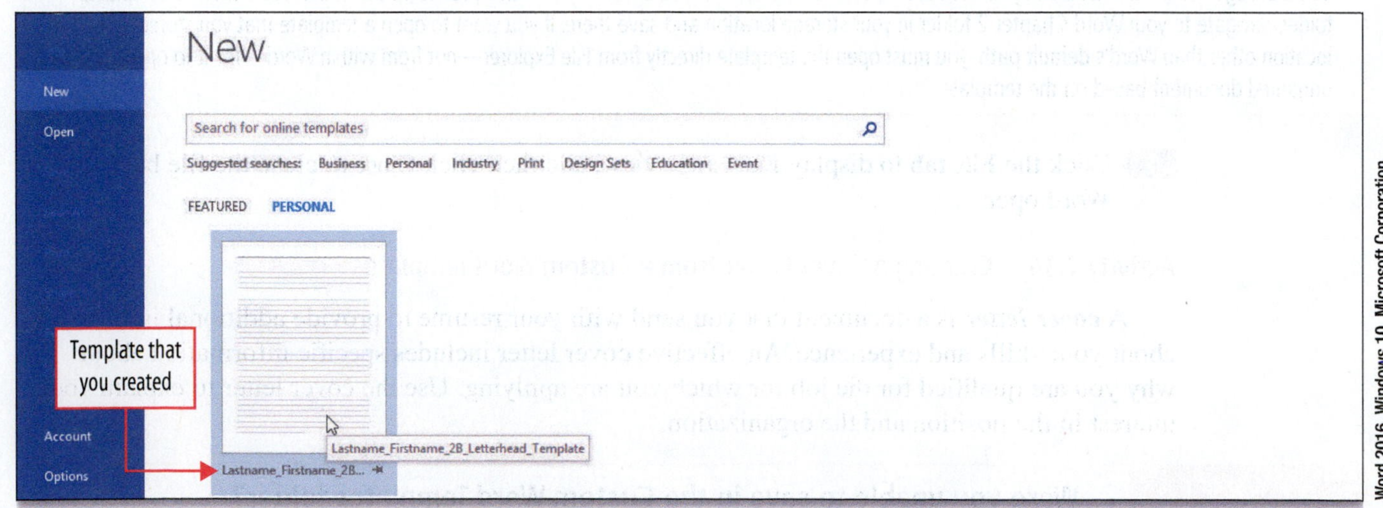

FIGURE 2.22

3 Click your letterhead template (or retrieve it from your storage location if you stored it elsewhere).

Word opens a copy of your 2B_Letterhead_Template in the form of a new Word document—the title bar indicates *Document* followed by a number. You are not opening the original template file, and changes that you make to this new document will not affect the contents of your stored 2B_Letterhead_Template file.

4 Display the **Save As** dialog box, and then navigate to your **Word Chapter 2** folder. Using your own first and last name, **Save** the file as **Lastname_Firstname_2B_Cover_Letter**

5 On the **Insert tab**, in the **Header & Footer** group, click **Footer**, at the bottom click **Edit Footer**, and then in the **Insert group**, click **Document Info**. Click **File Name**, and then click **Close Header and Footer**.

6 **Save** your document.

Objective 5 Correct and Reorganize Text

GO! Learn How Video W2-5

Business letters follow a standard format and contain the following parts: the current date, referred to as the ***dateline***; the name and address of the person receiving the letter, referred to as the ***inside address***; a greeting, referred to as the ***salutation***; the text of the letter, usually referred to as the ***body*** of the letter; a closing line, referred to as the ***complimentary closing***; and the ***writer's identification***, which includes the name or job title (or both) of the writer and which is also referred to as the ***writer's signature block***.

Some letters also include the initials of the person who prepared the letter, an optional ***subject line*** that describes the purpose of the letter, or a list of ***enclosures***—documents included with the letter.

2.1.3

Activity 2.15 | Adding AutoCorrect Entries

Word's ***AutoCorrect*** feature corrects commonly misspelled words automatically; for example, *teh* instead of *the*. If you have words that you frequently misspell, you can add them to the list for automatic correction.

1 Click the **File tab** to display **Backstage** view. On the left, click **Options** to display the **Word Options** dialog box.

2 On the left side of the **Word Options** dialog box, click **Proofing**, and then under **AutoCorrect options**, click the **AutoCorrect Options** button.

3 In the **AutoCorrect** dialog box, click the **AutoCorrect tab**. Under **Replace**, type **resumee** and under **With**, type **resume**

If another student has already added this AutoCorrect entry, a Replace button will display.

4 Click **Add**. If the entry already exists, click Replace instead, and then click Yes.

5 In the **AutoCorrect** dialog box, under **Replace**, type **computr** and under **With**, type **computer** Compare your screen with Figure 2.23.

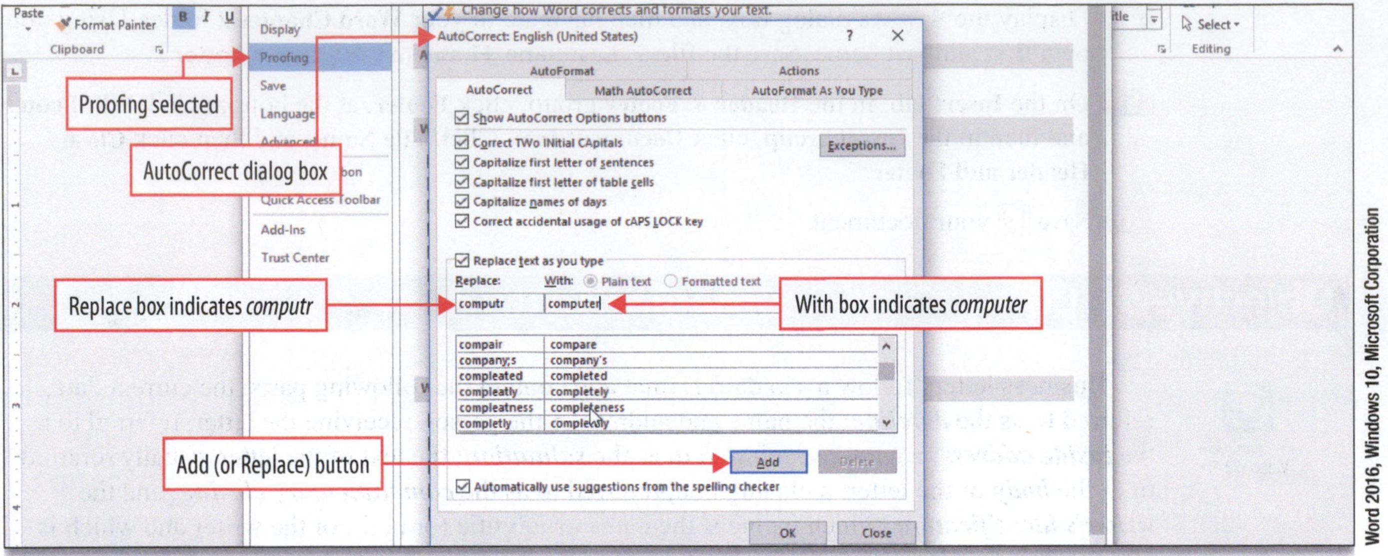

FIGURE 2.23

6 Click **Add** (or Replace) and then click **OK** two times to close the dialog boxes.

Activity 2.16 | Inserting the Current Date and Creating a Cover Letter

By using the ***Date & Time*** command, you can select from a variety of formats to insert the current date and time in a document.

For cover letters, there are a variety of accepted letter formats that you will see in reference manuals and Business Communications texts. The one used in this chapter is a block style cover letter following the style in Courtland Bovee and John Thill, *Business Communication Today*, Twelfth Edition, Pearson, 2014, p. 570.

1 Press Ctrl + End to move the insertion point to the blank line below the letterhead, and then press Enter three times.

2 On the **Insert tab**, in the **Text group**, click **Insert Date & Time**, and then click the third date format. Click **OK** to create the dateline.

Most Business Communication texts recommend that the dateline be positioned at least 0.5 inch (3 blank lines) below the letterhead; or, position the dateline approximately 2 inches from the top edge of the paper.

3 Press Enter four times, which leaves three blank lines. Type the following inside address on four lines, but do *not* press Enter following the last line:

Ms. Mary Walker-Huelsman, Director
Florida Port Community College Career Center
2745 Oakland Avenue
St. Petersburg, FL 33713

The recommended space between the dateline and inside address varies slightly among experts in Business Communication texts and office reference manuals. However, all indicate that the space can be from one to 10 blank lines depending on the length of your letter.

4 Press Enter two times to leave one blank line, and then compare your screen with Figure 2.24.

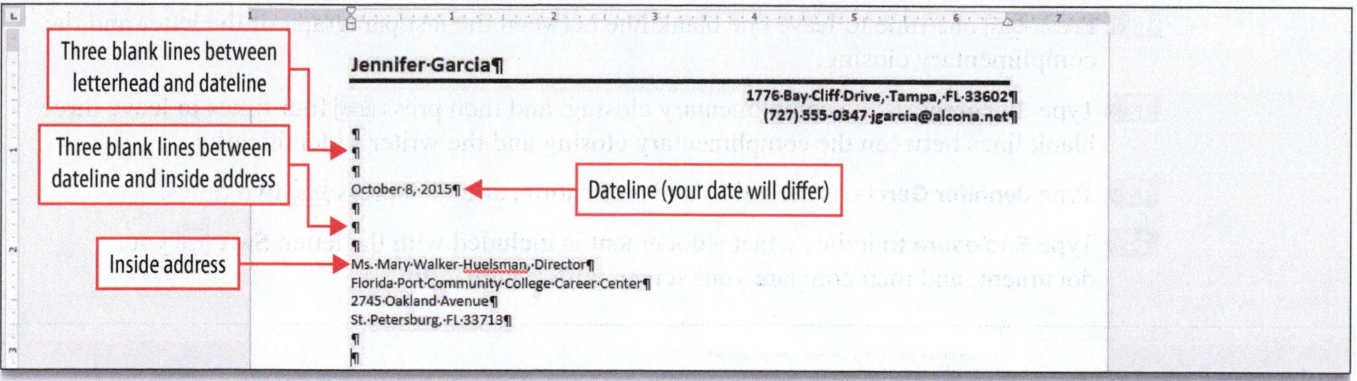

FIGURE 2.24

Word 2016, Windows 10, Microsoft Corporation

5 Type the salutation **Dear Ms. Walker-Huelsman:** and then press Enter two times.

Always leave one blank line above and below the salutation.

6 Type, exactly as shown, the following opening paragraph that includes an intentional word usage error: **I am seeking a position in witch I can use my** and press Spacebar. Type, exactly as shown, **computr** and then watch *computr* as you press Spacebar.

The AutoCorrect feature recognizes the misspelled word, and then changes *computr* to *computer* when you press Spacebar, Enter, or a punctuation mark.

7 Type the following, including the misspelled last word: **and communication skills. My education and experience, outlined on the enclosed resumee** and then type **,** (a comma). Notice that when you type the comma, AutoCorrect replaces *resumee* with *resume.*

8 Press Spacebar, and then complete the paragraph by typing **includes a Business Software Applications Specialist certificate from FPCC.** Compare your screen with Figure 2.25.

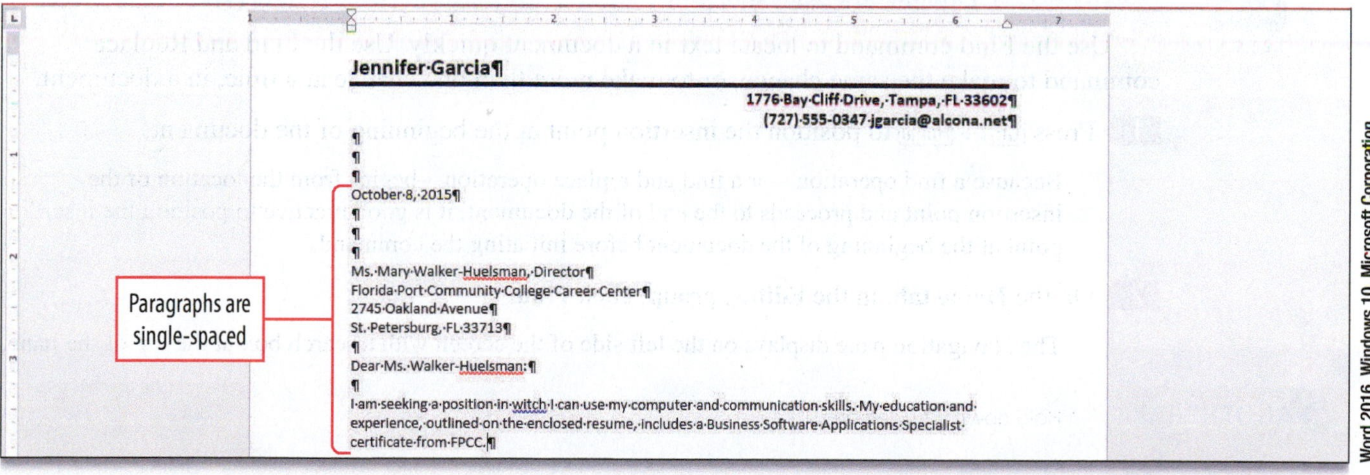

Word 2016, Windows 10, Microsoft Corporation

FIGURE 2.25

9 Press Enter two times. On the **Insert tab**, in the **Text group**, click the **Object button arrow**, and then click **Text from File**. From your student data files, locate and **Insert** the file **w02B_Cover_Letter_Text**.

Some of the words in the cover letter text display red or blue wavy underlines. These indicate potential spelling, grammar, or word usage errors, and will be addressed before the end of this project.

10 Scroll as necessary to display the lower half of the letter on your screen, and be sure your insertion point is positioned in the blank paragraph at the end of the document.

11 Press Enter one time to leave one blank line between the last paragraph of the letter and the complimentary closing.

12 Type **Sincerely,** as the complimentary closing, and then press Enter four times to leave three blank lines between the complimentary closing and the writer's identification.

13 Type **Jennifer Garcia** as the writer's identification, and then press Enter two times.

14 Type **Enclosure** to indicate that a document is included with the letter. **Save** your document, and then compare your screen with Figure 2.26.

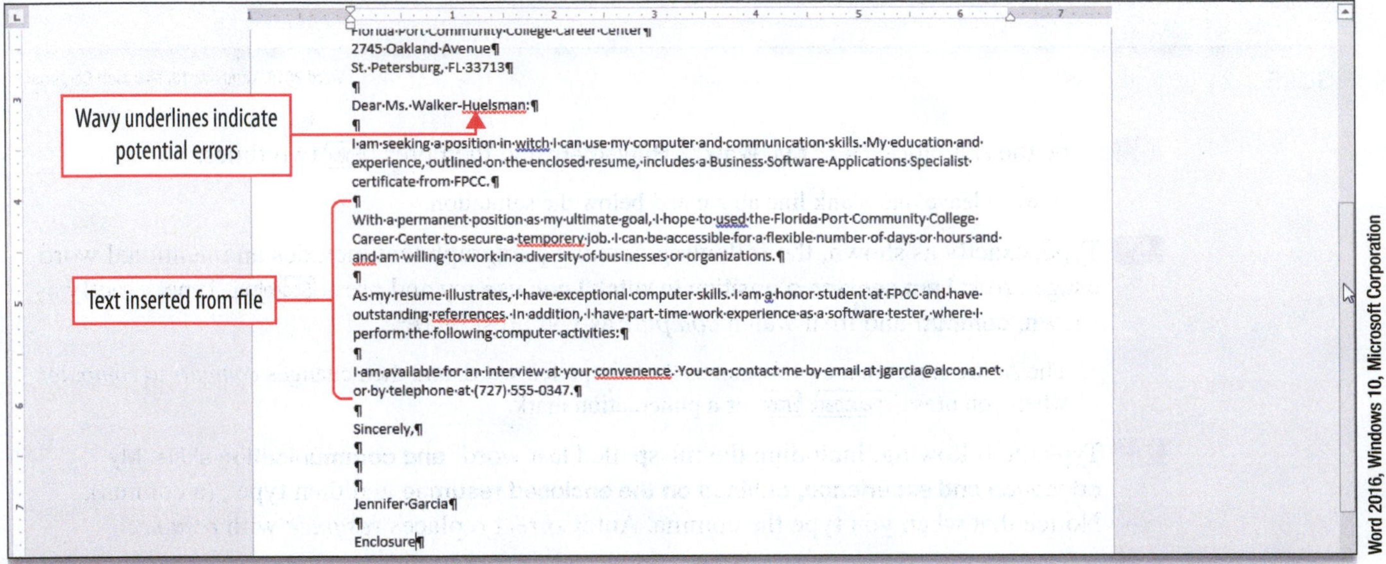

FIGURE 2.26

1.2.1, 2.1.1

Activity 2.17 | Finding and Replacing Text

Use the Find command to locate text in a document quickly. Use the Find and Replace command to make the same change, or to make more than one change at a time, in a document.

1 Press Ctrl + Home to position the insertion point at the beginning of the document.

Because a find operation—or a find and replace operation—begins from the location of the insertion point and proceeds to the end of the document, it is good practice to position the insertion point at the beginning of the document before initiating the command.

2 On the **Home tab**, in the **Editing group**, click **Find**.

The Navigation pane displays on the left side of the screen with a search box at the top of the pane.

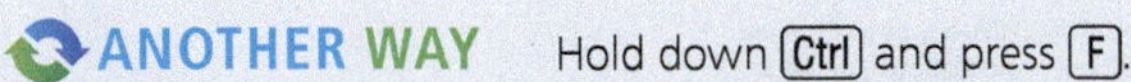

Hold down Ctrl and press F.

3 In the search box, type **ac** If necessary, scroll down slightly in your document to view the entire body text of the letter, and then compare your screen with Figure 2.27.

In the document, the search letters *ac* are selected and highlighted in yellow for both words that begin with the letters *ac* and also for the word *contact*, which contains this letter combination. In the Navigation pane, the three instances are shown in context—*ac* displays in bold.

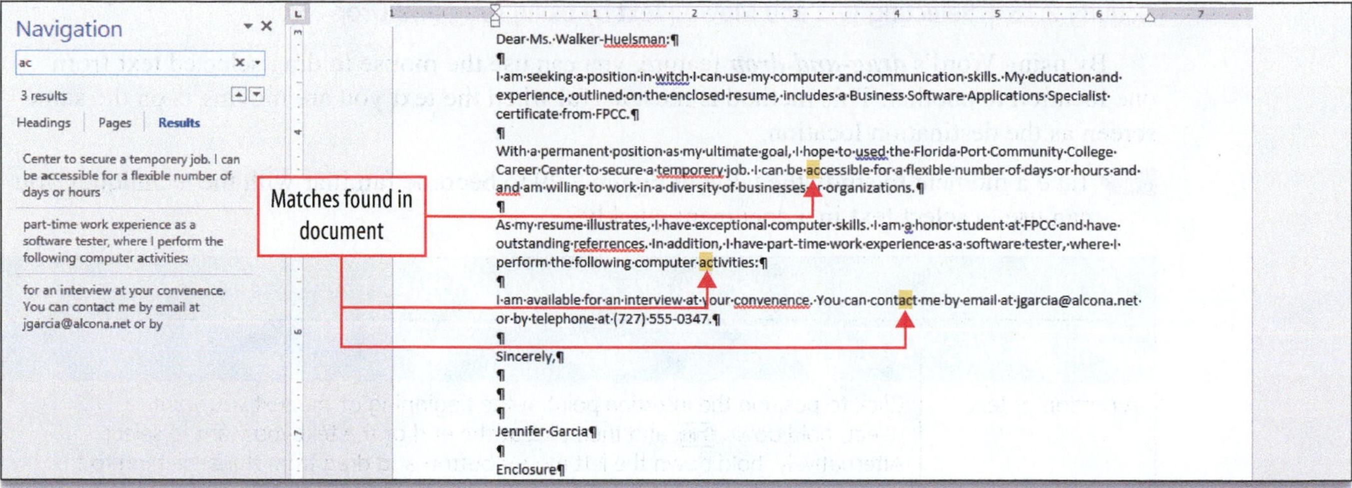

FIGURE 2.27

Word 2016, Windows 10, Microsoft Corporation

4 Click in the search box again, and type as necessary to display the word *accessible* in the search box.

One match for the search term displays in context in the Navigation pane and is highlighted in the document.

5 In the document, double-click the yellow highlighted word *accessible*, and then type **available** to replace the word.

6 **Close** the **Navigation** pane, and then on the **Home tab**, in the **Editing group**, click **Replace**.

7 In the **Find and Replace** dialog box, in the **Find what** box, replace the existing text by typing **FPCC** In the **Replace with** box, type **Florida Port Community College** and then compare your screen with Figure 2.28.

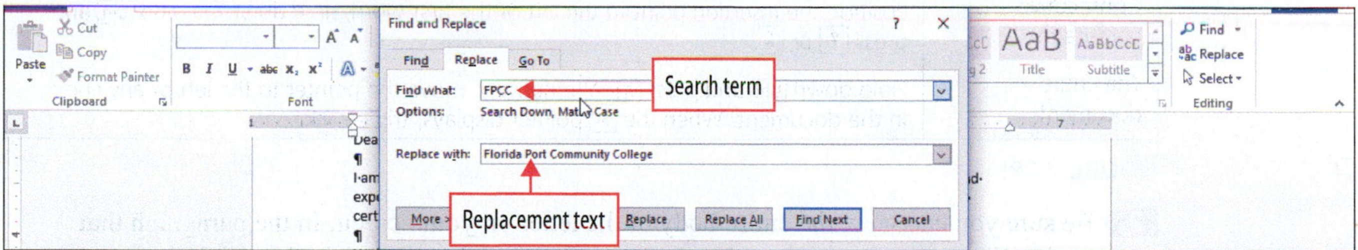

FIGURE 2.28

Word 2016, Windows 10, Microsoft Corporation

8 In the lower left corner of the dialog box, click **More** to expand the dialog box, and then under **Search Options**, select the **Match case** check box.

The acronym *FPCC* appears in the document two times. In a formal letter, the reader may not know what the acronym means, so you should include the full text instead of an acronym. In this instance, you must select the *Match case* check box so that the replaced text will match the case you typed in the Replace with box, and *not* display in all uppercase letters in the manner of *FPCC*.

9 In the **Find and Replace** dialog box, click **Replace All** to replace both instances of *FPCC*. Click **OK** to close the message box.

10 In the **Find and Replace** dialog box, clear the **Match case** check box, click **Less**, and then **Close** the dialog box.

The Find and Replace dialog box opens with the settings used the last time it was open. Therefore, it is good practice to reset this dialog box to its default settings each time you use it.

11 **Save** your document.

Activity 2.18 | Selecting Text and Moving Text by Using Drag and Drop

By using Word's ***drag-and-drop*** feature, you can use the mouse to drag selected text from one location to another. This method is most useful when the text you are moving is on the same screen as the destination location.

1 Take a moment to study the table in Figure 2.29 to become familiar with the techniques you can use to select text in a document quickly.

SELECTING TEXT IN A DOCUMENT	
TO SELECT THIS:	**DO THIS:**
A portion of text	Click to position the insertion point at the beginning of the text you want to select, hold down Shift, and then click at the end of the text you want to select. Alternatively, hold down the left mouse button and drag from the beginning to the end of the text you want to select.
A word	Double-click the word.
A sentence	Hold down Ctrl and click anywhere in the sentence.
A paragraph	Triple-click anywhere in the paragraph; or, move the pointer to the left of the paragraph, into the margin area. When the pointer displays, double-click.
A line	Move the pointer to the left of the line. When the pointer displays, click one time.
One character at a time	Position the insertion point to the left of the first character, hold down Shift, and press ← or → as many times as desired.
A string of words	Position the insertion point to the left of the first word, hold down Shift and Ctrl, and then press ← or → as many times as desired.
Consecutive lines	Position the insertion point to the left of the first word, hold down Shift and press ↑ or ↓.
Consecutive paragraphs	Position the insertion point to the left of the first word, hold down Shift and Ctrl and press ↑ or ↓.
The entire document	Hold down Ctrl and press A. Alternatively, move the pointer to the left of any line in the document. When the pointer displays, triple-click.

FIGURE 2.29

2 Be sure you can view the entire body of the letter on your screen. In the paragraph that begins *With a permanent position*, in the second line, locate and double-click *days*.

3 Point to the selected word to display the pointer.

4 Drag to the right until the dotted vertical line that floats next to the pointer is positioned to the right of the word *hours* in the same line, as shown in Figure 2.30.

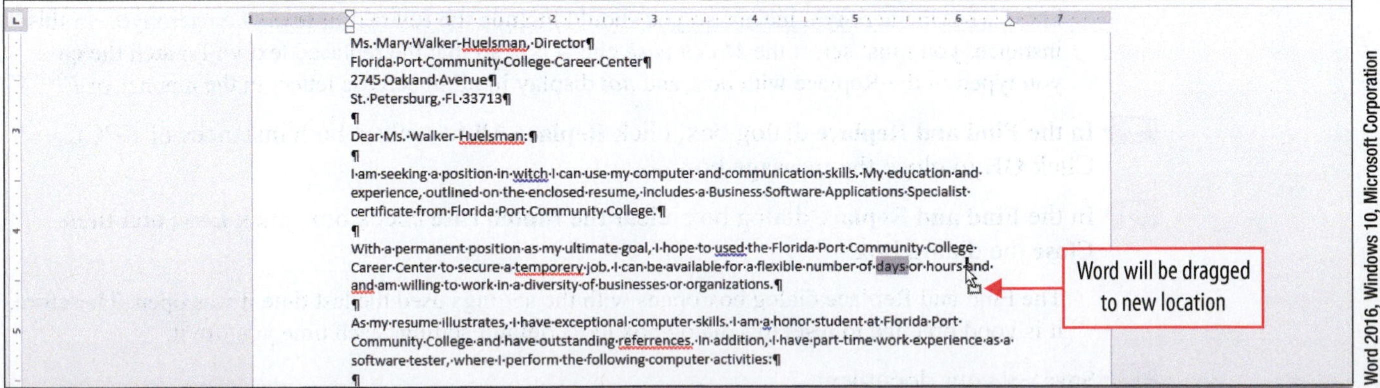

Ms.·Mary·Walker-Huelsman,·Director¶
Florida·Port·Community·College·Career·Center¶
2745·Oakland·Avenue¶
St.·Petersburg,·FL·33713¶
¶
Dear·Ms.·Walker-Huelsman:¶
¶
I·am·seeking·a·position·in·witch·I·can·use·my·computer·and·communication·skills.·My·education·and·experience,·outlined·on·the·enclosed·resume,·includes·a·Business·Software·Applications·Specialist·certificate·from·Florida·Port·Community·College.¶
¶
With·a·permanent·position·as·my·ultimate·goal,·I·hope·to·used·the·Florida·Port·Community·College·Career·Center·to·secure·a·temporery·job.·I·can·be·available·for·a·flexible·number·of·days·or·hours·and·and·am·willing·to·work·in·a·diversity·of·businesses·or·organizations.¶
¶
As·my·resume·illustrates,·I·have·exceptional·computer·skills.·I·am·a·honor·student·at·Florida·Port·Community·College·and·have·outstanding·referrences.·In·addition,·I·have·part-time·work·experience·as·a·software·tester,·where·I·perform·the·following·computer·activities:¶
¶

FIGURE 2.30

5 Release the mouse button to move the text. Select the word *hours* and drag it to the left of the word *or*—the previous location of the word *days*. Click anywhere in the document to deselect the text.

6 Examine the text that you moved, and add or remove spaces as necessary.

7 Hold down Ctrl, and then in the paragraph that begins *I am available*, click anywhere in the first sentence to select the entire sentence.

8 Release Ctrl. Drag the selected sentence to the end of the paragraph by positioning the small vertical line that floats with the pointer to the left of the paragraph mark. **Save** your document, and then compare your screen with Figure 2.31.

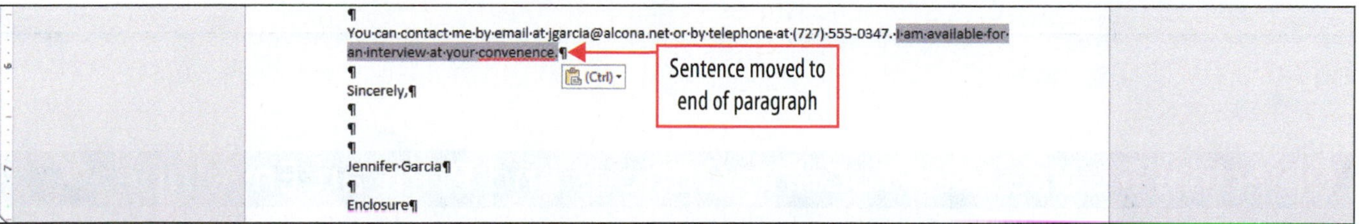

¶
You·can·contact·me·by·email·at·jgarcia@alcona.net·or·by·telephone·at·(727)-555-0347.·I·am·available·for·an·interview·at·your·convenence.¶
¶
(Ctrl)
Sincerely,¶
¶
¶
¶
Jennifer·Garcia¶
¶
Enclosure¶
Sentence moved to end of paragraph

Word 2016, Windows 10, Microsoft Corporation

FIGURE 2.31

3.1.4

Activity 2.19 | Inserting a Table into a Document and Applying a Table Style

1 Locate the paragraph that begins *You can contact me*, and then click to position the insertion point in the blank paragraph above that paragraph. Press Enter one time.

2 On the **Insert tab**, in the **Tables group**, click **Table**. In the **Table** grid, in the third row, click the second square to insert a 2x3 table.

3 In the first cell of the table, type **Microsoft Access** and then press Tab. Type **Test database queries** and then press Tab. Complete the table using the following information:

Microsoft Excel	**Enter software test data**
Microsoft Word	**Create and mail form letters**

4 Point slightly outside of the upper left corner of the table to display the **table move handle** button. With the pointer, click one time to select the entire table.

5 On the ribbon, under **Table Tools**, click the **Layout tab**. In the **Cell Size group**, click **AutoFit**, and then click **AutoFit Contents** to have Word choose the best column widths for the two columns based on the text you entered.

6 With the table still selected, under **Table Tools**, click the **Design tab**. In the **Table Styles group**, click **More**. Under **Plain Tables**, click the second style—**Table Grid Light**.

Use Table Styles to change the visual style of a table.

7 With the table still selected, on the **Home tab**, in the **Paragraph group**, click **Center** to center the table between the left and right margins. Click anywhere to deselect the table.

8 **Save** and then compare your screen with Figure 2.32.

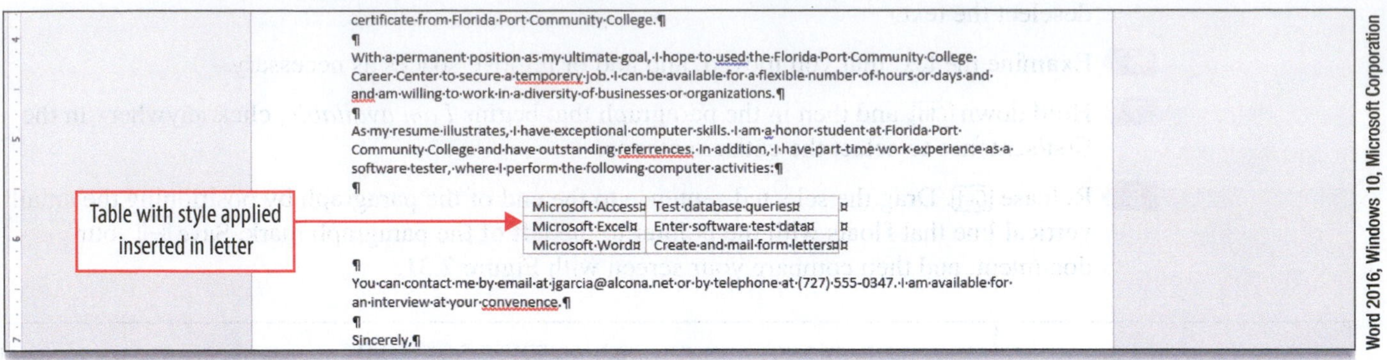
certificate·from·Florida·Port·Community·College.¶

¶

With·a·permanent·position·as·my·ultimate·goal,·I·hope·to·used·the·Florida·Port·Community·College·Career·Center·to·secure·a·temporery·job.·I·can·be·available·for·a·flexible·number·of·hours·or·days·and·and·am·willing·to·work·in·a·diversity·of·businesses·or·organizations.¶

¶

As·my·resume·illustrates,·I·have·exceptional·computer·skills.·I·am·a·honor·student·at·Florida·Port·Community·College·and·have·outstanding·referrences.·In·addition,·I·have·part-time·work·experience·as·a·software·tester,·where·I·perform·the·following·computer·activities:¶

¶

Microsoft·Access	Test·database·queries
Microsoft·Excel	Enter·software·test·data
Microsoft·Word	Create·and·mail·form·letters

¶

You·can·contact·me·by·email·at·jgarcia@alcona.net·or·by·telephone·at·(727)·555-0347.·I·am·available·for·an·interview·at·your·convenence.¶

¶

Sincerely,¶

FIGURE 2.32

Objective 6 Use the Proofing Options and Print an Envelope

GO! Learn How Video W2-6

Word compares the words you type to words in the Office dictionary and also compares the phrases and punctuation that you type to a list of grammar rules. This automatic proofing is set by default. Words that are not in the dictionary and words, phrases, and punctuation that differ from the grammar rules are marked with wavy underlines; for example, the misuse of *their*, *there*, and *they're*.

Word will not flag the word *sign* as misspelled even though you intended to type *sing a song* rather than *sign a song*, because both are words contained within Word's dictionary. Your own knowledge and proofreading skills are still required, even when using a sophisticated word processing program like Word.

Activity 2.20 | Checking for Spelling and Grammar Errors

There are two ways to respond to spelling and grammar errors flagged by Word. You can right-click a flagged word or phrase, and then from the shortcut menu choose a correction or action. Or, you can initiate the Spelling & Grammar command to display the Spelling and Grammar pane, which provides more options than the shortcut menus.

ALERT! **Activating Spelling and Grammar Checking**

If you do not see any wavy red or blue lines under words, the automatic spelling and/or grammar checking has been turned off on your system. To activate the spelling and grammar checking, display Backstage view, click Options, click Proofing, and then under *When correcting spelling in Microsoft Office programs*, select the first four check boxes. Under *When correcting spelling and grammar in Word*, select the first four check boxes, and then click the Writing Style arrow and click Grammar. Under *Exceptions for*, clear both check boxes. To display the flagged spelling and grammar errors, click the Recheck Document button, and then close the dialog box.

1 Position the body of the letter on your screen, and then examine the text to locate wavy underlines.

A list of grammar rules applied by a computer program like Word can never be exact, and a computer dictionary cannot contain all known words and proper names. Therefore, you will need to check any words flagged by Word with wavy underlines, and you will also need to proofread for content errors.

2 In the lower left corner of your screen, in the status bar, locate and point to but do not click the icon to display the ScreenTip *Word found proofing errors. Click or tap to correct them.* Compare your screen with Figure 2.33.

If this button displays, you know there are potential errors identified in the document.

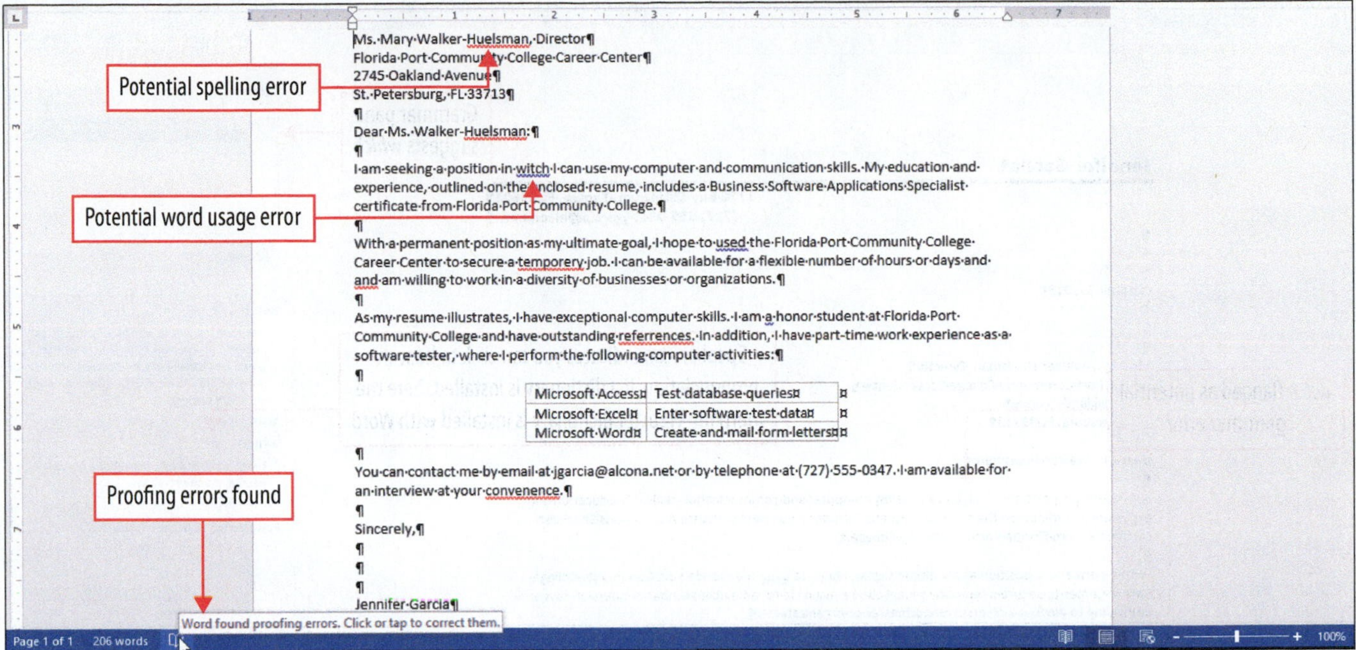

Word 2016, Windows 10, Microsoft Corporation

FIGURE 2.33

3 In the paragraph that begins *With a permanent*, in the second line, locate the word *temporery* with the wavy red underline. Point to the word and right-click, and then click **temporary** to correct the spelling error.

4 In the next line, locate the word *and* that displays with a wavy red underline, point to the word and right-click, and then on the shortcut menu, click **Delete Repeated Word** to delete the duplicate word.

5 Press Ctrl + Home to move the insertion point to the beginning of the document. Click the **Review tab**, and then in the **Proofing group**, click **Spelling & Grammar** to check the spelling and grammar of the text in the document.

The Spelling pane displays on the right, and the proper name *Huelsman* is flagged. Word's dictionary contains only very common proper names—unusual names like this one will typically be flagged as a potential spelling error. If this is a name that you frequently type, consider adding it to the dictionary.

ANOTHER WAY Press F7 to start the Spelling & Grammar command.

6 In the **Spelling** pane, click **Ignore All**. Compare your screen with Figure 2.34.

The word *witch* is highlighted as a grammar error, and in the Grammar pane, *which* is suggested.

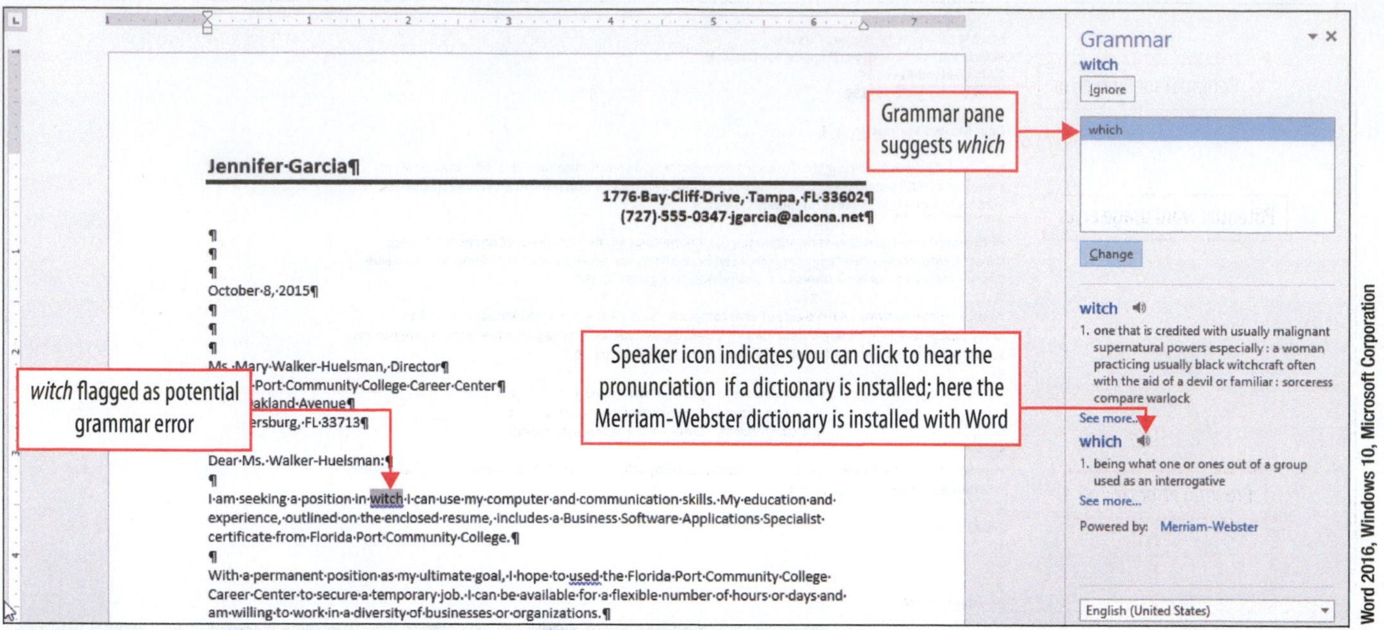

FIGURE 2.34

7 In the **Grammar** pane, click **Change** to change to the correct usage *which*.

The next marked word—a possible grammar error—displays.

8 Click **Change** to change *used* to *use*. Notice that the next error is a potential Spelling error. In the **Spelling** pane, change *referrences* to the suggestion *references*. Notice that the next error is a possible grammar error.

9 Click **Change** to change *a* to *an*. Continue the spelling and grammar check and correct the spelling of *convenence*.

10 When Word displays the message *Spelling and grammar check is complete*, click **OK**.

11 **Save** your document.

Activity 2.21 | Using the Thesaurus

A ***thesaurus*** is a research tool that lists ***synonyms***—words that have the same or similar meaning to the word you selected.

1 Scroll so that you can view the body of the letter. In the paragraph that begins *With a permanent*, double-click to select the word *diversity*, and then in the **Proofing** group, click **Thesaurus**.

The Thesaurus pane displays on the right with a list of synonyms; the list will vary in length depending on the selected word.

ANOTHER WAY Right-click the word, on the shortcut menu, point to Synonyms, and then click Thesaurus.

2 In the **Thesaurus** pane, under **variety (n.)**, point to the word *variety*, and then click the arrow that displays. Click **Insert** to change *diversity* to *variety*.

3 In the paragraph that begins *As my resume*, double-click the word *exceptional*, and then on the ribbon, click **Thesaurus** again.

4 In the **Thesaurus** pane, under **excellent (adj.)**, point to *excellent*, click the **arrow**, and then click **Insert**. Compare your screen with Figure 2.35.

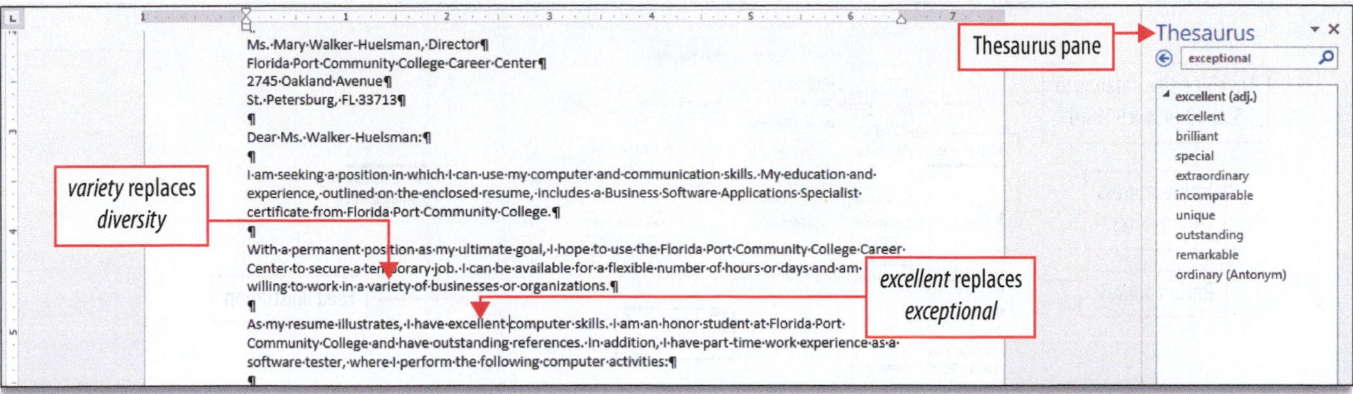

Word 2016, Windows 10, Microsoft Corporation

FIGURE 2.35

5 **Close** ☒ the **Thesaurus** pane.

6 Click the **File tab** to display **Backstage** view, and then on the **Info tab**, in the lower right portion of the screen, click **Show All Properties**. If you used your template, notice that it is indicated to the right of *Template*.

7 In the **Tags** box, type **cover letter** and in the **Subject** box, type your course name and section number. In the **Author** box, be sure your name is indicated and edit if necessary.

8 On the left, click **Print** to display **Print Preview**. If necessary, return to the document and make any necessary changes.

9 **Save** your document. If directed by your instructor to do so, submit your paper printout, your electronic image of your document that looks like a printed document, or your original Word file. In the upper right corner of the Word window, click **Close** ☒.

ALERT!

Because the next Activity is optional, if you are submitting your work in MyITLab, this is the file you will upload.

Activity 2.22 | Addressing and Printing an Envelope

Use Word's Envelopes command on the Mailings label to format and print an envelope.

NOTE

This Is an Optional Activity

This activity is optional. If you do not have an envelope and printer, or do not want to complete the activity at this time, then this project is complete.

1 Display your **2B_Cover_Letter**, and then select the four lines that comprise the inside address.

2 On the **Mailings tab**, in the **Create group**, click **Envelopes**. Notice that the **Delivery address** contains the selected inside address.

3 Click in the **Return address** box, and then type **Jennifer Garcia** and press Enter. Type **1776 Bay Cliff Drive** and then press Enter. Type **Tampa, FL 33602**

4 In the lower portion of the **Envelopes and Labels** dialog box, click **Options**, and then compare your screen with Figure 2.36.

The default envelope size is a standard business envelope referred to as a Size 10.

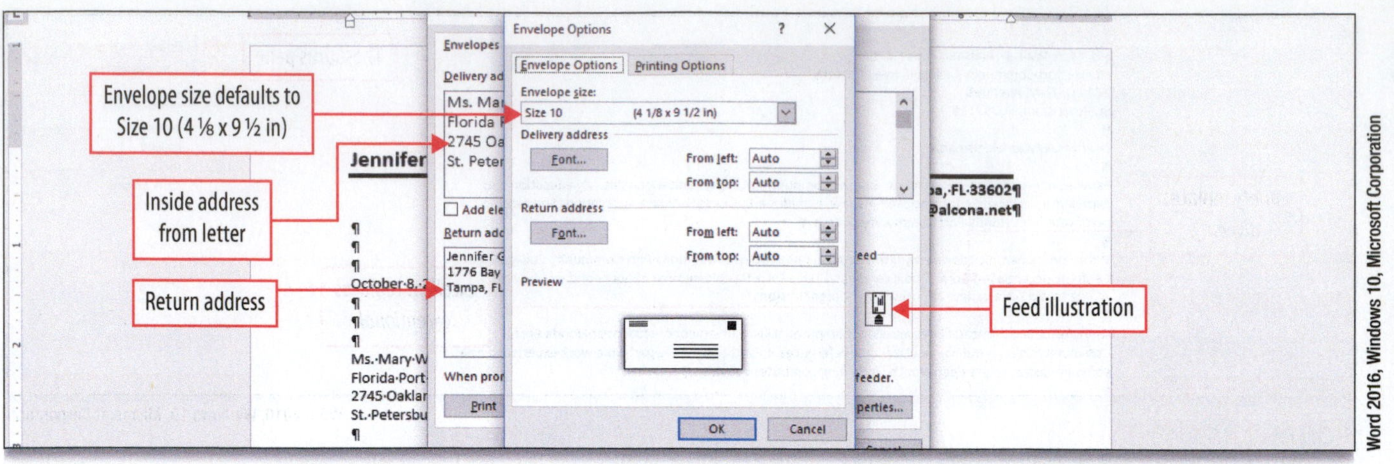

FIGURE 2.36

5 Click **OK** to close the **Envelope Options** dialog box. As shown under **Feed**, insert an envelope in your printer and then click **Print**.

Depending on the type and brand of printer you are using, your feed area may vary.

6 Close your **2B_Cover_Letter**, and then close Word.

END | You have completed Project 2B

GO! With Google

2 WORD

Objective | Create a Table in Google Docs

ALERT! **Working with Web-Based Applications and Services**

Computer programs and services on the web receive continuous updates and improvements, so the steps to complete this web-based activity may differ from the ones shown. You can often look at the screens and the information presented to determine how to complete the activity.

If you do not already have a Google account, you will need to create one before you begin this activity. Go to http://google.com and, in the upper right corner, click Sign In. On the Sign In screen, click Create Account. On the Create your Google Account page, complete the form, read and agree to the Terms of Service and Privacy Policy, and then click Next step. On the Welcome screen, click Get Started.

Activity | Creating a Table in Google Docs

In this Activity, you will use Google Docs to create a table within a document similar to Project 2B.

1. From the desktop, open your browser, navigate to **http://google.com**, and then click the **Google Apps** menu. Click **Drive**, and then if necessary, sign in to your Google account.

2. Open your **GO! Web Projects** folder—or click New to create and then open this folder if necessary.

3. In the left pane, click **NEW**, and then click **File upload**. In the **Open** dialog box, navigate to your Student Data Files for this chapter, and then in the **File List**, double-click to open **w02_2B_Web**.

4. When the upload is complete, in the **Google Drive file list**, point to the document name, right-click, point to **Open with**, and then click **Google Docs** to open it in Google Docs.

5. Click in the document and then press Ctrl + End to move to the end of the document, and then press Enter.

6. On the menu bar, click **Table**, point to **Insert table**, and then insert a **3x4 Table**.

7. Type **Position** and press Tab. Type **Type** and press Tab. Type **Location** and press Tab.

8. In the second row type **Paralegal** and press Tab. Type **Part-time** and press Tab. Type **Tampa** and press Tab. Compare your screen with Figure A.

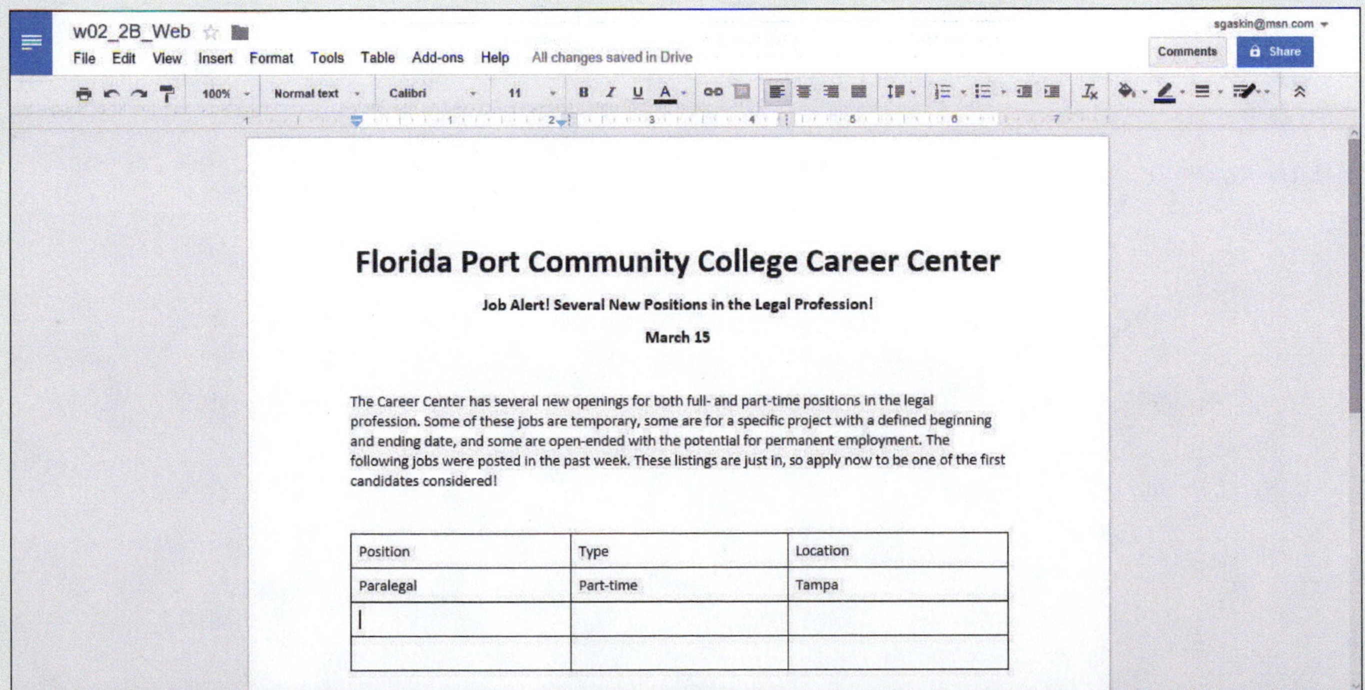

FIGURE A

(GO! With Google continues on the next page)

GO! With Google

9 Type **Legal Records Clerk** and press Tab. Type **Full-time, 2 months** and press Tab. Type **North Tampa** and press Tab.

11 Right-click in the last row of the table, and then click **Delete row**.

12 Drag to select all the cells in the first row, and then on the toolbar, click the **Normal text button arrow**, and then click **Heading 2**. With the three column titles still selected, on the toolbar, click **Center**.

13 Press Ctrl + Home to move to the top of the document, and then compare your screen with Figure B.

14 Submit the file as directed by your instructor. In the upper right, click your user name, and then click **Sign out**. **Close** your browser window. Your file is automatically saved in your Google Drive.

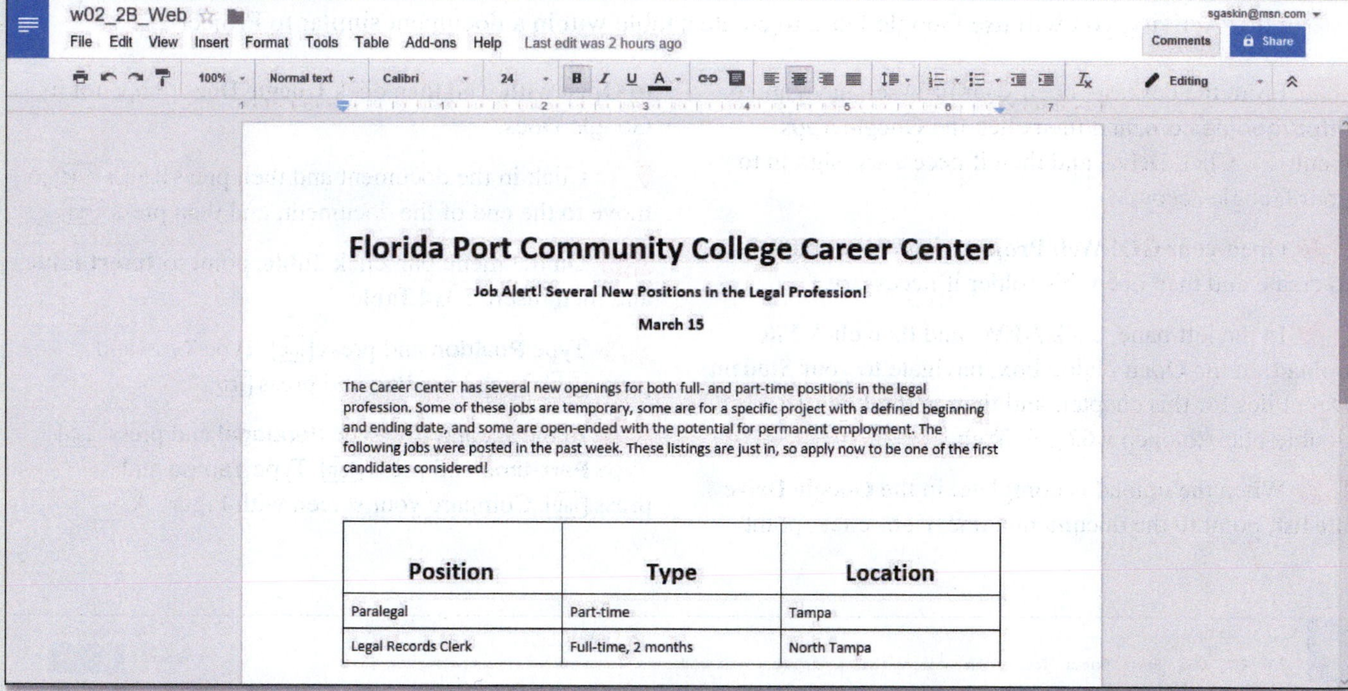

FIGURE B

GO! To Work

Andrew Rodriguez / Fotolia; FotolEdhar / Fotolia; apops / Fotolia; Yuri Arcurs / Fotolia

2 WORD

MICROSOFT OFFICE SPECIALIST (MOS) SKILLS IN THIS CHAPTER	
PROJECT 2A	**PROJECT 2B**
1.1.4 Insert text from a file or external source **3.1.3** Create a table by specifying rows and columns **3.2.3** Merge and split cells **3.2.4** Resize tables, rows, and columns	**1.2.1** Search for text **1.3.3** Apply document style sets **2.1.1** Find and replace text **2.1.3** Replace text by using AutoCorrect **3.1.4** Apply table styles

BUILD YOUR E-PORTFOLIO

An E-Portfolio is a collection of evidence, stored electronically, that showcases what you have accomplished while completing your education. Collecting and then sharing your work products with potential employers reflects your academic and career goals. Your completed documents from the following projects are good examples to show what you have learned: 2G, 2K, and 2L.

GO! FOR JOB SUCCESS

Video: Cover Letter and Resume Tips

Your instructor may assign this video to your class, and then ask you to think about, or discuss with your classmates, these questions:

FotolEdhar / Fotolia

A cover letter should contain information that is different from but complementary to the information and facts on your resume and be tailored to the specific job you are applying for. Name two different things that you could mention in a cover letter.

What type of information belongs in the Career Objective portion of your resume?

When is it best to use a chronological resume layout, and when is it appropriate to use a functional resume layout?

END OF CHAPTER

SUMMARY

Word tables enable you to present information in a logical and orderly format. Each cell in a Word table behaves like a document; as you type in a cell, wordwrap moves text to the next line.

A good source of information for resume formats is a business communications textbook. A simple two-column table created in Word is suitable to create an appropriate resume for a recent college graduate.

Use Word's Office Presentation Service to present a Word document to others who can watch in a web browser. Word automatically creates a link to your document that you can share with others via email.

A template is useful because it has a predefined document structure and defined settings such as font and margins. Create your own custom template or, from Word's opening screen, select from thousands of templates.

GO! LEARN IT ONLINE

Review the concepts, key terms, and MOS skills in this chapter by completing these online challenges, which you can find at **MyITLab**.

Matching and Multiple Choice: Answer matching and multiple-choice questions to test what you learned in this chapter.

Lessons on the GO: Learn how to use all the new apps and features as they are introduced by Microsoft.

MOS Prep Quiz: Answer questions to review the MOS skills that you practiced in this chapter.

GO! COLLABORATIVE TEAM PROJECT (Available in MyITLab and Instructor Resource Center)

If your instructor assigns this project to your class, you can expect to work with one or more of your classmates—either in person or by using Internet tools—to create work products similar to those that you created in this chapter. A team is a group of workers who work together to solve a problem, make a decision, or create a work product. Collaboration is when you work together with others as a team in an intellectual endeavor to complete a shared task or achieve a shared goal.

PROJECT GUIDE FOR WORD CHAPTER 2

Your instructor will assign Projects from this list to ensure your learning and assess your knowledge.

2 WORD

REVIEW AND ASSESSMENTS GUIDE FOR WORD CHAPTER 2			
Project	**Apply Skills from These Chapter Objectives**	**Project Type**	**Project Location**
2A MyITLab	Objectives 1–3 from Project 2A	**2A Instructional Project (Grader Project)** Guided instruction to learn the skills in Project 2A.	In MyITLab and in text
2B MyITLab	Objectives 4–6 from Project 2B	**2B Instructional Project (Grader Project)** Guided instruction to learn the skills in Project 2B.	In MyITLab and in text
2C	Objectives 1–3 from Project 2A	**2C Skills Review (Scorecard Grading)** A guided review of the skills from Project 2A.	In text
2D	Objectives 4–6 from Project 2B	**2D Skills Review (Scorecard Grading)** A guided review of the skills from Project 2B.	In text
2E MyITLab	Objectives 1–3 from Project 2A	**2E Mastery (Grader Project)** **Mastery and Transfer of Learning** A demonstration of your mastery of the skills in Project 2A with extensive decision making.	In MyITLab and in text
2F MyITLab	Objectives 4–6 from Project 2B	**2F Mastery (Grader Project)** **Mastery and Transfer of Learning** A demonstration of your mastery of the skills in Project 2B with extensive decision making.	In MyITLab and in text
2G MyITLab	Objectives 1–6 from Projects 2A and 2B	**2G Mastery (Grader Project)** **Mastery and Transfer of Learning** A demonstration of your mastery of the skills in Projects 2A and 2B with extensive decision making.	In MyITLab and in text
2H	Combination of Objectives from Projects 2A and2B	**2H GO! Fix It (Scorecard Grading)** **Critical Thinking** A demonstration of your mastery of the skills in Projects 2A and 2B by creating a correct result from a document that contains errors you must find.	Instructor Resource Center (IRC and MyITLab)
2I	Combination of Objectives from Projects 2A and 2B	**2I GO! Make It (Scorecard Grading)** **Critical Thinking** A demonstration of your mastery of the skills in Projects 2A and 2B by creating a result from a supplied picture.	IRC and MyITLab
2J	Combination of Objectives from Projects 2A and 2B	**2J GO! Solve It (Rubric Grading)** **Critical Thinking** A demonstration of your mastery of the skills in Projects 2A and 2B, your decision-making skills, and your critical-thinking skills. A task-specific rubric helps you self-assess your result.	IRC and MyITLab
2K	Combination of Objectives from Projects 2A and 2B	**2K GO! Solve It (Rubric Grading)** **Critical Thinking** A demonstration of your mastery of the skills in Projects 2A and 2B, your decision-making skills, and your critical-thinking skills. A task-specific rubric helps you self-assess your result.	In text
2L	Combination of Objectives from Projects 2A and 2B	**2L GO! Think (Rubric Grading)** **Critical Thinking** A demonstration of your understanding of the chapter concepts applied in a manner that you would outside of college. An analytic rubric helps you and your instructor grade the quality of your work by comparing it to the work an expert in the discipline would create.	In text
2M	Combination of Objectives from Projects 2A and 2B	**2M GO! Think (Rubric Grading)** **Critical Thinking** A demonstration of your understanding of the chapter concepts applied in a manner that you would outside of college. An analytic rubric helps you and your instructor grade the quality of your work by comparing it to the work an expert in the discipline would create.	IRC and MyITLab
2N	Combination of Objectives from Projects 2A and 2B	**2N You and GO! (Rubric Grading)** **Critical Thinking** A demonstration of your understanding of the chapter concepts applied in a manner that you would in a personal situation. An analytic rubric helps you and your instructor grade the quality of your work.	IRC and MyITLab
2O	Combination of Objectives from Projects 2A and 2B	**2O Collaborative Team Project for Word Chapter 2** **Critical Thinking** A demonstration of your understanding of concepts and your ability to work collaboratively in a group role-playing assessment, requiring both collaboration and self-management.	IRC and MyITLab

GLOSSARY

GLOSSARY OF CHAPTER KEY TERMS

AutoCorrect A feature that corrects common typing and spelling errors as you type, for example, changing *teh* to *the*.

Body The text of a letter.

Cell The box at the intersection of a row and column in a Word table.

Complimentary closing A parting farewell in a business letter.

Cover letter A document that you send with your resume to provide additional information about your skills and experience.

Date & Time A command with which you can automatically insert the current date and time into a document in a variety of formats.

Dateline The first line in a business letter that contains the current date and which is positioned just below the letterhead if a letterhead is used.

Drag-and-drop A technique by which you can move, by dragging, selected text from one location in a document to another.

Enclosures Additional documents included with a business letter.

Inside address The name and address of the person receiving the letter and positioned below the date line.

Letterhead The personal or company information that displays at the top of a letter.

No Paragraph Space Style The built-in paragraph style—available from the Paragraph Spacing command—that inserts *no* extra space before or after a paragraph and uses line spacing of 1.

Normal template The template that serves as a basis for all Word documents.

Office Presentation Service A Word feature to present your Word document to others who can watch in a web browser.

One-click Row/Column Insertion A Word table feature with which you can insert a new row or column by pointing to the desired location and then clicking.

Salutation The greeting line of a business letter.

Single spacing The common name for line spacing in which there is *no* extra space before or after a paragraph and uses line spacing of 1.

Skype A Microsoft product with which you can make voice calls, make video calls, transfer files, or send messages—including instant messages and text messages—over the Internet.

Style set A collection of character and paragraph formatting that is stored and named.

Subject line The optional line following the inside address in a business letter that states the purpose of the letter.

Synonyms Words with the same or similar meaning.

Table An arrangement of information organized into rows and columns.

Template An existing document that you use as a starting point for a new document; it opens a copy of itself, unnamed, and then you use the structure—and possibly some content, such as headings—as the starting point for new a document.

Thesaurus A research tool that provides a list of synonyms.

Writer's identification The name and title of the author of a letter, placed near the bottom of the letter under the complimentary closing—also referred to as the *writer's signature block*.

Writer's signature block The name and title of the author of a letter, placed near the bottom of the letter, under the complimentary closing—also referred to as the *writer's identification*.

CHAPTER REVIEW

Apply 2A skills from these Objectives:

1. Create a Table
2. Format a Table
3. Present a Word Document Online

Skills Review Project 2C Student Resume

In the following Skills Review, you will use a table to create a resume for Ashley Kent. Your completed resume will look similar to the one shown in Figure 2.37.

PROJECT FILES

For Project 2C, you will need the following files:

New blank Word document
w02C_Skills
w02C_Experience

You will save your document as:

Lastname_Firstname_2C_Student_Resume

PROJECT RESULTS

Build From Scratch

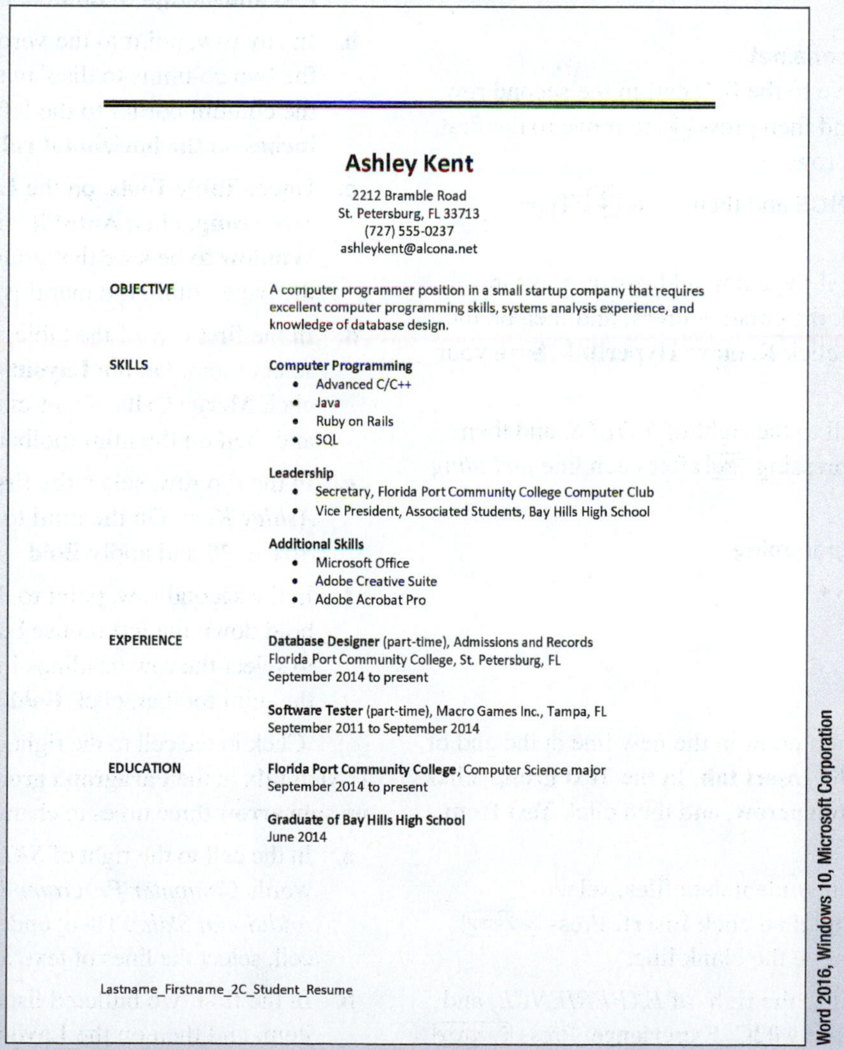

Ashley Kent

2212 Bramble Road
St. Petersburg, FL 33713
(727) 555-0237
ashleykent@alcona.net

OBJECTIVE	A computer programmer position in a small startup company that requires excellent computer programming skills, systems analysis experience, and knowledge of database design.
SKILLS	**Computer Programming** • Advanced C/C++ • Java • Ruby on Rails • SQL **Leadership** • Secretary, Florida Port Community College Computer Club • Vice President, Associated Students, Bay Hills High School **Additional Skills** • Microsoft Office • Adobe Creative Suite • Adobe Acrobat Pro
EXPERIENCE	**Database Designer** (part-time), Admissions and Records Florida Port Community College, St. Petersburg, FL September 2014 to present **Software Tester** (part-time), Macro Games Inc., Tampa, FL September 2011 to September 2014
EDUCATION	**Florida Port Community College**, Computer Science major September 2014 to present **Graduate of Bay Hills High School** June 2014

Lastname_Firstname_2C_Student_Resume

Word 2016, Windows 10, Microsoft Corporation

FIGURE 2.37

(Project 2C Student Resume continues on the next page)

Skills Review Project 2C Student Resume (continued)

1 Start Word and display a blank document. Be sure that formatting marks and rulers display. **Save** the document in your **Word Chapter 2** folder as **Lastname_Firstname_2C_Student_Resume**

a. Add the file name to the footer, and then close the footer area. Click the **Insert tab**, and then in the **Tables group**, click **Table**. In the **Table** grid, in the fourth row, click the second square to insert a **2x4** table.

b. In the first cell of the table, type **Ashley Kent** and then press Enter. Type the following text, pressing Enter after each line *except* the last line:

2212 Bramble Road
St. Petersburg, FL 33713
(727) 555-0237
ashleykent@alcona.net

c. Press ↓ to move to the first cell in the second row. Type **SKILLS** and then press ↓ to move to the first cell in the third row.

d. Type **EXPERIENCE** and then press ↓. Type **EDUCATION**

e. In the first cell, if the email address displays in blue, right-click the email address, and then on the shortcut menu, click **Remove Hyperlink**. **Save** your document.

2 Click in the cell to the right of *SKILLS*, and then type the following, pressing Enter after each line *including* the last line:

Computer Programming
Advanced C/C++
Java
Ruby on Rails
SQL

a. With the insertion point in the new line at the end of the cell, click the **Insert tab**. In the **Text group**, click the **Object button arrow**, and then click **Text from File**.

b. Navigate to your student data files, select **w02C_Skills**, and then click **Insert**. Press Backspace one time to remove the blank line.

c. Click in the cell to the right of *EXPERIENCE*, and then insert the file **w02C_Experience**. Press Backspace one time to remove the blank line.

d. Click in the cell to the right of *EDUCATION*, and then type the following, pressing Enter after all lines *except* the last line:

Florida Port Community College, Computer Science major
September 2014 to present
Graduate of Bay Hills High School
June 2014

3 Point to the upper left corner of the *SKILLS* cell, and then click the **Row Insertion** button. In the first cell of the new row, type **OBJECTIVE** and then press Tab.

a. Type **A computer programmer position in a small startup company that requires excellent computer programming skills, systems analysis experience, and knowledge of database design.**

b. In any row, point to the vertical border between the two columns to display the ✥ pointer. Drag the column border to the left to approximately **1.5 inches on the horizontal ruler**.

c. Under **Table Tools**, on the **Layout tab**, in the **Cell Size group**, click **AutoFit**, and then click **AutoFit Window** to be sure that your table stretches across the page within the margins.

d. In the first row of the table, drag across both cells to select them. On the **Layout tab**, in the **Merge group**, click **Merge Cells**. Right-click over the selected cell, and then on the mini toolbar, click **Center**.

e. In the top row, select the first paragraph of text—*Ashley Kent*. On the mini toolbar, increase the **Font Size** to **20** and apply **Bold**.

f. In the second row, point to the word *OBJECTIVE*, hold down the left mouse button, and then drag down to select the row headings in uppercase letters. On the mini toolbar, click **Bold**. **Save** your document.

4 Click in the cell to the right of *OBJECTIVE*. On the **Layout tab**, in the **Paragraph group**, click the **Spacing After up spin arrow** three times to change the spacing to **18 pt**.

a. In the cell to the right of *SKILLS*, apply **Bold** to the words *Computer Programming*, *Leadership*, and *Additional Skills*. Then, under each bold heading in the cell, select the lines of text, and create a bulleted list.

b. In the first two bulleted lists, click in the last bullet item, and then on the **Layout tab**, in the **Paragraph group**, set the **Spacing After** to **12 pt**.

(Project 2C Student Resume continues on the next page)

Skills Review Project 2C Student Resume (continued)

c. In the last bulleted list, click in the last bullet item, and then set the **Spacing After** to **18 pt**.

d. In the cell to the right of *EXPERIENCE*, apply **Bold** to *Database Designer* and *Software Tester*. Click in the line *September 2014 to present* and apply **Spacing After** of **12 pt**. Click in the line *September 2011 to September 2014* and apply **Spacing After** of **18 pt**.

e. In the cell to the right of *EDUCATION*, apply **Bold** to *Florida Port Community College* and *Graduate of Bay Hills High School*.

f. In the same cell, click in the line *September 2014 to present* and apply **Spacing After** of **12 pt**.

g. In the first row, click in the last line—*ashleykent@alcona.net*—and then change the **Spacing After** to **18 pt**. Click in the first line—*Ashley Kent*—and set the **Spacing Before** to **30 pt** and the **Spacing After** to **6 pt**.

5 Point to the upper left corner of the table, and then click the **table move handle** [⊞] to select the entire table. Under **Table Tools**, on the **Design tab**, in the **Borders group**, click the **Borders button arrow**, and then click **No Border**.

a. In the **Borders group**, click the **Borders button arrow** again, and then at the bottom of the gallery, click **Borders and Shading**. In the **Borders and Shading** dialog box, under **Setting**, click **Custom**. Under **Style**, scroll down slightly, and then click the style with two equal lines.

b. Click the **Width arrow**, and then click **1 1/2 pt**. Under **Preview**, click the top border of the preview box, and then click **OK**.

c. Click the **File tab** to display **Backstage** view, and then in the lower right portion of the screen, click **Show All Properties**. In the **Tags** box, type **resume, table** and in the **Subject** box, type your course name and section number. In the **Author** box, be sure your name is indicated and edit if necessary.

d. On the left, click **Print** to display **Print Preview**. If necessary, return to the document and make any necessary changes.

e. **Save** [💾] your document, and then if you want to do so, present your document online to a fellow classmate. If directed by your instructor to do so, submit your paper printout, your electronic image of your document that looks like a printed document, or your original Word file. Close Word.

END | You have completed Project 2C

CHAPTER REVIEW

Apply 2B skills from these Objectives:

4 Create a Custom Word Template
5 Correct and Reorganize Text
6 Use the Proofing Options and Print an Envelope

Skills Review Project 2D Cover Letter

In the following Skills Review, you will create a letterhead, save the letterhead as a custom Word template, and then use the letterhead to create a cover letter to accompany a resume. If you have an envelope and printer available, you will format and print an envelope. Your completed document will look similar to Figure 2.38.

PROJECT FILES

For Project 2D, you will need the following files:

New blank Word document
w02D_Cover_Letter_Text

You will save your documents as:

Lastname_Firstname_2D_Cover_Letter

PROJECT RESULTS

Build From Scratch

Sarah Villmosky
7279 Rambling Brook Way, St. Petersburg, FL 33713
(727) 555-0117 svillmosky@alcona.net

October 7, 2015

Ms. Mary Walker-Huelsman, Director
Florida Port Community College Career Center
2745 Oakland Avenue
St. Petersburg, FL 33713

Dear Ms. Walker-Huelsman:

I am seeking the assistance of the Career Center in my job search.

Having recently graduated from Florida Port Community College with an Associate of Arts in Media Studies, I am interested in working for a newspaper, a magazine, or a publishing company.

I have previous work experience in the publishing industry as a writer and section editor for the local activities section of the St. Petersburg News and Times. I have the following skills that I developed while working at the St. Petersburg News and Times. I believe these skills would be a good fit with a local or national newspaper or publication:

Editorial experience:	Writing, editing, interviewing
Computer proficiency:	CS InDesign, QuarkXPress, Microsoft Publisher
Education focus:	Media Studies and Journalism

I am willing to consider temporary positions that might lead to a permanent position. Please contact me at sarahvillmosky@alcona.net or by phone at (727) 555-0117. I am available immediately for an interview or for further training at the Career Center that you think would be beneficial in my job search.

Sincerely,

Sarah Villmosky

Enclosure

Lastname_Firstname_2D_Cover_Letter

FIGURE 2.38

(Project 2D Cover Letter continues on the next page)

Skills Review Project 2D Cover Letter (continued)

1 Start Word and display a blank document; be sure that formatting marks and rulers display. On the **Design tab**, in the **Document Formatting group**, click **Paragraph Spacing**, and then click **No Paragraph Space**.

a. Type **Sarah Villmosky** and then press Enter. Type **7279 Rambling Brook Way, St. Petersburg, FL 33713** and then press Enter.

b. Type **(727) 555-0117 svillmosky@alcona.net** and then press Enter. If the web address changes to blue text, right-click the web address, and then click **Remove Hyperlink**.

c. Select the first paragraph—*Sarah Villmosky*—and then on the mini toolbar, apply **Bold**, and change the **Font Size** to **16**.

d. Select the second and third paragraphs, and then on the mini toolbar, apply **Bold**, and change the **Font Size** to **12**.

e. Click anywhere in the first paragraph—*Sarah Villmosky*. On the **Home tab**, in the **Paragraph group**, click the **Borders button arrow**, and then click **Borders and Shading**. Under **Style**, click the first style—a single solid line. Click the **Width arrow**, and then click **3 pt**. In the **Preview** area, click the bottom border, and then click **OK**.

f. Click the **File tab**, click **Save As**, and then click **Browse** to display the **Save As** dialog box. In the lower portion of the dialog box, in the **Save as type** box, click the arrow, and then click **Word Template**. In the **File name** box, using your own name, type **Lastname_Firstname_2D_Letterhead_Template** and then click **Save** to save the custom Word template in the default path, which is the Templates folder on the hard drive of your computer.

g. Click the **File tab** to display **Backstage** view, and then click **Close** to close the file but leave Word open.

h. With Word open but no documents displayed, click the **File tab**, and then click **New**. Under **Suggested searches**, click **PERSONAL**, and then locate and click the letterhead template that you just created.

i. Click the **File tab**, click **Save As**, click **Browse** to display the **Save As** dialog box, navigate to your **Word Chapter 2** folder, and then using your own name **Save** the file as **Lastname_Firstname_2D_Cover_Letter**

j. On the **Insert tab**, in the **Header & Footer group**, click **Footer**, click **Edit Footer**, and then in the **Insert group**, click **Document Info**. Click **File Name**, and then click **Close Header and Footer**. Click **Save**.

2 Click the **File tab**. On the left, click **Options**. On the left side of the **Word Options** dialog box, click **Proofing**, and then under **AutoCorrect options**, click the **AutoCorrect Options** button.

a. In the **AutoCorrect** dialog box, click the **AutoCorrect tab**. Under **Replace**, type the misspelled word **assistence** and under **With**, type **assistance** Click **Add**. If the entry already exists, click Replace instead, and then click Yes. Click **OK** two times to close the dialog boxes.

b. Press Ctrl + End, and then press Enter three times. On the **Insert tab**, in the **Text group**, click **Date & Time**, and then click the third date format. Click **OK**.

c. Press Enter four times. Type the following inside address using four lines, but do *not* press Enter after the last line:

Ms. Mary Walker-Huelsman, Director
Florida Port Community College Career Center
2745 Oakland Avenue
St. Petersburg, FL 33713

d. Press Enter two times, type **Dear Ms. Walker-Huelsman:** and then press Enter two times. Type, exactly as shown with the intentional misspelling, and then watch *assistence* as you press Spacebar after typing it: **I am seeking the assistence**

e. Type **of the Career Center in my job search.** Press Enter two times.

f. On the **Insert tab**, in the **Text Group**, click the **Object button arrow**, and then click **Text from File**. From your student data files, locate and insert the file **w02D_Cover_Letter_Text**.

g. Scroll to view the lower portion of the page, and be sure your insertion point is in the empty paragraph mark at the end. Press Enter, type **Sincerely,** and then press Enter four times. Type **Sarah Villmosky** and press Enter two times. Type **Enclosure** and then **Save** your document.

h. Press Ctrl + Home. On the **Home tab**, in the **Editing group**, click **Find**. In the **Navigation** pane that opens on the left, click in the search box, and then type **journalism** In the letter, double-click the yellow highlighted word *Journalism* and type **Media Studies**

(Project 2D Cover Letter continues on the next page)

Skills Review Project 2D Cover Letter (continued)

i. **Close** the **Navigation** pane, and then on the **Home tab**, in the **Editing group**, click **Replace**. In the **Find and Replace** dialog box, in the **Find what** box, replace the existing text by typing **SPNT** In the **Replace with** box, type **St. Petersburg News and Times** Click **More** to expand the dialog box, select the **Match case** check box, click **Replace All**, and then click **OK**. Two replacements are made. **Close** the **Find and Replace** dialog box.

j. In the paragraph that begins *I am available*, hold down Ctrl, and then click anywhere in the first sentence. Drag the selected sentence to the end of the paragraph by positioning the small vertical line that floats with the point to the left of the paragraph mark.

3 Below the paragraph that begins *I have previous*, click to position the insertion point in the blank paragraph, and then press Enter one time. On the **Insert tab**, in the **Tables group**, click **Table**. In the **Table grid**, in the third row, click the second square to insert a **2×3** table. Type the following information in the table:

Editorial experience:	Writing, editing, interviewing
Computer proficiency:	CS InDesign, QuarkXPress, Microsoft Publisher
Education focus:	Media Studies and Journalism

a. Point outside of the upper left corner of the table and click the **table move handle** button to select the entire table. On the **Layout tab**, in the **Cell Size group**, click **AutoFit**, and then click **AutoFit Contents**.

b. With the table selected, on the **Table Tools Design tab**, in the **Table Styles group**, click **More**. Under **Plain Tables**, click the second style—**Table Grid Light**.

c. With the table still selected, on the **Home tab**, in the **Paragraphs group**, click **Center**. **Save** your document.

4 Press Ctrl + Home. On the **Review tab**, in the **Proofing group**, click **Spelling & Grammar**. For the spelling of *Villmosky*, in the **Spelling** pane, click **Ignore All**. For the spelling of *Huelsman*, click **Ignore All**.

a. For the grammar error *a*, click **Change**. Click **Change** to correct the misspelling of *intrested*. Click **Delete** to delete the duplicated word *for*. Change *activitys* to *activities*. Change *benificial* to *beneficial*. Click **OK** when the Spelling & Grammar check is complete.

b. In the paragraph that begins *I am willing*, in the third line, double-click the word *preparation*. In the **Proofing group**, click **Thesaurus**.

c. In the **Thesaurus** pane, point to *training*, click the arrow, and then click **Insert**. **Close** the **Thesaurus** pane.

d. Click **File tab**, and then in the lower right portion of the screen, click **Show All Properties**. In the **Tags** box, type **cover letter** and in the **Subject** box, type your course name and section number.

e. In the **Author** box, be sure your name is indicated and edit if necessary. On the left, click **Print**. If necessary, return to the document and make any necessary changes. Save your document. If directed by your instructor to do so, submit your paper printout, your electronic image of your document that looks like a printed document, or your original Word file. **Close** Word.

END | You have completed Project 2D

Mastering Word Project 2E Table of Job Listings

Apply 2A skills from these Objectives:

1. Create a Table
2. Format a Table
3. Present a Word Document Online

In the following Mastering Word project, you will create an announcement for new job postings at the Career Center. Your completed document will look similar to Figure 2.39.

PROJECT FILES

For Project 2E, you will need the following files:

New blank Word document

w02E_New_Jobs

You will save your document as:

Lastname_Firstname_2E_Job_Listings

PROJECT RESULTS

Build From Scratch

Florida Port Community College Career Center

Job Alert! New Positions for Computer Science Majors!

April 11

Florida Port Community College Career Center has new jobs available for both part-time and full-time positions in Computer Science. Some of these jobs are temporary, some are for a specific project with a defined beginning and ending date, and some are open-ended with the potential for permanent employment. The following jobs were posted in the past week. These listings are just in, so apply now to be one of the first candidates considered!

For further information about any of these new jobs, or a complete listing of jobs that are available through the Career Center, please call Mary Walker-Huelsman at (727) 555-0030 or visit our website at www.fpcc.pro/careers.

New Computer Science Listings for the Week of April 11

POSITION	TYPE	LOCATION
Computer Engineer	Full-time, two months	Clearwater
Project Assistant	Full-time, three months	Coral Springs
Software Developer	Full-time, open-ended	Tampa
UI Designer	Part-time, two months	St. Petersburg

To help prepare yourself before applying for these jobs, we recommend that you review the following articles on our website at www.fpcc.pro/careers.

Topic	Article Title
Research	Working in Computer Science Fields
Interviewing	Interviewing in Startup Companies

Lastname_Firstname_2E_Job_Listings

Word 2016, Windows 10, Microsoft Corporation

FIGURE 2.39

(Project 2E Table of Job Listings continues on the next page)

CONTENT-BASED ASSESSMENTS (MASTERY AND TRANSFER OF LEARNING)

Mastering Word | Project 2E Table of Job Listings (continued)

1 Start Word and display a blank document; display formatting marks and rulers. **Save** the document in your **Word Chapter 2** folder as **Lastname_Firstname_2E_Job_Listings** and then add the file name to the footer.

2 Type **Florida Port Community College Career Center** and press Enter. Type **Job Alert! New Positions for Computer Science Majors!** and press Enter. Type **April 11** and press Enter. **Insert** the file **w02E_New_Jobs**.

3 At the top of the document, select and **Center** the three title lines. Select the title *Florida Port Community College Career Center*, change the **Font Size** to **20 pt** and apply **Bold**. Apply **Bold** to the second and third title lines. Locate the paragraph that begins *For further*, and then below that paragraph, position the insertion point in the second blank paragraph. **Insert** a **3x4** table. Enter the following in the table:

POSITION	TYPE	LOCATION
Computer Engineer	Full-time, two months	Clearwater
Software Developer	Full-time, open-ended	Tampa
UI Designer	Part-time, two months	St. Petersburg

4 In the table, point to the upper left corner of the cell *Software Developer* to display the **Row Insertion** button, and then click to insert a new row. In the new row, type the following information so that the job titles remain in alphabetic order:

Project Assistant	Full-time, three months	Coral Springs

5 Select the entire table. On the **Table Tools Layout tab**, in the **Cell Size group**, click **AutoFit**, and then click **AutoFit Contents**. With the table still selected, on the **Home tab**, **Center** the table. With the table still selected, on the **Layout tab**, add **6 pt Spacing Before** and **6 pt Spacing After**.

6 With the table still selected, remove all table borders, and then add a **Custom 1 pt** solid line top border and bottom border. Select all three cells in the first row, apply **Bold**, and then **Center** the text. Click anywhere in the first row, and then on the **Table Tools Layout tab**, in the **Rows & Columns group**, insert a row above. Merge the three cells in the new top row, and then type **New Computer Science Listings for the Week of April 11** Notice that the new row keeps the formatting of the row from which it was created.

7 In the last blank paragraph at the bottom of the document, **Insert** a **2×3** table. Enter the following:

Topic	Article Title
Research	Working in Computer Science Fields
Interviewing	Interviewing in Startup Companies

8 Select the entire table. On the **Table Tools Layout tab**, in the **Cell Size group**, use the **AutoFit** button to **AutoFit Contents**. On the **Home tab**, **Center** the table. On the **Layout tab**, add **6 pt Spacing Before** and **6 pt Spacing After**. With the table still selected, remove all table borders, and then add a **Custom 1 pt** solid line top border and bottom border. Select the cells in the first row, apply **Bold**, and then **Center** the text.

9 Click the **File tab** to display **Backstage** view, and then in the lower right portion of the screen, click **Show All Properties**. In the **Tags** box type **new listings, computer science** and in the **Subject** box type your course name and section number. In the **Author** box, be sure your name is indicated and edit if necessary.

10 On the left, click **Print** to display **Print Preview**. If necessary, return to the document and make any necessary changes. **Save** your document, and then if you want to do so, present your document online to a fellow classmate. If directed by your instructor to do so, submit your paper printout, your electronic image of your document that looks like a printed document, or your original Word file. **Close** Word.

END | You have completed Project 2E

CONTENT-BASED ASSESSMENTS (MASTERY AND TRANSFER OF LEARNING)

MyITLab grader

Mastering Word Project 2F Career Tips Memo

Apply 2B skills from these Objectives:

4 Create a Custom Word Template
5 Correct and Reorganize Text
6 Use the Proofing Options and Print an Envelope

In the following Mastering Word project, you will create a memo that includes job tips for students and graduates using the services of the Florida Port Community College Career Center. Your completed document will look similar to Figure 2.40.

PROJECT FILES

For Project 2F, you will need the following files:

w02F_Memo_Template
w02F_Memo_Text

You will save your documents as:

Lastname_Firstname_2F_Career_Tips

PROJECT RESULTS

Florida Port Community College Career Center

Memo

DATE: January 12, 2019

TO: Florida Port Community College Students and Graduates

FROM: Mary Walker-Huelsman, Director

SUBJECT: Using the Career Center

Tips for Students and Recent Graduates of Florida Port Community College

It is no surprise that after you leave college, you will be entering one of the most competitive job markets on record. That doesn't mean it's impossible to get your dream job. It does, however, mean that it's critical that you know how to put your best self forward to job interviewers and that you highlight all of your academic, personal, and professional achievements in a way that will help you stand out from the crowd. An Associate degree from Florida Port Community College is just the first step on your journey to getting the professional career that you want.

Give 100 Percent to Every Job

Treat every job as a career. Be willing to go beyond your assignment and complete tasks not delegated to you. Take the initiative to see ways to contribute to the company. Be willing to stay if there is unfinished work. You never know who you will meet on any job. Making a positive impression every time will give you a network of people who may help you down the road. Networking is an established means professionals use to further their careers. You can always benefit from networking. You will distinguish yourself from potential competitors if you truly give 100 percent to each job. Always remember these job basics:

Job Item	Tip for Success
Time Management	Show up on time and don't hurry to leave
Attire	Dress appropriately for the job
Work Area	Keep your work area neat and organized

Use the Career Center

Here at the Career Center and on our website, we offer tips on how to write a stellar resume and a cover letter that puts your hard work up front and center. Have you volunteered somewhere? Have you participated at a club at school? Were you a TA or a tutor? Did you make the Dean's list or graduate with honors? These are the kinds of achievements interviewers want to see. Meet with your career guidance counselor and together, come up with a plan to find the jobs that you want and get the important interview.

Lastname_Firstname_2F_Career_Tips

Word 2016, Windows 10, Microsoft Corporation

FIGURE 2.40

(Project 2F Career Tips Memo continues on the next page)

CONTENT-BASED ASSESSMENTS (MASTERY AND TRANSFER OF LEARNING)

Mastering Word Project 2F Career Tips Memo (continued)

1 Start Word. From your student data files, open the file **02F_Memo_Template.**

2 Display the **Save As** dialog box. Navigate to your **Word Chapter 2** folder, and then in the **File name** box, using your own name, type **Lastname_Firstname_2F_Career_Tips**

3 Add the file name to the footer. At the top of your document, in the *DATE* paragraph, click to the right of the tab formatting mark, and then type **January 12, 2019** Use a similar technique to add the following information:

TO:	**Florida Port Community College Students and Graduates**
FROM:	**Mary Walker-Huelsman, Director**
SUBJECT:	**Using the CC**

4 Position the insertion point in the blank paragraph below the memo heading. **Insert** the file **w02F_Memo_Text**, and then press Backspace one time to remove the blank line at the end of the inserted text.

5 Press Ctrl + Home to move to the top of the document. By using either the **Spelling & Grammar** command on the Review tab or by right-clicking words that display blue or red wavy underlines, correct or ignore words flagged as spelling, grammar, or word usage errors. *Note*: If you are checking an entire document, it is usually preferable to move to the top of the document, and then use the Spelling & Grammar command so that you do not overlook any flagged words.

6 In the paragraph that begins *Treat every job*, in the second line of the paragraph, locate and double-click **donate**. On the **Review tab**, in the **Proofing group**, click **Thesaurus**, and then from the **Thesaurus** pane, change the word to *contribute*. In the last line of the same paragraph, point to **fundamentals**, right-click, point to **Synonyms**, and then click **basics**.

7 In the paragraph that begins *An Associate degree*, move the first sentence to the end of the paragraph.

8 At the end of the paragraph that begins *Treat every job*, click in the blank paragraph, and then **Insert** a **2x4** table. Type the following information in the table:

Job Item	**Tip for Success**
Time Management	**Show up on time and don't hurry to leave**
Attire	**Dress appropriately for the job**
Work Area	**Keep your work area neat and organized**

9 Select the entire table. **AutoFit Contents**, and then apply the **Grid Table 1 Light – Accent 1** table style—under **Grid Tables**, in the first row, the second style. **Center** the table.

10 Press Ctrl + Home to move to the top of your document. Using Match Case, replace all instances of *CC* with *Career Center*.

11 Click the **File tab**, and then click **Show All Properties**. As the **Tags**, type **memo, job tips** As the **Subject**, type your course name and section number. Be sure your name is indicated as the **Author**, and edit if necessary. View the Print Preview, and make any necessary changes. Save your document. If directed by your instructor to do so, submit your paper printout, your electronic image of your document that looks like a printed document, or your original Word file. **Close** Word.

END | You have completed Project 2F

CONTENT-BASED ASSESSMENTS (MASTERY AND TRANSFER OF LEARNING)

MyITLab grader

Apply 2A and 2B skills from these Objectives:

1 Create a Table
2 Format a Table
3 Present a Word Document Online
4 Create a Custom Word Template
5 Correct and Reorganize Text
6 Use the Proofing Options and Print an Envelope

Mastering Word Project 2G Application Letter and Resume

In the following Mastering Word project, you will create a letter and resume. Your completed document will look similar to Figure 2.41.

PROJECT FILES

For Project 2G, you will need the following files:

w02G_Letter_and_Resume
w02G_Letter_Text

You will save your documents as:

You will save your document as
Lastname_Firstname_2G_Letter_and_Resume

PROJECT RESULTS

William Franklin
4224 White Oak Road
Tampa, FL 33601
(813) 555-0112
wfranklin@alcona.net

October 7, 2015

Ms. Mary Walker-Huelsman, Director
Florida Port Community College Career Center
2745 Oakland Avenue
St. Petersburg, FL 33713

Dear Ms. Walker-Huelsman:

On the Florida Port Community College Alumni website, I see that the Career Center has a job listing that interests me and for which I have the necessary skills and education. Specifically, this is the position for a Business Programmer Analyst in enterprise cloud computing.

The job listing indicates that the company would like to fill this position very quickly. As you requested on the website, I am faxing both my resume and this cover letter. I will send a printed copy, and can also send the resume in PDF format if that would be more convenient.

The job description had several very explicit requirements. I would like to point out my qualifications in a few of the specified areas:

Education	Bachelor of Science, Business Management
Experience	Two years Computer Support experience at a major university
Required Certifications	MCITP, MCDST

I could be available to begin work in as few as two weeks. The job description does not specify exactly where this company does business. I currently live in Tampa, but would be willing to relocate.

Sincerely,

William Franklin

Lastname_Firstname_2G_Letter_and_Resume

William Franklin
4224 White Oak Road
Tampa, FL 33601
(813) 555-0112
wfranklin@alcona.net

OBJECTIVE To obtain a Business Programmer Analyst position that will use my technical and communications skills and computer support experience.

EDUCATION
Florida International University, Miami, FL
Bachelor of Science, Business Management
September 2014 to May 2016

Florida Port Community College, St. Petersburg, FL
Associate of Science, Business Computing
September 2012 to May 2014

RELEVANT EXPERIENCE
IT Analyst, Florida International University, Miami, FL
January 2014 to present
- Provide local and remote desktop support across campus
- Link computers via wireless router
- Provide support for Windows, Macintosh, and Linux computers
- Provide support for Windows Azure cloud platform
- Provide support for Microsoft and Adobe Creative Suite software products
- Analyze and resolve network problems

Computer Technician (part-time), Coast Off Road Racing, St Petersburg, FL
September 2012 to January 2014
- Installed computer hardware
- Installed, updated, and upgraded application software
- Installed, updated, and upgraded security software
- Performed all computer maintenance
- Updated device drivers for computer peripherals

CERTIFICATIONS
- Microsoft Certified IT Professional (MCITP)
- Microsoft Certified Desktop Support Technician (MCDST)
- Microsoft Office Specialist (MOS) in Word, Excel, Access, and Outlook
- Apple Certified Desktop Technician (ACDT)

Lastname_Firstname_2G_Letter_and_Resume

FIGURE 2.41

(Project 2G Application Letter and Resume continues on the next page)

Mastering Word Project 2G Application Letter and Resume (continued)

1 Start Word. From your student data files, open the file **w02G_Letter_and_Resume.**

2 Display the **Save As** dialog box. Navigate to your **Word Chapter 2** folder, and then in the **File name** box, using your own name, type **Lastname_Firstname_2G_Letter_and_Resume**

3 Add the file name to the footer. Be sure that rulers and formatting marks display. On **Page 1**, click in the blank paragraph below the letterhead, and then press Enter three times. Use the **Date & Time** command to insert the current date using the third format, and then press Enter four times. Type the following:

Ms. Mary Walker-Huelsman, Director
Florida Port Community College Career Center
2745 Oakland Avenue
St. Petersburg, FL 33713

4 Press Enter two times, type **Dear Ms. Walker-Huelsman:** and press Enter two times. **Insert** the text from the file **w02G_Letter_Text** and press Backspace one time to remove the blank line at the bottom of the selected text.

5 Press Ctrl + Home to move to the top of the document. By using either the **Spelling & Grammar** command on the **Review tab** or by right-clicking words that display blue or red wavy underlines, correct or ignore words flagged as spelling, grammar, or word usage errors. *Hint*: If you are checking an entire document, it is usually preferable to move to the top of the document, and then use the Spelling & Grammar command so that you do not overlook any flagged words.

6 Press Ctrl + Home to move to the top of the document again, and then replace all instances of **posting** with **listing**

7 In the paragraph that begins *The job description*, use the Thesaurus pane or the Synonyms command on the shortcut menu to change *specific* to *explicit* and *credentials* to *qualifications*.

8 In the paragraph that begins *I currently live in Tampa*, select the first sentence of the paragraph and drag it to the end of the same paragraph.

9 Click to position your insertion point in the *second* blank line below the paragraph that begins *The job description*. **Insert** a **2x3** table, and then type the text shown in Table 1.

TABLE 1

Education	Bachelor of Science, Business Management
Experience	Two years Computer Support experience at a major university
Required Certifications	MCITP, MCDST

10 Select the entire table. **AutoFit Contents**, and then apply the **Table Grid Light** table style—under **Plain Tables**, in the first row, the first style. **Center** the table.

11 In the resume on **Page 2**, insert a new second row in the table. In the first cell of the new row, type **OBJECTIVE** and then apply **Bold** to the text you just typed. Press Tab. Type **To obtain a Business Programmer Analyst position that will use my technical and communications skills and computer support experience.** In the same cell, add **12 pt Spacing After**.

12 Select the entire table. On the **Layout tab**, **AutoFit Contents**. Remove the table borders, and then display the **Borders and Shading** dialog box. With the table selected, create a **Custom** single solid line **1 1/2 pt** top border.

13 In the first row of the resume table, select both cells and then **Merge Cells**. **Center** the five lines and apply **Bold**. In the first row, select **William Franklin** and change the **Font Size** to **20 pt** and add **24 pt Spacing Before**. In the email address at the bottom of the first row, add **24 pt Spacing After**.

14 In the cell to the right of *RELEVANT EXPERIENCE*, below the line that begins *January 2014*, apply bullets to the six lines that comprise the job duties. Create a similar bulleted list for the duties as a Computer Technician. In the cell to the right of *CERTIFICATIONS*, select all four lines and create a bulleted list.

15 Click the **File tab**, and then click **Show All Properties**. As the **Tags**, type **cover letter, resume** As the **Subject**, type your course name and section number. Be sure your name is indicated as the **Author**, and edit if necessary. View the Print Preview, and make any necessary changes. If directed by your instructor to do so, submit your paper printout, your electronic image of your document that looks like a printed document, or your original Word file. **Close** Word.

END | You have completed Project 2G

CONTENT-BASED ASSESSMENTS (CRITICAL THINKING)

Apply a combination of the 2A and 2B skills.

GO! Fix It Project 2H New Jobs **MyITLab**

GO! Make It Project 2I Training **MyITLab**

GO! Solve It Project 2J Job Postings **MyITLab**

GO! Solve It Project 2K Agenda

Build From Scratch

PROJECT FILES

For Project 2K, you will need the following file:

Agenda template from Word's Online templates

You will save your document as:

Lastname_Firstname_2K_Agenda

On Word's opening screen, search for an online template using the search term **formal meeting agenda** Create the agenda and then save it in your Word Chapter 2 folder as **Lastname_Firstname_2K_Agenda** Use the following information to prepare an agenda for an FPCC Career Center meeting.

The meeting will be chaired by Mary Walker-Huelsman. It will be the monthly meeting of the Career Center's staff—Kevin Rau, Marilyn Kelly, André Randolph, Susan Nguyen, and Charles James. The meeting will be held on March 15, 2016, at 3:00 p.m. The old business agenda items (open issues) include 1) seeking more job listings related to the printing and food service industries; 2) expanding the alumni website, and 3) the addition of a part-time trainer. The new business agenda items will include 1) writing a grant so the center can serve more students and alumni; 2) expanding the training area with 20 additional workstations; 3) purchase of new computers for the training room; and 4) renewal of printing service contract.

Add the file name to the footer, add your name, your course name, the section number, and then add the keywords **agenda, monthly staff meeting** to the Properties area. Submit as directed.

Performance Level

Performance Criteria	Exemplary: You consistently applied the relevant skills.	Proficient: You sometimes, but not always, applied the relevant skills.	Developing: You rarely or never applied the relevant skills.
Select an agenda template	Agenda template is appropriate for the information provided for the meeting.	Agenda template is used, but does not fit the information provided.	No template is used for the agenda.
Add appropriate information to the template	All information is inserted in the appropriate places.	All information is included, but not in the appropriate places.	Information is missing.
Format template information	All text in the template is properly aligned and formatted.	All text is included, but alignment or formatting is inconsistent.	No additional formatting has been added.

END | You have completed Project 2K

OUTCOMES-BASED ASSESSMENTS

RUBRIC

The following outcomes-based assessments are *open-ended assessments*. That is, there is no specific correct result; your result will depend on your approach to the information provided. Make *Professional Quality* your goal. Use the following scoring rubric to guide you in *how* to approach the problem and then to evaluate *how well* your approach solves the problem.

The *criteria*—Software Mastery, Content, Format and Layout, and Process—represent the knowledge and skills you have gained that you can apply to solving the problem. The *levels of performance*—Professional Quality, Approaching Professional Quality, or Needs Quality Improvements—help you and your instructor evaluate your result.

	Your completed project is of Professional Quality if you:	Your completed project is Approaching Professional Quality if you:	Your completed project Needs Quality Improvements if you:
1-Software Mastery	Choose and apply the most appropriate skills, tools, and features and identify efficient methods to solve the problem.	Choose and apply some appropriate skills, tools, and features, but not in the most efficient manner.	Choose inappropriate skills, tools, or features, or are inefficient in solving the problem.
2-Content	Construct a solution that is clear and well organized, contains content that is accurate, appropriate to the audience and purpose, and is complete. Provide a solution that contains no errors of spelling, grammar, or style.	Construct a solution in which some components are unclear, poorly organized, inconsistent, or incomplete. Misjudge the needs of the audience. Have some errors in spelling, grammar, or style, but the errors do not detract from comprehension.	Construct a solution that is unclear, incomplete, or poorly organized, contains some inaccurate or inappropriate content, and contains many errors of spelling, grammar, or style. Do not solve the problem.
3-Format and Layout	Format and arrange all elements to communicate information and ideas, clarify function, illustrate relationships, and indicate relative importance.	Apply appropriate format and layout features to some elements, but not others. Overuse features, causing minor distraction.	Apply format and layout that does not communicate information or ideas clearly. Do not use format and layout features to clarify function, illustrate relationships, or indicate relative importance. Use available features excessively, causing distraction.
4-Process	Use an organized approach that integrates planning, development, self-assessment, revision, and reflection.	Demonstrate an organized approach in some areas, but not others; or, use an insufficient process of organization throughout.	Do not use an organized approach to solve the problem.

OUTCOMES-BASED ASSESSMENTS (CRITICAL THINKING)

Apply a combination of the 2A and 2B skills.

GO! Think Project 2L Workshops

PROJECT FILES

Build From Scratch

For Project 2L, you will need the following files:

New blank Word document
w02L_Workshop_Information

You will save your document as:

Lastname_Firstname_2L_Workshops

The Florida Port Community College Career Center offers a series of workshops for both students and alumni. Any eligible student or graduate can attend the workshops, and there is no fee. Currently, the Career Center offers a three-session workshop covering Excel and Word, a two-session workshop covering Business Communication, and a one-session workshop covering Creating a Resume.

Print the w02L_Workshop_Information file and use the information to complete this project. Create an announcement with a title, an introductory paragraph, and a table listing the workshops and the topics covered in each workshop. Use the file w02L_Workshop_Information for help with the topics covered in each workshop. Format the table cells appropriately. Add an appropriate footer and document properties. Save the document as **Lastname_Firstname_2L_Workshops** and submit it as directed.

END | You have completed Project 2L

Build from Scratch

GO! Think! Project 2M Schedule MyITLab

Build from Scratch

You and GO! Project 2N Personal Resume MyITLab

Build from Scratch

GO! Collaborative Team Project Project 2O Bell Orchid Hotels MyITLab

Creating Research Papers, Newsletters, and Merged Mailing Labels

OUTCOMES

Create a research paper that includes citations and a bibliography.

OBJECTIVES

1. Create a Research Paper
2. Insert Footnotes in a Research Paper
3. Create Citations and a Bibliography in a Research Paper
4. Use Read Mode and PDF Reflow

PROJECT 3B

OUTCOMES

Create a multiple-column newsletter and merged mailing labels.

OBJECTIVES

5. Format a Multiple-Column Newsletter
6. Use Special Character and Paragraph Formatting
7. Create Mailing Labels Using Mail Merge

Guschenkova/Fotolia

In This Chapter

Microsoft Word provides many tools for creating complex documents. For example, Word has tools that enable you to create a research paper that includes citations, footnotes, and a bibliography. You can also create multiple-column newsletters, format the nameplate at the top of the newsletter, use special character formatting to create distinctive title text, and add borders and shading to paragraphs to highlight important information.

In this chapter, you will edit and format a research paper, create a two-column newsletter, and optionally create a set of mailing labels to mail the newsletter to multiple recipients.

The projects in this chapter relate to **University Medical Center**, which is a patient-care and research institution serving the metropolitan area of Memphis, Tennessee. Because of its outstanding reputation in the medical community and around the world, University Medical Center is able to attract top physicians, scientists, and researchers in all fields of medicine and achieve a level of funding that allows it to build and operate state-of-the-art facilities. A program in biomedical research was recently added. Individuals throughout the eastern United States travel to University Medical Center for diagnosis and care.

PROJECT 3A Research Paper

PROJECT ACTIVITIES

In Activities 3.01 through 3.13, you will edit and format a research paper that contains an overview of a new area of study. This paper was created by Gerard Foster, a medical intern at University Medical Center, for distribution to his classmates studying various physiologic monitoring devices. Your completed document will look similar to Figure 3.1.

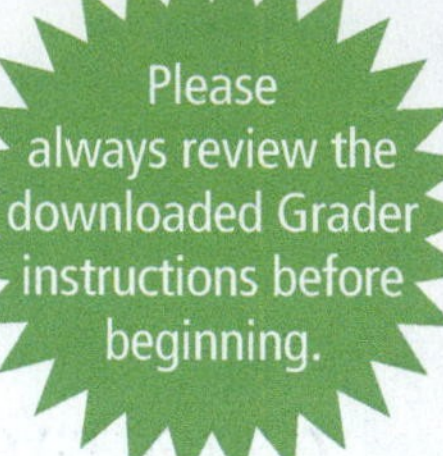

PROJECT FILES

If your instructor wants you to submit Project 3A in the MyITLab Grader system, log in to MyITLab, locate Grader Project 3A, and then download the files for this project.

For Project 3A, you will need the following file:
w03A_Quantitative_Technology

You will save your document as:
Lastname_Firstname_3A_Quantitative_Technology

GO! Walk Thru Project 3A

PROJECT RESULTS

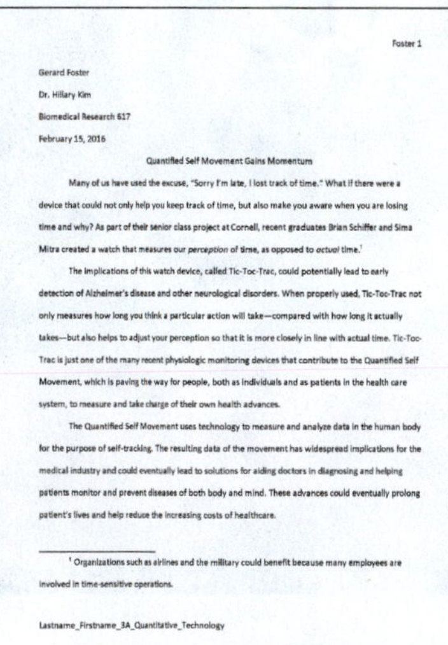

Foster 1

Gerard Foster

Dr. Hillary Kim

Biomedical Research 617

February 15, 2016

Quantified Self Movement Gains Momentum

Many of us have used the excuse, "Sorry I'm late, I lost track of time." What if there were a device that could not only help you keep track of time, but also make you aware when you are losing time and why? As part of their senior class project at Cornell, recent graduates Brian Schiffer and Sima Mitra created a watch that measures our *perception* of time, as opposed to *actual* time.[1]

The implications of this watch device, called Tic-Toc-Trac, could potentially lead to early detection of Alzheimer's disease and other neurological disorders. When properly used, Tic-Toc-Trac not only measures how long you think a particular action will take—compared with how long it actually takes—but also helps to adjust your perception so that it is more closely in line with actual time. Tic-Toc-Trac is just one of the many recent physiologic monitoring devices that contribute to the Quantified Self Movement, which is paving the way for people, both as individuals and as patients in the health care system, to measure and take charge of their own health advances.

The Quantified Self Movement uses technology to measure and analyze data in the human body for the purpose of self-tracking. The resulting data of the movement has widespread implications for the medical industry and could eventually lead to solutions for aiding doctors in diagnosing and helping patients monitor and prevent diseases of both body and mind. These advances could eventually prolong patient's lives and help reduce the increasing costs of healthcare.

[1] Organizations such as airlines and the military could benefit because many employees are involved in time-sensitive operations.

Lastname_Firstname_3A_Quantitative_Technology

Foster 2

There are many other practical uses of such intensive data tracking by using these physiologic monitoring devices. What if you could predict the perfect time to start studying in order to achieve the best grade on a test?

Gary Wolf, who along with Kevin Kelley started the Quantified Self Movement, theorizes that memorization is only a small part of learning and that there is an ideal moment to practice what one wants to memorize. They believe that if one practices too soon the time is wasted and if one practices too late the material is forgotten and then must be relearned. They conclude that the right time to practice is just at the moment one is about to forget. They point to the use of a computer to practice in which a *spaced repetition* program can predict when one is likely to forget an item and then schedule practice at the right time.

Accurate records and data have always been essential components of health care; however, the notion and widespread implications of using technology to help record and keep track of this data is still in its infancy.[2] New devices, apps, and websites to measure calorie input, body fat, heart rate, blood pressure, blood oxygen levels, water intake, sleep patterns and other diagnostics are being created every day. Dr. Eric Topol indicates that "the emergence of powerful tools to digitize human beings with full support of a digital infrastructure creates an unparalleled opportunity to inevitably and forever change the face of how health care is delivered" (Topol 5).

Doctors have long urged their patients to seek ways to better monitor and control their food intake and dietary habits. According to the Center for Disease Control and Prevention, obesity affects many adults (35.7% by some estimates) in the United States (Ogden). Doctors think that many diseases and conditions are exacerbated by an inappropriate diet and inadequate exercise. Medical professionals

[2] The Department of Health and Human Services indicates that the use of Health Information Technology will improve the quality of health care.

Lastname_Firstname_3A_Quantitative_Technology

Foster 3

are often at a standstill, because their patients claim they want to lose weight but cannot figure out how to control their diets, especially when they are unaware of how much they are eating or how little they are exercising.

Here is another instance where quantitative technology can make keeping track of intake and output simple and easy. Instead of having to write down every calorie, fat gram, and ounce of protein or carbohydrate consumed, there are now smartphone apps, tablet apps, and computer programs that will enable you to enter and store all that data easily and let you track how food has made you feel when you ate it. By analyzing the data at the end of a given week or month, an individual can make changes that will directly help him or her adjust food intake or exercise levels to reach a desired weight and to take the mystery out of why his or her current dietary plan may not be working.

The healthcare industry is taking notice. Many hospitals are planning for the effects of personalized medicine. There is a huge increase in the amount of data-driven information, and doctors and medical staffs are being encouraged to communicate with their patients about the data they track, some of which could permanently change the diagnoses and treatment of chronic conditions. Mining of data could even support research into the genomic basis of a disease (Glaser 28).

Lastname_Firstname_3A_Quantitative_Technology

Foster 4

Works Cited

Glaser, John P., and Claudia Salzberg. *The Strategic Application of Information Technology in Health Care Organizations*. San Francisco: Jossey-Bass, 2011. Print.

Ogden, C. L. *NCHS Data Brief Number 82*. 01 January 2012. Web. 17 January 2016.

Topol, Eric J. *The Creative Destruction of Medicine*. New York: Basic Books, 2012. Print.

Lastname_Firstname_3A_Quantitative_Technology

FIGURE 3.1 Project 3A Quantitative Technology

Objective 1 Create a Research Paper

GO! Learn How Video W3-1

When you write a research paper or a report for college or business, follow a format prescribed by one of the standard ***style guides***—a manual that contains standards for the design and writing of documents. The two most commonly used styles for research papers are those created by the ***Modern Language Association (MLA)*** and the ***American Psychological Association (APA)***; there are several others.

Activity 3.01 | Formatting the Spacing and First-Page Information for a Research Paper

ALERT!

To submit as an autograded project, log into MyITLab, download the files for this project, and then use those files instead of w03A_Quantitative_Technology.

When formatting the text for your research paper, refer to the standards for the style guide that you have chosen. In this Activity, you will create a research paper using the MLA style. The MLA style uses 1-inch margins, a 0.5" first line indent, and double spacing throughout the body of the document with no extra space above or below paragraphs.

1. Start Word. On the left, click **Open Other Documents**, click **Browse**, and then navigate to the student data files that accompany this chapter. Locate and open the document **w03A_Quantitative_Technology**. If necessary, display the formatting marks and rulers. In the location where you are storing your projects for this chapter, create a new folder named **Word Chapter 3** and then **Save** the file in the folder as **Lastname_Firstname_3A_Quantitative_Technology**

2. Press Ctrl + A to select the entire document. On the **Home tab**, in the **Paragraph group**, click **Line and Paragraph Spacing**, and then change the line spacing to **2.0**. On the **Layout tab**, in the **Paragraph group**, change the **Spacing After** to **0 pt**.

3. Press Ctrl + Home to deselect and move to the top of the document. Press Enter one time to create a blank paragraph at the top of the document, and then click to position the insertion point in the blank paragraph. Type **Gerard Foster** and press Enter.

4. Type **Dr. Hillary Kim** and press Enter. Type **Biomedical Research 617** and press Enter. Type **February 15, 2016** and press Enter.

5. Type **Quantified Self Movement Gains Momentum** and then press Ctrl + E, which is the keyboard shortcut to center a paragraph of text. Click **Save**, and then compare your screen with Figure 3.2.

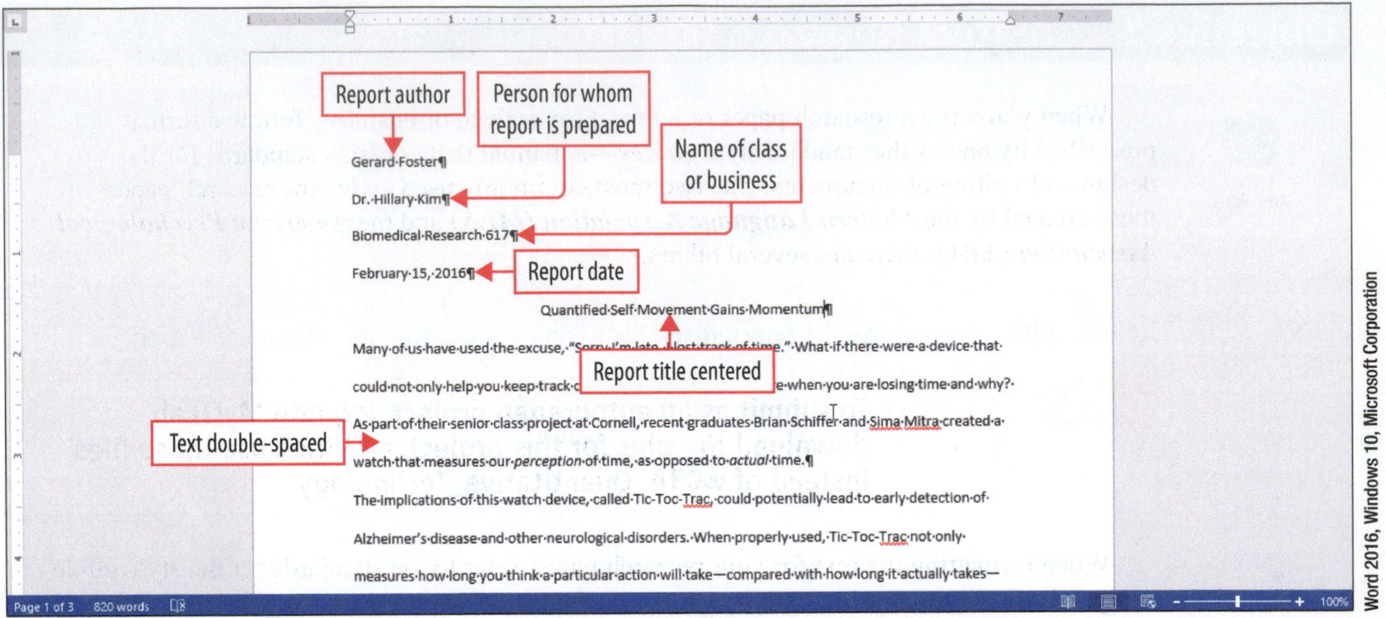

FIGURE 3.2

More Knowledge Creating a Document Heading for a Research Paper

On the first page of an MLA-style research paper, on the first line, type the report author. On the second line, type the person for whom the report is prepared—for example, your professor or supervisor. On the third line, type the name of the class or business. On the fourth line, type the date. On the fifth line, type the report title and center it.

Activity 3.02 | Formatting the Page Numbering and Paragraph Indents for a Research Paper

1.3.5, 2.2.3

1 On the **Insert tab**, in the **Header & Footer group**, click **Header**, and then at the bottom of the list, click **Edit Header**.

2 Type **Foster** and then press Spacebar.

Recall that the text you insert into a header or footer displays on every page of a document. Within a header or footer, you can insert many different types of information; for example, automatic page numbers, the date, the time, the file name, or pictures.

3 Under **Header and Footer Tools**, on the **Design tab**, in the **Header & Footer group**, click **Page Number**, and then point to **Current Position**. In the gallery, under **Simple**, click **Plain Number**. Compare your screen with Figure 3.3.

Word will automatically number the pages using this number format.

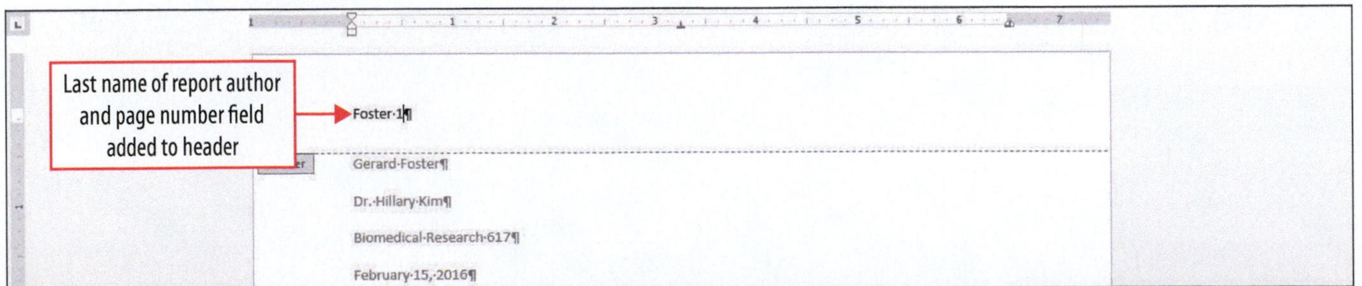

Word 2016, Windows 10, Microsoft Corporation

FIGURE 3.3

4 On the **Home tab**, in the **Paragraph group**, click **Align Right**. Double-click anywhere in the document to close the Header area.

5 Near the top of **Page 1**, locate the paragraph beginning *Many of us*, and then click to position the insertion point at the beginning of the paragraph. By moving the vertical scroll bar, scroll to view the end of the document, hold down Shift, and then click to the right of the last paragraph mark to select all of the text from the insertion point to the end of the document. Release Shift.

6 With the text selected, in the **Paragraph group**, click the **Dialog Box Launcher** button to display the **Paragraph** dialog box.

7 On the **Indents and Spacing tab**, under **Indentation**, click the **Special arrow**, and then click **First line**. In the **By** box, be sure **0.5"** displays. Click **OK**. Compare your screen with Figure 3.4.

The MLA style uses 0.5-inch indents at the beginning of the first line of every paragraph. *Indenting*—moving the beginning of the first line of a paragraph to the right or left of the rest of the paragraph—provides visual cues to the reader to help divide the document text and make it easier to read.

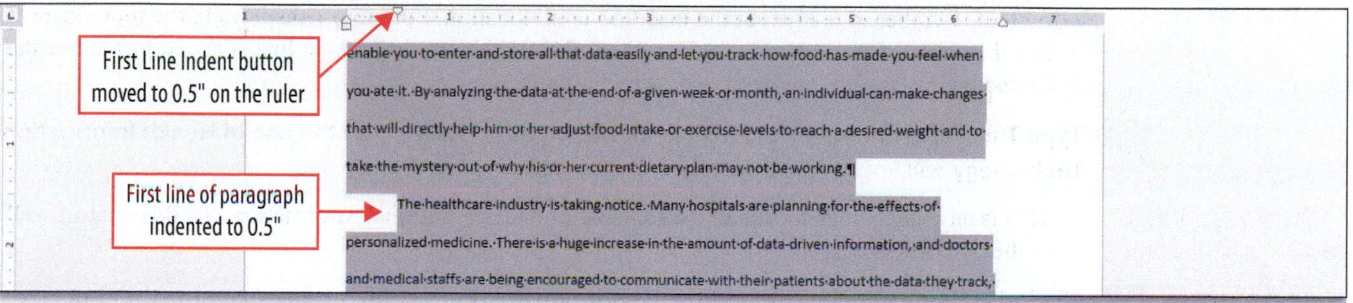

Word 2016, Windows 10, Microsoft Corporation

FIGURE 3.4

ANOTHER WAY On the ruler, point to the First Line Indent button, and then drag the button to 0.5" on the horizontal ruler.

8 Press Ctrl + Home to deselect and move to the top of the document. On the **Insert tab**, in **the Header & Footer group**, click **Footer**, and then at the bottom of the list click **Edit Footer**.

9 In the **Insert group**, click **Document Info**, and then click **File Name**. On the ribbon, click **Close Header and Footer**.

The file name in the footer is *not* part of the research report format, but it is included in projects in this chapter so that you and your instructor can identify your work.

10 **Save** your document.

***More* Knowledge**

Suppressing the Page Number on the First Page of a Document

Some style guidelines require that the page number and other header and footer information on the first page be hidden from view—***suppressed***. To hide the information contained in the header and footer areas on Page 1 of a document, double-click in the header or footer area. Then, under Header and Footer Tools, on the Design tab, in the Options group, select the Different First Page check box.

Objective 2 Insert Footnotes in a Research Paper

GO! Learn How
Video W3-2

Within report text, numbers mark the location of ***notes***—information that expands on the topic being discussed but that does not fit well in the document text. The numbers refer to ***footnotes***—notes placed at the bottom of the page containing the note, or to ***endnotes***—notes placed at the end of a document or chapter.

Activity 3.03 | Inserting Footnotes

MOS
4.1.1

You can add footnotes as you type your document or after your document is complete. Word renumbers the footnotes automatically, so footnotes do not need to be entered in order, and if one footnote is removed, the remaining footnotes automatically renumber.

1. Scroll to view the upper portion of **Page 2**, and then locate the paragraph that begins *Accurate records*. In the third line of the paragraph, click to position the insertion point to the right of the period after *infancy*.

2. On the **References tab**, in the **Footnotes group**, click **Insert Footnote**.

   Word creates space for a footnote in the footnote area at the bottom of the page and adds a footnote number to the text at the insertion point location. Footnote *1* displays in the footnote area, and the insertion point moves to the right of the number. A short black line is added just above the footnote area. You do not need to type the footnote number.

3. Type **The Department of Health & Human Services indicates that the use of Health Information Technology will improve the quality of health care.**

   This is an explanatory footnote; the footnote provides additional information that does not fit well in the body of the report.

4. Click the **Home tab**, and then in the **Font group** and **Paragraph group**, examine the font size and line spacing settings. Notice that the new footnote displays in 10 pt font size and is single-spaced, even though the font size of the document text is 11 pt and the text is double-spaced, as shown in Figure 3.5.

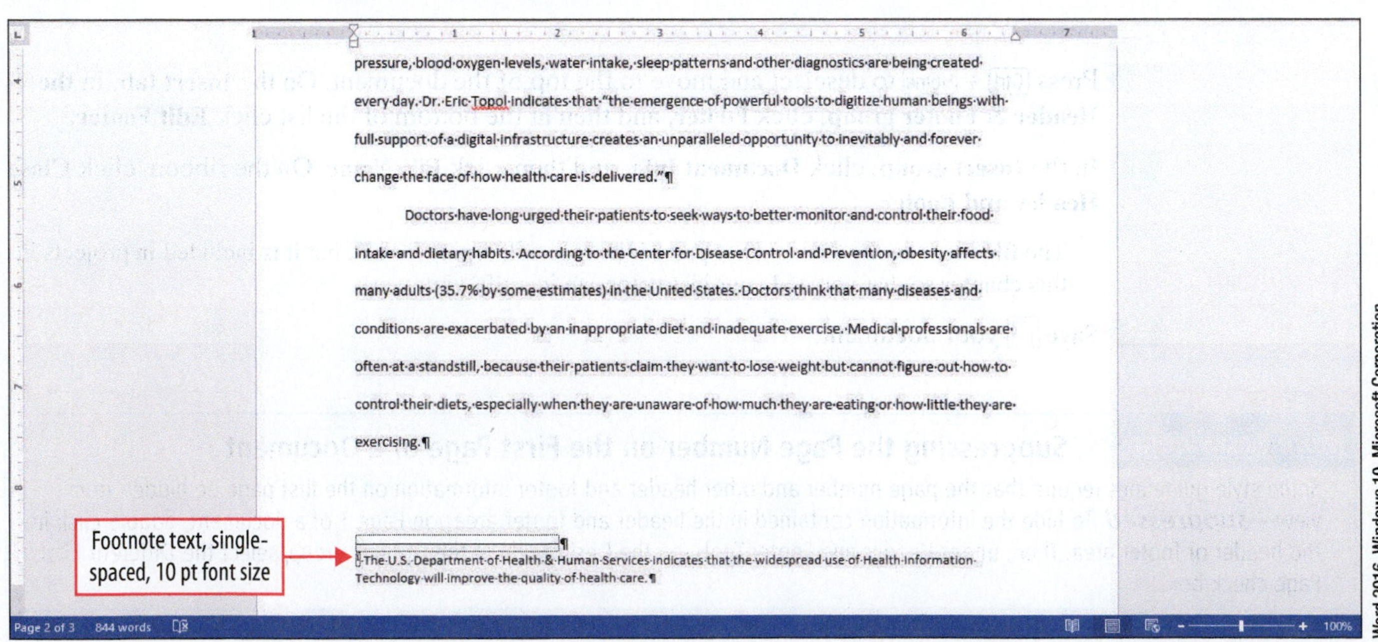

Word 2016, Windows 10, Microsoft Corporation

FIGURE 3.5

5 Scroll to view the top of **Page 1**, and then locate the paragraph that begins *Many of us*. At the end of the paragraph, click to position the insertion point to the right of the period following *time*.

6 On the **References tab**, in the **Footnotes group**, click **Insert Footnote**. Type **Organizations such as airlines and the military could benefit because many employees are involved in time-sensitive operations.** Notice that the footnote you just added becomes the new footnote *1*. Click **Save**, and then compare your screen with Figure 3.6.

The first footnote that you typed, which is on Page 2 and begins *The Department of Health*, is renumbered as footnote 2.

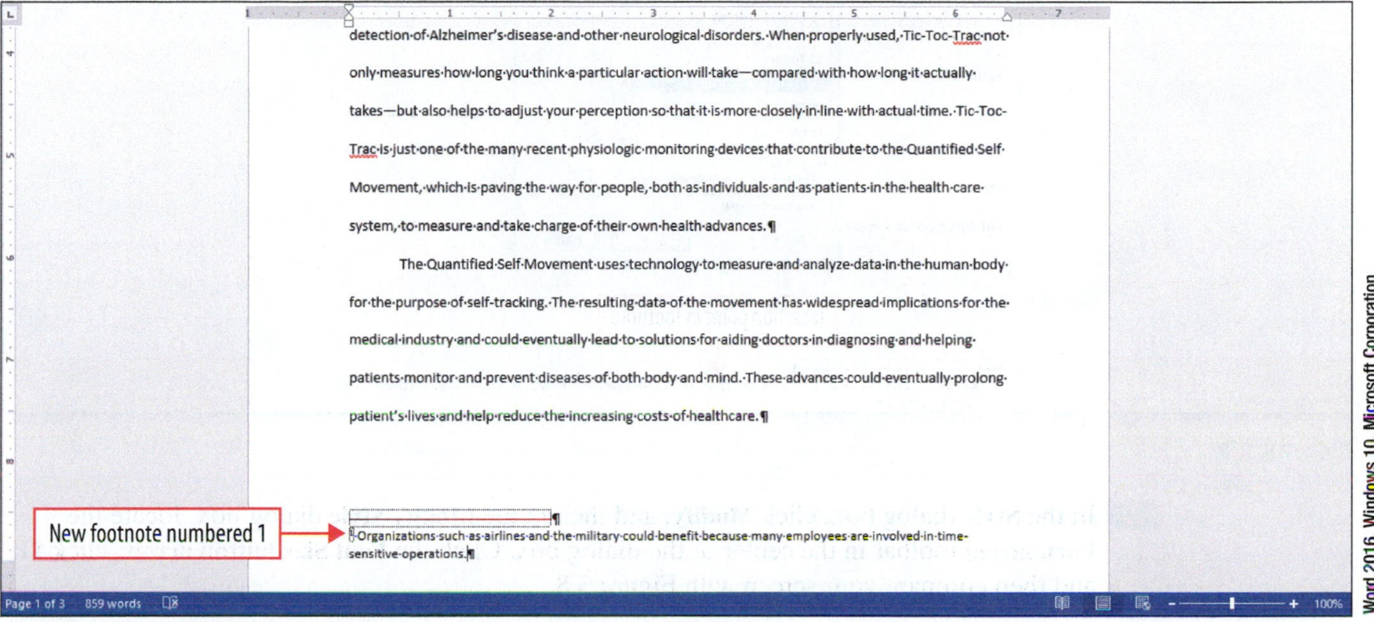

FIGURE 3.6

***More* Knowledge** **Using Symbols Rather Than Numbers for Notes**

Instead of using numbers to designate footnotes, you can use standard footnote symbols. The seven traditional symbols, available from the Footnote and Endnote dialog box, in order, are * (asterisk), † (dagger), ‡ (double dagger), § (section mark), || (parallels), ¶ (paragraph mark), and # (number or pound sign). This sequence can be continuous (this is the default setting), or it can begin anew with each page.

Activity 3.04 | Modifying a Footnote Style

4.1.2

Microsoft Word contains built-in paragraph formats called ***styles***—groups of formatting commands, such as font, font size, font color, paragraph alignment, and line spacing—that can be applied to a paragraph with one command.

The default style for footnote text is a single-spaced paragraph that uses a 10-point Calibri font and no paragraph indents. MLA style specifies double-spaced text in all areas of a research paper—including footnotes. According to the MLA style, first lines of footnotes must also be indented 0.5 inch and use the same font size as the report text.

1 At the bottom of **Page 1**, point anywhere in the footnote text you just typed, right-click, and then on the shortcut menu, click **Style**. Compare your screen with Figure 3.7.

The Style dialog box displays, listing the styles currently in use in the document, in addition to some of the word processing elements that come with special built-in styles. Because you right-clicked in the footnote text, the selected style is the Footnote Text style.

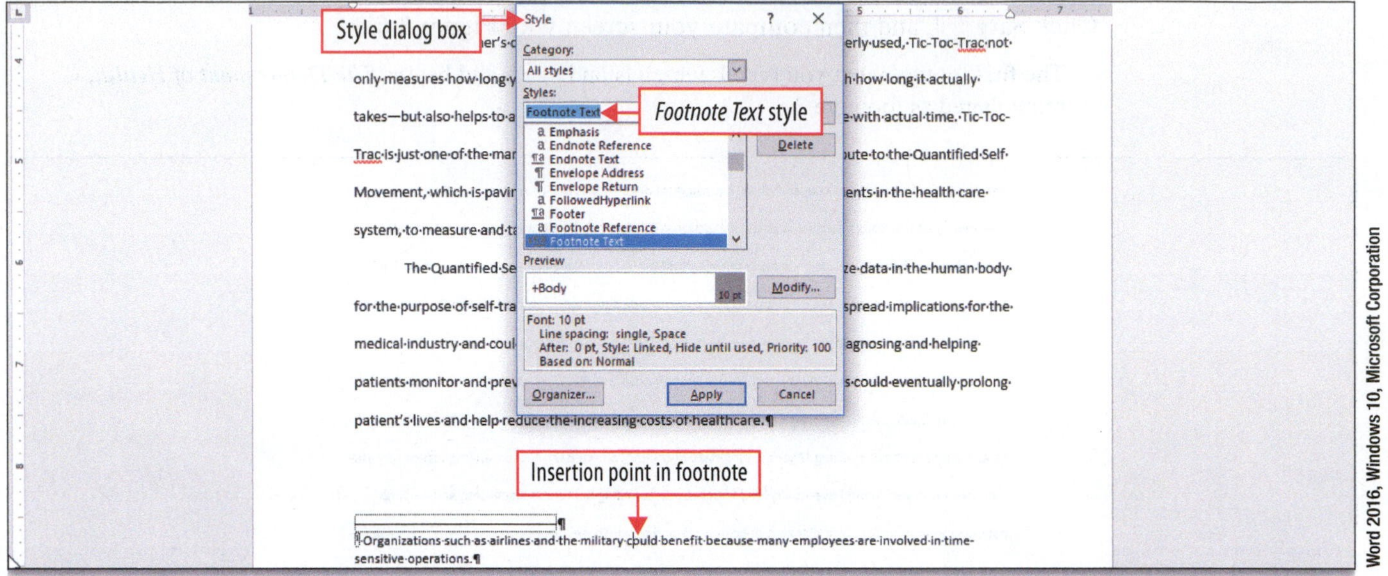

FIGURE 3.7

2 In the **Style** dialog box, click **Modify**, and then in the **Modify Style** dialog box, locate the **Formatting** toolbar in the center of the dialog box. Click the **Font Size button arrow**, click **11**, and then compare your screen with Figure 3.8.

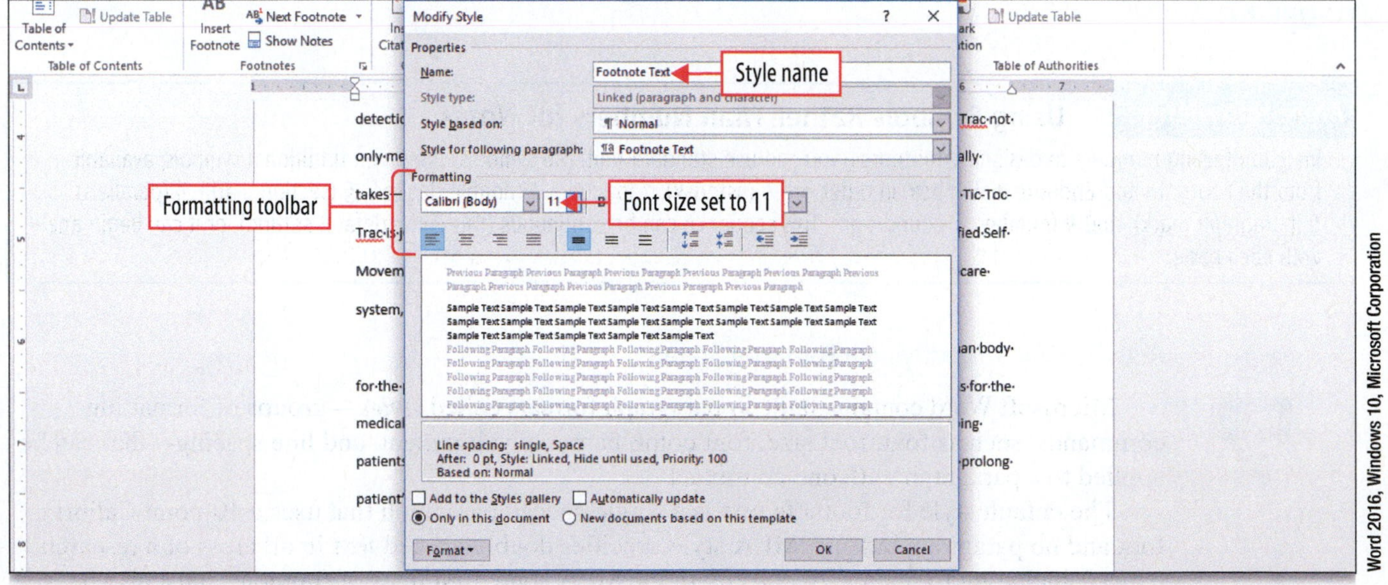

FIGURE 3.8

3 In the lower left corner of the dialog box, click **Format**, and then click **Paragraph**. In the **Paragraph** dialog box, on the **Indents and Spacing tab**, under **Indentation**, click the **Special arrow**, and then click **First line**.

4 Under **Spacing**, click the **Line spacing arrow**, and then click **Double**. Compare your dialog box with Figure 3.9.

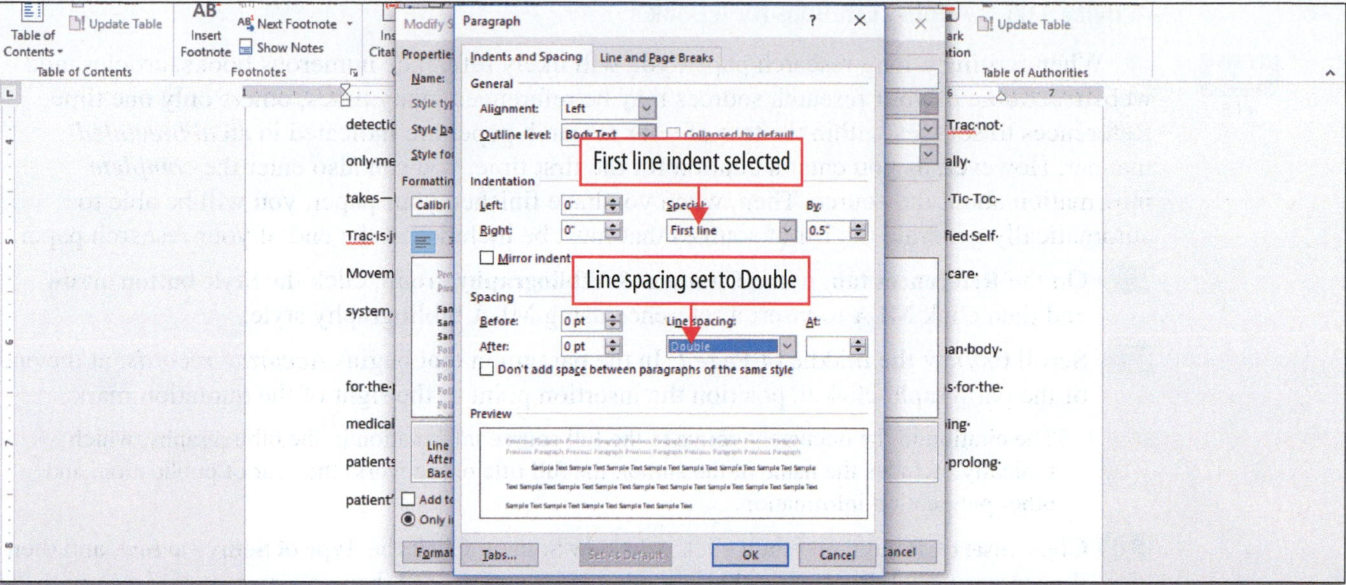

FIGURE 3.9

5 Click **OK** to close the **Paragraph** dialog box, click **OK** to close the **Modify Style** dialog box, and then click **Apply** to apply the new style and close the dialog box. Compare your screen with Figure 3.10.

Your inserted footnotes are formatted with the modified Footnote Text paragraph style; any new footnotes that you insert will also use this format.

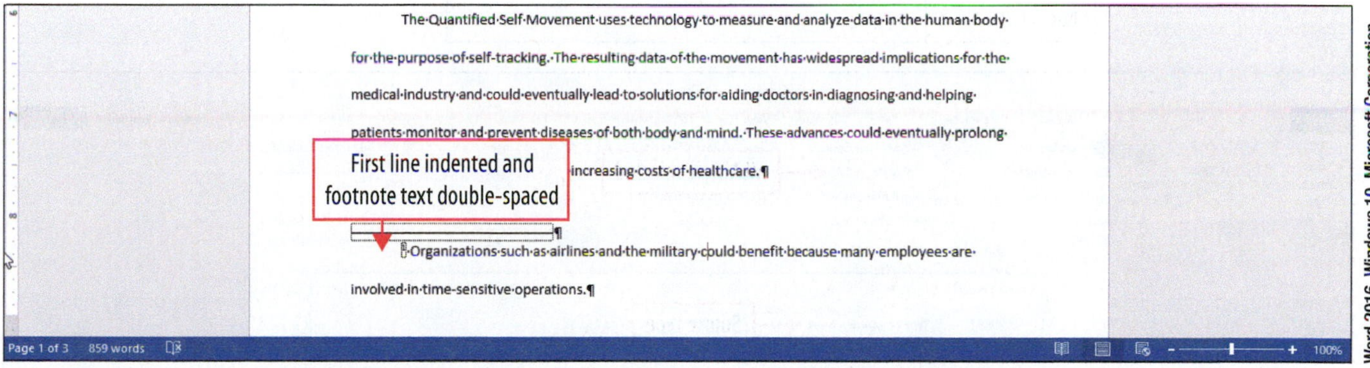

FIGURE 3.10

6 Scroll to view the bottom of **Page 2** to confirm that the new format was also applied to the second footnote, and then **Save** your document.

Objective 3 Create Citations and a Bibliography in a Research Paper

GO! Learn How
Video W3-3

Reports and research papers typically include information that you find in other sources, and these sources of information must be credited. When you use quotations from or detailed summaries of other people's work, you must specify the source of the information. A ***citation*** is a note inserted into the text of a report or research paper that refers the reader to a source in the bibliography. Create a ***bibliography*** at the end of a research paper to list the sources you have referenced. Such a list is typically titled ***Works Cited*** (in MLA style), *Bibliography*, *Sources*, or *References*.

Activity 3.05 | Adding Citations for a Book

When writing a long research paper, you will likely reference numerous books, articles, and websites. Some of your research sources may be referenced many times, others only one time. References to sources within the text of your research paper are indicated in an *abbreviated* manner. However, as you enter a citation for the first time, you can also enter the *complete* information about the source. Then, when you have finished your paper, you will be able to automatically generate the list of sources that must be included at the end of your research paper.

1 On the **References tab**, in the **Citations & Bibliography group**, click the **Style button arrow**, and then click **MLA** to insert a reference using MLA bibliography style.

2 Scroll to view the middle of **Page 2**. In the paragraph that begins *Accurate records*, at the end of the paragraph, click to position the insertion point to the right of the quotation mark.

The citation in the document points to the full source information in the bibliography, which typically includes the name of the author, the full title of the work, the year of publication, and other publication information.

3 Click **Insert Citation**, and then click **Add New Source**. Click the **Type of Source arrow**, and then if necessary, click **Book**. Add the following information, and then compare your screen with Figure 3.11:

Author	**Sopol, Eric J.**
Title	**The Creative Destruction of Medicine**
Year	**2012**
City	**New York**
Publisher	**Basic Books**
Medium	**Print**

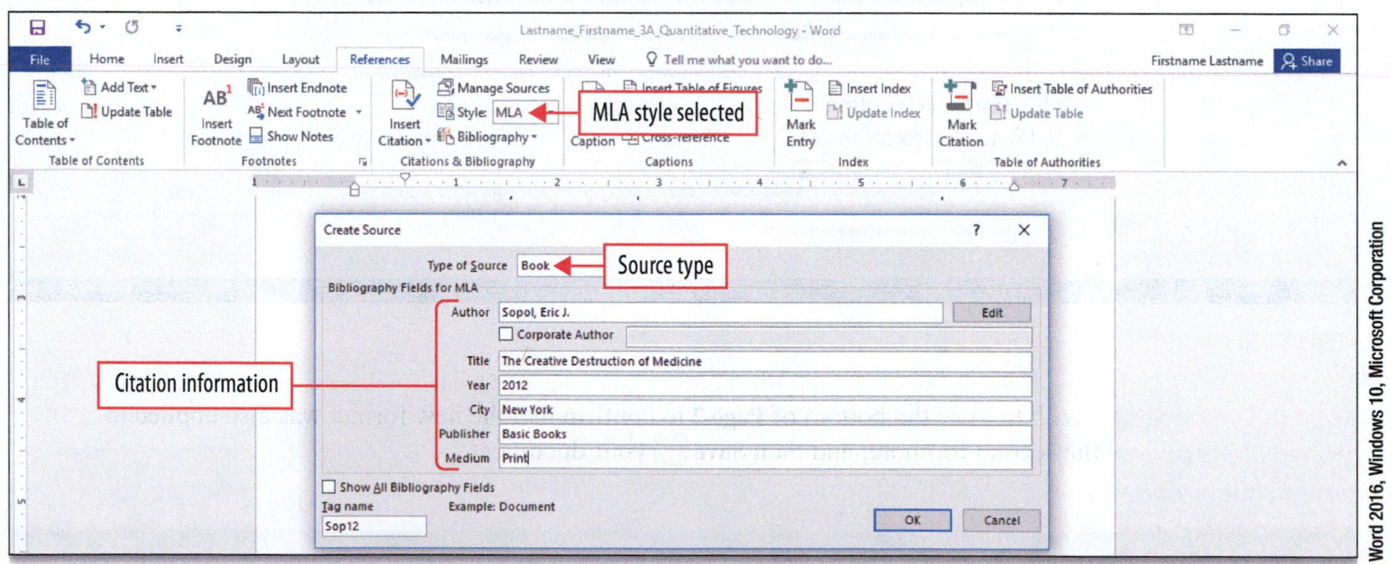

FIGURE 3.11

4 Click **OK** to insert the citation. Point to *(Sopol)* and click one time to select the citation.

In the MLA style, citations that refer to items on the *Works Cited* page are placed in parentheses and are referred to as ***parenthetical references***—references that include the last name of the author or authors and the page number in the referenced source, which you add to the reference. No year is indicated, and there is no comma between the name and the page number.

Both MLA and APA styles use parenthetical references for source citations rather than using footnotes.

5 **Save** the document.

NOTE Citing Corporate Authors and Indicating the Medium

If the author of a document is only identified as the name of an organization, select the Corporate Author check box and type the name of the organization in the Corporate Author box.

In the 7th edition of the *MLA Handbook for Writers of Research Papers*, the category Medium was added and must be included for any item on the Works Cited page. Entries for this category can include Print, Web, Performance, and Photograph, among many others.

Activity 3.06 | Editing Citations

4.1.4

1 In the lower right corner of the box that surrounds the selected reference, point to the small arrow to display the ScreenTip *Citation Options*. Click the **Citation Options arrow**, and then on the list of options, click **Edit Citation**.

2 In the **Edit Citation** dialog box, under **Add**, in the **Pages** box, type **5** to indicate that you are citing from page 5 of this source. Compare your screen with Figure 3.12.

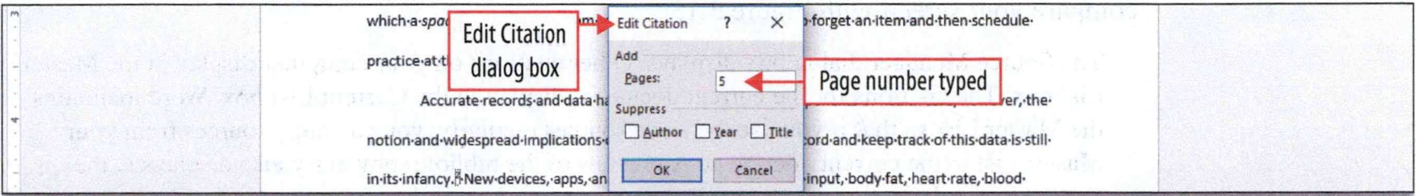

FIGURE 3.12

Word 2016, Windows 10, Microsoft Corporation

3 Click **OK** to display the page number of the citation. Click outside of the citation box to deselect it.

4 Type a period to the right of the citation, and delete the period to the left of the quotation mark.

In the MLA style, if the reference occurs at the end of a sentence, the parenthetical reference always displays to the left of the punctuation mark that ends the sentence.

5 Press Ctrl + End to move to the end of the document, and then click to position the insertion point after the letter *e* in *disease* and to the left of the period.

6 In the **Citations & Bibliography group**, click **Insert Citation**, and then click **Add New Source**. Click the **Type of Source arrow**, if necessary scroll to the top of the list, click **Book**, and then add the following information:

Author	**Glaser, John P., and Claudia Salzberg**
Title	**The Strategic Application of Information Technology in Health Care Organizations**
Year	**2011**
City	**San Francisco**
Publisher	**Jossey-Bass**
Medium	**Print**

ANOTHER WAY In the Create Source dialog box, if you prefer, you can enter each author name separately by using the Edit command to the right of the Author box. Initiate the command for each author of the work, and then Word will automatically format all the names properly and in the correct order in the Works Cited list.

NOTE **MLA Style for Two or More Authors**

According to MLA Style, to cite a book by two or more authors, reverse only the name of the first author, add a comma, and give the other name or names in normal form. Place a period after the last name.

7 Click **OK**. Click the inserted citation to select it, click the **Citation Options arrow**, and then click **Edit Citation**.

8 In the **Edit Citation** dialog box, under **Add**, in the **Pages** box, type **28** to indicate that you are citing from page 28 of this source. Click **OK**.

9 On the **References tab**, in the **Citations & Bibliography group**, click **Manage Sources**, and then compare your screen with Figure 3.13.

The Source Manager dialog box displays. Other citations on your computer display in the Master List box. The citations for the current document display in the Current List box. Word maintains the Master List so that if you use the same sources regularly, you can copy sources from your Master List to the current document. A preview of the bibliography entry also displays at the bottom of the dialog box.

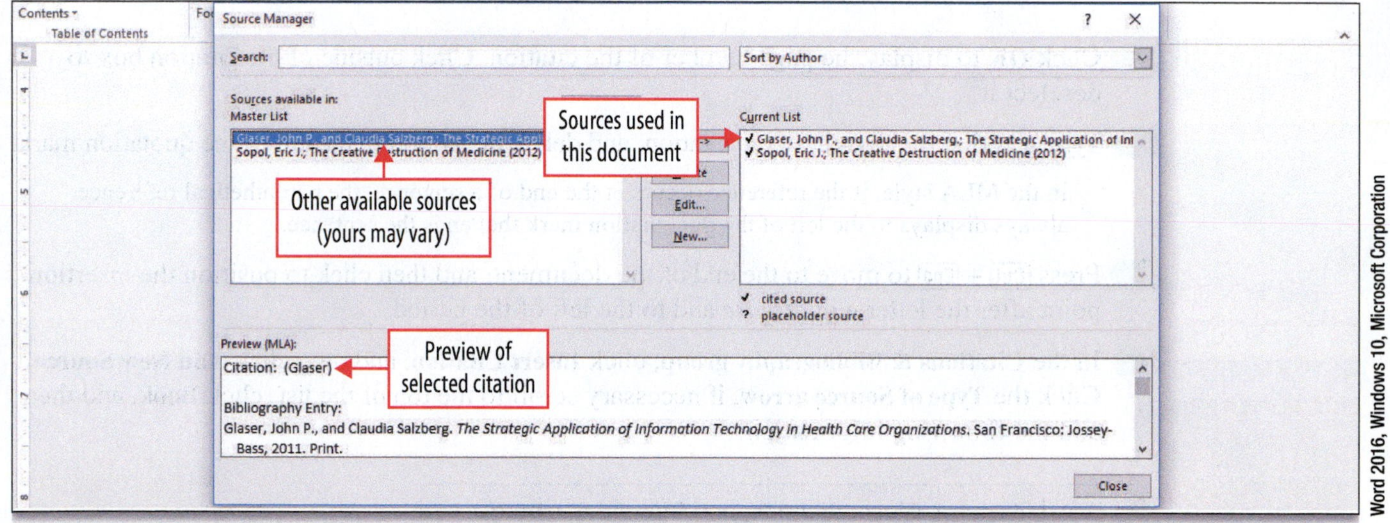

FIGURE 3.13

10 At the bottom of the **Source Manager** dialog box, click **Close**. Click anywhere in the document to deselect the parenthetical reference, and then **Save** your document.

Activity 3.07 | Adding Citations for a Website

MOS 4.1.3

1 In the lower portion of **Page 2**, in the paragraph that begins *Doctors have long urged*, in the third line, click to position the insertion point after the s in *States* and to the left of the period.

2 In the **Citations & Bibliography group**, click **Insert Citation**, and then click **Add New Source**. Click the **Type of Source arrow**, scroll down as necessary, and then click **Web site**. Type the following information:

Author	**Ogden, C. L.**
Name of Web Page	**NCHS Data Brief Number 82**
Year	**2012**
Month	**January**
Day	**01**
Year Accessed	**2016**
Month Accessed	**January**
Day Accessed	**17**
Medium	**Web**

3 Click **OK**. **Save**, and then compare your screen with Figure 3.14.

A parenthetical reference is added. Because the cited Web page has no page numbers, only the author name is used in the parenthetical reference.

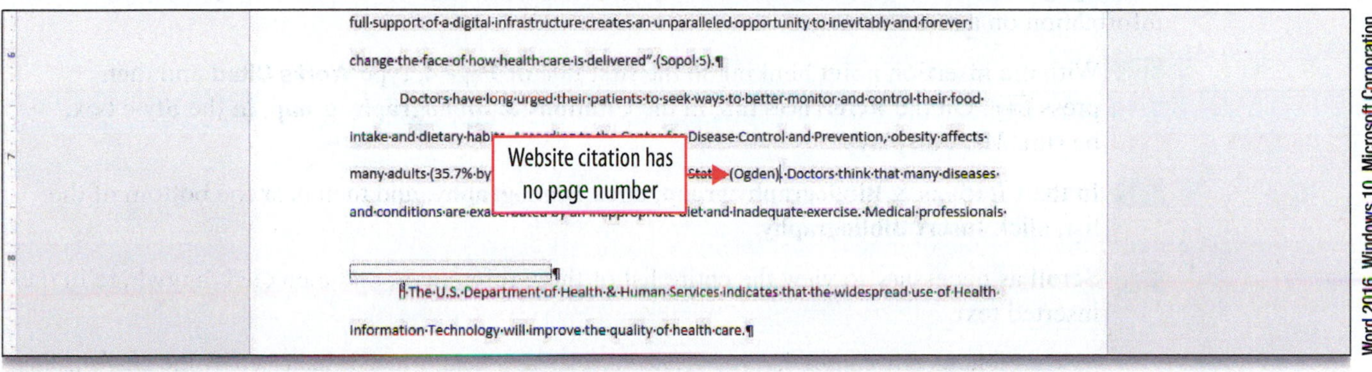

FIGURE 3.14

More Knowledge **Including URLs of Web Sources**

With the 7th edition of the *MLA Handbook for Writers of Research Papers*, including the URL of Web sources is recommended only when the reader would have difficulty finding the source without it or if your instructor requires it. Otherwise, readers will likely find the resource by using search tools. If you include the URL, enclose it in angle brackets and end with a period.

Activity 3.08 | Inserting Page Breaks

2.3.2

Your bibliography must begin on a new page, so at the bottom of the last page of your report, you must insert a manual page break.

1 Press Ctrl + End to move the insertion point to the end of the document.

If there is a footnote on the last page, the insertion point will display at the end of the final paragraph, but above the footnote—a footnote is always associated with the page that contains the footnote information.

2 Press Ctrl + Enter to insert a manual page break.

A ***manual page break*** forces a page to end at the insertion point location, and then places any subsequent text at the top of the next page. Recall that the new paragraph retains the formatting of the previous paragraph, so in this instance the first line is indented.

A ***page break indicator***, which shows where a manual page break was inserted, displays at the bottom of Page 3.

3 On the **Home tab**, in the **Paragraph group**, click the **Dialog Box Launcher** button to display the **Paragraph** dialog box.

4 On the **Indents and Spacing tab**, under **Indentation**, click the **Special arrow**, and then click **(none)**. Click **OK**, and then **Save** your document.

On the ruler, point to the First Line Indent button, and then drag the button to 0" on the horizontal ruler.

Activity 3.09 | Creating a Reference Page

4.1.3

At the end of a report or research paper, include a list of each source referenced. *Works Cited* is the reference page heading used in the MLA style guidelines. Other styles may refer to this page as a *Bibliography* (Business Style) or *References* (APA Style). Always display this information on a separate page.

1 With the insertion point blinking in the first line of **Page 4**, type **Works Cited** and then press Enter. On the **References tab**, in the **Citations & Bibliography group**, in the **Style** box, be sure *MLA* displays.

2 In the **Citations & Bibliography group**, click **Bibliography**, and then near the bottom of the list, click **Insert Bibliography**.

3 Scroll as necessary to view the entire list of three references, and then click anywhere in the inserted text.

The bibliography entries that you created display as a field, which is indicated by the gray shading. This field links to the Source Manager for the citations. The references display alphabetically by the author's last name.

4 In the bibliography, point to the left of the first entry—beginning *Glaser, John P.*—to display the pointer. Drag down to select all three references in the field but not the blank paragraph.

5 On the **Home tab**, in the **Paragraph group**, change the **Line spacing** to **2.0**, and then on the **Layout tab**, in the **Paragraph group**, change the **Spacing After** to **0 pt**.

The entries display according to MLA guidelines; the text is double-spaced, the extra space between paragraphs is removed, and each entry uses a ***hanging indent***—the first line of each entry extends 0.5 inch to the left of the remaining lines of the entry.

ANOTHER WAY Display the Paragraph dialog box. Under Spacing, click the Line spacing arrow, and then click Double. Under Spacing, in the After box, type 0.

6 At the top of **Page 4**, click anywhere in the title text *Works Cited*, and then press Ctrl + E to center the title. Compare your screen with Figure 3.15, and then **Save** your document.

In MLA style, the *Works Cited* title is centered.

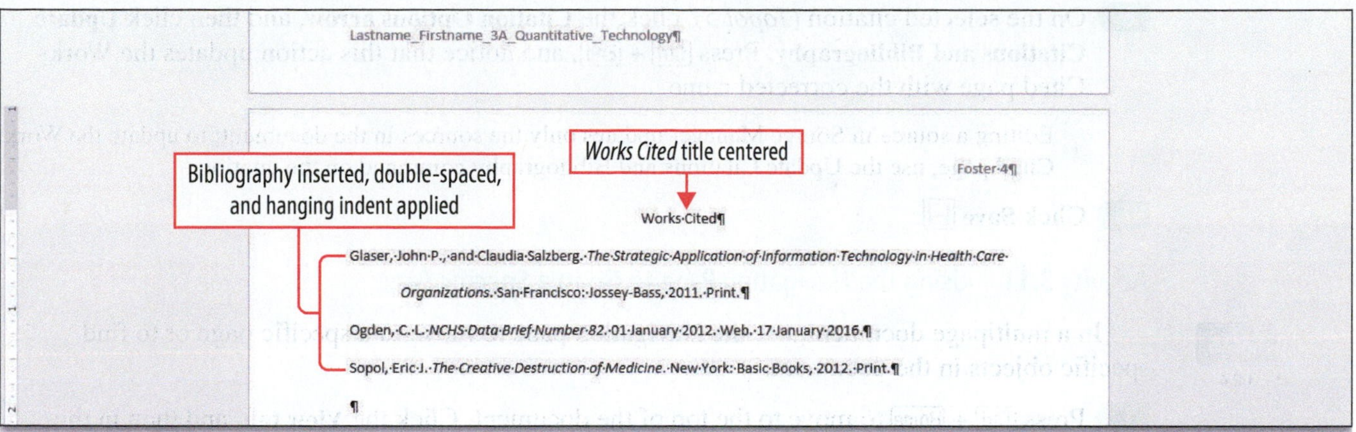

Word 2016, Windows 10, Microsoft Corporation

FIGURE 3.15

Activity 3.10 | Managing and Modifying Sources for a Document

Use the Source Manager to organize the sources cited in your document. For example, in the Source Manager dialog box, you can copy sources from the master list to the current list, delete a source, edit a source, or search for a source. You can also display a preview of how your citations will appear in your document.

1. On the **References tab**, in the **Citations & Bibliography group**, click **Manage Sources**.
2. On the left, in the **Master List**, click the entry for *Sopol, Eric J.* and then between the **Master List** and the **Current List**, click **Edit**.

   The name of this source should be *Topol* instead of *Sopol*.

3. In the **Edit Source** dialog box, in the **Author** box, delete *S* and type **T**
4. Click **OK**. When the message box indicates *This source exists in your master list and current document. Do you want to update both lists with these changes?* click **Yes**. Compare your screen with Figure 3.16.

   In the lower portion of the Source Manager dialog box, a preview of the corrected entry displays.

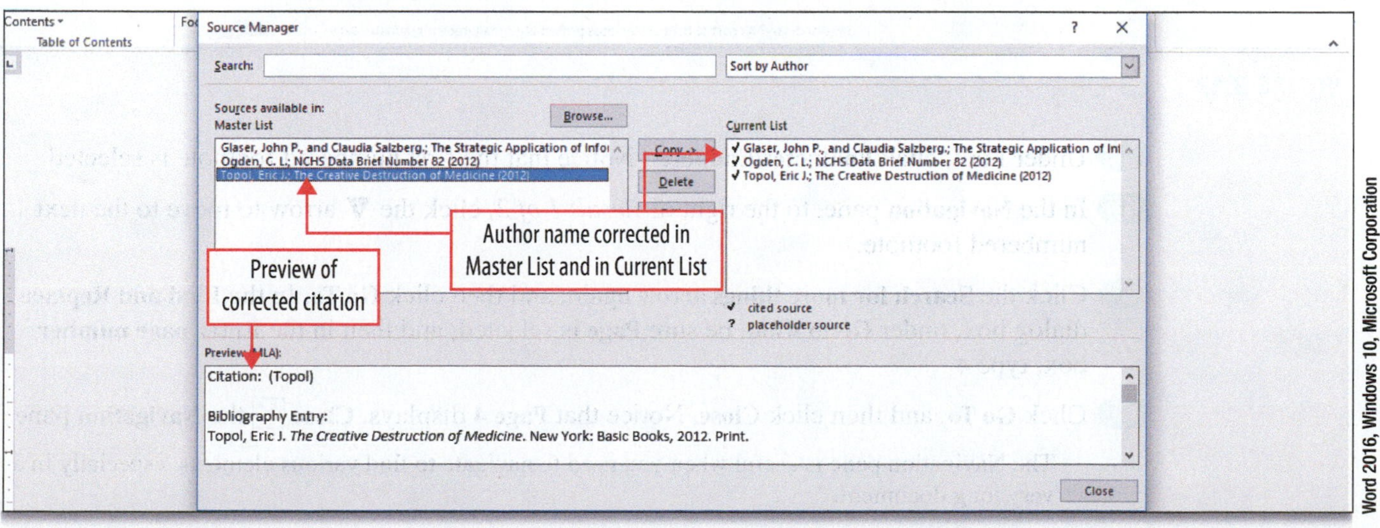

Word 2016, Windows 10, Microsoft Corporation

FIGURE 3.16

5. In the lower right corner, click **Close**. On your **Works Cited page**, notice that the author name is *not* corrected. Scroll to view the lower portion of **Page 2**, and notice that the author name *is* corrected and the citation is selected.

6 On the selected citation *(Topol 5)*, click the **Citation Options arrow**, and then click **Update Citations and Bibliography**. Press Ctrl + End, and notice that this action updates the Works Cited page with the corrected name.

Editing a source in Source Manager updates only the sources in the document; to update the Works Cited page, use the Update Citations and Bibliography command on the citation.

7 Click **Save**.

Activity 3.11 | Using the Navigation Pane to Go to a Specific Page

1.2.4

In a multipage document, use the Navigation pane to move to a specific page or to find specific objects in the document.

1 Press Ctrl + Home to move to the top of the document. Click the **View tab**, and then in the **Show group**, select the **Navigation Pane** check box.

2 In the **Navigation** pane, on the right end of the **Search document** box, click the **Search for more things arrow**, and then compare your screen with Figure 3.17.

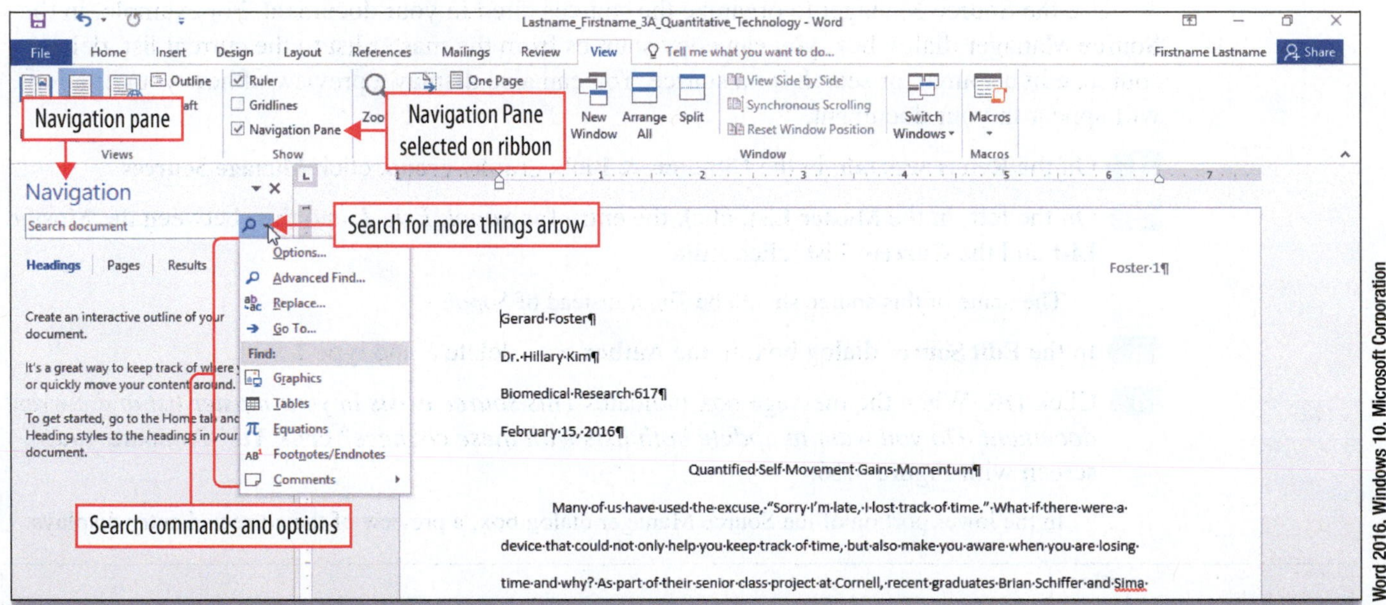

FIGURE 3.17

3 Under **Find**, click **Footnotes/Endnotes**. Notice that the first numbered footnote is selected.

4 In the **Navigation** pane, to the right of *Result 1 of 2*, click the ▼ arrow to move to the next numbered footnote.

5 Click the **Search for more things arrow** again, and then click **Go To**. In the **Find and Replace** dialog box, under **Go to what**, be sure **Page** is selected, and then in the **Enter page number** box, type **4**

6 Click **Go To**, and then click **Close**. Notice that **Page 4** displays. **Close** the **Navigation** pane.

The Navigation pane is useful when you need to navigate to find various elements, especially in a very long document.

ANOTHER WAY You can also initiate the Go To command from the ribbon or by using a keyboard shortcut. To do so, on the Home tab, in the Editing group, click the Find arrow, and then click Go To; or, hold down Ctrl and press G to display the Go To tab of the Find and Replace dialog box.

Activity 3.12 | Managing Document Properties

3.1.2

For a research paper, you may want to add additional document properties.

1. Press Ctrl + Home to return to the top of your document. Click the **File tab** to display **Backstage** view, and then in the lower right corner of the screen, click **Show All Properties**.
2. As the document **Title**, type **Quantified Self Movement Gains Momentum** and then as the **Tags**, type **quantified self, research paper**
3. Click in the **Comments** box and type **draft copy of report for class** and then in the **Categories** box, type **biomedical research**
4. In the **Subject** box, type your course name and section number. In the **Company** box, select and delete any existing text, and then type **University Medical Center**
5. Click in the **Manager** box and type **Dr. Hillary Kim** Be sure your name displays as the **Author** and edit if necessary.
6. At the top of the **Properties** list, click the text *Properties*, and then click **Advanced Properties**. In the dialog box, if necessary click the **Summary tab**, and then compare your screen with Figure 3.18.

   In the Advanced Properties dialog box, you can view and modify additional document properties.

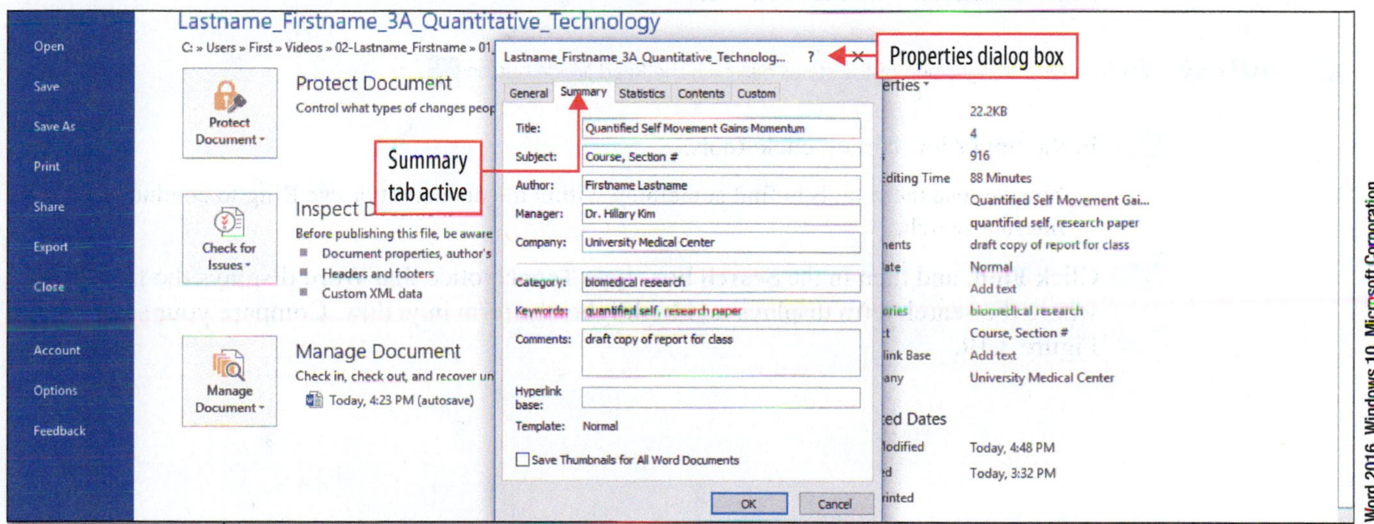

FIGURE 3.18

Word 2016, Windows 10, Microsoft Corporation

7. Click the **Statistics tab**.

   The document statistics show the number of revisions made to the document, the last time the document was edited, and the number of paragraphs, lines, words, and characters in the document. Additional information categories are available by clicking the Custom tab.

8. **Close** ✕ the dialog box, and then on the left, click **Save** to save and return to your document.

> ***More Knowledge*** **Inserting a Watermark**
>
> A **watermark** is a text or graphic element that displays behind document text. Until you know your research paper is final—for example, you have others reviewing it—you might want to display the word DRAFT on each page. To do so, on the Design tab, in the Page Background group, click Watermark, and then at the bottom, click Custom Watermark. In the Printed Watermark dialog box, click the Text watermark option button, click the Text arrow, and then click DRAFT. Click OK. To remove the watermark—after you are sure your research paper is final—click the Watermark command again, and then click Remove Watermark.

Objective 4 Use Read Mode and PDF Reflow

GO! Learn How Video W3-4

Read Mode optimizes the view of the Word screen for the times when you are *reading* Word documents on the screen and not creating or editing them. Microsoft's research indicates that two-thirds of user sessions in Word contain no editing—meaning that people are simply reading the Word document on the screen. The Column Layout feature of Read Mode reflows the document to fit the size of the device you are reading so that the text is as easy to read on a tablet device as on a 24-inch screen. The Object Zoom feature of Read Mode resizes graphics to fit the screen you are using, but you can click or tap to zoom in on the graphic.

PDF Reflow provides the ability to import PDF files into Word so that you can transform a PDF back into a fully editable Word document. This is useful if you have lost the original Word file or if someone sends you a PDF that you would like to modify. PDF Reflow is not intended to act as a viewer for PDF files—for that you will still want to use a PDF reader such as Adobe Reader. In Windows 10, the Microsoft Edge browser also serves as a PDF reader.

1.4.1

Activity 3.13 | Using Read Mode

1 If necessary, press Ctrl + Home to move to the top of your document. On the **View tab**, in the **Views group**, click **Read Mode**, and notice that Read Mode keeps footnotes displayed on the page associated with the footnote.

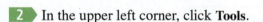

ANOTHER WAY On the right side of the status bar, click the Read Mode button .

2 In the upper left corner, click **Tools**.

You can use these tools to find something within the document or use Bing to conduct an Internet search.

3 Click **Find**, and then in the **Search** box, type **Topol** Notice that Word displays the first page where the search term displays and highlights the term in yellow. Compare your screen with Figure 3.19.

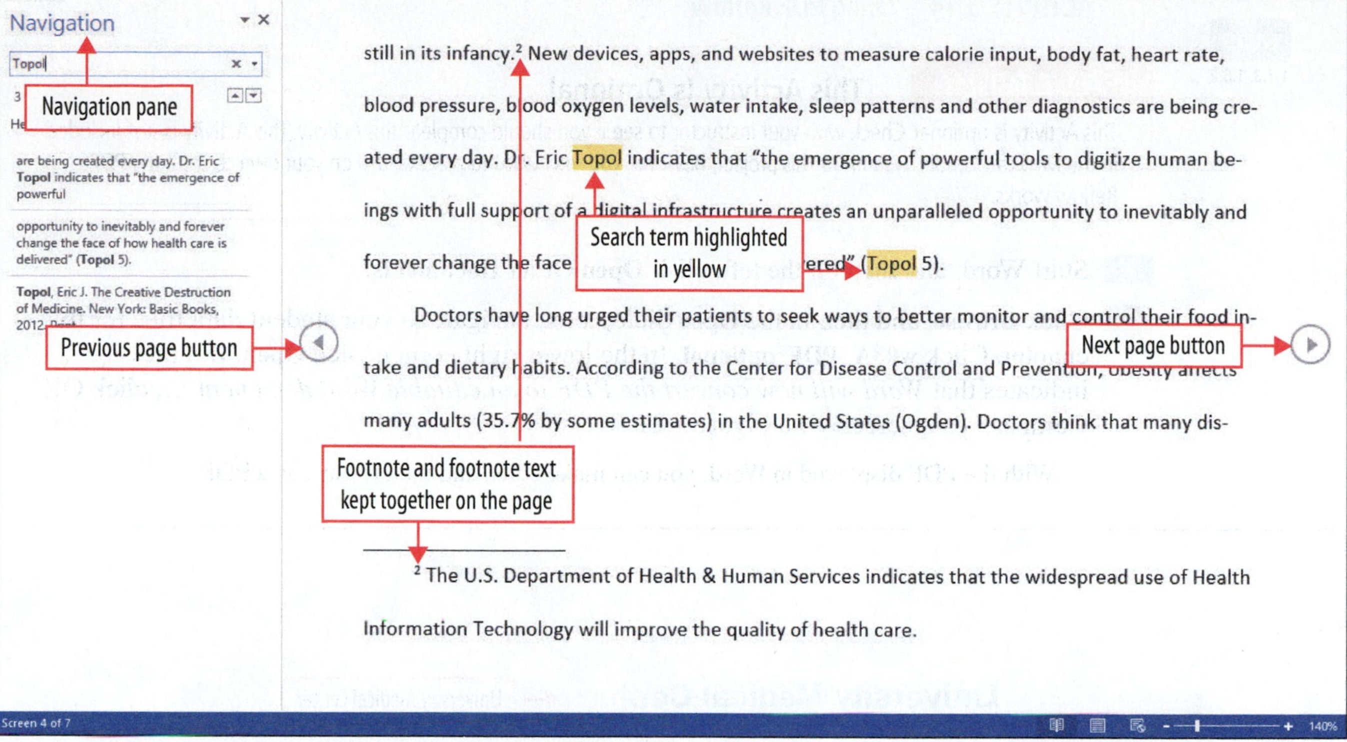

Word 2016, Windows 10, Microsoft Corporation

FIGURE 3.19

4 In the upper left corner, click **View**, and then take a moment to study the table in Figure 3.20.

VIEW COMMANDS IN READ MODE	
VIEW COMMAND	**ACTION**
Edit Document	Return to Print Layout view to continue editing the document.
Navigation Pane	Search for specific text or click a heading or page to move to that location.
Show Comments	See comments, if any, within the document.
Column Width	Change the display of the document to fit more or less text on each line.
Page Color	Change the colors used to show the document to make it easier to read. Some readers prefer a sepia (brownish-gray) shading as the background or a black background with white text.
Layout	Read in different layouts. Select Column Layout, which is the default, or Paper Layout, which mimics the 8.5 x 11 format but without the ribbon.

Word 2016, Windows 10, Microsoft Corporation

FIGURE 3.20

5 On the **View** menu, click **Edit Document** to return to **Print Layout** view. **Close** [X] the **Navigation** pane.

6 In the upper right corner of the Word window, click **Close** [X]. If directed by your instructor to do so, submit your paper printout, your electronic image of your document that looks like a printed document, or your original Word file. If you are submitting this Project as a MyITLab grader, submit this file.

***More* Knowledge** **Highlighting Text in a Word Document**

You can highlight text in a Word document. Select the text you want to highlight, and then on the Home tab, in the Font group, click the Text Highlight Color arrow. Click the color you want to use for your highlight to apply it to the selected text. Or, click the Text Highlight Color button arrow, click a color, and then use the pointer to select text that you want to highlight.

ACTIVITY 3.14 | Using PDF Reflow

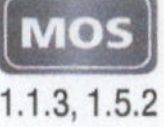

1.1.3, 1.5.2

ALERT! **This Activity Is Optional**

This Activity is optional. Check with your instructor to see if you should complete this Activity. This Activity is not included in the MyITLab Grader system for this project; however, you may want to practice this on your own to see how PDF Reflow works.

1. Start Word, and then on the left, click **Open Other Documents**.

2. Click **Browse**, and then in the **Open** dialog box, navigate to your student data files for this chapter. Click **w03A_PDF_optional**. In the lower right corner, click **Open**. If a message indicates that *Word will now convert the PDF to an editable Word document ...*, click OK. Compare your screen with Figure 3.21.

   With the PDF displayed in Word, you can make edits, and then re-save as a PDF.

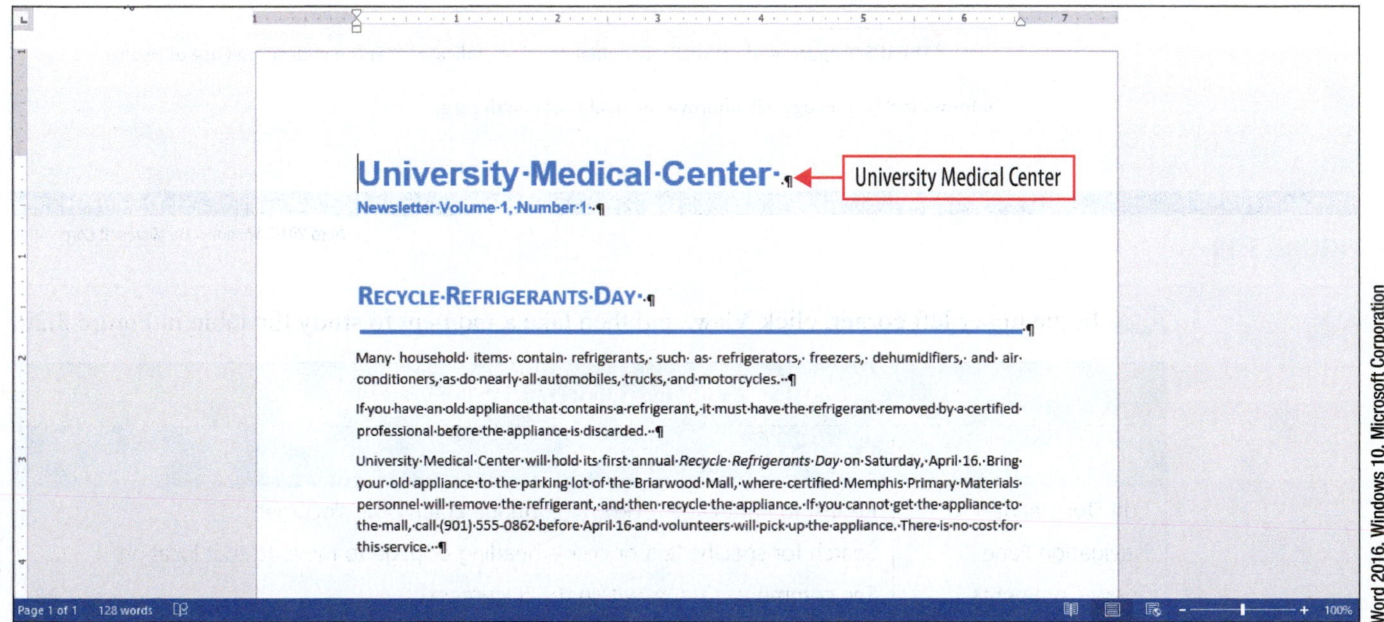

FIGURE 3.21

3. **Close** [X] Word.

***More* Knowledge** **Saving Documents in Alternative File Formats**

You can save a Word document in a variety of other document formats, including a PDF. To do so, with your Word document open, display the Save As dialog box. Click the Save as type arrow, and then click the desired file type. Commonly used file types are PDF and Rich Text Format.

END | You have completed Project 3A

GO! With Google

3 WORD

Objective Use the Research Bar in Google Docs

ALERT! Working with Web-Based Applications and Services

Computer programs and services on the web receive continuous updates and improvements, so the steps to complete this web-based Activity may differ from the ones shown. You can often look at the screens and the information presented to determine how to complete the Activity.

If you do not already have a Google account, you will need to create one before you begin this Activity. Go to http://google.com and, in the upper right corner, click Sign In. On the Sign In screen, click Create Account. On the Create your Google Account page, complete the form, read and agree to the Terms of Service and Privacy Policy, and then click Next step. On the Welcome screen, click Get Started.

Activity | Using the Research Bar in Google Docs

Google Docs provides a research tool that you can use to find studies and academic papers on many topics. You can narrow your search results by selecting "Scholar" from the menu in the search bar. After you find the study, you can insert it as a citation or a footnote. You can also choose to use the MLA, APA, or Chicago citation formatting.

1 From the desktop, open your browser, navigate to **http://google.com**, and then click the **Google Apps** menu [icon]. Click **Drive**, and then if necessary, sign in to your Google account.

2 Open your **GO! Web Projects** folder—or click NEW to create and then open this folder if necessary.

3 In the left pane, click **NEW**, and then click **File upload**. In the **Open** dialog box, navigate to your student data files for this chapter, and then in the **File List**, double-click to open **w03_3A_Web**.

4 Point to the uploaded file **w03_3A_Web**, and then right-click. On the shortcut menu, scroll as necessary, and then click **Rename**. Using your own last name and first name, type **Lastname_Firstname_WD_3A_Web** and use the default .docx extension. Click **OK** to rename the file.

5 Point to the file you just renamed, right-click, point to **Open with**, and then click **Google Docs**.

6 Press Ctrl + End to move to the end of the document, and then press Enter one time. Type **There are many studies related to the quantified self movement conducted by Melanie Swan, who is interested in crowdsourced health research.**

7 On the menu bar, click **Tools**, and then click **Research** to open the **Research pane** on the right. At the top of the **Research pane**, click the arrow to the right of *G*, click the arrow a second time to filter the results, and then on the list click **Scholar**.

8 In the search box at the top, delete any existing text, type **Melanie Swan** and then press Enter. *Point* to the first item in the list, and then compare your screen with Figure A.

(GO! With Google continues on the next page)

GO! With Google

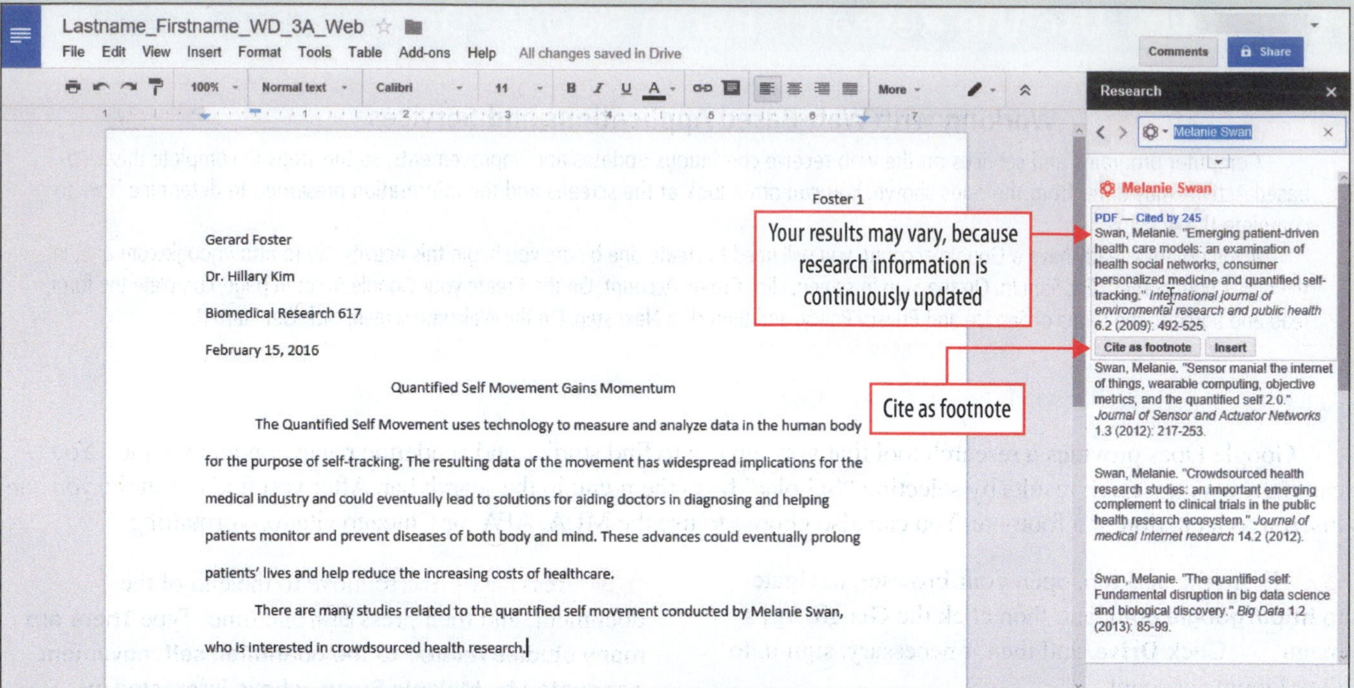

FIGURE A

9 Click **Cite as footnote**. Notice that a footnote number is inserted at the end of the sentence. Scroll down to view the bottom of the page, and then compare your screen with Figure B.

10 Submit the file as directed by your instructor. In the upper right, click your user name, and then click **Sign out**. **Close** your browser window. Your file is automatically saved in your Google Drive.

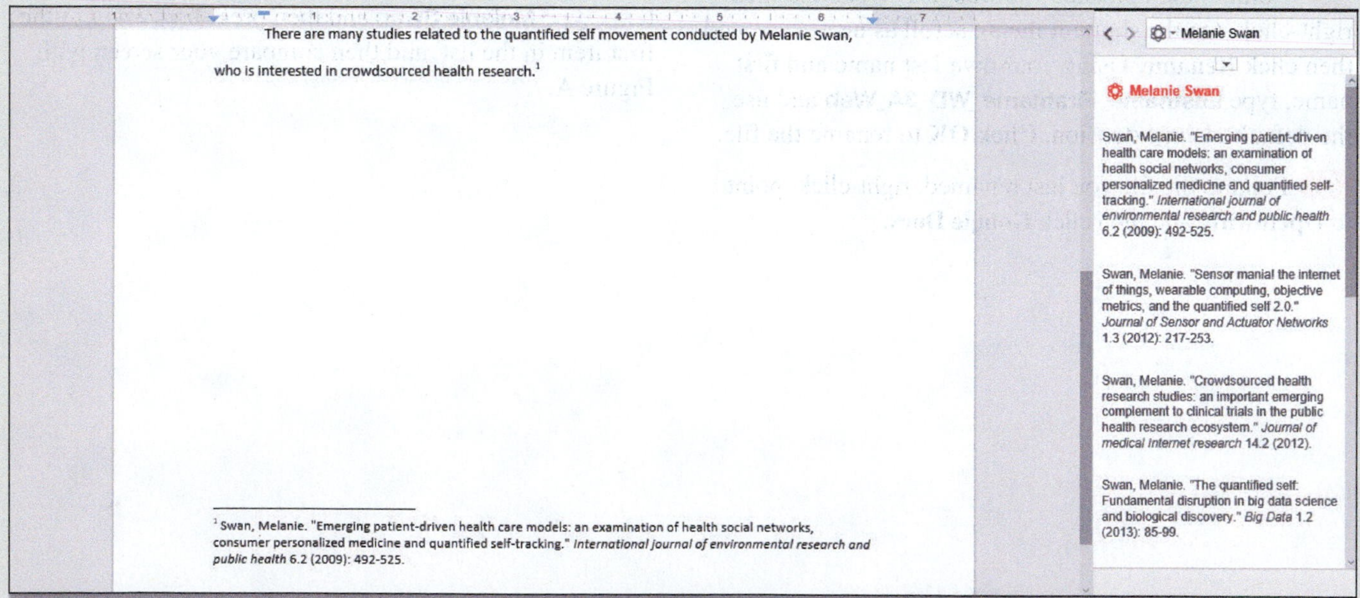

FIGURE B

PROJECT 3B

Newsletter with Optional Mailing Labels

Project 3B Training
Project 3B Grader

PROJECT ACTIVITIES

In Activities 3.15 through 3.29, you will edit a newsletter that University Medical Center is sending to the board of directors; optionally, you can create the necessary mailing labels. Your completed documents will look similar to Figure 3.22.

Please always review the downloaded Grader instructions before beginning.

PROJECT FILES

If your instructor wants you to submit Project 3B in the MyITLab Grader system, log in to MyITLab, locate Grader Project 3B, and then download the files for this project.

For Project 3B, you will need the following files:

w03B_Environment_Newsletter
w03B_Addresses (Optional if assigned)

You will save your documents as:

Lastname_Firstname_3B_Environment_Newsletter
Lastname_Firstname_3B_Mailing_Labels (Optional if assigned)

GO!
lk Thru
ject 3B

PROJECT RESULTS

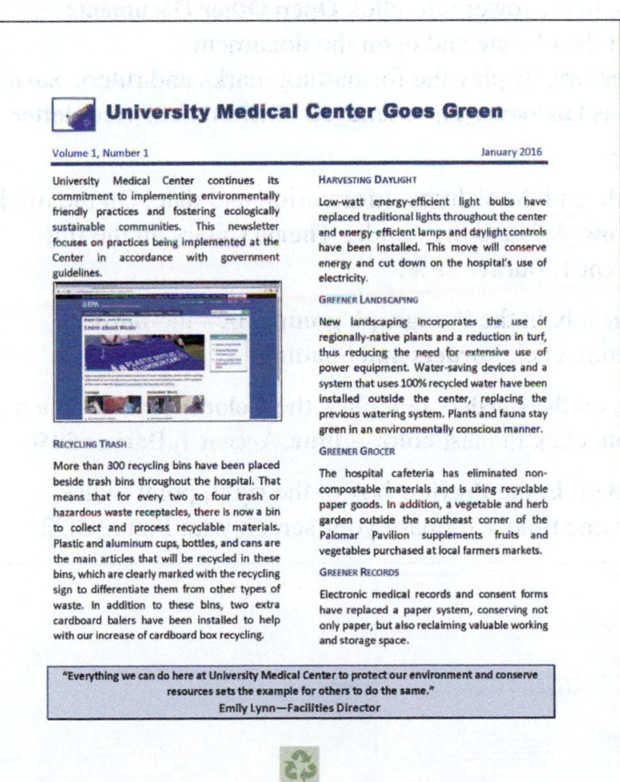

University Medical Center Goes Green

Volume 1, Number 1 January 2016

University Medical Center continues its commitment to implementing environmentally friendly practices and fostering ecologically sustainable communities. This newsletter focuses on practices being implemented at the Center in accordance with government guidelines.

RECYCLING TRASH

More than 300 recycling bins have been placed beside trash bins throughout the hospital. That means that for every two to four trash or hazardous waste receptacles, there is now a bin to collect and process recyclable materials. Plastic and aluminum cups, bottles, and cans are the main articles that will be recycled in these bins, which are clearly marked with the recycling sign to differentiate them from other types of waste. In addition to these bins, two extra cardboard balers have been installed to help with our increase of cardboard box recycling.

HARVESTING DAYLIGHT

Low-watt energy-efficient light bulbs have replaced traditional lights throughout the center and energy-efficient lamps and daylight controls have been installed. This move will conserve energy and cut down on the hospital's use of electricity.

GREENER LANDSCAPING

New landscaping incorporates the use of regionally-native plants and a reduction in turf, thus reducing the need for extensive use of power equipment. Water-saving devices and a system that uses 100% recycled water have been installed outside the center, replacing the previous watering system. Plants and fauna stay green in an environmentally conscious manner.

GREENER GROCER

The hospital cafeteria has eliminated non-compostable materials and is using recyclable paper goods. In addition, a vegetable and herb garden outside the southeast corner of the Palomar Pavilion supplements fruits and vegetables purchased at local farmers markets.

GREENER RECORDS

Electronic medical records and consent forms have replaced a paper system, conserving not only paper, but also reclaiming valuable working and storage space.

"Everything we can do here at University Medical Center to protect our environment and conserve resources sets the example for others to do the same."
Emily Lynn—Facilities Director

Lastname_Firstname_3B_Environment_Newsletter

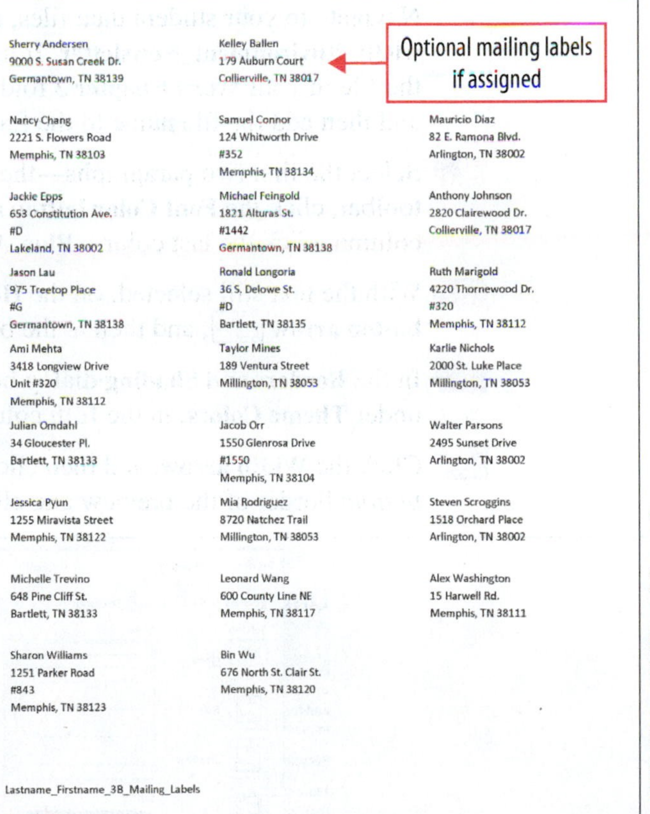

Sherry Andersen 9000 S. Susan Creek Dr. Germantown, TN 38139	Kelley Ballen 179 Auburn Court Collierville, TN 38017	
Nancy Chang 2221 S. Flowers Road Memphis, TN 38103	Samuel Connor 124 Whitworth Drive #352 Memphis, TN 38134	Mauricio Diaz 82 E. Ramona Blvd. Arlington, TN 38002
Jackie Epps 653 Constitution Ave. #D Lakeland, TN 38002	Michael Feingold 1821 Alturas St. #1442 Germantown, TN 38138	Anthony Johnson 2820 Clairewood Dr. Collierville, TN 38017
Jason Lau 975 Treetop Place #G Germantown, TN 38138	Ronald Longoria 36 S. Delowe St. #D Bartlett, TN 38135	Ruth Marigold 4220 Thornewood Dr. #320 Memphis, TN 38112
Ami Mehta 3418 Longview Drive Unit #320 Memphis, TN 38112	Taylor Mines 189 Ventura Street Millington, TN 38053	Karlie Nichols 2000 St. Luke Place Millington, TN 38053
Julian Omdahl 34 Gloucester Pl. Bartlett, TN 38133	Jacob Orr 1550 Glenrosa Drive #1550 Memphis, TN 38104	Walter Parsons 2495 Sunset Drive Arlington, TN 38002
Jessica Pyun 1255 Miravista Street Memphis, TN 38122	Mia Rodriguez 8720 Natchez Trail Millington, TN 38053	Steven Scroggins 1518 Orchard Place Arlington, TN 38002
Michelle Trevino 648 Pine Cliff St. Bartlett, TN 38133	Leonard Wang 600 County Line NE Memphis, TN 38117	Alex Washington 15 Harwell Rd. Memphis, TN 38111
Sharon Williams 1251 Parker Road #843 Memphis, TN 38123	Bin Wu 676 North St. Clair St. Memphis, TN 38120	

Lastname_Firstname_3B_Mailing_Labels

FIGURE 3.22 Project 3B Environment Newsletter

Objective 5 Format a Multiple-Column Newsletter

GO! Learn How Video W3-5

A ***newsletter*** is a periodical that communicates news and information to a specific group. Newsletters, as well as all newspapers and most magazines, use multiple columns for articles because text in narrower columns is easier to read than text that stretches across a page.

You can create a newsletter in Word by changing a single column of text into two or more columns. If a column does not end where you want it to, you can end the column at a location of your choice by inserting a ***manual column break***—an artificial end to a column to balance columns or to provide space for the insertion of other objects.

Activity 3.15 | Changing One Column of Text to Two Columns

ALERT! **To submit as an autograded project, log into MyITLab, download the files for this project, and then begin with those files instead of with w03B_Environment_Newsletter.**

2.3.1

Newsletters are usually two or three columns wide. When using 8.5 × 11-inch paper in portrait orientation, avoid creating four or more columns because they are so narrow that word spacing looks awkward, often resulting in one long word on a line by itself.

1. Start Word. On Word's opening screen, in the lower left, click **Open Other Documents**. Navigate to your student data files, and then locate and open the document **w03B_Environment_Newsletter**. If necessary, display the formatting marks and rulers. **Save** the file in your **Word Chapter 3** folder as **Lastname_Firstname_3B_Environment_Newsletter** and then add the file name to the footer.
2. Select the first two paragraphs—the title and the Volume information and date. On the mini toolbar, click the **Font Color button arrow**, and then under **Theme Colors**, in the fifth column, click the last color—**Blue, Accent 1, Darker 50%**.
3. With the text still selected, on the **Home tab**, in the **Paragraph group**, click the **Borders button arrow**, and then at the bottom, click **Borders and Shading**.
4. In the **Borders and Shading** dialog box, on the **Borders tab**, click the **Color arrow**, and then under **Theme Colors**, in the fifth column, click the last color—**Blue, Accent 1, Darker 50%**.
5. Click the **Width arrow**, and then click **3 pt**. In the **Preview** box at the right, point to the *bottom* border of the preview and click one time. Compare your screen with Figure 3.23.

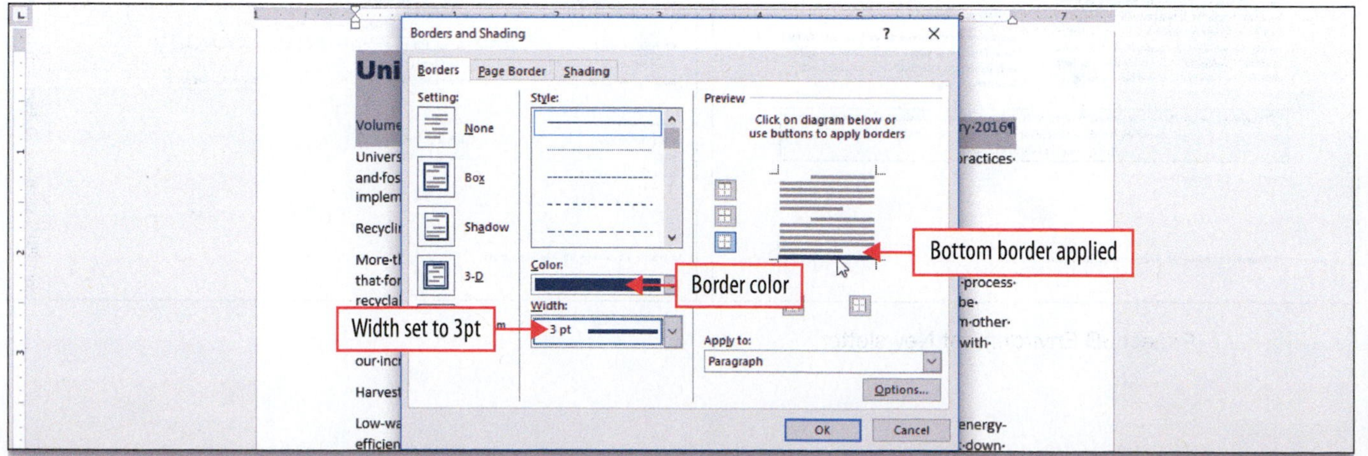

Word 2016, Windows 10, Microsoft Corporation

FIGURE 3.23

ANOTHER WAY In the Preview area, click the Bottom Border button.

6 In the **Borders and Shading** dialog box, click **OK**.

The line visually defines the newsletter's ***nameplate***—the banner on the front page of a newsletter that identifies the publication.

7 Below the Volume information, click at the beginning of the paragraph that begins *University Medical Center continues*. By using the vertical scroll box, scroll to view the lower portion of the document, hold down Shift, and then click after the paragraph mark at the end of the paragraph that begins *Electronic medical records* to select all of the text between the insertion point and the sentence ending with the word *space*. Be sure that the paragraph mark is included in the selection. Compare your screen with Figure 3.24.

Use Shift to define a selection that may be difficult to select by dragging.

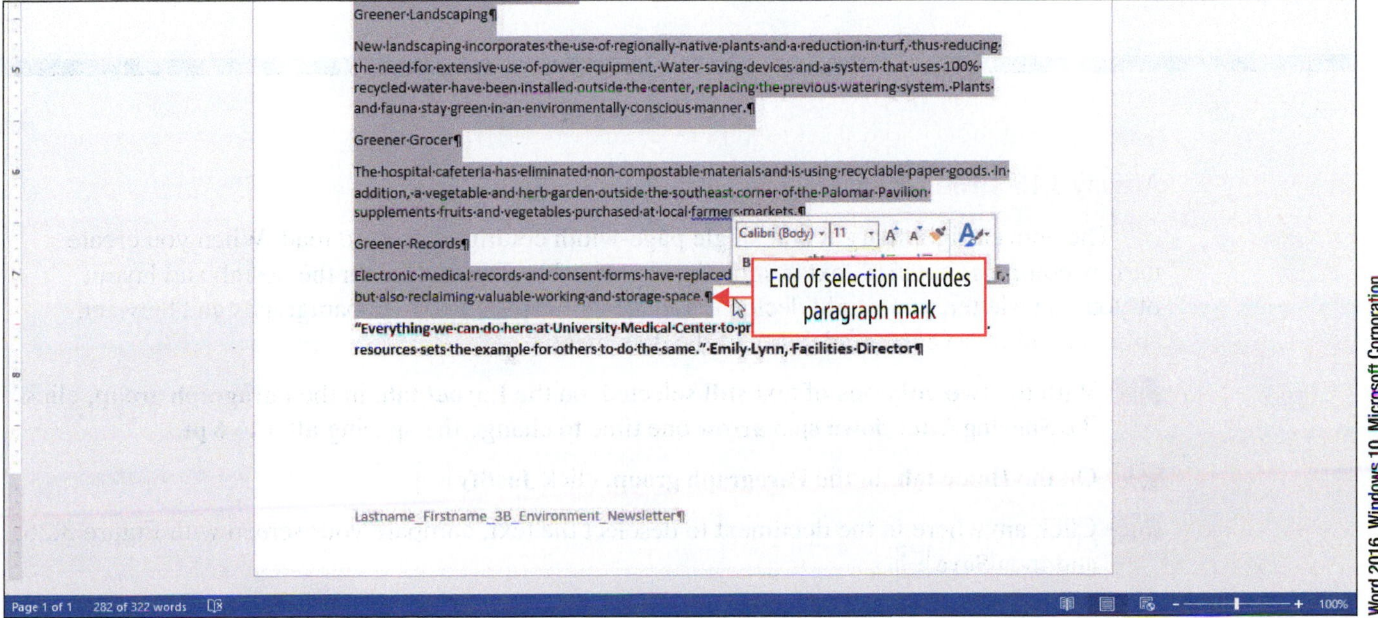

Greener·Landscaping¶
New·landscaping·incorporates·the·use·of·regionally·native·plants·and·a·reduction·in·turf,·thus·reducing·the·need·for·extensive·use·of·power·equipment.·Water-saving·devices·and·a·system·that·uses·100%·recycled·water·have·been·installed·outside·the·center,·replacing·the·previous·watering·system.·Plants·and·fauna·stay·green·in·an·environmentally·conscious·manner.¶
Greener·Grocer¶
The·hospital·cafeteria·has·eliminated·non-compostable·materials·and·is·using·recyclable·paper·goods.·In·addition,·a·vegetable·and·herb·garden·outside·the·southeast·corner·of·the·Palomar·Pavilion·supplements·fruits·and·vegetables·purchased·at·local·farmers·markets.¶
Greener·Records¶
Electronic·medical·records·and·consent·forms·have·replaced
but·also·reclaiming·valuable·working·and·storage·space.¶
"Everything·we·can·do·here·at·University·Medical·Center·to·pr
resources·sets·the·example·for·others·to·do·the·same."·Emily·Lynn,·Facilities·Director¶
Calibri (Body) 11
End of selection includes paragraph mark
Lastname_Firstname_3B_Environment_Newsletter¶
Page 1 of 1 282 of 322 words
100%

FIGURE 3.24

Word 2016, Windows 10, Microsoft Corporation

8 On the **Layout tab**, in the **Page Setup group**, click **Columns**, and then click **Two**. Compare your screen with Figure 3.25, and then **Save** your newsletter.

Word divides the selected text into two columns and inserts a ***section break*** at the end of the selection, dividing the one-column section of the document from the two-column section of the document. A ***section*** is a portion of a document that can be formatted differently from the rest of the document. A section break marks the end of one section and the beginning of another section.

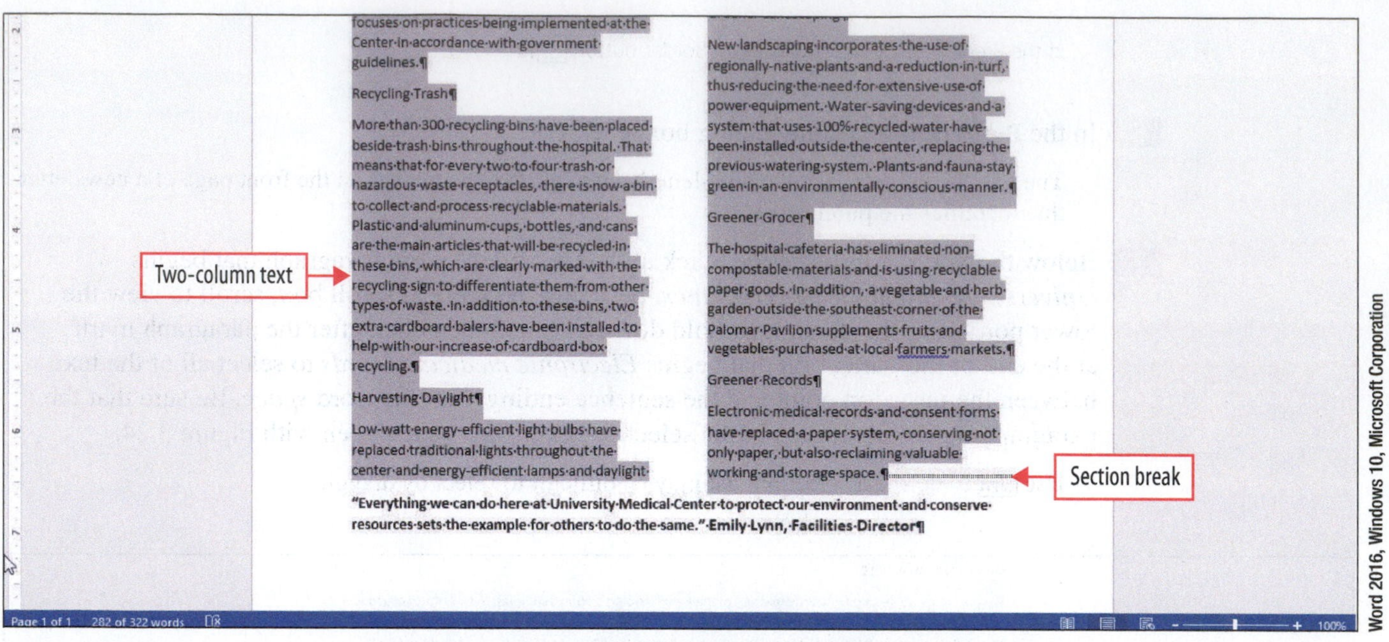

FIGURE 3.25

Activity 3.16 | Formatting Multiple Columns

The uneven right margin of a single page-width column is easy to read. When you create narrow columns, justified text is sometimes preferable. Depending on the design and layout of your newsletter, you might decide to reduce extra space between paragraphs and between columns to improve the readability of the document.

1. With the two columns of text still selected, on the **Layout tab**, in the **Paragraph group**, click the **Spacing After down spin arrow** one time to change the spacing after to **6 pt**.
2. On the **Home tab**, in the **Paragraph group**, click **Justify**.
3. Click anywhere in the document to deselect the text, compare your screen with Figure 3.26, and then **Save**.

focuses on practices being implemented at the Center in accordance with government guidelines.¶

Recycling Trash¶

More than 300 recycling bins have been placed beside trash bins throughout the hospital. That means that for every two to four trash or hazardous waste receptacles, there is now a bin to collect and process recyclable materials. Plastic and aluminum cups, bottles, and cans are the main articles that will be recycled in these bins, which are clearly marked with the recycling sign to differentiate them from other types of waste. In addition to these bins, two extra cardboard balers have been installed to help with our increase of cardboard box recycling.¶

Harvesting Daylight¶

Low-watt energy-efficient light bulbs have replaced traditional lights throughout the center and energy-efficient lamps and daylight controls have been installed. This move will conserve

New landscaping incorporates the use of regionally-native plants and a reduction in turf, thus reducing the need for extensive use of power equipment. Water-saving devices and a system that uses 100% recycled water have been installed outside the center, replacing the previous watering system. Plants and fauna stay green in an environmentally-conscious manner.¶

Greener Grocer¶

The hospital cafeteria has eliminated non-compostable materials and is using recyclable paper goods. In addition, a vegetable and herb garden outside the southeast corner of the Palomar Pavilion supplements fruits and vegetables purchased at local farmers markets.¶

Greener Records¶

Electronic medical records and consent forms have replaced a paper system, conserving not only paper, but also reclaiming valuable working and storage space.¶ Section Break (Continuous)

"Everything we can do here at University Medical Center to protect our environment and conserve resources sets the example for others to do the same." Emily Lynn, Facilities Director¶

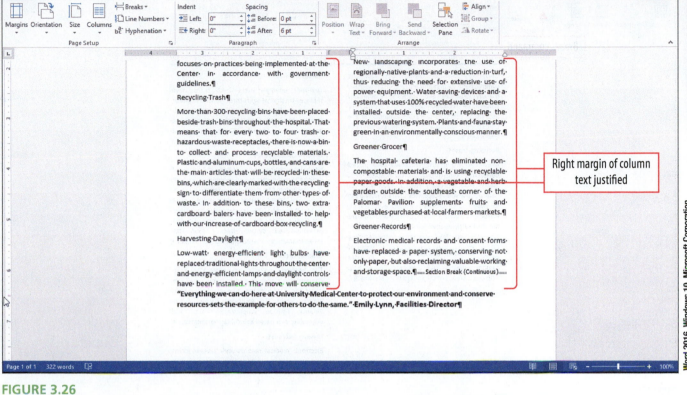

Right margin of column text justified

FIGURE 3.26

> ***More* Knowledge** **Justifying Column Text**
>
> Although many magazines and newspapers still justify text in columns, there are a variety of opinions about whether to justify the columns, or to use left alignment and leave the right edge uneven. Justified text tends to look more formal and cleaner, but in a word processing document, it also results in uneven spacing between words. It is the opinion of some authorities that justified text is more difficult to read, especially in a page-width document. Let the overall look and feel of your newsletter be your guide.

MOS 2.3.2

Activity 3.17 | Inserting a Column Break

1 Near the bottom of the first column, click to position the insertion point at the beginning of the line *Harvesting Daylight*.

2 On the **Layout tab**, in the **Page Setup group**, click **Breaks**. Under **Page Breaks**, click **Column**, and then if necessary, scroll to view the bottom of the first column.

A column break displays at the bottom of the first column; text to the right of the column break moves to the top of the next column.

3 Compare your screen with Figure 3.27, and then **Save**.

A ***column break indicator***—a dotted line containing the words *Column Break*—displays at the bottom of the column.

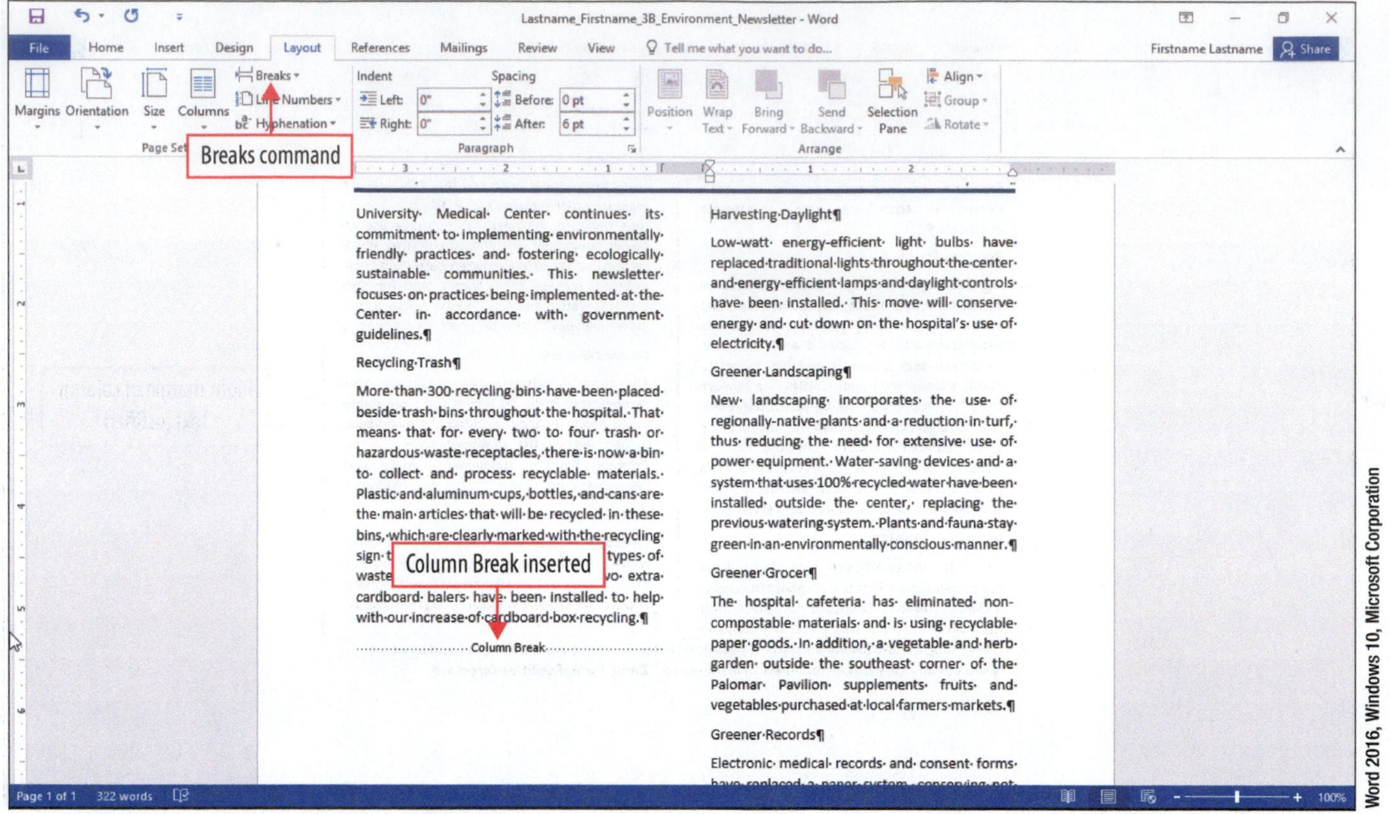

FIGURE 3.27

Activity 3.18 | Inserting an Online Picture

5.2.6, 5.2.7

You can search for and insert online pictures in your document without saving the images to your computer. Pictures can make your document visually appealing and more interesting.

1 Press Ctrl + End to move to the end of the document. Compare your screen with Figure 3.28.

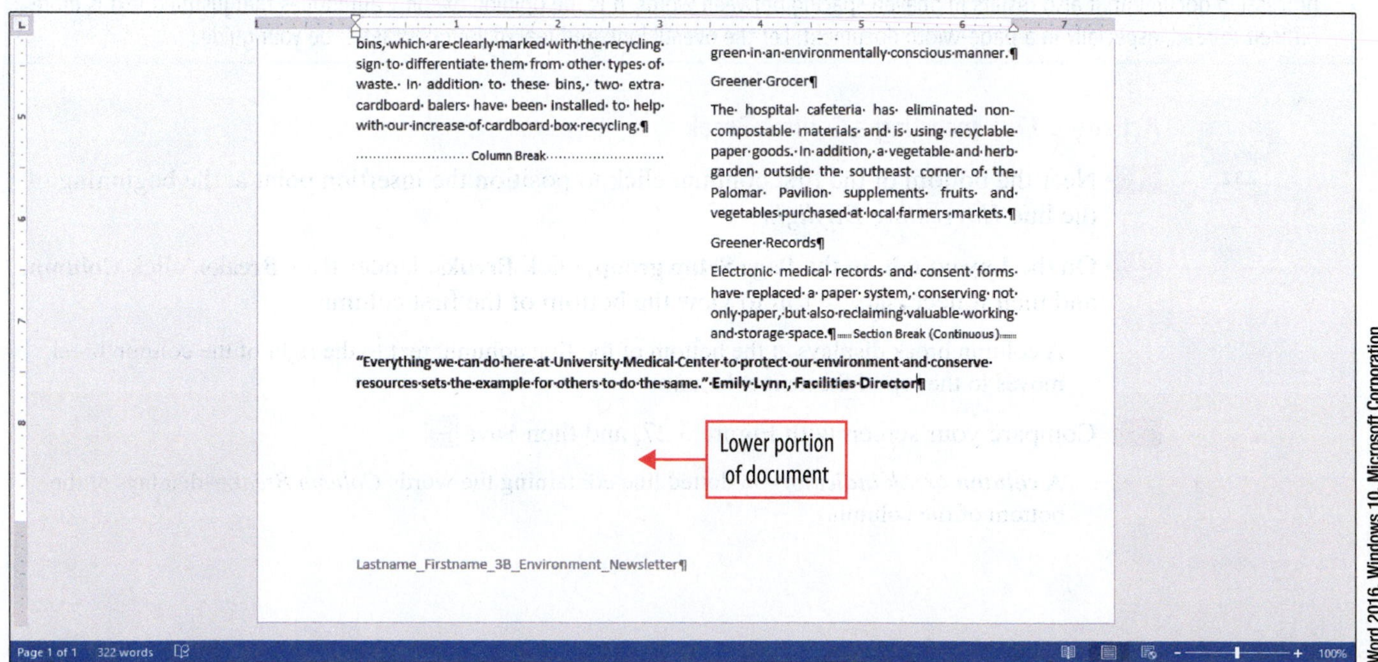

FIGURE 3.28

2 On the **Insert tab**, in the **Illustrations group**, click **Online Pictures**. With your insertion point blinking in the **Bing Image Search** box, type **green recycling symbol** and then press Enter. Compare your screen with Figure 3.29.

You can use various keywords to find images that are appropriate for your documents. The results shown indicate the images are licensed under ***Creative Commons***, which, according to **www.creativecommons.org** is "a nonprofit organization that enables the sharing and use of creativity and knowledge through free legal tools."

Creative Commons helps people share and use their photographs, but does not allow users to sell them. For your college assignments, you can use these images so long as you are not profiting by selling the images.

To find out more about Creative Commons, go to **https://creativecommons.org/about** and watch their video.

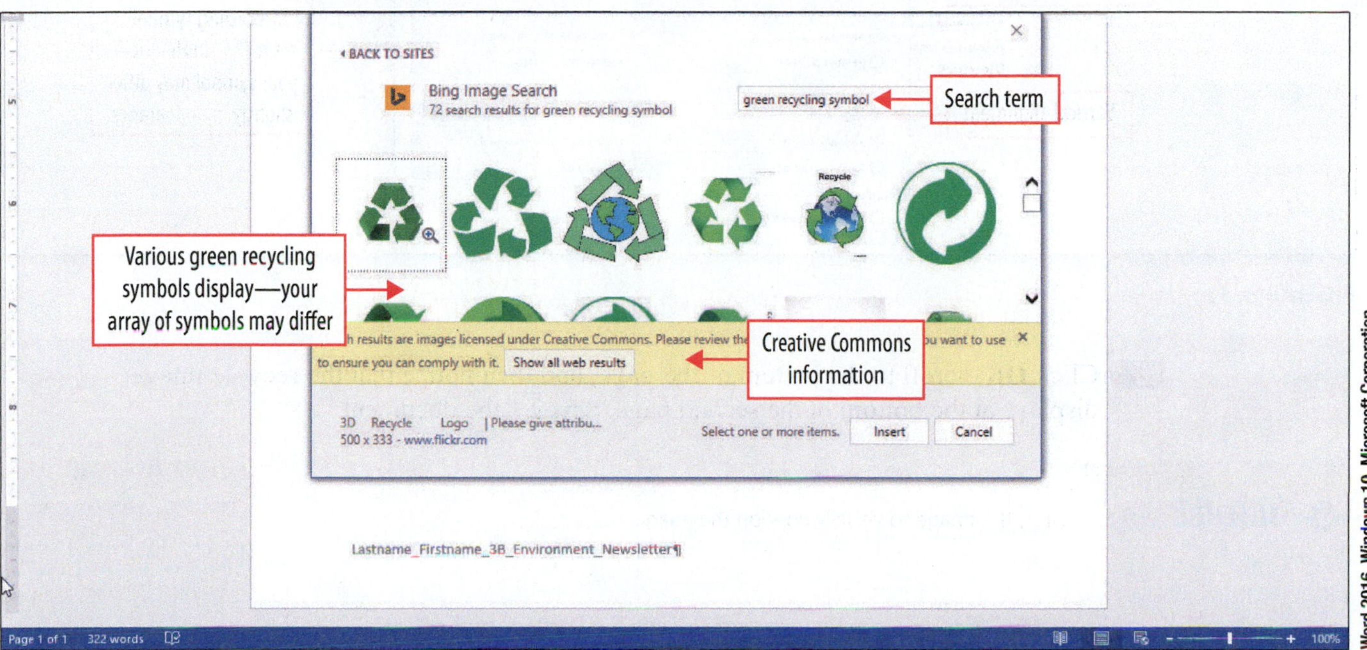

FIGURE 3.29

3 Click one of the green recycling symbols in the first row, and then in the lower right corner click **Insert**; your picture may display in a large size and create a new page.

4 With the picture selected, on the **Picture Tools Format tab**, in the **Size group**, click in the **Height** box. Type **0.5** and then press Enter. To the right of the picture, click **Layout Options**, and then click **Square**, which is the first button under **With Text Wrapping**. At the bottom of the **Layout Options gallery**, click **See more** to display the **Layout** dialog box. Compare your screen with Figure 3.30.

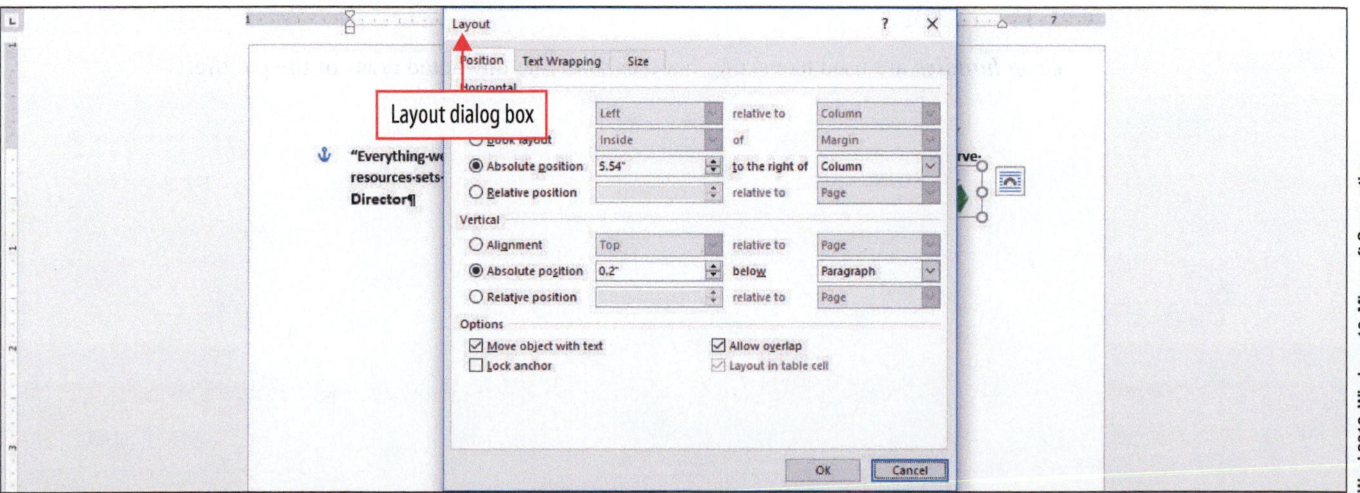

FIGURE 3.30

5 In the **Layout** dialog box, on the **Position tab**, under **Horizontal**, click the **Alignment** option button. Click the **Alignment arrow**, and then click **Centered**. Click the **relative to arrow** and then click **Page**. Under **Vertical**, click the **Alignment** option button. Click the **Alignment arrow**, and then click **Bottom**. Click the **relative to arrow**, and then click **Margin**. Compare your screen with Figure 3.31.

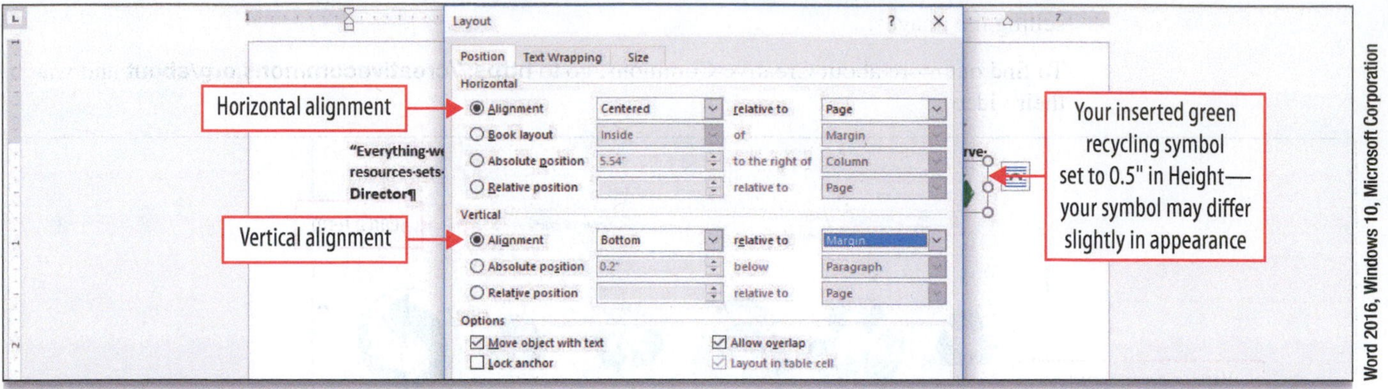

Word 2016, Windows 10, Microsoft Corporation

FIGURE 3.31

6 Click **OK**, scroll to the bottom of the page, and then notice that the recycle image displays at the bottom of the second page. **Save** the document.

ANOTHER WAY Drag the image to visually position the image.

Activity 3.19 | Cropping a Picture and Resizing a Picture by Scaling

MOS 5.2.4

In this Activity, you will insert a picture and edit the picture by cropping and scaling. When you ***crop*** a picture, you remove unwanted or unnecessary areas of the picture. When you ***scale*** a picture, you resize it to a percentage of its size.

1 Press Ctrl + Home to move to the top of the document. On the **Insert tab**, in the **Illustrations group**, click **Pictures**. In the **Insert Picture** dialog box, navigate to the location of your student data files, and then double-click **w03B_Recycling** to insert it.

2 With the picture selected, on the **Picture Tools Format tab**, in the **Size group**, click the upper portion of the **Crop** button to display crop handles around the picture. Compare your screen with Figure 3.32.

Crop handles are used like sizing handles to define unwanted areas of the picture.

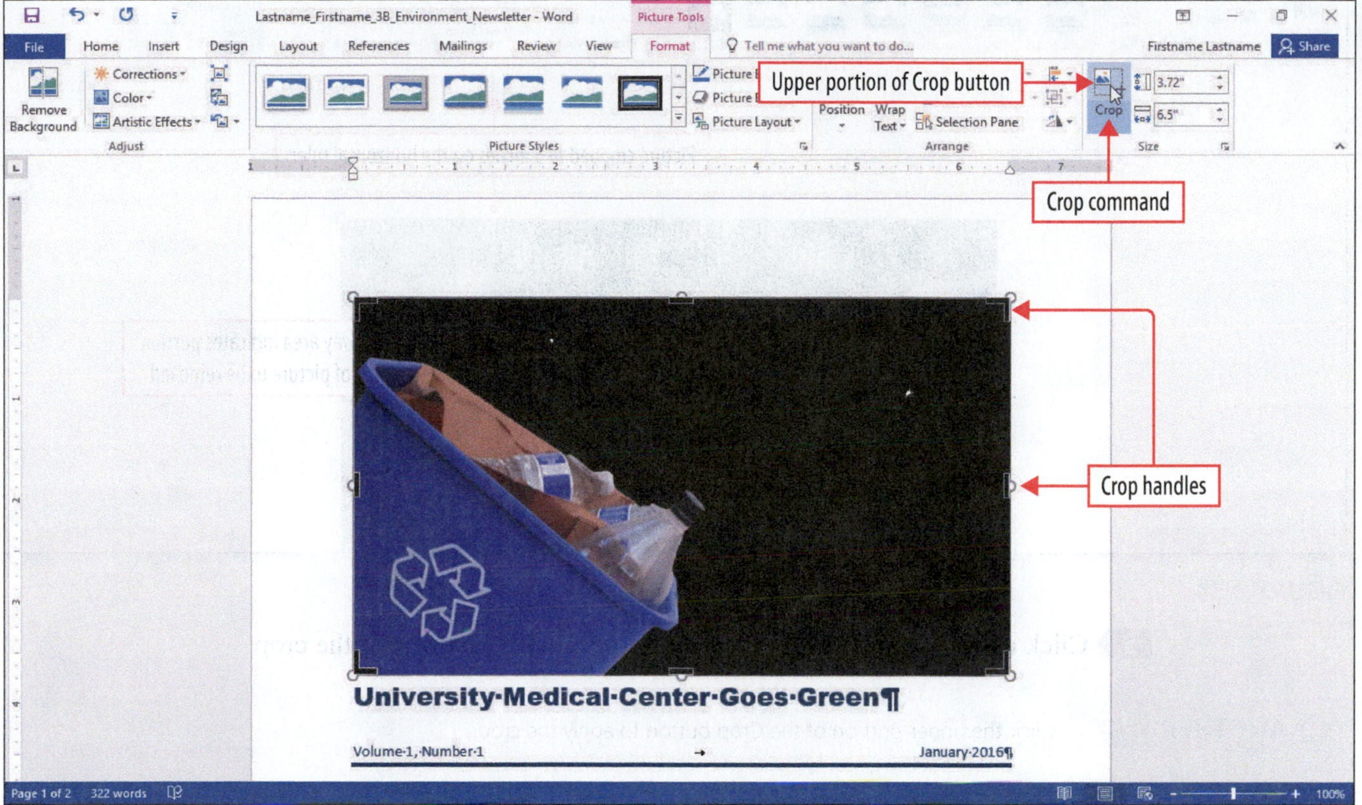

Word 2016, Windows 10, Microsoft Corporation

FIGURE 3.32

3 Point to the center right crop handle to display the ⊩ pointer. Compare your screen with Figure 3.33.

Use the ***crop pointer*** to crop areas of a picture.

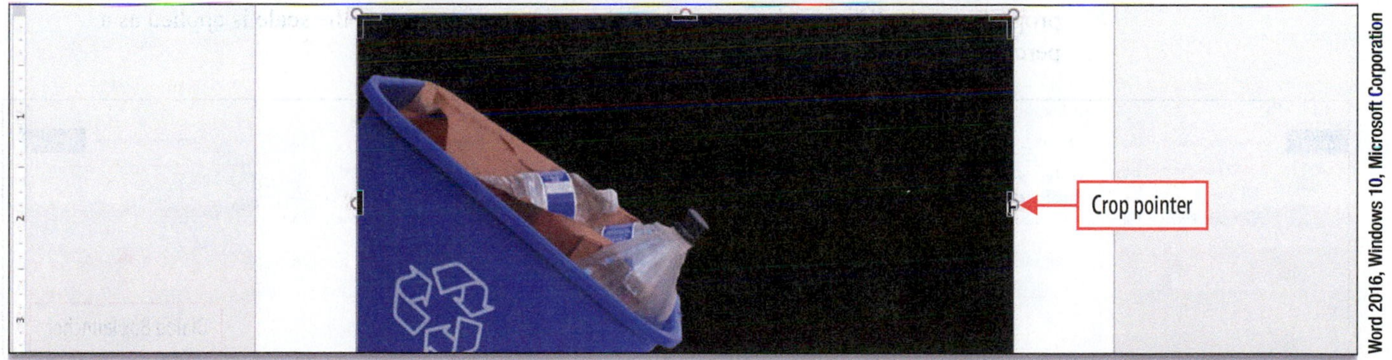

Word 2016, Windows 10, Microsoft Corporation

FIGURE 3.33

4 With the crop pointer displayed, hold down the left mouse button and drag to the left to approximately **5 inches on the horizontal ruler**, and then release the mouse button. Compare your screen with Figure 3.34.

The portion of the image to be removed displays in gray.

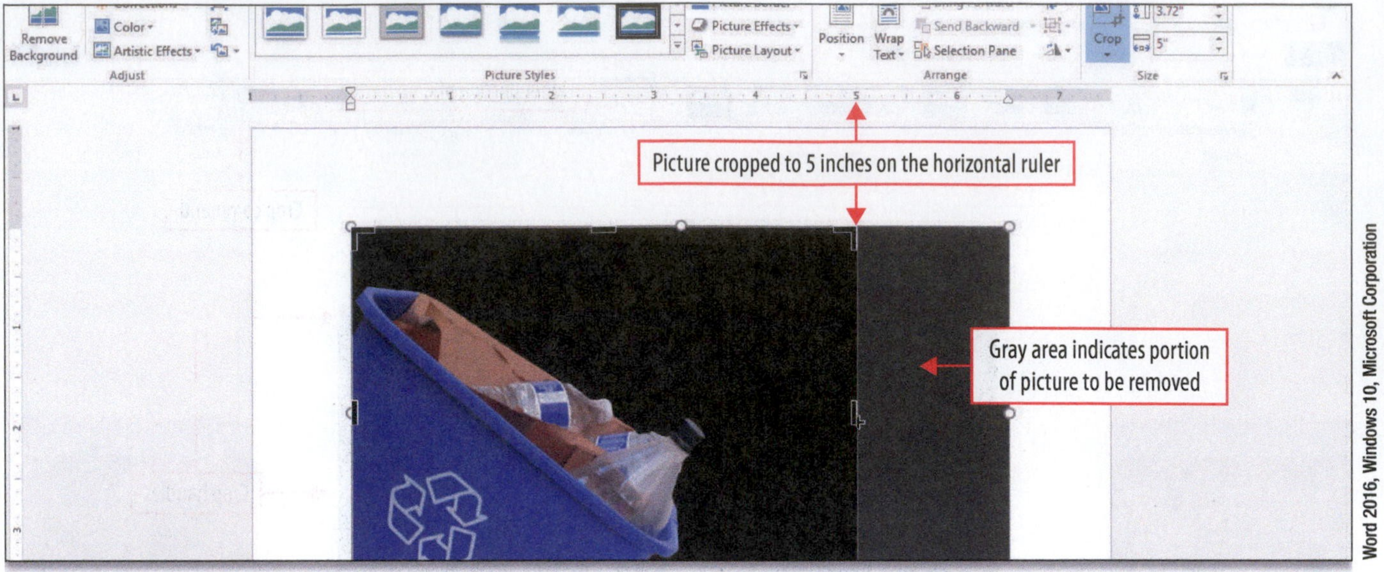

FIGURE 3.34

5 Click anywhere in the document outside of the image to apply the crop.

ANOTHER WAY Click the upper portion of the Crop button to apply the crop.

6 Click to select the picture again. On the **Picture Tools Format tab**, in the **Size group**, click the **Dialog Box Launcher** button.

7 In the **Layout** dialog box, on the **Size tab**, under **Scale**, be sure that the **Lock aspect ratio** and **Relative to original picture size** check boxes are selected. Under **Scale**, select the percentage in the **Height box**, type **10** and then press Tab. Compare your screen with Figure 3.35.

When *Lock aspect ratio* is selected, the height and width of the picture are sized proportionately and only one scale value is necessary. The second value—in this instance Width—adjusts proportionately. When *Relative to original picture size* is selected, the scale is applied as a percentage of the original picture size.

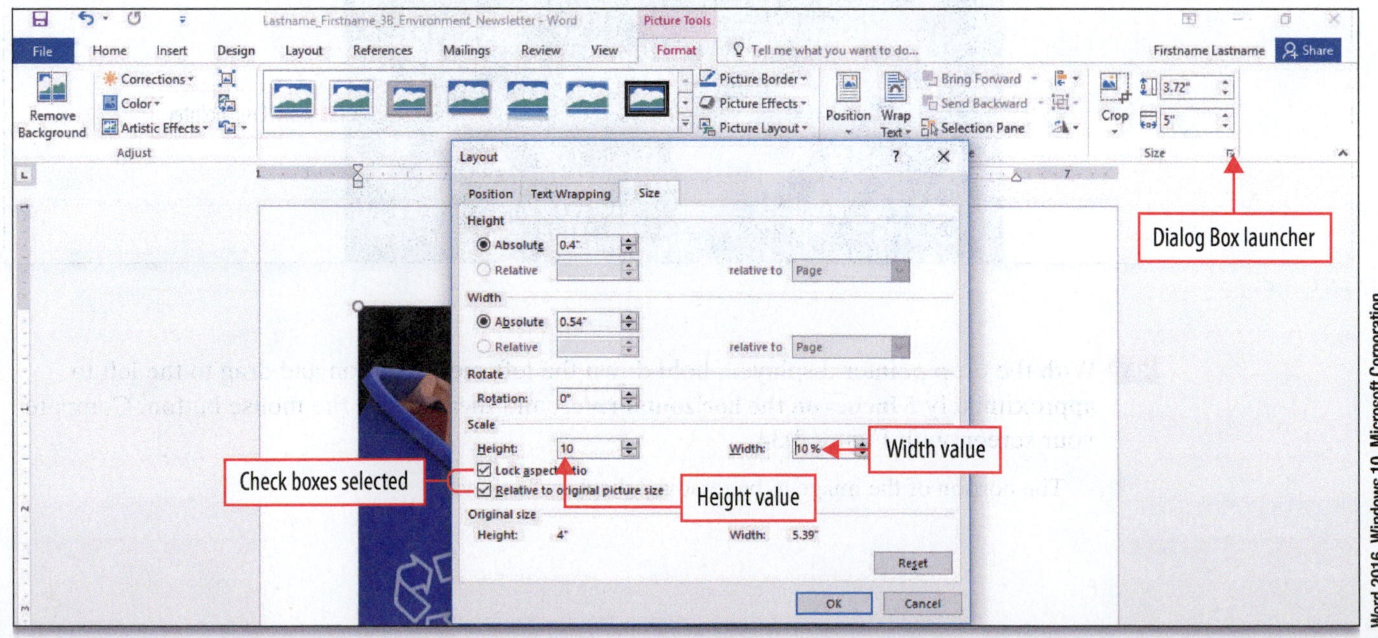

FIGURE 3.35

8 In the **Layout** dialog box, click the **Text Wrapping tab**. Under **Wrapping style**, click **Square**.

9 Click the **Position tab**, and then under **Horizontal**, click the **Alignment** option button. Be sure that the **Alignment** indicates **Left** and **relative to Column**. Under **Vertical**, click the **Alignment** option button, and then change the alignment to **Top relative to Margin**. Click **OK**, and then compare your screen with Figure 3.36.

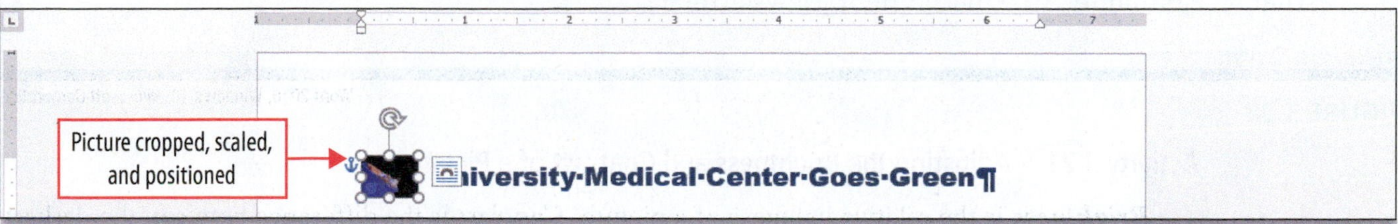

FIGURE 3.36

Word 2016, Windows 10, Microsoft Corporation

Activity 3.20 | Setting Transparent Color and Recoloring a Picture

1.4.2, 5.2.3

You can make one color in a picture transparent using the Set Transparent Color command. When you ***recolor*** a picture, you change all the colors in the picture to shades of a single color.

1 On the **View tab**, in the **Zoom group**, click **Zoom**, and then click **200%**. Click **OK**. Drag the scroll bars as necessary so that you can view the recycle bin picture at the top of the document.

2 If necessary, select the recycle bin picture. Click the **Picture Tools Format tab**. In the **Adjust group**, click **Color**, and then below the gallery, click **Set Transparent Color**. Move the pointer into the document to display the pointer.

3 Point anywhere in the black background of the recycle bin picture, and then click to apply the transparent color to the background. Compare your screen with Figure 3.37.

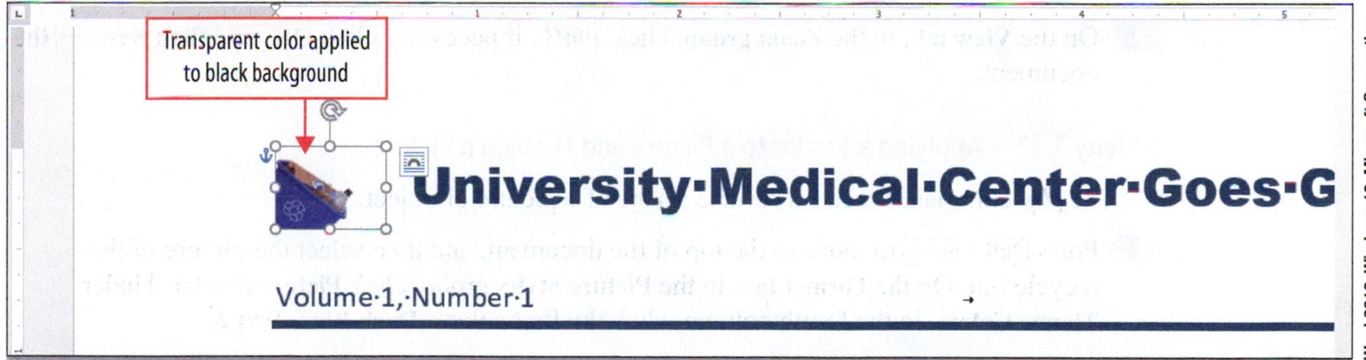

FIGURE 3.37

Word 2016, Windows 10, Microsoft Corporation

4 Press Ctrl + End to move to the end of your document, and then select the picture of the recycle symbol. On the **Format tab**, in the **Adjust group**, click **Color** to display a gallery of recoloring options. Under **Recolor**, in the last row, click the fourth option—**Olive Green, Accent color 3 Light**. Compare your screen with Figure 3.38, and then **Save** the document.

3 WORD

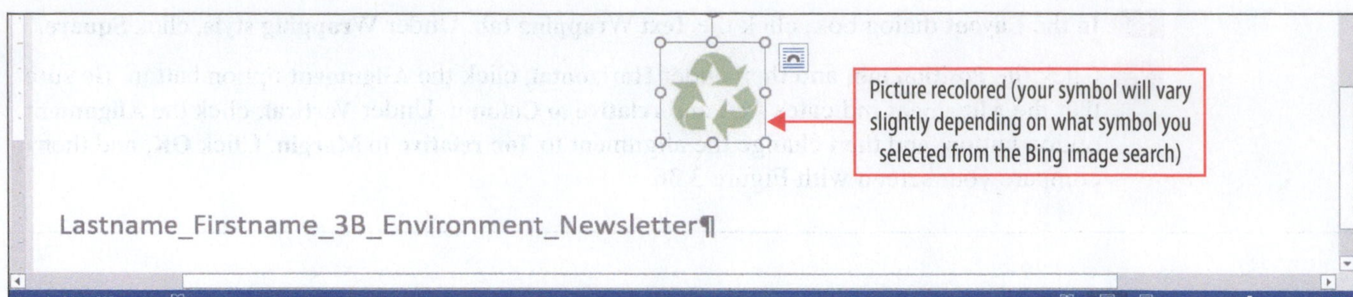

Word 2016, Windows 10, Microsoft Corporation

FIGURE 3.38

Activity 3.21 | Adjusting the Brightness and Contrast of a Picture

Brightness is the relative lightness of a picture. ***Contrast*** is the difference between the darkest and lightest area of a picture.

1. If necessary, select the recycle symbol. On the **Format tab**, in the **Adjust group**, click **Corrections**. Under **Brightness/Contrast**, point to several of the options to view the effect that the settings have on the picture.
2. Under **Brightness/Contrast**, in the last row, click the first setting—**Brightness: –40% Contrast: +40%**. Compare your screen with Figure 3.39.

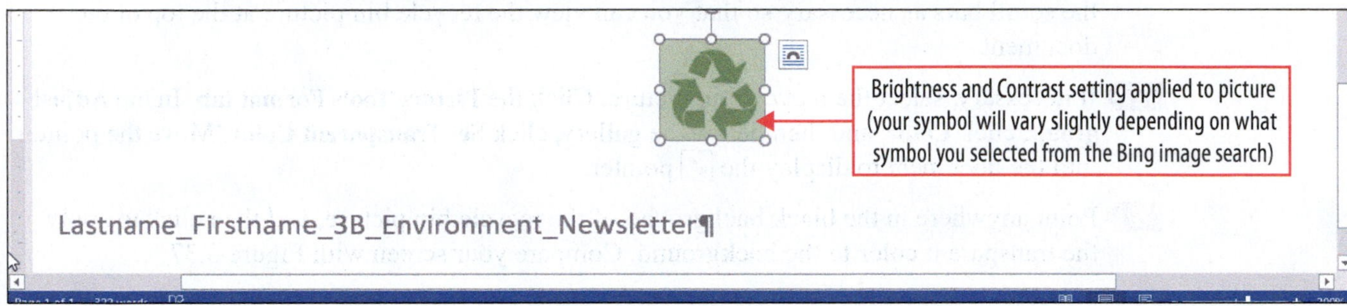

Word 2016, Windows 10, Microsoft Corporation

FIGURE 3.39

3. On the **View tab**, in the **Zoom group**, click **100%**, if necessary click **OK**, and then **Save** the document.

Activity 3.22 | Applying a Border to a Picture and Flipping a Picture

The ***flip*** commands create a reverse image of a picture or object.

1. Press Ctrl + Home to move to the top of the document, and then select the picture of the recycle bin. On the **Format tab**, in the **Picture Styles group**, click **Picture Border**. Under **Theme Colors**, in the fourth column, click the first color—**Dark Blue, Text 2**.
2. Click **Picture Border** again, and then point to **Weight**. Click **1 ½ pt** to change the thickness of the border.
3. On the **Format tab**, in the **Arrange group**, click **Rotate Objects**, and then click **Flip Horizontal**. Click anywhere in the document to deselect the picture. **Save**, and then compare your screen with Figure 3.40.

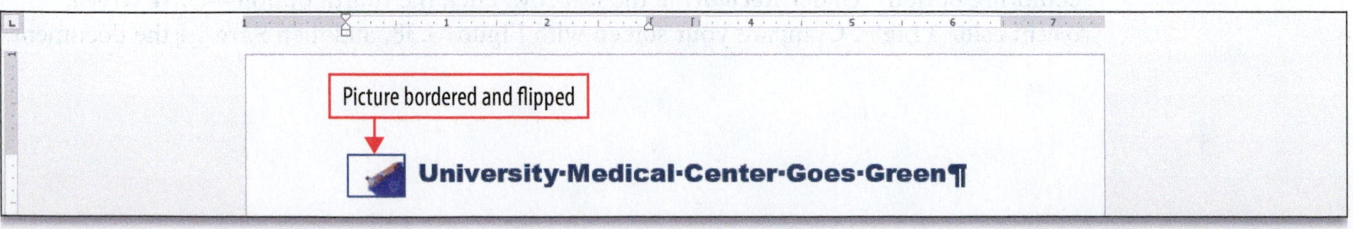

Word 2016, Windows 10, Microsoft Corporation

FIGURE 3.40

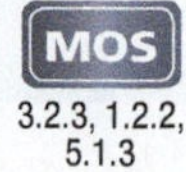

3.2.3, 1.2.2, 5.1.3

Activity 3.23 | Inserting and Formatting a Screenshot

A ***screenshot*** is an image of an active window on your computer that you can paste into a document. Screenshots are especially useful when you want to insert an image of a website into your Word document. You can insert a screenshot of any open window on your computer.

1. In the paragraph that begins *University Medical Center continues*, click after the period at the end of the paragraph. Start your web browser, and then navigate to **www.epa.gov** and press Enter.
2. From the taskbar, redisplay your **3B_Environment_Newsletter** document.
3. With the insertion point positioned at the end of the paragraph, on the **Insert tab**, in the **Illustrations group**, click **Screenshot**.

   All of your open windows display in the Available Windows gallery and are available to paste into the document.

ALERT! **If No Windows Display**

If no windows display when you click the Screenshot command, possibly your browser does not support this feature. Instead, on the menu that displays, click Screen Clipping, position the + pointer in the upper right corner of the web window, and then drag down to the lower right corner. Release the mouse button to insert the screenshot.

4. In the **Screenshot** gallery, click the browser window that contains the EPA site to insert the screenshot at the insertion point. If a message box displays asking if you want to hyperlink the screenshot, click No, and then notice that the image is inserted and is sized to fit between the margins of the first column. Compare your screen with Figure 3.41.

   By selecting No in the message box, you are inserting a screenshot without links to the actual website. Choose Yes if you want to link the image to the website.

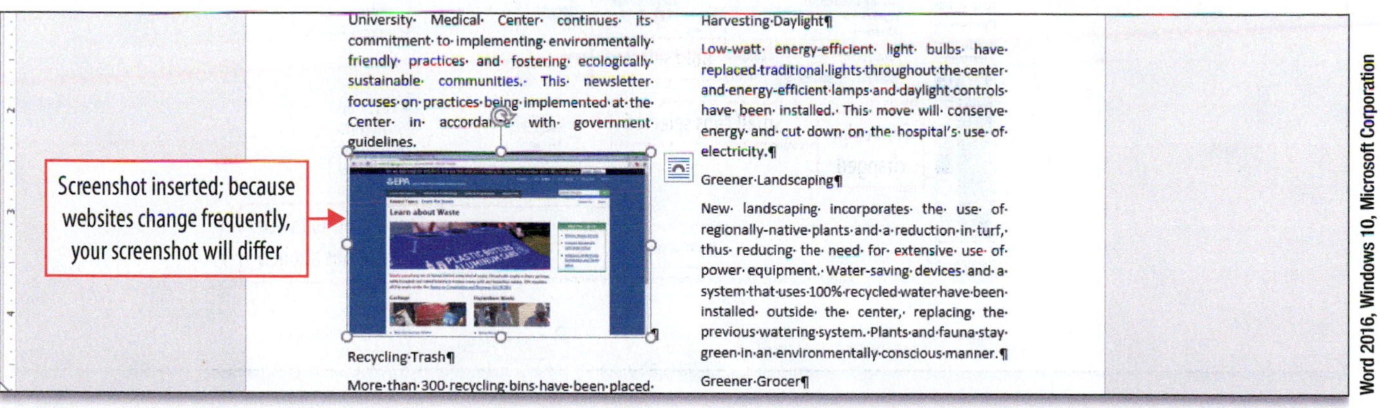

FIGURE 3.41

5. With the inserted screenshot selected, on the **Format tab**, in the **Picture Styles group**, click **Picture Border**, and then under **Theme Colors**, in the second column, click the first color—**Black, Text 1**.
6. **Save** the document.

More Knowledge **Inserting a Hyperlink in a Document**

You can create a link in your document for quick access to webpages and files. To insert a link in a document, first position the insertion point where you want the link to appear. On the Insert tab, in the Links group, click Hyperlink. In the Insert Hyperlink dialog box, in the Text to display box, type the text that will display in the document as a blue hyperlink. At the bottom, in the Address box, type the URL and then click OK.

Objective 6 Use Special Character and Paragraph Formatting

By using special text and paragraph formatting, you can emphasize text and make your newsletter look more professional. For example, you can place a border around one or more paragraphs or add shading to a paragraph. When adding shading, use light colors; dark shading can make the text difficult to read.

Activity 3.24 | Applying the Small Caps Font Effect

For headlines and titles, ***small caps*** is an attractive font effect. The effect changes lowercase letters to uppercase letters, but with the height of lowercase letters.

1. Under the screenshot, select the paragraph *Recycling Trash* including the paragraph mark.
2. Right-click the selected text, and then on the shortcut menu, click **Font** to display the **Font** dialog box. Click the **Font color arrow**, and then change the color to **Blue, Accent 1, Darker 50%**—in the fifth column, the last color.
3. Under **Font style**, click **Bold**. Under **Effects**, select the **Small caps** check box. Compare your screen with Figure 3.42.

   The Font dialog box provides more options than are available on the ribbon and enables you to make several changes at the same time. In the Preview box, the text displays with the selected formatting options applied.

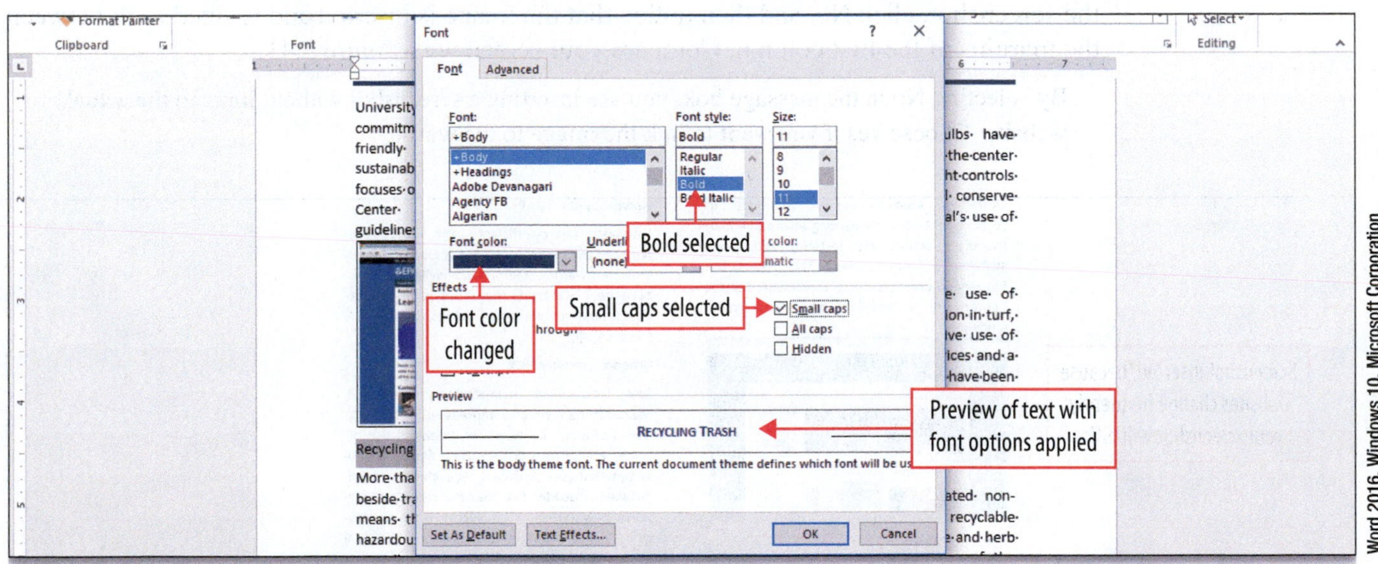

FIGURE 3.42

4. Click **OK**. With the text still selected, right-click, and then on the mini toolbar, double-click **Format Painter** so that you can apply the format multiple times. Then, in the second column, with the pointer, select each of the heading paragraphs—*Harvesting Daylight*, *Greener Landscaping*, *Greener Grocer*, and *Greener Records*—to apply the same formats. Press Esc to turn off Format Painter.
5. In the first column, below the screenshot, notice that the space between the *Recycling Trash* subheading and the screenshot is fairly small. Click anywhere in the *Recycling Trash* subheading, and then on the **Layout tab**, in the **Paragraph group**, click the **Before up spin arrow** two times to set the spacing to **12 pt**.
6. Compare your screen with Figure 3.43, and then **Save** your document.

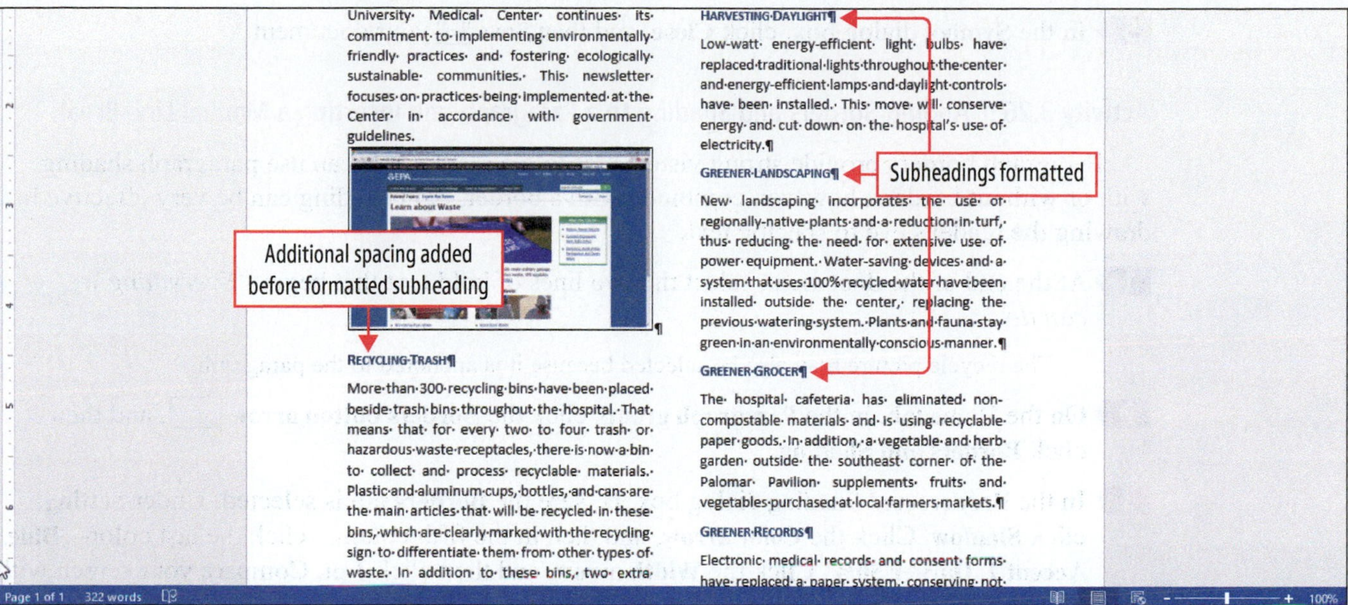

Word 2016, Windows 10, Microsoft Corporation

FIGURE 3.43

Activity 3.25 | Inserting Symbols and Special Characters

MOS 3.2.5

You can insert symbols and special characters in a Word document, including copyright symbols, trademark symbols, and em dashes. An ***em dash*** is a punctuation symbol used to indicate an explanation or emphasis.

1. Press Ctrl + End to move to the end of the document, and then after the name *Emily Lynn* delete the comma and the space that separates her name from her job title—*Facilities Director*.

2. With the insertion point positioned before the *F* in *Facilities*, on the **Insert tab**, in the **Symbols group**, click **Symbol**. Below the gallery, click **More Symbols** to display the **Symbol** dialog box.

   Here you can choose the symbol that you want to insert in your document.

3. In the **Symbol** dialog box, click the **Special Characters tab**. Scroll the list to view the types of special characters that you can insert; notice that some of the characters can be inserted using a Shortcut key.

4. Click **Em Dash**, and then in the lower right portion of the dialog box, click **Insert**. If necessary, drag the title bar of the Symbol window up or to the side, and then compare your screen with Figure 3.44.

   An em dash displays between the name *Lynn* and the word *Facilities*.

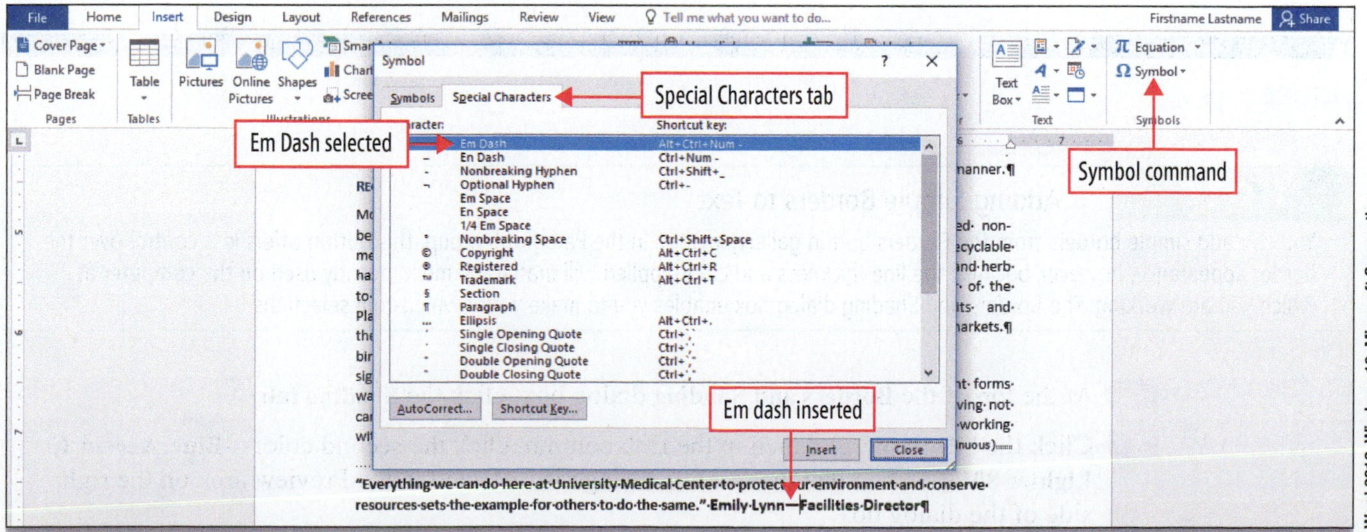

Word 2016, Windows 10, Microsoft Corporation

FIGURE 3.44

5 In the **Symbol** dialog box, click **Close**, and then **Save** your document.

Activity 3.26 | Adding Borders and Shading to a Paragraph and Inserting a Manual Line Break

Paragraph borders provide strong visual cues to the reader. You can use paragraph shading with or without borders; however, combined with a border, light shading can be very effective in drawing the reader's eye to specific text.

1 At the end of the document, select the two lines of bold text that begin *"Everything we can do.*

The recycle picture may also be selected because it is anchored to the paragraph.

2 On the **Home tab**, in the **Paragraph group**, click the **Borders button arrow**, and then click **Borders and Shading**.

3 In the **Borders and Shading** dialog box, be sure the **Borders tab** is selected. Under **Setting**, click **Shadow**. Click the **Color arrow**, and then in the fifth column, click the last color—**Blue, Accent 1, Darker 50%**. Click the **Width arrow**, and then click **1 pt**. Compare your screen with Figure 3.45.

In the lower right portion of the Borders and Shading dialog box, the *Apply to* box indicates *Paragraph*. The *Apply to* box directs where the border will be applied—in this instance, the border will be applied only to the selected paragraph.

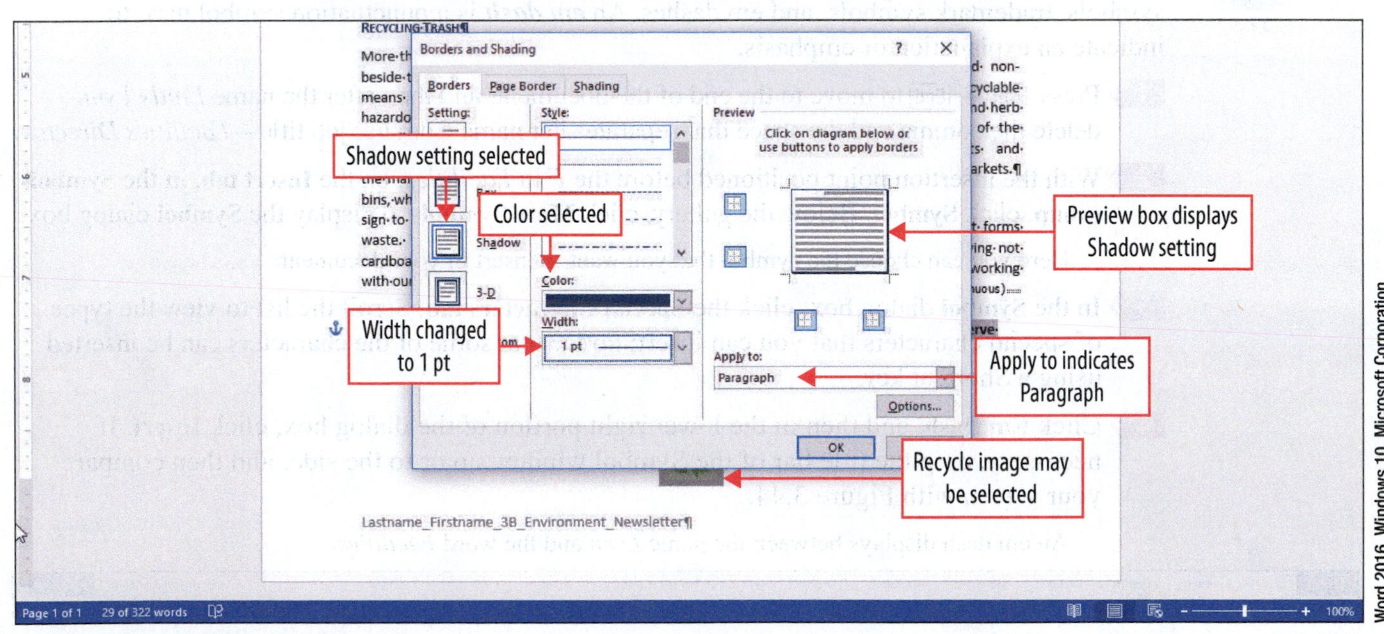

FIGURE 3.45

> **NOTE** Adding Simple Borders to Text
>
> You can add simple borders from the Borders button gallery, located in the Paragraph group. This button offers less control over the border appearance, however, because the line thickness and color applied will match the most recently used on the computer at which you are working. The Borders and Shading dialog box enables you to make your own custom selections.

4 At the top of the **Borders and Shading** dialog box, click the **Shading tab**.

5 Click the **Fill arrow**, and then in the fifth column, click the second color—**Blue, Accent 1, Lighter 80%**. Notice that the shading change is reflected in the Preview area on the right side of the dialog box.

6 Click **OK**. On the **Home tab**, in the **Paragraph group**, click **Center** [icon].

7 Click anywhere in the document to deselect, and then compare your screen with Figure 3.46.

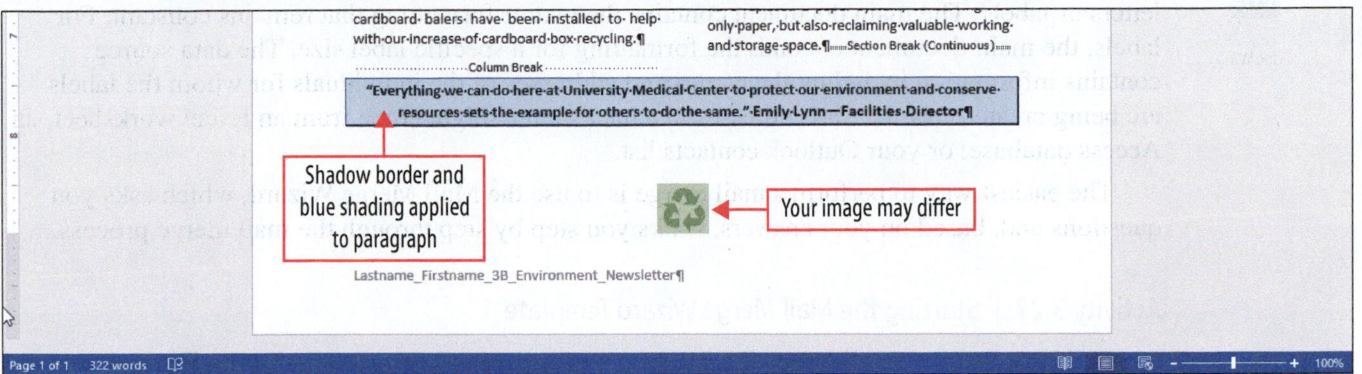

Word 2016, Windows 10, Microsoft Corporation

FIGURE 3.46

8 In the shaded paragraph, in the second line, click in front of the *E* in the name *Emily*. Hold down Shift and then press Enter.

Holding down Shift while pressing Enter inserts a ***manual line break***, which moves the text to the right of the insertion point to a new line while keeping the text in the same paragraph. A ***line break indicator***, in the shape of a bent arrow, indicates a manual line break.

9 Press Ctrl + Home to move the insertion point to the top of the document. Click the **File tab** to display **Backstage** view. On the right, at the bottom of the **Properties** list, click **Show All Properties**.

10 On the list of **Properties**, click to the right of **Tags**, and then type **newsletter, January**

11 Click to the right of **Subject**, and then type your course name and section number. Under **Related People**, be sure that your name displays as the author. If necessary, right-click the author name, click Edit Property, type your name, and click OK.

12 On the left, click **Print** to display the **Print Preview**, and then on the left click Save to save your document and return to the document window. In the upper right corner of the Word window, click **Close** [X]. If directed by your instructor to do so, submit your paper printout, your electronic image of your document that looks like a printed document, or your completed Word file. If you are submitting this Project as a MyITLab grader, submit this file.

ALERT!

The Remaining Activities in This Chapter Are Optional

Activities 3.27, 3.28, and 3.29, in which you create a set of mailing labels for the newsletter, are optional. Check with your instructor to see if you should complete these three Activities. These Activities *are* included in the MyITLab Grader system as a separate Grader exercise.

Objective 7 Create Mailing Labels Using Mail Merge

GO! Learn How Video W3-7

Word's ***mail merge*** feature joins a ***main document*** and a ***data source*** to create customized letters or labels. The main document contains the text or formatting that remains constant. For labels, the main document contains the formatting for a specific label size. The data source contains information including the names and addresses of the individuals for whom the labels are being created. Names and addresses in a data source might come from an Excel worksheet, an Access database, or your Outlook contacts list.

The easiest way to perform a mail merge is to use the Mail Merge Wizard, which asks you questions and, based on your answers, walks you step by step through the mail merge process.

Activity 3.27 | Starting the Mail Merge Wizard Template

In this Activity, you will open the data source for the mail merge, which is an Excel worksheet containing names and addresses.

1. Start Word and display a new blank document. Display formatting marks and rulers. **Save** the document in your **Word Chapter 3** folder as **Lastname_Firstname_3B_Mailing_Labels**

2. With your new document open on the screen, from the taskbar, open **File Explorer**. Navigate to the student data files that accompany this chapter, and then double-click the Word file **w03B_Addresses** to open it in Excel. Compare your screen with Figure 3.47.

   This Excel worksheet contains the addresses. Each row of information that contains data for one person is referred to as a ***record***. The column headings, for example *First Name* and *Last Name*, are referred to as ***fields***.

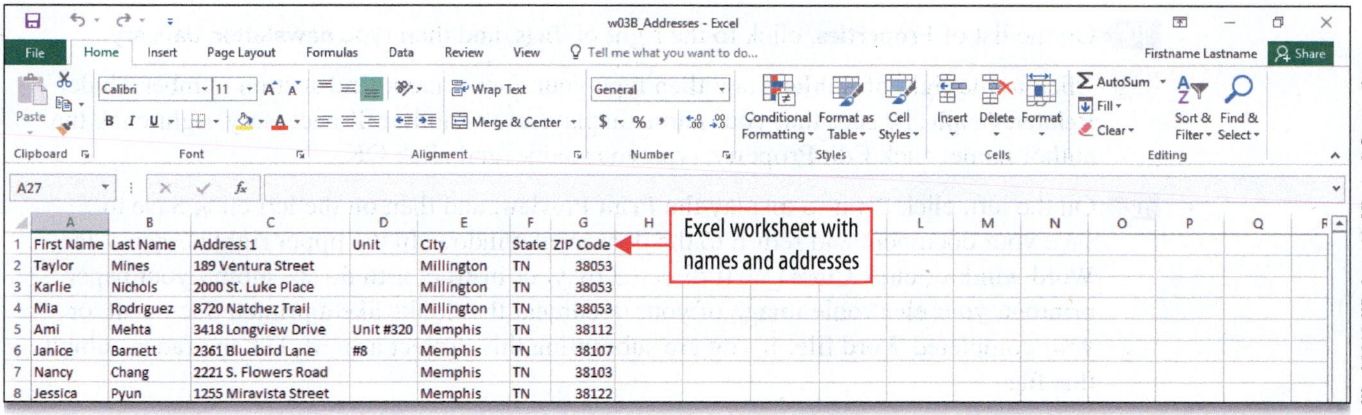

Word 2016, Windows 10, Microsoft Corporation

FIGURE 3.47

3. **Close** Excel and if necessary, close the File Explorer window. Be sure that your blank **Lastname_Firstname_3B_Mailing_Labels** document displays.

4. Click the **Mailings tab**. In the **Start Mail Merge group**, click **Start Mail Merge**, and then click **Step-by-Step Mail Merge Wizard** to display the **Mail Merge** pane on the right.

5. In the **Mail Merge** pane, under **Select document type**, click **Labels**. At the bottom of the **Mail Merge** pane, click **Next: Starting document** to display Step 2 of 6.

6. Under **Select starting document**, be sure **Change document layout** is selected, and then under **Change document layout**, click **Label options**.

7 In the **Label Options** dialog box, under **Printer information**, click the **Tray arrow**, and then if necessary, click **Default tray (Automatically Select)**—the exact wording may vary depending on your printer, but select the *Default* or *Automatic* option so that you can print the labels on regular paper rather than manually inserting labels in the printer.

8 Under **Label information**, click the **Label vendors arrow**, and then click **Avery US Letter**. Under **Product number**, scroll about halfway down the list, and then click **5160 Easy Peel Address Labels**. Compare your screen with Figure 3.48.

The Avery 5160 address label is a commonly used label. The precut sheets contain three columns of 10 labels each—for a total of 30 labels per sheet.

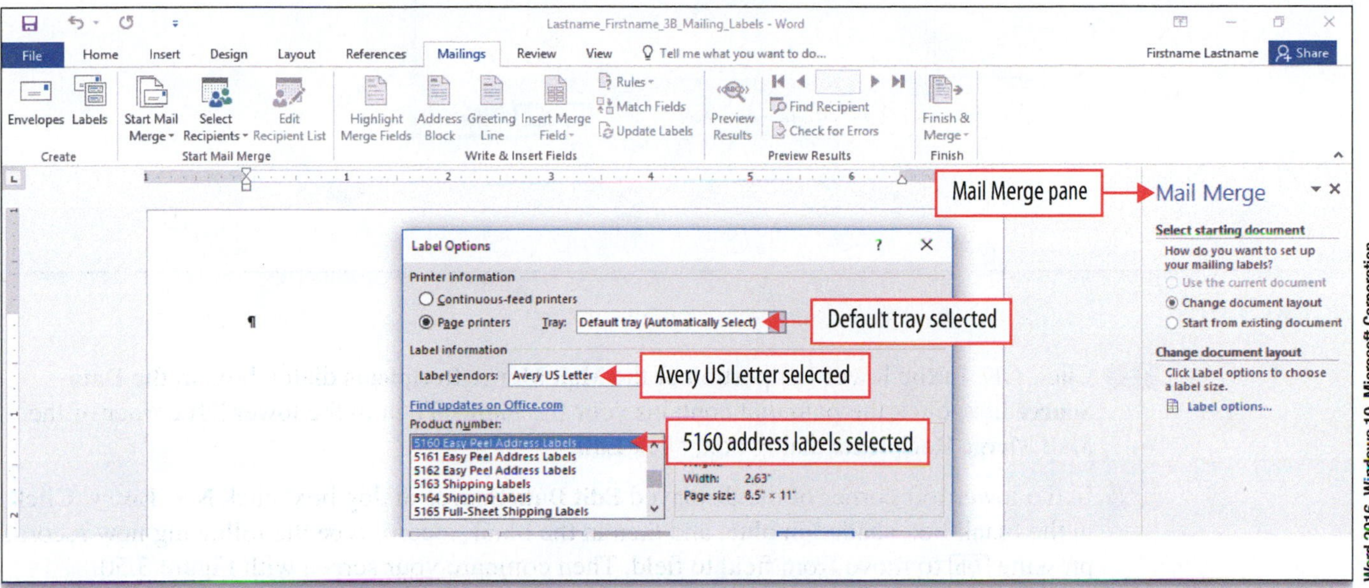

FIGURE 3.48

9 At the bottom of the **Label Options** dialog box, click **OK**. If a message box displays, click OK to set up the labels. If the gridlines do not display, on the Table Tools Layout tab, in the Table group, click View Gridlines. At the bottom of the **Mail Merge** pane, click **Next: Select recipients**.

The label page is set up with three columns and ten rows. Here, in Step 3 of the Mail Merge Wizard, you must identify the recipients—the data source. For your recipient data source, you can choose to use an existing list—for example, a list of names and addresses that you have in an Access database, an Excel worksheet, or your Outlook contacts list. If you do not have an existing data source, you can type a new list at this point in the wizard.

10 In the **Mail Merge** pane, under **Select recipients**, be sure the **Use an existing list** option button is selected. Under **Use an existing list**, click **Browse**.

11 In the **Select Data Source** dialog box, navigate to the student data files that accompany this chapter, click the Excel file **w03B_Addresses** one time to select it, and then click **Open** to display the **Select Table** dialog box. Compare your screen with Figure 3.49.

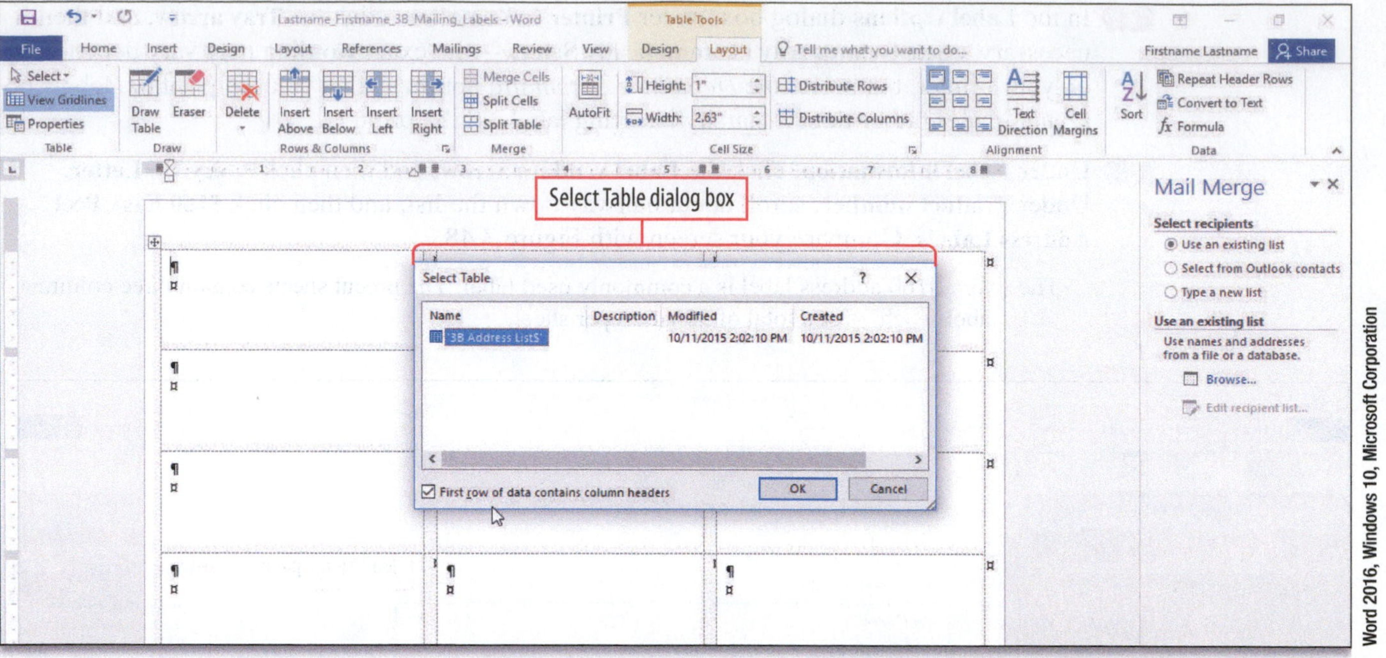

FIGURE 3.49

12 Click **OK**. In the lower left portion of the **Mail Merge Recipients** dialog box, in the **Data Source** box, click the path that contains your file name. Then in the lower left corner of the **Mail Merge Recipients** dialog box, click **Edit**.

13 In the lower left corner of the displayed **Edit Data Source** dialog box, click **New Entry**. Click in the blank box shaded in blue, and then in the blank record, type the following new record, pressing Tab to move from field to field. Then compare your screen with Figure 3.50.

FIRST_NAME	LAST_NAME	ADDRESS_1	UNIT	CITY	STATE	ZIP CODE
Sharon	Williams	1251 Parker Road	#843	Memphis	TN	38123

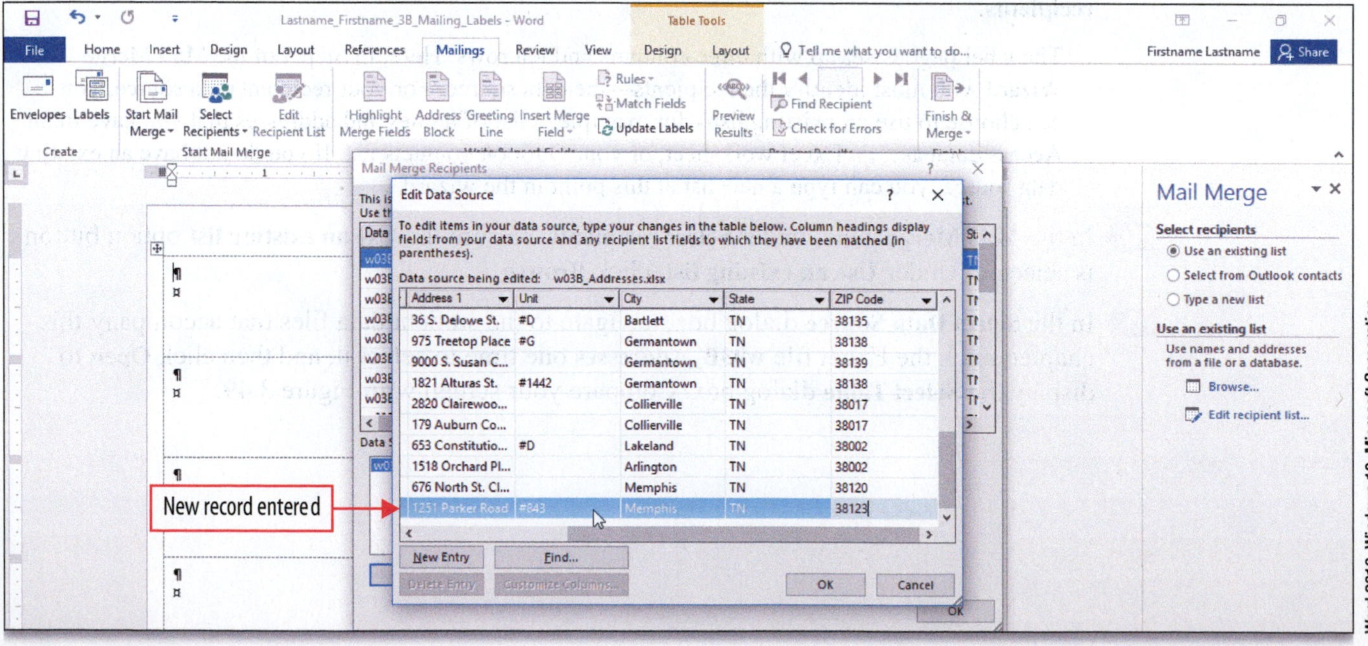

FIGURE 3.50

14 In the lower right corner of the **Edit Data Source** dialog box, click **OK**, and then in the displayed message, click **Yes**. Scroll to the end of the recipient list to confirm that the record for *Sharon Williams* that you just added is in the list. At the bottom of the **Mail Merge Recipients** dialog box, click **OK**.

Activity 3.28 | Completing the Mail Merge

Not only can you add and edit names and addresses while completing the Mail Merge, but you can also match your column names with preset names used in Mail Merge.

1 At the bottom of the **Mail Merge** pane, click **Next: Arrange your labels**.

2 Under **Arrange your labels**, click **Address block**. In the **Insert Address Block** dialog box, under **Specify address elements**, examine the various formats for names. If necessary, under *Insert recipient's name in this format*, select the *Joshua Randall Jr.* format. Compare your dialog box with Figure 3.51.

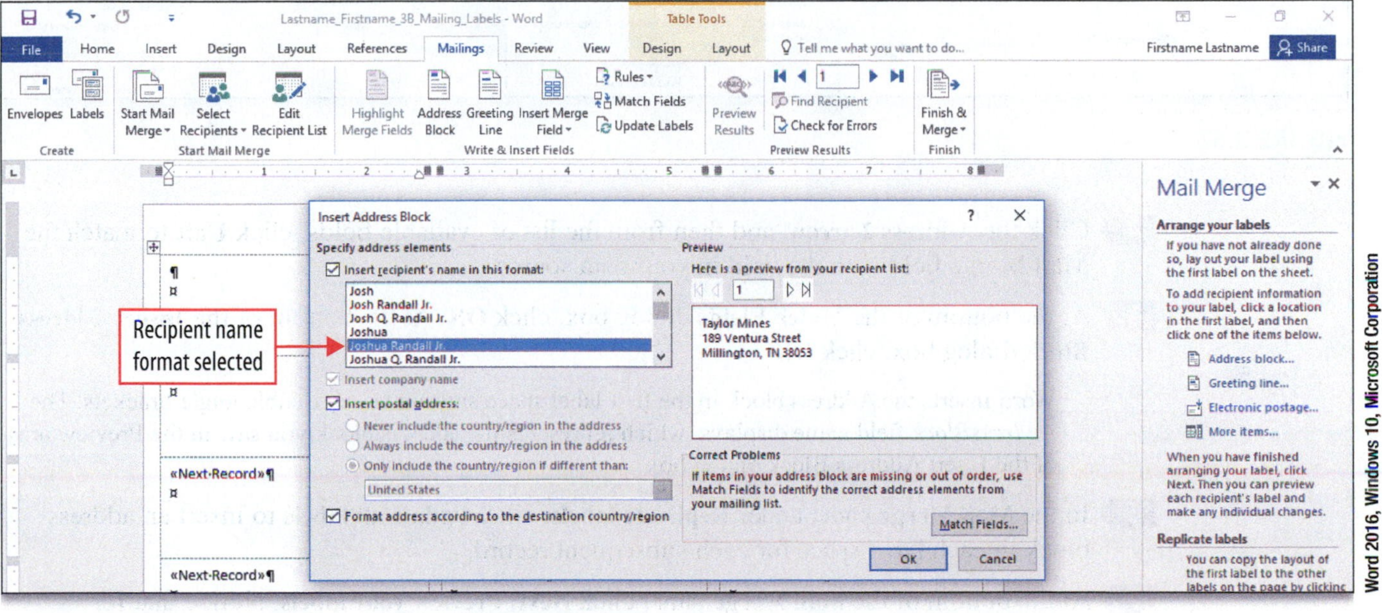

FIGURE 3.51

3 In the lower right corner of the **Insert Address Block** dialog box, click **Match Fields**, and then compare your screen with Figure 3.52.

If your field names are descriptive, the Mail Merge program will identify them correctly, as is the case with most of the information in the *Required for Address Block* section. However, the Address 2 field is unmatched—in the source file, this column is named *Unit*.

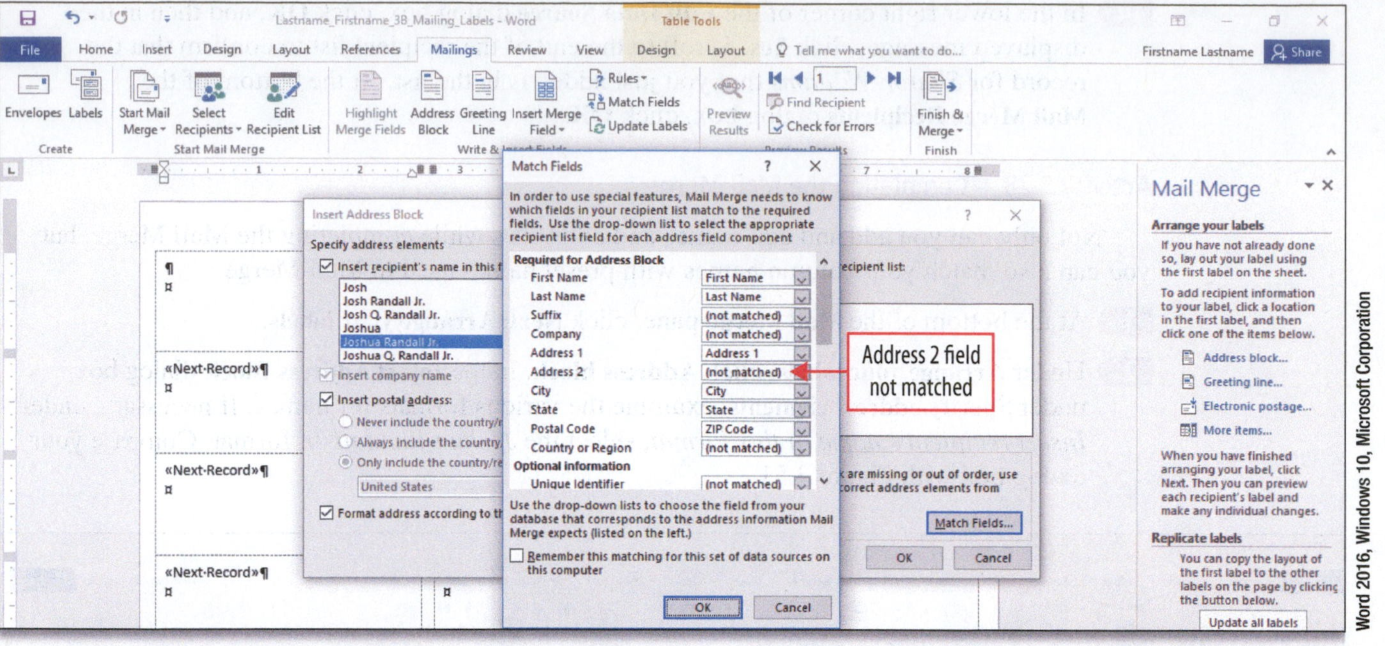

FIGURE 3.52

4 Click the **Address 2 arrow**, and then from the list of available fields, click **Unit** to match the Mail Merge field with the field in your data source.

5 At the bottom of the **Match Fields** dialog box, click **OK**. At the bottom of the **Insert Address Block** dialog box, click **OK**.

Word inserts the Address block in the first label space surrounded by double angle brackets. The *AddressBlock* field name displays, which represents the address block you saw in the Preview area of the Insert Address Block dialog box.

6 In the **Mail Merge** pane, under **Replicate labels**, click **Update all labels** to insert an address block in each label space for each subsequent record.

7 At the bottom of the **Mail Merge** pane, click **Next: Preview your labels**. Notice that for addresses with four lines, the last line of the address is cut off.

8 Press Ctrl + A to select all of the label text, click the **Layout tab**, and then in the **Paragraph group**, click in the **Spacing Before** box. Type **3** and press Enter.

9 Click in any label to deselect, and notice that 4-line addresses are no longer cut off. Compare your screen with Figure 3.53.

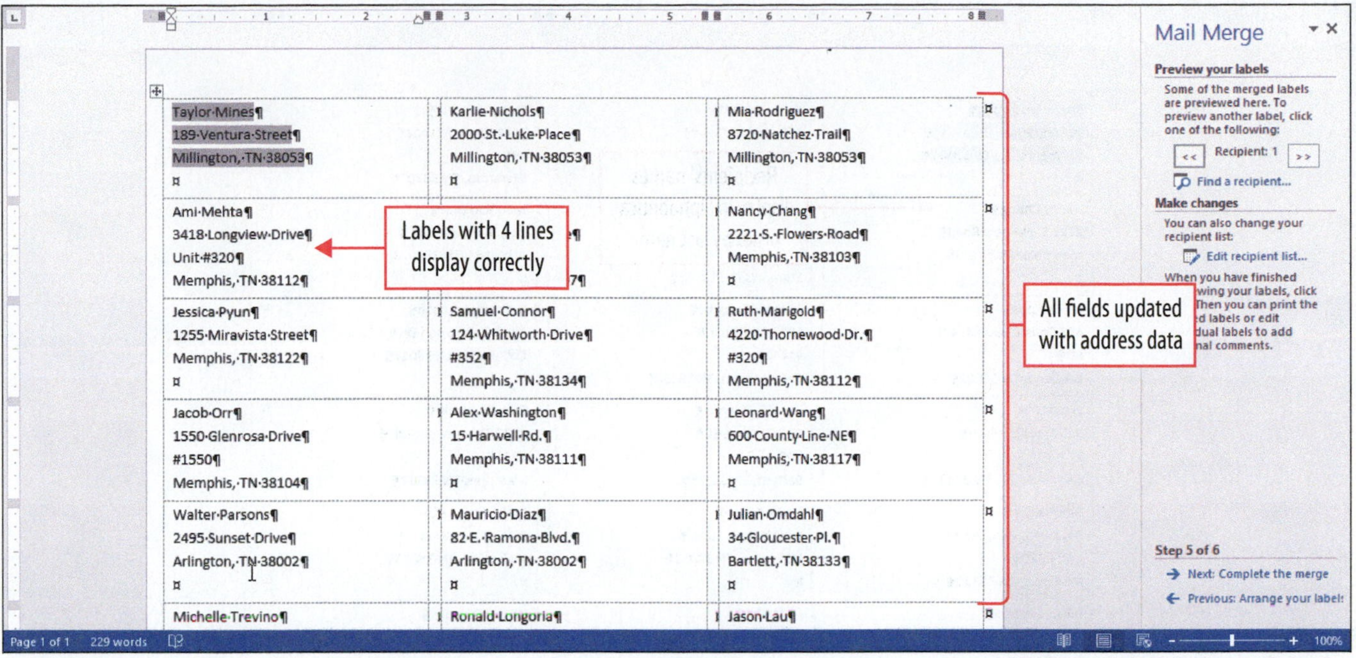

Word 2016, Windows 10, Microsoft Corporation

FIGURE 3.53

10 At the bottom of the **Mail Merge** pane, click **Next: Complete the merge.**

Step 6 of the Mail Merge displays. At this point you can print or edit your labels, although this is done more easily in the document window.

11 **Save** your labels, and then on the right, **Close** the **Mail Merge** pane.

Activity 3.29 | Previewing and Printing Mail Merge Results

If you discover that you need to make further changes to your labels, you can still make them even though the Mail Merge task pane is closed.

1 Add the file name to the footer, close the footer area, and then move to the top of **Page 2**. Click anywhere in the empty table row, and then click the **Table Tools Layout tab**. In the **Rows & Columns group**, click **Delete**, and then click **Delete Rows**.

Adding footer text to a label sheet replaces the last row of labels on a page with the footer text, and moves the last row of labels to the top of the next page. In this instance, a blank second page is created, which you can delete by deleting the blank row.

2 Notice that the labels do not display in alphabetical order. Click the **Mailings tab**, and then in the **Start Mail Merge group**, click **Edit Recipient List** to display the list of names and addresses.

3 In the **Mail Merge Recipients** dialog box, click the **Last Name** field heading, and notice that the names are sorted alphabetically by the recipient's last name.

Mailing labels are often sorted by either last name or by ZIP Code.

4 Click the **Last Name** field heading again, and notice that the last names are sorted in descending order. Click the **Last Name** field one more time to return to ascending order, and then click **OK**. Press Ctrl + Home, and then compare your screen with Figure 3.54.

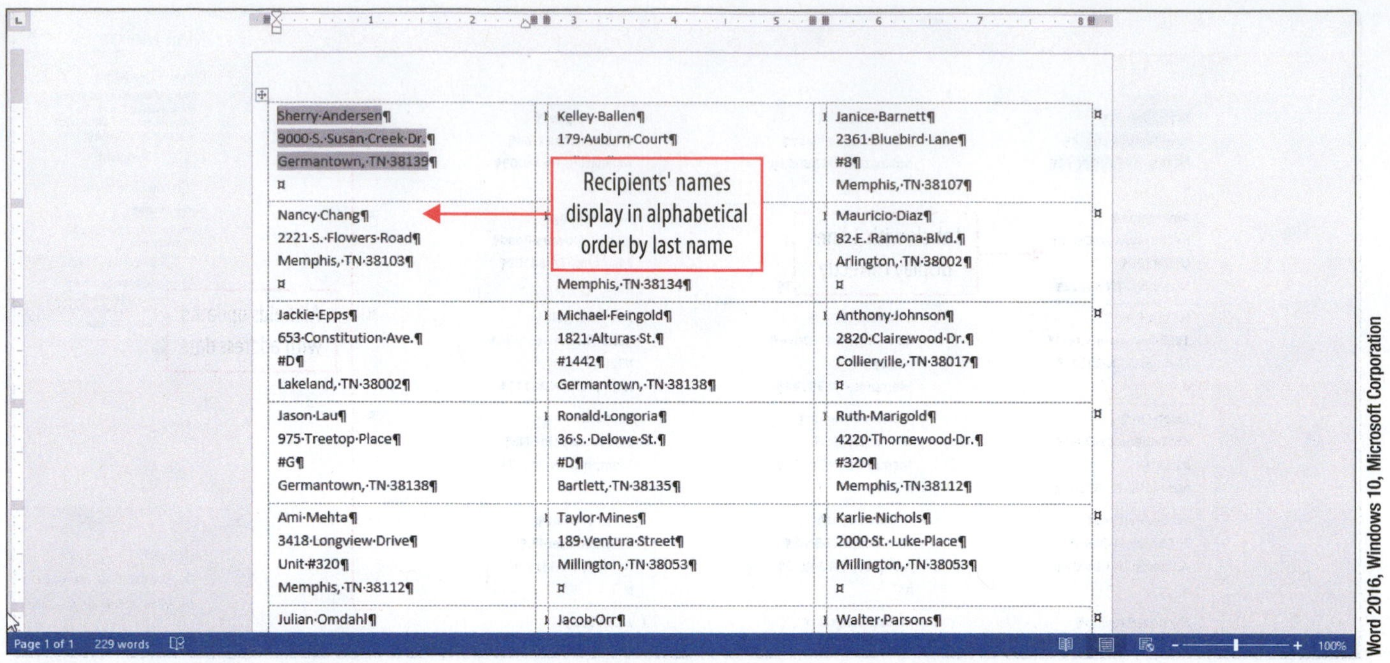

Sherry Andersen
9000 S. Susan Creek Dr.
Germantown, TN 38139
Kelley Ballen
179 Auburn Court
Janice Barnett
2361 Bluebird Lane
#8
Memphis, TN 38107
Nancy Chang
2221 S. Flowers Road
Memphis, TN 38103
Recipients' names display in alphabetical order by last name
Memphis, TN 38134
Mauricio Diaz
82 E. Ramona Blvd.
Arlington, TN 38002
Jackie Epps
653 Constitution Ave.
#D
Lakeland, TN 38002
Michael Feingold
1821 Alturas St.
#1442
Germantown, TN 38138
Anthony Johnson
2820 Clairewood Dr.
Collierville, TN 38017
Jason Lau
975 Treetop Place
#G
Germantown, TN 38138
Ronald Longoria
36 S. Delowe St.
#D
Bartlett, TN 38135
Ruth Marigold
4220 Thornewood Dr.
#320
Memphis, TN 38112
Ami Mehta
3418 Longview Drive
Unit #320
Memphis, TN 38112
Taylor Mines
189 Ventura Street
Millington, TN 38053
Karlie Nichols
2000 St. Luke Place
Millington, TN 38053
Julian Omdahl
Jacob Orr
Walter Parsons
Page 1 of 1
229 words
100%
Word 2016, Windows 10, Microsoft Corporation

FIGURE 3.54

5 Click the **File tab**. On the right, at the bottom of the **Properties** list, click **Show All Properties**. On the list of **Properties**, click to the right of **Tags**, and then type **labels**

6 Click to the right of **Subject**, and then type your course name and section number. Be sure that your name displays as the author. If necessary, right-click the author name, click Edit Property, type your name, and click OK.

7 On the left, click **Save**. In the upper right corner of the Word window, click **Close** [×]. If directed by your instructor to do so, submit your Lastname_Firstname_3B_Mailing_Labels file as a paper printout, an electronic image of your document that looks like a printed document, or your completed Word file.

If you print, the labels will print on whatever paper is in the printer; unless you have preformatted labels available, the labels will print on a sheet of paper. Printing the labels on plain paper enables you to proofread the labels before you print them on more expensive label sheets.

END | You have completed Project 3B

GO! With Google

Objective Format a Single-Column Newsletter in Google Docs

ALERT! **Working with Web-Based Applications and Services**

Computer programs and services on the web receive continuous updates and improvements, so the steps to complete this web-based activity may differ from the ones shown. You can often look at the screens and the information presented to determine how to complete the activity.

If you do not already have a Google account, you will need to create one before you begin this activity. Go to http://google.com and, in the upper right corner, click Sign In. On the Sign In screen, click Create Account. On the Create your Google Account page, complete the form, read and agree to the Terms of Service and Privacy Policy, and then click Next step. On the Welcome screen, click Get Started.

Activity | Formatting a Single-Column Newsletter in Google Docs

In this Activity, you will use Google Docs to edit a single-column newsletter similar to the one you edited in Project 3B. You can create columns in a Google Doc by inserting a table with two columns, and then typing in the two columns.

1 From the desktop, open your browser, navigate to **http://google.com**, and then click the **Google Apps** menu. Click **Drive**, and then if necessary, sign in to your Google account.

2 Open your **GO! Web Projects** folder—or click New to create and then open this folder if necessary.

3 In the left pane, click **NEW**, and then click **File upload**. In the **Open** dialog box, navigate to your student data files for this chapter, and then in the **File List**, double-click to open **w03_3B_Web**.

4 Point to the uploaded file **w03_3B_Web**, and then right-click. On the shortcut menu, scroll as necessary, and then click **Rename**. Using your own last name and first name, type **Lastname_Firstname_WD_3B_Web** (leave the file extension .docx) and then click **OK** to rename the file.

5 Right-click the file you just renamed, point to **Open with**, and then click **Google Docs.**

6 Drag to select the newsletter title—*University Medical Center Goes Green*. On the toolbar, click the **Font size arrow**, and then click **18**. With the newsletter title still selected, on the toolbar, click the **Text color arrow**, and then in the second row, click the third from last color—**blue**.

7 Apply the same **Font Color** to the five subheadings—*Recycling Trash*, *Harvesting Daylight*, *Greener Landscaping*, *Greener Grocer*, and *Greener Records*. Compare your screen with Figure A.

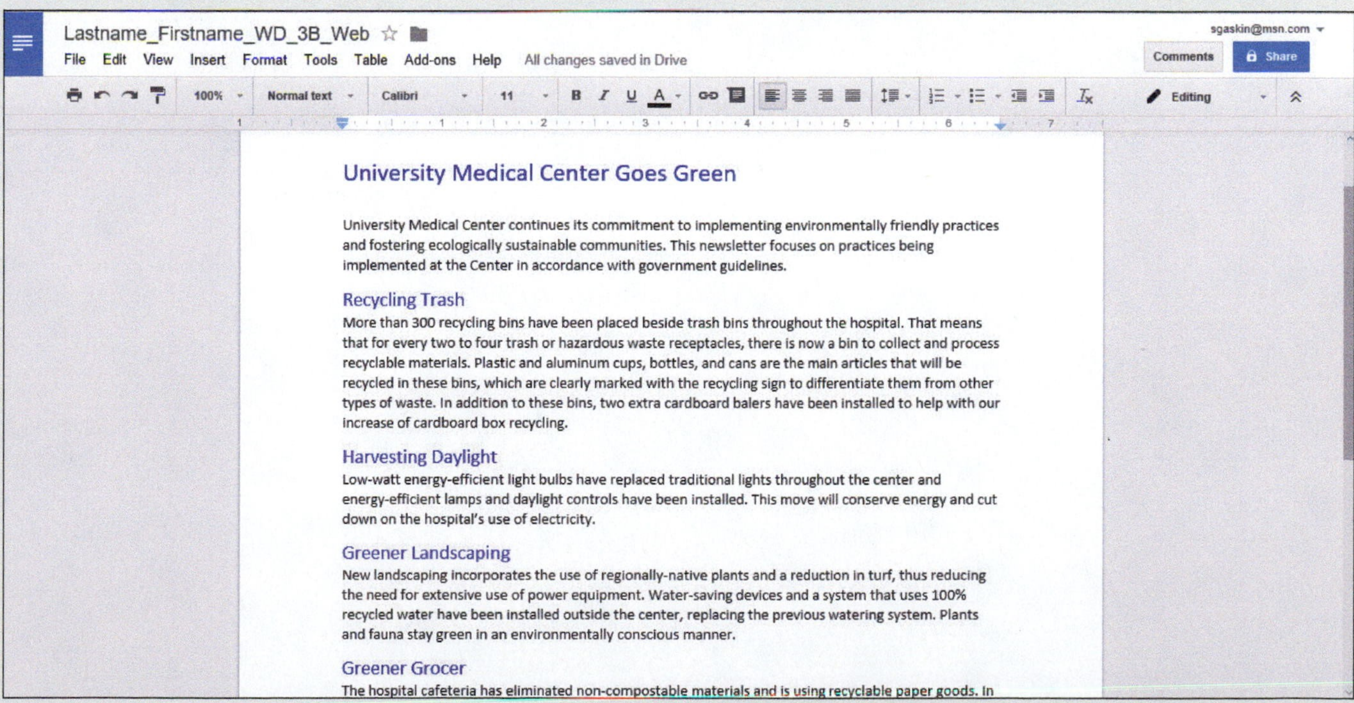

FIGURE A

(GO! With Google continues on the next page)

GO! With Google

8 Press Ctrl + End to move to the end of the document, and then press Enter. On the menu bar, click **Insert**, and then click **Image**. In the **Insert image** dialog box, in the upper right, click **Search**, and then click in the Google search box. Type **green recycle symbol** and then press Enter.

9 Click an image of a green recycle symbol similar to the one you used in Project 3B, and then at the bottom click **Select**.

10 Click the inserted image to select it, point to a corner of the image to display the sizing arrow, and then drag to resize the image until it displays at the bottom of the first page. On the toolbar, click the **Center** icon to center the image. Click anywhere in the text to deselect the image.

11 Submit the file as directed by your instructor. In the upper right, click your user name, and then click **Sign out**. **Close** your browser window. Your file is automatically saved in your Google Drive.

GO! To Work

Andrew Rodriguez / Fotolia; FotolEdhar/ Fotolia; apops/ Fotolia; Yuri Arcurs/ Fotolia

3 WORD

MICROSOFT OFFICE SPECIALIST (MOS) SKILLS IN THIS CHAPTER	
PROJECT 3A	**PROJECT 3B**
1.2.4 Move to a specific location in a document	**1.1.3** Open a PDF in Word for editing
1.3.5 Insert page numbers	**1.2.2** Insert hyperlinks
1.4.1 Change document views	**1.4.2** Customize views by using zoom settings
1.4.5 Add document properties	**1.5.2** Save documents in alternative file formats
2.2.3 Set line and paragraph spacing and indentation	**2.1.4** Insert special characters
4.1.1 Insert footnotes and endnotes	**2.2.1** Apply font formatting
4.1.2 Modify footnote and endnote properties	**2.3.1** Format text in multiple columns
4.1.3 Create bibliography citation sources	**2.3.2** Insert page, section, or column breaks
4.1.4 Modify bibliography citation sources	**5.1.3** Insert a screen shot or screen clipping
4.1.5 Insert citations for bibliographies	**5.2.3** Remove picture backgrounds
	5.2.4 Format objects
	5.2.6 Wrap text around objects
	5.2.7 Position objects

BUILD YOUR E-PORTFOLIO

An E-Portfolio is a collection of evidence, stored electronically, that showcases what you have accomplished while completing your education. Collecting and then sharing your work products with potential employers reflects your academic and career goals. Your completed documents from the following projects are good examples to show what you have learned: 3G, 3K, 3L.

GO! FOR JOB SUCCESS

Video: Email Etiquette

Your instructor may assign this video to your class, and then ask you to think about, or discuss with your classmates, these questions:

FotolEdhar / Fotolia

Why do you think it is important to follow specific etiquette when composing email?

Why is it important to include a greeting and sign every email that you send?

What are the differences between sending a business email and a personal email, and what are three specific things you should never do in a business email?

GO! COLLABORATIVE TEAM PROJECT

If your instructor assigns this project to your class, you can expect to work with one or more of your classmates—either in person or by using Internet tools—to create work products similar to those that you created in this chapter. A team is a group of workers who work together to solve a problem, make a decision, or create a work product. Collaboration is when you work together with others as a team in an intellectual endeavor to complete a shared task or achieve a shared goal.

END OF CHAPTER

SUMMARY

Word assists you in formatting a research paper for college or business by providing built-in styles and formats for the most commonly used footnote and citation styles for research papers—MLA and APA.

Word helps you create the bibliography for your research paper by recording all of your citations in the Source Manager, and then generating the bibliography—in MLA, called Works Cited—for you.

Newsletters are often used by organizations to communicate information to a specific group. A newsletter can be formatted in two columns with a nameplate at the top that identifies the publication.

The Mail Merge Wizard enables you to easily merge a main document and a data source to create customized letters or labels. The data source can be an Excel spreadsheet, an Access database, or Outlook contacts.

GO! LEARN IT ONLINE

Review the concepts, key terms, and MOS skills in this chapter by completing these online challenges, which you can in **MyITLab**.

Matching and Multiple Choice: Answer matching and multiple-choice questions to test what you learned in this chapter.

Lessons on the GO!: Learn how to use all the new apps and features as they are introduced by Microsoft.

MOS Prep Quiz: Answer questions to review the MOS skills that you practiced in this chapter.

PROJECT GUIDE FOR WORD CHAPTER 3

Your instructor will assign Projects from this list to ensure your learning and assess your knowledge.

REVIEW AND ASSESSMENTS GUIDE FOR WORD CHAPTER 3			
Project	**Apply Skills from These Chapter Objectives**	**Project Type**	**Project Location**
3A **MyITLab**	Objectives 1–4 from Project 3A	**3A Instructional Project (Grader Project)** Guided instruction to learn the skills in Project 3A	In MyITLab and in text
3B **MyITLab**	Objectives 5–7 from Project 3B	**3B Instructional Project (Grader Project)** Guided instruction to learn the skills in Project 3B	In MyITLab and in text
3C	Objectives 1–4 from Project 3A	**3C Skills Review** A guided review of the skills from Project 3A.	In text
3D	Objectives 5–7 from Project 3B	**3D Skills Review** A guided review of the skills from Project 3B.	In text
3E **MyITLab**	Objectives 1–4 from Project 3A	**3E Mastery (Grader Project)** **Mastery and Transfer of Learning** A demonstration of your mastery of the skills in Project 3A with extensive decision making.	In MyITLab and in text
3F **MyITLab**	Objectives 5–7 from Project 3B	**3F Mastery (Grader Project)** **Mastery and Transfer of Learning** A demonstration of your mastery of the skills in Project 3B with extensive decision making.	In MyITLab and in text
3G **MyITLab**	Objectives 1–7 from Projects 3A and 3B	**3G Mastery (Grader Project)** **Mastery and Transfer of Learning** A demonstration of your mastery of the skills in Projects 3A and 3B with extensive decision making.	In MyITLab and in text
3H	Combination of Objectives from Projects 3A and 3B	**3H GO! Fix It** **Critical Thinking** A demonstration of your mastery of the skills in Projects 3A and 3B by creating a correct result from a document that contains errors you must find.	Instructor Resource Center (IRC) and MyITLab
3I	Combination of Objectives from Projects 3A and 3B	**3I GO! Make It** **Critical Thinking** A demonstration of your mastery of the skills in Projects 3A and 3B by creating a result from a supplied picture.	IRC and MyITLab
3J	Combination of Objectives from Projects 3A and 3B	**3J GO! Solve It** **Critical Thinking** A demonstration of your mastery of the skills in Projects 3A and 3B, your decision-making skills, and your critical-thinking skills. A task-specific rubric helps you self-assess your result.	IRC and MyITLab
3K	Combination of Objectives from Projects 3A and 3B	**3K GO! Solve It** **Critical Thinking** A demonstration of your mastery of the skills in Projects 3A and 3B, your decision-making skills, and your critical-thinking skills. A task-specific rubric helps you self-assess your result.	In text
3L	Combination of Objectives from Projects 3A and 3B	**3L GO! Think** **Critical Thinking** A demonstration of your understanding of the chapter concepts applied in a manner that you would outside of college. An analytic rubric helps you and your instructor grade the quality of your work by comparing it to the work an expert in the discipline would create.	In text
3M	Combination of Objectives from Projects 3A and 3B	**3M GO! Think** **Critical Thinking** A demonstration of your understanding of the chapter concepts applied in a manner that you would outside of college. An analytic rubric helps you and your instructor grade the quality of your work by comparing it to the work an expert in the discipline would create.	IRC and MyITLab
3N	Combination of Objectives from Projects 3A and 3B	**3N You and GO!** **Critical Thinking** A demonstration of your understanding of the chapter concepts applied in a manner that you would in a personal situation. An analytic rubric helps you and your instructor grade the quality of your work.	IRC and MyITLab
3O	Combination of Objectives from Projects 3A and 3B	**3O Cumulative Team Project for Word Chapter 3** **Critical Thinking** A demonstration of your understanding of concepts and your ability to work collaboratively in a group role-playing assessment, requiring both collaboration and self-management.	IRC and MyITLab
Capstone Project for Word Chapters 1–3	Combination of Objectives from Projects 1A, 1B, 2A, 2B, 3A, and 3B	A demonstration of your mastery of the skills in Chapters 1–3 with extensive decision making. **(Grader Project)**	IRC and MyITLab

GLOSSARY

GLOSSARY OF CHAPTER KEY TERMS

American Psychological Association (APA) One of two commonly used style guides for formatting research papers.

Bibliography A list of cited works in a report or research paper; also referred to as Works Cited, Sources, or References, depending upon the report style.

Brightness The relative lightness of a picture.

Citation A note inserted into the text of a research paper that refers the reader to a source in the bibliography.

Column break indicator A dotted line containing the words *Column Break* that displays at the bottom of the column.

Contrast The difference between the darkest and lightest area of a picture.

Crop A command that removes unwanted or unnecessary areas of a picture.

Crop handles Handles used to define unwanted areas of a picture.

Crop pointer The pointer used to crop areas of a picture.

Data source A document that contains a list of variable information, such as names and addresses, that is merged with a main document to create customized form letters or labels.

Em dash A punctuation symbol used to indicate an explanation or emphasis.

Endnote In a research paper, a note placed at the end of a document or chapter.

Fields In a mail merge, the column headings in the data source.

Flip A command that creates a reverse image of a picture or object.

Footnote In a research paper, a note placed at the bottom of the page.

Hanging indent An indent style in which the first line of a paragraph extends to the left of the remaining lines and that is commonly used for bibliographic entries.

Line break indicator A nonprinting character in the shape of a bent arrow that indicates a manual line break.

Mail merge A feature that joins a main document and a data source to create customized letters or labels.

Main document In a mail merge, the document that contains the text or formatting that remains constant.

Manual column break An artificial end to a column to balance columns or to provide space for the insertion of other objects.

Manual line break A break that moves text to the right of the insertion point to a new line while keeping the text in the same paragraph.

Manual page break The action of forcing a page to end and placing subsequent text at the top of the next page.

Modern Language Association (MLA) One of two commonly used style guides for formatting research papers.

Nameplate The banner on the front page of a newsletter that identifies the publication.

Newsletter A periodical that communicates news and information to a specific group.

Note In a research paper, information that expands on the topic, but that does not fit well in the document text.

Page break indicator A dotted line with the text *Page Break* that indicates where a manual page break was inserted.

Parenthetical references References that include the last name of the author or authors, and the page number in the referenced source.

PDF Reflow The ability to import PDF files into Word so that you can transform a PDF back into a fully editable Word document.

Read Mode A view in Word that optimizes the Word screen for the times when you are reading Word documents on the screen and not creating or editing them.

Recolor A feature that enables you to change all colors in the picture to shades of a single color.

Record Each row of information that contains data for one person.

Scale A command that resizes a picture to a percentage of its size.

Screenshot An image of an active window on your computer that you can paste into a document.

Section A portion of a document that can be formatted differently from the rest of the document.

Section break A double dotted line that indicates the end of one section and the beginning of another section.

Small caps A font effect that changes lowercase letters to uppercase letters, but with the height of lowercase letters.

Style A group of formatting commands, such as font, font size, font color, paragraph alignment, and line spacing, that can be applied to a paragraph with one command.

Style guide A manual that contains standards for the design and writing of documents.

Suppress A Word feature that hides header and footer information, including the page number, on the first page of a document.

Watermark A text or graphic element that displays behind document text.

Works Cited In the MLA style, a list of cited works placed at the end of a research paper or report.

CHAPTER REVIEW

3 WORD

Apply 3A skills from these Objectives:

1. Create a Research Paper
2. Insert Footnotes in a Research Paper
3. Create Citations and a Bibliography in a Research Paper
4. Use Read Mode and PDF Reflow

Skills Review Project 3C Diet and Exercise Report

In the following Skills Review, you will edit and format a research paper that contains information about the effects of diet and exercise. This paper was created by Rachel Holder, a medical intern at University Medical Center, for distribution to her classmates studying physiology. Your completed document will look similar to the one shown in Figure 3.55.

PROJECT FILES

For Project 3C, you will need the following file:

w03C_Diet_Exercise

You will save your document as:

Lastname_Firstname_3C_Diet_Exercise

PROJECT RESULTS

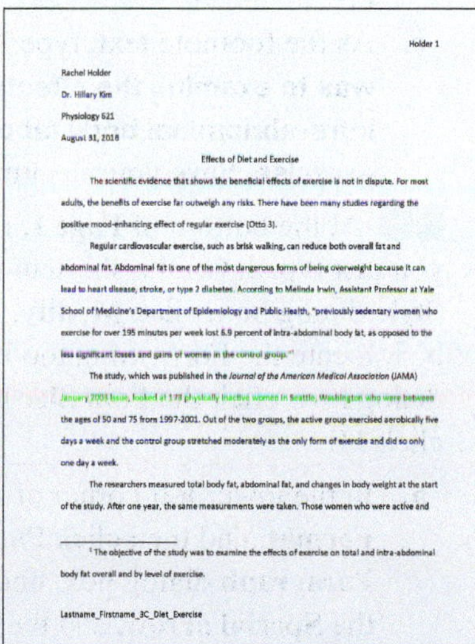

Holder 1

Rachel Holder

Dr. Hillary Kim

Physiology 621

August 31, 2016

Effects of Diet and Exercise

The scientific evidence that shows the beneficial effects of exercise is not in dispute. For most adults, the benefits of exercise far outweigh any risks. There have been many studies regarding the positive mood-enhancing effect of regular exercise (Otto 3).

Regular cardiovascular exercise, such as brisk walking, can reduce both overall fat and abdominal fat. Abdominal fat is one of the most dangerous forms of being overweight because it can lead to heart disease, stroke, or type 2 diabetes. According to Melinda Irwin, Assistant Professor at Yale School of Medicine's Department of Epidemiology and Public Health, "previously sedentary women who exercise for over 195 minutes per week lost 6.9 percent of intra-abdominal body fat, as opposed to the less significant losses and gains of women in the control group."[1]

The study, which was published in the *Journal of the American Medical Association* (JAMA) January 2003 issue, looked at 173 physically inactive women in Seattle, Washington who were between the ages of 50 and 75 from 1997-2001. Out of the two groups, the active group exercised aerobically five days a week and the control group stretched moderately as the only form of exercise and did so only one day a week.

The researchers measured total body fat, abdominal fat, and changes in body weight at the start of the study. After one year, the same measurements were taken. Those women who were active and

[1] The objective of the study was to examine the effects of exercise on total and intra-abdominal body fat overall and by level of exercise.

Lastname_Firstname_3C_Diet_Exercise

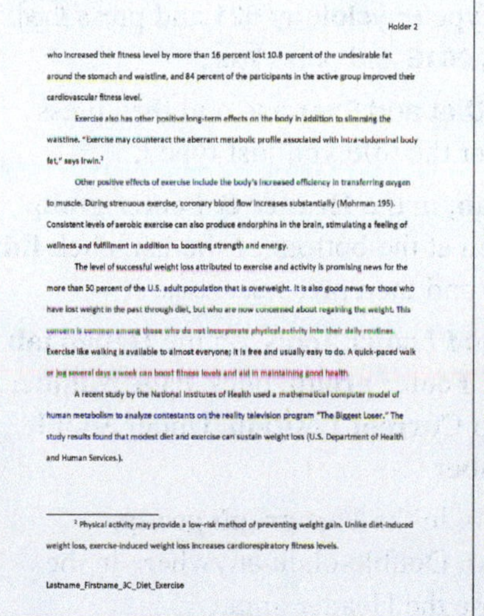

Holder 2

who increased their fitness level by more than 16 percent lost 10.8 percent of the undesirable fat around the stomach and waistline, and 84 percent of the participants in the active group improved their cardiovascular fitness level.

Exercise also has other positive long-term effects on the body in addition to slimming the waistline. "Exercise may counteract the aberrant metabolic profile associated with intra-abdominal body fat," says Irwin.[2]

Other positive effects of exercise include the body's increased efficiency in transferring oxygen to muscle. During strenuous exercise, coronary blood flow increases substantially (Mohrman 195). Consistent levels of aerobic exercise can also produce endorphins in the brain, stimulating a feeling of wellness and fulfillment in addition to boosting strength and energy.

The level of successful weight loss attributed to exercise and activity is promising news for the more than 50 percent of the U.S. adult population that is overweight. It is also good news for those who have lost weight in the past through diet, but who are now concerned about regaining the weight. This concern is common among those who do not incorporate physical activity into their daily routines. Exercise like walking is available to almost everyone; it is free and usually easy to do. A quick-paced walk or jog several days a week can boost fitness levels and aid in maintaining good health.

A recent study by the National Institutes of Health used a mathematical computer model of human metabolism to analyze contestants on the reality television program "The Biggest Loser." The study results found that modest diet and exercise can sustain weight loss (U.S. Department of Health and Human Services.).

[2] Physical activity may provide a low-risk method of preventing weight gain. Unlike diet-induced weight loss, exercise-induced weight loss increases cardiorespiratory fitness levels.

Lastname_Firstname_3C_Diet_Exercise

Word 2016, Windows 10, Microsoft Corporation

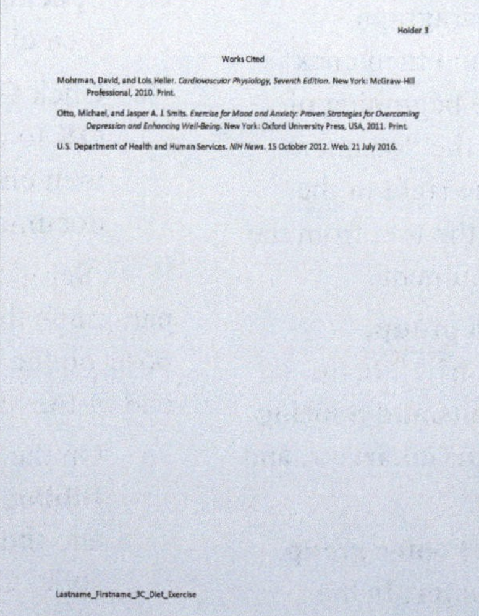

Holder 3

Works Cited

Mohrman, David, and Lois Heller. *Cardiovascular Physiology, Seventh Edition*. New York: McGraw-Hill Professional, 2010. Print.

Otto, Michael, and Jasper A. J. Smits. *Exercise for Mood and Anxiety: Proven Strategies for Overcoming Depression and Enhancing Well-Being*. New York: Oxford University Press, USA, 2011. Print.

U.S. Department of Health and Human Services. *NIH News*. 15 October 2012. Web. 21 July 2016.

Lastname_Firstname_3C_Diet_Exercise

FIGURE 3.55

(Project 3C Diet and Exercise Report continues on the next page)

Skills Review Project 3C Diet and Exercise Report (continued)

1 Start Word. On Word's opening screen, in the lower left, click **Open Other Documents**. Navigate to your student data files, and then locate and open the document **w03C_Diet_Exercise**. Display the formatting marks and rulers. Save the file in your **Word Chapter 3** folder as **Lastname_Firstname_3C_Diet_Exercise**

a. Press Ctrl + A to select all the text. On the **Home tab**, in the **Paragraph group**, click **Line and Paragraph Spacing**, and then change the line spacing to **2.0**. On the **Layout tab**, in the **Paragraph group**, change the **Spacing After** to **0 pt**.

b. Press Ctrl + Home, press Enter to create a blank line at the top of the document, and then click to position the insertion point in the new blank line. Type **Rachel Holder** and press Enter. Type **Dr. Hillary Kim** and press Enter. Type **Physiology 621** and press Enter. Type **August 31, 2016** and press Enter.

c. Type **Effects of Diet and Exercise** and then press Ctrl + E to center the title you just typed.

2 On the **Insert tab**, in the **Header & Footer group**, click **Header**, and then at the bottom of the list, click **Edit Header**. Type **Holder** and then press Spacebar.

a. Under **Header and Footer Tools**, on the **Design tab**, in the **Header & Footer group**, click **Page Number**, and then point to **Current Position**. Under **Simple**, click **Plain Number**.

b. On the **Home tab**, in the **Paragraph group**, click **Align Right**. Double-click anywhere in the document to close the Header area.

c. Near the top of **Page 1**, locate the paragraph beginning *The scientific evidence*, and then click to position the insertion point at the beginning of that paragraph. Scroll to the end of the document, hold down Shift, and then click to the right of the last paragraph mark to select all of the text from the insertion point to the end of the document.

d. On the **Home tab**, in the **Paragraph group**, click the **Dialog Box Launcher** button. In the **Paragraph** dialog box, on the **Indents and Spacing tab**, under **Indentation**, click the **Special arrow**, and then click **First line**. Click **OK**.

e. On the **Insert tab**, in the **Header & Footer group**, click **Footer**, and then click **Edit Footer**. In the **Insert group**, click **Document Info**, and then click **File Name**. Click **Close Header and Footer**.

3 Scroll to view the top of **Page 2**, locate the paragraph that begins *Exercise also has*, and then at the end of that paragraph, click to position the insertion point to the right of the period following *Irwin*. On the **References tab**, in the **Footnotes group**, click **Insert Footnote**.

a. As the footnote text, type **Physical activity may provide a low-risk method of preventing weight gain. Unlike diet-induced weight loss, exercise-induced weight loss increases cardiorespiratory fitness levels.**

b. In the upper portion of **Page 1**, locate the paragraph that begins *Regular cardiovascular exercise*. Click to position the insertion point at the end of the paragraph and insert a footnote.

c. As the footnote text, type **The objective of the study was to examine the effects of exercise on total and intra-abdominal body fat overall and by level of exercise. Save** your document.

4 At the bottom of **Page 1**, right-click in the footnote you just typed. On the shortcut menu, click **Style**. In the **Style** dialog box, click **Modify**. In the **Modify Style** dialog box, locate the Formatting toolbar in the center of the dialog box, click the **Font Size button arrow**, and then click **11**.

a. In the lower left corner of the dialog box, click **Format**, and then click **Paragraph**. In the **Paragraph** dialog box, under **Indentation**, click the **Special arrow**, and then click **First line**. Under **Spacing**, click the **Line spacing button arrow**, and then click **Double**.

b. Click **OK** to close the **Paragraph** dialog box, click **OK** to close the **Modify Style** dialog box, and then click **Apply** to apply the new style. **Save** your document.

5 Scroll to view the top of **Page 1**, and then in the paragraph that begins *The scientific evidence*, click to position the insertion point to the left of the period at the end of the paragraph.

a. On the **References tab**, in the **Citations & Bibliography group**, click the **Style button arrow**, and then click **MLA** to insert a reference using MLA style. Click **Insert Citation**, and then click **Add New Source**. Click the **Type of Source arrow**, scroll as

(Project 3C Diet and Exercise Report continues on the next page)

Skills Review Project 3C Diet and Exercise Report continued)

necessary to locate and click **Book**, and then add the following information:

Author	**Otto, Michael, and Jasper A. J. Smits**
Title	**Exercise for Mood and Anxiety: Proven Strategies for Overcoming Depression and Enhancing Well-Being**
Year	**2011**
City	**New York**
Publisher	**Oxford University Press, USA**
Medium	**Print**

b. Click **OK** to insert the citation. In the paragraph, click to select the citation, click the **Citation Options arrow**, and then click **Edit Citation.** In the **Edit Citation** dialog box, under **Add**, in the **Pages** box, type **3** and then click **OK**.

c. On the upper portion of **Page 2**, in the paragraph that begins *Other positive effects*, in the second line, click to position the insertion point to the left of the period following *substantially*. In the **Citations & Bibliography group**, click **Insert Citation**, and then click **Add New Source**. Click the **Type of Source arrow**, click **Book**, and then add the following information:

Author	**Lohrman, David, and Lois Heller**
Title	**Cardiovascular Physiology, Seventh Edition**
Year	**2010**
City	**New York**
Publisher	**McGraw-Hill Professional**
Medium	**Print**

d. Click **OK**. Click to select the citation in the paragraph, click the **Citation Options arrow**, and then click **Edit Citation**. In the **Edit Citation** dialog box, under **Add**, in the **Pages** box, type **195** and then click **OK**.

6 Press Ctrl + End to move to the end of the last paragraph in the document. Click to the left of the period following *loss*. In the **Citations & Bibliography group**, click **Insert Citation**, and then click **Add New Source**. Click the **Type of Source arrow**, click **Web site**, and then select the **Corporate Author** check box. Add the following information:

Corporate Author	**U.S. Department of Health and Human Services**
Name of Web Page	**NIH News**
Year	**2012**
Month	**October**
Day	**15**
Year Accessed	**2016**
Month Accessed	**July**
Day Accessed	**21**
Medium	**Web**

a. Click **OK**. Press Ctrl + End to move the insertion point to the end of the document. Press Ctrl + Enter to insert a manual page break. On the **Home tab**, in the **Paragraph group**, click the **Dialog Box Launcher** button. In the **Paragraph** dialog box, on the **Indents and Spacing tab**, under **Indentation**, click the **Special arrow**, and then click **(none)**. Click **OK**.

b. Type **Works Cited** and then press Enter. On the **References tab**, in the **Citations & Bibliography group**, be sure **MLA** displays in the **Style** box. In the **Citations & Bibliography group**, click **Bibliography**, and then at the bottom, click **Insert Bibliography**.

c. In the bibliography, move the pointer to the left of the first entry—beginning *Lohrman*—to display the pointer. Drag down to select all three references in the field. On the **Home tab**, in the **Paragraph group**, set the **Line spacing** to **2.0**. On the **Layout tab**, set the **Spacing After** to **0 pt**.

d. Click anywhere in the *Works Cited* title, and then press Ctrl + E to center the title. **Save** your document.

7 On the **References tab**, in the **Citations & Bibliography group**, click **Manage Sources**. On the left, on the **Master List**, click the entry for *Lohrman, David*, and then click **Edit**. In the **Edit Source** dialog box, in the **Author** box, change the *L* in *Lohrman* to **M** Click **OK**, click **Yes**, and then click **Close**.

a. On **Page 2**, in the paragraph that begins *Other positive effects*, in the second line, on the selected citation, click the **Citation Options arrow**, and then click **Update Citations and Bibliography**.

(Project 3C Diet and Exercise Report continues on the next page)

Skills Review Project 3C Diet and Exercise Report (continued)

b. Click the **File tab**, and then in the lower right corner, click **Show All Properties**. Add the following information:

Title	**Diet and Exercise**
Tags	**weight loss, exercise, diet**
Comments	**Draft copy of report for class**
Categories	**biomedical research**
Company	**University Medical Center**
Manager	**Dr. Hillary Kim**

c. In the **Subject** box, type your course name and section number. Be sure that your name displays as the Author and edit if necessary. On the left, click **Save** to redisplay your document. On the **View tab**, in the **Views group**, click **Read Mode**. In the upper left, click **Tools**, click **Find**, and then in the search box, type **Yale** and notice that the text you searched for is highlighted in the document.

d. In the upper left, click **View**, and then click **Edit Document** to return to Print Layout view. **Close** the **Navigation** pane. **Save** your document, and view the Print Preview. If directed by your instructor to do so, submit your paper printout, your electronic image of your document that looks like a printed document, or your original Word file. **Close** Word.

END | You have completed Project 3C

Apply 3B skills from these Objectives:

5 Format a Multiple-Column Newsletter

6 Use Special Character and Paragraph Formatting

7 Create Mailing Labels Using Mail Merge

Skills Review Project 3D Career Newsletter

In the following Skills Review, you will format a newsletter regarding professional development opportunities offered by University Medical Center, and you will create mailing labels for staff interested in these opportunities. Your completed document will look similar to Figure 3.56.

PROJECT FILES

For Project 3D, you will need the following files:

w03D_Career_Newsletter

w03D_Career_Sign (optional)

w03D_Medical_Symbol

w03D_Addresses (Optional: Use only if you are completing the Mailing Labels portion of this project)

You will save your documents as:

Lastname_Firstname_3D_Career_Newsletter

Lastname_Firstname_3D_Mailing_Labels (Optional: Create only if you are completing the Mailing Labels portion of this project)

PROJECT RESULTS

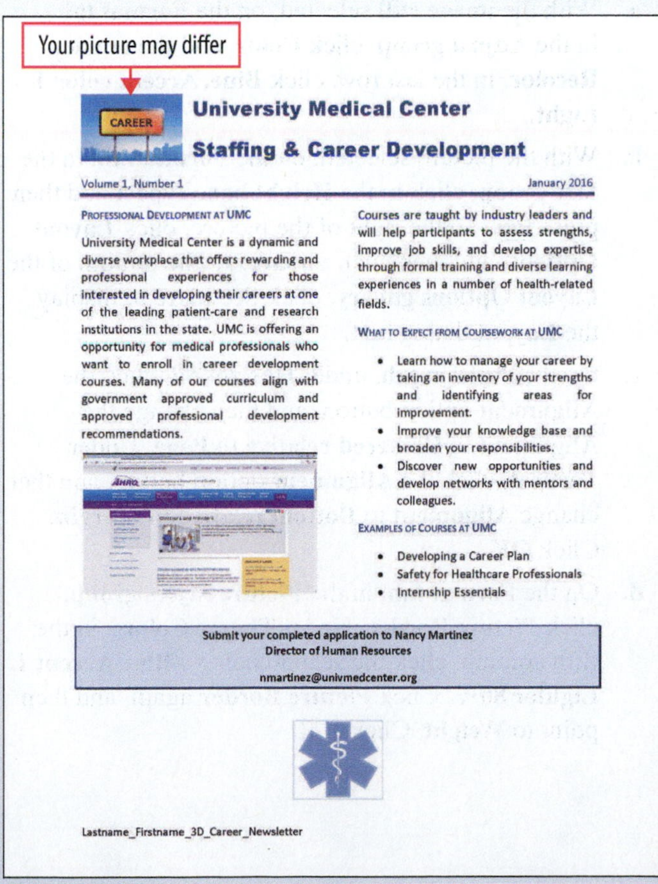

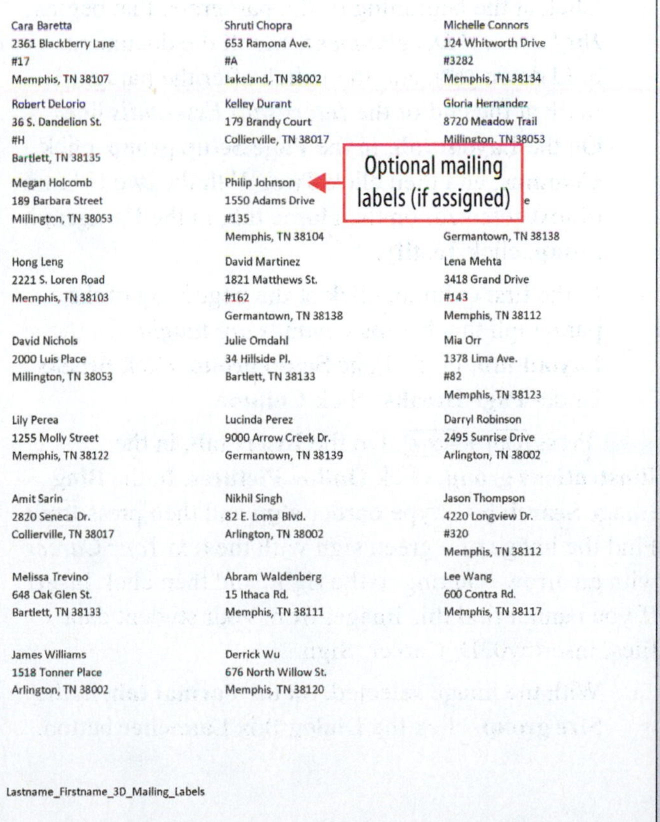

FIGURE 3.56

(Project 3D Career Newsletter continues on the next page)

Skills Review Project 3D Career Newsletter (continued)

1 Start Word. On Word's opening screen, in the lower left, click **Open Other Documents**. Navigate to your student files, and then locate and open **w03D_Career_Newsletter**. Save the file in your **Word Chapter 3** folder as **Lastname_Firstname_3D_Career_Newsletter** and then add the file name to the footer.

a. Select the first two lines of the document. On the mini toolbar, change the **Font** to **Arial Black** and the **Font Size** to **18**. Select the first three lines of the document. Click the **Font Color button arrow**, and then under **Theme Colors**, in the fifth column, click the last color—**Blue, Accent 1, Darker 50%**.

b. With the text still selected, on the **Home tab**, in the **Paragraph group**, click the **Borders button arrow**, and then at the bottom, click **Borders and Shading**. In the **Borders and Shading** dialog box, on the **Borders tab**, click the **Color arrow**, and then under **Theme Colors**, in the fifth column, click the last color—**Blue, Accent 1, Darker 50%**.

c. Click the **Width arrow**, and then click **3 pt**. In the **Preview** box, click the bottom border. Click **OK**.

d. Click at the beginning of the paragraph that begins *Professional Development*. Scroll the document, hold down Shift, and then click after the paragraph mark at the end of the *Internship Essentials* line. On the **Layout tab**, in the **Page Setup group**, click **Columns**, and then click **Two**. With the two columns of text selected, on the **Home tab**, in the **Paragraph group**, click **Justify**.

e. In the first column, click at the beginning of the paragraph that begins *Courses are taught*. On the **Layout tab**, in the **Page Setup group**, click **Breaks**. Under **Page Breaks**, click **Column**.

2 Press Ctrl + Home. On the **Insert tab**, in the **Illustrations group**, click **Online Pictures**. In the **Bing Image Search** box, type **career sign** and then press Enter. Find the image of a green sign with the text *Your Career* with an arrow pointing to the right, and then click **Insert**. If you cannot find this image, from your student data files, insert w03D_Career_Sign.

a. With the image selected, on the **Format tab**, in the **Size group**, click the **Dialog Box Launcher** button. In the **Layout** dialog box, on the **Size tab**, under **Scale**, be sure the **Lock aspect ratio** and **Relative to original picture size** check boxes are selected. Under **Scale**, select the percentage in the **Height box**, type **90** and then press Tab.

b. In the **Layout** dialog box, click the **Text Wrapping tab**. Under **Wrapping style**, click **Square**.

c. Click the **Position tab**, and then under **Horizontal**, click the **Alignment** option button. Be sure that the **Alignment** indicates **Left** and **relative to Column**. Under **Vertical**, click the **Alignment** option button, and then change the alignment to **Top relative to Margin**. Click **OK**. Compare the picture size and placement with Figure 3.56 and adjust the size of the image if necessary. **Save** your newsletter.

3 Press Ctrl + End to move to the end of the document. On the **Insert tab**, in the **Illustrations group**, click **Pictures**, and then from your student data files, insert the picture **w03D_Medical_Symbol**.

a. With the image still selected, on the **Format tab**, in the **Adjust group**, click **Color**, and then under **Recolor**, in the last row, click **Blue, Accent color 1 Light**.

b. With the picture selected, on the **Format tab**, in the **Size group**, click in the **Height** box. Type **1** and then press Enter. To the right of the picture, click **Layout Options**, and then click **Square**. At the bottom of the **Layout Options gallery**, click **See more** to display the **Layout** dialog box.

c. On the **Position tab**, under **Horizontal**, click the **Alignment** option button, and then change the **Alignment** to **Centered relative to Page**. Under **Vertical**, click the **Alignment** option button, and then change **Alignment** to **Bottom relative to Margin**. Click **OK**.

d. On the **Format tab**, in the **Picture Styles group**, click **Picture Border**. Under **Theme Colors**, in the fifth column, click the second color—**Blue Accent 1, Lighter 80%**. Click **Picture Border** again, and then point to **Weight**. Click **1 pt**.

(Project 3D Career Newsletter continues on the next page)

Skills Review Project 3D Career Newsletter (continued)

4 In the paragraph that begins *University Medical Center is a dynamic*, click after the period at the end of the paragraph, and then press Enter one time. With the insertion point in the new blank paragraph, open your web browser, and then navigate to **www.ahrq.gov/clinic/**

a. From the taskbar, redisplay your **3D_Career_Newsletter** document. With the insertion point positioned at the end of the first paragraph in the body of the newsletter, on the **Insert tab**, in the **Illustrations group**, click **Screenshot**. In the **Screenshot** gallery, click the browser window that contains the website you just opened.

b. Select the subheading **Professional Development at UMC** including the paragraph mark. Right-click the selected text, and then on the shortcut menu, click **Font**. In the **Font** dialog box, click the **Font color arrow**, and then in the fifth column, click the last color—**Blue, Accent 1, Darker 50%**. Under **Font style**, click **Bold**, and then under **Effects**, select **Small caps**. Click **OK**.

c. With the text still selected, right-click, and then on the mini toolbar, double-click **Format Painter**. In the second column, with the pointer, select each of the subheadings—**What to Expect from Coursework at UMC** and **Examples of Courses at UMC**. Press Esc to turn off Format Painter.

5 Press Ctrl + End to move to the end of the document, and then select the two lines of bold text—the graphic will also be selected. On the **Home tab**, in the **Paragraph group**, click the **Borders button arrow**, and then click **Borders and Shading**.

a. In the **Borders and Shading** dialog box, on the **Borders tab**, under **Setting**, click **Shadow**. Click the **Color arrow**, and then in the fifth column, click the last color—**Blue, Accent 1, Darker 50%**. Click the **Width arrow**, and then click **1 pt**.

b. In the **Borders and Shading** dialog box, click the **Shading tab**. Click the **Fill arrow**, and then in the fifth column, click the second color—**Blue, Accent 1, Lighter 80%**. Click **OK**. On the **Home tab**, in the **Paragraph group**, click **Center**. In the shaded paragraph, click in front of the *D* in the word *Director*. Hold down Shift and then press Enter.

c. Press Ctrl + Home, and then click the **File tab**. At the bottom of the **Properties** list, click **Show All Properties**. Click to the right of **Tags**, and then type **newsletter, careers** Click to the right of **Subject**, and then type your course name and section number. Under **Related People**, if necessary, type your name in the Author box. Display the **Print Preview** and make any necessary corrections. **Save** the document; close Word and close your browser window.

6 (NOTE: The remainder of this project, which is the creation of mailing labels, is optional. Complete if assigned by your instructor.) Start Word and display a new blank document. **Save** the document in your **Word Chapter 3** folder as **Lastname_Firstname_3D_Mailing_Labels**.

a. Click the **Mailings tab**. In the **Start Mail Merge group**, click **Start Mail Merge**, and then click **Step-by-Step Mail Merge Wizard**. In the **Mail Merge** pane, under **Select document type**, click **Labels**. At the bottom of the **Mail Merge** pane, click **Next: Starting document**.

b. Under **Select starting document**, under **Change document layout**, click **Label options**. In the **Label Options** dialog box, under **Printer information**, be sure that the **Default tray** is selected.

c. Under **Label information**, click the **Label vendors arrow**, and then click **Avery US Letter**. Under **Product number**, scroll about halfway down the list, and then click **5160 Easy Peel Address Labels**. At the bottom of the **Label Options** dialog box, click **OK**. At the bottom of the **Mail Merge** pane, click **Next: Select recipients**.

d. In the **Mail Merge** pane, under **Select recipients**, under **Use an existing list**, click **Browse**. In the **Select Data Source** dialog box, navigate to the student data files that accompany this chapter, click the Excel file **w03D_Addresses** one time to select it, and then click **Open** to display the **Select Table** dialog box. Click **OK**.

7 In the lower left portion of the **Mail Merge Recipients** dialog box, in the **Data Source** box, click the path that contains your file name. Then, at the bottom of the **Mail Merge Recipients** dialog box, click **Edit**. In the lower left corner of the displayed **Edit Data Source** dialog box, click **New Entry**. In the blank record, which

(Project 3D Career Newsletter continues on the next page)

Skills Review Project 3D Career Newsletter (continued)

is shaded, type the following, pressing Tab to move from field to field:

First Name	Mia
Last Name	Orr
Address 1	1378 Lima Ave.
Unit	#82
City	Memphis
State	TN
ZIP Code	38123

a. In the lower right corner of the **Edit Data Source** dialog box, click **OK**, and then in the displayed message, click **Yes**. At the bottom of the **Mail Merge Recipients** dialog box, click **OK**.

b. At the bottom of the **Mail Merge** pane, click **Next: Arrange your labels**. Under **Arrange your labels**, click **Address block**. In the lower right corner of the **Insert Address Block** dialog box, click **Match Fields**.

c. Click the **Address 2 arrow**, and then from the list of available fields, click **Unit**. Click **OK** two times.

d. In the **Mail Merge** pane, under **Replicate labels**, click **Update all labels**. At the bottom of the **Mail Merge** pane, click **Next: Preview your labels**. Press Ctrl + A to select all of the label text, click the **Layout tab**, and then in the **Paragraph group**, click in the **Spacing Before** box. Type **3** and press Enter. At the bottom of the **Mail Merge** pane, click **Next: Complete the merge**.

e. Click the **Mailings tab**, and then in the **Start Mail Merge group**, click **Edit Recipient List** to display the list of names and addresses. In the **Mail Merge Recipients** dialog box, click the **Last Name** field heading to sort the names. Click **OK**. **Close** the **Mail Merge** pane.

f. Scroll the document and then click anywhere in the empty table row at the bottom. Click the **Table Tools Layout tab**. In the **Rows & Columns group**, click **Delete**, and then click **Delete Rows**. Add the file name to the footer, close the footer area, and then click the **File tab**. Click **Show All Properties**. As the **Tags**, type **labels** and as the **Subject**, type your course name and section number. Be sure your name displays as the **Author**, and then **Save** your file.

g. If directed by your instructor to do so, submit your paper printout, your electronic image of your document, or your original Word file. **Close** Word.

END | You have completed Project 3D

Mastering Word Project 3E Skin Protection Report

Apply 3A skills from these Objectives:

1. Create a Research Paper
2. Insert Footnotes in a Research Paper
3. Create Citations and a Bibliography in a Research Paper
4. Use Read Mode and PDF Reflow

In the following Mastering Word project, you will edit and format a research paper that contains information about skin protection and the use of sunblocks and sunscreens. This paper was created by Rachel Holder, a medical intern at University Medical Center, for distribution to her classmates studying dermatology. Your completed document will look similar to the one shown in Figure 3.57.

PROJECT FILES

For Project 3E, you will need the following file:

w03E_Skin_Protection

You will save your document as:

Lastname_Firstname_3E_Skin_Protection

PROJECT RESULTS

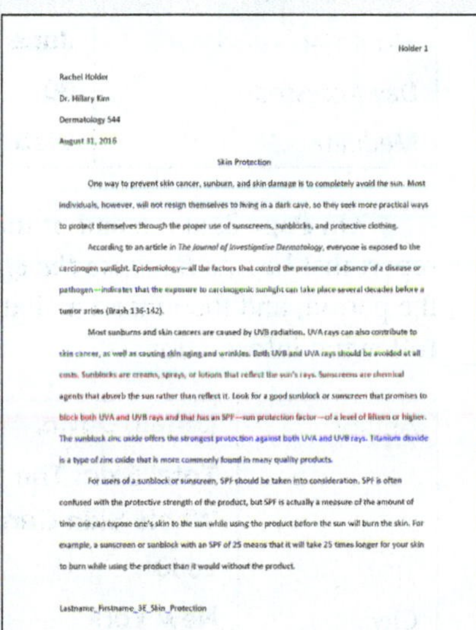

Holder 1

Rachel Holder

Dr. Hillary Kim

Dermatology 544

August 31, 2016

Skin Protection

One way to prevent skin cancer, sunburn, and skin damage is to completely avoid the sun. Most individuals, however, will not resign themselves to living in a dark cave, so they seek more practical ways to protect themselves through the proper use of sunscreens, sunblocks, and protective clothing.

According to an article in *The Journal of Investigative Dermatology*, everyone is exposed to the carcinogen sunlight. Epidemiology—all the factors that control the presence or absence of a disease or pathogen—indicates that the exposure to carcinogenic sunlight can take place several decades before a tumor arises (Brash 136-142).

Most sunburns and skin cancers are caused by UVB radiation. UVA rays can also contribute to skin cancer, as well as causing skin aging and wrinkles. Both UVB and UVA rays should be avoided at all costs. Sunblocks are creams, sprays, or lotions that reflect the sun's rays. Sunscreens are chemical agents that absorb the sun rather than reflect it. Look for a good sunblock or sunscreen that promises to block both UVA and UVB rays and that has an SPF—sun protection factor—of a level of fifteen or higher. The sunblock zinc oxide offers the strongest protection against both UVA and UVB rays. Titanium dioxide is a type of zinc oxide that is more commonly found in many quality products.

For users of a sunblock or sunscreen, SPF should be taken into consideration. SPF is often confused with the protective strength of the product, but SPF is actually a measure of the amount of time one can expose one's skin to the sun while using the product before the sun will burn the skin. For example, a sunscreen or sunblock with an SPF of 25 means that it will take 25 times longer for your skin to burn while using the product than it would without the product.

Lastname_Firstname_3E_Skin_Protection

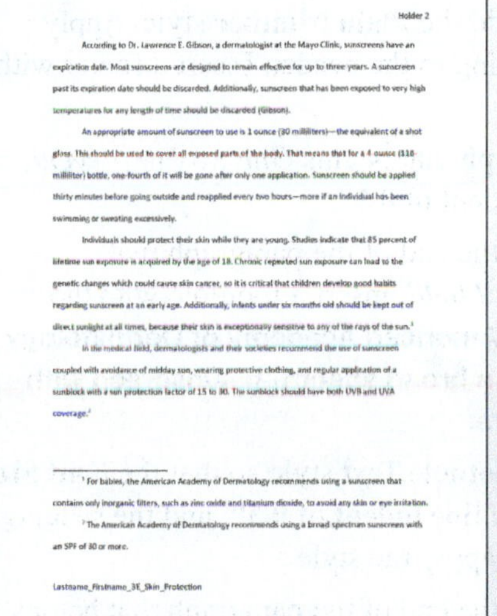

Holder 2

According to Dr. Lawrence E. Gibson, a dermatologist at the Mayo Clinic, sunscreens have an expiration date. Most sunscreens are designed to remain effective for up to three years. A sunscreen past its expiration date should be discarded. Additionally, sunscreen that has been exposed to very high temperatures for any length of time should be discarded (Gibson).

An appropriate amount of sunscreen to use is 1 ounce (30 milliliters)—the equivalent of a shot glass. This should be used to cover all exposed parts of the body. That means that for a 4 ounce (118 milliliter) bottle, one-fourth of it will be gone after only one application. Sunscreen should be applied thirty minutes before going outside and reapplied every two hours—more if an individual has been swimming or sweating excessively.

Individuals should protect their skin while they are young. Studies indicate that 85 percent of lifetime sun exposure is acquired by the age of 18. Chronic repeated sun exposure can lead to the genetic changes which could cause skin cancer, so it is critical that children develop good habits regarding sunscreen at an early age. Additionally, infants under six months old should be kept out of direct sunlight at all times, because their skin is exceptionally sensitive to any of the rays of the sun.[1]

In the medical field, dermatologists and their societies recommend the use of sunscreen coupled with avoidance of midday sun, wearing protective clothing, and regular application of a sunblock with a sun protection factor of 15 to 30. The sunblock should have both UVB and UVA coverage.[2]

[1] For babies, the American Academy of Dermatology recommends using a sunscreen that contains only inorganic filters, such as zinc oxide and titanium dioxide, to avoid any skin or eye irritation.

[2] The American Academy of Dermatology recommends using a broad spectrum sunscreen with an SPF of 30 or more.

Lastname_Firstname_3E_Skin_Protection

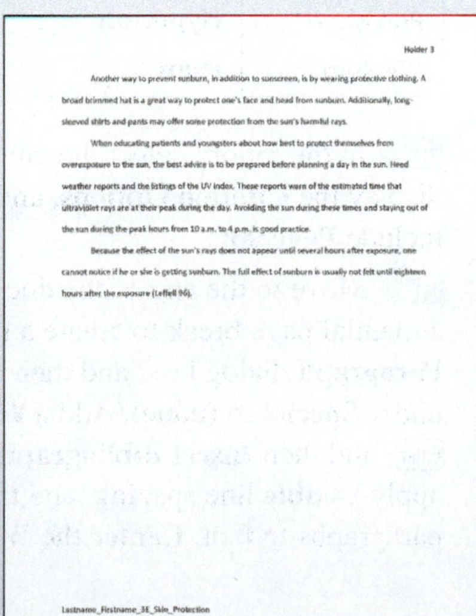

Holder 3

Another way to prevent sunburn, in addition to sunscreen, is by wearing protective clothing. A broad brimmed hat is a great way to protect one's face and head from sunburn. Additionally, long-sleeved shirts and pants may offer some protection from the sun's harmful rays.

When educating patients and youngsters about how best to protect themselves from overexposure to the sun, the best advice is to be prepared before planning a day in the sun. Heed weather reports and the listings of the UV index. These reports warn of the estimated time that ultraviolet rays are at their peak during the day. Avoiding the sun during these times and staying out of the sun during the peak hours from 10 a.m. to 4 p.m. is good practice.

Because the effect of the sun's rays does not appear until several hours after exposure, one cannot notice if he or she is getting sunburn. The full effect of sunburn is usually not felt until eighteen hours after the exposure (Leffell 96).

Lastname_Firstname_3E_Skin_Protection

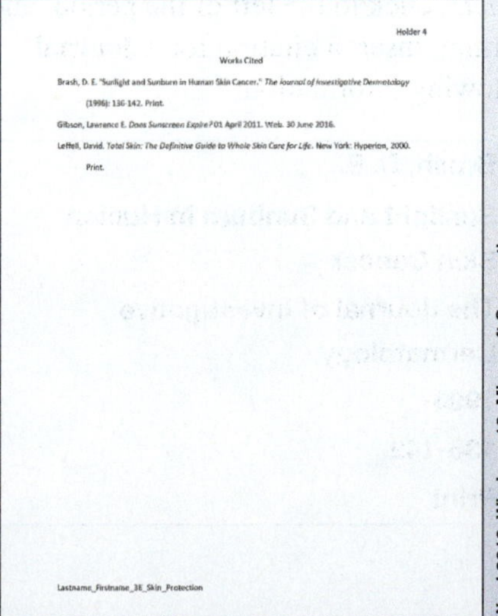

Holder 4

Works Cited

Brash, D. E. "Sunlight and Sunburn in Human Skin Cancer." *The Journal of Investigative Dermatology* (1996): 136-142. Print.

Gibson, Lawrence E. *Does Sunscreen Expire?* 01 April 2011. Web. 30 June 2016.

Leffell, David. *Total Skin: The Definitive Guide to Whole Skin Care for Life*. New York: Hyperion, 2000. Print.

Lastname_Firstname_3E_Skin_Protection

FIGURE 3.57

(Project 3E Skin Protection Report continues on the next page)

Mastering Word Project 3E Skin Protection Report (continued)

1 Start Word, and on the left click **Open Other Documents**. From your student data files, locate and open the document **w03E_Skin_Protection**. Display formatting marks and rulers. Save the file in your **Word Chapter 3** folder as **Lastname_Firstname_3E_Skin_Protection**

2 Select all the text, change the **Line Spacing** to **2.0**, and then change the **Spacing After** to **0 pt**.

3 At the top of the document, insert a new blank paragraph, and then in the new paragraph, type **Rachel Holder** Press Enter. Type **Dr. Hillary Kim** and press Enter. Type **Dermatology 544** and press Enter. Type **August 31, 2016** and press Enter. Type **Skin Protection** and then press Ctrl + E to center the title you just typed.

4 Insert a header, type **Holder** and then press Spacebar. Display the **Page Number gallery**, and then in the **Current Position**, add the **Plain Number** style. Apply **Align Right** formatting to the header. Insert a footer with the file name.

5 To the paragraph that begins *One way to prevent*, apply a **First line** indent of **0.5"**.

6 On **Page 2**, at the end of the paragraph that begins *In the medical field*, insert a footnote with the following text: **The American Academy of Dermatology recommends using a broad spectrum sunscreen with an SPF of 30 or more.**

7 Modify the **Footnote Text** style so that the **Font Size** is **11**, there is a **First line indent** of **0.5"**, and the spacing is **Double**, and then apply the style.

8 On **Page 1**, at the end of the paragraph that begins *According to an article*, click to the left of the period, and then using **MLA** format, insert a citation for a **Journal Article** with the following information:

Author	**Brash, D. E.**
Title	**Sunlight and Sunburn in Human Skin Cancer**
Journal Name	**The Journal of Investigative Dermatology**
Year	**1996**
Pages	**136-142**
Medium	**Print**

9 In the report, select the citation you just created, display the **Citation Options**, and then edit the citation to include **Pages 136-142**

10 At the top of **Page 2**, at the end of the paragraph that begins *According to Dr.*, click to the left of the period, and then insert a citation for a **Web site** with the following information:

Author	**Gibson, Lawrence E.**
Name of Web Page	**Does Sunscreen Expire?**
Year	**2011**
Month	**April**
Day	**01**
Year Accessed	**2016**
Month Accessed	**June**
Day Accessed	**30**
Medium	**Web**

11 On **Page 3**, at the end of the last paragraph of the report that begins *Because the effect*, click to the left of the period, and then insert a citation for a **Book** with the following information:

Author	**Leffell, David.**
Title	**Total Skin: The Definitive Guide to Whole Skin Care for Life**
Year	**2000**
City	**New York**
Publisher	**Hyperion**
Medium	**Print**

12 In the report, select the citation you just created, display the **Citation Options**, and then edit the citation to include **Page 96**

13 Move to the end of the document, and then insert a manual page break to create a new page. Display the **Paragraph** dialog box, and then change the **Indentation** under **Special** to **(none)**. Add a **Works Cited** title, press Enter, and then **Insert Bibliography**. Select the references, apply **Double** line spacing, and then set the **Spacing After** paragraphs to **0 pt**. **Center** the *Works Cited* title.

(Project 3E Skin Protection Report continues on the next page)

Mastering Word Project 3E Skin Protection Report (continued)

14 Update the **Document Properties** with the following information:

Title	**Skin Protection**
Tags	**sunscreen, sun exposure**
Comments	**Draft copy of report for class**
Categories	**Dermatology**
Company	**University Medical Center**
Manager	**Dr. Hillary Kim**

15 In the **Subject** box, type your course name and section number. Be sure that your name displays as the **Author** and edit if necessary. On the left, click **Print** to view the **Print Preview**. Click **Save** to redisplay your document. If directed by your instructor to do so, submit your paper printout, your electronic image of your document that looks like a printed document, or your original Word file. **Close** Word.

END | You have completed Project 3E

CONTENT-BASED ASSESSMENTS (MASTERY AND TRANSFER OF LEARNING)

MyITLab grader

Apply 3B skills from these Objectives:

5 Format a Multiple-Column Newsletter
6 Use Special Character and Paragraph Formatting
7 Create Mailing Labels Using Mail Merge

Mastering Word Project 3F Dogs Newsletter and Mailing Labels

In the following Mastering Word project, you will format a newsletter with information about the therapy dogs handled by volunteers at the University Medical Center. Optionally, you will create mailing labels so that the newsletter can be sent to the volunteer staff. Your completed documents will look similar to Figure 3.58.

PROJECT FILES

For Project 3F, you will need the following files:

w03F_Dogs_Newsletter
w03F_Dog
w03F_Addresses (Optional: Use only if you are completing the Mailing Labels portion of this project)

You will save your documents as:

Lastname_Firstname_3F_Dogs_Newsletter
Lastname_Firstname_3F_Mailing_Labels (Optional: Create only if you are completing the Mailing Labels portion of this project)

PROJECT RESULTS

Your symbol may differ

University Medical Center

Health Improvement Newsletter

Volume 3 Spring 2016

DOGS FOR HEALING

At University Medical Center, therapy dogs have been a welcomed asset to patient care and recovery since 2004. UMC works with several non-profit organizations to bring dedicated volunteers and their canine teams into the hospital to visit children, adults, and seniors. Information regarding service dog regulations, training, and laws is available on the ADA website.

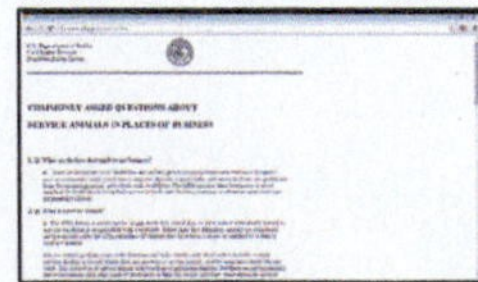

BENEFITS TO PATIENTS

Medical research shows that petting a dog or other domestic animal relaxes patients and helps ease symptoms of stress from illness or from the hospital setting. Studies have shown that such therapies contribute to decreased blood pressure and heart rate, and can help with patient respiratory rate.

CUDDLES

Cuddles, a 4 year-old Labrador, is one of our most popular therapy dogs and is loved by both young and senior patients. You'll see Cuddles in the Children's wing on Mondays with his owner, Jason, who trained him since he was a tiny pup.

BRANDY

Brandy is a 6-year-old Beagle who brings smiles and giggles to everyone she meets. Over the past several years, Brandy has received accolades and awards for her service as a therapy dog. Brandy is owned by Melinda Sparks, a 17-year veteran employee of University Medical Center. Brandy and Melinda can be seen making the rounds on Wednesdays in the Children's wing and on Mondays and Fridays.

To request a visit from a therapy dog, or to learn how to become involved with therapy dog training, call Carole Yates at extension 2365.

Lastname_Firstname_3F_Dogs_Newsletter

Optional mailing labels (if assigned)

Mary Ackerman
82 E. Roxie Blvd.
Arlington, TN 38002

Anthony Borman
2820 Lincoln Ave.
Collierville, TN 38017

Jerry Camden

Jacqueline Epps
653 Vista Ave.
#D
Lakeland, TN 38002

Renee Farnsworth
36 S. Levin St.
#D
Bartlett, TN 38135

Germantown, TN 38139

Emily Gold
888 Packard Court
Lakeland, TN 38002

Abel Heaphy
55 Amigo Lane
#4
Collierville, TN 38017

Katie Hughes
34 Sadler Pl.
Bartlett, TN 38133

Bin Lee
676 Silver St.
Memphis, TN 38120

Anh Ly
1255 Chestnut Street
Memphis, TN 38122

Priya Malik
975 Ricardo Place
#G
Germantown, TN 38138

Leland Marcus
600 Garfield Ave.
Memphis, TN 38117

Walter McKidd
2495 Holly Drive
Arlington, TN 38002

Sharon Moreno
1330 Golden Ave.
Memphis, TN 38120

Thai Nguyen
179 Sierra Court
Collierville, TN 38017

Thomas Norris
492 Mahogany Street
Bartlett, TN 38135

Daniel Scofield
1518 Price Place
Arlington, TN 38002

Erica Scott
124 Susan Drive
#352
Memphis, TN 38134

Andrew Sharma
1550 Beverly Drive
#1550
Memphis, TN 38104

Sara Thompson
4220 Glendora Dr.
#320
Memphis, TN 38112

Simone Thompson
648 Michaela St.
Bartlett, TN 38133

David Turnbull
1821 Chelsea St.
#1442
Germantown, TN 38138

Jackson Williams
15 Atlantic Rd.
Memphis, TN 38111

Miranda Yanos
1256 Loma Ave.
#34
Memphis, TN 38123

Lastname_Firstname_3F_Mailing_Labels

FIGURE 3.58

(Project 3F Dogs Newsletter and Mailing Labels continues on the next page)

Mastering Word Project 3F Dogs Newsletter and Mailing Labels (continued)

1 Start Word. From your student files, open **w03F_Dogs_Newsletter**. **Save** the file in your **Word Chapter 3** folder as **Lastname_Firstname_3F_Dogs_Newsletter** and then add the file name to the footer. Select the first three lines of the document, and then change the **Font Color** to **Olive Green, Accent 3, Darker 25%**—in the seventh column, the fifth color. With the text selected, display the **Borders and Shading** dialog box. Apply a **3 pt** bottom border using the color **Black, Text 1**.

2 Click at the beginning of the newsletter title *University Medical Center*. Insert an online picture from **Bing Image Search** by searching for **physician symbol** and then insert one of the symbols that is not bordered or framed.

3 Set the image **Height** to **1"**. Change the **Brightness/Contrast** to **Brightness: 0% (Normal) Contrast: +40%**.

4 Change the **Text Wrapping** to **Square**. Change the **Horizontal Alignment** to **Left relative** to **Margin** and the **Vertical Alignment** to **Top relative** to **Margin**. If necessary, drag a corner of the inserted physician symbol to decrease its size so that the newsletter title displays on two lines.

5 Starting with the paragraph that begins *Dogs for Healing*, select all of the text from that point to the end of the document. Change the **Spacing After** to **10 pt**, format the text in two columns, and apply **Justify** alignment. Insert a **Column** break before the subheading *Cuddles*.

6 Click at the beginning of the sentence that begins with *Brandy is a 6-year-old Beagle*. From your student data files, insert the picture **w03F_Dog**. Rotate the picture using **Flip Horizontal**.

7 Change the picture **Width** to **1** and then apply the **Square** layout option. Change the **Horizontal Alignment** to **Right relative** to **Margin** and the **Vertical Alignment** to **Top relative** to **Line**. Apply a **Black, Text 1 Picture Border** and change the **Weight** to **2 ¼ pt**.

8 Start your web browser and if necessary, maximize the window. Navigate to **www.ada.gov/qasrvc.htm** From the taskbar, redisplay your **Lastname_Firstname_3F_Dogs_Newsletter** file, click at the end of the paragraph below the *Dogs for Healing* subheading. Insert a **Screenshot** of the website. Apply a **Black, Text 1 Picture Border** and change the **Weight** to **1 pt**.

9 Select the subheading **Dogs for Healing** including the paragraph mark. By using the **Font** dialog box, change the **Size** to **16**, apply **Bold**, apply the **Small caps** effect, and change the **Font color** to **Olive Green, Accent 3, Darker 50%**—in the seventh column, the last color. Apply the same formatting to the subheadings **Benefits to Patients**, **Cuddles**, and **Brandy**.

10 Select the last paragraph in the newsletter including the paragraph mark, and then apply a **1 pt Shadow** border, in **Black, Text 1**. Shade the paragraph with a **Fill** color of **Olive Green, Accent 3, Lighter 80%**—in the seventh column, the second color.

11 Click the **File tab**, and then click **Show All Properties**. As the **Tags**, type **dogs, newsletter** As the **Subject**, type your course name and section number. Under **Related People**, if necessary, type your name in the Author box. **Print Preview** the document and make any necessary corrections.

12 On the left, click **Print** to view the **Print Preview**. Click **Save** to redisplay your document. If directed by your instructor to do so, submit your paper printout, your electronic image of your document that looks like a printed document, or your original Word file. **Close** Word.

END | You have completed Project 3F

ALERT!

Optional Project to Produce Mailing Labels

Your instructor may ask you to complete the optional project on the following page to produce mailing labels. Check with your instructor to see if you should complete the mailing labels. This project is not included in the MyITLab Grader system.

CONTENT-BASED ASSESSMENTS (MASTERY AND TRANSFER OF LEARNING)

1 Start Word and display a new blank document. **Save** the document in your **Word Chapter 3** folder as **Lastname_Firstname_3F_Mailing_Labels** From your student files, **Open** the file **w03F_Addresses. Save** the address file in your **Word Chapter 3** folder as **Lastname_Firstname_3F_Addresses.**

2 Start the **Step-by-Step Mail Merge Wizard** to create **Labels**. Display the **Label Options** dialog box, and be sure that the **Default tray** is selected and that the label vendor is **Avery US Letter**. The **Product number** is **5160 Easy Peel Address Labels**. Select the **Use an existing list** option, click **Browse**, and then in the **Select Data Source** dialog box, navigate to your student data files and open **w03F_Addresses.** In the **Select Table** dialog box, click **OK**. Add the following record to your file:

First Name	**Miranda**
Last Name	**Yanos**
Address 1	**1256 Loma Ave.**
Unit	**#34**
City	**Memphis**
State	**TN**
ZIP Code	**38123**

3 Insert an **Address block** and match the fields. Match the **Address 2** field to the **Unit** field, and then update the labels. Preview the labels, and then select the entire document. Change the **Spacing Before** to **3** and then **Complete the merge**. Delete the last row from the bottom of the table, and then add the file name to the footer.

4 Display the document properties. As the **Tags** type **labels** and as the **Subject** type your course name and section number. Be sure your name displays in the **Author box**, and then **Save** your file. As directed by your instructor, print or submit electronically. **Close** Word and close your browser window.

END | You have completed the optional portion of this project

CONTENT-BASED ASSESSMENTS (MASTERY AND TRANSFER OF LEARNING)

Mastering Word | Project 3G Research Paper, Newsletter, and Mailing Labels

Apply 3A and 3B skills from these Objectives:

1 Create a Research Paper
2 Insert Footnotes in a Research Paper
3 Create Citations and a Bibliography in a Research Paper
4 Use Read Mode and PDF Reflow
5 Format a Multiple-Column Newsletter
6 Use Special Character and Paragraph Formatting
7 Create Mailing Labels Using Mail Merge

In the following Mastering Word project, you will edit and format a research paper and a newsletter. Optionally, you will create mailing labels. Your completed documents will look similar to Figure 3.59.

PROJECT FILES

For Project 3G, you will need the following files:

w03G_Newsletter_and_Research_Paper
w03G_Addresses (Optional: For use if you are completing the Mailing Labels portion of this project)

You will save your documents as:

Lastname_Firstname_3G_Research_Paper_and_Newsletter
Lastname_Firstname_3G_Mailing_Labels (Optional: Create only if you are completing the Mailing Labels portion of this project)

PROJECT RESULTS

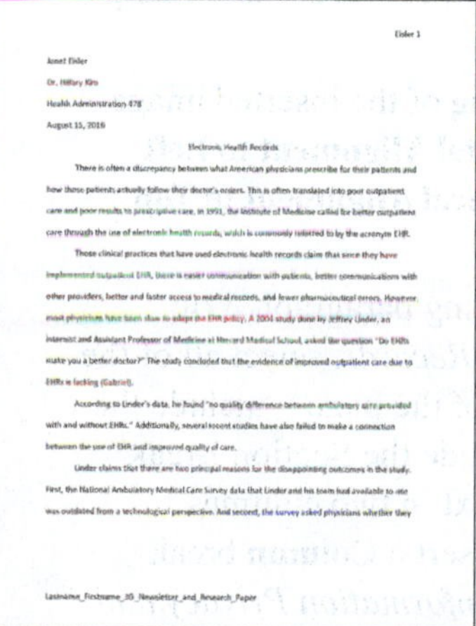

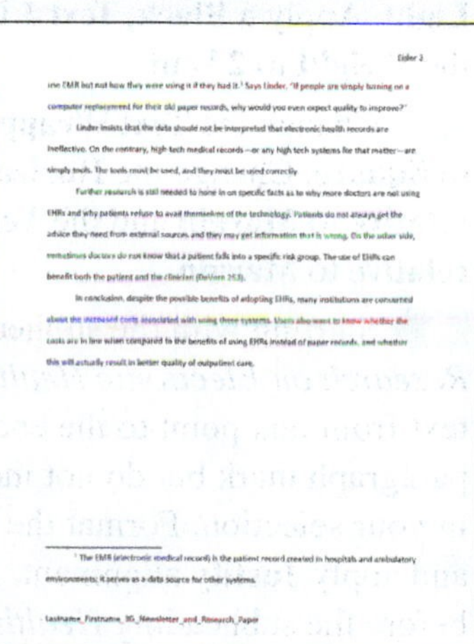

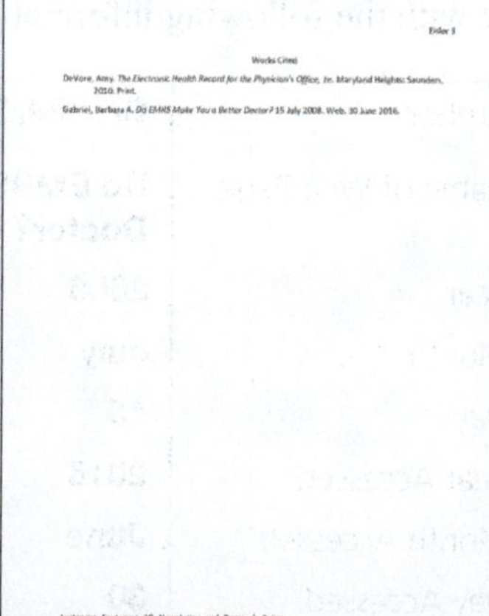

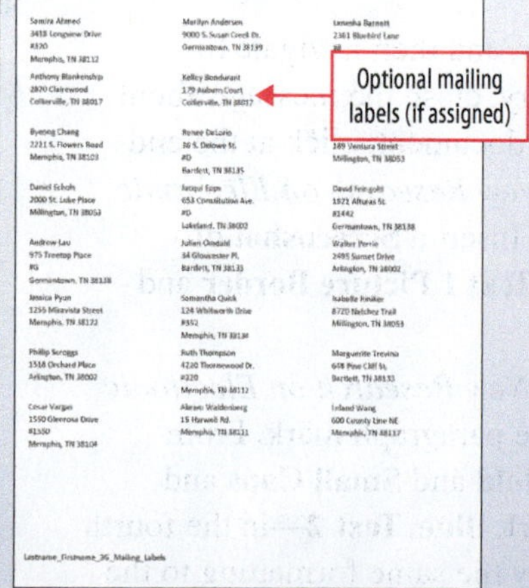

FIGURE 3.59

Word 2016, Windows 10, Microsoft Corporation

(Project 3G Research Paper, Newsletter, and Mailing Labels continues on the next page)

Mastering Word Project 3G Research Paper, Newsletter, and Mailing Labels (continued)

1 From your student files, open **w03G_Newsletter_and_Research_Paper**. **Save** the file in your **Word Chapter 3** folder as **Lastname_Firstname_3G_Newsletter_and_Research_Paper** and then add the file name to the footer. Click anywhere on Page 2, and because this is a separate section, add the File Name to the footer again so that it appears in both sections of the document. Redisplay **Page 1**, select the first three lines of the newsletter heading, and then apply a **3 pt** bottom border in **Black, Text 1**.

2 Click at the beginning of the newsletter title *University Medical Center*. Insert an online picture from **Bing Image Search** by searching for **microscope** and then insert an image of a black—or a black and white—microscope. Set the **Height** of the image to **.7"** and then **Recolor** the picture by applying **Blue, Accent color 1 Light**. Apply a **Black, Text 1 Picture Border** and change the **Weight** to **2 ¼ pt**.

3 Change the **Text Wrapping** of the inserted image to **Square**. Change the **Horizontal Alignment** to **Left relative** to **Margin** and the **Vertical Alignment** to **Top relative** to **Margin**.

4 Starting with the subheading paragraph *New Research on Electronic Health Records*, select all of the text from that point to the end of the page—include the paragraph mark but do not include the Section Break in your selection. Format the text in two columns, and apply **Justify** alignment. Insert a **Column** break before the subheading *Health Information Privacy and Security*.

5 Start your web browser, and then navigate to **www.healthit.gov** If necessary, close the message about subscribing. Redisplay your document, click at the end of the paragraph below the *New Research on Electronic Health Records* subheading. Insert a **Screenshot** of the website. Apply a **Black, Text 1 Picture Border** and change the **Weight** to **1 pt**.

6 Select the subheading *New Research on Electronic Health Records* including the paragraph mark. From the **Font** dialog box, apply **Bold** and **Small Caps** and change the **Font color** to **Dark Blue, Text 2**—in the fourth column, the first color. Apply the same formatting to the subheadings *Doctors Define Meaningful Use*, *Health Information and Privacy and Security* and *Research Sources Aid in EHR Implementation*. Select the *Doctors Define Meaningful Use* subheading and then change the **Spacing Before** to **18 pt**.

7 Select the last paragraph in the newsletter—the text in bold italic that begins *Ensuring the privacy* including the paragraph mark but not the Section Break lines—and then apply a **1 pt Shadow** border using **Black, Text 1**. Shade the paragraph with the **Fill** color **Dark Blue, Text 2, Lighter 80%**—in the fourth column, the second color. **Center** the text. **Save** your document.

8 On **Page 2**, beginning with **Janet Eisler**, select all of the text on the page. With the text on Page 2 selected, change the **Line Spacing** to **2.0**, and then change the **Spacing After** to **0 pt**. To the paragraph that begins *There is often a discrepancy*, apply a **First line** indent of **0.5"** inches.

9 At the bottom of **Page 2**, in the next to last line of text, after the period at the end of the sentence that ends *if they had it*, insert a footnote with the following text: **The EMR (electronic medical record) is the patient record created in hospitals and ambulatory environments; it serves as a data source for other systems.**

10 Modify the **Footnote Text** style to set the **Font Size** to **11** and the format of the Footnote Text paragraph to include a **First line** indent of **0.5"** and **Double** spacing. Apply the new style to the footnote text.

11 On **Page 2**, at the end of the paragraph that begins *Those clinical practices*, click to the left of the period, and then using **MLA** format, insert a citation for a **Web site** with the following information:

Author	**Gabriel, Barbara A.**
Name of Web Page	**Do EMRS Make You a Better Doctor?**
Year	**2008**
Month	**July**
Day	**15**
Year Accessed	**2016**
Month Accessed	**June**
Day Accessed	**30**
Medium	**Web**

(Project 3G Research Paper, Newsletter, and Mailing Labels continues on the next page)

Mastering Word Project 3G Research Paper, Newsletter, and Mailing Labels (continued)

12 On **Page 3**, at the end of the paragraph that begins *Further research*, click to the left of the period, and then using **MLA** format, insert a citation for a **Book** with the following information:

Author	**DeVore, Amy.**
Title	**The Electronic Health Record for the Physician's Office, 1e**
Year	**2010**
City	**Maryland Heights**
Publisher	**Saunders**
Medium	**Print**

13 In the report, select the citation you just created, display the **Citation Options**, and then edit the citation to include **Pages 253**

14 On **Page 4**, click in the blank paragraph. On the **References tab**, click **Bibliography**, and then click **Insert Bibliography**.

15 Update the **Document Properties** with the following information:

Title	**Electronic Health Records**
Tags	**EMR, health records**
Subject	(insert your course name and section number)
Company	**University Medical Center**
Manager	**Dr. Hillary Kim**

16 On the left, click **Print** to display the **Print Preview**, and then click **Save** to redisplay your document. If directed by your instructor to do so, submit your paper printout, your electronic image of your document that looks like a printed document, or your original Word file. **Close** Word.

END | You have completed Project 3G

ALERT! **Optional Project to Produce Mailing Labels**

Your instructor may ask you to complete the optional project on the next page to produce mailing labels. Check with your instructor to see if you should complete the mailing labels. This project is not included in the MyITLab Grader system.

CONTENT-BASED ASSESSMENTS (MASTERY AND TRANSFER OF LEARNING)

1 Start Word and display a new blank document. **Save** the document in your **Word Chapter 3** folder as **Lastname_Firstname_3G_Mailing_Labels**

2 Start the **Step-by-Step Mail Merge Wizard** to create **Labels**. Display the **Label Options** dialog box, and be sure that the **Default tray** is selected and that the label vendor is **Avery US Letter**. The **Product number** is **5160 Easy Peel Address Labels**. Select the **Use an existing list option**, click **Browse**, and then in the **Select Data Source** dialog box, navigate to your student data files and open **w03G_Addresses**. In the **Select Table** dialog box, click **OK**. Add the following record to your file:

First Name	**Mason**
Last Name	**Zepeda**
Address 1	**134 Atlantic Ave.**
Unit	**#21**
City	**Memphis**
State	**TN**
ZIP Code	**38123**

3 Insert an **Address block** and match the fields. Match the **Address 2** field to the **Unit** field, and then update the labels. Preview the labels, and then select the entire document. Change the **Spacing Before** to **3** and then **Complete the merge**. Delete the last row from the bottom of the table, and then add the file name to the footer.

4 Display the document properties. As the **Tags** type **labels** and as the **Subject** type your course name and section number. Be sure your name displays in the **Author box**, and then **Save** your file. As directed by your instructor, print or submit your work electronically. Close all open windows.

END | You have completed the optional portion of this project

Apply a combination of the 3A and 3B skills.

CONTENT-BASED ASSESSMENTS (CRITICAL THINKING)

GO! Fix It Project 3H Hospital Materials **MyITLab**

GO! Make It Project 3I Health Newsletter **MyITLab**

GO! Solve It Project 3J Colds and Flu **MyITLab**

GO! Solve It Project 3K Cycling Newsletter

PROJECT FILES

For Project 3K, you will need the following file:

w03K_Cycling_Newsletter

You will save your document as:

Lastname_Firstname_3K_Cycling_Newsletter

The University Medical Center Emergency Department publishes a monthly newsletter focusing on safety and injury prevention. The topic for the current newsletter is bicycle safety. From your student data files, open **w03K_Cycling_Newsletter**, add the file name to the footer, and then save the file in your **Word Chapter 3** folder as **Lastname_Firstname_3K_Cycling_Newsletter**

Using the techniques that you practiced in this chapter, format the document in two-column newsletter format. Format the nameplate so that it is clearly separate from the body of the newsletter and is easily identified as the nameplate. Insert column breaks as necessary and apply appropriate formatting to subheadings. Insert and format at least one online picture that is appropriate to the topic, and insert a screenshot of a relevant website. Apply a border and shading to the last paragraph so that it is formatted attractively.

Add your name, your course name and section number, and the keywords **agenda, monthly staff meeting** to the Properties area. Submit as directed.

(Project 3K Cycling Newsletter continues on the next page)

CONTENT-BASED ASSESSMENTS (CRITICAL THINKING)

GO! Solve It Project 3K Cycling Newsletter (continued)

Performance Level

Performance Criteria	Exemplary: You consistently applied the relevant skills	Proficient: You sometimes, but not always, applied the relevant skills	Developing: You rarely or never applied the relevant skills
Format nameplate	The nameplate is formatted attractively and in a manner that clearly indicates that it is the nameplate.	The nameplate includes some formatting but is not clearly separated from the body of the newsletter.	The newsletter does not include a nameplate.
Insert and format at least one online picture	An appropriate online picture image is included. The image is sized and positioned appropriately.	A clip art image is inserted but is either inappropriate, or is formatted or positioned poorly.	No clip art image is included.
Border and shading added to a paragraph	The last paragraph displays an attractive border with shading that enables the reader to read the text.	A border or shading is displayed but not both; or the shading is too dark to enable the reader to easily read the text.	No border or shading is added to a paragraph.
Insert a screenshot	A screenshot is inserted in one of the columns; the screenshot is related to the content of the article.	A screenshot is inserted in the document but does not relate to the content of the article.	No screenshot is inserted.

END | You have completed Project 3K

OUTCOMES-BASED ASSESSMENTS

RUBRIC

The following outcomes-based assessments are *open-ended assessments*. That is, there is no specific correct result; your result will depend on your approach to the information provided. Make *Professional Quality* your goal. Use the following scoring rubric to guide you in *how* to approach the problem and then to evaluate *how well* your approach solves the problem.

The *criteria*—Software Mastery, Content, Format and Layout, and Process—represent the knowledge and skills you have gained that you can apply to solving the problem. The *levels of performance*—Professional Quality, Approaching Professional Quality, or Needs Quality Improvements—help you and your instructor evaluate your result.

	Your completed project is of Professional Quality if you:	Your completed project is Approaching Professional Quality if you:	Your completed project Needs Quality Improvements if you:
1-Software Mastery	Choose and apply the most appropriate skills, tools, and features and identify efficient methods to solve the problem.	Choose and apply some appropriate skills, tools, and features, but not in the most efficient manner.	Choose inappropriate skills, tools, or features, or are inefficient in solving the problem.
2-Content	Construct a solution that is clear and well organized, contains content that is accurate, appropriate to the audience and purpose, and is complete. Provide a solution that contains no errors in spelling, grammar, or style.	Construct a solution in which some components are unclear, poorly organized, inconsistent, or incomplete. Misjudge the needs of the audience. Have some errors in spelling, grammar, or style, but the errors do not detract from comprehension.	Construct a solution that is unclear, incomplete, or poorly organized; contains some inaccurate or inappropriate content; and contains many errors in spelling, grammar, or style. Do not solve the problem.
3-Format & Layout	Format and arrange all elements to communicate information and ideas, clarify function, illustrate relationships, and indicate relative importance.	Apply appropriate format and layout features to some elements, but not others. Overuse features, causing minor distraction.	Apply format and layout that does not communicate information or ideas clearly. Do not use format and layout features to clarify function, illustrate relationships, or indicate relative importance. Use available features excessively, causing distraction.
4-Process	Use an organized approach that integrates planning, development, self-assessment, revision, and reflection.	Demonstrate an organized approach in some areas, but not others; or, use an insufficient process of organization throughout.	Do not use an organized approach to solve the problem.

OUTCOMES-BASED ASSESSMENTS

Apply a combination of the 3A and 3B skills.

GO! Think Project 3L Influenza Report

PROJECT FILES

Build from Scratch

For Project 3L, you will need the following file:

New blank Word document

You will save your document as:

Lastname_Firstname_3L_Influenza

As part of the ongoing research conducted by University Medical Center in the area of community health and contagious diseases, Dr. Hillary Kim has asked Sarah Stanger to create a report on influenza—how it spreads, and how it can be prevented in the community.

Create a new Word document and save it as **Lastname_Firstname_3L_Influenza** Conduct your research and then create the report in MLA format. The report should include at least two footnotes, at least two citations, and should include a *Works Cited* page.

The report should contain an introduction, and then information about what influenza is, how it spreads, and how it can be prevented. A good place to start is at **http://health.nih.gov/topic/influenza**.

Add the file name to the footer. Add appropriate information to the Document Properties and submit as directed.

END | You have completed Project 3L

Build From Scratch

GO! Think! Project 3M Volunteer Newsletter MyITLab

Build from Scratch

You and GO! Project 3N College Newsletter MyITLab

GO! Collaborative Team Project Project 3O Bell Orchid Hotels MyITLab

Using Styles and Creating Multilevel Lists and Charts

4

WORD 2016

PROJECT 4A

OUTCOMES

Edit a handout using styles and arrange text into an organized list.

OBJECTIVES

1. Apply and Modify Styles
2. Create New Styles
3. Manage Styles
4. Create a Multilevel List

PROJECT 4B

OUTCOMES

Change a style set and create and format a chart.

OBJECTIVES

5. Change the Style Set of a Document and Apply a Template
6. Insert a Chart and Enter Data into a Chart
7. Change a Chart Type
8. Format a Chart

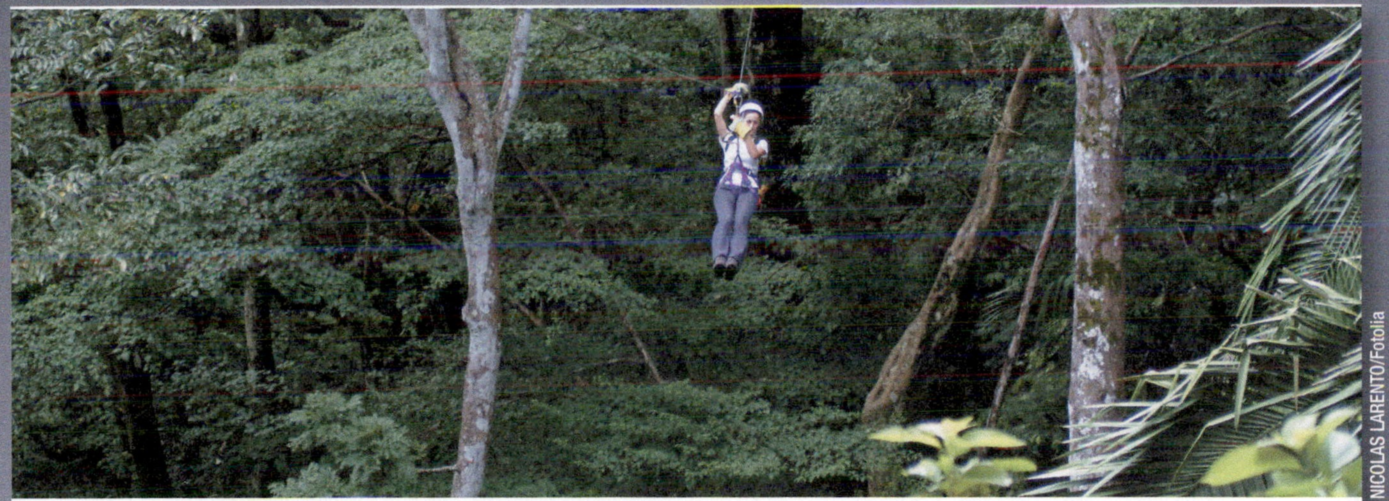

NICOLAS LARENTO/Fotolia

In This Chapter

In this chapter, you will apply styles, create multilevel lists, attach a template to a document, and display numerical data in charts. The theme and style set features provide a simple way to coordinate colors, fonts, and effects used in a document. For example, if you publish a monthly newsletter, you can apply styles to article headings and modify lists to ensure that all editions of the newsletter maintain a consistent and professional look. Charts display numerical data in a visual format. Formatting chart elements adds interest and assists the reader in interpreting the displayed data.

The projects in this chapter relate to **Costa Rican Treks**, a tour company named for the small country in Central America with a diverse ecosystem. Costa Rican Treks offers exciting but affordable adventure tours for individuals and groups. Travelers go off the beaten path to explore amazing remote places in this scenic country. If you prefer to experience the heart of Costa Rica on the water, try the kayaking or rafting tours. Costa Rican Treks also offers hiking and Jeep tours. Whatever you prefer—mountain, sea, volcano—our trained guides are experts in the history, geography, culture, and flora and fauna of Costa Rica.

PROJECT 4A Customer Handout

PROJECT ACTIVITIES

In Activities 4.01 through 4.11, you will create a handout for Costa Rican Treks customers who are interested in scuba diving tours. You will use styles and multilevel list formats so that the document is attractive and easy to read. Your completed document will look similar to Figure 4.1.

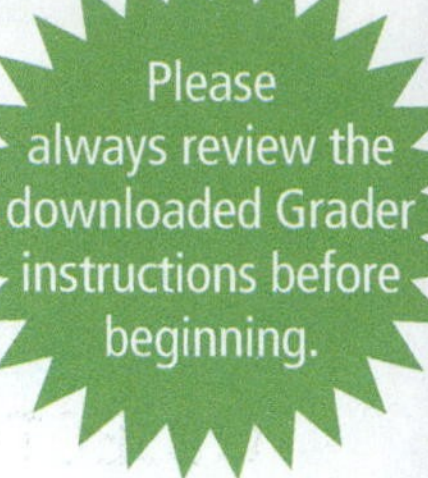

If your instructor wants you to submit Project 4A in the MyITLab Grader system, log in to MyITLab, locate Grader Project 4A, and then download the files for this project.

For Project 4A, you will need the following file: **w04A_Customer_Handout**

You will save your document as: **Lastname_Firstname_4A_Customer_Handout**

PROJECT RESULTS

GO! Walk Thru Project 4A

Costa Rican Treks

REQUIREMENTS FOR SCUBA DIVING TRIPS

Costa Rican Treks offers several tours that include scuba diving. For any tours where equipment will be rented, facilitators must ensure that several pieces of safety equipment are available for each participant.

Please notify us when you book a tour if you would like us to supply any of the following scuba gear for you. We are happy to do so at a reasonable price.

Equipment

1 Air Tank
- ➢ The air tank holds high-pressure breathing gas. Typically, each diver needs just one air tank. Contrary to common perception, the air tank does not hold pure oxygen; rather, it is filled with compressed air that is about 21 percent oxygen and 79 percent nitrogen.
  - ✦ Examples: Aluminum, steel, pony

2 Buoyancy Compensator
- ➢ The buoyancy compensator controls the overall buoyancy of the diver so that descending and ascending can be controlled.
  - ✦ Examples: Wings, stab jacket, life jacket

3 Regulator
- ➢ A regulator controls the pressure of the breathing gas supplied to the diver to make it safe and comfortable to inhale.
  - ✦ Examples: Constant flow, twin-hose

4 Weights
- ➢ Weights add just enough weight to help the diver descend rather than float. The right amount of weight will not cause the diver to sink.
  - ✦ Examples: Weight belt, integrated weight systems

Attire

1 Dry Suits
- ➢ A dry suit is intended to insulate and protect the diver's skin. Dry suits are different from wet suits in that they prevent water from entering the suits.
  - ✦ Examples: Membrane, neoprene, hybrid

2 Wet Suits
- ➢ A wet suit insulates and protects, whether in cool or warm water. Wet suits differ from dry suits in that a small amount of water gets between the suit and the diver's skin.
  - ✦ Examples: Two millimeter, 5 millimeter, 7 millimeter, Titanium

Lastname_Firstname_4A_Customer_Handout

FIGURE 4.1 Project 4A Customer Handout

NOTE	If You Are Using a Touchscreen
	Tap an item to click it.
	Press and hold for a few seconds to right-click; release when the information or commands display.
	Touch the screen with two or more fingers and then pinch together to zoom out or stretch your fingers apart to zoom in.
	Slide your finger on the screen to scroll—slide left to scroll right and slide right to scroll left.
	Slide to rearrange—similar to dragging with a mouse.
	Swipe to select—slide an item a short distance with a quick movement—to select an item and bring up commands, if any.

4 WORD

Objective 1 Apply and Modify Styles

GO! Learn How Video W4-1

A ***style*** is a group of formatting commands, such as font, font size, font color, paragraph alignment, and line spacing. You can retrieve a style by name and apply it to text with one click.

Using styles to format text has several advantages over using ***direct formatting***—the process of applying each format separately; for example, bold, then font size, then font color, and so on. Styles are faster to apply, result in a consistent look, and can be automatically updated in all instances in a document, which can be especially useful in long documents.

2.2.6

Activity 4.01 | Applying Styles to Paragraphs

ALERT! **To submit as an autograded project, log into MyITLab and download the files for this project, and begin with those files instead of w04A_Customer_Handout.**

Styles that are grouped together comprise a ***style set***. A style set is a group of styles that are designed to work together. Specific styles—for example, *Title* or *Heading 1*—that display in the Styles gallery on the ribbon can be applied to any selected text.

1. Start Word. From your student files, locate and open the document **w04A_Customer_Handout.**
2. Press F12 to display the Save As dialog box. In the **Save As** dialog box, navigate to the location where you are saving your files for this chapter. Create a new folder named **Word Chapter 4** and then **Save** the document as **Lastname_Firstname_4A_Customer_Handout**
3. Scroll to the bottom of **Page 1**, right-click in the footer area, and then click **Edit Footer.** On the ribbon, under **Header & Footer Tools**, on the **Design tab**, in the **Insert group**, click **Document Info**, and then click **File Name**. **Close** the footer area. If necessary, display the rulers and formatting marks.
4. Press Ctrl + Home to move to the top of the document.

5 On the **Home tab**, in the **Styles group**, notice that the **Normal** style is selected—outlined in blue. Compare your screen with Figure 4.2.

The ***Normal*** style is the default style in Word for a new blank document. Normal style formatting includes the Calibri font, 11 point font size, line spacing at 1.08, and 8 pt spacing after a paragraph.

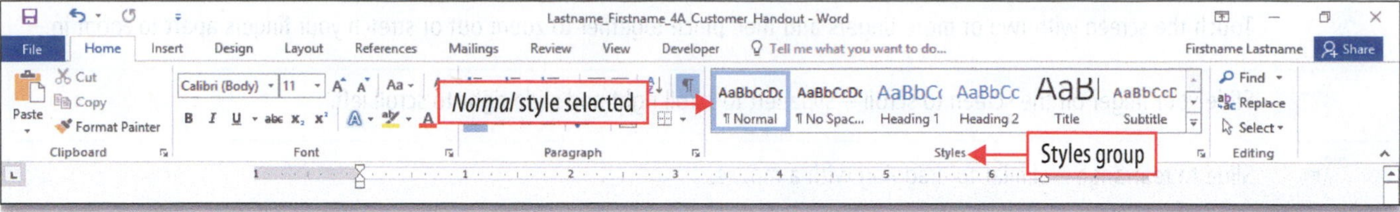

FIGURE 4.2 Word 2016, Windows 10, Microsoft Corporation

6 Including the paragraph mark, select the first paragraph, which forms the title of the document—*Costa Rican Treks*. On the **Home tab**, in the **Styles group**, click the **More** button to display the Styles gallery. Point to the style named **Title**, and then compare your screen with Figure 4.3.

Live Preview displays how the text will look with the Title style applied.

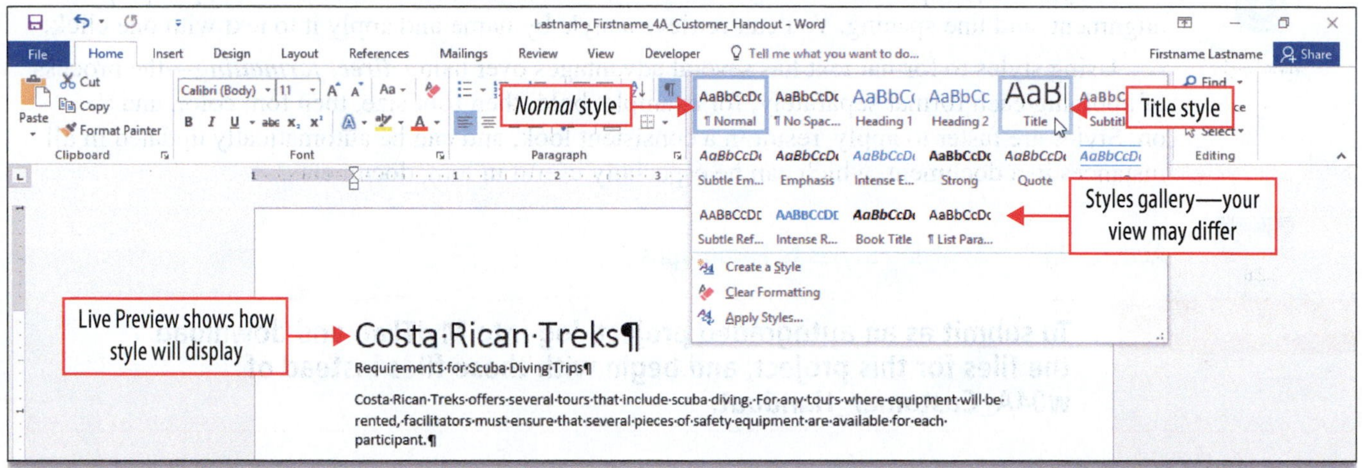

FIGURE 4.3 Word 2016, Windows 10, Microsoft Corporation

7 Click **Title**, and then click anywhere in the document to deselect the title.

The Title style includes the 28 point Calibri Light font, single line spacing and 0 pt spacing after the paragraph.

8 Select the second paragraph, which begins *Requirements for*, and is the subtitle of the document. In the **Styles group**, click **More**, and then in the gallery, click **Subtitle**.

The Subtitle style includes a Black, Text 1 Lighter 35% font color and expanding of the text by 0.75 pt.

9 Select the third and fourth paragraphs, beginning with *Costa Rican Treks offers* and ending with the text *at a reasonable price*. In the **Styles group**, click **More**, and then in the gallery, click **Emphasis**. Click anywhere to deselect the text, and then compare your screen with Figure 4.4.

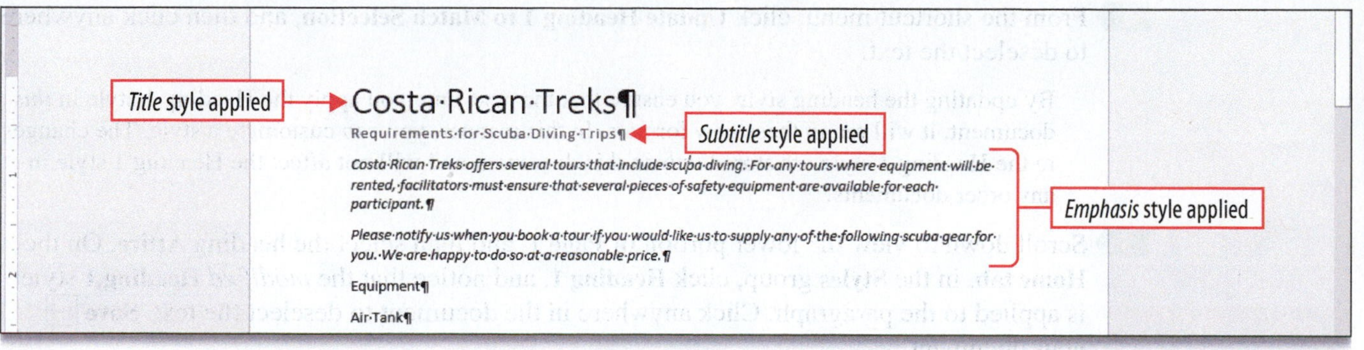

FIGURE 4.4 Word 2016, Windows 10, Microsoft Corporation

10 **Save** your document.

Activity 4.02 | Modifying Existing Style Attributes

Expert 2.2.b

You are not limited to the exact formatting of a style—you can change it to suit your needs. For example, you might like the formatting of a style with the exception of the font size. If you plan to use a customized style repeatedly in a document, it's a good idea to modify the style to look exactly the way you want it. You can either save the modified style as a new style or you can update the existing style to match the new formatting.

1 Select the heading *Equipment*. Using the technique you practiced, apply the **Heading 1** style.

The Heading 1 style includes the 16 point Calibri Light font, the Accent 1 font color, 12 pt spacing before the paragraph and 0 pt spacing after the paragraph.

A small black square displays to the left of the paragraph indicating that the Heading 1 style also includes the ***Keep with next*** and ***Keep lines together*** formatting—Word commands that keep a heading with its first paragraph of text together on the page, or prevent a single line from displaying by itself at the bottom of a page or at the top of a page.

2 With the paragraph selected, on the mini toolbar, change the **Font Size** to **18**.

3 On the mini toolbar, click **Styles**. In the **Styles** gallery, right-click **Heading 1**, and then compare your screen with Figure 4.5.

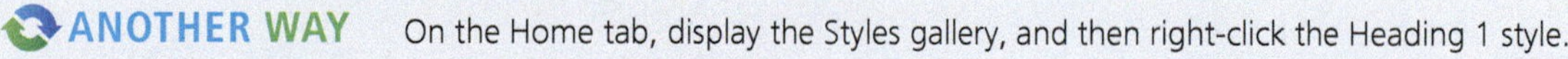

On the Home tab, display the Styles gallery, and then right-click the Heading 1 style.

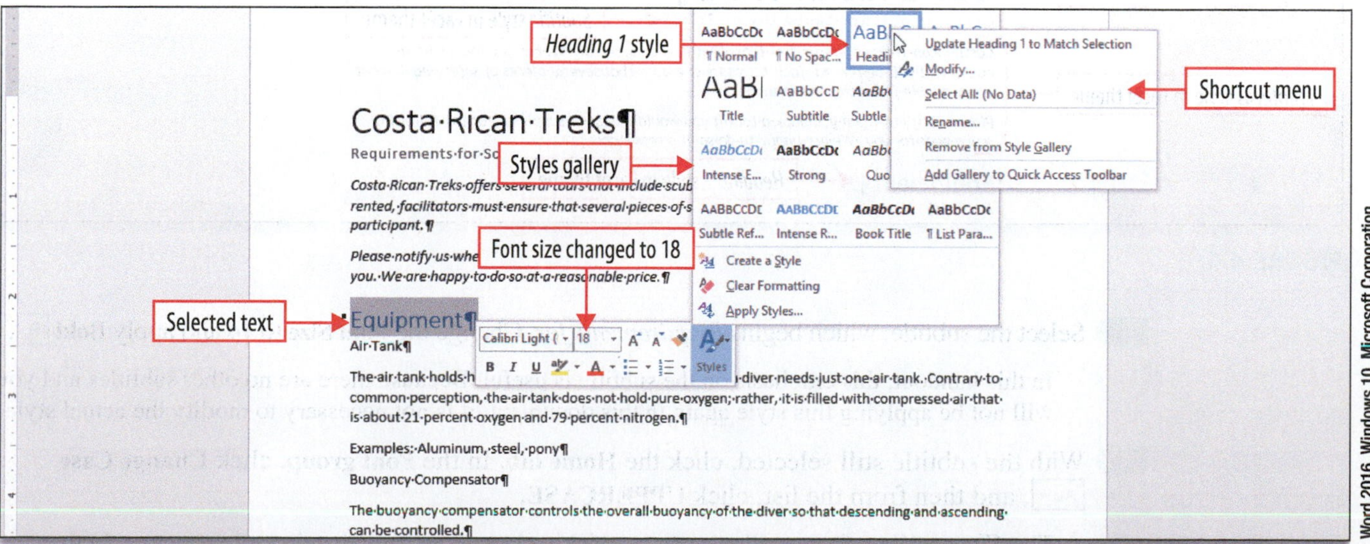

FIGURE 4.5

4 From the shortcut menu, click **Update Heading 1 to Match Selection**, and then click anywhere to deselect the text.

By updating the heading style, you ensure that the next time you apply the Heading 1 style in *this* document, it will retain these new formats. In this manner, you can customize a style. The changes to the Heading 1 style are stored *only* in this document and will not affect the Heading 1 style in any other documents.

5 Scroll down to view the lower portion of **Page 1**, and then select the heading **Attire**. On the **Home tab**, in the **Styles** group, click **Heading 1**, and notice that the *modified* **Heading 1** style is applied to the paragraph. Click anywhere in the document to deselect the text. **Save** your document.

Activity 4.03 | Changing the Document Theme

1.3.2

Recall that a theme is a predefined combination of colors, fonts, and effects; the *Office* theme is the default theme applied to new blank documents. Styles use the font scheme, color scheme, and effects associated with the current theme. If you change the theme, the styles adopt the fonts, colors, and effects of the new theme.

1 Press Ctrl + Home. Click the **Design tab**, and then in the **Document Formatting group**, click **Themes**. In the gallery, point to the various themes and notice the changes in your document.

Live Preview enables you to see the effects a theme has on text with styles applied.

2 Click **Facet**, and then compare your screen with Figure 4.6.

The Facet theme's fonts, colors, and effects display in the document. All the styles will now use the Facet theme.

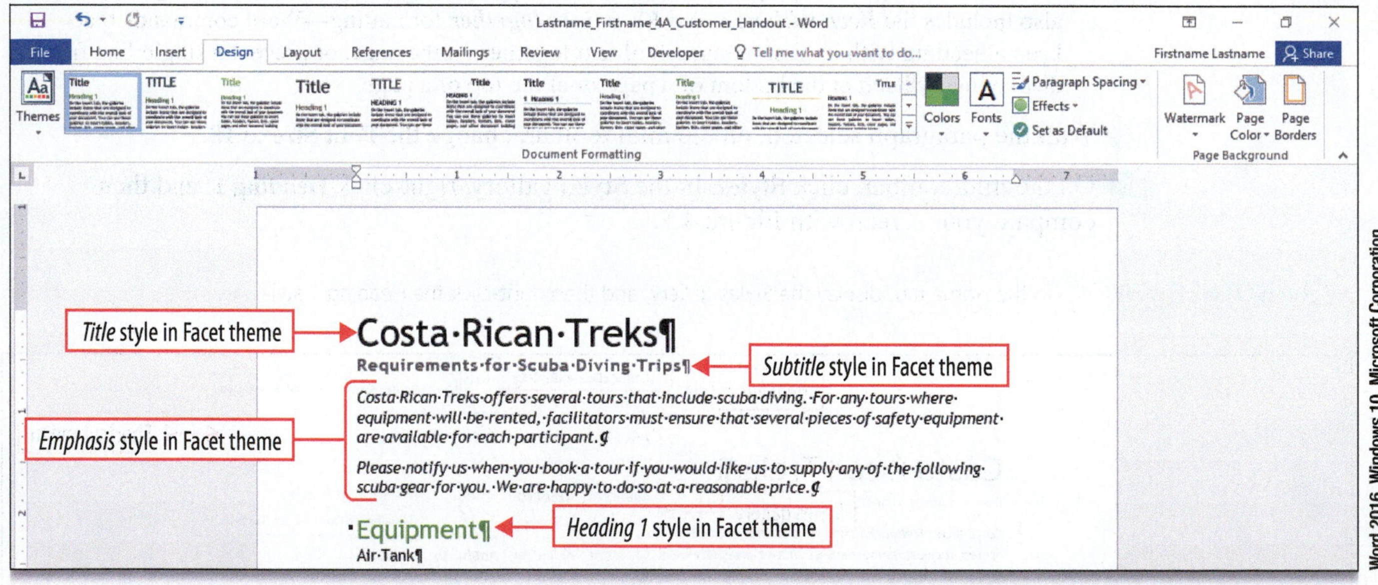
Title style in Facet theme
Costa·Rican·Treks¶
Requirements·for·Scuba·Diving·Trips¶
Subtitle style in Facet theme
Costa·Rican·Treks·offers·several·tours·that·include·scuba·diving.·For·any·tours·where·equipment·will·be·rented,·facilitators·must·ensure·that·several·pieces·of·safety·equipment·are·available·for·each·participant.¶
Emphasis style in Facet theme
Please·notify·us·when·you·book·a·tour·if·you·would·like·us·to·supply·any·of·the·following·scuba·gear·for·you.·We·are·happy·to·do·so·at·a·reasonable·price.¶
Equipment¶
Heading 1 style in Facet theme
Air·Tank¶
Word 2016, Windows 10, Microsoft Corporation

FIGURE 4.6

3 Select the subtitle, which begins *Requirements for*. Change the **Font Size** to **14** and apply **Bold** B.

In this handout, this emphasis on the subtitle is useful. Because there are no other subtitles and you will not be applying this style again in this document, it is not necessary to modify the actual style.

4 With the subtitle still selected, click the **Home tab**. In the **Font group**, click **Change Case** Aa, and then from the list, click **UPPERCASE**.

The ***Change Case*** feature allows you to quickly change the capitalization of characters. In the selection, all characters now display in uppercase letters.

5 Select the third and fourth paragraphs, beginning with *Costa Rican Treks offers* and ending with the text *at a reasonable price*. On the mini toolbar, change the **Font Size** to **12**, and then click **Styles**. In the **Styles** gallery, right-click **Emphasis**, and then click **Update Emphasis to Match Selection**. Click anywhere to deselect the text. **Save** your document.

4 WORD

Objective 2 Create New Styles

GO! Learn How Video W4-2

You can create a new style based on formats that you specify. For example, if you frequently use a 12 point Verdana font with bold emphasis and double spacing, you can create a style to apply those settings to a paragraph with a single click, instead of using multiple steps each time you want that specific formatting. Any new styles that you create are stored with the document and are available any time that the document is open.

Activity 4.04 | Creating Custom Styles and Assigning Shortcut Keys

2.2.1

You can assign a shortcut key to a style, which allows you to apply the style using the keyboard instead of clicking the style in the Styles gallery.

1 Select the paragraph that begins *Examples: Aluminum*, and then on the mini toolbar, change the **Font Size** to **12**, click **Bold** [B], and then click **Italic** [I].

2 With the paragraph still selected, on the **Home tab**, in the **Styles group**, click the **More** button. In the lower portion of the gallery, click **Create a Style**.

ANOTHER WAY On the mini toolbar, click Styles, and then click Create a Style.

3 In the **Create New Style from Formatting** dialog box, in the **Name** box, type **Examples** and then compare your screen with Figure 4.7.

Select a name for your new style that will remind you of the type of text to which the style applies. A preview of the style displays in the Paragraph style preview box.

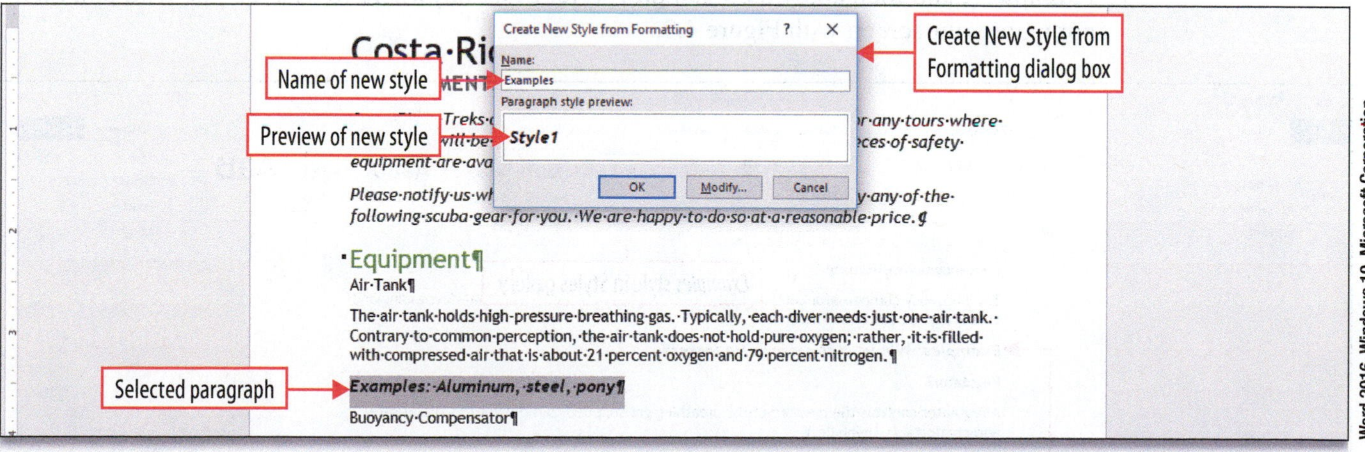

Word 2016, Windows 10, Microsoft Corporation

FIGURE 4.7

4 At the bottom of the dialog box, click **Modify**.

5 In the **Create New Style from Formatting** dialog box, at the bottom left, click **Format**, and then click **Shortcut key**.

6 In the **Customize Keyboard** dialog box, with the insertion point in the **Press new shortcut key** box, press Alt + E. Compare your screen with Figure 4.8.

The Command box indicates that the shortcut key will be assigned to the Examples style. The text *Alt+E* indicates the keys that have been pressed. A message indicates that the shortcut key is currently unassigned.

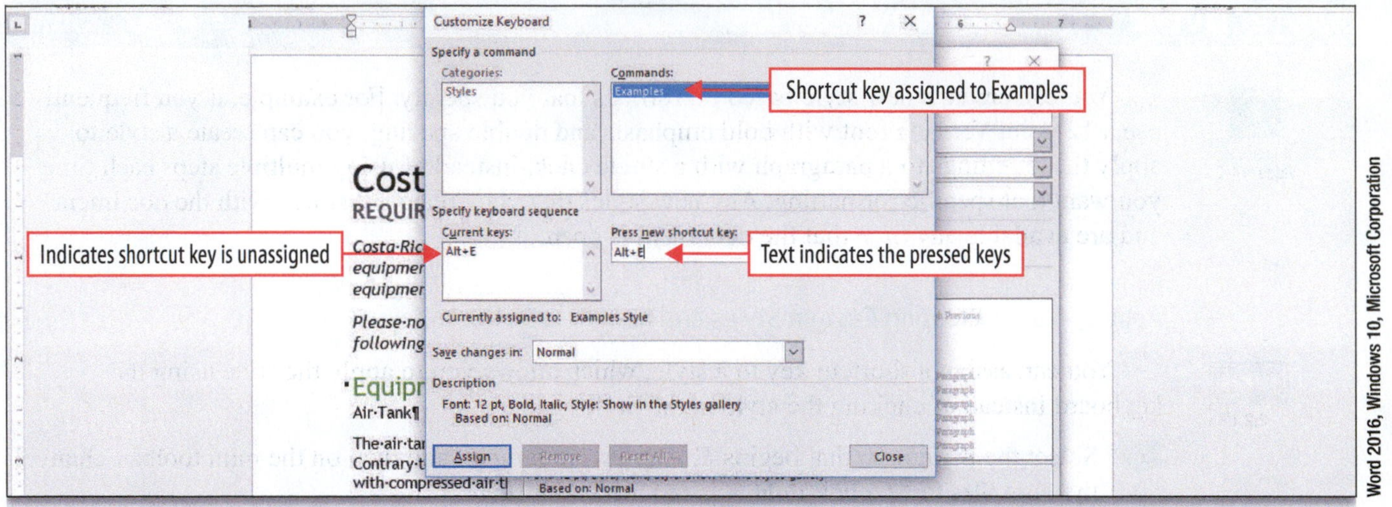

FIGURE 4.8

7 In the **Customize Keyboard** dialog box, click **Assign**. Click **Close**, and then in the **Create New Style from Formatting** dialog box, click **OK**.

The *Examples* style is added to the available styles for this document and displays in the Styles gallery. The shortcut key Alt + E is assigned to the *Examples* style.

8 Scroll down as necessary and select the paragraph that begins *Examples: Wings*. Press Alt + E to apply the new style *Examples*.

9 Using the technique you just practiced, select the four remaining paragraphs that begin *Examples:*, and then apply the **Examples** style. Click anywhere to deselect the text, and then compare your screen with Figure 4.9.

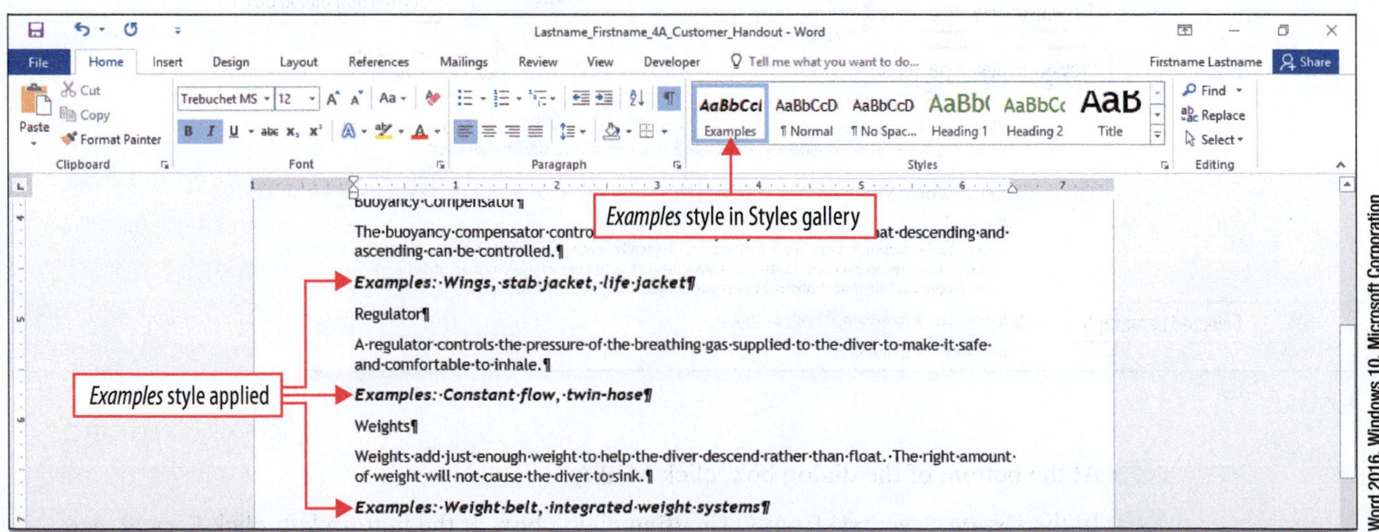

FIGURE 4.9

10 **Save** your document.

More Knowledge **Creating a Custom Style Set**

If you modify existing styles or create new styles, you can create a custom style set by saving the revised style set as a template. In this manner, you can apply the style set to other documents. On the Design tab, in the Document Formatting group, display the Styles gallery, and then click Save as a New Style Set. In the Save as a New Style Set dialog box, navigate to the location where you wish to save the file—the default location is the QuickStyles folder on your hard drive. Assign an appropriate file name, and then click Save. The file is saved as a Word template with the file extension .dotx.

4 WORD

Objective 3 Manage Styles

GO! Learn How Video W4-3

You can accomplish most of the tasks related to applying, modifying, and creating styles easily by using the Styles gallery. However, if you create and modify many styles in a document, you will find it useful to work in the ***Styles window***. The Styles window is a pane that displays a list of styles and contains tools to manage styles. Additionally, by viewing available styles in the Styles window, you can see the exact details of all the formatting that is included with each style.

Activity 4.05 | Customizing Settings for Existing Styles

1 Press Ctrl + Home, and then click anywhere in the title *Costa Rican Treks*. On the **Home tab**, in the lower right corner of the **Styles** group, click the **Dialog Box Launcher** to display the **Styles** window. Compare your screen with Figure 4.10.

The Styles window displays the same group of available styles found in the Styles gallery, including the new *Examples* style that you created.

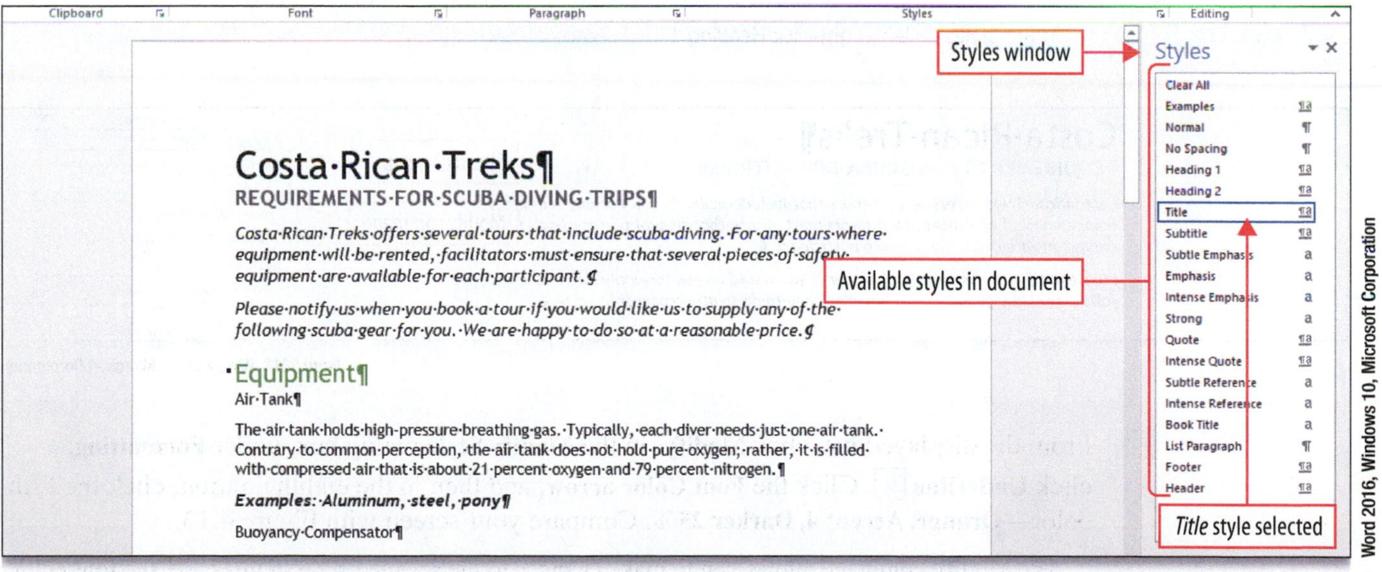

Clipboard
Font
Paragraph
Styles
Editing
Styles window
Styles
Clear All
Examples
Normal
No Spacing
Heading 1
Heading 2
Title
Subtitle
Subtle Emphasis
Emphasis
Intense Emphasis
Strong
Quote
Intense Quote
Subtle Reference
Intense Reference
Book Title
List Paragraph
Footer
Header
Costa·Rican·Treks¶
REQUIREMENTS·FOR·SCUBA·DIVING·TRIPS¶
Costa·Rican·Treks·offers·several·tours·that·include·scuba·diving.·For·any·tours·where· equipment·will·be·rented,·facilitators·must·ensure·that·several·pieces·of·safety· equipment·are·available·for·each·participant.¶
Please·notify·us·when·you·book·a·tour·if·you·would·like·us·to·supply·any·of·the· following·scuba·gear·for·you.·We·are·happy·to·do·so·at·a·reasonable·price.¶
Available styles in document
Equipment¶
Air·Tank¶
The·air·tank·holds·high-pressure·breathing·gas.·Typically,·each·diver·needs·just·one·air·tank.· Contrary·to·common·perception,·the·air·tank·does·not·hold·pure·oxygen;·rather,·it·is·filled· with·compressed·air·that·is·about·21·percent·oxygen·and·79·percent·nitrogen.¶
Examples:·Aluminum,·steel,·pony¶
Buoyancy·Compensator¶
Title style selected

FIGURE 4.10

2 In the **Styles** window, point to **Title** to display a ScreenTip with the details of the formats associated with the style. In the **ScreenTip**, under **Style**, notice that *Style Linked* is indicated.

3 Move your mouse pointer into the document to close the ScreenTip. In the **Styles** window, examine the symbols to the right of each style, as shown in Figure 4.11.

A ***character style***, indicated by the symbol **a**, contains formatting characteristics that you apply to text—for example, font name, font size, font color, bold emphasis, and so on.

A ***paragraph style***, indicated by the symbol **¶**, includes everything that a character style contains, plus all aspects of a paragraph's appearance—for example, text alignment, tab stops, line spacing, and borders.

A ***linked style***, indicated by the symbol **¶a**, behaves as either a character style or a paragraph style, depending on what you select.

List styles, which apply formats to a list, and ***table styles***, which apply a consistent look to the borders, shading, and so on of a table, are also available but do not display here.

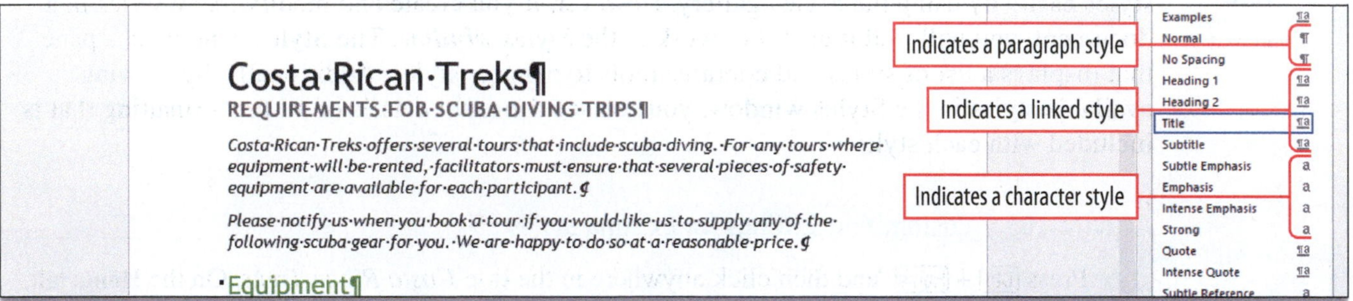

FIGURE 4.11 Word 2016, Windows 10, Microsoft Corporation

4 In the **Styles** window, point to **Heading 1**, and then click the **arrow** to display a list of commands. Compare your screen with Figure 4.12.

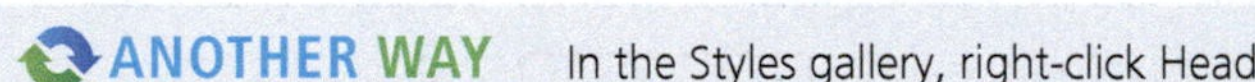
ANOTHER WAY In the Styles gallery, right-click Heading 1.

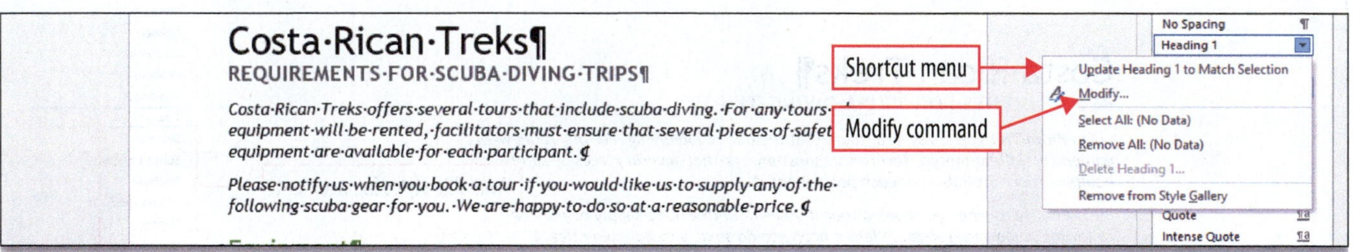

FIGURE 4.12 Word 2016, Windows 10, Microsoft Corporation

5 From the displayed list, click **Modify**. In the **Modify Style** dialog box, under **Formatting**, click **Underline** [U]. Click the **Font Color arrow**, and then in the eighth column, click the fifth color—**Orange, Accent 4, Darker 25%**. Compare your screen with Figure 4.13.

The Modify command allows you to make changes to the selected style In this case, the font color is changed and underline formatting is added to the style.

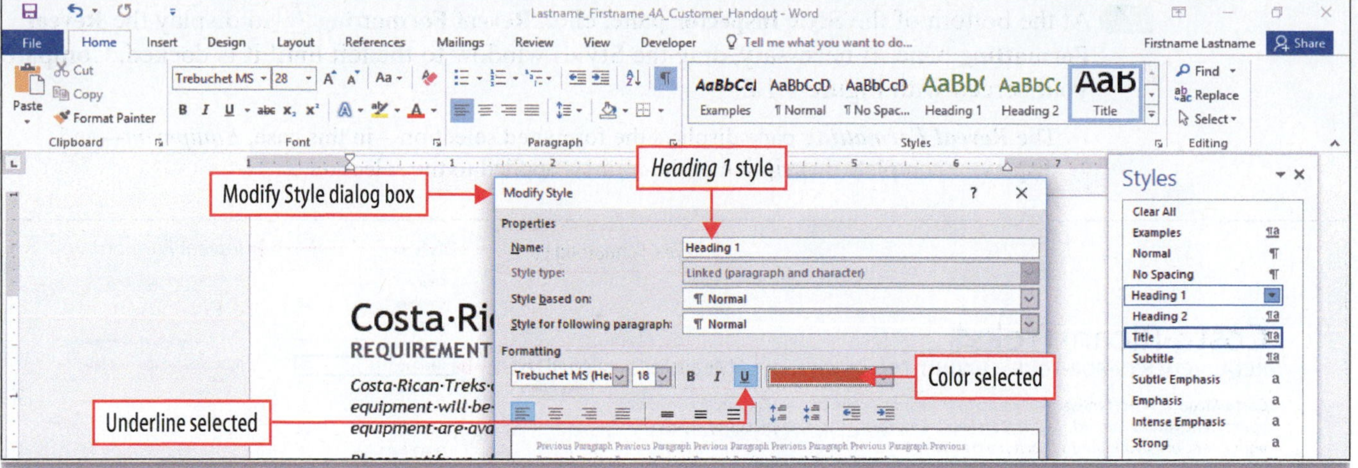

FIGURE 4.13

Word 2016, Windows 10, Microsoft Corporation

6 Click **OK** to close the Modify Styles dialog box. Scroll as necessary, and then notice that both headings—*Equipment* and *Attire*—are underlined and display in an orange font color. **Save** your document.

More Knowledge **Using Styles in Other Documents**

By default, styles that you create are stored in the current document only. However, you can make the style available in other documents. To do so, in the Modify Styles dialog box, select the New documents based on this template option button, which deselects the Only in this document option button.

Activity 4.06 | Viewing Style Formats

1 Scroll to view the upper portion of **Page 1**, and then select the heading **Equipment**. Notice that in the Styles window *Heading 1* is selected.

2 At the bottom right of the **Styles** window, click **Options**. In the **Style Pane Options** dialog box, in the **Select styles to show** box, click the **arrow** to display specific selection styles.

The selected option—in this case, the default option *Recommended*—determines the styles that display in the Styles window. The Recommended option causes the most commonly used styles to display.

3 At the bottom of the **Style Pane Options** dialog box, click **Cancel** to close the dialog box.

4 Near the bottom of the **Styles** window, select the **Show Preview** check box.

The ***Show Preview*** feature causes a visual representation of each style to display in the Styles window.

5 Clear the **Show Preview** check box.

6 At the bottom of the **Styles** window, click **Style Inspector**. In the **Style Inspector** pane, notice the name of the style applied to the selected text displays.

The ***Style Inspector*** pane displays the name of the style with formats applied and contains paragraph-level and text-level formatting options that allow you to modify the style or reset to default formats.

7 At the bottom of the **Style Inspector** pane, click **Reveal Formatting** to display the **Reveal Formatting** pane. If necessary, drag the Styles window to the left until it is docked. Compare your screen with Figure 4.14.

The ***Reveal Formatting*** pane displays the formatted selection—in this case, *Equipment*—and displays a complete description of the formats applied to the selection.

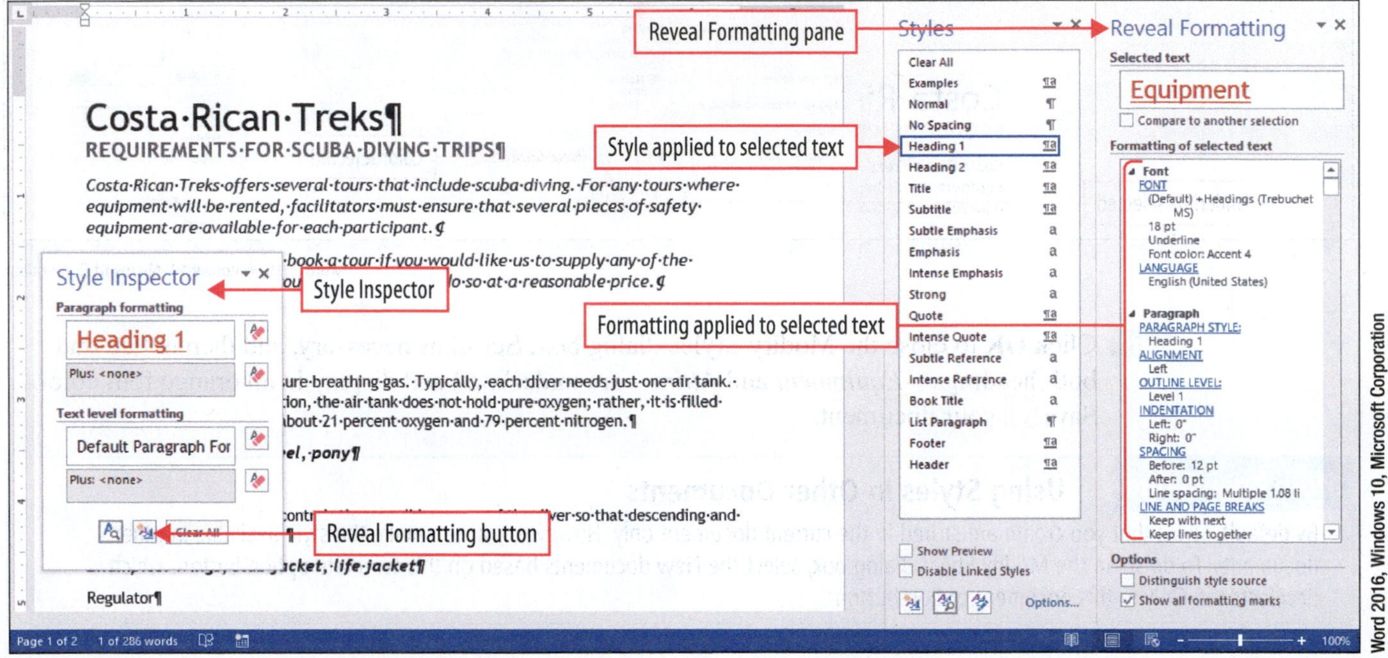

FIGURE 4.14

8 **Close** the Style Inspector pane, the Reveal Formatting pane, and the Styles window. **Save** your document.

Activity 4.07 | Clearing Existing Formats

2.2.4

There may be instances where you want to remove all formatting from existing text—for example, when you create a multilevel list.

1 Scroll to view the upper portion of **Page 1**, and then select the paragraph that begins *Examples: Aluminum*. On the **Home tab**, in the **Font group**, click **Clear All Formatting**. Compare your screen with Figure 4.15.

The Clear All Formatting command removes all formatting of the applied style from the selected text. Text returns to the *Normal* style formatting for the current theme.

ANOTHER WAY Select the desired text, and then at the top of the Styles window, click the Clear All command.

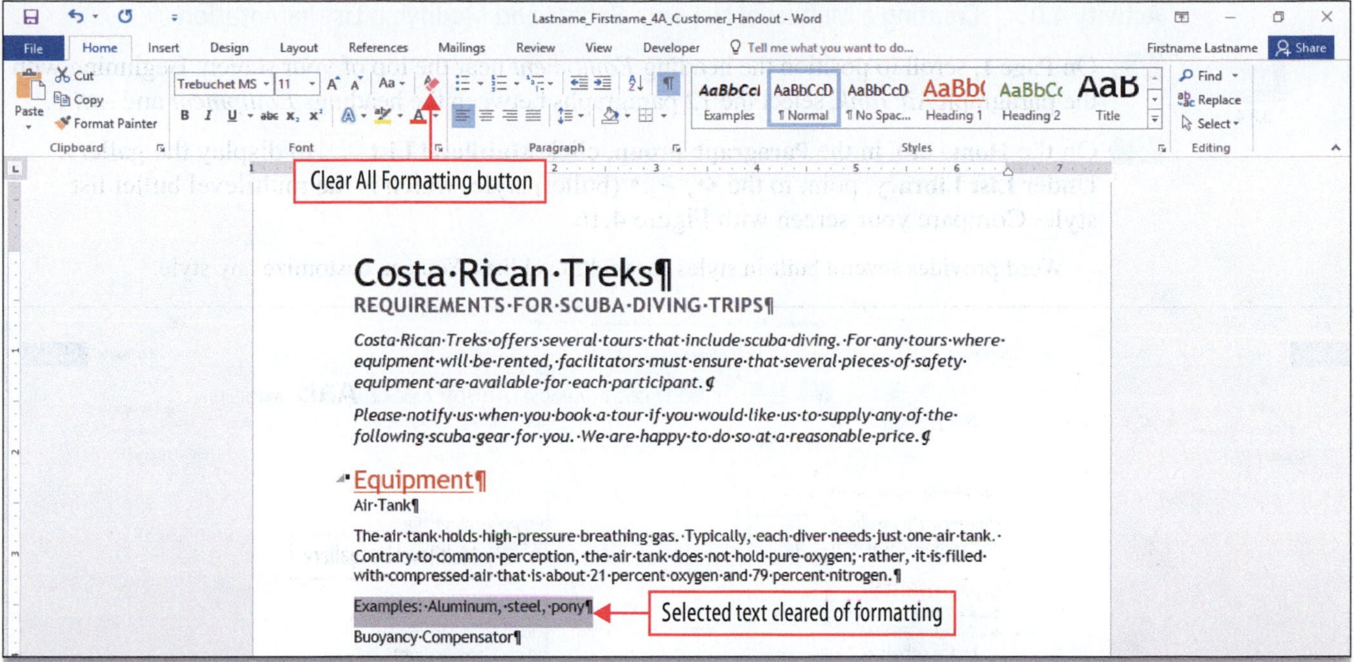

Lastname_Firstname_4A_Customer_Handout - Word
Clear All Formatting button
Costa·Rican·Treks¶
REQUIREMENTS·FOR·SCUBA·DIVING·TRIPS¶
Costa·Rican·Treks·offers·several·tours·that·include·scuba·diving.·For·any·tours·where·equipment·will·be·rented,·facilitators·must·ensure·that·several·pieces·of·safety·equipment·are·available·for·each·participant.¶
Please·notify·us·when·you·book·a·tour·if·you·would·like·us·to·supply·any·of·the·following·scuba·gear·for·you.·We·are·happy·to·do·so·at·a·reasonable·price.¶
Equipment¶
Air·Tank¶
The·air·tank·holds·high-pressure·breathing·gas.·Typically,·each·diver·needs·just·one·air·tank.·Contrary·to·common·perception,·the·air·tank·does·not·hold·pure·oxygen;·rather,·it·is·filled·with·compressed·air·that·is·about·21·percent·oxygen·and·79·percent·nitrogen.¶
Examples:·Aluminum,·steel,·pony¶
Selected text cleared of formatting
Buoyancy·Compensator¶

FIGURE 4.15 Word 2016, Windows 10, Microsoft Corporation

2 With the text still selected, in the **Styles group**, right-click **Examples**, and then click **Update Examples to Match Selection**.

All instances of text formatted with the Examples style now display with the Normal style formatting.

3 **Save** your document.

Activity 4.08 | Removing a Style

If a style that you created is no longer needed, you can remove it from the Styles gallery.

1 In the **Styles group**, right-click **Examples**, and then click **Remove from Style Gallery**.

The Examples style is removed from the Styles gallery. The style is no longer needed because all the paragraphs that are examples of scuba gear will be included in a multilevel list. Although the Examples style is removed from the Styles gallery, it is not deleted from the document.

2 **Save** your document.

> ***More Knowledge*** **Removing Built-in Styles**
>
> Built-in styles are predefined in Word whenever you open a new document. Although you can remove a built-in style from a single document, the built-in style is not deleted from the Word program; the built-in style will be available in all other documents.

Objective 4 Create a Multilevel List

GO! Learn How Video W4-4

When a document includes a list of items, you can format the items as a bulleted list, as a numbered list, or as a ***multilevel list***. Use a multilevel list when you want to add a visual hierarchical structure to the items in the list.

Activity 4.09 | Creating a Multilevel List with Bullets and Modifying List Indentation

3.3.4

1 On **Page 1**, scroll to position the heading *Equipment* near the top of your screen. Beginning with the paragraph *Air Tank*, select the 12 paragraphs between the headings *Equipment* and *Attire*.

2 On the **Home tab**, in the **Paragraph group**, click **Multilevel List** to display the gallery. Under **List Library**, point to the ❖, ➢, • (bullet) style, which is the multilevel bullet list style. Compare your screen with Figure 4.16.

Word provides several built-in styles for multilevel lists. You can customize any style.

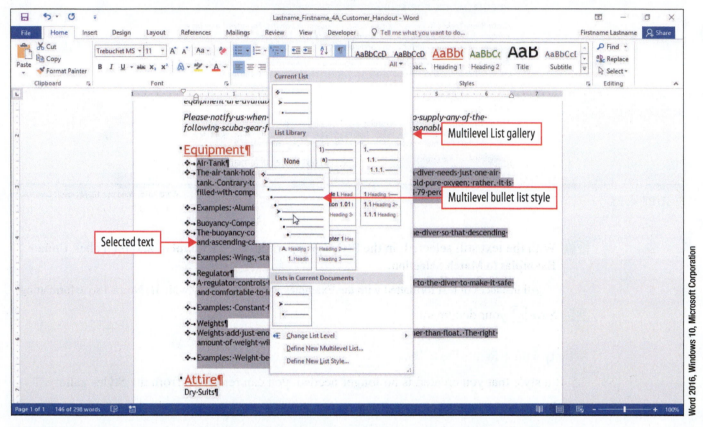

Word 2016, Windows 10, Microsoft Corporation

FIGURE 4.16

3 Click the **multilevel bullet list** style. Compare your screen with Figure 4.17.

All the items in the list display at the first level; the items are not visually indented to show different levels.

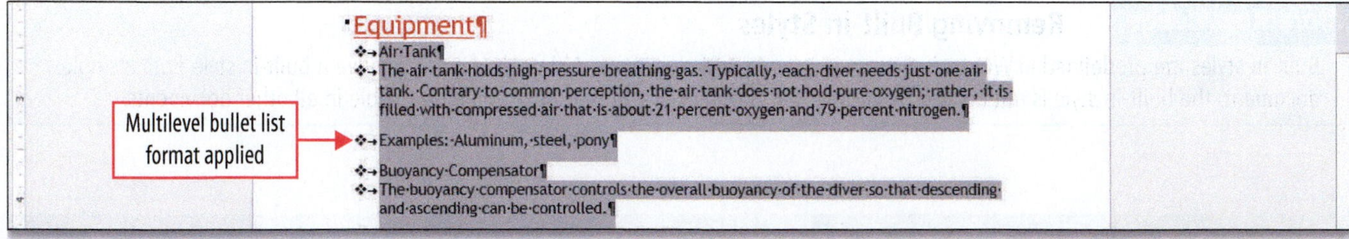

Word 2016, Windows 10, Microsoft Corporation

FIGURE 4.17

4 Click anywhere in the second list item, which begins *The air tank*. In the **Paragraph group**, click **Increase Indent**, and then compare your screen with Figure 4.18.

The list item displays at the second level, which uses the ➢ symbol. The Increase Indent command demotes an item to a lower level; the Decrease Indent command promotes an item to a higher level. To change the list level using the Increase Indent command or Decrease Indent command, it is not necessary to select the entire paragraph.

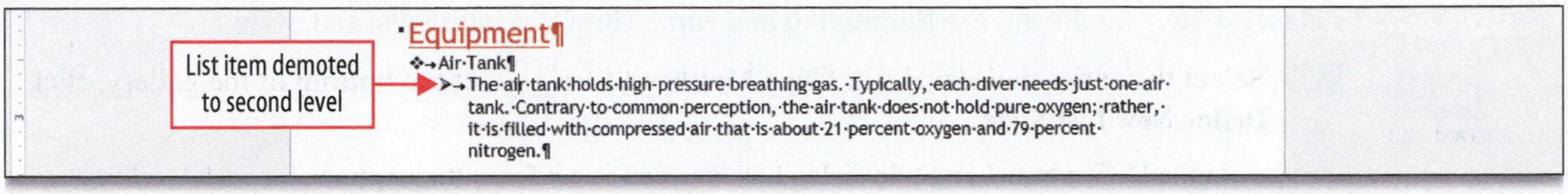

List item demoted to second level

·Equipment¶
❖→Air·Tank¶
➢→The·air·tank·holds·high·pressure·breathing·gas.·Typically,·each·diver·needs·just·one·air·tank.·Contrary·to·common·perception,·the·air·tank·does·not·hold·pure·oxygen;·rather,·it·is·filled·with·compressed·air·that·is·about·21·percent·oxygen·and·79·percent·nitrogen.¶

FIGURE 4.18 Word 2016, Windows 10, Microsoft Corporation

ANOTHER WAY Select the item, and press Tab to demote the item or press Shift + Tab to promote it.

5 Click in the third item in the list, which begins *Examples: Aluminum*. In the **Paragraph group**, click **Increase Indent** two times, and then compare your screen with Figure 4.19.

The list item displays at the third level, which uses the ▪ symbol.

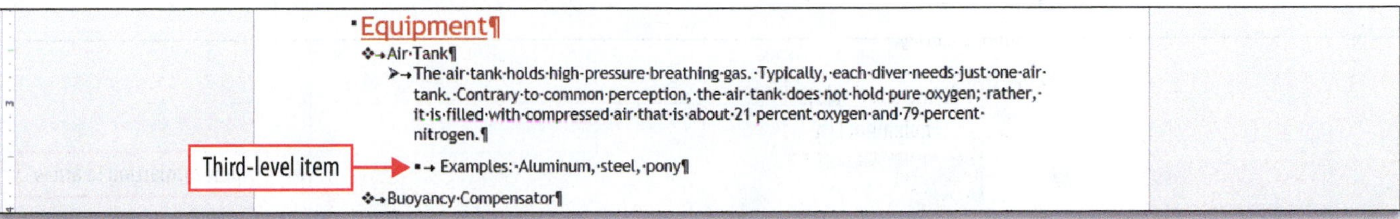

FIGURE 4.19 Word 2016, Windows 10, Microsoft Corporation

6 Using the technique you just practiced, continue setting levels for the remainder of the multilevel list as follows: Apply the second-level indent for the descriptive paragraphs that begin *The buoyancy*, *A regulator*, and *Weights add*. Apply the third-level indent for the paragraphs that begin *Examples*.

7 Compare your screen with Figure 4.20. If necessary, adjust your list by clicking Increase Indent or Decrease Indent so that your list matches the one shown in Figure 4.20.

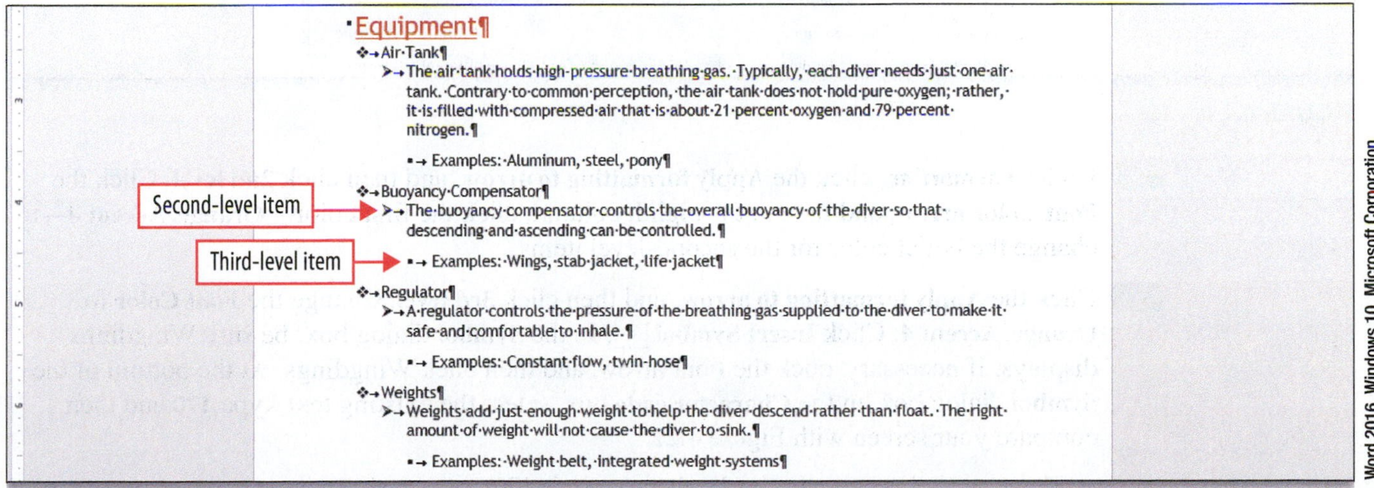

Word 2016, Windows 10, Microsoft Corporation

FIGURE 4.20

8 **Save** your document.

More Knowledge **Selecting List Items**

To select several items in a document that are ***contiguous***—adjacent to one another—click the first item, hold down Shift, and then click the last item. To select several items that are ***noncontiguous***—not adjacent to one another—hold down Ctrl, and then click each item. After items are selected, you can format all the selected items at one time.

Activity 4.10 | Modifying the Numbering and Formatting in a Multilevel List Style

3.3.2 and 3.3.3

1 Select the entire multilevel list. Click **Multilevel List**. At the bottom of the gallery, click **Define New List Style**.

In the Define New List Style dialog box, you can select formatting options for each level in your list. By default, the dialog box displays formatting options starting with the *1st level*.

2 Under **Properties**, in the **Name** box, type **Equipment List** Under **Formatting**, in the small toolbar above the preview area, to the right of *Bullet:* ❖, click the **Numbering Style arrow**.

3 In the list, scroll to the top of the list, and then click the **1, 2, 3** style. Click the **Font Color arrow**, which currently displays black, and then in the eighth column, click the fifth color—**Orange, Accent 4, Darker 25%**. Compare your screen with Figure 4.21.

The numbering style and font color change will be applied only to first-level items. The style changes are visible in the preview area.

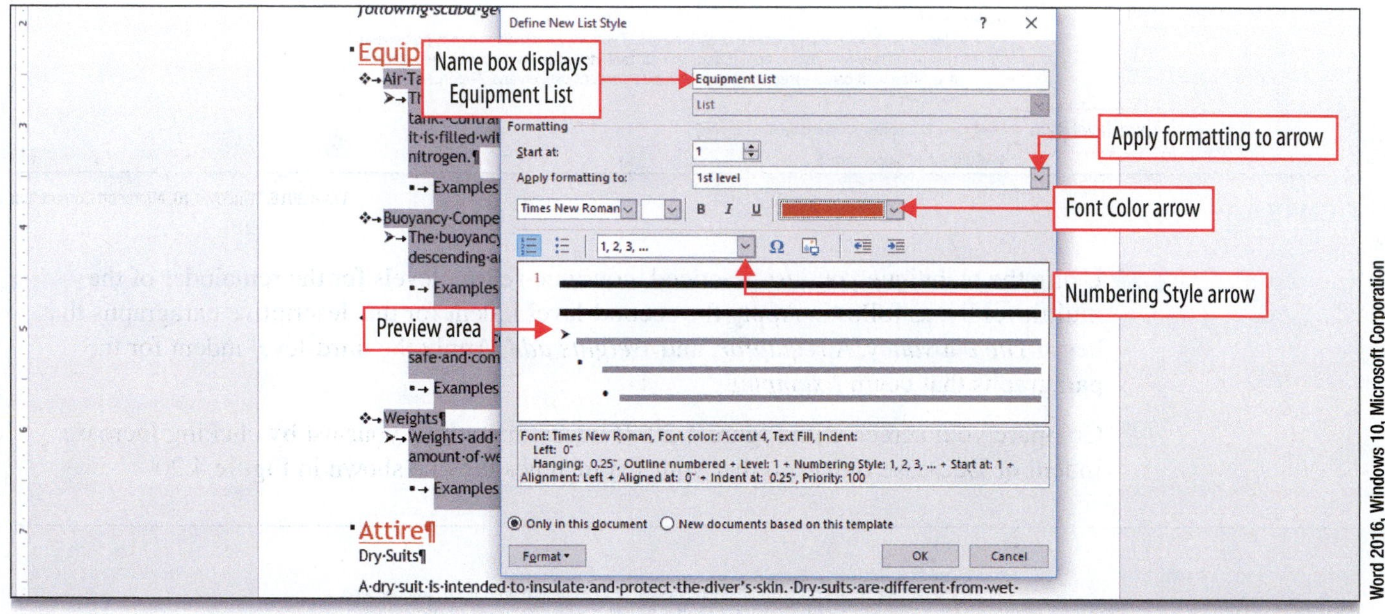

FIGURE 4.21

4 Under **Formatting**, click the **Apply formatting to arrow**, and then click **2nd level**. Click the **Font Color arrow**, and then in the eighth column, click the first color—**Orange, Accent 4**—to change the bullet color for the second-level items.

5 Click the **Apply formatting to arrow**, and then click **3rd level**. Change the **Font Color** to **Orange, Accent 4**. Click **Insert Symbol** Ω. In the **Symbol** dialog box, be sure Wingdings displays. If necessary, click the Font arrow, and then click Wingdings. At the bottom of the **Symbol** dialog box, in the **Character code** box, select the existing text, type **170** and then compare your screen with Figure 4.22.

The ✦ symbol, represented by the character code 170, is selected.

If you do not know the character code, in the Symbol dialog box, locate and click the desired symbol.

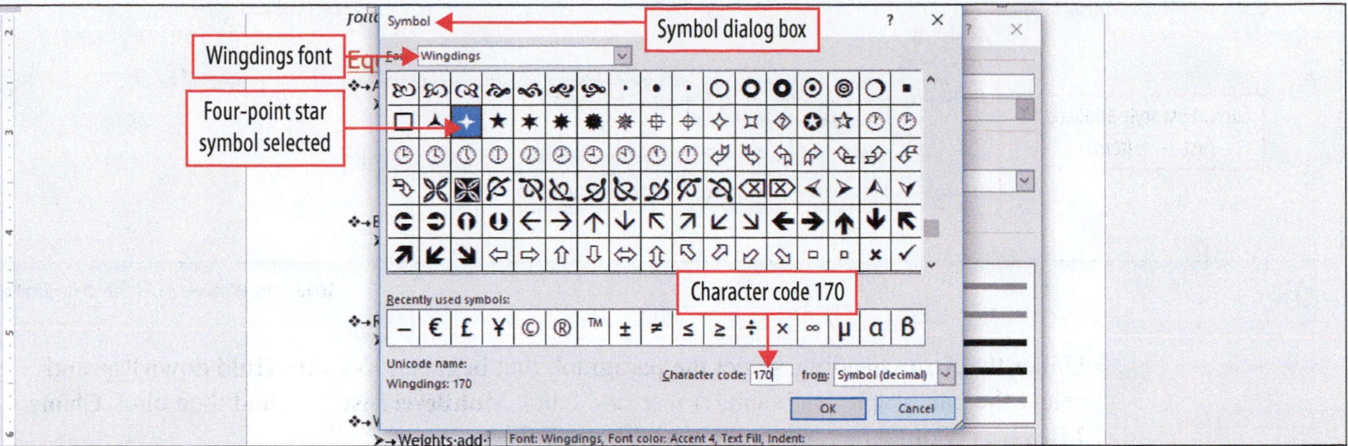

Word 2016, Windows 10, Microsoft Corporation

FIGURE 4.22

6 Click **OK** to apply the selected symbol and close the Symbol dialog box.

Third-level items will display with the ✦ symbol and orange font color.

7 In the **Define New List Style** dialog box, notice the preview of your changes, and then click **OK** to close the dialog box. Click anywhere to deselect the text, and then compare your screen with Figure 4.23.

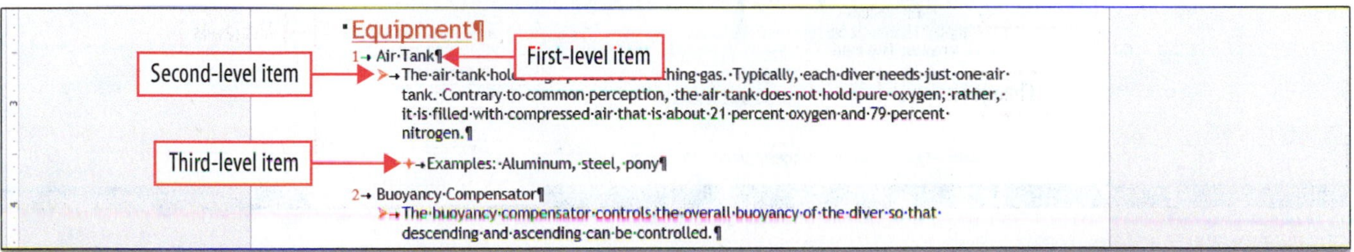

Word 2016, Windows 10, Microsoft Corporation

FIGURE 4.23

8 Select the entire list. With all 12 paragraphs selected, click the **Layout tab**, and then in the **Paragraph group**, click the **Spacing After down spin arrow** to **6 pt**. **Save** your changes.

Activity 4.11 | Applying the Current List Style and Changing the List Levels

After you define a new list style, you can apply the style to other similar items in your document.

1 Scroll to display the heading *Attire* and all remaining paragraphs in the document. Beginning with the paragraph *Dry Suits*, select the remaining paragraphs of the document.

2 Click the **Home tab**, and then in the **Paragraph group**, click **Multilevel List**. In the gallery, under **List Styles**, point to the list style that you created to display the ScreenTip *Equipment List*, and then click the **Equipment List** style. Compare your screen with Figure 4.24.

Each paragraph is formatted as a first-level item.

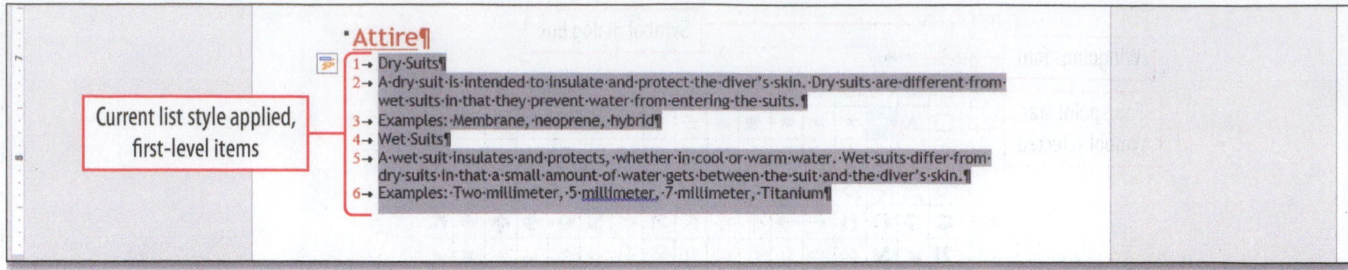

FIGURE 4.24

Word 2016, Windows 10, Microsoft Corporation

3 Under the *Attire* heading, select the paragraph that begins *A dry suit*. Hold down Ctrl and select the paragraph that begins *A wet suit*. Click **Multilevel List**, and then click **Change List Level**. Compare your screen with Figure 4.25.

Hold down Ctrl to select nonadjacent text.

All available list levels display for the selected paragraphs. You can increase or decrease the list level for selected items in a list by assigning the desired level.

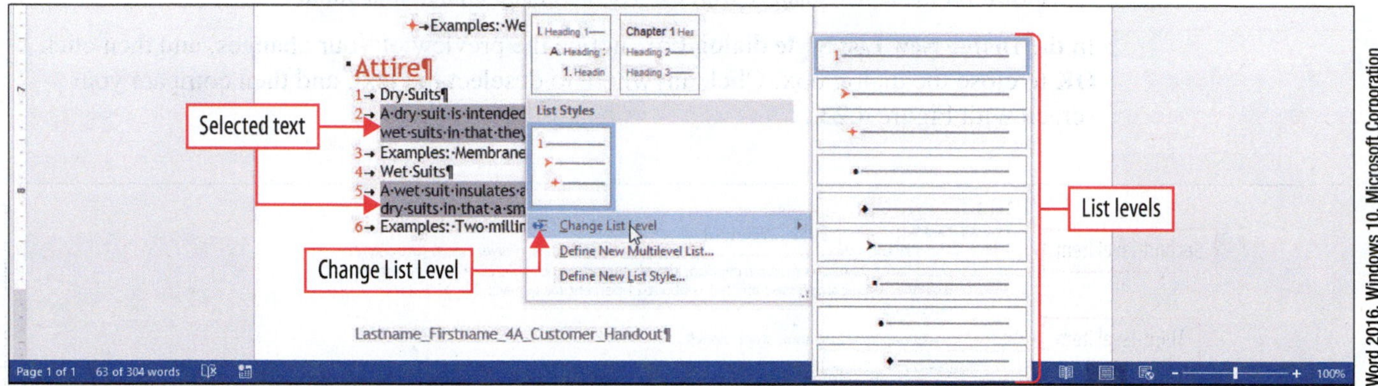

FIGURE 4.25

Word 2016, Windows 10, Microsoft Corporation

4 From the levels list, point to the second level to display the ScreenTip **Level 2**. Click the **Level 2** list level.

5 Select the paragraph that begins *Examples: Membrane*, hold down Ctrl, and then select the paragraph that begins *Examples: Two millimeter*. Using the technique you just practiced, assign the third list level that displays the symbol ✦—**Level 3**.

6 Select the entire list. With all six paragraphs selected, click the **Layout tab**, and then in the **Paragraph group**, click the **Spacing After down spin arrow** to **6 pt**. Deselect the text, and then compare your screen with Figure 4.26.

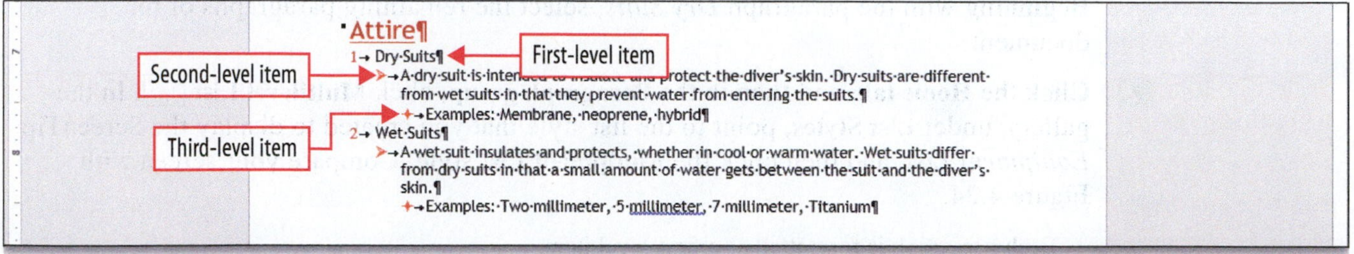

FIGURE 4.26

Word 2016, Windows 10, Microsoft Corporation

7 Click the **File tab** to display **Backstage** view. On the right, at the bottom of the **Properties** list, click **Show All Properties**. In the **Tags** box, type **scuba diving** and then in the **Subject** box, type your course name and section number. If necessary, edit the author name to display your name.

8 On the left, click **Print** to display **Print Preview**. If necessary, return to the document and make any necessary changes.

9 **Save** your document. In the upper right corner of the Word window, click **Close** ×. If directed by your instructor to do so, submit your paper printout, your electronic image of your document that looks like a printed document, or your original Word file.

END | You have completed Project 4A

PROJECT 4B Planning Memo with a Chart

PROJECT ACTIVITIES

In Activities 4.12 through 4.23, you will edit a memo to all the company tour guides regarding an upcoming planning session for the types of tours the company will offer in the coming year. The group will discuss information gathered from customer research to provide an appropriate mix of tour types that will appeal to a wide audience. You will add a chart to illustrate plans for tour types in the coming year. Your completed document will look similar to Figure 4.27.

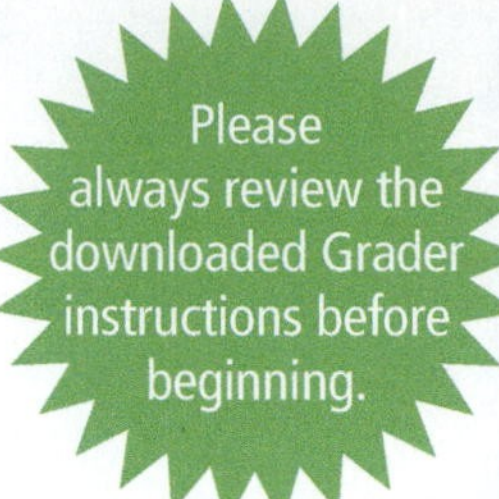

PROJECT FILES

If your instructor wants you to submit Project 4B in the MyITLab grader system, log in to MyITLab, locate Grader Project 4B, and then download the files for this project.

For Project 4B, you will need the following files:
w04B_Planning_Memo
w04B_Custom_Styles

You will save your file as:
Lastname_Firstname_4B_Planning_Memo

PROJECT RESULTS

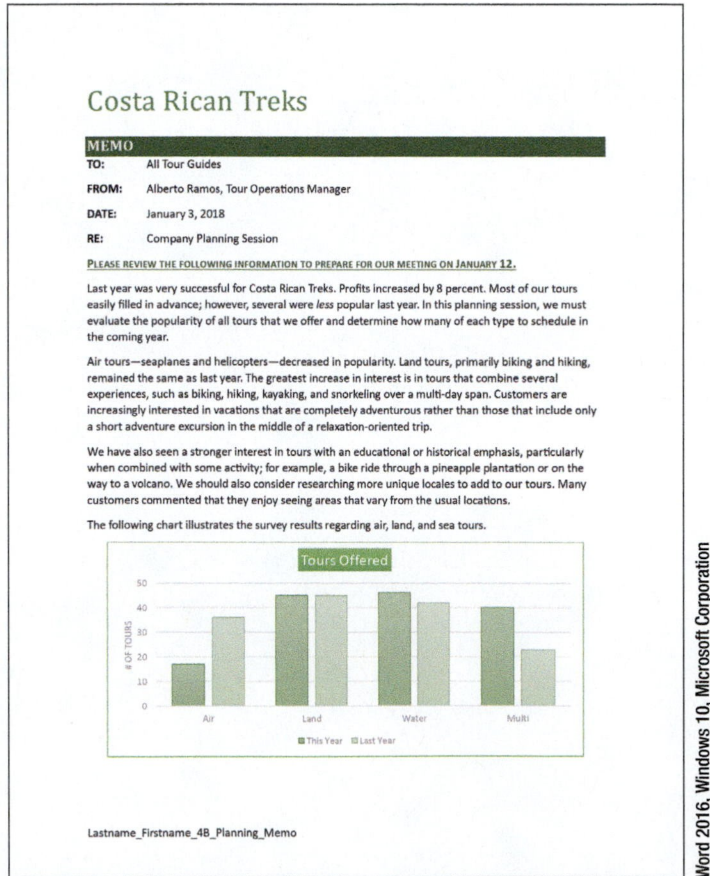
Costa Rican Treks

MEMO

TO: All Tour Guides

FROM: Alberto Ramos, Tour Operations Manager

DATE: January 3, 2018

RE: Company Planning Session

PLEASE REVIEW THE FOLLOWING INFORMATION TO PREPARE FOR OUR MEETING ON JANUARY 12.

Last year was very successful for Costa Rican Treks. Profits increased by 8 percent. Most of our tours easily filled in advance; however, several were *less* popular last year. In this planning session, we must evaluate the popularity of all tours that we offer and determine how many of each type to schedule in the coming year.

Air tours—seaplanes and helicopters—decreased in popularity. Land tours, primarily biking and hiking, remained the same as last year. The greatest increase in interest is in tours that combine several experiences, such as biking, hiking, kayaking, and snorkeling over a multi-day span. Customers are increasingly interested in vacations that are completely adventurous rather than those that include only a short adventure excursion in the middle of a relaxation-oriented trip.

We have also seen a stronger interest in tours with an educational or historical emphasis, particularly when combined with some activity; for example, a bike ride through a pineapple plantation or on the way to a volcano. We should also consider researching more unique locales to add to our tours. Many customers commented that they enjoy seeing areas that vary from the usual locations.

The following chart illustrates the survey results regarding air, land, and sea tours.

Lastname_Firstname_4B_Planning_Memo

Word 2016, Windows 10, Microsoft Corporation

FIGURE 4.27 Project 4B Planning Memo

Objective 5 Change the Style Set of a Document and Apply a Template

GO! Learn How Video W4-5

Recall that a style set is a group of styles that is designed to work together. A style set is useful when you want to change the look of all the styles in a document in one step rather than modifying individual styles. You can modify the document using a built-in style set or by attaching a template.

Activity 4.12 | Formatting a Memo

A ***memo***, also referred to as a ***memorandum***, is a written message to someone working in the same organization. Among organizations, memo formats vary, and there are many acceptable memo formats. Always consult trusted references or the preferences set by your organization when deciding on the proper formats for your professional memos.

ALERT! **To submit as an autograded project, log into MyITLab and download the files for this project, and begin with those files instead of w04B_Planning_Memo.**

1. Start Word. From your student files, locate and open the file **w04B_Planning_Memo**.
2. **Save** the document in your **Word Chapter 4** folder as **Lastname_Firstname_4B_Planning_Memo** and then **Insert** the **File name** in the footer. If necessary, display the rulers and formatting marks.
3. Select the first paragraph of the document—*Costa Rican Treks*. On the **Home tab**, in the **Styles group**, click the **More** button, and then in the gallery, click **Title**.
4. Select the second paragraph, the heading **MEMO**, and then apply the **Heading 1** style.
5. Select the text **TO:**—include the colon—hold down Ctrl, and then select the text **FROM:**, **DATE:**, and **RE:**. On the mini toolbar, apply **Bold** to these four memo headings.
6. Select the paragraph that begins *Please review*. In the **Styles** group, click the **More** button. In the gallery, use the ScreenTips to locate and then click **Intense Reference**. Click anywhere to deselect the text. **Save** your document. Compare your screen with Figure 4.28.

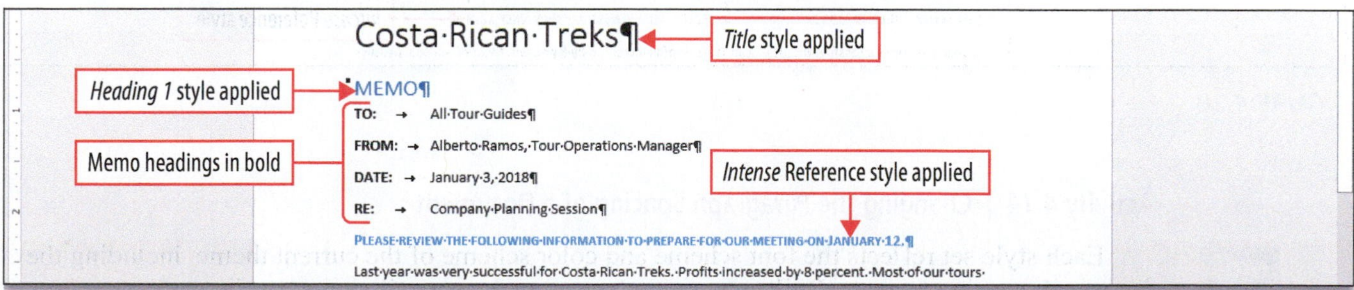

FIGURE 4.28 Word 2016, Windows 10, Microsoft Corporation

Activity 4.13 | Changing the Style Set of a Document

MOS 1.3.3

By changing a style set, you can apply a group of styles to a document in one step.

1. Click the **Design tab**. In the **Document Formatting group**, click the **More** button. Compare your screen with Figure 4.29.

   All available style sets display in the Style Set gallery. The default style set is named Word. The style set currently applied to a document displays under This Document.

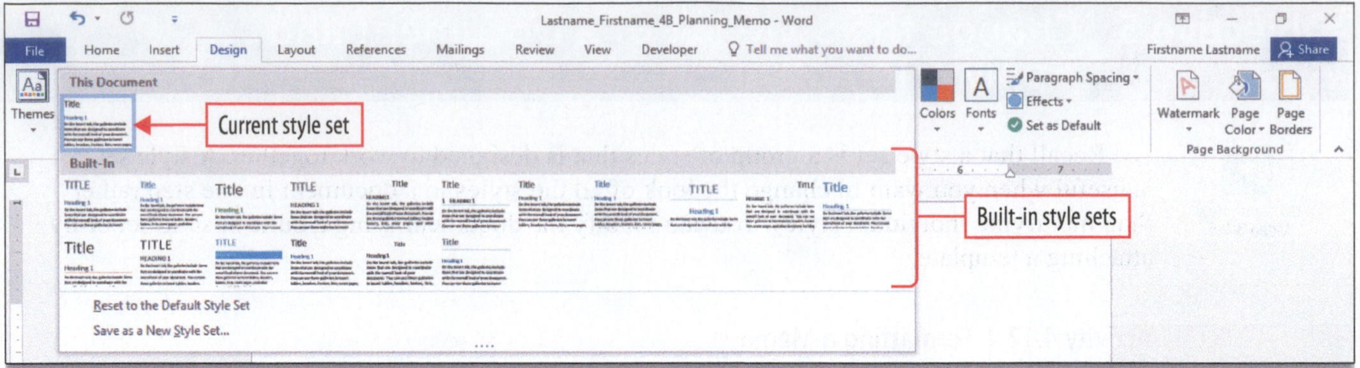

FIGURE 4.29

Word 2016, Windows 10, Microsoft Corporation

2 In the gallery, under **Built-In**, use the ScreenTips to locate and then click the **Minimalist** style set. Compare your screen with Figure 4.30, and then **Save** your document.

Minimalist is the name of a particular style set. Applying the *Minimalist* style set, which includes a default font size of 10.5, causes styles—such as Title, Heading 1, and Intense Reference—to display a different format.

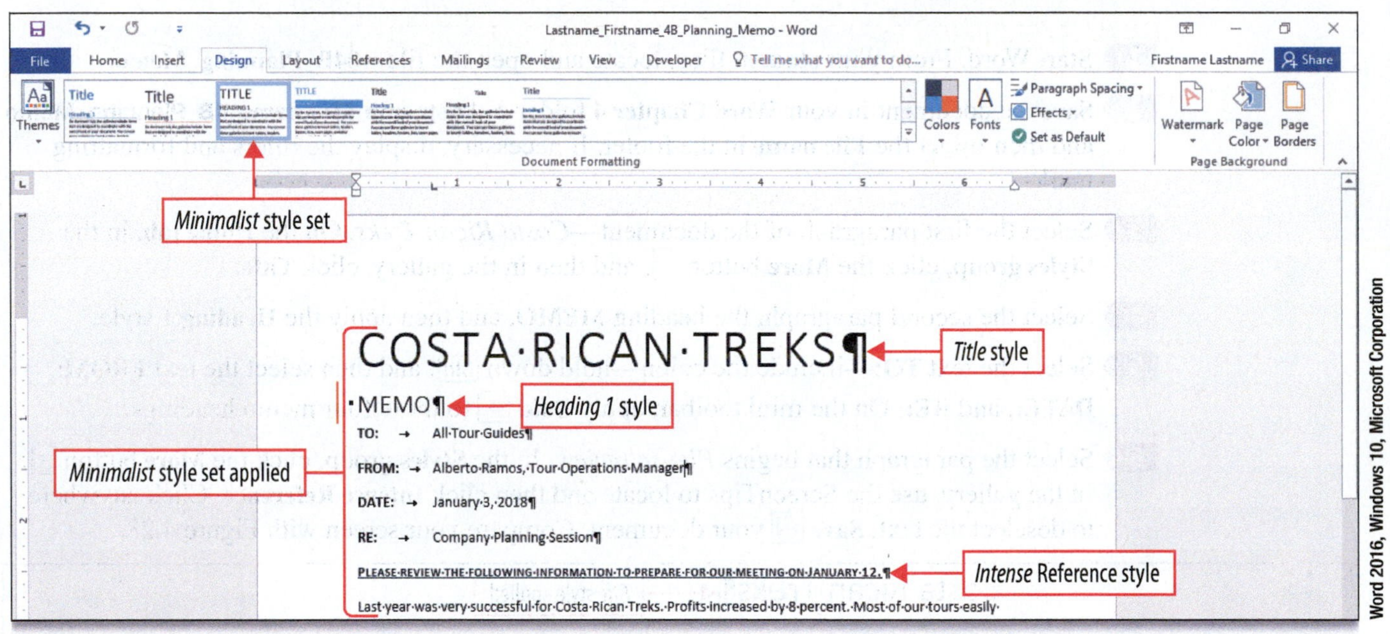

Word 2016, Windows 10, Microsoft Corporation

FIGURE 4.30

Activity 4.14 | Changing the Paragraph Spacing of a Document

2.2.3

Each style set reflects the font scheme and color scheme of the current theme, including the paragraph spacing formats. Built-in paragraph spacing formats allow you to change the paragraph spacing and line spacing for an entire document in one step.

1 On the **Design tab**, in the **Document Formatting group**, click **Paragraph Spacing**. Compare your screen with Figure 4.31, and then take a moment to study the table shown in Figure 4.32.

Word provides six built-in styles for paragraph spacing. The *Minimalist* style set uses custom paragraph spacing that includes line spacing of 1.3, 0 pt spacing before, and 8 pt spacing after a paragraph.

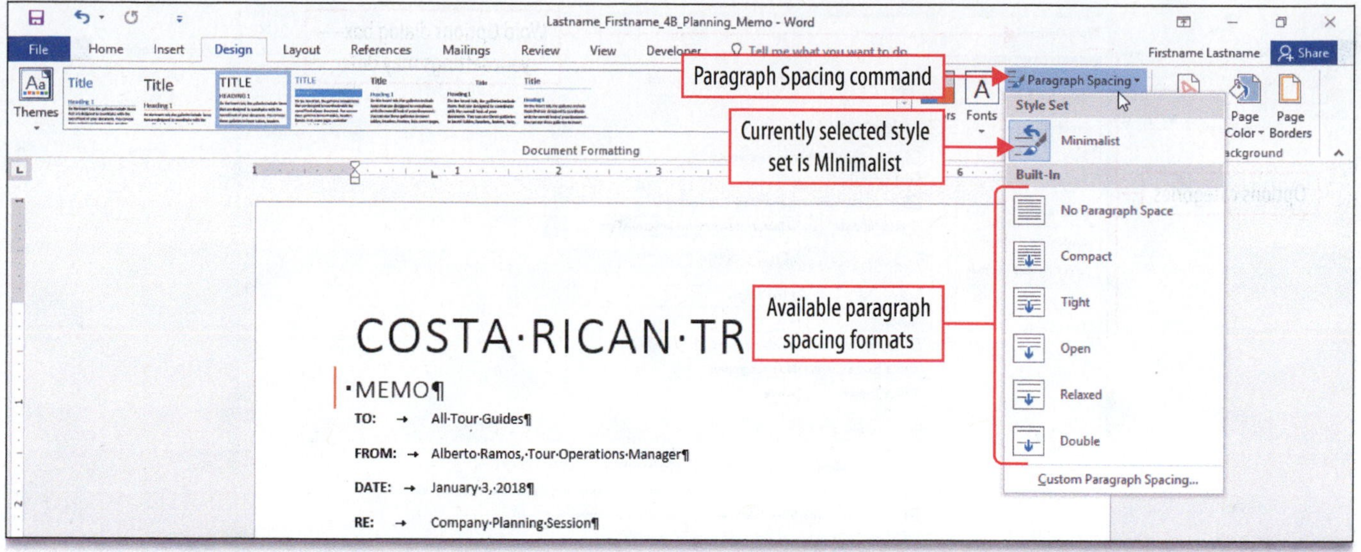

FIGURE 4.31

Word 2016, Windows 10, Microsoft Corporation

PARAGRAPH SPACING FORMATS			
OPTION	SPACING BEFORE	SPACING AFTER	LINE SPACING
No paragraph spacing	0 pt	0 pt	1
Compact	0 pt	4 pt	1
Tight	0 pt	6 pt	1.15
Open	0 pt	10 pt	1.15
Relaxed	0 pt	6 pt	1.5
Double	0 pt	8 pt	2

Word 2016, Windows 10, Microsoft Corporation

FIGURE 4.32

2 In the gallery, point to **Open**. Notice that the ScreenTip describes the paragraph spacing format and that Live Preview displays how the document would look with this paragraph spacing format applied. Click **Open**.

3 **Save** your document.

Activity 4.15 | Customizing the Ribbon and Attaching a Template to a Document

1.1.7

Word Options form a collection of settings that you can change to customize Word. In this Activity, you will customize the ribbon and attach a template. Recall that a template is an existing document—for example, the Normal template—that you use as a starting point for a new document. You can apply a template to an existing document to change the appearance of the document.

1 Press Ctrl + Home. Click the **File tab**, and then on the left, click **Options** to display the **Word Options** dialog box. Compare your screen with Figure 4.33, and then take a few moments to study the table in Figure 4.34.

In an organizational environment such as a college or business, you may not have access or permission to change some or all of the settings.

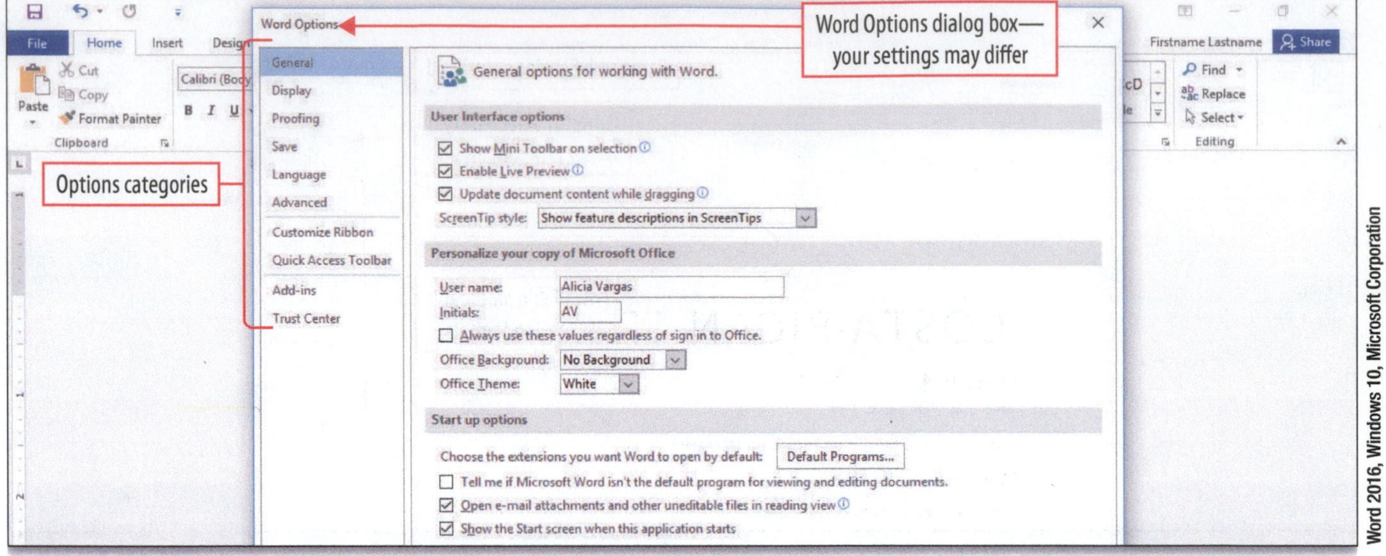

Word 2016, Windows 10, Microsoft Corporation

FIGURE 4.33

WORD OPTIONS	
CATEGORY	**OPTIONS TO:**
General	Set up Word for your personal way of working—for example, changing the Office Background—and personalize Word with your name and initials.
Display	Control the way content displays pages on the screen and when it prints.
Proofing	Control how Word corrects and formats your text—for example, how AutoCorrect and spell checker perform.
Save	Specify where you want to save your Word documents by default and set the AutoRecover time for saving information.
Language	Set the default language and add additional languages for editing documents.
Advanced	Control advanced features, including editing and printing options.
Customize Ribbon	Add commands to existing tabs, create new tabs, and set up your own keyboard shortcuts.
Quick Access Toolbar	Customize the Quick Access Toolbar by adding commands.
Add-Ins	View and manage add-in programs that come with the Word software or ones that you add to Word.
Trust Center	Control privacy and security when working with files from other sources or when you share files with others.

Word 2016, Windows 10, Microsoft Corporation

FIGURE 4.34

2 In the **Word Options** dialog box, on the left, click **Customize Ribbon**.

The Word Options dialog box displays a list of popular commands on the left and main tabs display on the right. Under Main Tabs, the checkmarks to the left of the tab names indicate tabs that are currently available on the ribbon.

3 In the **Word Options** dialog box, in the **Main Tabs** list, select the **Developer** check box. Compare your screen with Figure 4.35.

The Developer tab extends the capabilities of Word—including commands for using existing templates.

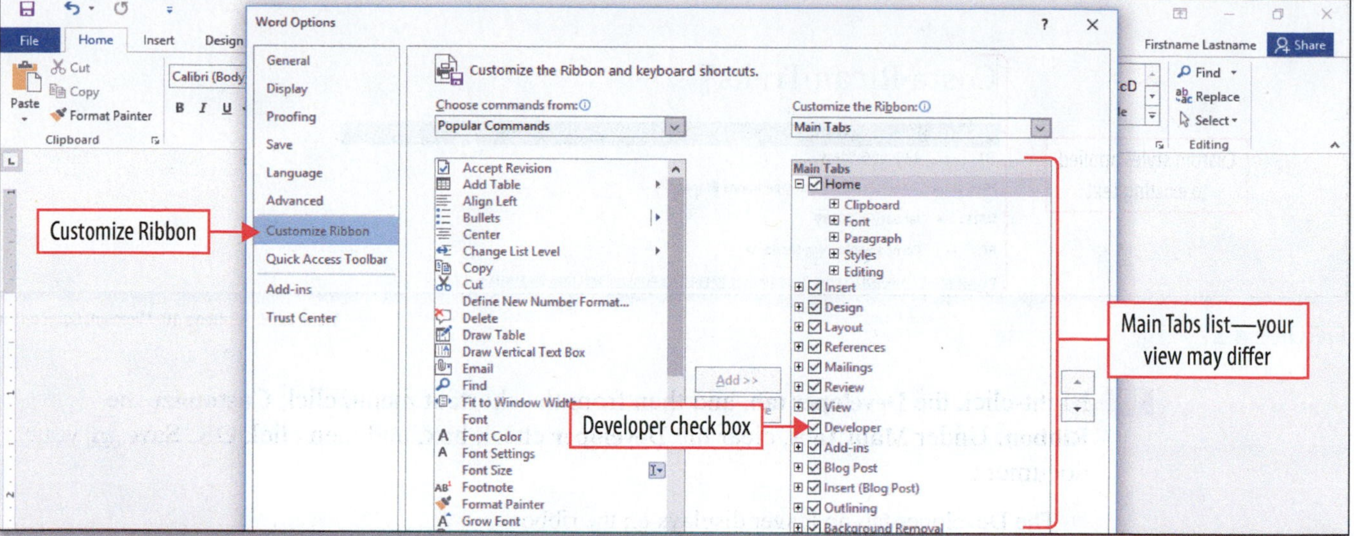

FIGURE 4.35

Word 2016, Windows 10, Microsoft Corporation

4 Click **OK** to close the **Word Options** dialog box.

The Developer tab displays on the ribbon to the right of the VIEW tab.

5 Click the **Developer tab**, and then in the **Templates group**, click **Document Template**.

6 In the **Templates and Add-ins** dialog box, to the right of the **Document template** box, click **Attach** to display the **Attach Template** dialog box.

7 In the **Attach Template** dialog box, navigate to the location of your student files, click **w04B_Custom_Styles**, and then click **Open**.

The file w04B_Custom_Styles is a Word template that contains styles created by the marketing director to be used in all Costa Rican Treks documents.

8 In the **Templates and Add-ins** dialog box, to the left of **Automatically update document styles**, select the check box, and then compare your screen with Figure 4.36.

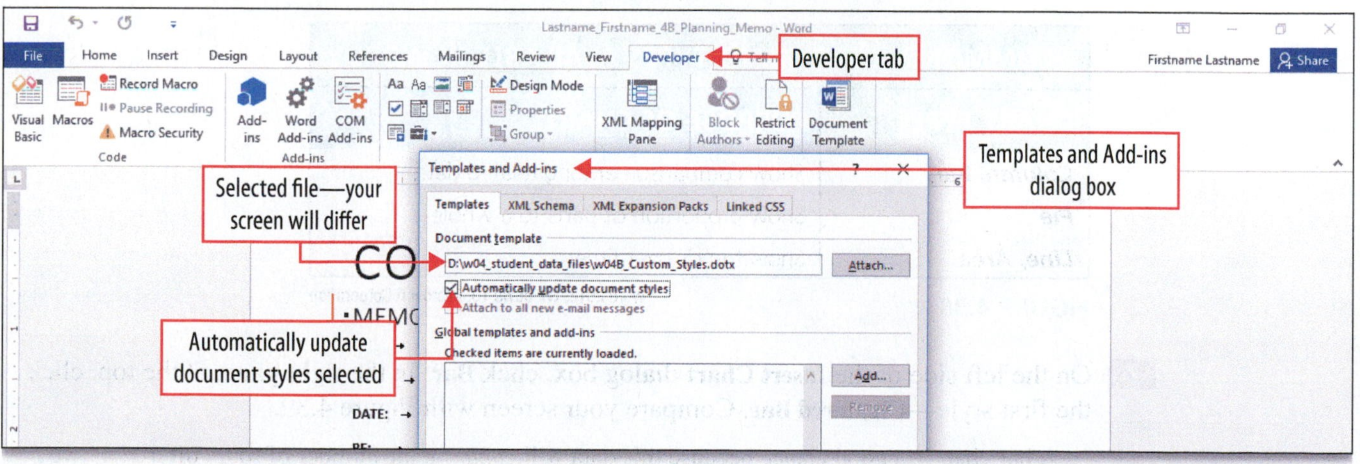

FIGURE 4.36

Word 2016, Windows 10, Microsoft Corporation

9 In the **Templates and Add-ins** dialog box, click **OK**. Compare your screen with Figure 4.37.

All styles contained in the w04B_Custom_Styles template are applied to your Lastname_Firstname_4B_Planning_Revised document.

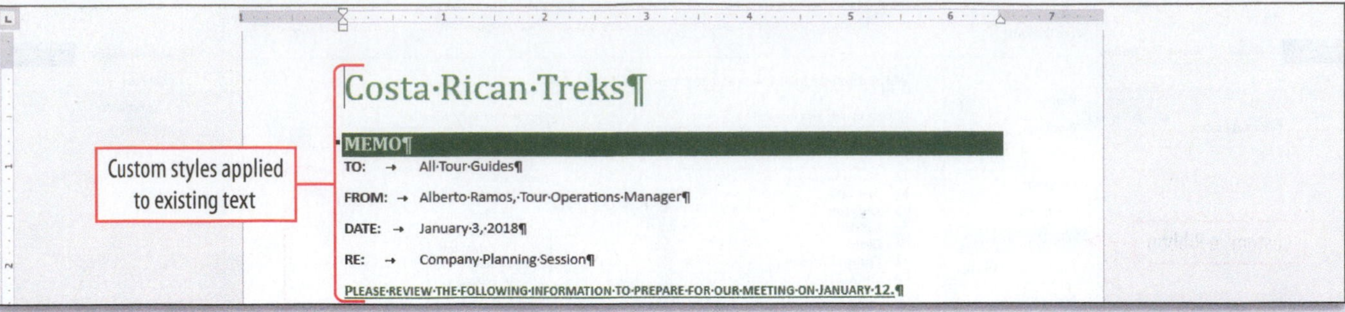

Costa·Rican·Treks¶
MEMO¶
TO: → All·Tour·Guides¶
FROM: → Alberto·Ramos,·Tour·Operations·Manager¶
DATE: → January·3,·2018¶
RE: → Company·Planning·Session¶
PLEASE·REVIEW·THE·FOLLOWING·INFORMATION·TO·PREPARE·FOR·OUR·MEETING·ON·JANUARY·12.¶
Custom styles applied to existing text

FIGURE 4.37

Word 2016, Windows 10, Microsoft Corporation

10 Right-click the **Developer tab**, and then from the shortcut menu, click **Customize the Ribbon**. Under **Main Tabs**, clear the **Developer** check box, and then click **OK**. **Save** your document.

The Developer tab no longer displays on the ribbon.

Objective 6 Insert a Chart and Enter Data into a Chart

GO! Learn How Video W4-6

A ***chart*** is a visual representation of ***numerical data***—numbers that represent facts. Word provides the same chart tools that are available in Excel. A chart that you create in Word is stored in a worksheet, and the worksheet is saved with the Word document. Charts make numbers easier for the reader to understand.

Activity 4.16 | Inserting a Chart

1 Press Ctrl + End to move the insertion point to the end of the document. Click the **Insert tab**, and then in the **Illustrations group**, click **Chart** to display the **Insert Chart** dialog box. Take a moment to examine the chart types described in the table shown in Figure 4.38.

The available chart types display on the left side of the Insert Chart dialog box. The most commonly used chart types are column, bar, pie, line, and area.

COMMONLY USED CHART TYPES AVAILABLE IN WORD	
CHART TYPE	PURPOSE OF CHART
Column, Bar	Show comparison among related data
Pie	Show proportion of parts to a whole
Line, Area	Show trends over time

FIGURE 4.38

Word 2016, Windows 10, Microsoft Corporation

2 On the left side of the **Insert Chart** dialog box, click **Bar**. In the right pane, at the top, click the first style—**Clustered Bar**. Compare your screen with Figure 4.39.

A bar chart is a good choice because this data will *compare* the number of tours offered in two different years.

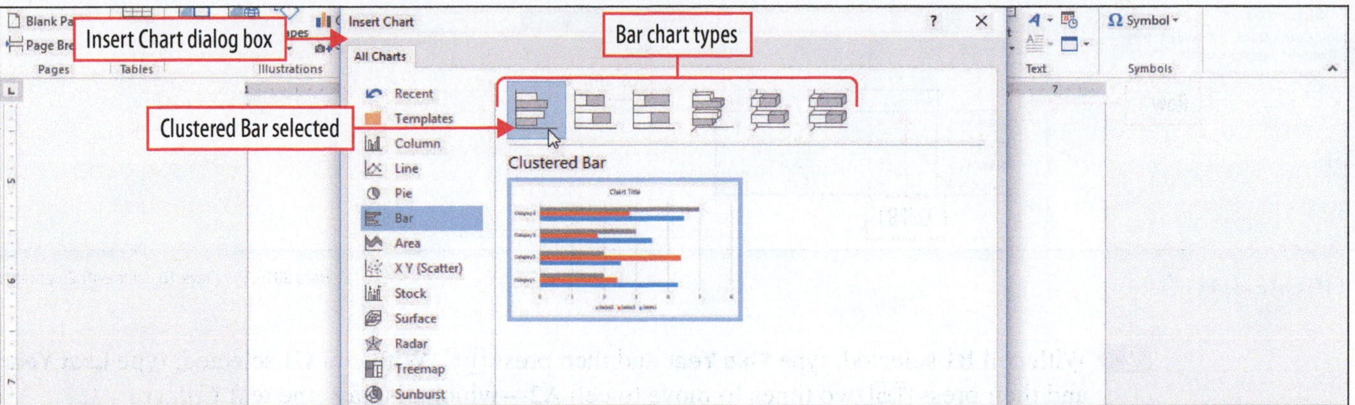

FIGURE 4.39

Word 2016, Windows 10, Microsoft Corporation

3 Click **OK** to insert the chart in your document and open the related *Chart in Microsoft Word* worksheet. Compare your screen with Figure 4.40.

The chart displays on Page 2 of your Word document. Sample data displays in the worksheet.

The process of inserting a chart in your document in this manner is referred to as ***embedding***—the object, in this case a chart, becomes part of the Word document. When you edit the data in the worksheet, the chart in your Word document updates automatically.

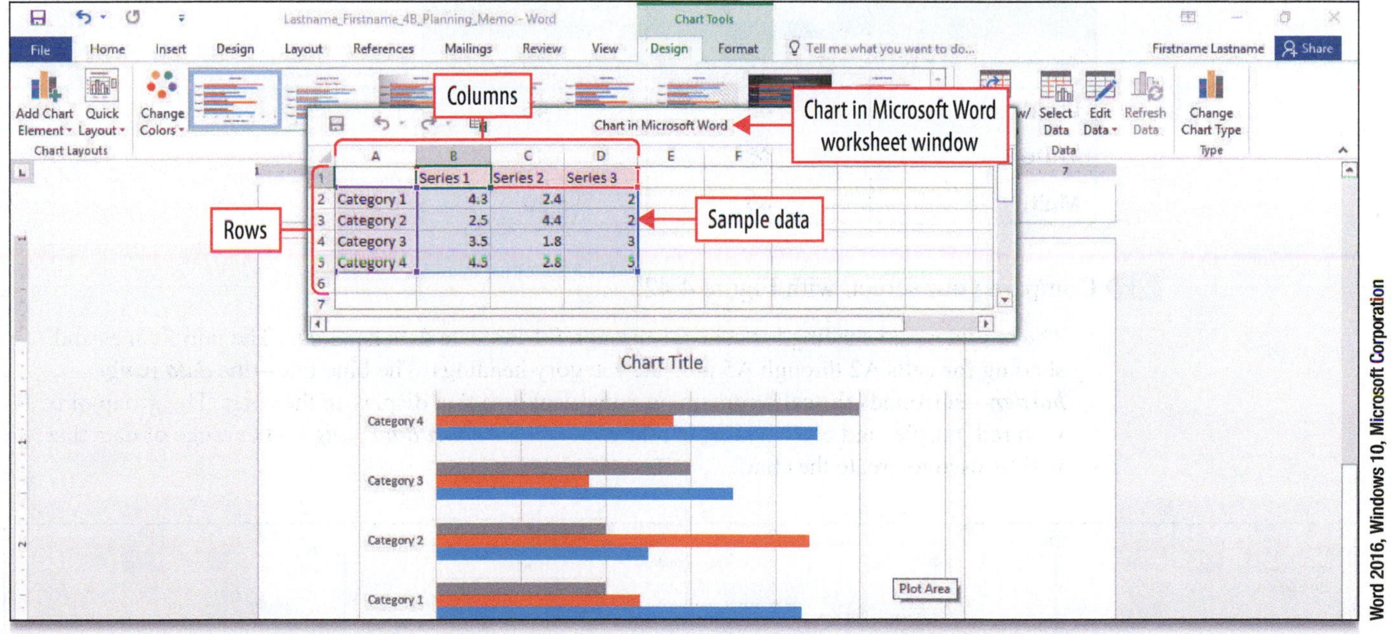

FIGURE 4.40

Word 2016, Windows 10, Microsoft Corporation

Activity 4.17 | Entering Chart Data

You can replace the sample data in the worksheet with specific tour data for your chart.

1 In the **Chart in Microsoft Word** worksheet, point to the small box where **column B** and **row 1** intersect—referred to as cell **B1**—and click. Compare your screen with Figure 4.41.

A ***cell*** is the location where a row and column intersect. The cells are named by their column and row headings. For example, cell B1, containing the text *Series 1*, is in column B and row 1.

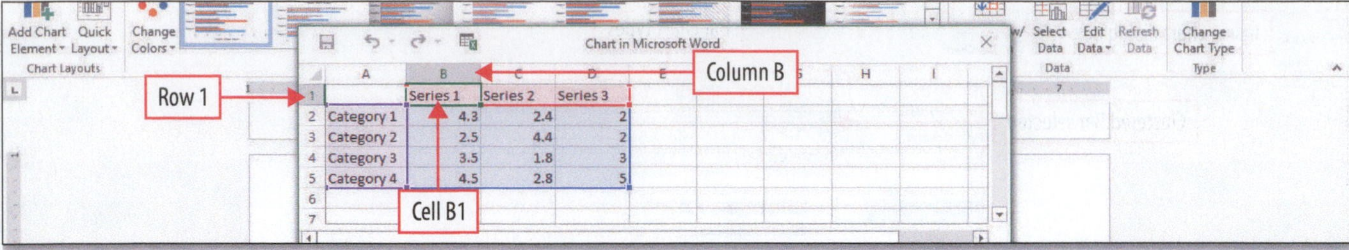

FIGURE 4.41

Word 2016, Windows 10, Microsoft Corporation

2 With cell **B1** selected, type **This Year** and then press Tab. With cell **C1** selected, type **Last Year** and then press Tab two times to move to cell **A2**—which displays the text *Category 1*.

3 With cell **A2** selected, type **Air** and then press Tab to move to cell **B2**. Type **17** and then press Tab. In cell **C2** type **36** and then press Tab two times to move to **row 3**.

As you enter data in the worksheet, the chart is automatically updated in the Word document. When entering a large amount of data in a cell, it may not fully display. If necessary, the data worksheet or chart can be modified to display the data completely.

4 Without changing any values in column D—Series 3, type the following data in columns A, B, and C. After typing *10* in C5, press Tab to select cell D5.

	THIS YEAR	LAST YEAR
Air	17	36
Land	**45**	**45**
Water	**46**	**42**
Multi	**35**	**10**

5 Compare your screen with Figure 4.42.

The red lines and shading for cells B1 through D1 indicate data headings. The purple lines and shading for cells A2 through A5 indicate category headings. The blue line—the ***data range border***—surrounds the cells containing numerical data that display in the chart. The group of cells with red, purple, and blue shading is referred to as the ***chart data range***—the range of data that will be used to create the chart.

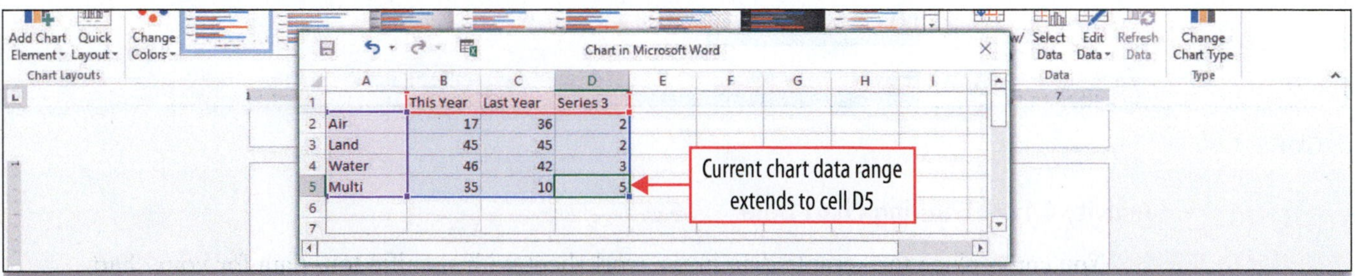

FIGURE 4.42

Word 2016, Windows 10, Microsoft Corporation

6 In the **Chart in Microsoft Word** worksheet, point to the lower right corner of the blue border to display the pointer, and then drag to the left to select only cells **A1** through **C5**. Compare your screen with Figure 4.43.

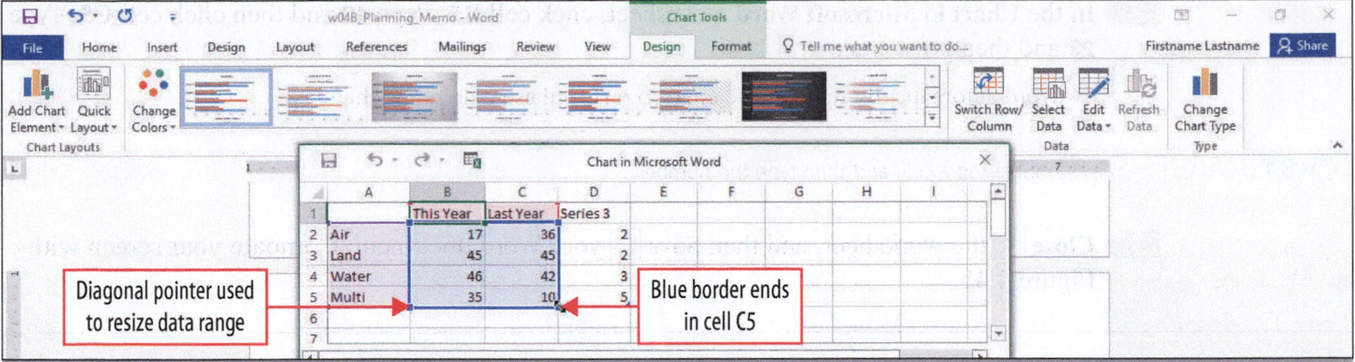

FIGURE 4.43

Word 2016, Windows 10, Microsoft Corporation

7 Release the mouse button to change the selected range of data used in the chart. In the upper right corner of the worksheet window, click **Close** ☒. Click the chart border to select the chart. **Save** your Word document, and then compare your screen with Figure 4.44.

The ***chart area*** refers to the entire chart and all its elements. The categories—the tour type names—display along the left side of the chart on the ***category axis***. The scale—based on the numerical data—displays along the lower edge of the chart on the ***value axis***.

Data markers, the bars in your chart, are the shapes representing each of the cells that contain data, referred to as the ***data points***. A ***data series*** consists of related data points represented by a unique color. For example, this chart has two data series—*This Year* and *Last Year*. The ***legend*** identifies the colors assigned to each data series or category.

With the chart selected, the Chart Tools display on the ribbon and include two additional tabs—Design and Format—to provide commands with which you can modify and format chart elements.

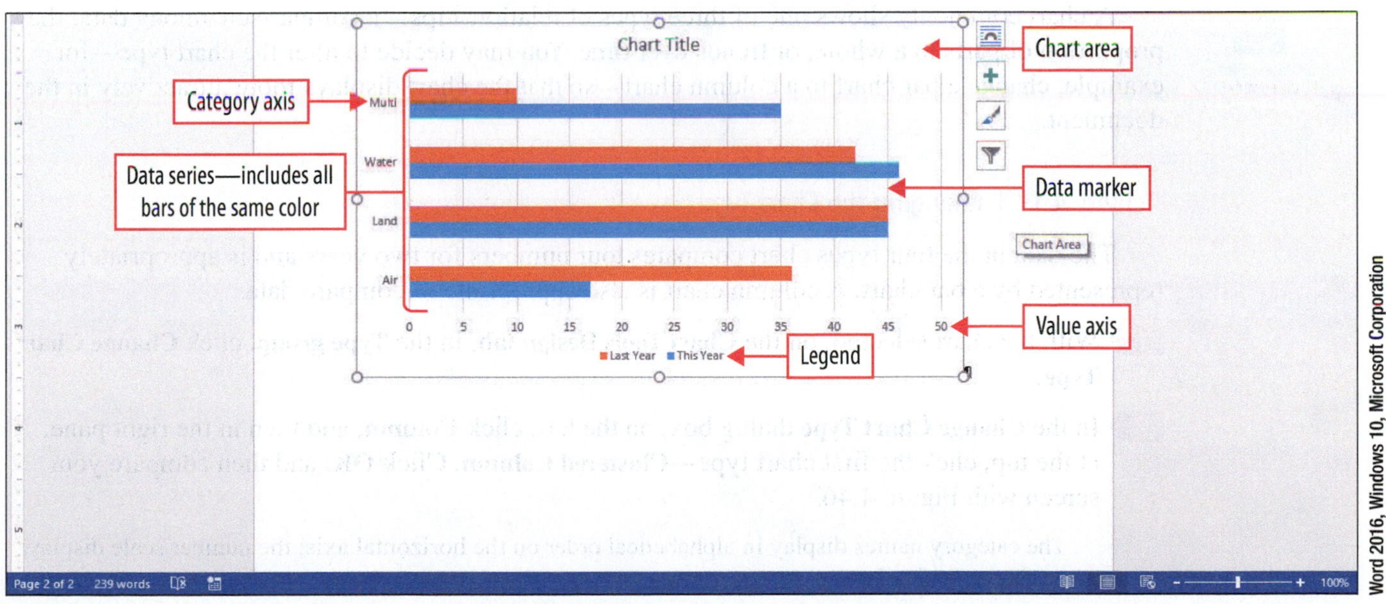

Word 2016, Windows 10, Microsoft Corporation

FIGURE 4.44

Activity 4.18 | Editing Chart Data

You can edit data points to update a chart.

1 Be sure your chart is selected; if necessary, click the chart border to select it. On the ribbon, under **Chart Tools**, click the **Design tab**, and then in the **Data group**, click the upper portion of the **Edit Data** button to redisplay the embedded Chart in Microsoft Word worksheet.

2 In the **Chart in Microsoft Word** worksheet, click cell **B5**. Type **40** and then click cell **C5**. Type **23** and then press Enter.

Word automatically updates the chart to reflect these data point changes.

BY TOUCH Double-tap a cell, and then type the number.

3 **Close** the worksheet, and then **Save** your Word document. Compare your screen with Figure 4.45.

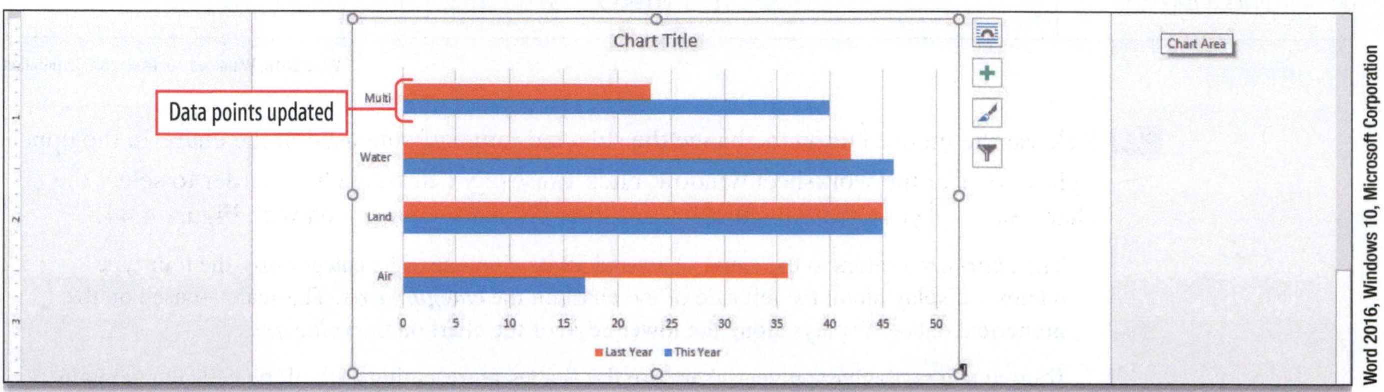

FIGURE 4.45

Objective 7 Change a Chart Type

A chart commonly shows one of three types of relationships—a comparison among data, the proportion of parts to a whole, or trends over time. You may decide to alter the chart type—for example, change a bar chart to a column chart—so that the chart displays more attractively in the document.

Activity 4.19 | Changing the Chart Type

The data in the tour types chart compares tour numbers for two years and is appropriately represented by a bar chart. A column chart is also appropriate to compare data.

1 With the chart selected, on the **Chart Tools Design tab**, in the **Type group**, click **Change Chart Type**.

2 In the **Change Chart Type** dialog box, on the left, click **Column**, and then in the right pane, at the top, click the first chart type—**Clustered Column**. Click **OK**, and then compare your screen with Figure 4.46.

The category names display in alphabetical order on the horizontal axis; the number scale displays on the vertical axis.

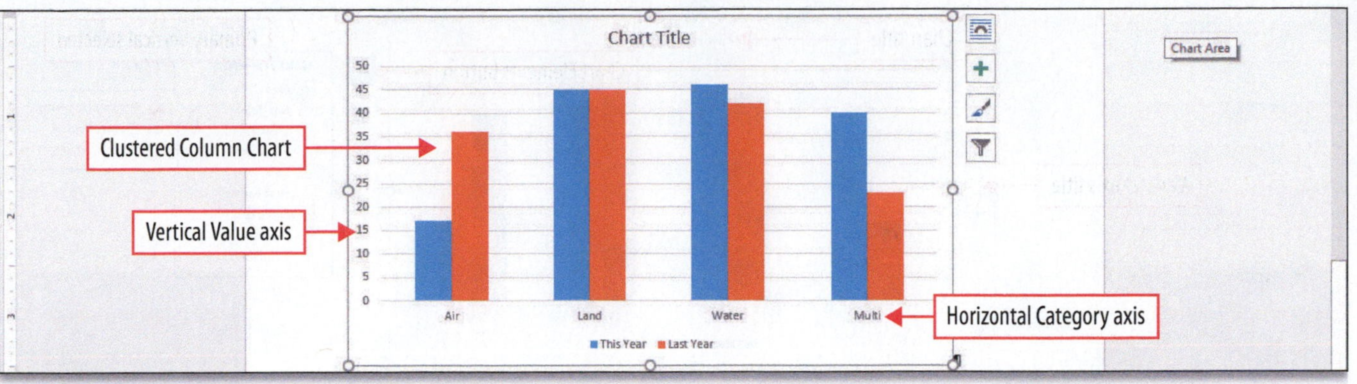

FIGURE 4.46

Word 2016, Windows 10, Microsoft Corporation

3 **Save** your document.

Activity 4.20 | Adding Chart Elements

Add chart elements to help the reader understand the data in your chart. For example, you can add a title to the chart and to individual axes, or add ***data labels***, which display the value represented by each data marker.

1 Four buttons—*Layout Options*, *Chart Elements*, *Chart Styles*, and *Chart Filters*—display to the right of the chart. Take a moment to read the descriptions of each button in the table in Figure 4.47.

AVAILABLE CHART BUTTONS		
CHART BUTTON	ICON	PURPOSE
Layout Options		To set how a chart interacts with the text around it
Chart Elements		To add, remove, or change chart elements—such as a chart title, legend, gridlines, and data labels
Chart Styles		To apply a style and color scheme to a chart
Chart Filters		To define what data points and names display on a chart

Word 2016, Windows 10, Microsoft Corporation

FIGURE 4.47

2 Click **Chart Elements**, and then select the **Axis Titles** check box. To the right of Axis Titles, click the arrow, and then clear the **Primary Horizontal** check box to remove the primary horizontal title text box from the chart. Compare your screen with Figure 4.48.

By default, when you select Axis Titles, both the primary horizontal axis title and primary vertical axis title text boxes display in the chart. In this case, because the chart title identifies the categories, the primary horizontal axis title is not needed.

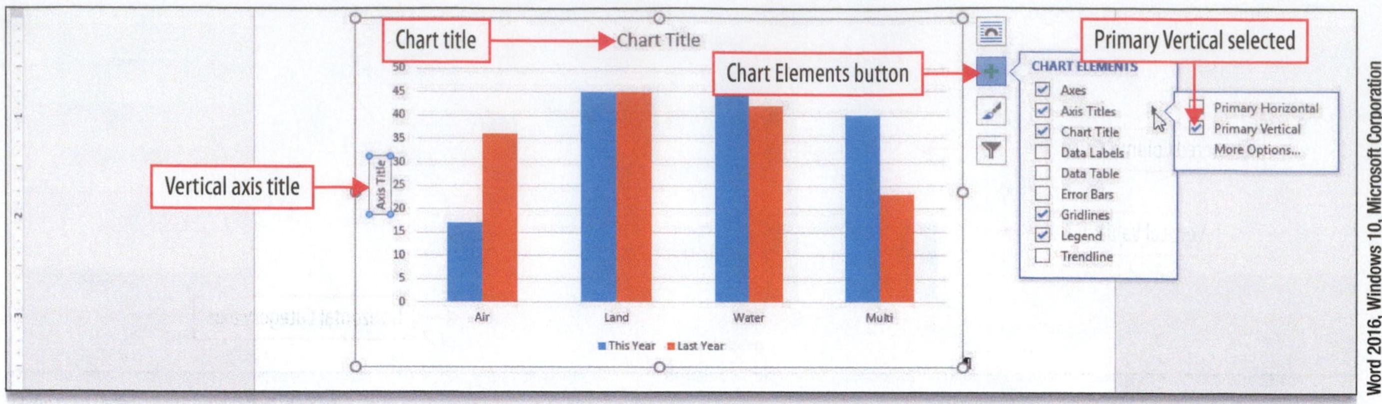

FIGURE 4.48

ANOTHER WAY Under Chart Tools, on the Design tab, in the Chart Layouts group, click Add Chart Element.

3 To the left of the vertical axis, notice that the **Axis Title** is selected. If the title is not selected, click the Axis title so that it is surrounded by a solid border. Type **# of Tours** and notice that the text displays vertically in the text box. Click outside the axis title to deselect the title.

4 Above the chart, click the text box that displays *Chart Title*, and then type **Tours Offered**

5 Click in an empty corner of the chart to deselect the title text box. **Save** your document.

Objective 8 Format a Chart

GO! Learn How Video W4-8

You can format a chart to change the appearance of chart elements.

Activity 4.21 | Applying a Chart Style and Changing the Chart Color

A ***chart style*** refers to the overall visual look of a chart in terms of its graphic effects, colors, and backgrounds. For example, you can have flat or beveled columns, colors that are solid or transparent, and backgrounds that are dark or light.

1 To the right of the chart, click **Chart Styles**. With **Style** selected, scroll down and click the fifth style—**Style 5**.

2 At the top of the **Chart Styles** list, click **Color**. Under **Monochromatic**, in the sixth row, click the green color scheme—**Color 10**. Compare your screen with Figure 4.49.

ANOTHER WAY Under Chart Tools, on the Design tab, in the Chart Styles group, click Change Colors to display the Color Gallery.

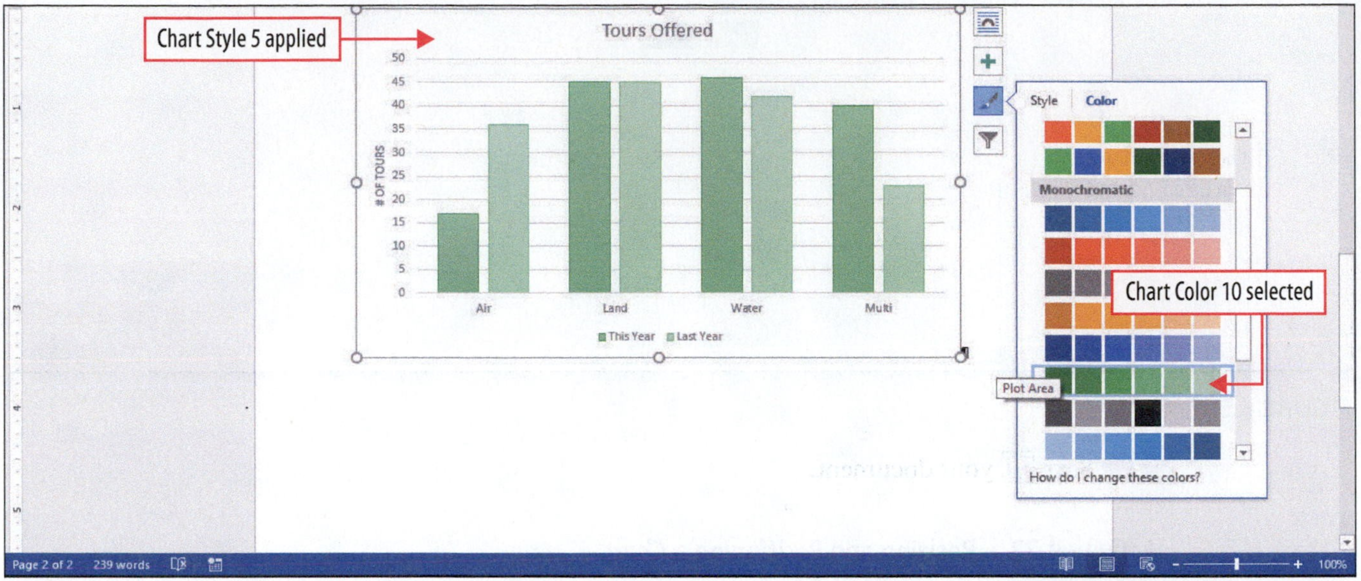

Word 2016, Windows 10, Microsoft Corporation

FIGURE 4.49

3 Click in the document to close the Chart Styles list, and then **Save** your document.

Activity 4.22 | Formatting Chart Elements

Individual chart elements can also be formatted to enhance the appearance of the chart.

1 Select the chart title. On the **Chart Tools Format tab**, in the **Shape Styles group**, click the **More** button. In the gallery, in the fifth row, click the last style—**Moderate Effect – Green, Accent 6**. Click in an empty corner of the chart to deselect the chart title, and then compare your screen with Figure 4.50.

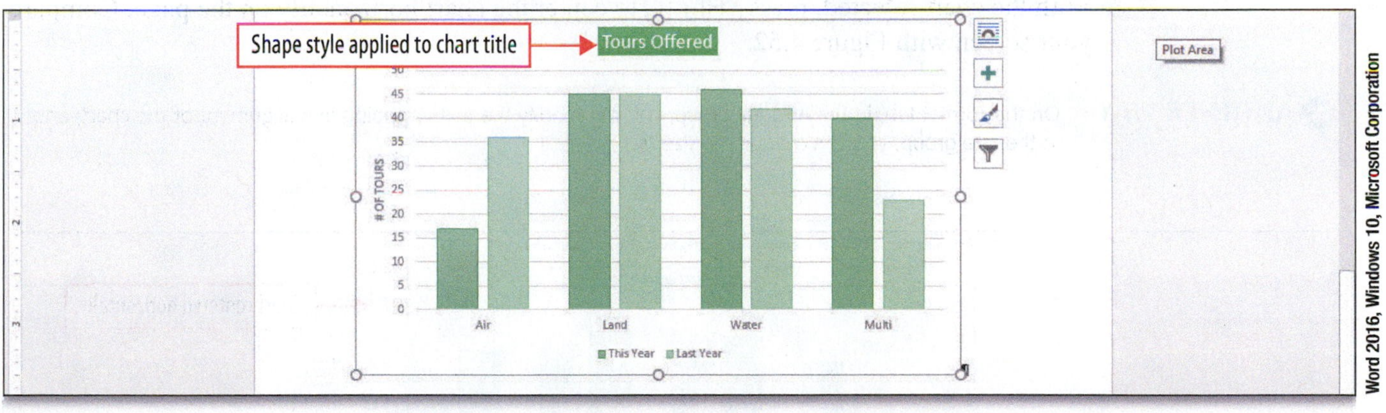

Word 2016, Windows 10, Microsoft Corporation

FIGURE 4.50

2 Click the border of the chart. On the **Format tab**, in the **Shape Styles group**, click **Shape Outline**, and then in the last column, click the first color—**Green, Accent 6**. Deselect the chart, and then compare your screen with Figure 4.51.

A border surrounds the entire chart.

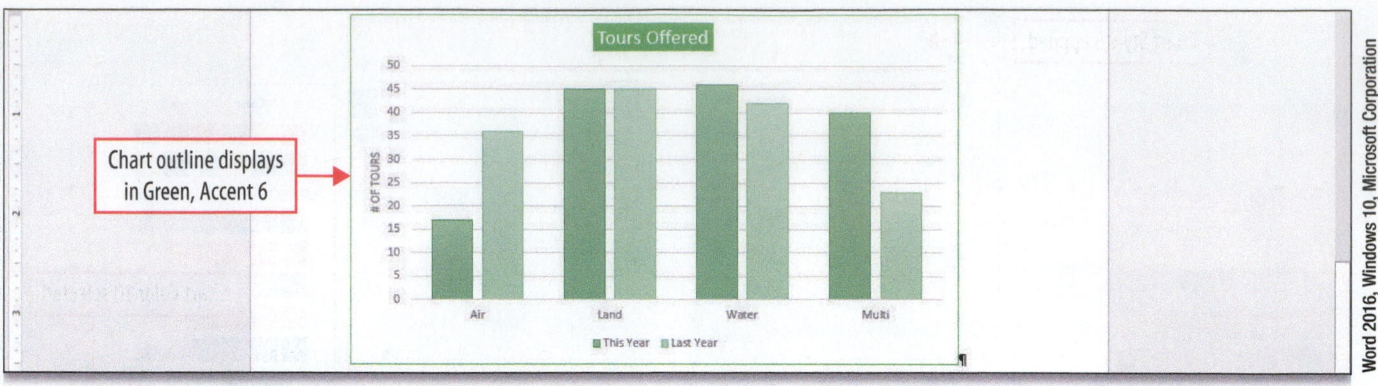

FIGURE 4.51

3 **Save** your document.

Activity 4.23 | Resizing and Positioning a Chart

You can resize and position both the chart and individual chart elements. You can also position the chart on the page relative to the left and right margins.

1 Click the chart to select it. To the right of the chart, click **Layout Options**.

When you insert a chart, the default text wrapping setting is In Line with Text.

2 Near the bottom of the gallery, click **See more** to display the Layout dialog box.

The Layout dialog box allows you to change the position, text wrapping, and size of a chart.

3 In the **Layout** dialog box, click the **Size tab**, and then under **Height**, click the **Absolute down spin arrow** to **2.7**. Click **OK** to close the dialog box.

When you change the position, text wrapping, or size of a chart, the chart may display differently in the document. In this case, the chart displays at the bottom of Page 1.

4 With the chart selected, press Ctrl + E to center the chart horizontally on the page. Compare your screen with Figure 4.52.

ANOTHER WAY On the Format tab, in the Arrange group, you can modify the text wrapping and alignment of the chart; and in the Size group, you can change the size.

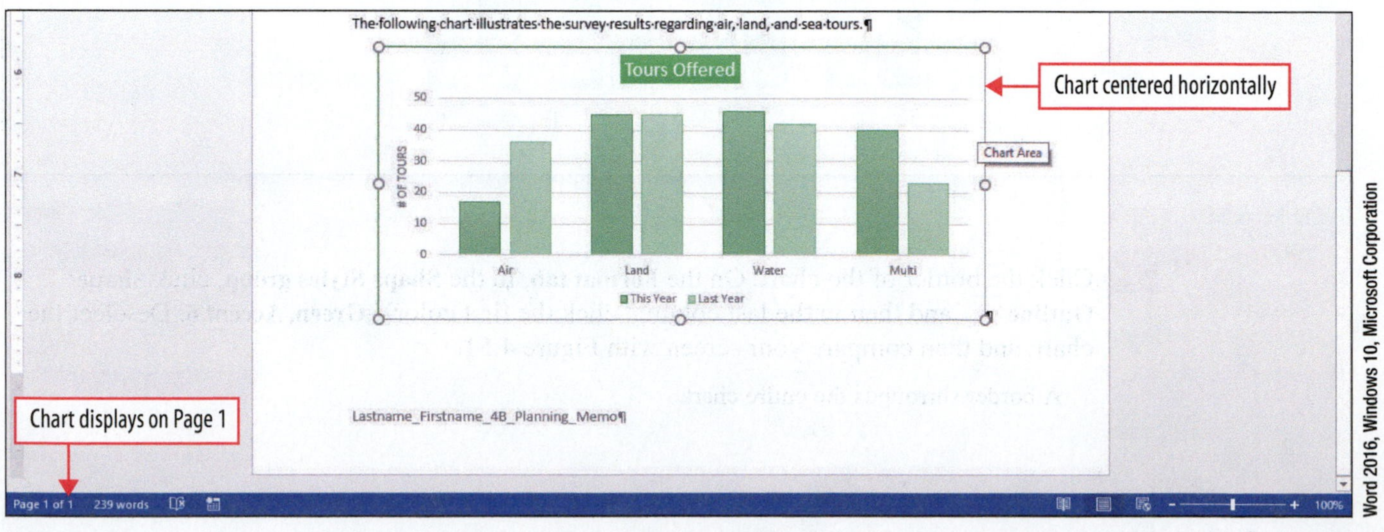

FIGURE 4.52

5 Press Ctrl + Home. Click the **File tab** to display **Backstage** view. On the right, at the bottom of the **Properties** list, click **Show All Properties**. In the **Tags** box, type **tours data** and in the **Subject** box type your course name and section number. If necessary, edit the author name to display your name.

6 On the left, click **Print** to display **Print Preview**. If necessary, return to the document and make any necessary changes.

7 **Save** your document. In the upper right corner of the Word window, click **Close**. If directed by your instructor to do so, submit your paper printout, your electronic image of your document that looks like a printed document, or your original Word file.

More **Knowledge**

Saving a Chart Template as a Template

Right-click the border of the chart, and then from the shortcut menu, click Save as Template. Then, save the chart in the location in which you are saving your templates. The chart template will be saved with the file extension .crtx.

END | You have completed Project 4B

GO! To Work

Andrew Rodriguez / Fotolia; FotolEdhar/ Fotolia; apops/ Fotolia; Yuri Arcurs/ Fotolia

4 WORD

Microsoft Office Specialist (MOS) Skills in this Chapter	
PROJECT 4A	**PROJECT 4B**
1.3.2 Apply document themes **2.2.1** Create paragraph and character styles **2.2.4** Clear formatting **2.2.6** Apply built-in styles to text **3.3.2** Change bullet characters or number formats for a list level **3.3.3** Define a custom bullet character or number format **3.3.4** Increase or decrease list levels	**1.1.7** Display hidden ribbon tabs **1.3.3** Apply document style sets **2.2.3** Set line and paragraph spacing and indentation

BUILD YOUR E-PORTFOLIO

An E-Portfolio is a collection of evidence, stored electronically, that showcases what you have accomplished while completing your education. Collecting and then sharing your work products with potential employers reflects your academic and career goals. Your completed documents from the following projects are good examples to show what you have learned: 4G, 4K, and 4L.

GO! FOR JOB SUCCESS

Discussion: Big Data

Your instructor may assign these questions to your class, and then ask you to think about them or discuss them with your classmates:

"Big data" describes information that a company has that is so massive in the number of records that it is difficult to analyze using standard database techniques. It often refers to information that a company collects in the course of doing business that is not usually used for any other purpose than to process transactions. An example is airline ticket sales: The information airlines collect in a ticket sale includes names, addresses, travel preferences, destinations, credit cards, seating preferences, and so forth. Analyzing this information could result in information that would be useful in updating flight schedules, changing seat layouts, and marketing plans.

FotolEdhar / Fotolia

What are some other industries that collect large amounts of data about customers during the course of a normal transaction?

What other industries would benefit from data such as that collected during an airline ticket sale?

Do you think it is ethical for businesses to sell the information they collect to other businesses?

END OF CHAPTER

SUMMARY

Use built-in and customized theme and style features to coordinate colors, fonts, effects, and other formatting elements. Apply themes and styles to maintain a consistent and professional appearance in documents.

A multilevel list displays information in an organized, hierarchical structure. You can create and save a custom multilevel list style, and apply it to other lists within the same document or in other documents.

A custom theme that is saved as a Word template can be attached to other documents. This is a quick and easy method to change the appearance of an existing document and provide consistency among related documents.

Because a chart displays numbers in a visual format, readers can easily understand the data. Add and format chart elements to enhance the chart's appearance.

GO! LEARN IT ONLINE

Review the concepts, key terms, and MOS skills in this chapter by completing these online challenges, which you can find at **MyITLab**.

Matching and Multiple Choice: Answer matching and multiple-choice questions to test what you learned in this chapter.

Lessons on the GO!: Learn how to use all the new apps and features as they are introduced by Microsoft.

MOS Prep Quiz: Answer questions to review the MOS skills that you practiced in this chapter.

PROJECT GUIDE FOR WORD CHAPTER 4

Your instructor will assign Projects from this list to ensure your learning and assess your knowledge.

PROJECT GUIDE FOR WORD CHAPTER 4			
Project	**Apply Skills from These Chapter Objectives**	**Project Type**	**Project Location**
4A **MyITLab**	Objectives 1-4 from Project 4A	**4A Instructional Project (Grader Project)** Guided instruction to learn the skills in Project 4A.	In MyITLab and in text
4B **MyITLab**	Objectives 5-8 from Project 4B	**4B Instructional Project (Grader Project)** Guided instruction to learn the skills in Project 4B.	In MyITLab and in text
4C	Objectives 1-4 from Project 4A	**4C Skills Review (Scorecard Grading)** A guided review of the skills from Project 4A.	In text
4D	Objectives 5-8 from Project 4B	**4D Skills Review (Scorecard Grading)** A guided review of the skills from Project 4B.	In text
4E **MyITLab**	Objectives 1-4 from Project 4A	**4E Mastery (Grader Project)** **Mastery and Transfer of Learning** A demonstration of your mastery of the skills in Project 4A with extensive decision making.	In MyITLab and in text
4F **MyITLab**	Objectives 5-8 from Project 4B	**4F Mastery (Grader Project)** **Mastery and Transfer of Learning** A demonstration of your mastery of the skills in Project 4B with extensive decision making.	In MyITLab and in text
4G **MyITLab**	Objectives 1-8 from Project 4A and 4B	**4G Mastery (Grader Project)** **Mastery and Transfer of Learning** A demonstration of your mastery of the skills in Projects 4A and 4B with extensive decision making.	In MyITLab and in text
4H	Combination of Objectives from Projects 4A and 4B	**4H GO! Fix It (Scorecard Grading)** **Critical Thinking** A demonstration of your mastery of the skills in Projects 4A and 4B by creating a correct result from a document that contains errors you must find.	Instructor Resource Center (IRC) and MyITLab
4I	Combination of Objectives from Projects 4A and 4B	**4I GO! Make It (Scorecard Grading)** **Critical Thinking** A demonstration of your mastery of the skills in Projects 4A and 4B by creating a result from a supplied picture.	IRC and MyITLab
4J	Combination of Objectives from Projects 4A and 4B	**4J GO! Solve It (Rubric Grading)** **Critical Thinking** A demonstration of your mastery of the skills in Projects 4A and 4B, your decision-making skills, and your critical thinking skills. A task-specific rubric helps you self-assess your result.	IRC and MyITLab
4K	Combination of Objectives from Projects 4A and 4B	**4K GO! Solve It (Rubric Grading)** **Critical Thinking** A demonstration of your mastery of the skills in Projects 4A and 4B, your decision-making skills, and your critical thinking skills. A task-specific rubric helps you self-assess your result.	In text
4L	Combination of Objectives from Projects 4A and 4B	**4L GO! Think (Rubric Grading)** **Critical Thinking** A demonstration of your understanding of the chapter concepts applied in a manner that you would outside of college. An analytic rubric helps you and your instructor grade the quality of your work by comparing it to the work an expert in the discipline would create.	In text
4M	Combination of Objectives from Projects 4A and 4B	**4M GO! Think (Rubric Grading)** **Critical Thinking** A demonstration of your understanding of the chapter concepts applied in a manner that you would outside of college. An analytic rubric helps you and your instructor grade the quality of your work by comparing it to the work an expert in the discipline would create.	IRC and MyITLab
4N	Combination of Objectives from Projects 4A and 4B	**4N You and GO! (Rubric Grading)** **Critical Thinking** A demonstration of your understanding of the chapter concepts applied in a manner that you would in a personal situation. An analytic rubric helps you and your instructor grade the quality of your work.	IRC and MyITLab

GLOSSARY

GLOSSARY OF CHAPTER KEY TERMS

Area chart A chart type that shows trends over time.

Bar chart A chart type that shows a comparison among related data.

Category axis The area of the chart that identifies the categories of data.

Cell The intersection of a column and row.

Change Case A formatting command that allows you to quickly change the capitalization of selected text.

Character style A style, indicated by the symbol **a**, that contains formatting characteristics that you apply to text, such as font name, font size, font color, bold emphasis, and so on.

Chart A visual representation of numerical data.

Chart area The entire chart and all its elements.

Chart data range The group of cells with red, purple, and blue shading that is used to create a chart.

Chart Elements A Word feature that displays commands to add, remove, or change chart elements, such as the legend, gridlines, and data labels.

Chart Filters A Word feature that displays commands to define what data points and names display on a chart.

Chart style The overall visual look of a chart in terms of its graphic effects, colors, and backgrounds.

Chart Styles A Word feature that displays commands to apply a style and color scheme to a chart.

Column chart A chart type that shows a comparison among related data.

Contiguous Items that are adjacent to one another.

Data labels The part of a chart that displays the value represented by each data marker.

Data markers The shapes in a chart representing each of the cells that contain data.

Data points The cells that contain numerical data used in a chart.

Data range border The blue line that surrounds the cells containing numerical data that display in in the chart.

Data series In a chart, related data points represented by a unique color.

Direct formatting The process of applying each format separately, for example, bold, then font size, then font color, and so on.

Embedding The process of inserting an object, such as a chart, into a Word document so that it becomes part of the document.

Keep lines together A formatting feature that prevents a single line from displaying by itself at the bottom of a page or at the top of a page.

Keep with next A formatting feature that keeps a heading with its first paragraph of text together on the page.

Layout Options A Word feature that displays commands to control the manner in which text wraps around a chart or other object.

Legend The part of a chart that identifies the colors assigned to each data series or category.

Line chart A chart type that shows trends over time.

Linked style A style, indicated by the symbol **¶a**, that behaves as either a character style or a paragraph style, depending on what you select.

List style A style that applies a format to a list.

Memorandum (Memo) A written message sent to someone working in the same organization.

Multilevel list A list in which the items display in a visual hierarchical structure.

Noncontiguous Items that are not adjacent to one another.

Normal The default style in Word for new documents and which includes default styles and customizations that determine the basic look of a document; for example, it includes the Calibri font, 11-pt font size, line spacing at 1.08, and 8-pt spacing after a paragraph.

Numerical data Numbers that represent facts.

Paragraph style A style, indicated by ¶, that includes everything that a character style contains, plus all aspects of a paragraph's appearance; for example, text alignment, tab stops, line spacing, and borders.

Pie chart A chart type that shows the proportion of parts to a whole.

Reveal Formatting A pane that displays the formatted selection and includes a complete description of formats applied.

Show Preview A formatting feature that displays a visual representation of each style in the Styles window.

Style A group of formatting commands, such as font, font size, font color, paragraph alignment, and line spacing, that can be applied to selected text with one command.

Style Inspector A pane that displays the name of the selected style with formats applied and contains paragraph- and text-level formatting options.

Style set A group of styles that are designed to work together.

Styles window A pane that displays a list of styles and contains tools to manage styles.

Table style A style that applies a consistent look to borders, shading, and so on of a table.

Value axis The area of a chart that displays a numerical scale based on the numerical data in a chart.

Word Options A collection of settings that you can change to customize Word.

CHAPTER REVIEW

Apply 4A skills from these Objectives:

1. Apply and Modify Styles
2. Create New Styles
3. Manage Styles
4. Create a Multilevel List

Skills Review Project 4C Training Classes

In the following Skills Review, you will add styles and a multilevel list format to a document that describes training classes for Costa Rican Treks tour guides. Your completed document will look similar to Figure 4.53.

PROJECT FILES

For Project 4C, you will need the following file:

w04C_Training_Classes

You will save your document as:

Lastname_Firstname_4C_Training_Classes

PROJECT RESULTS

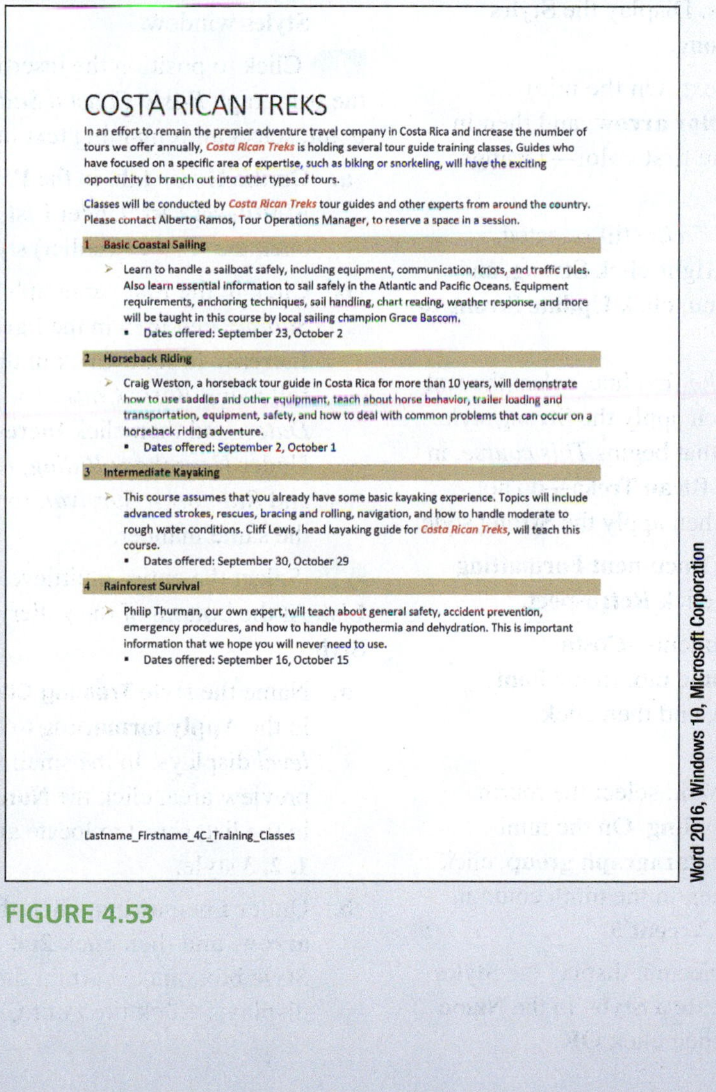

COSTA RICAN TREKS

In an effort to remain the premier adventure travel company in Costa Rica and increase the number of tours we offer annually, *Costa Rican Treks* is holding several tour guide training classes. Guides who have focused on a specific area of expertise, such as biking or snorkeling, will have the exciting opportunity to branch out into other types of tours.

Classes will be conducted by *Costa Rican Treks* tour guides and other experts from around the country. Please contact Alberto Ramos, Tour Operations Manager, to reserve a space in a session.

1 Basic Coastal Sailing

- Learn to handle a sailboat safely, including equipment, communication, knots, and traffic rules. Also learn essential information to sail safely in the Atlantic and Pacific Oceans. Equipment requirements, anchoring techniques, sail handling, chart reading, weather response, and more will be taught in this course by local sailing champion Grace Bascom.
  - Dates offered: September 23, October 2

2 Horseback Riding

- Craig Weston, a horseback tour guide in Costa Rica for more than 10 years, will demonstrate how to use saddles and other equipment, teach about horse behavior, trailer loading and transportation, equipment, safety, and how to deal with common problems that can occur on a horseback riding adventure.
  - Dates offered: September 2, October 1

3 Intermediate Kayaking

- This course assumes that you already have some basic kayaking experience. Topics will include advanced strokes, rescues, bracing and rolling, navigation, and how to handle moderate to rough water conditions. Cliff Lewis, head kayaking guide for *Costa Rican Treks*, will teach this course.
  - Dates offered: September 30, October 29

4 Rainforest Survival

- Philip Thurman, our own expert, will teach about general safety, accident prevention, emergency procedures, and how to handle hypothermia and dehydration. This is important information that we hope you will never need to use.
  - Dates offered: September 16, October 15

Lastname_Firstname_4C_Training_Classes

Word 2016, Windows 10, Microsoft Corporation

FIGURE 4.53

(Project 4C Training Classes continues on the next page)

Skills Review Project 4C Training Classes (continued)

1 Start Word. Navigate to the student data files that accompany this chapter, and then open the file **w04C_Training_Classes**. **Save** the document in your **Word Chapter 4** folder as **Lastname_Firstname_4C_Training_Classes** Scroll to the bottom of the page, right-click in the footer area, and then click **Edit Footer**. On the ribbon, in the **Insert group**, click **Document Info**, and then click **File Name**. **Close** the footer area.

a. Select the first paragraph—*Costa Rican Treks*. On the **Home tab**, in the **Styles group**, click **More**, and then in the gallery, click **Title**.

b. In the second paragraph, in the second line, select the text **Costa Rican Treks**. Display the **Styles** gallery, and then click **Strong**.

c. Right-click the selected text. On the mini toolbar, click the **Font Color arrow**, and then in the sixth column, click the first color—**Orange, Accent 2**.

d. With the text *Costa Rican Treks* still selected, display the **Styles** gallery, right-click **Strong**, and then from the shortcut menu, click **Update Strong to Match Selection**.

e. In the third paragraph, in the first line, select the text **Costa Rican Treks**, and then apply the **Strong** style. In the eleventh paragraph that begins *This course*, in the third line, select **Costa Rican Treks**—do not include the comma—and then apply the **Strong** style.

2 On the **Design tab**, in the **Document Formatting group**, click **Themes**, and then click **Retrospect**.

a. Select the title of the document—**Costa Rican Treks**. Click the **Home tab**. In the **Font group**, click **Change Case**, and then click **UPPERCASE**.

b. Including the paragraph mark, select the fourth paragraph **Basic Coastal Sailing**. On the mini toolbar, apply **Bold**. In the **Paragraph group**, click the **Shading arrow**, and then in the ninth column, click the first color—**Tan, Accent 5**.

c. With the paragraph still selected, display the **Styles** gallery, and then click **Create a Style**. In the **Name** box, type **Class Title** and then click **OK**.

d. Scroll down as necessary, select the paragraph **Horseback Riding**, and then apply the **Class Title** style.

e. Using the same technique, apply the **Class Title** style to the paragraphs *Intermediate Kayaking* and *Rainforest Survival*.

3 Press Ctrl + Home. In the **Styles group**, click the **Dialog Box Launcher**.

a. In the **Styles** window, point to **Strong**, click the **arrow**, and then click **Modify**.

b. In the **Modify Style** dialog box, under **Formatting**, click **Italic**. Click **OK** to close the dialog box and update all instances of the *Strong* style. **Close** the **Styles** window.

4 Click to position the insertion point to the left of the paragraph *Basic Coastal Sailing*, and then from this point, select all remaining text in the document.

a. On the **Home tab**, in the **Paragraph group**, click **Multilevel List**. Under **List Library**, locate and then click the ❖, ➢, • (bullet) style.

b. Click in the first paragraph following *Basic Coastal Sailing*, and then in the **Paragraph group**, click **Increase Indent**. Click in the second paragraph following *Basic Coastal Sailing*, which begins *Dates*, and then click **Increase Indent** two times. Under *Horseback Riding*, *Intermediate Kayaking*, and *Rainforest Survival*, format the paragraphs in the same manner.

5 Select the entire multilevel list. Click **Multilevel List**. At the bottom of the gallery, click **Define New List Style**.

a. Name the style **Training Class** Under **Formatting**, in the **Apply formatting to** box, be sure *1st level* displays. In the small toolbar above the preview area, click the **Numbering Style arrow**, in the list, scroll to locate and then click the **1, 2, 3** style.

b. Under **Formatting**, click the **Apply formatting to arrow**, and then click **2nd level**. In the **Numbering Style** box, make certain the **Bullet:** ➢ style displays. Click the **Font Color arrow**, and then

(Project 4C Training Classes continues on the next page)

Skills Review Project 4C Training Classes (continued)

in the ninth column, click the fifth color—**Tan, Accent 5, Darker 25%**. Click **OK** to close the dialog box.

c. Press Ctrl + Home. Click the **File tab**, and then click **Show All Properties**. In the **Tags** box, type **training classes** and then in the Subject box, type your course name and section number. If necessary, edit the author name to display your name.

d. On the left, click **Print**. If necessary, return to the document and make any necessary changes. **Save** your document. If directed by your instructor to do so, submit your paper printout, your electronic image of your document that looks like a printed document, or your original Word file. **Close** Word.

END | You have completed Project 4C

CHAPTER REVIEW

Skills Review Project 4D Strategy Session

Apply 4B skills from these Objectives:

5 Change the Style Set of a Document and Apply a Template
6 Insert a Chart and Enter Data into a Chart
7 Change a Chart Type
8 Format a Chart

In the following Skills Review, you will create a memo for Maria Tornio, President of Costa Rican Treks, which details the company's financial performance and provides strategies for the upcoming year. Your completed document will look similar to Figure 4.54.

PROJECT FILES

For Project 4D, you will need the following files:

w04D_Strategy_Session
w04D_Memo_Styles

You will save your document as:

Lastname_Firstname_4D_Strategy_Session

PROJECT RESULTS

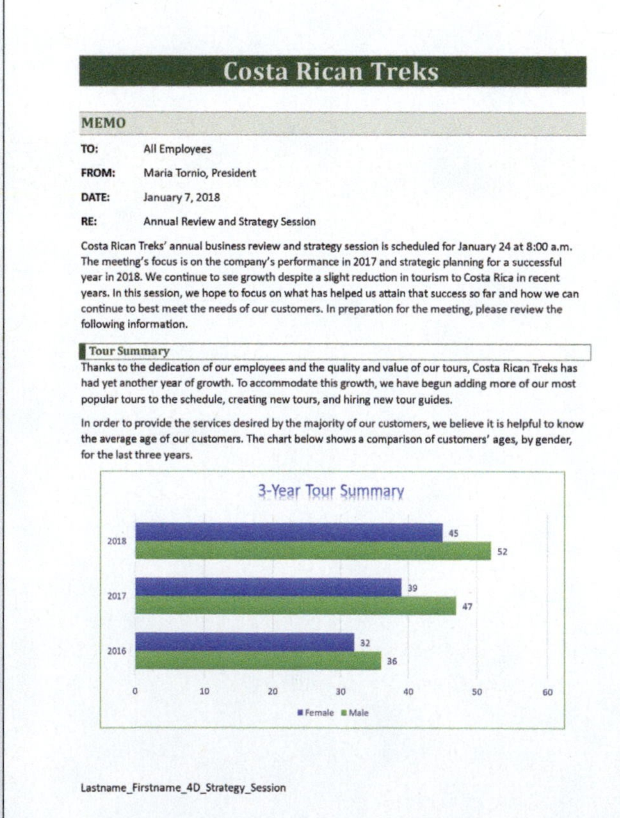

Costa Rican Treks

MEMO

TO: All Employees

FROM: Maria Tornio, President

DATE: January 7, 2018

RE: Annual Review and Strategy Session

Costa Rican Treks' annual business review and strategy session is scheduled for January 24 at 8:00 a.m. The meeting's focus is on the company's performance in 2017 and strategic planning for a successful year in 2018. We continue to see growth despite a slight reduction in tourism to Costa Rica in recent years. In this session, we hope to focus on what has helped us attain that success so far and how we can continue to best meet the needs of our customers. In preparation for the meeting, please review the following information.

Tour Summary

Thanks to the dedication of our employees and the quality and value of our tours, Costa Rican Treks has had yet another year of growth. To accommodate this growth, we have begun adding more of our most popular tours to the schedule, creating new tours, and hiring new tour guides.

In order to provide the services desired by the majority of our customers, we believe it is helpful to know the average age of our customers. The chart below shows a comparison of customers' ages, by gender, for the last three years.

Lastname_Firstname_4D_Strategy_Session

Local Industry Assessment

There are numerous outdoor adventure companies in Costa Rica. Travelers have many options to choose from. Our greatest assets in the past have been satisfied customers who become repeat customers, referrals, and our excellent relationships with local concierges and travel agencies. These qualities have helped us become one of the better-known sources for adventure tours in Costa Rica.

In the coming year we also plan to expand our online marketing efforts. More travelers are researching their own trips online rather than using travel agencies. We have begun developing fliers that will be sent to travel agents throughout the United States and Canada. In addition, our website is being redesigned, and through that we will offer a discussion board, articles, and some discounts and prizes for referrals and newsletter subscriptions. As always, we will continue to closely monitor our customers' reviews and make adjustments as necessary, such as offering specialized tours that differ from others offered by our competitors.

Customer Feedback

After every trip, our guides ask all participants to fill out a survey indicating their satisfaction and suggestions. We've consistently received excellent ratings on the informative nature of our tours, an appropriate level of activity and adventure, organization and planning, and the types of tours offered.

The most interesting aspect of this year's reviews was that our customers value the affordability of our tours. In general, they stated that ours had the best combination of quality and affordability of those they researched. We had been considering offering some luxury tours that would include things like extravagant accommodations and gourmet meals, but based on our research, our customers choose us because our tours are so reasonably priced. Our corporate identity is such that we should maintain it by not venturing into more expensive options right now. In the future, we can revisit this concept if interest exists.

Lastname_Firstname_4D_Strategy_Session

Word 2016, Windows 10, Microsoft Corporation

FIGURE 4.54

(Project 4D Strategy Session continues on the next page)

Skills Review Project 4D Strategy Session (continued)

1 Start Word. From your student files, locate and then open the file **w04D_Strategy_Session. Save** the document in your **Word Chapter 4** folder as **Lastname_Firstname_4D_Strategy_Session** Scroll to the bottom of **Page 1**, right-click in the footer area, and then click **Edit Footer**. On the ribbon, in the **Insert group**, click **Document Info**, and then click **File Name. Close** the footer area.

a. Select the first paragraph—**Costa Rican Treks**. On the **Home tab**, in the **Styles** group, click the **More** button, and then click **Title**. Select the second paragraph—**MEMO**, display the **Styles** gallery, and then click **Heading 1**.

b. Select the memo heading **TO:**—include the colon—hold down Ctrl and then select the memo headings **FROM:, DATE:**, and **RE:**. On the mini toolbar, click **Bold**.

c. Select the paragraph **Tour Summary**, press and hold Ctrl, and then select the paragraphs **Local Industry Assessment** and **Customer Feedback**. Apply the **Heading 2** style.

d. Click the **Design tab**, and then in the **Document Formatting group**, click the **More** button. In the gallery, under **Built-In**, in the first row, click the first style set—**Basic (Elegant)**. In the **Document Formatting group**, click **Paragraph Spacing**, and then click **Open**.

2 Click the **File tab**, and then click **Options**. In the **Word Options** dialog box, click **Customize Ribbon**. In the **Main Tabs** list, select the **Developer** check box, and then click **OK**.

a. On the **Developer tab**, in the **Templates group**, click **Document Template**. In the **Templates and Add-ins** dialog box, click **Attach**. In the **Attach Template** dialog box, navigate to your student files, click **w04D_Memo_Styles**, and then click **Open**. Select the **Automatically update document styles** check box, and then click **OK**.

b. On the **File tab**, click **Options**. In the **Word Options** dialog box, click **Customize Ribbon**. In the **Main Tabs** list, click to deselect the **Developer** check box, and then click **OK**.

c. On **Page** 1, below *Tour Summary*, locate the paragraph that begins *In order to provide*. Position the insertion point at the end of the paragraph, and then press Enter.

3 Click the **Insert tab**, and then in the **Illustrations group**, click **Chart**.

a. On the left side of the **Insert Chart** dialog box, be sure **Column** is selected. At the top of the right pane, click the first chart type—**Clustered Column**—and then click **OK**.

b. In the **Chart in Microsoft Word** worksheet, click cell **B1**, type **Male** and then press Tab. With cell **C1** selected, type **Female** and then click cell **A2**.

c. With cell **A2** selected, type **2016** and then press Tab. In cell **B2**, type **36**, press Tab, and then in cell **C2**, type **32** Press Tab two times to move to **row 3**.

d. Using the technique you just practiced, and without changing the values in **column D**, enter the following data:

	MALE	FEMALE
2016	36	32
2017	**47**	**39**
2018	**52**	**43**

e. Point to the lower right corner of the blue border to display the ⇘ pointer, and then drag to the left and up to select only cells **A1** through **C4**.

f. **Close** the Chart in Microsoft Word worksheet, and then **Save** your document. Scroll as necessary to display the entire chart.

4 If necessary, click in an empty area of the chart to select it. Under **Chart Tools**, on the **Design tab**, in the **Data group**, click the upper portion of the **Edit Data** button to redisplay the worksheet.

a. In the worksheet, click cell **C4**, type **45** press Enter, and then **Close** the worksheet.

b. With the chart selected, under **Chart Tools**, on the **Design tab**, in the **Type group**, click **Change Chart Type**.

(Project 4D Strategy Session continues on the next page)

Skills Review Project 4D Strategy Session (continued)

c. In the **Change Chart Type** dialog box, on the left, click **Bar**, and then on the right, at the top, click the first chart type—**Clustered Bar**. Click **OK**.

5 Select the text **Chart Title**, and then type **3-Year Tour Summary**

a. Click in an empty area of the chart, and then to the right of the chart, click **Chart Elements**. Select the **Data Labels** check box.

b. Click **Chart Styles**. Scroll down, and then click the fifth style—**Style 5**. At the top of the list, click **Color**, and then under **Colorful**, in the fourth row, click the color scheme **Color 4** to display the chart with blue and green data markers.

c. Select the chart title. Click the **Format tab**, and then in the **WordArt Styles group**, click the **More** button. In the gallery, in the second row, click the second style—**Gradient Fill – Blue, Accent 1, Reflection**. Click in an empty corner area of the chart. On the **Format tab**, in the **Shape Styles group**, click **Shape Outline**, and then in the last column, click the first color—**Green, Accent 6**.

d. Click **Layout Options**, and then click **See more**. In the **Layout** dialog box, Click the **Size tab** and under **Height**, change the **Absolute down spin arrow** to **3.3"** Click **OK** to close the dialog box. Press Ctrl + E to center the chart.

e. Click the **File tab**, and then click **Show All Properties**. In the **Tags** box, type **strategy session** and in the **Subject** box, type your course name and section number. If necessary, edit the author name to display your name.

f. On the left, click **Print**. If necessary, return to the document and make any necessary changes. **Save** your document. If directed by your instructor to do so, submit your paper printout, your electronic image of your document that looks like a printed document, or your original Word file. **Close** Word.

END | You have completed Project 4D

CONTENT-BASED ASSESSMENTS (MASTERY AND TRANSFER OF LEARNING)

Mastering Word Project 4E Trip Tips

Apply 4A skills from these Objectives:

1. Apply and Modify Styles
2. Create New Styles
3. Manage Styles
4. Create a Multilevel List

In the following Mastering Word project, you will create a handout that details tips for tour participants for Alberto Ramos, Tour Operations Manager of Costa Rican Treks. Your completed document will look similar to Figure 4.55.

PROJECT FILES

For Project 4E, you will need the following file:

w04E_Trip_Tips

You will save your document as:

Lastname_Firstname_4E_Trip_Tips

PROJECT RESULTS

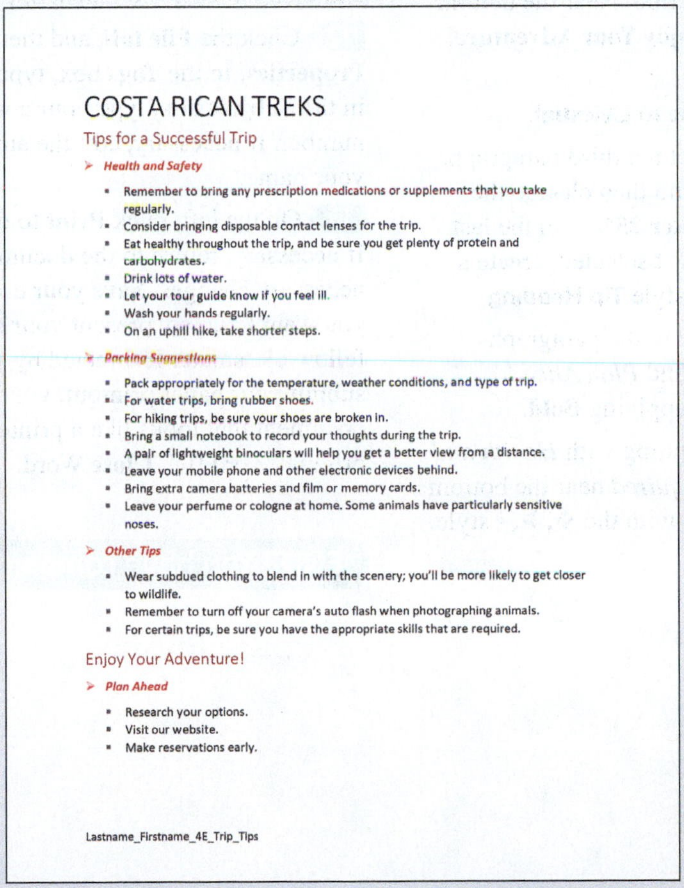

COSTA RICAN TREKS

Tips for a Successful Trip

➢ *Health and Safety*

- Remember to bring any prescription medications or supplements that you take regularly.
- Consider bringing disposable contact lenses for the trip.
- Eat healthy throughout the trip, and be sure you get plenty of protein and carbohydrates.
- Drink lots of water.
- Let your tour guide know if you feel ill.
- Wash your hands regularly.
- On an uphill hike, take shorter steps.

➢ *Packing Suggestions*

- Pack appropriately for the temperature, weather conditions, and type of trip.
- For water trips, bring rubber shoes.
- For hiking trips, be sure your shoes are broken in.
- Bring a small notebook to record your thoughts during the trip.
- A pair of lightweight binoculars will help you get a better view from a distance.
- Leave your mobile phone and other electronic devices behind.
- Bring extra camera batteries and film or memory cards.
- Leave your perfume or cologne at home. Some animals have particularly sensitive noses.

➢ *Other Tips*

- Wear subdued clothing to blend in with the scenery; you'll be more likely to get closer to wildlife.
- Remember to turn off your camera's auto flash when photographing animals.
- For certain trips, be sure you have the appropriate skills that are required.

Enjoy Your Adventure!

➢ *Plan Ahead*

- Research your options.
- Visit our website.
- Make reservations early.

Lastname_Firstname_4E_Trip_Tips

Word 2016, Windows 10, Microsoft Corporation

FIGURE 4.55

(Project 4E Trip Tips continues on the next page)

Mastering Word Project 4E Trip Tips (continued)

1 Start Word. From your student files, open the document **w04E_Trip_Tips**. Save the file in your **Word Chapter 4** folder as **Lastname_Firstname_4E_Trip_Tips** and then insert the file name in the footer.

2 Select the first paragraph—**Costa Rican Treks**. Apply the **Title** style, and then change the case to **UPPERCASE**.

3 Select the second paragraph that begins *Tips for*, apply the **Heading 2** style. Change the **Font Size** to **16**, change the **Font Color** to **Green, Accent 6, Darker 50%**—in the last column, the last color, and then change the **Spacing After** to **6 pt**.

4 With the second paragraph selected, update the **Heading 2** style to match the selection. Near the bottom of **Page** 1, select the paragraph **Enjoy Your Adventure!** Apply the **Heading 2** style.

5 Change the document **Theme** to **Celestial**.

6 Near the top of **Page** 1, select the third paragraph, **Health and Safety**. Apply **Italic**, and then change the **Font Color** to **Red, Accent 6, Darker 25%**—in the last column, the fifth color. With the text selected, create a new style and then name the new style **Tip Heading**

7 Apply the **Tip Heading** style to the paragraphs *Packing Suggestions*, *Other Tips*, and *Plan Ahead*. **Modify** the **Tip Heading** style by applying **Bold**.

8 Select the block of text beginning with *Health and Safety* and ending with *that are required* near the bottom of **Page** 1. Apply a **Multilevel List** with the ❖, ➢, • style.

9 Select the paragraphs below each *Tip Heading* paragraph, and then increase the indent one time.

10 Select the entire list, and then display the **Define New List Style** dialog box. Name the style **Tips List** and change the **1st level** to **Bullet: ➢**. Set the color to **Red, Accent 6**—in the last column, the first color. Set the **2nd level** by inserting a symbol using the **WingDings character code 167**. Change the color of the bullet to **Gray-25%, Background 2, Darker 75%**—in the third column, the fifth color.

11 At the bottom of **Page 1**, beginning with *Plan Ahead*, select the last four paragraphs. Apply the **Tips List** multilevel list style. Select the last three paragraphs, and then increase the indent one time.

12 Click the **File tab**, and then click **Show All Properties**. In the **Tags** box, type **trip tips list** and then in the **Subject** box, type your course name and section number. If necessary, edit the author name to display your name.

13 On the left, click **Print** to display **Print Preview**. If necessary, return to the document and make any necessary changes. **Save** your document, and then if you want to do so, present your document online to a fellow classmate. If directed by your instructor to do so, submit your paper printout, your electronic image of your document that looks like a printed document, or your original Word file. **Close** Word.

END | You have completed Project 4E

CONTENT-BASED ASSESSMENTS (MASTERY AND TRANSFER OF LEARNING)

4 WORD

Mastering Word Project 4F Hiking FAQ

Apply 4B skills from these Objectives:

5 Change the Style Set of a Document and Apply a Template
6 Insert a Chart and Enter Data into a Chart
7 Change a Chart Type
8 Format a Chart and Save a Chart as a Template

In the following Mastering Word project, you will create a document that provides frequently asked questions and includes a chart about hiking trips offered by Costa Rican Treks. Your completed document will look similar to Figure 4.56.

PROJECT FILES

For Project 4F, you will need the following files:

w04F_Hiking_FAQ
w04F_Hiking_Styles

You will save your document as:

Lastname_Firstname_4F_Hiking_FAQ

PROJECT RESULTS

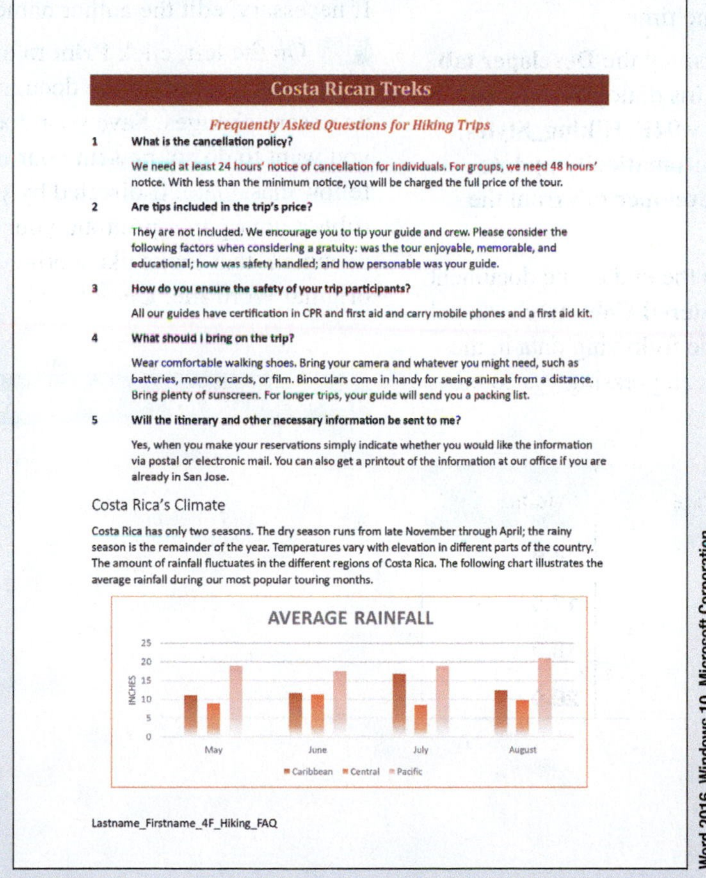

Costa Rican Treks

Frequently Asked Questions for Hiking Trips

1 **What is the cancellation policy?**

We need at least 24 hours' notice of cancellation for individuals. For groups, we need 48 hours' notice. With less than the minimum notice, you will be charged the full price of the tour.

2 **Are tips included in the trip's price?**

They are not included. We encourage you to tip your guide and crew. Please consider the following factors when considering a gratuity: was the tour enjoyable, memorable, and educational; how was safety handled; and how personable was your guide.

3 **How do you ensure the safety of your trip participants?**

All our guides have certification in CPR and first aid and carry mobile phones and a first aid kit.

4 **What should I bring on the trip?**

Wear comfortable walking shoes. Bring your camera and whatever you might need, such as batteries, memory cards, or film. Binoculars come in handy for seeing animals from a distance. Bring plenty of sunscreen. For longer trips, your guide will send you a packing list.

5 **Will the itinerary and other necessary information be sent to me?**

Yes, when you make your reservations simply indicate whether you would like the information via postal or electronic mail. You can also get a printout of the information at our office if you are already in San Jose.

Costa Rica's Climate

Costa Rica has only two seasons. The dry season runs from late November through April; the rainy season is the remainder of the year. Temperatures vary with elevation in different parts of the country. The amount of rainfall fluctuates in the different regions of Costa Rica. The following chart illustrates the average rainfall during our most popular touring months.

FIGURE 4.56

(Project 4F Hiking FAQ continues on the next page)

CONTENT-BASED ASSESSMENTS (MASTERY AND TRANSFER OF LEARNING)

Mastering Word Project 4F Hiking FAQ (continued)

1 Start Word. From your student files for this chapter, open the file **w04F_Hiking_FAQ**, and then **Save** the document in your **Word Chapter 4** folder as **Lastname_Firstname_4F_Hiking_FAQ** Insert the file name in the footer.

2 Format the first paragraph *Costa Rican Treks* with the **Heading 1** style, and then change the **Font Size** to **18**. Select the second paragraph, and then apply the **Heading 2** style.

3 Select the paragraph **Costa Rica's Climate**, and then apply the **Subtitle** style.

4 Change the **Style Set** to **Basic (Stylish)** and change the **Paragraph Spacing** style to **Compact**.

5 Select all the numbered paragraphs, and then apply **Bold**. For each single paragraph following a numbered paragraph, increase the indent one time.

6 Customize the ribbon to display the **Developer tab**. Display the **Templates and Add-ins** dialog box. From your student files, attach the file **w04F_Hiking_Styles**, and then include the option to **Automatically update document styles**. Remove the **Developer tab** from the ribbon.

7 Move the insertion point to the end of the document, and then press Enter. **Insert** a **Clustered Column** chart, and then beginning in cell **B1**, type the following data in the Chart in Microsoft Word worksheet, pressing Tab to move from one cell to the next:

	Caribbean	Central	Pacific
May	11	8.9	18.9
June	11.7	11.3	17.5
July	16.8	8.5	18.9
August	12.3	9.8	20.9

8 **Close** the worksheet. Change the chart title to **Average Rainfall** Display a **Primary Vertical Axis Title** with the title **Inches**

9 Change the **Chart Style** to **Style 9**, and then change the chart **Color** scheme to **Color 6**—under **Monochromatic**, in the second row, the orange color scheme. Select the chart border, and then change the chart **Shape Outline** to **Orange, Accent 2**.

10 Display the **Layout** dialog box, and then change the **Absolute Height** of the chart to **2.4"**. **Center** the chart horizontally on the page.

11 Click the **File tab**, and then click **Show All Properties**. In the **Tags** box, type **FAQ** and then in the **Subject** box, type your course name and section number. If necessary, edit the author name to display your name.

12 On the left, click **Print** to display **Print Preview**. If necessary, return to the document and make any necessary changes. **Save** your document, and then if you want to do so, present your document online to a fellow classmate. If directed by your instructor to do so, submit your paper printout, your electronic image of your document that looks like a printed document, or your original Word file. **Close** Word.

END | You have completed Project 4F

MyITLab grader

CONTENT-BASED ASSESSMENTS (MASTERY AND TRANSFER OF LEARNING)

Mastering Word Project 4G Expense Reduction

Apply 4A and 4B skills from these Objectives:

1. Apply and Modify Styles
2. Create New Styles
3. Manage Styles
4. Create a Multilevel List
5. Change the Style Set of a Document and Apply a Template
6. Insert a Chart and Enter Data into a Chart
7. Change a Chart Type
8. Format a Chart and Save a Chart as a Template

In the following Mastering Word project, you will create a memo that includes ideas for reducing expenses for Paulo Alvarez, Vice President of Finance for Costa Rican Treks. Your completed document will look similar to Figure 4.57.

PROJECT FILES

For Project 4G, you will need the following file:

w04G_Expense_Reduction

You will save your document as:

Lastname_Firstname_4G_Expense_Reduction

PROJECT RESULTS

COSTA RICAN TREKS

MEMO

TO: Maria Tornio, President; Alberto Ramos, Tour Operations Manager

FROM: Paulo Alvarez, Vice President Finance

DATE: August 12, 2018

SUBJECT: Expense Reductions

I have examined company expenses and have several recommendations for implementing cost-saving measures. Please review the attachment, which covers operating, marketing, and employee-related expenses. It is important that we make well-informed decisions in selecting vendors and continue to leverage our standing as a premiere tour operator in negotiating contracts. We should also analyze the effectiveness of our advertising strategy and determine which efforts are yielding the best results. Finally, we must determine the types of employee expenses and allowances that can be reduced with minimal effect on tour operations.

I have scheduled a meeting on August 18 at 2 p.m. in Conference Room B so that we can discuss our plan. Please let me know what other members of our team should be invited.

Lastname_Firstname_4G_Expense_Reduction

1. Employee Related Savings
   A. Mobile phone plans reduced to smaller plans with focus on emergency-only calls
   B. Reduction in vehicle allowance
2. Operations Related Cost Savings
   A. Vendor contract negotiations
   B. Research less expensive local and long-distance phone services
3. Marketing Related Cost Savings
   A. Evaluate current marketing strategies and advertisements, evaluate effectiveness, and focus on most successful ventures
   B. Utilize Web site, electronic newsletter, and other electronic formats as much as possible

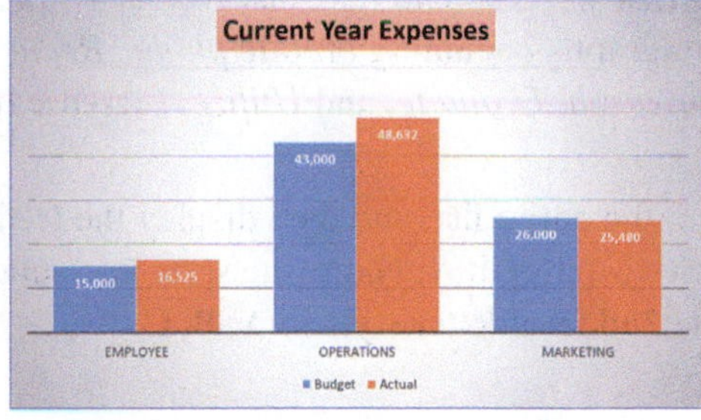

Lastname_Firstname_4G_Expense_Reduction

FIGURE 4.57

Word 2016, Windows 10, Microsoft Corporation

(Project 4G Expense Reduction continues on the next page)

Mastering Word Project 4G Expense Reduction (continued)

1 Start Word. From your student files, open the file **w04G_Expense_Reduction**, and then save the document in your **Word Chapter 4** folder as **Lastname_Firstname_4G_Expense_Reduction** Insert the file name in the footer.

2 Apply the **Title** style to the first paragraph. Apply the **Strong** style to the second paragraph *Memo*, With *Memo* selected, change the **Font Size** to **26**, and then change the text to **UPPERCASE**.

3 Select the text **TO:**—include the colon, but do not include the formatting marks—and then apply **Bold** and change the **Font Color** to **Orange, Accent 2, Darker 25%**. Save the selection as a new style with the name **Memo Heading**

4 Apply the **Memo Heading** style to the memo headings *FROM:*, *DATE:*, and *SUBJECT:*.

5 Change the **Style Set** to **Basic (Elegant)**, and then change the **Paragraph Spacing** style to **Relaxed**. On **Page 1**, beginning with the heading *TO:*, change the **Font Size** of all the remaining text in the document to **12**.

6 Select the text on **Page 2**, and then apply a **Multilevel List** with the **Current List** format **1., a., i.** For the paragraphs beginning *Mobile phone*, *Reduction*, *Vendor*, *Research*, *Evaluate*, and *Utilize*, **Increase Indent** one time.

7 Select the entire list, and then display the **Define New List Style** dialog box. Name the style **Reduction List** Change the **2nd level** letter style to **A, B, C**.

8 Press Ctrl + End to move to the end of the document. Insert a **Clustered Column** chart and type the following chart data in columns A, B, and C:

	Budget	Actual
Employee	15,000	16,525
Operations	43,000	48,632
Marketing	26,000	25,480

9 Select the chart data range **A1** through **C4**, and then **Close** the worksheet. Apply the **Style 4** chart style. Format the chart **Shape Outline** as **Blue, Accent 5**.

10 Change the **Chart Title** to **Current Year Expenses** and then apply the **Subtle Effect – Orange, Accent 2** shape style to the title. **Center** the chart horizontally on the page.

11 Click the **File tab**, and then click **Show All Properties**. In the **Tags** box, type **expenses** and then in the **Subject** box, type your course name and section number. If necessary, edit the author name to display your name.

12 On the left, click **Print** to display **Print Preview**. If necessary, return to the document and make any necessary changes. **Save** your document, and then if you want to do so, present your document online to a fellow classmate. If directed by your instructor to do so, submit your paper printout, your electronic image of your document that looks like a printed document, or your original Word file. **Close** Word.

END | You have completed Project 4G

CONTENT-BASED ASSESSMENTS (CRITICAL THINKING)

Apply a combination of the 4A and 4B skills.

GO! Fix It | Project 4H New Tours | MyITLab

GO! Make It | Project 4I Newsletter | MyITLab

GO! Solve It | Project 4J Fall Newsletter | MyITLab

GO! Solve It | Project 4K Custom Adventure

PROJECT FILES

For Project 4K, you will need the following file:

w04K_Custom_Adventure

You will save your document as:

Lastname_Firstname_4K_Custom_Adventure

Open the file **w04K_Custom_Adventures** and save it in your **Word Chapter 4** folder as **Lastname_Firstname_4K_Custom_Adventure** Change the theme, and apply existing styles to the first two and last two paragraphs of the document. Create a new style for *Choose a Region*, and apply the new style to *Choose Your Favorite Activities* and *Develop Your Skills*. Define a multilevel list style and apply the style to all lists in the document. Adjust paragraph and text formats to display the information appropriately in a one-page document. Include the file name in the footer, add appropriate document properties, and submit as directed by your instructor.

Performance Level

Performance Criteria	Exemplary: You consistently applied the relevant skills	Proficient: You sometimes, but not always, applied the relevant skills	Developing: You rarely or never applied the relevant skills
Change theme and apply existing styles	All existing styles are applied correctly using an appropriate theme.	Existing styles are applied correctly but an appropriate theme is not used.	One or more styles are not applied correctly.
Create a new style	A new style is created and applied correctly.	A new style is created but not applied correctly.	A new style is not created.
Create a multilevel list	A multilevel list style is created and applied correctly.	A multilevel list style is applied correctly but the default style is used.	A multilevel list style is not applied correctly.
Format attractively and appropriately	Document formatting is attractive and appropriate.	The document is adequately formatted but is unattractive or difficult to read.	The document is formatted inadequately.

END | You have completed Project 4K

OUTCOMES-BASED ASSESSMENTS (CRITICAL THINKING)

RUBRIC

The following outcomes-based assessments are open-ended assessments. That is, there is no specific correct result; your result will depend on your approach to the information provided. Make *Professional Quality* your goal. Use the following scoring rubric to guide you in how to approach the problem and then to evaluate how well your approach solves the problem.

The *criteria*—Software Mastery, Content, Format and Layout, and Process—represent the knowledge and skills you have gained that you can apply to solving the problem. The *levels of performance*—Professional Quality, Approaching Professional Quality, or Needs Quality Improvements—help you and your instructor evaluate your result.

	Your completed project is of Professional Quality if you:	Your completed project is Approaching Professional Quality if you:	Your completed project Needs Quality Improvements if you:
1-Software Mastery	Choose and apply the most appropriate skills, tools, and features and identify efficient methods to solve the problem.	Choose and apply some appropriate skills, tools, and features, but not in the most efficient manner.	Choose inappropriate skills, tools, or features, or are inefficient in solving the problem.
2-Content	Construct a solution that is clear and well organized, contains content that is accurate, appropriate to the audience and purpose, and is complete. Provide a solution that contains no errors of spelling, grammar, or style.	Construct a solution in which some components are unclear, poorly organized, inconsistent, or incomplete. Misjudge the needs of the audience. Have some errors in spelling, grammar, or style, but the errors do not detract from comprehension.	Construct a solution that is unclear, incomplete, or poorly organized, contains some inaccurate or inappropriate content, and contains many errors of spelling, grammar, or style. Do not solve the problem.
3-Format and Layout	Format and arrange all elements to communicate information and ideas, clarify function, illustrate relationships, and indicate relative importance.	Apply appropriate format and layout features to some elements, but not others. Overuse features, causing minor distraction.	Apply format and layout that does not communicate information or ideas clearly. Do not use format and layout features to clarify function, illustrate relationships, or indicate relative importance. Use available features excessively, causing distraction.
4-Process	Use an organized approach that integrates planning, development, self-assessment, revision, and reflection.	Demonstrate an organized approach in some areas, but not others; or, use an insufficient process of organization throughout.	Do not use an organized approach to solve the problem.

OUTCOMES-BASED ASSESSMENTS (CRITICAL THINKING)

Apply a combination of the 4A and 4B skills.

GO! Think Project 4L Training

PROJECT FILES

For Project 4L, you will need the following file:

New blank Word document

You will save your file as:

Lastname_Firstname_4L_Training

Alberto Ramos, Tour Operations Manager, wants to send a memo to all tour guides concerning upcoming training opportunities.

DATE	TRAINING	LOCATION	LENGTH
June 6	Horseback Riding	Barbille Stables	4 hours
June 17	Orienteering	Manuel Antonio Park	8 hours
June 29	Basic Coastal Sailing	Playa Hermosa	6 hours
July 7	White Water Rafting	Pacuare River	5 hours

Using this information, create a memo inviting tour guides to attend as many training sessions as possible. Include a custom multilevel list for the four training sessions. Insert a chart to compare class length. Format the entire memo in a manner that is professional and easy to read and understand. Save the document as **Lastname_Firstname_4L_Training** Insert the file name in the footer and add appropriate document properties. Submit as directed by your instructor.

END | You have completed Project 4L

GO! Think Project 4M Waterfalls Handout MyITLab

You and GO! Project 4N Cover Letter MyITLab

Using Advanced Table Features

OUTCOMES

Create a product summary by using an advanced table.

OBJECTIVES

1. Create and Apply a Custom Table Style
2. Format Cells
3. Use Advanced Table Features
4. Modify Table Properties

PROJECT 5B

OUTCOMES

Create a custom table that includes a nested table and an Excel spreadsheet.

OBJECTIVES

5. Use Freeform Drawing Tools in a Table
6. Use Nested Tables
7. Insert an Excel Spreadsheet

Kaspars Grinvalds/Shutterstock

In This Chapter

A table provides a convenient way to organize text. In addition to using the Table command, there are other methods for inserting a table in a document. For example, you can draw a table, convert existing text into a table format, or insert Excel spreadsheets. Formatting a table makes data easier to read and provides a professional appearance. You can create and apply custom table styles, merge and split cells, and change the way text displays within the cells. The Organizer feature enables you to copy custom styles from one document to another.

The projects in this chapter relate to **Chesterfield Creations**, a manufacturer of high-quality leather and fabric accessories for men and women. Products include wallets, belts, handbags, key chains, backpacks, business cases, laptop sleeves, and travel bags. The Toronto-based company distributes its products to department stores and specialty shops throughout the United States and Canada. Chesterfield Creations also has a website from which over 60 percent of its products are sold. The company pays shipping costs for both delivery and returns, and bases its operating philosophy on exceptional customer service.

PROJECT 5A

Product Summary

PROJECT ACTIVITIES

In Activities 5.01 through 5.13, you will create, modify, and format tables containing new product information to produce a document that will be distributed to the Chesterfield Creations sales team. Chesterfield Creations is introducing new products for the spring season. Charles Ferguson, Marketing Vice President, has asked you to create a document that summarizes the new product lines. Your completed document will look similar to Figure 5.1.

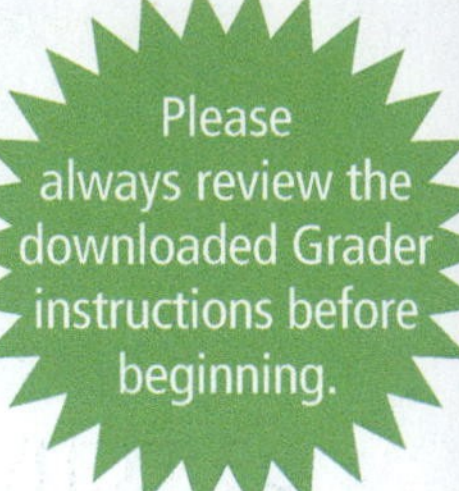

PROJECT FILES

If your instructor wants you to submit Project 5A in the MyITLab Grader system, log in to MyITLab, locate Grader Project 5A, and then download the files for this project.

For Project 5A, you will need the following files:

w05A_Product_Summary
w05A_Chesterfield_Document_Styles

You will save your file as:

Lastname_Firstname_5A_Product_Summary

PROJECT RESULTS

Chesterfield Creations

New Spring Product Summary

Chesterfield Creations is proud to introduce new products to our line of leather and fabric-covered accessories for men and women for spring. These products were carefully designed to meet the needs of our customers, who crave the best in quality, durability, functionality, and aesthetics.

We are pleased to announce the following additions to our Illumina Collection. These fabric-covered accessories are specifically designed for the woman who desires to match her existing Illumina products.

1: Illumina Collection

Item	Description	Price
Checkbook Cover	This cover will hold a standard checkbook or pocket calendar, and includes a place for a pen.	$ 15
Cosmetic Case	This case has a plastic lining and zippered top. It fits easily into a larger purse.	$ 25
Eyeglass Case	Soft on the outside, this sturdy case is lined with a soft, non-scratch fabric.	$ 25
Jewelry Box	Designed for travel, this compact box contains a small mirror and individual compartments to store your jewelry securely.	$ 35
Cell Phone Case	While small enough to fit in a purse, you can attach this case to your belt or purse with the elegant silver clip.	$ 40
	Illumina Accessories Discounted Total Price	**$ 119**

For business executive, we have added several items to our Momentum Collection. These leather accessories offer the same durability and quality as our Momentum briefcases and travel bags.

2: Momentum Collection

Item	Description	Price
Key Case	Special features of this case include eight key hooks, a double snap closure, a valet ring, and a small pocket for receipts or other small papers.	$ 35
Tablet Case	Keep your tablet safe with the Velcro closure. You can carry the case in your briefcase, clip it on to your pants or pocket, or slip it through a belt loop.	$ 40
Passport Wallet	Slots for six credit cards, a currency pocket, and two clear sleeves to contain your ID and passport are included in this distinctive wallet.	$ 45
	Momentum Accessories Discounted Total Price	**$ 102**

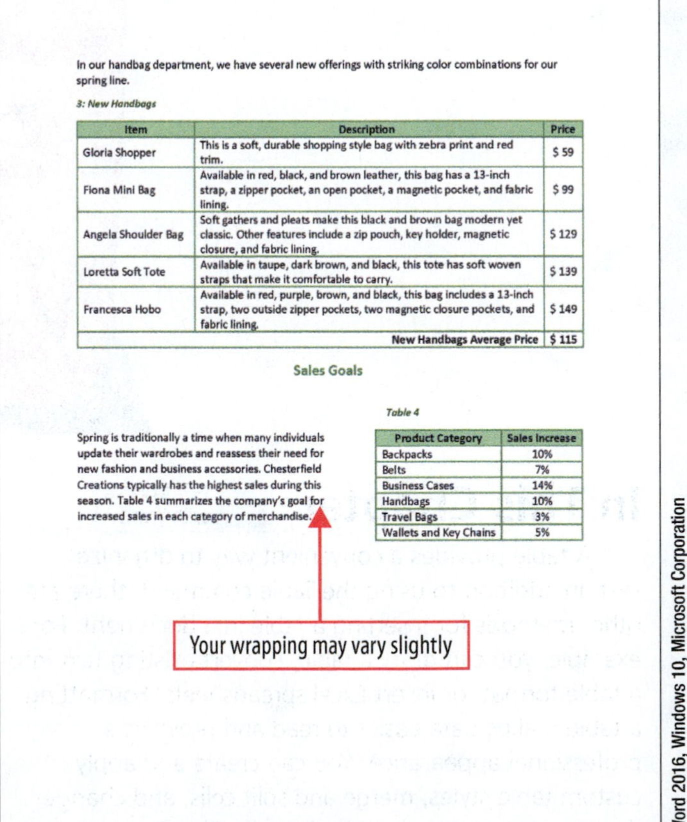

In our handbag department, we have several new offerings with striking color combinations for our spring line.

3: New Handbags

Item	Description	Price
Gloria Shopper	This is a soft, durable shopping style bag with zebra print and red trim.	$ 59
Fiona Mini Bag	Available in red, black, and brown leather, this bag has a 13-inch strap, a zipper pocket, an open pocket, a magnetic pocket, and fabric lining.	$ 99
Angela Shoulder Bag	Soft gathers and pleats make this black and brown bag modern yet classic. Other features include a zip pouch, key holder, magnetic closure, and fabric lining.	$ 129
Loretta Soft Tote	Available in taupe, dark brown, and black, this tote has soft woven straps that make it comfortable to carry.	$ 139
Francesca Hobo	Available in red, purple, brown, and black, this bag includes a 13-inch strap, two outside zipper pockets, two magnetic closure pockets, and fabric lining.	$ 149
	New Handbags Average Price	**$ 115**

Sales Goals

Spring is traditionally a time when many individuals update their wardrobes and reassess their need for new fashion and business accessories. Chesterfield Creations typically has the highest sales during this season. Table 4 summarizes the company's goal for increased sales in each category of merchandise.

Table 4

Product Category	Sales Increase
Backpacks	10%
Belts	7%
Business Cases	14%
Handbags	10%
Travel Bags	3%
Wallets and Key Chains	5%

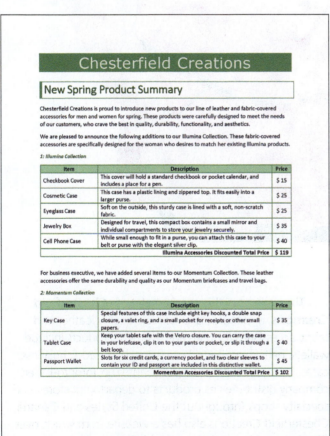

FIGURE 5.1 Project 5A Product Summary

Objective 1 Create and Apply a Custom Table Style

GO! Learn How Video W5-1

A ***style*** is a group of formatting commands—such as font, font size, and font color—that can be applied with a single command. Styles in an existing document can be copied to another document.

You can create a ***table style*** and apply it any table you create to give your tables a consistent format. A table style can include formatting for the entire table and also for specific table elements such as rows and columns. You can use the ***Split Table*** feature to divide an existing table into two tables in which the selected row—where the insertion point is located—becomes the first row of the second table.

Activity 5.01 | Copy a Style from a Template to a Document by Using the Style Organizer

1.1.2 Expert

Chesterfield Creations has a Word template in which several common document styles used in their corporate communications are stored, and employees routinely copy styles from this template to create new corporate documents.

To copy a style from another document or from a template, use the ***Organizer***—a dialog box where you can modify a document by copying styles stored in another document or template.

ALERT! **To submit as an autograded project, log into MyITLab, download the files for this project, and begin with those files instead of a new blank document.**

1. Start Word, on the left click **Open Other Documents**, click **Browse**, and then in the **Open** dialog box, navigate to the student data files that accompany this chapter. Locate and open the file **w05A_Product_Summary**. If necessary, display the rulers and formatting marks. If any words are flagged as spelling or grammar errors, right-click, and then click **Ignore All**.
2. Click the **File tab**, on the left click **Save As**, click **Browse** and then in the **Save As** dialog box, navigate to the location where you are saving your files for this chapter. Create a new folder named **Word Chapter 5** Save the document as **Lastname_Firstname_5A_Product_Summary** and then using the techniques you have practiced, insert the **File Name** in the footer.
3. Press Ctrl + Home to be sure you are at the top of the document. On the **Home tab**, in the **Styles group**, *point to* but do not click, **Heading 1**. Notice that Live Preview displays the first paragraph of the document in the default blue text and font size for the Heading 1 style.
4. *Point to*, but do not click, the **Title** style. Notice that Live Preview displays the first paragraph of the document in the default black text and font size for the Title style.
5. On the **Home tab**, in the **Styles group**, click the **Dialog Box Launcher**, and then at the bottom of the dialog box, click the third button, **Manage Styles**.
6. In the **Manage Styles** dialog box, in the lower left corner, click **Import/Export** to display the **Organizer** dialog box. Compare your screen with Figure 5.2.

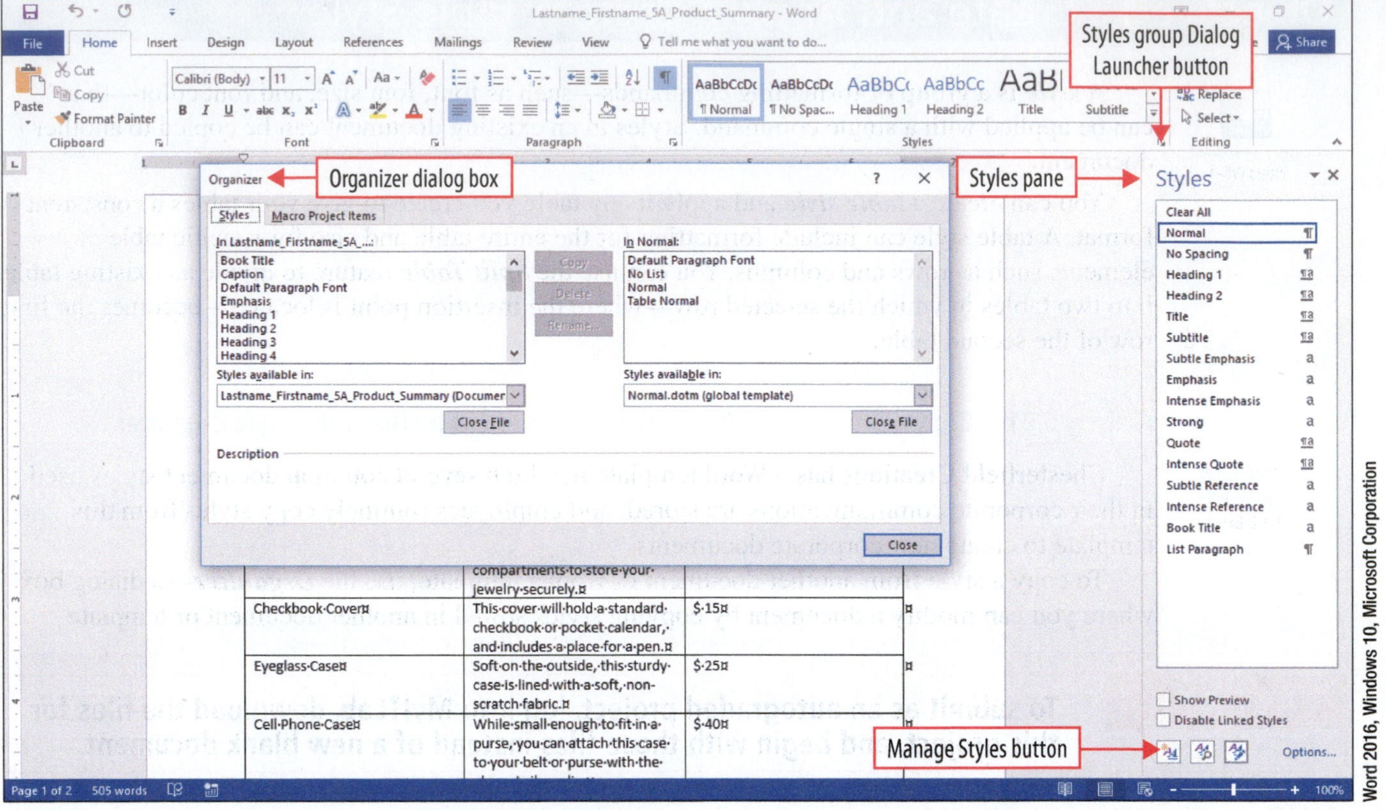

Word 2016, Windows 10, Microsoft Corporation

FIGURE 5.2

7 On the **left side** of the **Organizer** dialog box, in the **Styles available in:** box, be sure your *Lastname_Firstname_5A_Product_Summary (Document)* displays.

8 On the right side of the dialog box, under the **Styles available in:** box, click **Close File**, and notice that the button changes to an **Open File** button.

This action closes the default template from which you can copy styles and displays the Open File command so that you can select a different template or document from which you can copy styles into your displayed document.

9 Click **Open File**, navigate to your student data files, click one time to select the file **w05A_Chesterfield_Document_Styles**, and then in the lower right corner, click **Open**. Compare your screen with Figure 5.3.

This action places the styles contained in the *w05A_Chesterfield_Document_Styles (Template)* into the Organizer so that you can use the various styles in your 5A_Product_Summary document.

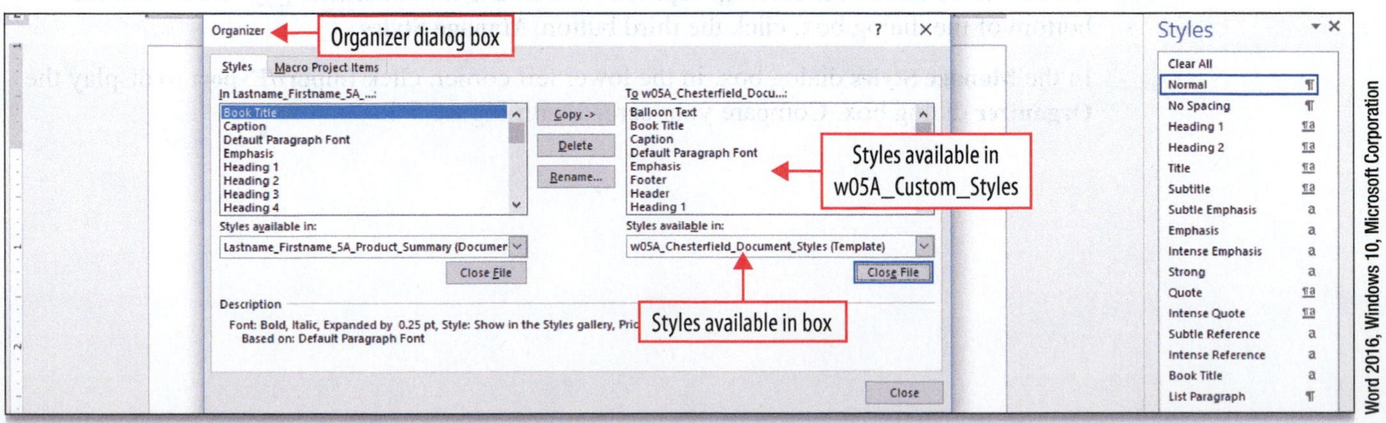

FIGURE 5.3

10 In the upper right portion of the dialog box, in the **To w05A_Chesterfield_Document_Styles** box, scroll down, and then click **Heading 2**. Hold down Ctrl, scroll down, and then click **Title**.

Two styles are selected. Use this technique to select one or more styles to copy to another document.

11 In the center of the **Organizer** dialog box, locate the **Copy** button, and notice that it displays a left-pointing arrow. With the two styles selected on the left, click **Copy**. When a message displays asking if you want to overwrite the existing style entry Heading 2, click **Yes to All**.

This action copies the Heading 2 and Title styles from the w05A_Chesterfield_Document_Styles template file to your 5A_Product_Summary document so that you will be able to use these styles in your document.

12 In the lower right corner, click **Close** to close the dialog box. With your **Lastname_Firstname_5A_Product_Summary** document displayed, if necessary, on the right, **Close** the **Styles** pane.

13 Be sure your insertion point is at the top of the document—to the left of the title *Chesterfield Creations*. On the **Home tab**, in the **Styles group**, click the More button and then point to but do not click, **Title**. Compare your screen with Figure 5.4.

Live Preview displays how the document title would look if the new Title style is applied.

The new Heading 2 and Title styles are copied to your *Lastname_Firstname_5A_Product_Summary* document. These two styles, both of which display green formatting, are now available to you in this document to apply.

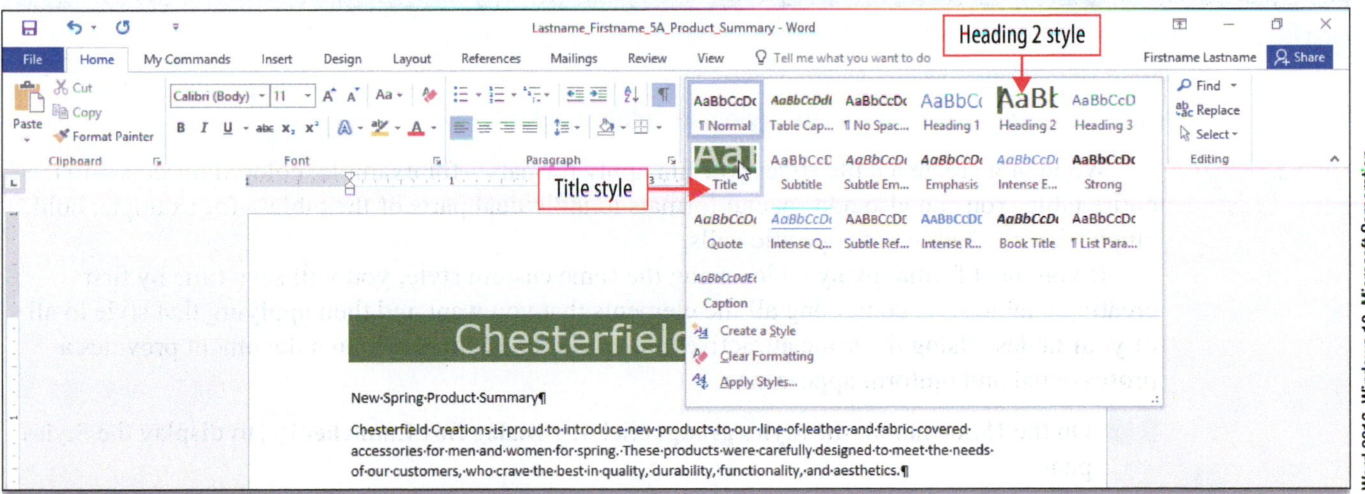

FIGURE 5.4

14 Select the first paragraph of the document—the company name *Chesterfield Creations*. On the **Home tab**, in the **Styles group**, click **Title**.

15 Select the second paragraph that begins *New Spring*, and then in the **Styles group**, click **Heading 2**. Click anywhere in the third paragraph, and then compare your screen with Figure 5.5.

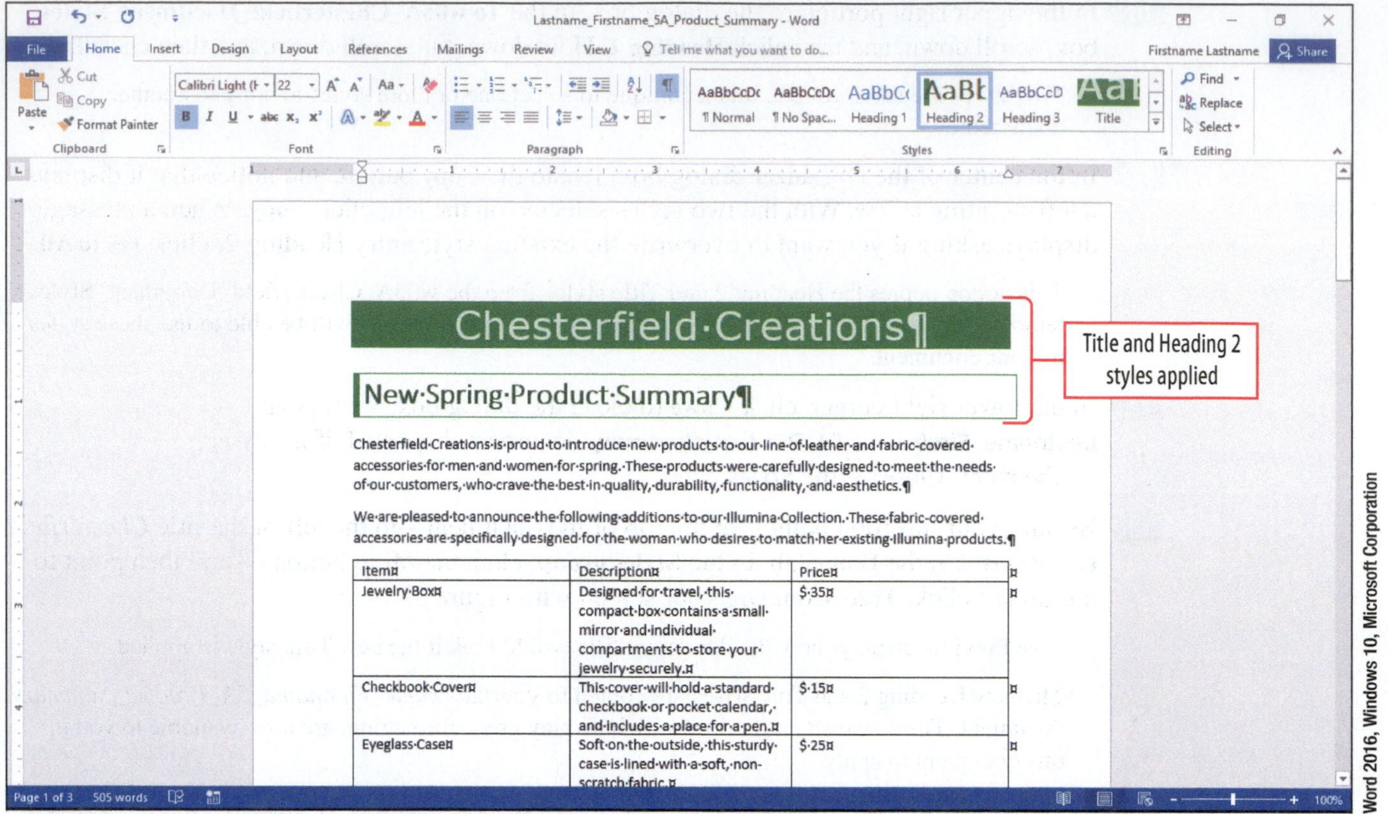

FIGURE 5.5

Activity 5.02 | Creating a Table Style and Splitting a Table

3.2.5

When you create a table style, you can apply formats—for example, colored borders—to the entire table. You can also add special formats to individual parts of the table—for example, bold emphasis and shading—to specific cells.

If you must format many tables using the same custom style, you will save time by first creating a table style containing all the elements that you want and then applying that style to all of your tables. Using the same attractive table style for all the tables in a document provides a professional and uniform appearance.

1. On the **Home tab**, in the **Styles group**, click the **Dialog Box Launcher** to display the **Styles** pane.

2. At the bottom of the **Styles** pane, click the first button, **New Style**. In the **Create New Style from Formatting** dialog box, under **Properties**, in the **Name** box, type **Chesterfield Creations** Click the **Style type arrow**, and then click **Table**.

   A sample table displays in the preview area. Use the Create New Style from Formatting dialog box to create a new style to apply a set of formats to a table.

3. Under **Formatting**, click the **Border button arrow**, and then click **All Borders**. Click the **Line Weight arrow**, and then click **1 pt**. Click the **Border Color arrow**, and then under **Theme Colors**, in the last column, click the fifth color—**Green, Accent 6, Darker 25%**. Compare your screen with Figure 5.6.

   Under *Formatting*, in the *Apply formatting to* box, the formatting will be applied to the whole table. By default, at the bottom of the dialog box, Word indicates that this style is available only in this document.

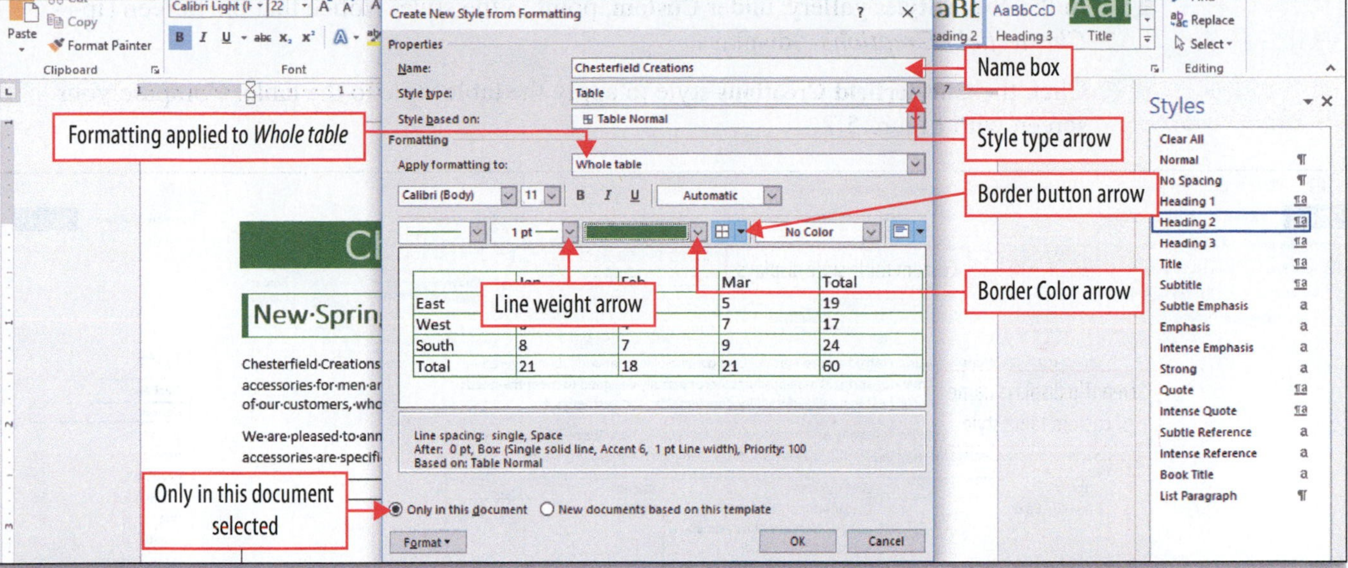

FIGURE 5.6

Word 2016, Windows 10, Microsoft Corporation

4 Click **OK** to close the dialog box, and then **Close** the **Styles** pane.

5 Scroll down as necessary to view the first table in your document. In the seventh row of the first table, click to position the insertion point in the first cell, which contains the text *Item*. On the ribbon, click the **Table Tools Layout tab**, and then in the **Merge group**, click **Split Table**.

The original table splits into two separate tables and a new blank paragraph displays above the second table.

6 If necessary, click to position the insertion point in the blank paragraph above the second table, and then press Enter. Type **For the business executive, we have added several items to our Momentum Collection. These leather accessories offer the same durability and quality as our Momentum briefcases and travel bags.**

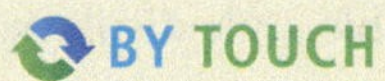
BY TOUCH

Tap in the blank paragraph, and then on the taskbar, tap the Touch Keyboard button. Tap the appropriate keys to type the text, and then on the Touch Keyboard, tap the X button.

7 **Save** your document.

***More* Knowledge**

Creating a Custom Table Style from the Table Styles Gallery

If the insertion point is in an existing table, you can create a custom table style from the Table Styles gallery. Under Table Tools, on the Design tab, in the Table Styles group, click More, and then click New Table Style to display the Create New Style from Formatting dialog box.

Activity 5.03 | Applying and Modifying a Table Style

3.1.4

You can apply a table style to an existing table. Additionally, you can modify an existing style or make formatting changes after a style has been applied to a table.

1 Scroll as necessary to view the first table in the document, and then click in the top left cell, which contains the text *Item*.

You can apply a table style when the insertion point is positioned anywhere within a table.

2 Under **Table Tools**, on the **Design tab**, in the **Table Styles group**, click **More**.

3 In the **Table Styles** gallery, under **Custom**, point to the style. Notice that the ScreenTip—*Chesterfield Creations*—displays.

4 Click the **Chesterfield Creations** style to apply the table style to the table. Compare your screen with Figure 5.7.

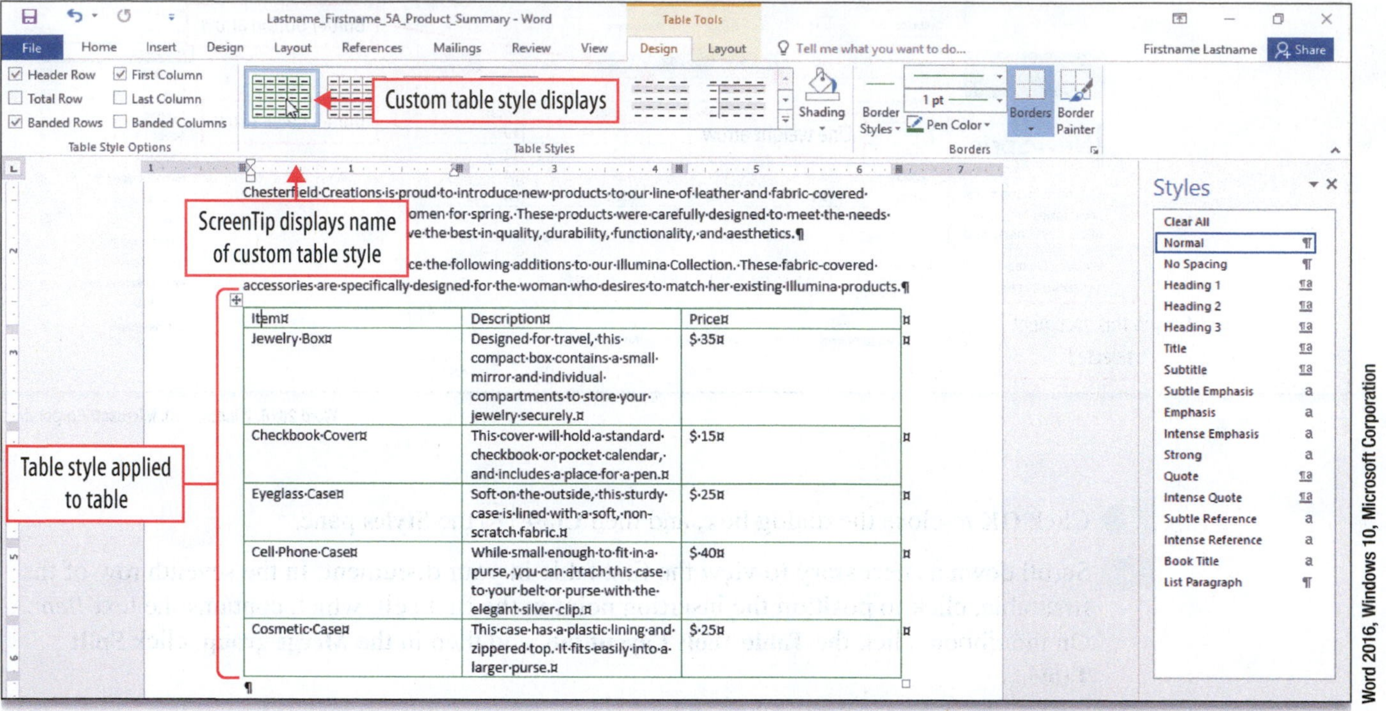

FIGURE 5.7

5 Scroll as necessary, and then click to position the insertion point anywhere in the second table of the document—the table spans two pages. Under **Table Tools**, on the **Design tab**, in the **Table Styles group**, click **More**, and then under **Custom**, click the **Chesterfield Creations** style.

On the ribbon, in the Table Styles group, at the left, the *Chesterfield Creations* table style displays.

6 On the ribbon, in the **Table Styles** gallery, right-click the **Chesterfield Creations** style. A shortcut menu displays commands for working with styles as described in the table in Figure 5.8.

TABLE STYLE COMMANDS

COMMAND	DESCRIPTION
Apply (and Clear Formatting)	Table style applied; text formatting reverts to Normal style.
Apply and Maintain Formatting	Table style applied, including text formatting.
New Table Style	Create a new, custom table style.
Modify Table Style	Edit the table style.
Delete Table Style	Remove the style from the Table Styles gallery.
Set as Default	Style is used as the default for all tables created in the document.
Add Gallery to Quick Access Toolbar	Table Styles gallery is added to the Quick Access Toolbar.

FIGURE 5.8

7 On the shortcut menu, click **Modify Table Style**. In the **Modify Style** dialog box, under **Formatting**, click the **Apply formatting to arrow**, and then click **Header row**.

You can apply formatting to specific table elements. In the *Chesterfield Creations* style, you want to change formats that apply only to the ***header row***—the first row of a table containing column titles.

8 Click **Bold** [B], and then click the **Fill Color arrow** [No Color]. Under **Theme Colors**, in the last column, click the fourth color—**Green, Accent 6, Lighter 40%**. Compare your screen with Figure 5.9.

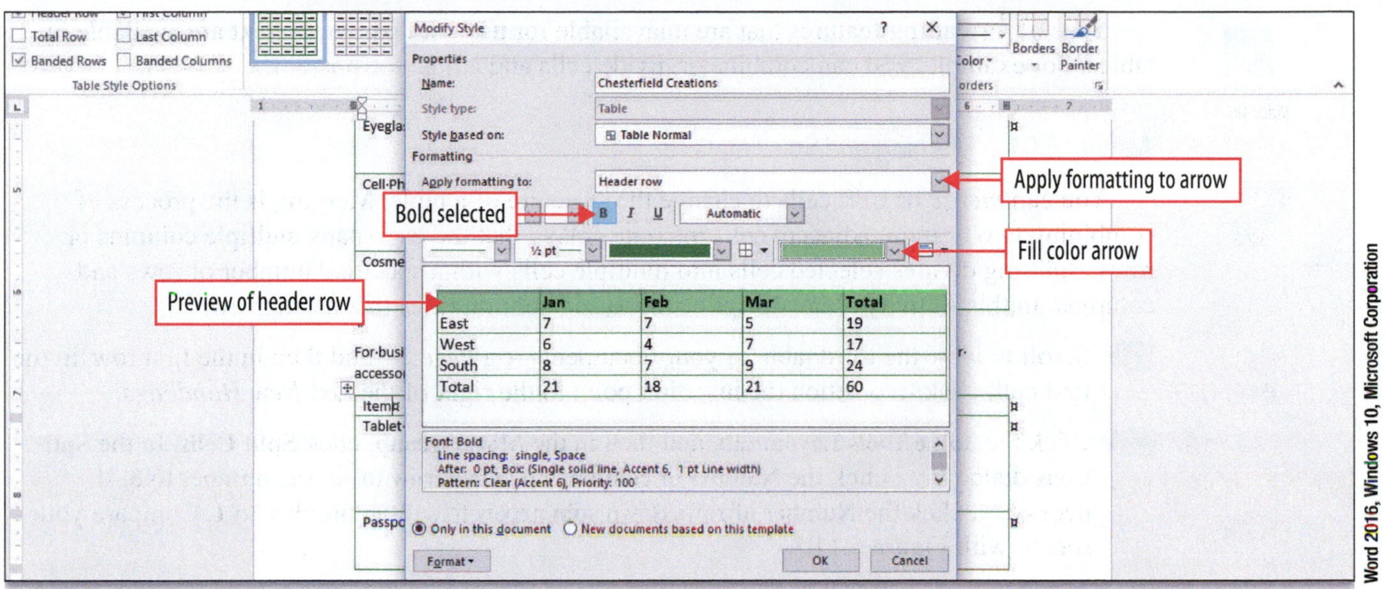

FIGURE 5.9

9 Click **OK** to close the dialog box, and then press Ctrl + Home. If necessary, **Close** [X] the **Styles** pane. On the **View tab**, in the **Zoom group**, click **Multiple Pages**. Compare your screen with Figure 5.10.

The additional formatting is applied to the header rows in the first and second tables.

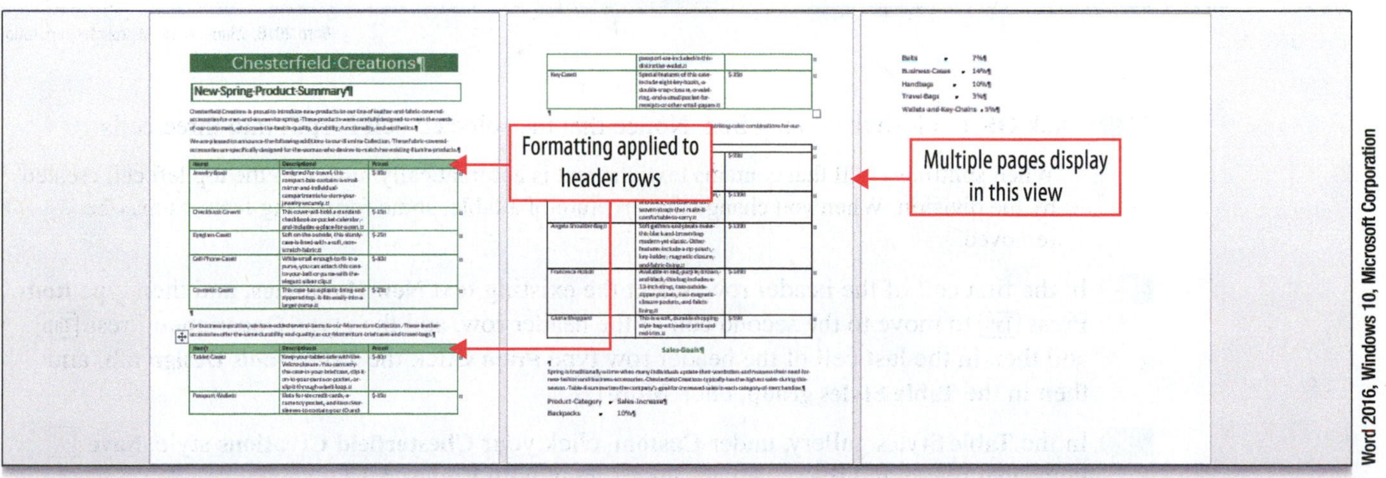

FIGURE 5.10

10 On the **View tab**, in the **Zoom group**, click **100%**, and then **Save** your document.

More Knowledge **Repeating Header Rows**

When a table is large enough to cause part of the table to display on a second page, the header row of the table can be repeated on the second page. With the insertion point in the header row, on the Layout tab, in the Table group, click the Properties button. In the Table Properties dialog box, click the Row tab, and then under Options, click *Repeat as header row at the top of each page*.

Objective 2 Format Cells

GO! Learn How Video W5-2

Special formatting features that are unavailable for use with paragraph text are available in tables. For example, you can combine or divide cells and adjust the positioning of text.

Activity 5.04 | Merging and Splitting Cells

3.2.3

You can ***merge*** or ***split*** cells to change the structure of a table. Merging is the process of combining two or more adjacent cells into one cell so that the text spans multiple columns or rows. Splitting divides selected cells into multiple cells with a specified number of rows and columns. In this Activity, you will split cells to add column titles to a header row.

1. Scroll to view the third table of your document—on **Page 2**—and then in the first row, in the first cell, click to position the insertion point to the right of the text *New Handbags*.

2. Click the **Table Tools Layout tab**, and then in the **Merge group**, click **Split Cells**. In the **Split Cells** dialog box, click the **Number of columns up spin arrow** to set the number to **3**. If necessary, click the **Number of rows down spin arrow** to set the number to **1**. Compare your screen with Figure 5.11.

   Because you want this header row to match the header rows in the other two product tables, you will split the cell into multiple cells and add column titles.

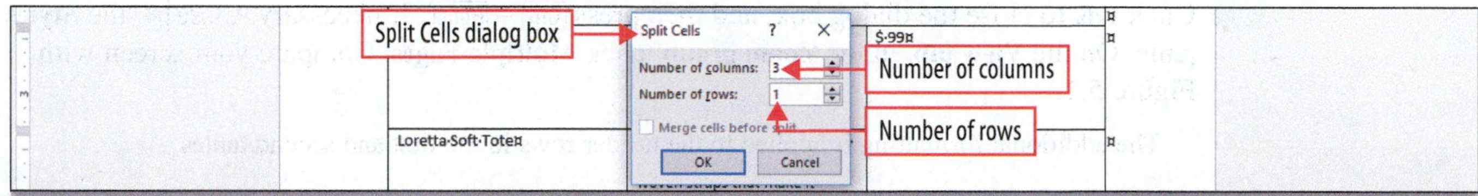

FIGURE 5.11

Word 2016, Windows 10, Microsoft Corporation

3. Click **OK** to close the dialog box. Notice that the selected cell is split into three cells.

   When splitting a cell that contains text, the text is automatically moved to the top left cell created by the division. When you change the structure of a table, some formatting features may be removed.

4. In the first cell of the header row, select the existing text **New Handbags**, and then type **Item** Press Tab to move to the second cell of the header row, and then type **Description** Press Tab, and then in the last cell of the header row type **Price** Click the **Table Tools Design tab**, and then in the **Table Styles group**, click **More**.

5. In the **Table Styles** gallery, under **Custom**, click your **Chesterfield Creations** style. **Save** your document, and then compare your screen with Figure 5.12.

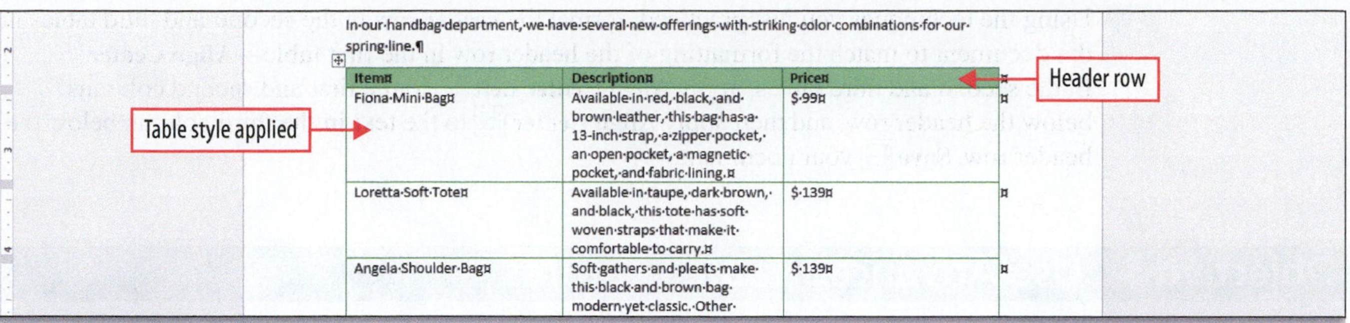

FIGURE 5.12

Word 2016, Windows 10, Microsoft Corporation

> ***More Knowledge*** **Splitting Multiple Cells**
>
> You can modify the number of rows or columns for any group of adjacent cells in a table. Select the cells you want to modify, and then on the Layout tab, in the Merge group, click the Split Cells button. In the Split Cells dialog box, change the number of columns or rows to the desired values.

Activity 5.05 | Positioning Text Within Cells

Within a cell, you can align text horizontally—left, center, or right. Within a cell, you can also align text vertically—top, center, or bottom. The default setting is to align text at the top left of a cell. Changing cell alignments often makes a table easier to read and look more symmetrical.

1. Press Ctrl + Home to move to the top **Page 1**. In the first table, in the left margin, point to the header row to display the pointer, and then click one time to select the header row.

2. Click the **Table Tools Layout tab**, and then in the **Alignment group**, click **Align Center**.

   All text in the header row is centered horizontally and vertically within the cell.

3. Below the header row, drag to select all the cells in the first and second columns, and then in the **Alignment group**, click **Align Center Left**.

   The selected text is left aligned and centered vertically within the cells.

4. Below the header row, drag to select all the cells in the third column, and then in the **Alignment group**, click **Align Center**. Click anywhere in the table to deselect the text, and then compare your screen with Figure 5.13.

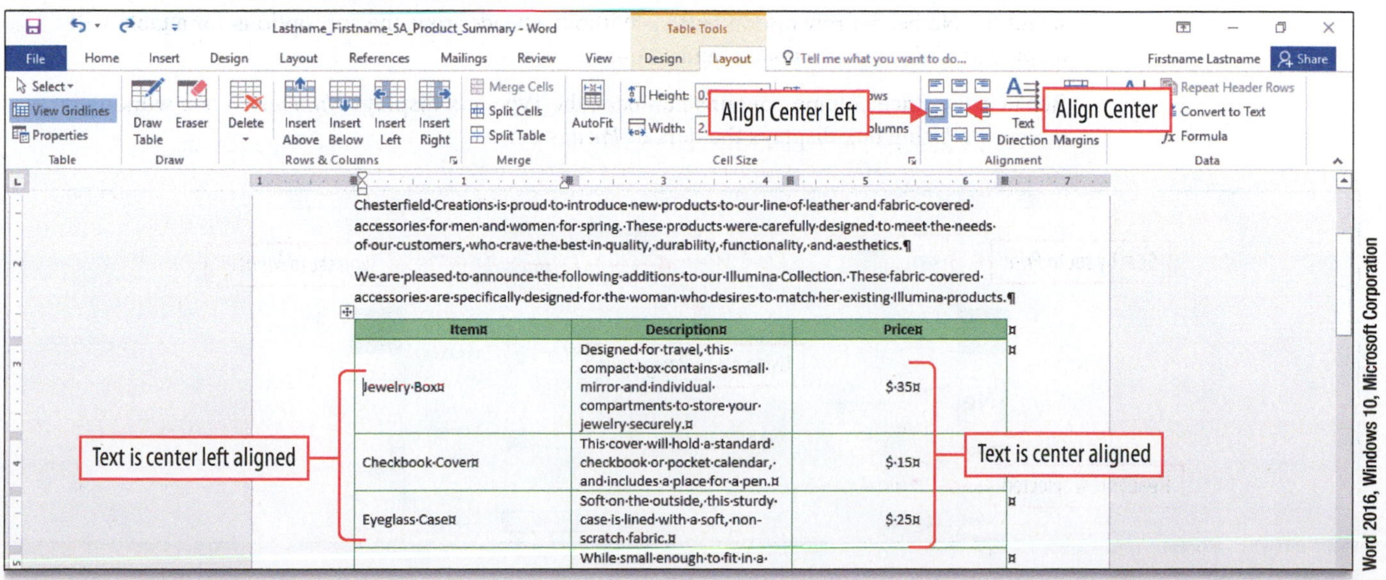

Word 2016, Windows 10, Microsoft Corporation

FIGURE 5.13

5 Using the techniques you just practiced, format the **header row** in the second and third tables in the document to match the formatting of the header row in the first table—**Align Center**. In the second and third tables, apply **Align Center Left** to the first and second columns below the header row, and then apply **Align Center** to the text in the third column below the header row. **Save** your document.

Objective 3 Use Advanced Table Features

GO! Learn How Video W5-3

Word tables have some capabilities similar to those in an Excel spreadsheet; for example, sorting data and performing simple calculations. Additionally, you can convert existing text to a table format and resize tables in several ways.

Activity 5.06 | Sorting Tables by Category

5.06

In this Activity, you will sort the data in the three product tables by price and item to make it easier for the sales team to reference specific items.

1 Press Ctrl + Home to display **Page 1**, and then click to position the insertion point anywhere in the first table.

Recall that data in a table can be sorted in ascending order—from the smallest to the largest number or alphabetically from A to Z; or, a table can be sorted in descending order—from the largest to the smallest number or alphabetically from Z to A. Regardless of the columns that are selected in the sort, all cells in each row are moved to keep the data intact.

2 On the **Table Tools Layout tab**, in the **Data group**, click **Sort**.

The Sort dialog box displays, in which you can sort alphabetically, by number, or by date. The Sort feature can be applied to entire tables, to selected data within tables, to paragraphs, or to body text that is separated by characters such as tabs or commas. You can sort information using a maximum of three columns.

3 In the **Sort** dialog box, under **Sort by**, click the **Sort by arrow**. Notice that your three headings display on the list, and then click **Price**. Compare your screen with Figure 5.14.

This action will sort the data in the table by the product's price. When a table has a header row, Word displays each column's header text in the *Sort by* list. By default, the Header row option is selected at the bottom left of the Sort dialog box. If a table does not have a header row, you can select the No header row option button. Without a header row, the sort options for a table will display as *Column 1*, *Column 2*, and so on.

Because the Price column contains numbers, the Type box displays *Number*. When working in tables, the Using box displays the default *Paragraphs*.

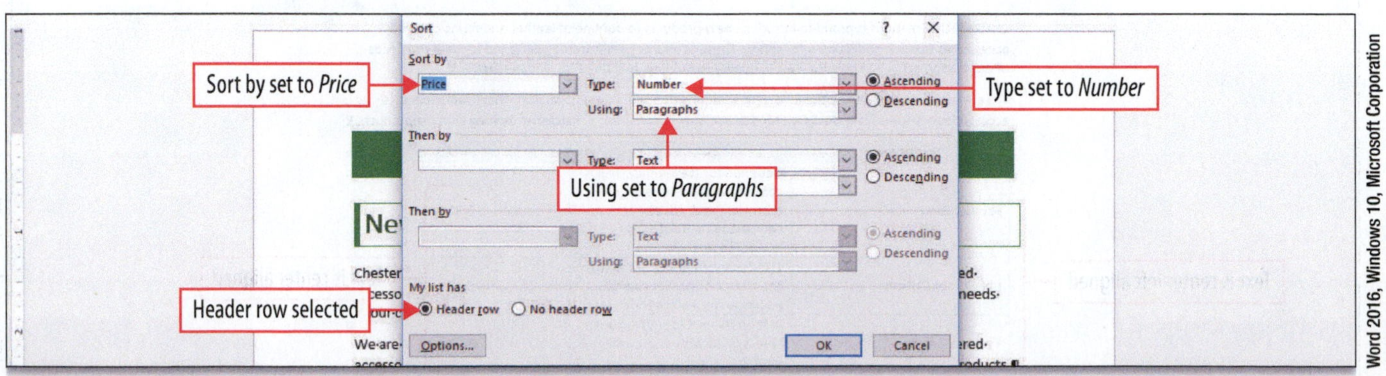

FIGURE 5.14

4 Under **Then by**, click the first **Then by arrow**, and then click **Item**. Notice that the **Type** box displays *Text*.

It is important to designate the columns in the order that you want them sorted. Word will first sort the data by price in ascending order. If two or more items have the same price, Word will arrange those items in alphabetical order by Item name.

5 Click **OK** to close the dialog box and notice that the two items with the same price of **$25** are listed in alphabetical order by Item name. Click anywhere outside of the table to deselect the table, and then compare your screen with Figure 5.15.

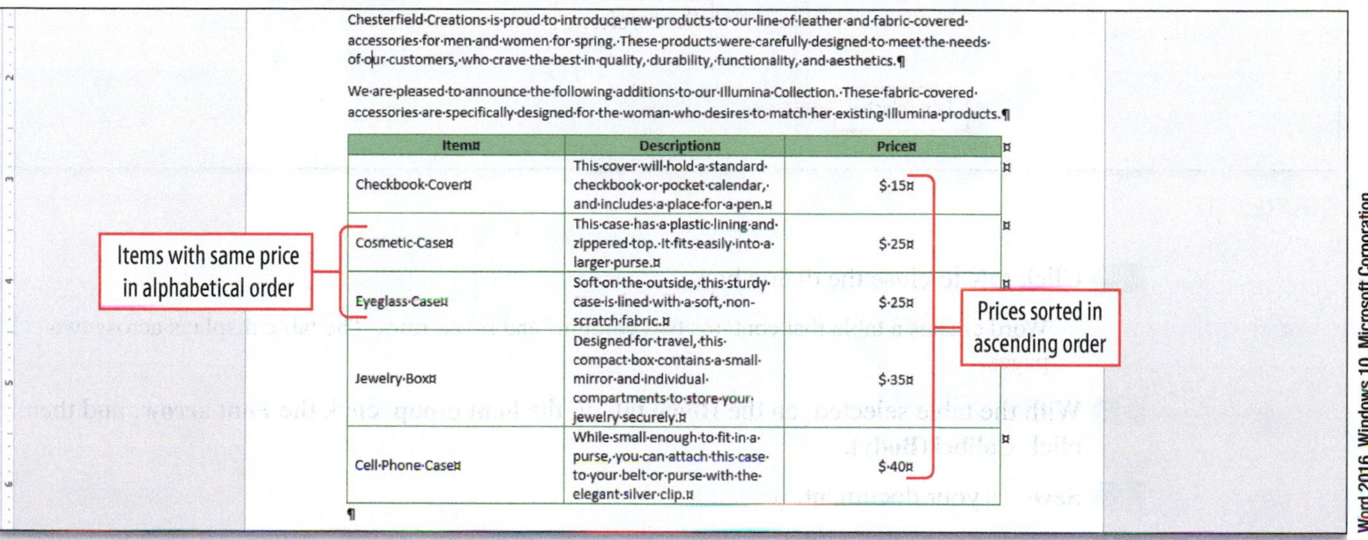

Item	Description	Price
Checkbook Cover	This cover will hold a standard checkbook or pocket calendar, and includes a place for a pen.	$15
Cosmetic Case	This case has a plastic lining and zippered top. It fits easily into a larger purse.	$25
Eyeglass Case	Soft on the outside, this sturdy case is lined with a soft, non-scratch fabric.	$25
Jewelry Box	Designed for travel, this compact box contains a small mirror and individual compartments to store your jewelry securely.	$35
Cell Phone Case	While small enough to fit in a purse, you can attach this case to your belt or purse with the elegant silver clip.	$40

FIGURE 5.15

6 Scroll to view the bottom of **Page 1**, and then click to position the insertion point anywhere in the second table of the document. On the **Table Tools Layout tab**, in the **Data group**, click **Sort**.

The Sort by box displays *Price*, and the Then by box displays *Item*. In the Sort dialog box, Word retains the last sort options used in a document.

7 Click **OK**, and notice that the table is sorted similarly to the first table.

8 On **Page 2**, click to position the insertion point anywhere in the third table of the document. On the **Table Tools Layout tab**, click **Sort**, and then click **OK**. Notice that the table is sorted in the same manner as the previous tables.

9 **Save** your document.

Activity 5.07 | Converting Text to a Table and Modifying Fonts Within a Table

MOS 3.1.1

You can convert existing text, such as a list of information, to a table. In this Activity, you will convert text to a table and then change the font of the table text.

1 Scroll to view the bottom of **Page 2** and the top of **Page 3**.

2 Beginning with the paragraph that begins *Product Category*, drag down to select all the remaining text in the document. Be sure to include the text on *Page 3*—you should have seven paragraphs selected.

3 On the **Insert tab**, in the **Tables group**, click **Table**, and then at the bottom click **Convert Text to Table** to display the **Convert Text to Table** dialog box. Compare your screen with Figure 5.16.

Word uses characters such as tabs, commas, or hyphens to determine the number of columns. The selected text consists of seven paragraphs—or rows—with each paragraph containing a single tab.

By default, Word uses the tab formatting mark to separate each paragraph into two parts—forming the two columns of the table. Under the *Separate text at* section of the dialog box, you can define the character Word uses to separate the text into columns. You can also change the number of columns or rows, based on the text you are converting.

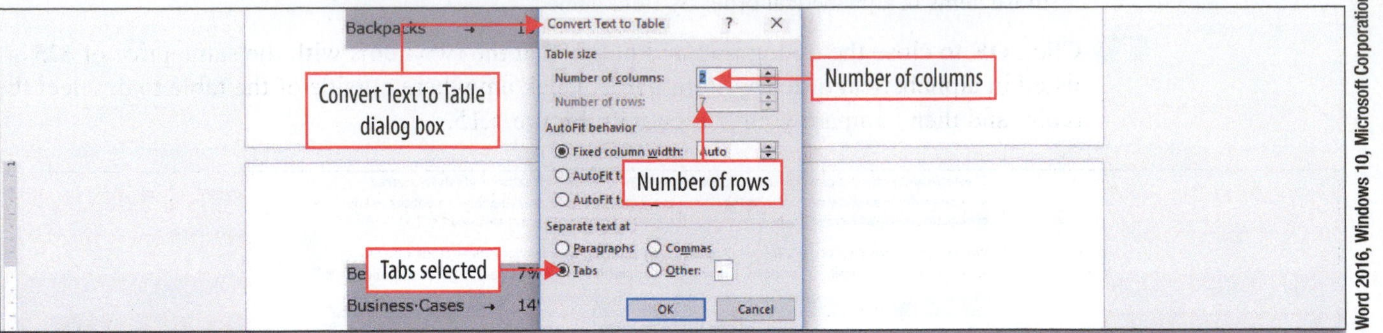

FIGURE 5.16

4 Click **OK** to close the dialog box.

Word creates a table that contains two columns and seven rows. The table displays across two pages.

5 With the table selected, on the **Home tab**, in the **Font group**, click the **Font arrow**, and then click **Calibri (Body)**.

6 **Save** your document.

***More* Knowledge** **Converting a Table to Text**

To convert an existing table to text, on the Layout tab, in the Data group, click the Convert to Text button, and then in the Convert Table to Text dialog box, select the type of text separator you want to use.

Activity 5.08 | Setting Table Column Widths and Resizing Columns by Using AutoFit

3.2.4

Word provides several methods for resizing a table. The ***AutoFit*** command automatically adjusts column widths or the width of the entire table. The ***AutoFit Contents*** command resizes the column widths to accommodate the maximum field size. You can change a row height or column width by dragging a border or by designating specific width and height settings. In this Activity, you will modify column widths.

1 Press Ctrl + Home to move to the top of **Page 1**. In the first table in the document, point to the top border of the first column—*Item*—and when the ⬇ pointer displays, click one time to select the entire column.

2 On the **Table Tools Layout tab**, in the **Cell Size group**, click in the **Width** box to select the existing text, type **1.5"** and then press Enter. Using the same technique, select the second column in the table—**Description**—and then in the **Cell Size group**, click in the **Width** box to select the existing text. Type **4.5"** and then press Enter.

3 Select the last column in the table—**Price**—and then using the techniques you just practiced, set the width of the column to **0.5"** and compare your screen with Figure 5.17.

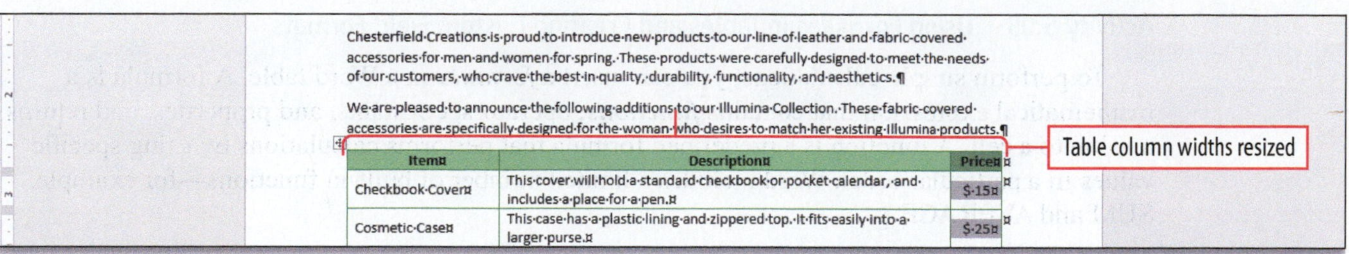

FIGURE 5.17 Word 2016, Windows 10, Microsoft Corporation

4 In the second and third tables of the document, using the techniques you just practiced, change the **Width** of the first column to **1.5"** and the **Width** of the second column to **4.5"** and the **Width** of the third column to **0.5"**

All product tables now have the same structure—the first, second, and third column widths in all tables are identical.

ANOTHER WAY Use the spin box arrows to change the Width or Height.

5 At the bottom of **Page 1**, below the second table, click to position the insertion point to the left of the paragraph that begins *In our handbag department*, and then press Ctrl + Enter to insert a page break.

6 At the bottom of **Page 2**, click to position your insertion point anywhere in the last table of the document—the table you created by converting text to a table. On the **Table Tools Layout tab**, in the **Cell Size group**, click **AutoFit**, and then click **AutoFit Contents**. Compare your screen with Figure 5.18.

The AutoFit Contents command resizes a table by changing the column widths to fit the existing data. In this table, the widths of both columns were decreased.

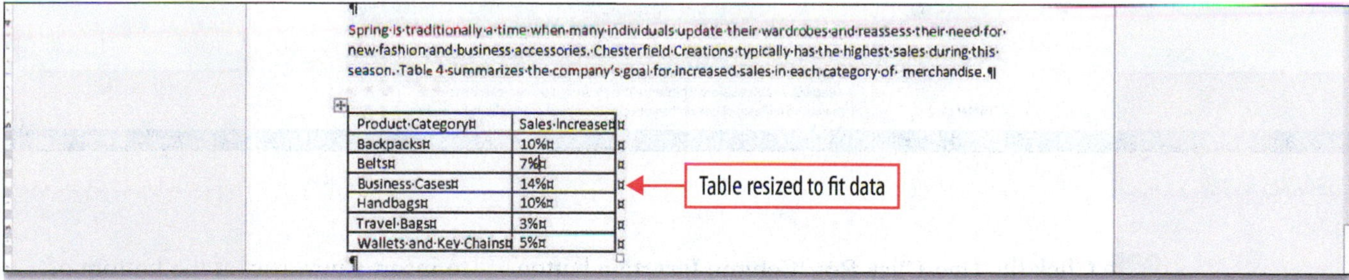

FIGURE 5.18 Word 2016, Windows 10, Microsoft Corporation

7 Click to position the insertion point anywhere in the table, and then on the **Table Tools Design tab**, in the **Table Styles group**, click **More**. In the **Table Styles** gallery, under **Custom**, click **Chesterfield Creations**.

8 Select the **header row**, and then on the **Table Tools Layout tab**, in the **Alignment group**, click **Align Center**. Select the remaining cells in the second column, and then click **Align Center**. **Save** your changes.

More Knowledge

Using the Sizing Handle

At the lower right of a table, drag the sizing handle to change the entire table to the desired size.

Activity 5.09 | Using Formulas in Tables and Creating Custom Field Formats

To perform simple calculations, you can insert a ***formula*** in a Word table. A formula is a mathematical expression that contains ***functions***, operators, constants, and properties, and returns a value to a cell. A function is a predefined formula that performs calculations by using specific values in a particular order. Word includes a limited number of built-in functions—for example, SUM and AVERAGE.

1 Press Ctrl + Home to move to the top of **Page 1**, scroll as necessary to view all of the first table, and then click anywhere in the first table of the document. Point to the bottom left corner of the table to display the **One-Click Row/Column Insertion** button. Compare your screen with Figure 5.19.

The One-Click Row/Column Insertion button provides a quick method to insert a row or column in a table.

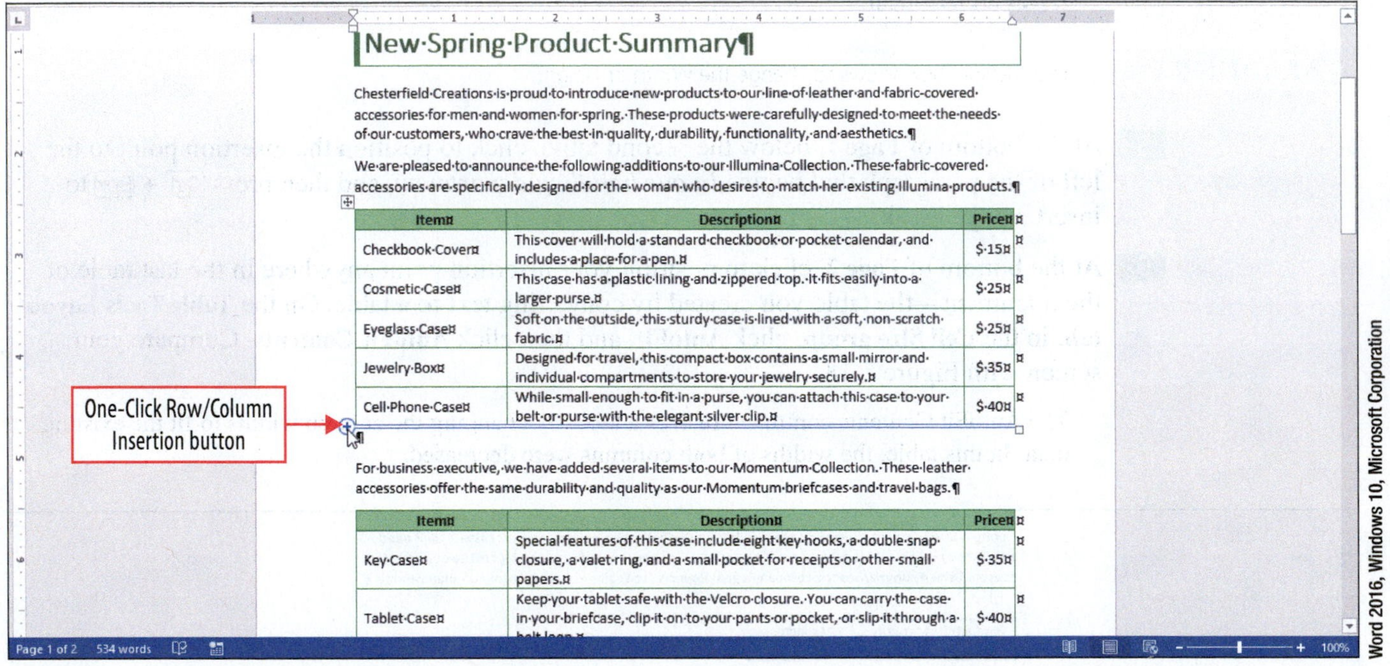

FIGURE 5.19

2 Click the **One-Click Row/Column Insertion** button to insert a new row at the bottom of the table.

ANOTHER WAY On the Layout tab, in the Rows & Columns group, click Insert Below.

3 In the new row, select the first two cells, and then on the **Table Tools Layout tab**, in the **Merge group**, click **Merge Cells**. In the merged cell, type **Illumina Accessories Total Price** Select the text you just typed, and then from the mini toolbar, apply **Bold** B. On the **Table Tools Layout tab**, in the **Alignment group**, click **Align Center Right**. Press Tab to move to the last cell in the table. Compare your screen with Figure 5.20.

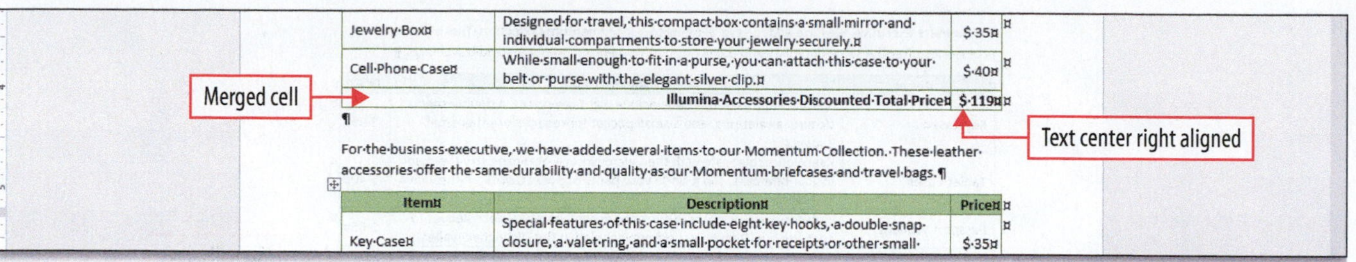

Jewelry·Box
Designed·for·travel,·this·compact·box·contains·a·small·mirror·and·individual·compartments·to·store·your·jewelry·securely.
$·35
Cell·Phone·Case
While·small·enough·to·fit·in·a·purse,·you·can·attach·this·case·to·your·belt·or·purse·with·the·elegant·silver·clip.
$·40
Merged cell
Illumina·Accessories·Discounted·Total·Price
$·119
Text center right aligned
For·the·business·executive,·we·have·added·several·items·to·our·Momentum·Collection.·These·leather·accessories·offer·the·same·durability·and·quality·as·our·Momentum·briefcases·and·travel·bags.¶
Item
Description
Price
Key·Case
Special·features·of·this·case·include·eight·key·hooks,·a·double·snap·closure,·a·valet·ring,·and·a·small·pocket·for·receipts·or·other·small·
$·35

FIGURE 5.20 Word 2016, Windows 10, Microsoft Corporation

4 On the **Table Tools Layout tab**, in the **Data group**, click **Formula**. In the **Formula** dialog box, under **Number format**, click the **Number format arrow**, and then click **#,##0**—the first option. Click to position the insertion point to the left of the characters displayed in the **Number format** text, and then type **$** Compare your screen with Figure 5.21.

The Formula dialog box contains the default formula =SUM(ABOVE). All formulas begin with an equal sign [=]. This formula includes the SUM function and calculates the total of the numbers in all of the cells above the current cell—up to the first empty cell or a cell that contains text—and places the result in the current cell. You can specify a special number format—in this instance, a whole number preceded by a dollar sign.

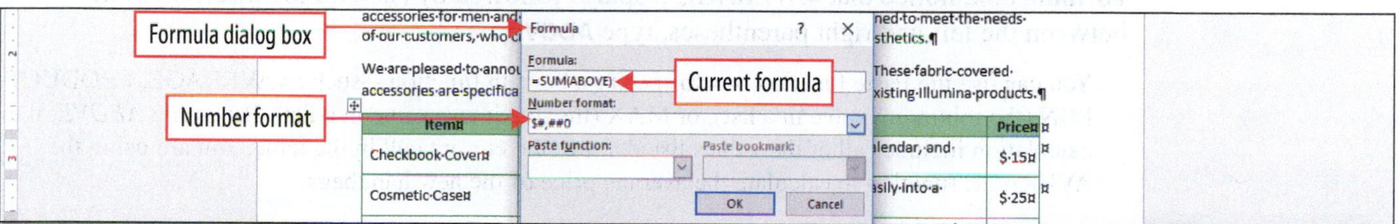

FIGURE 5.21 Word 2016, Windows 10, Microsoft Corporation

5 Click **OK** to close the dialog box. Notice that *$ 140* displays in the active cell, so a customer buying each piece of the Illumina series would pay *$ 140* for the entire set of accessories.

A formula is a type of ***field***—a placeholder for data. The displayed number is a formula field representing the value calculated by the formula.

6 Select the inserted text, and then from the mini toolbar, apply **Bold** [B].

7 Position the insertion point anywhere in the second table. Point to the lower left border of the table, and then click the **One-Click Row/Column Insertion** button. In the new row, select the first two cells, right-click, and then from the shortcut menu, click **Merge Cells**. In the merged cell, type **Momentum Accessories Total Price** and then apply **Bold** [B] and **Align Center Right** [icon]. Press [Tab].

8 On the **Table Tools Layout tab**, in the **Data group**, click **Formula**. In the **Formula** dialog box, under **Number format**, click the **Number format arrow**, and then click **#,##0**. Click to position the insertion point to the left of the characters in the **Number format** text, and then type **$** Click **OK**. Compare your screen with Figure 5.22.

A customer buying each piece of the Momentum series would pay *$ 120* for the entire set of accessories.

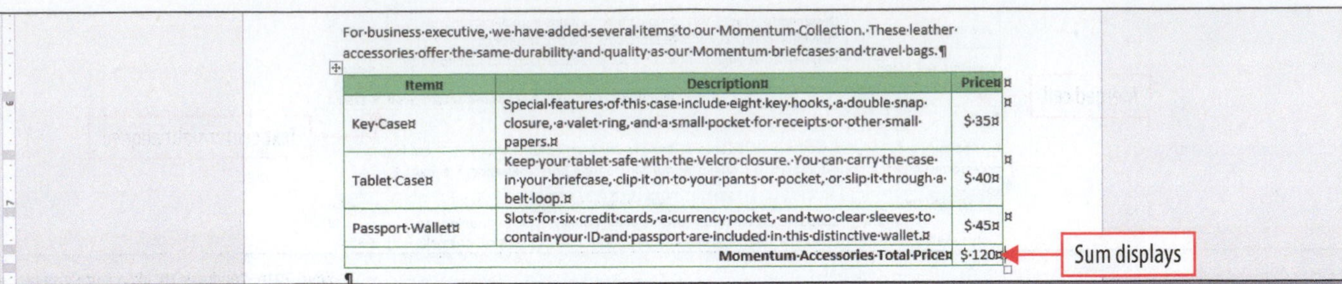

For business executive, we have added several items to our Momentum Collection. These leather accessories offer the same durability and quality as our Momentum briefcases and travel bags.
Item
Description
Price
Key Case
Special features of this case include eight key hooks, a double snap closure, a valet ring, and a small pocket for receipts or other small papers.
$ 35
Tablet Case
Keep your tablet safe with the Velcro closure. You can carry the case in your briefcase, clip it on to your pants or pocket, or slip it through a belt loop.
$ 40
Passport Wallet
Slots for six credit cards, a currency pocket, and two clear sleeves to contain your ID and passport are included in this distinctive wallet.
$ 45
Momentum Accessories Total Price
$ 120
Sum displays

Word 2016, Windows 10, Microsoft Corporation

FIGURE 5.22

9 Select **$ 120** and apply **Bold** [B].

10 In the third table of the document, use the technique you just practiced to insert a new row at the bottom of the table. Select the first two cells and merge them. In the merged cell, type **New Handbags Average Price** and then apply **Bold** [B] and **Align Center Right**.

11 Press [Tab] to position the insertion point in the last cell of the table, and then click **Formula**. In the **Formula** dialog box, in the **Formula** box, delete the existing text, and then type **=** Under **Paste function**, click the **Paste function arrow**, and then click **AVERAGE**. In the **Formula** box, notice that *=AVERAGE* displays followed by *()*. With the insertion point between the left and right parentheses, type **ABOVE**

You can use the Paste function box to specify a built-in function—such as AVERAGE, PRODUCT, MIN (the minimum value in a list), or MAX (the maximum value in a list). By typing *ABOVE*, the calculation includes all of the values listed above the current cell in the table. You are using the AVERAGE function to calculate the average price of the new handbags.

12 In the **Formula** dialog box, under **Number format**, click the **Number format arrow**, and then click **#,##0**. Click to position the insertion point to the left of the **Number format** text, and then type **$** Compare your screen with Figure 5.23.

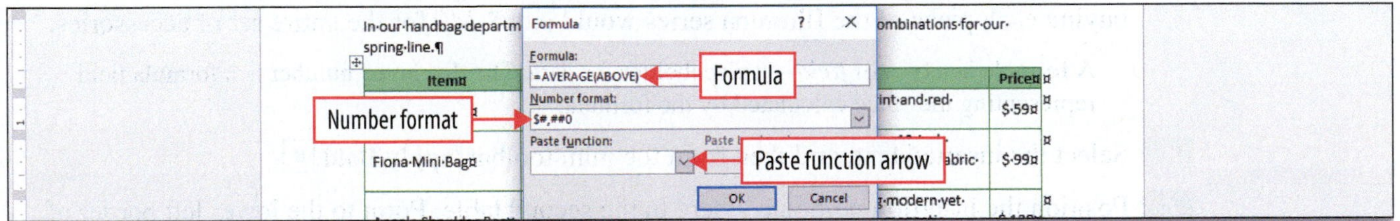

Word 2016, Windows 10, Microsoft Corporation

FIGURE 5.23

13 Click **OK** to close the **Formula** dialog box. Select the inserted text, and then apply **Bold** [B]. **Save** your changes.

The average price of the five handbags—*$ 117*—displays in the active cell.

> ***More* Knowledge** **Inserting Rows and Columns in a Table**
>
> To insert a new row in an existing table, point to the left of the border between two existing rows, and then click the One-Click Row/Column Insertion button. To insert a new column, point above the border between two existing columns, and then click the One-Click Row/Column Insertion button. To insert a column at the extreme right of the table, point to the top right corner of the table, and then click the One-Click Row/Column Insertion button.

Activity 5.10 | Updating Formula Fields in Tables

You can edit an existing formula in a table. Additionally, if you change a value in a table, you must manually update the field containing the formula.

1 On **Page 1**, in the first table, in the last row, click to position the insertion point to the left of the word *Total*, type **Discounted** and then press Spacebar.

2 Press Tab to select the cell containing the formula, right-click over the selected cell, and then on the shortcut menu, click **Edit Field**. In the **Field** dialog box, under **Field properties**, click **Formula**.

3 In the **Formula** dialog box, in the **Formula** box, be sure the insertion point displays to the right of the formula =*SUM(ABOVE)*, and then type ***.85** Compare your screen with Figure 5.24.

Formulas are not restricted to the built-in functions. You can also create your own. Customers purchasing the entire Illumina collection of accessories receive a 15 percent discount. The modified formula reflects this discounted price. The total price is multiplied by 85 percent (.85), representing 100 percent minus the 15 percent discount.

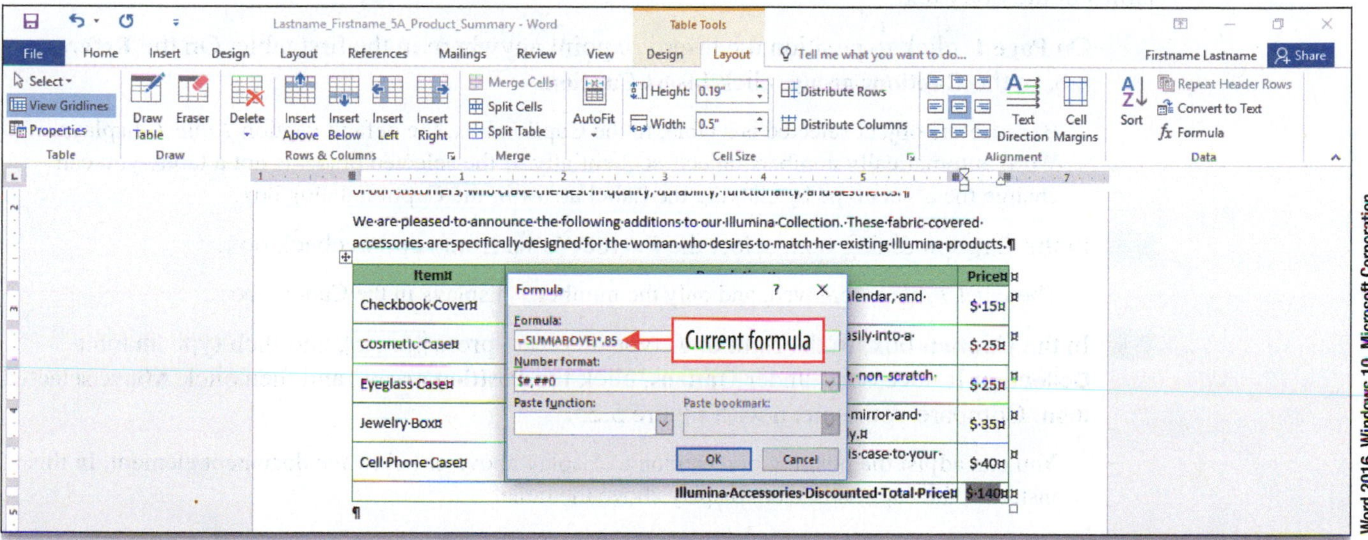

FIGURE 5.24

4 Click **OK**, and notice that a new, lower price—*$ 119*—displays in the active cell.

5 In the second table, in the last row, click to position the insertion point to the left of the word *Total*, type **Discounted** and then press Spacebar.

6 Press Tab, right-click over the selected cell, and then on the shortcut menu, click **Edit Field**. In the **Field** dialog box, under **Field properties**, click the **Formula** button.

7 In the **Formula** dialog box, in the **Formula** box, if necessary click to position the insertion point to the right of the displayed formula =*SUM(ABOVE)*, and then type ***.85** Click **OK**.

The discounted total for the Momentum collection of accessories—*$ 102*—displays in the active cell.

8 In the third table, in the last column, below the **header row**, click in the third cell—the price of the Angela Shoulder Bag. Select only the number **139**, and then type **129**

Unlike Excel, when you change a value that is used in a formula, the resulting calculation is not automatically updated.

9 In the bottom right cell of the table, select the text. Right-click the selection, and then on the shortcut menu, click **Update Field**.

The value *$ 115* displays in the active cell and represents a formula field. If a number used in the calculation is changed, you must use the Update Field command to recalculate the value.

10 **Save** your changes.

NOTE Summing Rows

The default formula is =SUM(ABOVE), assuming the cell above the selected cell contains a number. If there is a number in the cell to the left of the selected cell and no number in the cell above, the default is =SUM(LEFT). If you want to sum the entire range, be sure to avoid leaving a cell empty within a range. If there is no value, then enter a 0 (zero).

Activity 5.11 | Adding Captions, Excluding Labels from Captions, and Setting Caption Positions

4.1.6, 4.1.7
3.2.2 Expert

Captions are labels that you can add to Word objects such as a picture or table. As you add captions to objects within a document, Word automatically numbers the captions sequentially. It is good practice to add a caption to each table in a document to make it easier to refer to specific tables in the body text.

1 On **Page 1**, click to position the insertion point anywhere in the first table. On the **References tab**, in the **Captions group**, click **Insert Caption**.

Because the object selected is a table, in the Caption box, the default caption *Table 1* displays. Word automatically numbers objects sequentially. If the selected object is not a table, you can change the object type by clicking the Label arrow in the Caption dialog box.

2 In the **Caption** dialog box, select the **Exclude label from caption** check box.

The label *Table* is removed, and only the number *1* displays in the Caption box.

3 In the **Caption** box, to the right of *1*, type a colon : press Spacebar, and then type **Illumina Collection** If necessary, under **Options**, click the **Position arrow**, and then click **Above selected item**. Compare your screen with Figure 5.25.

You can adjust the position of a caption to display above or below the document element. In this instance, the caption is set to display above the table.

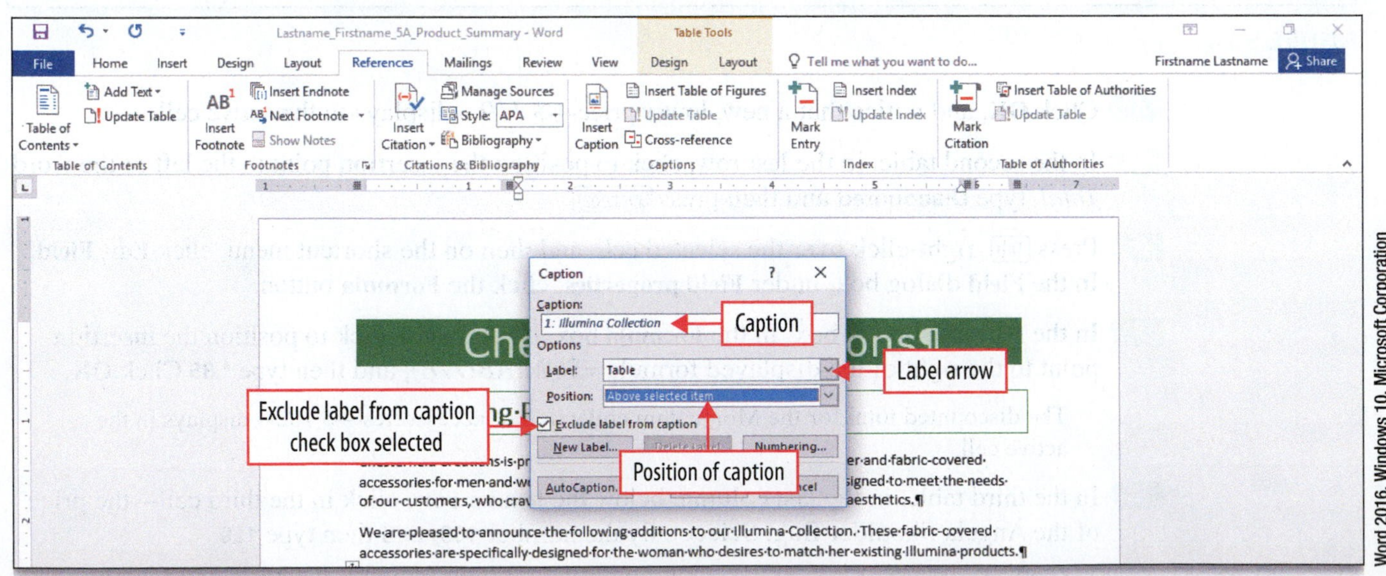

FIGURE 5.25

4 Click **OK** to close the **Caption** dialog box. Notice that the caption displays above the table.

5 Using the technique you just practiced, add captions to the second and third tables. For the second table caption, insert the caption **2: Momentum Collection** above the table. For the third table, insert the caption **3: New Handbags** above the table.

6 **Save** your changes.

Objective 4 Modify Table Properties

GO! Learn How Video W5-4

Tables, like all other Word objects, have properties that you can alter. For example, you can change how text wraps around tables and define cell spacing. Modify table properties to improve the overall appearance of your document.

Activity 5.12 | Moving a Table and Wrapping Text a Around Tables

MOS 5.2.6

If you have a long document with several tables and body text, you can apply text wrapping to have the text flow around the table. This can create a shorter document and improve the overall readability of the document.

1 Press Ctrl + End to move to the bottom of **Page 2**, and then scroll up slightly to view the text above the two-column table.

2 Point to the upper left corner of the table to display the **table move handle** and the pointer, hold down the left mouse button, and then drag the table until the top border is aligned with the top of the paragraph that begins *Spring is*, and the right border is at approximately **6.5" on the horizontal ruler**. Compare your screen with Figure 5.26. If your table position does not match the figure, on the Quick Access Toolbar click Undo and begin again.

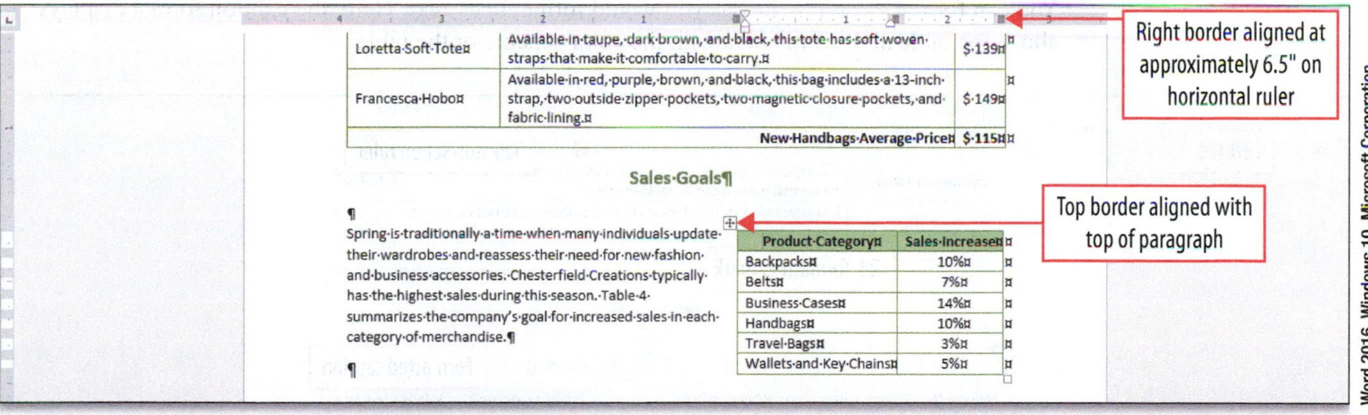

FIGURE 5.26

3 Click to position the insertion point anywhere in the table. On the **Table Tools Layout tab**, in the **Table group**, click **Properties**. In the **Table Properties** dialog box, on the **Table tab**, under **Text wrapping**, be sure **Around** is selected, and then click the **Positioning** button.

4 In the **Table Positioning** dialog box, under **Distance from surrounding text**, in the **Left** box, select the existing text, and then type **0.5"** Compare your screen with Figure 5.27.

You can define how close existing text displays in relation to the top, bottom, left, or right of a table. By changing the Left box value to 0.5, the text will display one-half inch from the left border of the table.

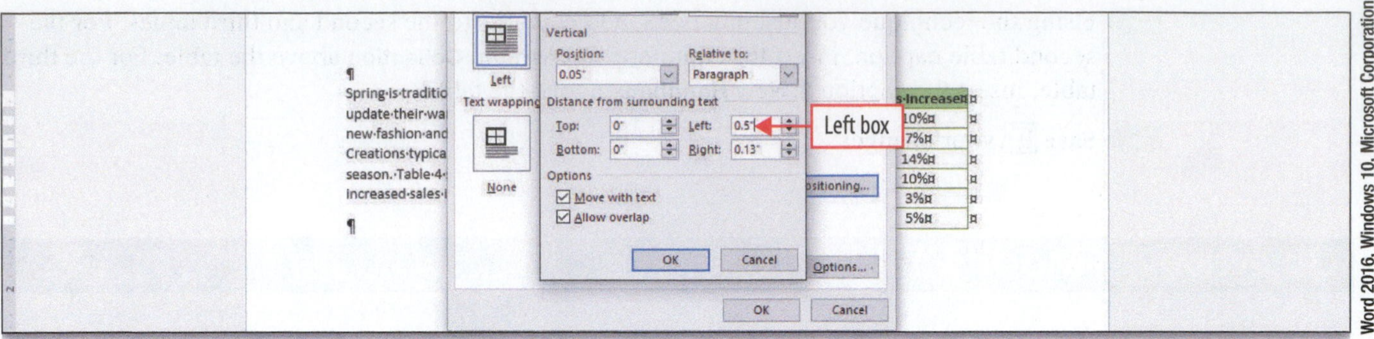

FIGURE 5.27

5 Click **OK** two times to close the dialog boxes.

Activity 5.13 | Changing Caption Formats and Creating a Caption Style

4.1.7

1 With the insertion point in the table, on the **References tab**, in the **Captions group**, click **Insert Caption**. In the **Caption** dialog box, clear the **Exclude label from caption** check box. With *Table 4* displayed in the **Caption** box and *Above selected item* displayed in the **Position** box, click **OK** to close the dialog box and insert the caption at the left margin.

2 Select the caption. From the mini toolbar, change the **Font Size** to **10**, apply **Bold**, and then change the **Font Color** to **Green, Accent 6, Darker 50%**—in the last column, the last color.

3 At the left end of the horizontal ruler, if necessary, click the **Tab Alignment** button to display the **Left tab** button. To set a left tab stop, on the horizontal ruler, click at **4.0 inches on the horizontal ruler**. Click to the left of the caption, and then press Tab. Compare your screen with Figure 5.28.

You can format a caption, just as you would format body text. Here, the caption format displays above the table and coordinates with the color scheme of the table.

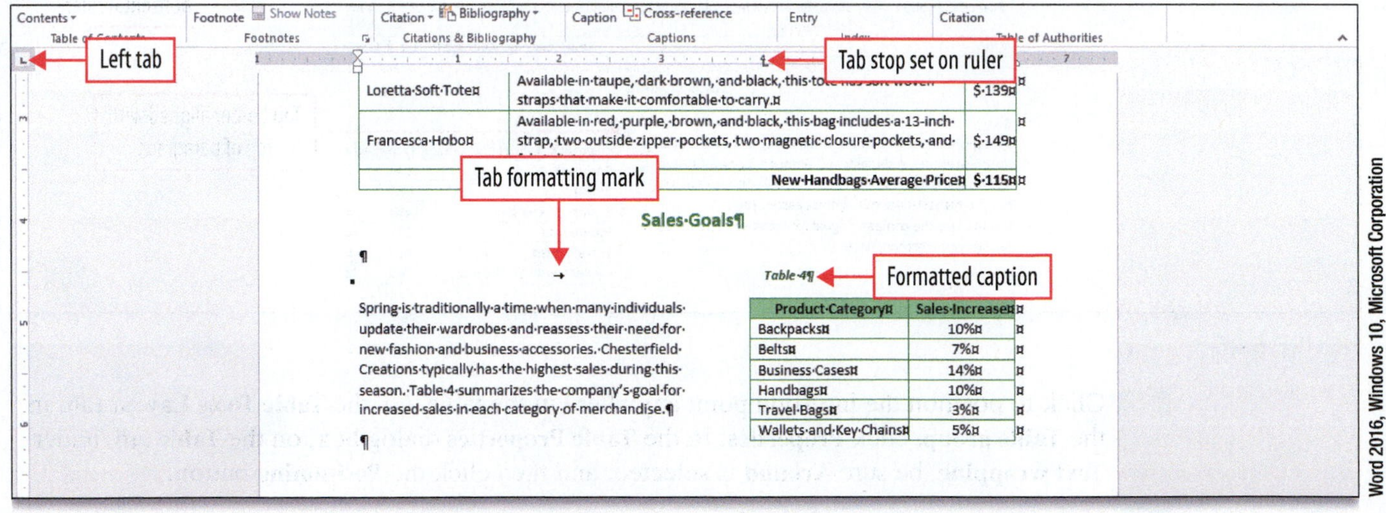

FIGURE 5.28

4 Select the caption *Table 4*. On the mini toolbar, click **Styles**, and then in the **Styles** gallery, click **Create a Style**.

5 In the **Create New Style from Formatting** dialog box, in the **Name** box, type **Table Caption** and then click **OK**.

6 Press Ctrl + Home. Select the first table caption, and then on the mini toolbar, click **Styles**. In the **Styles** gallery, click the **Table Caption** style. In the same manner, apply the **Table Caption** style to the remaining two captions in the document.

7 Press Ctrl + Home. Click the **File tab** to display **Backstage** view. On the right, at the bottom of the **Properties** list, click **Show All Properties**. As the **Tags**, type **product summary, tables** In the **Subject** box, type your course name and section number. If necessary, edit the author name to display your name.

8 **Save** your document. In the upper right corner of the Word window, click **Close** ✕. If directed by your instructor to do so, submit your paper printout, your electronic image of your document that looks like a printed document, or your original Word file.

END | You have completed Project 5A

Expense Form

PROJECT ACTIVITIES

In Activities 5.14 through 5.24, you will create an expense form from a freeform table, use nested tables to display expense codes, and insert an Excel spreadsheet. Rachel Anders, Chief Financial Officer for Chesterfield Creations, has asked you to design an expense reimbursement form to be used by the company's sales representatives. Your completed document will look similar to Figure 5.29.

Please always review the downloaded Grader instructions before beginning.

PROJECT FILES

If your instructor wants you to submit Project 5B in the MyITLab grader system, log in to MyITLab, locate Grader Project 5B, and then download the files for this project.

For Project 5B, you will need the following files:
w05B_Expense_Form
w05B_Logo

You will save your file as:
Lastname_Firstname_5B_Expense_Form

PROJECT RESULTS

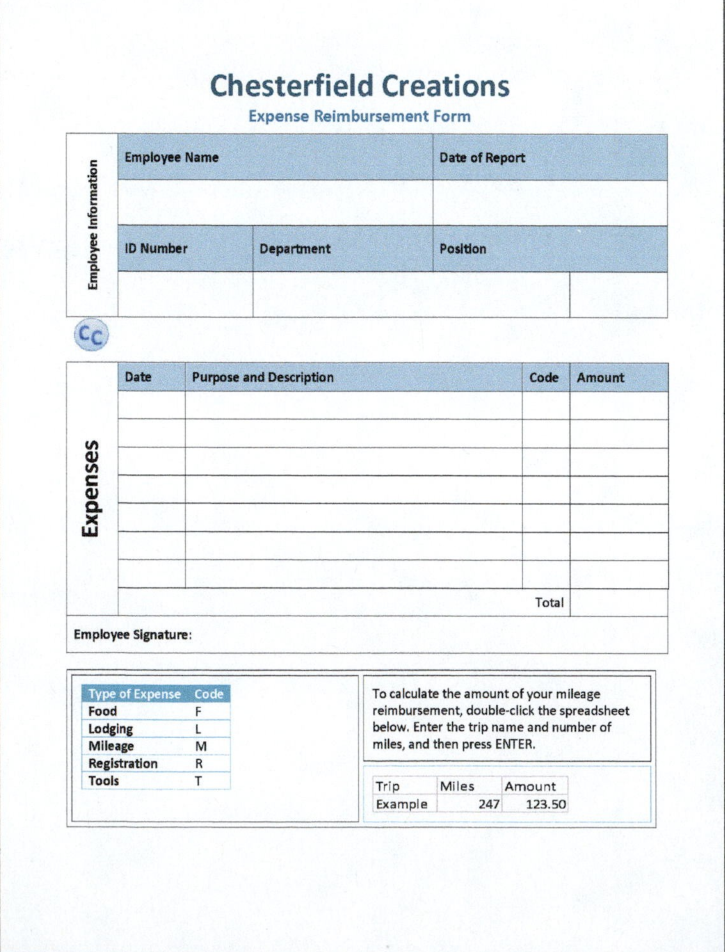

Chesterfield Creations
Expense Reimbursement Form

Employee Information	Employee Name		Date of Report	
	ID Number	Department	Position	

Expenses	Date	Purpose and Description	Code	Amount
			Total	

Employee Signature:

Type of Expense	Code
Food	F
Lodging	L
Mileage	M
Registration	R
Tools	T

To calculate the amount of your mileage reimbursement, double-click the spreadsheet below. Enter the trip name and number of miles, and then press ENTER.

Trip	Miles	Amount
Example	247	123.50

Word 2016, Windows 10, Microsoft Corporation

FIGURE 5.29 Project 5B Expense Form

Objective 5 Use Freeform Drawing Tools in a Table

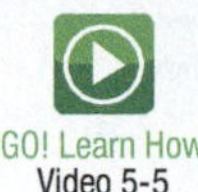

When you insert a table into a Word document, the result is a table structure that consists of rows and columns of a *uniform* size. However, sometimes you must modify the table structure to create rows and columns of *varying* sizes, such as on a purchase order or employee expense form. Word provides freeform drawing tools that work like an electronic pencil and eraser to draw the table objects. After the table is drawn, you can use the features on the Design and Layout tabs to refine the table format.

Activity 5.14 | Drawing a Freeform Table

1 Start Word. On the left, click **Open Other Documents**, click **Browse**, and then in the **Open** dialog box, navigate to the student data files that accompany this chapter and open **w05B_Expense_Form**. Click the **File tab**, on the left click **Save As**, and then in the **Save As** dialog box, navigate to your **Word Chapter 5** folder. Using your own name, save the file as **Lastname_Firstname_5B_Expense_Form** and then add the **File Name** to the footer.

Here, the outside border and some of the horizontal and vertical lines have already been drawn. Some text is entered and some formatting applied.

The outside table border spans the document width from the left margin to the right margin and extends to approximately 6 inches on the vertical ruler.

2 Click anywhere inside the table. On the **Table Tools Layout tab**, in the **Draw group**, click **Draw Table**. Move your mouse pointer into the document to display the **Draw** pointer . Compare your screen with Figure 5.30.

When drawing a table from scratch, plan to begin with the outside border of the table, starting at the top left corner and dragging the Draw pointer down and to the right. After the table is drawn, the Draw pointer continues to display, the Layout tab is active, and in the Draw group, the Draw Table button is turned on.

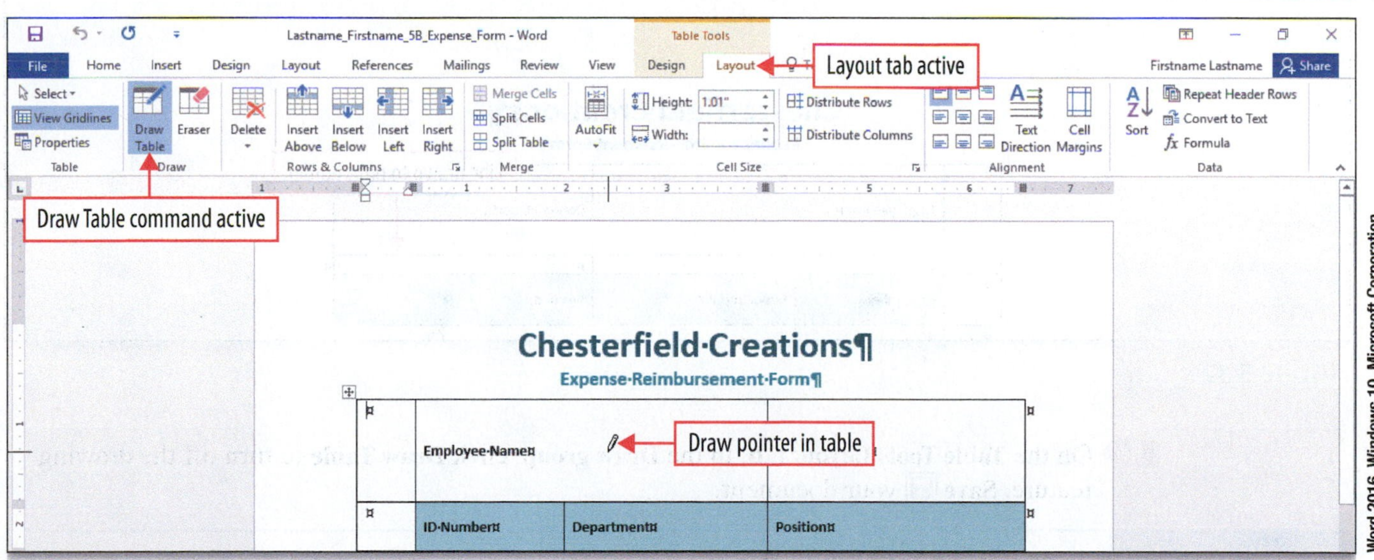

FIGURE 5.30

3 Position the tip of the pointer slightly above the cell containing the text *ID Number*, as shown in Figure 5.31.

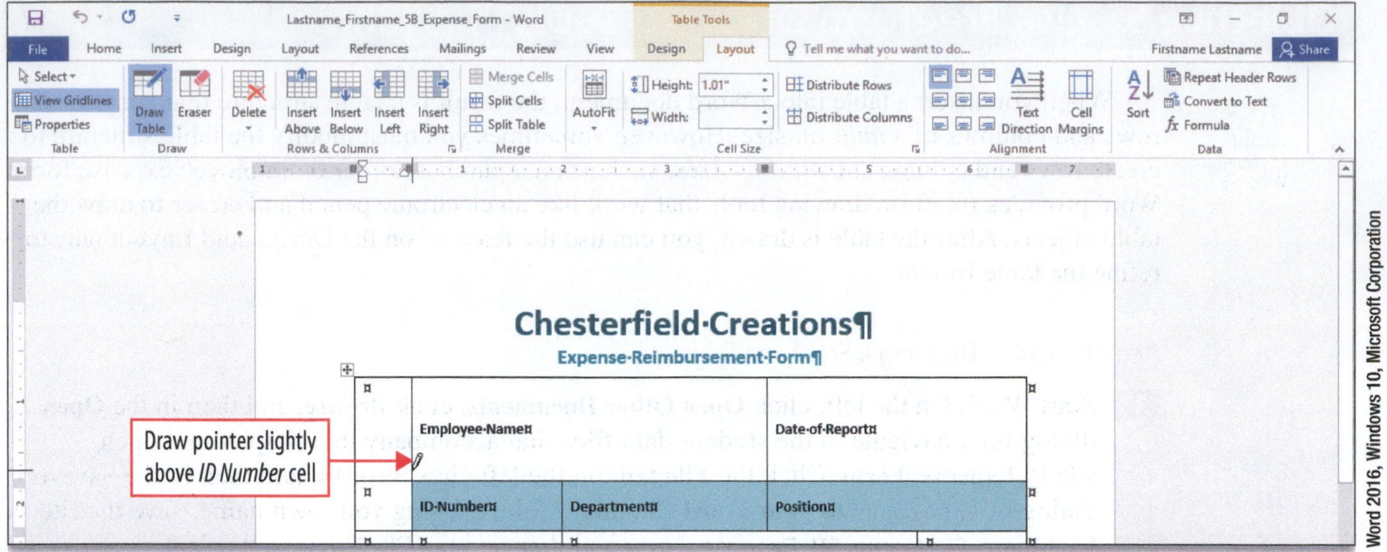

FIGURE 5.31

4 Hold down the left mouse button, and then drag to the right to draw a horizontal line extending to the right border of the table. Notice that as soon as you begin to draw, Word begins to form a straight line—you need not draw precisely because Word will do the work for you. Compare your screen with Figure 5.32.

You can draw horizontal and vertical lines inside the table to create cells of various sizes. Here, your table requires a section for entering employee information and another section for listing expenses incurred. Each section requires cells that vary in size.

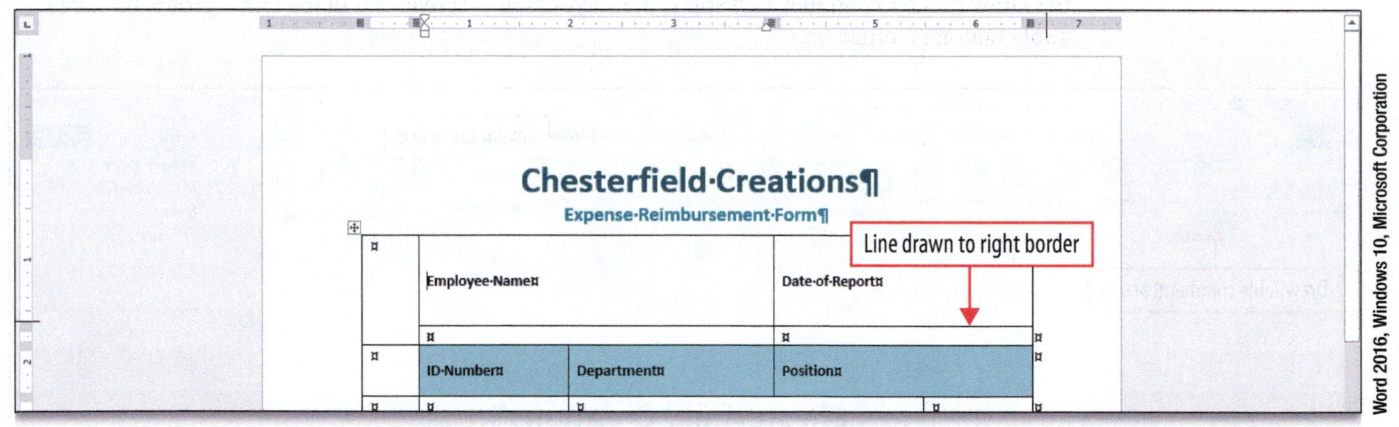

FIGURE 5.32

5 On the **Table Tools Layout tab**, in the **Draw group**, click **Draw Table** to turn off the drawing feature. **Save** your document.

More Knowledge

Wrapping Text When Drawing a Table

To cause existing text to flow around the table you are drawing, click the Draw Table command, and then press and hold Ctrl as you draw the table.

Activity 5.15 | Adding and Removing Rows and Columns and Merging Cells

1 In the fifth row of the table, point to the cell containing the word *Date* and be sure that your I mouse pointer displays, indicating that the Draw feature is off.

2 Above the cell with the text *Expenses*, point to the left border of the table to display the **Insert Row/Column** button. Compare your screen with Figure 5.33.

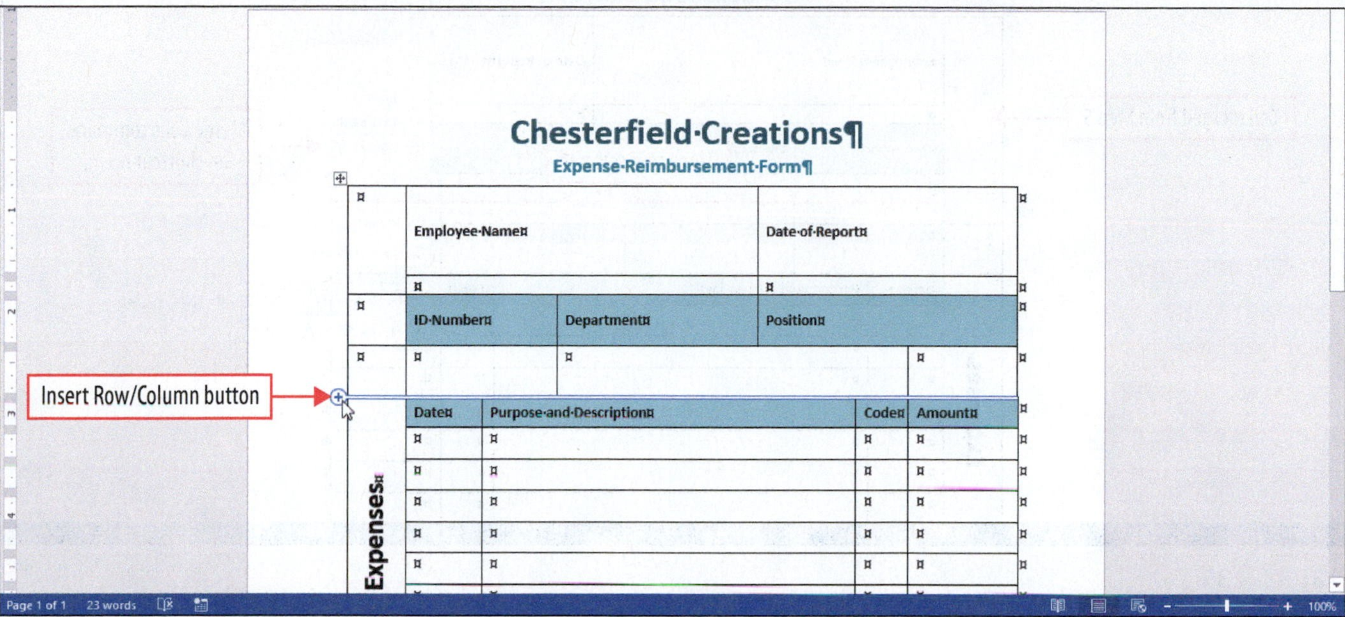

Word 2016, Windows 10, Microsoft Corporation

FIGURE 5.33

3 Click one time to insert a row above the Date row.

4 In the upper left corner of the table, click in the first cell, and then drag down to select the first cell in the second and third rows, as shown in Figure 5.34.

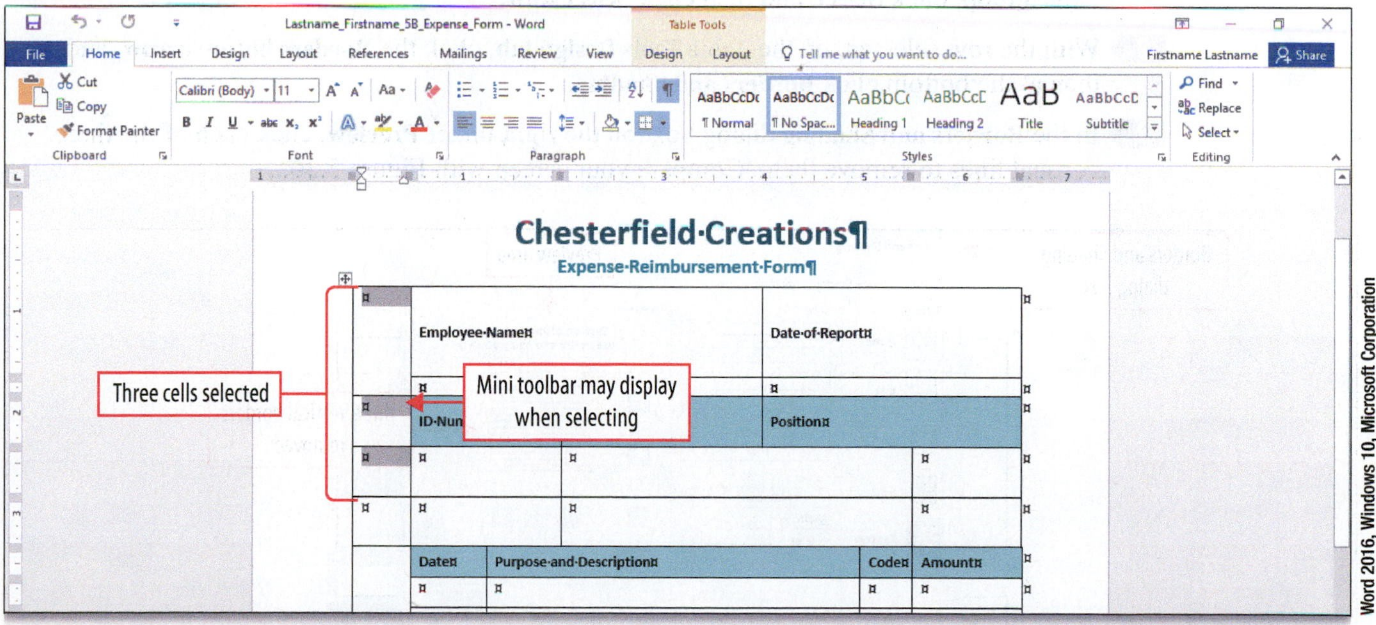

Word 2016, Windows 10, Microsoft Corporation

FIGURE 5.34

5 With the three cells selected, on the **Table Tools Layout tab**, in the **Merge group**, click **Merge Cells**.

6 In the row you inserted above *Date*, select the second, third, and fourth cells, right-click over the selection, and then compare your screen with Figure 5.35.

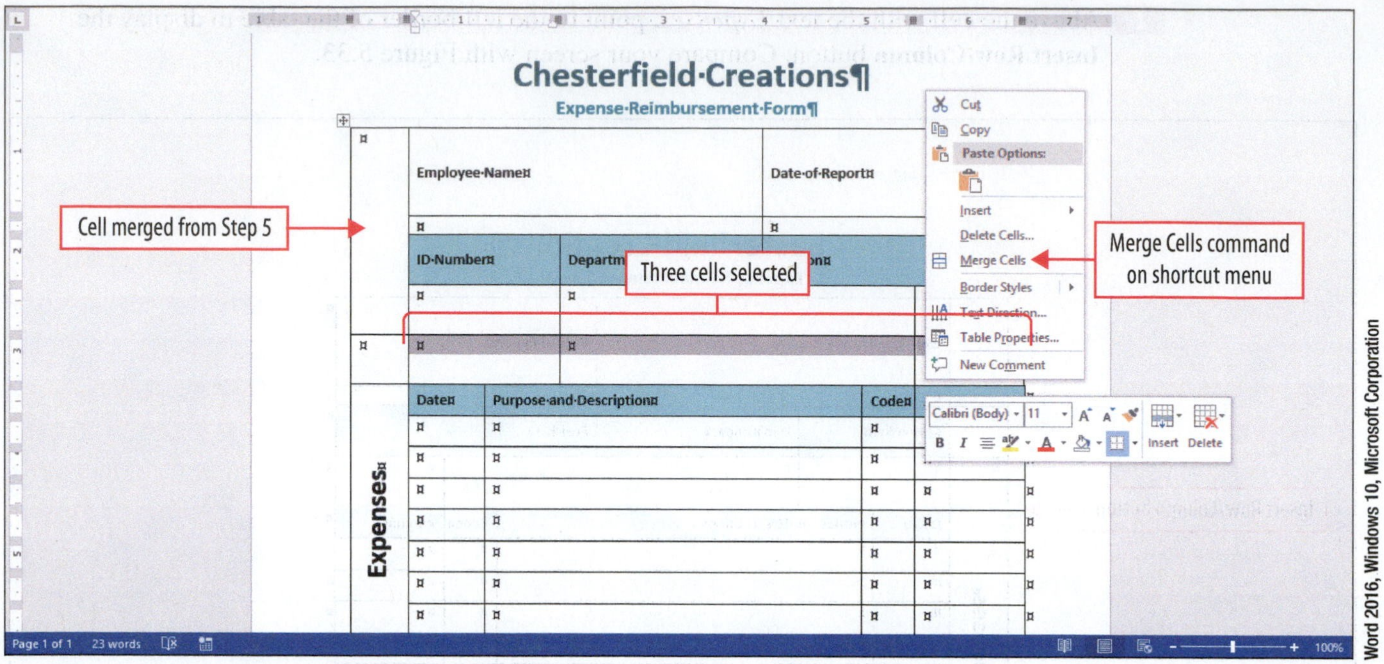

FIGURE 5.35

7 On the shortcut menu, click **Merge Cells**, and then click **Save**.

You can access the Merge Cells command from the ribbon or from the shortcut menu.

Activity 5.16 | Removing Cell Borders

1 Click in the newly merged cell above the *Date* cell. On the **Table Tools Layout tab**, in the **Table group**, click **Select**, and then click **Select Row**.

2 With the row selected, on the **Table Tools Design tab**, click the **Borders button arrow**, and then at the bottom click **Borders and Shading**.

3 In the **Borders and Shading** dialog box, on the right under **Preview**, click each of the three vertical lines to remove them. Compare your screen with Figure 5.36.

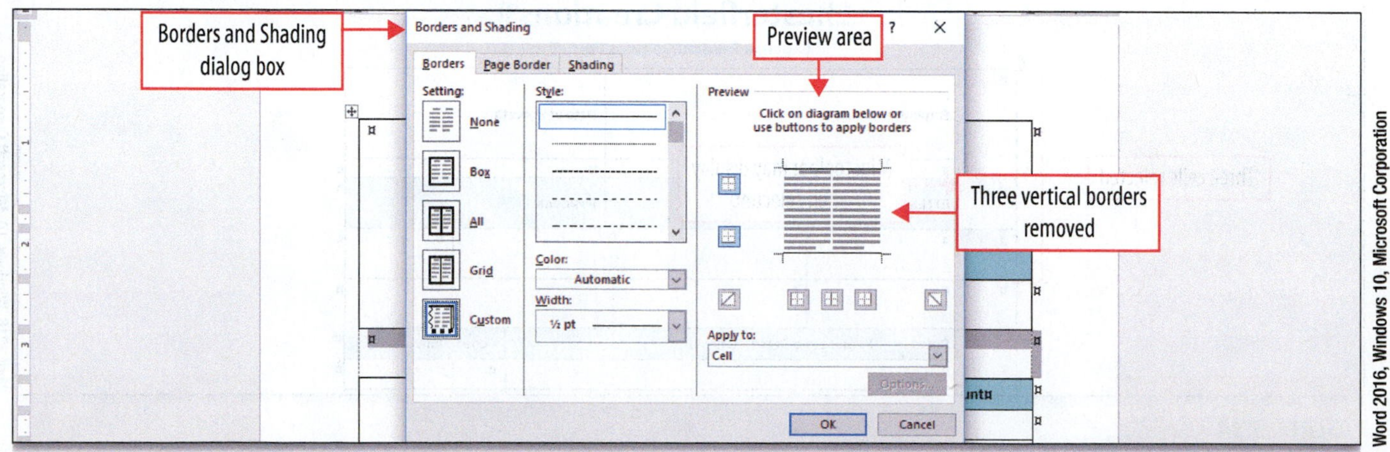

FIGURE 5.36

ANOTHER WAY User the Eraser tool to erase lines directly in the table.

4 Click **OK**, and then click anywhere in the table to deselect the row. On the **Table Tools Layout tab**, in the **Table group**, if necessary, click **View Gridlines**—if the button is shaded, then Gridlines are already active and dotted lines display on the borders you just removed. If necessary, activate gridlines, and then compare your screen with Figure 5.37.

Gridlines—the dashed lines—are nonprinting cell borders that can be used as a guide for viewing table cells. They are useful when positioning content in a table when you are not using a table border.

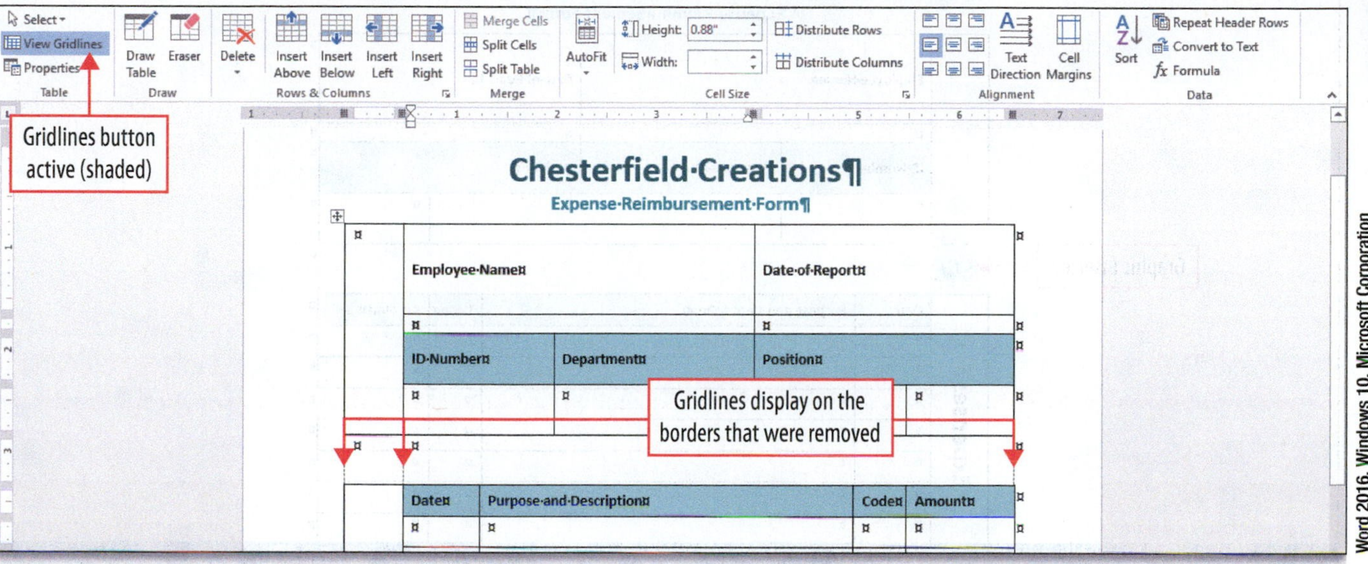

FIGURE 5.37

5 Click the **File tab**, and then click **Print**. In the **Print Preview**, notice how removing the cell borders gives the appearance of having two separate tables.

6 In the upper left corner, click **Back**. By removing borders, the border will not print but the cells are retained so that you can insert text or formatting.

7 **Save** your document.

More Knowledge **Deleting Table Elements**

You can delete cells, columns, rows, or an entire table. Select the cell, column, row, or table that you want to delete. On the Table Tools Layout tab, in the Rows & Columns group, click the Delete button, and then click the appropriate button—Delete Rows, Delete Columns, Delete Table, or Delete Cells. If deleting cells, the Delete Cells dialog box displays so that you can select how adjacent cells should be moved.

Activity 5.17 | Inserting Text and Graphics Into a Table

5.1.2

You can insert text and objects, such as pictures and WordArt, into table cells.

1 Press Ctrl + Home to move to the top of your document.

2 In the table, in the first column, click to position your insertion point in the second cell—the cell from which you removed the left and right borders and just above the *Expenses* cell.

3 On the **Insert tab**, in the **Illustrations group**, click **Pictures**. In the **Insert Picture** dialog box, navigate to your student data files for this chapter, select the file **w05B_Logo**, and then click **Insert**. Notice that the picture—the company logo—is inserted in the cell. Compare your screen with Figure 5.38.

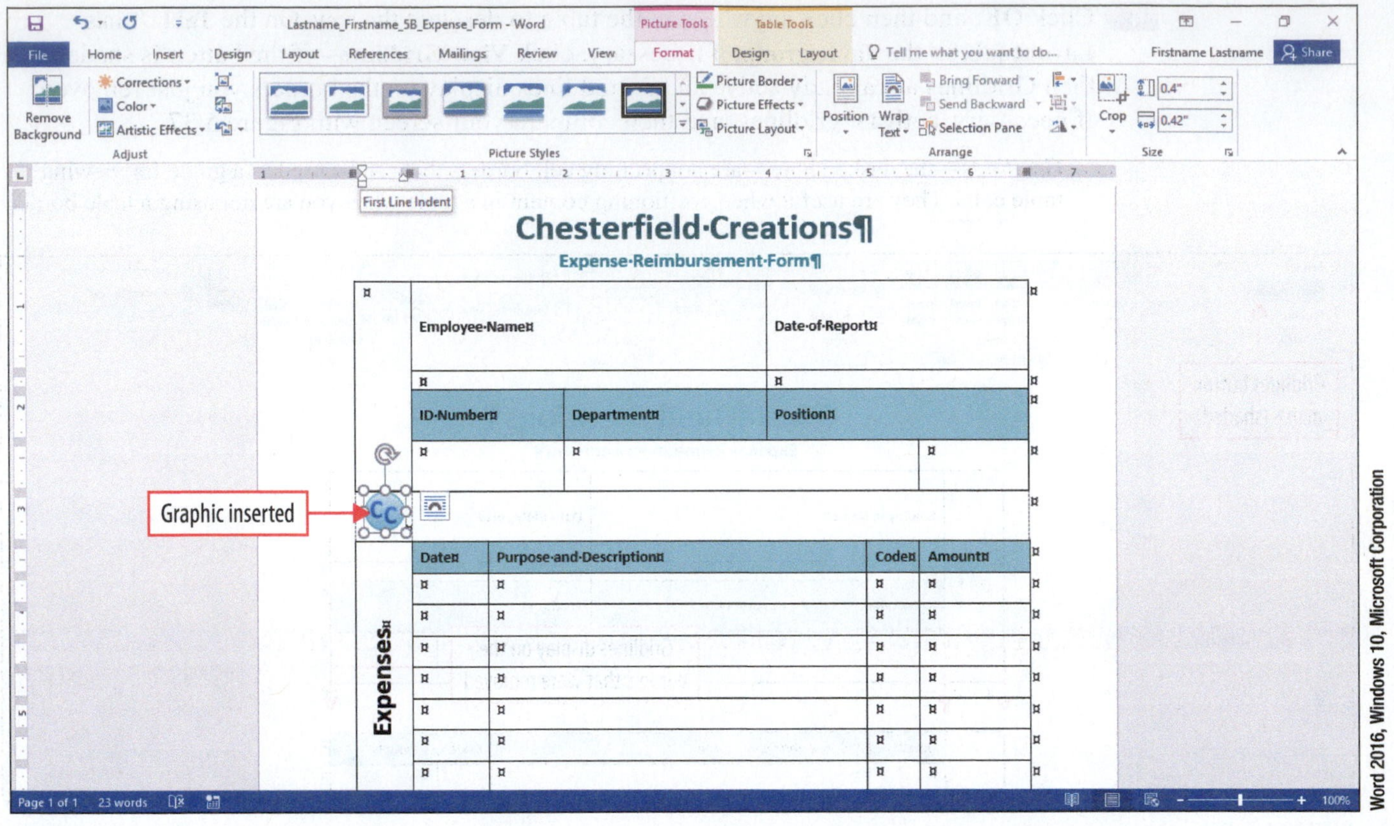

Word 2016, Windows 10, Microsoft Corporation

FIGURE 5.38

4 With the graphic selected, on the **Picture Tools Format tab**, in the **Size group**, click in the **Shape Width** box to select the existing text, type **0.4** and press Enter.

Using this method to reduce the size of the image automatically reduces the row height and column width proportionally.

5 At the bottom of the table, click in the first empty cell above the text *Employee Signature*. Type **Total** and then on **Table Tools Layout tab**, in the **Alignment group**, click **Align Center Right**.

6 Click outside of the table to deselect the cell. **Save** your document, and then compare your screen with Figure 5.39.

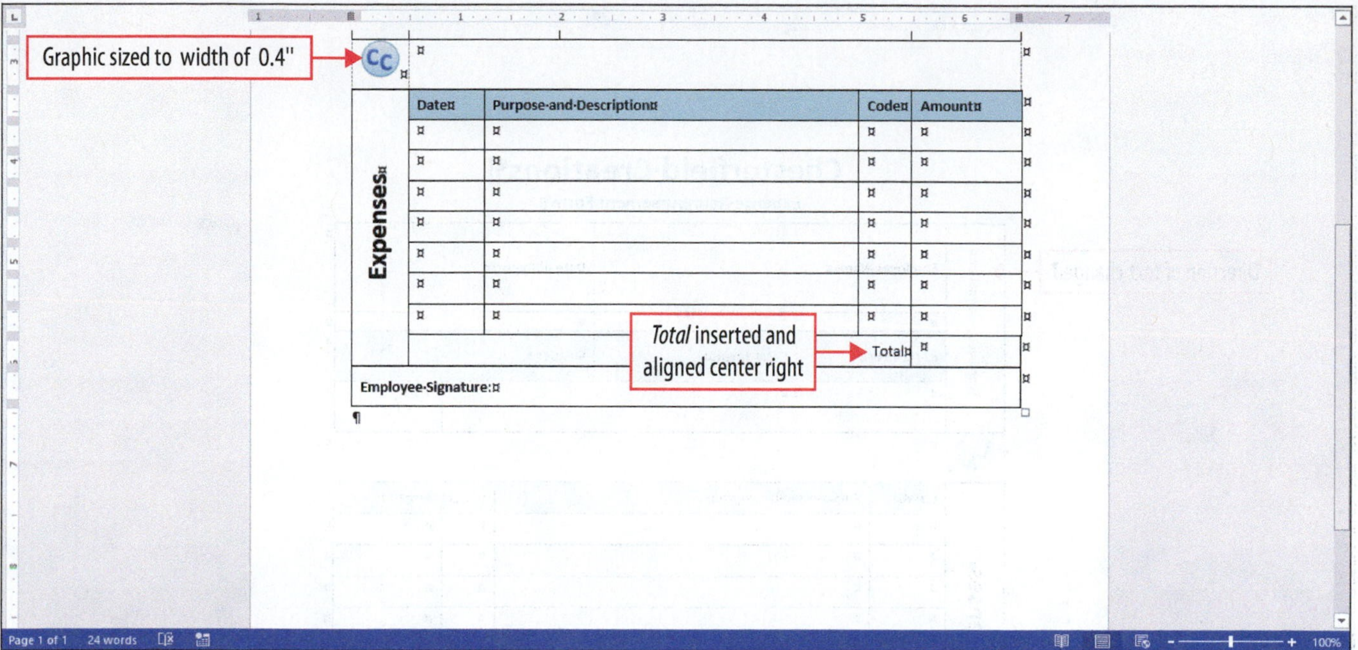

FIGURE 5.39

Word 2016, Windows 10, Microsoft Corporation

More Knowledge **Inserting a Single Cell**

If you want to add a single cell to a table—not an entire row or column—click the cell adjacent to where you want to add the cell. On the Table Tools Layout tab, in the Rows & Columns group, click the Dialog Box Launcher. In the Insert Cells dialog box, select the option that specifies how adjacent cells should be moved to accommodate the new cell, and then click OK.

Activity 5.18 | Changing Text Direction

You can change the text direction within a cell in a Word table. This is effective for column titles that do not fit at the top of narrow columns or for row headings that cover multiple rows.

1. Click to position the insertion point in the first cell of the table. On the **Table Tools Layout tab**, in the **Alignment group**, click **Text Direction** two times to set the text direction to vertical from the bottom, and then in the second row of buttons, click the center button—**Align Center**. Notice that the insertion point displays horizontally and at the bottom of the cell.

   Use the Text Direction button to change the positioning of text within a cell, and then select the appropriate alignment button. The appearance of the Text Direction button changes to indicate the direction of the text within the currently selected cell.

2. Type **Employee Information**

3. Press Ctrl + Home to move to the top of your document and deselect the text. **Save** your document, and then compare your screen with Figure 5.40.

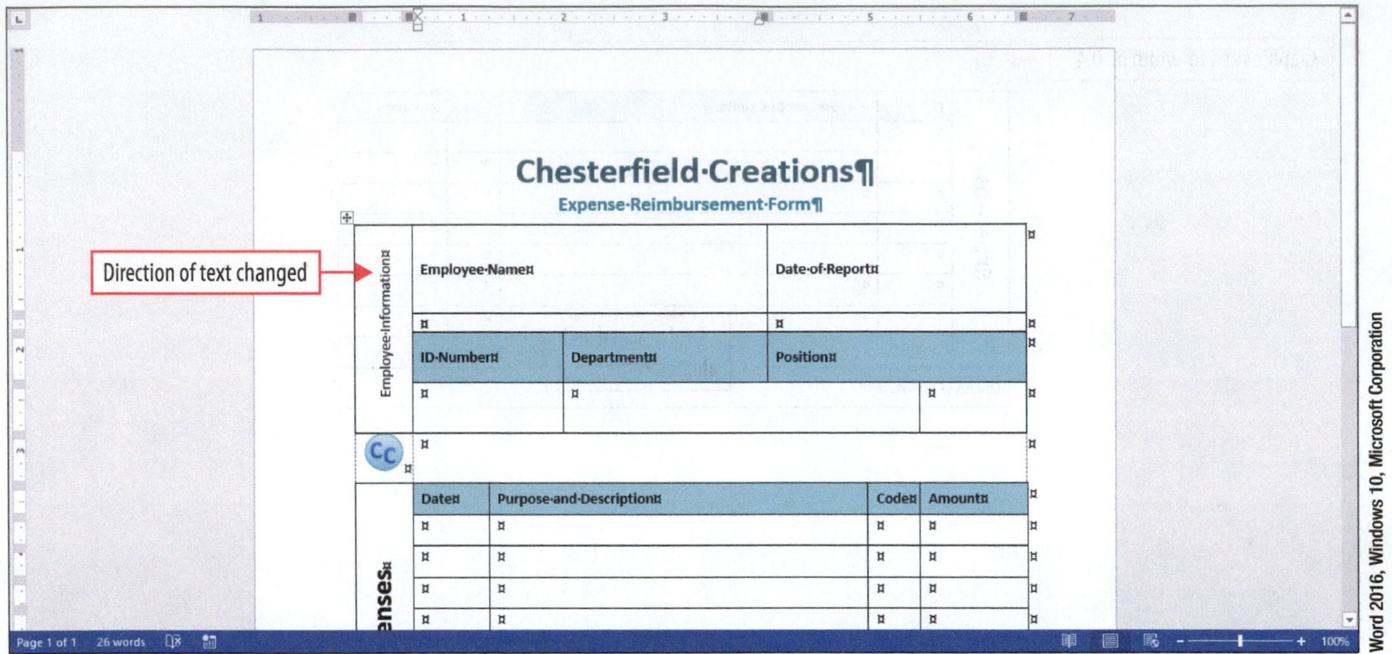

FIGURE 5.40

Activity 5.19 | Distributing Rows and Columns

When you draw a freeform table, you may want some rows to be the same height or some columns to be the same width. The ***Distribute Columns*** command adjusts the width of the selected columns so that they are equal. Similarly, the ***Distribute Rows*** command adjusts the height of the selected rows to be equal.

1 In the first four rows of the table, select all of the cells to the right of the first column. On the **Table Tools Layout tab**, in the **Cell Size group**, click **Distribute Rows**. Click outside of the table to deselect the cells, and then compare your screen with Figure 5.41.

This action distributes the height of the selected rows equally between them.

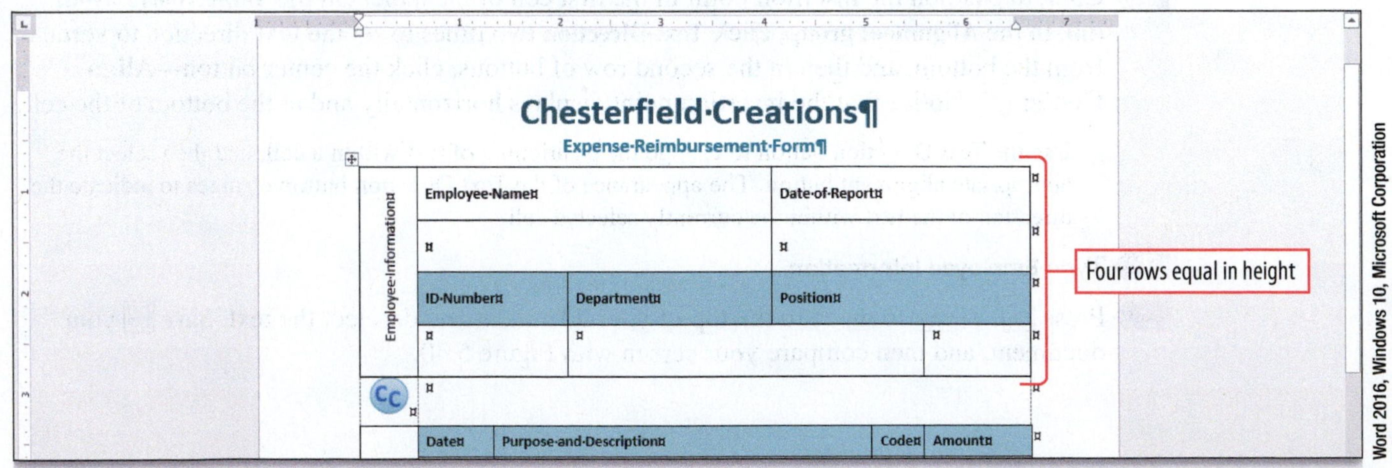

FIGURE 5.41

2 **Save** your document.

Activity 5.20 | Shading Table Cells

In this Activity, you will add shading to cells.

1 In the first row of the table, select the second and third cells—the cells containing *Employee Name* and *Date of Report*—and then compare your screen with Figure 5.42.

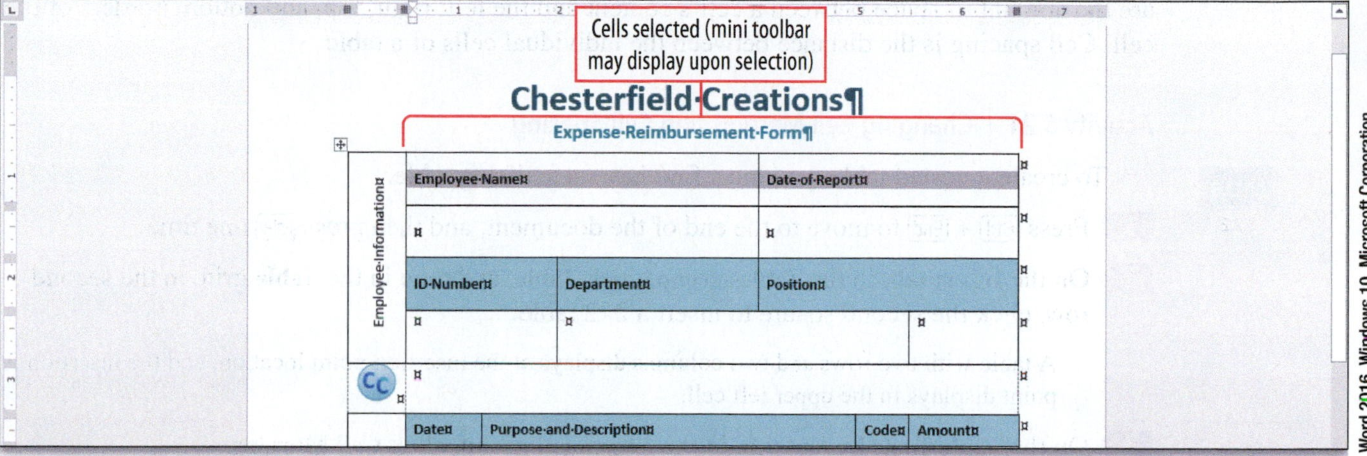

FIGURE 5.42

2 On the **Table Tools Design tab**, in the **Table Styles group**, click the **Shading button arrow**, and then under **Theme Colors**, in the next to last column, click the third color—**Aqua, Accent 5, Lighter 60%**.

3 Click outside of the table to deselect the cells, and then compare your screen with Figure 5.43.

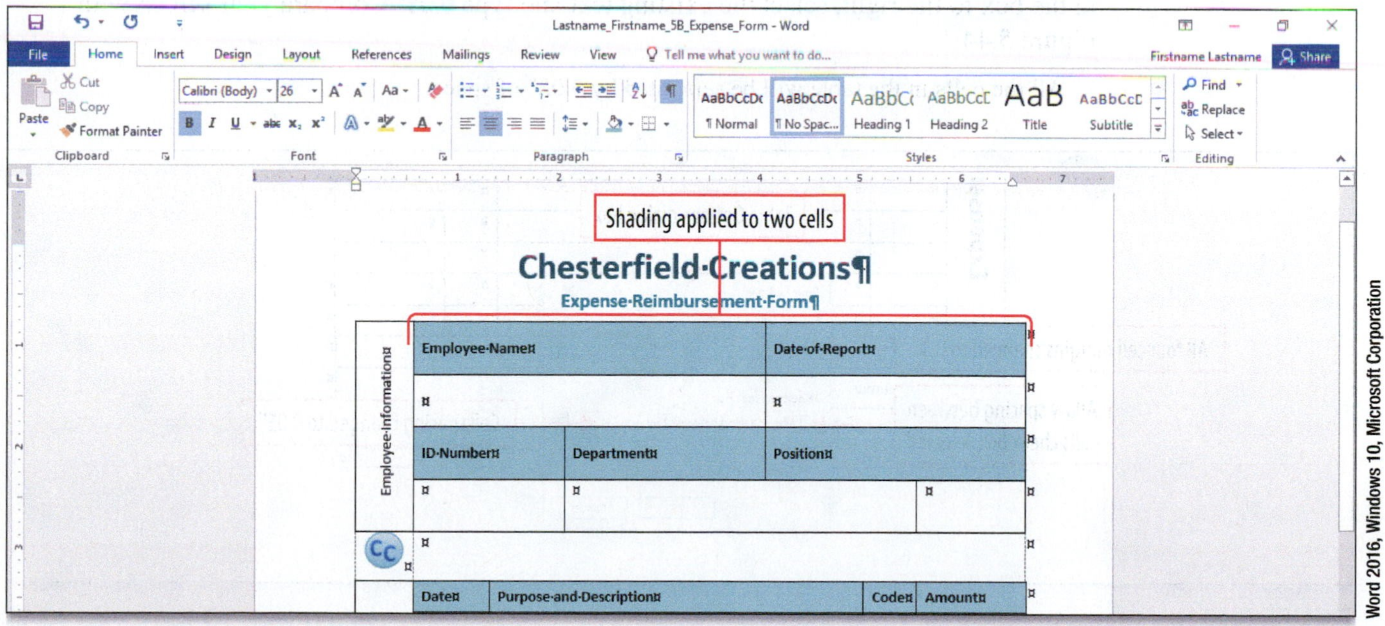

FIGURE 5.43

4 **Save** your document.

Objective 6 Use Nested Tables

GO! Learn How Video W5-6

A ***nested table*** is a table within a table. You can insert a table in any cell of an existing table. Using nested tables can enhance the readability of the displayed data. You can also improve the appearance of data within tables by changing ***cell margins*** and ***cell spacing***. Cell margins are the amount of space between a cell's content and the left, right, top, and bottom borders of the cell. Cell spacing is the distance between the individual cells of a table.

Activity 5.21 | Changing Cell Margins and Cell Spacing

3.2.2

To create a nested table, you must first have an existing table.

1. Press Ctrl + End to move to the end of the document, and then press Enter one time.

2. On the **Insert tab**, in the **Tables group**, click **Table**, and then in the **Table** grid, in the second row, click the second square to insert a 2×2 table.

   A table with two rows and two columns displays at the insertion point location, and the insertion point displays in the upper left cell.

3. On the **Table Tools Layout tab**, in the **Alignment group**, click **Cell Margins**.

   The Table Options dialog box displays. Here you can set the cell margins and cell spacing for a table.

4. In the **Table Options** dialog box, under **Default cell margins**, for *each* of the four cell margins—**Top**, **Bottom**, **Left**, and **Right**—select the existing text and type **0.1"**

   The contents of each cell within the table will be displayed 0.1" from each cell border.

5. Under **Default cell spacing**, select the **Allow spacing between cells** check box, and then in the box to the right, select the existing text and type **0.05"** Compare your screen with Figure 5.44.

   All the cells in the table will be separated by 0.05" of space.

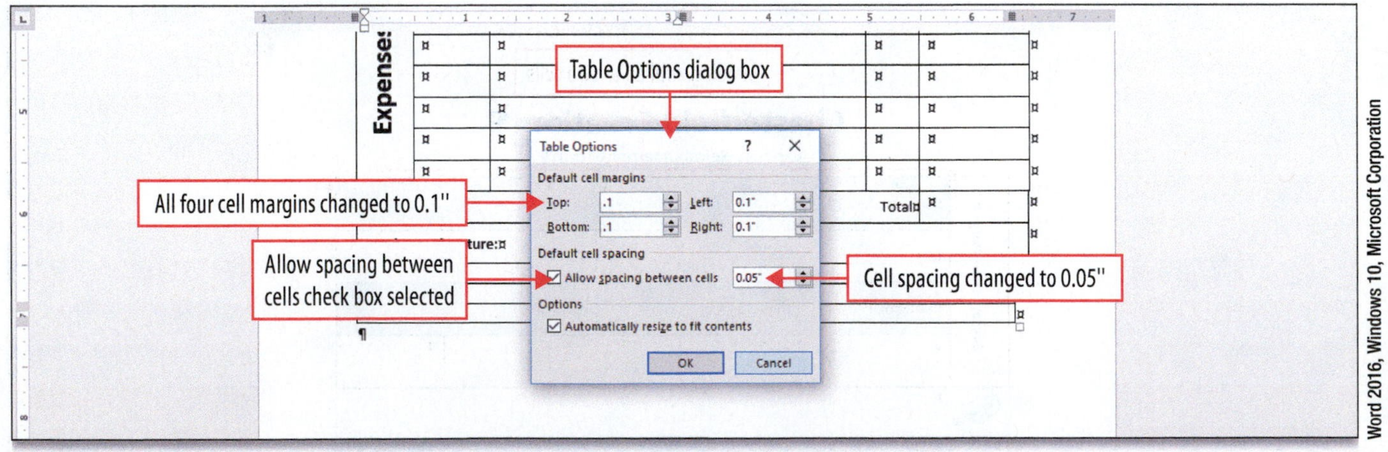

FIGURE 5.44

6. Click **OK** to accept the settings and close the **Table Options** dialog box.

Activity 5.22 | Using the Border Painter

1. In the new table, select the two cells in the first column, and then on the **Table Tools Layout tab**, in the **Merge group**, click **Merge Cells**. Compare your screen with Figure 5.45.

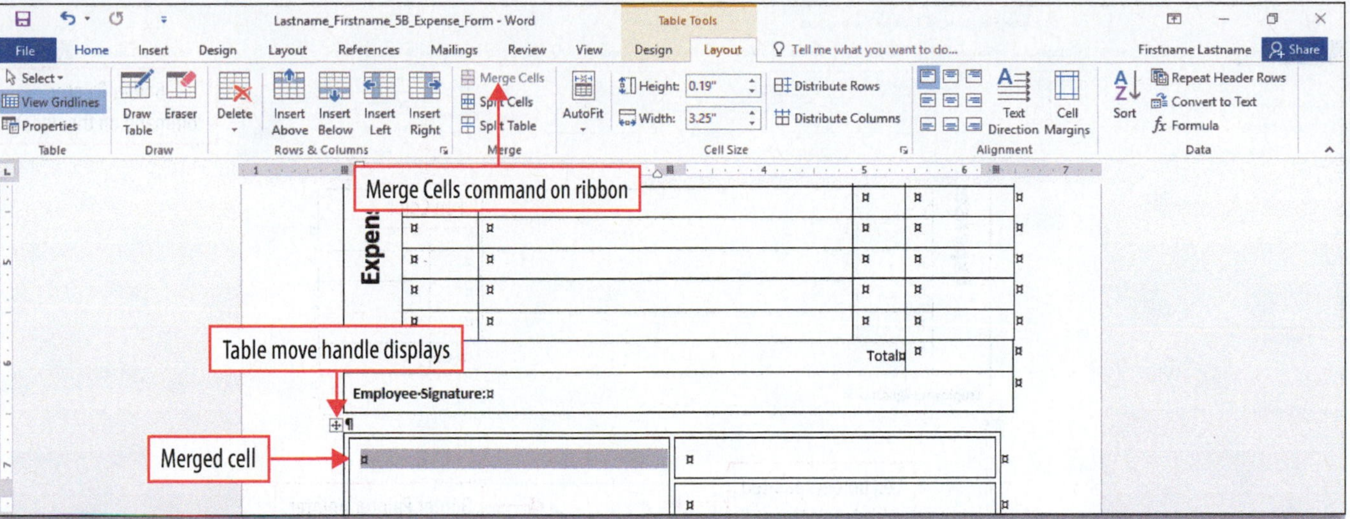

FIGURE 5.45 Word 2016, Windows 10, Microsoft Corporation

2 Point slightly outside of the upper left corner of the table to display the **table move handle** ⊞. With the pointer displayed, click the **table move handle** ⊞ one time to select the entire table.

ANOTHER WAY On the Table Tools Layout tab, in the Table group, click Select, and then click Select Table.

3 On the **Table Tools Layout tab**, in the **Table group**, if necessary, click the **View Gridlines** button to turn on the feature—when the feature is active, the button is shaded. On the **Table Tools Design tab**, in the **Borders group**, click the **Borders button arrow**, and then click **No Border**.

4 In the second column, click to position the insertion point in the second cell. On the **Table Tools Design tab**, in the **Borders group**, click **Pen Color**, and then under **Theme Colors**, in the next to last column, click the first color—**Aqua, Accent 5**.

By default, in the Borders group, when you change the Border Style, Pen Color, or Line Weight, the ***Border Painter*** feature becomes active. The Border Painter applies selected formatting to specific borders of a table. When the Border Painter is turned on, the pointer takes the shape of a small brush.

5 In the second column, in the lower cell, click each of the four borders of the cell with the **Border Painter** pointer. Notice that the border color changes to the selected color. Compare your screen with Figure 5.46.

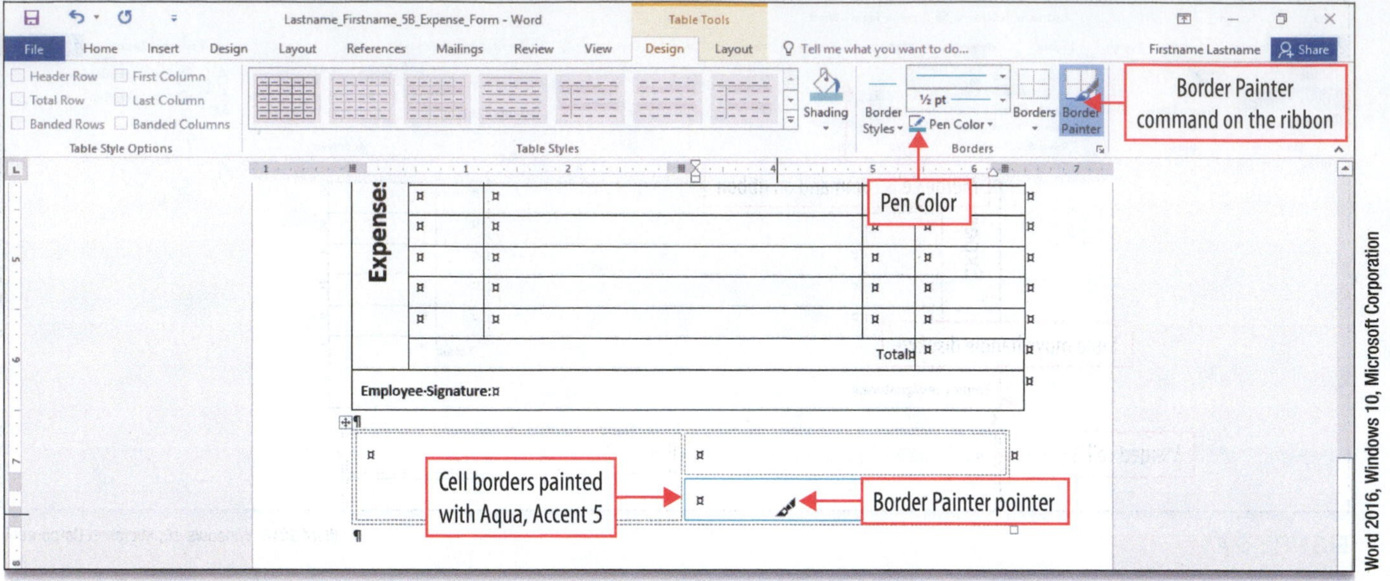

FIGURE 5.46

6 In the **Borders group**, click the **Pen Color arrow**, and then click **Automatic**. In the same group, click **Border Painter** to turn off the feature. **Save** your document.

Activity 5.23 | Inserting a Nested Table

In this Activity, you will create a nested table to display the codes that are used on the expense form.

1 Click to position the insertion point in the first cell of the second table. On the **Insert tab**, in the **Tables group**, click **Table**, and then in the **Table** grid, in the sixth row, click the second cell.

A table containing two columns and six rows is created—nested—within the first cell of the table.

2 In the first cell of the nested table, type **Type of Expense** Press Tab, and then type **Code**

3 In the same manner, enter the following data in the remaining cells of the table:

TYPE OF EXPENSE	CODE
Food	F
Lodging	L
Mileage	M
Registration	R
Tools	T

4 Be sure your insertion point is still active in the nested table. On the **Table Tools Layout tab**, in the **Cell Size group**, click **AutoFit**, and then click **AutoFit Contents** to resize the nested table to fit the existing text.

5 On the **Table Tools Design tab**, in the **Table Styles group**, click **More**. In the **Table Styles** gallery, scroll down, and then under **List Tables**, in the third row, click the sixth style—**List Table 3 – Accent 5**. Compare your screen with Figure 5.47.

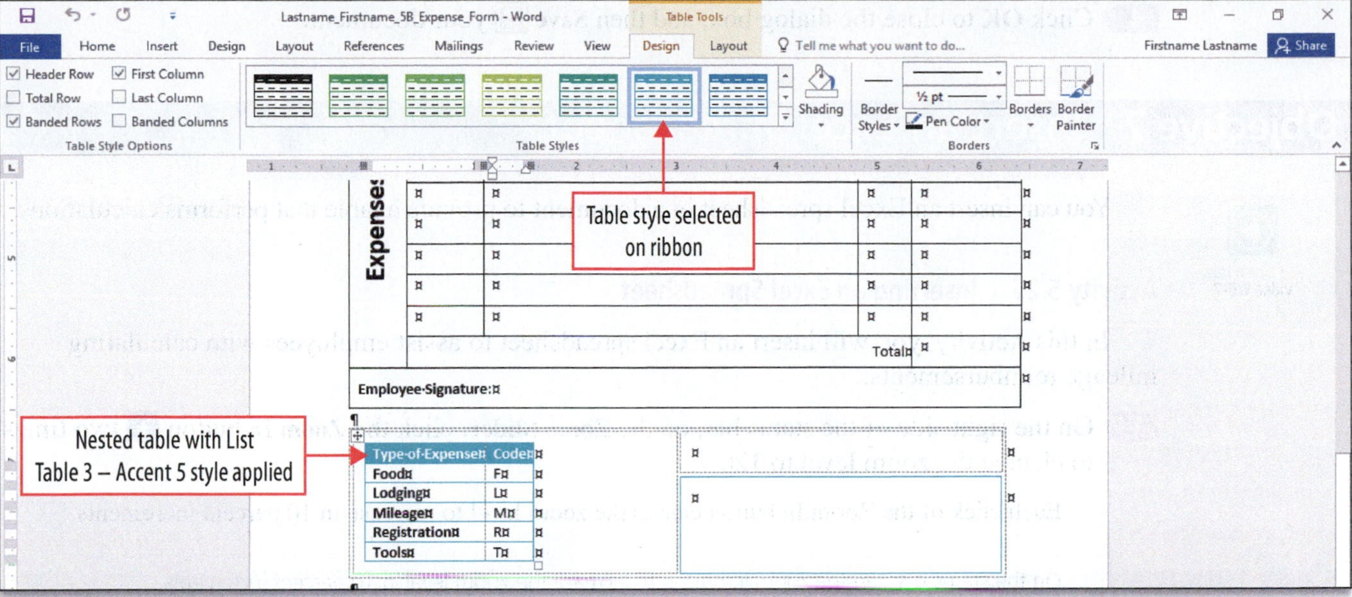

FIGURE 5.47

Word 2016, Windows 10, Microsoft Corporation

Activity 5.24 | Adding Alternative Text to a Table

4.3.2, 5.2.8

Alternative text—text associated with an image that serves the same purpose and conveys the same essential information as the image—can be added to the properties of an object—for example, a table, chart, or picture. This is useful for a person with vision or cognitive impairments who may not be able to view or understand the object as it displays in the document. The title of the object—in this instance, the table—can be read to the person with the disability. If applicable, the description can also be read to provide more information.

1. With the insertion point in the table, on the **Table Tools Layout tab**, in the **Table group**, click **Properties**.
2. In the **Table Properties** dialog box, click the **Alt Text tab**.
3. In the **Title** box, type **Expense Codes** In the **Description** box, type **The table contains the codes to be used when completing the expense form.** Compare your screen with Figure 5.48.

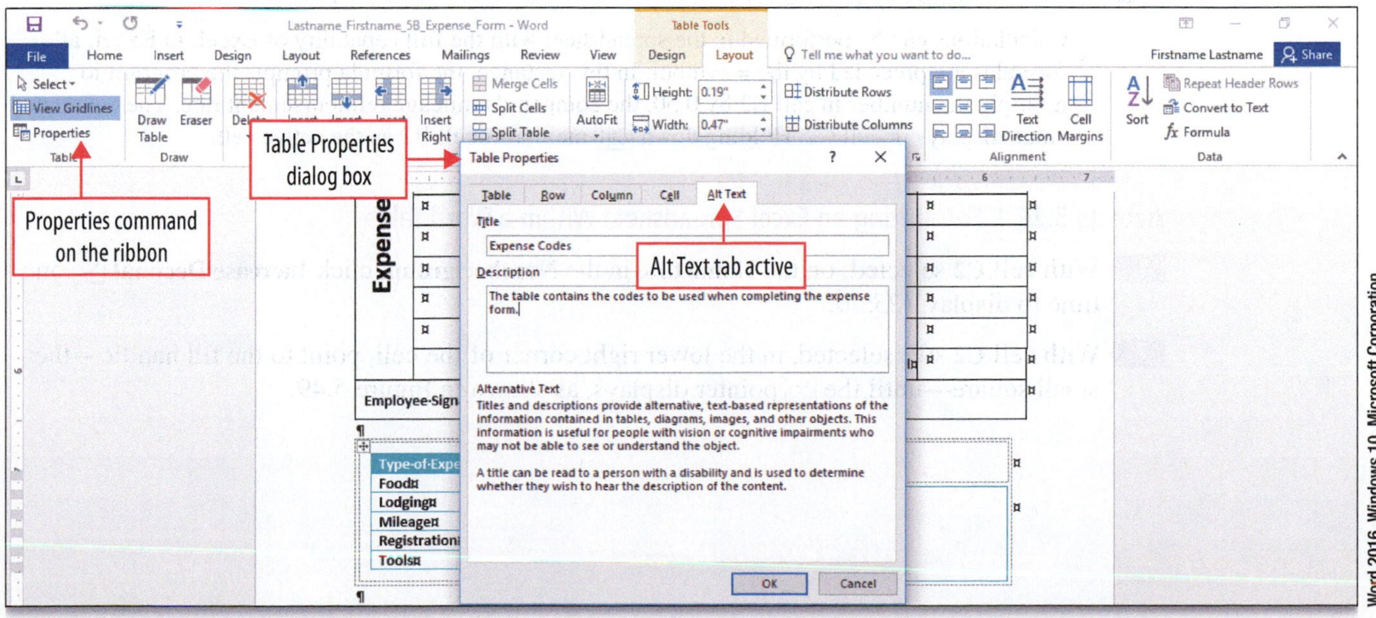

FIGURE 5.48

Word 2016, Windows 10, Microsoft Corporation

4 Click **OK** to close the dialog box, and then **Save** your document.

Objective 7 Insert an Excel Spreadsheet

GO! Learn How
Video W5-7

You can insert an Excel spreadsheet in a document to provide a table that performs calculations.

Activity 5.25 | Inserting an Excel Spreadsheet

In this Activity, you will insert an Excel spreadsheet to assist employees with calculating mileage reimbursements.

1 On the right side of the status bar, on the **Zoom Slider**, click the **Zoom In** button two times to change the zoom level to 120%.

Each click of the Zoom In button causes the zoom level to increase in 10 percent increments.

BY TOUCH On the status bar, tap the Zoom In button to increase the zoom level in 10 percent increments.

2 In the second table, which contains the nested table, in the second column, click to position the insertion point in the top cell. Type **To calculate the amount of your mileage reimbursement, double-click the spreadsheet below. Enter the trip name and number of miles, and then press ENTER.**

3 Click to position the insertion point in the remaining empty cell. On the **Insert tab**, in the **Tables group**, click **Table**, and then click **Excel Spreadsheet**.

An Excel spreadsheet and part of the table display on **Page 2** of the document.

4 In cell **A1**, type **Trip** and then press Tab. In cell **B1**, type **Miles** and then press Tab. In cell **C1**, type **Amount**

5 Click in cell **A2**, type **Example** and then press Tab. In cell **B2**, type **247** and then press Tab. In cell **C2**, type **=b2*0.5**

The formula is based on a mileage reimbursement rate of 50 cents per mile.

6 Hold down Ctrl and press Enter, and notice that the value *123.5* displays in cell **C2**.

Calculations can be performed in the spreadsheet with the full capability of Excel. In Excel, all formulas are preceded by the = symbol. In this instance, the formula prompts the program to multiply the number in cell B2 by 0.50, the company's mileage reimbursement rate. The calculated value displays in cell C2. Holding down Ctrl maintains cell B2 as the active cell.

Activity 5.26 | Formatting an Excel Spreadsheet Within a Word Table

1 With cell **C2** selected, on the **Home tab**, in the **Number group**, click **Increase Decimal** one time to display *123.50*.

2 With cell **C2** still selected, in the lower right corner of the cell, point to the fill handle—the small square—until the + pointer displays, as shown in Figure 5.49.

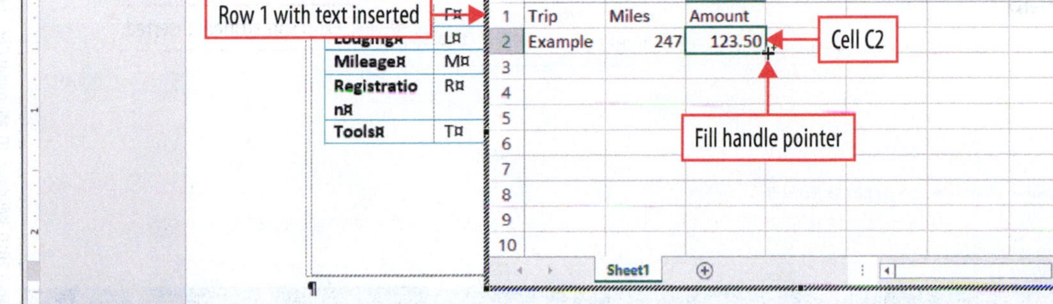

FIGURE 5.49

3 With the [+] pointer displayed, drag down to cell **C3**. Notice that the number *0.00* displays.

Dragging the fill handle copies the formula in C2 to the cell below. Excel changes the cell references in the formula to match the row number—for example, in cell C3 the formula is copied as =B3*0.5. Because you have not yet entered any data in row 3, the Amount column displays a value of 0.00.

4 On the right edge of the spreadsheet, point to the middle sizing handle until the [⇔] pointer displays. Compare your screen with Figure 5.50.

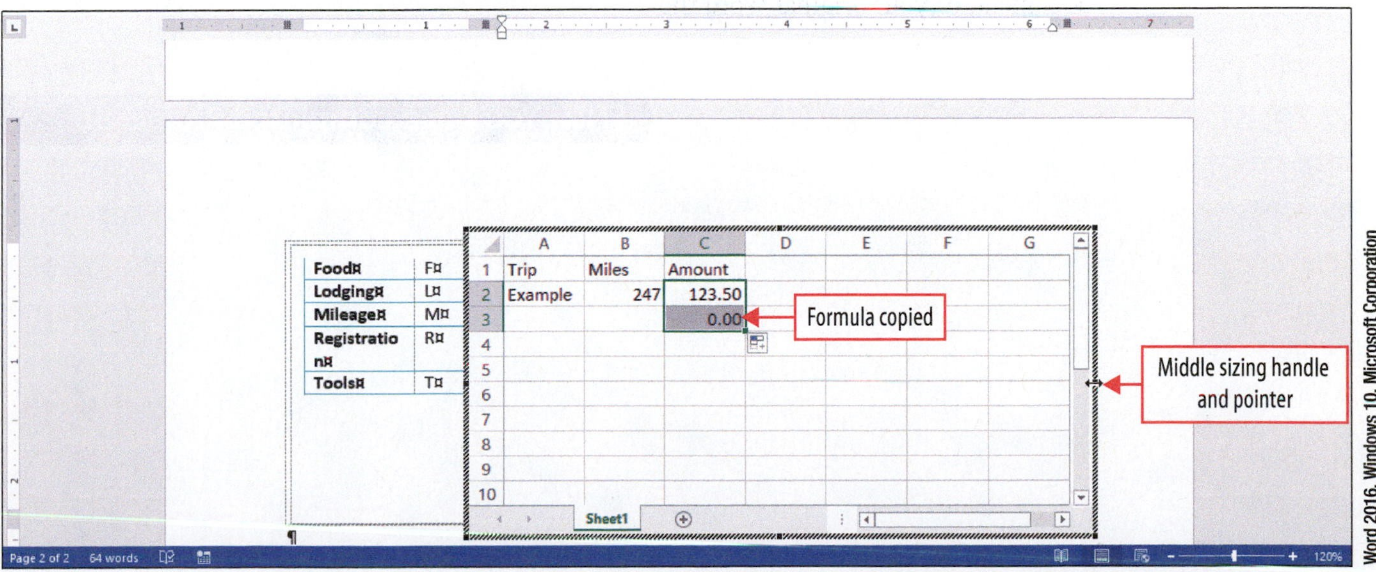

FIGURE 5.50

5 Drag to the left until only **columns A, B, and C** display—there will be a slight amount of space to the right of column C to accommodate the scroll bar.

6 At the bottom of the spreadsheet, point to the middle sizing handle until the [pointer icon] pointer displays. Drag upward until only **rows 1 through 3** display and then release the mouse button. Compare your screen with Figure 5.51.

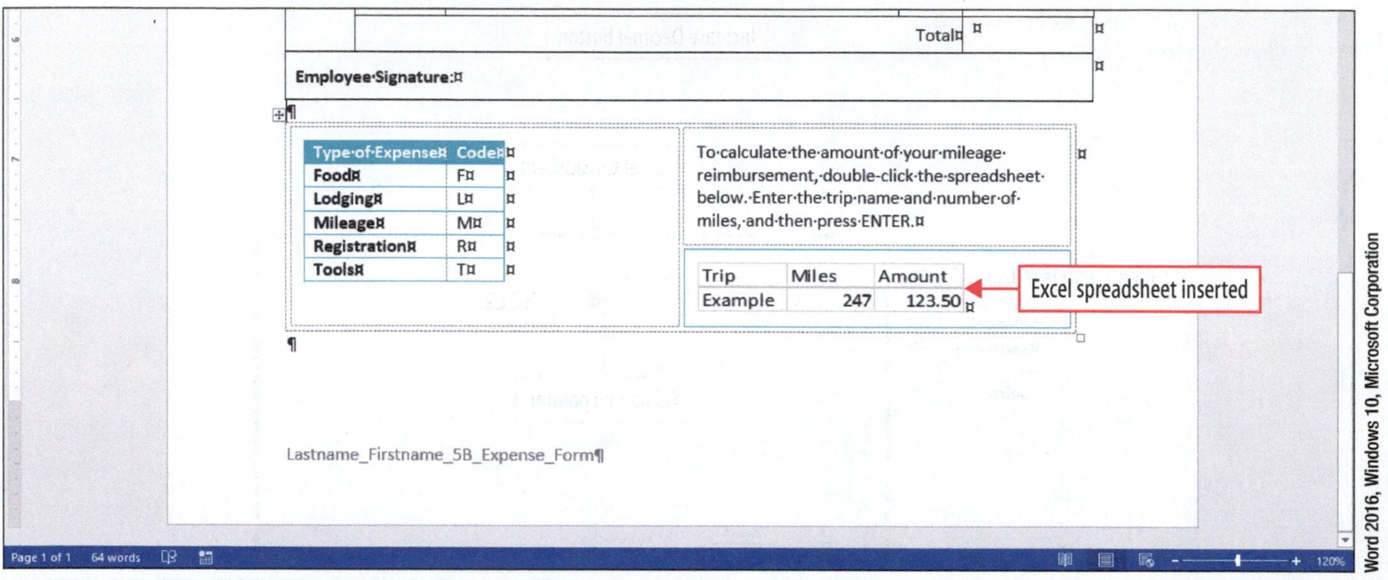

FIGURE 5.51

7 To close the Excel spreadsheet, click in a blank area of the document.

8 Press Ctrl + Home, and then **Save** your document.

9 Click the **File tab** to display **Backstage** view, and then show all properties. In the **Tags** box, type **expense form, nested table** In the **Subject** box, type your course name and section number. If necessary, edit the author name to display your name.

10 On the left, click **Save** to save your document and return to the Word window. In the upper right corner of the Word window, click **Close** [X]. If directed by your instructor to do so, submit your paper printout, your electronic image of your document that looks like a printed document, or your original Word file.

END | You have completed Project 5B

GO! To Work

Andrew Rodriguez / Fotolia; FotolEdhar/ Fotolia; apops/ Fotolia; Yuri Arcurs/ Fotolia

5 WORD

MICROSOFT OFFICE SPECIALIST (MOS) SKILLS IN THIS CHAPTER	
PROJECT 5A	**PROJECT 5B**
3.1.1 Convert text to tables **3.1.4** Apply table styles **3.2.1** Sort table data **3.2.3** Merge and split cells **3.2.4** Resize tables, rows, and columns **3.2.5** Split tables **4.1.6** Insert figure and table captions **4.1.7** Modify caption properties **5.2.6** Wrap text around objects **1.1.2** Expert: Copy custom styles, macros, and building blocks to other documents or templates **3.2.2** Expert: Insert and modify captions	**3.2.2** Configure cell margins and spacing **4.3.2** Add alt-text to document elements **5.2.8** Add alternative text to objects for accessibility

BUILD YOUR E-PORTFOLIO

An E-Portfolio is a collection of evidence, stored electronically, that showcases what you have accomplished while completing your education. Collecting and then sharing your work products with potential employers reflects your academic and career goals. Your completed documents from the following projects are good examples to show what you have learned: 5G, 5K, and 5L.

GO! FOR JOB SUCCESS

Discussion: 3D Printing

Your instructor may assign this discussion to your class, and then ask you to think about, or discuss with your classmates, these questions.

3D printing is a manufacturing process where three-dimensional objects are created from a digital file. You are familiar with laser printers that read digital files, like a Word document, and place ink on paper. 3D "printers" are machines that lay down layers of materials based on instructions from a digital file. The result is an object, like a part for an automobile, instead of a document. Research 3d printing on the Internet to help you think about the following questions.

FotolEdhar / Fotolia

What are some industries that could benefit from trying out completely new products by using a 3D printer without having to build new manufacturing plants?

What are some medical devices that could be improved by being made specifically for you or a friend or family member by using a 3D printer?

If a 3D printer could be sent into space and receive instructions from earth, what are some objects it could create that would help scientists understand space objects?

END OF CHAPTER

SUMMARY

Creating and applying a table style standardizes the appearance of multiple tables in a document. The style can include formatting for the entire table and for specific elements—such as rows and columns.

Word has advanced tools that enable you to present table data efficiently and attractively—such as changing alignment within cells, merging and splitting cells, sorting data, and changing text direction.

The Draw Table and Table Eraser features function as an electronic pencil and eraser. By drawing and erasing borders, you can create a table with rows and columns of varying sizes—for example, in a form.

Insert a nested table or modify the cell margins and cell spacing to improve readability of data within a table. To perform simple or complex calculations within a document, insert an Excel spreadsheet.

GO! LEARN IT ONLINE

Review the concepts, key terms, and MOS skills in this chapter by completing these online challenges, which you can find at **MyITLab**.

Matching and Multiple Choice: Answer matching and multiple-choice questions to test what you learned in this chapter.

Lessons on the GO!: Learn how to use all the new apps and features as they are introduced by Microsoft.

MOS Prep Quiz: Answer questions to review the MOS skills that you practiced in this chapter.

PROJECT GUIDE FOR WORD CHAPTER 5

Your instructor will assign Projects from this list to ensure your learning and assess your knowledge.

PROJECT GUIDE FOR WORD CHAPTER 5			
Project	**Apply Skills from These Chapter Objectives**	**Project Type**	**Project Location**
5A **MyITLab**	Objectives 1–4 from Project 5A	**5A Instructional Project (Grader Project)** Guided instruction to learn the skills in Project 5A.	In MyITLab and in text
5B **MyITLab**	Objectives 5–7 from Project 5B	**5B Instructional Project (Grader Project)** Guided instruction to learn the skills in Project 5B.	In MyITLab and in text
5C	Objectives 1–4 from Project 5A	**5C Skills Review (Scorecard Grading)** A guided review of the skills from Project 5A.	In text
5D	Objectives 5–7 from Project 5B	**5D Skills Review (Scorecard Grading)** A guided review of the skills from Project 5B.	In text
5E **MyITLab**	Objectives 1–4 from Project 5A	**5E Mastery (Grader Project)** **Mastery and Transfer of Learning** A demonstration of your mastery of the skills in Project 5A with extensive decision making.	In MyITLab and in text
5F **MyITLab**	Objectives 5–7 from Project 5B	**5F Mastery (Grader Project)** **Mastery and Transfer of Learning** A demonstration of your mastery of the skills in Project 5B with extensive decision making.	In MyITLab and in text
5G **MyITLab**	Objectives 1–7 from Projects 5A and 5B	**5G Mastery (Grader Project)** **Mastery and Transfer of Learning** A demonstration of your mastery of the skills in Projects 5A and 5B with extensive decision making.	In MyITLab and in text
5H	Combination of Objectives from Projects 5A and 5B	**5H GO! Fix It (Scorecard Grading)** **Critical Thinking** A demonstration of your mastery of the skills in Projects 5A and 5B by creating a correct result from a document that contains errors you must find.	Instructor Resource Center (IRC) and MyITLab
5I	Combination of Objectives from Projects 5A and 5B	**5I GO! Make It (Scorecard Grading)** **Critical Thinking** A demonstration of your mastery of the skills in Projects 5A and 5B by creating a result from a supplied picture.	IRC and MyITLab
5J	Combination of Objectives from Projects 5A and 5B	**5J GO! Solve It (Rubric Grading)** **Critical Thinking** A demonstration of your mastery of the skills in Projects 5A and 5B, your decision-making skills, and your critical thinking skills. A task-specific rubric helps you self-assess your result.	IRC and MyITLab
5K	Combination of Objectives from Projects 5A and 5B	**5K GO! Solve It (Rubric Grading)** **Critical Thinking** A demonstration of your mastery of the skills in Projects 5A and 5B, your decision-making skills, and your critical thinking skills. A task-specific rubric helps you self-assess your result.	In text
5L	Combination of Objectives from Projects 5A and 5B	**5L GO! Think (Rubric Grading)** **Critical Thinking** A demonstration of your understanding of the chapter concepts applied in a manner that you would outside of college. An analytic rubric helps you and your instructor grade the quality of your work by comparing it to the work an expert in the discipline would create.	In text
5M	Combination of Objectives from Projects 5A and 5B	**5M GO! Think (Rubric Grading)** **Critical Thinking** A demonstration of your understanding of the chapter concepts applied in a manner that you would outside of college. An analytic rubric helps you and your instructor grade the quality of your work by comparing it to the work an expert in the discipline would create.	IRC and MyITLab
5N	Combination of Objectives from Projects 5A and 5B	**5N You and GO! (Rubric Grading)** **Critical Thinking** A demonstration of your understanding of the chapter concepts applied in a manner that you would in a personal situation. An analytic rubric helps you and your instructor grade the quality of your work.	IRC and MyITLab

GLOSSARY

GLOSSARY OF CHAPTER KEY TERMS

Alternative text Text associated with an image that serves the same purpose and conveys the same essential information as the image.

AutoFit A table feature that automatically adjusts column widths or the width of the entire table.

AutoFit Contents A table feature that resizes the column widths to accommodate the maximum field size.

Border Painter A table feature that applies selected formatting to specific borders of a table.

Caption A title that is added to a Word object and numbered sequentially.

Cell margins The amount of space between a cell's content and the left, right, top, and bottom borders of the cell.

Cell spacing The distance between the individual cells in a table.

Distribute Columns A command that adjusts the width of the selected columns so that they are equal.

Distribute Rows A command that causes the height of the selected rows to be equal.

Field A placeholder for data.

Formula A mathematical expression that contains functions, operators, constants, and properties and returns a value to a cell.

Function A predefined formula that performs calculations by using specific values in a particular order.

Gridlines Nonprinting lines that indicate cell borders.

Header row The first row of a table containing column titles.

Merge A table feature that combines two or more adjacent cells into one cell so that the text spans across multiple columns or rows.

Nested table A table inserted in a cell of an existing table.

Organizer A dialog box where you can modify a document by using styles stored in another document or template.

Split A table feature that divides selected cells into multiple cells with a specified number of rows and columns.

Split Table A table feature that divides an existing table into two tables in which the selected row—where the insertion point is located—becomes the first row of the second table.

Style A group of formatting commands—such as font, font size, and font color—that can be applied with a single command.

Table style A style that includes formatting for the entire table and specific table elements, such as rows and columns.

CHAPTER REVIEW

Apply 5A skills from these Objectives:

1. Create and Apply a Custom Table Style
2. Format Cells
3. Use Advanced Table Features
4. Modify Table Properties

Skills Review Project 5C Sales Conference

In the following Skills Review, you will format tables and insert formulas to create a memo regarding a conference for sales managers at Chesterfield Creations. Your completed document will look similar to Figure 5.52.

PROJECT FILES

For Project 5C, you will need the following files:

w05C_Sales_Conference

w05C_Sales_Styles

You will save your file as:

Lastname_Firstname_5C_Sales_Conference

PROJECT RESULTS

Chesterfield Creations

TO: All Sales Managers

FROM: Charles Ferguson, Marketing Vice President

DATE: March 3, 2018

RE: Annual Sales Conference

This past year was highly successful for Chesterfield Creations. In preparation for the annual sales conference to be held March 20 at our corporate headquarters in Toronto, I would like to review our accomplishments during the past year.

After conducting extensive customer research and launching our large line of new products, we expanded our customer base to include leisure and adventure travelers as well as fashion-forward men and women.

We have had a huge increase in online sales due to a more attractive, user-friendly website and new online marketing strategies. Chesterfield Creations products are being sold in 40 additional retail stores in Canada and the United States, as noted in the tables below. We owe this success to the diligence of our extraordinary sales team.

Table 1: New Canadian Stores

Province	# of Stores
Nova Scotia	1
British Columbia	2
Quebec	3
Ontario	6
Total Stores	12

Table 2: New US Stores

State	# of Stores
New Hampshire	1
Michigan	2
Virginia	3
New York	6
Florida	7
California	9
Total Stores	28

Lastname_Firstname_5C_Sales_Conference

Throughout the conference, we will be honoring many of you for the efforts you've made to secure new clients and maintain existing relationships. Several of you will also have the opportunity to share specific success stories from the past year that will inspire all of us.

Conference Information

Table 3 lists the topics and speakers for the conference. If you have not yet made your reservation, please contact me at c.ferguson@chesterfieldcreations.com. I look forward to seeing you at the conference on March 20.

Table 3

Topic	Speaker
Competitive Analysis	Huong Nguyen
Overall Industry Trends	Roslyn Godfrey
Product Training	Joseph D'Angelo
Sales Skills Development	Charles Ferguson
Team Building	Alejandra Domene

Lastname_Firstname_5C_Sales_Conference

Word 2016, Windows 10, Microsoft Corporation

FIGURE 5.52

(Project 5C Sales Conference continues on the next page)

Skills Review Project 5C Sales Conference (continued)

1 Start Word. From your student data files for this chapter, open the file **w05C_Sales_Conference**. Save the document in your **Word Chapter 5** folder, using your own name, as **Lastname_Firstname_5C_Sales_Conference** Insert the file name in the footer. Display the rulers and formatting marks. If any words are flagged as spelling errors, **Ignore All**.

- **a.** On the **Home tab**, in the **Styles group**, click the **Dialog Box Launcher** button.
- **b.** At the bottom of the **Styles pane**, click the third button—**Manage Styles**.
- **c.** In the lower left corner of the **Manage Styles** dialog box, click **Import/Export** to display the **Organizer** dialog box.
- **d.** On the left side of the **Organizer** dialog box, be sure that your *Lastname_Firstname_5C_Sales_Conference* file displays. On the right side of the **Organizer**, click the **Close File** button. Click the **Open File** button, navigate to your student data files for this chapter, click one time to select the file **w05C_Sales_Styles**, and then click **Open**.
- **e.** On the right side of the **Organizer**, scroll as necessary, select **Heading 2**, press and hold Ctrl, scroll down as necessary, and then select **Title**. In the middle of the **Organizer** dialog box, **Copy**. **Close** the **Organizer**. **Save** your document.

2 Select the first paragraph—**Chesterfield Creations**, and then apply the **Title** style.

- **a.** On the **Home tab**, in the **Styles group**, if necessary click the **Dialog Box Launcher** to display the **Styles** pane. At the bottom of the **Styles** pane, click the first button—**New Style**. In the **Create New Style from Formatting** dialog box, under **Properties**, in the **Name** box, type **Sales Conference** Click the **Style type arrow**, and then click **Table**.
- **b.** Under **Formatting**, click the **Border button arrow**, and then click **All Borders**. Click the **Line Weight arrow**, and then click **1 pt**. Click the **Border Color arrow**, and then in the sixth column, click the first color—**Orange, Accent 2**.
- **c.** Under **Formatting**, click the **Apply formatting to arrow**, and then click **Header row**. Click the **Fill Color arrow**, and then in the sixth column, click the third color—**Orange, Accent 2, Lighter 60%**. Click **OK**. **Close** the **Styles** pane.
- **d.** In the sixth row of the table, click in the first cell that contains the text *State*. On the **Table Tools Layout tab**, in the **Merge group**, click the **Split Table** button.

3 In the first table, click in the first cell. Click the **Table Tools Design tab**, and then in the **Table Styles group**, click the **Sales Conference** table style. In a similar manner, in the second table click in the first cell, and then apply the **Sales Conference** table style.

- **a.** On the **Table Tools Design tab**, in the **Table Styles group**, right-click the **Sales Conference** table style, and then click **Modify Table Style**. Click the **Apply formatting to arrow**, and then click **Header row**. Apply **Bold**, and then click **OK**.
- **b.** In the first table, position the insertion point to the right of *Province*. On the **Table Tools Layout tab**, in the **Merge group**, click **Split Cells**, and then click **OK**. In the first row, click in the second cell, and type **# of Stores**
- **c.** Select the **header row**, and then on the **Table Tools Layout tab**, in the **Alignment group**, click **Align Center**. In the first column, select all cells below the header row, and then click **Align Center Left**. In the second column, select all cells below the header row, and then click **Align Center**.
- **d.** In the second table, position the insertion point to the right of *State*. On the **Table Tools Layout tab**, in the **Merge group**, click **Split Cells**, and then click **OK**. In the first row, click in the second cell, and type **# of Stores**
- **e.** Select the **header row**, and then on the **Table Tools Layout tab**, in the **Alignment group**, click **Align Center**. In the first column, select all cells below the header row, and then click **Align Center Left**. In the second column, select all cells below the header row, and then click **Align Center**.

4 Click anywhere in the first table, and then on the **Table Tools Layout tab**, in the **Data group**, click **Sort**. Click the **Sort by arrow**, click **# of Stores**, and then click **OK**. Click anywhere in the second table, and then in the **Data group**, click **Sort**. In the **Sort** dialog box, click the **Sort by arrow**, click **# of Stores**, and then click **OK**.

5 Near the bottom of **Page 1**, select the paragraph **Conference Information**, and then apply the **Heading 2** style.

(Project 5C Sales Conference continues on the next page)

Skills Review Project 5C Sales Conference (continued)

a. On **Page 2**, locate the paragraph that begins *Topic*, and then beginning with this paragraph, select the six paragraphs at the end of the document.

b. On the **Insert tab**, in the **Tables group**, click **Table**, and then click **Convert Text to Table**. Click **OK** to close the dialog box.

6 Click to position your insertion point anywhere in the table you inserted. On the **Table Tools Design tab**, in the **Table Styles group**, click the **Sales Conference** table style.

a. On the **Table Tools Layout tab**, in the **Cell Size group**, click **AutoFit**, and then click **AutoFit Contents**.

b. Select the **header row**, and then in the **Alignment group**, click **Align Center**. Select the remaining cells in the table, and then click **Align Center Left**.

7 On **Page 1**, in the first table, click to position the insertion point in the first cell of the last row—the cell containing *Ontario*. On the **Table Tools Layout tab**, in the **Cell Size group**, click **AutoFit**, and then click **AutoFit Contents**. Point to the bottom left corner of the table, and then click the **One-Click Row/Column Insertion** button.

a. In the new last row of the table, click in the first cell, and then type **Total Stores** Select the text, and apply **Bold**. In the **Alignment group**, click **Align Center Right**. Press Tab, and then in the **Data group**, click **Formula**.

b. In the **Formula** dialog box, with *=SUM(ABOVE)* displayed, click the **Number format arrow**, and then click **0**. Click **OK**. Select the inserted text, and apply **Bold**.

8 In the second table, click to position the insertion point in the first cell of the last row—the cell containing the text *California*. On the **Table Tools Layout tab**, in the **Cell Size group**, click **AutoFit**, and then click **AutoFit Contents**. Point to the bottom left corner of the table, and then click the **One-Click Row/Column Insertion** button.

a. In the new last row, click in the first cell, and then type **Total Stores** Select the text, and apply **Bold**. In the **Alignment group**, click **Align Center Right**. Press Tab, and then in the **Data group**, click **Formula**.

b. In the **Formula** dialog box, with *=SUM(ABOVE)* displayed, click the **Number format arrow**, and then click **0**. Click **OK**. Select the inserted text, and apply **Bold**.

c. In the first table, in the second column, click in the fifth cell. Select *5*, and then type **6** In the last cell of the table, select **11**, right-click the selection, and then click **Update Field**.

d. In the second table, in the second column, click in the sixth cell. Select *8*, and then type **7** In the last cell of the table, select **29**, right-click the selection, and then click **Update Field**.

9 Click to position the insertion point anywhere in the first table. On the **References tab**, in the **Captions group**, click **Insert Caption**. In the **Caption** dialog box, with the insertion point to the right of *Table 1,* type a colon **:** and press Spacebar. Type **New Canadian Stores** If necessary, under **Options**, click the **Position arrow**, and then click **Above selected item**. Click **OK**.

a. Click to position the insertion point anywhere in the second table. In the **Captions group**, click **Insert Caption**. In the **Caption** dialog box, with the insertion point to the right of *Table 2*, type a colon **:** and then press Spacebar. Type **New US Stores** If necessary, under **Options**, click the **Position arrow**, and then click **Above selected item**. Click **OK**.

b. On **Page 2**, click to position the insertion point anywhere in the last table. On the **Table Tools Layout tab**, in the **Table group**, click **Properties**. In the **Table Properties** dialog box, if necessary, under **Text wrapping**, click **Around**, and then click **Positioning**.

c. In the **Table Positioning** dialog box, under **Distance from surrounding text**, click the **Left up spin arrow** to **0.5"**. Click **OK** two times to close the dialog boxes. Display the **Table Move Handle**, and then drag the table up and to the right until the top border is even with the first line of the last paragraph and the right border is aligned with the right margin.

d. Click anywhere in the table. On the **References tab**, in the **Captions group**, click **Insert Caption**. In the **Caption** dialog box, with *Table 3* displayed, click **OK**. Select the caption, and then on the **Home tab**, in the **Paragraph group**, click **Align Right**. In the last paragraph of the document, select the text **Listed below are**, and then to replace the selected text, type **Table 3 lists**

(Project 5C Sales Conference continues on the next page)

CHAPTER REVIEW

Skills Review Project 5C Sales Conference (continued)

10 On **Page 1**, click to position the insertion point anywhere in the first table. On the **Table Tools Layout tab**, in the **Table group**, click **Properties**. In the **Table Properties** dialog box, under **Alignment**, click **Center**, and then click **OK**. Click to position the insertion point anywhere in the second table. In the **Table group**, click **Properties**. In the **Table Properties** dialog box, under **Alignment**, click **Center**, and then click **OK**. Select the captions for *Table 1* and *Table 2*, and then press Ctrl + E to center the captions over the tables.

11 Press Ctrl + Home. Click the **File tab**, and then click **Show All Properties**. As the **Tags**, type **sales conference** In the **Subject** box, type your course name and section number. If necessary, edit the author name to display your name.

12 **Save** your document. In the upper right corner of the Word window, click **Close**. If directed by your instructor to do so, submit your paper printout, your electronic image of your document that looks like a printed document, or your original Word file.

END | You have completed Project 5C

CHAPTER REVIEW

Skills Review Project 5D Student Interns

Apply 5B skills from these Objectives:

5 Draw a Freeform Table
6 Use Nested Tables
7 Insert an Excel Spreadsheet

In the following Skills Review, you will create a payment form for recording the work performed by and payment due to student interns at Chesterfield Creations. Your completed document will look similar to Figure 5.53.

PROJECT FILES

For Project 5D, you will need the following files:

w05D_Student_Interns
w05D_Logo

You will save your file as:

Lastname_Firstname_5D_Student_Interns

PROJECT RESULTS

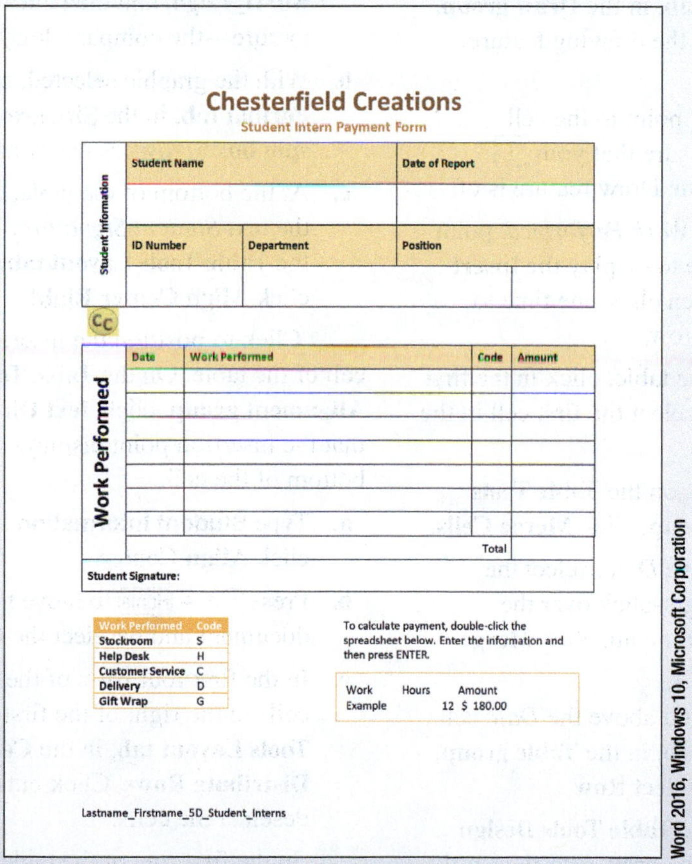

Chesterfield Creations
Student Intern Payment Form

Student Information	Student Name		Date of Report
	ID Number	Department	Position

Work Performed	Date	Work Performed	Code	Amount
			Total	
Student Signature:				

Work Performed	Code
Stockroom	S
Help Desk	H
Customer Service	C
Delivery	D
Gift Wrap	G

To calculate payment, double-click the spreadsheet below. Enter the information and then press ENTER.

Work	Hours	Amount
Example	12	$ 180.00

Lastname_Firstname_5D_Student_Interns

Word 2016, Windows 10, Microsoft Corporation

FIGURE 5.53

(Project 5D Student Interns continues on the next page)

Skills Review Project 5D Student Interns (continued)

1 Start Word. Navigate to the student files for this chapter and open the file **w05D_Student_Interns**. **Save** the document in your **Word Chapter 5** folder as **Lastname_Firstname_5D_Student_Interns** Insert the file name in the footer. Display the rulers and formatting marks.

a. Click anywhere inside the table. On the **Table Tools Layout tab**, in the **Draw group**, click **Draw Table**. Position the tip of the draw pointer slightly above the cell containing the text *ID Number*.

b. Hold down the left mouse button, and then drag to the right to draw a horizontal line extending to the right border of the table.

c. On the **Table Tools Layout tab**, in the **Draw group**, click **Draw Table** to turn off the drawing feature. **Save** your document.

2 In the fifth row of the table, point to the cell containing the word *Date* and be sure that your [I] pointer displays, indicating that the Draw feature is off.

a. Above the cell with the text *Work Performed*, point to the left border of the table to display the **Insert Row/Column** button, and then click one time to insert a row above the *Date* row.

b. In the upper left corner of the table, click in the first cell, and then drag down to select the first cell in the second and third rows.

c. With the three cells selected, on the **Table Tools Layout tab**, in the **Merge group**, click **Merge Cells**.

3 In the row you inserted above *Date*, select the second, third, and fourth cells, right-click over the selection, and then on the shortcut menu, click **Merge Cells**.

a. Click in the newly merged cell above the *Date* cell. On the **Table Tools Layout tab**, in the **Table group**, click **Select**, and then click **Select Row**.

b. With the row selected, on the **Table Tools Design tab**, click the **Borders button arrow**, and then at the bottom click **Borders and Shading**.

c. In the **Borders and Shading** dialog box, on the right under **Preview**, click each of the three vertical lines to remove them.

d. Click **OK**, and then click anywhere in the table to deselect the row. On the **Table Tools Layout tab**, in the **Table group**, if necessary, click **View Gridlines**—if the button is shaded, then Gridlines are already active and dotted lines display on the borders you just removed. If necessary, activate gridlines.

e. **Save** your document.

4 Press Ctrl + Home to move to the top of your document. In the table, in the first column, click to position your insertion point in the second cell—the cell from which you removed the left and right borders and just above the *Work Performed* cell.

a. On the **Insert tab**, in the **Illustrations group**, click **Pictures**. Navigate to the location where your student data files are stored, select the file **w05D_Logo**, and then click **Insert**. Notice that the picture—the company logo—is inserted in the cell.

b. With the graphic selected, on the **Picture Tools Format tab**, in the **Size group**, click the **Shape Width spin box arrows** as necessary to set the width to **0.4"**.

c. At the bottom of the table, click in the cell above the text *Student Signature*. Type **Total** and then on the **Table Tools Layout tab**, in the **Alignment group**, click **Align Center Right**.

5 Click to position the insertion point in the first cell of the table. On the **Table Tools Layout tab**, in the **Alignment group**, click **Text Direction** two times. Notice that the insertion point displays horizontally and at the bottom of the cell.

a. Type **Student Information** In the **Alignment group**, click **Align Center**.

b. Press Ctrl + Home to move to the top of your document and deselect the text.

c. In the first four rows of the table, select all of the cells to the right of the first column. On the **Table Tools Layout tab**, in the **Cell Size group**, click **Distribute Rows**. Click outside of the table to deselect the cells.

6 In the first row of the table, select the second and third cells—the cells containing *Student Name* and *Date of Report*.

a. On the **Table Tools Design tab**, in the **Table Styles group**, click the **Shading button arrow**, and then under **Theme Colors**, in the next to last column, click the third color—**Gold, Accent 5, Lighter 60%**. Click outside of the table to deselect the cell.

(Project 5D Student Interns continues on the next page)

Skills Review Project 5D Student Interns (continued)

7 Press Ctrl + End to move to the end of the document, and then press Enter one time. On the **Insert tab**, in the **Tables group**, click the **Table** button, and then in the **Table** grid, in the second row, click the second square to insert a 2 × 2 table.

a. On the **Table Tools Layout tab**, in the **Alignment group**, click **Cell Margins**.

b. In the **Table Options** dialog box, under **Default cell margins**, use the spin box arrows to set **Top, Bottom, Left, and Right** to **0.1"**.

c. Under **Default cell spacing**, select the **Allow spacing between cells** check box, and then in the box to the right, use the spin box arrows to set the spacing to **0.05"**. Click **OK**.

8 In the new table, select the two cells in the first column, and then on the **Table Tools Layout tab**, in the **Merge group**, click **Merge Cells**.

a. Point slightly outside of the upper left corner of the table to display the **table move handle**, and then click the **table move handle** to select the entire table.

b. On the **Table Tools Layout tab**, in the **Table group**, if necessary, click the **View Gridlines** button to turn on the feature—when the feature is active, the button is shaded. On the **Table Tools Design tab**, in the **Borders group**, click the **Borders button arrow**, and then click **No Border**.

c. In the second column, click to position the insertion point in the second cell. On the **Table Tools Design tab**, in the **Borders group**, click **Pen Color**, and then under **Theme Colors**, in the next to last column, click the first color—**Gold, Accent 5**.

d. In the second column, in the lower cell, click each of the four borders of the cell with the **Border Painter** pointer. Notice that the border color changes to the selected color.

e. In the **Borders group**, click the **Pen Color arrow**, and then click **Automatic**. In the same group, click **Border Painter** to turn off the feature.

9 Click to position the insertion point in the first cell of the last table. On the **Insert tab**, in the **Tables group**, click **Table**, and then in the **Table** grid, in the sixth row, click the second cell.

a. In the first cell of the nested table, type **Work Performed** Press Tab, and then type **Code**

b. In the same manner, enter the following data in the remaining cells of the table:

WORK PERFORMED	CODE
Stockroom	S
Help Desk	H
Customer Service	C
Delivery	D
Gift Wrap	G

c. Be sure your insertion point is still active in the nested table. On the **Table Tools Layout tab**, in the **Cell Size group**, click **AutoFit**, and then click **AutoFit Contents** to resize the nested table to fit the existing text.

d. On the **Table Tools Design tab**, in the **Table Styles group**, click **More**. In the **Table Styles** gallery, scroll down, and then under **List Tables**, in the third row, click the sixth style—**List Table 3 – Accent 5**.

10 With the insertion point in the table, on the **Table Tools Layout tab**, in the **Table group**, click **Properties**. In the **Table Properties** dialog box, click the **Alt Text tab**.

a. In the **Title** box, type **Work Codes** In the **Description** box, type **The table contains the codes to be used when completing the expense form.** Click **OK**.

b. On the right side of the status bar, on the **Zoom Slider**, click the **Zoom In** button two times to change the zoom level to 120%.

c. In the second column, click to position the insertion point in the top cell. Type **To calculate payment, double-click the spreadsheet below. Enter the information and then press ENTER.**

11 Click to position the insertion point in the remaining empty cell. On the **Insert tab**, in the **Tables group**, click **Table**, and then click **Excel Spreadsheet**.

a. In cell **A1**, type **Work** and then press Tab. In cell **B1**, type **Hours** and then press Tab. In cell **C1**, type **Amount**

(Project 5D Student Interns continues on the next page)

Skills Review Project 5D Student Interns (continued)

b. Click in cell **A2**, type **Example** and then press Tab. In cell **B2,** type **12** and then press Tab. In cell **C2**, type **=b2*15**

c. Hold down Ctrl and press Enter.

d. With cell **C2** selected, on the **Home tab**, in the **Number group**, click **Accounting Number Format** $ one time to display *$180.00*.

e. With cell **C2** still selected, in the lower right corner of the cell, point to the fill handle—the small square—until the + pointer displays.

f. With the + pointer displayed, drag down to cell **C3**.

g. On the right edge of the spreadsheet, point to the middle sizing handle until the ⟺ pointer displays. Drag to the left until only **columns A, B, and C** display—there will be a slight amount of space to the right of cell C to accommodate the scroll bar.

h. At the bottom of the spreadsheet, point to the middle sizing handle until the ⇕ pointer displays. Drag upward until only **rows 1 through 3** display and then release the mouse button. Press Ctrl + Home, and then **Save**.

12 Press Ctrl + Home. Click the **File tab**, and then click **Show All Properties**. As the **Tags**, type **student interns** In the **Subject** box, type your course name and section number. If necessary, edit the author name to display your name.

13 On the left, click **Save**. In the upper right corner of the Word window, click **Close**. If directed by your instructor to do so, submit your paper printout, your electronic image of your document that looks like a printed document, or your original Word file.

END | You have completed Project 5D

Mastering Word Project 5E Travel Bags

Apply 5A skills from these Objectives:

1. Create and Apply a Custom Table Style
2. Format Cells
3. Use Advanced Table Features
4. Modify Table Properties

In the following Mastering Word project, you will create a memo to all Chesterfield Creations sales managers announcing the Flair Collection of travel bags. Your completed document will look similar to Figure 5.54.

PROJECT FILES

For Project 5E, you will need the following file:

w05E_Travel_Bags

You will save your file as:

Lastname_Firstname_5E_Travel_Bags

PROJECT RESULTS

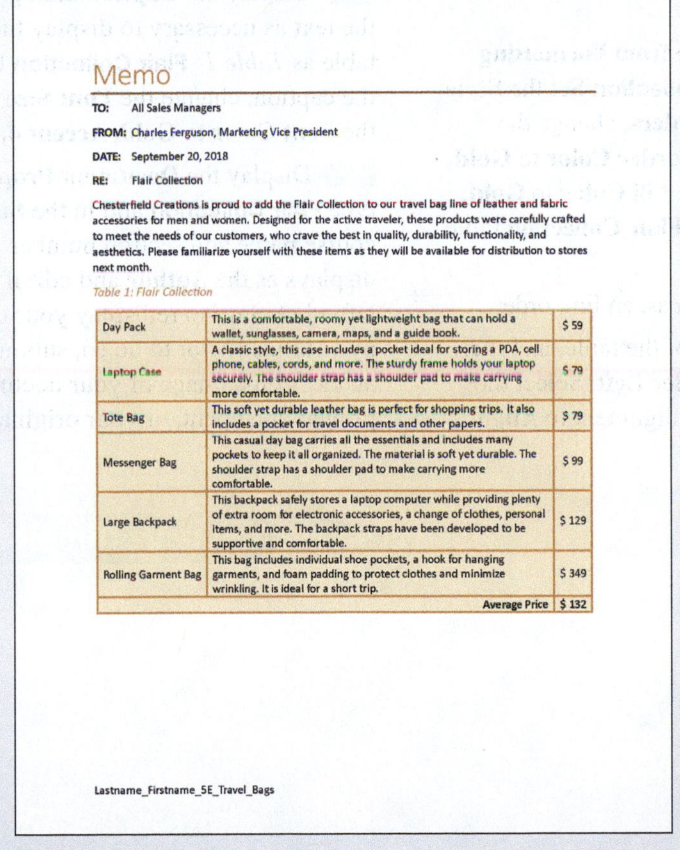

Memo

TO: All Sales Managers

FROM: Charles Ferguson, Marketing Vice President

DATE: September 20, 2018

RE: Flair Collection

Chesterfield Creations is proud to add the Flair Collection to our travel bag line of leather and fabric accessories for men and women. Designed for the active traveler, these products were carefully crafted to meet the needs of our customers, who crave the best in quality, durability, functionality, and aesthetics. Please familiarize yourself with these items as they will be available for distribution to stores next month.

Table 1: Flair Collection

Day Pack	This is a comfortable, roomy yet lightweight bag that can hold a wallet, sunglasses, camera, maps, and a guide book.	$ 59
Laptop Case	A classic style, this case includes a pocket ideal for storing a PDA, cell phone, cables, cords, and more. The sturdy frame holds your laptop securely. The shoulder strap has a shoulder pad to make carrying more comfortable.	$ 79
Tote Bag	This soft yet durable leather bag is perfect for shopping trips. It also includes a pocket for travel documents and other papers.	$ 79
Messenger Bag	This casual day bag carries all the essentials and includes many pockets to keep it all organized. The material is soft yet durable. The shoulder strap has a shoulder pad to make carrying more comfortable.	$ 99
Large Backpack	This backpack safely stores a laptop computer while providing plenty of extra room for electronic accessories, a change of clothes, personal items, and more. The backpack straps have been developed to be supportive and comfortable.	$ 129
Rolling Garment Bag	This bag includes individual shoe pockets, a hook for hanging garments, and foam padding to protect clothes and minimize wrinkling. It is ideal for a short trip.	$ 349
	Average Price	$ 132

Lastname_Firstname_5E_Travel_Bags

FIGURE 5.54

(Project 5E Travel Bags continues on the next page)

Mastering Word Project 5E Travel Bags (continued)

1 Start Word. Navigate to your student data files for this chapter, and then open the file **w05E_Travel_Bags**. Using your own name, save the document in your **Word Chapter 5** folder as **Lastname_Firstname_5E_Travel_Bags** Insert the file name in the footer, and display the rulers and formatting marks.

2 Select the first paragraph, and then apply the **Title** style. For each of the next four paragraphs, select the headings **To:** and **From:** and **Date:** and **Re:** being sure to include the colon, and then apply the **Strong** style.

3 Select the paragraph that begins **Rolling Garment Bag** and the remaining five paragraphs in the document. Convert the selected text to a table with 3 columns and 6 rows.

4 Display the **Create New Style from Formatting** dialog box. Name the style **Flair Collection** Set the **Style** to **Table**. Set the borders to **All Borders**, change the **Line Weight** to **1½pt**, change the **Border Color** to **Gold, Accent 4, Darker 25%**. Change the **Fill Color** to **Gold, Accent 4, Lighter 80%**. Apply the **Flair Collection** table style to the table.

5 Sort the table by **Column 3** in ascending order.

6 Select the first two columns of the table, and then change the alignment to **Align Center Left**. Select the third column, and then change the alignment to **Align Center**.

7 Resize the table to **AutoFit Contents**. Change the width of the second column to **4.5"**.

8 At the bottom of the table, insert a new row. Select the first and second cells, and then merge the cells. Change the alignment to **Align Center Right**, type **Average Price** and then apply **Bold**.

9 In the last cell of the table, click **Formula**. Change the formula to **=AVERAGE(ABOVE)** Change the **Number format** to **#,##0** and then to the left of the number format, type **$** Click **OK**. Select the displayed value, and apply **Bold**.

10 Display the **Table Properties** dialog box, and then change the table alignment to **Center**.

11 Display the **Caption** dialog box, and then modify the text as necessary to display the caption above the table as *Table 1:* **Flair Collection** In the document, select the caption, change the **Font Size** to **12**, and then change the **Font Color** to **Gold, Accent 4, Darker 25%**.

12 Display the **Document Properties**. As the **Tags** type **Flair Collection** and in the **Subject** box, type your course name and section number. Be sure that your name displays as the **Author** and edit if necessary. On the left, click **Save** to redisplay your document. If directed by your instructor to do so, submit your paper printout, an electronic image of your document that looks like a printed document, or your original Word file. **Close** Word.

END | You have completed Project 5E

CONTENT-BASED ASSESSMENTS (MASTERY AND TRANSFER OF LEARNING)

Apply 5B skills from these Objectives:

5 Draw a Freeform Table
6 Use Nested Tables
7 Insert an Excel Spreadsheet

Mastering Word Project 5F Buyer Program

In the following Mastering Word project, you will create a flyer explaining the Frequent Buyer program to Chesterfield Creations customers. Your completed document will look similar to Figure 5.55.

PROJECT FILES

For Project 5F, you will need the following files:

w05F_Buyer_Program
w05F_Frequent_Buyer

You will save your file as:

Lastname_Firstname_5F_Buyer_Program

PROJECT RESULTS

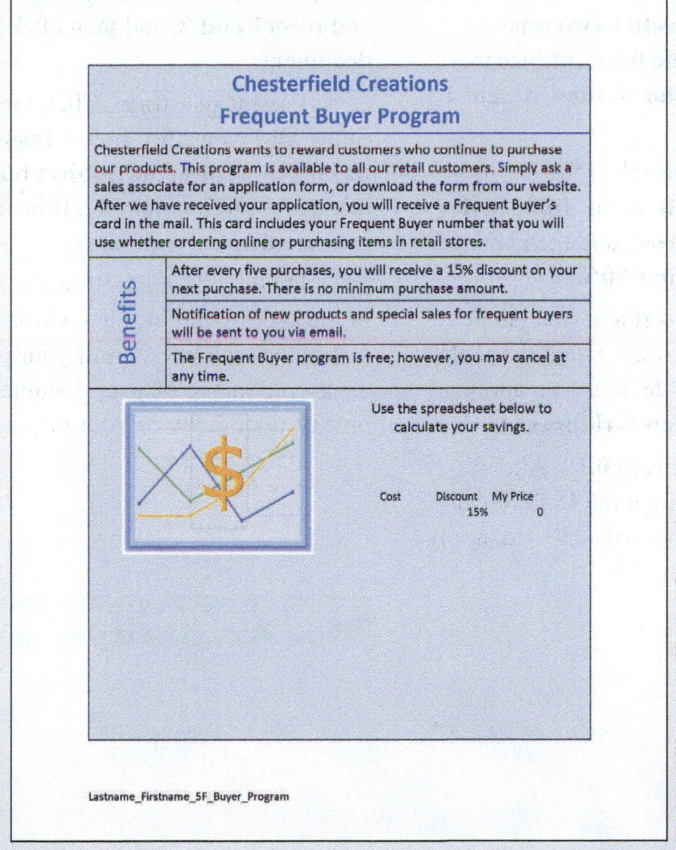

FIGURE 5.55

(Project 5F Buyer Program continues on the next page)

Mastering Word Project 5F Buyer Program (continued)

1 Start Word. Navigate to your student data files for this chapter, and then open the file **w05F_Buyer_Program**. Using your own name, save the document in your **Word Chapter 5** folder as **Lastname_Firstname_5F_Buyer_Program** Insert the file name in the footer, and display rulers and formatting marks.

2 In the first row of the table, type **Chesterfield Creations** Press Enter, and then type **Frequent Buyer Program** (do not press Enter). Select the text you just typed, change the **Font Size** to **22 pt**, apply **Bold**, and then change the **Font Color** to **Blue, Accent 1, Darker 25%**. Click **Align Center**.

3 In the third row, click in the first cell, and then apply **Align Center**. Click **Text Direction** two times. Type **Benefits** Select the text, change the **Font Size** to **24 pt**, and then change the **Font Color** to **Blue, Accent 1, Darker 25%**.

4 Click the **table move handle** to select the entire table. On the **Table Tools Design tab**, in the **Table Styles group**, click the **Shading button arrow**, and then change the **Shading** to **Blue, Accent 1, Lighter 80%**.

5 In the last row of the table, insert a nested table that contains two rows and two columns. Click the **table move handle** to select the nested table, and then apply **No Border**. If necessary, turn on **View Gridlines**.

6 Change all **Default cell margins** to **0.1"**. Allow spacing between cells, and then change the **Default cell spacing** to **0.3"**. With the nested table still selected, apply **Align Center**.

7 Select the two cells in the first column, and then **Merge Cells**. Click in the newly merged cell, and then from your student data files, insert the picture **w05F_Frequent_Buyer**. Change the height of the picture to **2"**.

8 In the nested table, in the first cell of the second column, type **Use the spreadsheet below to calculate your savings.**

9 In the second cell of the second column, insert an **Excel Spreadsheet**. In cell **A1**, type **Cost** In cell **B1**, type **Discount** In cell **C1**, type **My Price** In cell **B2**, type **15%** and then in cell **C2**, type **=a2*.85** and press Enter. (The result is 0 because no data is entered.) Resize the spreadsheet to display only **columns A through C** and **rows 1 and 2**, and then click in a blank area of the document.

10 Press Ctrl + Home. Click the **File tab**, and then click **Show All Properties**. In the **Tags** box, type **frequent buyer program** In the **Subject** box, type your course name and section number. If necessary, change the author name to display your name.

11 On the left, click **Save**. In the upper right corner of the Word window, click **Close**. If directed by your instructor to do so, submit your paper printout, your electronic image of your document that looks like a printed document, or your original Word file.

END | You have completed Project 5F

Mastering Word Project 5G Gift Special

Apply 5A and 5B skills from these Objectives:

1. Create and Apply a Custom Table Style
2. Format Cells
3. Use Advanced Table Features
4. Modify Table Properties
5. Draw a Freeform Table
6. Use Nested Tables
7. Insert an Excel Spreadsheet

In the following Mastering Word project, you will create a flyer that provides descriptions of new products available for gift giving at Chesterfield Creations. Your completed document will look similar to Figure 5.56.

PROJECT FILES

For Project 5G, you will need the following file:

w05G_Gift_Special

You will save your file as:

Lastname_Firstname_5G_Gift_Special

PROJECT RESULTS

NEW GIFT IDEAS FOR THE BUSINESS PROFESSIONAL

Just in time for the gift-giving season, Chesterfield Creations is pleased to add three computer bags to our Mainline Collection designed for the business professional. These bags offer the same durability and quality as our other business bags but with an extra dose of style and sophistication to carry all of the gadgets on which we all rely.

Item	Description	Price
Compact Bag	Special features include a pocket for items such as tickets and other travel information, and the most comfortable shoulder strap on the market. The computer sleeve has extra padding for the ultimate protection.	$ 149
Streamlined Tote	Available in a choice of five colors, the front pocket provides ample storage for tickets and other documents, metal feet protect the bag from dirty surfaces, extra padding in the computer sleeve stores your laptop securely, and the removable pouch can hold personal items.	$ 199
Large Tote	Similar to our other computer totes, this item has plenty of extra room for notebooks, pens, presentation information, personal items, and electronic accessories.	$ 209
	Average Price	**$ 186**
As a sales incentive during December, these items will be available at a 25% discount.	Retail Price Discount 25% Sale Price 0	

Lastname_Firstname_5G_Gift_Special

Word 2016, Windows 10, Microsoft Corporation

FIGURE 5.56

(Project 5G Gift Special continues on the next page)

Mastering Word Project 5G Gift Special (continued)

1 Start Word, and then from your student data files, open the file **w05G_Gift_Special**. Save the document in your **Word Chapter 5** folder as **Lastname_Firstname_5G_Gift_Special** Insert the file name in the footer, and display rulers and formatting marks.

2 Select the first paragraph, and then apply the **Heading 1** style. Select the second paragraph, and then change the **Font Size** to **12**.

3 Select the remaining three paragraphs of the document, change the **Font Size** to **14**, and then with the text still selected, **Convert Text to Table** with three columns and three rows.

4 Display the **Styles** pane, and then click the **New Style** button. In the **Create New Style from Formatting** dialog box, create a new style named **Gift** Set the **Style type** to **Table**. Apply the style to **All Borders**. Set the **Line Weight** to **1½ pt**, and then set the **Border Color** to **Green, Accent 6, Darker 25%**. Change the **Fill Color** to **Green, Accent 6, Lighter 80%**. Apply the **Gift** style to the entire table.

5 Click in the first cell of the table. On the **Table Tools Layout tab**, in the **Table group**, click **Select**, and then click **Select Column**. Change the column **Width** to **1.2"**. Change the second column **Width** to **4.5"**, and the third column **Width** to **0.7"**. Position the insertion point anywhere in the first row, and then click **Insert Above**.

6 In the first cell of the table, type **Item** and then press Tab. Type **Description** Press Tab and then type **Price** Select the **header row**, apply **Bold**, and then click **Align Center**.

7 Change the row **Height** of rows 2, 3, and 4 to **1.5"**, **1.8"**, and **1.4"**, respectively.

8 In the first column, select all the cells below the header row. Apply **Bold**, click **Align Center**, and then click **Text Direction** two times. In the second column, select all the cells below the header row, and then click **Align Center Left**. In the last column, select all the cells below the header row, and click **Align Center**.

9 Point to the lower left corner of the table, and then click the **One-Click Row/Column Insertion** button. In the last row, change the **Height** to **0.4"**.

10 Select the first and second cells, and then **Merge Cells**. Click **Text Direction** one time, and then click **Align Center Right**. Type **Average Price** and then apply **Bold**.

11 In the last cell of the table, insert the **Formula**: **=AVERAGE(ABOVE)** Change the **Number format** to **#,##0**, to the left of the number format, type **$** and then click **OK**. Select the displayed value, and then apply **Bold**.

12 Point to the lower left corner of the table, and then click the **One-Click Row/Column Insertion** button. Select both cells in the last row, and then **Merge Cells**. Insert a nested table containing one row and two columns. Select both cells, and then apply **No Border**. If necessary, display Gridlines.

13 From the **Table Tools Layout tab**, change all **Cell Margins** to **0.1"**, set **Allow spacing between cells** to **0.02"**. Apply **Align Center**.

14 In the first cell of the nested table, type **As a sales incentive during December, these items will be available at a 25% discount.** Be sure to include the period.

15 In the second cell of the nested table, insert an **Excel Spreadsheet**. In cell **A1**, type **Retail Price** and then in cell **A2**, type **Discount** In cell **A3**, type **Sale Price**. In cell **B2**, type **25%** and then in cell **B3**, type **=b1*.75** Press Enter. Resize the spreadsheet to display only **columns A and B** and **rows 1 through 3**, and then click in a blank area of the document.

16 Press Ctrl + Home. Click the **File tab**, and then click **Show All Properties**. In the **Tags** box, type **holiday special, Mainline** In the **Subject** box, type your course name and section number. If necessary, edit the author name to display your name. **Save** your document. Print the document or submit electronically as directed by your instructor. **Close** Word.

END | You have completed Project 5G

CONTENT-BASED ASSESSMENTS (CRITICAL THINKING)

Apply a combination of the 5A and 5B skills.

GO! Fix It | Project 5H Safety Program | MyITLab

GO! Make It | Project 5I Product Flyer | MyITLab

Build from Scratch

GO! Solve It | Project 5J Planning Committee | MyITLab

GO! Solve It | Project 5K Wallet Collection

PROJECT FILES

For Project 5K, you will need the following file:

w05K_Wallet_Collection

You will save your file as:

Lastname_Firstname_5K_Wallet_Collection

From your student data files, open the file **w05K_Wallet_Collection** and save it to your **Word Chapter 5** folder as **Lastname_Firstname_5K_Wallet_Collection** Using the information for the specific wallets, convert the text to a table. Insert a header row, add appropriate column headings, and then sort the table by price and item name. Create a formula to display the average price of the items. Create and apply a table style. Adjust paragraph, text, table, and cell formats to display attractively in a one-page document. Insert the file name in the footer and add appropriate document properties. Print your document or submit electronically as directed by your instructor.

Performance Level

Performance Criteria	Exemplary: You consistently applied the relevant skills	Proficient: You sometimes, but not always, applied the relevant skills	Developing: You rarely or never applied the relevant skills
Convert text to table	All appropriate text is displayed in a table.	At least one item of text is not displayed in a table.	No text is displayed in a table.
Sort the table	The data in the table is sorted by both price and item name.	The data in the table is sorted only by price or item name.	The data in the table is not sorted.
Create a formula	The average price is calculated using a formula and displays in a new row.	The average price displays in a new row, but a formula is not used.	The average price does not display in a new row.
Create and apply a table style	A new table style is created and applied to the table.	A table style is applied to the table, but it is a built-in style—not new.	No table style is applied to the table.
Format the document	All items in the document are formatted appropriately.	At least one item in the document is not formatted appropriately.	No items in the document are formatted.

END | You have completed Project 5K

OUTCOMES-BASED ASSESSMENTS (CRITICAL THINKING)

RUBRIC

The following outcomes-based assessments are open-ended assessments. That is, there is no specific correct result; your result will depend on your approach to the information provided. Make *Professional Quality* your goal. Use the following scoring rubric to guide you in *how* to approach the problem and then to evaluate *how well* your approach solves the problem.

The *criteria*—Software Mastery, Content, Format and Layout, and Process—represent the knowledge and skills you have gained that you can apply to solving the problem. The *levels of performance*—Professional Quality, Approaching Professional Quality, or Needs Quality Improvements—help you and your instructor evaluate your result.

	Your completed project is of Professional Quality if you:	Your completed project is Approaching Professional Quality if you:	Your completed project Needs Quality Improvements if you:
1-Software Mastery	Choose and apply the most appropriate skills, tools, and features and identify efficient methods to solve the problem.	Choose and apply some appropriate skills, tools, and features, but not in the most efficient manner.	Choose inappropriate skills, tools, or features, or are inefficient in solving the problem.
2-Content	Construct a solution that is clear and well organized, contains content that is accurate, appropriate to the audience and purpose, and is complete. Provide a solution that contains no errors of spelling, grammar, or style.	Construct a solution in which some components are unclear, poorly organized, inconsistent, or incomplete. Misjudge the needs of the audience. Have some errors in spelling, grammar, or style, but the errors do not detract from comprehension.	Construct a solution that is unclear, incomplete, or poorly organized, contains some inaccurate or inappropriate content, and contains many errors of spelling, grammar, or style. Do not solve the problem.
3-Format and Layout	Format and arrange all elements to communicate information and ideas, clarify function, illustrate relationships, and indicate relative importance.	Apply appropriate format and layout features to some elements, but not others. Overuse features, causing minor distraction.	Apply format and layout that does not communicate information or ideas clearly. Do not use format and layout features to clarify function, illustrate relationships, or indicate relative importance. Use available features excessively, causing distraction.
4-Process	Use an organized approach that integrates planning, development, self-assessment, revision, and reflection.	Demonstrate an organized approach in some areas, but not others; or, use an insufficient process of organization throughout.	Do not use an organized approach to solve the problem.

OUTCOMES-BASED ASSESSMENTS (CRITICAL THINKING)

Apply a combination of the 5A and 5B skills.

GO! Think Project 5L Company Picnic

PROJECT FILES

Build from Scratch

For Project 5L, you will need the following file:

New blank Word document

You will save your file as:

Lastname_Firstname_5L_Company_Picnic

Every year, Chesterfield Creations holds a picnic for employees and their families. This year the picnic will be held on June 16 from 10 a.m. to 4 p.m. at High Park in Toronto. Lunch and snacks are provided. There will be music and an assortment of games for young and old. In addition, other park activities are available for a fee—such as pony rides and miniature golf.

Using this information, create a flyer to distribute to employees as an email attachment. Create a document that explains the picnic and lists the schedule of events in a table format. Insert a second table that lists fees for specific activities. Use a formula to provide the total cost for these events. Create a table style and apply it to both tables. Format the flyer, including table and cell properties, so that it is attractive and easy to read. Save the file as **Lastname_Firstname_5L_Company_Picnic** Insert the file name in the footer and add appropriate document properties. Print the document or submit as directed by your instructor.

END | You have completed Project 5L

Build from Scratch

GO! Think Project 5M Employee Newsletter MyITLab

Build from Scratch

You and GO! Project 5N Personal Budget MyITLab

Using Building Blocks and Markup Tools

PROJECT 6A

OUTCOMES

Create reusable content and construct a document with building blocks and theme templates.

OBJECTIVES

1. Create Custom Building Blocks
2. Create and Save a Theme Template
3. Create a Document by Using Building Blocks

PROJECT 6B

OUTCOMES

Collaborate with others to edit, review, and finalize a document.

OBJECTIVES

4. Use Comments in a Document
5. Track Changes in a Document
6. View Side by Side, Compare, and Combine Documents

Stokkete/Fotolia

In This Chapter

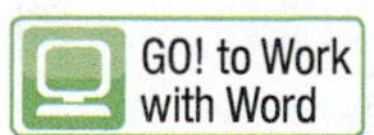

In this chapter, you will work with building blocks—objects that can be reused in multiple documents. You will customize predefined building blocks and create your own reusable content. You will create a theme—by defining the colors, fonts, and effects—to give documents a customized appearance. You will build a new document from the custom building blocks and theme. Word includes features to review revisions and comments made in a document. This makes it easy to work with a team to collaborate on documents. You will insert comments, track changes, review changes made by others, and then accept or reject those changes.

The projects in this chapter relate to **Mountain View Public Library**, which serves the Claremont, Tennessee, community at three locations—the Main library, the East Branch, and the West Branch. The library's extensive collection includes books, audio books, music CDs, video DVDs, magazines, and newspapers—for all ages. The Mountain View Public Library also provides sophisticated online and technology services, youth programs, and frequent appearances by both local and nationally known authors. The citizens of Claremont support the Mountain View Public Library with local taxes, donations, and special events fees.

PROJECT 6A

Newsletter with Reusable Content and Custom Theme

PROJECT ACTIVITIES

In Activities 6.01 through 6.12, you will assist Ami Sanjay, Director of Library Services at Mountain View Public Library, in designing a custom look for documents that the library produces by creating a custom theme and building blocks for content that can be reused. Your completed documents will look similar to Figure 6.1.

PROJECT FILES

If your instructor wants you to submit Project 6A in the MyITLab Grader system, log into MyITLab, locate Grader Project 6A, and then download the files for the project.

Build from Scratch

For Project 6A, you will need the following files:	You will save your files as:
New blank document	Lastname_Firstname_6A_Building_Blocks
w06A_Building_Blocks	Lastname_Firstname_6A_February_Newsletter
w06A_February_Newsletter	Lastname_Firstname_6A_Library_Theme

GO! Walk Thru Project 6A

PROJECT RESULTS

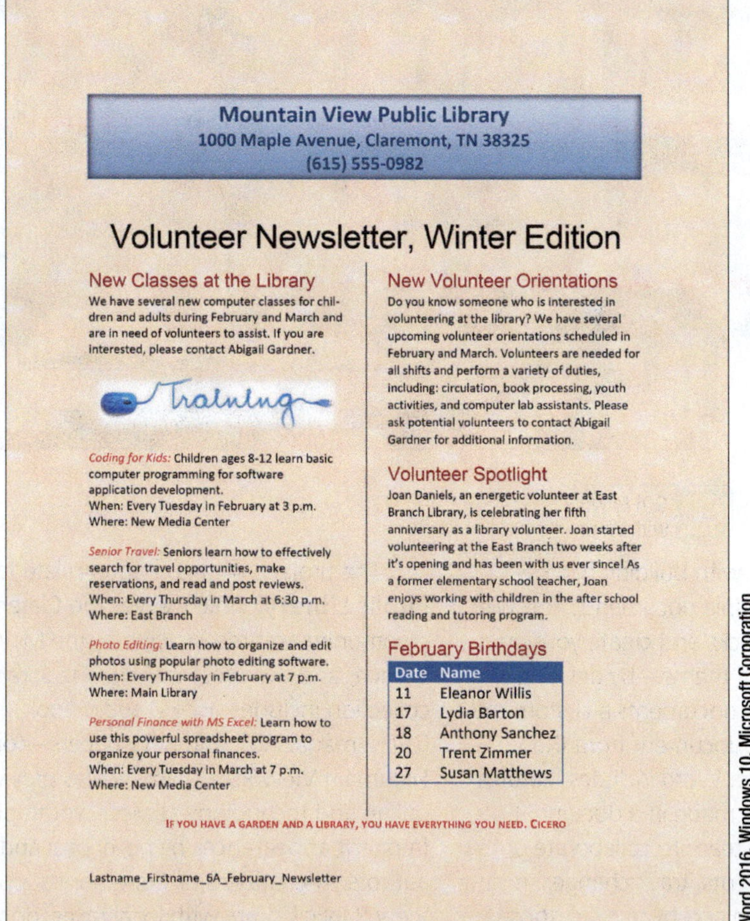

Mountain View Public Library
1000 Maple Avenue, Claremont, TN 38325
(615) 555-0982

Volunteer Newsletter, Winter Edition

New Classes at the Library

We have several new computer classes for children and adults during February and March and are in need of volunteers to assist. If you are interested, please contact Abigail Gardner.

Coding for Kids: Children ages 8-12 learn basic computer programming for software application development.
When: Every Tuesday in February at 3 p.m.
Where: New Media Center

Senior Travel: Seniors learn how to effectively search for travel opportunities, make reservations, and read and post reviews.
When: Every Thursday in March at 6:30 p.m.
Where: East Branch

Photo Editing: Learn how to organize and edit photos using popular photo editing software.
When: Every Thursday in February at 7 p.m.
Where: Main Library

Personal Finance with MS Excel: Learn how to use this powerful spreadsheet program to organize your personal finances.
When: Every Tuesday in March at 7 p.m.
Where: New Media Center

New Volunteer Orientations

Do you know someone who is interested in volunteering at the library? We have several upcoming volunteer orientations scheduled in February and March. Volunteers are needed for all shifts and perform a variety of duties, including: circulation, book processing, youth activities, and computer lab assistants. Please ask potential volunteers to contact Abigail Gardner for additional information.

Volunteer Spotlight

Joan Daniels, an energetic volunteer at East Branch Library, is celebrating her fifth anniversary as a library volunteer. Joan started volunteering at the East Branch two weeks after it's opening and has been with us ever since! As a former elementary school teacher, Joan enjoys working with children in the after school reading and tutoring program.

February Birthdays

Date	Name
11	Eleanor Willis
17	Lydia Barton
18	Anthony Sanchez
20	Trent Zimmer
27	Susan Matthews

IF YOU HAVE A GARDEN AND A LIBRARY, YOU HAVE EVERYTHING YOU NEED. CICERO

Lastname_Firstname_6A_February_Newsletter

Word 2016, Windows 10, Microsoft Corporation

FIGURE 6.1 Project 6A February Newsletter

Objective 1 Create Custom Building Blocks

GO! Learn How Video W6-1

Building blocks are reusable pieces of content or other document parts—for example, headers, footers, page number formats—that are stored in galleries. The Headers gallery, the Footers gallery, the Page Numbers gallery, and the Bibliographies gallery, some of which you have already used, are all examples of building block galleries. You can also create your own building blocks for content that you use frequently.

ALERT! Completing This Project in One Working Session

If you are working in a school lab, plan to complete Project 6A in one working session. Building blocks are stored on the computer at which you are working. Thus, in a school lab, if you close Word before completing the project, the building blocks might be deleted and will not be available for your use—you will have to re-create them. On your own computer, you can close Word, and the building blocks will remain until you purposely delete them.

Activity 6.01 | Format a Text Box

ALERT! To submit as an autograded project, log into MyITLab and download the files for this Project, and begin with those files instead of w06A_Building_Blocks and w06A_February_Newsletter.

Recall that a ***text box*** is a movable, resizable container for text or graphics. In this Activity, you will format a text box that the library can use for any documents requiring the library's contact information.

1 Start Word, and then from your student data files, open **w06A_Building_Blocks**. If necessary, display the rulers and formatting marks. Click the **File tab** and then click **Save As**. In the **Save As** dialog box, navigate to the location where you are saving your files for this chapter. Create a folder named **Word Chapter 6** and then **Save** the document as **Lastname_Firstname_6A_Building_Blocks**

2 Click the outer edge of the text box to select it. On the **Format tab**, in the **Shape Styles group**, click **More** ▾. In the **Shape Styles** gallery, in the fourth row, click the fifth style—**Subtle Effect – Gold, Accent 4**. Compare your screen with Figure 6.2.

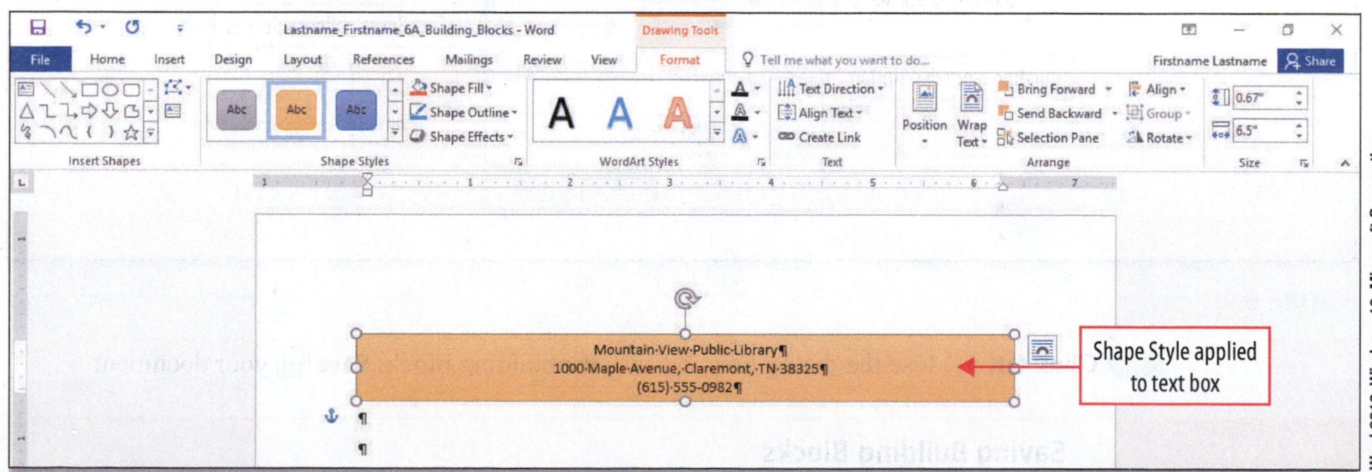

FIGURE 6.2

Word 2016, Windows 10, Microsoft Corporation

3 On the **Format tab**, in the **Shape Styles group**, click **Shape Effects**. Point to **Shadow**, and then under **Inner**, in the second row, click the second style—**Inside Center**.

4 In the text box, select the first paragraph, change the **Font Size** to **20**, and then apply **Bold** [B]. Select the second and third paragraphs, change the **Font Size** to **16**, and then apply **Bold** [B]. Notice the height of the text box automatically adjusts to accommodate the text.

5 Click the outer edge of the text box so that none of the text is selected, but that the text box itself is selected and displays sizing handles. Compare your screen with Figure 6.3 and then **Save** your document.

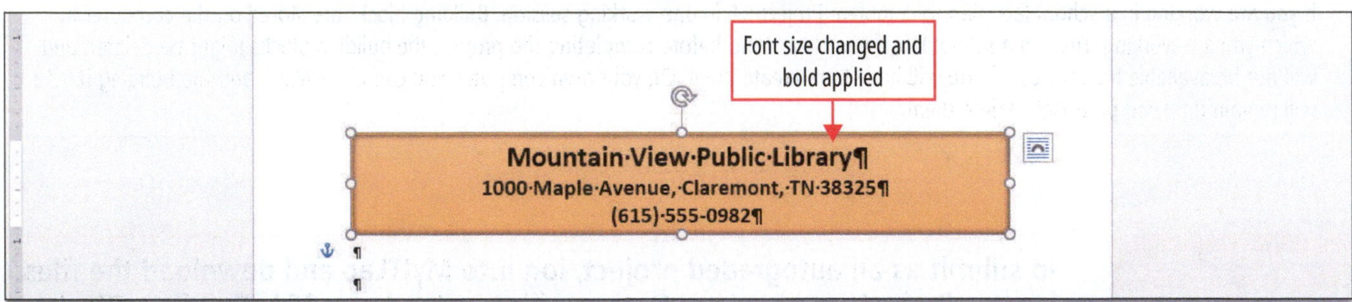

Word 2016, Windows 10, Microsoft Corporation

FIGURE 6.3

Activity 6.02 | Adding a Building Block to a Gallery

Expert 4.1.1

1 With the text box selected, on the **Insert tab**, in the **Text group**, click **Text Box**, and then click **Save Selection to Text Box Gallery**. In the **Create New Building Block** dialog box, in the **Name** box, type **Library Information** Notice that the **Gallery** box displays *Text Boxes*.

By selecting the Text Boxes gallery, this building block will display in the gallery of other text box building blocks.

2 In the **Description** box, type **Library contact information for publications** and then compare your screen with Figure 6.4.

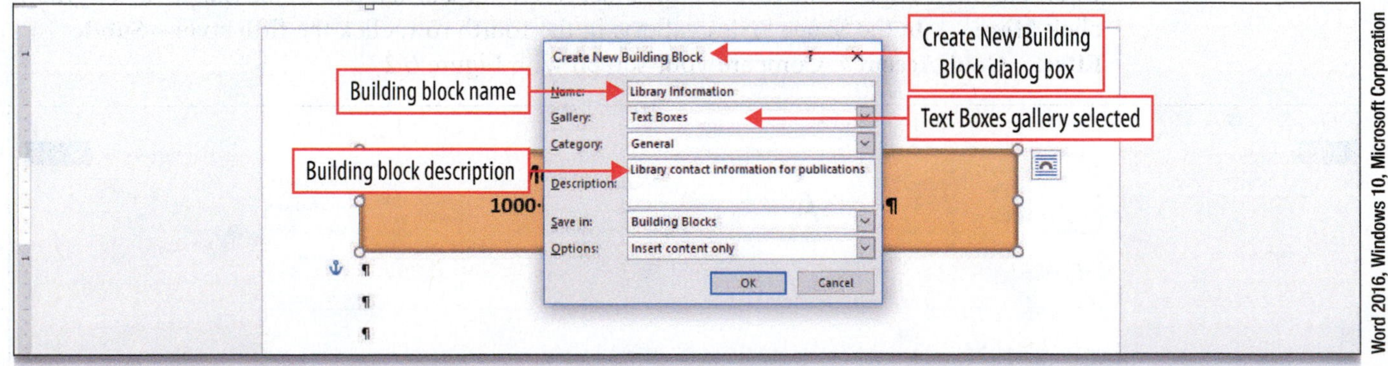

Word 2016, Windows 10, Microsoft Corporation

FIGURE 6.4

3 Click **OK** to close the dialog box and save the building block. **Save** your document.

> **ALERT!** **Saving Building Blocks**
>
> Building blocks that you create in a gallery are saved on the computer at which you are working.

Activity 6.03 | Using the Building Blocks Organizer to View and Edit Building Blocks

Expert 4.1.2

The ***Building Blocks Organizer*** enables you to view—in a single location—all of the available building blocks from all galleries.

1 On the **Insert tab**, in the **Text group**, click **Quick Parts**.

Quick Parts are the reusable pieces of content that are available to insert into a document, including building blocks, document properties, and fields.

2 From the list, click **Building Blocks Organizer**. In the **Building Blocks Organizer** dialog box, in the upper left corner, click **Name** to sort the building blocks alphabetically by name.

Here you can view all of the building blocks available in Word. In this dialog box, you can also delete a building block, edit its properties—for example, change the name, description, or gallery location—or select and insert it into a document.

3 By using the scroll bar in the center of the **Building Blocks Organizer** dialog box, scroll down until you see your building block that begins *Library*, and then click to select it. Compare your screen with Figure 6.5.

In the preview area on the right, notice that under the preview of the building block, the name and description that you entered displays.

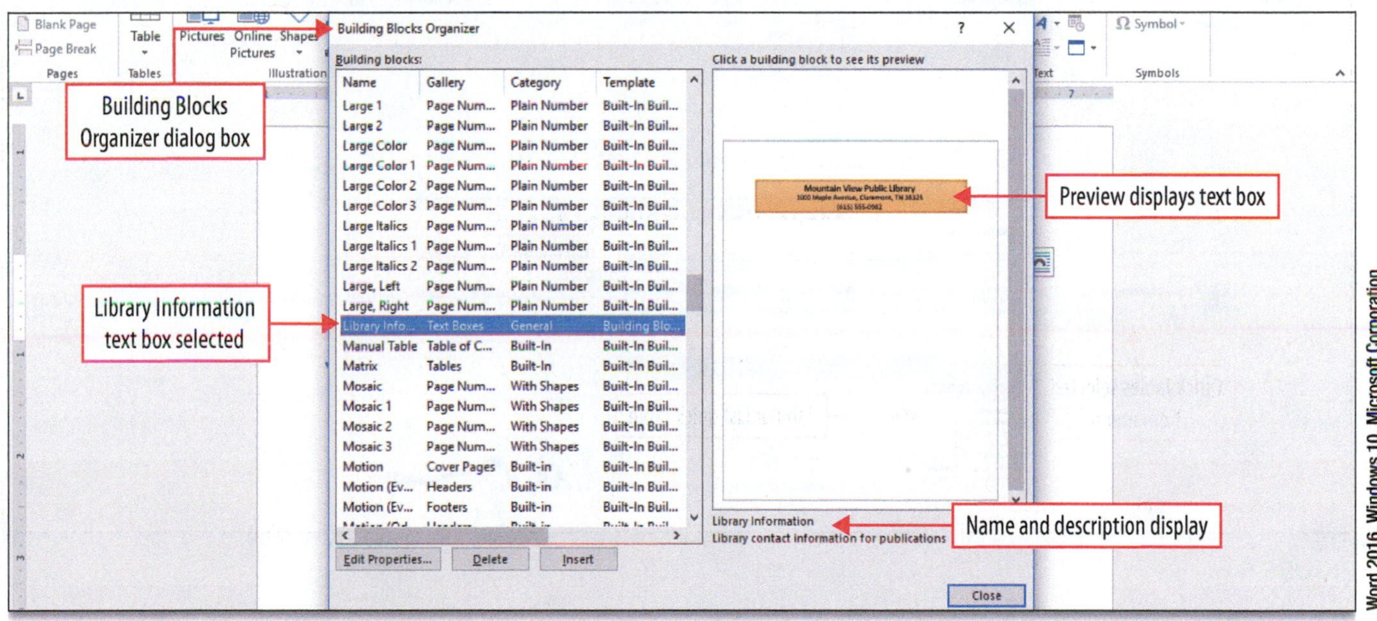

FIGURE 6.5

4 In the **Building Blocks Organizer** dialog box, click **Edit Properties**.

5 Be sure *Building Blocks* is selected in the *Save in* list, and then in the **Modify Building Block** dialog box, click in the **Description** box.

6 In the **Description** box, select the word **contact**, and then press Delete.

You can edit building block properties in the Modify Building Block dialog box. In this case, you are changing the description of the text box building block.

7 In the **Modify Building Block** dialog box, click **OK**. In the **Microsoft Word** message box, when asked if you want to redefine the building block entry, click **Yes**. In the lower right corner of the **Building Blocks Organizer** dialog box, click **Close**, and then **Save** your document.

More Knowledge **Copying a Building Block to the Normal Template**

To copy a building block to the Normal Template so that it is available to other documents, in the Modify Building Block dialog box, click the Save in arrow, click Normal, and then click OK.

Activity 6.04 | Saving a Custom Building Block as a Quick Table

Expert 4.1.1

Quick Tables are tables that are stored as building blocks. Word includes many predesigned Quick Tables, and you can also create your own tables and save them as Quick Tables in the Quick Tables gallery. In this Activity, you will modify an existing Quick Table and then save it as a new building block.

1. Below the text box, position the insertion point in the second blank paragraph. On the **Insert tab**, in the **Tables group**, click **Table**, and then at the bottom of the list, point to **Quick Tables**. In the **Quick Tables** gallery, scroll down to locate **Tabular List**, as shown in Figure 6.6.

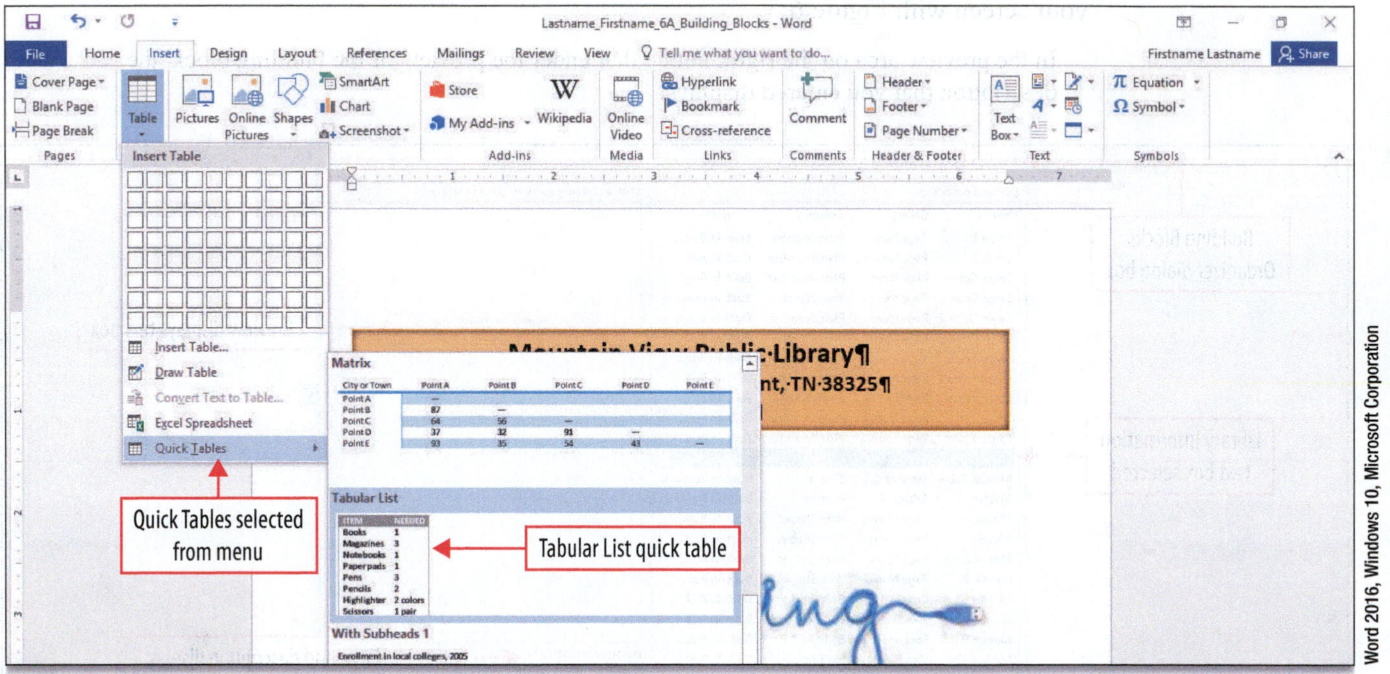

FIGURE 6.6

2. Click **Tabular List**. In the first row of the table, click in the first cell, select the text **ITEM**, and then type **Date** to replace the text.
3. Press Tab to move to the second cell, and with **NEEDED** selected, type **Name**
4. Select all the remaining text in the table, and then press Delete to delete the text. Compare your screen with Figure 6.7.

   Because this table will be used as a building block to enter birthday information, the sample text is not needed.

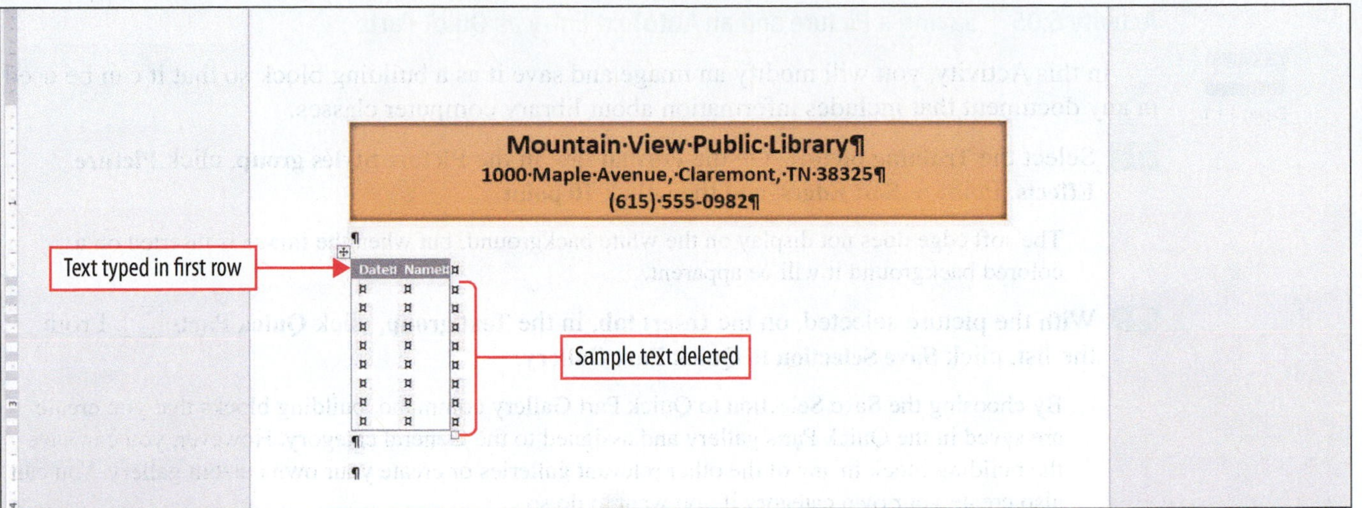

Word 2016, Windows 10, Microsoft Corporation

FIGURE 6.7

ALERT! **Viewing Gridlines**

If the table borders do not display, under Table Tools, click the Layout tab, and then in the Table group, click View Gridlines.

5 Click in the table, point slightly outside the upper left corner of the table, and then click the **table move handle** to select the entire table.

6 With the table selected, on the **Insert tab**, in the **Tables group**, click **Table**. In the displayed list, point to **Quick Tables**, and then at the bottom of the list, click **Save Selection to Quick Tables Gallery**.

7 In the **Create New Building Block** dialog box, in the **Name** box, type **Birthday Table** and then click in the **Description** box. Type **Use for staff birthdays in publications** and then compare your screen with Figure 6.8.

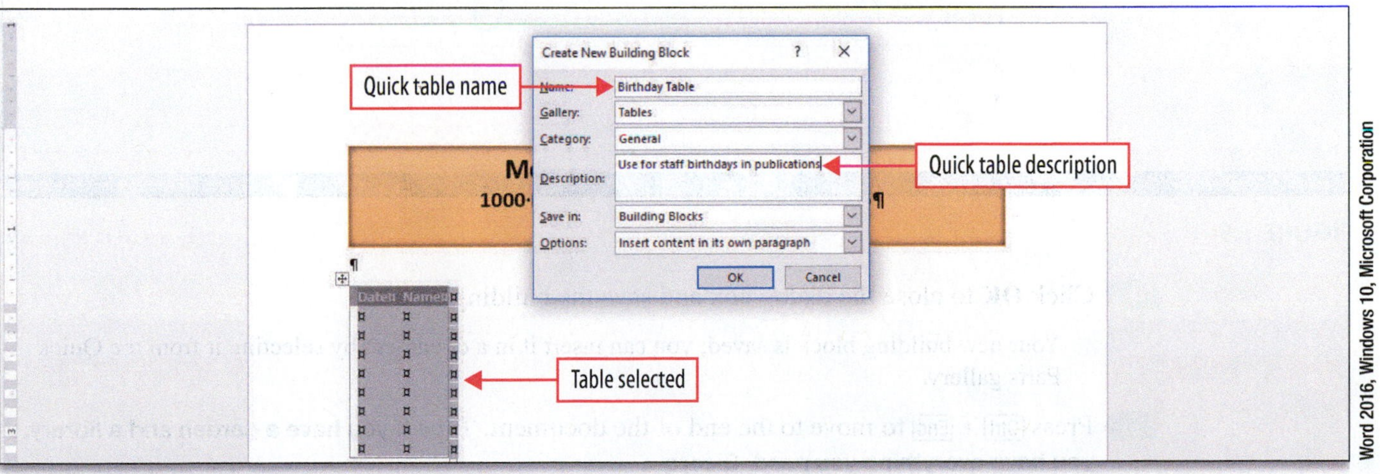

Word 2016, Windows 10, Microsoft Corporation

FIGURE 6.8

8 Click **OK** to save the table in the **Quick Tables** gallery. **Save** your document.

Activity 6.05 | Saving a Picture and an AutoText Entry as Quick Parts

Expert 4.1.1

In this Activity, you will modify an image and save it as a building block so that it can be used in any document that includes information about library computer classes.

1. Select the **Training picture**. On the **Format tab**, in the **Picture Styles group**, click **Picture Effects**. Point to **Soft Edges**, and then click **10 point**.

   The soft edge does not display on the white background, but when the image is inserted on a colored background it will be apparent.

2. With the picture selected, on the **Insert tab**, in the **Text group**, click **Quick Parts**. From the list, click **Save Selection to Quick Part Gallery**.

   By choosing the Save Selection to Quick Part Gallery command, building blocks that you create are saved in the Quick Parts gallery and assigned to the General category. However, you can save the building block in any of the other relevant galleries or create your own custom gallery. You can also create your own category if you want to do so.

3. In the **Create New Building Block** dialog box, in the **Name** box, type **Training Image** and then click in the **Description** box. Type **Library training image** and then compare your screen with Figure 6.9.

   You can create and then select any content and save it as a building block in this manner.

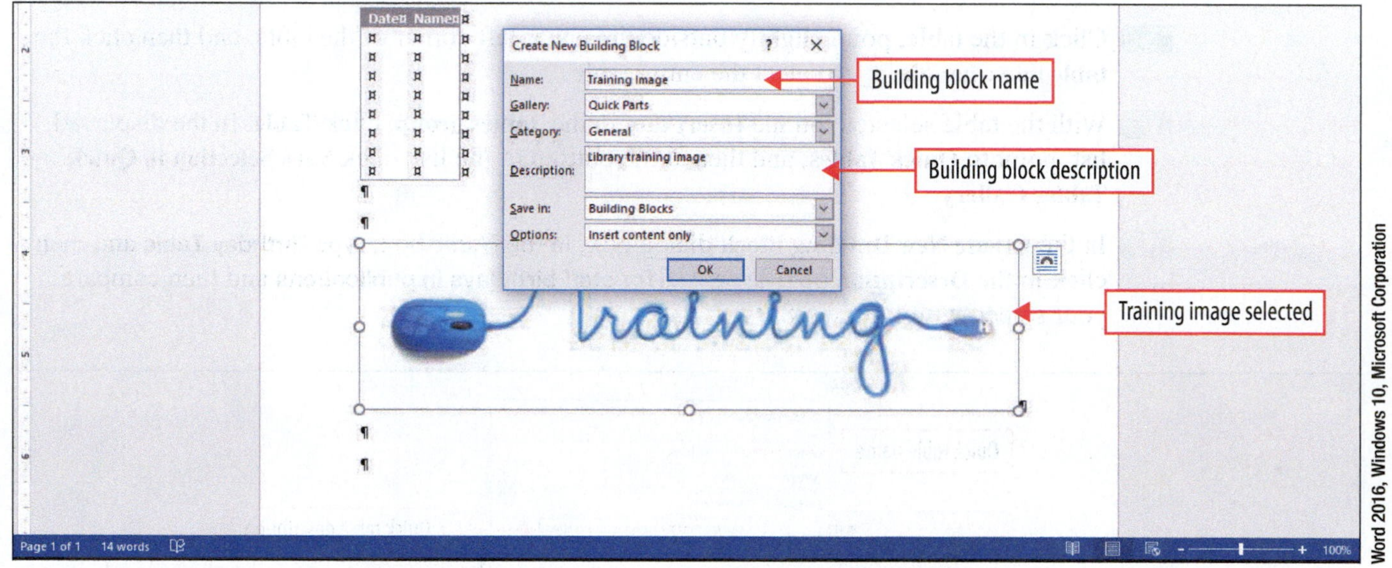

FIGURE 6.9

4. Click **OK** to close the dialog box and save the building block.

   Your new building block is saved; you can insert it in a document by selecting it from the Quick Parts gallery.

5. Press Ctrl + End to move to the end of the document. Type **If you have a garden and a library, you have everything you need. Cicero**

6. Select the text you just typed. On the **Insert tab**, in the **Text group**, click **Quick Parts**. From the list, click **AutoText**, and then click **Save Selection to AutoText Gallery**.

7. In the **Create New Building Block** dialog box, in the **Name** box, type **Library Quote** and then in the **Description** box, type **Quote for newsletter**

8. Verify that the **Gallery** displays **AutoText**. Click the **Save in box arrow**, and then click **Building Blocks**. Compare your screen with Figure 6.10.

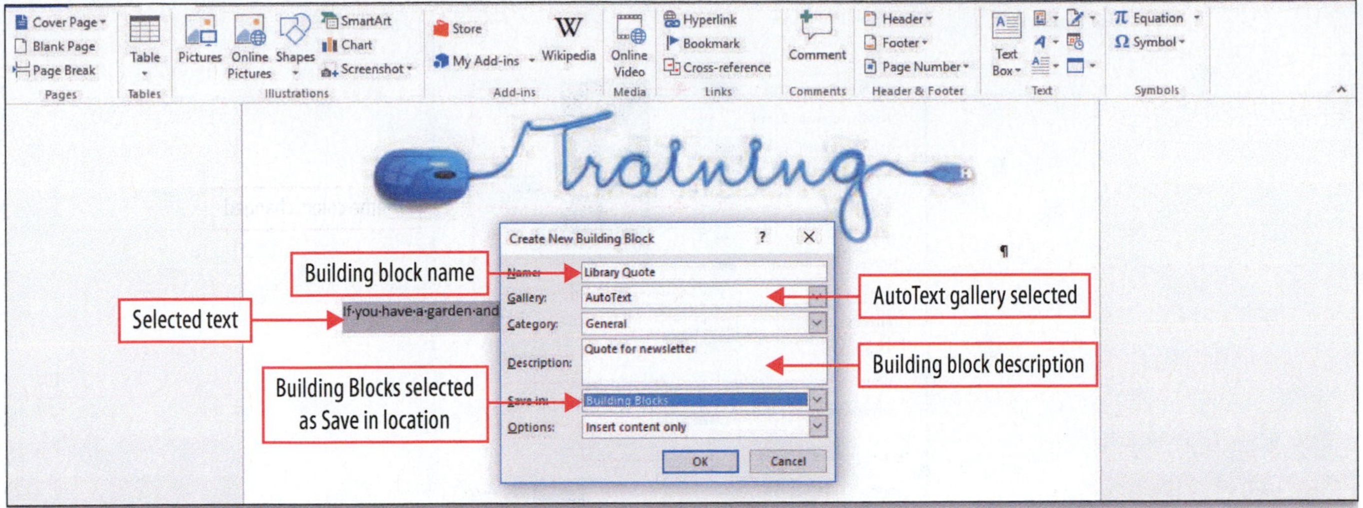

Word 2016, Windows 10, Microsoft Corporation

FIGURE 6.10

9 Click **OK** to close the dialog box, and then press Ctrl + Home. **Save** your document. On the **File tab**, click **Close** to close the document and leave Word open. If a message box displays asking if you want to save the building blocks, click Yes.

Objective 2 Create and Save a Theme Template

GO! Learn How Video W6-2

Recall that a ***theme*** is a predefined combination of colors, fonts, and line and fill effects that look good together and is applied to an entire document by a single selection. Word comes with a group of predefined themes—the default theme is named *Office*. You can also create your own theme by selecting any combination of colors, fonts, and effects, which, when saved, creates a ***theme template***. A theme template, which stores a set of colors, fonts, and effects—lines and fill effects—can be shared with other Office programs, such as Excel and PowerPoint.

Activity 6.06 | Creating Custom Theme Colors and Theme Fonts

Expert 4.2.1, 4.2.2

1 Press Ctrl + N to display a new blank document.

2 On the **Design tab**, in the **Document Formatting group**, click **Themes**. In the **Themes** gallery, click **Organic**.

3 On the **Design tab**, in the **Document Formatting group**, click **Colors**. In the **Theme Colors** gallery, take a moment to examine the various color schemes, scrolling as necessary, and then at the bottom of the list, click **Customize Colors**.

4 In the **Create New Theme Colors** dialog box, click the **Text/Background – Dark 1 arrow**, and then under **Theme Colors**, in the seventh column, click the fifth color—**Blue-Gray, Accent 3, Darker 25%**. Using the same technique, change **Accent 1** to **Red, Accent 4**—in the eighth column, the first color—and then change **Accent 4** to **Blue-Gray, Accent 3, Lighter 40%**—in the seventh column, the fourth color. In the **Name** box, delete the existing text. Type **Newsletter Colors** and then compare your screen with Figure 6.11.

A set of theme colors contains four text/background colors, six accent colors, and two hyperlink colors. You can select a new color for any category and save the combination of colors with a new name. In this case, you are changing the colors for the Text/Background – Dark 1, Accent 1, and Accent 4 categories, and saving the color combination with the name Newsletter Colors. The Sample box displays both the original and modified theme color schemes.

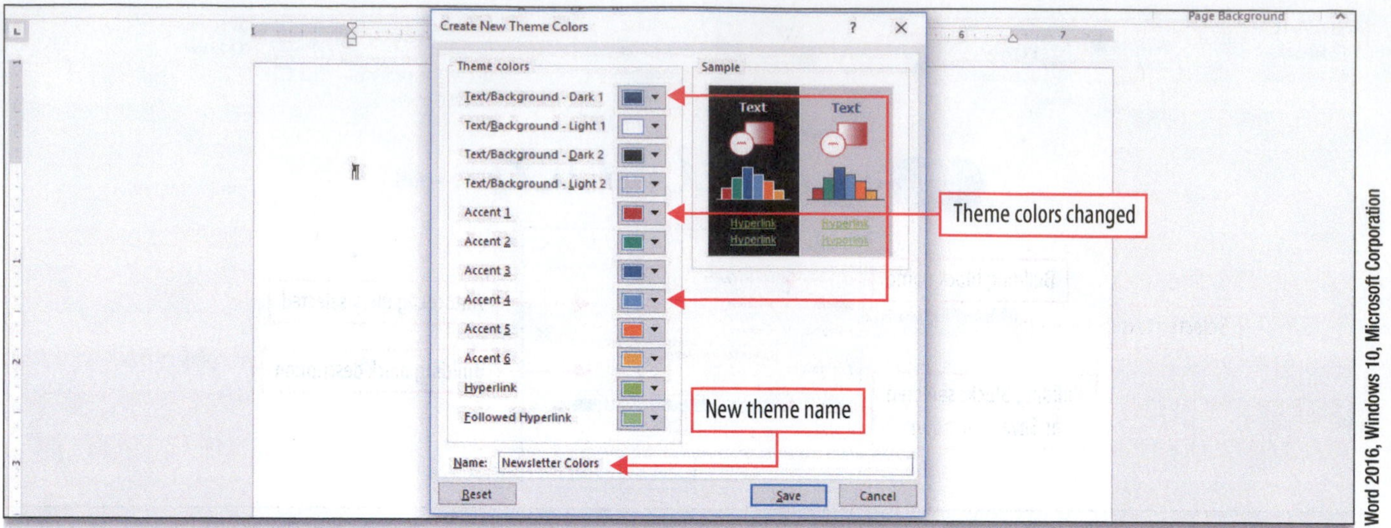

FIGURE 6.11

5 Click **Save** to close the **Create New Theme Colors** dialog box. In the **Document Formatting group**, click **Fonts** [A], and then at the bottom of the list, click **Customize Fonts**.

Theme fonts contain a heading font—the upper font—and a body text font—the lower font. You can use an existing set of Built-In fonts for your new theme, or define new sets of fonts.

6 In the **Create New Theme Fonts** dialog box, click the **Heading font arrow**, scroll as necessary to locate and then click **Arial**. Click the **Body font arrow**, scroll as necessary, and then click **Calibri**. In the **Name** box, delete the existing text, and then type **Newsletter Fonts**

The custom Theme Fonts—Newsletter Fonts—include the Arial heading font and the Calibri body text font.

7 Click **Save** to close the **Create New Theme Fonts** dialog box.

Activity 6.07 | Saving a Custom Theme Template

Expert 4.2.3

To use your custom theme in other Microsoft Office files, you can save it as a theme template.

1 In the **Document Formatting group**, click **Themes**, and then at the bottom of the **Themes** gallery, click **Save Current Theme** to display the **Save Current Theme** dialog box. Compare your screen with Figure 6.12.

By default, saving a new theme displays the Templates folder, which includes the Document Themes folder, containing separate folders for Theme Colors, Theme Effects, and Theme Fonts. The Save as type box specifies the file type *Office Theme*.

If you save your theme in the Templates folder, it is available to the Office programs on the computer at which you are working. In a college or organization, you may not have permission to update this folder, but on your own computer, you can save your themes here if you want to do so.

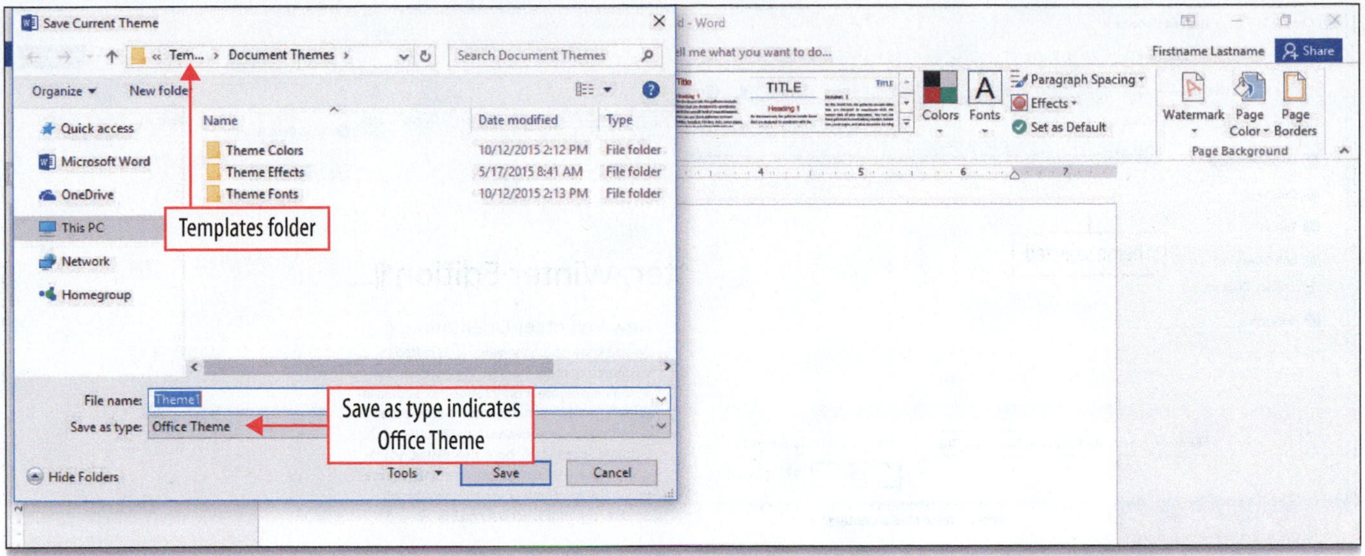

FIGURE 6.12

Word 2016, Windows 10, Microsoft Corporation

2 In the **Save Current Theme** dialog box, navigate to your **Word Chapter 6** folder. In the **File name** box, type **Lastname_Firstname_6A_Library_Theme** and then click **Save**.

3 Click the **File tab**, and then click **Close**. Do not save changes. Keep Word open for the next Activity.

Objective 3 Create a Document by Using Building Blocks

GO! Learn How Video W6-3

One of the benefits of creating building blocks and theme templates is that they can be used repeatedly to create individual documents. The building blocks ensure consistency in format and structure, and the theme template provides consistency in colors, fonts, and effects.

Activity 6.08 | Applying a Custom Theme and a Page Color

1.3.2, 1.3.6

In this Activity, you will apply a theme template and format text in columns.

1 From your student data files, open **w06A_February_Newsletter**. **Save** the file in your **Word Chapter 6 folder** as **Lastname_Firstname_6A_February_Newsletter** and then insert a footer with the file name. **Close** the footer area. If necessary, display the rulers and formatting marks.

This document contains a newsletter formatted in two columns with several styles applied.

2 On the **Design tab**, in the **Document Formatting group**, click **Themes**, and then click **Browse for Themes**. In the **Choose Theme or Themed Document** dialog box, navigate to your **Word Chapter 6** folder, and then click your file **Lastname_Firstname_6A_Library_Theme**. Compare your screen with Figure 6.13.

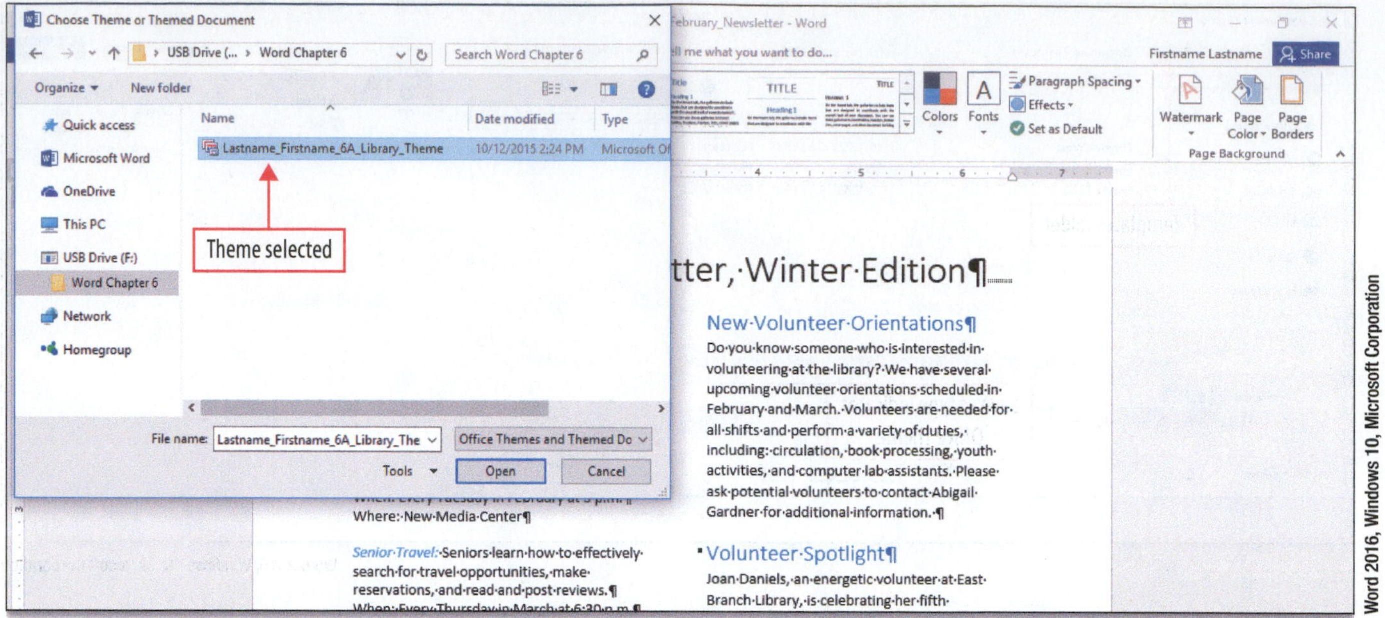

FIGURE 6.13

3 Click **Open** to apply the theme, and notice that the text with the heading styles applied is formatted with the color of the custom theme that you created.

4 On the **Design tab**, in the **Page Background group**, click **Page Color**, and then click **Fill Effects**. In the **Fill Effects** dialog box, click the **Texture tab**, and then in the fourth row, click the third texture–**Parchment**. Compare your screen with Figure 6.14.

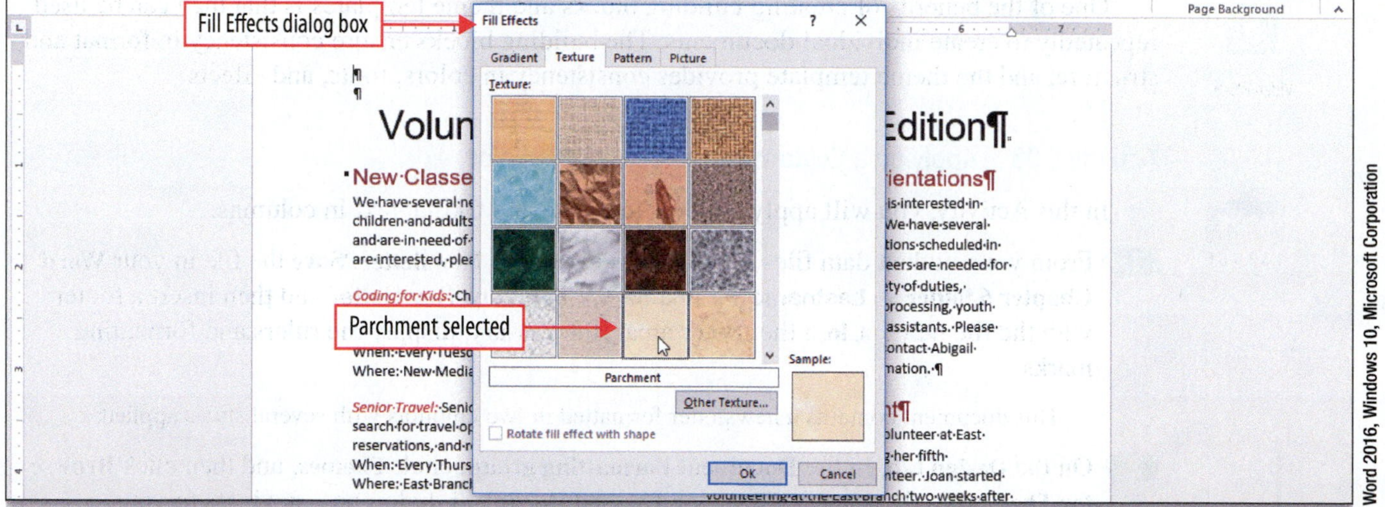

FIGURE 6.14

5 Click **OK** to apply the textured background.

6 Click anywhere in the two-column area of the document. On the **Layout tab**, in the **Page Setup group**, click the **Columns arrow**, and then click **More Columns** to display the **Columns** dialog box.

You can modify column formats in the Columns dialog box. For example, you can change the number of columns, the width of the columns, the spacing after columns, and insert a line to separate the columns.

7 In the **Columns** dialog box, above the **Preview** area, click the **Line between** check box so that it is selected, and then click **OK** to insert a line between the two columns of the newsletter. Compare your screen with Figure 6.15, and then **Save** your document.

FIGURE 6.15 Word 2016, Windows 10, Microsoft Corporation

Activity 6.09 | Inserting Quick Parts

In this Activity, you will insert the text box and picture Quick Parts that you created.

1 Press Ctrl + Home. On the **Insert tab**, in the **Text group**, click **Text Box**. To the right of the **Text Box** gallery, drag the vertical scroll box to the bottom of the gallery, and then under **General**, click the **Library Information** building block.

The theme colors of your custom theme are applied to the building block.

2 In the first column, click at the end of the paragraph that begins *We have several new* and then press Enter. On the **Insert tab**, in the **Text group**, click **Quick Parts**, and notice that your Training Image building block displays. Compare your screen with Figure 6.16.

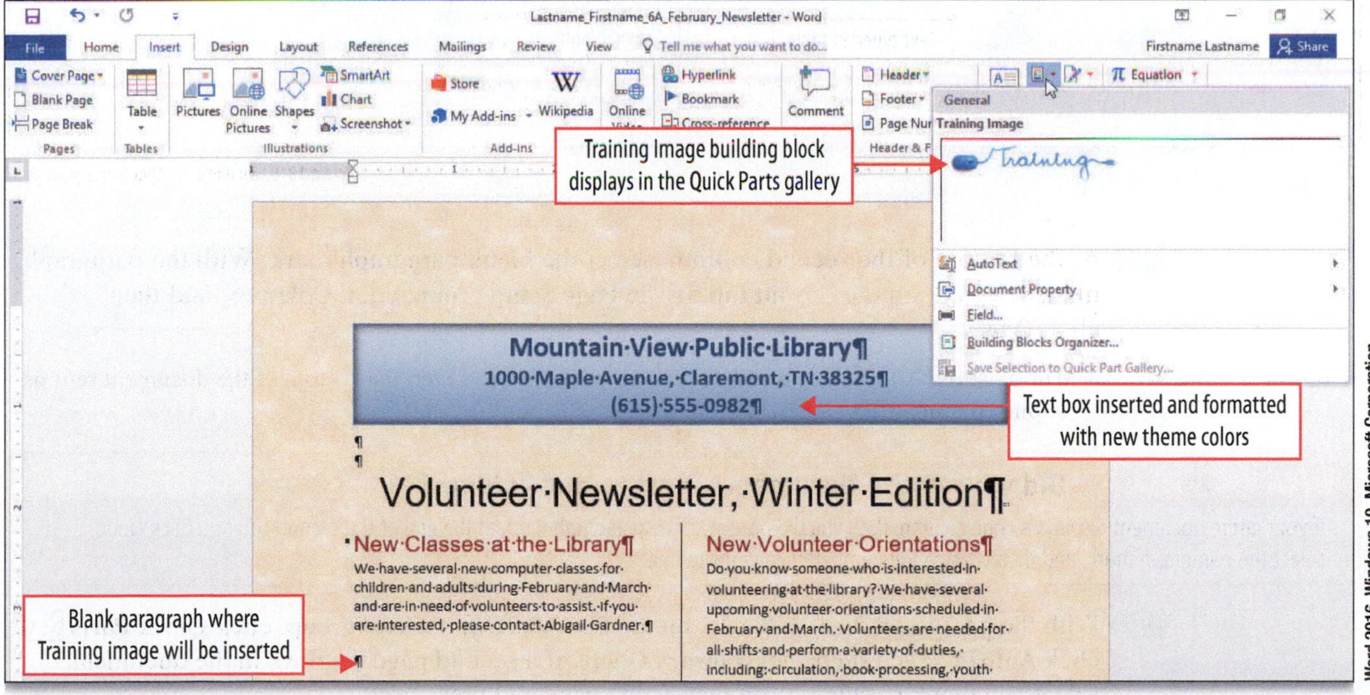

Word 2016, Windows 10, Microsoft Corporation

FIGURE 6.16

3 Under **General**, click the **Training Image** building block to insert it, and then **Save** your document.

Activity 6.10 | Inserting a Quick Table and an AutoText Quick Part

In this Activity, you will complete the newsletter by inserting the Quick Table and the AutoText that you created.

1 In the second column, click in the blank paragraph below *February Birthdays*. On the **Insert tab**, in the **Tables group**, click **Table**, point to **Quick Tables**, scroll to the bottom of the list, and then under **General**, click **Birthday Table**.

2 In the second row of the table, click in the first cell. Type **11** and then press [Tab]. Type **Eleanor Willis** and then press [Tab]. Use the same technique to type the following text in the table:

17	Lydia Barton
18	Anthony Sanchez
20	Trent Zimmer
27	Susan Matthews

3 Select the last three empty rows of the table. On the mini toolbar, click **Delete**, and then click **Delete Rows**. Click the **table move handle** [⊞] to select the entire table, and then on the mini toolbar, change the **Font Size** to **14**. Click outside the table so that it is not selected, and then compare your screen with Figure 6.17.

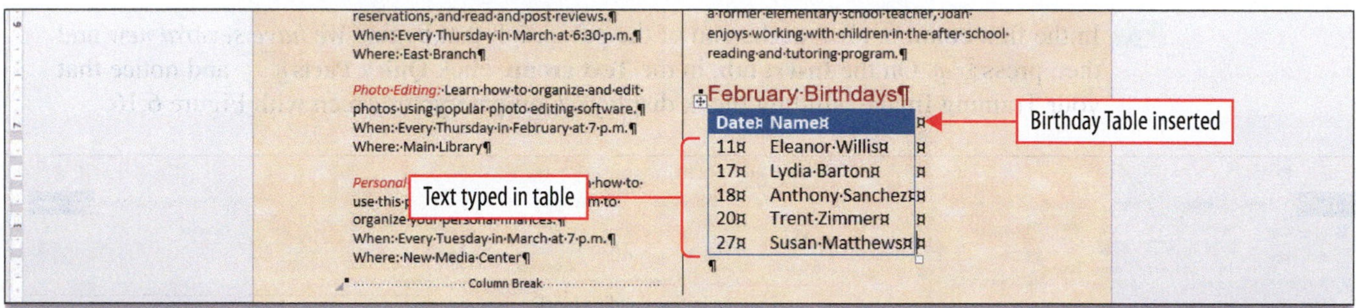

FIGURE 6.17

Word 2016, Windows 10, Microsoft Corporation

4 At the bottom of the second column, select the blank paragraph mark. With the paragraph mark selected, on the **Layout tab**, in the **Page Setup group**, click **Columns**, and then click **One**.

The existing text remains formatted in two columns; however, the bottom of the document returns to one column—full page width.

> **ALERT!** **Did your entire document revert to one column?**
>
> If your entire document displays as one column, then you did not select the paragraph mark at the end of the second column. Click Undo, select the paragraph mark, and then change the number of columns to one.

5 With the paragraph mark selected, on the **Insert tab**, in the **Text group**, click **Quick Parts** [icon], click **AutoText**, and then click **Library Quote**. If a second page displays in the document, select any blank paragraphs on the second page and press [Delete].

6 Select the inserted text. On the mini toolbar, click **Styles**, and then click **Intense Reference**. Press [Ctrl] + [E] to center the text, and then deselect the text. Compare your screen with Figure 6.18.

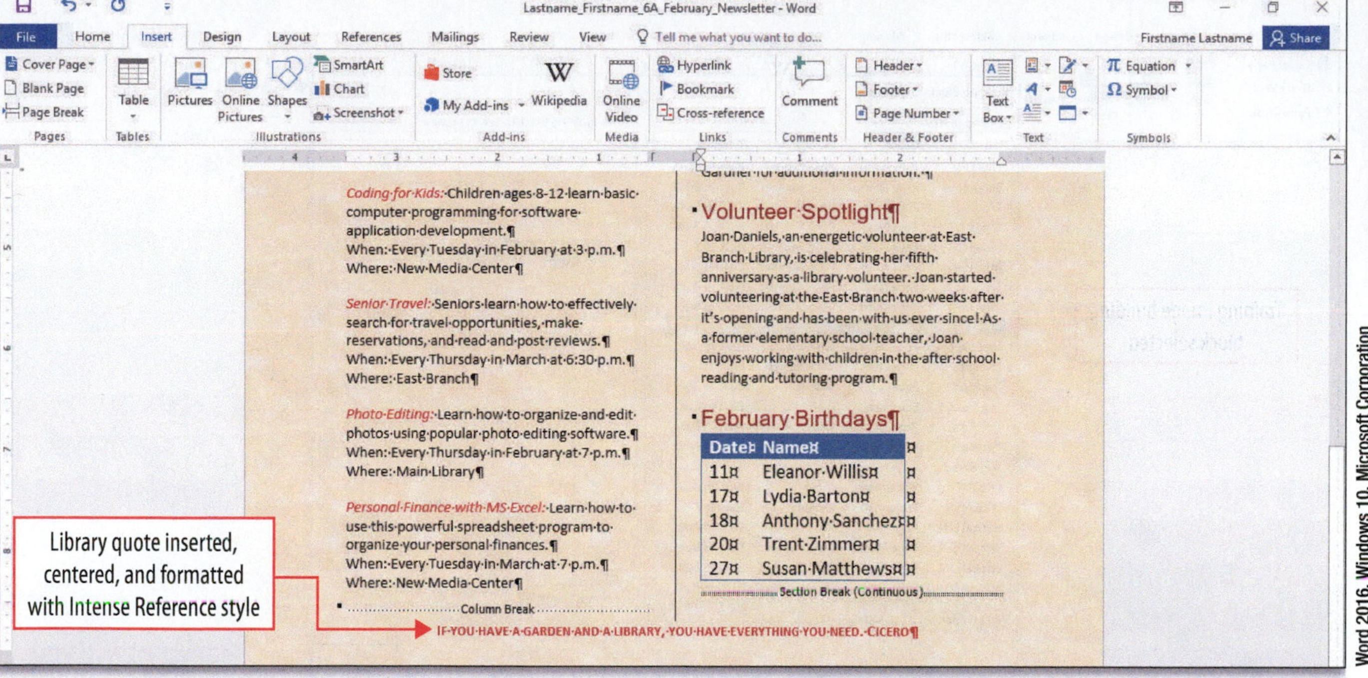

FIGURE 6.18

7 **Save** your document.

Expert 2.1.3

Activity 6.11 | Manually Hyphenating a Document

1 Press Ctrl + Home. On the **Layout tab**, in the **Page Setup group**, click **Hyphenation**, and then click **Manual** to display the **Manual Hyphenation: English (United States)** dialog box.

Hyphenation is a tool in Word that controls how words are split between two lines. By selecting Manual, you can control which words are hyphenated.

2 In the **Manual Hyphenation: English (United States)** dialog box, in the **Hyphenate at** box, with *chil-dren* displayed, click **Yes** to accept the hyphenated word.

3 When a message displays indicating that the hyphenation is complete, click **OK**. **Save** your document.

Activity 6.12 | Deleting Custom Building Blocks, Theme Colors, and Theme Fonts

Expert 4.1.2

You can delete user-created building blocks, theme colors, and theme fonts if they are no longer needed. If you are sharing a computer with others, you must restore Word to its default settings. In this Activity, you will delete the building blocks, theme colors, and theme fonts that you created.

1 On the **Insert tab**, in the **Text group**, click **Quick Parts**. Right-click the **Training Image** building block, and then click **Organize and Delete**. Compare your screen with Figure 6.19.

The Training Image building block is selected in the Building Blocks Organizer dialog box. A preview of the building block displays on the right. The name and description of the building block display below the preview.

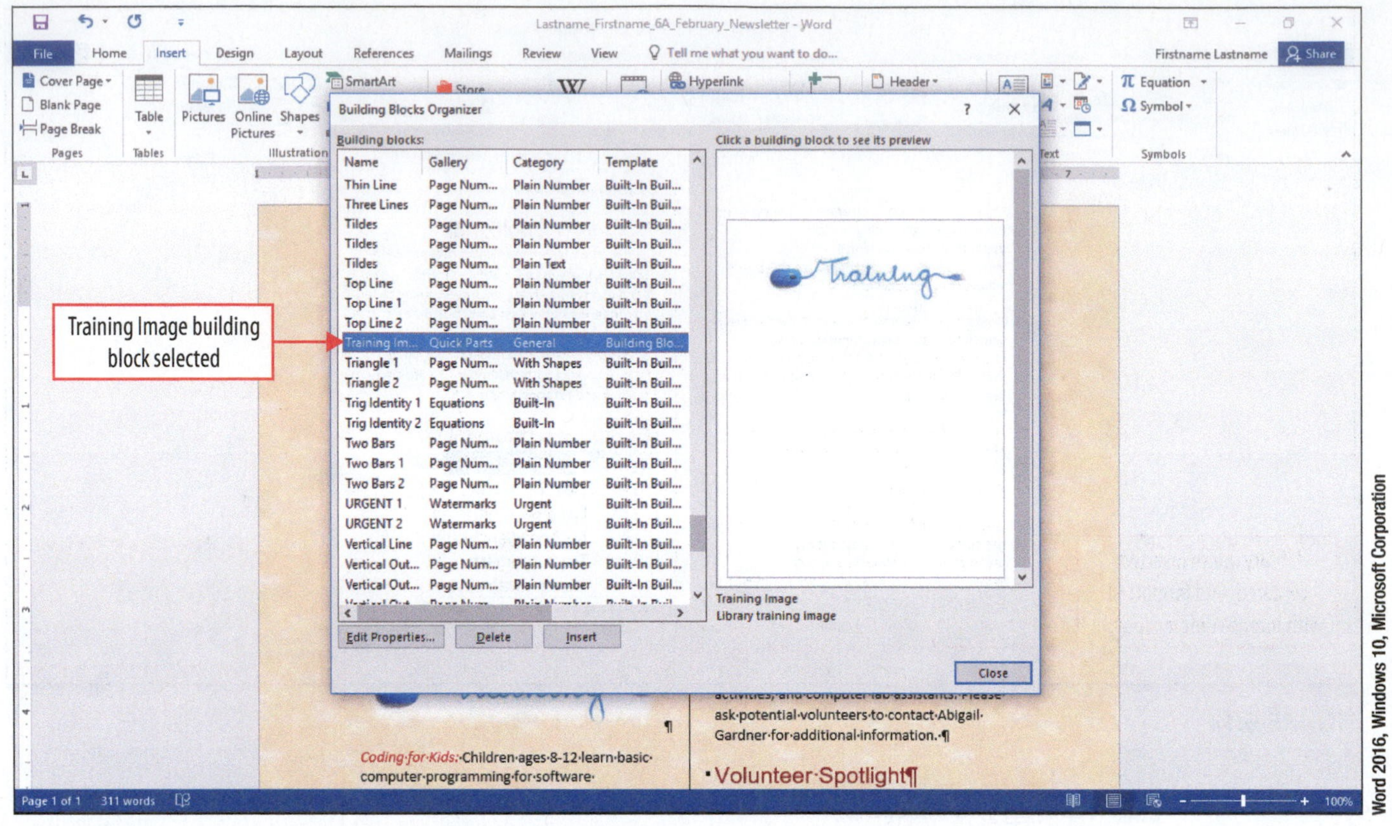

FIGURE 6.19

2 Click **Delete**. When a message displays to confirm the deletion, click **Yes**.

> ***More* Knowledge** **Deleting Building Blocks**
>
> To delete a building block, you must have an open document so that the Quick Parts command is active.

3 In the **Building Blocks Organizer** dialog box, in the upper left corner, click **Name** to sort the building blocks alphabetically by name.

4 By using the scroll bar in the center of the **Building Blocks Organizer** dialog box, scroll down until you see your building block that begins *Birthday*, and then click to select it. Click **Delete**, and then click **Yes** to confirm the deletion.

5 Using the same technique, scroll to locate your building block *Library Information*, and then **Delete** it. **Delete** the **Library Quote** building block. **Close** the **Building Blocks Organizer** dialog box.

6 On the **Design tab**, in the **Document Formatting group**, click **Colors**. At the top of the **Theme Colors** gallery, right-click **Newsletter Colors**, and then click **Delete**. When a message displays to confirm the deletion, click **Yes**. Using the same technique, display the **Theme Fonts** gallery, and then **Delete** the **Newsletter Fonts**.

Because the theme—including the custom theme colors and theme fonts—has been saved, you no longer need the Newsletter Colors and Newsletter Fonts to display in the respective lists.

7 Click the **File tab**, and then click **Show All Properties**. In the **Tags** box, type **library newsletter** and in the **Subject** box, type your course name and section number. If necessary, edit the author name to display your name.

8 **Save** your document. In the upper right corner of the Word window, click **Close** [×]. When a message displays regarding changes to building blocks, click **Save** to accept the changes. If directed by your instructor to do so, submit your paper printout, your electronic image of your document that looks like a printed document, or your original Word file.

***More* Knowledge** **Printing Page Backgrounds**

To print the background color or fill effect of a document, display the Word Options dialog box, select Display, and under Printing Options, select the Print background colors and images check box. Click OK.

END | You have completed Project 6A

PROJECT 6B Events Schedule with Tracked Changes

PROJECT ACTIVITIES

In Activities 6.13 through 6.22, you will assist Abigail Gardner, Director of Programs and Youth Services, in using the markup tools in Word to add comments and make changes to a schedule of events. You will accept or reject each change, and then compare and combine your document with another draft version to create a final document. Your completed documents will look similar to Figure 6.20.

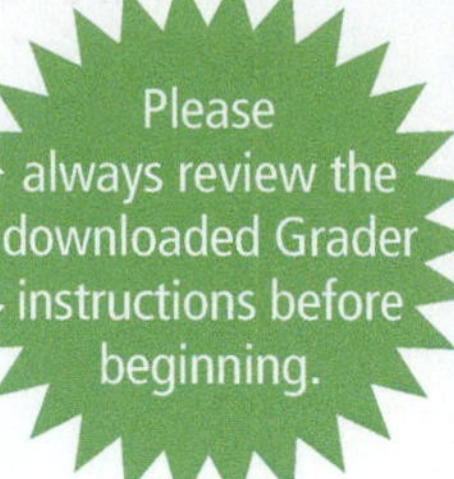

PROJECT FILES

If your instructor wants you to submit Project 6B in the MyITLab Grader system, log into MyITLab, locate Grader Project 6B, and then download the files for the project.

For Project 6B, you will need the following files:

w06B_Events_Schedule
w06B_Schedule_Revisions

You will save your files as:

Lastname_Firstname_6B_Events_Schedule
Lastname_Firstname_6B_Schedule_Revisions
Lastname_Firstname_6B_Schedule_Combined (shown)

PROJECT RESULTS

Mountain View Public Library

Children's Department

September Events

Mountain View Public Library offers many special events to area children at our three branches. Attending one of these activities is a wonderful way to promote a love of reading that will last a lifetime.

Meet the Author

This month's author is Isabelle Saunders, author of *Splendid Dreams*. She will read her story, answer questions, and sign copies of her book. Ms. Saunders will appear at the Main Library on September 23 at 7:00 p.m. All ages are welcome to attend.

Toddler Story Time

Toddler story time is geared toward children who are 2-3 years old. Composed of stories and songs, and usually geared toward the seasons, it is a wonderful opportunity to foster a love of reading. This event is held at the Main Library on Mondays at 10:00 a.m., the East Branch on Wednesdays at 10:30 a.m., and the West Branch on Fridays at 9:30 a.m.

Preschool Story Time

Preschool story time is designed for children ages 3-5. This is a great setting for children to learn to sit and listen as the librarian reads several books. Children are encouraged to respond to questions about each book. The youngsters are assisted in selecting and checking out other books by the featured authors. Preschool story time is held at 1:00 p.m. at the Main Library on Mondays.

Baby Story Time

Specifically designed for children under 2 years old, baby story time provides an opportunity for your child to hear several stories and participate in songs and finger plays. Additional time is provided to play with toys, listen to music, and for you to interact with other parents. This one-hour program is held at the Main Library on Tuesdays at 9:30 a.m., the East Branch on Thursdays at 10:30 a.m., and the West Branch on Fridays at 2:30 p.m.

Story and Craft

This month's story and craft time will be held at the West Branch at 4:00 p.m. on September 16. The theme will be butterflies. Children ages 5-12 are welcome to attend. To reserve your place, please call Abigail Gardner at (615) 555-0982 to register.

Animal Adventures

Safari Steve from Wildlife Friends will bring in many small animals for children to look at, touch, and learn about. This event is suitable for families and will be held at the Main Library at 7:00 p.m. on September 24.

Lastname_Firstname_6B_Schedule_Combined

Internet Safety

This seminar is geared for teenagers, ages 13-17. It will cover a variety of techniques for maintaining safety while on the Internet. This event will be held at the East Branch location at 7:30 p.m. on September 25.

Seek and Find at the Library

Led by librarian Annette Liebig, this session explains how to find a specific book, magazine, audio book, CD, DVD, or other items at the library. Appropriate for children ages 8 and up, this seminar will be held at 7:00 p.m. on September 27 at our West Branch location.

Lastname_Firstname_6B_Schedule_Combined

FIGURE 6.20 Project 6B Events Schedule

Objective 4 Use Comments in a Document

GO! Learn How
Video W6-4

Building a final document often involves more than one person. One person usually drafts the original and becomes the document ***author***—or *owner*—and then others add their portions of text and comment on, or propose changes to, the text of others. A ***reviewer*** is someone who reviews and marks changes on a document.

A ***comment*** is a note that an author or reviewer adds to a document. Comments are a good way to communicate when more than one person is involved with the writing, reviewing, and editing process. Comments are like sticky notes attached to the document—they can be viewed and read by others but are not part of the document text.

Activity 6.13 | Inserting and Replying to Comments

Expert 1.3.4

For the library's monthly schedule of events, Abigail Gardner has created a draft document; edits and comments have been added by others. In this Activity, you will insert a comment to suggest confirming a scheduled guest.

1 Start Word. From your student files, locate and open the file **w06B_Events_Schedule**. Save the file in your **Chapter 6 folder** as **Lastname_Firstname_6B_Events_Schedule**

2 Insert the file name in the footer, and then close the footer area. If necessary, display the rulers and formatting marks.

3 Click the **Review tab**. In the **Tracking group**, verify that **Simple Markup** displays as shown in Figure 6.21. If a different markup style displays, click the arrow, and then click Simple Markup.

In ***Simple Markup*** view, ***revisions***—changes made to a document—are indicated by vertical red lines in the left margin, and comments that have been made are indicated by icons in the right margin.

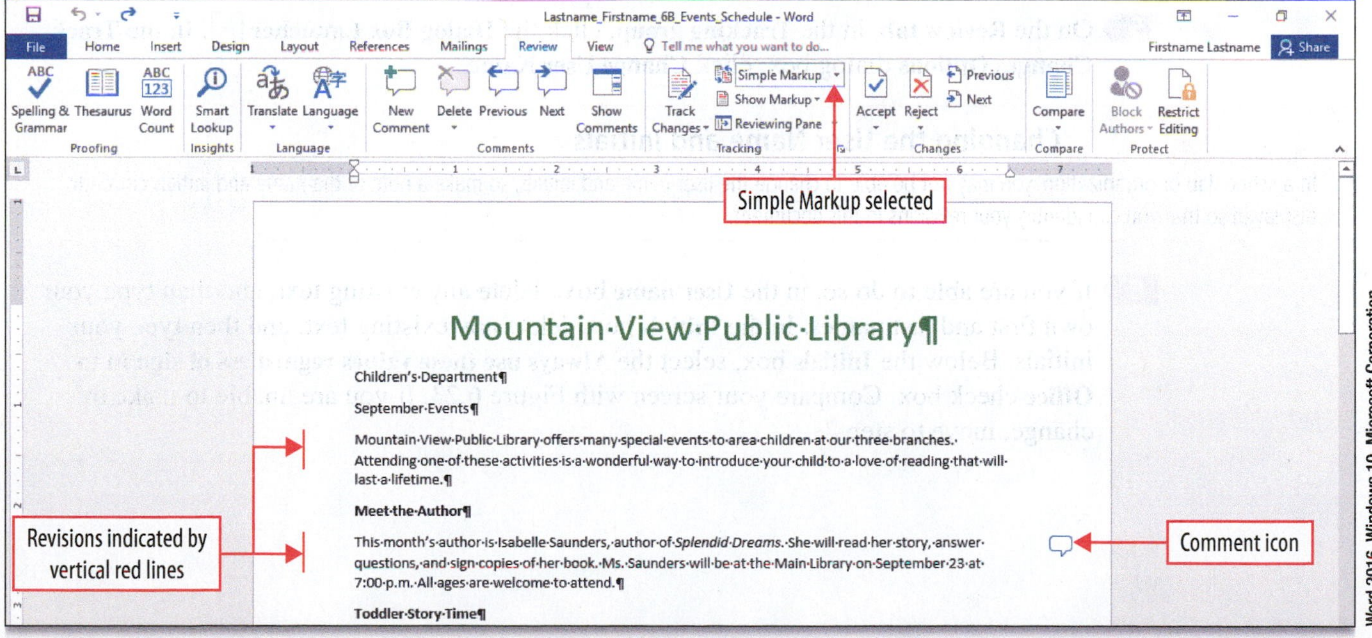

FIGURE 6.21

4 If necessary, press Ctrl + Home. On the **Review tab**, in the **Comments group**, click **Show Comments** so that it is selected. Compare your screen with Figure 6.22.

The comments display in ***balloons*** in the nonprinting ***markup area***. A balloon is the outlined shape in which a comment or formatting change displays The markup area is the space to the right or left of the document where comments and also formatting changes—for example, applying italic—display. Each comment includes the name of the reviewer who made the comment. Each reviewer's comments are identified by a distinct color.

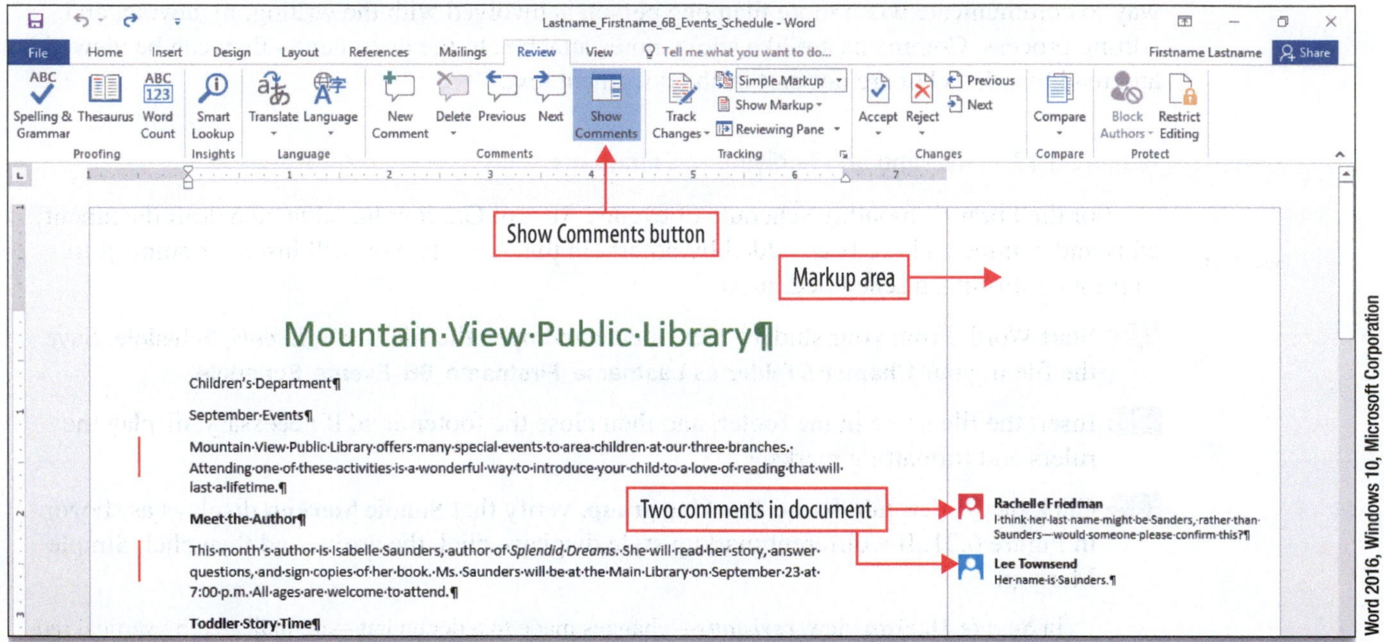

Word 2016, Windows 10, Microsoft Corporation

FIGURE 6.22

5 On the **Review tab**, in the **Tracking group**, click the **Dialog Box Launcher**. In the **Track Changes Options** dialog box, click **Change User Name**.

ALERT! **Changing the User Name and Initials**

In a school lab or organization, you may not be able to change the user name and initials, so make a note of the name and initials currently displayed so that you can identify your revisions in this document.

6 If you are able to do so, in the **User name** box, delete any existing text, and then type your own first and last names. In the **Initials** box, delete any existing text, and then type your initials. Below the **Initials** box, select the **Always use these values regardless of sign in to Office** check box. Compare your screen with Figure 6.23. If you are unable to make this change, move to step 7.

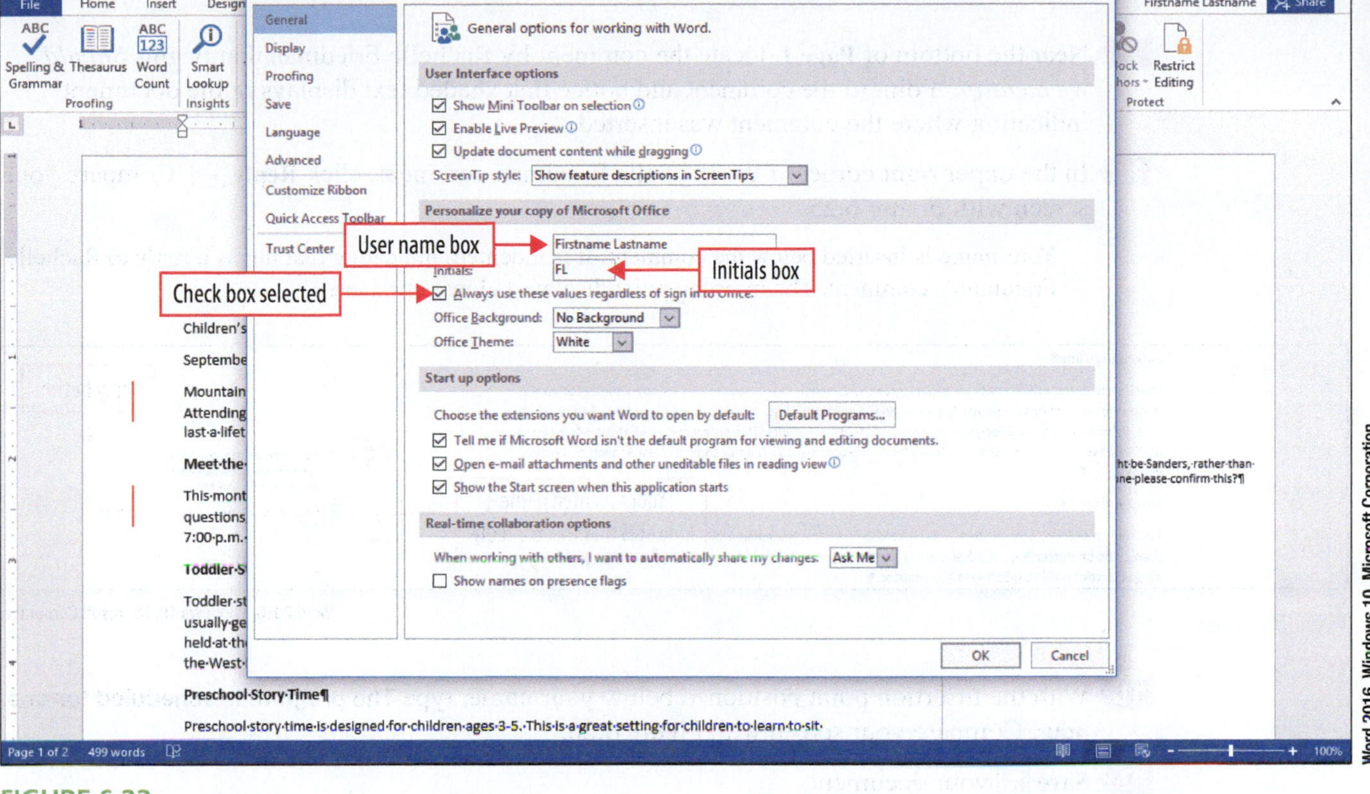

FIGURE 6.23

7 Click **OK** two times to close the dialog boxes.

8 On **Page 1**, select the fifth paragraph **Meet the Author**. On the **Review tab**, in the **Comments group**, click **New Comment**, and notice that a new comment balloon displays in the markup area with the user name configured on your computer. Type **Check with Barry Smith to confirm.** Compare your screen with Figure 6.24.

You can insert a comment at a specific location in a document or to selected text, such as an entire paragraph. Your name—or the name configured for the computer at which you are working—displays at the beginning of the comment.

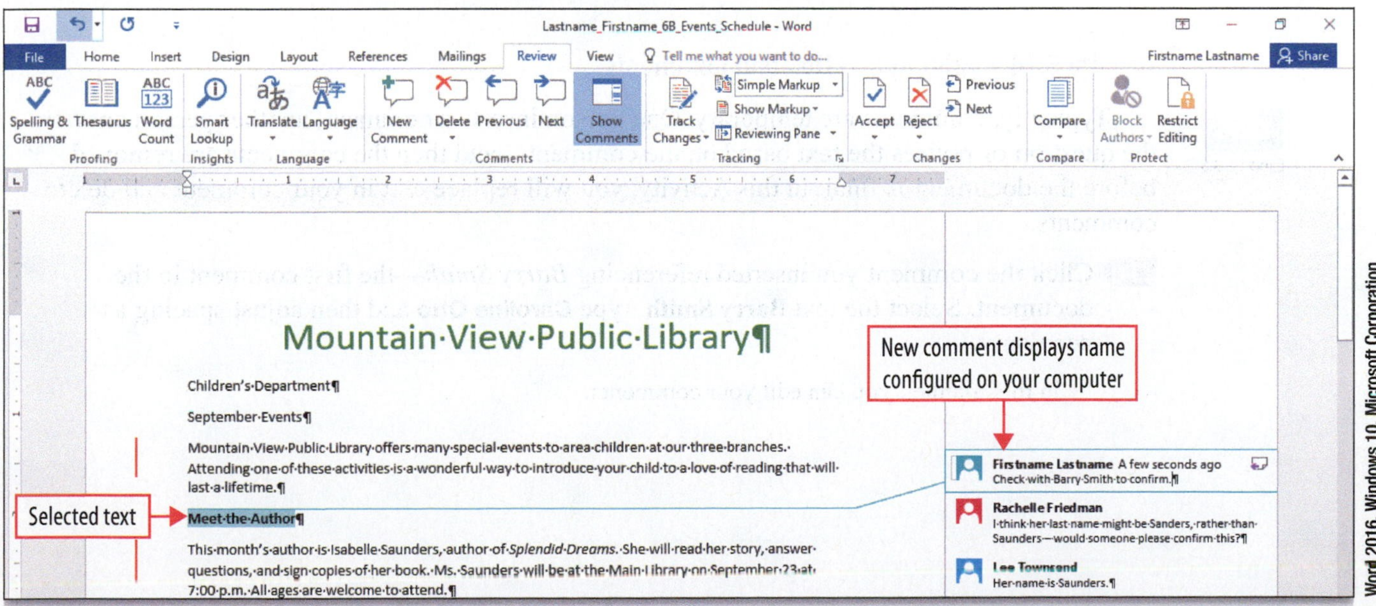

FIGURE 6.24

ANOTHER WAY On the Insert tab, in the Comments group, click Comment.

9. Near the bottom of **Page 1**, locate the comment by Rachelle Friedman that begins *Should we mention*. Point to the comment and notice that shaded text displays in the document indicating where the comment was inserted.

10. In the upper right corner of the Rachelle Friedman comment, click **Reply**. Compare your screen with Figure 6.25.

    Your name is inserted below the comment. It is indented, indicating that this is a *reply* to Rachelle Friedman's comment. The insertion point displays below your name.

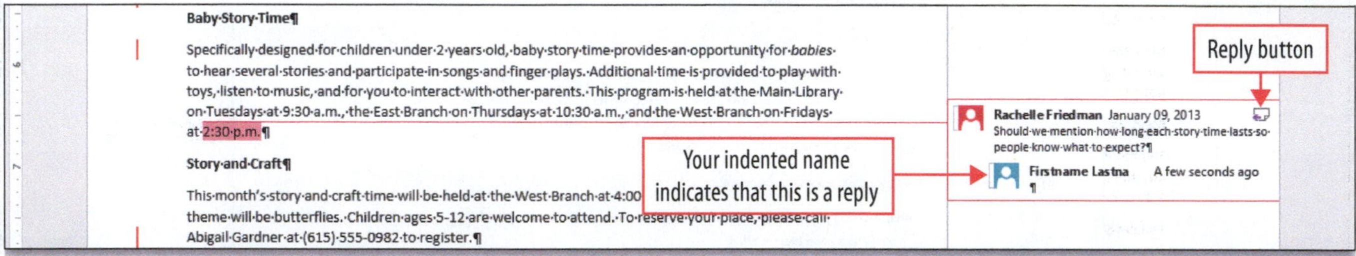

FIGURE 6.25 Word 2016, Windows 10, Microsoft Corporation

11. With the insertion point positioned below your name, type **The program is scheduled for one hour.** Compare your screen with Figure 6.26.

12. **Save** your document.

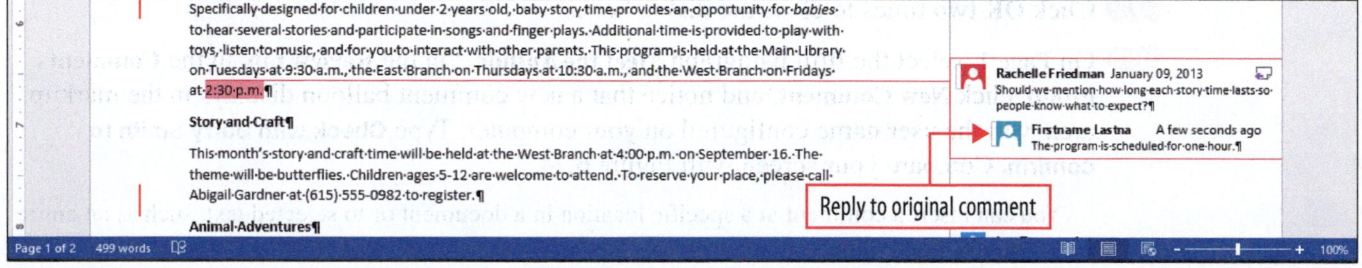

FIGURE 6.26 Word 2016, Windows 10, Microsoft Corporation

Activity 6.14 | Editing and Deleting Comments

Expert 1.3.5

Typically, comments are temporary. One person inserts a comment, another person answers the question or revises the text based on the comment—and then the comments are removed before the document is final. In this Activity, you will replace text in your comment and delete comments.

1. Click the comment you inserted referencing *Barry Smith*—the first comment in the document. Select the text **Barry Smith**, type **Caroline Otto** and then adjust spacing as necessary.

    In this manner, you can edit your comments.

2 Immediately below your comment, click the comment created by Rachelle Friedman, which begins **I think her last name**, and notice the following comment created by *Lee Townsend*. Compare your screen with Figure 6.27.

Because the question asked by Rachelle Friedman has been answered by Lee Townsend, both comments can be deleted.

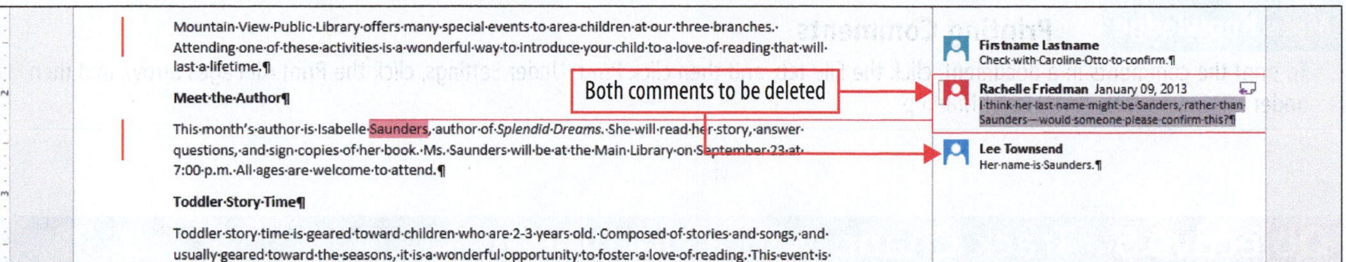

FIGURE 6.27

Word 2016, Windows 10, Microsoft Corporation

3 With your insertion point positioned in the comment by *Rachelle Friedman*, on the **Review tab**, in the **Comments group**, click the upper portion of the **Delete** button to delete the comment.

4 Point to the comment by *Lee Townsend*, right-click, and then from the shortcut menu, click **Delete Comment**.

Use either technique to delete a comment.

5 In the **Comments group**, click **Next**. In the markup area, notice that the comment by *Rachelle Friedman* is selected. Compare your screen with Figure 6.28.

In the Comments group, you can use the Next and Previous buttons in this manner to navigate through the comments in a document.

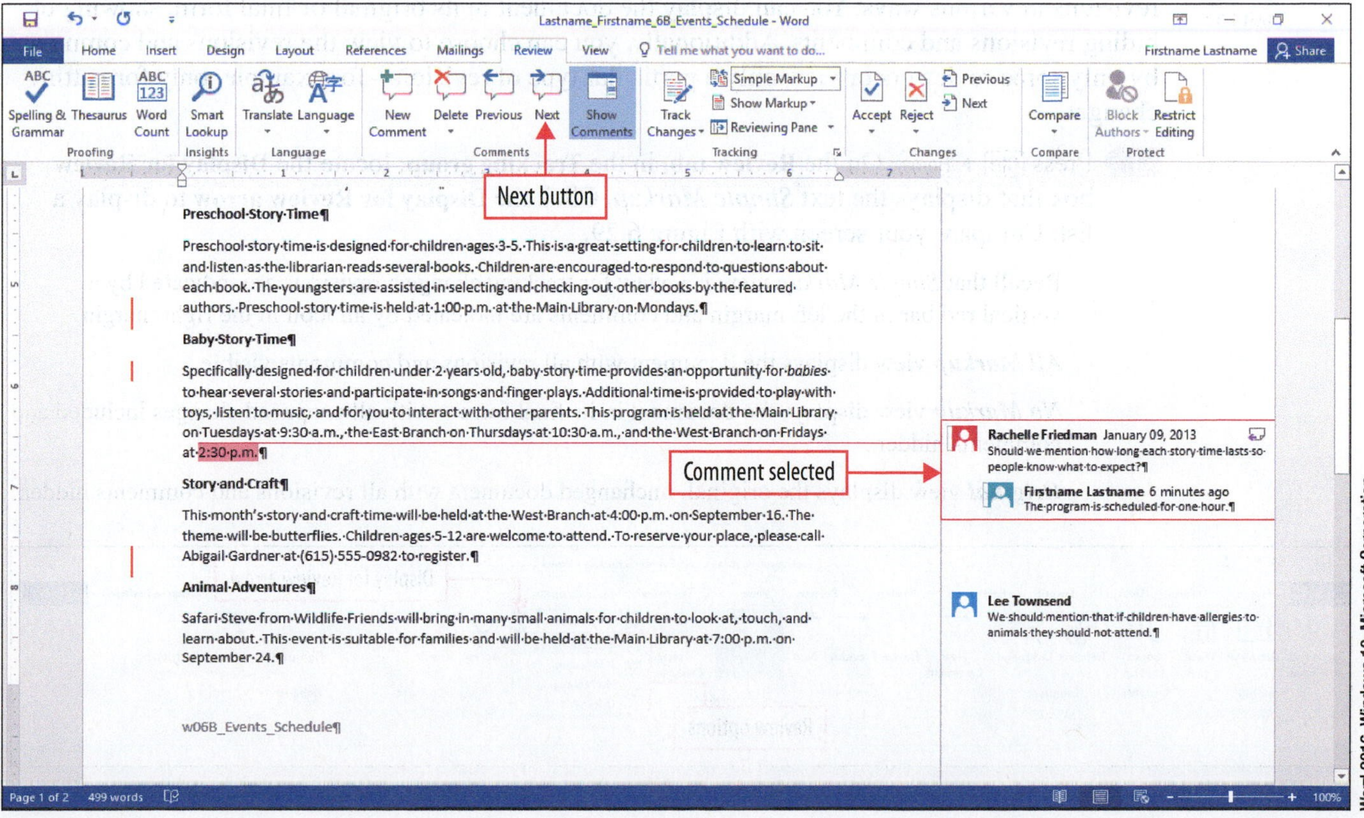

Word 2016, Windows 10, Microsoft Corporation

FIGURE 6.28

6 In the **Comments group**, click **Next** two times to select the comment by Lee Townsend that begins **We should mention**, and then use any technique you have practiced to **Delete** the comment.

7 **Save** your document.

> ***More* Knowledge** **Printing Comments**
>
> To print the comments in a document, click the File tab, and then click Print. Under Settings, click the Print All Pages arrow, and then under Document Info, click List of Markup.

Objective 5 Track Changes in a Document

GO! Learn How Video W6-5

When you turn on the ***Track Changes*** feature, it makes a record of—*tracks*—the changes made to a document. As you revise the document with your changes, Word uses markup to visually indicate insertions, deletions, comments, formatting changes, and content that has moved.

Each reviewer's revisions and comments display in a different color. This is useful if, for example, you want to quickly scan only for edits made by your supervisor or only for edits made by a coworker. After the document has been reviewed by the appropriate individuals, you can locate the changes and accept or reject the revisions on a case-by-case basis or globally in the entire document.

Activity 6.15 | Viewing All Tracked Changes in a Document and Setting Tracking and Markup Options

Expert 1.3.1

After one or more reviewers have made revisions and inserted comments, you can view the revisions in various ways. You can display the document in its original or final form, showing or hiding revisions and comments. Additionally, you can choose to view the revisions and comments by only some reviewers or view only a particular type of revision—for example, only formatting changes.

1 Press Ctrl + Home. On the **Review tab**, in the **Tracking group**, locate the **Display for Review** box that displays the text *Simple Markup*. Click the **Display for Review arrow** to display a list. Compare your screen with Figure 6.29.

Recall that *Simple Markup* view is a view for tracking changes; revisions are indicated by a vertical red bar in the left margin and comments are indicated by an icon in the right margin.

All Markup view displays the document with all revisions and comments visible.

No Markup view displays the document in its final form—with all proposed changes included and comments hidden.

Original view displays the original, unchanged document with all revisions and comments hidden.

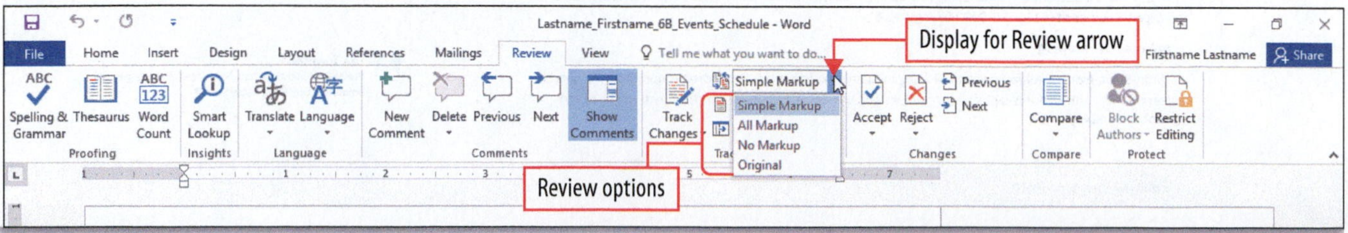

FIGURE 6.29

Word 2016, Windows 10, Microsoft Corporation

2 On the list, click **No Markup**. Notice that all comments and indicated changes are hidden. The document displays with all proposed changes included.

When you are editing a document in which you are proposing changes, this view is useful because the revisions of others or the markup of your own revisions is not distracting.

3 In the **Tracking group**, click the **Display for Review arrow**, and then from the list, click **All Markup**. Compare your screen with Figure 6.30.

At the stage where you, the document owner, must decide which revisions to accept or reject, you will find this view to be the most useful. The document displays with revisions—changes are shown as ***markup***. Markup refers to the formatting Word uses to denote the revisions visually. For example, when a reviewer changes text, the original text displays with strikethrough formatting by default. When a reviewer inserts new text, the new text is underlined. A ***vertical change bar*** displays in the left margin next to each line of text that contains a revision. In All Markup view, the vertical change bar displays in black; in Simple Markup view, it displays in red. In All Markup view, shaded text indicates where a comment has been inserted.

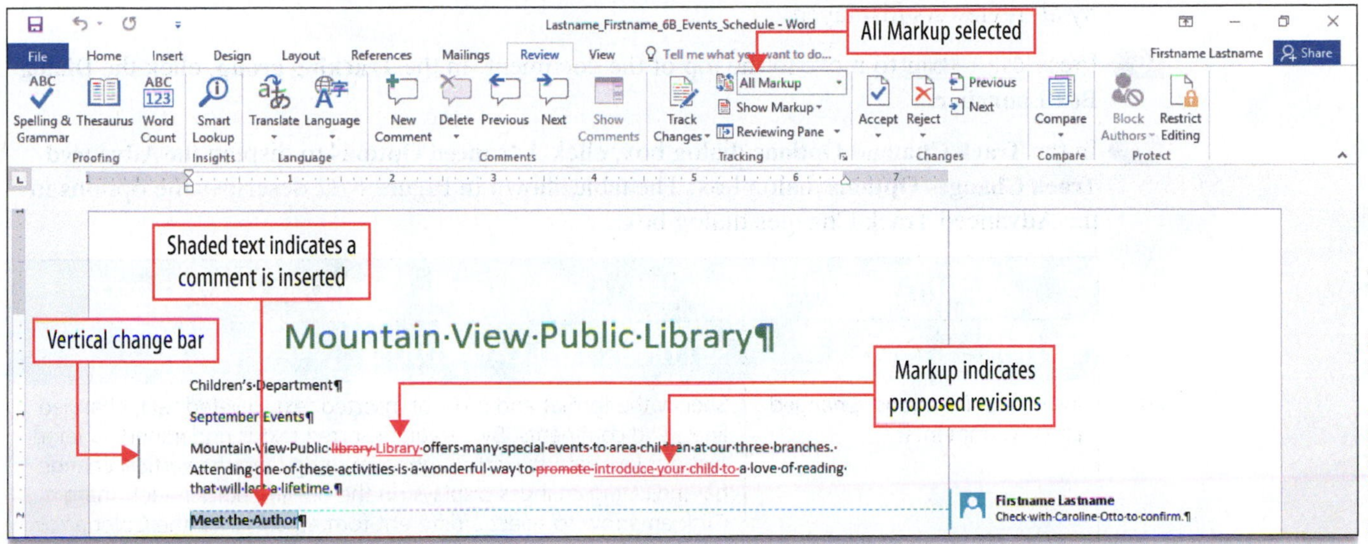

FIGURE 6.30

BY TOUCH Tap any vertical change bar to toggle between Simple Markup view and All Markup view.

4 In the **Tracking group**, click **Show Markup**, and then point to **Specific People** to see the name of each individual who proposed changes to this document. Compare your screen with Figure 6.31.

Here you can turn off the display of revisions by one or more reviewers. For example, you might want to view only the revisions proposed by a supervisor—before you consider the revisions proposed by others—by clearing the check box for all reviewers except the supervisor.

In the Show Markup list, you can also determine which changes display by deselecting one or more of the options. ***Ink*** refers to marks made directly on a document by using a stylus on a Tablet PC.

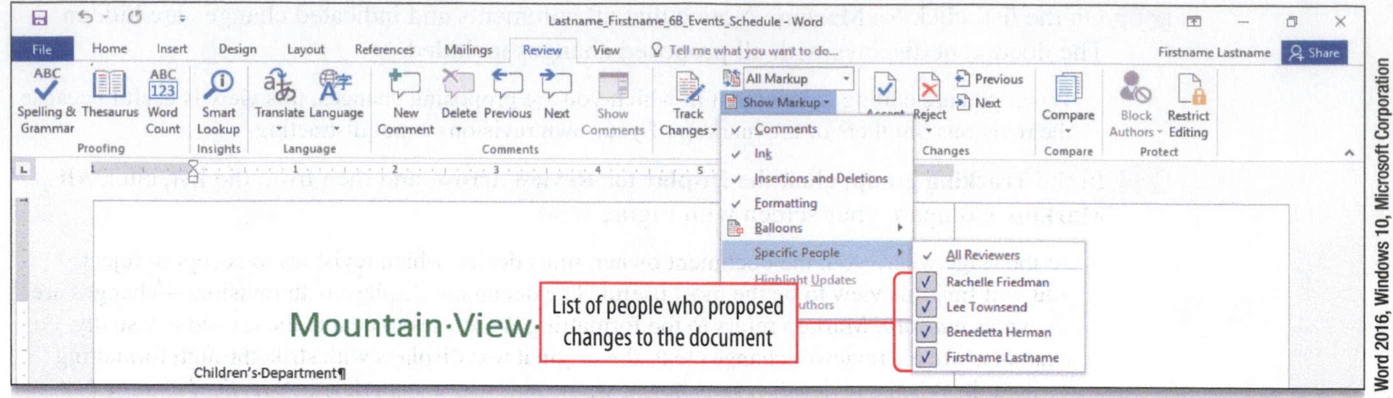

Word 2016, Windows 10, Microsoft Corporation

FIGURE 6.31

5 Click anywhere in the document to close the **Show Markup** list and leave all revision types by all reviewers displayed.

6 Press Ctrl + Home to move to the top of the document. In the **Tracking group**, click the **Dialog Box Launcher**.

7 In the **Track Changes Options** dialog box, click **Advanced Options** to display **the Advanced Track Changes Options** dialog box. The table shown in Figure 6.32 describes the options in the Advanced Track Changes dialog box.

SETTINGS IN THE ADVANCED TRACK CHANGES OPTIONS DIALOG BOX	
OPTION	**SETTINGS YOU CAN ADJUST**
Insertions, Deletions, Changed Lines, Comments	Specify the format and color of inserted text, deleted text, changed lines, and comments. By default, inserted text is underlined, deleted text displays with strikethrough formatting, and the vertical change bar indicating changes displays on the outside border—left margin. Click an arrow to select a different format, and click the Color arrow to select a different color. The default, by author, indicates that Word will assign a different color to each person who inserts comments or tracks changes.
Moved from, Moved To	Specify the format of moved text. The default is green with double strikethrough in the moved content and a double underline below the content in its new location. To turn off this feature, clear the Track moves check box.
Inserted cells, Deleted Cells	Specify the color that will display in a table if cells are inserted, deleted, merged, or split.
Track formatting markup area	Specify the location and width of the markup area. By default, the location is at the right margin and the preferred width for balloons is set to 3.7". You can also control the display of connecting lines to text.

FIGURE 6.32

8 In the **Advanced Track Changes Options** dialog box, locate and verify that the Track formatting check box is selected. Below the check box, select the value in the **Preferred width** box, type **3** and then click **OK**.

This action will cause the markup area to display with a width of 3 inches.

9 Click **OK** again, and then **Save** your document.

Use the Advanced Track Changes Options dialog box in this manner to set Track Changes to display the way that works best for you.

Activity 6.16 | Using the Reviewing Pane

The ***Reviewing Pane***, which displays in a separate scrollable window, shows all of the changes and comments that currently display in your document. In this Activity, you will use the Reviewing Pane to view a summary of all changes and comments in the document.

1 On the **Review tab**, in the **Tracking group**, click the **Reviewing Pane arrow**. From the list, click **Reviewing Pane Vertical**, and then compare your screen with Figure 6.33.

The Reviewing Pane displays at the left of the document. Optionally, you can display the Reviewing Pane horizontally at the bottom of the document window. The summary section at the top of the Reviewing Pane displays the number of revisions that remain in your document.

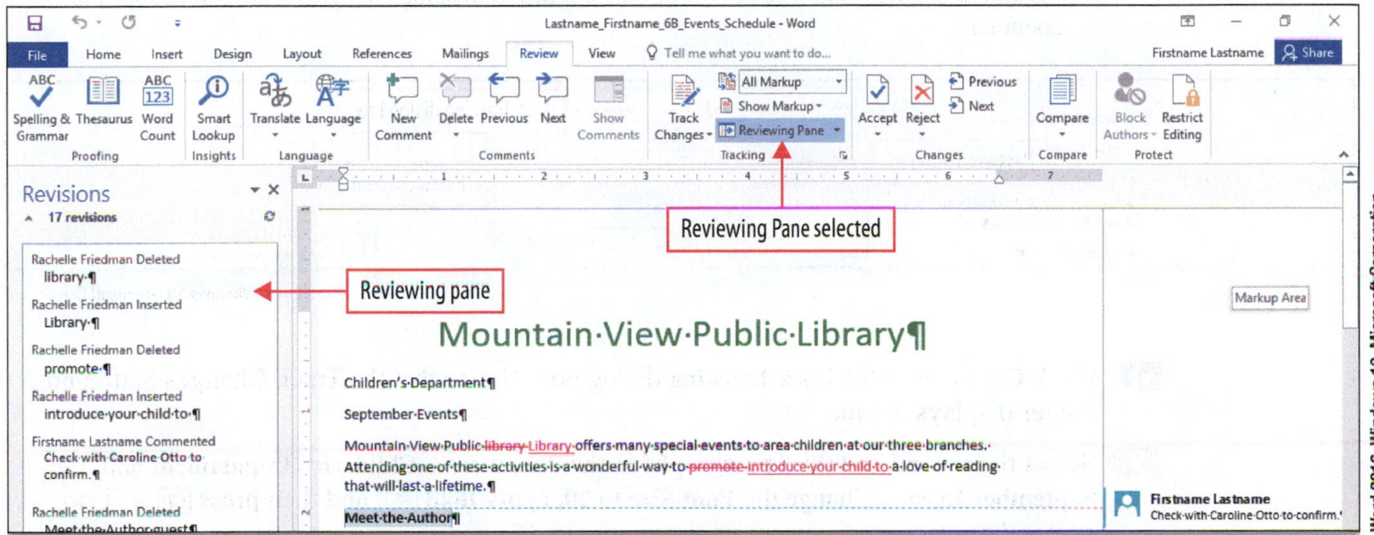

FIGURE 6.33

2 Take a moment to read the entries in the **Reviewing Pane**.

In the Reviewing Pane, you can view each type of revision, view the name of the reviewer associated with each item, and read long comments that do not display in the comments in the markup area. The Reviewing Pane is also useful for ensuring that all tracked changes have been *removed* from your document when it is ready for final distribution.

3 At the top of the **Reviewing Pane**, click **Close** .

ALERT! **Completing the Remainder of This Project in One Working Session**

Plan to complete the remaining activities in this project in one working session. For purposes of instruction, some revisions in documents must be made within a restricted time frame. If you must take a break, save the document, and then close Word. When you return to complete the project, reopen your file Lastname_Firstname_6B_Events_Schedule. If you are sharing a computer, be sure the user name and initials are the same as in the previous activities.

Activity 6.17 | Tracking Changes and Locking Tracking to Restrict Editing

Expert 1.3.2, 1.3.3

The Track Changes feature is turned off by default; you must turn on the feature each time you want to begin tracking changes in a document.

1 Press Ctrl + Home, if necessary, to move to the top of the document. On the **Review tab**, in the **Tracking group**, click the upper portion of the **Track Changes** button to enable tracking. Notice that the button displays in blue to indicate that the feature is turned on.

2 In the **Tracking group**, click the **Track Changes arrow**, and then click **Lock Tracking**.

The ***Lock Tracking*** feature prevents reviewers from turning off Track Changes and making changes that are not visible in markup.

3 In the **Lock Tracking** dialog box, in the **Enter password (optional)** box, type **1234** and then press Tab. In the **Reenter to confirm** box, type **1234** and then compare your screen with Figure 6.34.

The Tracking Changes feature will remain turned on, regardless of who edits the document—the author or reviewers. The password only applies to tracking changes; it does not protect the document.

FIGURE 6.34

Word 2016, Windows 10, Microsoft Corporation

4 Click **OK** to close the **Lock Tracking** dialog box. Notice that the Track Changes button no longer displays in blue.

5 Select the second and third paragraphs in the document—**Children's Department** and **September Events**. Change the **Font Size** to **20**, apply **Bold** B, and then press Ctrl + E to center the selection. Compare your screen with Figure 6.35.

As you make each change, the markup displays in the markup area, and the vertical change bar displays to the left of the paragraph. The types of changes—formatted text and center alignment—are indicated in the balloons in the markup area and lines point to the location of the revisions.

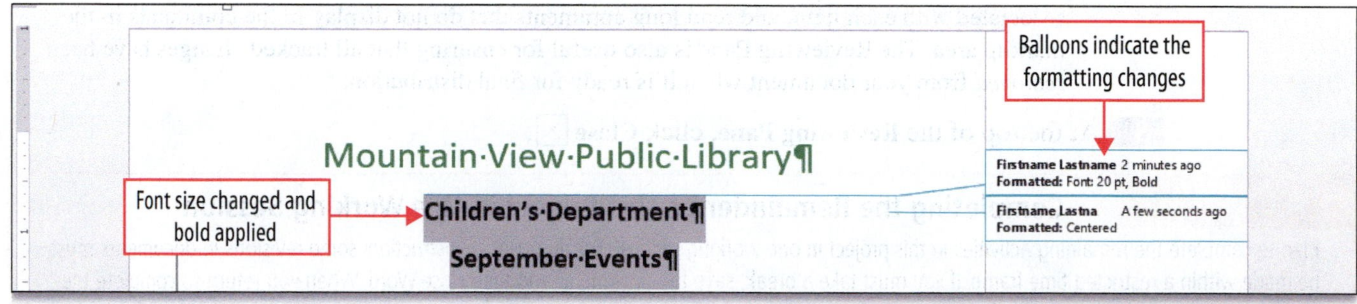

FIGURE 6.35

Word 2016, Windows 10, Microsoft Corporation

6 Locate the paragraph below *Baby Story Time* that begins *Specifically designed*. In the third line, click to position the insertion point to the left of *program*, type **one-hour** and then press Spacebar.

The inserted text is underlined and displays with your designated color.

7 Point to the inserted text, and then compare your screen with Figure 6.36.

A ScreenTip displays, showing the revision that was made, which reviewer made the change, and the date and time of the change.

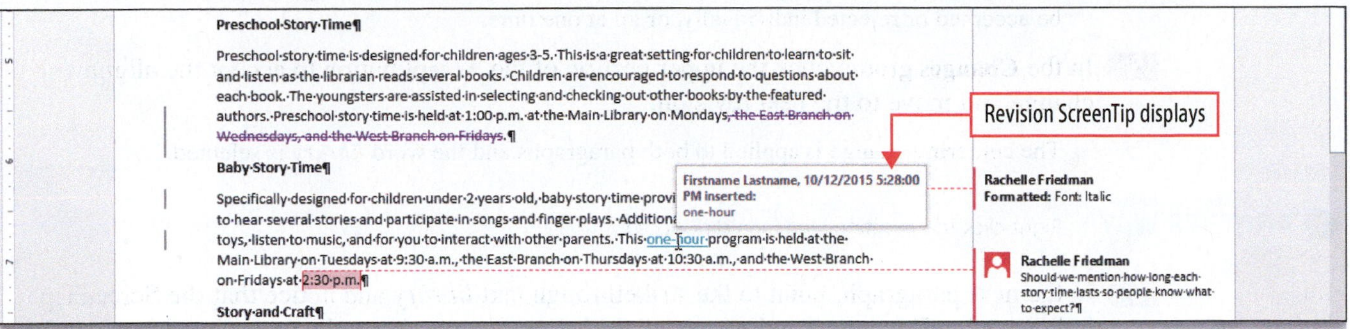

FIGURE 6.36

Word 2016, Windows 10, Microsoft Corporation

8 In the markup area, read the comment that begins *Should we mention*. Use any technique you practiced to **Delete** the comment. **Save** your document.

Having responded to this suggestion by inserting appropriate text, you can delete the comment. When developing important documents, having others review the document can improve its content and appearance.

> ***More* Knowledge** **Sharing a Document Using OneDrive**
>
> Use the Share command to allow reviewers to insert comments or edit a document that has been saved to OneDrive. To share a saved document, open the document. Click the File tab, click Share, and then click Save to Cloud. Open the OneDrive folder to which you want to save the file, and then click Save.

Activity 6.18 | Accepting or Rejecting Changes in a Document

Expert 1.3.2

After all reviewers have made their proposed revisions and added their comments, the document owner must decide which changes to accept and incorporate into the document and which changes to reject. Unlike revisions, it is not possible to accept or reject comments; instead, the document owner reads the comments, takes appropriate action or makes a decision, and then deletes each comment. In this Activity, you will accept and reject changes to create a final document.

1 Press Ctrl + Home.

When reviewing comments and changes in a document, it is good practice to start at the beginning of the document to be sure you do not miss any comments or revisions.

2 On the **Review tab**, in the **Tracking group**, click the **Track Changes arrow**, and then click **Lock Tracking**. In the **Unlock Tracking** dialog box, in the Password box, type **1234** and then click **OK**.

Because you are finalizing the changes in a document, it is necessary to unlock tracking. After entering the password, you have unlocked tracking. In the Tracking group, the Track Changes button displays in blue, which indicates that the feature is turned on.

3 On the **Review tab**, in the **Changes group**, click **Next**—be careful to select **Next** in the **Changes group**, *not* the Comments group. Notice that the second and third paragraphs in the document are selected.

In the Changes group, the Next button and the Previous button enable you to navigate from one revision or comment to the next or previous one.

4 In the **Changes group**, click the **Accept arrow**—the lower portion of the Accept button, and then click **Accept This Change**.

The text formatting is accepted for the selection, the related balloon no longer displays in the markup area, and the two paragraphs are still selected. When reviewing a document, changes can be accepted or rejected individually, or all at one time.

5 In the **Changes group**, click the upper portion of the **Accept** button to accept the alignment change and move to the next revision.

The centering change is applied to both paragraphs and the word *library* is selected.

ANOTHER WAY Right-click the selection, and then click Accept.

6 In the next paragraph, point to the strikethrough text *library* and notice that the ScreenTip indicates that Rachelle Friedman deleted *library*. Then, point to the underline directly below *Library* to display a ScreenTip. Compare your screen with Figure 6.37.

When a reviewer replaces text—for example, when Rachelle replaced *library* with *Library*—the inserted text displays with an underline and in the color designated for the reviewer. The original text displays with strikethrough formatting.

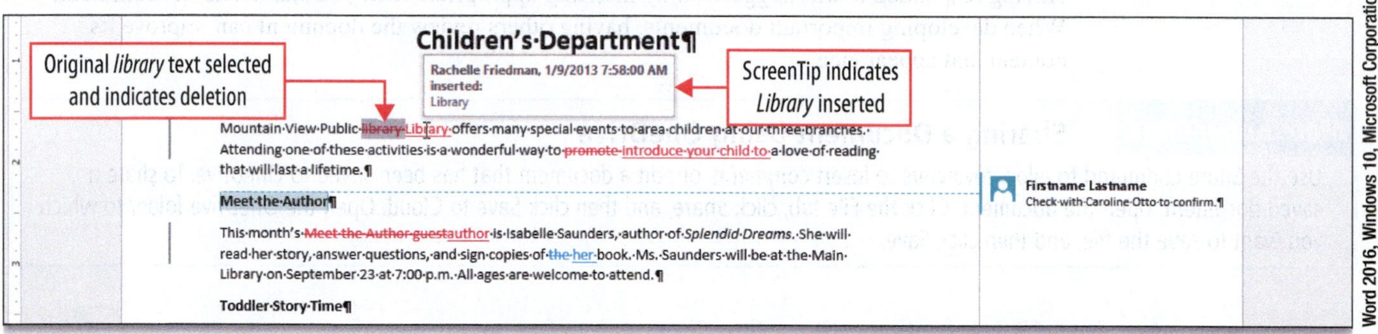

FIGURE 6.37

7 In the **Changes group**, click **Accept** two times to accept the deletion of *library* and the insertion of *Library*.

The next change, the deletion of *promote*, is selected.

8 With the suggested deletion—**promote**—selected, in the **Changes group**, click **Reject**, and then point to the selected text **introduce your child to**, to display a ScreenTip. Compare your screen with Figure 6.38.

The original text *promote* is reinserted in the sentence. As the document owner, you decide which proposed revisions to accept; you are not required to accept every change in a document.

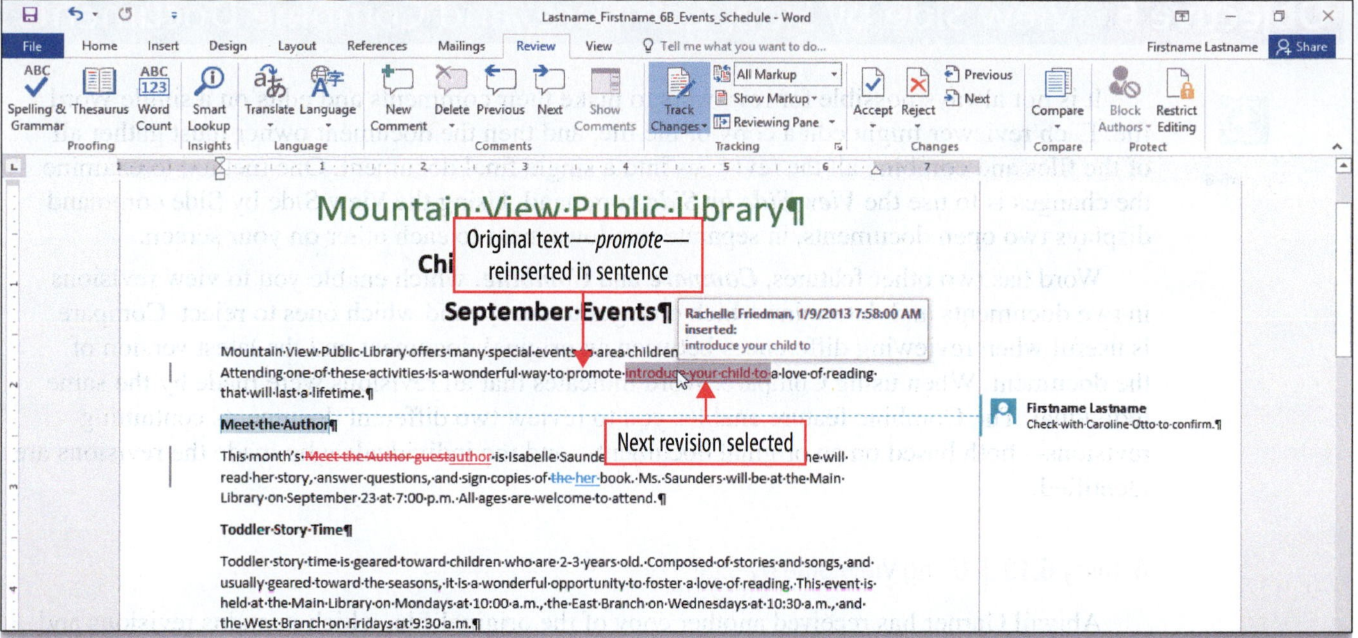

FIGURE 6.38

Word 2016, Windows 10, Microsoft Corporation

9 Click **Reject** again to reject the insertion of *introduce your child to* and to select the next change.

10 In the **Changes group**, click the **Accept arrow**. From the list, click **Accept All Changes and Stop Tracking**.

All remaining changes in the document are accepted and Track Changes is turned off.

11 Press Ctrl + Home, verify that the remaining comment displays, and then compare your screen with Figure 6.39.

12 **Save** your document; leave it open for the next Activity.

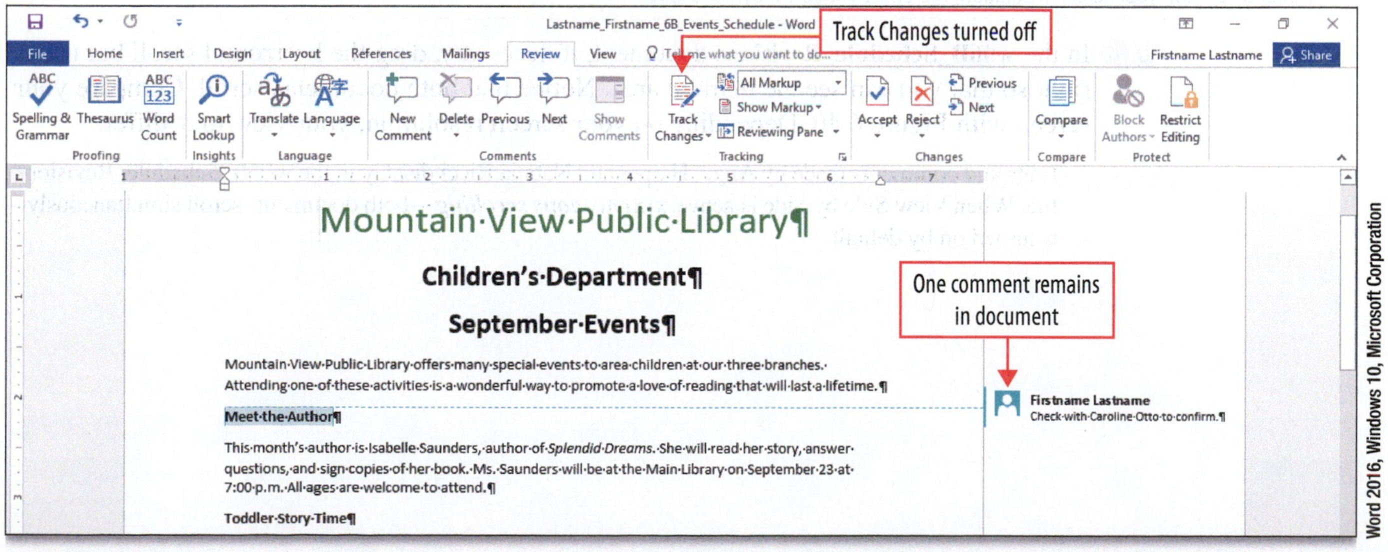

FIGURE 6.39

Word 2016, Windows 10, Microsoft Corporation

Objective 6 View Side by Side, Compare, and Combine Documents

GO! Learn How Video W6-6

It is not always possible for reviewers to make their comments and edits on a single Word file. Each reviewer might edit a copy of the file, and then the document owner must gather all of the files and combine all the revisions into a single final document. One method to examine the changes is to use the ***View Side by Side*** command. Using the View Side by Side command displays two open documents, in separate windows, next to each other on your screen.

Word has two other features, ***Compare*** and ***Combine***, which enable you to view revisions in two documents and determine which changes to accept and which ones to reject. Compare is useful when reviewing differences between an original document and the latest version of the document. When using Compare, Word indicates that all revisions were made by the same individual. The Combine feature enables you to review two different documents containing revisions—both based on an original document—and the individuals who made the revisions are identified.

Activity 6.19 | Using View Side by Side

Abigail Garner has received another copy of the original file, which contains revisions and comments from two additional reviewers—Angie Harper and Natalia Ricci. In this Activity, you will use View Side by Side to compare the new document with the version you finalized in the previous Activity.

1. With your file **Lastname_Firstname_6B_Events_Schedule** open and the insertion point at the top of the document, **Open** from your student data files **w06B_Schedule_Revisions**.
2. On the **View tab**, in the **Window group**, click **View Side by Side** to display both documents.

   This view enables you to see whether there have been any major changes to the original document that should be discussed by the reviewers before making revisions. Both documents contain the same basic text.

> **ALERT!** **Why Doesn't the Entire Window Display?**
>
> Depending upon your screen resolution, the entire window may not display.

3. In the **w06B_Schedule_Revisions** document, if necessary, drag the horizontal scroll bar to the right so that you can see the markup area. Notice that both documents scroll. Compare your screen with Figure 6.40. Depending on your screen resolution, your view may differ.

   Edits and comments made by Angie Harper and Natalia Ricci display in the w06B_Schedule_Revisions file. When View Side by Side is active, ***synchronous scrolling***—both documents scroll simultaneously—is turned on by default.

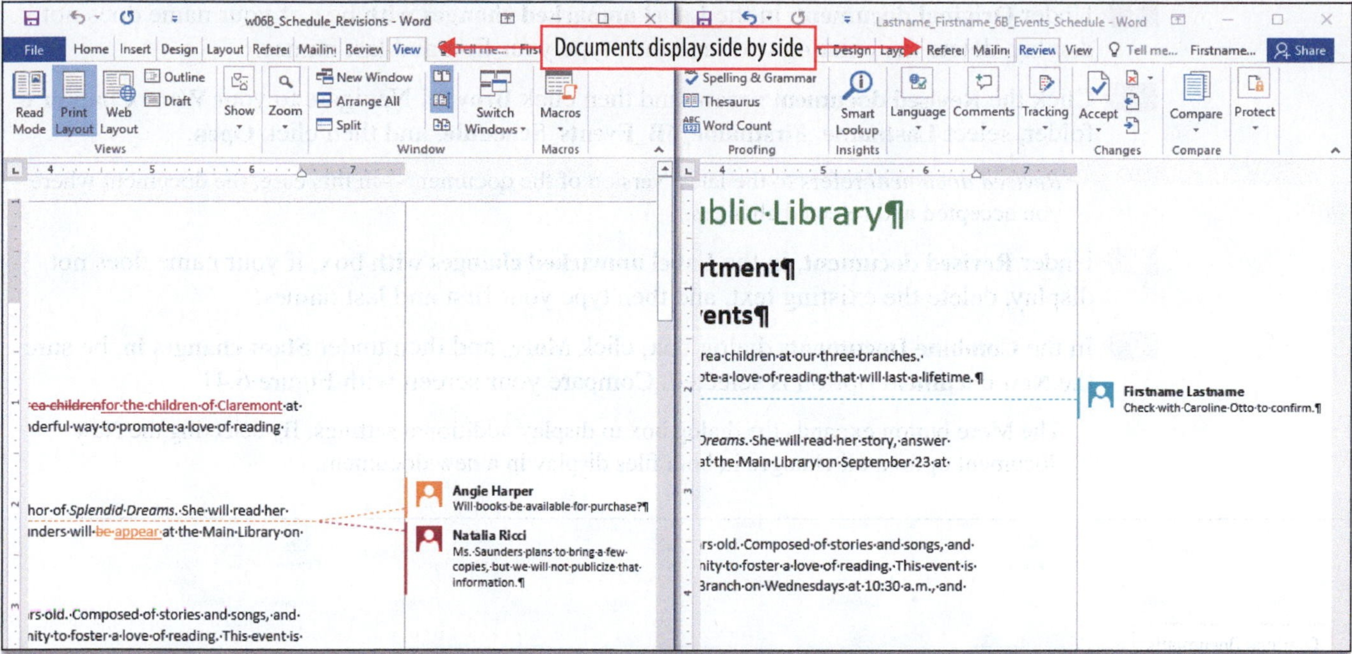

FIGURE 6.40

Word 2016, Windows 10, Microsoft Corporation

4 In the **w06B_Schedule_Revisions** document, in the **Window group**, click **View Side by Side** to restore program windows to their original size.

5 In the **w06B_Schedule_Revisions** document, select the first paragraph, and then on the mini toolbar, click **Styles**. In the **Styles** gallery, click **Heading 1**.

6 Display the **Save As** dialog box, and then **Save** the file in your **Word Chapter 6 folder** as **Lastname_Firstname_6B_Schedule_Revisions**

7 **Close** the **Lastname_Firstname_6B_Schedule_Revisions** document. Notice that your **Lastname_Firstname_6B_Events_Schedule** document displays.

8 Press Ctrl + W to close your **Lastname_Firstname_6B_Events_Schedule**, without closing Word.

Activity 6.20 | Combining Documents and Resolving Multi-Document Style Conflicts

Expert 1.1.4

In this Activity, you will combine the document containing revisions and comments by Angie Harper and Natalia Ricci with your finalized version of the events schedule. Then, you will accept or reject the additional revisions to create a final document ready for distribution to the public.

1 On the **Review tab**, in the **Compare group**, click **Compare**. From the list, click **Combine** to display the **Combine Documents** dialog box.

When using the Combine feature, it is not necessary to have an open document.

2 In the **Combine Documents** dialog box, click the **Original document arrow**, and then click **Browse**. In the **Open** dialog box, navigate to your **Word Chapter 6** folder, select the file **Lastname_Firstname_6B_Schedule_Revisions**, and then click **Open**.

Recall that this file includes revisions and comments from two additional reviewers. *Original document* usually refers to a document without revisions or, in this case, the document that you have not yet reviewed. The file also includes the formatting change you made to the first paragraph.

To the right of the Original document box, click Browse.

3. Under **Original document**, in the **Label unmarked changes with** box, if your name does not display, delete the existing text, and then type your first and last names.

4. Click the **Revised document arrow**, and then click **Browse**. Navigate to your **Word Chapter 6** folder, select **Lastname_Firstname_6B_Events_Schedule**, and then click **Open**.

   Revised document refers to the latest version of the document—in this case, the document where you accepted and rejected changes.

5. Under **Revised document**, in the **Label unmarked changes with** box, if your name does not display, delete the existing text, and then type your first and last names.

6. In the **Combine Documents** dialog box, click **More**, and then under **Show changes in**, be sure the **New document** option is selected. Compare your screen with Figure 6.41.

   The More button expands the dialog box to display additional settings. By selecting the New document option, all changes in both files display in a new document.

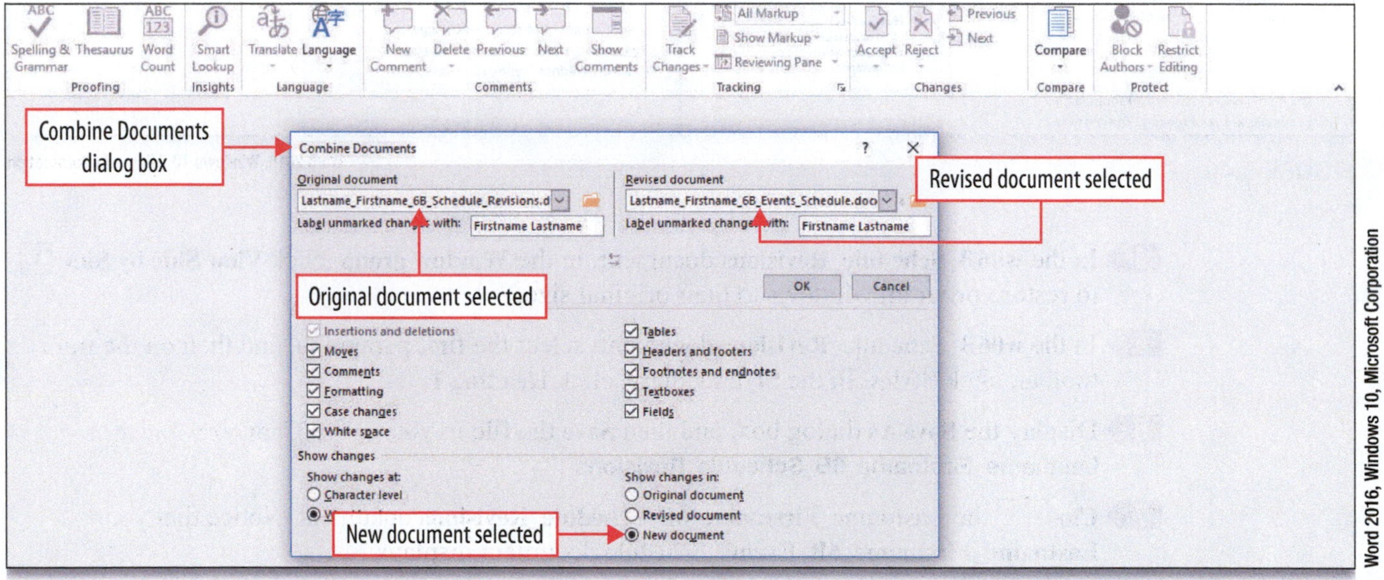

FIGURE 6.41

Word 2016, Windows 10, Microsoft Corporation

7. In the **Combine Documents** dialog box, click **Less**, and then click **OK**. In the message box indicating that Word can only store one style of formatting changes in the final merged document, under **Keep formatting changes**, select **The other document (Lastname_Firstname_6B_Events_Schedule)** option button.

   When combining two documents, style conflicts can exist when formatting changes are made to the same text in different versions of the document in the same time frame. In this case, the conflict exists because both files contain a formatting change applied to the first paragraph. The message box allows you to select the document that contains the formatting change you want to display in the combined document.

8. In the message box, click **Continue with Merge**. Compare your screen with Figure 6.42.

   The Tri-Pane Review Panel displays with the combined document in the left pane, the original document in the top right pane, and the revised document in the bottom right pane. The Reviewing Pane displays to the left of your screen, indicating all accepted changes in your Lastname_Firstname_6B_Events_Schedule file with your user name.

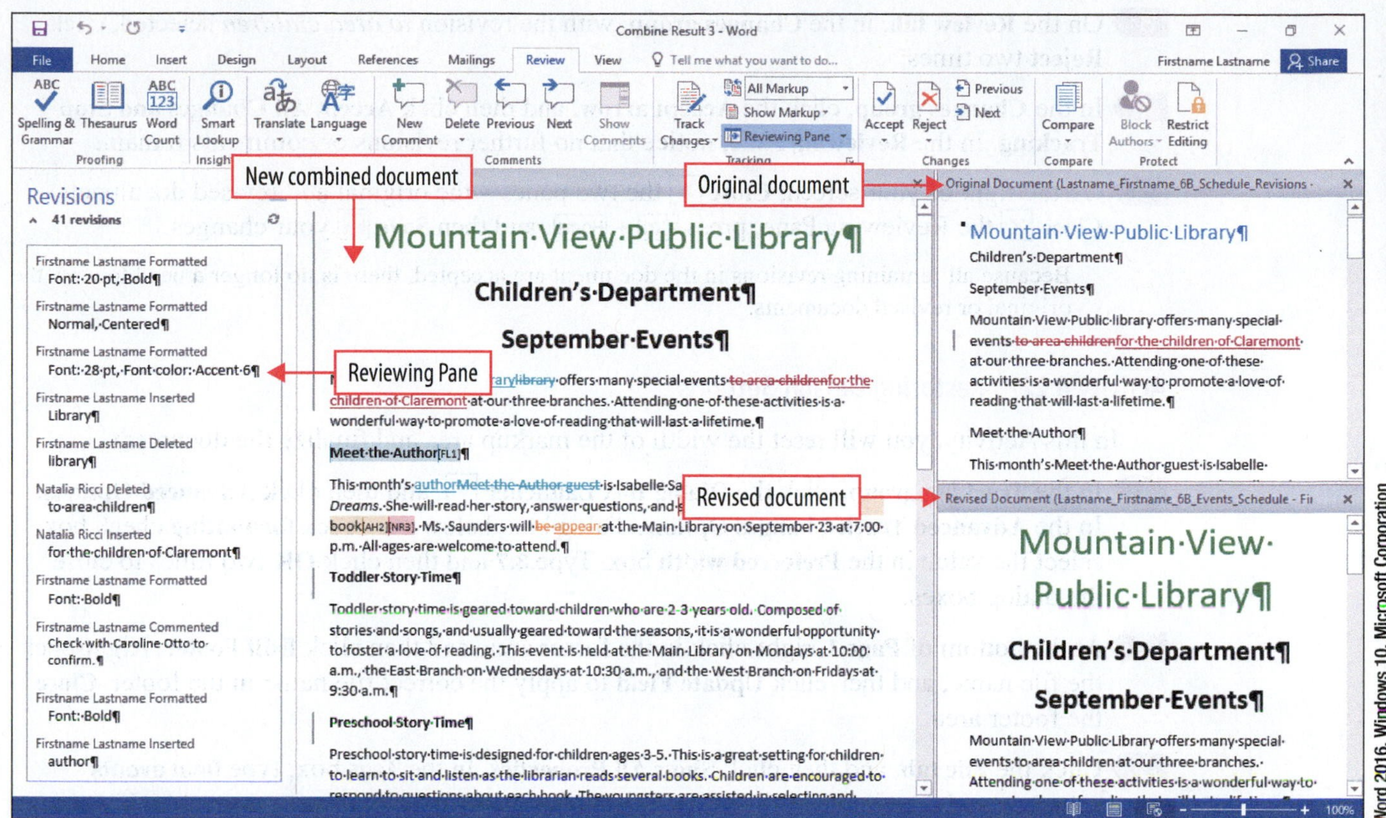

Word 2016, Windows 10, Microsoft Corporation

FIGURE 6.42

ALERT! **Should Both Documents Display?**

If only the combined document displays, in the Compare group, click Compare, click Show Source Documents, and then click Show Both. If the Reviewing Pane does not display, in the Tracking group, click the Reviewing Pane arrow, and then click Reviewing Pane Vertical.

9. If necessary, click to position the insertion point at the beginning of the **Combined Document**. **Save** the document in your **Word Chapter 6** folder as **Lastname_Firstname_6B_Schedule_Combined**

Activity 6.21 | Accepting and Rejecting Changes in a Combined Document

1. With the **Lastname_Firstname_6B_Schedule_Combined** document active, on the **Review tab**, in the **Comments group**, click the **Delete arrow**, and then click **Delete All Comments in Document**. If necessary, press Ctrl + Home.

2. In the **Changes group**, click **Next**, and then click **Accept** to accept the first change. Continue to click **Accept** until the revision *to area children* is selected. Compare your screen with Figure 6.43.

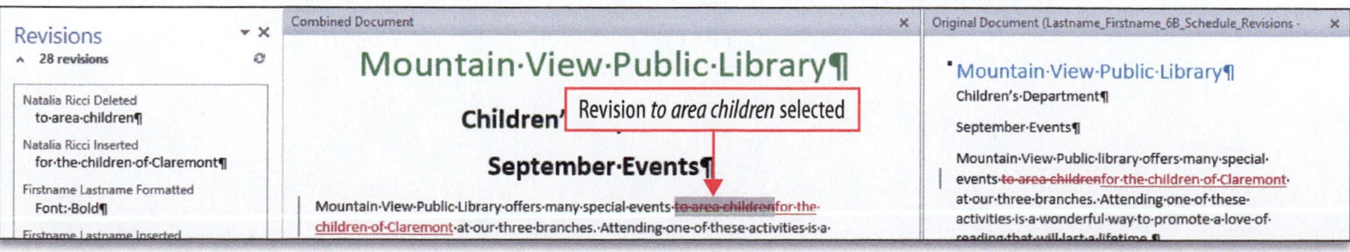

FIGURE 6.43

Word 2016, Windows 10, Microsoft Corporation

3 On the **Review tab**, in the **Changes group**, with the revision *to area children* selected, click **Reject** two times.

4 In the **Changes group**, click the **Accept arrow**, and then click **Accept All Changes and Stop Tracking**. In the **Reviewing Pane**, notice that no further revisions or comments remain.

5 On the right of your screen, **Close** [×] the two panes—the original and revised documents. **Close** [×] the Reviewing Pane, press Ctrl + Home, and then **Save** your changes.

Because all remaining revisions in the document are accepted, there is no longer a need to view the original or revised documents.

Activity 6.22 | Restoring Default Settings

In this Activity, you will reset the width of the markup area and finalize the document.

1 In the **Tracking group**, click the **Dialog Box Launcher**, and then click **Advanced Options**. In the **Advanced Track Changes Options** dialog box, below the **Track formatting** check box, select the value in the **Preferred width** box. Type **3.7** and then click **OK** two times to close the dialog boxes.

2 At the bottom of **Page 1**, right-click in the footer area, and then click **Edit Footer**. Right-click the file name, and then click **Update Field** to apply the correct file name in the footer. **Close** the footer area.

3 Click the **File tab**, and then click **Show All Properties**. In the **Tags** box, type **final events schedule** and then in the **Subject** box, type your course name and section number. If necessary, edit the author name to display your name, and then **Save** your document.

4 In the upper right corner of the Word window, click **Close** [×]. If directed by your instructor to do so, submit your paper printout, your electronic image of your document that looks like a printed document, or your original Word file.

ALERT! **If you are submitting this project in the MyITLab Grader system, submit your Lastname_Firstname_Schedule_Combined document.**

END | You have completed Project 6B

GO! To Work

Andrew Rodriguez / Fotolia; FotolEdhar/ Fotolia; apops/ Fotolia; Yuri Arcurs/ Fotolia

6 WORD

MICROSOFT OFFICE SPECIALIST (MOS) SKILLS IN THIS CHAPTER			
PROJECT 6A		**PROJECT 6B**	
1.3.2	Apply document themes	**Expert 1.1.4**	Compare and combine multiple documents
1.3.6	Format page background elements	**Expert 1.3.2**	Manage tracked changes
Expert 2.1.3	Set advanced page setup layout options	**Expert 1.3.3**	Lock or unlock tracking
Expert 4.1.1	Create QuickParts	**Expert 1.3.4**	Add comments
Expert 4.1.2	Manage building blocks	**Expert 1.3.5**	Manage comments
Expert 4.2.1	Create custom color sets		
Expert 4.2.2	Create custom font sets		
Expert 4.2.3	Create custom themes		

BUILD YOUR E-PORTFOLIO

An E-Portfolio is a collection of evidence, stored electronically, that showcases what you have accomplished while completing your education. Collecting and then sharing your work products with potential employers reflects your academic and career goals. Your completed documents from the following projects are good examples to show what you have learned: 6G, 6K, and 6L.

GO! FOR JOB SUCCESS

Discussion: The Internet of Things

Your instructor may assign these questions to your class, and then ask you to think about them or discuss them with your classmates:

Physical objects can be embedded with electronics and software that allow connectivity and data exchange with manufacturers, operators, and each other. These connected objects make up The Internet of Things. Examples include cars that send data on fuel efficiency to the manufacturer and devices that remind patients to take medications and report medical information to their doctors.

Amazon has introduced the Dash Button, which allows customers to order refills of household supplies simply by pressing the button when the item runs low, no computer or Amazon app required. One area where the Internet of Things has huge potential is in sensors that can create an alert when there is danger, such as sensors in a bridge that can signal when the structure is weakening.

FotolEdhar / Fotolia

If you owned a business, what are some ways that the Internet of Things could increase energy efficiency?

What are some items in your household that would be convenient to reorder with the push of a button?

What is another example of when danger could be averted by sensors inside a "thing"?

END OF CHAPTER

SUMMARY

Inserting building blocks—such as text boxes, pictures, Quick Tables, and AutoText—can save time and provide consistency in your documents. Use built-in document elements or create your own building blocks.

A theme template, defined by colors, fonts, and effects, enhances the appearance of a document. Attach a theme template to multiple documents to create documents that have a coordinated appearance.

The Track Changes feature enables a group of individuals to work together on a document. Reviewers can insert comments; reply to comments made by others; insert, edit, delete, and move text; and format documents.

The author of the document can accept or reject revisions. The author can compare two different versions of a document that has been revised using the Track Changes feature or combine them in a new document.

GO! LEARN IT ONLINE

Review the concepts, key terms, and MOS skills in this chapter by completing these online challenges, which you can find at **MyITLab**.

Matching and Multiple Choice: Answer matching and multiple choice questions to test what you learned in this chapter.

Lessons on the GO!: Learn how to use all the new apps and features as they are introduced by Microsoft.

MOS Prep Quiz: Answer questions to review the MOS skills that you practiced in this chapter.

PROJECT GUIDE FOR WORD CHAPTER 6

Your instructor will assign projects from this list to ensure your learning and assess your knowledge.

Project Guide for Word Chapter 6			
Project	**Apply Skills from These Chapter Objectives**	**Project Type**	**Project Location**
6A	Objectives 1–3 from Project 6A	**6A Instructional Project (Grader Project)** Guided instruction to learn the skills in Project 6A.	In MyITLab and in text
6B	Objectives 4–6 from Project 6B	**6B Instructional Project (Grader Project)** Guided instruction to learn the skills in Project 6B.	In MyITLab and in text
6C	Objectives 1–3 from Project 6A	**6C Skills Review (Scorecard Grading)** A guided review of the skills from Project 6A.	In text
6D	Objectives 4–6 from Project 6B	**6D Skills Review (Scorecard Grading)** A guided review of the skills from Project 6B.	In text
6E MyITLab	Objectives 1–3 from Project 6A	**6E Mastery (Grader Project)** **Mastery and Transfer of Learning** A demonstration of your mastery of the skills in Project 6A with extensive decision making.	In MyITLab and in text
6F MyITLab	Objectives 4–6 from Project 6B	**6F Mastery (Grader Project)** **Mastery and Transfer of Learning** A demonstration of your mastery of the skills in Project 6B with extensive decision making.	In MyITLab and in text
6G MyITLab	Objectives 1–6 from Project 6A and 6B	**6G Mastery (Grader Project)** **Mastery and Transfer of Learning** A demonstration of your mastery of the skills in Projects 6A and 6B with extensive decision making.	In MyITLab and in text
6H	Combination of Objectives from Projects 6A and 6B	**6H GO! Fix It (Scorecard Grading)** **Critical Thinking** A demonstration of your mastery of the skills in Projects 6A and 6B by creating a correct result from a document that contains errors you must find.	Instructor Resource Center (IRC) and MyITLab
6I	Combination of Objectives from Projects 6A and 6B	**6I GO! Make It (Scorecard Grading)** **Critical Thinking** A demonstration of your mastery of the skills in Projects 6A and 6B by creating a result from a supplied picture.	IRC and MyITLab
6J	Combination of Objectives from Projects 6A and 6B	**6J GO! Solve It (Rubric Grading)** **Critical Thinking** A demonstration of your mastery of the skills in Projects 6A and 6B, your decision-making skills, and your critical thinking skills. A task-specific rubric helps you self-assess your result.	IRC and MyITLab
6K	Combination of Objectives from Projects 6A and 6B	**6K GO! Solve It (Rubric Grading)** **Critical Thinking** A demonstration of your mastery of the skills in Projects 6A and 6B, your decision-making skills, and your critical thinking skills. A task-specific rubric helps you self-assess your result.	In text
6L	Combination of Objectives from Projects 6A and 6B	**6L GO! Think (Rubric Grading)** **Critical Thinking** A demonstration of your understanding of the chapter concepts applied in a manner that you would outside of college. An analytic rubric helps you and your instructor grade the quality of your work by comparing it to the work an expert in the discipline would create.	In text
6M	Combination of Objectives from Projects 6A and 6B	**6M GO! Think (Rubric Grading)** **Critical Thinking** A demonstration of your understanding of the chapter concepts applied in a manner that you would outside of college. An analytic rubric helps you and your instructor grade the quality of your work by comparing it to the work an expert in the discipline would create.	IRC and MyITLab
6N	Combination of Objectives from Projects 6A and 6B	**6N You and GO! (Rubric Grading)** **Critical Thinking** A demonstration of your understanding of the chapter concepts applied in a manner that you would in a personal situation. An analytic rubric helps you and your instructor grade the quality of your work.	IRC and MyITLab
Capstone Project for Word Chapters 4–6	Combination of Objectives from Projects A and B	A demonstration of your mastery of the skills in Chapters 4–6 with extensive decision making. **(Grader Project)**	IRC and MyITLab

GLOSSARY

GLOSSARY OF CHAPTER KEY TERMS

All Markup A Track Changes view that displays the document with all revisions and comments visible.

Author The owner, or creator, of the original document.

Balloon The outline shape in which a comment or formatting change displays.

Building blocks Reusable pieces of content or other document parts—for example, headers, footers, and page number formats—that are stored in galleries.

Building Blocks Organizer A feature that enables you to view—in a single location—all of the available building blocks from all the different galleries.

Combine A Track Changes feature that allows you to review two different documents containing revisions, both based on an original document.

Comment A note that an author or reviewer adds to a document.

Compare A Track Changes feature that enables you to review differences between an original document and the latest version of the document.

Hyphenation A tool in Word that controls how words are split between two lines.

Ink Revision marks made directly on a document by using a stylus on a Tablet PC.

Lock Tracking A feature that prevents reviewers from turning off Track Changes and making changes that are not visible in markup.

Markup The formatting Word uses to denote a document's revisions visually.

Markup area The space to the right or left of a document where comments and formatting changes display in balloons.

No Markup A Track Changes view that displays the document in its final form—with all proposed changes included and comments hidden.

Original A Track Changes view that displays the original, unchanged document with all revisions and comments hidden.

Quick Parts All of the reusable pieces of content that are available to insert into a document, including building blocks, document properties, and fields.

Quick Tables Tables that are stored as building blocks.

Reviewer An individual who reviews and marks changes on a document.

Reviewing Pane A separate scrollable window that shows all of the changes and comments that currently display in a document.

Revisions Changes made to a document.

Simple Markup The default Track Changes view that indicates revisions by vertical red lines in the left margin and displays comment icons in the right margin.

Synchronous scrolling The setting that causes two documents to scroll simultaneously.

Text box A movable, resizable container for text or graphics.

Theme A predesigned set of colors, fonts, and line and fill effects that look good together and is applied to an entire document by a single selection.

Theme template A stored, user-defined set of colors, fonts, and effects that can be shared with other Office programs.

Track Changes A feature that makes a record of the changes made to a document.

Vertical change bar A line that displays in the left margin next to each line of text that contains a revision.

View Side by Side A view that displays two open documents, in separate windows, next to each other on the screen.

Apply 6A skills from these Objectives:

1. Create Custom Building Blocks
2. Create and Save a Theme Template
3. Create a Document by Using Building Blocks

Skills Review Project 6C Literacy Program

In the following Skills Review, you will create and save building blocks and create a theme to be used in a flyer seeking volunteers for Mountain View Public Library's Adult Literacy Program. Your completed documents will look similar to Figure 6.44.

PROJECT FILES

For Project 6C, you will need the following files:

New blank Word document
w06C_Literacy_Program
w06C_Literacy_Blocks
w06C_Literacy_Image

You will save your files as:

Lastname_Firstname_6C_Literacy_Blocks
Lastname_Firstname_6C_Literacy_Program
Lastname_Firstname_6C_Literacy_Theme

PROJECT RESULTS

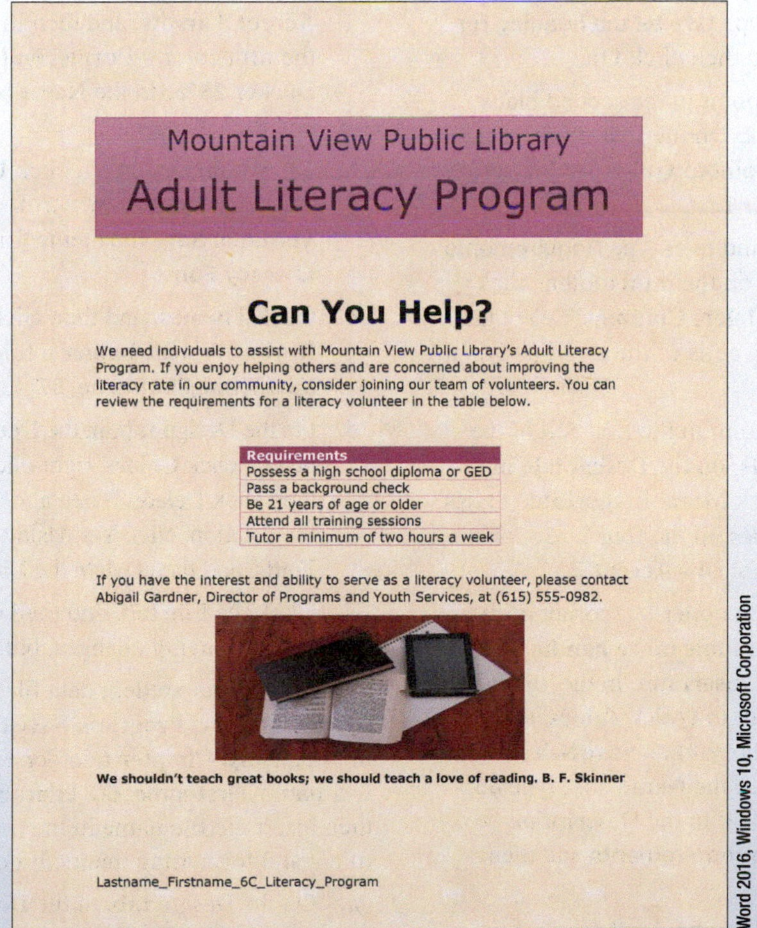

Word 2016, Windows 10, Microsoft Corporation

FIGURE 6.44

(Project 6C Literacy Program continues on the next page)

Skills Review Project 6C Literacy Program (continued)

1 Start Word. From your student data files, open **w06C_Literacy_Blocks** and if necessary, display the ruler and formatting marks. **Save** the file in your **Word Chapter 6** folder as **Lastname_Firstname_6C_Literacy_Blocks** and then insert the file name in the footer.

a. Select the text box at the top of the page. On the **Format tab**, in the **Shape Styles group**, click **More**. In the fourth row, click the third style—**Subtle Effect – Orange, Accent 2**.

b. Select both lines of text, change the **Font Color** to **Orange, Accent 2, Darker 50%**. Select the first line of text, and then change the **Font Size** to **24**. Select the second line of text, and then change the **Font Size** to **36**.

c. Click the outside edge of the text box to select it. On the **Insert tab**, in the **Text group**, click **Text Box**, and then click **Save Selection to Text Box Gallery**. In the **Name** box, type **Literacy Heading** and then click in the **Description** box. Type **Use as the heading for literacy documents** and then click **OK**.

2 Position the insertion point in the second blank paragraph below the text box. On the **Insert tab**, in the **Tables group**, click **Table**, point to **Quick Tables**, scroll down, and then click **Tabular List**.

a. Select the text **ITEM**, and then type **Requirements** Press Tab. Right-click, on the mini toolbar click **Delete**, and then click **Delete Columns**. Select the text in all the remaining cells of the table, and then press Delete.

b. Position the insertion point in the first cell of the table. Under **Table Tools**, on the **Design tab**, in the **Table Styles group**, click **More**. In the **Table Styles** gallery, under **List Tables**, in the fourth row, click the third style—**List Table 4 – Accent 2**.

c. Point slightly outside the upper left corner of the table, and then click the **table move handle** to select the entire table. On the **Insert tab**, in the **Tables group**, click **Table**. Point to **Quick Tables**, and then at the bottom of the gallery, click **Save Selection to Quick Tables Gallery**. In the **Name** box, type **Job Information** and then click in the **Description** box. Type **Use for listing job requirements** and then click **OK**.

d. Press Ctrl + End. Type **We shouldn't teach great books; we should teach a love of reading. B. F. Skinner** and then select the text you just typed. On the **Insert tab**, in the **Text group**, click **Quick Parts**, click **AutoText**, and then click **Save Selection to AutoText Gallery**. In the **Create New Building Block** dialog box, in the **Name** box, type **Literacy Quote** and then in the **Description** box, type **Quote for program** Click the **Save in arrow**, and then click **Building Blocks**. Click **OK**.

e. **Save** your changes. Click the **File tab**, and then click **Close** to close the document, but leave Word open. If a message box displays, asking if you want to save the building blocks, click Yes.

3 Press Ctrl + N to display a new blank document.

a. On the **Design tab**, in the **Document Formatting group**, click **Colors**, and then click **Customize Colors**. Click the **Accent 2 arrow**, and then under **Theme Colors**, in the last column, click the first color—**Purple, Followed Hyperlink**. Click the **Accent 3 arrow**, and then in the last column, click the fifth color—**Purple, Followed Hyperlink, Darker 25%**. In the Name box, type **Literacy Colors** and then click Save.

b. Click **Fonts**, and then click **Customize Fonts**. Click the **Body font arrow**, scroll down, and then click **Verdana**. **Save** the theme fonts with the name **Literacy Fonts**

c. Click **Themes**, and then click **Save Current Theme**. In your **Word Chapter 6** folder, **Save** the theme as **Lastname_Firstname_6C_Literacy_Theme**

d. On the **Design tab**, in the **Document Formatting group**, click **Colors**, right-click **Literacy Colors**, and then click **Delete**. When a message displays to confirm the deletion, click **Yes**. Using the same technique, click **Fonts**, and then **Delete** the **Literacy Fonts**.

e. Click the **File tab**, and then **Close** the document without saving changes, but leave Word open.

4 From your student data files, open **w06C_Literacy_Program**. **Save** the file in your **Word Chapter 6** folder as **Lastname_Firstname_6C_Literacy_Program** and then insert the file name in the footer. Display rulers and formatting marks, if necessary.

a. On the **Design tab**, in the **Document Formatting group**, click **Themes**, and then click **Browse for Themes**. In your **Word Chapter 6** folder, select your

(Project 6C Literacy Program continues on the next page)

Skills Review Project 6C Literacy Program (continued)

Lastname_Firstname_6C_Literacy_Theme file, and then click **Open** to apply the theme.

b. In the **Page Background group**, click **Page Color**, and then click **Fill Effects**. In the **Fill Effects** dialog box, click the **Texture tab**, and then in the fourth row, click the third texture—**Parchment**. Click **OK**.

c. With the insertion point at the top of the document, press Enter, and then position the insertion point in the first blank paragraph. On the **Insert tab**, in the **Text group**, click **Text Box**. Scroll to the bottom of the gallery, and then under **General**, click your **Literacy Heading** building block.

d. At the end of the paragraph that ends *in the table below*, position the insertion point after the period, and then press Enter two times.

5 On the **Insert tab**, in the **Tables group**, click **Table**, point to **Quick Tables**, scroll toward the bottom of the gallery, and then under **General**, click **Job Information**.

a. Position the insertion point in the second row of the table. Type the following text in the table, pressing Tab after each line to move to the next row:

Possess a high school diploma or GED
Pass a background check
Be 21 years of age or older
Attend all training sessions
Tutor a minimum of two hours a week

b. Select the last three empty rows of the table. On the mini toolbar, click **Delete**, and then click **Delete Rows**. Point slightly outside the upper left corner of the table, and then click the **table move handle** to select the entire table. **Center** the table on the page.

6 Press Ctrl + End, press Enter, and then press Ctrl + E. On the **Insert tab**, in the **Illustrations group**, click **Pictures**. In the **Insert Picture** dialog box, navigate to your student data files, select the file **w06C_Literacy_Image**, and then click **Insert**.

a. Position the insertion point to the right of the picture, and then press Enter. On the **Insert tab**, in the **Text group**, click **Quick Parts**, click **AutoText**, and then click **Literacy Quote**. Select the inserted text, change the **Font Size** to **10**, and then apply **Bold**. If necessary, at the end of the document, delete the blank paragraph.

b. Press Ctrl + Home. Click the **File tab**, and then click **Show All Properties**. In the **Tags** box, type **literacy program, volunteers** and in the **Subject** box, type your course name and section number. If necessary, edit the author name to display your name, and then **Save** the document.

c. On the **Insert tab**, in the **Text group**, click **Quick Parts**, and then click **Building Blocks Organizer**. In the **Building Blocks Organizer** dialog box, in the upper left corner, click **Name** to sort the building blocks alphabetically by name. Locate your building block **Job Information**, click to select it, click **Delete**, and then click **Yes** to confirm the deletion. Using the same technique, scroll to locate and then **Delete** your building blocks **Literacy Heading** and **Literacy Quote**. **Close** the dialog box, and then **Save** the document.

7 In the upper right corner of the Word window, click **Close**. If a message displays regarding changes to building blocks, click **Save** to accept the changes. If directed by your instructor to do so, submit your paper printout, your electronic image of your document that looks like a printed document, or your original Word file.

END | You have completed Project 6C

Apply 6B skills from these Objectives:

4 Use Comments in a Document

5 Track Changes in a Document

6 View Side by Side, Compare, and Combine Documents

Skills Review Project 6D User Guide

In the following Skills Review, you will edit a user guide for Mountain View Public Library by creating and deleting comments, inserting text, applying formatting, and accepting changes made by others. Your completed documents will look similar to Figure 6.45.

PROJECT FILES

For Project 6D, you will need the following files:

w06D_User_Guide

w06D_Reviewed_Guide

You will save your files as:

Lastname_Firstname_6D_User_Guide

Lastname_Firstname_6D_Combined_Guide

PROJECT RESULTS

Mountain View Public Library

User Guide

Welcome to Mountain View Public Library! We have a vast collection of fiction and non-fiction items. Additionally, we offer special events and classes through the year on a variety of topics. If you're new to using a library, sign up for a 45-minute library tour. The tour is offered several times a week.

OBTAIN A LIBRARY CARD

If you haven't yet done so, you should fill out an application for a library card. Even young children can get their own cards. With your library card number, you can access your complete account online. You'll be able to conduct searches, put materials on hold for pickup within the next two weeks, see which materials you have checked out and when they are due, renew materials, and much more. You can even set your profile to receive email alerts three days prior to when an item is due.

Materials must be returned before the library closes on the day they are due. Items returned after the due dates are considered overdue and a fine starts accruing immediately. Fines stop accruing when the item is returned. Most items can be borrowed for three weeks, with the exception of new release DVDs and CDs, which can be borrowed for two weeks. Items can be renewed repeatedly as long as no one has placed a hold request on them. If there is a hold request, the renewal will be denied.

ORGANIZATION OF MATERIAL

When you begin browsing the library's bookshelves, you'll notice that fiction books are arranged in alphabetical order, while each non-fiction book includes a number on its spine. This number is based on the Dewey Decimal System, which was invented by Melivil Dewey. These numbers and letters are used to organize topics at the library.

When you look up an item on the computer or ask a librarian to locate it, notice the numbers and letters that identify that item. Then find the area in the library where that number is located. Each topic has a certain number combination that is the beginning of each identification number within the section. For example, the number for "Mammals" is 599, so all books about dogs start with 599. Books aren't the only materials in the library that are marked with numbers—cassettes, CDs, DVDs, and videos all have numbers, too.

SEARCHING FOR ITEMS

If you're not sure what you're looking for, you can just enjoy a leisurely stroll through the library, or you can check out the New Releases shelf. There is also a New Releases section on the library's website.

One of the easiest ways to find an item is to search on the computer, either at home or in the library. You can browse by subject or search by title, author, or subject. If you are not certain how something is spelled, use the Find It feature on the library's website. It has been programmed to help find items even if they are misspelled.

Lastname_Firstname_6D_Combined_Guide

If you are looking for a specific issue of a newspaper or magazine or a specific article, you'll need to know the title and date of the magazine. To view a magazine or newspaper that is more than 20 years old, you may have to use microfilm, which will require some help from a librarian.

RESEARCHING MATERIAL

Libraries are often used for school research projects. An encyclopedia would be a great place to start. Write down lists of people, places, and events related to your subject, plus any related subjects or book lists. Then consider the requirements of your project:

- How many pages do you need to write?
- How many and what type of resources are you supposed to use?
- Do you need to make a bibliography?

Bring your instructor's assignment with you to the library. Give yourself plenty of time to do your research, and remember to consult resources other than just books. There is a fee if you need to make copies or print documents.

COMPUTER ACCESS

The branches of Mountain View Public Library are wonderful places to bring your laptop and do work or conduct research. We offer free wireless access. The library is not responsible for any loss of information or damage to your laptop or PDA that might result from using the wireless network.

All branches of the Mountain View Public Library have computer stations where you can work online. There is a signup sheet near the computers. If there are people waiting, the librarian may issue a time limit.

COMMUNITY EVENTS

You might be surprised to learn that the library is more than just a place to read and check out books, CDs, DVDs, magazines, and newspapers. Many events are hosted by the library nearly every day, for all ages and interests. You can either click the Events Calendar on the library's website or pick up this month's flyer at your local branch.

The library branches also have several meeting rooms that can be used by the community when not already in use by the library. These are generally intended for civic and cultural activities presented by non-profit organizations. Please submit an application to the library if you want to reserve a room.

To find out more information about any library services, please contact us at (615) 555-0982.

Lastname_Firstname_6D_Combined_Guide

Word 2016, Windows 10, Microsoft Corporation

FIGURE 6.45

(Project 6D User Guide continues on the next page)

Skills Review Project 6D User Guide (continued)

1 **Start** Word. Navigate to your student files and open the file **w06D_User_Guide. Save** the document in your **Word Chapter 6** folder as **Lastname_Firstname_6D_User_Guide** and then insert the file name in the footer.

a. On the **Review tab**, in the **Tracking group**, click the **Dialog Box Launcher**. In the **Track Changes Options** dialog box, click **Change User Name**. If you are able to do so, in the **User name** box, delete any existing text, and then type your own first and last names. In the **Initials** box, delete any existing text, and then type your initials. Below the **Initials** box, select the **Always use these values regardless of sign in to Office** check box. Click **OK** two times.

b. On the **Review tab**, in the **Tracking group**, click the **Display for Review arrow**, and then click **All Markup**. In the paragraph beginning *Materials must be*, select the text **DVDs and CDs, which can be borrowed for two weeks**. On the **Review tab**, in the **Comments group**, click **New Comment**. In the comment, type **Check with Angie Harper to confirm that it is two weeks.**

c. Press Ctrl + Home. Click to position the insertion point in the text for the *Benedetta Herman* comment that begins *I thought*, and then in the **Comments group**, click **Delete**. Using the same technique, delete the *Caroline Marina* comment that begins *We offer*.

d. Locate your comment, and then replace *Angie Harper* with **Caroline Marina**

2 To enable tracking, in the **Tracking group**, click **Track Changes** so that it displays in blue. Select the first paragraph—the title—and then apply **Center**. Select the second paragraph—**User Guide**— change the **Font Size** to **18**, change the **Font Color** to **Blue, Accent 1**—in the fifth column, the first color—and then apply **Center**.

a. In the paragraph that begins *When you begin browsing*, in the third line, replace the text *Melville* with **Melvil** and then delete the related *Benedetta Herman* comment. On **Page 2**, in the paragraph that begins *The branches of*, in the second line, delete the sentence *We have many comfortable desks and chairs.*

b. Press Ctrl + End. Press Enter, and then type **To find out more information about any library services, please contact us at (615) 555-0982.** Select the text you just typed, change the **Font Size** to **12**, and apply **Italic**. Delete the *Benedetta Herman* comment that begins *Please add.*

c. Press Ctrl + Home. On the **Review tab**, in the **Changes group**, click the **Accept arrow**, and then click **Accept All Changes and Stop Tracking**.

d. **Save** your document. Click the **File tab**, and then **Close** the document but leave Word open.

3 On the **Review tab**, in the **Compare group**, click **Compare**, and then click **Combine**. In the **Combine Documents** dialog box, click the **Original document arrow**, and then click **Browse**. Navigate to your student files, select the file **w06D_Reviewed_Guide**, and then click **Open**.

a. Click the **Revised document arrow**, and then click **Browse**. Navigate to your **Word Chapter 6** folder, select the file **Lastname_Firstname_6D_User_Guide**, and then click **Open**.

b. In the **Combine Documents** dialog box, click **More**, and then under **Show changes in**, select the **New document** option, if necessary. Click **Less**, and then click **OK**. If necessary, on the right of your screen, close the Original Document Pane and the Revised Document Pane, and then on the left, close the Reviewing Pane.

c. With the insertion point positioned at the beginning of the **Combined Document**, click **Save**, and then save the document in your **Word Chapter 6** folder as **Lastname_Firstname_6D_Combined_Guide**

4 On the **Review tab**, in the **Changes group**, click the **Accept arrow**, and then click **Accept All Changes and Stop Tracking**.

a. On **Page 2**, locate the *Angie Harper* comment. Select the two sentences that begin **Be aware**, and end **wireless device. Delete** the two sentences.

b. On the **Review tab**, in the **Comments group**, click the **Delete arrow**, and then click **Delete All Comments in Document**.

(Project 6D User Guide continues on the next page)

Skills Review | Project 6D User Guide (continued)

5 Right-click in the footer area, and then click **Edit Footer**. Right-click the existing text, and then from the shortcut menu, click **Update Field**. **Close** the footer area.

a. On the **Design tab**, in the **Page Background group**, click **Page Color**, and then click **Fill Effects**. In the **Fill Effects** dialog box, click the **Texture tab**, scroll as necessary, and then in the next-to-last row, click the first texture—**Blue tissue paper**. Click **OK**.

b. Press Ctrl + Home. Click the **File tab**, and then click **Show All Properties**. In the **Tags** box, type **user guide** and in the **Subject** box, type your course name and section number. If necessary, edit the author name to display your name.

c. **Save** your document and **Close** Word.

6 If directed by your instructor to do so, submit your paper printout, your electronic image of your document that looks like a printed document, or your original Word file.

END | You have completed Project 6D

Mastering Word Project 6E Seminar Agenda

Apply 6A skills from these Objectives:

1 Create Custom Building Blocks
2 Create and Save a Theme Template
3 Create a Document by Using Building Blocks

In the following Mastering Word project, you will create and save building blocks and create a theme for an agenda for Mountain View Public Library's seminar on Public Libraries and the Internet. Your completed documents will look similar to Figure 6.46.

PROJECT FILES

For Project 6E, you will need the following files:

New blank Word document
w06E_Seminar_Agenda
w06E_Seminar_Blocks

You will save your files as:

Lastname_Firstname_6E_Seminar_Blocks
Lastname_Firstname_6E_Seminar_Agenda
Lastname_Firstname_6E_Seminar_Theme

PROJECT RESULTS

Public Libraries and the Internet

Spring Seminar for Employees

Mountain View Public Library's spring seminar is scheduled for April 12 at the Main library. All branches of the library will be closed until 5 p.m. so that employees can attend the sessions. As you know, there have been recent computer upgrades at the library. It is essential that we remain informed on the latest trends in technology so that we can best assist our patrons. The schedule below indicates the topics that will be covered. Lunch will be provided. Please contact Benedetta Herman if you can attend this exciting event.

AGENDA

Time	Topic	Location	Speaker
9:30 – 10 a.m.	Continental Breakfast	Community Room	
10 a.m. – Noon	Virtual Reference Desks	Computer Lab A	Irene Grant
Noon – 1 p.m.	Lunch	Community Room	
1 p.m. – 3 p.m.	Innovative Internet Librarians	Computer Lab A	Josh McCarthy

Lastname_Firstname_6E_Seminar_Agenda

FIGURE 6.46

(Project 6E Seminar Agenda continues on the next page)

CONTENT-BASED ASSESSMENTS (MASTERY AND TRANSFER OF LEARNING)

Mastering Word Project 6E Seminar Agenda (continued)

1 **Start** Word. From your student data files, open **w06E_Seminar_Blocks**. Be sure rulers and formatting marks display. Save the document in your **Word Chapter 6** folder as **Lastname_Firstname_6E_Seminar_Blocks** and then insert the file name in the footer.

2 To the text box, apply the shape style **Colored Fill - Orange, Accent 2**. In the text box, change the text **Font Size** to **28** and then apply **Bold** and **Center**. Select and then save the text box in the Text Box gallery with the name **Internet Seminar** and the description **Use in Internet Seminar documents**

3 Click in the second blank paragraph below the text box, display the **Quick Tables** gallery, and then insert a **Double Table**. Above the table, delete the text *The Greek Alphabet*. Replace the text *Letter name* with **Time** and then press Tab. Change *Uppercase* to **Topic** and then Change *Lowercase* to **Location**

4 Change *Letter name* to **Speaker** and then delete the remaining columns and any remaining text. Apply the table style **List Table 4 – Accent 2**. Save the table in the **Quick Tables** gallery with the name **Seminar Schedule** and the description **Use for seminar schedules**

5 **Save** your changes, and then **Close** the document but leave Word open. Start a new blank document.

6 Display the **Create New Theme Colors** dialog box. Change **Accent 1** to **Green, Accent 6, Darker 25%**, and then change **Accent 2** to **Green, Accent 6**. **Save** the Theme Colors as **Internet Colors** and then save the current theme in your **Word Chapter 6** folder as **Lastname_Firstname_6E_Seminar_Theme**

7 **Close** your theme file but leave Word open. Do not save changes.

8 **Open** the file **w06E_Seminar_Agenda**, save it in your **Word Chapter 6** folder as **Lastname_Firstname_6E_Seminar_Agenda** and then insert the file name in the footer. In the first blank paragraph, display the **Text Box** gallery, and then insert your **Internet Seminar** text box.

9 Apply your **Lastname_Firstname_6E_Seminar_Theme** to the document.

10 Select the text **Spring Seminar for Employees**, apply the **Heading 1** style, and then apply **Center**. Change the **Spacing After** to **6 pt**. Select the text **AGENDA**, apply the **Heading 2** style, apply **Center**, and then change the **Spacing After** to **12 pt**.

11 Position the insertion point in the blank paragraph following *AGENDA*, and then insert your **Seminar Schedule** quick table. In the table, enter the text shown in Table 1 below.

12 In the table, delete empty rows. Select the table, and then **AutoFit** the table to contents. Center the table on the page.

13 Display the file properties. In the **Tags** box, type **seminar, agenda** and in the **Subject** box, type your course name and section number. If necessary, edit the author name to display your name. **Save** the document.

14 Display the **Building Blocks Organizer** dialog box, and then **Delete** your building blocks **Internet Seminar** and **Seminar Schedule**. Close the **Building Blocks Organizer** dialog box. Display the **Theme Colors** list, and then **Delete** the **Internet Colors**.

15 **Close** Word. When a message displays regarding changes to building blocks, click **Save** to accept the changes. If directed by your instructor to do so, submit your paper printout, your electronic image of your document that looks like a printed document, or your original Word file.

16 If you are submitting this project in the MyITLab Grader system, submit your **Lastname_Firstname_Seminar_Agenda** file.

Time	Topic	Location	Speaker
9:30 a.m. – 10 a.m.	Continental Breakfast	Community Room	
10 a.m. – Noon	Virtual Reference Desks	Computer Lab A	Irene Grant
Noon – 1 p.m.	Lunch	Community Room	
1 p.m. – 3 p.m.	Innovative Internet Librarians	Computer Lab A	Josh McCarthy

TABLE 1

(Return to Step 12)

END | You have completed Project 6E

CONTENT-BASED ASSESSMENTS (MASTERY AND TRANSFER OF LEARNING)

Apply 6B skills from these Objectives:

4 Use Comments in a Document
5 Track Changes in a Document
6 View Side by Side, Compare, and Combine Documents

Mastering Word Project 6F Library Classes

In the following Mastering Word project, you will edit a user guide for Mountain View Public Library by creating and deleting comments, inserting text, applying formatting, and accepting changes made by others. Your completed documents will look similar to Figure 6.47.

PROJECT FILES

For Project 6F, you will need the following files:

w06F_Library_Classes
w06F_Classes_Reviewed

You will save your files as:

Lastname_Firstname_6F_Library_Classes
Lastname_Firstname_6F_Classes_Combined

PROJECT RESULTS

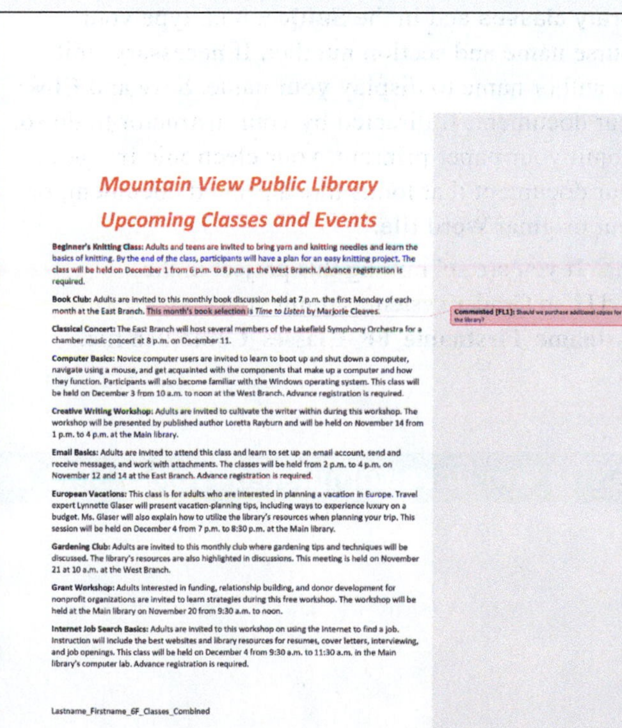

FIGURE 6.47

Word 2016, Windows 10, Microsoft Corporation

(Project 6F Library Classes continues on the next page)

Mastering Word Project 6F Library Classes (continued)

1 **Start** Word, and then open the file **w06F_Library_Classes**. **Save** the file in your **Word Chapter 6** folder as **Lastname_Firstname_6F_Library_Classes** and then insert the file name in the footer.

2 On the **Review tab**, in the **Tracking group**, display the **Track Changes Options** dialog box, and then click **Change User Name**. Under **Personalize your copy of Microsoft Office**, type your name in the **User name** box, and then type your initials in the **Initials** box, if necessary. Immediately below Initials, be sure the check box is selected. In the **Tracking group**, change **Display for Review** to **All Markup**.

3 In the *Book Club* paragraph, select the text **This month's book selection**. Insert a new comment with the text **Should we purchase additional copies for the library?** Delete the *Abigail Gardner* and the *Caroline Marina* comments regarding spelling.

4 Turn on **Track Changes**. Select the first two paragraphs, and then apply the **Book Title** style. Change the **Font Size** to **28**, change the **Font Color** to **Orange, Accent 2, Darker 25%**, and then apply **Center**.

5 On **Page 2**, locate the paragraph that begins *Microsoft Word*. **Delete** the text *101*, and then press Ctrl + End. Press Enter, and then type **To register for a class or to obtain more information, contact Abigail Gardner at (615) 555-0982.** Select the sentence you just typed, and then apply **Italic** and **Center**.

6 Press Ctrl + Home, and then **Accept All Changes and Stop Tracking**. **Save** your document, click the **File tab**, and then **Close** the document but leave Word open.

7 Display the **Combine Documents** dialog box. For the **Original document**, from your student data files, select the file **w06F_Classes_Reviewed**. For the **Revised document**, in your **Word Chapter 6** folder, select the file **Lastname_Firstname_6F_Library_Classes**. Verify that the **New document** option is selected and then click **OK**.

8 **Save** the combined document in your **Word Chapter 6** folder as **Lastname_Firstname_6F_Classes_Combined** and if necessary, close all open panes. **Accept All Changes and Stop Tracking**.

9 Insert the file name in the footer, and then **Close** the footer area.

10 Display the properties. In the **Tags** box, type **library classes** and in the **Subject** box, type your course name and section number. If necessary, edit the author name to display your name. **Save** and **Close** your document. If directed by your instructor to do so, submit your paper printout, your electronic image of your document that looks like a printed document, or your original Word file.

11 If you are submitting this project in the MyITLab Grader system, submit your **Lastname_Firstname_6F_Classes_Combined** file.

END | You have completed Project 6F

CONTENT-BASED ASSESSMENTS (MASTERY AND TRANSFER OF LEARNING)

Apply 6A and 6B skills from these Objectives:

1. Create Custom Building Blocks
2. Create and Save a Theme Template
3. Create a Document by Using Building Blocks
4. Use Comments in a Document
5. Track Changes in a Document
6. View Side by Side, Compare, and Combine Documents

Mastering Word Project 6G Website Flyer

In the following Mastering Word project, you will create a document to announce the launch of Mountain View Public Library's new website by creating and inserting building blocks, creating a custom theme, inserting text, applying formatting, and accepting changes made by others. Your completed documents will look similar to Figure 6.48.

PROJECT FILES

For Project 6G, you will need the following files:

New blank Word document
w06G_Website_Flyer

You will save your files as:

Lastname_Firstname_6G_Website_Blocks
Lastname_Firstname_6G_Website_Flyer
Lastname_Firstname_6G_Website_Theme

PROJECT RESULTS

Mountain View Public Library
Information Technology Department

LIBRARY TO LAUNCH NEW WEBSITE

After much strategizing and collaboration, Mountain View Public Library's new website will be launched next Monday. After evaluating feedback from library employees and patrons, we designed a website that is easy to use, attractive, and full of information.

The website is now much more accessible to all users, including those with visual and hearing impairments. There is also a special section just for children, with learning games and resources tailored to young people.

The Events Calendar can be searched by specific dates, subjects, or intended age groups. Participants can even register for classes online. There is a section where patrons can bookmark events and classes that are of interest and request that a reminder be sent prior to the date.

Individual library patron pages have been vastly improved. Library members can access account information, including materials that are checked out, on hold, or overdue. Items can also be renewed online. A simplified search engine allows patrons to easily locate materials. There's also a section for creating a reading list and recording when books have been read.

Meetings to demonstrate the new website features will be held this week as indicated below. The IT Department urges you to attend one of these meetings so you can be trained in navigating the website and answer questions from patrons as they use the redesigned site.

Location	Day	Time
East Branch	Tuesday	2 p.m.
Main Library	Monday	9 a.m.
West Branch	Friday	3 p.m.

The Internet is becoming the town square for the global village of tomorrow. Bill Gates

Lastname_Firstname_6G_Website_Flyer

Word 2016, Windows 10, Microsoft Corporation

FIGURE 6.48

(Project 6G Website Flyer continues on the next page)

Mastering Word Project 6G Website Flyer (continued)

1 **Start** Word, and then display a new document. Save the document in your **Word Chapter 6** folder as **Lastname_Firstname_6G_Website_Blocks** and be sure rulers and formatting marks display.

2 Display the **Quick Tables** gallery, and insert a **Tabular List**. In the first cell, replace the text **ITEM** with **Location** and in the second cell, replace the text **NEEDED** with **Day**

3 Insert a third column in the table to the right of the *Day* column. In the first cell of the third column, type **Time** and then delete all remaining text in the table. Apply the **List Table 3 – Accent 2** table style and then **Save** the table in the **Quick Tables** gallery with the name **Training Schedule** and the **Description Use to display schedules for training**

4 Press Ctrl + End. Press Enter two times, and then type **The Internet is becoming the town square for the global village of tomorrow. Bill Gates** and then save the quote in the **AutoText** gallery with the name **Internet Quote** and the **Description Use in website documents** Change the **Save in** location to **Building Blocks**.

5 **Save** your changes. Click the **File tab**, and then **Close** the document but leave Word open.

6 Display a new blank document. Display the **Create New Theme Colors** dialog box, change **Accent 2** to **Blue, Accent 5, Darker 25%**—in the ninth column, the fifth color—and then save the theme colors with the name **Website Colors**

7 Display the **Create New Theme Fonts** dialog box, change the **Body font** to **Verdana**, and then save the theme fonts with the name **Website Fonts**

8 Save the current theme in your **Word Chapter 6** folder as **Lastname_Firstname_6G_Website_Theme**

9 **Delete** the **Website Colors** and **Website Fonts**. **Close** the document without saving changes, but leave Word open.

10 From your student data files, open the file **w06G_Website_Flyer**. Save the file in your **Word Chapter 6** folder as **Lastname_Firstname_6G_Website_Flyer** and then insert a footer with the file name. Apply your custom theme—**Lastname_Firstname_6G_Website_Theme**.

11 Select the first two paragraphs of the document. Change the **Font Size** to **22**, change the **Font Color** to **Blue, Accent 5**, and then apply **Bold** and **Center**.

12 Press Ctrl + End, and then insert the **Training Schedule** Quick Table. Beginning in the first cell of the second row, type the following text in the table:

East Branch	**Tuesday**	**2 p.m.**
Main Library	**Monday**	**9 a.m.**
West Branch	**Friday**	**3 p.m.**

13 Delete all empty rows in the table. Select the table, and then **AutoFit Contents**. **Center** the table horizontally in the document.

14 Press Ctrl + End, and then press Enter. Insert the **Internet Quote** AutoText. Select the inserted text, change the **Font Size** to **9**, change the **Font Color** to **Blue, Accent 5**—in the ninth column, the first color; and then apply **Bold** and **Center**. If necessary, at the end of the document, delete the blank paragraph.

15 Press Ctrl + Home, and then **Accept All Changes**. Change the **Page Color** to the **Blue tissue paper** fill effect—on the **Texture tab**, in the next to last row, the first texture.

16 Display the document properties. In the **Tags** box, type **website flyer** and then in the **Subject** box, type your course name and section number. If necessary, edit the author name to display your name. **Save** your document. **Delete** the **Training Schedule** and **Internet Quote** building blocks. **Close** Word and if prompted, save changes.

17 If directed by your instructor to do so, submit your paper printout, your electronic image of your document that looks like a printed document, or your original Word file.

18 If you are submitting this project in the MyITLab Grader system, submit your **Lastname_Firstname_6G_Website_Flyer** file.

END | You have completed Project 6G

CONTENT-BASED ASSESSMENTS (CRITICAL THINKING)

Apply a combination of the 6A and 6B skills.

GO! Fix It	Project 6H Internship Memo	MyITLab
GO! Make It	Project 6I Request Form	MyITLab
GO! Solve It	Project 6J Employee Newsletter	MyITLab
GO! Solve It	Project 6K Library Rules	

PROJECT FILES

For Project 6K, you will need the following files:

New blank Word document
w06K_Library_Rules

You will save your files as:

Lastname_Firstname_6K_Rules_Blocks
Lastname_Firstname_6K_Library_Rules

Display a new blank document and save it in your **Word Chapter 6** folder as **Lastname_Firstname_6K_Rules_Blocks** Insert a text box that includes the text **Mountain View Public Library** on the first line and **Library Rules** on the second line. Format the text box and the text, and then save the text box as a building block. Save and close the file but leave Word open.

From your student files, open the document **w06K_Library_Rules**. Accept all changes. Save the file to your **Word Chapter 6** folder as **Lastname_Firstname_6K_Library_Rules** Modify the theme colors and format the text to improve readability. Insert the building block you created. Adjust the building block and text to create an attractive, one-page document. Insert the file name in the footer and add appropriate document properties. Submit the document as directed.

Performance Level

Performance Criteria	Exemplary: You consistently applied the relevant skills	Proficient: You sometimes, but not always, applied the relevant skills	Developing: You rarely or never applied the relevant skills
Create a text box building block	A text box containing the correct information is saved as a building block.	A text box is saved as a building block but contains incorrect information.	No text box is saved as a building block.
Accept changes	All changes are accepted.	Some changes are accepted but others are not.	No changes are accepted.
Modify theme colors and format text	The theme colors are modified and the text is formatted attractively.	The theme colors are not modified or the text is not formatted attractively.	The theme colors are not modified and the text is not formatted.
Insert building blocks	The building block is inserted and positioned appropriately.	The building block is not positioned inappropriately.	The building block is not inserted.

END | You have completed Project 6K

OUTCOMES-BASED ASSESSMENTS (CRITICAL THINKING)

RUBRIC

The following outcomes-based assessments are open-ended assessments. That is, there is no specific correct result; your result will depend on your approach to the information provided. Make *Professional Quality* your goal. Use the following scoring rubric to guide you in *how* to approach the problem and then to evaluate *how well* your approach solves the problem.

The *criteria*—Software Mastery, Content, Format and Layout, and Process—represent the knowledge and skills you have gained that you can apply to solving the problem. The *levels of performance*—Professional Quality, Approaching Professional Quality, or Needs Quality Improvements—help you and your instructor evaluate your result.

	Your completed project is of Professional Quality if you:	Your completed project is Approaching Professional Quality if you:	Your completed project Needs Quality Improvements if you:
1-Software Mastery	Choose and apply the most appropriate skills, tools, and features and identify efficient methods to solve the problem.	Choose and apply some appropriate skills, tools, and features, but not in the most efficient manner.	Choose inappropriate skills, tools, or features, or are inefficient in solving the problem.
2-Content	Construct a solution that is clear and well organized, contains content that is accurate, appropriate to the audience and purpose, and is complete. Provide a solution that contains no errors of spelling, grammar, or style.	Construct a solution in which some components are unclear, poorly organized, inconsistent, or incomplete. Misjudge the needs of the audience. Have some errors in spelling, grammar, or style, but the errors do not detract from comprehension.	Construct a solution that is unclear, incomplete, or poorly organized, contains some inaccurate or inappropriate content, and contains many errors of spelling, grammar, or style. Do not solve the problem.
3-Format and Layout	Format and arrange all elements to communicate information and ideas, clarify function, illustrate relationships, and indicate relative importance.	Apply appropriate format and layout features to some elements, but not others. Overuse features, causing minor distraction.	Apply format and layout that does not communicate information or ideas clearly. Do not use format and layout features to clarify function, illustrate relationships, or indicate relative importance. Use available features excessively, causing distraction.
4-Process	Use an organized approach that integrates planning, development, self-assessment, revision, and reflection.	Demonstrate an organized approach in some areas, but not others; or, use an insufficient process of organization throughout.	Do not use an organized approach to solve the problem.

OUTCOMES-BASED ASSESSMENTS (CRITICAL THINKING)

6 WORD

GO! Think Project 6L Fundraising Flyer

Build from Scratch

PROJECT FILES

For Project 6L, you will need the following file:

New blank Word document

You will save your files as:

Lastname_Firstname_6L_Fundraising_Flyer

The Mountain View Public Library is conducting a fundraising campaign with a goal of $200,000 needed to upgrade the computer lab at the Main library and fund library programs. Donations can be sent to 1000 Maple Avenue, Claremont, TN 38325. Benedetta Herman, Director of Library Services, is chairing the fundraising committee and can be reached at (615) 555-0982. Donor levels include:

TYPE OF RECOGNITION	AMOUNT OF GIFT
Bronze Book Club	$ 100 or more
Silver Book Club	$ 500 or more
Gold Book Club	$ 1,000 or more

Create a document that includes a text box containing the name and address of the library and an appropriate quotation. Save both objects as building blocks. Create a flyer explaining the campaign and how donors will be acknowledged. Customize the theme, add appropriate text, and insert your building blocks. Include a Quick Table to display the recognition types. Format the flyer in a professional manner. Save the file as **Lastname_Firstname_6L_Fundraising_Flyer** and insert the file name in the footer and appropriate properties. Submit the document as directed.

END | You have completed Project 6L

Build from Scratch

GO! Think Project 6M Reading Certificate MyITLab

Build from Scratch

You and GO! Project 6N Personal Calendar MyITLab

Creating Web Content and Using Advanced Editing Tools

OUTCOMES

Create and manage web content in Microsoft Word.

PROJECT 7B

OUTCOMES

Use advanced editing tools and manage document versions and file formats.

OBJECTIVES

1. Format a Word Document to Create a Webpage
2. Insert and Modify Hyperlinks in a Word Document
3. Create a Webpage and Blog Post

OBJECTIVES

4. Manage Document Versions
5. Collect and Paste Images and Text
6. Locate Supporting Information and Insert Equations
7. Use Advanced Find and Replace Options
8. Save in Other File Formats

Arman Zhenikeyev/Fotolia

In This Chapter

GO! To Work with Word

In this chapter, you will use text, graphic, and document formatting features in Word to create documents saved as attractive, professional-looking webpages that include hyperlinks. You will also create blog posts, which can contain text, images, and links to related blogs or webpages. You will modify Word option settings to create document versions that are automatically saved. You will use Word's research features and the Clipboard to collect and organize information in documents. You will also insert equations in documents and use Find and Replace to edit text. Finally, you will save documents in other useful file formats.

The projects in this chapter relate to **Oregon Wireless Specialties**, a supplier of accessories and software for all major brands of cell phones, smartphones, tablet computers, music players, and laptop computers. The company sells distinctive products in its stores, which are located throughout Oregon and the northwestern United States. Items are also available on its website. For online orders, the company offers its retail and wholesale customers low shipping costs and full credit on returns. Oregon Wireless Specialties takes pride in offering unique categories of accessories such as waterproof and ruggedized gear.

Webpage and Blog

PROJECT ACTIVITIES

In Activities 7.01 through 7.11, you will assist Nanci Scholtz, Vice President of Marketing for Oregon Wireless Specialties, in creating a new home page for the online store and a new blog post for the company's customer service blog. Your completed documents will look similar to Figure 7.1.

PROJECT FILES

If your instructor wants you to submit Project 7A in the MyITLab grader system, log in to MyITLab, locate Grader Project 7A, and then download the files for this project.

For Project 7A, you will need the following files:	You will save your file as:
w07A_Webpage_Blog w07A_Features_Guide	Lastname_Firstname_7A_Webpage_Blog

PROJECT RESULTS

GO! Walk Thru Project 7A

Oregon Wireless Specialties

625 Market Street, Portland, OR 97206
(503) 555-7702

Oregon Wireless Specialties provides accessories for all major brands of cell phones, tablets, music players, notebooks, and laptop computers. We sell thousands of unique products in our retail store and through this website, and we take pride in offering unique categories of accessories, such as waterproof and ruggedized gear. Take a look at our Top 10 sellers and new arrivals, or search our site to find the accessories you need.

Our selection includes the latest wireless phone accessories—faceplates, batteries, holsters, chargers, cases, ringtones, and hands-free enablers—for every budget. If you are still looking for the right wireless phone for you, read our useful Guide to Popular Cell Phone Features. A brief list of these features is listed here.

- Bluetooth-enabled
- Camera
- Color Display
- Downloadable Ringtones
- MP3 Player
- Photo Caller ID
- Removable Memory Card
- Speakerphone
- Video Recorder
- Voice-activated Dialing

Lastname_Firstname_7A_Webpage_Blog

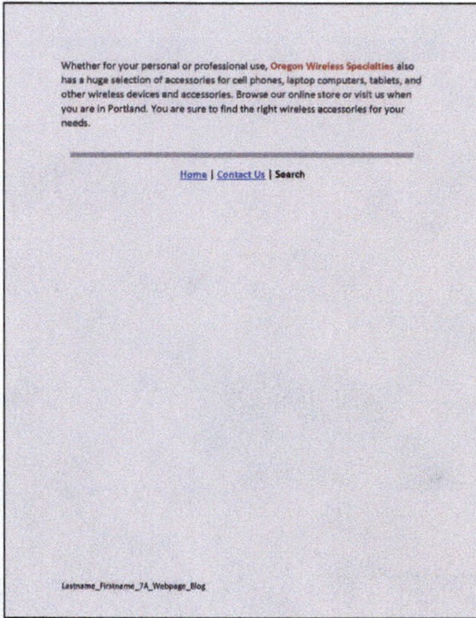

Whether for your personal or professional use, Oregon Wireless Specialties also has a huge selection of accessories for cell phones, laptop computers, tablets, and other wireless devices and accessories. Browse our online store or visit us when you are in Portland. You are sure to find the right wireless accessories for your needs.

Home | Contact Us | Search

Lastname_Firstname_7A_Webpage_Blog

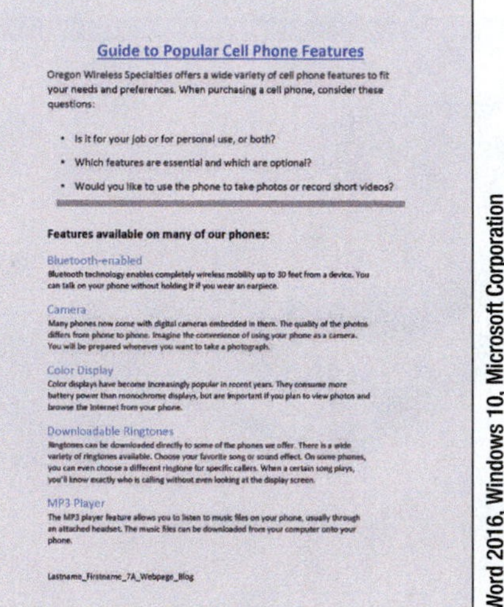

Guide to Popular Cell Phone Features

Oregon Wireless Specialties offers a wide variety of cell phone features to fit your needs and preferences. When purchasing a cell phone, consider these questions:

- Is it for your job or for personal use, or both?
- Which features are essential and which are optional?
- Would you like to use the phone to take photos or record short videos?

Features available on many of our phones:

Bluetooth-enabled
Bluetooth technology enables completely wireless mobility up to 30 feet from a device. You can talk on your phone without holding it if you wear an earpiece.

Camera
Many phones now come with digital cameras embedded in them. The quality of the photos differs from phone to phone. Imagine the convenience of using your phone as a camera. You will be prepared whenever you want to take a photograph.

Color Display
Color displays have become increasingly popular in recent years. They consume more battery power than monochrome displays, but are important if you plan to view photos and browse the Internet from your phone.

Downloadable Ringtones
Ringtones can be downloaded directly to some of the phones we offer. There is a wide variety of ringtones available. Choose your favorite song or sound effect. On some phones, you can even choose a different ringtone for specific callers. When a certain song plays, you'll know exactly who is calling without even looking at the display screen.

MP3 Player
The MP3 player feature allows you to listen to music files on your phone, usually through an attached headset. The music files can be downloaded from your computer onto your phone.

Lastname_Firstname_7A_Webpage_Blog

Photo Caller ID
All our phones come equipped with caller ID, but some have a photo caller ID feature. These enable you to view the photo of the person calling you. Photos must be pre-assigned to contacts for this feature to work.

Removable Memory Card
Some phones come with a slot for a removable memory card. This is useful if you intend to use your phone to store photos, keep extensive contact information, or browse the Internet.

Speakerphone
Speakerphones enable you to talk on the phone without speaking directly into the microphone and holding the phone in your hand. They are particularly helpful when more than one person needs to participate in a conversation.

Video Recorder
With a video recorder, you can record short videos onto your cell phone. The videos can then be viewed on your phone or sent to others by e-mail.

Voice-activated Dialing
This feature allows you to call a contact by speaking the name. For each contact, you must record yourself saying the person's name. Voice-activated dialing is helpful when you want to keep your hands free while driving or completing a task.

Lastname_Firstname_7A_Webpage_Blog

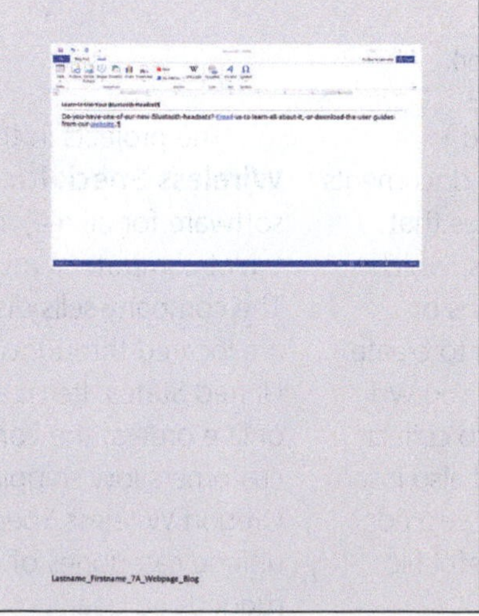

Lastname_Firstname_7A_Webpage_Blog

FIGURE 7.1 Project 7A Webpage and Blog

7 WORD

NOTE	If You Are Using a Touchscreen
	Tap an item to click it.
	Press and hold for a few seconds to right-click; release when the information or commands display.
	Touch the screen with two or more fingers and then pinch together to zoom out or stretch your fingers apart to zoom in.
	Slide your finger on the screen to scroll—slide left to scroll right and slide right to scroll left.
	Slide to rearrange—similar to dragging with a mouse.
	Swipe to select—slide an item a short distance with a quick movement—to select an item and bring up commands, if any.

Objective 1 Format a Word Document to Create a Webpage

GO! Learn How Video W7-1

You can create a ***webpage*** from a Word document. A webpage is a file coded in ***HyperText Markup Language***—referred to as ***HTML***—that can be viewed on the Internet by using a ***web browser***. A web browser—also referred to as simply a ***browser***—is software that interprets HTML files, formats them into webpages, and then displays them. HTML is a markup language that communicates color and graphics in a format that all computers can understand.

ALERT!

To submit as an autograded project, log into MyITLab, download the files for this project, and begin with those files instead of w07A_Webpage_Blog and w07A_Features_Guide.

Activity 7.01 | Formatting a Document for a Webpage and Applying a Background Color

1.3.6

In this Activity, you will begin the formatting of a Word document for Web viewing so that it can be saved as a webpage and added to the company's website. You will change the background color of the document so that when it is viewed as a webpage, an attractive background color displays.

1. Start Word, on the left click **Open Other Documents**, click **Browse**, and then in the **Open** dialog box, navigate to the student data files that accompany this chapter. Locate and open the file **w07A_Webpage_Blog**. If necessary, display formatting marks and rulers.

2. Click the **File tab**, on the left click **Save As**, click **Browse**, and then in the **Save As** dialog box, navigate to the location where you are saving your files for this chapter. Create a new folder named **Word Chapter 7** and open the folder. In the **File name** box, using your own name, type **Lastname_Firstname_7A_Webpage_Blog** and click **Save** or press Enter. Compare your screen with Figure 7.2.

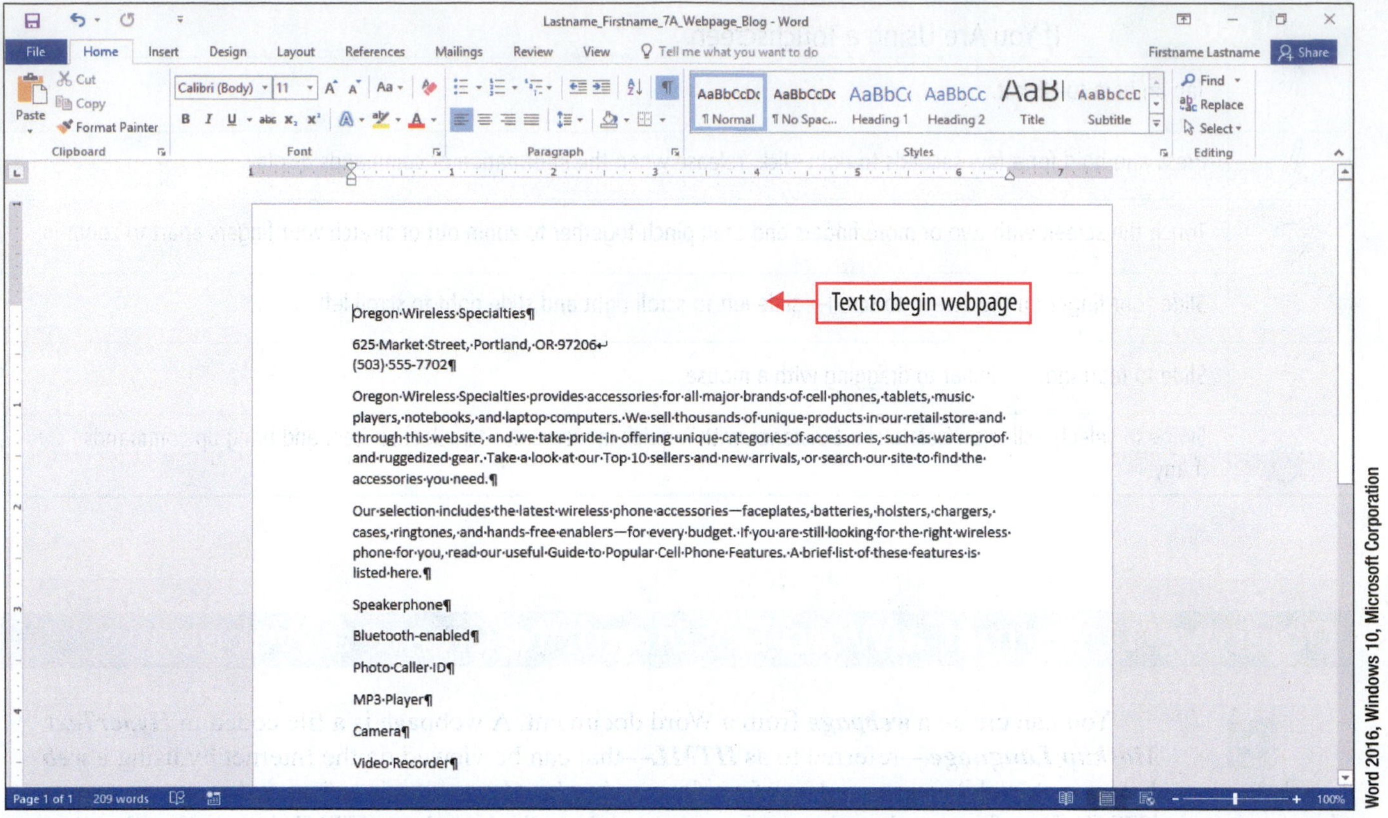

FIGURE 7.2

3 Click the **Insert tab**, and then in the **Header & Footer group**, click **Footer**. At the bottom of the list, click **Edit Footer**. On the ribbon, in the **Insert group**, click **Document Info**, and then click **File Name**. Compare your screen with Figure 7.3.

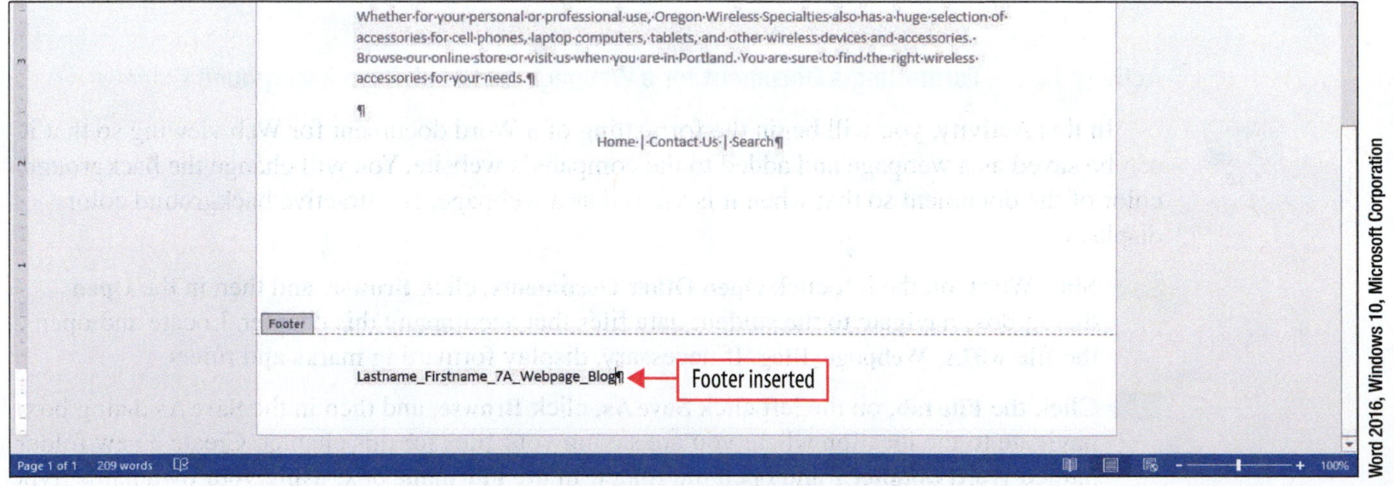

FIGURE 7.3

4 On the ribbon, click **Close Header and Footer**.

5 Select the first paragraph of the document—the company name *Oregon Wireless Specialties*. On the mini toolbar, apply **Bold** [B], and then change the **Font Size** to **48**.

6 Select the two lines that contain the company address and telephone number. On the mini toolbar, apply **Bold** [B], and then change the **Font Size** to **24**.

7 Select the first and second paragraphs that you just formatted, and then press Ctrl + E to center the paragraphs. Click anywhere to deselect the text, and then compare your screen with Figure 7.4.

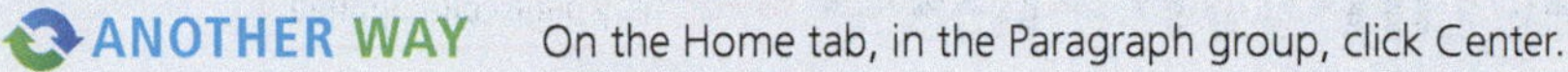

On the Home tab, in the Paragraph group, click Center.

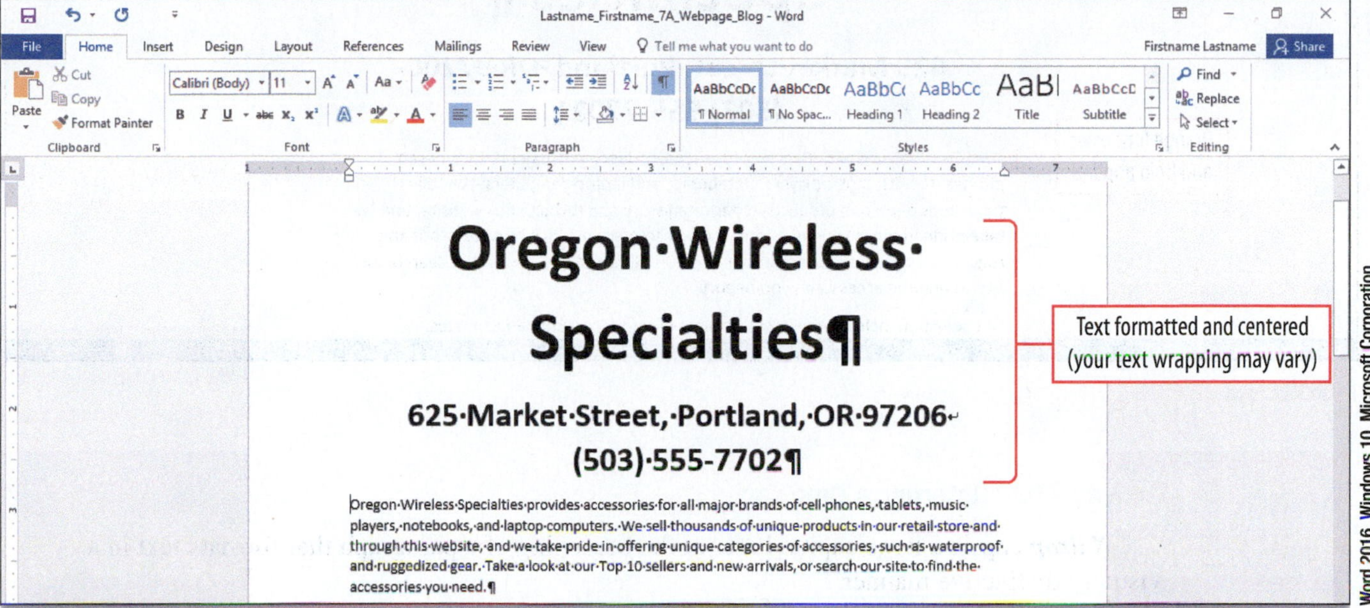

FIGURE 7.4

8 Beginning with the paragraph that begins **Oregon Wireless Specialties provides**, select all the remaining text in the document—including the centered paragraph at the end of the document—and then change the **Font Size** to **14**.

9 At the beginning of the third paragraph, select the text **Oregon Wireless Specialties**. Apply **Bold** B, click the **Font Color arrow** A, and then under **Theme Colors**, in the sixth column, click the last color—**Orange, Accent 2, Darker 50%**.

10 Press Ctrl + End. In the paragraph that begins *Whether*, select the text **Oregon Wireless Specialties**. Apply **Bold** B, and then click **Font Color** A to apply the same font color.

Recall that the Font Color button retains its most recently used setting.

11 Select the last paragraph—*Home* | *Contact Us* | *Search*—and apply **Bold** B. Click anywhere to deselect the text.

12 Press Ctrl + Home. Click the **Design tab**. In the **Page Background group**, click **Page Color**, and then in the third column, click the first color—**Gray – 25%, Background 2**. **Save** your document, and then compare your screen with Figure 7.5.

FIGURE 7.5

Activity 7.02 | Inserting a Drop Cap

A ***drop cap*** is a large capital letter at the beginning of a paragraph that formats text in a visually distinctive manner.

1. At the beginning of the third paragraph in the document, select the orange letter **O**. Click the **Insert tab**. In the **Text group**, click **Drop Cap** and then click **Drop Cap Options**. Compare your screen with Figure 7.6.

   Here you can select either the ***Dropped*** position, which enlarges the letter and drops it into the text, or the ***In margin*** position, which drops the enlarged letter into the left margin. The Drop Cap dialog box provides a visual example of each position.

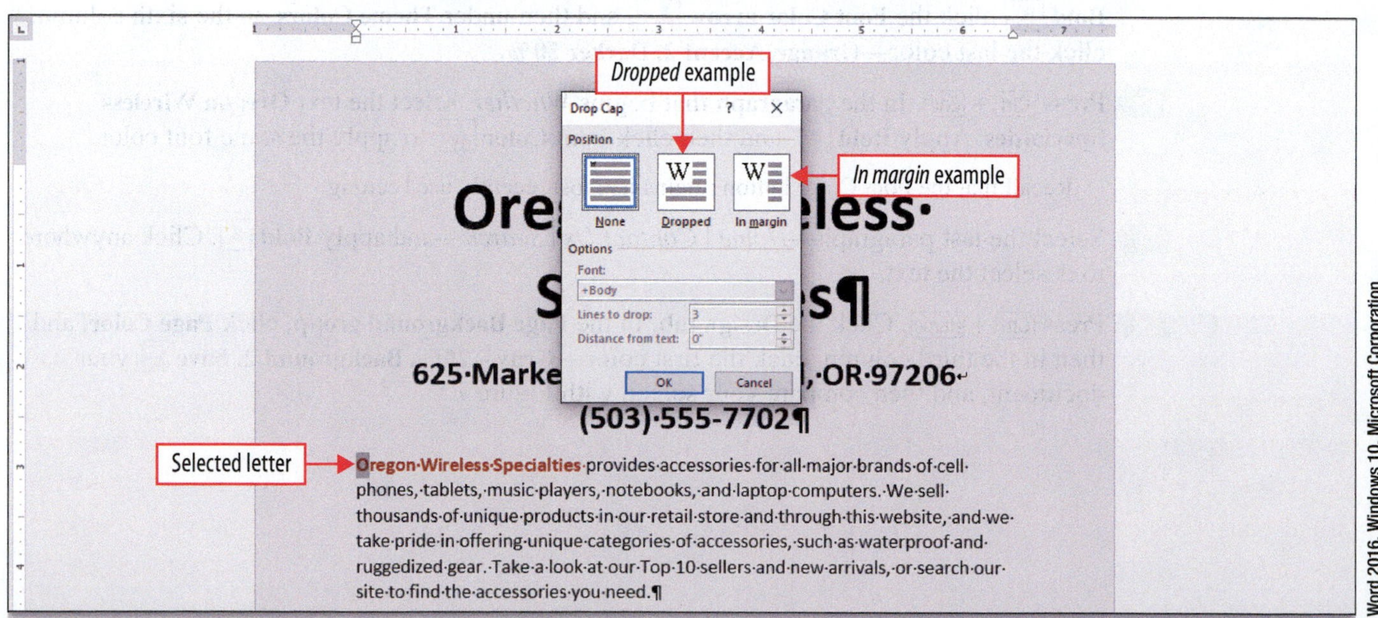

FIGURE 7.6

2 In the **Drop Cap** dialog box, under **Position**, click **Dropped**. Under **Options**, click the **Lines to drop down spin arrow** one time to change the number of lines by which to drop to **2** lines. Compare your screen with Figure 7.7.

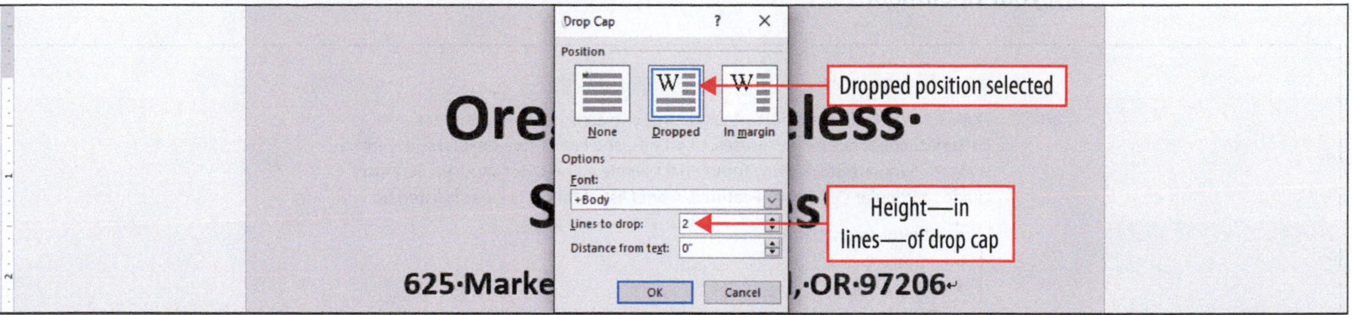

FIGURE 7.7

Word 2016, Windows 10, Microsoft Corporation

3 In the **Drop Cap** dialog box, click **OK**.

Sizing handles display around the border of the dropped letter indicating that it is selected.

4 Click anywhere in the document to deselect the drop cap, and then **Save** your document.

Activity 7.03 | Sorting Paragraphs

Sorting is the action of ordering data, usually in alphabetical or numeric order. ***Ascending*** refers to sorting alphabetically from A to Z or ordering numerically from the smallest to the largest. ***Descending*** refers to sorting alphabetically from Z to A or ordering numerically from the largest to the smallest.

1 Scroll to display the ten paragraphs that comprise the cell phone features—beginning with *Speakerphone* and ending with *Downloadable Ringtones*. Click to position the insertion point to the left of *Speakerphone*, and then select the ten paragraphs.

BY TOUCH Tap Speakerphone, and then drag the selection handle to the end of the last paragraph, *Downloadable Ringtones*.

2 On the **Home tab**, in the **Paragraph group**, click **Sort** to display the **Sort Text** dialog box. Compare your screen with Figure 7.8.

Here you can select what you want to sort by, which in this instance is *Paragraphs*; the type of data to sort, which in this instance is *Text*; and the type of sort—ascending or descending.

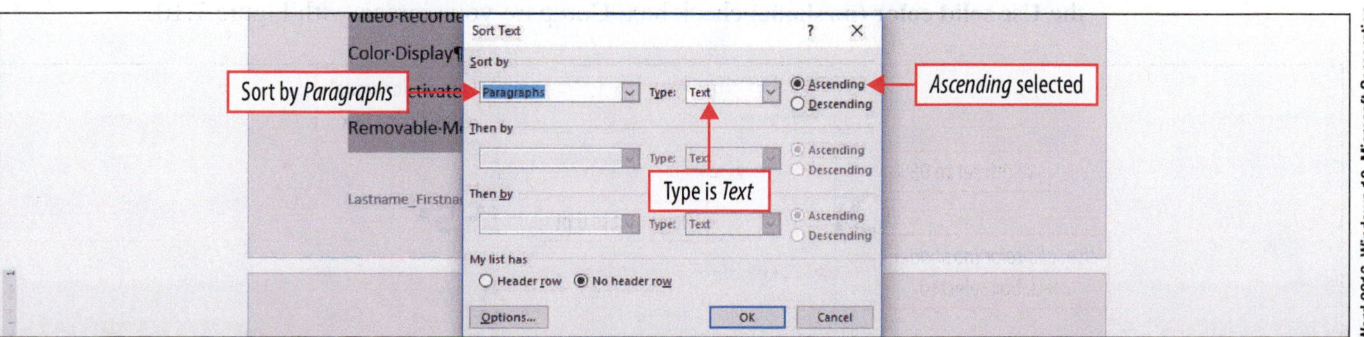

FIGURE 7.8

Word 2016, Windows 10, Microsoft Corporation

3 Click **OK** to accept the default settings. Notice that the paragraphs are arranged alphabetically.

4 With the paragraphs still selected, in the **Paragraph group**, click the **Bullets** button, and then click anywhere to deselect the bulleted text. Compare your screen with Figure 7.9. **Save** your document.

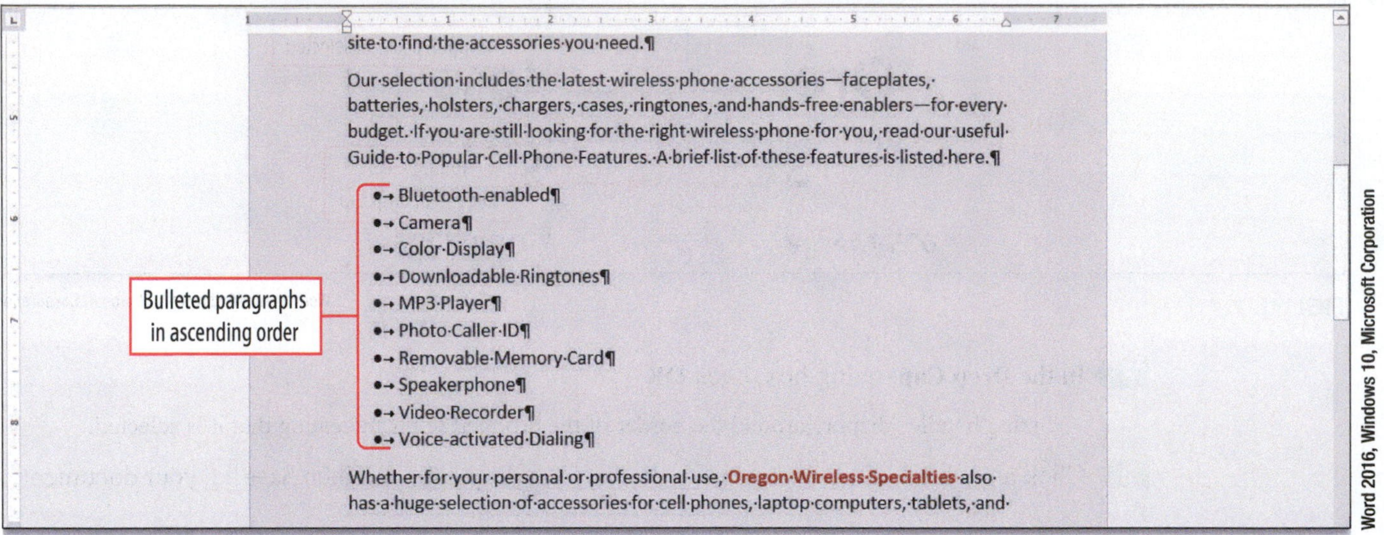

FIGURE 7.9

Activity 7.04 | Inserting a Horizontal Line

5.1.1

A horizontal line can add visual interest to and differentiate sections of a webpage.

1 Press Ctrl + Home. In the second paragraph, click to position the insertion point to the right of the telephone number.

2 Press Enter one time. On the **Home tab**, in the **Paragraph group**, click the **Borders button arrow**, and then click **Horizontal Line**. Notice a horizontal line is inserted in the document.

ANOTHER WAY On the Insert tab, in the Illustrations group, click Shapes, and then under Lines, click the first shape—Line.

3 Click the horizontal line to select it—sizing handles display on the ends and in the middle. Point to the selected line, right-click, and then on the shortcut menu, click **Picture** to display the **Format Horizontal Line** dialog box.

4 In the **Format Horizontal Line** dialog box, click the **Width down spin arrow** as necessary to set **95%** and then click the **Height up spin arrow** as necessary to set **6 pt**. Under **Color**, select the **Use solid color (no shade)** check box. Compare your screen with Figure 7.10.

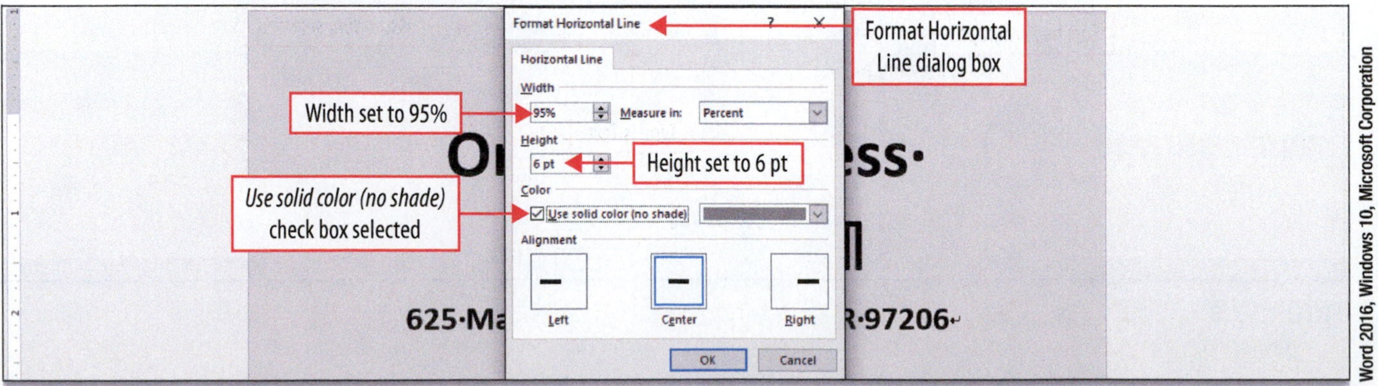

FIGURE 7.10

5 Click **OK**. Point to the line, right-click, and then click **Copy**.

6 In the blank paragraph immediately above the last paragraph of the document that begins *Home*, click to position the insertion point. Right-click, and then under **Paste Options**, click the first option—**Keep Source Formatting**—to insert a copy of the horizontal line with the same formatting. **Save** your document.

Objective 2 Insert and Modify Hyperlinks in a Word Document

GO! Learn How Video W7-2

Hyperlinks are text, buttons, pictures, or other objects in a document that, when clicked, access other sections of the active document or another file. A web browser—for example, Google Chrome or Microsoft Edge developed by Microsoft for Windows 10—enables you to transfer files, play sound or video files that are embedded in webpages, and follow hyperlinks to other webpages and files.

Activity 7.05 | Inserting a Hyperlink

1.2.1

By inserting hyperlinks, individuals who view your webpage can move to other webpages inside your ***website*** or to pages in another website. A website is a group of related webpages published to a specific location on the Internet. The most common type of hyperlink is a ***text link***—a link applied to a selected word or phrase. Text links usually display as blue underlined text.

1 Press Ctrl + End, and notice that the last paragraph consists of a series of words and phrases.

Websites commonly have a ***navigation bar***—a series of text links across the top or bottom of a webpage that, when clicked, will link to another webpage in the same website.

2 Select the first word in the paragraph—**Home**—and then on the **Insert tab**, in the **Links group**, click **Hyperlink**. Under **Link to**, click **Existing File or Web Page**, if necessary. Compare your screen with Figure 7.11.

In the Insert Hyperlink dialog box, the Text to display box indicates the selected word *Home*.

ANOTHER WAY Right-click the selected text, and then from the shortcut menu, click Hyperlink.

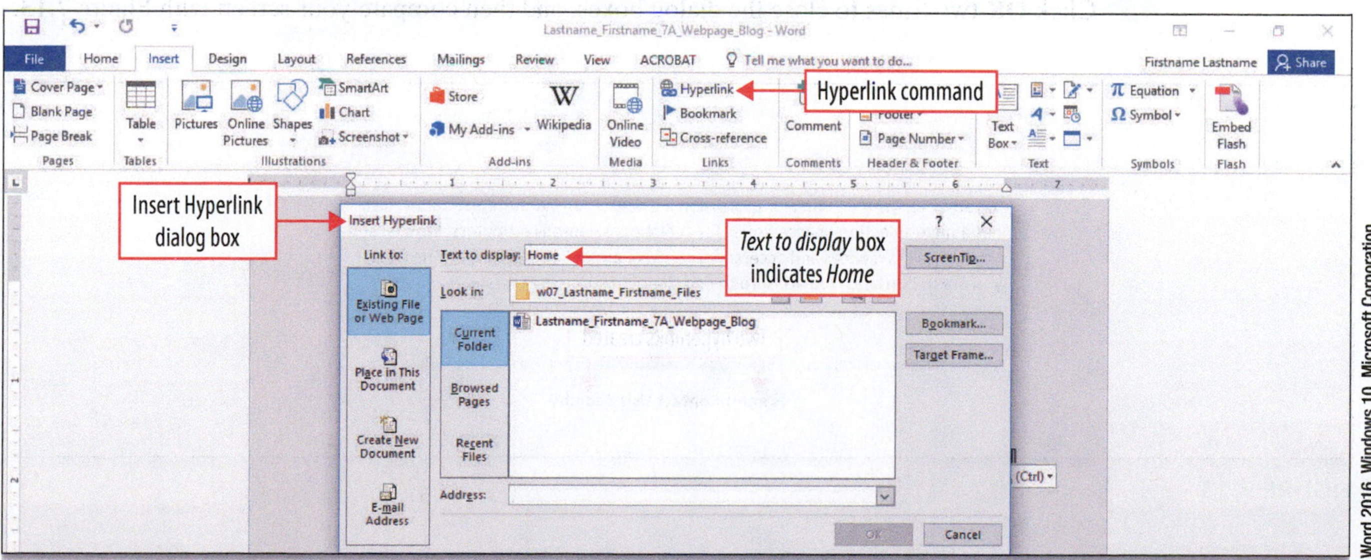

FIGURE 7.11

3 Click in the **Address** box, delete any existing text, and then type **www.owspecialties.biz** As you begin typing the Internet address, notice that the text http:// is automatically inserted at the left of the box. If another address displays while you are typing, continue typing to replace it. When you are finished typing, if any other characters display, delete them.

If another address displays as you type, it is a result of the AutoComplete feature, which displays the most recently used web address from your computer.

4 In the upper right corner of the dialog box, click **ScreenTip**. In the **Set Hyperlink ScreenTip** dialog box, in the **ScreenTip text** box, type **Oregon Wireless Specialties** Compare your screen with Figure 7.12.

Text that you type here will display as a ScreenTip when an individual viewing your site points to this hyperlink.

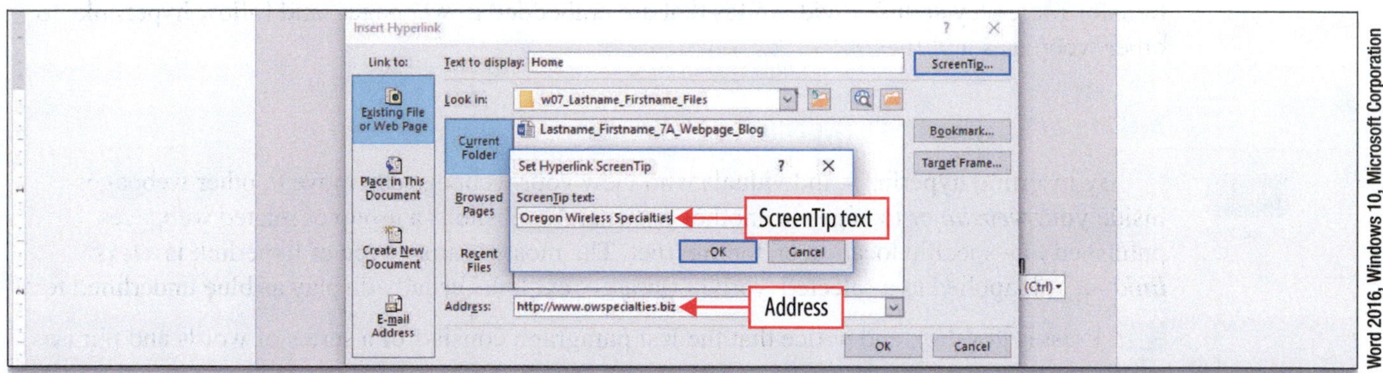

FIGURE 7.12

5 In the **Set Hyperlink ScreenTip** dialog box, click **OK**. In the **Insert Hyperlink** dialog box, click **OK**.

The hyperlink is recorded, and the selected text is blue and underlined.

6 In the same paragraph, select the word **Search**. Using the techniques you practiced, display the **Insert Hyperlink** dialog box, and then in the **Address** box, type **www.owspecialties.biz/search** As the **ScreenTip text**, type **Search OWS**

7 Click **OK** two times to close the dialog boxes, and then compare your screen with Figure 7.13.

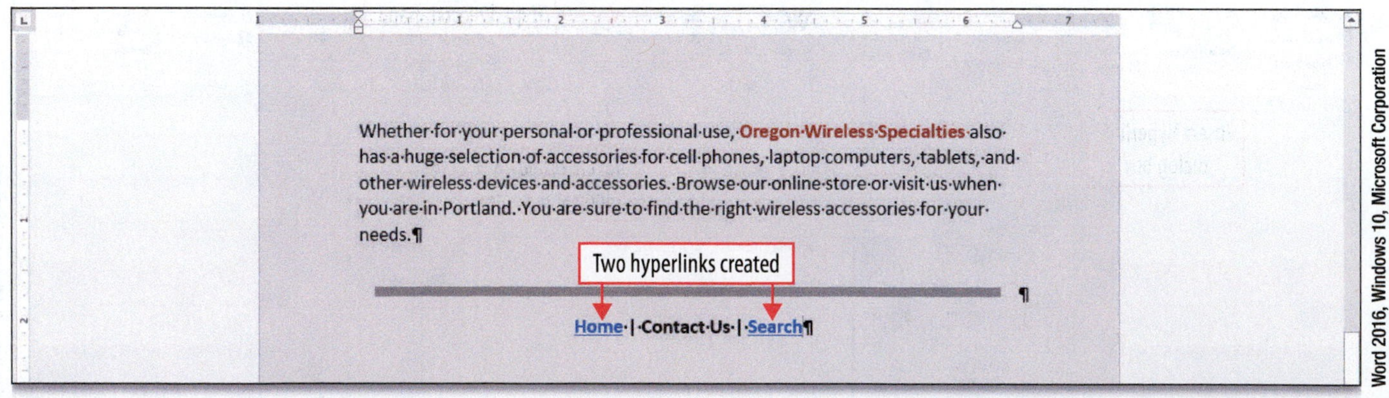

FIGURE 7.13

8 **Save** the document.

Activity 7.06 | Inserting a Hyperlink That Opens a New Email Message

Another common type of hyperlink is an ***email address link***, which opens a new message window so that an individual viewing your site can send an email message.

1 At the end of the document, select the text **Contact Us**, and then display the **Insert Hyperlink** dialog box. Under **Link to**, click **E-mail Address**.

2 In the **E-mail address** box, type **jlovrick@owspecialties.biz** As the **ScreenTip text**, type **Operations Manager** and then compare your screen with Figure 7.14.

As you type an email address, Word automatically inserts *mailto:*. Other email addresses may display in the Recently used e-mail addresses box.

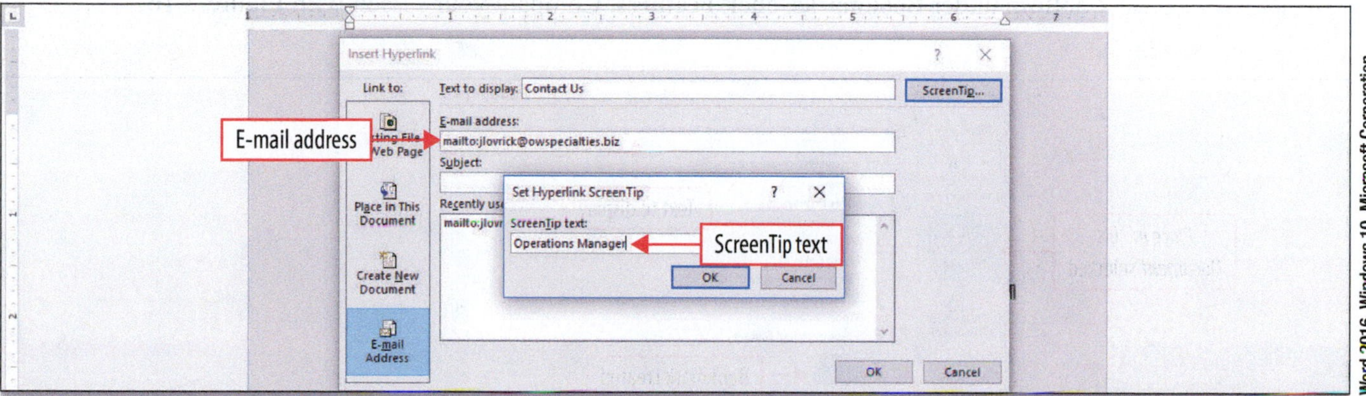

FIGURE 7.14

3 Click **OK** two times to close the dialog boxes, and then click **Save**.

The hyperlink is recorded, and the selected text changes to blue and is underlined.

Activity 7.07 | Using PDF Reflow to Create Additional Webpage Content

In this Activity, you will use PDF Reflow to import a PDF file into Word, and then create a hyperlink to the added information.

1 Press Ctrl + End, and then press Ctrl + Enter to create a new page. On the **Insert tab**, in the **Text group**, click the **Object button arrow**, and then click **Text from File**.

2 In the **Insert File** dialog box, navigate to the student data files that accompany this chapter, and then select the PDF file **w07A_Features_Guide**. Compare your screen with Figure 7.15.

The icon indicates that the document is saved as a ***PDF*** file—your icon may differ depending on what program you have selected to open PDFs on your system.

Recall that PDF stands for ***Portable Document Format***, a technology that creates an image that preserves the look of your file but that cannot be easily changed or edited. You can, however, open and edit a PDF file in Word.

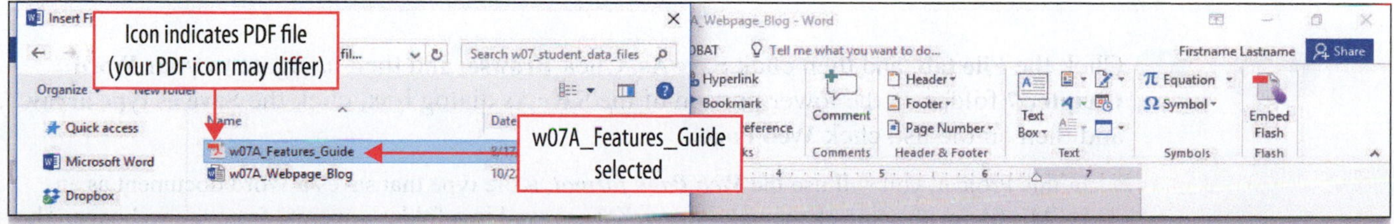

FIGURE 7.15

Word 2016, Windows 10, Microsoft Corporation

3 In the **Insert File** dialog box, with the file **w07A_Features_Guide** selected, click **Insert**. In the **Microsoft Word** message box, click **OK** to convert the PDF file to a Word document.

The text from the PDF document is inserted into your Word document. The conversion may result in some extraneous spaces in front of paragraph marks, but this will not affect your result.

4 Scroll as necessary, and then select the text *Features available on many of our phones:*. On the **Insert tab**, in the **Links group**, click **Bookmark**. As the **Bookmark name**, type **Features** and then click **Add**.

5 Scroll up slightly, and then select the text **Guide to Popular Cell Phone Features**. On the **Insert tab**, in the **Links group**, click **Hyperlink**.

6 Under **Link to**, click **Place in This Document**. Under **Select a place in this document**, at the bottom under **Bookmarks**, click **Features**. Compare your screen with Figure 7.16.

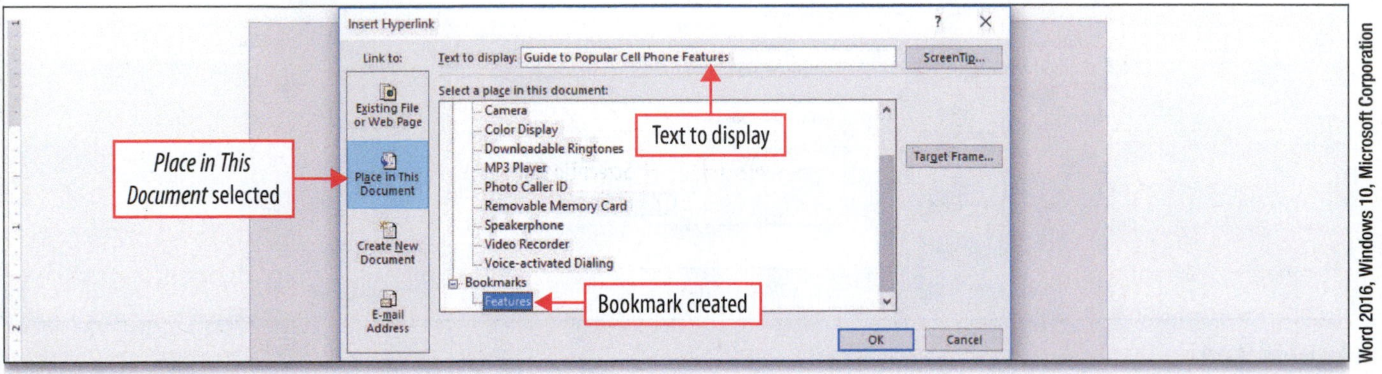

FIGURE 7.16

7 In the upper right corner of the **Insert Hyperlink** dialog box, click **ScreenTip**, type **Features Guide** as the **ScreenTip text**, and then click **OK** two times to close the dialog boxes.

8 Click the **File tab**, if necessary, click **Info**, and then click **Show All Properties**. In the **Tags** box, type **website, features** In the **Subject** box, type your course name and section number. If necessary, edit the author name to display your name. On the left, click **Save**.

Objective 3 Create a Webpage and Blog Post

Activity 7.08 | Saving a Word Document as a Webpage and Testing Webpages in a Browser

GO! Learn How Video W7-3

In this Activity, you will save your document as a webpage and then display and test your webpage in your browser.

ALERT! Be Sure You Are Connected to the Internet

Be sure you are connected to the Internet so that you can test your webpage. If you cannot connect now, just read through the steps, and then test your page when you are connected.

1.5.2

1 Click the **File tab**, and then click **Save As**. Click **Browse**, and then navigate to your **Word Chapter 7** folder. In the lower portion of the **Save As** dialog box, click the **Save as type arrow**, and then on the list, click **Web Page**.

In this Project, you will use the ***Web Page format***, a file type that saves a Word document as an HTML file, with some elements of the webpage saved in a folder, separate from the webpage. The format is useful if you want to access individual elements, such as pictures, separately.

2 Near the bottom center of the **Save As** dialog box, click **Change Title**. In the **Enter Text** dialog box, in the **Page title** box, type **Oregon Wireless Specialties** and then compare your screen with Figure 7.17.

By creating this title, when the document is viewed as a webpage with a browser, *Oregon Wireless Specialties* will display on the title bar. Because Internet search engines locate the content of webpages by title, it is important to create a title that describes the content of the webpage.

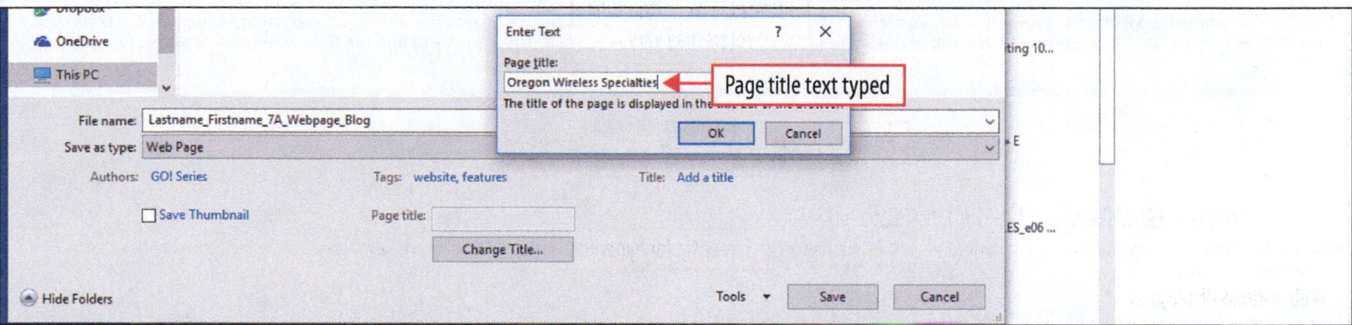

FIGURE 7.17

Word 2016, Windows 10, Microsoft Corporation

3 Click **OK**, and then in the lower right corner of the **Save As** dialog box, click **Save**. If the **Microsoft Word Compatibility Checker** dialog box displays, click **Continue**.

Because you saved the document as a webpage, the document displays in Web Layout view, and on the status bar, the Web Layout button is active. The Zoom level may change to display text according to the size of your screen.

4 In the upper right corner of the Word window, click **Close** [×]. If a message box displays regarding the Clipboard, click **No**.

5 On the Windows taskbar, click **File Explorer**, navigate to your **Word Chapter 7 folder**, and then in the **File list**, be sure you can view the **Type** column. Double-click the **HTML file** for your Lastname_Firstname_7A_Webpage_Blog to open it in your default browser.

6 Scroll down slightly, if necessary, and then point to the text *Home* to display the pointer, and the ScreenTip that you created. Compare your screen with Figure 7.18.

At the bottom left of your screen, the web address assigned to the hyperlink displays as another ScreenTip.

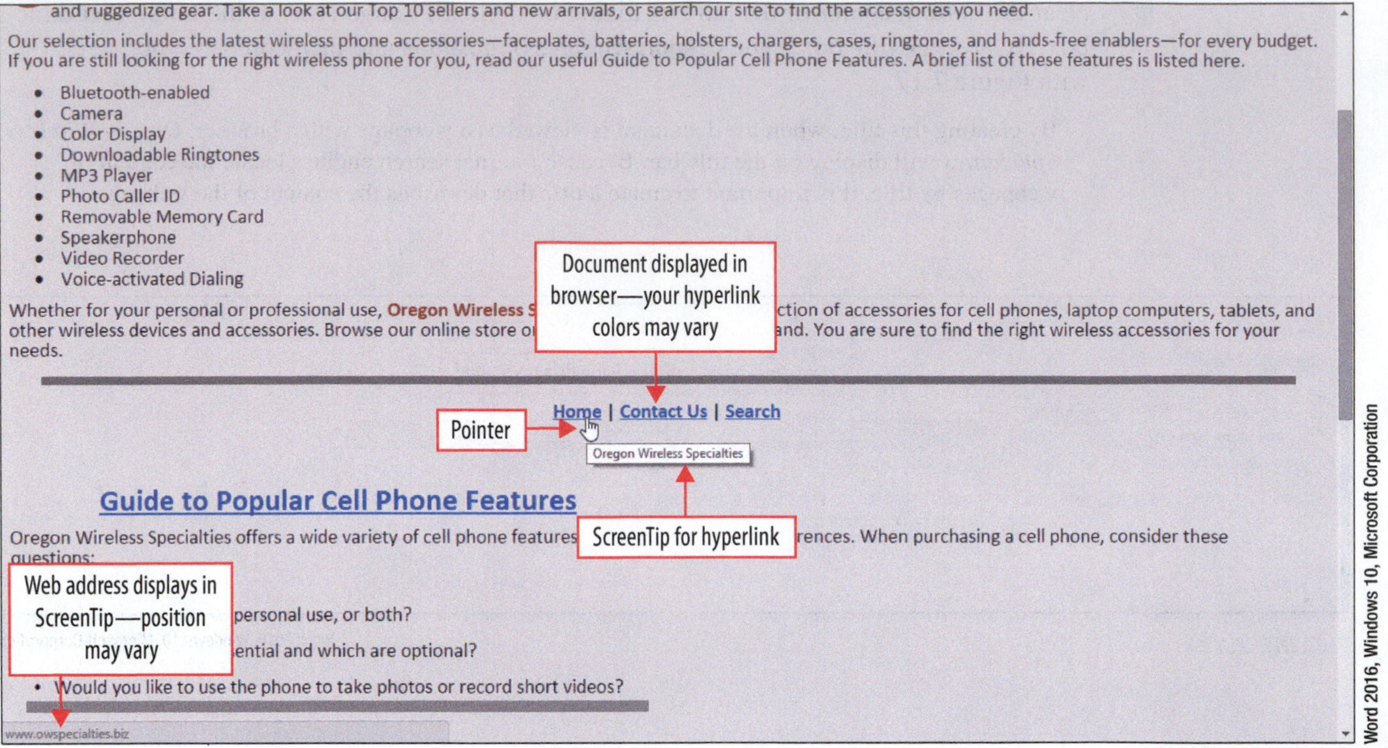

Word 2016, Windows 10, Microsoft Corporation

FIGURE 7.18

7 On the same line, *point to*, but do not click, the text *Contact Us* and *Search* to display the ScreenTips you created.

8 Locate and then click the **Guide to Popular Cell Phone Features** link to display the linked area of the page. Compare your screen with Figure 7.19.

The browser displays the Features Guide portion of the webpage.

BY TOUCH Tap the Guide to Popular Cell Phone Features link.

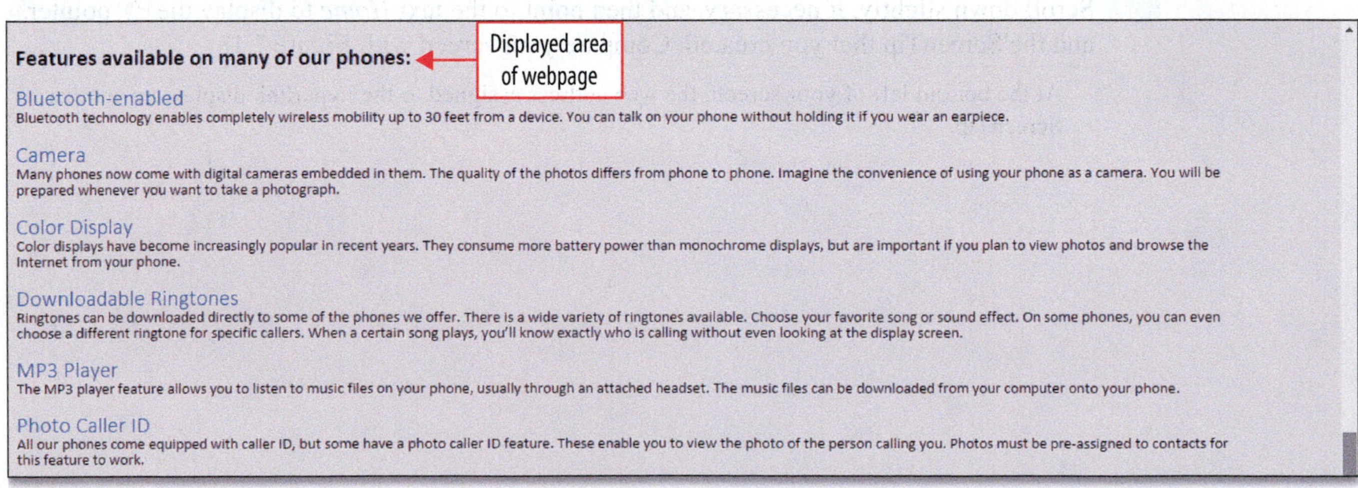

Word 2016, Windows 10, Microsoft Corporation

FIGURE 7.19

9 **Close** [X] the browser window. If necessary, close any File Explorer windows.

Activity 7.09 | Editing and Removing Hyperlinks

You can modify the hyperlinks in your webpage—for example, to change an address or ScreenTip—and you can also remove a hyperlink.

1 Start Word. On the left, under **Recent Documents**, click your *Word document*—not your webpage—named **Lastname_Firstname_7A_Webpage_Blog**.

2 On the **View tab**, in the **Views group**, click **Print Layout**. Scroll to view the top of **Page 2**. In the navigation bar, right-click the **Contact Us** link, and then on the shortcut menu, click **Edit Hyperlink**.

3 In the upper right corner of the **Edit Hyperlink** dialog box, click **ScreenTip**, and then edit the ScreenTip text to indicate **Click here to send a message to our Operations Manager** Compare your screen with Figure 7.20.

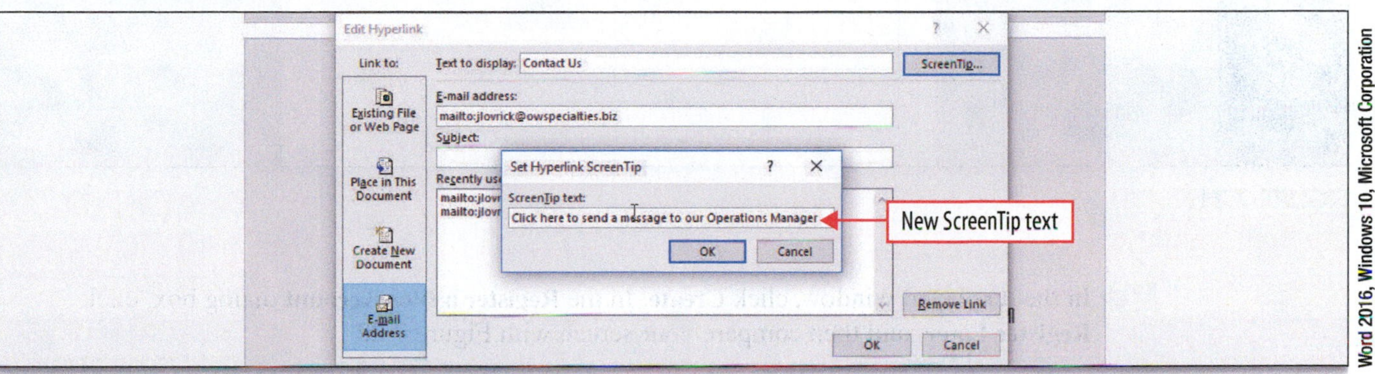

Word 2016, Windows 10, Microsoft Corporation

FIGURE 7.20

4 Click **OK** two times to close the dialog boxes.

5 In the navigation bar, right-click the **Search** link, and then click **Remove Hyperlink**.

The link is removed, but the link can be added again at a later time when Oregon Wireless Specialties decides how customers will be able to search the website.

6 Press Ctrl + Home, **Save** your document, and leave it open for the next Activity.

Activity 7.10 | Creating a Blog Post from a Template

A ***blog***, short for *Web log*, is a website that displays dated entries. Blogs are fast-changing websites and usually contain many hyperlinks—links to other blogs, to resource sites about the topic, or to photos and videos. A ***blog post*** is an individual article entered in a blog with a time and date stamp.

1 Click the **File tab**, and then click **New**. On the right, locate and click the **Blog post** template. Compare your screen with Figure 7.21.

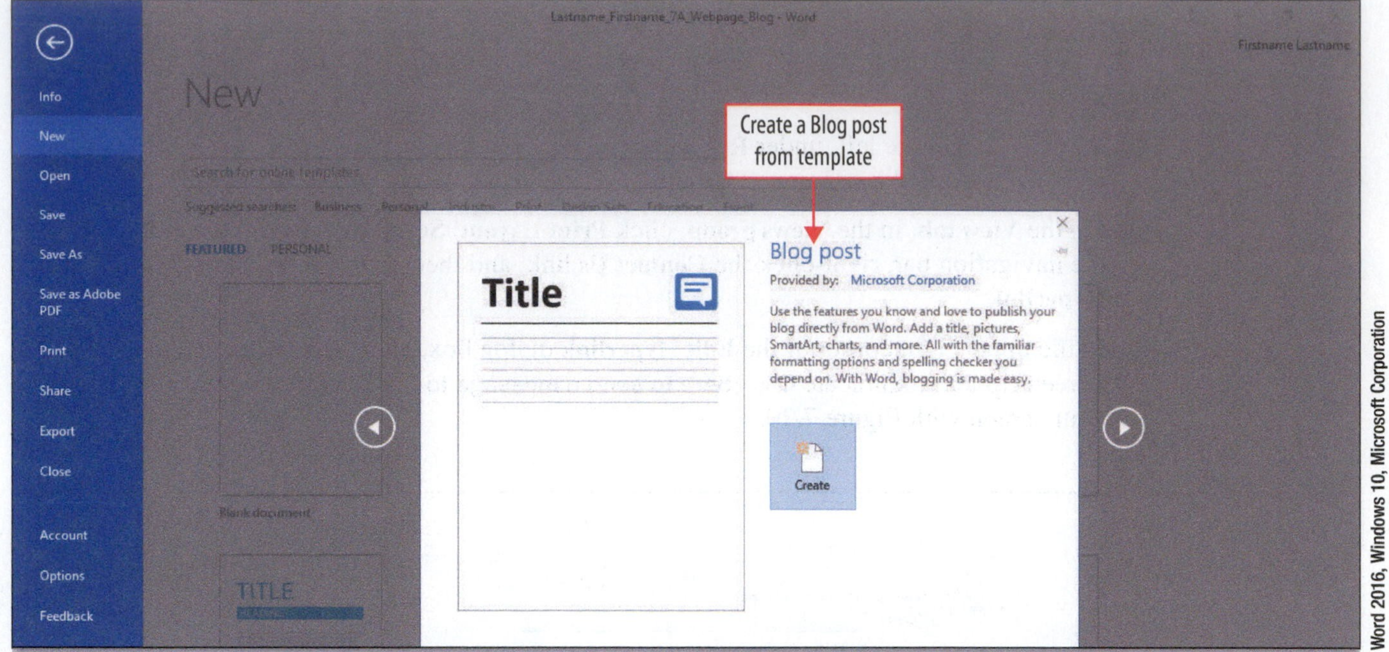

Word 2016, Windows 10, Microsoft Corporation

FIGURE 7.21

2 In the displayed window, click **Create**. In the **Register a Blog Account** dialog box, click **Register Later**, and then compare your screen with Figure 7.22.

A new document formatted as a blog post displays, and the Blog Post and Insert tabs display on the ribbon. In the document, you can enter a title for the blog post and then type the text. Some of the commands are inactive until you register at an actual blog site.

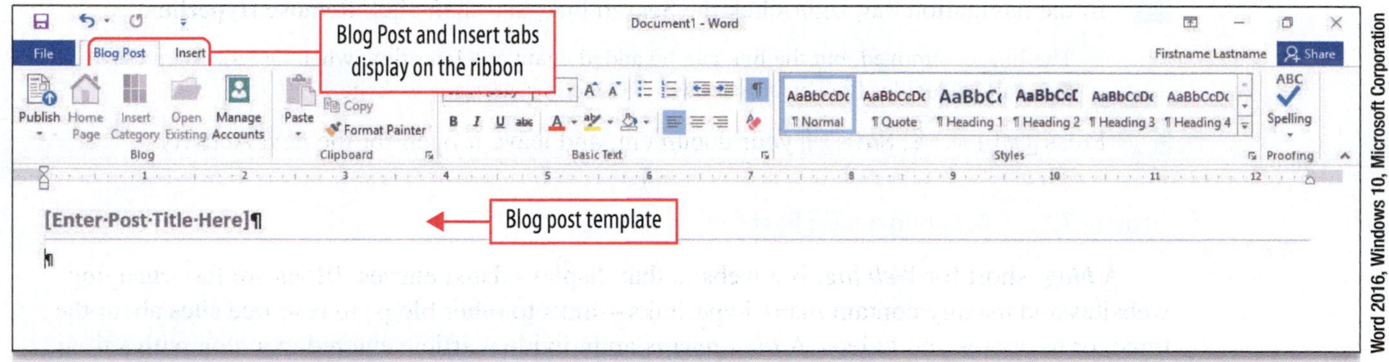

Word 2016, Windows 10, Microsoft Corporation

FIGURE 7.22

3 At the top of the document, click anywhere in the text *Enter Post Title Here* field to select the placeholder text, and then type **Learn to Use Your Bluetooth Headset**

4 Under the line, click in the body text area, and then type the following text:

Do you have one of our new Bluetooth headsets? Email us to learn all about it, or download the user guides from our website.

5 Select all the text you typed in the previous step, and then on the mini toolbar, change the **Font** to **Verdana** and the **Font Size** to **16**. Compare your screen with Figure 7.23.

Although it is not required to do so, you can use Word's formatting tools to change the font, size, color, or alignment of text.

FIGURE 7.23

Word 2016, Windows 10, Microsoft Corporation

Activity 7.11 | Inserting Hyperlinks in a Blog Post

1.2.2

Blog posts are not limited to text. You can link to pictures, graphics, other websites, and email addresses.

1 In the second sentence, select the text **Email**. Click the **Insert tab**, and then in the **Links group**, click **Hyperlink**.

ANOTHER WAY Right-click the selected text, and then on the shortcut menu, click Hyperlink.

2 In the **Insert Hyperlink** dialog box, under **Link to**, click **E-mail Address**, if necessary. In the **E-mail address** box, type **jlovrick@owspecialties.biz** Compare your screen with Figure 7.24.

Recall that when you create an email hyperlink, Word automatically inserts *mailto:*. Because this is the same email address you typed previously, it may display in the Recently used e-mail addresses: box.

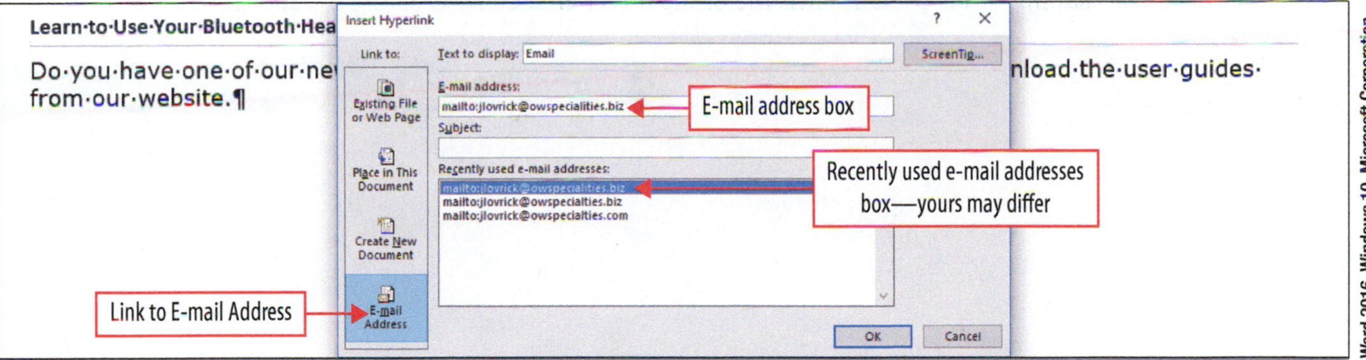

Word 2016, Windows 10, Microsoft Corporation

FIGURE 7.24

3 Click **OK**. Notice that the text *Email* displays with hyperlink formatting.

4 In the last sentence, select the text **website**, and then using the technique you practiced, create a hyperlink to an existing webpage. As the **Address**, type **www.owspecialties.biz** With *http://* and your typed text displayed, if any other characters display, delete them. As the **ScreenTip**, type **Oregon Wireless Specialties** Click **OK** two times to close the dialog boxes.

5 From the taskbar, redisplay your **Lastname_Firstname_7A_Webpage_Blog** document. Press Ctrl + End, and then press Ctrl + Enter to create a new page.

6 With the insertion point in front of the centered paragraph on the new page, on the **Insert tab**, in the **Illustrations group**, click **Screenshot**.

7 Click the screenshot that displays the blog post to insert it as an image in your document—instead of saving it as a separate document. Compare your screen with Figure 7.25.

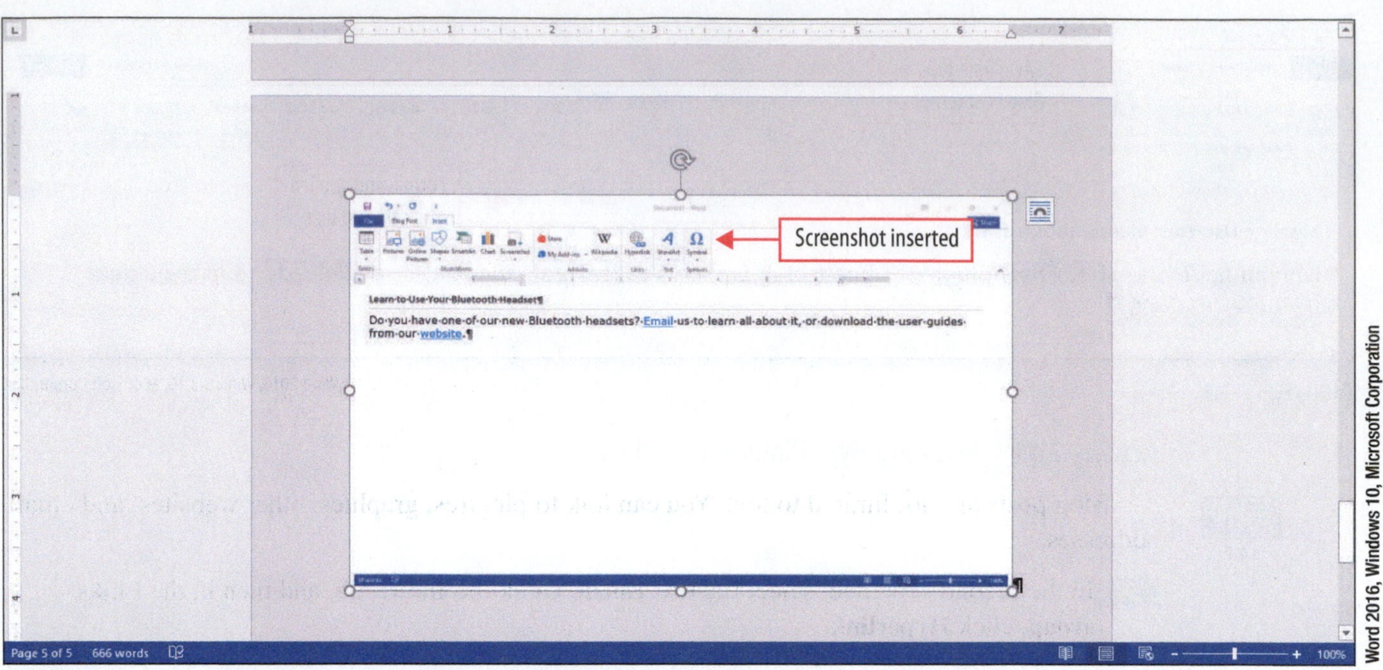
Screenshot inserted
Learn to Use Your Bluetooth Headset
Do you have one of our new Bluetooth headsets? Email us to learn all about it, or download the user guides from our website.
Page 5 of 5 666 words
Word 2016, Windows 10, Microsoft Corporation

FIGURE 7.25

8 Press Ctrl + Home.

9 **Save** your document. In the upper right corner of the Word window, click **Close**, and then **Close** the blog document without saving. If directed by your instructor to do so, submit your paper printout, your electronic image of your document that looks like a printed document, or your original Word file. Unless directed by your instructor, you need not submit or keep the HTML file or the folder created by creating a webpage.

END | You have completed Project 7A

PROJECT 7B FAQ List

Project 7B Training
Project 7B Grader

7 WORD

PROJECT ACTIVITIES

In Activities 7.12 through 7.24, you will examine Word settings, gather supporting information, insert an equation, and use find and replace options to create a draft version of an FAQ list. Additionally, you will save the file in a different format. Nanci Scholtz, Vice President of Marketing for Oregon Wireless Specialties, is compiling a list of Frequently Asked Questions, or FAQs, from customers who shop from the online site. She plans to include the information in a separate webpage on the company's website. Your completed documents will look similar to Figure 7.26.

PROJECT FILES

If your instructor wants you to submit Project 7B in the MyITLab grader system, log in to MyITLab, locate Grader Project 7B, and then download the files for this project.

For Project 7B, you will need the following files:
w07B_FAQ_List
w07B_Image
w07B_Packaging

You will save your files as:
Lastname_Firstname_7B_FAQ_List
Lastname_Firstname_7B_FAQ_RTF
(will not be submitted for grading)

Please always review the downloaded Grader instructions before beginning.

PROJECT RESULTS

GO! Walk Thru Project 7B

Frequently Asked Questions

Oregon Wireless Specialties is proud of its excellent customer service. If you cannot find an answer to your question here, please contact Nanci Scholtz at nscholtz@owspecialties.biz.

How frequently do you add new products to your website?

Oregon Wireless Specialties constantly evaluates the popularity of all items on our website and adds new products to ensure that our customers have the best selection possible to meet their needs.

Do you accept suggestions for new accessories for cell phones, PDAs, MP3 players, and so on?

We welcome any suggestions for new additions to our inventory. Please send your requests to Nanci Scholtz at nscholtz@owspecialties.com.

How do you package the items I order?

Padded mailers provide excellent protection when shipping small, fragile items. For large orders, we use heavy duty corrugated cardboard boxes. Items are packed with foam or bubble wrap to provide padding and cushioning.

Will I receive tracking information for my shipment?

Whether you choose UPS or USPS Express Mail® shipping, you will receive tracking information.

No weighing or calculating needed up to 70 lbs. Flat Rate affordable pricing offers one rate to any state.

How can I check the status of my order?

You can check the status of your order online at www.owspecialties.com/orders or contact Nanci Scholtz at nscholtz@owspecialties.com.

Do you ship internationally?

Oregon Wireless Specialties ships to the United States, Canada, and Mexico.

The item I received is defective. How can I get a replacement?

All of our products are quality tested and meet rigorous standards. We apologize if you received a defective item. Please contact Josette Lovrick, Operations Manager, at jlovrick@owspecialties.com for an immediate replacement.

I would like a refund for the item(s) I purchased. Is this possible?

Yes! Within 30 days of the date of purchase, you can return any item for a refund. Please go to www.owspecialties.com/returns for further details on receiving refunds. Provide your order number, date of purchase, reason for requesting the return, and your contact information.

Lastname_Firstname_7B_FAQ_List

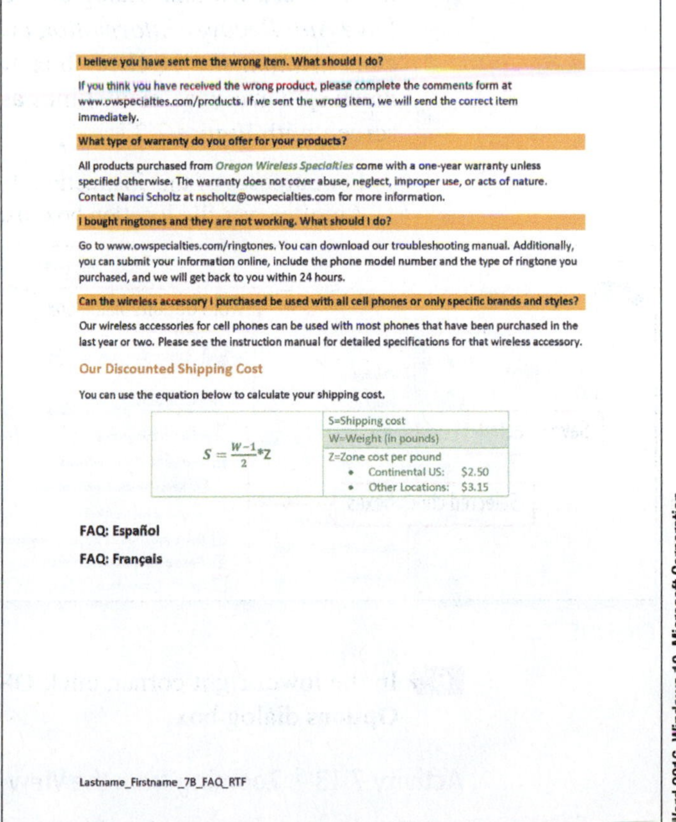

I believe you have sent me the wrong item. What should I do?

If you think you have received the wrong product, please complete the comments form at www.owspecialties.com/products. If we sent the wrong item, we will send the correct item immediately.

What type of warranty do you offer for your products?

All products purchased from *Oregon Wireless Specialties* come with a one-year warranty unless specified otherwise. The warranty does not cover abuse, neglect, improper use, or acts of nature. Contact Nanci Scholtz at nscholtz@owspecialties.com for more information.

I bought ringtones and they are not working. What should I do?

Go to www.owspecialties.com/ringtones. You can download our troubleshooting manual. Additionally, you can submit your information online, include the phone model number and the type of ringtone you purchased, and we will get back to you within 24 hours.

Can the wireless accessory I purchased be used with all cell phones or only specific brands and styles?

Our wireless accessories for cell phones can be used with most phones that have been purchased in the last year or two. Please see the instruction manual for detailed specifications for that wireless accessory.

Our Discounted Shipping Cost

You can use the equation below to calculate your shipping cost.

$S = \frac{W-1}{2} * Z$	S=Shipping cost W=Weight (in pounds) Z=Zone cost per pound • Continental US: $2.50 • Other Locations: $3.15

FAQ: Español

FAQ: Français

Lastname_Firstname_7B_FAQ_RTF

FIGURE 7.26 Project 7B FAQ List

Word 2016, Windows 10, Microsoft Corporation

Objective 4 Manage Document Versions

GO! Learn How Video W7-4

When you install Microsoft Office, default settings are created for many features. For example, when working on an unsaved document, Word saves a temporary version every ten minutes. This time can be adjusted to suit your needs. Recall that Word settings are modified in the Word Options dialog box.

ALERT! **To submit as an autograded project, log into MyITLab, download the files for this project, and begin with those files instead of w07B_FAQ_List.**

Activity 7.12 | Changing the Auto Save Frequency

In this Activity, you will change the save frequency for the ***AutoRecover*** option, which helps prevent losing unsaved changes by automatically creating a backup version of the current document.

1. Start Word, and then on the left, click **Open Other Documents**. Click **Browse**, navigate to the student data files that accompany this chapter, and then open the file **w07B_FAQ_List**. If necessary, display the rulers and formatting marks.
2. Be sure your document displays in **Print Layout** view. Click the **File tab**, on the left click **Save As**, click **Browse**, and then in the **Save As** dialog box, navigate to your **Word Chapter 7** folder. Using your own name, save the document as **Lastname_Firstname_7B_FAQ_List**
3. At the bottom of **Page 1**, right-click in the footer area, and then click **Edit Footer**. On the ribbon, in the **Insert group**, click **Document Info**, and then click **File Name**. **Close** the footer area.
4. Click the **File tab**, and then on the left click **Options** to display the **Word Options** dialog box.
5. In the **Word Options** dialog box, on the left, click **Save**. Under **Save documents**, verify that the *Save AutoRecover information every* check box and the *Keep the last autosaved version if I close without saving* check box are selected. Click the **Save AutoRecover information every down spin arrow** as many times as necessary to set the minutes to **1**, and then compare your screen with Figure 7.27.

   For purposes of this instruction, Word will save a version of this document every minute. The AutoRecover file location box displays the location where the temporary versions are stored.

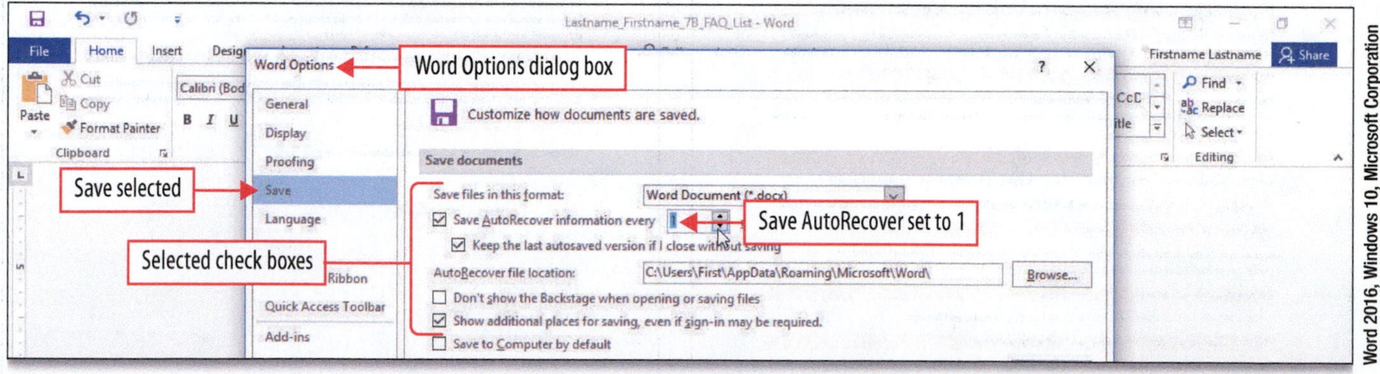

FIGURE 7.27

6. In the lower right corner, click **OK** to save the change you made and to close the **Word Options** dialog box.

Activity 7.13 | Zooming from the View Tab

By changing the way in which documents display on your screen, you make your editing tasks easier and more efficient. For example, you can display multiple pages of a long document or increase the zoom level to make reading easier or to examine specific text more closely.

1 Press Ctrl + Home, and then click at the end of the first paragraph—*FAQ*. Press Enter to insert a new blank paragraph.

2 Type **Oregon Wireless Specialties is proud of its excellent customer service. If you cannot find an answer to your question here, please contact Nanci Scholtz at nscholtz@owspecialties.biz.**

3 Click the **View tab**, and then in the **Zoom group**, click **Zoom**. In the **Zoom** dialog box, under **Zoom to**, click the **200%** option button, and then compare your screen with Figure 7.28.

In the Zoom dialog box, you can select from among several preset zoom levels, select a specific number of pages to view at one time, or use the Percent box to indicate a specific zoom level.

ANOTHER WAY Use the Zoom slider on the status bar to change the Zoom percentage.

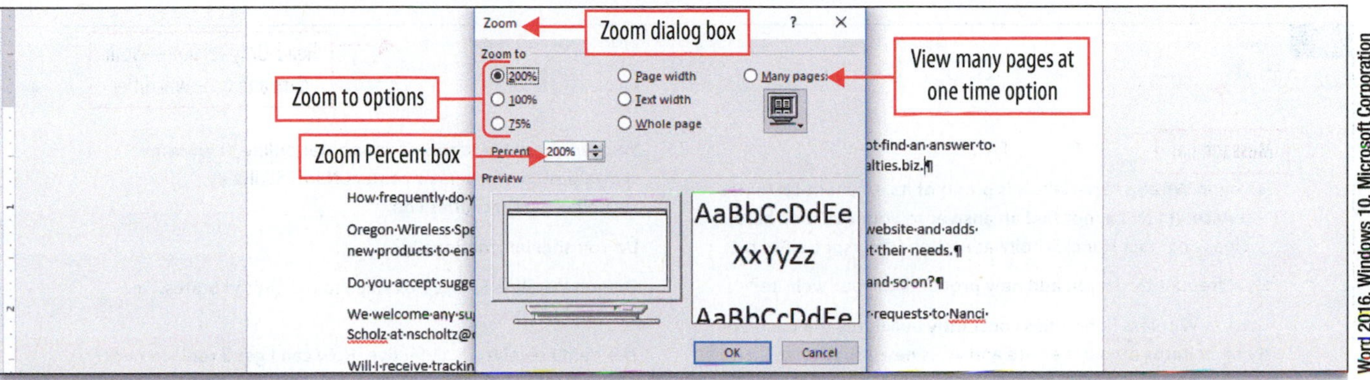

FIGURE 7.28

4 Click **OK**, and notice that the document displays in a magnified view.

5 Scroll as necessary, and in the paragraph that begins *We welcome*, notice that the email address has an extra character—an *i*— to the right of the letter *l*—the text should display as *owspecialties*. Click to position the insertion point to the right of *l*, and then press Delete one time to delete the *i*.

A magnified view is useful when you must make a close inspection of characters—for example, when typing email addresses or scientific formulas.

6 On the **View tab**, in the **Zoom group**, click **Multiple Pages** to display both **Page 1** and **Page 2** on your screen.

The ***Multiple Pages*** zoom setting decreases the magnification. Although the displayed text is smaller, you have an overall view of the page arrangement.

7 On the **View tab**, in the **Zoom group**, click **100%** to return to the default zoom setting.

Activity 7.14 | Managing Document Versions

1.1.3 Expert

You can examine an older version of your current document that was automatically saved—for example, to check the wording of a paragraph.

1 Click the **File tab**, and then on the left, if necessary, click **Info**. To the right of the **Manage Document** box, take a moment to review the list.

The list displays the most recently saved versions of the current document. Recall that you changed the AutoSave frequency to 1 minute. Several versions may display depending on the amount of time it has taken you to reach this step in the Project.

2 Click the **Manage Document** button, and then click **Recover Unsaved Documents** to display the **Open** dialog box.

In the Open dialog box, the *UnsavedFiles* folder displays the file names of all old documents that have never been saved. From this dialog box, you can select the file you want to display. Note: This folder may be empty on your computer.

3 In the lower right corner, click **Cancel** to close the **Open** dialog box. Click the **File tab**. To the right of the **Manage Document** button, at the bottom of the list, click the last file name to display the oldest version of the current document. Compare your screen with Figure 7.29.

A temporary, autosaved version of the current document opens as a Read-Only document. A message bar displays indicating that a newer version is available. You can replace a current document with a previous version by clicking the Restore button on the message bar.

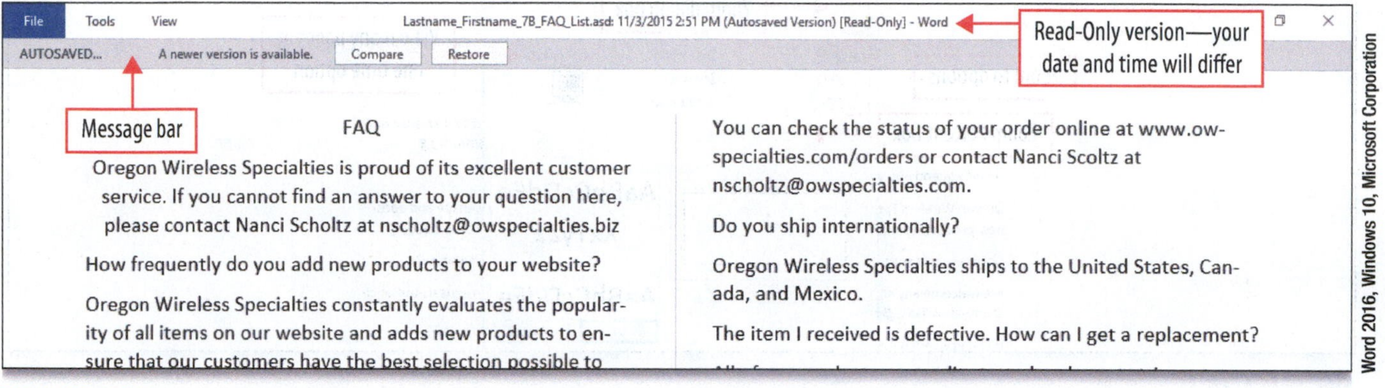

FIGURE 7.29

4 In the upper right corner, click **Close** ☒. In the **Microsoft Word** message box, click **Don't Save**.

All recent versions of the current document display in the Manage Document list.

5 At the bottom of the **Manage Document** list, right-click the last file name, and then on the shortcut menu, click **Delete This Version**. In the message box, click **Yes** to confirm the deletion.

The oldest version of the current document is deleted.

6 On the left, click **Options**, and then in the **Word Options** dialog box, on the left click **Save**. Click the **Save AutoRecover information every up spin arrow** as many times as necessary to set the minutes to **10**, and then click **OK** to close the **Word Options** dialog box and restore the default setting. **Save** your document.

Objective 5 Collect and Paste Images and Text

GO! Learn How Video W7-5

As you are writing, you may want to gather material—for example, text or pictures related to your topic. This supporting information may be located in another document or on the Internet. Recall that you can use the Clipboard to collect a group of graphics or selected text blocks and then paste them into a document.

Activity 7.15 | Collecting Images and Text from Multiple Documents

2.1.2

In this Activity, you will copy images and text from two different documents and then paste them into your current document.

1 Press Ctrl + Home. On the **Home tab**, in the lower right corner of the **Clipboard group**, click the **Dialog Box Launcher** to display the **Clipboard** pane. If necessary, at the top of the pane, click **Clear All** to delete anything currently on the Clipboard.

2 Be sure that only your **Lastname_Firstname_7B_FAQ_List** document and the **Clipboard** display; if necessary, close any other open windows. Click the **File tab**, on the left click **Open**, click **Browse**, and then in the **Open** dialog box, from your student data files, locate and open the file **w07B_Image**. If necessary, in the **Clipboard group**, click the **Dialog Box Launcher** to display the pane.

3 With the **w07B_Image** document displayed, select the **Frequently Asked Questions** graphic. Right-click the graphic, and then click **Copy**. Compare your screen with Figure 7.30.

The image in your w07B_Image document displays on the Clipboard pane—or yours may display *(preview not available)* as shown here.

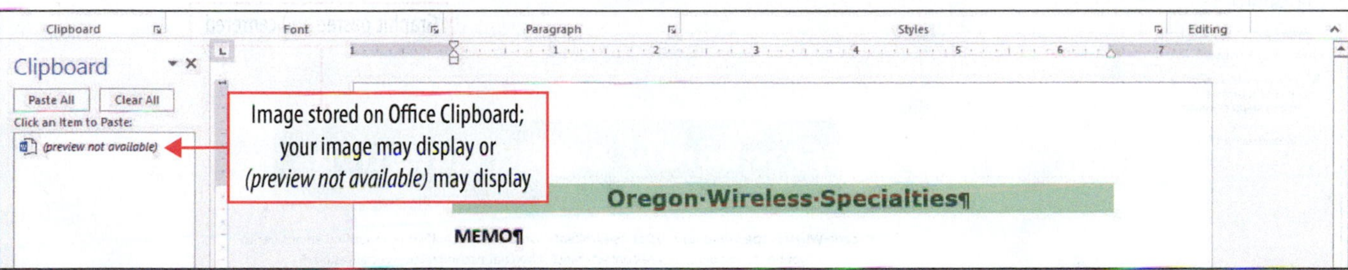

FIGURE 7.30

4 **Close** the **w07B_Image** file.

5 From your student files, open the file **w07B_Packaging**. If necessary, on the **Home tab**, in the **Clipboard group**, click the **Dialog Box Launcher** to display the **Clipboard** pane. Without selecting the paragraph mark at the end, select the entire paragraph that begins *Padded mailers*, and then **Copy** the selection to the Clipboard. Compare your screen with Figure 7.31.

The first few lines of the copied text display on the Clipboard. When copying multiple items to the Clipboard, the most recently copied item displays at the top of the list.

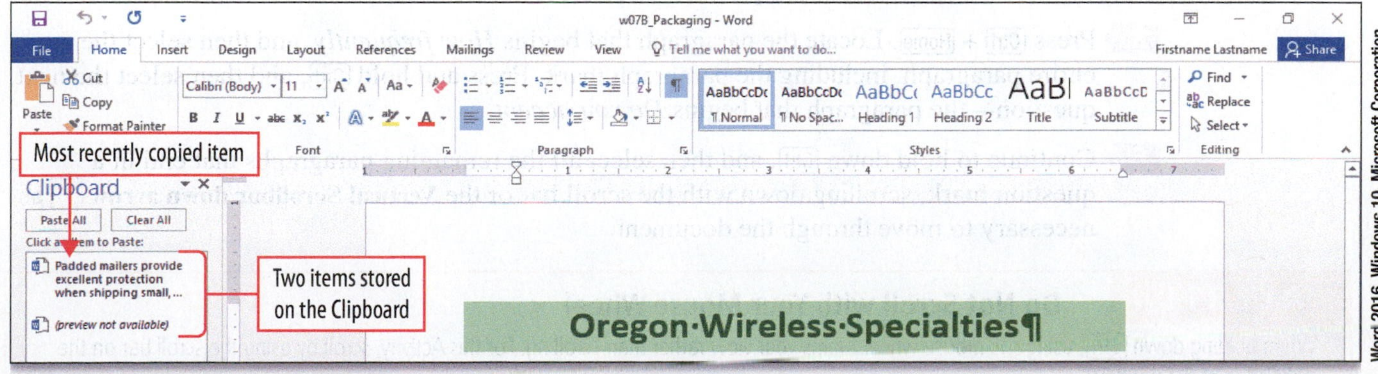

FIGURE 7.31

6 Close [X] the **w07B_Packaging** document.

Activity 7.16 | Pasting Information from the Clipboard Pane

2.1.2

After you have collected text items or images on the Clipboard, you can paste them into a document in any order.

1 Press Ctrl + Home. Without selecting the paragraph mark, select only the text **FAQ**, and then press Delete. In the **Clipboard** pane, click the graphic **Frequently Asked Questions** or the text *(preview not available)*, whichever displays in your Clipboard pane.

The graphic is inserted in the blank paragraph.

2 Locate the sixth text paragraph of the document, which begins *Will I receive*. Click to position the insertion point to the left of the paragraph, press Enter, and then press ↑. In the new paragraph, type **How do you package the items I order?** and then press Enter.

3 In the **Clipboard** pane, click the text entry that begins *Padded mailers* to paste the entire block of text at the insertion point. Compare your screen with Figure 7.32.

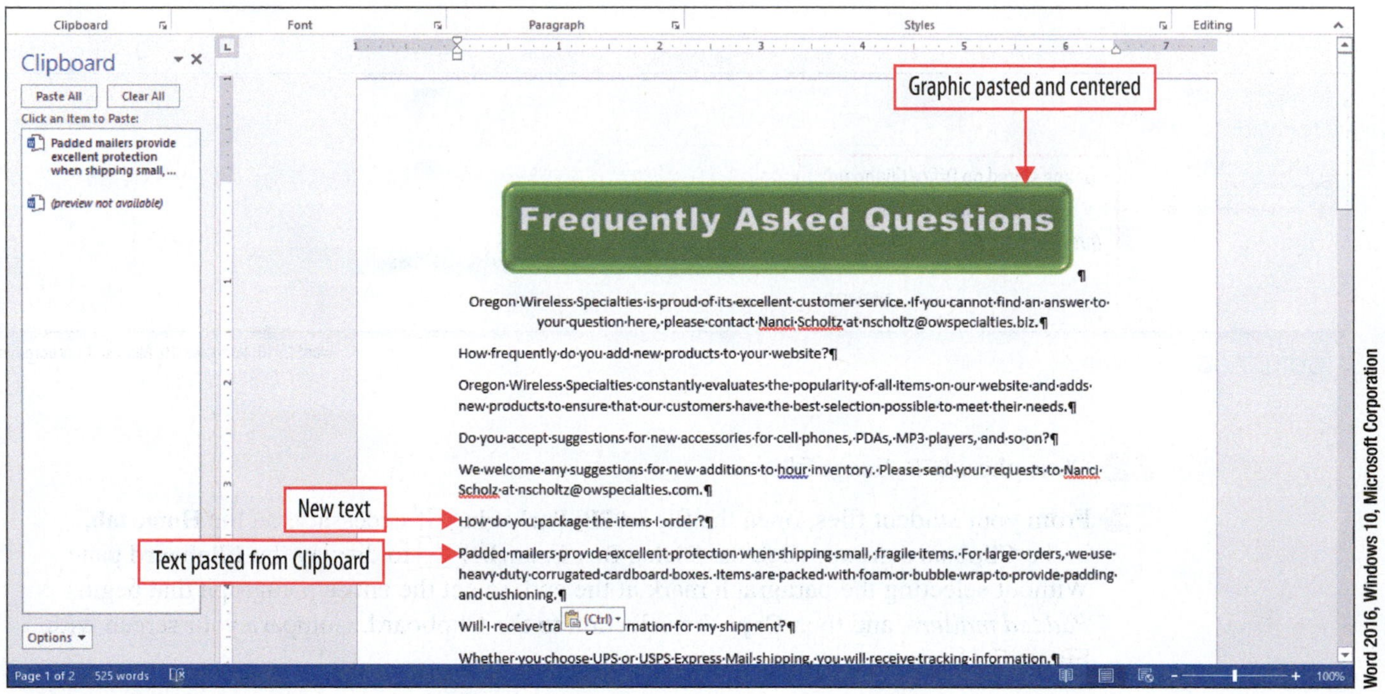

FIGURE 7.32

4 At the top of the **Clipboard** pane, click **Clear All** to remove all items from the Clipboard, and then **Close** [X] the **Clipboard** pane.

5 Press Ctrl + Home. Locate the paragraph that begins *How frequently*, and then select the entire paragraph, including the paragraph mark. Press and hold Ctrl, and then select the next question—the paragraph that begins *Do you accept*.

6 Continue to hold down Ctrl, and then select all the remaining paragraphs that end in a question mark, scrolling down with the scroll bar or the **Vertical Scrollbar down arrow** [▼] as necessary to move through the document.

ALERT! **Do Not Scroll with Your Mouse Wheel**

When holding down Ctrl, using the mouse wheel zooms your view rather than scrolling. For this Activity, scroll by using the scroll bar on the right edge of the window.

7 With all the questions selected, apply **Bold** [B]. On the **Home tab**, in the **Paragraph group**, click the **Shading arrow**, and then in the eighth column, click the first color—**Gold, Accent 4**.

8 Click anywhere to deselect the text, scroll through the document to be sure you have shaded each of the 12 questions, and then scroll so that the *Frequently Asked Questions* graphic displays at the top of your screen. Compare your screen with Figure 7.33.

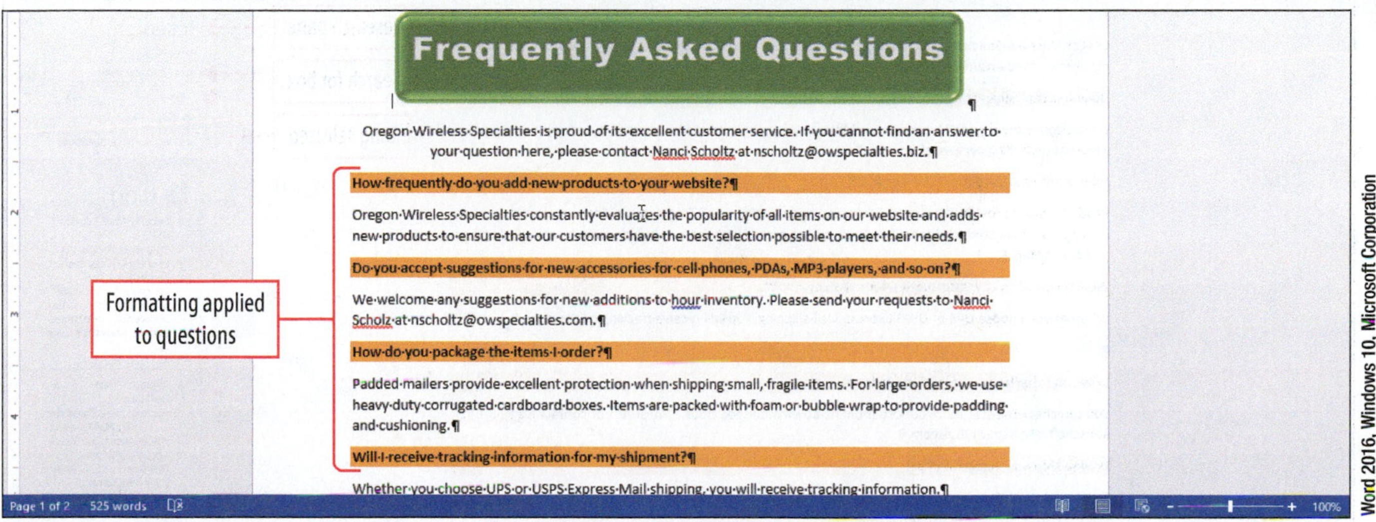

FIGURE 7.33

9 **Save** your document.

Objective 6 Locate Supporting Information and Insert Equations

GO! Learn How Video W7-6

While composing a document, you can use the Research pane to locate additional information about your topic. For example, you can look up additional facts on the Internet, replace words with synonyms to improve readability, or translate a phrase into another language. Additionally, Word provides tools to enter simple or complex equations in a document.

You can also use ***Smart Lookup***, which is a feature powered by Bing and that enables you to select text, and then Smart Lookup uses the surrounding content to provide results that are relevant to the context of the text.

Activity 7.17 | Using Smart Lookup and the Research Pane to Locate Information

In this Activity, you will use Smart Lookup and the Research Sites feature in the Research pane to search for additional information for and make changes to the FAQ list.

1 In the middle of **Page 1**, locate the paragraph that begins *Whether you choose*, and then click to position the insertion point at the end of the paragraph. Press Enter to insert a blank paragraph.

2 With the insertion point in the blank paragraph, press and hold Alt and click the left mouse button to display the Research pane on the right.

The Research pane displays at the right of your screen.

3 In the **Research** pane, under **Search for**, in the second box, click the **arrow**, and then click **Bing**. In the first box, type **usps express mail** press Enter, and then compare your screen with Figure 7.34.

In the second box, you can specify the type of reference source from which you want to locate information. For example, you might want to use the Microsoft search engine Bing as a reference source.

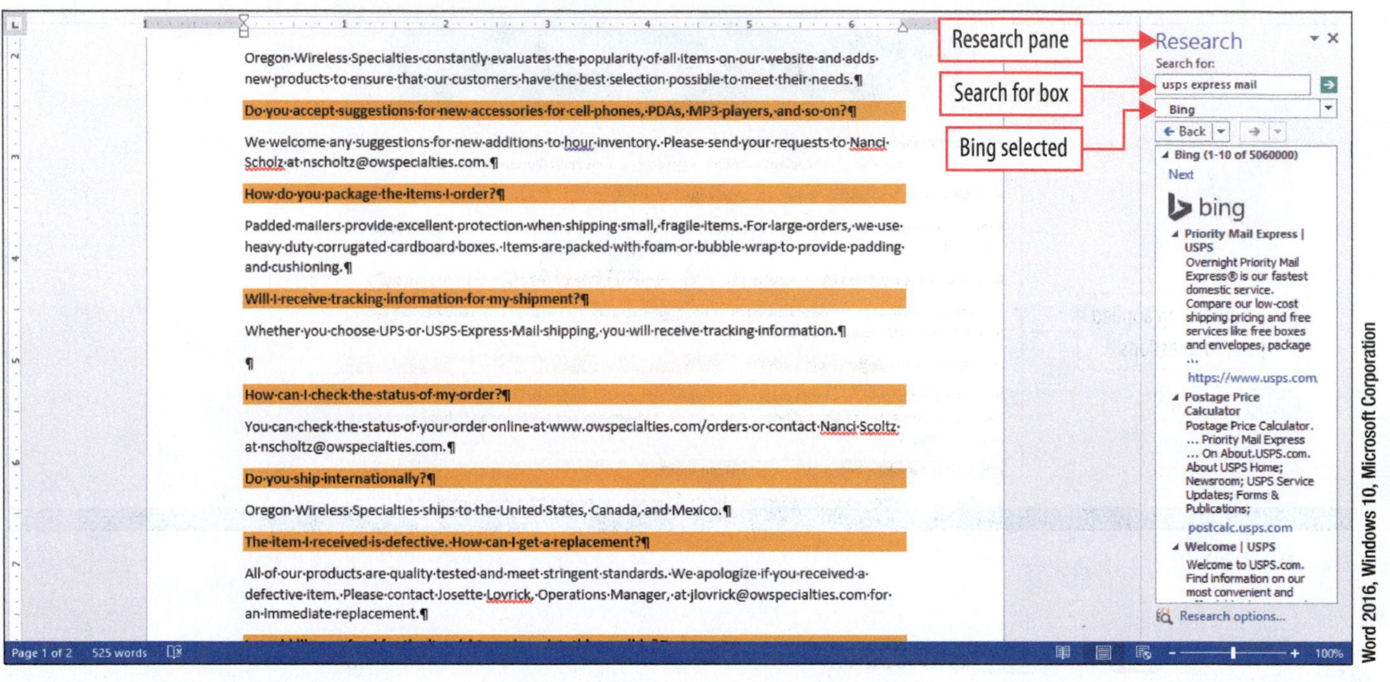

FIGURE 7.34

4 On the list of results, locate the item regarding **Priority Mail Express**, and then click the related link that contains *usps.com*. If necessary **Maximize** the browser window, and then compare your screen with Figure 7.35.

The related webpage displays in your browser.

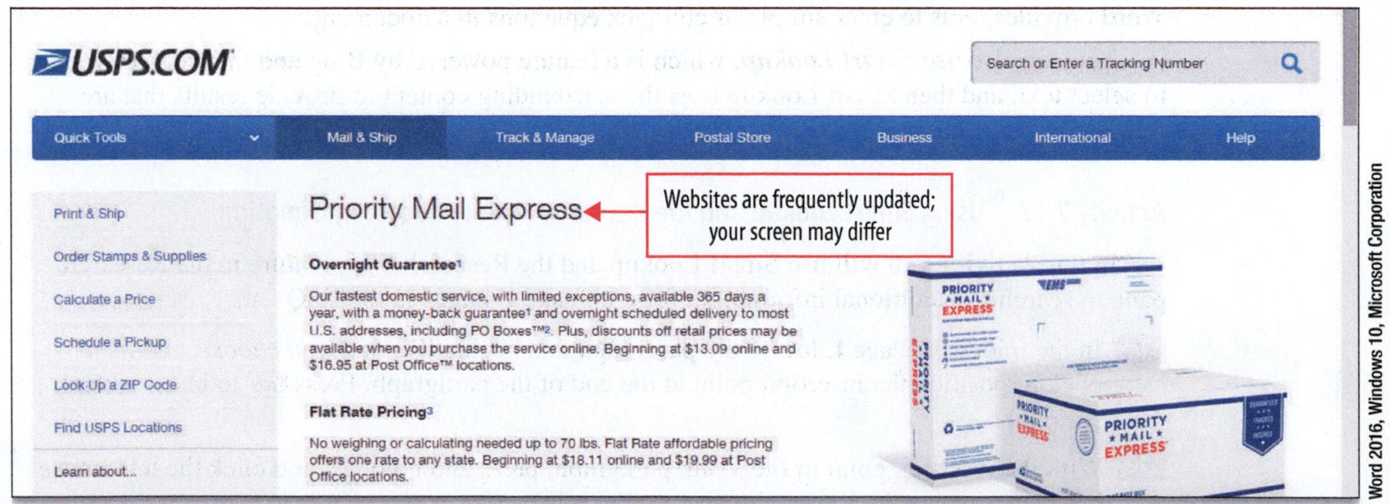

FIGURE 7.35

5 On the webpage, locate the paragraph that explains flat rate pricing.

6 From the taskbar, redisplay your **Lastname_Firstname_7B_FAQ_List** document. With the insertion point in the blank line below the paragraph that begins *Whether you choose*, type **No weighing or calculating needed up to 70 lbs. Flat Rate affordable pricing offers one rate to any state**. Compare your screen with Figure 7.36.

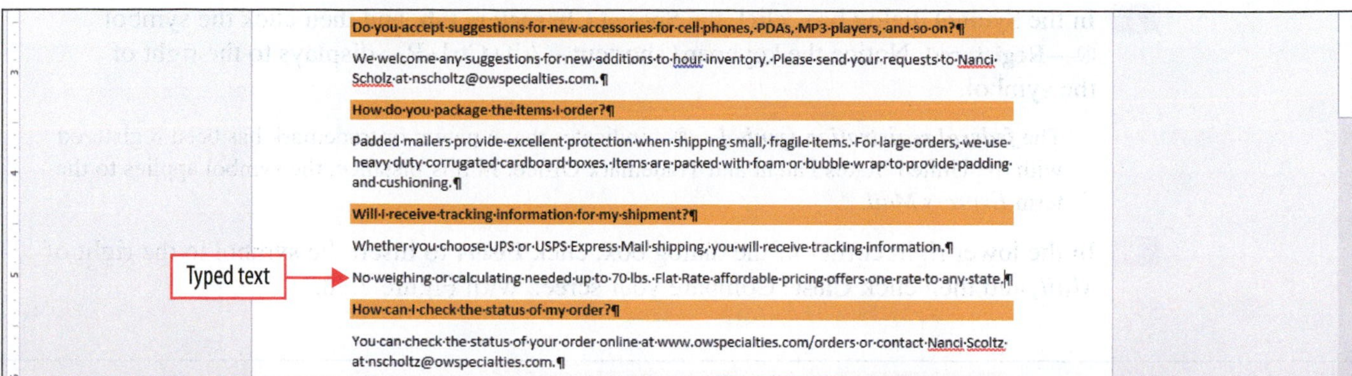

FIGURE 7.36

7 Close ☒ the **Research** pane. Under the third question, select the text **bubble wrap**, right-click, and then click **Smart Lookup**. In the pane that displays, if necessary click **Got it** to accept the privacy information, and then compare your screen with Figure 7.37.

Use Smart Lookup when you want to learn more about a term or to fact-check your information.

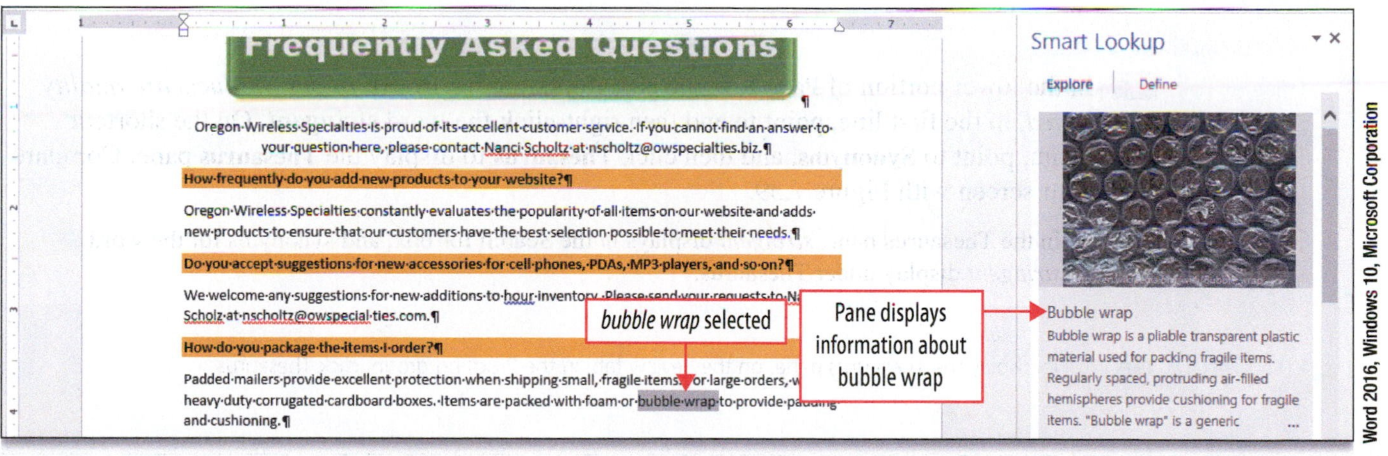

FIGURE 7.37

8 Close ☒ the pane, and then **Save** 🖫 your document.

NOTE Be Careful of Copyright Issues

Nearly everything you find on the Internet is protected by copyright law, which protects authors of original works, including text, art, photographs, and music. If you want to use text or graphics that you find online, you must get permission. One of the exceptions to the law is the use of small amounts of information for educational purposes, which falls under Fair Use guidelines. As a general rule, however, if you want to use someone else's material, always get permission first.

Activity 7.18 | Inserting Special Characters and Using the Thesaurus

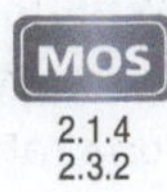

2.1.4
2.3.2

1 Above the text you just inserted, in the paragraph that begins *Whether you choose*, position the insertion point immediately to the right of *Express Mail*. Click the **Insert tab**. In the **Symbols group**, click **Symbol**, and then on the list, click **More Symbols**.

Here you will find characters that are not available on your keyboard.

2 In the **Symbol** dialog box, click the **Special Characters tab**, and then click the symbol **®—Registered**. Notice the keyboard shortcut—Alt+Ctrl+R—displays to the right of the symbol.

The ***federal registration symbol***—®—indicates that a patent or trademark has been registered with the United States Patent and Trademark Office. In this instance, the symbol applies to the term *Express Mail*.

3 In the lower right corner of the dialog box, click **Insert** to insert the symbol to the right of *Mail*, and then click **Close**. Compare your screen with Figure 7.38.

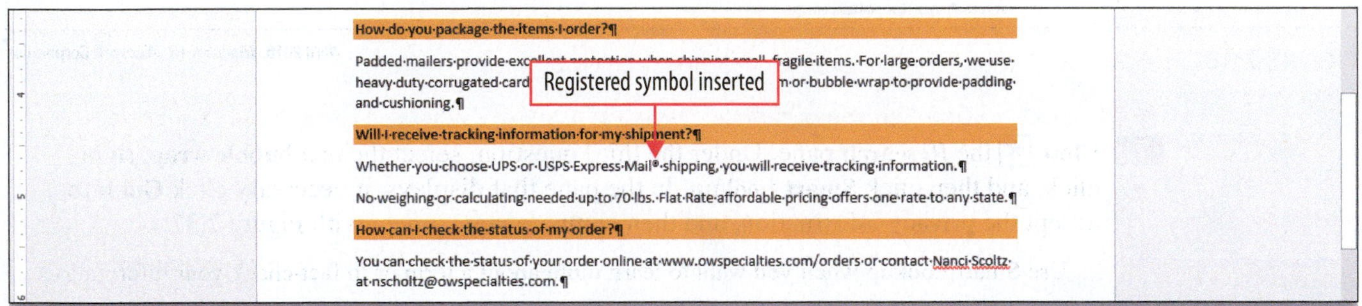

FIGURE 7.38

Word 2016, Windows 10, Microsoft Corporation

4 In the lower portion of **Page 1**, in the paragraph that begins *All of our products are quality tested*, in the first line, point to and then right-click the word **stringent**. On the shortcut menu, point to **Synonyms**, and then click **Thesaurus** to display the **Thesaurus** pane. Compare your screen with Figure 7.39.

In the Thesaurus pane, *stringent* displays in the Search for box, and synonyms for the word *stringent* display under Thesaurus.

ANOTHER WAY To display the Thesaurus pane, on the Review tab, in the Proofing group, click Thesaurus.

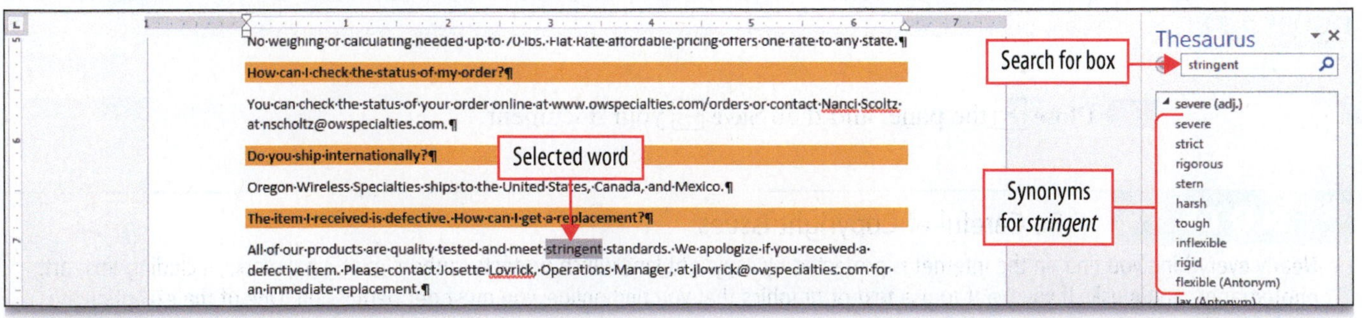

FIGURE 7.39

Word 2016, Windows 10, Microsoft Corporation

5 In the **Thesaurus** pane, point to *rigorous*, click the **arrow**, and then click **Insert** to replace *stringent* with *rigorous*.

6 **Close** [X] the **Thesaurus** pane. At the bottom of **Page 1**, click to position the insertion point to the left of the shaded paragraph that begins *I believe you have sent me*. Press Ctrl + Enter, which is the keyboard shortcut to insert a page break. **Save** your document.

Because the document contains questions and answers, it is good document design to keep the question and answer together on the same page.

ANOTHER WAY On the Layout tab, in the Page Setup group, click Breaks, and then under Page Breaks, click Page.

Activity 7.19 | Translating Text

You can translate a word or phrase into a different language. Because Oregon Wireless Specialties has customers outside the United States, the FAQ will include text for Spanish-speaking and French-speaking customers that can eventually be linked to FAQ pages written in those languages. In this Activity, you will add Spanish and French text to the FAQ list.

1 Press Ctrl + End, press Enter, and then type **FAQ: Spanish**

2 Select the text **Spanish**. Click the **Review tab**. In the **Language group**, click **Translate**, and then click **Translate Selected Text**.

3 If a message displays, click **Yes** to open the **Research** pane.

4 In the **Research** pane, verify that *Spanish* displays in the **Search for** box, and that *Translation* displays in the second box.

In the Search for box, you can type a word or phrase that you want to translate.

5 If necessary, under **Translation**, click the **From arrow**, and then click **English (United States)**. Click the **To arrow**, and then click **Spanish (Spain)**. Compare your screen with Figure 7.40.

The translated text—español—displays in the Translation area of the pane.

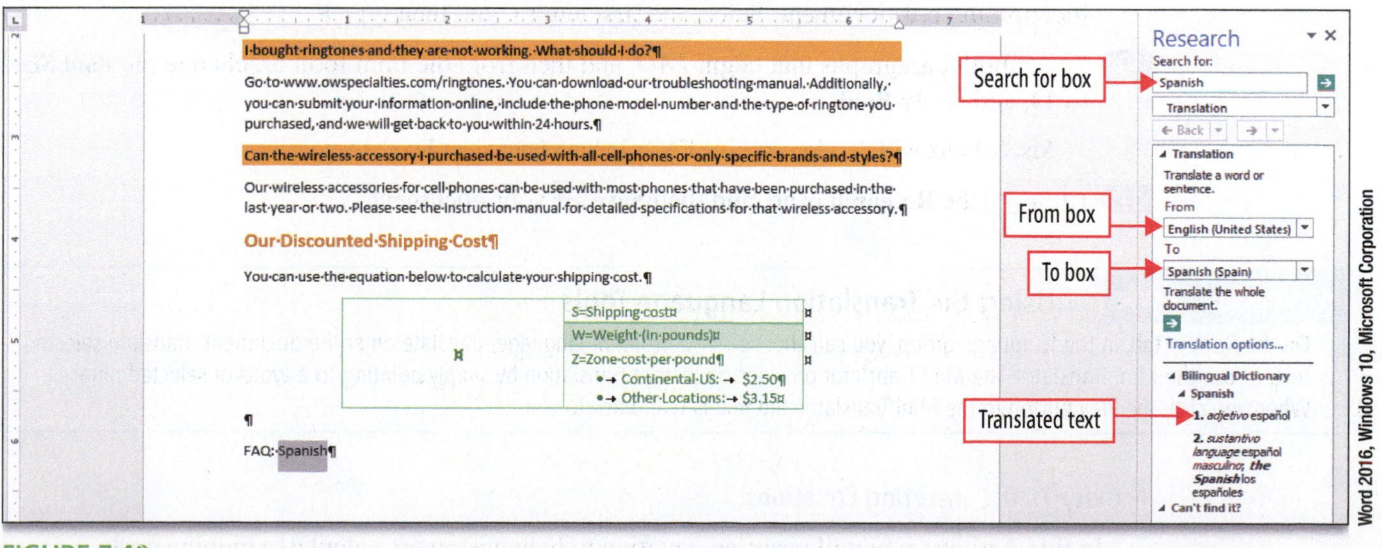

FIGURE 7.40

6 In the lower portion of the **Research** pane, select the translated text **español**, right-click, and then click **Copy**. In your document, right-click the selected text **Spanish**, and then under **Paste Options**, click **Keep Text Only**. In the pasted text, select the first letter **e**, type **E** and then compare your screen with Figure 7.41.

Word uses a machine translation service—not a human being—to translate text, which can result in slight discrepancies in the translated phrases. The main idea is captured, but an accurate translation may differ slightly.

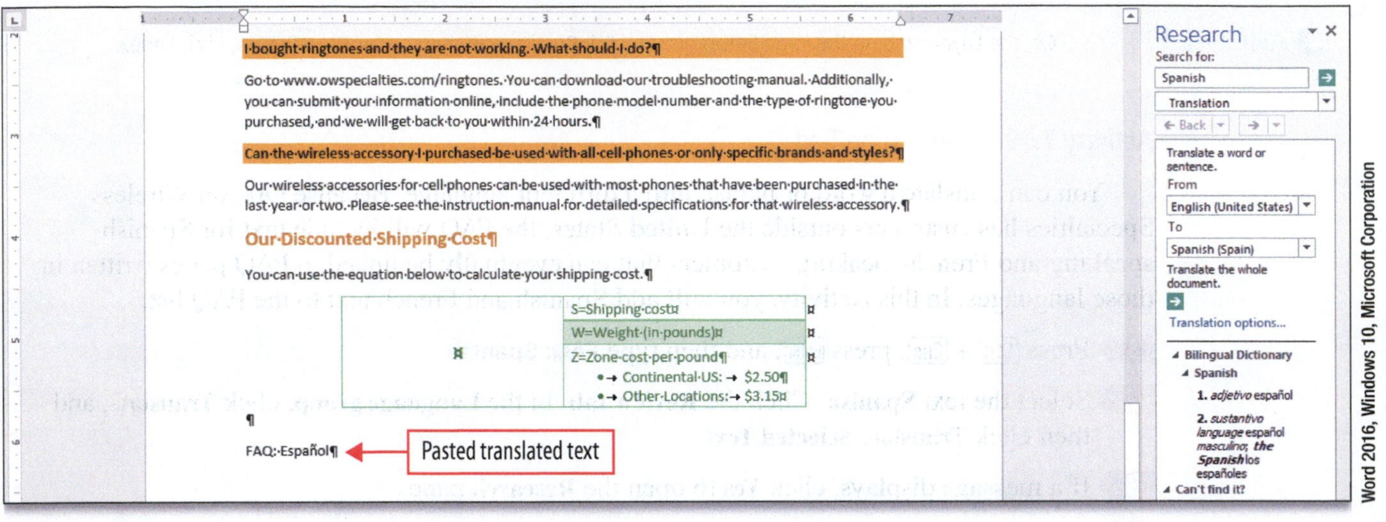

FIGURE 7.41

7 Position the insertion point at the end of the paragraph. Press Enter, type **FAQ: French** and then select the word *French*.

8 In the **Research** pane, in the **Search for** box, type **French** Click the **To arrow**, and then click **French (France)**.

9 Using the technique you just practiced, insert the French text *français* at the insertion point location in your document. Select the first letter **f**, and then type **F**

10 Select both paragraphs that begin *FAQ*, and then from the mini toolbar, change the **Font Size** to **14**, and apply **Bold**.

Ms. Scholtz will develop specific FAQs in both languages here.

11 **Close** the **Research** pane, and then **Save** your document.

> ***More* Knowledge** **Using the Translation Language Tools**
>
> On the Review tab, in the Language group, you can choose the translation language, translate an entire document, translate selected text, or use the Mini Translator. The Mini Translator provides an instant translation by simply pointing to a word or selected phrase. When you click the Play button in the Mini Translator, the text is read back to you.

Activity 7.20 | Inserting Equations

In this Activity, you will insert an equation to help customers calculate shipping costs.

1 In the lower portion of **Page 2**, click in the large left cell of the table. Click the **Insert tab**, and then in the **Symbols group**, click the **Equation arrow**. In the list, take a moment to view the **Built-In** equations, and then at the bottom of the list, click **Insert New Equation**.

An equation placeholder displays in the table cell. On the ribbon, under Equation Tools, the Design tab displays, which includes built-in formulas and components you can modify to meet your needs.

2 With the equation placeholder selected, type **S=** On the ribbon, under **Equation Tools**, on the **Design tab**, in the **Structures group**, click **Fraction**. In the **Fraction** gallery, under **Fraction**, click the first format—**Stacked Fraction**.

A fraction with a top and bottom placeholder displays to the right of the text you just typed.

3 In the fraction, click the top placeholder, and then type **W-1** Click the bottom placeholder, and then type **2** Click to the right of the fraction, type ***Z** and then compare your screen with Figure 7.42.

The ***variables***—letters that represent values—in the equation are described in the second cell of the table. In this equation, the customer will pay a reduced shipping cost based on the weight and destination, and if the weight is one pound or less, the customer pays no shipping cost.

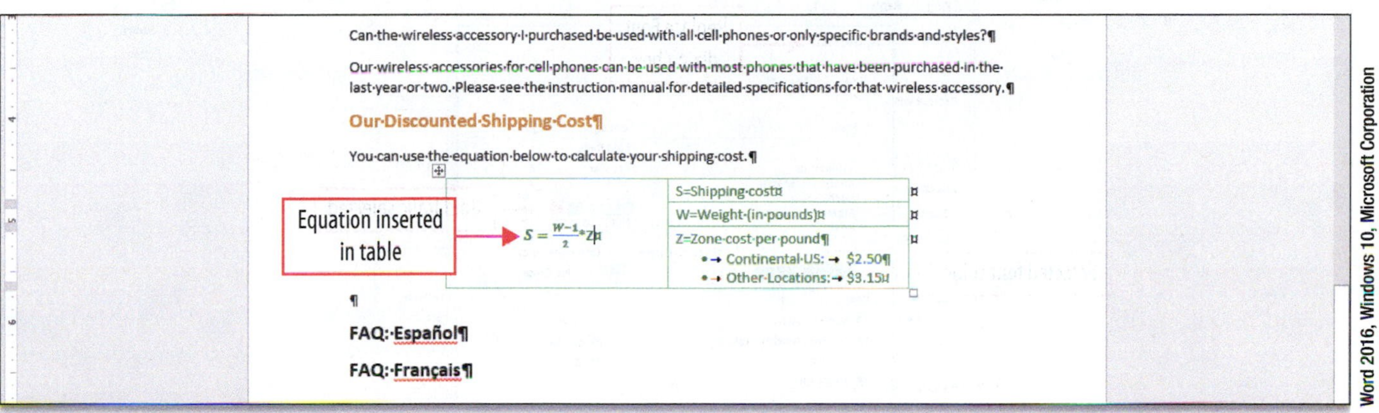

FIGURE 7.42

4 Select the entire equation, and then on the **Home tab**, change the **Font Size** to **14** and if necessary, apply **Bold**. **Save** your document.

Objective 7 Use Advanced Find and Replace Options

GO! Learn How Video W7-7

From the Find and Replace dialog box, you can locate occurrences of words that sound the same although spelled differently, find phrases that are capitalized in exactly the same way, and find different forms of a word—such as *work*, *worked*, and *working*.

Activity 7.21 | Using Find and Replace to Change Text Formatting

1.2.1
2.1.1
2.1.1 Expert

You can change the formatting of a word or phrase that is repeated throughout a document by using the Find and Replace dialog box. In this Activity, you will change the formatting of the company name that appears numerous times in the FAQ list.

1 Press Ctrl + Home. On the **Home tab**, in the **Editing group**, click **Replace** to display the **Find and Replace** dialog box.

2 In the **Find what** box, type **Oregon Wireless Specialties** and then in the **Replace with** box, type the exact same text **Oregon Wireless Specialties**

3 Below the **Replace with** box, click **More** to expand this dialog box.

The More button exposes advanced settings with which you can refine this command. At the bottom of the expanded dialog box, the Format button provides additional options for text, paragraph, tab, and style formats. The Special button provides options for location or replacing special characters.

4 Near the bottom of the **Find and Replace** dialog box, under **Replace**, click **Format**, and then on the list, click **Font**.

5 In the **Replace Font** dialog box, under **Font style**, click **Bold Italic**. Click the **Font color arrow**, and then in the last column, click the fifth color—**Green, Accent 6, Darker 25%**. Compare your screen with Figure 7.43.

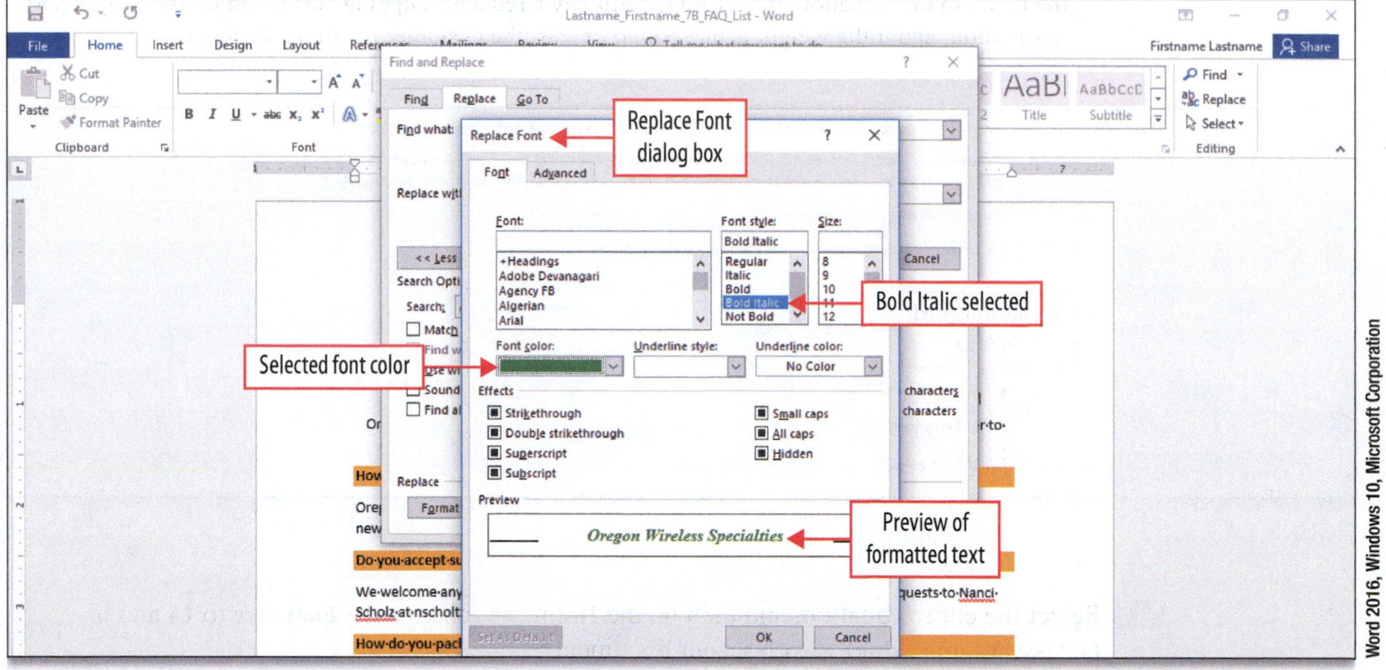

FIGURE 7.43

6 Click **OK** to close the **Replace Font** dialog box, and then in the middle of the **Find and Replace** dialog box, click **Replace All**. When a Microsoft Word message displays indicating that you have made *4* replacements, click **OK**. Leave the expanded dialog box displayed for the next Activity.

This action finds each instance of the text *Oregon Wireless Specialties*, and then replaces the font format with bold italic in the green color that you selected.

Activity 7.22 | Using Wildcards to Find and Replace Text

1.2.1
2.1.1 Expert

Use a ***wildcard*** in the Find and Replace dialog box when you are not certain of the exact term you want to find. A wildcard is a special character such as * or ? that can be inserted with a Find what term. For example, searching a document for the term b*k could find *blink*, *book*, *brick*, or any other word in the document that begins with b and ends with k.

Using a wildcard can save time when you do not know the specific characters in the search term. In this Activity, you will use a wildcard to search for email and webpage addresses that may be spelled incorrectly.

1 In the **Find and Replace** dialog box, in the **Find what** box, delete the existing text, and then type **Sc*z**

2 Press Tab to move to and select the text in the **Replace with** box. Type **Scholtz** and then at the bottom of the **Find and Replace** dialog box, click **No Formatting** to remove the formatting settings from the previous activity.

3 Under **Search Options**, select the **Use wildcards** check box. Compare your screen with Figure 7.44.

The name *Scholtz* may have been spelled incorrectly. By using the Find command to locate each instance that begins with *Sc* and ends with *z*, you can find, and then verify, the correct spelling of her name in every instance.

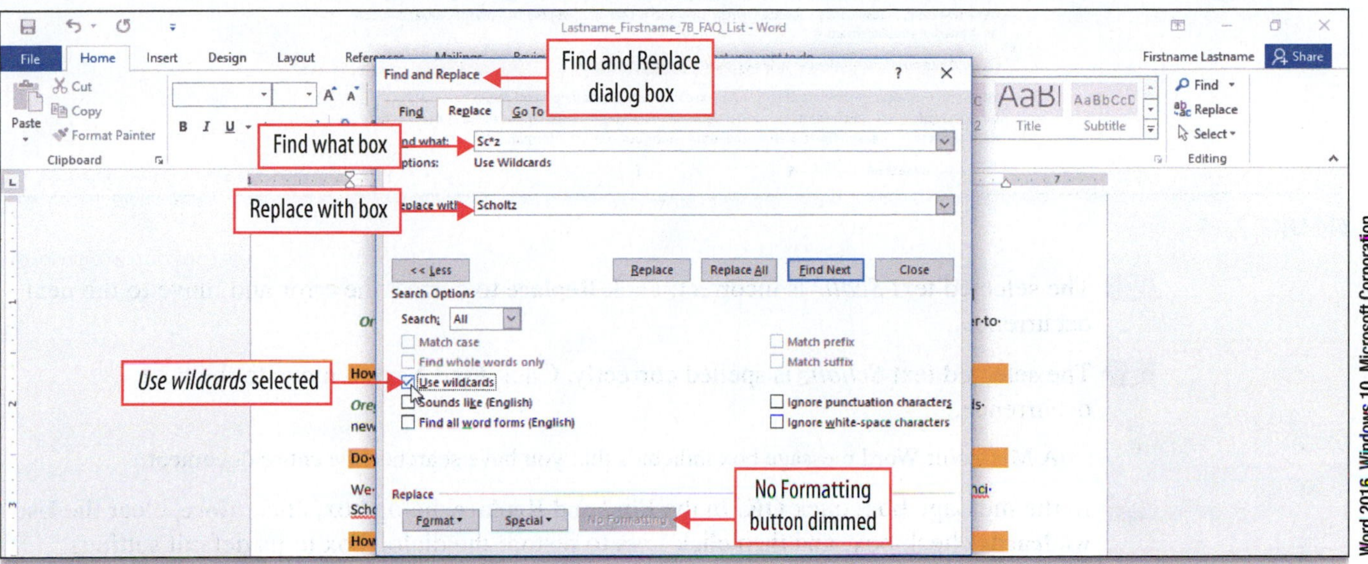

FIGURE 7.44

4 In the **Find and Replace** dialog box, click **Less** so that the dialog box is smaller, and then drag the title bar of the **Find and Replace** dialog box to the upper left corner of your screen so that it is not blocking the document. Click **Find Next**. Notice that the first instance of the text *Scholtz* is selected in the document.

This instance is spelled correctly—no changes are required.

5 In the **Find and Replace** dialog box, click **Find Next** again, and notice that in this occurrence the name is not spelled correctly.

6 Click **Replace**, and then compare your screen with Figure 7.45.

The misspelling is corrected, and Word selects the next occurrence of text that begins with *Sc* and ends with *z*.

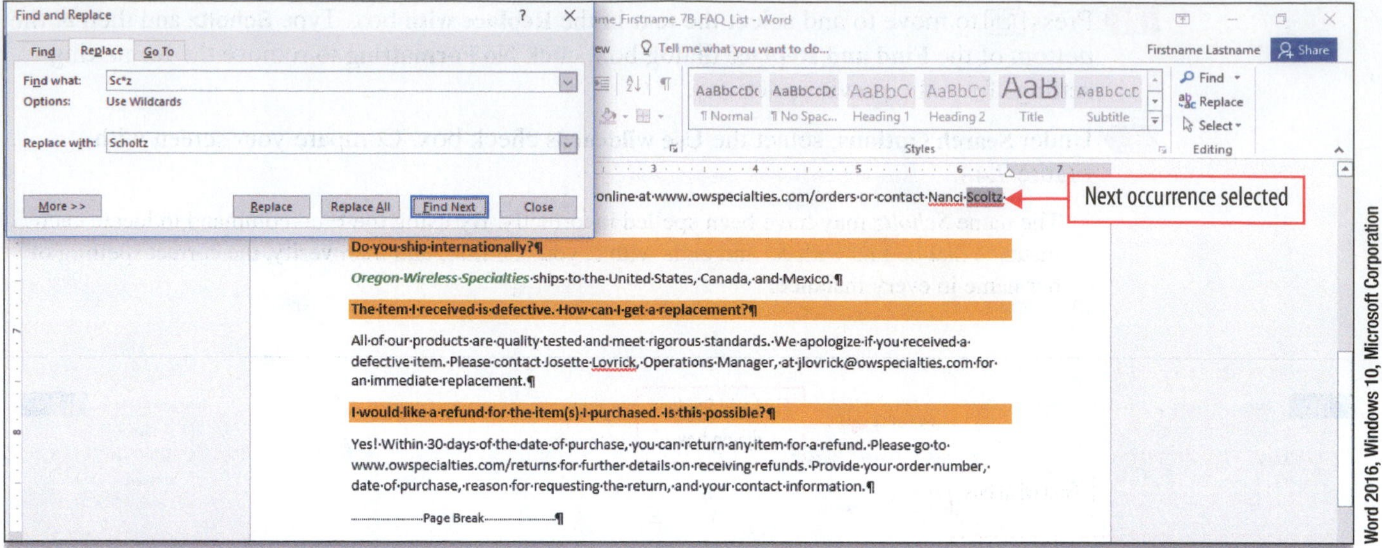

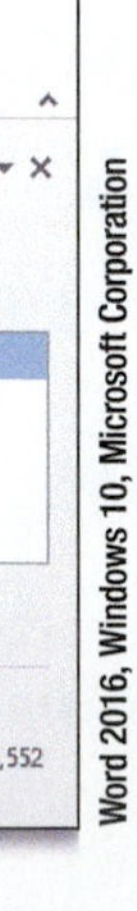

FIGURE 7.45

7 The selected text *Scoltz* is incorrect; click **Replace** to correct the error and move to the next occurrence.

8 The selected text *Scholtz* is spelled correctly. Click **Find Next** to move to the next occurrence.

A Microsoft Word message box indicates that you have searched the entire document.

9 In the message box, click **OK**. In the **Find and Replace** dialog box, click **More**, clear the **Use wildcards** check box, and then click **Less** to restore the dialog box to its default settings. **Close** the **Find and Replace** dialog box, and then **Save** the document.

Activity 7.23 | Checking Spelling and Grammar in the Document

1 Press Ctrl + Home. On the **Review tab**, in the **Proofing group**, click **Spelling & Grammar**. Compare your screen with Figure 7.46.

The Spelling pane displays on the right, indicating the first suggested error—Nanci. It is good practice to position the insertion point at the beginning of the document when checking the entire document for errors in spelling and grammar.

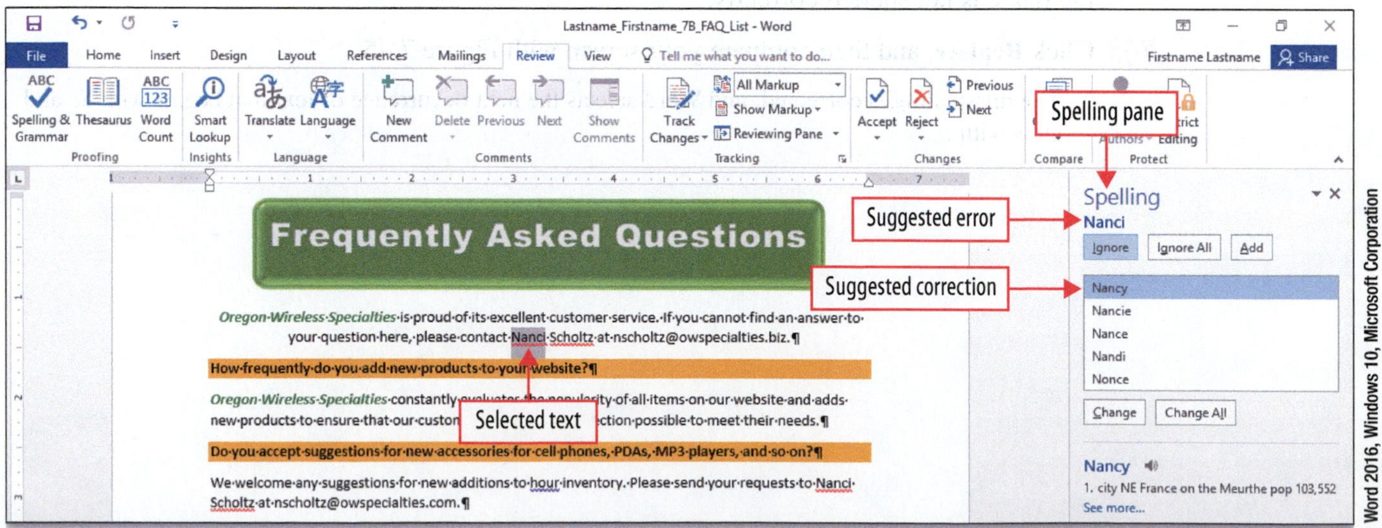

FIGURE 7.46

ALERT! **Spelling and Grammar Selection May Differ**

Flagged errors depend on the Proofing settings in the Word Options dialog box or on the actions of others who might have used the computer at which you are working. Not all of the potential errors listed in this Activity may appear in your spelling and grammar check. Your document may also display errors not indicated here. If you encounter flagged words or phrases that are not included here, take appropriate action.

2 If *Nanci* is indicated as a spelling error, in the **Spelling** pane, click **Ignore All**.

All occurrences of *Nanci* are ignored, and the word *Scholtz* displays with a red underline as a potential spelling error.

3 If *Scholtz* is indicated as a spelling error, click **Ignore All**.

All occurrences of *Scholtz* are ignored, and the next potential error—*hour*—is selected. Because this is a possible contextual error, the pane displays as a *Grammar* pane.

4 In the **Grammar** pane, if *hour* is highlighted, with *our* selected, click **Change**. If *hour* is not identified as an error, correct it by deleting h.

In this case, Word identified *hour* as a word that is spelled correctly but used in the wrong context.

5 Click **Ignore All** as necessary to ignore web addresses and the proper names *Josette* and *Lovrick*.

6 Continue to the end of the document, and click **Ignore** for the foreign words.

A Microsoft Word message box indicates that the spelling and grammar check is complete.

7 Click **OK** to close the message box. Press Ctrl + Home.

8 Click the **File tab**, if necessary, on the left click **Info**, and then click **Show All Properties**. In the **Tags** box, type **faq list** In the **Subject** box, type your course name and section number. If necessary, edit the author name to display your name.

9 On the left, click **Save** to save your document and return to the Word window.

10 If you are completing the next Optional Activity, leave your document open and go to Step 1 of Activity 7.24. If you are not completing the Optional Activity, in the upper right corner of the Word window, click **Close**. If directed by your instructor to do so, submit your paper printout, your electronic image of your document that looks like a printed document, or your original Word file.

Objective 8 Save in Other File Formats

GO! Learn How Video W7-8

If you send a Word document to someone who uses a word processing program other than Microsoft Word, he or she may not be able to read the document. If you expect that your document must be read or edited in another word processing program, save your Word document in ***Rich Text Format***, or ***RTF***. Rich Text Format is a universal document format that can be read by nearly all word processing programs and retains most text and paragraph formatting. Saving a document as an RTF file adds the .rtf extension to the document file name. An RTF file that you might receive can be easily converted to the Word document file format.

ALERT! **This Activity Is Optional**

This Activity is optional. Check with your instructor to see if you should complete this Activity. This Activity is not included in the MyITLab Grader system for this project; however, you may want to practice this on your own to see how to save a document in RTF format.

Activity 7.24 | Saving a Document in RTF Format

1.5.2

When you save a Word document as an RTF file, all but the most complex formatting is translated into a format usable by most word processing programs. Nanci Scholtz is sending the FAQ list to her sales managers for review before saving it as a webpage. In this Activity, you will save the FAQ list as an RTF file to ensure that all the managers can review the document.

1. With your document displayed, click the **File tab**, on the left click **Save As**, click **Browse** to display the **Save As** dialog box, and then navigate to your **Word Chapter 7** folder. In the lower portion of the **Save As** dialog box, click the **Save as type arrow**, and then on the list, click **Rich Text Format**.

2. In the **File name** box, type **Lastname_Firstname_7B_FAQ_RTF** Compare your screen with Figure 7.47.

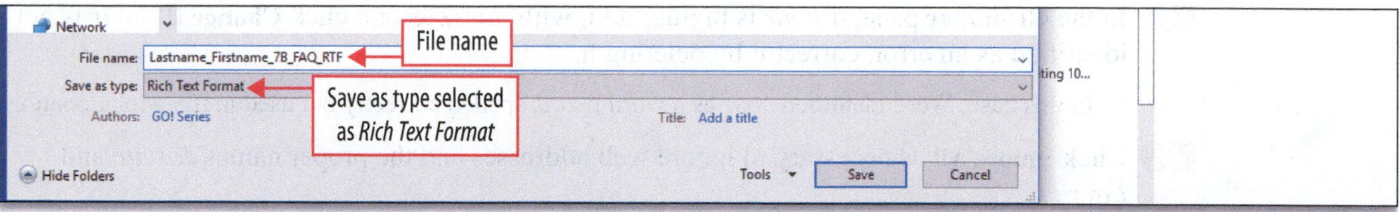

FIGURE 7.47 Word 2016, Windows 10, Microsoft Corporation

3. Click **Save**. Scroll to the bottom of **Page 1**, and then double-click the footer. Right-click the file name, and then from the shortcut menu, click **Update Field** to update the file name and format. **Close** the footer area.

4. Click the **File tab**, if necessary, click **Info**, and then click **Show All Properties**. In the **Tags** box, delete the existing text, type **faq, rtf** and then on the left, click **Save**.

5. **Close** [X] Word; submit this file if directed to do so.

> ***More Knowledge*** **Saving in PDF or XPS Formats**
>
> In Microsoft Word, you can save documents in other formats such as PDF—Portable Document Format—and XPS—XML Paper Specification. Click the File tab, click Export, and then click the Create a PDF/XPS button. In the Publish as PDF or XPS dialog box, click the Save as type arrow, click PDF or XPS Document, and then click Publish.

END | You have completed Project 7B

GO! To Work

Andrew Rodriguez / Fotolia; FotolEdhar / Fotolia; apops / Fotolia; Yuri Arcurs / Fotolia

7 WORD

Microsoft Office Specialist (MOS) Skills in this Chapter	
PROJECT 7A	**PROJECT 7B**
1.2.2 Insert hyperlinks **1.3.6** Format background elements **1.5.2** Save documents in alternative file formats **5.1.1** Insert shapes	**1.2.1** Search for text **1.5.2** Save documents in alternative file formats **2.1.1** Find and replace text **2.1.1** Cut, copy, and paste text **2.1.4** Insert special characters **2.3.2** Insert page, section, or column breaks **1.1.3** Expert: Manage document versions **2.1.1** Expert: Find and replace text by using wildcards and special characters **2.1.2** Expert: Find and replace formatting and styles

GO! FOR JOB SUCCESS

Discussion: Emotional Intelligence

Your instructor may assign this discussion to your class, and then ask you to think about, or discuss with your classmates, these questions:

Emotional intelligence is the awareness of and ability to control one's own emotions and interact with others empathetically in a way that makes them comfortable. People who are emotionally intelligent are both personally and socially competent. Emotional intelligence is critical to success in business because it affects your ability to manage behaviors, navigate social and business situations, and make decisions that yield positive results. The components of emotional intelligence include self-awareness, self-regulation, motivation, empathy, and social skills.

FotolEdhar / Fotolia

Who among your family, friends, teachers, and colleagues do you believe possess all or most of these qualities?

How many of these qualities do you think you demonstrate, and which could you develop further?

What business or political leaders have you heard or read about who demonstrate a quality like empathy but lack qualities like self-control or self-awareness?

END OF CHAPTER

SUMMARY

Documents saved in Web Page format—enhanced with elements such as drop caps, horizontal lines, and hyperlinks—can be viewed in a browser. A Blog post template provides a simple format to create a message.

The AutoRecover feature automatically creates backup versions of the current document, which helps prevent losing unsaved changes. Setting the AutoSave frequency determines how often a document is saved.

The Clipboard, the Research pane, and the Research pane are Word features you use to gather information from a variety of sources—including other documents and websites—using a search engine, such as Bing.

The Find and Replace feature includes advanced options for formatting text and searching for specific text using wildcards. Saving a file in Rich Text Format enables individuals without Word to read the document.

GO! LEARN IT ONLINE

Review the concepts, key terms, and MOS skills in this chapter by completing these online challenges, which you can find at **MyITLab**.

Matching and Multiple Choice: Answer matching and multiple choice questions to test what you learned in this chapter.

Lessons on the GO!: Learn how to use all the new apps and features as they are introduced by Microsoft.

MOS PREP Quiz: Answer questions to review the MOS skills that you practiced in this chapter.

PROJECT GUIDE FOR WORD CHAPTER 7

Your instructor will assign Projects from this list to ensure your learning and assess your knowledge.

PROJECT GUIDE FOR WORD CHAPTER 7			
Project	**Apply Skills from These Chapter Objectives**	**Project Type**	**Project Location**
7A **MyITLab**	Objectives 1–3 from Project 7A	**7A Instructional Project (Grader Project)** A guided review of the skills from Project 7A.	In MyITLab and in text
7B **MyITLab**	Objectives 4–8 from Project 7B	**7B Instructional Project (Grader Project)** A guided review of the skills from Project 7B.	In MyITLab and in text
7C	Objectives 1–3 from Project 7A	**7C Chapter Review (Scorecard Grading)** A guided review of the skills from Project 7A.	In text
7D	Objectives 4–8 from Project 7B	**7D Chapter Review (Scorecard Grading)** A guided review of the skills from Project 7B.	In text
7E **MyITLab**	Objectives 1–3 from Project 7A	**7E Mastery (Grader Project)** **Mastery and Transfer of Learning** A demonstration of your mastery of the skills in Project 7A with extensive decision making.	In MyITLab and in text
7F **MyITLab**	Objectives 4–8 from Project 7B	**7F Mastery (Grader Project)** **Mastery and Transfer of Learning** A demonstration of your mastery of the skills in Project 7B with extensive decision making.	In MyITLab and in text
7G **MyITLab**	Objectives 1–8 from Projects 7A and 7B	**7G Mastery (Grader Project)** **Mastery and Transfer of Learning** A demonstration of your mastery of the skills in Projects 7A and 7B with extensive decision making.	In MyITLab and in text
7H	Combination of Objectives from Projects 7A and 7B	**7H GO! Fix It (Scorecard Grading)** A demonstration of your mastery of the skills in Projects 7A and 7B by creating a correct result from a document that contains errors you must find.	Instructor Resource Center (IRC) and MyITLab
7I	Combination of Objectives from Projects 7A and 7B	**7I GO! Make It (Scorecard Grading)** **Critical Thinking** A demonstration of your mastery of the skills in Projects 7A and 7B by creating a result from a supplied picture.	IRC and MyITLab
7J	Combination of Objectives from Projects 7A and 7B	**7J GO! Solve It (Rubric Grading)** **Critical Thinking** A demonstration of your mastery of the skills in Projects 7A and 7B, your decision-making skills, and your critical thinking skills. A task-specific rubric helps you self-assess your result.	IRC and MyITLab
7K	Combination of Objectives from Projects 7A and 7B	**7K GO! Solve It (Rubric Grading)** **Critical Thinking** A demonstration of your mastery of the skills in Projects 7A and 7B, your decision-making skills, and your critical thinking skills. A task-specific rubric helps you self-assess your result.	In text
7L	Combination of Objectives from Projects 7A and 7B	**7L GO! Think (Rubric Grading)** **Critical Thinking** A demonstration of your understanding of the chapter concepts applied in a manner that you would outside of college. An analytic rubric helps you and your instructor grade the quality of your work by comparing it to the work an expert in the discipline would create.	In text
7M	Combination of Objectives from Projects 7A and 7B	**7M GO! Think (Rubric Grading)** **Critical Thinking** A demonstration of your understanding of the chapter concepts applied in a manner that you would outside of college. An analytic rubric helps you and your instructor grade the quality of your work by comparing it to the work an expert in the discipline would create.	IRC and MyITLab
7N	Combination of Objectives from Projects 7A and 7B	**7N You and GO! (Rubric Grading)** **Critical Thinking** A demonstration of your understanding of the chapter concepts applied in a manner that you would in a personal situation. An analytic rubric helps you and your instructor grade the quality of your work.	IRC and MyITLab

GLOSSARY

GLOSSARY OF CHAPTER KEY TERMS

Ascending The order of text sorted alphabetically from A to Z or numbers sorted from the smallest to the largest.

AutoRecover A feature that helps prevent losing unsaved changes by automatically creating a backup version of the current document.

Blog A website that displays dated entries, short for *Web log*.

Blog post An individual article entered in a blog with a time and date stamp.

Descending The order of text sorted alphabetically from Z to A or numbers sorted from the largest to the smallest.

Drop cap A large capital letter at the beginning of a paragraph that formats text in a visually distinctive manner.

Dropped The position of a drop cap when it is within the text of the paragraph.

Email address link A hyperlink that opens a new message window so that an individual viewing a website can send an email message.

Federal registration symbol The symbol ® that indicates that a patent or trademark is registered with the United States Patent and Trademark Office.

Hyperlinks Text, buttons, pictures, or other objects that, when clicked, access other sections of the active document or another file.

Hypertext Markup Language (HTML) The markup language that communicates color and graphics in a format that all computers can understand.

In margin The position of a drop cap when it is in the left margin of a paragraph.

Multiple Pages A zoom setting that decreases the magnification to display several pages of a document.

Navigation bar A series of text links across the top or bottom of a webpage that, when clicked, will link to another webpage on the same website.

Portable Document Format (PDF) A technology that creates an image that preserves the look of your file but that cannot be easily changed or edited.

Rich Text Format (RTF) A universal file format, using the *.rtf* file extension, that can be read by many word processing programs.

Smart Lookup A feature powered by Bing and that enables you to select text, and then have Bing provide search results that are relevant to the surrounding context of the text.

Sorting The action of ordering data, usually in alphabetical or numeric order.

Text link A hyperlink applied to a selected word or phrase.

Variable In an equation, a letter that represents a value.

Web browser (Browser) Software that interprets HTML files, formats them into webpages, and then displays them.

Web Page format A file type that saves a Word document as an HTML file, with some elements of the webpage saved in a folder, separate from the webpage itself.

Webpage A file coded in HTML that can be viewed on the Internet using a web browser.

Website A group of related webpages published to a specific location on the Internet.

Wildcard A special character such as * or ? that is used to search for an unknown term.

CHAPTER REVIEW

Apply 7A skills from these Objectives:

1. Format a Word Document to Create a Webpage
2. Insert and Modify Hyperlinks in a Word Document
3. Create a Webpage and Blog Post

Skills Review Project 7C Awards Information

In the following Skills Review, you will modify and add hyperlinks to the webpage containing nomination information for the Employee of the Year Award that is given to outstanding individuals at Oregon Wireless Specialties. You will also create a blog post related to the nomination process. Your completed documents will look similar to Figure 7.48, although your text wrapping may vary.

PROJECT FILES

For Project 7C, you will need the following files:

w07C_Awards_Information
w07C_Nomination_Form

You will save your files as:

Lastname_Firstname_7C_Awards_Information
Lastname_Firstname_7C_Nomination_Form
Lastname_Firstname_7C_Awards_Blog

PROJECT RESULTS

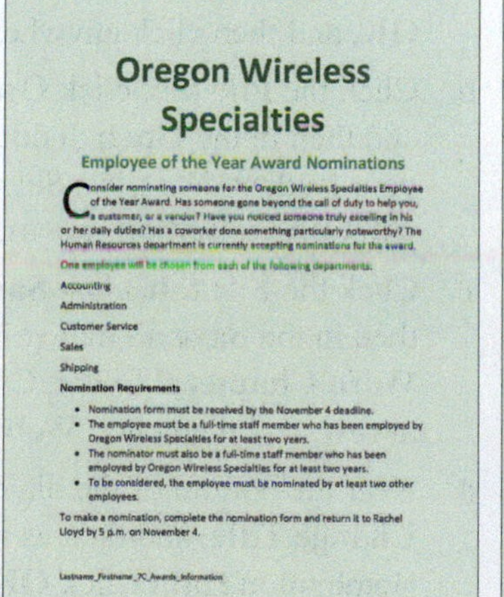
Oregon Wireless Specialties

Employee of the Year Award Nominations

Consider nominating someone for the Oregon Wireless Specialties Employee of the Year Award. Has someone gone beyond the call of duty to help you, a customer, or a vendor? Have you noticed someone truly excelling in his or her daily duties? Has a coworker done something particularly noteworthy? The Human Resources department is currently accepting nominations for the award.

One employee will be chosen from each of the following departments:

Accounting
Administration
Customer Service
Sales
Shipping

Nomination Requirements

- Nomination form must be received by the November 4 deadline.
- The employee must be a full-time staff member who has been employed by Oregon Wireless Specialties for at least two years.
- The nominator must also be a full-time staff member who has been employed by Oregon Wireless Specialties for at least two years.
- To be considered, the employee must be nominated by at least two other employees.

To make a nomination, complete the nomination form and return it to Rachel Lloyd by 5 p.m. on November 4.

Lastname_Firstname_7C_Awards_Information

Nomination Form Contact Rachel Lloyd

Lastname_Firstname_7C_Awards_Information

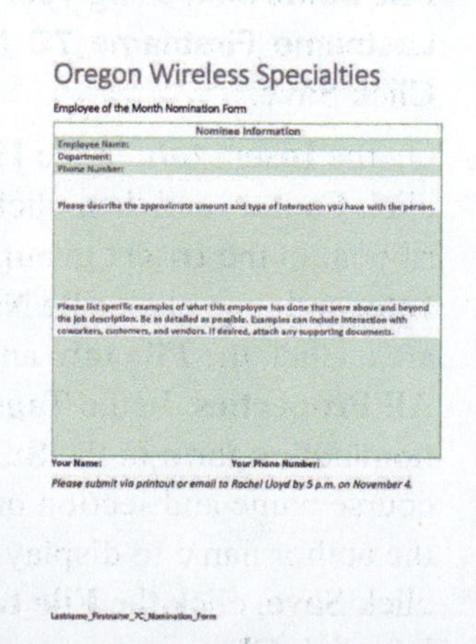
Oregon Wireless Specialties

Employee of the Month Nomination Form

Nominee Information

Employee Name:
Department:
Phone Number:

Please describe the approximate amount and type of interaction you have with the person.

Please list specific examples of what this employee has done that were above and beyond the job description. Be as detailed as possible. Examples can include interaction with coworkers, customers, and vendors. If desired, attach any supporting documents.

Your Name: Your Phone Number:

Please submit via printout or email to Rachel Lloyd by 5 p.m. on November 4.

Lastname_Firstname_7C_Nomination_Form

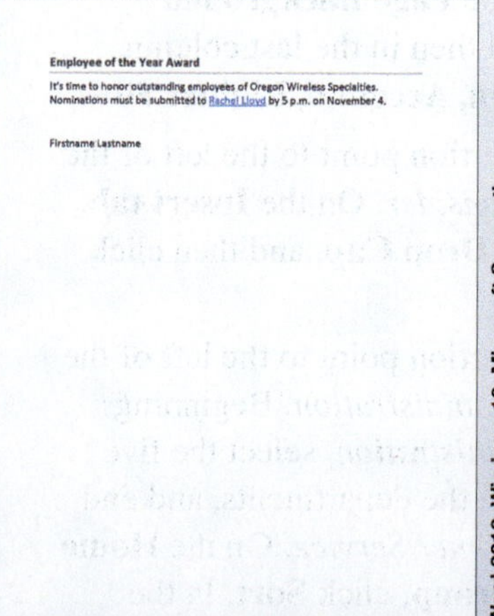
Employee of the Year Award

It's time to honor outstanding employees of Oregon Wireless Specialties. Nominations must be submitted to Rachel Lloyd by 5 p.m. on November 4.

Firstname Lastname

Word 2016, Windows 10, Microsoft Corporation

FIGURE 7.48

(Project 7C Awards Information continues on the next page)

Skills Review Project 7C Awards Information (continued)

1 Start Word, on the left click **Open Other Documents**, click **Browse**, and then in the **Open** dialog box, navigate to the student data files that accompany this chapter. Open the file **w07C_Awards_Information.** Click the **File tab**, click **Save As**, click **Browse**, and then in the **Save As** dialog box, navigate to your **Word Chapter 7** folder. In the lower portion of the dialog box, click the **Save as type arrow**. On the list, click **Web Page**. Near the bottom of the dialog box, click **Change Title**, and then in the **Enter Text** dialog box, in the **Page title** box, type **Awards Information** Click **OK**. In the **File name** box, using your own name, type **Lastname_Firstname_7C_Awards_Information** and then press Enter.

a. On the **Insert tab**, in the **Header & Footer group**, click **Footer**, and then click **Edit Footer**. On the ribbon, in the **Insert group**, click **Document Info**, and then click **File Name**. **Close** the footer area.

b. Select the first paragraph—*Oregon Wireless Specialties*. On the mini toolbar, change the **Font Size** to **48**, apply **Bold**, click the **Font Color arrow**, and then in the last column, click the last color—**Green, Accent 6, Darker 50%**.

c. Select the second paragraph, which begins *Employee*. Change the **Font Size** to **24**, apply **Bold**, click the **Font Color arrow**, and then in the last column, click the fifth color—**Green, Accent 6, Darker 25%**.

d. Select the first and second paragraphs, and then press Ctrl + E. Select the remaining text in the document, and then change the **Font Size** to **14**. Click anywhere to deselect the text.

2 On the **Design tab**, in the **Page Background group**, click **Page Color**, and then in the last column, click the second color—**Green, Accent 6, Lighter 80%**.

a. Click to position the insertion point to the left of the paragraph that begins *Consider*. On the **Insert tab**, in the **Text group**, click **Drop Cap**, and then click **Dropped**.

b. Click to position the insertion point to the left of the paragraph that begins *Administration*. Beginning with the paragraph *Administration*, select the five paragraphs that comprise the departments, and end with the paragraph *Customer Service*. On the **Home tab**, in the **Paragraph group**, click **Sort**. In the **Sort Text** dialog box, click **OK**.

c. Select the paragraph **Nomination Requirements** and apply **Bold**. Click to position the insertion point to the left of the paragraph that begins *Nomination form must be*. Beginning with the paragraph *Nomination form*, select the four paragraphs that comprise the requirements, and end with the paragraph that begins *To be considered*. On the **Home tab**, in the **Paragraph group**, click **Bullets**, and then click anywhere to deselect the text. **Save** your document.

3 In the paragraph that begins *To make a nomination*, click to position the insertion point to the right of the period at the end of the sentence, and then press Enter. On the **Home tab**, in the **Paragraph group**, click the **Borders button arrow**, and then click **Horizontal Line**.

a. Point to the inserted line, right-click, and then click **Picture**. In the **Format Horizontal Line** dialog box, change the **Height** to **6 pt**, and then under **Color**, select the **Use solid color (no shade)** check box. Click **OK**, and then click anywhere to deselect the line.

b. Click the **File tab**, click **Open**, click **Browse**, and then in the **Open** dialog box, navigate to your student data files. Select the file **w07C_Nomination_Form**, and then click **Open**.

c. Click the **File tab**, click **Save As**, click **Browse**, and then in the **Save As** dialog box, navigate to your **Word Chapter 7** folder. Click the **Save as type arrow**, and then click **Web Page**.

d. Near the bottom of the dialog box, click **Change Title**, and then as the **Page title**, type **Nomination Form** Click **OK**, and then in the **File name** box, using your own name, type **Lastname_Firstname_7C_Nomination_Form** Click **Save**.

e. On the **Insert tab**, in the **Header & Footer group**, click **Footer**, and then click **Edit Footer**. On the ribbon, in the **Insert group**, click **Document Info**, and then click **File Name**. **Close** the footer area. Click the **File tab**, and then click **Show All Properties**. In the **Tags** box, type **awards, nomination form** In the **Subject** box, type your course name and section number. If necessary, edit the author name to display your name. On the left, click **Save**, click the **File tab** again, and then on the left click **Close**.

(Project 7C Awards Information continues on the next page)

Skills Review Project 7C Awards Information (continued)

4 With your **Lastname_Firstname_7C_Awards_Information** document displayed, press Ctrl + End. Select the text **Nomination Form**. On the **Insert tab**, in the **Links group**, click **Hyperlink**. In the **Insert Hyperlink** dialog box, under **Link to**, click **Existing File or Web Page**, if necessary.

a. In the **Look in** box, if necessary, navigate to your **Word Chapter 7** folder, in the list below, click your **Lastname_Firstname_7C_Nomination_Form** HTML document, and then click **ScreenTip**. In the **ScreenTip text** box, type **Nomination Form** and then click **OK** two times.

b. Select the text **Rachel Lloyd**, and then display the **Insert Hyperlink** dialog box. Under **Link to**, click **E-mail Address**. In the **E-mail address** box, type **rlloyd@owspecialties.com** As the **ScreenTip text**, type **Human Relations Director** and then click **OK** two times.

c. At the bottom of the webpage, point to *Rachel Lloyd* to display the ScreenTip. Right-click the **Rachel Lloyd** hyperlink, and then click **Edit Hyperlink**. Click **ScreenTip**, and then edit the **ScreenTip text** to indicate **Click here to send an email message** Click **OK** two times, and then point to the **Rachel Lloyd** link to display the ScreenTip.

d. Press Ctrl + Home. Click the **File tab**, and then click **Show All Properties**. In the **Tags** box, type **awards information, webpage** In the **Subject** box, type your course name and section number. If necessary, edit the author name to display your name.

e. On the left, click **Save**, click the **File tab** again, and then on the left click **Close**.

5 Click the **File tab**, and then click **New**. On the right, click the **Blog post** template, and then in the displayed window, click **Create**. In the **Register a Blog Account** dialog box, click **Register Later**.

a. Click the **File tab**, on the left click **Save As**, click **Browse**, and then in the **Save As** dialog box, navigate to your **Word Chapter 7** folder. Using your own name, **Save** the file as **Lastname_Firstname_7C_Awards_Blog**

b. Click anywhere in the **Enter Post Title Here** field to select the placeholder text, and then type **Employee of the Year Award** Click under the line in the body text area, and then type **It's time to honor outstanding employees of Oregon Wireless Specialties. Nominations must be submitted to Rachel Lloyd by 5 p.m. on November 4.**

c. Select all the body text, and then change the **Font Size** to **14**. In the second sentence, select the text **Rachel Lloyd**. Click the **Insert tab**, and then in the **Links group**, click **Hyperlink**. Under **Link to**, click **E-mail Address**, and then in the **E-mail address** box, type **rlloyd@owspecialties.com** Click **OK**.

d. Click to position the insertion point at the end of the paragraph, press Enter two times, and then type your first and last names.

e. Press Ctrl + Home. Click the **File tab**, and then click **Show All Properties**. In the **Tags** box, type **awards nomination, blog** In the **Subject** box, type your course name and section number. If necessary, edit the author name to display your name. On the left click **Save**. On the status bar, change the document view to Print Layout. **Close** Word.

6 Print, or submit electronically, the three files—the blog post and two webpages—as directed by your instructor.

END | You have completed Project 7C

Skills Review Project 7D Outdoor Accessories

Apply 7B skills from these Objectives:

4 Manage Document Versions
5 Collect and Paste Images and Text
6 Locate Supporting Information and Insert Equations
7 Use Advanced Find and Replace Options
8 Save in Other File Formats

In the following Skills Review, you will create a document for Nanci Scholtz, Marketing Vice President of Oregon Wireless Specialties, which details the waterproof and ruggedized accessories sold by the company. Your completed documents will look similar to Figure 7.49.

PROJECT FILES

For Project 7D, you will need the following files:

w07D_Outdoor_Accessories
w07D_Product_Info
w07D_Product_Images

You will save your files as:

Lastname_Firstname_7D_Outdoor_Accessories
Lastname_Firstname_7D_Accessories_RTF (optional to submit)

PROJECT RESULTS

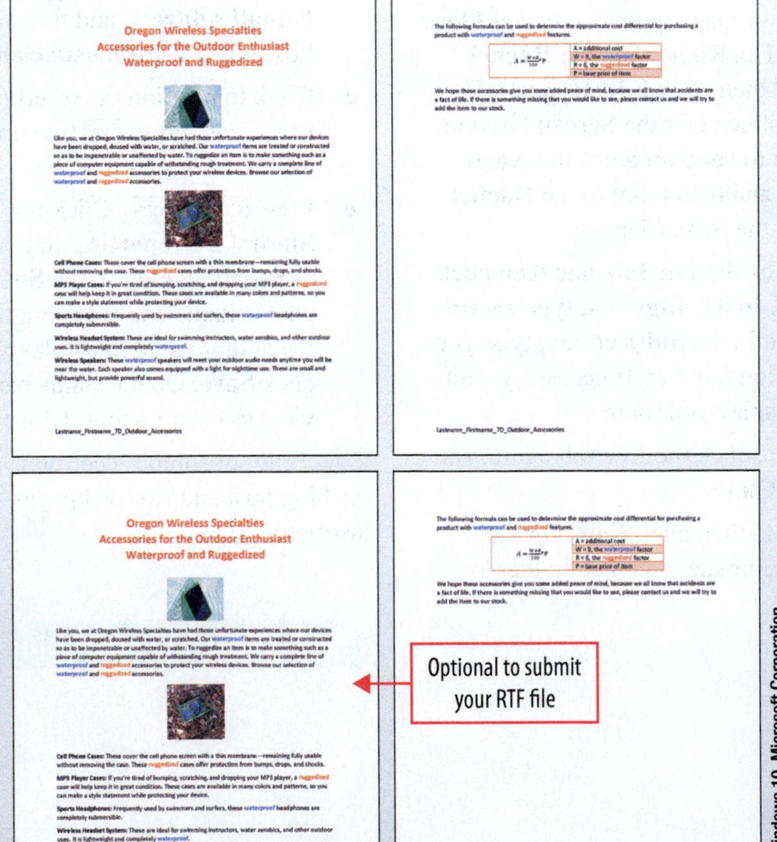

FIGURE 7.49

(Project 7D Outdoor Accessories continues on the next page)

Skills Review Project 7D Outdoor Accessories (continued)

1 Start Word, on the left click **Open Other Documents**, click **Browse**, and then in the **Open** dialog box, navigate to the student data files that accompany this chapter. Open the file **w07D_Outdoor_Accessories**. Click the **File tab**, click **Save As**, click **Browse**, navigate to your **Word Chapter 7** folder, and then using your own name, save the document as **Lastname_Firstname_7D_Outdoor_Accessories**

- **a.** Right-click in the footer area, and then click **Edit Footer**. On the ribbon, in the **Insert group**, click **Document Info**, and then click **File Name**. **Close** the footer area.
- **b.** Click the **View tab**. In the **Zoom group**, click **Zoom**. In the **Zoom** dialog box, under **Zoom to**, click **200%**, and then click **OK**. In the first row of the table, click to position the insertion point to the left of *cost*, and then press Backspace one time to remove the extra space. On the **View tab**, in the **Zoom group**, click **100%**.
- **c.** Select the first three paragraphs. On the mini toolbar, change the **Font Size** to **20**, apply **Bold**, click the **Font Color arrow**, and then in the sixth column, click the fifth color—**Orange, Accent 2, Darker 25%**. Press Ctrl + E to center the three paragraphs.
- **d.** Click the **Home tab**, and then in the **Clipboard group**, click the **Dialog Box Launcher** to display the **Clipboard** pane. If necessary, at the top of the pane, click **Clear All** to delete anything on the Clipboard.
- **e.** From your student files, open **w07D_Product_Images**. If necessary, display the **Clipboard** pane. Point to the first graphic—a cell phone in water—right-click, and then click **Copy**. Using the same technique, **Copy** the second graphic—a cell phone on the ground. **Close** the **w07D_Product_Images** file.
- **f.** From your student files, open **w07D_Product_Info**. Press Ctrl + A to select all of the text, right-click the selected text, click **Copy**, and then **Close** the **w07D_Product_Info** file.

2 Above the paragraph that begins *Like you*, position the insertion point in the blank paragraph. In the **Clipboard** pane, click the **water** graphic, which is the item at the bottom of the Clipboard, and then press Ctrl + E.

- **a.** Click to position the insertion point at the end of the paragraph that begins *Like you*, and then press Enter. In the **Clipboard** pane, click the **ground** graphic, which is the second item on the Clipboard, and then press Ctrl + E.
- **b.** Click to position the insertion point to the left of the paragraph that begins *The following formula*. In the **Clipboard** pane, click the text entry that begins *Cell Phone Cases* to paste the entire block of text at the insertion point. In the **Clipboard** pane, click **Clear All**, and then **Close** the **Clipboard** pane.
- **c.** In the paragraph that begins *Cell Phone Cases*, click to position the insertion point to the right of *membrane*. Click the **Insert tab**. In the **Symbols group**, click **Symbol**, and then click **More Symbols**. In the **Symbol** dialog box, click the **Special Characters tab**, and then click the first character—**Em Dash**. Click **Insert**, and then **Close** the **Symbol** dialog box. Type **remaining** and then **Save** the document.

3 In the paragraph that begins *Like you*, position the insertion point at the end of the first sentence—following the period after *scratched*. Press Spacebar, and then type **Our waterproof items are** Press and hold Alt and then press the left mouse button.

- **a.** In the **Research** pane, in the **Search for** box, delete any existing text, and then type **waterproof** In the second box, click the **arrow**. From the list, click **Encarta Dictionary: English (North America)**. Under **Encarta Dictionary**, locate the text *impervious to water*. Indented and immediately below the definition, select the text that begins *treated or constructed* and ends with *by water*. Right-click the selection, and then on the shortcut menu click **Copy**.
- **b.** Click in your document at the point you stopped typing—after *are*, right-click, and then from the shortcut menu, under **Paste Options**, click **Keep Text Only** to insert the copied text in the document. Type a period after the added text, and then press Spacebar. Type **To ruggedize an item is**
- **c.** In the **Research** pane, in the **Search for** box, replace *waterproof* with **ruggedize** and then press Enter. Under **Encarta Dictionary**,

(Project 7D Outdoor Accessories continues on the next page)

Skills Review Project 7D Outdoor Accessories (continued)

locate and then select the entire definition that begins *to make something* and ends with *rough treatment*. Right-click the selection, and then click **Copy**.

d. Click in the document at the point you stopped typing, right-click, and then under **Paste Options**, click **Keep Text Only**. Type a period after the added text. **Close** the **Research** pane.

e. Near the bottom of **Page 1**, click to the left of the paragraph that begins *The following formula*, and then press Ctrl + Enter. On **Page 2**, click in the first cell of the table, and then on the **Insert tab**, in the **Symbols group**, click **Equation**. In the inserted equation placeholder, type **A=** Under **Equation Tools**, on the **Design tab**, in the **Structures group**, click **Fraction**, and then click the first format—**Stacked Fraction**.

f. In the fraction, click in the top placeholder, and then type **W+R** Click in the bottom placeholder, and then type **100** Click to the right of the fraction, and then type ***P** **Save** your document.

4 Press Ctrl + Home. Click the **Home tab**, and then in the **Editing group**, click **Replace**. In the **Find and Replace** dialog box, in the **Find what** box, type **waterproof** and then in the **Replace with** box, type the same text **waterproof**

a. Below the **Replace with** box, click **More**. Under **Search Options**, select the **Match case** check box. At the bottom, under **Replace**, click **Format**, and then on the list, click **Font**.

b. In the **Replace Font** dialog box, under **Font style**, click **Bold**. Click the **Font color arrow**, and then in the ninth column, click the first color—**Blue, Accent 5**.

c. Click **OK** to close the **Replace Font** dialog box, and then in the **Find and Replace** dialog box, click **Replace All**. When a **Microsoft Word** message box displays indicating that you have made 8 replacements, click **OK**.

d. **Close** the dialog box, press Ctrl + Home, and then redisplay the **Replace** dialog box. Using the same technique, replace all instances of *ruggedized* and select **Match case**. For the replaced text, change the **Font style** to **Bold** and change the **Font color** to **Orange, Accent 2**—in the sixth column, the first color. When a **Microsoft Word** message box displays indicating that you have made 6 replacements, click **OK**.

e. In the **Find and Replace** dialog box, **Delete** the text in the **Find what** box, and then clear the **Match case** check box. **Delete** the text in the **Replace with** box, click **No Formatting**, and then click **Less**. **Close** the **Find and Replace** dialog box.

5 Press Ctrl + Home. Click the **Review tab**, and then in the **Proofing group**, click **Spelling & Grammar**.

a. For any grammar errors, select the suggestion if necessary, and then click **Change**. Click **Ignore Once** for any other errors. When a message indicates that the spelling and grammar check is complete, click **OK** to close the dialog box. Note: If Word does not identify *their* as a grammar error, change the word to *there*.

b. Click the **File tab**, and then click **Show All Properties**. In the **Tags** box, type **waterproof, ruggedized** In the **Subject** box, type your course name and section number. If necessary, edit the author name to display your name. On the left, click **Save**.

c. Click the **File tab**, and then click **Save As**. Click **Browse**, if necessary navigate to your **Word Chapter 7** folder. In the lower portion of the **Save As** dialog box, click the **Save as type arrow**, and then from the list, click **Rich Text Format**. In the **File name** box, type **Lastname_Firstname_7D_Accessories_RTF** and then click **Save**.

d. Scroll to the bottom of the document, and then double-click in the footer area. Right-click the file name, and then on the shortcut menu, click **Update Field**. **Close** the footer area.

e. Click the **File tab**, if necessary, click **Show All Properties**. In the **Tags** box, position the insertion point to the right of the existing text. Type **,rtf** and then on the left, click **Save**.

6 Print or submit electronically the two files—the Word document and the RTF file—as directed by your instructor. **Close** Word.

END | You have completed Project 7D

CONTENT-BASED ASSESSMENTS (MASTERY AND TRANSFER OF LEARNING)

Mastering Word Project 7E Accessories

Apply 7A skills from these Objectives:

1. Format a Word Document to Create a Webpage
2. Insert and Modify Hyperlinks in a Word Document
3. Create a Webpage and Blog Post

In the following Mastering Word project, you will create a webpage for Nanci Scholtz, Marketing Vice President of Oregon Wireless Specialties, which describes the types of cell phone accessories available for purchase. You will also create a blog post announcing savings on purchases. Your completed documents will look similar to Figure 7.50, although text wrapping may vary.

PROJECT FILES

For Project 7E, you will need the following file:

w07E_Accessories

You will save your file as:

Lastname_Firstname_7E_Accessories

PROJECT RESULTS

Oregon Wireless Specialties

Cell Phone Accessories

Are you looking for a particular cell phone accessory? Oregon Wireless Specialties offers an extensive selection of items in our retail stores and online. Take your time and browse through our collection of high-quality products that will enhance the use of your phone.

All of our accessories come with a one-year warranty. We also offer price matching—if you find an accessory for a lower price elsewhere, we will match the price.

Shop for items by clicking the type of accessory in which you are interested. We also offer an option to search by phone brand or service provider.

- Antennas
- Batteries
- Belt Clips and Holsters
- Bluetooth/Hands Free
- Car Kits
- Cases and Pouches
- Chargers
- Data Cables
- Faceplates and Covers
- Headsets
- Memory Cards
- Phone Holders

Please contact our customer service department with any questions. We're happy to help you find the best accessories for your needs. Sign up for our newsletter to receive a coupon for 15% off your next order.

Lastname_Firstname_7E_Accessories

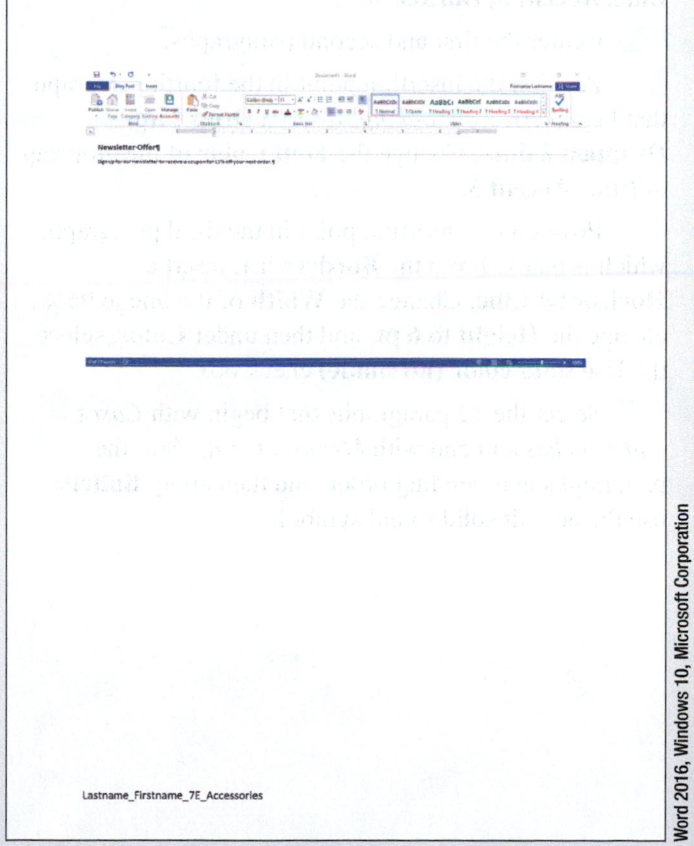

Newsletter Offer¶

Sign up for our newsletter to receive a coupon for 15% off your next order.¶

Lastname_Firstname_7E_Accessories

Word 2016, Windows 10, Microsoft Corporation

FIGURE 7.50

(Project 7E Accessories continues on the next page)

Mastering Word Project 7E Accessories (continued)

1 Start Word, on the left click **Open Other Documents**, click **Browse**, and then in the **Open** dialog box, navigate to the student data files that accompany this chapter. Open the document **w07E_Accessories**. Click the **File tab**, on the left click **Save As**, click **Browse**, and then in the **Save As** dialog box, navigate to your **Word Chapter 7** folder.

2 Using your own name, save the file as **Lastname_Firstname_7E_Accessories** Insert the file name in the footer.

3 Select the first paragraph *Oregon Wireless Specialties*. Change the **Font Size** to **28**, apply **Bold**, and then change the **Font Color** to **Blue, Accent 5**.

4 Select the second paragraph. Change the **Font Size** to **20**, apply **Bold**, and then change the **Font Color** to **Blue, Accent 5, Darker 50%**.

5 Center the first and second paragraphs.

6 Position the insertion point in the fourth paragraph that begins *Are you looking*. Insert a **Drop Cap, Dropped 2 lines**. Change the **Font Color** of the drop cap to **Blue, Accent 5**.

7 Position the insertion point in the third paragraph, which is blank. From the **Borders** list, insert a **Horizontal Line**. Change the **Width** of the line to **95%**, change the **Height** to **6 pt**, and then under **Color**, select the **Use solid color (no shade)** check box.

8 Select the 12 paragraphs that begin with *Cases and Pouches* and end with *Memory Cards*. Sort the paragraphs in ascending order, and then apply **Bullets**; use the default solid round symbol.

9 In the bulleted list, select the text **Cases and Pouches**. Insert a hyperlink to an existing file, and type **Phone_Cases** in the **Address** box. As the **ScreenTip** text, type **Cases**

10 In the last paragraph of the document, select the text **customer service department**. Insert a hyperlink to the email address **service@owspecialties.biz** As the **ScreenTip** text, type **Contact** Select the text **Sign up**, and then insert a hyperlink to the email address **newsletter@owspecialties.biz** As the **ScreenTip** text, type **Newsletter**

11 **Save**, but do not close, the current document. Create a new **Blog post**, and then click **Register Later**. In the title placeholder, type **Newsletter Offer** In the body text area, type **Sign up for our newsletter to receive a coupon for 15% off your next order.**

From the taskbar, redisplay your **Lastname_Firstname_7E_Accessories** document. Press Ctrl + End, and then press Ctrl + Enter to create a new page.

12 On the **Insert tab**, in the **Illustrations group**, click **Screenshot**, and then click the screen image of your blog post.

13 Press Ctrl + Home. On the **Quick Access Toolbar**, click **Save**. Click the **File tab**, and then click **Close**. Close Word without saving the blog post. If directed by your instructor to do so, submit your paper printout, your electronic image of your document that looks like a printed document, or your original Word file.

END | You have completed Project 7E

CONTENT-BASED ASSESSMENTS (MASTERY AND TRANSFER OF LEARNING)

Mastering Word Project 7F Sale Flyer

Apply 7B skills from these Objectives:

4 Manage Document Versions
5 Collect and Paste Images and Text
6 Locate Supporting Information and Insert Equations
7 Use Advanced Find and Replace Options
8 Save in Other File Formats

In the following Mastering Word project, you will create an RTF document for Nanci Scholtz, Marketing Vice President of Oregon Wireless Specialties, which announces an upcoming sale. Your completed document will look similar to Figure 7.51.

PROJECT FILES

For Project 7F, you will need the following files:

w07F_Sale_Flyer
w07F_Sale_List

You will save your file as:

Lastname_Firstname_7F_Sale_Flyer

PROJECT RESULTS

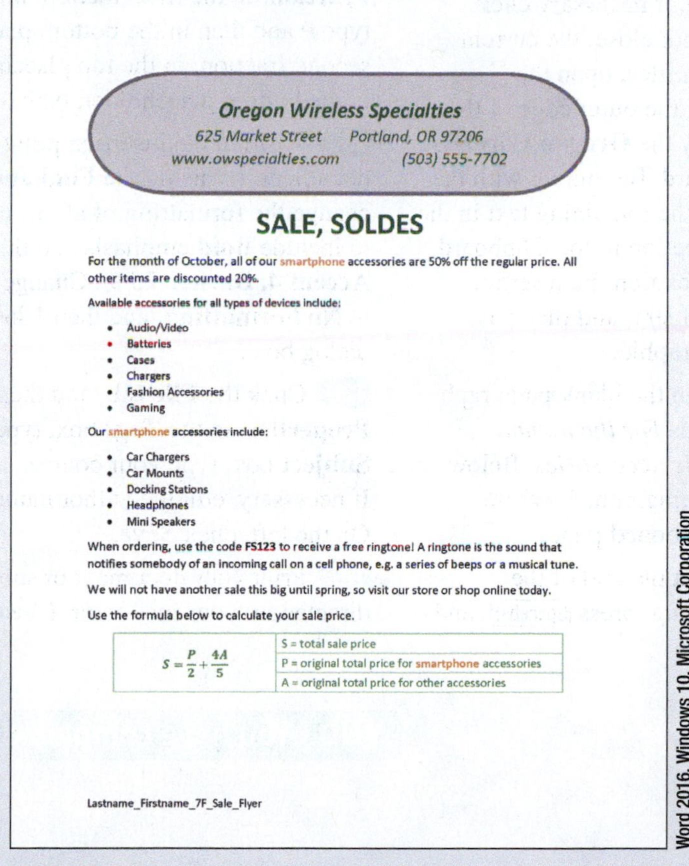

Oregon Wireless Specialties
625 Market Street Portland, OR 97206
www.owspecialties.com (503) 555-7702

SALE, SOLDES

For the month of October, all of our smartphone accessories are 50% off the regular price. All other items are discounted 20%.

Available accessories for all types of devices include:

- Audio/Video
- Batteries
- Cases
- Chargers
- Fashion Accessories
- Gaming

Our smartphone accessories include:

- Car Chargers
- Car Mounts
- Docking Stations
- Headphones
- Mini Speakers

When ordering, use the code FS123 to receive a free ringtone! A ringtone is the sound that notifies somebody of an incoming call on a cell phone, e.g. a series of beeps or a musical tune.

We will not have another sale this big until spring, so visit our store or shop online today.

Use the formula below to calculate your sale price.

$S = \frac{P}{2} + \frac{4A}{5}$	S = total sale price
	P = original total price for smartphone accessories
	A = original total price for other accessories

Lastname_Firstname_7F_Sale_Flyer

Word 2016, Windows 10, Microsoft Corporation

FIGURE 7.51

(Project 7F Sale Flyer continues on the next page)

Mastering Word Project 7F Sale Flyer (continued)

1 Start Word, on the left click **Open Other Documents**, click **Browse**, and then in the **Open** dialog box, navigate to the student data files that accompany this chapter. Open the document **w07F_Sale_Flyer**. Click the **File tab**, on the left click **Save As**, click **Browse**, and then in the **Save As** dialog box, navigate to your **Word Chapter 7** folder.

2 Using your own name, save the file as **Lastname_Firstname_7F_Sale_Flyer** and then insert the file name in the footer.

3 Using **Zoom** as necessary, in the table cell that contains the text *S = total sale price*, position the insertion point to the left of the equal sign, and then delete the extra space.

4 Display the **Clipboard** pane, if necessary click **Clear All**, and then **Save**, but do not close, the current document. From your student data files, open the document **w07F_Sale_List**. Click the outer edge of the graphic to select it; and then **Copy** the **Oregon Wireless Specialties** graphic to the Clipboard. Beginning with the text *Available accessories*, select the remaining text in the document, and then **Copy** the selection to the Clipboard. **Close** the **w07F_Sale_List** file. Position the insertion point at the beginning of the document, and then paste the Oregon Wireless Specialties graphic.

5 Position the insertion point in the blank paragraph following the paragraph that begins *For the month*. **Paste** the text that begins *Available accessories*. Below the pasted text, delete the blank paragraph. Clear the Clipboard, and then close the **Clipboard** pane.

6 Position the insertion point at the end of the paragraph that begins *When ordering*, press Spacebar, and then type **A ringtone is**

7 Display the **Research** pane, in the **Search for** box, type **ringtone** Use **Encarta Dictionary** to search for the definition. In the **Research** pane, select and copy the text that begins *the sound that notifies*, and ends with *a musical tune*. Position the insertion point to the right of *A ringtone is*, and then paste the text in the document. Type a period.

8 At the top of the document, select the text **SALE**. Translate the selected text to **French (France)**. Following the word *SALE*, type a comma and a space and then type the French word **SOLDES**

9 In the first cell of the table, insert an **Equation** placeholder. In the placeholder, type **S=** Insert a **Stacked Fraction**, type **+–** and then insert a second **Stacked Fraction**. In the first fraction, in the top placeholder, type **P** and then in the bottom placeholder, type **2** In the second fraction, in the top placeholder, type **4A** and then in the bottom placeholder, type **5**

10 Position the insertion point at the beginning of the document. By using the **Find and Replace** dialog box, change the formatting of all occurrences of **smartphone** to include **Bold** emphasis and the font color **Gold, Accent 4, Darker 25%**. Change the **Replace with** box to **No Formatting**, and then **Close** the **Find and Replace** dialog box.

11 Click the **File tab**, and then click **Show All Properties**. In the **Tags** box, type **sale flyer** In the **Subject** box, type your course name and section number. If necessary, edit the author name to display your name. On the left, click **Save**.

12 Print your document or submit electronically as directed by your instructor. **Close** Word.

END | You have completed Project 7F

CONTENT-BASED ASSESSMENTS (MASTERY AND TRANSFER OF LEARNING)

Apply 7A and 7B skills from these Objectives:

1. Format a Word Document to Create a Webpage
2. Insert and Modify Hyperlinks in a Word Document
3. Create a Webpage and Blog Post
4. Manage Document Versions
5. Collect and Paste Images and Text
6. Locate Supporting Information and Insert Equations
7. Use Advanced Find and Replace Options
8. Save in Other File Formats

Mastering Word Project 7G Returns Policy

In the following Mastering Word project, you will create a webpage and blog post for Josette Lovrick, Operations Manager of Oregon Wireless Specialties, which explains the return and exchange policy for the company. Your completed documents will look similar to Figure 7.52.

PROJECT FILES

For Project 7G, you will need the following files:

w07G_Returns_Policy

w07G_Returns_Image

w07G_Shipping_Policy

You will save your file as:

Lastname_Firstname_7G_Returns_Policy

PROJECT RESULTS

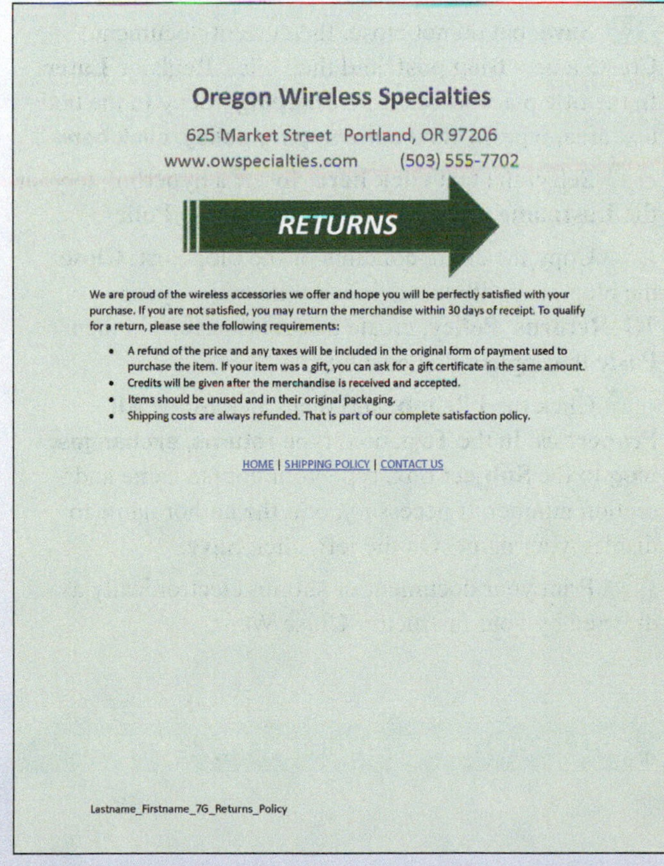

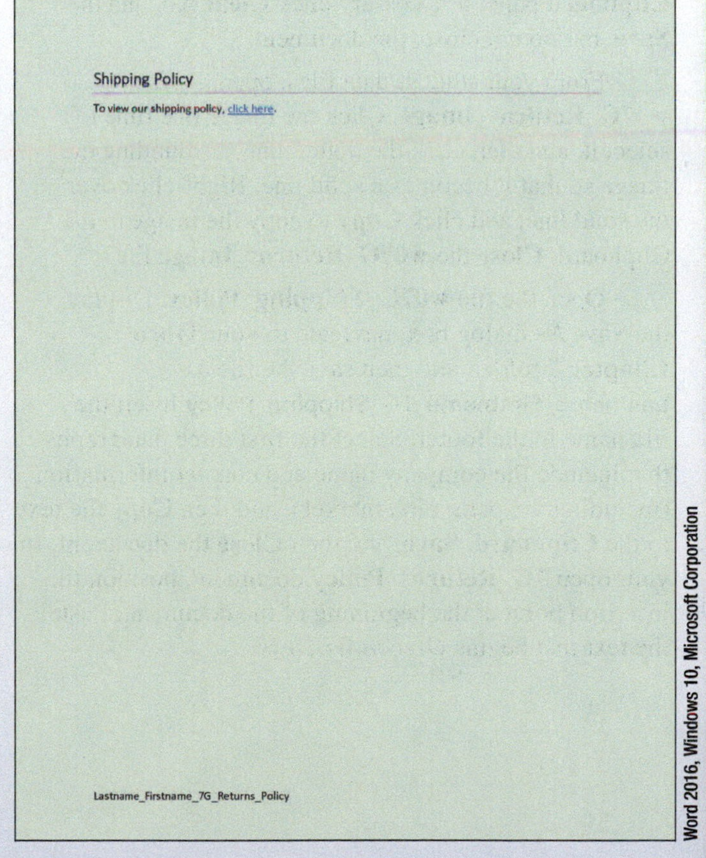

FIGURE 7.52

Word 2016, Windows 10, Microsoft Corporation

(Project 7G Returns Policy continues on the next page)

Mastering Word Project 7G Returns Policy (continued)

1 Start Word, on the left click **Open Other Documents**, click **Browse**, and then in the **Open** dialog box, navigate to the student data files that accompany this chapter. Open the document **w07G_Returns_Policy**. Click the **File tab**, on the left click **Save As**, click **Browse**, and then in the **Save As** dialog box, navigate to your **Word Chapter 7** folder.

2 Using your own name, save the file as **Lastname_Firstname_7G_Returns_Policy** and then insert the file name in the footer.

3 By using the **Zoom** feature to view the text, in the first paragraph, to the left of **30**, delete the second space.

4 Change the **Page Color** to **Green, Accent 6, Lighter 80%**.

5 Position the insertion point to the left of the paragraph that begins *Items*. Select the next four paragraphs that list the requirements for a return. Sort the paragraphs in ascending order, and then apply **Bullets** using the default solid round symbol. Display the **Clipboard** pane, if necessary click **Clear All**, and then **Save**, but do not close, the document.

6 From your student data files, open the file **w07G_Returns_Image**. Click the image one time to select it, and then click the dotted line surrounding the image so that it becomes a solid line. Right-click over the solid line, and click **Copy** to copy the image to the Clipboard. **Close** the **w07G_Returns_Image** file.

7 Open the file **w07G_Shipping_Policy**. Display the **Save As** dialog box, navigate to your **Word Chapter 7** folder, and then save the file as **Lastname_Firstname_7G_Shipping_Policy** Insert the file name in the footer. Select the first three paragraphs that include the company name and contact information (including the paragraph marker), and then **Copy** the text to the **Clipboard**. **Save**, and then **Close** the document. In your open **7G_Returns_Policy** document, position the insertion point at the beginning of the document. Paste the text that begins *Oregon Wireless*.

8 Above the paragraph that begins *We are proud*, position the insertion point in the blank paragraph. Paste the image, and then center the image horizontally on the page. **Close** the **Clipboard** pane.

9 At the bottom of the document, select **HOME**, and then insert a hyperlink to an **Existing File or Web Page** using the address **www.owspecialties.biz**

10 In the same paragraph, select the text **SHIPPING POLICY**, and then insert a hyperlink to your file that you saved **Lastname_Firstname_7G_Shipping_Policy**.

11 In the same paragraph, select the text **CONTACT US**, and then insert a hyperlink to the email address **service@owspecialties.biz**

12 In the second bulleted paragraph that begins *Credits*, replace the text *approved* with the synonym *accepted*.

13 Move to the top of your document. Display the **Grammar** pane, and then accept the corrected changes for *sea, there,* and *hour*.

14 **Save**, but do not close, the current document. Create a new **Blog post**, and then click **Register Later**. In the title placeholder, type **Shipping Policy** In the body text area, type **To view our shipping policy, click here.**

15 Select the text **click here**. Insert a hyperlink to your file **Lastname_Firstname_7G_Shipping_Policy**.

16 Copy the entire contents of the blog post. **Close** the blog post without saving. At the end of your **7G_Returns_Policy**, create a second page, and then **Paste** the copied blog post text.

17 Click the **File tab**, and then click **Show All Properties**. In the **Tags** box, type **returns, exchanges, blog** In the **Subject** box, type your course name and section number. If necessary, edit the author name to display your name. On the left, click **Save**.

18 Print your document or submit electronically as directed by your instructor. **Close** Word.

END | You have completed Project 7G

CONTENT-BASED ASSESSMENTS (CRITICAL THINKING)

Apply a combination of the 7A and 7B skills.

GO! Fix It Project 7H Company Overview MyITLab

GO! Make It Project 7I Screen Protectors MyITLab

GO! Solve It Project 7J Wholesalers MyITLab

GO! Solve It Project 7K Staff Increase

PROJECT FILES

For Project 7K, you will need the following files:

New blank Word document
w07K_Staff_Increase

From Scratch icon

You will save your files as:

Lastname_Firstname_7K_Staff_Schedule
Lastname_Firstname_7K_Staff_Increase

Open a new blank document, and then save it in your **Word Chapter 7** folder as an RTF file with the file name **Lastname_Firstname_7K_Staff_Schedule** Use the following information to create an attractive document.

The document should include an *Employee Schedule for December*. Four additional sales associates must be scheduled at the Portland store during the holiday season for the following times: Monday through Friday 9 a.m. to 3 p.m. and 3 p.m. to 9 p.m., Saturday 10 a.m. to 6 p.m., and Sunday 11 a.m. to 5 p.m. Employees will work the same hours throughout December. No employee can be scheduled for two different time periods. Using fictitious employee names, arrange the time periods in an alphabetical list that includes the employee names as bulleted items. Add appropriate document properties, including the tags **schedule, December**

Sales Manager Yolanda Richards is sending a memo to President Roslyn Thomas with the *Employee Schedule for December* included as a hyperlink. Open the file **w07K_Staff_Increase** and save it as **Lastname_Firstname_7K_Staff_Increase** Using the existing text, add appropriate hyperlinks to the schedule you created and to contact Ms. Reynolds at **yreynolds@owspecialties** Add appropriate properties, including the tags **staff, increase** Proofread your document and make any necessary corrections. Insert the file names in the footers. Print both files—the RTF file and the memo—or submit electronically as directed by your instructor.

(Project 7K Staff Increase continues on the next page)

Performance Level

Performance Criteria	Exemplary: You consistently applied the relevant skills	Proficient: You sometimes, but not always, applied the relevant skills	Developing: You rarely or never applied the relevant skills
Save in RTF format	The schedule is saved in RTF format with the appropriate file name.	The schedule is saved in RTF format but has an incorrect file name.	The schedule is saved in the wrong format.
Insert lists	Sorted, bulleted lists are inserted in the schedule.	Lists are inserted in the schedule but they are not sorted.	No lists are inserted in the schedule.
Insert hyperlinks	Hyperlinks are inserted in the memo for the schedule and contact information, using existing text.	Hyperlinks are inserted in the memo but at the wrong locations or include incorrect text.	No hyperlinks are inserted in the memo.
Insert and format text	The schedule contains the correct information and is formatted attractively.	The schedule contains the correct information, but the format is not consistent or attractive.	The schedule does not contain the correct information.
Correct errors	Both documents have no spelling or grammar errors.	One document contains spelling or grammar errors.	Both documents contain spelling or grammar errors.

END | You have completed Project 7K

RUBRIC

The following outcomes-based assessments are open-ended assessments. That is, there is no specific correct result; your result will depend on your approach to the information provided. Make *Professional Quality* your goal. Use the following scoring rubric to guide you in *how* to approach the problem and then to evaluate *how well* your approach solves the problem.

The *criteria*—Software Mastery, Content, Format and Layout, and Process—represent the knowledge and skills you have gained that you can apply to solving the problem. The *levels of performance*—Professional Quality, Approaching Professional Quality, or Needs Quality Improvements—help you and your instructor evaluate your result.

	Your completed project is of Professional Quality if you:	Your completed project is Approaching Professional Quality if you:	Your completed project Needs Quality Improvements if you:
1-Software Mastery	Choose and apply the most appropriate skills, tools, and features and identify efficient methods to solve the problem.	Choose and apply some appropriate skills, tools, and features, but not in the most efficient manner.	Choose inappropriate skills, tools, or features, or are inefficient in solving the problem.
2-Content	Construct a solution that is clear and well organized, contains content that is accurate, appropriate to the audience and purpose, and is complete. Provide a solution that contains no errors of spelling, grammar, or style.	Construct a solution in which some components are unclear, poorly organized, inconsistent, or incomplete. Misjudge the needs of the audience. Have some errors in spelling, grammar, or style, but the errors do not detract from comprehension.	Construct a solution that is unclear, incomplete, or poorly organized, contains some inaccurate or inappropriate content, and contains many errors of spelling, grammar, or style. Do not solve the problem.
3-Format and Layout	Format and arrange all elements to communicate information and ideas, clarify function, illustrate relationships, and indicate relative importance.	Apply appropriate format and layout features to some elements, but not others. Overuse features, causing minor distraction.	Apply format and layout that does not communicate information or ideas clearly. Do not use format and layout features to clarify function, illustrate relationships, or indicate relative importance. Use available features excessively, causing distraction.
4-Process	Use an organized approach that integrates planning, development, self-assessment, revision, and reflection.	Demonstrate an organized approach in some areas, but not others; or, use an insufficient process of organization throughout.	Do not use an organized approach to solve the problem.

OUTCOMES-BASED ASSESSMENTS (CRITICAL THINKING)

Apply a combination of the 7A and 7B skills.

GO! Think Project 7L Phone Jewelry

From Scratch icon

PROJECT FILES

For Project 7L, you will need the following file:

New blank Word document

You will save your file as:

Lastname_Firstname_7L_Phone_Jewelry

The marketing director at Oregon Wireless Specialties wants to create a flyer to advertise its latest product line—cell phone bling and a variety of jewelry accessories. The categories include butterfly, tiger, seashore, carnation, and mountain. This document will be reviewed by others because it includes Spanish and French translations of the styles.

Create a flyer with basic information about the new product line. Include a brief paragraph describing cell phone bling and accessories. Use the Research pane to locate descriptive information, adding a hyperlink to the website where you obtained the data. Display the individual styles in an organized list. Use Word's translate feature to create two additional style lists—in Spanish and French. Be sure the document has an attractive design and is easy to read. Correct all spelling and grammar errors, excluding the translated text.

Save the file in Rich Text Format, with the file name **Lastname_Firstname_7L_Phone_Jewelry** Add appropriate information in the Properties area and insert the file name in the footer. Print your file or submit electronically as directed by your instructor.

END | You have completed Project 7L

From Scratch icon

GO! Think Project 7M Memory Cards MyITLab

From Scratch icon

You and GO! Project 7N Personal Webpage MyITLab

Creating Merged Documents

OUTCOMES
Filter records and create envelopes.

PROJECT 8B

OUTCOMES
Create and modify a data source and create a directory.

OBJECTIVES

1. Merge a Data Source and a Main Document
2. Use Mail Merge to Create Envelopes

OBJECTIVES

3. Edit and Sort a Data Source
4. Match Fields and Apply Rules
5. Create a Data Source and a Directory

SOMATUSCAN/Fotolia

In This Chapter

GO! to Work with Word

In this chapter, you will use data sources with mail merge to create letters, envelopes, postcards, and a directory. Mail merge provides a time-saving and convenient way to produce personalized mass mailings, such as customized letters and envelopes. You can construct your own table of data or use an existing file. You can also sort and filter the data to specify what information will be used. For example, you might want to send individual letters to customers who purchased a specific cruise. You can also use a data source with mail merge to generate a directory—for example, a list of company employees and their phone extensions.

The projects in this chapter relate to **Caribbean Customized**, which specializes in exciting cruises in the Caribbean, including excursions to islands and the mainland in North and Central America. With its tropical beauty and cultural diversity, the Caribbean region offers lush jungles, freshwater caves, miles of white sand beaches, ancient ruins, and charming cities. Ships are innovative and include rock-climbing walls and extensive spa facilities. A variety of accommodations are available on each ship to meet the needs and budgets of a wide array of travelers. The food and entertainment are rated as exceptional by all.

PROJECT 8A

Customer Letters

PROJECT ACTIVITIES

Caribbean Customized is launching a new rewards program for its valued customers. Lucinda Parsons, the president of the company, has asked you to create a document describing the Emerald Program that can be sent to all customers who previously booked multiple cruises. In Activities 8.01 through 8.07, you will create a customized form letter and envelope. This will enable the company to send a personalized letter to the targeted group of customers. Your completed documents will look similar to Figure 8.1.

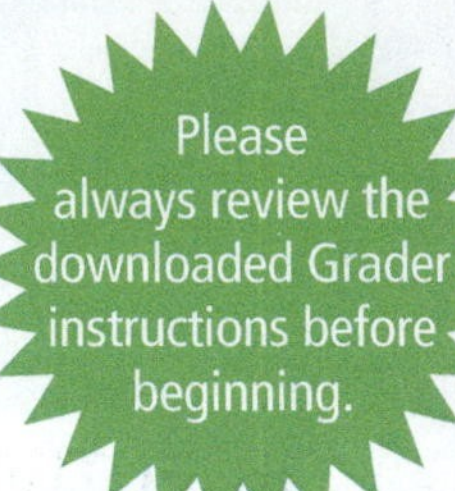

PROJECT FILES

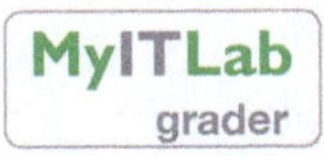

If your instructor wants you to submit Project 8A in the MyITLab Grader system, log into MyITLab, locate Grader Project 8A, and then download the files for the project.

For Project 8A, you will need the following files:

w08A_Customers
w08A_Letters_Main

You will save your documents as:

Lastname_Firstname_8A_Letters_Main (not shown in Figure)
Lastname_Firstname_8A_Letters_Merged
Lastname_Firstname_8A_Envelopes_Main (not shown in Figure)
Lastname_Firstname_8A_Envelopes_Merged

PROJECT RESULTS

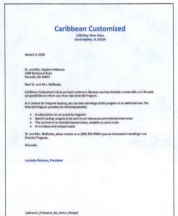

Caribbean Customized

Caribbean Customized

Caribbean Customized

FIGURE 8.1 Project 8A Customer Letters

Objective 1 Merge a Data Source and a Main Document

GO! Learn How
Video W8-1

Recall that ***mail merge*** is a Word feature that joins a ***data source*** with a ***main document*** to create a customized document, such as mailing labels. The data source, containing categories of information such as names and addresses, can be stored in a variety of formats—a Word table, an Excel worksheet, an Access table or query, or an Outlook contact list. Placeholders for the customized information from the data source are inserted in the main document. You can use the Mail Merge Wizard or the commands on the Mailings tab to create personalized letters, envelopes, labels, or directories.

Expert 2.2.1

Activity 8.01 | Creating and Applying a Character Style

ALERT!

To submit as an autograded project, log into MyITLab and download the files for this Project, and begin with those files instead of w08A_Letters_Main.

A ***character style*** contains formatting characteristics that you apply to text—for example, font name, font size, font color, and bold emphasis. You can create a style to apply consistent formatting throughout a document.

1. Start Word. Navigate to your student data files that accompany this chapter, and then open **w08A_Letters_Main**. Be sure that the formatting marks and rulers display in your document. Display the **Save As** dialog box, create a **New Folder** with the name **Word Chapter 8** and then save your file as **Lastname_Firstname_8A_Letters_Main**

   This letter contains information regarding the Emerald Program developed by Caribbean Customized.

2. Select the second and third paragraphs of the document containing the company address. On the **Home tab**, in the **Styles group**, click the **Dialog Box Launcher** [icon] to display the Styles pane.

3. At the bottom of the **Styles** pane, click the **New Style** button [icon]. In the **Create New Style from Formatting** dialog box, under **Properties**, in the **Name** box, type **Letter Emphasis** and then click the **Style type arrow**. Click **Character**.

4. Under **Formatting**, change the **Font Size** to **12**, and then apply **Bold** [B] and **Italic** [I]. Click the **Font Color arrow**, and then in the fifth column, click the last color—**Blue, Accent 1, Darker 50%**. Compare your screen with Figure 8.2.

   A preview of the style formatting applied to the first line of the selected text displays.

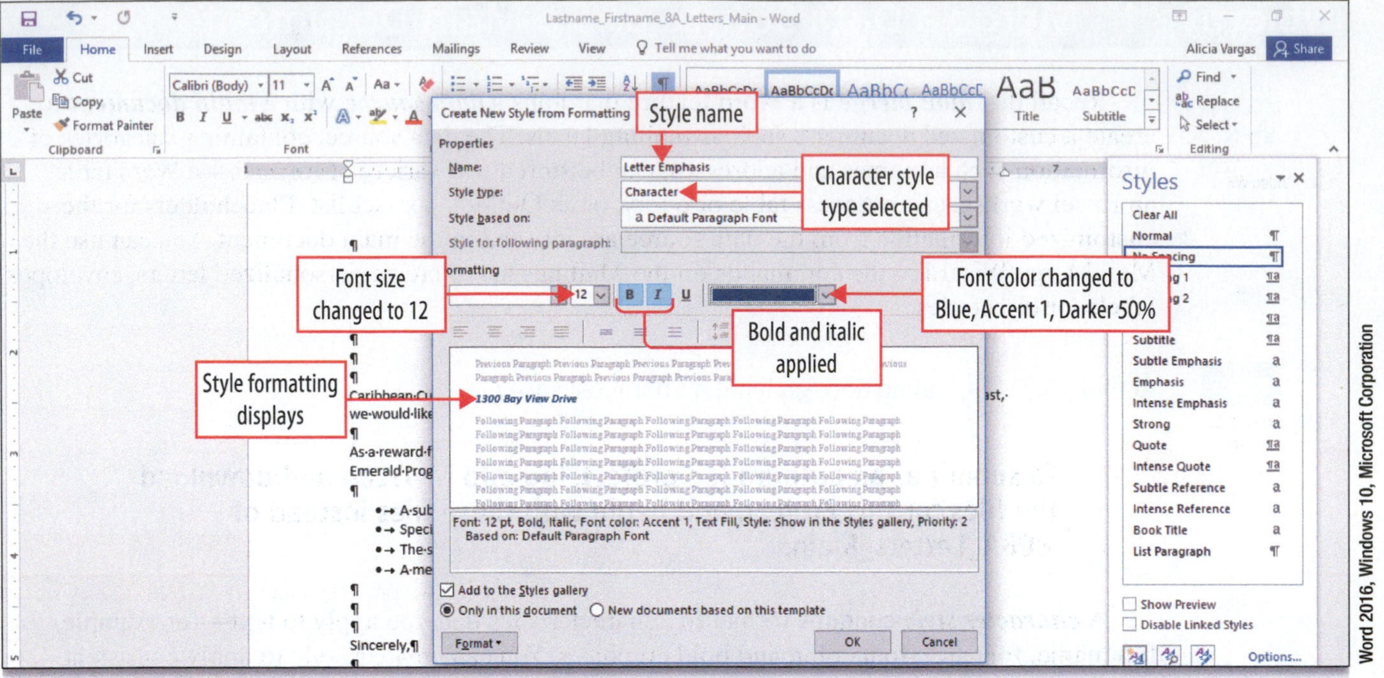

FIGURE 8.2

5 Click **OK** to create the style, and then **Close** ☒ the **Styles** pane.

6 Press Ctrl + End, and then select the text **Lucinda Parsons, President**. On the mini toolbar, click **Styles**, and then in the **Styles** gallery, point to **Letter Emphasis**. Compare your screen with Figure 8.3.

The style that you created displays in the Styles gallery and can be applied to text in this document.

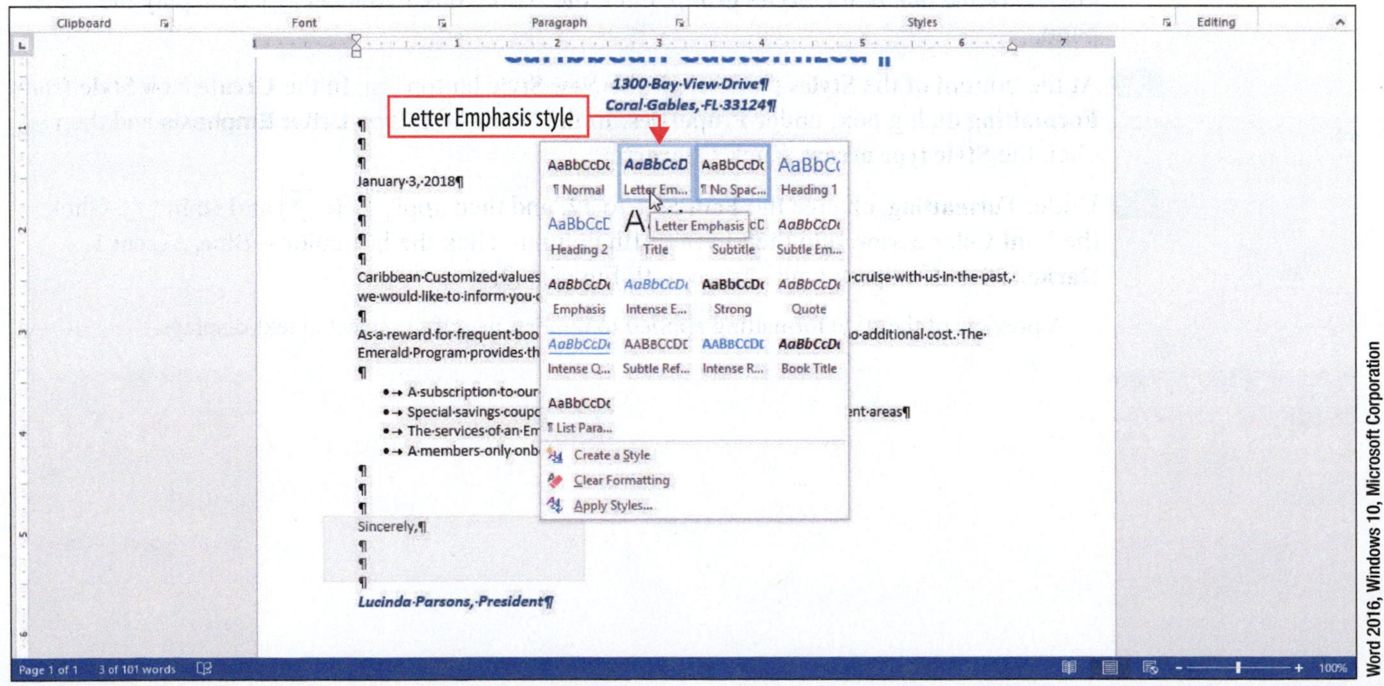

FIGURE 8.3

7 Click **Letter Emphasis**, and then **Save** your changes.

Activity 8.02 | Selecting a Mail Merge Data Source and Defining the Main Document

Expert 3.3.3

A data source is composed of ***fields***, categories—or columns—of data, and ***records***. A record is a row of information that contains the data for one entity—for example, information about one customer. In this Activity, you will select an Excel file as a data source and you will use the commands on the Mailings tab to define the main document.

1. Click the **Mailings tab**. In the **Start Mail Merge group**, click **Start Mail Merge**, and then click **Letters**.
2. On the **Mailings tab**, in the **Start Mail Merge group**, click **Select Recipients**, and then click **Use an Existing List**.
3. In the **Select Data Source** dialog box, navigate to the student data files for this chapter, locate and select **w08A_Customers**, and then click **Open**.

   The file w08A_Customers file is an Excel workbook that includes names and addresses for current and potential customers.
4. In the **Select Table** dialog box, if necessary, select 'Customer Information$', which is the name of the worksheet in the w08A_Customers file that contains the customer mailing data. At the lower left of the dialog box, verify that the **First row of data contains column headers** check box is selected and select it if it is not. Compare your screen with Figure 8.4.

   The worksheet contains column headers in row 1. The column headers will comprise the field names used in the mail merge.

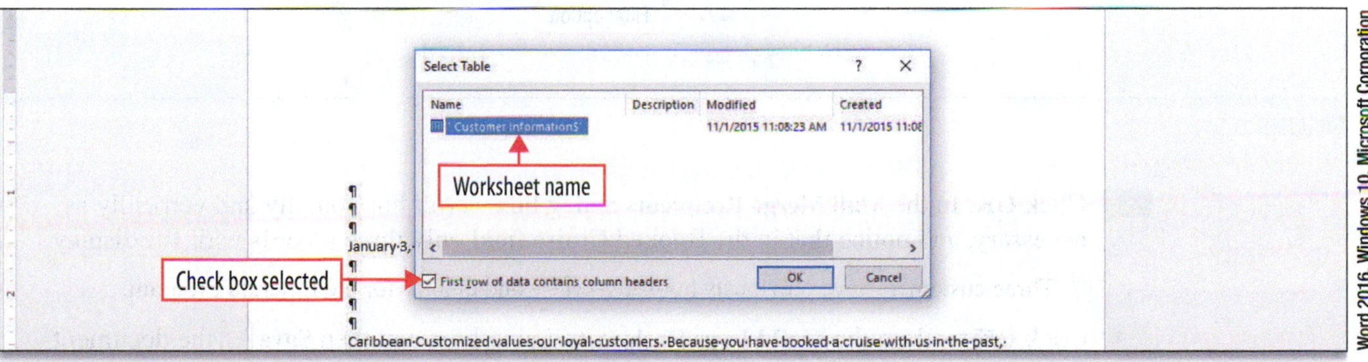

FIGURE 8.4

5. Click **OK**, and then **Save** your document.

   Although visually nothing appears to happen, when you designate a data source, the file—in this instance, the Excel file—is linked to the main document based on the current locations of both files.

> ***More* Knowledge** **Using Outlook as a Data Source**
>
> You can use an Outlook Contacts list as a data source. To use the Contacts list, on the Mailings tab, in the Start Mail Merge group, click Select Recipients. Then, from the list, click Choose from Outlook Contacts. In the Choose Profile dialog box, select the folder where your Outlook Contacts list is stored, and then click OK.

Activity 8.03 | Filtering Records

Expert 3.3.4

You can ***filter*** a data source to apply a set of criteria to display specific records—for example, information only for customers that live in a particular state. Because the Emerald Program is available only to individuals who have previously toured with Caribbean Customized, you will filter the data source to display only existing customers.

1 On the **Mailings tab**, in the **Start Mail Merge group**, click **Edit Recipient List**. In the **Mail Merge Recipients** dialog box, under **Refine recipient list**, click **Filter**.

2 In the **Filter and Sort** dialog box, on the **Filter Records tab**, click the **Field arrow**, scroll as necessary, and then click **Booked Cruise**. Click the **Comparison arrow**, and then if necessary, click Equal to. In the **Compare to** box, type **Yes** and then compare your screen with Figure 8.5.

The data source will be filtered to display only those records where the Booked Cruise field is equal to Yes.

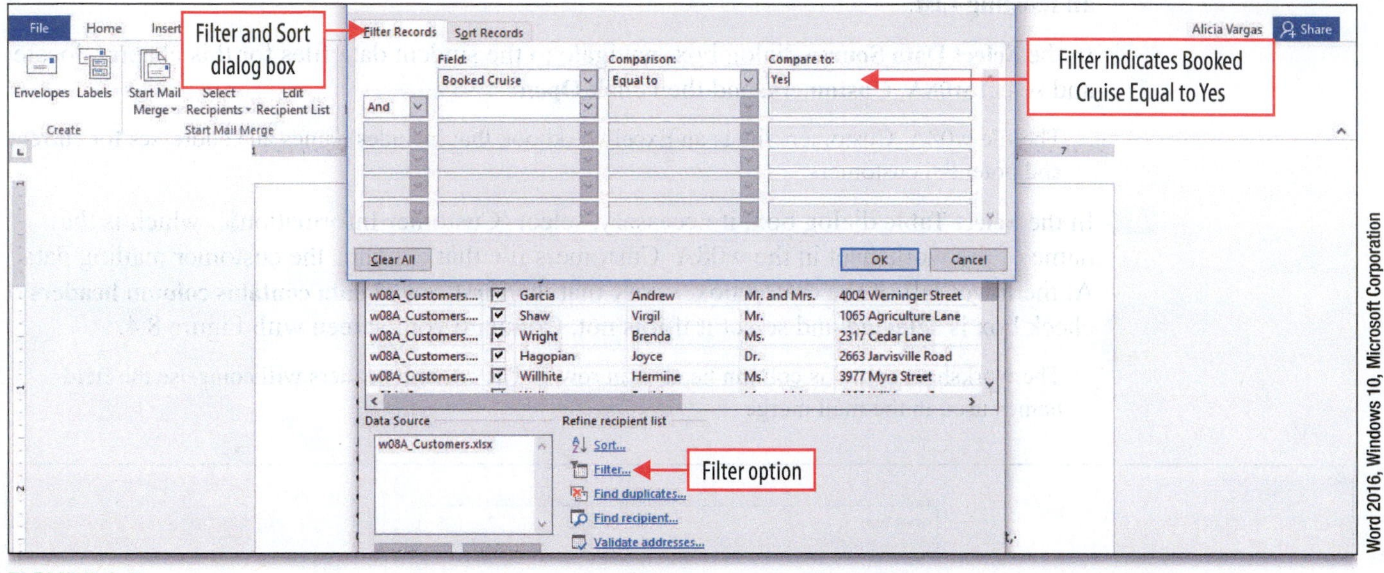

FIGURE 8.5

3 Click **OK**. In the **Mail Merge Recipients** dialog box, scroll horizontally and vertically as necessary, and notice that in the Booked Cruise field only three records with *Yes* display.

Three customers have previously booked a cruise and qualify for the Emerald Program.

4 Click **OK** to close the **Mail Merge Recipients** dialog box, and then **Save** the document.

Activity 8.04 | Inserting Merge Fields

Expert 3.3.5

You are creating a ***form letter***—a letter with standardized wording that can be sent to many different people. Each letter can be customized by inserting ***merge fields***—placeholders that represent specific information in the data source. In this Activity, you will insert appropriate merge fields.

1 Click in the blank paragraph above the paragraph that begins *Caribbean Customized values*. On the **Mailings tab**, in the **Write & Insert Fields group**, click **Address Block**. In the **Insert Address Block** dialog box, take a moment to examine the various settings associated with this dialog box, and then click **OK**. In the document, notice that the **Address Block merge field** is inserted. Compare your screen with Figure 8.6.

A standard feature of a business letter is the ***inside address***—the name and address of the recipient of the letter. The ***Address Block*** is a predefined merge field that includes the recipient's name, street address, city, state, and postal code. The Insert Address Block dialog box provides options for changing the way the inside address displays. You are inserting the Address Block merge field as a placeholder for the inside address. Each merge field in a main document is surrounded by double angle brackets—characters used to distinguish where data will be populated.

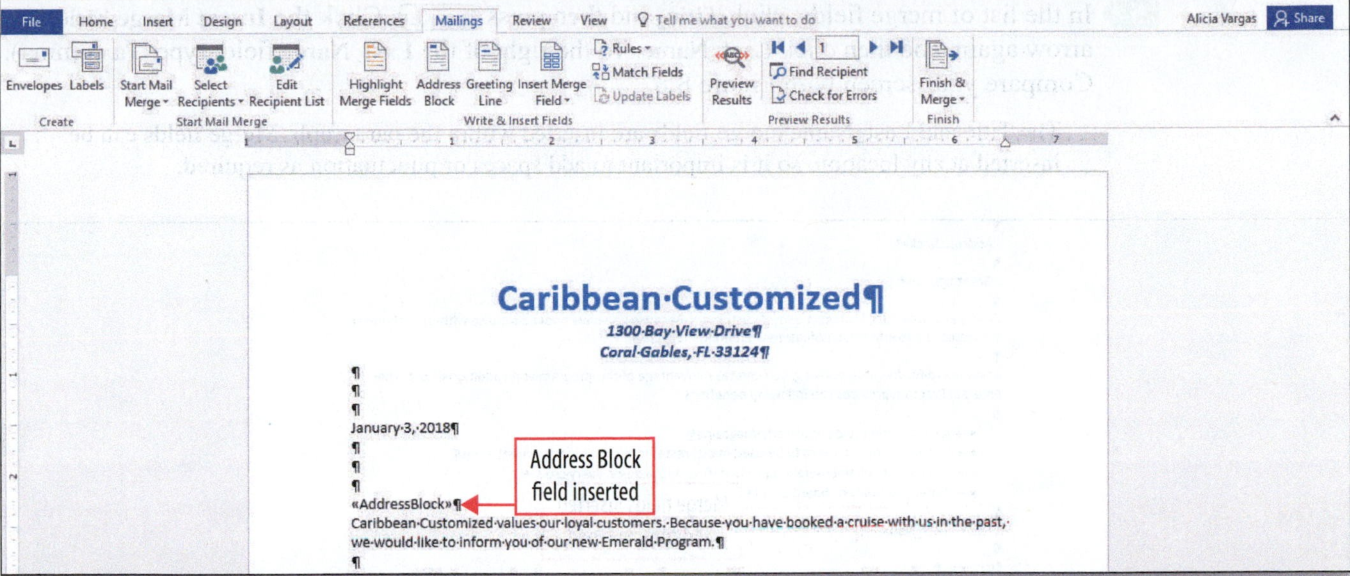

FIGURE 8.6

Word 2016, Windows 10, Microsoft Corporation

2 Press Enter two times, and then in the **Write & Insert Fields group**, click **Greeting Line**. In the **Insert Greeting Line** dialog box, under **Greeting line format**, in the box on the right—the **Punctuation** box—click the **Punctuation arrow**, and then click **:** (the colon). Compare your screen with Figure 8.7.

Another standard feature of a business letter is the ***salutation***—or greeting line. The ***Greeting Line*** is a predefined merge field that includes an introductory word, such as *Dear*, and the recipient's name. When using a business letter format, a colon usually follows the salutation. The Insert Greeting Line dialog box allows you to choose the introductory word and punctuation that display in the salutation.

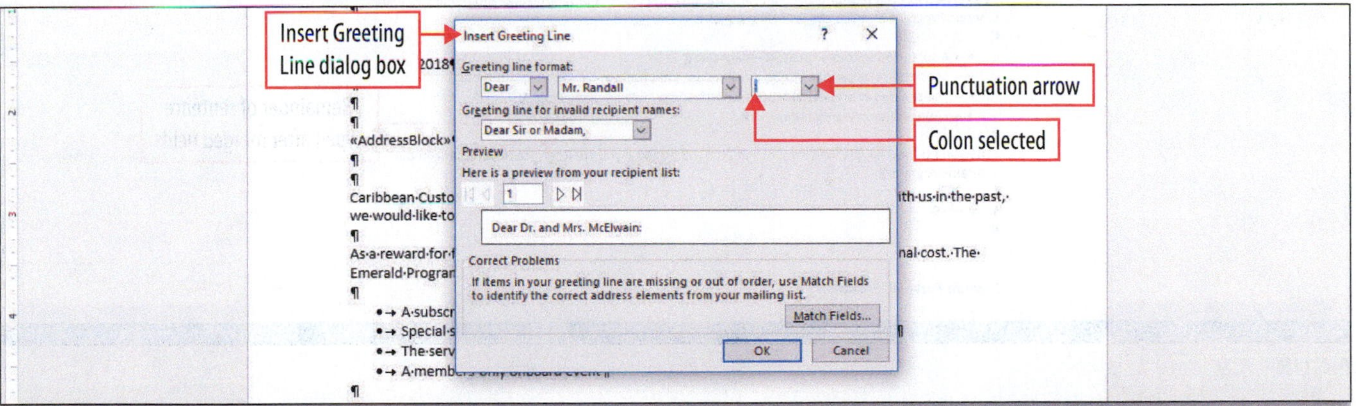

FIGURE 8.7

Word 2016, Windows 10, Microsoft Corporation

3 Click **OK**, and then press Enter to insert a blank line.

The Greeting Line merge field is inserted in the document and is used as a placeholder for the salutation.

4 Scroll down, and then position the insertion point in the *second* blank line below the bulleted text. On the **Mailings tab**, in the **Write & Insert Fields group**, click the **Insert Merge Field** arrow. Be careful to click the arrow, not the button.

5 In the list of merge fields, click **Title**, and then press Spacebar. Click the **Insert Merge Field** arrow again, and then click **Last_Name**. To the right of the **Last_Name** field, type **,** (a comma). Compare your screen with Figure 8.8.

The Title and Last_Name merge fields are inserted within the paragraph. Merge fields can be inserted at any location, so it is important to add spaces or punctuation as required.

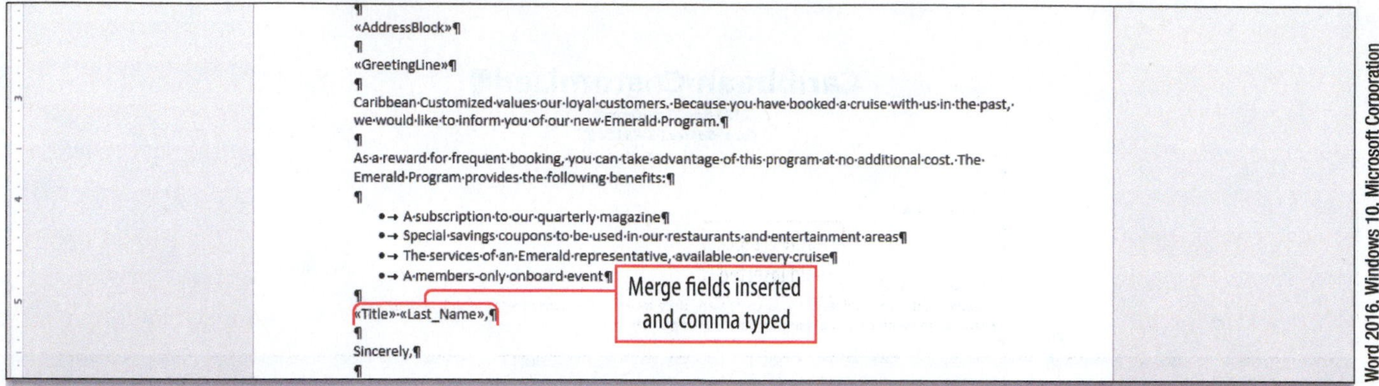

FIGURE 8.8

6 Press Spacebar, and then type **please contact us at (305) 555-0768 if you are interested in enrolling in our Emerald Program.** Compare your screen with Figure 8.9.

Formatting and editing of your main document is complete.

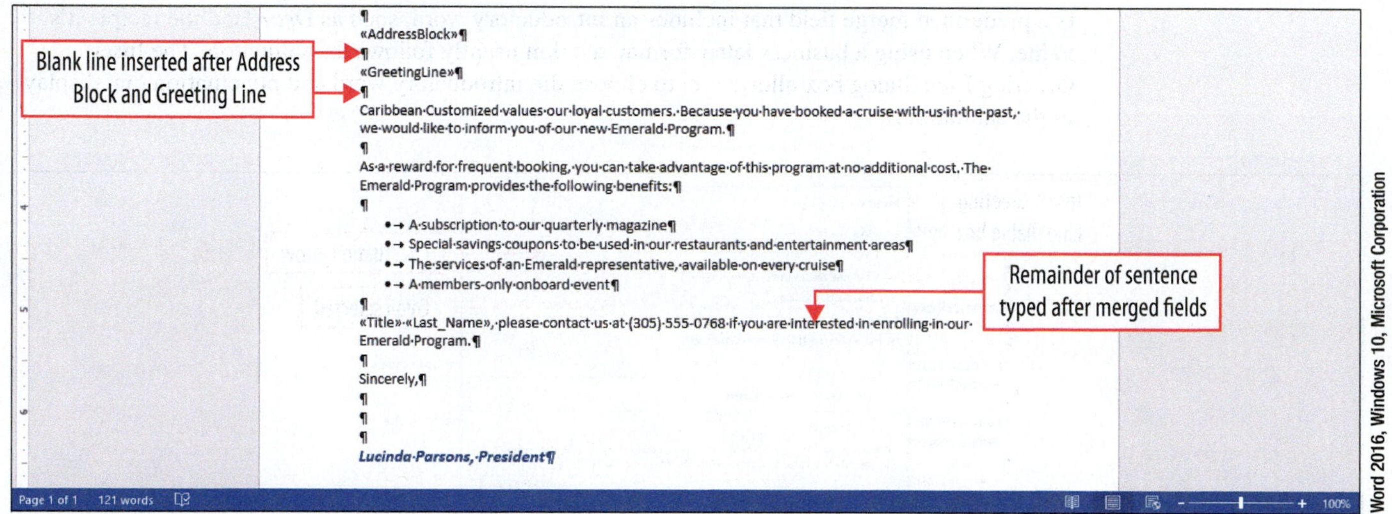

FIGURE 8.9

7 **Save** your document.

Activity 8.05 | Previewing Results and Validating Merged Data

Expert 3.3.6

After the merge fields are added to the form letter, you can preview the letters one at a time. Before you complete the merge process, it is a good idea to scan the letters to check for spelling, punctuation, and spacing errors. If you find an error, correct it in the main document before completing the merge. You can use the Check for Errors feature to specify how to handle errors that may occur during the merge process.

1 Press Ctrl + Home. On the **Mailings tab**, in the **Preview Results group**, click **Preview Results**. Notice that the merge fields are replaced with specific information from the data source. Compare your screen with Figure 8.10.

Previewing the merged results allows you to see how each record will display in the letter. By default, the displayed information—in this instance, the customer information—is from record 1, as indicated in the Go to Record box.

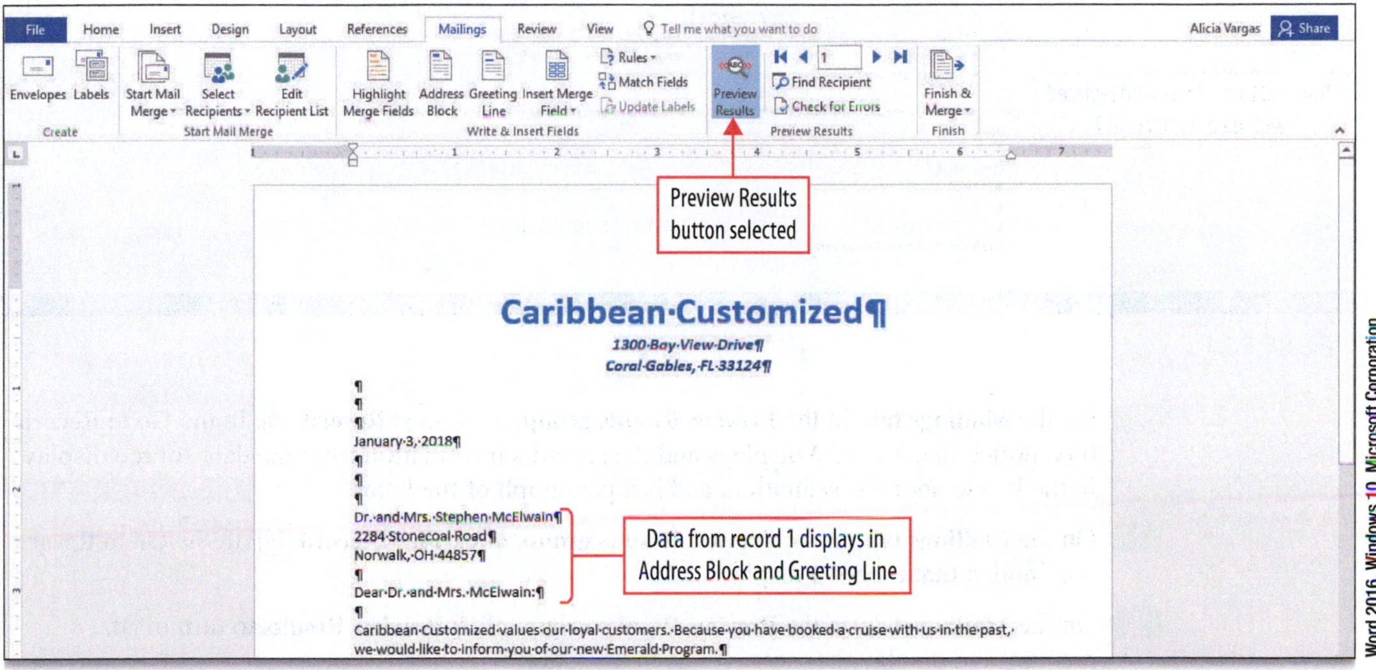

FIGURE 8.10

2 On the **Mailings tab**, in the **Preview Results group**, click **Next Record** ▶, and then scroll your document so that the date displays at the top of the document and the signature line is visible at the bottom. Compare your screen with Figure 8.11.

In the Go to Record box, record 2 displays. You can use the navigation buttons to preview how other letters will display after the merge. In the paragraph following the bulleted list, the *Title* and *Last_Name* merge fields are replaced with data from record 2.

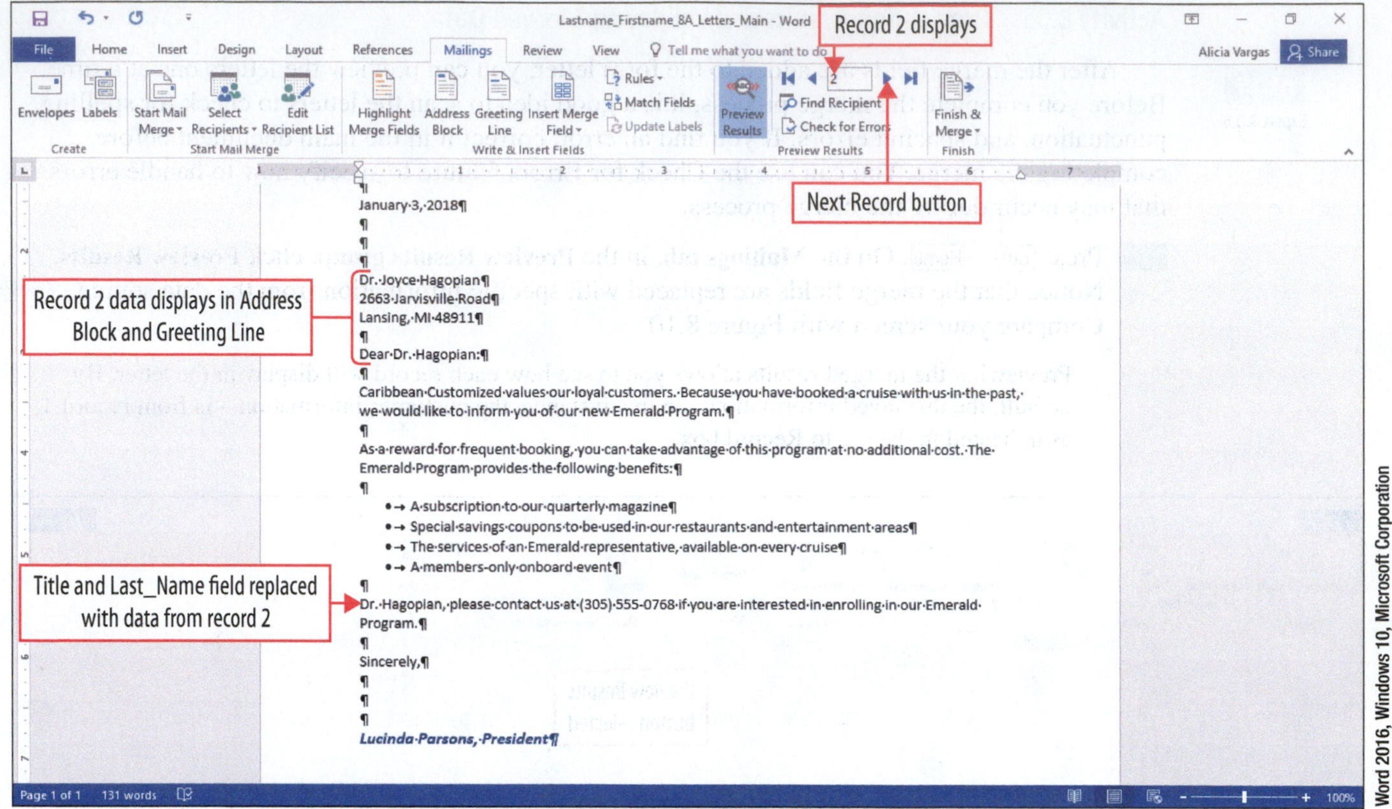

FIGURE 8.11

3 On the **Mailings tab**, in the **Preview Results group**, click **Last Record**. In the **Go to Record** box, notice that record **3** displays and the record's information from the data source displays in the inside address, salutation, and last paragraph of the letter.

4 On the **Mailings tab**, in the **Preview Results group**, click **First Record**. In the **Go to Record** box, notice that record **1** displays.

5 On the **Mailings tab**, in the **Preview Results group**, click **Preview Results** to turn off the preview and display the merge fields in the letter.

6 On the **Mailings tab**, in the **Preview Results group**, click **Check for Errors**.

7 In the **Checking and Reporting Errors** dialog box, click to select the first option that begins **Simulate the merge**, and then click **OK**.

By simulating the merge, you can designate how to handle errors that might occur during the final merge process. If there are any errors, the *Invalid Merge Field* dialog box displays with the options to *Remove Field* or to *Choose a matching field from the Fields in Data Source list*. In this instance, there are no errors reported.

8 Click **OK** to close the Microsoft Word message box.

Activity 8.06 | Merging to a New Document

Expert 3.3.3

Recall that your form letter is the main document containing the merge fields. You can print the letters directly from the main document or merge all of the letters into one Word document that you can edit. You will finish the merge process by merging the data source and the main document to a new, single document that contains the individual letters. This new document will no longer be connected to the data source.

1 On the **Mailings tab**, in the **Finish group**, click **Finish & Merge**, and then click **Edit Individual Documents** to display the **Merge to New Document** dialog box. Compare your screen with Figure 8.12.

Although *All* is selected by default, you can use the Merge to New Document dialog box to specify which records you want to merge to a new document.

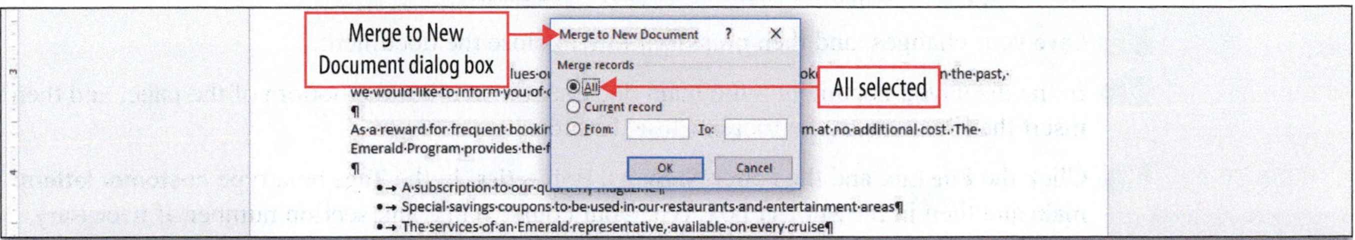

FIGURE 8.12

Word 2016, Windows 10, Microsoft Corporation

2 In the **Merge to New Document** dialog box, click **OK** and then scroll the document to view the results of the merge.

A new merged document displays with *Letters1 – Word* in the title bar. Based on the filtered recipient list, three letters display.

3 Press Ctrl + Home, and then scroll to view the bottom of **Page 1**. Compare your screen with Figure 8.13.

The status bar indicates that there are three pages—the individual letters. Each page, or letter, is separated by a Next Page section break.

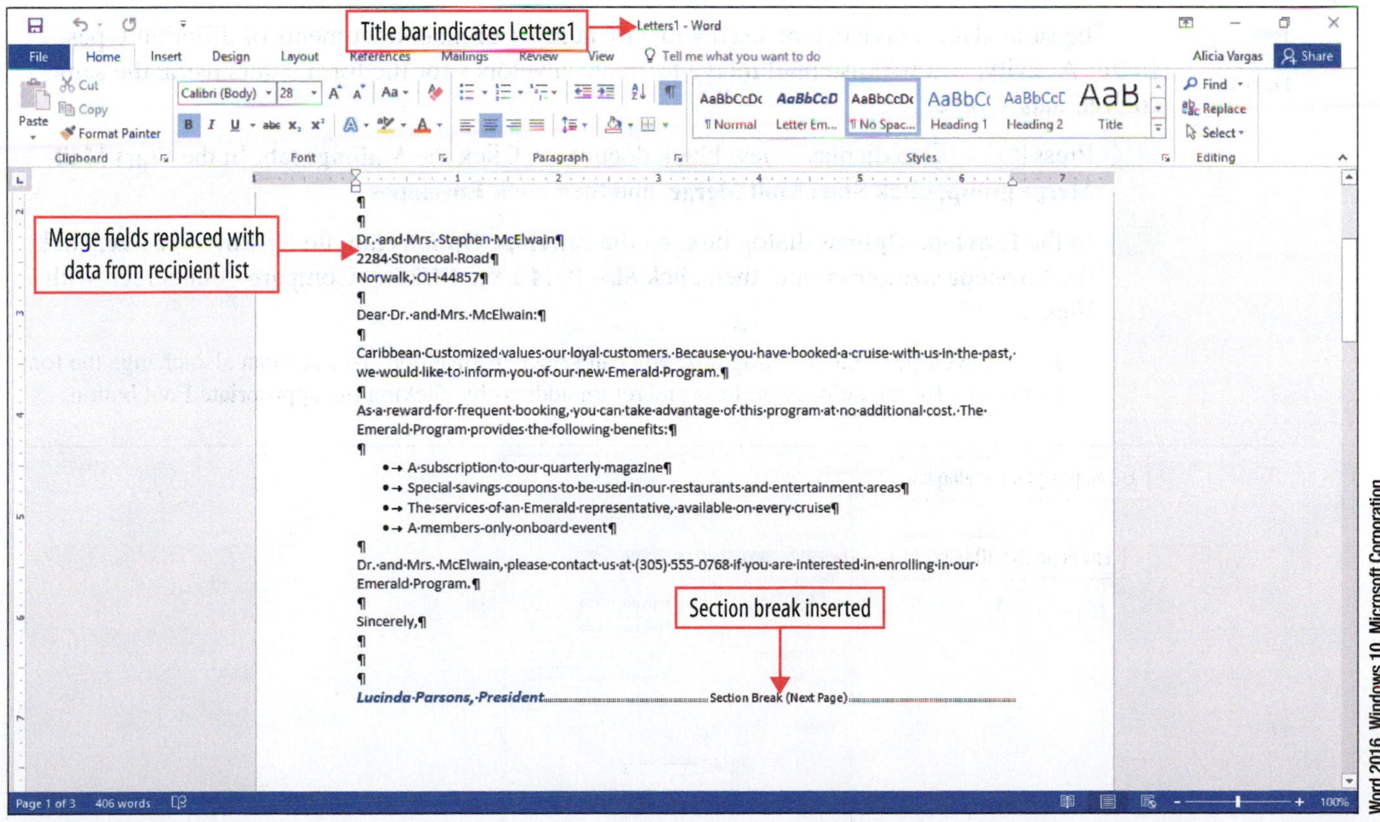

Word 2016, Windows 10, Microsoft Corporation

FIGURE 8.13

4 Display the **Save As** dialog box. Navigate to your **Word Chapter 8** folder, and then **Save** the document as **Lastname_Firstname_8A_Letters_Merged** At the bottom of **Page 1**, right-click in the footer area, click **Edit Footer**, and then insert the file name. **Close** the footer area.

5 Click the **File tab**, and then click **Show All Properties**. In the **Tags** box, type **customer letters, merged** and then in the **Subject** box, type your course name and section number. If necessary, edit the author name to display your name.

6 **Save** your changes, and then press Ctrl + W to close the document.

7 In the displayed document—the main document—scroll to the bottom of the page, and then insert the file name in the footer. **Close** the footer area.

8 Click the **File tab**, and then click **Show All Properties**. In the **Tags** box, type **customer letters, main** and then in the **Subject** box, type your course name and section number. If necessary, edit the author name to display your name.

9 **Save** your document. Press Ctrl + W to close the document but leave Word open.

Objective 2 Use Mail Merge to Create Envelopes

GO! Learn How Video W8-2

You can use mail merge to create envelopes from a data source, and you can specify the envelope size and text formatting. Additionally, you can include electronic postage, if the appropriate software is installed on your computer.

Activity 8.07 | Using Mail Merge to Create Envelopes

Expert 3.3.3

The same data source can be used with any number of main documents of different types. In this Activity, you will use mail merge to create envelopes for the form letters using the same filtered data source.

1 Press Ctrl + N to display a new blank document. Click the **Mailings tab**. In the **Start Mail Merge group**, click **Start Mail Merge**, and then click **Envelopes**.

2 In the **Envelope Options** dialog box, on the **Envelope Options tab**, under **Envelope size**, click the **Envelope size arrow**, and then click **Size 10 (4 1/8 x 9 1/2 in)**. Compare your screen with Figure 8.14.

In the Envelope Options dialog box, you can select an envelope size. You can also change the font formatting for the delivery address and return address by clicking the appropriate Font button.

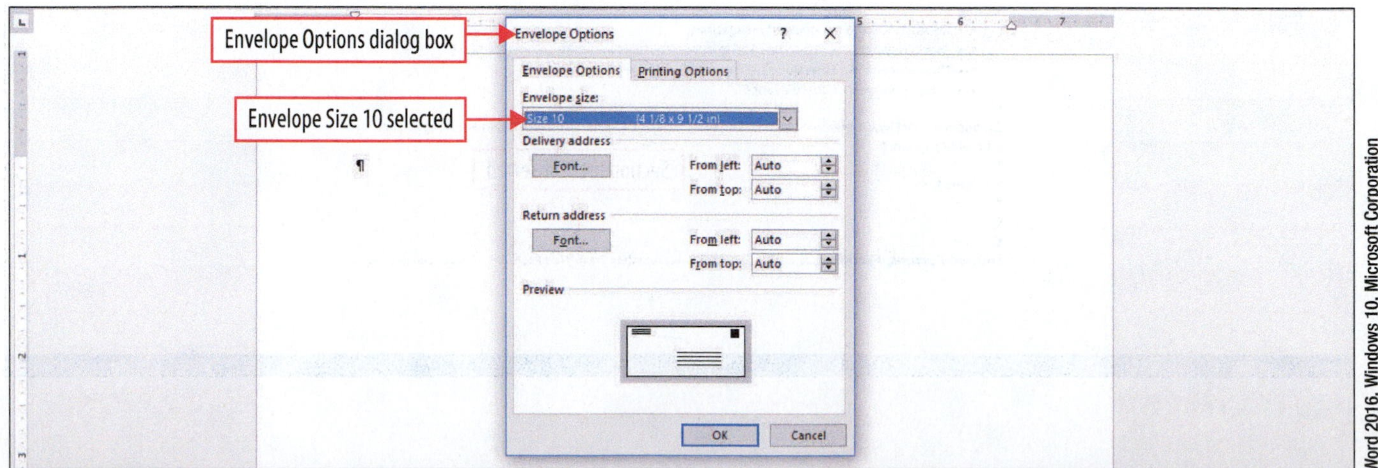

FIGURE 8.14

3 Click **OK** to display your Word document with the Envelope Size 10 margins and paper size applied. Display the **Save As** dialog box, and then navigate to your **Word Chapter 8** folder. Save the document as **Lastname_Firstname_8A_Envelopes_Main** and **Zoom** your document so that it displays at **100%**.

4 On the **Mailings tab**, in the **Start Mail Merge group**, click **Select Recipients**, and then click **Use an Existing List**. In the **Select Data Source** dialog box, navigate to your student data files for this chapter, select the file **w08A_Customers**, and then click **Open**.

5 In the **Select Table** dialog box, with **'Customer Information$'** and **First row of data contains column headers** check box selected, click **OK**.

6 On the **Mailings tab**, in the **Start Mail Merge group**, click **Edit Recipient List**. In the **Mail Merge Recipients** dialog box, under **Refine recipient list**, click **Filter**.

7 In the **Filter and Sort** dialog box, on the **Filter Records tab**, click the **Field arrow**, scroll as necessary, and then click **Booked Cruise**. Click the **Comparison arrow**, and then click **Equal to**. In the **Compare to** box, type **Yes** Compare your screen with Figure 8.15.

The data source will be filtered to display only those records where the Booked Cruise field is equal to Yes.

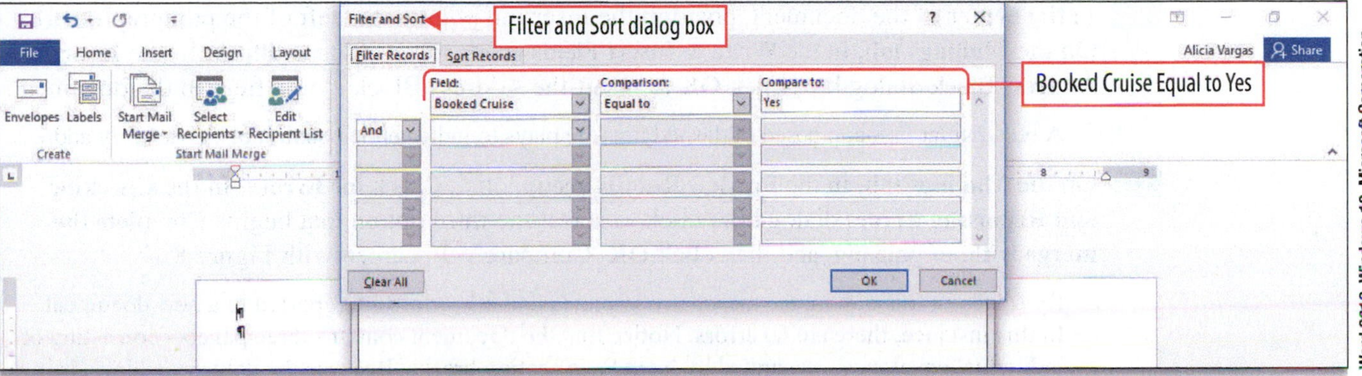

FIGURE 8.15

8 Click **OK** two times to close the dialog boxes.

9 In the upper left corner of the envelope, if a return address displays, delete the existing text. Type the following return address, pressing Enter after the first and second lines. Compare your screen with Figure 8.16.

Caribbean Customized
1300 Bay View Drive
Coral Gables, FL 33124

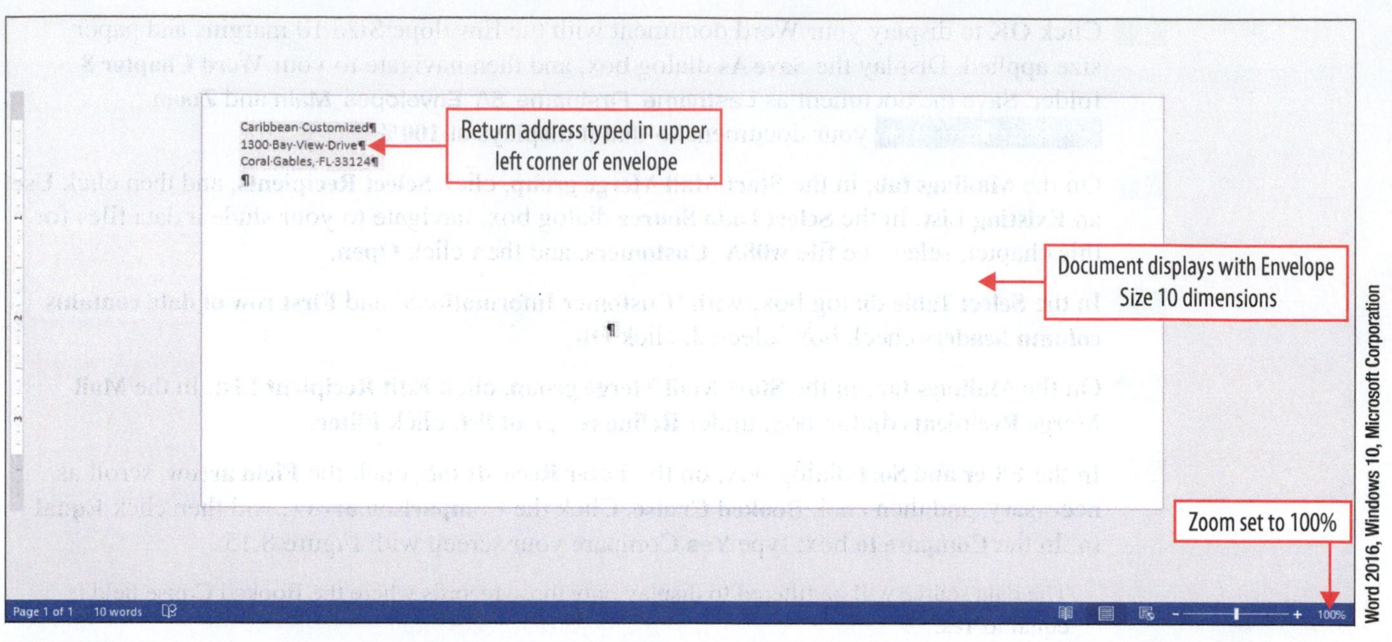

FIGURE 8.16

10 In the center of the document, position the insertion point to the left of the paragraph mark. On the **Mailings tab**, in the **Write & Insert Fields group**, click **Address Block**. In the **Insert Address Block** dialog box, click **OK** to insert the Address Block merge field in the document.

A rectangular box composed of dashed lines displays to indicate the position of the delivery address.

11 On the **Mailings tab**, in the **Preview Results group**, click **Check for Errors**. In the **Checking and Reporting Errors** dialog box, click to select the third option that begins **Complete the merge without pausing**, and then click **OK**. Compare your screen with Figure 8.17.

By selecting this option, the merge is completed and any errors are reported in a new document. In this instance, there are no errors. Notice that the document contains three pages—consisting of individual envelopes—separated by Next Page section breaks. Because the delivery address is in a text box, Word positions the section breaks below the return address.

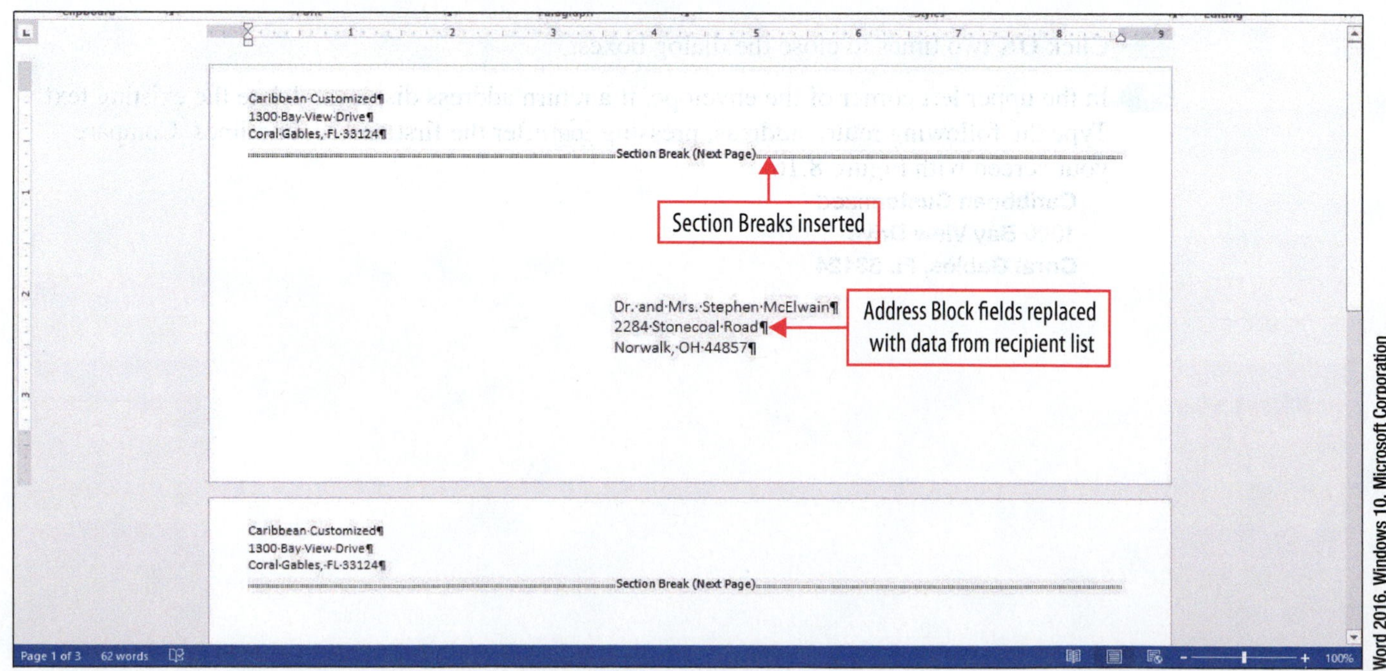

FIGURE 8.17

12 Display the **Save As** dialog box, navigate to your **Word Chapter 8** folder, and then **Save** the document as **Lastname_Firstname_8A_Envelopes_Merged** Insert the file name in the footer, and then close the footer. Click the **File tab**, and then click **Show All Properties**. In the **Tags** box, type **customer envelopes, merged** and then in the **Subject** box, type your course name and section number. If necessary, edit the author name to display your name. **Save** your document.

13 **Close** your merged document. In the main document, insert the file name in the footer, and then close the footer. Click the **File tab**, and then click **Show All Properties**. In the **Tags** box, type **customer envelopes, main** and then in the **Subject** box, type your course name and section number. If necessary, edit the author name to display your name. **Save** and **Close** your document and then submit as directed by your instructor.

ALERT! **If you are submitting your merged letters and envelopes in MyITLab, complete Steps 14 through 16.**

14 To submit your merged letters and envelopes in MyITLab, you will combine your merged letters and merged envelopes into one file. **Open** your **Lastname_Firstname_8A_Envelopes_Merged** file. Press Ctrl + A to select all of the merged envelopes. On the **Home tab**, in the **Clipboard group**, click **Copy**.

15 Click the **File tab**, and then **Open** your **Lastname_Firstname_8A_Letters_Merged** file. Press Ctrl + End to move to the end of the last merged letter. On the **Home tab**, in the **Clipboard group**, click **Paste** to paste the three merged envelopes at the end of the document.

16 **Save** your document, **Close** all open documents, and then submit your **Lastname_Firstname_8A_Letters_Merged** file in MyITLab.

***More* Knowledge** **Printing an Envelope or Label from Selected Data**

To print a single envelope or label from selected data, in any document, select the name and address you want to use. On the Mailings tab, in the Create group, click Envelopes for an envelope or Labels for a label. In the Envelopes and Labels dialog box, you can edit the delivery address and make other changes, and then click Print.

END | You have completed Project 8A

PROJECT 8B

Cruise Postcards

PROJECT ACTIVITIES

Build From Scratch

Caribbean Customized is offering a special cruise to loyal customers. Maria Ramirez, Cruise Consultant, has asked you to create postcards to advertise the cruise. In Activities 8.08 through 8.17, you will use mail merge to create the postcards. You will also create a contact list for customers who are going on the cruise. Your completed files will look similar to Figure 8.18.

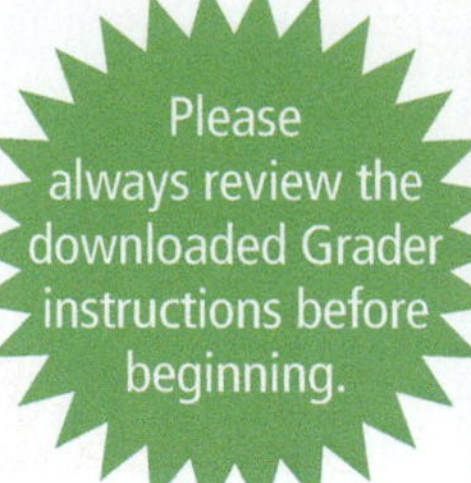

PROJECT FILES

If your instructor wants you to submit Project 8B in the MyITLab Grader system, log into MyITLab, locate Grader Project 8B, and then download the files for the project.

For Project 8B, you will need the following files:

Two new blank Word documents
w08B_Cruise_Clients
w08B_Cruise
w08B_Appreciation_Cruise
w08B_Directory_Data

You will save your files as:

Lastname_Firstname_8B_Postcards_Main (not shown in Figure)
Lastname_Firstname_8B_Postcards_Merged
Lastname_Firstname_8B_Directory_Main (not shown in Figure)
Lastname_Firstname_8B_Directory_Merged

PROJECT RESULTS

GO! Walk Thru Project 8B

Caribbean Customized

Customer Appreciation Cruise

Emergency Contact List

Customer	Contact	Relationship	Phone Number
Mrs. Nema Eros	Ms. Maria Salva	Sister	(773) 555-9244
Mr. Charles Guernon	Mrs. Janet Deimler	Daughter	(410) 555-7163
Mrs. Bridget Reinhard	Mr. Herman Reinhard	Husband	(218) 555-2279
Dr. Ursula Tezuka	Dr. Julius Tezuka	Brother	(208) 555-7128
Mr. Ernest Zambrano	Mr. Tony Zambrano	Son	(310) 555-8643

Lastname_Firstname_8B_Directory_Merged

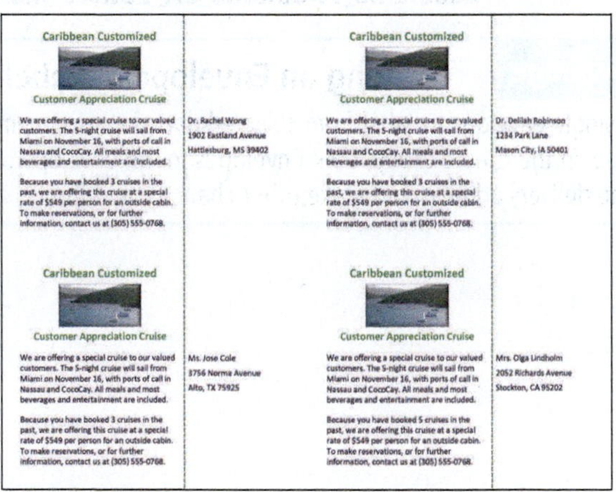

Caribbean Customized
Customer Appreciation Cruise
We are offering a special cruise to our valued customers. The 5-night cruise will sail from Miami on November 16, with ports of call in Nassau and CocoCay. All meals and most beverages and entertainment are included.
Because you have booked 3 cruises in the past, we are offering this cruise at a special rate of $549 per person for an outside cabin. To make reservations, or for further information, contact us at (305) 555-0768.
Dr. Rachel Wong
1902 Eastland Avenue
Hattiesburg, MS 39402

Caribbean Customized
Customer Appreciation Cruise
We are offering a special cruise to our valued customers. The 5-night cruise will sail from Miami on November 16, with ports of call in Nassau and CocoCay. All meals and most beverages and entertainment are included.
Because you have booked 3 cruises in the past, we are offering this cruise at a special rate of $549 per person for an outside cabin. To make reservations, or for further information, contact us at (305) 555-0768.
Dr. Delilah Robinson
1234 Park Lane
Mason City, IA 50401

Caribbean Customized
Customer Appreciation Cruise
We are offering a special cruise to our valued customers. The 5-night cruise will sail from Miami on November 16, with ports of call in Nassau and CocoCay. All meals and most beverages and entertainment are included.
Because you have booked 3 cruises in the past, we are offering this cruise at a special rate of $549 per person for an outside cabin. To make reservations, or for further information, contact us at (305) 555-0768.
Ms. Jose Cole
3756 Norma Avenue
Alto, TX 75925

Caribbean Customized
Customer Appreciation Cruise
We are offering a special cruise to our valued customers. The 5-night cruise will sail from Miami on November 16, with ports of call in Nassau and CocoCay. All meals and most beverages and entertainment are included.
Because you have booked 5 cruises in the past, we are offering this cruise at a special rate of $549 per person for an outside cabin. To make reservations, or for further information, contact us at (305) 555-0768.
Mrs. Olga Lindholm
2052 Richards Avenue
Stockton, CA 95202

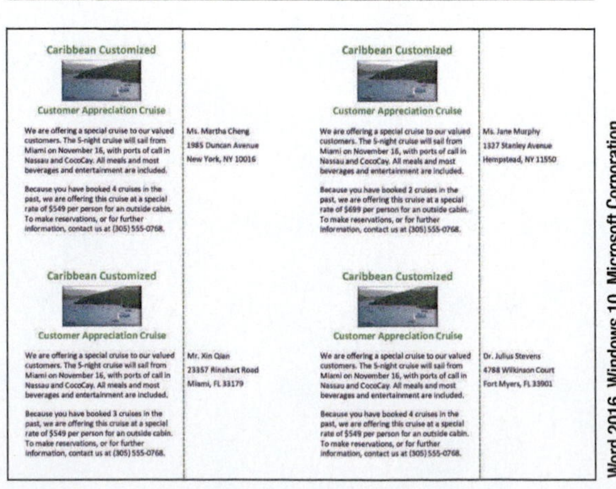

Caribbean Customized
Customer Appreciation Cruise
We are offering a special cruise to our valued customers. The 5-night cruise will sail from Miami on November 16, with ports of call in Nassau and CocoCay. All meals and most beverages and entertainment are included.
Because you have booked 4 cruises in the past, we are offering this cruise at a special rate of $549 per person for an outside cabin. To make reservations, or for further information, contact us at (305) 555-0768.
Ms. Martha Cheng
1985 Duncan Avenue
New York, NY 10016

Caribbean Customized
Customer Appreciation Cruise
We are offering a special cruise to our valued customers. The 5-night cruise will sail from Miami on November 16, with ports of call in Nassau and CocoCay. All meals and most beverages and entertainment are included.
Because you have booked 2 cruises in the past, we are offering this cruise at a special rate of $699 per person for an outside cabin. To make reservations, or for further information, contact us at (305) 555-0768.
Ms. Jane Murphy
1327 Stanley Avenue
Hempstead, NY 11550

Caribbean Customized
Customer Appreciation Cruise
We are offering a special cruise to our valued customers. The 5-night cruise will sail from Miami on November 16, with ports of call in Nassau and CocoCay. All meals and most beverages and entertainment are included.
Because you have booked 3 cruises in the past, we are offering this cruise at a special rate of $549 per person for an outside cabin. To make reservations, or for further information, contact us at (305) 555-0768.
Mr. Xin Qian
23357 Rinehart Road
Miami, FL 33179

Caribbean Customized
Customer Appreciation Cruise
We are offering a special cruise to our valued customers. The 5-night cruise will sail from Miami on November 16, with ports of call in Nassau and CocoCay. All meals and most beverages and entertainment are included.
Because you have booked 4 cruises in the past, we are offering this cruise at a special rate of $549 per person for an outside cabin. To make reservations, or for further information, contact us at (305) 555-0768.
Dr. Julius Stevens
4788 Wilkinson Court
Fort Myers, FL 33901

FIGURE 8.18 Project 8B Cruise Postcards

Objective 3 Edit and Sort a Data Source

GO! Learn How Video W8-3

During the merge process, you can modify information in the data source and arrange the records in a particular order. For example, you may want to add new records or display the records in alphabetical or numerical order based on a specific field.

Activity 8.08 | Using an Access Database as a Mail Merge Data Source

Devon Marshall, Database Coordinator for Caribbean Customized, has asked to you create a postcard mail merge using a table in an Access ***database***. A database is an organized collection of facts about people, events, things, or ideas related to a particular topic or purpose.

ALERT! **To submit as an autograded project, log into MyITLab and download the files for this Project, and begin with those files instead of a new blank document.**

1. Start Word and display a new blank document. If necessary, display the rulers and formatting marks. On the **Mailings tab**, in the **Start Mail Merge group**, click **Start Mail Merge**, and then click **Labels**.

2. In the **Label Options** dialog box, under **Label information**, click the **Label vendors arrow**, and then click **Avery US Letter**. Under **Product number**, scroll as necessary, and then click **3263 Postcards**. Compare your screen with Figure 8.19.

   A description of the selected label displays under Label information on the right side of the Label Options dialog box. In addition to labels, some product numbers are designated as business cards, name tags, or—in this instance—postcards.

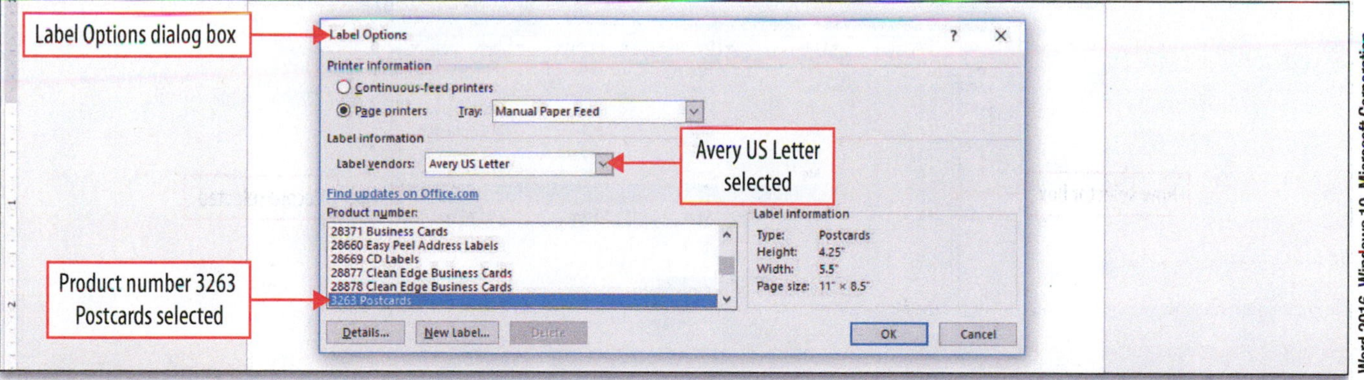

FIGURE 8.19

ALERT! **The Product Number Does Not Display**

If the Avery US Letter 3263 label option does not display, in the Label Options dialog box, click the New Label button to create a custom postcard template. Set the Top Margin and Side Margin to 0. Set the Label Height to 4.25 and the Label Width to 5.5. Set the Vertical Pitch to 4.25 and the Horizontal Pitch to 5.5. Set the Number Across and Number Down to 2. Set the Page Size to Letter Landscape (11 × 8½).

3. In the **Label Options** dialog box, click **OK**. Verify that the gridlines—dashed lines—display in the document. If necessary, click the Table Tools Layout tab, and then in the Table group, click View Gridlines to display the gridlines.

   The postcard template is a table consisting of four cells.

4 On the **Mailings tab**, in the **Start Mail Merge group**, click **Select Recipients**, and then click **Use an Existing List**. In the **Select Data Source** dialog box, navigate to your student data files for this chapter, select **w08B_Cruise_Clients**, and then click **Open**.

In the second, third, and fourth cells, notice that the <Next Record> field displays. When you are using a label template, the <Next Record> field indicates that the contents of the first label will be propagated to the remaining cells of the table during the mail merge process.

5 Display the **Save As** dialog box. Navigate to your **Word Chapter 8** folder, and then **Save** the document as **Lastname_Firstname_8B_Postcards_Main**

Activity 8.09 | Managing a Recipient List by Editing a Data Source

MOS Expert 3.3.4

In this Activity, you will edit the data source.

1 On the **Mailings tab**, in the **Start Mail Merge group**, click **Edit Recipient List**. In the **Mail Merge Recipients** dialog box, under **Data Source**, click **w08B_Cruise_Clients.accdb**, and then click **Edit**.

You can edit a data source during the merge process by changing existing data or by adding or deleting records.

2 In the **ID** field, scroll as necessary, and locate the cell containing *7*. To the left of the cell in the ID field, click the row selector box—the small square to the left of the row. Compare your screen with Figure 8.20.

Clicking the row selector box selects an entire record. This is useful if you want to delete a record.

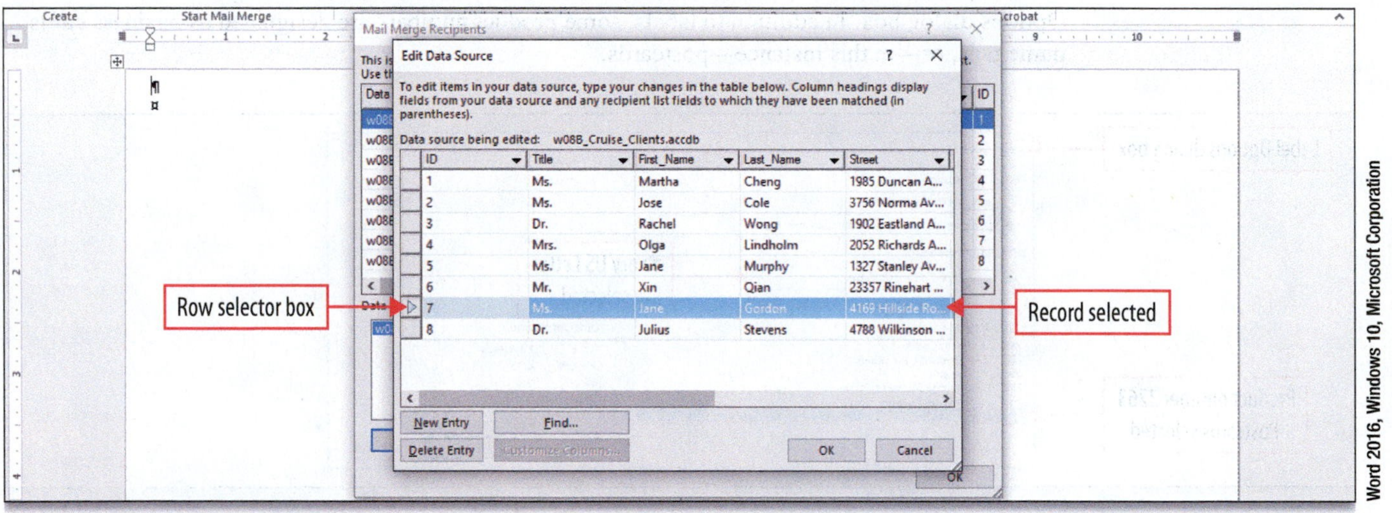

FIGURE 8.20

3 In the **Edit Data Source** dialog box, click **Delete Entry**. In the **Microsoft Word** message box, click **Yes** to confirm the deletion of the record.

4 In the **Edit Data Source** dialog box, click **New Entry**. Notice that a new record line displays below the last current record with ID *0*. Compare your screen with Figure 8.21.

In the new record line, you can add new client information to the data source.

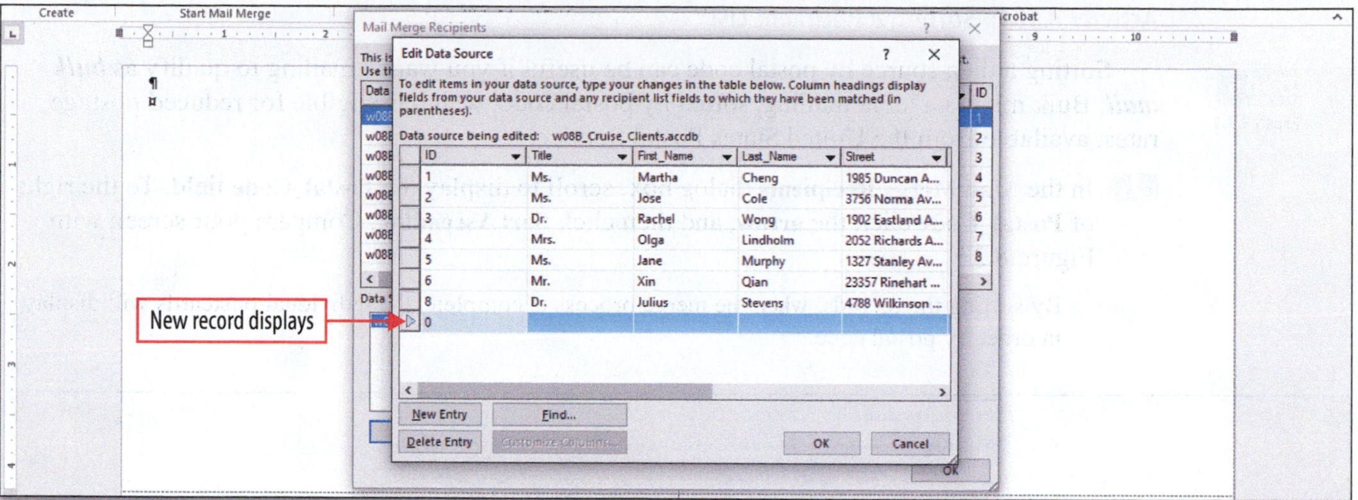

FIGURE 8.21

Word 2016, Windows 10, Microsoft Corporation

5 In the new record line, in the **ID** field, position the insertion point to the right of **0**. Type **9** and then press Tab. In the **ID** field, notice that *9* displays, without the default *0*.

It is not necessary to delete the default 0 when entering data in cells containing numbers. In this instance, the ID, Postal_Code, and Cruises_Booked fields all contain numbers and display the default 0 value.

6 In the cell in the **Title** field, type **Dr.** and then press Tab. Type the following text in the remaining cells of the row, pressing Tab after each entry *except* the last entry.

First_Name	Last_Name	Street	City	State	Postal_Code	Cruises_Booked
Delilah	**Robinson**	**1234 Park Lane**	**Mason City**	**IA**	**50401**	**3**

7 Click **OK**. In the **Microsoft Word** message box, click **Yes** to update your recipient list and save the changes to w08B_Cruise_Clients. Compare your screen with Figure 8.22 and leave the **Mail Merge Recipients** dialog box open for the next Activity.

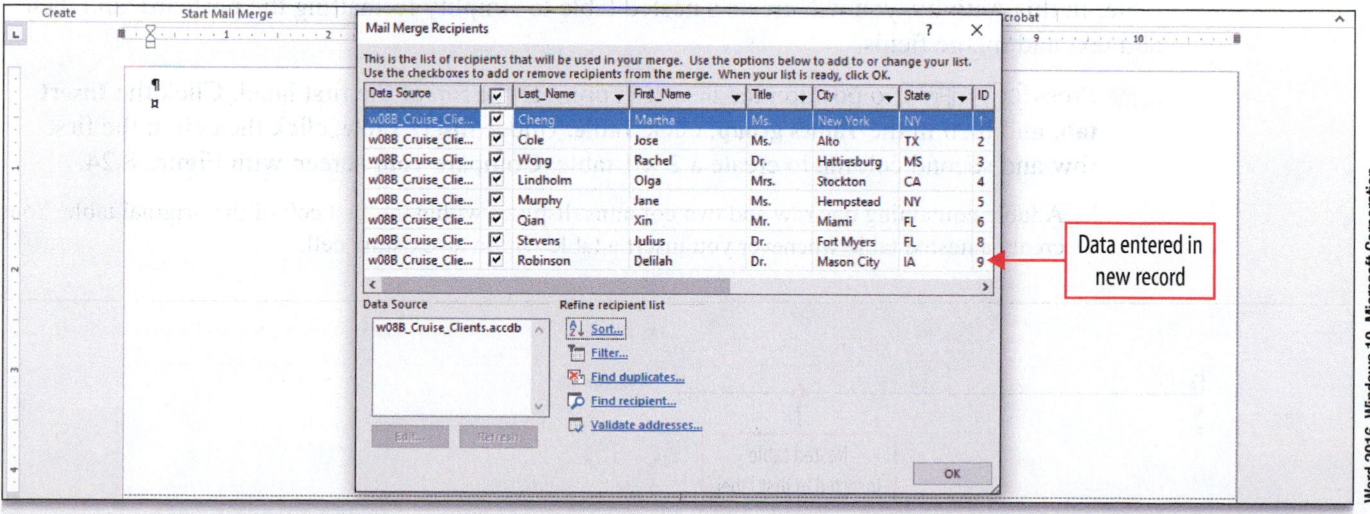

FIGURE 8.22

Word 2016, Windows 10, Microsoft Corporation

Activity 8.10 | Sorting a Recipient List

Expert 3.3.4

Sorting a data source by postal code can be useful if you want a mailing to qualify as ***bulk mail***. Bulk mail is a large mailing, sorted by postal code, which is eligible for reduced postage rates, available from the United States Postal Service.

1 In the **Mail Merge Recipients** dialog box, scroll to display the **Postal_Code** field. To the right of **Postal_Code** click the **arrow**, and then click **Sort Ascending**. Compare your screen with Figure 8.23.

By sorting the records, when the merge process is complete, the individual postcards will display in order by postal code.

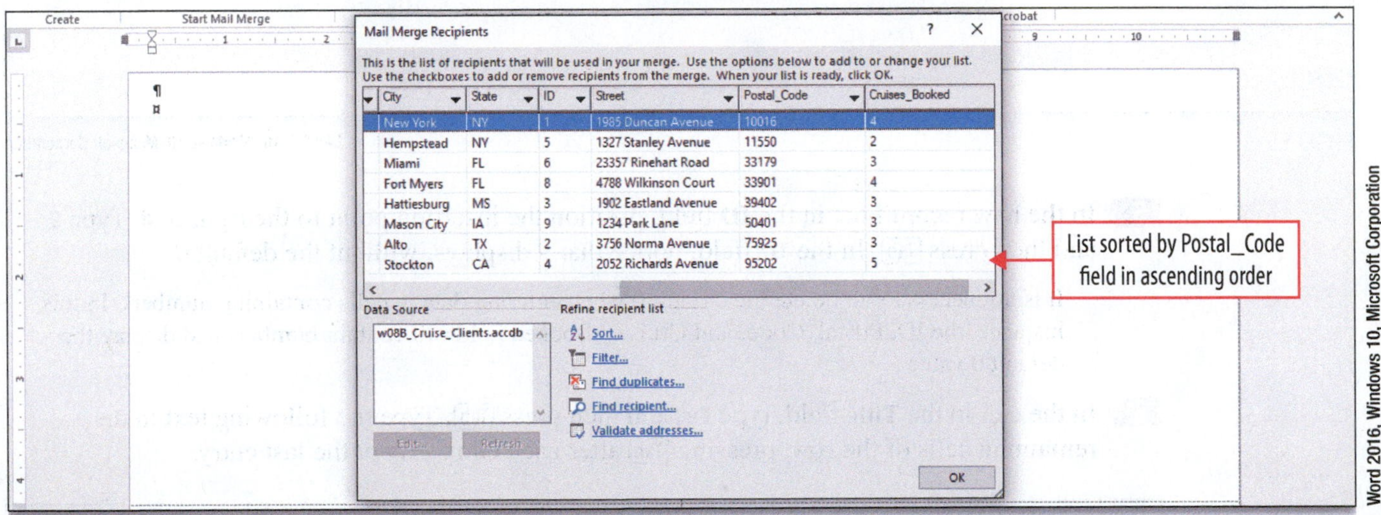

FIGURE 8.23

2 Click **OK**, and then **Save** your changes.

Activity 8.11 | Creating a Nested Table in the Main Document

In Word documents, you can create a ***nested table***—a table inserted in a cell of an existing table. In this Activity, you will create a nested table to simplify formatting the postcard, and then add text and merge fields.

1 Press Ctrl + Home to position the insertion point at the top of the first label. Click the **Insert tab**, and then in the **Tables group**, click **Table**. Under **Insert Table**, click the cell in the first row and second column to create a 2 × 1 table. Compare your screen with Figure 8.24.

A table containing one row and two columns displays within the first cell of the original table. You create a nested table whenever you insert a table within an existing cell.

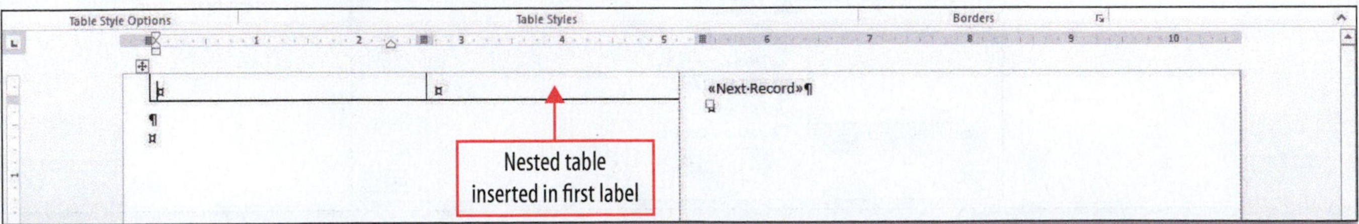

FIGURE 8.24

Word 2016, Windows 10, Microsoft Corporation

2 With the insertion point in the first cell of the nested table, drag to the right to select both cells in the new nested table. Under **Table Tools**, on the **Design tab**, in the **Borders group**, click the **Borders button arrow**, and then click **No Border**.

3 With the cells still selected, click the **Table Tools Layout tab**, and then in the **Cell Size group**, click in the **Table Row Height** box, type **4.25** and then press Enter. Compare your screen with Figure 8.25.

The row height of the nested table matches the height of the label.

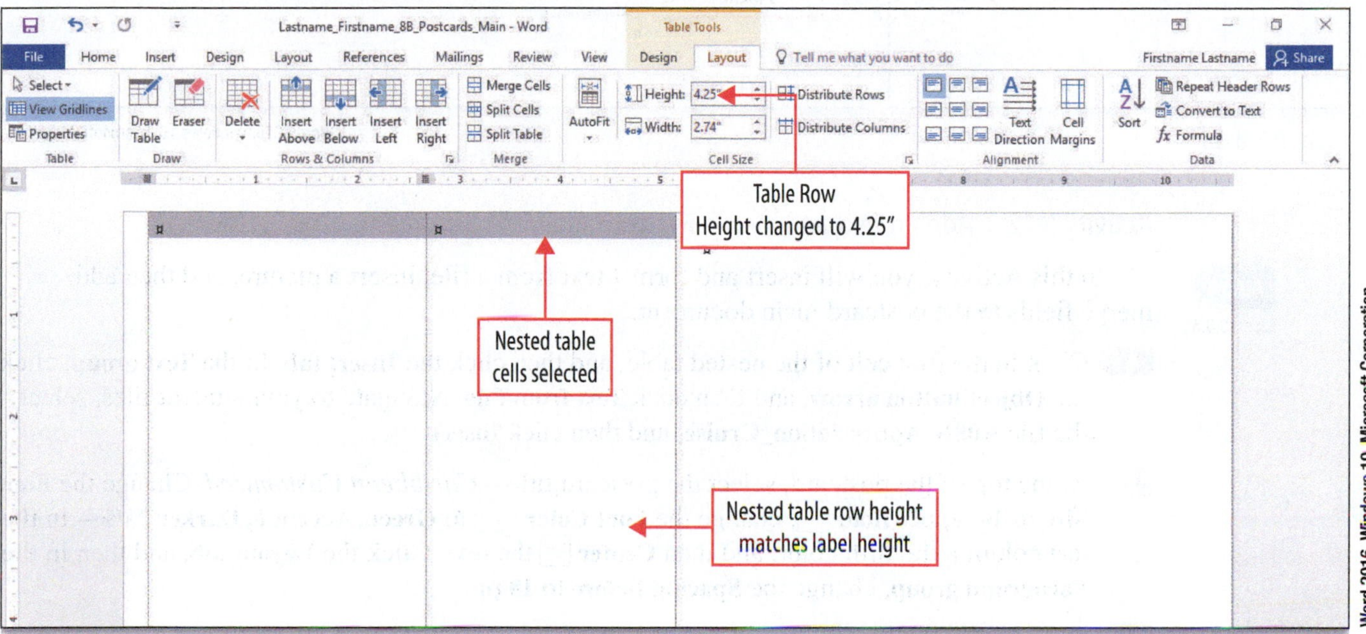

FIGURE 8.25

4 Position the insertion point in the second cell of the nested table. Under **Table Tools**, click the **Design tab**. In the **Borders group**, click the **Line Style arrow**, and then click the third line style—the dashed border. Click the **Line Weight arrow** ½ pt, and then click **1 1/2 pt**. Click the **Pen Color button arrow**, and then under **Theme Colors**, in the last column, click the last color—**Green, Accent 6, Darker 50%**. In the **Borders group**, click the **Borders button arrow**, and then click **Left Border**. Compare your screen with Figure 8.26.

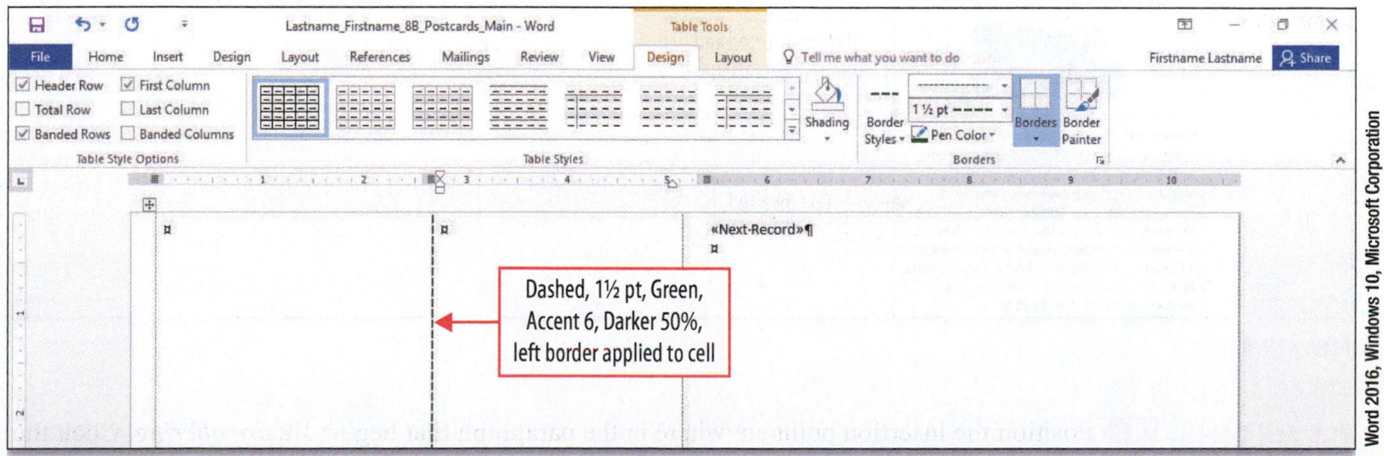

FIGURE 8.26

5 Point to the dashed green border in the nested table to display the resize pointer, and then drag to the right until the border aligns at approximately **3 inches on the horizontal ruler**. Compare your screen with Figure 8.27, and then **Save** your document.

This border will visually separate the message from the delivery address in the completed postcards.

FIGURE 8.27

Word 2016, Windows 10, Microsoft Corporation

Activity 8.12 | Adding Text and Merge Fields to the Main Document

Expert 3.3.5

In this Activity, you will insert and format text from a file, insert a picture, and then add merge fields to the postcard main document.

1 Click in the first cell of the nested table, and then click the **Insert tab**. In the **Text group**, click the **Object button arrow**, and then click **Text from File**. Navigate to your student files, select the file **w08B_Appreciation_Cruise**, and then click **Insert**.

2 At the top of the postcard, select the postcard title—*Caribbean Customized*. Change the **Font Size** to **16**, apply **Bold**, change the **Font Color** to **Green, Accent 6, Darker 25%**—in the last column, the fifth color, and then **Center** the text. Click the **Layout tab**, and then in the **Paragraph group**, change the **Spacing Before** to **18 pt**.

3 Click in the blank paragraph below the postcard title. Click the **Insert tab**, and then in the **Illustrations group**, click **Pictures**. From your student files, insert **w08B_Cruise**, and then on the **Picture Tools Format tab**, in the **Picture Styles group**, click **Picture Effects**. Point to **Bevel**, and then in the first row, click the first style—**Circle**. With the picture selected, press Ctrl + E to center the picture. Compare your screen with Figure 8.28.

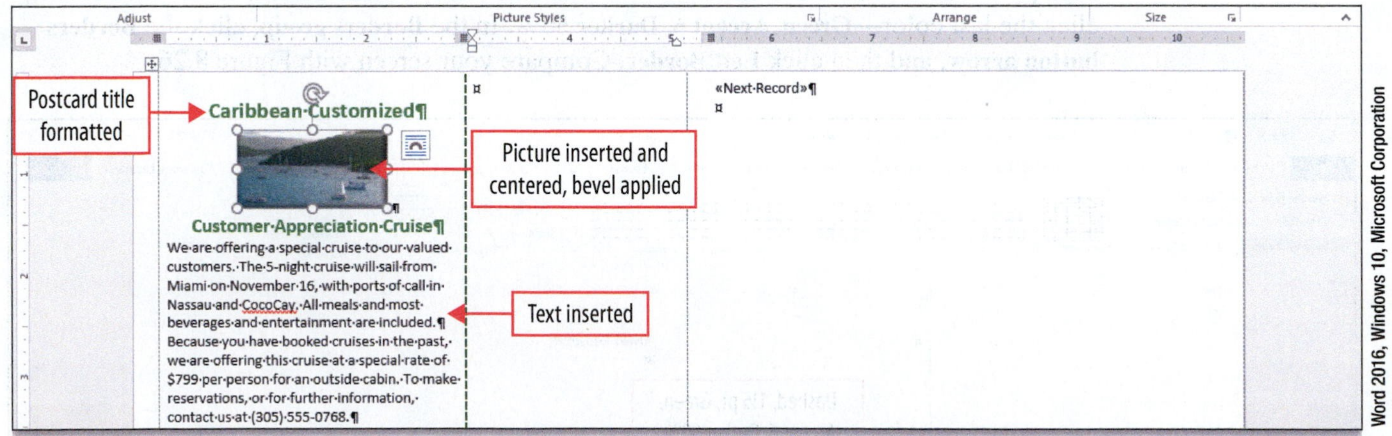

FIGURE 8.28

Word 2016, Windows 10, Microsoft Corporation

4 Position the insertion point anywhere in the paragraph that begins *We are offering*. Click the **Layout tab**. In the **Paragraph group**, click the **Spacing Before spin box up arrow** to **12 pt**, and then click the **Spacing After spin box up arrow** to **12 pt**.

5 In the paragraph that begins *Because you have booked*, position the insertion point to the right of *booked*, and then press Spacebar. Click the **Mailings tab**. In the **Write & Insert Fields group**, click the **Insert Merge Field button arrow**, and then click **Cruises_Booked**. Compare your screen with Figure 8.29.

The Cruises_Booked field contains the number of cruises previously booked by each customer. By inserting this merge field, you can personalize the postcards.

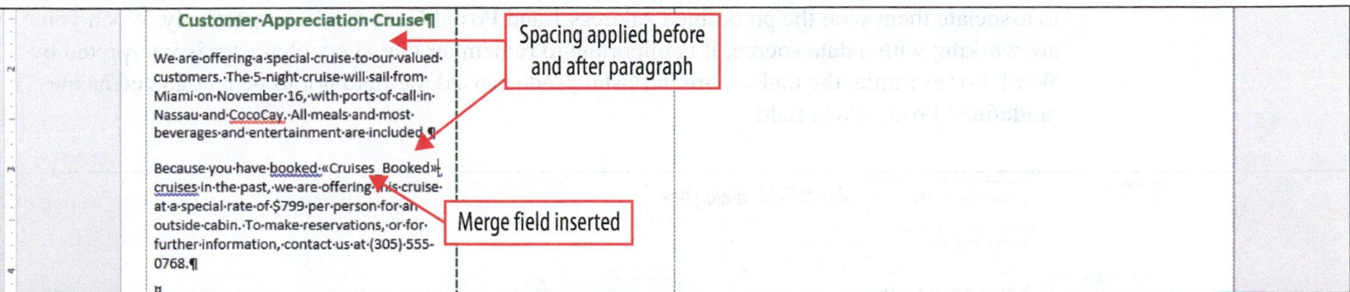

FIGURE 8.29

6 **Save** your changes.

Objective 4 Match Fields and Apply Rules

GO! Learn How Video W8-4

The data source that you use in a mail merge may not include the same field names that are used in the Address Block or Greeting Line merge fields. The ***Match Fields*** feature maps the predefined field names to the field names in your data source. You can apply ***rules***—conditional Word fields—that allow you to determine how the merge process is completed. This allows you to personalize the final document in additional ways—for example, inserting a specific date in a letter based on the department field in a data source with employee information.

Activity 8.13 | Matching Fields to a Data Source

The Address Block and Greeting Line merge fields include specific field names—such as Last Name, Address 1, and Postal Code. In this Activity, you will use the Match Fields feature to map the Address Block fields to your data source fields to display the delivery address correctly.

1 In the nested table, click to the right of the green dashed border to position the insertion point in the second cell of the nested table. On the **Mailings tab**, in the **Write & Insert Fields group**, click **Address Block**. Compare your screen with Figure 8.30.

In the Preview box, only the name, city, and state of the customer display.

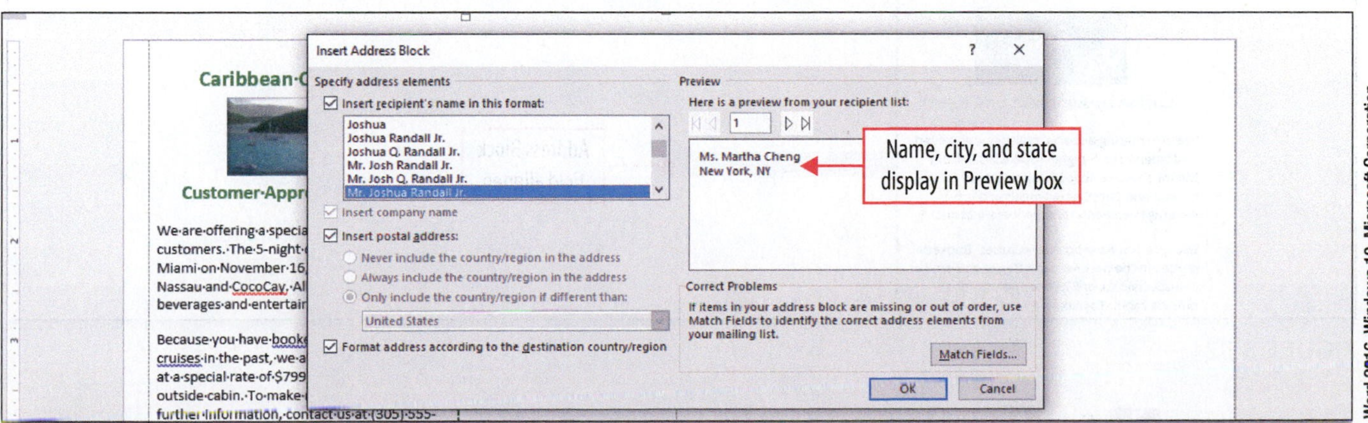

FIGURE 8.30

2 In the **Insert Address Block** dialog box, under **Correct Problems**, click **Match Fields**. In the **Match Fields** dialog box, click the **Address 1 arrow**, and then from the displayed list, click **Street**.

3 Click the **Postal Code arrow**, and then click **Postal_Code**. Compare your screen with Figure 8.31.

Word did not recognize the Street and Postal_Code fields in the data source, so it was necessary to associate them with the predefined Address 1 and Postal Code fields, respectively. When you are working with a data source, it is important to remember that *every* character is interpreted by Word. For example, the underscore in Postal_Code caused the field not to be recognized as the predefined Postal Code field.

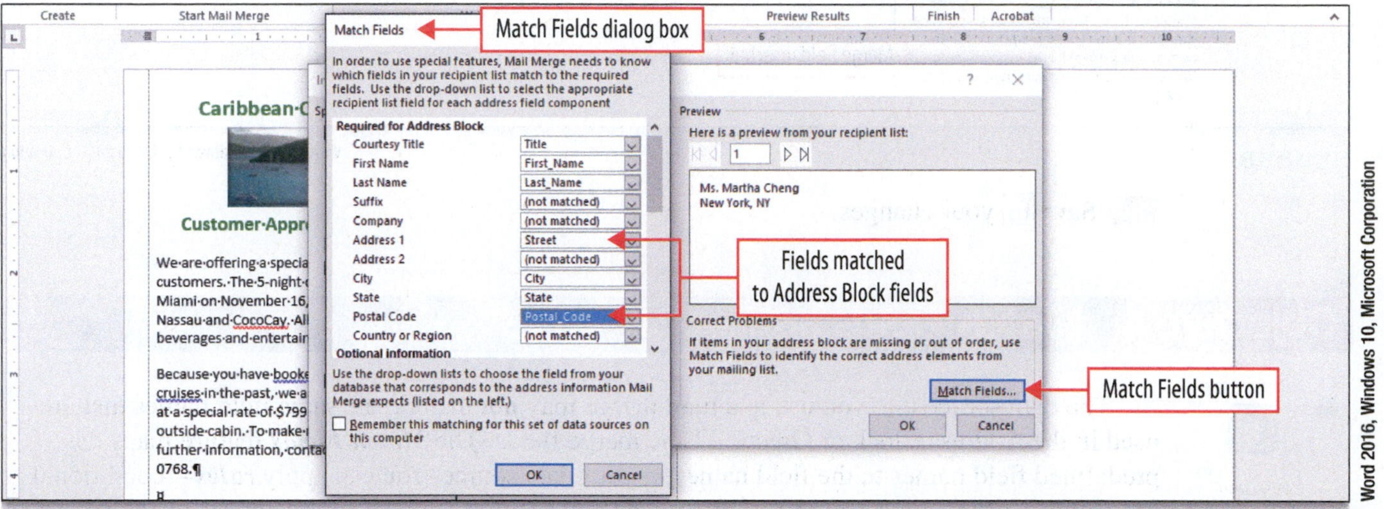

FIGURE 8.31

4 Click **OK**. In the **Microsoft Word** message box, when asked if you want to match this field to a Unique Identifier, click **Yes**. Notice that the Preview box displays the complete mailing address.

5 Click **OK** to insert the Address Block merge field in the document.

6 With the insertion point in the second cell of the nested table, under **Table Tools**, click the **Layout tab**. In the **Alignment group**, click **Align Center Left**, and then compare your screen with Figure 8.32.

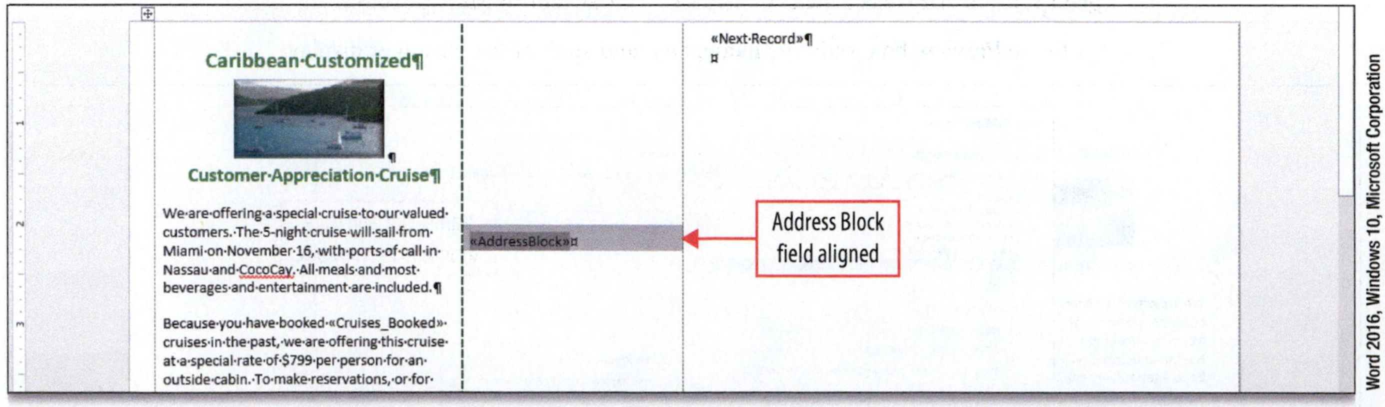

FIGURE 8.32

7 **Save** your changes.

Activity 8.14 | Applying Rules to a Merge

You can apply rules to add a decision-making element to the mail merge process. In this Activity, you will add a rule that will place different cruise prices in the individual postcards, based on the number of cruises the customer has booked.

1 In the first cell of the nested table, in the last paragraph, delete the text *$799*. Do *not* delete the surrounding space formatting marks.

2 With the insertion point positioned between the two space formatting marks, on the **Mailings tab**, in the **Write & Insert Fields group**, click **Rules**, and then click **If...Then...Else**.

3 In the **Insert Word Field: IF** dialog box, under **IF**, click the **Field name arrow**, scroll as necessary, and then click **Cruises_Booked**. Click the **Comparison arrow**, and then click **Greater than or equal**. In the **Compare to** box, type **3** In the **Insert this text** box, type **$549** In the **Otherwise insert this text** box, type **$699** Compare your screen with Figure 8.33.

The If...Then...Else rule allows you to set a condition so that specific text is inserted if the condition is met, and different text is inserted if the condition is not satisfied. In this instance, if the number of cruises booked is greater than or equal to 3, during the merge process, Word will insert the text $549. Otherwise, Word will insert the text $699.

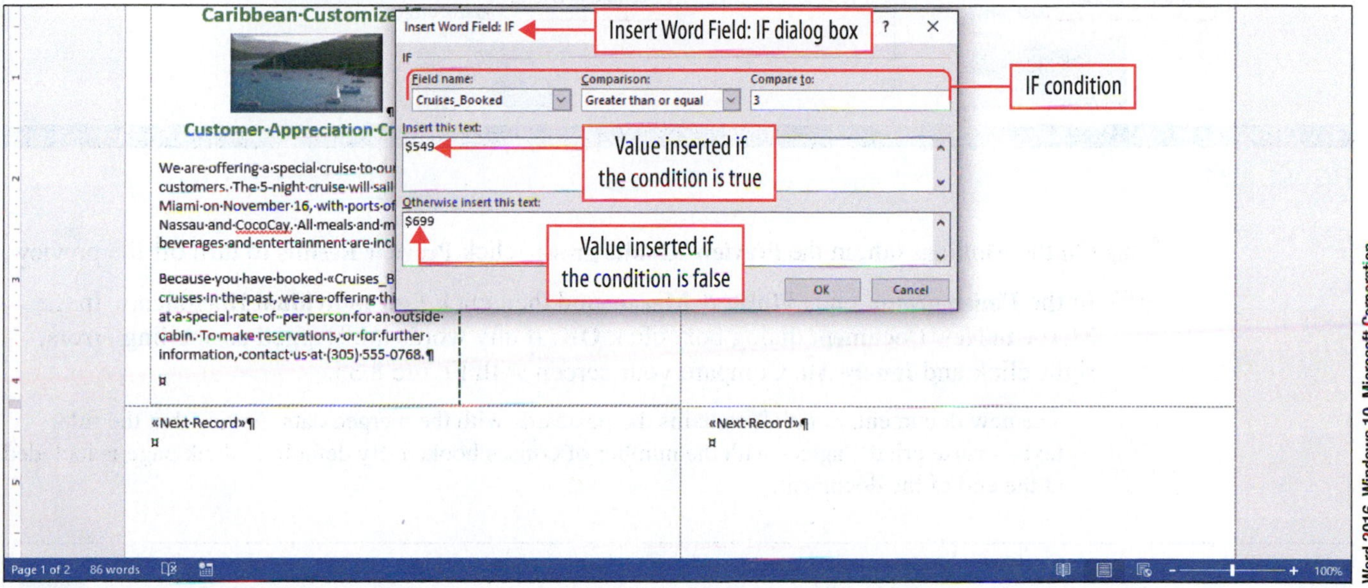

FIGURE 8.33

4 Click **OK**. Notice that $549 is inserted as the default value for the rule.

5 On the **Mailings tab**, in the **Write & Insert Fields group**, click **Update Labels**. In the **Preview Results group**, click **Preview Results**.

The number of cruises booked, the text for the rule, and the mailing addresses display for each record. Compare your screen with Figure 8.34.

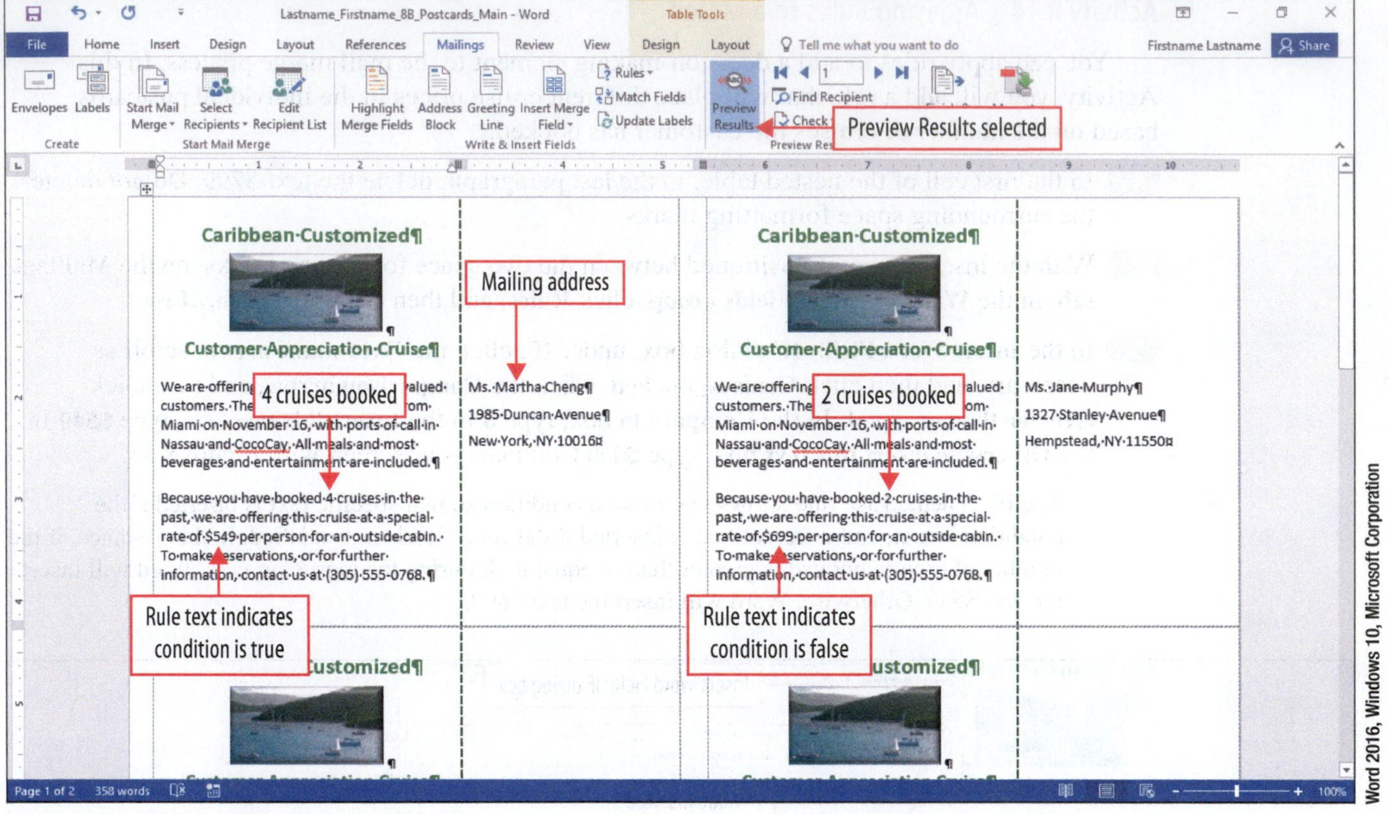

FIGURE 8.34

6 On the **Mailings tab**, in the **Preview Results group**, click **Preview Results** to turn off the preview.

7 In the **Finish group**, click **Finish & Merge**, and then click **Edit Individual Documents**. In the **Merge to New Document** dialog box, click **OK**. If any words are flagged as spelling errors, right-click and **Ignore All**. Compare your screen with Figure 8.35.

The new document, *Labels1*, contains the postcards with the merged data. Notice that the rule text—cruise price—agrees with the number of cruises booked. By default, a blank page is included at the end of the document.

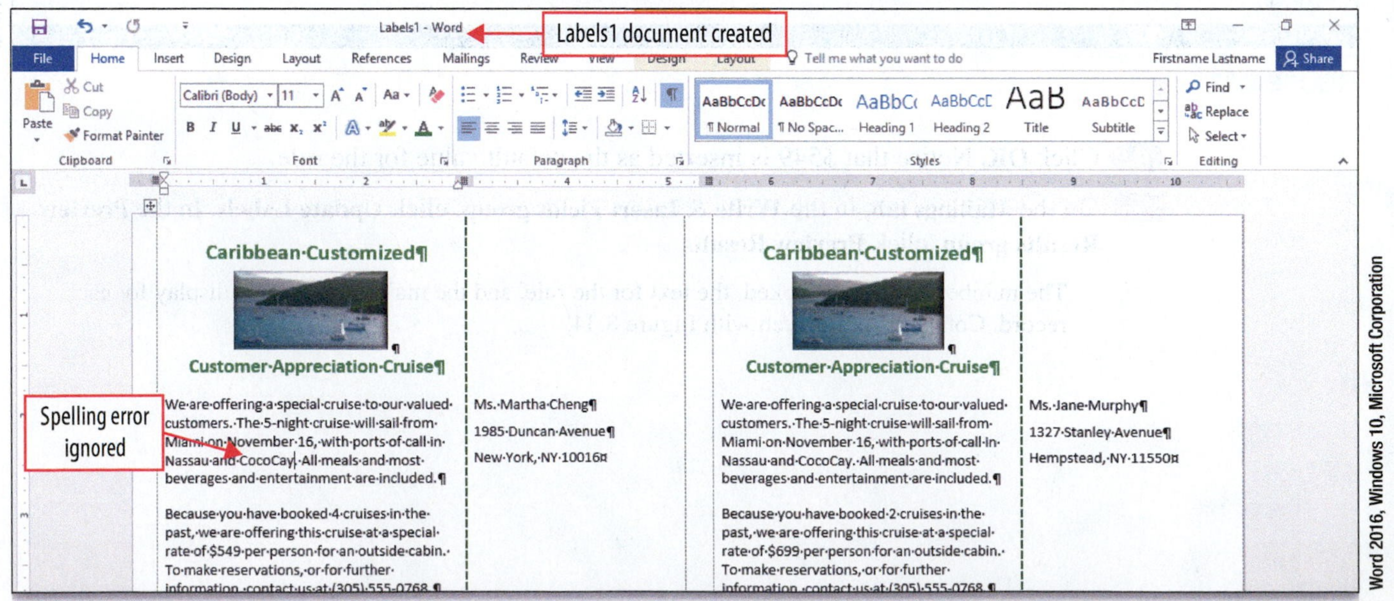

FIGURE 8.35

8 WORD

8 Display the **Save As** dialog box. Navigate to your **Word Chapter 8** folder, and then save the document as **Lastname_Firstname_8B_Postcards_Merged**

9 Click the **File tab**, and then click **Show All Properties**. In the **Tags** box, type **cruise postcards, merged** In the **Subject** box, type your course name and section number, and then if necessary, edit the author name to display your name. **Save** your document, and then press Ctrl + W to close the file.

10 With your main document displayed, click the **File tab**, and then click **Show All Properties**. In the **Tags** box, type **cruise postcards, main** In the **Subject** box, type your course name and section number, and then if necessary, edit the author name to display your name. **Save** your document, and then press Ctrl + W to close the document but leave Word open.

Objective 5 Create a Data Source and a Directory

GO! Learn How Video W8-5

Previously in this chapter, you used mail merge to create documents that contain individual components—such as letters, envelopes, and postcards. You can also use mail merge to create a ***directory***—a single list of selected data records using specified fields from a data source. For example, a directory might contain the names, departments, and phone numbers for company employees.

Activity 8.15 | Formatting a Directory Main Document

Maria Ramirez, Cruise Consultant, has asked you to create a directory that lists emergency contact information, which is recorded on paper forms, for customers booked on the Customer Appreciation Cruise.

ALERT! **To submit as an autograded project, log into MyITLab and download the files for this Project, and begin with those files instead of a new blank document.**

1 Press Ctrl + N to display a new document, or if necessary, start Word and open a new blank document. Display the **Save As** dialog box, navigate to your **Word Chapter 8** folder, and save the document as **Lastname_Firstname_8B_Directory_Main**

2 On the **Layout tab**, in the **Page Setup group**, click **Margins**, and then click **Narrow**.

The Narrow margin setting adjusts all margins to 0.5".

3 Click the **Mailings tab**. In the **Start Mail Merge group**, click **Start Mail Merge**, and then click **Directory**. Click **Select Recipients**, and then click **Use an Existing List**. Navigate to your student data files, select **w08B_Directory_Data**, and then click **Open**. In the **Select Table** dialog box, click **OK**.

4 To set a left tab stop, at the left end of the horizontal ruler, verify that the **Left Tab** button displays. On the ruler, click at **2.5 inches on the horizontal ruler**. To set two additional left tab stops, click at **4.5 inches** and then at **5.5 inches on the horizontal ruler**. Compare your screen with Figure 8.36.

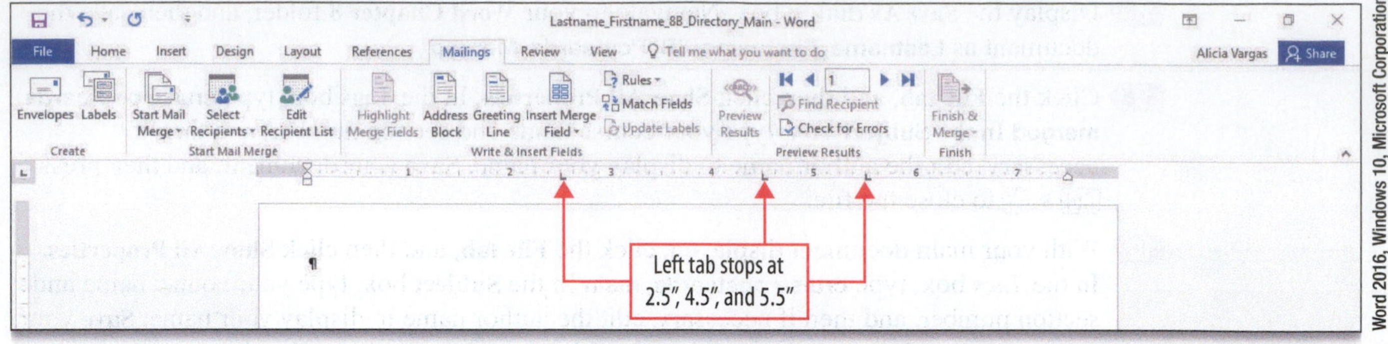

FIGURE 8.36

5 On the **Mailings tab**, in the **Write & Insert Fields group**, click the **Insert Merge Field** arrow. In the list, click **Title**, and then press Spacebar. Click the **Insert Merge Field arrow** again, click **First_Name**, and then press Spacebar. Click the **Insert Merge Field arrow** again, click **Last_Name**, and then press Tab.

6 Click the **Insert Merge Field** arrow, click **Contact_Name**, and then press Tab. Use the same technique to insert the **Relationship** field, being sure to press Tab after you insert the field. Then, insert the **Home_Phone** field and press Enter. Compare your screen with Figure 8.37.

All of the merge fields from the data source are inserted on the first line of the document. When the directory is created, all the information for one record—a customer—will display on a single line. The tab between the fields will display the data in columns, creating a professional appearance. Pressing Enter after the last field adds a new paragraph so that when the data is merged, each record will display on a separate line.

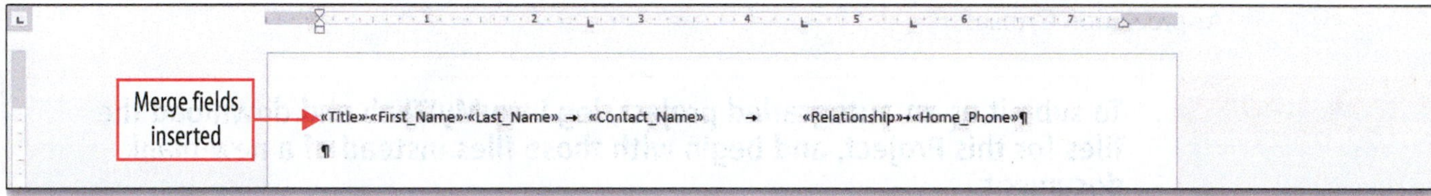

FIGURE 8.37

Word 2016, Windows 10, Microsoft Corporation

7 **Save** your changes.

Activity 8.16 | Merging Files to Create a Directory

When completing the merge process for a directory, all of the data represented by the merge fields is displayed in a single document.

1 On the **Mailings tab**, in the **Preview Results group**, click **Preview Results**.

Because you are creating a directory, only one record—the first record—displays.

2 On the **Mailings tab**, in the **Finish group**, click **Finish & Merge**, and then click **Edit Individual Documents**. In the **Merge to New Document** dialog box, click **OK**. Compare your screen with Figure 8.38.

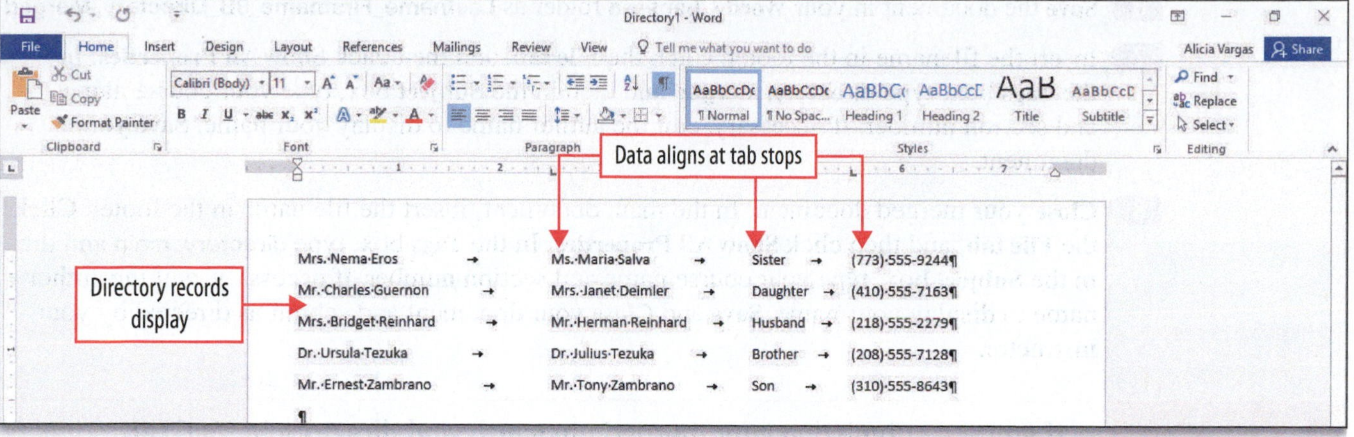

FIGURE 8.38

Word 2016, Windows 10, Microsoft Corporation

Activity 8.17 | Editing a Directory

In the final merged directory, you can add additional elements, such as a title and headings, to improve the appearance of the final document.

1 With the insertion point at the beginning of the document, press Enter, and then press ↑.

2 Type the following text, pressing Enter after each line, including the last line:

Caribbean Customized
Customer Appreciation Cruise
Emergency Contact List

3 Select the first paragraph, and then change the **Font Size** to **28**. On the **Layout tab**, in the **Paragraph group**, change the **Spacing Before** to **24 pt**. Select the second and third paragraphs, and then change the **Font Size** to **16**.

4 Position the insertion point in the blank paragraph immediately above the first customer record. Type **Customer** press Tab, and then type **Contact** Press Tab, type **Relationship** press Tab, and then type **Phone Number**

5 Select the column heading text that you just typed. On the mini toolbar, apply **Bold** B and **Underline** U. Deselect the text, and then compare your screen with Figure 8.39.

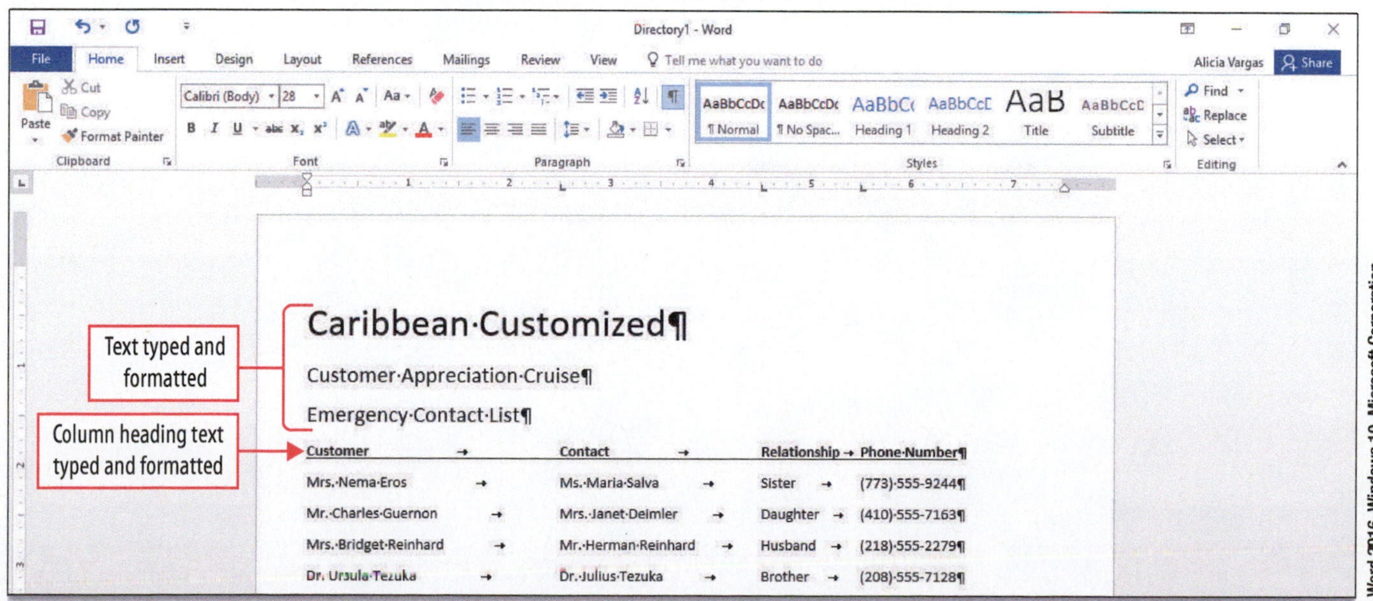

Word 2016, Windows 10, Microsoft Corporation

FIGURE 8.39

6 **Save** the document in your **Word Chapter 8** folder as **Lastname_Firstname_8B_Directory_Merged**

7 Insert the filename in the footer. Click the **File tab**, and then click **Show All Properties**. In the **Tags** box, type **directory, merged** and then in the **Subject** box, type your course name and section number. If necessary, edit the author name to display your name. **Save** your document.

8 **Close** your merged document. In the main document, insert the file name in the footer. Click the **File tab**, and then click **Show All Properties**. In the **Tags** box, type **directory, main** and then in the **Subject** box, type your course name and section number. If necessary, edit the author name to display your name. **Save** and **Close** your document and submit as directed by your instructor.

ALERT! **If you are submitting your merged postcards and directory in MyITLab, complete Steps 9 through 12.**

9 To submit your merged postcards and directory in MyITLab, you will combine your merged postcards and merged directory into one file. **Open** your **Lastname_Firstname_8B_Postcards_Merged** file. Press Ctrl + A to select all of the merged postcards. On the **Home tab**, in the **Clipboard group**, click **Copy**.

10 Click the **File tab**, and then **Open** your **Lastname_Firstname_8B_Directory_Merged** file. Press Ctrl + End to move to the end of the document. On the **Layout tab**, in the **Page Setup group**, click **Breaks**, and then under **Section Breaks**, click **Next Page** to insert a new section in the document.

11 On the **Home tab**, in the **Clipboard group**, click **Paste** to paste the merged postcards at the end of the document.

12 **Save** your document, **Close** all open documents, and then submit your **Lastname_Firstname_8A_Directory_Merged** file in MyITLab.

END | You have completed Project 8B

GO! To Work

Andrew Rodriguez / Fotolia; FotolEdhar / Fotolia; apops / Fotolia; Yuri Arcurs / Fotolia

8 WORD

MICROSOFT OFFICE SPECIALIST (MOS) SKILLS IN THIS CHAPTER	
PROJECT 8A	**PROJECT 8B**
Expert 2.2.1 Create paragraph and character styles **Expert 3.3.3** Perform mail merges **Expert 3.3.4** Manage recipient lists **Expert 3.3.5** Insert merged fields **Expert 3.3.6** Preview merge results	**Expert 3.3.4** Manage recipient lists **Expert 3.3.5** Insert merged fields

BUILD YOUR E-PORTFOLIO

An E-Portfolio is a collection of evidence, stored electronically, that showcases what you have accomplished while completing your education. Collecting and then sharing your work products with potential employers reflects your academic and career goals. Your completed documents from the following projects are good examples to show what you have learned: 8G, 8K, and 8L.

GO! FOR JOB SUCCESS

Discussion: Project Management

Your instructor may assign these questions to your class, and then ask you to think about them or discuss them with your classmates:

Project management is a discipline that identifies and plans for the resources required to complete a defined set of tasks to achieve a stated goal. Project managers develop timelines, coordinate resources, organize and motivate cross-functional groups working on the project, and forecast and monitor costs. Size and complexity of projects vary: Construction and architecture projects might entail building a new highway or skyscraper; software projects develop new software products or upgrades of existing products. Administrative projects might include meeting and event planning.

FotolEdhar / Fotolia

Project managers must have skills in a variety of areas, including accounting, management, forecasting, and writing. What are some other skills that would be valuable in project management?

What "soft" skills do you think are required to be a successful project manager?

To assure that the corporate strategy translates into projects actually being implemented, many organizations have implemented a Project Management Office, which assures alignment between strategy and projects so that the right projects move forward at the right time and right budget. What do you think are some other benefits to both executives and project managers of using a Project Management Office?

END OF CHAPTER

SUMMARY

The mail merge feature joins a main document with a data source—for example, an Excel spreadsheet or an Access table—to create personalized documents such as letters, envelopes, mailing labels, and directories.

Filter the data source to display specific records or sort the data source to display records in a specific order. Predefined merge fields or individual merge fields determine the placement of data in the document.

Match Fields maps predefined field names to the field names in the data source. Apply a rule to check criteria—for example, to insert a specific date based on a particular field—when completing the merge process.

When performing a mail merge, you can edit a data source to add new records, delete records, and customize the field names. A directory is a single list of records using specified fields from a data source.

GO! LEARN IT ONLINE

Review the concepts and key terms in this chapter by completing these online challenges, which you can find at **MyITLab**.

Matching and Multiple Choice: Answer matching and multiple choice questions to test what you learned in this chapter.

Lessons on the GO!: Learn how to use all the new apps and features as they are introduced by Microsoft.

MOS Prep Quiz: Answer questions to review the MOS skills that you practiced in this chapter.

PROJECT GUIDE FOR WORD CHAPTER 8

Your instructor may assign one or more of these projects to help you review the chapter and assess your mastery and understanding of the chapter.

Project Guide for Word Chapter 8			
Project	**Apply Skills from These Chapter Objectives**	**Project Type**	**Project Location**
8A MyITLab	Objectives 1–2 from Project 8A	**8A Instructional Project (Grader Project)** Guided instruction to learn the skills in Project 8A.	In MyITLab and in text
8B MyITLab	Objectives 3–5 from Project 8B	**8B Instructional Project (Grader Project)** Guided instruction to learn the skills in Project 8B.	In MyITLab and in text
8C	Objectives 1–2 from Project 8A	**8C Skills Review (Scorecard Grading)** A guided review of the skills from Project 8A.	In text
8D	Objectives 3–5 from Project 8B	**8D Skills Review (Scorecard Grading)** A guided review of the skills from Project 8B.	In text
8E MyITLab	Objectives 1–2 from Project 8A	**8E Mastery (Grader Project)** **Mastery and Transfer of Learning** A demonstration of your mastery of the skills in Project 8A with extensive decision making.	In MyITLab and in text
8F MyITLab	Objectives 3–5 from Project 8B	**8F Mastery (Grader Project)** **Mastery and Transfer of Learning** A demonstration of your mastery of the skills in Project 8B with extensive decision making.	In MyITLab and in text
8G MyITLab	Objectives 1–5 from Project 8A and 8B	**8G Mastery (Grader Project)** **Mastery and Transfer of Learning** A demonstration of your mastery of the skills in Projects 8A and 8B with extensive decision making.	In MyITLab and in text
8H	Combination of Objectives from Projects 8A and 8B	**8H GO! Fix It (Scorecard Grading)** **Critical Thinking** A demonstration of your mastery of the skills in Projects 8A and 8B by creating a correct result from a document that contains errors you must find.	Instructor Resource Center (IRC) and MyITLab
8I	Combination of Objectives from Projects 8A and 8B	**8I GO! Make It (Scorecard Grading)** **Critical Thinking** A demonstration of your mastery of the skills in Projects 8A and 8B by creating a result from a supplied picture.	IRC and MyITLab
8J	Combination of Objectives from Projects 8A and 8B	**8J GO! Solve It (Rubric Grading)** **Critical Thinking** A demonstration of your mastery of the skills in Projects 8A and 8B, your decision-making skills, and your critical thinking skills. A task-specific rubric helps you self-assess your result.	IRC and MyITLab
8K	Combination of Objectives from Projects 8A and 8B	**8K GO! Solve It (Rubric Grading)** **Critical Thinking** A demonstration of your mastery of the skills in Projects 8A and 8B, your decision-making skills, and your critical thinking skills. A task-specific rubric helps you self-assess your result.	In text
8L	Combination of Objectives from Projects 8A and 8B	**8L GO! Think (Rubric Grading)** **Critical Thinking** A demonstration of your understanding of the chapter concepts applied in a manner that you would outside of college. An analytic rubric helps you and your instructor grade the quality of your work by comparing it to the work an expert in the discipline would create.	In text
8M	Combination of Objectives from Projects 8A and 8B	**8M GO! Think (Rubric Grading)** **Critical Thinking** A demonstration of your understanding of the chapter concepts applied in a manner that you would outside of college. An analytic rubric helps you and your instructor grade the quality of your work by comparing it to the work an expert in the discipline would create.	IRC and MyITLab
8N	Combination of Objectives from Projects 8A and 8B	**8N You and GO! (Rubric Grading)** **Critical Thinking** A demonstration of your understanding of the chapter concepts applied in a manner that you would in a personal situation. An analytic rubric helps you and your instructor grade the quality of your work.	IRC and MyITLab

GLOSSARY

GLOSSARY OF CHAPTER KEY TERMS

Address Block A predefined merge field that includes the recipient's name and address.

Bulk mail A large mailing, sorted by postal code, that is eligible for reduced postage rates, available from the United States Postal Service.

Character style A type of style that contains formatting that can be applied to selected text and does not include formatting that affects paragraphs.

Data source A list of variable information, such as names and addresses, that is merged with a main document to create customized form letters or labels.

Database An organized collection of facts about people, events, things, or ideas related to a particular topic or purpose.

Directory A single list of records using specified fields from a data source.

Fields In a mail merge, a category—or column—of data.

Filter A set of criteria applied to fields in a data source to display specific records.

Form letter A letter with standardized wording that can be sent to many different people.

Greeting Line A predefined merge field that includes an introductory word, such as *Dear*, and the recipient's name.

Inside address The name and address of the person receiving the letter; positioned below the date line.

Mail merge A Word feature that joins a main document and a data source to create customized letters or labels.

Main document In a mail merge, the document that contains the text or formatting that remains constant.

Match Fields A Word feature that maps predefined field names to the field names in a data source.

Merge field In a mail merge, a placeholder that represents specific information in the data source.

Nested table A table inserted in a cell of an existing table.

Record All of the categories of data pertaining to one person, place, thing, event, or idea, and which is formatted as a row in a database table.

Rules Conditional Word fields that allow you to determine how the merge process is completed.

Salutation The greeting line of a letter, such as *Dear Sir*.

CHAPTER REVIEW

Apply 8A skills from these Objectives:

1 Merge a Data Source and a Main Document
2 Use Mail Merge to Create Envelopes

Skills Review Project 8C Eastern Cruise

In the following Skills Review, you will create a form letter, customized for current customers, that announces a new cruise offered by Caribbean Customized. You will also create envelopes to accompany the merged letters. Your completed documents will look similar to Figure 8.40.

PROJECT FILES

For Project 8C, you will need the following files:

New blank Word document
w08C_Eastern_Letter
w08C_Eastern_Customers

You will save your documents as:

Lastname_Firstname_8C_Eastern_Main (not shown in Figure)
Lastname_Firstname_8C_Eastern_Merged
Lastname_Firstname_8C_EasternEnv_Main (not shown in Figure)
Lastname_Firstname_8C_EasternEnv_Merged

PROJECT RESULTS

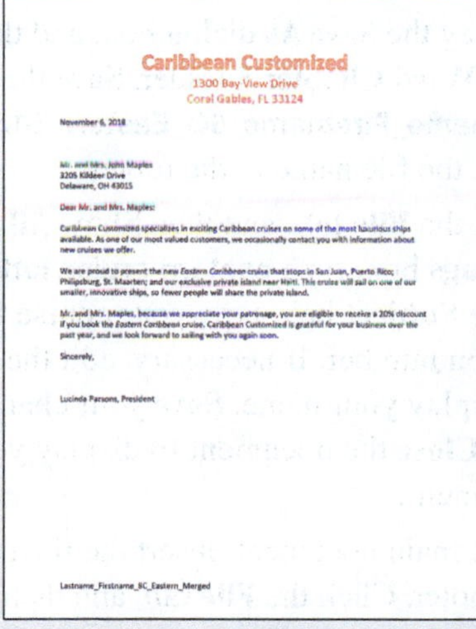

Caribbean Customized
1300 Bay View Drive
Coral Gables, FL 33124

November 6, 2018

Mr. and Mrs. John Maples
3205 Kildeer Drive
Delaware, OH 43015

Dear Mr. and Mrs. Maples:

Caribbean Customized specializes in exciting Caribbean cruises on some of the most luxurious ships available. As one of our most valued customers, we occasionally contact you with information about new cruises we offer.

We are proud to present the new *Eastern Caribbean* cruise that stops in San Juan, Puerto Rico; Philipsburg, St. Maarten; and our exclusive private island near Haiti. This cruise will sail on one of our smaller, innovative ships, so fewer people will share the private island.

Mr. and Mrs. Maples, because we appreciate your patronage, you are eligible to receive a 20% discount if you book the *Eastern Caribbean* cruise. Caribbean Customized is grateful for your business over the past year, and we look forward to sailing with you again soon.

Sincerely,

Lucinda Parsons, President

Lastname_Firstname_8C_Eastern_Merged

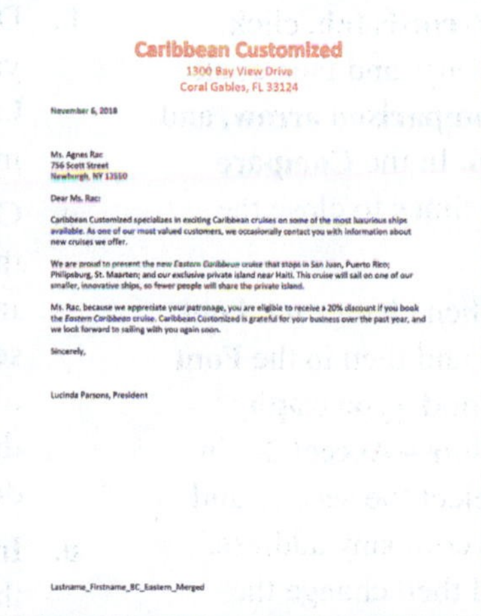

Caribbean Customized
1300 Bay View Drive
Coral Gables, FL 33124

November 6, 2018

Ms. Agnes Rac
756 Scott Street
Newburgh, NY 12550

Dear Ms. Rac:

Caribbean Customized specializes in exciting Caribbean cruises on some of the most luxurious ships available. As one of our most valued customers, we occasionally contact you with information about new cruises we offer.

We are proud to present the new *Eastern Caribbean* cruise that stops in San Juan, Puerto Rico; Philipsburg, St. Maarten; and our exclusive private island near Haiti. This cruise will sail on one of our smaller, innovative ships, so fewer people will share the private island.

Ms. Rac, because we appreciate your patronage, you are eligible to receive a 20% discount if you book the *Eastern Caribbean* cruise. Caribbean Customized is grateful for your business over the past year, and we look forward to sailing with you again soon.

Sincerely,

Lucinda Parsons, President

Lastname_Firstname_8C_Eastern_Merged

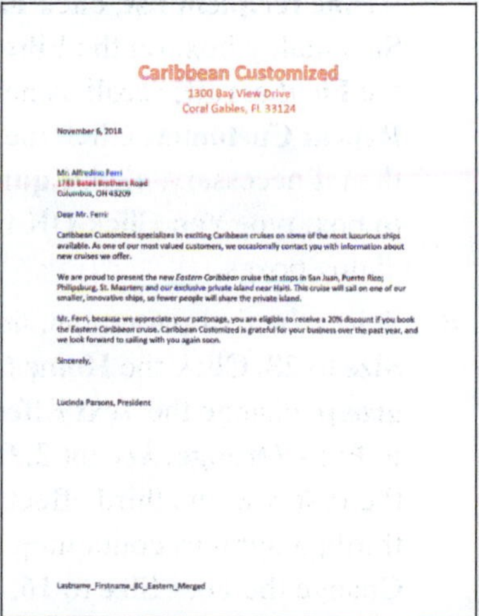

Caribbean Customized
1300 Bay View Drive
Coral Gables, FL 33124

November 6, 2018

Mr. Alfredino Ferri
1783 Bates Brothers Road
Columbus, OH 43209

Dear Mr. Ferri:

Caribbean Customized specializes in exciting Caribbean cruises on some of the most luxurious ships available. As one of our most valued customers, we occasionally contact you with information about new cruises we offer.

We are proud to present the new *Eastern Caribbean* cruise that stops in San Juan, Puerto Rico; Philipsburg, St. Maarten; and our exclusive private island near Haiti. This cruise will sail on one of our smaller, innovative ships, so fewer people will share the private island.

Mr. Ferri, because we appreciate your patronage, you are eligible to receive a 20% discount if you book the *Eastern Caribbean* cruise. Caribbean Customized is grateful for your business over the past year, and we look forward to sailing with you again soon.

Sincerely,

Lucinda Parsons, President

Lastname_Firstname_8C_Eastern_Merged

Caribbean Customized
1300 Bay View Drive
Coral Gables, FL 33124

Mr. and Mrs. John Maples
3205 Kildeer Drive
Delaware, OH 43015

Lastname_Firstname_8C_EasternEnv_Merged

Caribbean Customized
1300 Bay View Drive
Coral Gables, FL 33124

Ms. Agnes Rac
756 Scott Street
Newburgh, NY 12550

Lastname_Firstname_8C_EasternEnv_Merged

Caribbean Customized
1300 Bay View Drive
Coral Gables, FL 33124

Mr. Alfredino Ferri
1783 Bates Brothers Road
Columbus, OH 43209

Lastname_Firstname_8C_EasternEnv_Merged

FIGURE 8.40

(Project 8C Eastern Cruise continues on the next page)

Skills Review Project 8C Eastern Cruise (continued)

1 Start Word. Navigate to your student files, open the file **w08C_Eastern_Letter**, and then **Save** the document in your **Word Chapter 8** folder as **Lastname_Firstname_8C_Eastern_Main** If necessary display the rulers and formatting marks. For any words flagged as a spelling error, click Ignore All.

a. Click the **Mailings tab**. In the **Start Mail Merge group**, click **Start Mail Merge**, and then click **Letters**. In the **Start Mail Merge group**, click **Select Recipients**, and then click **Use an Existing List**. In the **Select Data Source** dialog box, navigate to your student data files, select the file **w08C_Eastern_Customers**, and then click **Open**.

b. In the **Select Table** dialog box, verify that **'Cruise Customers$'** and the **First row of data contains column headers** check box are selected. Click **OK**. On the **Mailings tab**, in the **Start Mail Merge group**, click **Edit Recipient List**.

c. In the **Mail Merge Recipients** dialog box, under **Refine recipient list**, click **Filter**. In the **Filter and Sort** dialog box, on the **Filter Records tab**, click the **Field arrow**, scroll as necessary, and then click **Repeat Customer**. Click the **Comparison arrow**, and then if necessary, click **Equal to**. In the **Compare to** box, type **Yes** Click **OK** two times to close the dialog boxes.

d. Select the first paragraph, and then change the **Font Size** to **28**. Click the **Home tab**, and then in the **Font group**, change the **Text Effects and Typography** to **Fill – Orange, Accent 2, Outline – Accent 2**—in the first row, the third effect. Select the second and third paragraphs containing the company address. Change the **Font Size** to **16**, and then change the **Font Color** to **Orange, Accent 2, Darker 25%**—in the sixth column, the fifth color. Select the first three paragraphs, and then press Ctrl + E.

e. In the blank paragraph following the date, click to position the insertion point, and then press Enter three times. Click the **Mailings tab**, and then in the **Write & Insert Fields group**, click **Address Block**. In the **Insert Address Block** dialog box, click **OK**.

f. Press Enter two times, and then in the **Write & Insert Fields group**, click **Greeting Line**. In the **Insert Greeting Line** dialog box, under **Greeting line format**, in the box on the right—the **Punctuation** box, click the **Punctuation arrow**, and then click **:** (the colon). Click **OK**, and then press Enter.

2 In the paragraph that begins *Because*, select the word **Because**, and then press Delete. On the **Mailings tab**, in the **Write & Insert Fields group**, click the **Insert Merge Field** arrow, and then click **Title**. Press Spacebar, and then click the **Insert Merge Field arrow** again. Click **Last_Name** and then type **, because** Press Spacebar and then **Save** your changes.

a. On the **Mailings tab**, in the **Preview Results group**, click **Check for Errors**. In the **Checking and Reporting Errors** dialog box, select the option that begins **Simulate the merge**, and then click **OK**. In the **Microsoft Word** message box, click **OK**. On the **Mailings tab**, in the **Finish group**, click **Finish & Merge**, and then click **Edit Individual Documents**. In the **Merge to New Document** dialog box, click **OK**.

b. Display the **Save As** dialog box, and then navigate to your **Word Chapter 8** folder. Save the document as **Lastname_Firstname_8C_Eastern_Merged** and then insert the file name in the footer.

c. Click the **File tab**, and then **Show All Properties**. In the **Tags** box, type **eastern cruise letters, merged** In the **Subject** box, type your course name and section number. If necessary, edit the author name to display your name. **Save** your changes, and then **Close** the document to display your main document.

d. In the main document, insert the file name in the footer. Click the **File tab**, and then **Show All Properties**. In the **Tags** box, type **eastern cruise letters, main** In the **Subject** box, type your course name and section number. If necessary, edit the author name to display your name. **Save** your document, and then press Ctrl + W to close the document but leave Word open.

3 Press Ctrl + N to open a new document. Click the **Mailings tab**. In the **Start Mail Merge group**, click **Start Mail Merge**, and then click **Envelopes**. In the **Envelope Options** dialog box, on the **Envelope**

(Project 8C Eastern Cruise continues on the next page)

Skills Review Project 8C Eastern Cruise (continued)

Options tab, under **Envelope size**, click **Size 10 (4 1/8 x 9 1/2 in)**. Click **OK** and then **Save** the document in your **Word Chapter 8** folder, with the file name **Lastname_Firstname_8C_EasternEnv_Main**

a. On the **Mailings tab**, in the **Start Mail Merge group**, click **Select Recipients**, and then click **Use an Existing List**. In the **Select Data Source** dialog box, navigate to your student data files, select **w08C_Eastern_Customers**, and then click **Open**. In the **Select Table** dialog box, verify that **'Cruise Customers$'** and the **First row of data contains column headers** check box are selected, and then Click **OK**.

b. On the **Mailings tab**, in the **Start Mail Merge group**, click **Edit Recipient List**. In the **Mail Merge Recipients** dialog box, click **Filter**. In the **Filter and Sort** dialog box, on the **Filter Records tab**, click the **Field arrow**, scroll as necessary, and then click **Repeat Customer**. Click the **Comparison arrow**, and then if necessary, click **Equal to**. In the **Compare to** box, type **Yes** Click **OK** two times to close the dialog boxes.

c. Type the following return address, pressing Enter after the first and second lines.

Caribbean Customized

1300 Bay View Drive

Coral Gables, FL 33124

d. In the center of the document, position the insertion point to the left of the paragraph mark. On the **Mailings tab**, in the **Write & Insert Fields group**, click **Address Block**. In the **Insert Address Block** dialog box, click **OK**. On the **Mailings tab**, in the **Preview Results group**, click **Check for Errors**. In the **Checking and Reporting Errors** dialog box, select the third option that begins **Complete the merge without pausing**, and then click **OK**.

4 **Save** the document in your **Word Chapter 8** folder, with the file name **Lastname_Firstname_8C_EasternEnv_Merged** Insert the file name in the footer. Click the **File tab**, and then click **Show All Properties**. In the **Tags** box, type **customer envelopes, merged** In the **Subject** box, type your course name and section number. If necessary, edit the author name to display your name. **Save** your document, and then press Ctrl + W to close the file and display the main document.

5 In the main document, insert the file name in the footer. Click the **File tab**, and then **Show All Properties**. In the **Tags** box, type **customer envelopes, main** In the **Subject** box, type your course name and section number. If necessary, edit the author name to display your name. **Save** your document.

6 If directed by your instructor to do so, submit your paper printout, your electronic image of your document that looks like a printed document, or your original Word file. **Close** Word.

END | You have completed Project 8C

CHAPTER REVIEW

Apply 8B skills from these Objectives:

3 Edit and Sort a Data Source
4 Match Fields and Apply Rules
5 Create a Data Source and a Directory

Skills Review Project 8D Name Tags

In the following Skills Review, you will use mail merge to create name tags for customers taking the Western Caribbean cruise by selecting a label option, editing records, and sorting the data source. You will create a new data source and match fields to create a list of Southern Caribbean cruise employees and their addresses. Your completed documents will look similar to the ones shown in Figure 8.41.

Build from Scratch

PROJECT FILES

For Project 8D, you will need the following files:

Two new blank Word documents
w08D_Cruise_Customers
w08D_List

You will save your documents as:

Lastname_Firstname_8D_NameTags_Main (not shown in Figure)
Lastname_Firstname_8D_NameTags_Merged
Lastname_Firstname_8D_Employee_List

PROJECT RESULTS

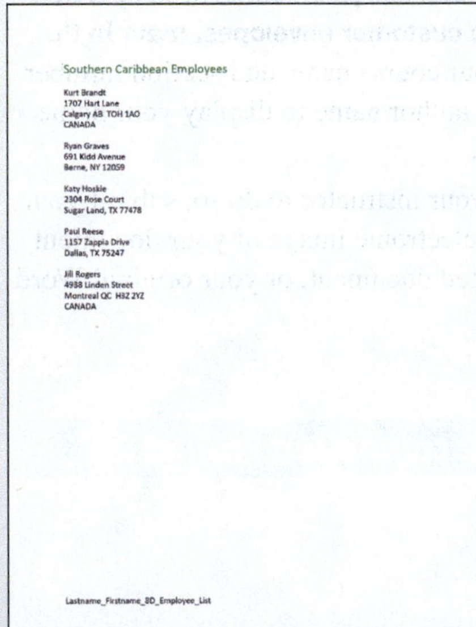

FIGURE 8.41

(Project 8D Name Tags continues on the next page)

Skills Review Project 8D Name Tags (continued)

1 Start Word and display a new blank document. If necessary, display the rulers and formatting marks.

a. Click the **Mailings tab**. In the **Start Mail Merge group**, click **Start Mail Merge**, and then click **Labels**. In the **Label Options** dialog box, under **Label information**, click the **Label vendors arrow** and select **Avery US Letter**, and then in the **Product number** box, scroll as necessary and click **5392 Name Badges Insert Refills**. Click **OK**. Click the **Table Tools Layout tab**, and then in the **Table group**, if necessary, click View Gridlines to display gridlines. Navigate to your **Word Chapter 8** folder, and then **Save** the document as **Lastname_Firstname_8D_NameTags_Main**

b. On the **Mailings tab**, in the **Start Mail Merge group**, click **Select Recipients**, and then click **Use an Existing List**. In the **Select Data Source** dialog box, navigate to your student data files for this chapter, select **w08D_Cruise_Customers**, and then click **Open**.

c. On the **Mailings tab**, in the **Start Mail Merge group**, click **Edit Recipient List**. In the **Mail Merge Recipients** dialog box, at the lower left, under **Data Source**, click **w08D_Cruise_Customers**, and then click **Edit**.

d. In the **Edit Data Source** dialog box, click **New Entry**. In the new record line, in the **First_Name** field, type **Lawrence** and then press Tab. In the **Last_Name** field, type **Forbus** and then press Tab. In the **Country** field, type **USA** and then click **OK**. In the **Microsoft Word** message box, click **Yes** to update your recipient list.

e. In the **Mail Merge Recipients** dialog box, immediately to the right of **Last_Name**, click the **arrow**, and then click **Sort Ascending**. Click **OK**.

2 Select the entire table, click the **Table Tools Layout tab**, and then in the **Alignment group**, click **Align Center**.

a. Click in the first cell of the table. Type **Caribbean Customized** and then press Enter two times. Select the text you just typed, change the **Font Size** to **16**, apply **Bold**, and then change the **Font Color** to **Green, Accent 6, Darker 25%**—in the last column, the fifth color.

b. Click to position the insertion point in the third blank paragraph. Click the **Mailings tab**. In the **Write & Insert Fields group**, click the **Insert Merge Field button arrow**, and then click **First_Name**. Press Spacebar, click the **Insert Merge Field button arrow**, and then click **Last_Name**. Press Enter two times. Select the merge fields you just inserted, change the **Font Size** to **20**, and then change the **Font Color** to **Green, Accent 6, Darker 50%**—in the last column, the last color.

c. In the last blank paragraph, click to position the insertion point. Type **Southern Caribbean Cruise** select the text, change the **Font Size** to **16**, and then apply **Italic**.

d. On the **Mailings tab**, in the **Write & Insert Fields group**, click **Update Labels**. In the **Finish group**, click **Finish & Merge**, and then click **Edit Individual Documents**. In the **Merge to New Document** dialog box, click **OK**.

e. **Save** the document in your **Word Chapter 8** folder, as **Lastname_Firstname_8D_NameTags_Merged**

f. Click the **File tab**, and then click **Show All Properties**. In the **Tags** box, type **name tags, merged** In the **Subject** box, type your course name and section number. If necessary, edit the author name to display your name. **Save** your document, and then press Ctrl + W to close the file.

g. With the main document displayed, click the **File tab**, and then click **Show All Properties**. In the **Tags** box, type **name tags, main** and then in the **Subject** box, type your course name and section number. If necessary, edit the author name to display your name. **Save** your document. **Close** the document but leave Word open.

3 Press Ctrl + N to display a new document. On the **Home tab**, in the **Styles group**, change the style to **No Spacing**.

a. Click the **Mailings tab**, in the **Start Mail Merge group**, click **Start Mail Merge**, and then click **Directory**. On the **Mailings tab**, in the **Start Mail Merge group**, click **Select Recipients**, and then click **Use an Existing List**. Navigate to your student data files, select **w08D_List**, and then click **Open**. In the **Select Table** dialog box, click **OK**.

(Project 8D Name Tags continues on the next page)

Skills Review Project 8D Name Tags (continued)

b. On the **Mailings tab**, in the **Write & Insert Fields group**, click **Address Block**. In the **Insert Address Block** dialog box, under **Correct Problems**, click **Match Fields**. In the **Match Fields** dialog box, click the **State arrow**, and then from the displayed list, click **State/Province**. Click **OK** two times to close the dialog boxes.

c. Position the insertion point to the right of the *Address Block* merge field, if necessary, and then press Enter two times. On the **Mailings tab**, in the **Finish group**, click **Finish & Merge**, and then click **Edit Individual Documents**. In the **Merge to New Document** dialog box, click **OK**.

4 With the insertion point at the beginning of the document, press Enter two times and then press Ctrl + Home. Type **Southern Caribbean Employees** and then select the text that you typed. Change the **Font Size** to **16**, and then change the **Font Color** to **Green, Accent 6, Darker 25%**—in the last column, the fifth color.

a. Display the **Save As** dialog box. Navigate to your **Word Chapter 8** folder, and save the document as **Lastname_Firstname_8D_Employee_List** Insert the file name in the footer.

b. Click the **File tab**, and then click **Show All Properties**. In the **Tags** box, type **employee list** and then in the **Subject** box, type your course name and section number. If necessary, edit the author name to display your name. **Save** your document, and then **Close** the document. **Close** Word without saving the main document.

5 If directed by your instructor to do so, submit your paper printout, your electronic image of your document that looks like a printed document, or your original Word file. **Close** Word.

END | You have completed Project 8D

CONTENT-BASED ASSESSMENTS (MASTERY AND TRANSFER OF LEARNING)

Mastering Word Project 8E Hospitality Team

Apply 8A skills from these Objectives:

1. Merge a Data Source and a Main Document
2. Use Mail Merge to Create Envelopes

In the following Mastering Word project, you will use mail merge to filter a data source and customize a form letter to employees who have been selected for the hospitality team for the Ultimate Southern cruise. Your completed documents will look similar to the ones shown in Figure 8.42.

PROJECT FILES

For Project 8E, you will need the following files:

New blank Word document
w08E_Hospitality_Team
w08E_Hospitality

You will save your documents as:

Lastname_Firstname_8E_Hospitality_Main (not shown in Figure)
Lastname_Firstname_8E_Hospitality_Merged
Lastname_Firstname_8E_HospitalityEnv_Main (not shown in Figure)
Lastname_Firstname_8E_HospitalityEnv_Merged

PROJECT RESULTS

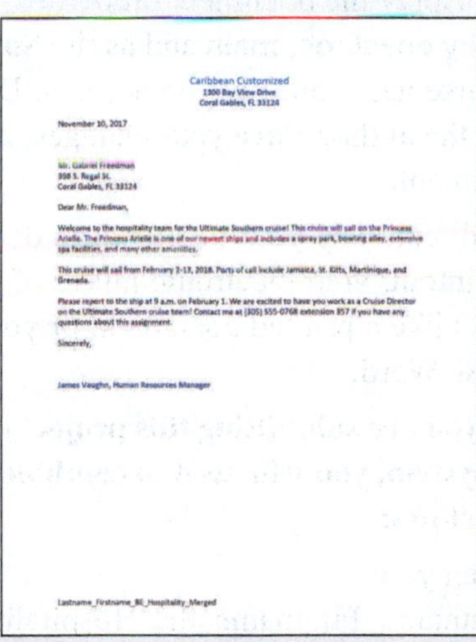

Caribbean Customized
1300 Bay View Drive
Coral Gables, FL 33124

November 10, 2017

Mr. Gabriel Freedman
398 S. Regal St.
Coral Gables, FL 33124

Dear Mr. Freedman,

Welcome to the hospitality team for the Ultimate Southern cruise! This cruise will sail on the Princess Arielle. The Princess Arielle is one of our newest ships and includes a spray park, bowling alley, extensive spa facilities, and many other amenities.

This cruise will sail from February 2-13, 2018. Ports of call include Jamaica, St. Kitts, Martinique, and Grenada.

Please report to the ship at 9 a.m. on February 1. We are excited to have you work as a Cruise Director on the Ultimate Southern cruise team! Contact me at (305) 555-0768 extension 357 if you have any questions about this assignment.

Sincerely,

James Vaughn, Human Resources Manager

Lastname_Firstname_8E_Hospitality_Merged

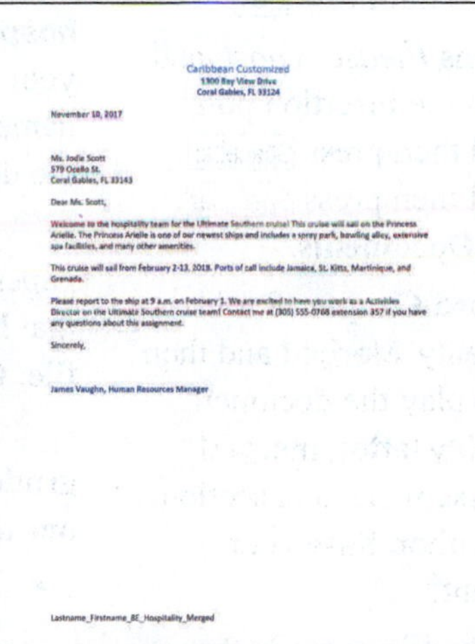

Caribbean Customized
1300 Bay View Drive
Coral Gables, FL 33124

November 10, 2017

Ms. Jodie Scott
579 Ocello St.
Coral Gables, FL 33143

Dear Ms. Scott,

Welcome to the hospitality team for the Ultimate Southern cruise! This cruise will sail on the Princess Arielle. The Princess Arielle is one of our newest ships and includes a spray park, bowling alley, extensive spa facilities, and many other amenities.

This cruise will sail from February 2-13, 2018. Ports of call include Jamaica, St. Kitts, Martinique, and Grenada.

Please report to the ship at 9 a.m. on February 1. We are excited to have you work as a Activities Director on the Ultimate Southern cruise team! Contact me at (305) 555-0768 extension 357 if you have any questions about this assignment.

Sincerely,

James Vaughn, Human Resources Manager

Lastname_Firstname_8E_Hospitality_Merged

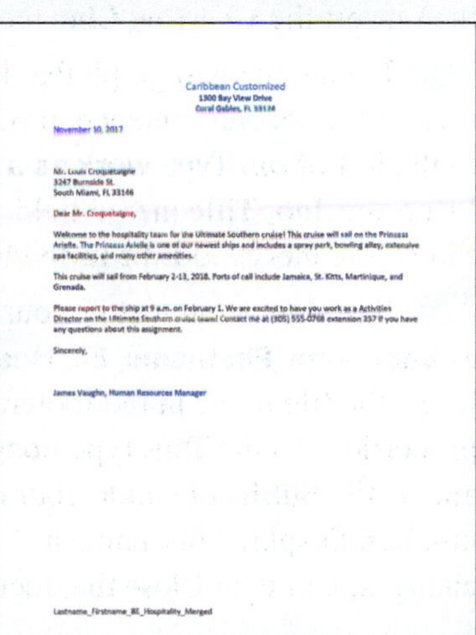

Caribbean Customized
1300 Bay View Drive
Coral Gables, FL 33124

November 10, 2017

Mr. Louis Croquetaigne
3247 Burnside St.
South Miami, FL 33146

Dear Mr. Croquetaigne,

Welcome to the hospitality team for the Ultimate Southern cruise! This cruise will sail on the Princess Arielle. The Princess Arielle is one of our newest ships and includes a spray park, bowling alley, extensive spa facilities, and many other amenities.

This cruise will sail from February 2-13, 2018. Ports of call include Jamaica, St. Kitts, Martinique, and Grenada.

Please report to the ship at 9 a.m. on February 1. We are excited to have you work as a Activities Director on the Ultimate Southern cruise team! Contact me at (305) 555-0768 extension 357 if you have any questions about this assignment.

Sincerely,

James Vaughn, Human Resources Manager

Lastname_Firstname_8E_Hospitality_Merged

Caribbean Customized
1300 Bay View Drive
Coral Gables, FL 33124

Mr. Gabriel Freedman
398 S. Regal St.
Coral Gables, FL 33124

Lastname_Firstname_8E_HospitalityEnv_Merged

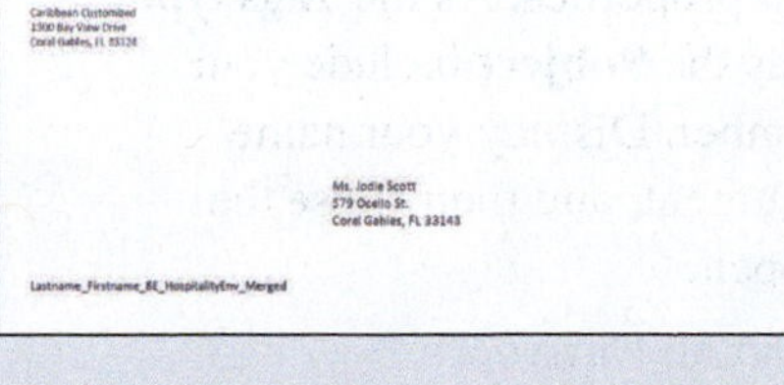

Caribbean Customized
1300 Bay View Drive
Coral Gables, FL 33124

Ms. Jodie Scott
579 Ocello St.
Coral Gables, FL 33143

Lastname_Firstname_8E_HospitalityEnv_Merged

Caribbean Customized
1300 Bay View Drive
Coral Gables, FL 33124

Mr. Louis Croquetaigne
3247 Burnside St.
South Miami, FL 33146

Lastname_Firstname_8E_HospitalityEnv_Merged

FIGURE 8.42

(Project 8E Hospitality Team continues on the next page)

CONTENT-BASED ASSESSMENTS (MASTERY AND TRANSFER OF LEARNING)

Mastering Word Project 8E Hospitality Team (continued)

1 Start Word. Navigate to your student files, and open the file **w08E_Hospitality**. If necessary, display the rulers and formatting marks. **Save** the document to your **Word Chapter 8** folder as **Lastname_Firstname_8E_Hospitality_Main**

2 Select the two lines of the company address, apply **Bold**, and then change the **Font Color** to **Blue, Accent 1, Darker 50%**. Create a **Character Style** named **Letter Emphasis** and then apply the **Letter Emphasis** style to the last line in the letter—**James Vaughn, Human Resources Manager**.

3 Create a **Letters** mail merge document. As the data source, from your student data files, select the file **w08E_Hospitality_Team**, and then select the worksheet **'Employee Information$'**. **Filter** the data source so that the **Job Title** field is **Not equal to Fitness Instructor**

4 Position the insertion point in the blank paragraph following the date, press Enter three times, and then insert the **Address Block** merge field. Press Enter two times, and then insert the **Greeting Line** merge field. Press Enter.

5 Locate the paragraph that begins *Please report*, and then in the second sentence, position the insertion point to the left of *on*. Type **work as a** and then press Spacebar. Insert the **Job_Title** merge field, and then press Spacebar. Finish the merge to **Edit Individual Documents**.

6 **Save** the document in your **Word Chapter 8** folder as **Lastname_Firstname_8E_Hospitality_Merged** and then insert the file name in the footer. Display the document properties. As the **Tags** type **hospitality letter, merged** and as the **Subject** include your course name and section number. Display your name as the author. **Save** your changes, and then **Close** the document.

7 In the main document, insert the file name in the footer. Display the document properties. As the **Tags** type **hospitality letter, main** and as the **Subject** include your course name and section number. Display your name as the author. **Save** your document, and then **Close** the document, but leave Word open.

8 In a new document, start an **Envelopes** mail merge using **Size 10 (4 1/8 x 9 1/2 in)**. **Save** the document to your **Word Chapter 8** folder as **Lastname_Firstname_8E_HospitalityEnv_Main**

9 As the data source, from your student data files, select the file **w08E_Hospitality_Team**, and then select the worksheet **'Employee Information$'**. **Filter** the data source so that the **Job Title** field is **Not equal to Fitness Instructor**

10 Type the following return address on three lines:

Caribbean Customized
1300 Bay View Drive
Coral Gables, FL 33124

11 In the center of the document, insert the **Address Block** merge field. Finish the merge to **Edit Individual Documents**.

12 **Save** the document to your **Word Chapter 8** folder as **Lastname_Firstname_8E_HospitalityEnv_Merged** and then insert the file name in the footer. Display the document properties. As the **Tags** type **hospitality envelope, merged** and as the **Subject** include your course name and section number. Display your name as the author. **Save** your changes, and then **Close** the document.

13 In the main document, insert the file name in the footer. Display the document properties. As the **Tags** type **hospitality envelope, main** and as the **Subject** include your course name and section number. Display your name as the author. **Save** your changes, and then **Close** the document.

14 If directed by your instructor to do so, submit your paper printout, your electronic image of your document that looks like a printed document, or your original Word file. **Close** Word.

15 **If you are submitting this project in the MyITLab grader system, you will need to combine the two files into one as follows:**

- Open your Lastname_Firstname_8E_HospitalityEnv_Merged document, select the entire document, and then Copy the selection.
- Open your Lastname_Firstname_8E_Hospitality_Merged document, and then press Ctrl + End. Paste the three merged envelopes to the end of the document.
- Save your document, and then Close all open documents. Submit your Lastname_Firstname_8E_Hospitality_Merged file in MyITLab.

END | You have completed Project 8E

Mastering Word Project 8F Cruise Ships

Apply 8B skills from these Objectives:

3. Edit and Sort a Data Source
4. Match Fields and Apply Rules
5. Create a Data Source and a Directory

Build from Scratch

In the following Mastering Word project, you will use mail merge and sort a data source to create jewel case labels for DVDs containing information about Caribbean Customized cruises and ships. Additionally, you will create a directory listing customer information. Your completed files will look similar to the ones shown in Figure 8.43.

PROJECT FILES

For Project 8F, you will need the following files:

Two new blank Word documents
w08F_Ships_Data
w08F_Eastern_Data

You will save your documents as:

Lastname_Firstname_8F_Ships_Main (not shown in Figure)
Lastname_Firstname_8F_Ships_Merged
Lastname_Firstname_8F_Cruise_Roster

PROJECT RESULTS

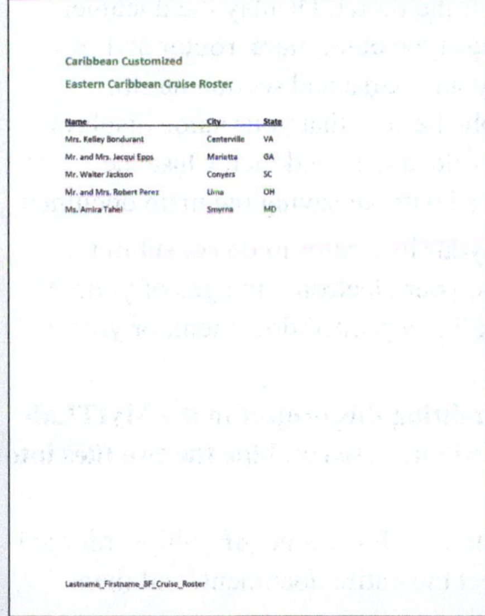

Caribbean Customized

Eastern Caribbean Cruise Roster

Name	City	State
Mrs. Kelley Bondurant	Centerville	VA
Mr. and Mrs. Jacqui Epps	Marietta	GA
Mr. Walter Jackson	Conyers	SC
Mr. and Mrs. Robert Perez	Lima	OH
Ms. Amira Tahei	Smyrna	MD

Lastname_Firstname_8F_Cruise_Roster

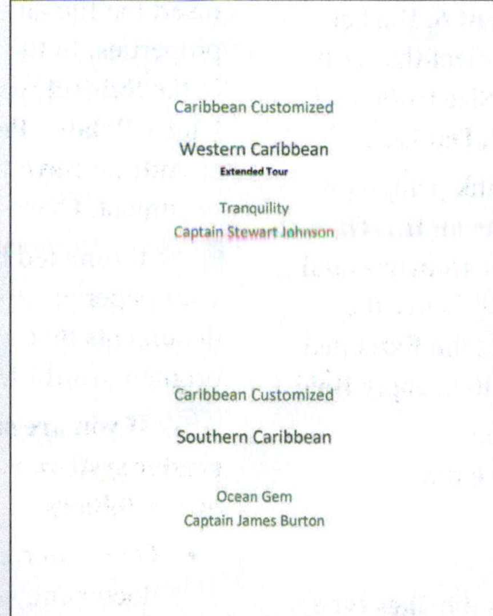

Caribbean Customized
Western Caribbean
Extended Tour
Tranquility
Captain Stewart Johnson

Caribbean Customized
Southern Caribbean
Ocean Gem
Captain James Burton

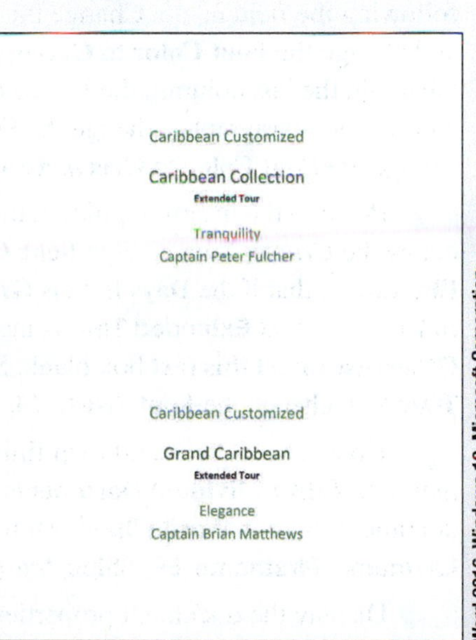

Caribbean Customized
Caribbean Collection
Extended Tour
Tranquility
Captain Peter Fulcher

Caribbean Customized
Grand Caribbean
Extended Tour
Elegance
Captain Brian Matthews

FIGURE 8.43

(Project 8F Cruise Ships continues on the next page)

CONTENT-BASED ASSESSMENTS (MASTERY AND TRANSFER OF LEARNING)

Mastering Word Project 8F Cruise Ships (continued)

1 Start Word and display a new blank document. Start a **Labels** mail merge using **Avery US Letter**, and change the **Product number** to **8962 DVD Labels**. From your student data files, select **w08F_Ships_Data** as the data source.

2 **Save** the main document in your **Word Chapter 8** folder as **Lastname_Firstname_8F_Ships_Main**

3 Change the **Alignment** for the entire table to **Align Center**. In the first cell, type **Caribbean Customized** and then press Enter two times. Insert the **Cruise_Name** merge field, and then press Enter three times. Insert the **Ship** merge field and press Enter. Type **Captain** and then press Spacebar. Insert the **Captain** merge field.

4 Select the first paragraph, change the **Font Size** to **22**, and change the **Font Color** to **Green, Accent 6, Darker 25%**—in the last column, the fifth color.

5 Select the third paragraph, which contains the *Cruise_Name* field. Be sure to include the paragraph mark following the field name. Change the **Font Size** to **24**, and change the **Font Color** to **Green, Accent 6, Darker 50%**—in the last column, the last color. Select the sixth and seventh paragraphs, change the **Font Size** to **20**, and change the **Font Color** to **Green, Accent 6, Darker 25%**.

6 Position the insertion point in the blank paragraph below the *Cruise_Name* merge field. Create an **If…Then…Else** rule so that if the **Days** field is **Greater than or equal to 7** then the text **Extended Tour** is inserted. Leave the **Otherwise insert this text** box blank. Select the **Extended Tour** text, change the **Font Size** to **14**, and then apply **Bold**.

7 Update the labels, and then finish the merge to **Edit Individual Documents**. **Save** the document to your **Word Chapter 8** folder as **Lastname_Firstname_8F_Ships_Merged**

8 Display the document properties. As the **Tags** type **cruises, merged** and as the **Subject** include your course name and section number. Display your name as the author. **Save** your document, and then **Close** the document.

9 In the main document, display the document properties. As the **Tags** type **cruises, main** and as the **Subject** include your course name and section number. Display your name as the author. **Save** your document, and then **Close** the document but leave Word open.

10 Start a new blank document and start a **Directory** mail merge. From your student data files, use **w08F_Eastern_Data** as the data source. Sort the data source to display the **Last** field in ascending order.

11 On the horizontal ruler, set left tabs at the **2.5-inch mark** and **3.5-inch mark**. Insert the **Title** merge field, press Spacebar, insert the **First** merge field, press Spacebar, and then insert the **Last** merge field. Press Tab, insert the **City** merge field, press Tab, insert the **State** merge field, and then press Enter. Finish the merge to **Edit Individual Documents**.

12 With the insertion point at the beginning of the document, press Enter. In the first paragraph, type **Caribbean Customized** and then press Enter. Type **Eastern Caribbean Cruise Roster** and then press Enter two times. Select the first two paragraphs, change the **Font Size** to **16**, apply **Bold**, and then change the **Font Color** to **Green, Accent 6, Darker 25%**.

13 In the blank line above the merge fields, type **Name** press Tab, type **City** press Tab, type **State** and then select the text you typed and apply **Bold** and **Underline**.

14 **Save** the document to your **Word Chapter 8** folder as **Lastname_Firstname_8F_Cruise_Roster** and then insert the file name in the footer. Display the document properties. In the **Tags** type **customers, roster** and in the **Subject** type your course and section number. Under **Related People**, be sure that your name displays as **Author**. **Save** your document and then **Close** the document. **Close** Word without saving the main document.

15 If directed by your instructor to do so, submit your paper printouts, your electronic images of your documents that look like a printed document, or your original Word files.

16 **If you are submitting this project in the MyITLab grader system, you will need to combine the two files into one as follows:**

- Open your Lastname_Firstname_8F_Ships_Merged document, select the entire document, and then Copy the selection.
- Open your Lastname_Firstname_8F_Cruise_Roster document, and then press Ctrl + End. On the Layout tab, in the Page Setup group, click Breaks, and then under Section Breaks, click Next Page. Paste the merged labels to the end of the document.
- Save your document, and then Close all open documents. Submit your Lastname_Firstname_8F_Cruise_Roster file in MyITLab.

END | You have completed Project 8F

CONTENT-BASED ASSESSMENTS (MASTERY AND TRANSFER OF LEARNING)

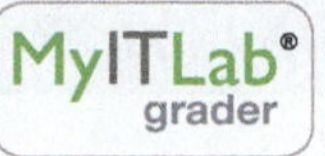

Mastering Word Project 8G Entertainers

Apply 8A and 8B skills from these Objectives:

1. Merge a Data Source and a Main Document
2. Use Mail Merge to Create Envelopes
3. Edit and Sort a Data Source
4. Match Fields and Apply Rules
5. Create a Data Source and a Directory

In the following Mastering Word project, you will create a letter to recruit entertainers for next year's Caribbean Customized cruises. You will filter the data source, match fields, and insert merge fields to modify the form letter. Your completed documents will look similar to the ones shown in Figure 8.44.

PROJECT FILES

For Project 8G, you will need the following files:

Two new blank Word documents
w08G_Entertainers
w08G_Entertainers_Letter

You will save your documents as:

Lastname_Firstname_8G_Entertainers_Main (not shown in Figure)
Lastname_Firstname_8G_Entertainers_Merged
Lastname_Firstname_8G_Entertainers_Directory

PROJECT RESULTS

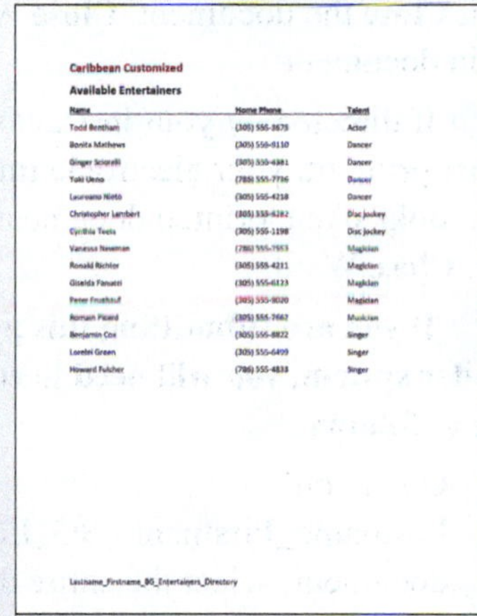
Caribbean Customized

Available Entertainers

Name	Home Phone	Talent
Todd Bentham	(305) 555-3675	Actor
Bonita Mathews	(305) 555-0110	Dancer
Ginger Sciorelli	(305) 555-4381	Dancer
Yuki Ueno	(786) 555-7736	Dancer
Laureano Nieto	(305) 555-4218	Dancer
Christopher Lambert	(305) 555-6282	Disc Jockey
Cynthia Teets	(305) 555-1198	Disc Jockey
Vanessa Newman	(786) 555-7553	Magician
Ronald Richter	(305) 555-4211	Magician
Giselda Fanucci	(305) 555-6123	Magician
Peter Fruehauf	(305) 555-9020	Magician
Romain Picard	(305) 555-7667	Musician
Benjamin Cox	(305) 555-8822	Singer
Lorelei Green	(305) 555-6499	Singer
Howard Fulcher	(786) 555-4833	Singer

Lastname_Firstname_8G_Entertainers_Directory

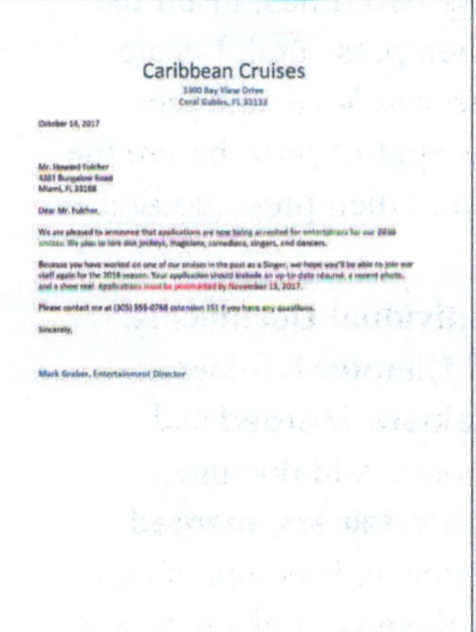
Caribbean Cruises
1300 Bay View Drive
Coral Gables, FL 33132

October 14, 2017

Mr. Howard Fulcher
4281 Bungalow Road
Miami, FL 33168

Dear Mr. Fulcher,

We are pleased to announce that applications are now being accepted for entertainers for our 2018 cruises. We plan to hire disk jockeys, magicians, comedians, singers, and dancers.

Because you have worked on one of our cruises in the past as a Singer, we hope you'll be able to join our staff again for the 2018 season. Your application should include an up-to-date résumé, a recent photo, and a show reel. Applications must be postmarked by November 15, 2017.

Please contact me at (305) 555-0768 extension 151 if you have any questions.

Sincerely,

Mark Graber, Entertainment Director

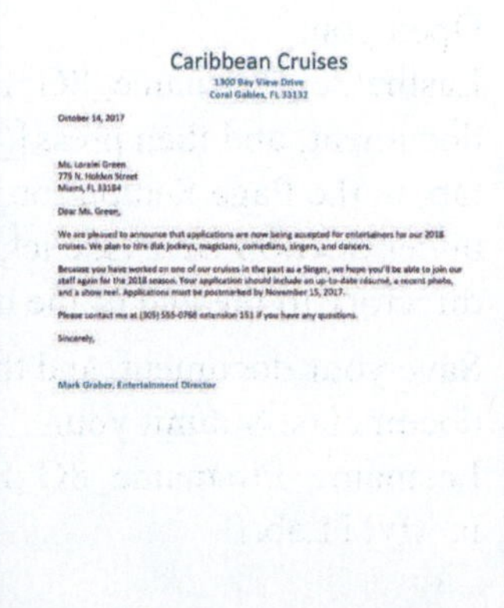
Caribbean Cruises
1300 Bay View Drive
Coral Gables, FL 33132

October 14, 2017

Ms. Loralei Green
775 N. Holden Street
Miami, FL 33184

Dear Ms. Green,

We are pleased to announce that applications are now being accepted for entertainers for our 2018 cruises. We plan to hire disk jockeys, magicians, comedians, singers, and dancers.

Because you have worked on one of our cruises in the past as a Singer, we hope you'll be able to join our staff again for the 2018 season. Your application should include an up-to-date résumé, a recent photo, and a show reel. Applications must be postmarked by November 15, 2017.

Please contact me at (305) 555-0768 extension 151 if you have any questions.

Sincerely,

Mark Graber, Entertainment Director

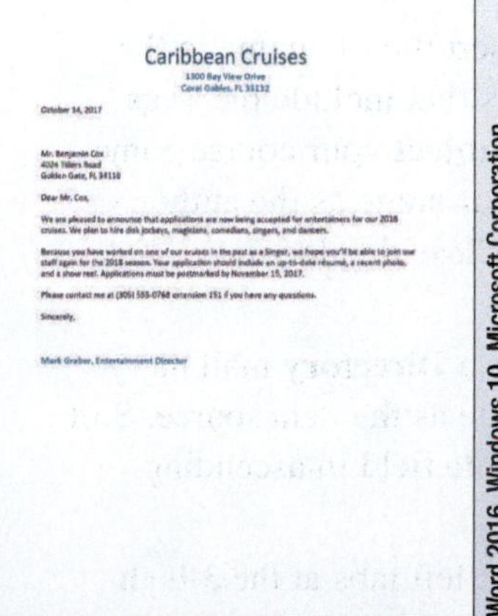
Caribbean Cruises
1300 Bay View Drive
Coral Gables, FL 33132

October 14, 2017

Mr. Benjamin Cox
4024 Tillers Road
Golden Gate, FL 34116

Dear Mr. Cox,

We are pleased to announce that applications are now being accepted for entertainers for our 2018 cruises. We plan to hire disk jockeys, magicians, comedians, singers, and dancers.

Because you have worked on one of our cruises in the past as a Singer, we hope you'll be able to join our staff again for the 2018 season. Your application should include an up-to-date résumé, a recent photo, and a show reel. Applications must be postmarked by November 15, 2017.

Please contact me at (305) 555-0768 extension 151 if you have any questions.

Sincerely,

Mark Graber, Entertainment Director

FIGURE 8.44

(Project 8G Entertainers continues on the next page)

Mastering Word Project 8G Entertainers (continued)

1 Start Word. Navigate to your student files, and open the file **w08G_Entertainers_Letter**. **Save** the document to your **Word Chapter 8** folder as **Lastname_Firstname_8G_Entertainers_Main** and if necessary, display the rulers and formatting marks.

2 Select the two-line company address. Apply **Bold**, change the **Font Size** to **12**, and change the **Font Color** to **Teal, Accent 5, Darker 25%**. Create a **Character** style named **Address** and then apply the style to the last line of the document—*Mark Graber, Entertainment Director*.

3 Start a **Letters** mail merge using your student data file **w08G_Entertainers** as the data source. Sort the data source to display the **Postal Code** field in ascending order, and then filter the list to create letters for entertainers whose **Role** is **Singer**

4 Position the insertion point in the blank paragraph following the date, and press Enter three times. Insert the **Address Block** merge field, matching the field **Street** with the **Address 1** field. Press Enter two times, insert the **Greeting Line** merge field, and then press Enter. Locate the paragraph that begins *Because you have*, and then position the insertion point to the right of *past*, before the comma. Press Spacebar, type **as a** and then press Spacebar. Insert the **Role** merge field.

5 Finish the merge to **Edit Individual Documents**. **Save** the document in your **Word Chapter 8** folder as **Lastname_Firstname_8G_Entertainers_Merged** and then insert the file name in the footer. Add document properties that include the **Tags entertainers, merged** and as the **Subject** your course name and section number. Display your name as the author. **Save** your changes, and then **Close** the document.

6 In the main document, insert the file name in the footer. Add document properties that include the **Tags entertainers, main** and as the **Subject** your course name and section number. Display your name as the author. **Save** your document, and then **Close** the document, but leave Word open.

7 In a new document, create a **Directory** mail merge using the **w08G_Entertainers** file as the data source. Sort the data source to display the **Role** field in ascending order.

8 On the horizontal ruler, set left tabs at the **3-inch mark** and the **5-inch mark**. Insert the **First_Name** merge field, press Spacebar, and then insert the **Last_Name** merge field. Press Tab, insert the **Home_Phone** merge field, press Tab, and then insert the **Role** merge field. Press Enter. Finish the merge to **Edit Individual Documents**.

9 At the top of the document, insert a blank line. In the blank line, type **Caribbean Customized** and then press Enter. Type **Available Entertainers** and then press Enter. Type **Name** press Tab, type **Home Phone** press Tab, and then type **Talent**

10 Select the first two paragraphs, change the **Font Size** to **16**, and apply **Bold**. Select the third paragraph, and apply **Bold** and **Underline**.

11 **Save** the document in your **Word Chapter 8** folder as **Lastname_Firstname_8G_Entertainers_Directory** and then insert the file name in the footer. Add document properties that include the **Tags directory, merged** and as the **Subject** your course name and section number. Display your name as the author. **Save** your changes, and then **Close** the document. **Close** Word without saving the main document.

12 If directed by your instructor to do so, submit your paper printout, your electronic image of your document that looks like a printed document, or your original Word file. **Close** Word.

13 **If you are submitting this project in the MyITLab grader system, you will need to combine the two files into one as follows:**

- Open your Lastname_Firstname_8G_Entertainers_Directory document, select the entire document, and then Copy the selection.
- Open your Lastname_Firstname_8G_Entertainers_Merged document, and then press Ctrl + End. On the Layout tab, in the Page Setup group, click Breaks, and then under Section Breaks, click Next Page. Paste the directory to the end of the document.
- Save your document, and then Close all open documents. Submit your Lastname_Firstname_8G_Entertainers_Merged file in MyITLab.

END | You have completed Project 8G

CONTENT-BASED ASSESSMENTS

Apply a combination of the 8A and 8B skills.

GO! Fix It Project 8H Marketing Plan MyITLab

Build from Scratch

GO! Make It Project 8I Business Cards MyITLab

GO! Solve It Project 8J Planning Session MyITLab

GO! Solve It Project 8K Shipping Information

Build From Scratch

PROJECT FILES

For Project 8K, you will need the following files:

New blank Word document

w08K_Shipping_Information

You will save your document as:

Lastname_Firstname_8K_Shipping_Merged

Using mail merge, create labels using Avery US Letter 5352 Mailing Labels. Use **w08K_Shipping_Information** as the data source, sort the data in ascending order by Zip_Code, and apply a filter to display only individuals on the Southern cruise. Include the Address Block merge field and match fields as necessary. Format the document so that the labels display attractively and then merge the labels. Save the merged document to your **Word Chapter 8** folder as **Lastname_Firstname_8K_Shipping_Merged** and then submit your file as directed by your instructor. Do not save the main document.

Performance Level

Performance Criteria	Exemplary: You consistently applied the relevant skills	Proficient: You sometimes, but not always, applied the relevant skills	Developing: You rarely or never applied the relevant skills
Select a mailing label	The correct mailing label is selected.	A mailing label template is used, but an incorrect label is selected.	No label template is used.
Sort and filter the data source	The data source is sorted and filtered	The data source is not sorted or it is not filtered.	The data source is neither sorted nor filtered.
Match fields in the Address Block	All fields are matched and display correctly in the Address Block.	The Address Block is inserted but the fields are not matched.	No fields are matched or the Address Block is not inserted.
Insert text and merge fields in labels	The labels are merged and formatted appropriately.	The labels are merged but are not formatted appropriately.	The labels are not merged.

END | You have completed Project 8K

OUTCOMES-BASED ASSESSMENTS (CRITICAL THINKING)

RUBRIC

The following outcomes-based assessments are *open-ended assessments*. That is, there is no specific correct result; your result will depend on your approach to the information provided. Make *Professional Quality* your goal. Use the following scoring rubric to guide you in *how* to approach the problem and then to evaluate *how well* your approach solves the problem.

The *criteria*—Software Mastery, Content, Format and Layout, and Process—represent the knowledge and skills you have gained that you can apply to solving the problem. The *levels of performance*—Professional Quality, Approaching Professional Quality, or Needs Quality Improvements—help you and your instructor evaluate your result.

	Your completed project is of Professional Quality if you:	Your completed project is Approaching Professional Quality if you:	Your completed project Needs Quality Improvements if you:
1-Software Mastery	Choose and apply the most appropriate skills, tools, and features and identify efficient methods to solve the problem.	Choose and apply some appropriate skills, tools, and features, but not in the most efficient manner.	Choose inappropriate skills, tools, or features, or are inefficient in solving the problem.
2-Content	Construct a solution that is clear and well organized, contains content that is accurate, appropriate to the audience and purpose, and is complete. Provide a solution that contains no errors of spelling, grammar, or style.	Construct a solution in which some components are unclear, poorly organized, inconsistent, or incomplete. Misjudge the needs of the audience. Have some errors in spelling, grammar, or style, but the errors do not detract from comprehension.	Construct a solution that is unclear, incomplete, or poorly organized, contains some inaccurate or inappropriate content, and contains many errors of spelling, grammar, or style. Do not solve the problem.
3-Format and Layout	Format and arrange all elements to communicate information and ideas, clarify function, illustrate relationships, and indicate relative importance.	Apply appropriate format and layout features to some elements, but not others. Overuse features, causing minor distraction.	Apply format and layout that does not communicate information or ideas clearly. Do not use format and layout features to clarify function, illustrate relationships, or indicate relative importance. Use available features excessively, causing distraction.
4-Process	Use an organized approach that integrates planning, development, self-assessment, revision, and reflection.	Demonstrate an organized approach in some areas, but not others; or, use an insufficient process of organization throughout.	Do not use an organized approach to solve the problem.

8 WORD

OUTCOMES-BASED ASSESSMENTS (CRITICAL THINKING)

Apply a combination of the 8A and 8B skills.

GO! Think Project 8L Health Insurance

Build From Scratch

PROJECT FILES

For Project 8L, you will need the following files:

New blank Word document
w08L_Insurance_Data

You will save your documents as:

Lastname_Firstname_8L_Insurance_Main
Lastname_Firstname_8L_Insurance_Merged

Caribbean Customized is changing to a new health insurance provider—MediCertain—at the beginning of the year. MediCertain offers more coverage at a lower rate and a variety of plans for employees. James Vaughn, Human Resources Manager, is conducting information sessions for employees during November in Conference Room D at 9:30 a.m. The Administrative department will meet on November 1; all other departments will meet on November 3. The enrollment period begins November 10 and ends November 30.

Create a memo to department managers from Mr. Vaughn, informing them of the new provider and the scheduled time for the department's information session. Save the document as **Lastname_Firstname_8L_Insurance_Main**

Start a Letters mail merge using the memo that you created and use the data source w08L_Insurance_Data. Insert appropriate merge fields in the memo, and create a rule to display the date of the session based on the department. Format the memo in a professional manner. Save the merged document as **Lastname_Firstname_8L_Insurance_Merged** and then add appropriate properties to the merged and main documents. Submit your files as directed by your instructor.

END | You have completed Project 8L

Build from Scratch

GO! Think Project 8M Training MyITLab

Build From Scratch

You and GO! Project 8N Invitation MyITLab

Creating Forms, Customizing Word, and Preparing Documents for Review and Distribution

OUTCOMES

Create and protect a customized form with content controls.

PROJECT
9B

OUTCOMES

Customize Word and prepare documents for review and distribution.

OBJECTIVES

1. Create a Customized Form
2. Convert Text to a Table and Insert Content Controls in a Table
3. Modify and Protect a Form
4. Complete a Form

OBJECTIVES

5. Create a Custom Ribbon Tab
6. Create Style, Color, and Font Sets
7. Convert a Table to Text
8. Prepare a Document for Review and Distribution

Krzysztof Slusarczyk/Shutterstock

In This Chapter

In this chapter, you will create a form, which is a structured document that includes fields—such as check boxes—that assist the person entering information into the form. You can save a form as a template, protect a form from unauthorized changes, and then make the form available to others for completion in Word. In this chapter, you will also create a custom ribbon tab to improve your productivity when using Word. Using advanced graphic features—for example, stacking and grouping—you will enhance the appearance of a document. You will also prepare a document for distribution. For example, when a document that requires a signature is sent electronically, the recipient can digitally sign the file. Removing document properties and personal information is another way to prepare a document for distribution.

The projects in this chapter relate to **Laurales Herbs and Spices**. After ten years as an Executive Chef, Laura Morales started her own business, which offers quality products for cooking, eating, and entertaining for purchase in retail stores and online. In addition to herbs and spices, there is a wide variety of condiments, confections, jams, sauces, oils, and vinegars. Later this year, Laura will add a line of tools, cookbooks, and gift baskets. The company name is a combination of Laura's first and last names and also is the name of an order of plants related to cinnamon.

PROJECT 9A Survey Form

PROJECT ACTIVITIES

In Activities 9.01 through 9.14, you will create a form to measure customer satisfaction. Chelsea Warren, Marketing Vice President, wants to get feedback from customers regarding the quality of products and services offered by Laurales Herbs and Spices. You will customize the form and save it as a template so that it can be completed by individual users. To test the form prior to distribution, you will enter customer information in the survey form. Your completed document will look similar to Figure 9.1.

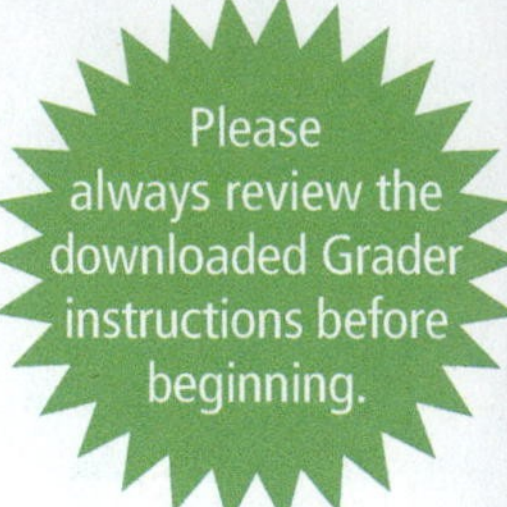

PROJECT FILES

If your instructor wants you to submit Project 9A in the MyITLab Grader system, log into MyITLab, locate Grader Project 9A, and then download the files for the project.

For Project 9A, you will need the following file:
w09A_Customer_Survey

You will save your documents as:
Lastname_Firstname_9A_Survey_Completed
Lastname_Firstname_9A_Customer_Survey
(you will not submit this file)

PROJECT RESULTS

GO! Walk Thru Project 9A

Laurales Herbs and Spices
1550 Columbus Avenue
San Francisco, CA 94133
(877) 555-0144 www.laurales.com

Customer Satisfaction Survey

Thank you for your recent order. Please help us to continue to improve the quality of our products and services by completing this satisfaction survey. We are grateful for your business and want to make certain that we meet or exceed your expectations. As a token of appreciation, if you return this survey, we will send you an e-coupon for five dollars off your next purchase.

Name: **Firstname Lastname**

Email address: **Lastname@laurales.com**

Today's Date: December 13, 2015

1. How did you learn about our company? Friend
2. What was the **primary** reason for placing the order with us? Excellent service!
3. How did you choose to have your items shipped? UPS
4. Did the items arrive on or before the stated delivery date? ☒ Yes ☐ No
5. Please rate the quality of each product you received.

	Excellent	Average	Poor
Cheeses	☐	☒	☐
Chocolates	☐	☐	☐
Herbs	☒	☐	☐
Oils	☐	☐	☐
Spices	☒	☐	☐
Vinegars	☐	☐	☐

6. Comments:

   I am eager to try your vinegars.

Please send your form to cwarren@laurales.com. Thank you for your time and feedback.

Lastname_Firstname_9A_Survey_Completed

Word 2016, Windows 10, Microsoft Corporation

FIGURE 9.1 Project 9A Survey Form

Objective 1 Create a Customized Form

GO! Learn How Video W9-1

A ***form*** is a structured document that has ***static text***—descriptive text such as headings and labels—and reserved spaces, or ***content controls***, for information to be entered by the person filling in the form. A content control is a data entry field in a form in which a particular type of information, such as a name or date, is supplied by the person entering information into the form. For example, you can create a survey form that provides a place to enter text or choose a specific entry from a list. You can also protect the form to restrict changes made by the person completing the form.

Activity 9.01 | Displaying the Developer Tab

MOS 1.1.7 Expert

Content controls are inserted in forms that will be filled in electronically. Content controls are accessed from the Developer tab; by default, the Developer tab does not display on the ribbon.

ALERT!

To submit as an autograded project, log into MyITLab, download the files for this project, and begin with those files instead of w09A_Customer_Survey.

1. Start Word, on the left click **Open Other Documents**, click **Browse**, and then in the **Open** dialog box, navigate to the student data files that accompany this chapter. Open the file **w09A_Customer_Survey**.

2. Click the **File tab**, on the left click **Save As**, click **Browse**, and then in the **Save As** dialog box, navigate to the location where you are saving your files for this chapter. Create a new folder named **Word Chapter 9** Using your own name, save the file as **Lastname_Firstname_9A_Customer_Survey** and if necessary, display the rulers and formatting marks. Compare your screen with Figure 9.2.

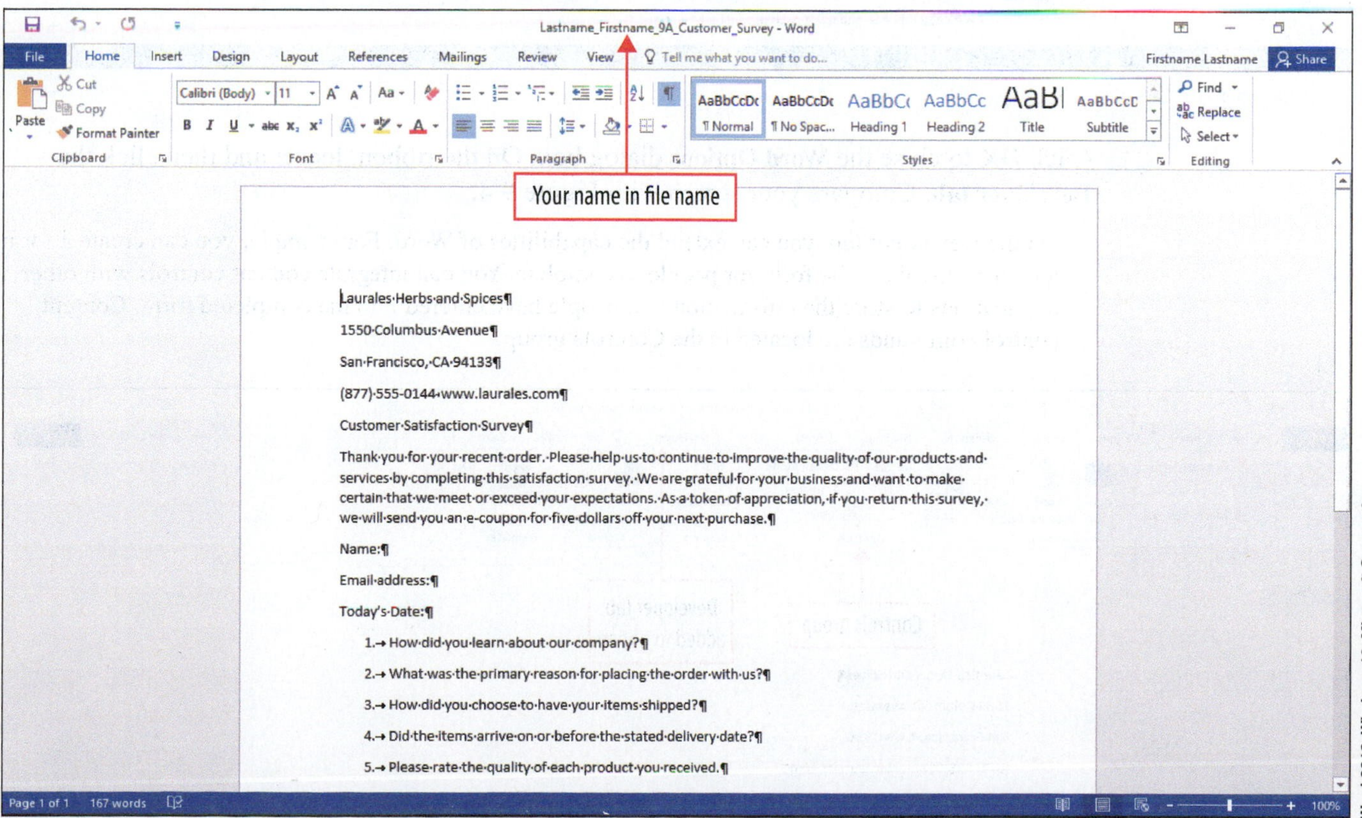

Word 2016, Windows 10, Microsoft Corporation

FIGURE 9.2

3 Click the **File tab**, and then click **Options**. In the **Word Options** dialog box, on the left, click **Customize Ribbon**.

4 On the right, in the **Main Tabs** list, locate and then click to select the **Developer** check box. Compare your screen with Figure 9.3.

Main tabs that display on the ribbon are indicated with a check mark.

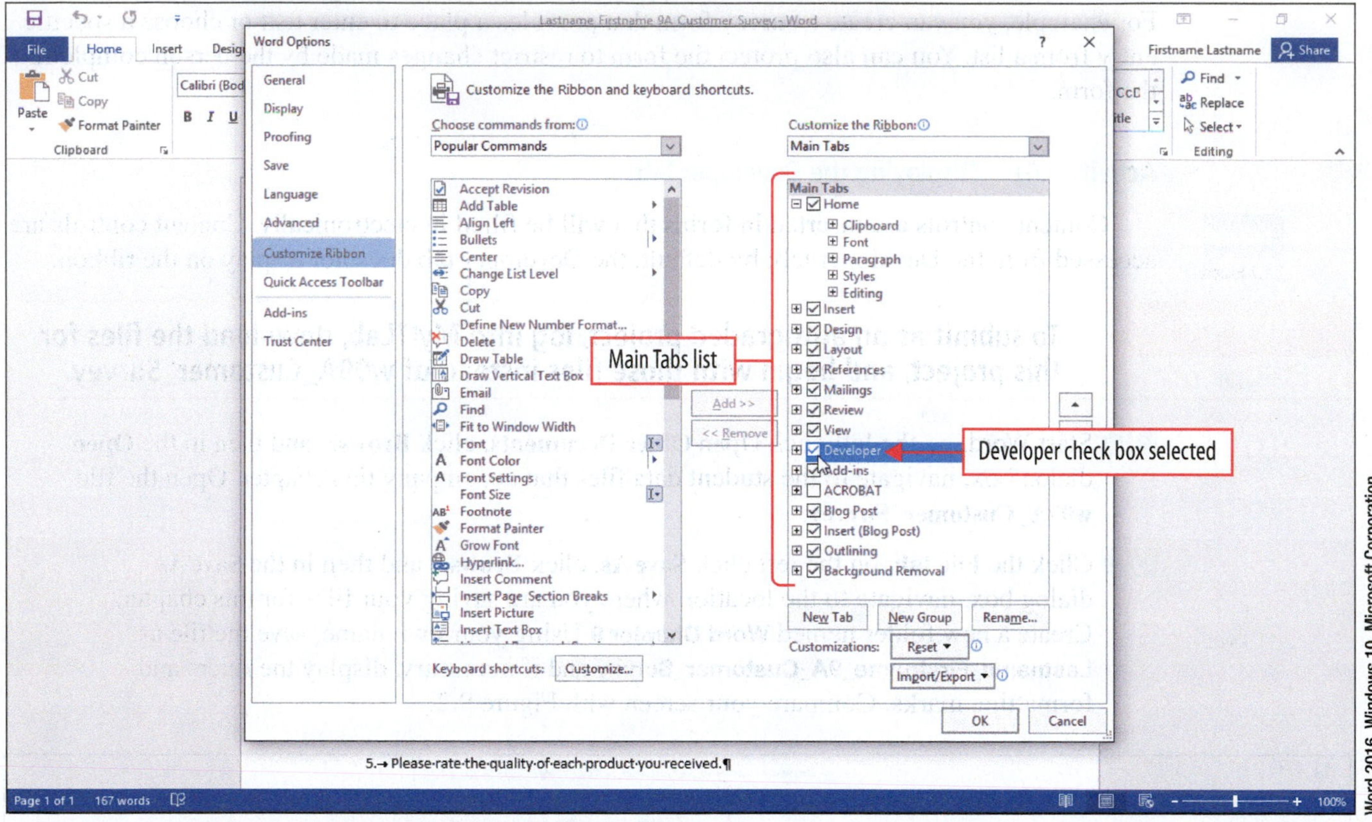

FIGURE 9.3

5 Click **OK** to close the **Word Options** dialog box. On the ribbon, locate and then click the **Developer tab**. Compare your screen with Figure 9.4.

On the Developer tab, you can extend the capabilities of Word. For example, you can create a form and then distribute the form for people to complete. You can integrate content controls with other applications to store the information that people have entered into the completed form. Content control commands are located in the Controls group.

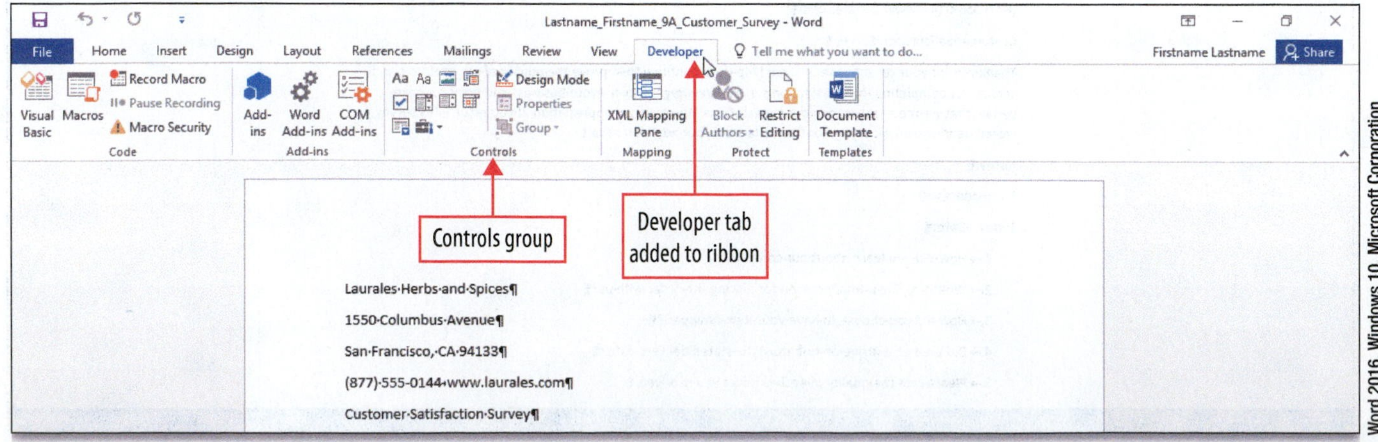

FIGURE 9.4

6 Select the first three paragraphs of the document, click the **Home tab**, and then in the **Styles group**, click **No Spacing**.

7 Select the first paragraph of the document—*Laurales Herbs and Spices*. On the mini toolbar, change the **Font Size** [11] to **18**, apply **Bold** [B], click the **Font Color button arrow** [A], and then in the eighth column, click the fifth color—**Gold, Accent 4, Darker 25%**. Press Ctrl + E to center the paragraph.

8 Select the next three paragraphs—the address, phone, and website information. On the mini toolbar, change the **Font Size** [11] to **14**, and then click **Font Color** [A]. Press Ctrl + E to center the paragraphs.

Recall that the Font Color button will retain its most recently used color.

9 Select the fifth paragraph—*Customer Satisfaction Survey*. On the mini toolbar, change the **Font Size** [11] to **14**, apply **Bold** [B], click the **Font Color button arrow** [A], and then in the eighth column, click the last color—**Gold, Accent 4, Darker 50%**. **Save** your document.

Activity 9.02 | Inserting a Plain Text Content Control

4.1.4 Expert

The ***Plain Text content control*** inserts a field in the form that enables the person completing the form to insert ***unformatted text***—plain text—in the document. You will add several plain text content controls to the form so that the customer filling out the form can provide personal information and comments.

1 Locate the paragraph *Name*, and then scroll as necessary so that the paragraph displays near the top of your screen. Click to position the insertion point to the right of *Name:*—after the colon, and then press Tab.

2 On the ribbon, click the **Developer tab**, and then in the **Controls group**, click **Design Mode**.

Turning on ***Design Mode*** enables you to edit content controls in a document.

3 In the **Controls group**, click **Plain Text Content Control** [Aa]. At the insertion point, notice that a field with the default text *Click or tap here to enter text.* displays. Compare your screen with Figure 9.5.

The default text serves as a placeholder and also assists the person filling in the form to know what to do.

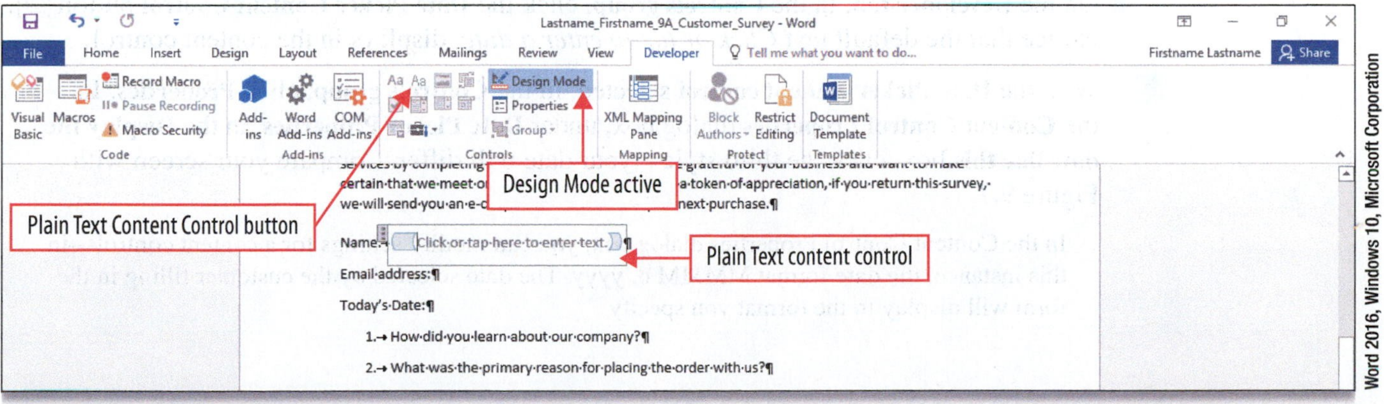

FIGURE 9.5

4 Locate the paragraph *Email address*. Click to position the insertion point to the right of the colon, press Tab, and then in the **Controls group**, click **Plain Text Content Control** [Aa].

5 Press Ctrl+ End to move to the end of the document. Above the last paragraph that begins *Please send*, click to position the insertion point in the blank paragraph.

6 Press Tab two times, and then in the **Controls group**, click **Plain Text Content Control** . Click in a blank area of the document to deselect the content control, and then compare your screen with Figure 9.6.

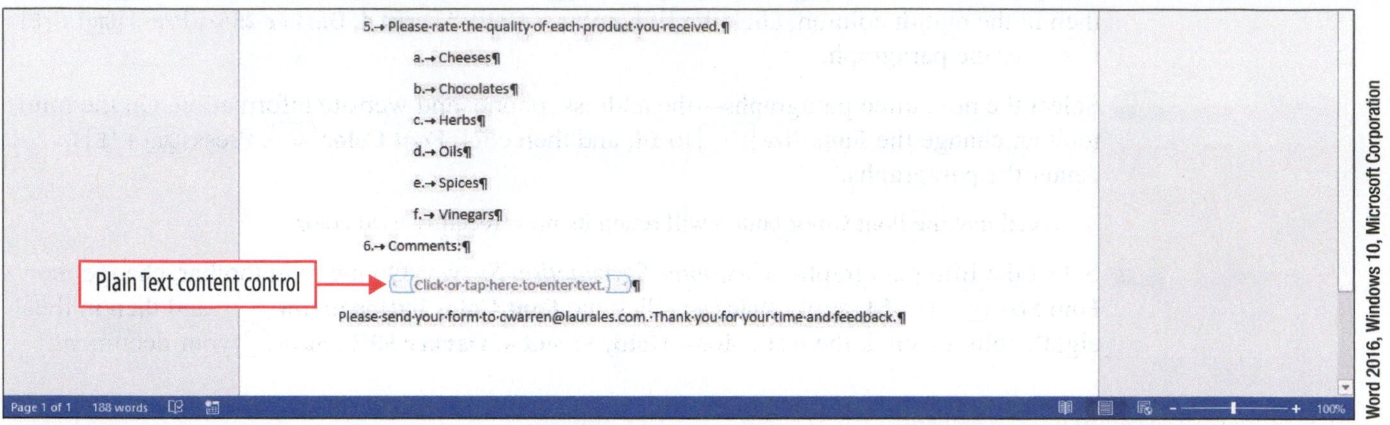

FIGURE 9.6

7 **Save** your document.

***More* Knowledge** **Inserting a Rich Text Content Control**

The Controls group includes a ***Rich Text content control*** that enables the person filling in the form to add text with most types of formatting, such as formats available on the mini toolbar. The Rich Text content control also allows for the insertion of tables and graphics.

Activity 9.03 | Inserting a Date Picker Content Control and Modifying Field Properties

4.1.4 Expert

The ***Date Picker content control*** allows the person filling out the form to select a date from a calendar. In this Activity, you will insert the Date Picker content control and then specify the format for displaying the date.

1 Locate the paragraph *Today's Date*. Click to position the insertion point to the right of the colon, and then press Tab.

2 On the **Developer tab**, in the **Controls group**, click the **Date Picker Content Control** button . Notice that the default text *Click or tap to enter a date.* displays in the content control.

3 With the **Date Picker content control** selected, in the **Controls group**, click **Properties**. In the **Content Control Properties** dialog box, under **Date Picker Properties**, in the **Display the date like this** box, click the third style—your date will differ. Compare your screen with Figure 9.7.

In the Content Control Properties dialog box, you can modify settings for a content control—in this instance, the date format MMMM d, yyyy. The date selected by the customer filling in the form will display in the format you specify.

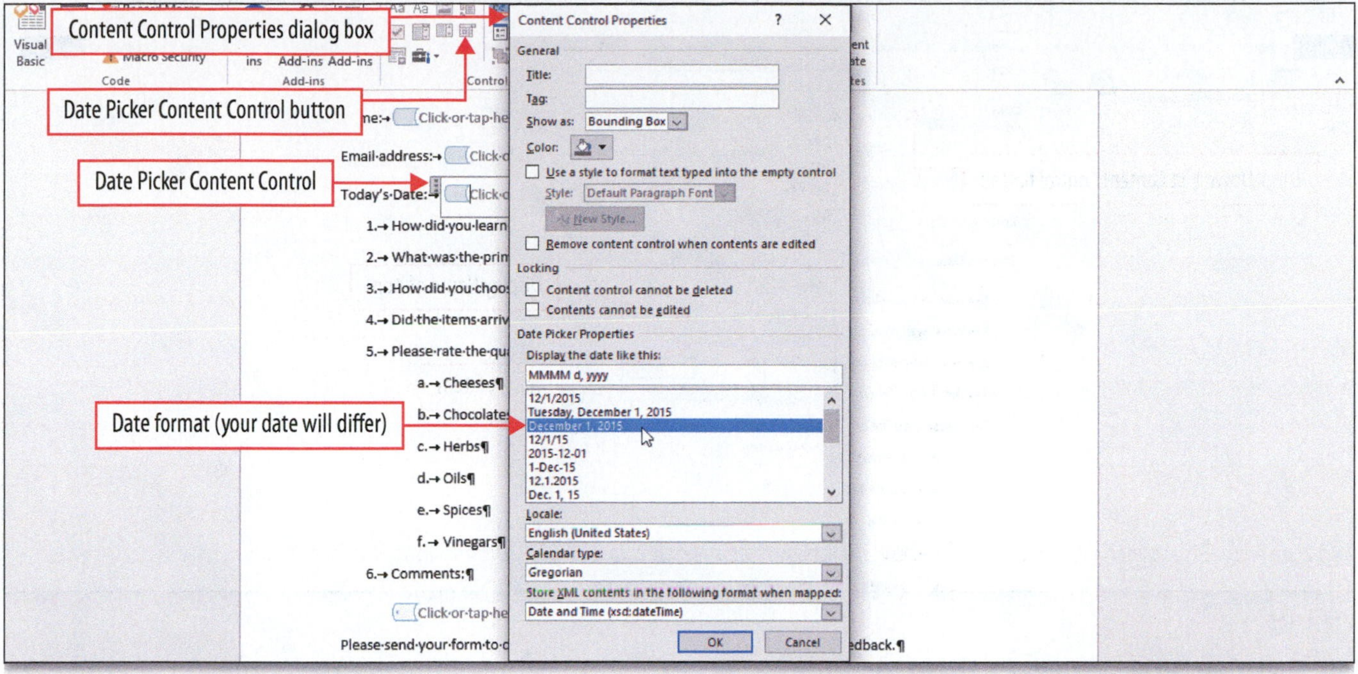

Word 2016, Windows 10, Microsoft Corporation

FIGURE 9.7

4 Click **OK** to close the **Content Control Properties** dialog box, and then **Save** your document.

Activity 9.04 | Inserting a Drop-Down List Content Control

4.1.4 Expert

The ***Drop-Down List content control*** allows the person filling in the form to select a specific item from a list, which is created by the designer of the form. By providing a list, you limit the available choices and ensure acceptable responses. You will use the Drop-Down List content control to solicit information regarding company awareness and shipping options.

1 Locate the paragraph that begins *1. How did you learn about*. Click to position the insertion point to the right of the question mark, and then press Tab.

2 In the **Controls group**, click **Drop-Down List Content Control**. With the **Drop-Down List content control** selected, in the **Controls group**, click **Properties**.

3 In the lower portion of the **Content Control Properties** dialog box, under **Drop-Down List Properties**, click **Add**. In the **Add Choice** dialog box, click in the **Display Name** box, type **Internet** and notice that as you type, the text in the **Value** box changes to match what you type in the **Display Name** box. Compare your screen with Figure 9.8.

The Add button enables you to specify the items that will be included in the Drop-Down List content control. Each item in the list is identified by a name and a value. The display name is the text that will display to customers filling out the form when they view the list.

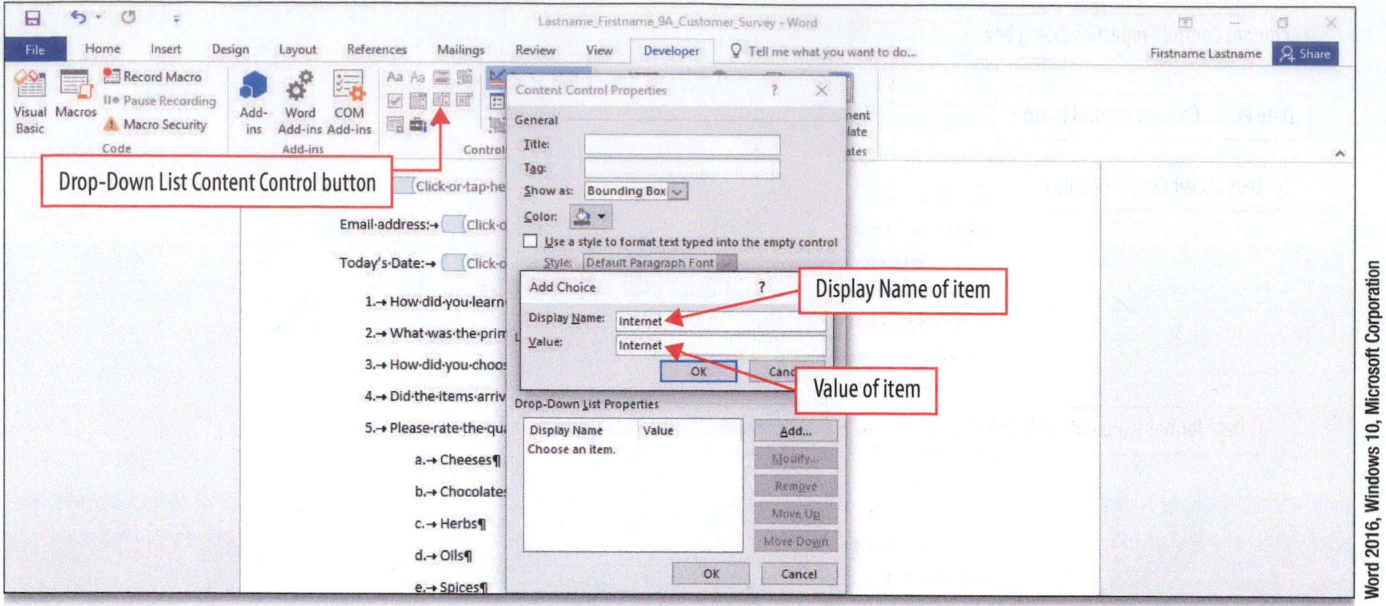

FIGURE 9.8

4 In the **Add Choice** dialog box, click **OK**. In the lower portion of the **Content Control Properties** dialog box, click **Add**. In the **Add Choice** dialog box, click in the **Display Name** box, type **Magazine** and then click **OK**.

5 Using the technique you just practiced, **Add** the choices **Television** and **Friend**

6 In the **Content Control Properties** dialog box, under **Drop-Down List Properties**, click **Friend**, and then click **Move Up** three times. Compare your screen with Figure 9.9.

It is helpful for the person filling out the form if the items in the list are in alphabetical order. You can use the Move Up and Move Down buttons to modify the order of the items.

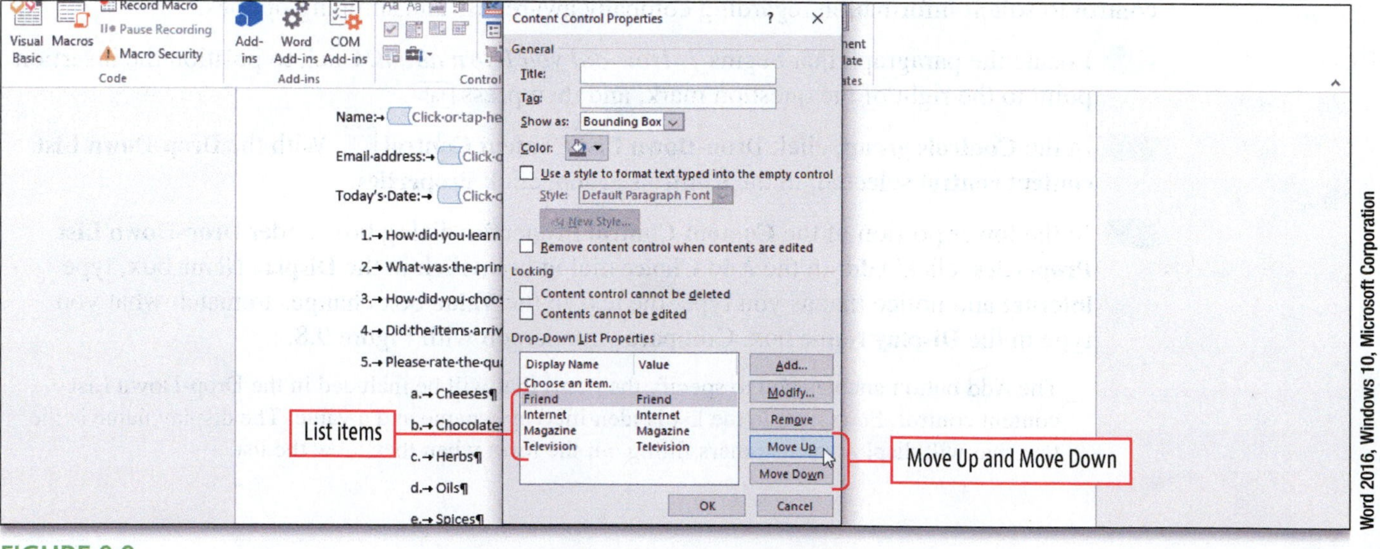

FIGURE 9.9

7 Click **OK**, and then on the **Developer tab**, in the **Controls group**, click **Design Mode** to turn off Design Mode. In the inserted **Drop-Down List content control**, click the **Drop-Down List arrow**, and then compare your screen with Figure 9.10.

The listed items are the various ways that a customer might have learned about the company. When Design Mode is turned off, you can view the document as it will be seen by the person filling in the form. The term *Choose an item.* displays by default.

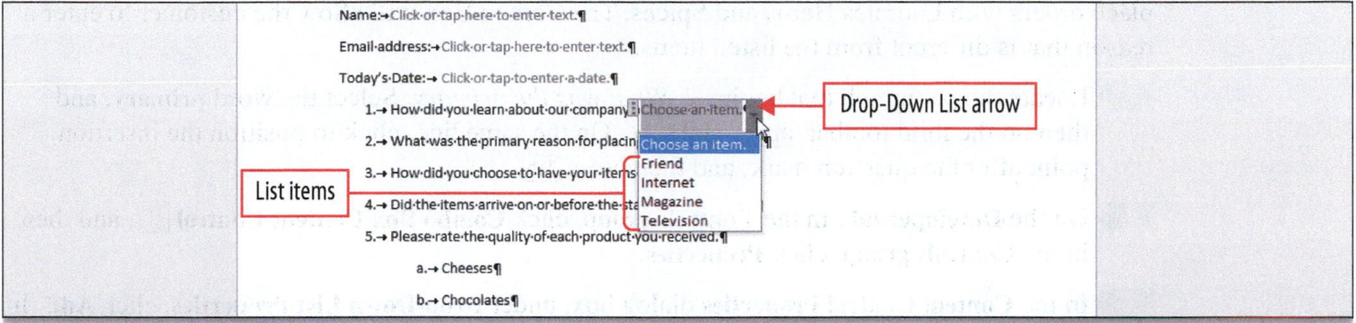

FIGURE 9.10

Word 2016, Windows 10, Microsoft Corporation

Activity 9.05 | Inserting an Additional Drop-Down List Content Control

4.1.4 Expert

1 Click anywhere in the question text to deselect the Drop-Down List content control. On the **Developer tab**, in the **Controls group**, click **Design Mode** to turn on Design Mode.

2 Locate the paragraph that begins *3. How did you choose*. Click to position the insertion point to the right of the question mark, and then press Tab.

3 In the **Controls group**, click **Drop-Down List Content Control**, and then in the **Controls group**, click **Properties**.

4 In the **Content Control Properties** dialog box, click **Add**. By using the techniques you have practiced, add three choices for this control—one each for **FedEx** and **UPS** and **USPS** and then compare your **Content Control Properties** dialog box with Figure 9.11.

The three items in the list represent the shipping providers used by Laurales Herbs and Spices.

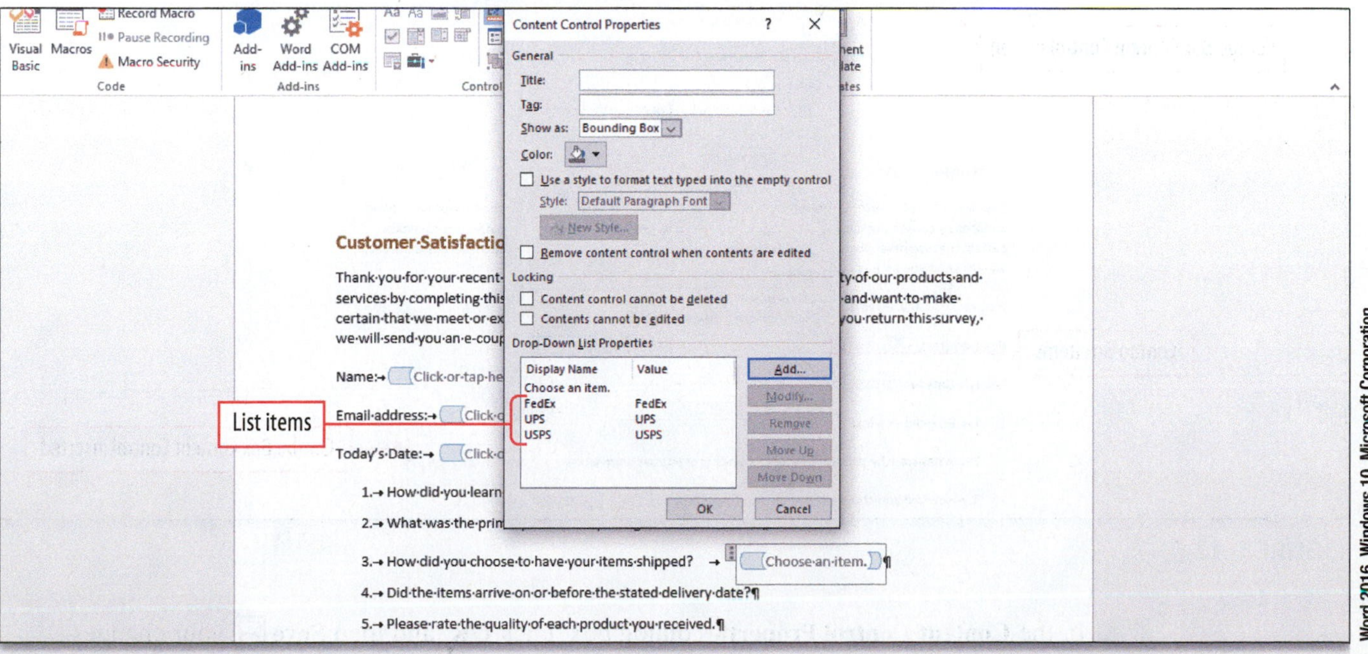

FIGURE 9.11

Word 2016, Windows 10, Microsoft Corporation

5 In the **Content Control Properties** dialog box, click **OK**, and then **Save** your document.

Activity 9.06 | Inserting a Combo Box Content Control

4.1.4 Expert

A ***Combo Box content control***, which is similar to a Drop-Down List content control, enables the customer filling out the form to select from an existing list and also to enter in new text. In this Activity, you will add a Combo Box content control that asks customers to indicate why they place orders with Laurales Herbs and Spices. The Combo Box will allow the customer to enter a reason that is different from the listed items.

1 Locate the paragraph that begins *2. What was the primary*. Select the word **primary**, and then on the mini toolbar, apply **Bold** [B]. On the same line, click to position the insertion point after the question mark, and then press Tab.

2 On the **Developer tab**, in the **Controls group**, click **Combo Box Content Control**, and then in the **Controls group**, click **Properties**.

3 In the **Content Control Properties** dialog box, under **Drop-Down List Properties**, click **Add**. In the **Add Choice** dialog box, in the **Display Name** box, type **Price** and then click **OK**.

4 In a similar manner, **Add** the choices **Quality** and **Selection**

5 In the **Content Control Properties** dialog box, under **Drop-Down List Properties**, click the default text *Choose an item.* and then click **Modify**.

6 In the **Modify Choice** dialog box, in the **Display Name** box, click to position the insertion point to the left of the period, and then press Spacebar. Type **or type another reason** and then click **OK**. Compare your screen with Figure 9.12.

Recall that a Combo Box content control allows the person filling out the form to insert new text. In this instance, you want to provide the customer with the option to enter a reason that is not already listed for choosing Laurales Herbs and Spices.

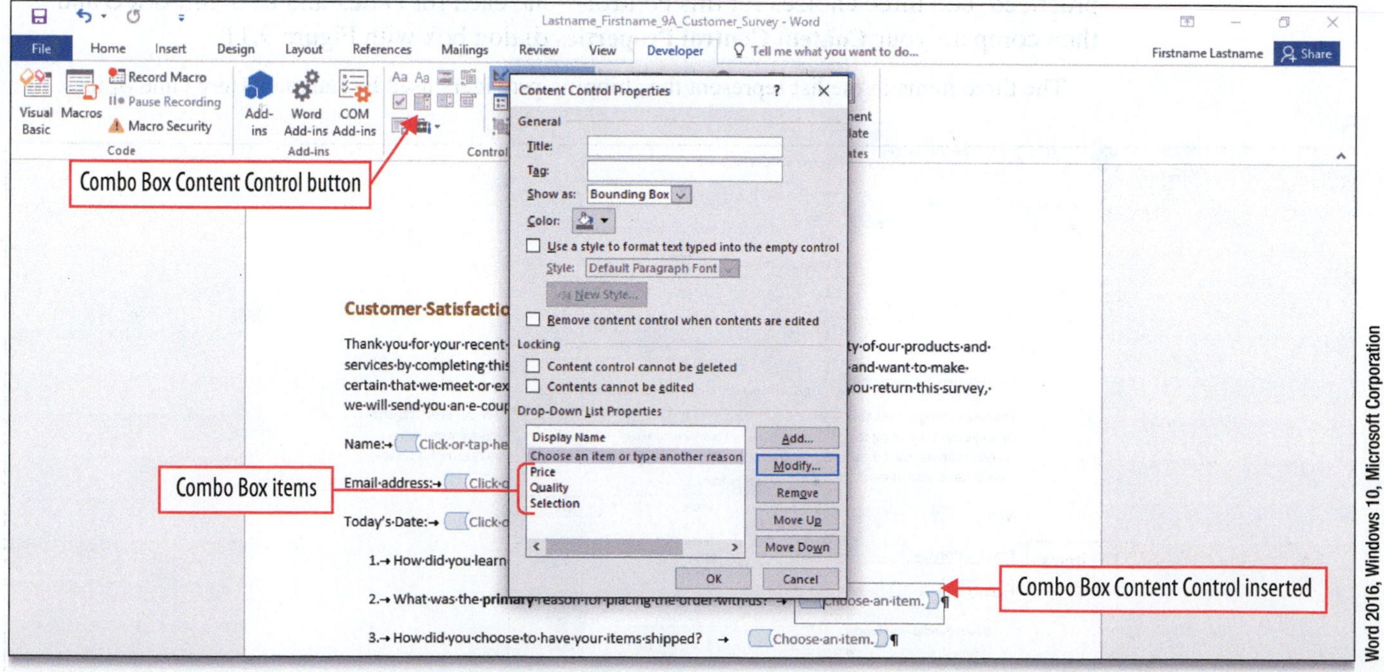

FIGURE 9.12

7 In the **Content Control Properties** dialog box, click **OK**, and then **Save** your changes.

Activity 9.07 | Inserting and Modifying a Check Box Form Field

Legacy controls are fields you use in designing a form for persons who possess older versions of Word. A ***Check Box form field*** is a legacy control that enables the customer to select, or not select, a specific option. For purposes of this instruction, you are adding content controls and legacy controls in the same form. In this Activity, you will add two check box form fields and then modify their properties.

1. Locate the paragraph that begins *4. Did the items arrive*. Click to position the insertion point to the right of the question mark, and then press Tab.
2. On the **Developer tab**, in the **Controls group**, click **Legacy Tools**, and then under **Legacy Forms**, point to **Check Box Form Field**. Compare your screen with Figure 9.13.

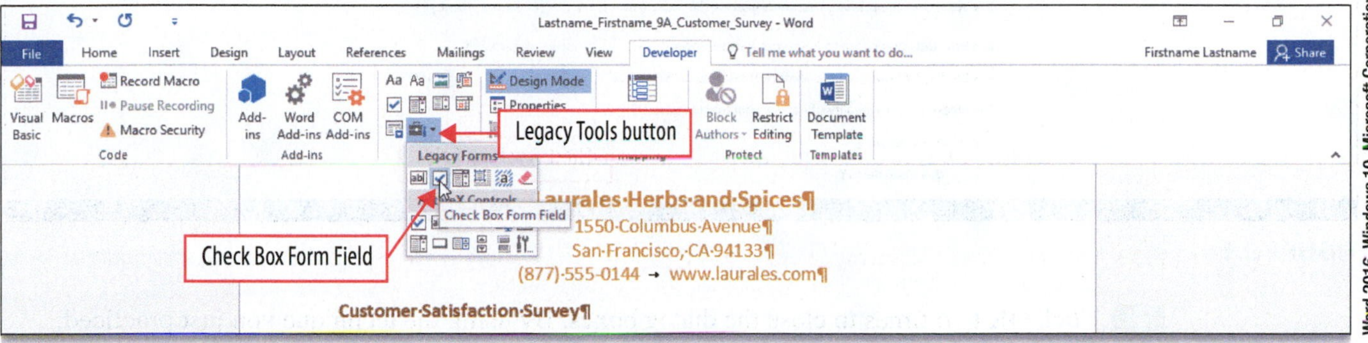

FIGURE 9.13

3. Click **Check Box Form Field**. With the insertion point to the right of the inserted check box, press Spacebar two times, and then type **Yes**
4. With the insertion point to the right of *Yes*, press Tab two times. In the **Controls group**, click **Legacy Tools**, and then under **Legacy Forms**, click **Check Box Form Field**. With the insertion point to the right of the check box, press Spacebar two times, and then type **No**

   A check box can be selected or deselected when the person using the form clicks the field.

5. Click the first check box, and then in the **Controls** group, click **Properties**. In the **Check Box Form Field Options** dialog box, in the lower left corner, click **Add Help Text**.
6. In the **Form Field Help Text** dialog box, click the **Help Key (F1) tab**, click in the **Type your own** box, and then type **Click here for Yes** Compare your screen with Figure 9.14.

   As the customer completes the form, the text for the check box form field will display in a Help message box when the F1 key is pressed.

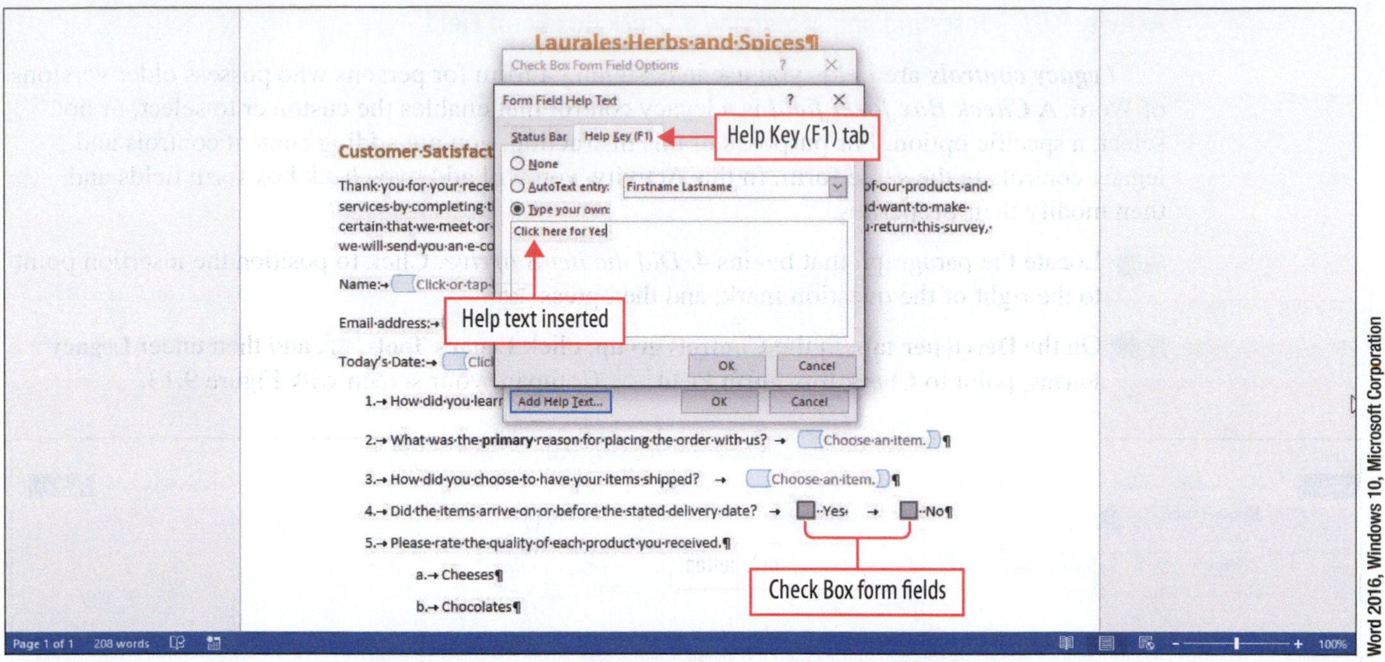

FIGURE 9.14

7 Click **OK** two times to close the dialog boxes. By using the technique you just practiced, select the second check box, display the **Form Field Help Text** dialog box, click the **Help Key (F1) tab**, and then type **Click here for No** Click **OK** two times to close the dialog boxes. **Save** your document.

More Knowledge **Deleting Form Fields and Content Controls**

To delete a form field or content control, select the field you want to remove, and then press Del.

Objective 2 Convert Text to a Table and Insert Content Controls in a Table

GO! Learn How Video W9-2

You can select any text and convert it to a table.

Activity 9.08 | Converting Text to a Table

3.1.1

1 Select the six paragraphs formatted with lowercase letters—beginning with *a. Cheeses* and ending with *f. Vinegars*. Click the **Home tab**, in the **Paragraph group**, click **Numbering** to turn off the numbered format. Click the **Insert tab**, in the **Tables group**, click **Table**, and then click **Convert Text to Table**.

2 In the **Convert Text to Table** dialog box, under **Separate text at**, be sure the **Paragraphs** option button is selected. Click **OK**, and then compare your screen with Figure 9.15.

Recall that a table is a useful tool to display information in an organized format.

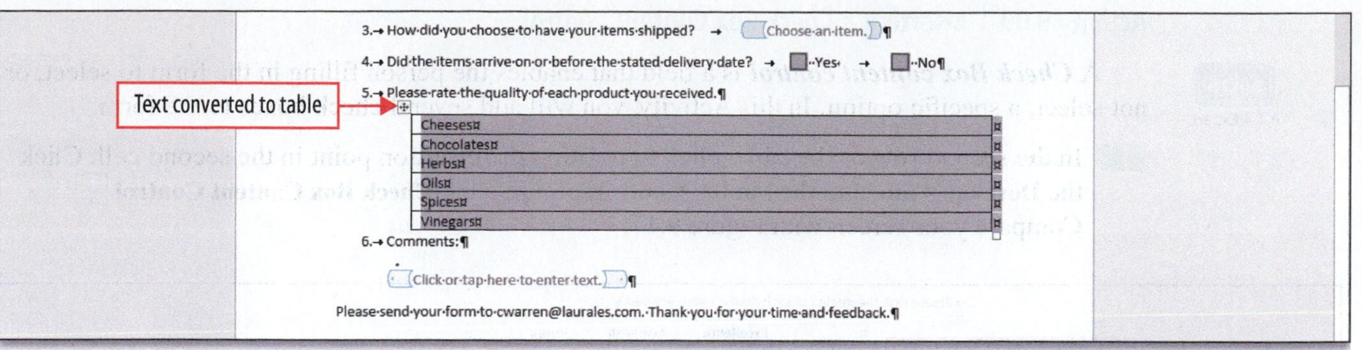

FIGURE 9.15

Word 2016, Windows 10, Microsoft Corporation

3 In the first cell of the table, click to position the insertion point to the right of *Cheeses*. Point slightly above the top right corner of the cell, and then click the **One-Click Row/Column Insertion** button three times to insert three additional table columns.

4 Click in the first cell of the table, and then under **Table Tools**, click the **Layout tab**. In the **Rows & Columns group**, click **Insert Above** to insert a new row at the top of the table.

5 In the first row of the table, click to position the insertion point in the second cell. Type **Excellent** press Tab, type **Average** press Tab, and then type **Poor**

6 Under **Table Tools**, click the **Design tab**, in the **Table Styles group**, click **More**. In the **Table Styles** gallery, under **Grid Tables**, in the second row, click the fifth style—**Grid Table 2 - Accent 4**. Click the **Table Tools Layout tab**, in the **Table group**, if necessary click **View Gridlines** to display dotted gridlines around the table.

7 Slightly outside the upper left corner of the table, point to the table move handle. With the pointer, click one time to select the entire table. On the **Table Tools Layout tab**, in the **Cell Size group**, in the **Height** box, type **0.2** In the **Cell Size group**, in the **Width** box, type **1** and then press Enter.

8 On the **Table Tools Layout tab**, in the **Table group**, click **Properties**. In the **Table Properties** dialog box, on the **Table tab**, under **Alignment**, click **Center**. Click **OK**, deselect the table, and then compare your screen with Figure 9.16.

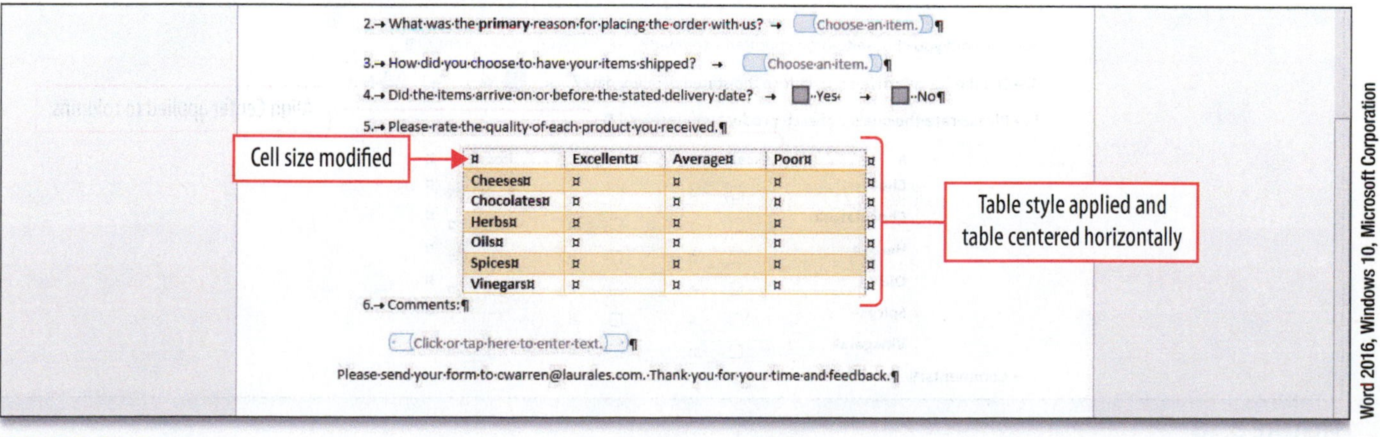

Word 2016, Windows 10, Microsoft Corporation

FIGURE 9.16

9 **Save** your document.

Activity 9.09 | Inserting a Check Box Content Control

4.1.4 Expert

A ***Check Box content control*** is a field that enables the person filling in the form to select, or not select, a specific option. In this Activity, you will add several check boxes to the form.

1 In the second row of the table, click to position the insertion point in the second cell. Click the **Developer tab**, and then in the **Controls group**, click **Check Box Content Control**. Compare your screen with Figure 9.17.

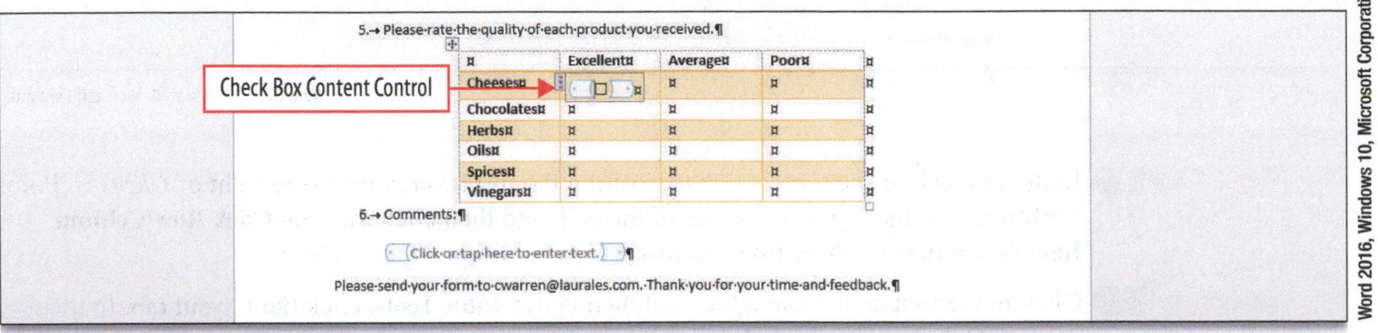

FIGURE 9.17

2 In the current cell, with the insertion point to the left of the check box, on the content control, click **Select Field** to select the Check Box content control. Right-click the selection, and then click **Copy**. In the second row, click in the third cell, and then press Ctrl + V to paste the Check Box content control in the cell. Press Tab, and then press Ctrl + V to paste the Check Box content control.

You can copy and paste content controls in the same manner as text and graphics.

3 In a similar manner, paste the **Check Box Content Control** in the remaining empty cells of the table.

4 Point slightly above the second column of the table to display the pointer, and then drag to the right to select the second, third, and fourth columns of the table. On the **Table Tools Layout tab**, in the **Alignment group**, click **Align Center**. Press Ctrl + End, and then compare your screen with Figure 9.18. **Save** your document.

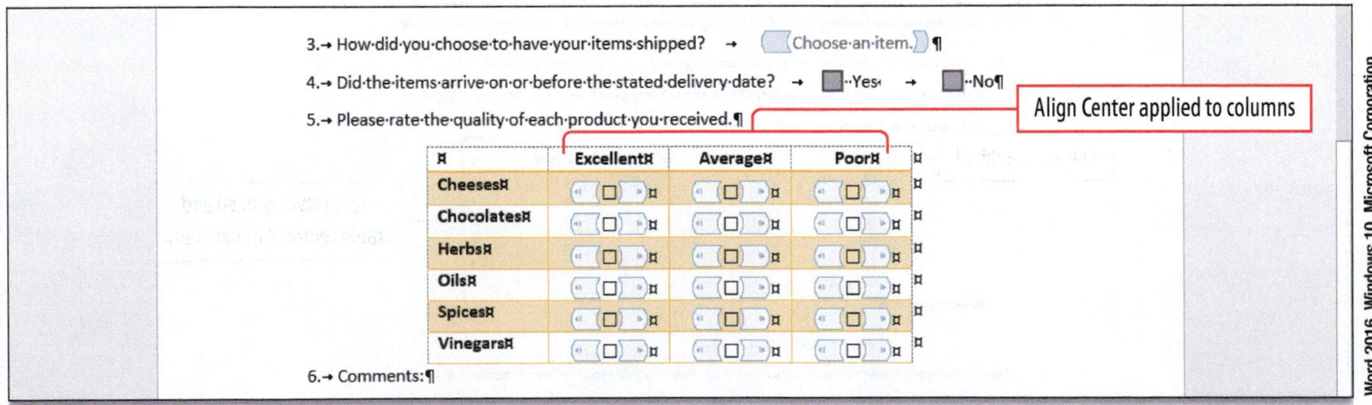

FIGURE 9.18

> ***More* Knowledge** **Inserting Other Controls**
>
> The Picture content control enables you to insert an image—for example, a photo for identification. Use the Building Block Gallery content control to insert a building block in a content control—which enables you to add specific text. The Repeat Section content control contains other controls and repeats the contents as needed.

9 WORD

Objective 3 Modify and Protect a Form

GO! Learn How Video W9-3

You can manage the information provided by the person filling in the form by modifying the properties of content controls. In addition, when a form is distributed, you can protect it so that the static text and content controls cannot be edited or removed by the person filling out the form.

Activity 9.10 | Editing Text in a Content Control

You can customize the placeholder text that displays in content controls.

1. Locate the paragraph that begins *Name*, and then in the same paragraph, click anywhere in the text *Click or tap here to enter text* to select the **Plain Text content control** that you inserted earlier.

2. In the **Plain Text content control**, select the existing text *Click or tap here to enter text.*, and then type **Enter your first and last name.**

3. To the right of the text *Email address*, in the **Plain Text content control**, select the existing text, and then type **Enter your email address.** Click in a blank area of the document to deselect the content control, and then compare your screen with Figure 9.19.

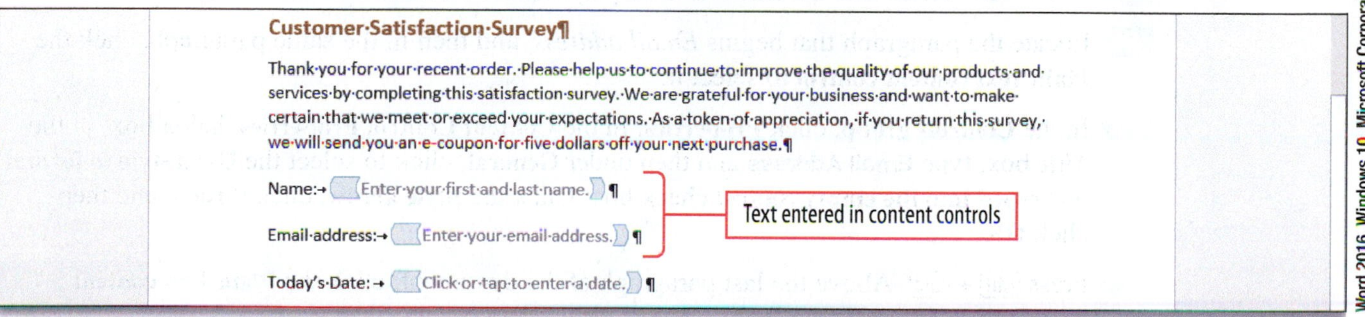

FIGURE 9.19

Word 2016, Windows 10, Microsoft Corporation

4. Below the paragraph *Comments*, in the **Plain Text content control**, select the existing text, and then type **Enter your comments. Save** your document.

Activity 9.11 | Modifying Content Control Properties

MOS 3.3.2 Expert

You can designate the characteristics of a content control by modifying its properties. In this Activity, you will assign a title and style to plain text content controls.

1. Locate the paragraph that begins *Name*, and then in the same paragraph, click anywhere in the **Plain Text content control** to select it.

2. Click the **Developer tab**, and then in the **Controls group**, click **Properties.**

3. In the **Content Control Properties** dialog box, in the **Title** box, type **Name**

   Assigning a title that displays on the content control makes it easier to identify it.

4. In the **Content Control Properties** dialog box, under **General**, select the **Use a style to format text typed into the empty control** check box. Click the **Style arrow**, and then click **Strong**. Compare your screen with Figure 9.20.

   Styles for a content control work in the same manner as other text in a document. In addition to the displayed styles, you can create a new style. In this instance, when the customer types his or her name, the text will be formatted with the Strong style.

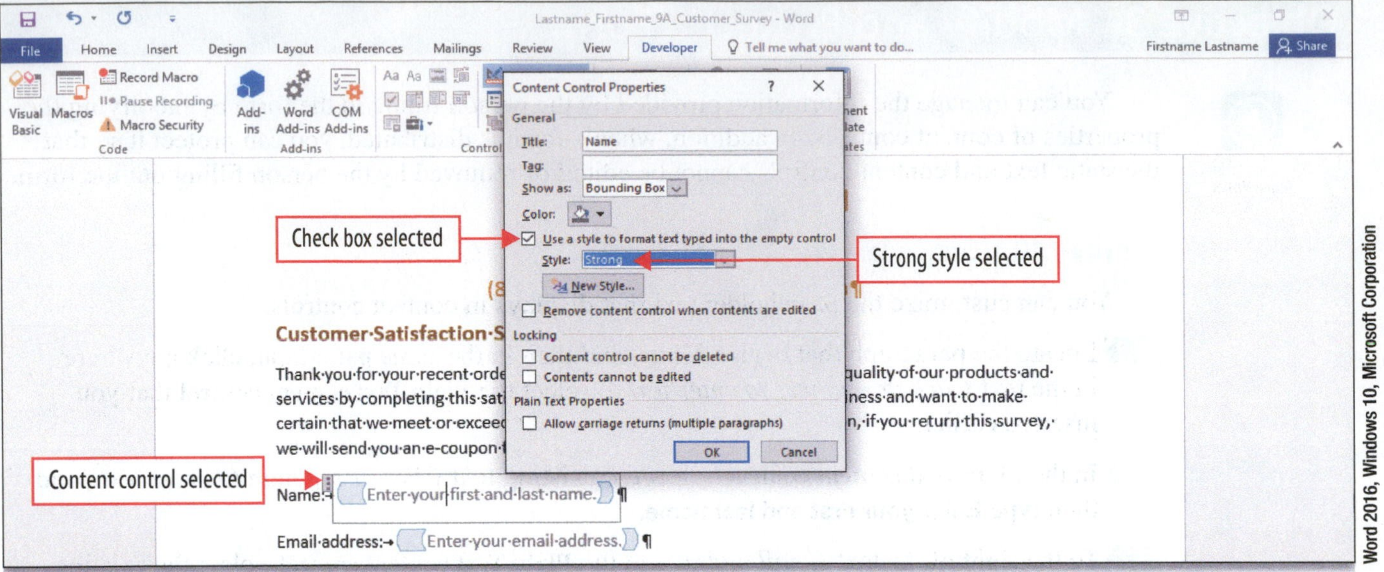

FIGURE 9.20

5 Click **OK**. Notice that the title *Name* displays on the Plain Text content control.

6 Locate the paragraph that begins *Email address*, and then in the same paragraph, click the **Plain Text content control** to select it.

7 In the **Controls group**, click **Properties**. In the **Content Control Properties** dialog box, in the **Title** box, type **Email Address** and then under **General**, click to select the **Use a style to format text typed into the empty control** check box. Click the **Style arrow**, click **Strong**, and then click **OK**.

8 Press Ctrl + End. Above the last paragraph of the document, click the **Plain Text content control** to select it.

9 In the **Controls group**, click **Properties**. In the **Content Control Properties** dialog box, in the **Title** box, type **Comments** and then under **General**, click to select the **Use a style to format text typed into the empty control** check box. Click the **Style arrow**, click **Quote**, and then click **OK**.

The customer's comments will be formatted with the Quote style.

10 **Save** your document.

Activity 9.12 | Restricting Editing and Using a Password to Protect a Form

1.2.1 Expert
1.2.3 Expert

The purpose of providing a form is to have individuals enter data only in the content controls you have created without editing other text or modifying any formats in the form document. To do so, Word enables you to protect the form to restrict the entry of data only into the control fields you have created. In this Activity, you will apply restrictions and add a password to safeguard the form.

1 Press Ctrl + Home to move to the top of your form. On the **Developer tab**, in the **Controls group**, click **Design Mode** to turn off Design Mode.

When you finish designing a form, you must turn off Design Mode before you can restrict the form and distribute the form for use.

2 On the **Developer tab**, in the **Protect group**, click **Restrict Editing** to display the **Restrict Editing** pane.

By restricting the formatting and editing, you can control the changes the person filling out the form can make in the form. Item 1, if selected, restricts formatting changes. Item 2 defines how the document can be edited.

3 In the **Restrict Editing** pane, under **2. Editing restrictions**, click to select the **Allow only this type of editing in the document** check box.

4 Click the **Allow only this type of editing in the document arrow**, and then click **Filling in forms**. Compare your screen with Figure 9.21.

This option restricts the use of the document so that the person filling in the form can only fill in the content controls in the document.

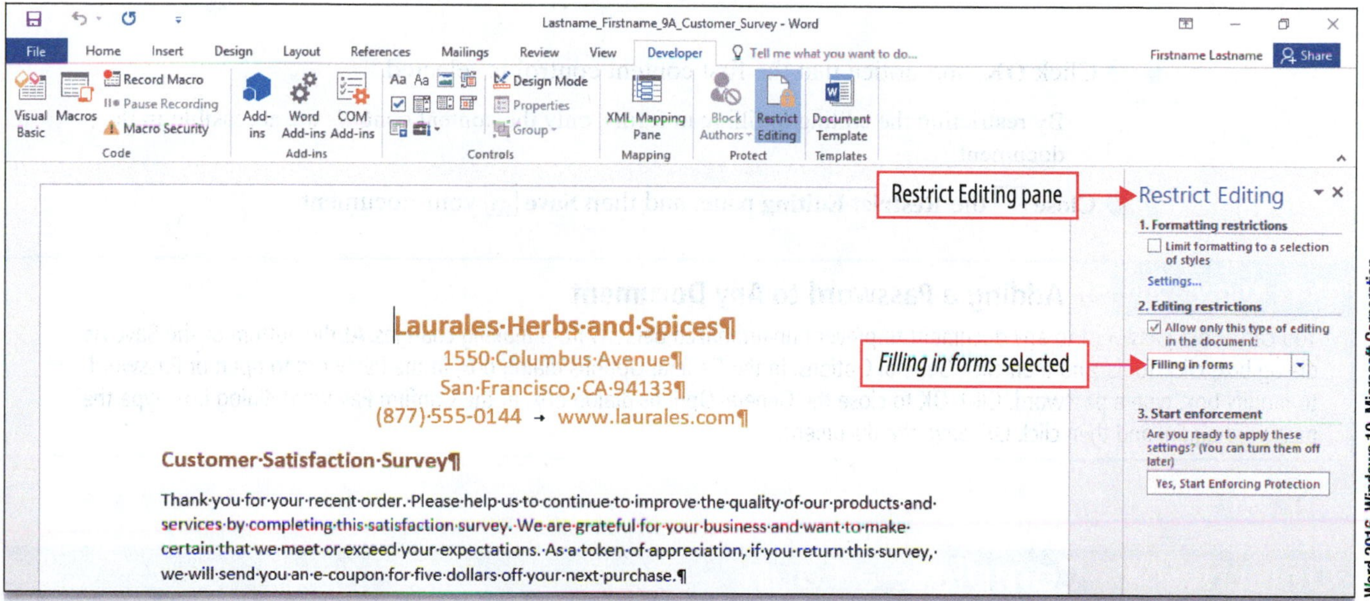

FIGURE 9.21

5 In the **Restrict Editing** pane, under **3. Start enforcement**, click **Yes, Start Enforcing Protection**.

Before you begin enforcing protection, you should always confirm that all elements of the document display correctly.

6 In the **Start Enforcing Protection** dialog box, in the **Enter new password (optional)** box, type **survey15** Notice that as you type, the characters are replaced with bullets.

A ***password*** is a code to gain access to a file—in this instance, the customer survey document.

7 In the **Reenter password to confirm** box, type **survey15** and then compare your screen with Figure 9.22.

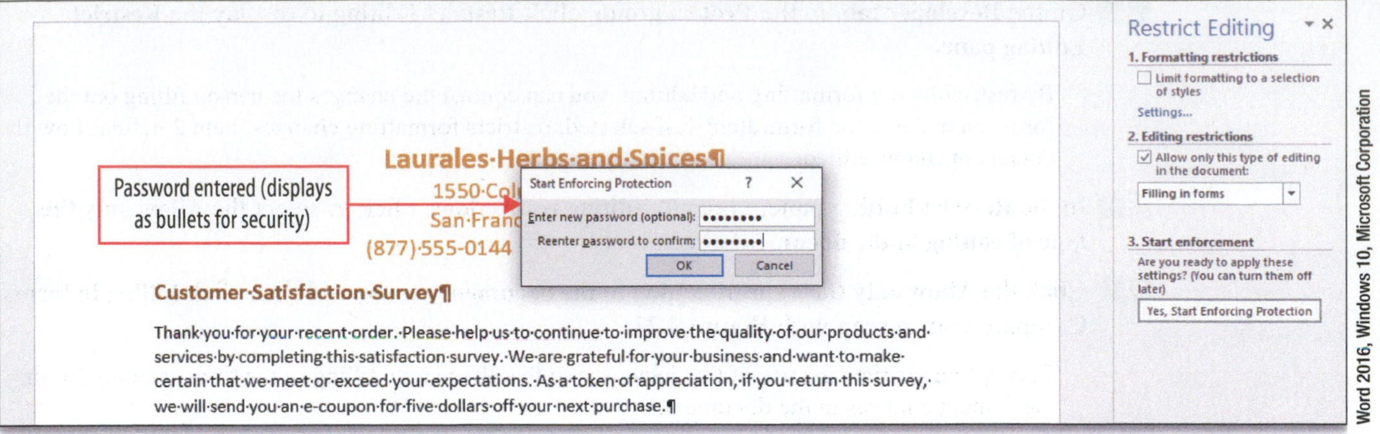

FIGURE 9.22

8 Click **OK**, and notice that the first content control is selected.

By restricting the editing to filling in forms, only the content controls are accessible in the document.

9 **Close** the **Restrict Editing** pane, and then **Save** your document.

***More* Knowledge** **Adding a Password to Any Document**

You can add a password to any document to prevent unauthorized persons from making changes. At the bottom of the Save As dialog box, click Tools, and then click General Options. In the General Options dialog box, in the Password to open or Password to modify box, type a password. Click OK to close the General Options dialog box. In the Confirm Password dialog box, type the password again, and then click OK. Save the document.

Objective 4 Complete a Form

GO! Learn How Video W9-4

After the form is protected, it can be distributed to others by sending it as an email attachment, and then the recipient can complete the form in Word. Typically, you create a form and then save it as a ***template*** so that it can be used repeatedly without changing the original document. A template is a predefined structure that contains basic document settings, such as fonts, margins, and available styles, and can also store elements such as building blocks and content controls.

Activity 9.13 | Completing a Form

In this Activity, you will complete the customer satisfaction survey. In actual use, be sure to save your form as a template so that it can re-used.

1 Click the **File tab**, click **Save As**, click **Browse**, and then in the **Save As** dialog box, navigate to your **Word Chapter 9** folder.

2 Click in the **File name** box to select the text, and then using your own name, type **Lastname_Firstname_9A_Survey_Completed** Click **Save**.

3 In the paragraph that begins *Name*, with the **Plain Text content control** selected, using your own name, type **Firstname Lastname** and then compare your screen with Figure 9.23.

Your name is formatted with the Strong style—the style you selected in the Content Control Properties dialog box.

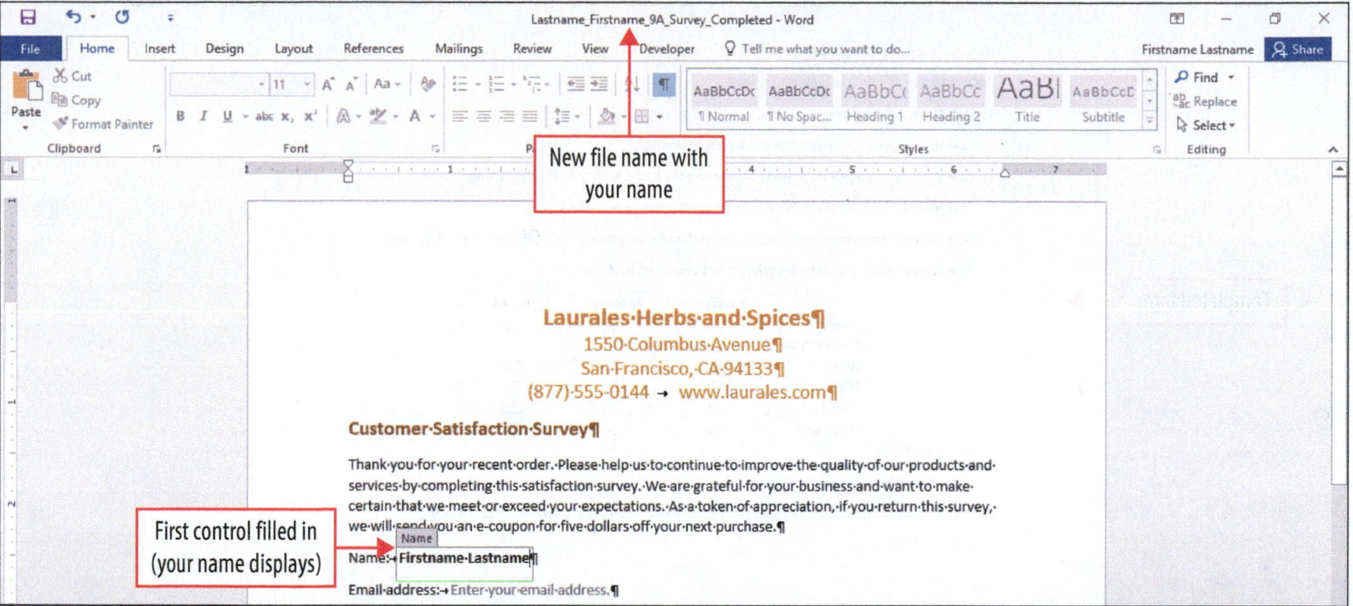

FIGURE 9.23

Word 2016, Windows 10, Microsoft Corporation

4 Press Tab, and then in the paragraph that begins *Email address*, in the **Plain Text content control**, using your own last name, type **Lastname@laurales.com**

Because the form is protected—only filling in information is allowed—you can move from one content control to the next by pressing Tab.

5 Press Tab, click the **Date Picker content control arrow** to display the calendar, and then at the bottom of the calendar, click **Today**.

The date displays with the format you selected in the Content Control Properties dialog box. In the Date Picker content control, you can navigate in the calendar to select any date.

6 Press Tab. To the right of the paragraph that begins with *1*, click the **Drop-Down List content control arrow**, and then click **Friend**.

7 Press Tab. To the right of the paragraph that begins *2*, click the **Combo Box content control arrow**, click **Choose an item or type another reason.** and then type **Excellent service!**

Recall that you modified the default text in the list to read *Choose an item or type another reason.* The user of the form can type a response that differs from the listed items.

8 Press Tab. To the right of the paragraph that begins *3*, click the **Drop-Down List content control arrow**, and then click **UPS**.

9 Locate the paragraph that begins *4*, click the **Check Box form field** to select **Yes**. Press F1 to display the **Help** dialog box. Take a moment to read the help text, and then click **OK** to close the **Help** dialog box.

10 In the table, in the **Cheeses** row, in the **Average** column, click the check box. In the **Herbs** row, in the **Excellent** column, click the check box. In the **Spices** row, in the **Excellent** column, click the check box.

11 Below the paragraph that begins *6. Comments*, click the **Plain Text content control** that indicates *Enter your comments* and then type **I am eager to try your vinegars.** Click in a blank area of the document to deselect the content control, and then compare your screen with Figure 9.24.

The text is formatted with the Quote style—the style you selected in the Content Control Properties dialog box.

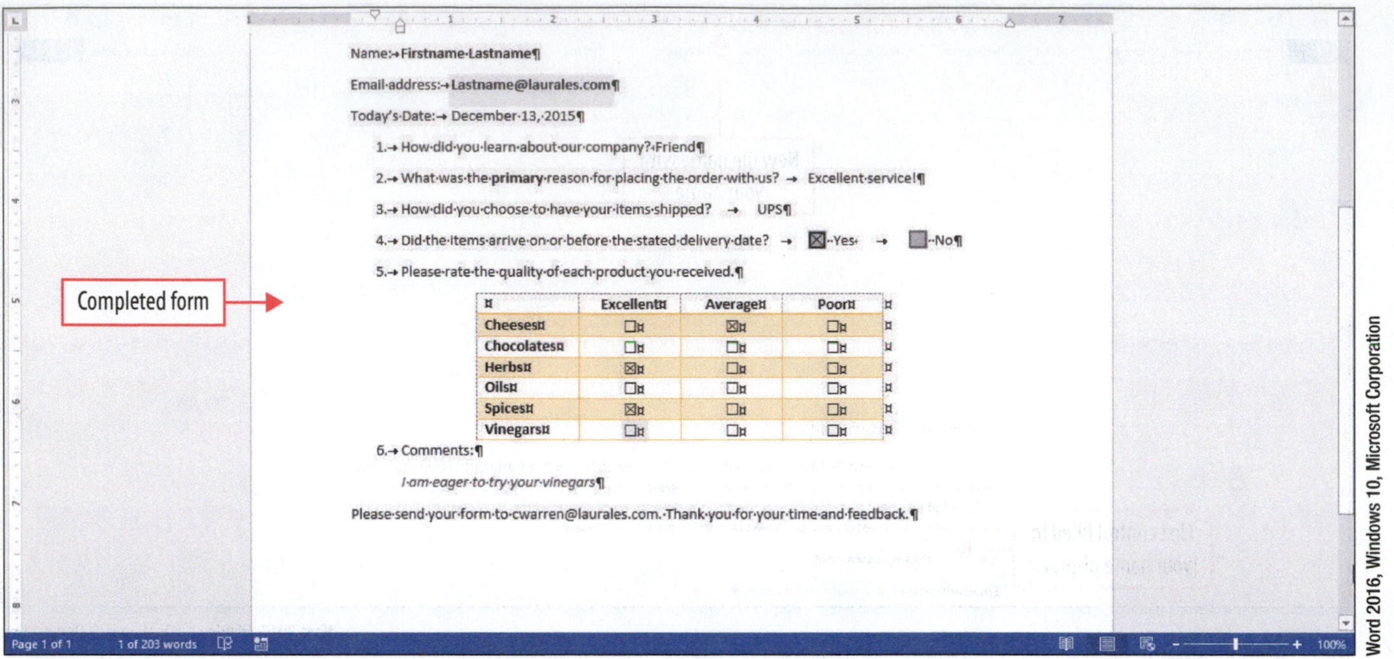

FIGURE 9.24

12 Click the **File tab**, and then click **Show All Properties**. In the **Tags** box, type **customer survey, tested** In the **Subject** box, type your course name and section number. If necessary, edit the author name to display your name. On the left, click **Save** to save your document and return to the Word window.

> ***More Knowledge*** **Linking a Form to a Database**
>
> To link data that is entered in a form to a database, the best option is to use a form in a Microsoft Access database. To link a form designed in Word to a database requires extensive programming skills.

Activity 9.14 | Unlocking a Form

1 Click the **Developer tab**, in the **Protect group**, click **Restrict Editing** to display the **Restrict Editing** pane. At the bottom of the **Restrict Editing** pane, click **Stop Protection**. In the **Unprotect Document** dialog box, in the **Password** box, type **survey15** and then click **OK**.

Recall that the form is protected with a password. You must know the password to unlock the form.

2 **Close** [X] the **Restrict Editing** pane, and then insert the file name in the footer.

3 Click the **File tab**, on the left click **Options**. In the **Word Options** dialog box, on the left click **Customize Ribbon**. In the **Main Tabs** list, locate and then click to clear the **Developer** check box. Click **OK**, and notice that the Developer tab no longer displays on the ribbon.

4 **Save** your document. In the upper right corner of the Word window, click **Close** [X]. If directed by your instructor to do so, submit your paper printout, your electronic image of your document that looks like a printed document, or your original Word file.

END | You have completed Project 9A

PROJECT

9B Moving Agreement

PROJECT ACTIVITIES

In Activities 9.15 through 9.22, you will create a document pertaining to an upcoming office move. Laurales Herbs and Spices is relocating its administrative offices. To help ensure that no items are lost or damaged, Rachel Enders, who is in charge of the move, has asked each employee to sign an agreement indicating that everything has been properly packed, labeled, and is ready to be moved. You will customize the ribbon to increase your efficiency in creating the agreement and insert a signature line. Your completed document will look similar to Figure 9.25.

PROJECT FILES

If your instructor wants you to submit Project 9B in the MyITLab Grader system, log into MyITLab, locate Grader Project 9B, and then download the files for the project.

For Project 9B, you will need the following files:

w09B_Moving_Agreement
w09B_Logo_Photo
w09B_Paid_Time_Off_optional
(you will need this file only if assigned the optional Activities at the end of the project)
w09B_Language_optional

You will save your documents as:

Lastname_Firstname_9B_Moving_Agreement
Lastname_Firstname_9B_Paid_Time_Off_optional
(this file results from optional Activities at the end of the project; submit this file only if assigned by your instructor)
Lastname_Firstname_9B_Language_optional
(this file results from optional Activities at the end of the project; submit this file only if assigned by your instructor)

PROJECT RESULTS

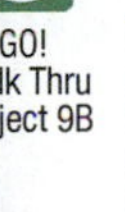

Laurales Herbs and Spices

MOVING AGREEMENT

The administrative division of Laurales Herbs and Spices is relocating to a new building next week. At our last meeting, you were given detailed instructions on how to prepare your workspace for the move. Below is a brief summary. Print this form. When you have finished packing, sign and date the consent form below and return it to Rachel Enders through interoffice mail. This will assure that all your belongings get to the new location.

1. Remove all items from drawers and cabinets.
2. Place items in boxes provided by the movers.
3. Label the boxes with your full name.
4. Use masking tape to label all furniture and equipment.
5. Sign the consent form and return to Rachel Enders.

I have cleared my workspace, packed and labeled all boxes, furniture, and equipment, and give permission for all items to be moved to the new location.

X
Employee Name
Administration

Date

Lastname_Firstname_9B_Moving_Agreement

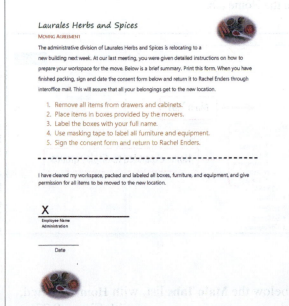

FIGURE 9.25 Project 9B Moving Agreement

Objective 5 Create a Custom Ribbon Tab

The ribbon consists of tabs, and each tab contains groups of related commands. You can personalize Word and improve your efficiency by adding commands that you use frequently to an existing tab or by creating a new custom tab.

Activity 9.15 | Creating a Custom Ribbon Tab

ALERT! **To submit as an autograded project, log into MyITLab, download the files for this project, and begin with those files instead of w09B_Moving_Agreement.**

1. Start Word, on the left click **Open Other Documents**, click **Browse**, and then in the **Open** dialog box, navigate to the student data files that accompany this chapter. Open the file **w09B_Moving_Agreement**.
2. Click the **File tab**, on the left click **Save As**, click **Browse**, and then in the **Save As** dialog box, navigate to your **Word Chapter 9** folder. Using your own name, save the file as **Lastname_Firstname_9B_Moving_Agreement** and if necessary, display the rulers and formatting marks.
3. Select the paragraph *Moving Agreement*, and then on the **Home tab**, in the **Font group**, click the **Dialog Box Launcher** to display the **Font** dialog box.
4. On the **Font tab**, under **Font style**, click **Bold**. Under **Effects**, select the **Small caps** check box. Click **OK**.
5. Click the **File tab**, and then click **Options**. In the **Word Options** dialog box, on the left click **Customize Ribbon**, and then compare your screen with Figure 9.26.

   The Customize Ribbon tab of the Word Options dialog box displays a list of Popular Commands on the left and a list of Main Tabs on the right. Under Main Tabs, recall that the check marks to the left of tab names indicate tabs that are currently available on the ribbon. You can expand or collapse the view of tabs and groups by clicking + or − respectively. By default, Home is selected and expanded to display the groups on the Home tab.

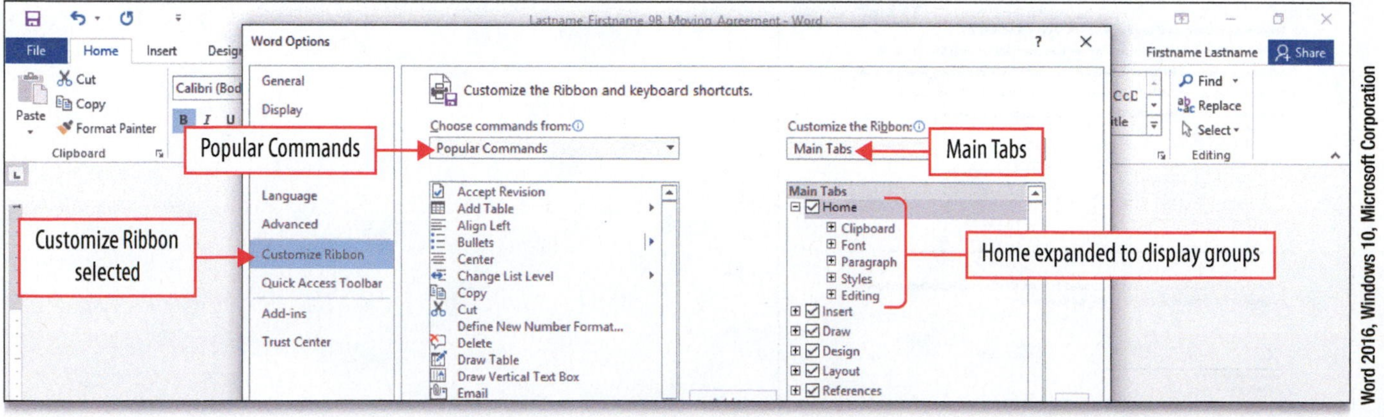

FIGURE 9.26

6. In the **Word Options** dialog box, on the right below the **Main Tabs** list, with **Home** selected, in the lower right corner, click **New Tab**, and then compare your screen with Figure 9.27.

   In the Main Tabs list, *New Tab (Custom)* displays in expanded view with *New Group (Custom)* indented and selected.

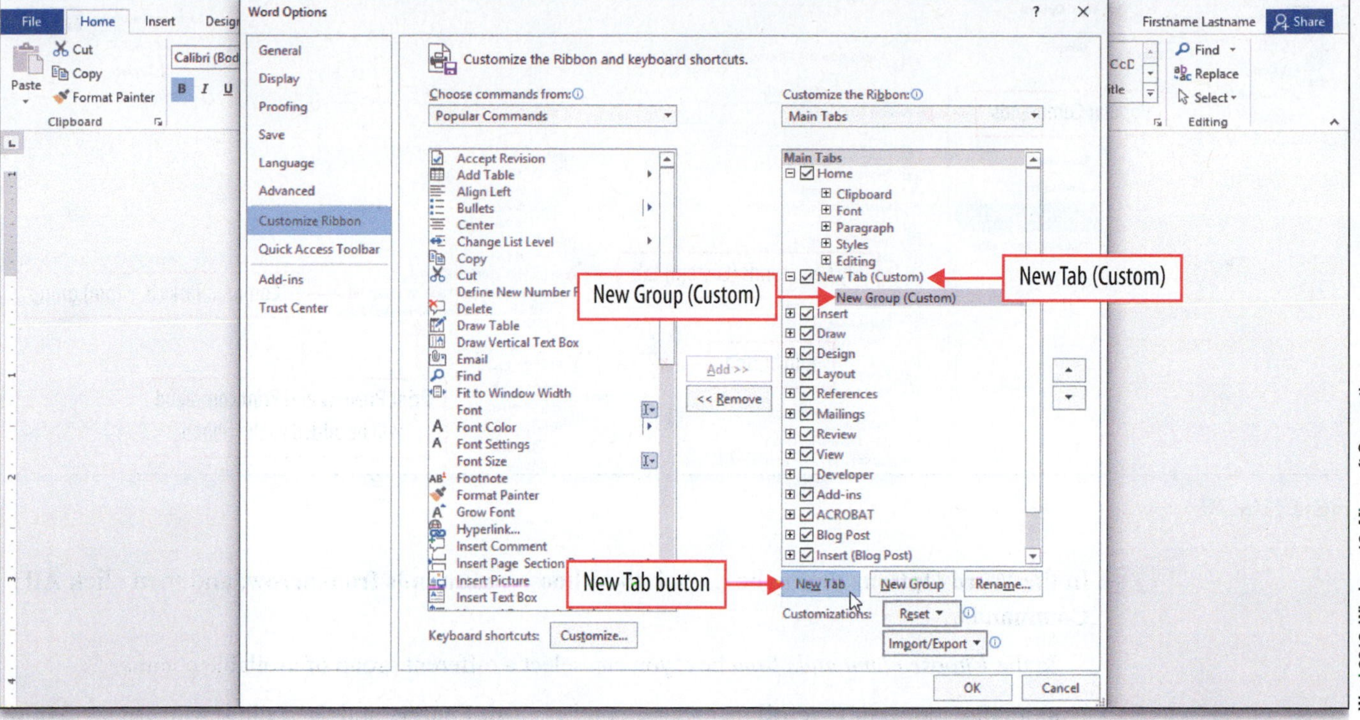

FIGURE 9.27

Word 2016, Windows 10, Microsoft Corporation

7 On the list, click **New Tab (Custom)** to select it, and then in the lower right corner of the **Word Options** dialog box, click **Rename**. In the **Rename** dialog box, in the **Display name** box, type **My Commands** and then click **OK**.

8 On the list, click **New Group (Custom)** to select it, and then at the bottom right of the **Word Options** dialog box, click **Rename**. In the **Rename** dialog box, in the **Display name** box, type **Common Tasks** and then click **OK**. Leave the **Word Options** dialog box open for the next Activity.

Activity 9.16 | Adding Commands to a Ribbon Tab

Commands are arranged within groups on a tab. You can add any command directly to a tab, but it is good practice to add related commands to a group.

1 In the **Word Options** dialog box, near the top on the left, locate the **Choose commands from** box, and notice that *Popular Commands* displays.

2 In the list under **Popular Commands**, scroll as necessary, click **Print Preview and Print**, and then to the right of the list, click **Add**. In the **Main Tabs** list, notice that **Print Preview and Print** displays below the **Common Tasks (Custom)** group you created. Compare your screen with Figure 9.28.

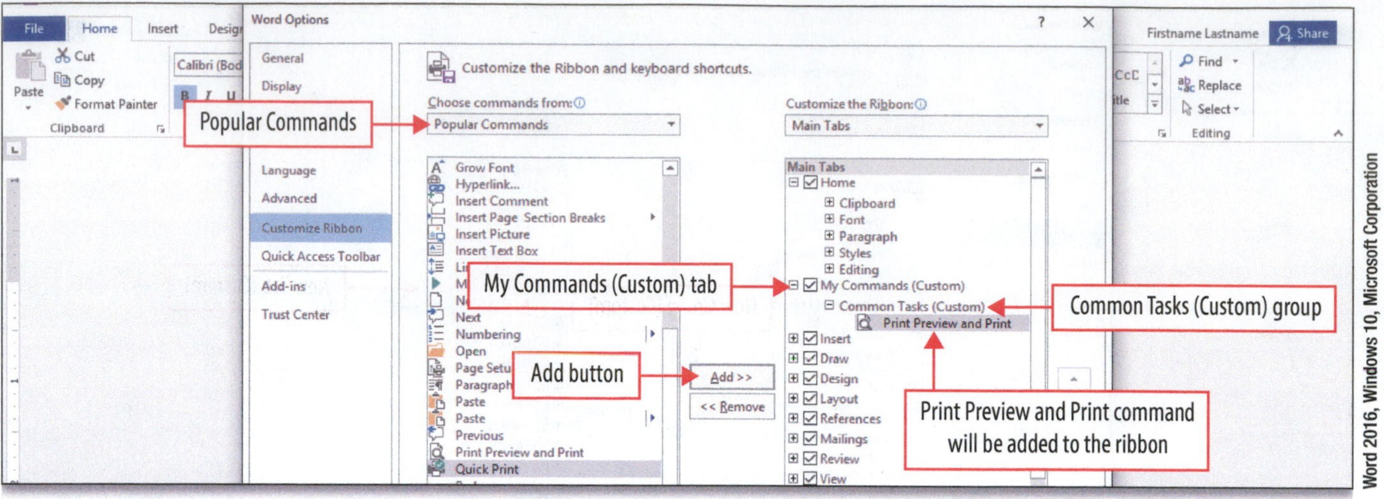

FIGURE 9.28

3 In the **Word Options** dialog box, click the **Choose commands from arrow**, and then click **All Commands**.

In the *Choose commands from* box, you can select a different group of available commands.

4 Under **All Commands**, scroll as necessary, click **Edit Footer**, and then click **Add**. In the **Main Tabs** list, notice that in the **Common Tasks (Custom)** group, **Edit Footer** displays below **Print Preview and Print**.

5 Click the **Choose commands from arrow**, and then click **File Tab**.

6 In the **File Tab** list, click **Close File**, and then click **Add**.

The Close command closes a document and keeps Word open.

7 In the **Main Tabs** list, with **Close File** selected, to the right of the **Main Tabs** list, click **Move Up** [▲] two times. Click **Edit Footer**, click **Move Up** [▲] one time, and then compare your screen with Figure 9.29.

The commands are displayed in alphabetical order. You can use the Move Up and Move Down buttons to arrange tabs, groups, and commands in any order.

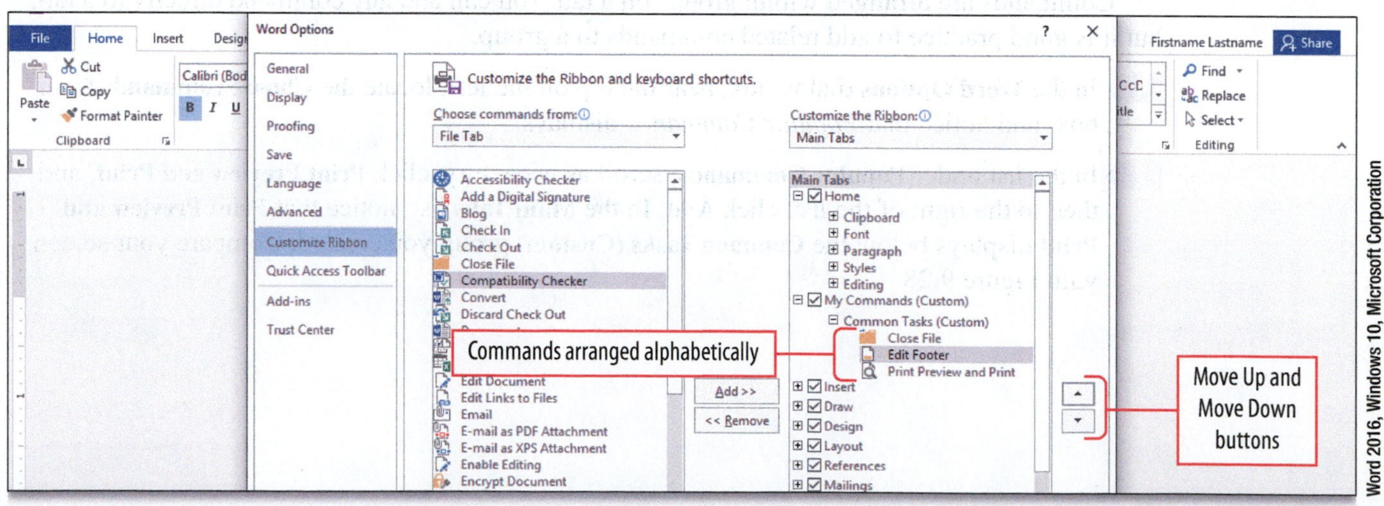

FIGURE 9.29

8 In the lower right corner, click **OK** to close the **Word Options** dialog box, and notice that your custom tab *My Commands* displays to the right of the **Home tab** on the ribbon.

9 Click the **My Commands tab**, and notice that the **Common Tasks group** displays on the left and includes the three commands you added.

10 On the **My Commands tab**, in the **Common Tasks group**, click **Edit Footer**. In the **Insert group**, click **Document Info**, and then click **File Name** to insert the file name in the footer. **Close** the footer area.

11 If necessary, select the paragraph **Moving Agreement**, and then change the **Font Color** to **Green, Accent 6, Darker 50%**—in that last column, the last color.

12 **Save** your document.

Objective 6 Create Style, Color, and Font Sets

GO! Learn How
Video W9-6

You can create custom elements for your documents, and this is commonly done in large organizations where every document must have the same look and feel. For example, if you visit the website for Microsoft or for Apple or for Google, you will notice that every page presents a similar style of fonts, colors, and layouts. This visual consistency demonstrates how a company wants to present itself to the public.

Think about the various publications at your college—the college catalog, the course schedule, the website pages, news releases. You will probably notice that your college attempts to use similar fonts, colors—for example, the school colors—and layouts for its publications.

Activity 9.17 | Creating a Custom Font Set

4.2.2 Expert

1 Click anywhere to deselect the subtitle. On the **Design tab**, in the **Document Formatting group**, click **Fonts**, and then at the bottom, click **Customize Fonts**.

2 In the **Create New Theme Fonts** dialog box, click the **Heading font arrow**, scroll down the alphabetic list, and then click **Segoe Print**.

Segoe, typically pronounced SEE-goh, is a family of fonts that Microsoft uses for its online and printed materials. In August of 2012, Microsoft updated its corporate logo for the first time in 25 years with a new logo using one of the Segoe fonts.

3 Click the **Body font arrow**, scroll down as necessary, and then click **Segoe UI Semilight**.

4 In the **Name** box, select the existing text, type **Laurales 9B** and then compare your screen with Figure 9.30.

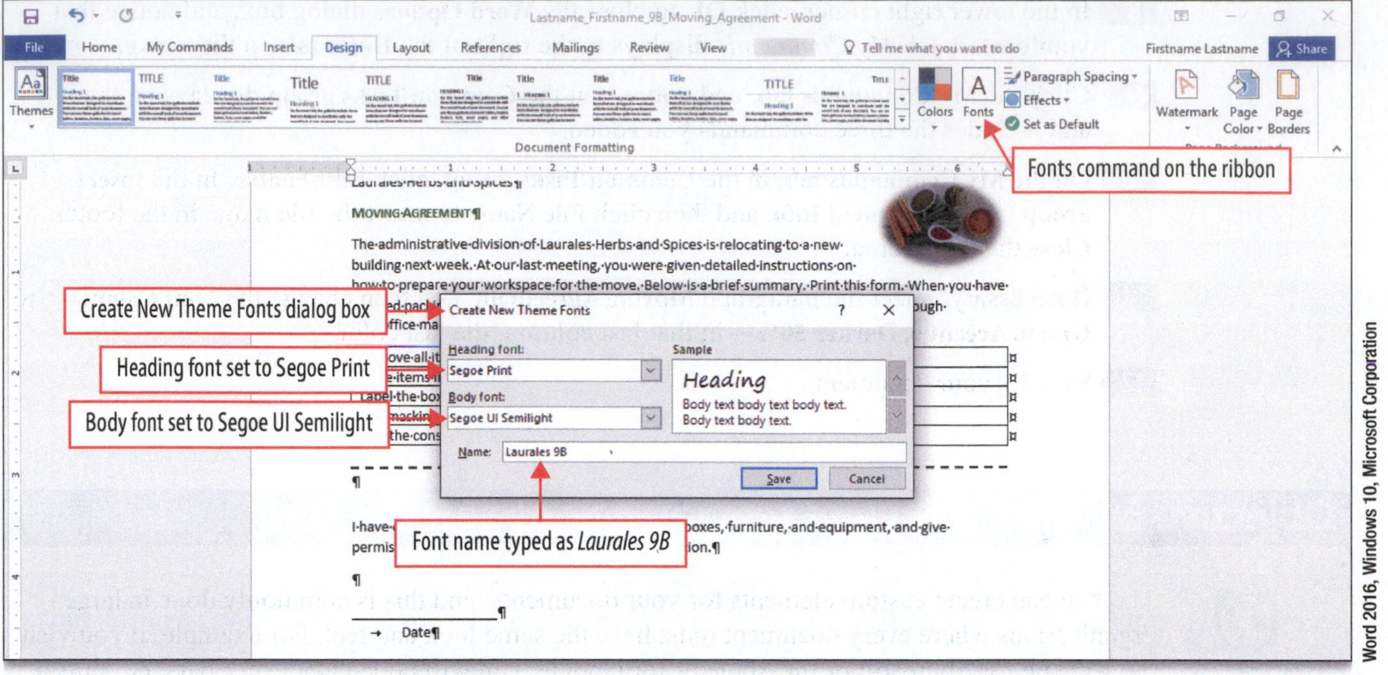

FIGURE 9.30

5 At the bottom of the **Create New Theme Fonts** dialog box, click **Save**, and notice that the Body font—Segoe UI Semilight—is applied to the body text.

6 At the top of the document, select the paragraph *Laurales Herbs and Spices*, and then on the **Home tab**, in the **Font group**, click the **Font Color arrow**. Under **Theme Colors** in the fifth column, click the first color—**Blue, Accent 1**.

7 With the paragraph still selected, in the **Styles group**, click the **More** button, and then click **Heading 1**. Click anywhere in the document to deselect the title, and then compare your screen with Figure 9.31.

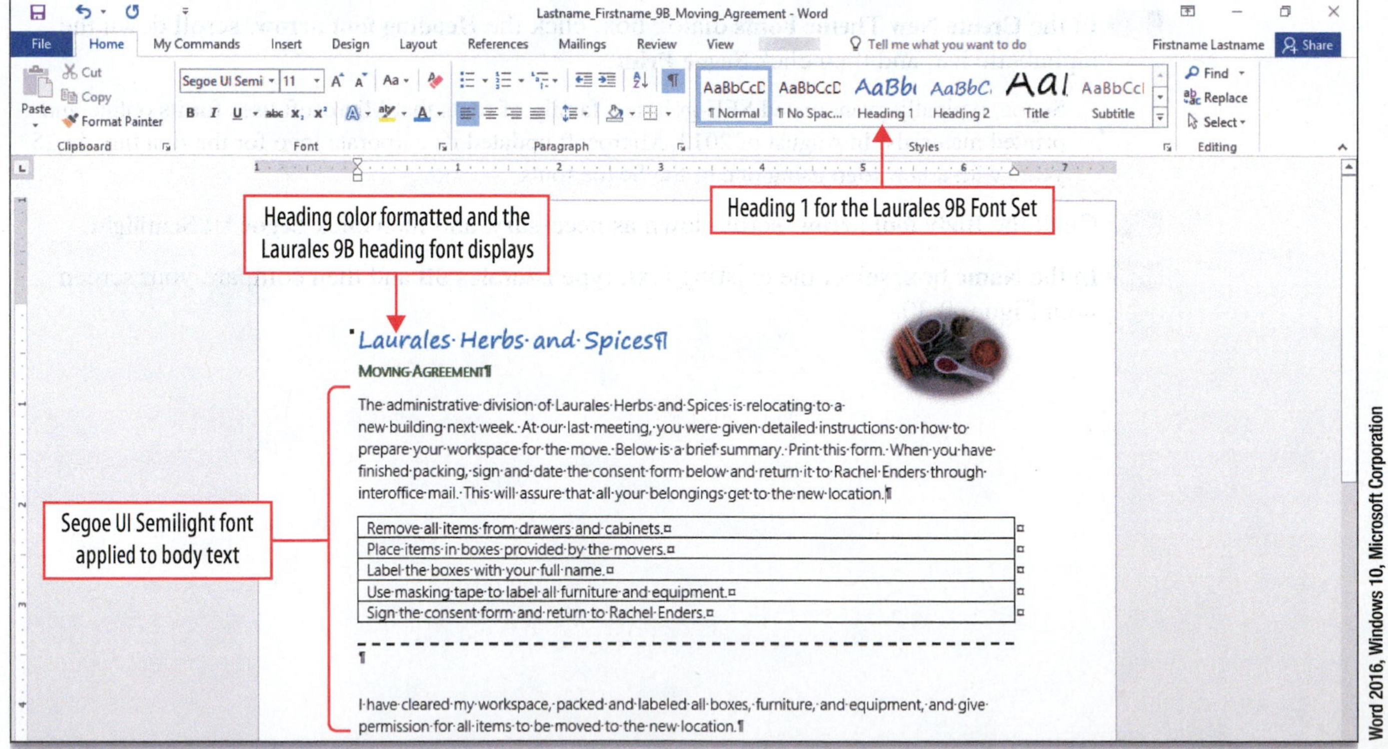

FIGURE 9.31

More Knowledge Deleting a Custom Font Set

To delete a custom font set, on the Design tab, in the Document Formatting group, click Fonts, point to the font set name, right-click, click Delete, and then click Yes.

9 WORD

Activity 9.18 | Creating a Custom Color Set

4.2.1 Expert

1. On the **Design tab**, in the **Document Formatting group**, click **Colors**, and then at the bottom, click **Customize Colors**.
2. In the **Create New Theme Colors** dialog box, click the **Accent 1 arrow**. Below the color palette, click **More Colors**, in the **Colors** dialog box, click the **Standard tab**, and then in the seventh (widest) row, click the first color. Compare your screen with Figure 9.32.

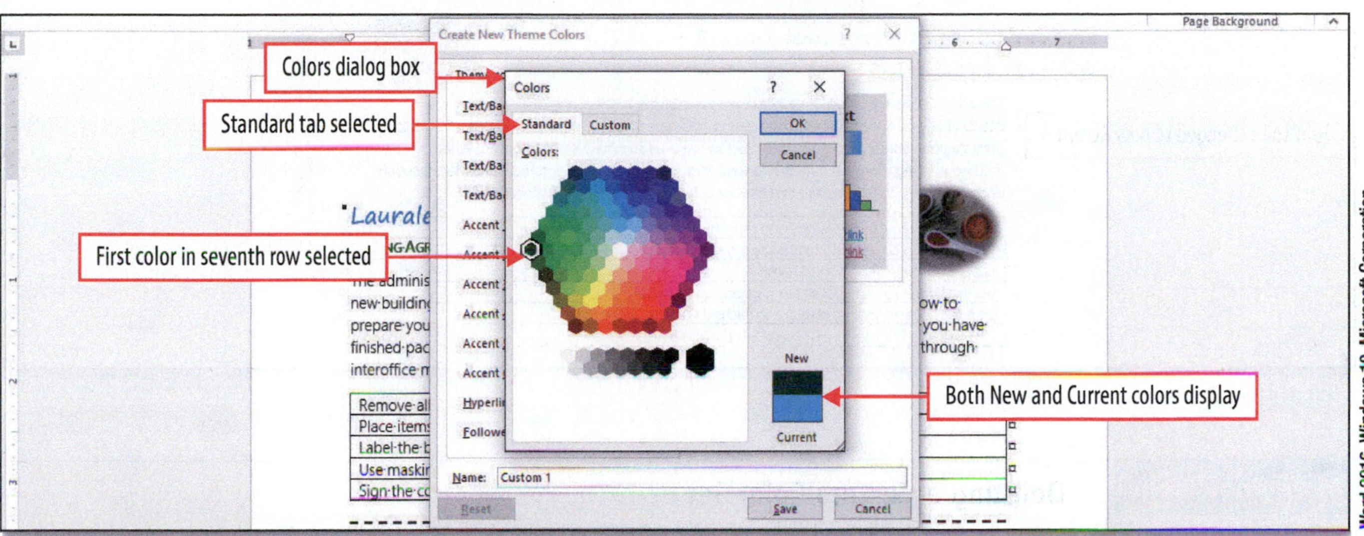

FIGURE 9.32

3. Click **OK**, and then in the **Create New Theme Colors** dialog box, click the **Accent 6 arrow**. Click **More Colors**, click the **Standard tab**, and then in the last row, click the third color. Compare your screen with Figure 9.33.

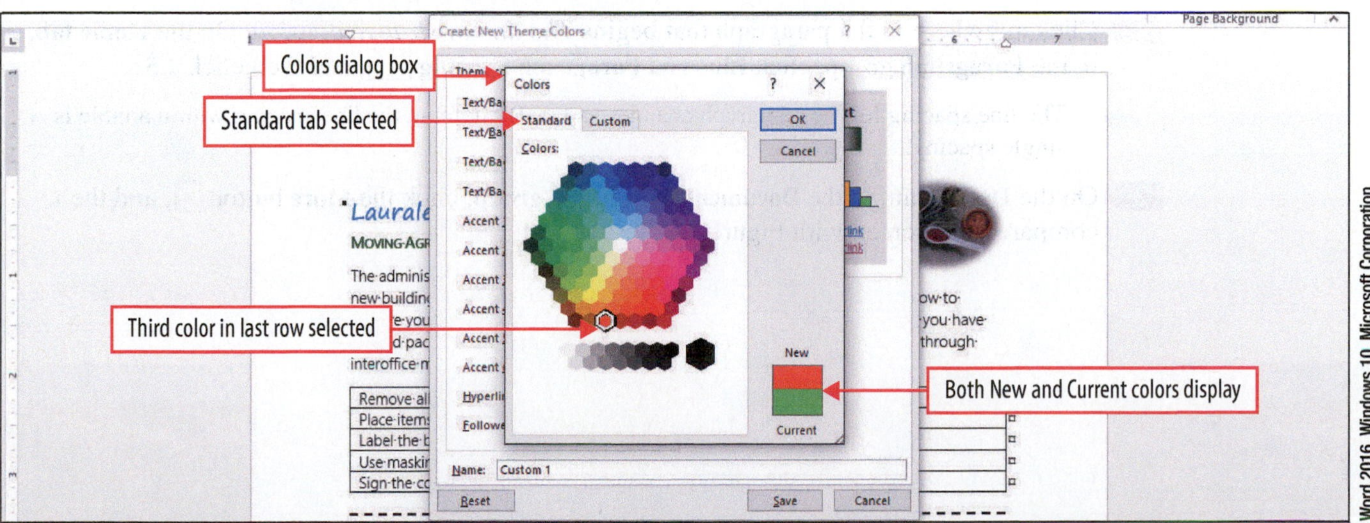

FIGURE 9.33

4 Click **OK**, and then at the bottom of the dialog box, in the **Name** box, type **Laurales 9B** Click **Save**. Notice the change in color for the title *Laurales Herbs and Spices* and the heading *Moving Agreement*. Compare your screen with Figure 9.34.

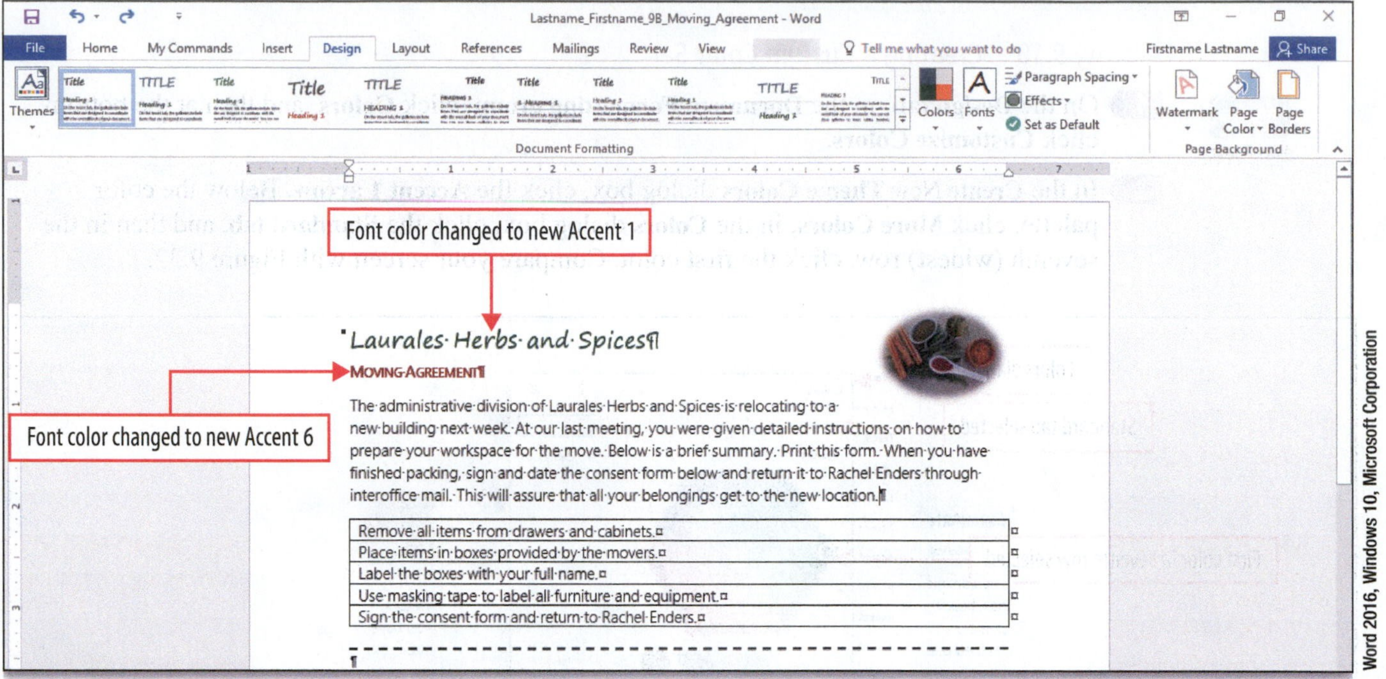

FIGURE 9.34

More Knowledge — Deleting a Custom Color Set

To delete a custom color set, on the Design tab, in the Document Formatting group, click Colors, point to the color set name, right-click, and then click Delete, and then click Yes.

Activity 9.19 | Creating a Custom Style Set

4.2.4 Expert

A ***style set*** is a group of settings for the Font and Paragraph properties of your document. In this Activity, you will create a style set that uses line spacing of 1.5 lines.

1 Click anywhere in the paragraph that begins *The administrative division*. On the **Home tab**, in the **Paragraph group**, click **Line and Paragraph Spacing**, and then click **1.5**.

The line spacing for the paragraph changes to 1.5. By default, the line spacing within a table is single spacing.

2 On the **Design tab**, in the **Document Formatting group**, click the **More** button, and then compare your screen with Figure 9.35.

Save as a New Style Set command

Line spacing set to 1.5

FIGURE 9.35

3 At the bottom of the gallery, click **Save as a New Style Set**, and then in the **File name** box, type **Laurales 9B**

For each user, style sets are stored in the username area of the C drive on the computer.

> **ALERT!**
>
> **If you are working in a college lab and are unable to store your style set, move to the next Activity. The formatting you have applied will remain—you just won't have the style set available to you for other documents.**

4 Click **Save** to save the style and close the dialog box. On the **Design tab**, in the **Document Formatting group**, click the **More** button, and then under **Custom**, point to the first style. Compare your screen with Figure 9.36.

So long as you are using this computer with the same signed-on user, this Style Set will be available to you.

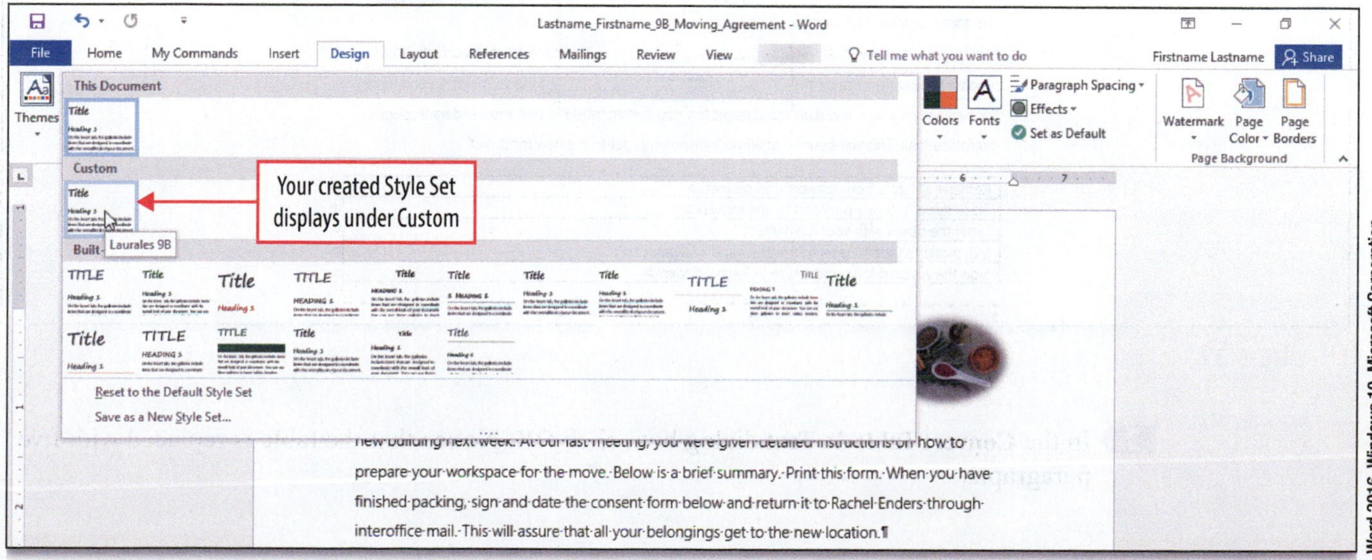

FIGURE 9.36

5 Click in a blank area of the document to close the gallery without making any selections, and then **Save** your document.

More Knowledge **Deleting a Custom Style Set**

To delete a custom style set, on the Design tab, in the Document Formatting group, click the More button. Under Custom, point to the custom style, right-click, click Delete, and then click Yes.

Objective 7 Convert a Table to Text

GO! Learn How Video W9-7

You can convert a Word table to text if you decide a table is not an appropriate format for the information. For example, a table with only one column might be easier to read if formatted as text.

Activity 9.20 | Converting a Table to Text

3.1.2

1 Click anywhere in the table. On the **Table Tools Layout tab**, in the **Data group**, click **Convert to Text**.

2 In the **Convert Table To Text** dialog box, under **Separate text with**, if necessary, click the **Paragraph marks** option button, and then compare your screen with Figure 9.37.

You can choose how the content of the table cells will be separated—by paragraph marks, tabs, commas, or any other single character.

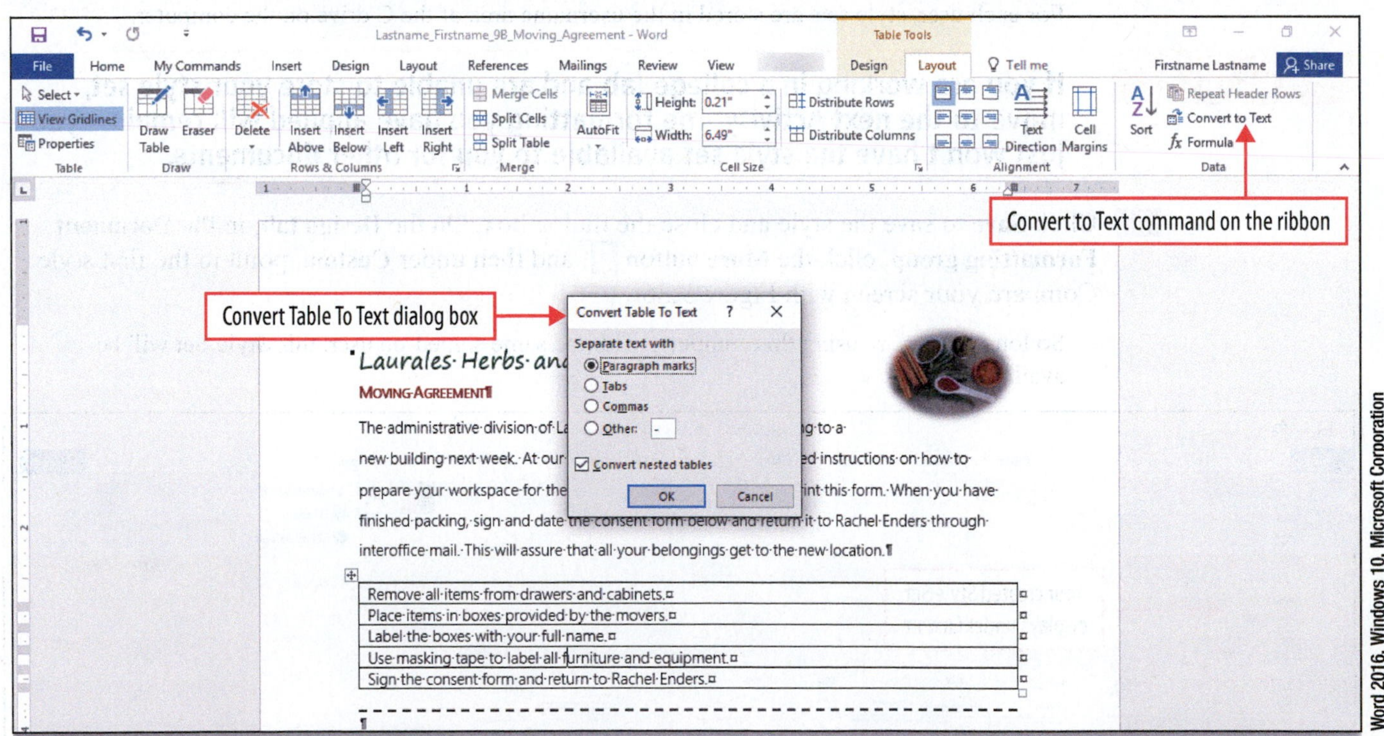

Word 2016, Windows 10, Microsoft Corporation

FIGURE 9.37

3 In the **Convert Table To Text** dialog box, click **OK**. Notice that the table is replaced with five paragraphs.

4 With all five paragraphs selected, on the **Home tab**, in the **Font group**, change the **Font Size** to **14**, apply **Bold**, and then change the **Font Color** to **Gold, Accent 4, Darker 50%**—in the eighth column, the last color.

5 On the **Home tab**, in the **Paragraph group**, click **Numbering**. Press Ctrl + Home, and then compare your screen with Figure 9.38.

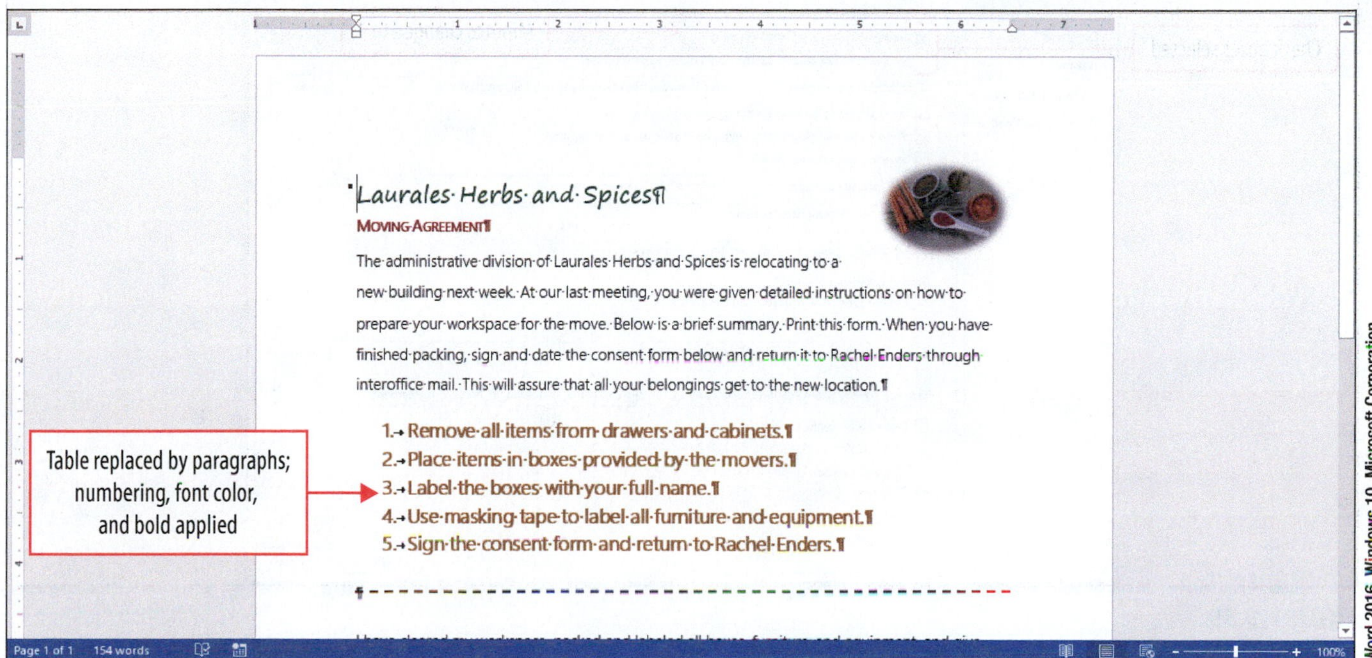

Laurales Herbs and Spices
MOVING AGREEMENT
The administrative division of Laurales Herbs and Spices is relocating to a new building next week. At our last meeting, you were given detailed instructions on how to prepare your workspace for the move. Below is a brief summary. Print this form. When you have finished packing, sign and date the consent form below and return it to Rachel Enders through interoffice mail. This will assure that all your belongings get to the new location.
1. Remove all items from drawers and cabinets.
2. Place items in boxes provided by the movers.
3. Label the boxes with your full name.
4. Use masking tape to label all furniture and equipment.
5. Sign the consent form and return to Rachel Enders.
Table replaced by paragraphs; numbering, font color, and bold applied
Page 1 of 1
154 words
100%
Word 2016, Windows 10, Microsoft Corporation

FIGURE 9.38

6 **Save** your document.

Objective 8 Prepare a Document for Review and Distribution

Activity 9.21 | Managing Document Versions and Inserting a Signature Line

GO! Learn How Video W9-8

1.1.3 Expert

AutoRecover, if turned on, automatically saves versions of your file while you are working on it, and also helps to recover unsaved documents. The AutoRecover option in Word helps you protect your files in case your computer hardware fails or if you accidentally close a file without saving.

A ***signature line*** is an element you can add to a document that specifies who should sign the document. In this Activity, you will add a signature line indicating that an employee signature is required to confirm that items are ready to be moved.

1 Click the **File tab**, on the left click **Options**, and then in the **Word Options** dialog box, on the left, click **Save**.

2 Be sure the **Save AutoRecover information every** box is selected—the default is 10 minutes. Also, be sure the **Keep the last autosaved version if I close without saving** box is selected.

With these two check boxes selected, you will never lose more than 10 minutes of work, and if you accidently close a file without saving your latest changes, you can recover the last autosaved version.

3 By clicking the down spin box arrow, change the number of minutes to **1**, and then compare your screen with Figure 9.39.

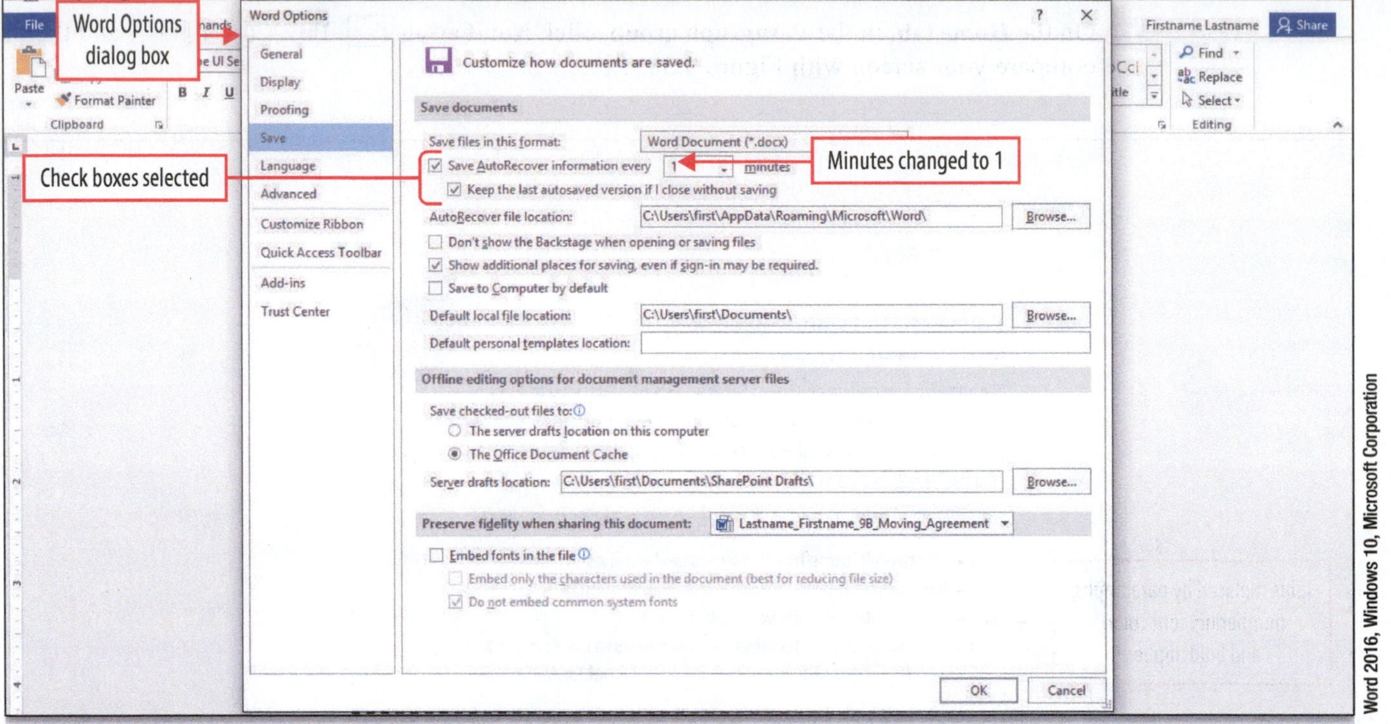

FIGURE 9.39

4 In the lower right corner, click **OK** to close the **Word Options** dialog box.

5 In your document, below the paragraph that begins *I have cleared*, click to position the insertion point in the empty paragraph.

6 Click the **Insert tab**. In the **Text group**, click the **Add a Signature Line button arrow**, and then click **Microsoft Office Signature Line**.

7 In the **Signature Setup** dialog box, in the **Suggested signer** box, type **Employee Name** In the **Suggested signer's title** box, type **Administration** and then compare your screen with Figure 9.40.

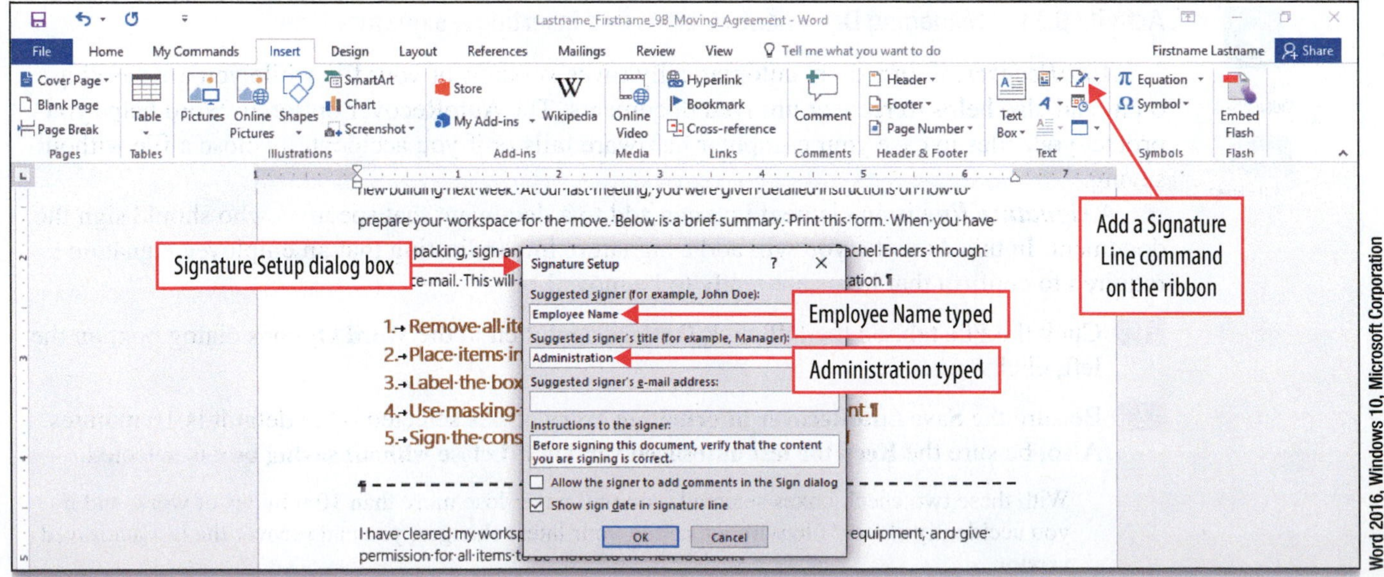

FIGURE 9.40

8 Click **OK** to insert the signature line in the document. Compare your screen with Figure 9.41.

The signer can sign a hard copy—a printed copy. Or, the signer can sign the document electronically by inserting an image of a signature or by using a ***stylus***—a pen-like device—with a ***tablet PC***—a computer with a monitor that enables you to write on the screen.

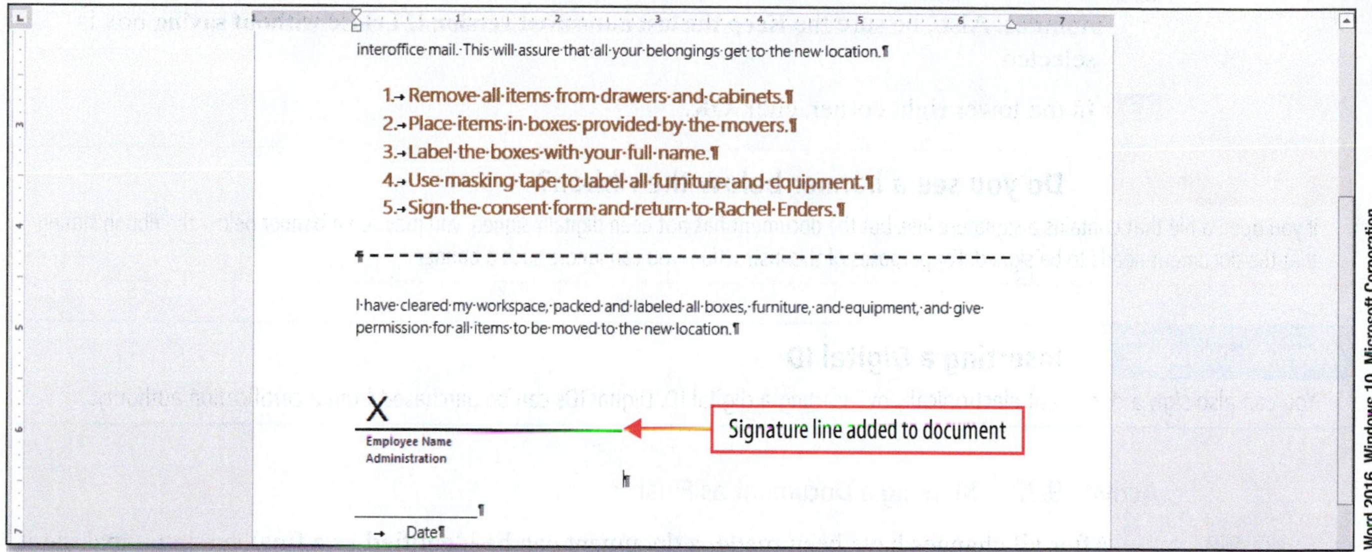

FIGURE 9.41

9 Click the **File tab**, on the left be sure that **Info** is selected, and then to the right, under **Info**, click **Manage Document**. Compare your screen with Figure 9.42.

Here you can recover unsaved documents, or open a version of the document that has been saved in the last minute. In the Figure, several minutes have elapsed so there are several versions—yours may differ.

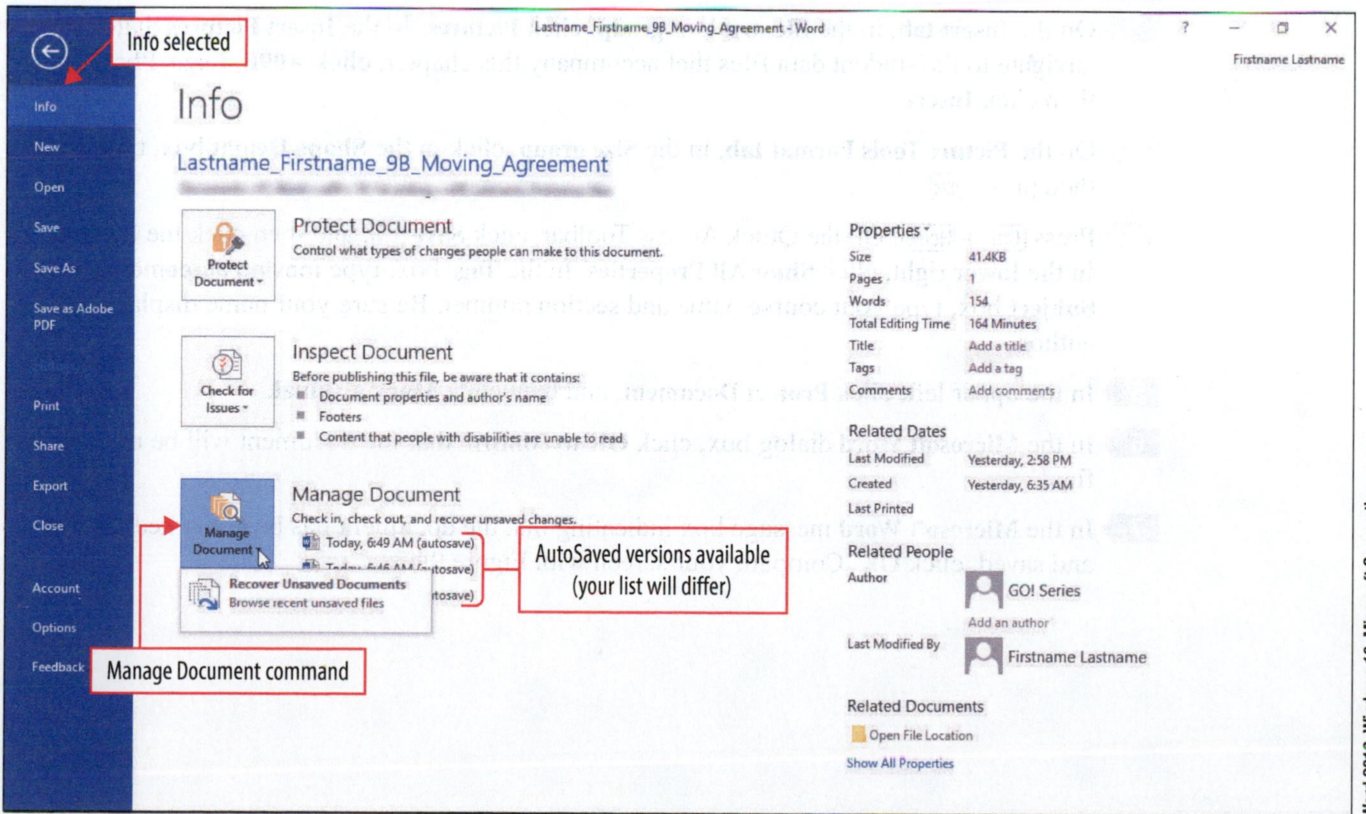

FIGURE 9.42

10 In the upper left, click **Back**, and then click **Save**.

11 Click the **File tab**, on the left click **Options**, and then in the **Word Options** dialog box, on the left, click **Save**.

12 In the Save AutoRecover information every box, set the minutes back to the default of **10** minutes. Also, be sure the **Keep the last autosaved version if I close without saving** box is selected.

13 In the lower right corner, click **OK**.

ALERT! **Do you see a banner below the ribbon?**

If you open a file that contains a signature line, but the document has not been digitally signed, you may see a banner below the ribbon stating that the document needs to be signed. For purposes of this instruction, you can ignore such a banner.

***More* Knowledge** **Inserting a Digital ID**

You can also sign a document electronically by inserting a digital ID. Digital IDs can be purchased from a certification authority.

Activity 9.22 | Marking a Document as Final

1.2.2 Expert

After all changes have been made, a document can be identified as a final version—making it a ***read-only file***. A read-only file can be viewed but not changed.

The Mark as Final command is not a security feature; anyone can remove the Mark as Final status from the document and edit it. However, marking a document as final lets people with whom you are sharing the document know that you consider this to be a complete version of the document. Marking a document as final also prevents others from making inadvertent changes if they are just reading the document on their screen.

1 Press Ctrl + End to move to the end of your document, and then press Enter three times.

2 On the **Insert tab**, in the **Illustrations group**, click **Pictures**. In the **Insert Pictures** dialog box, navigate to the student data files that accompany this chapter, click **w09B_Logo_Photo**, and then click **Insert**.

3 On the **Picture Tools Format tab**, in the **Size group**, click in the **Shape Height** box, type **1** and then press Enter.

4 Press Ctrl + Home. On the Quick Access Toolbar, click **Save**, and then click the **File tab**. In the lower right, click **Show All Properties**. In the **Tags** box, type **moving agreement** In the **Subject** box, type your course name and section number. Be sure your name displays as the author.

5 In the upper left, click **Protect Document**, and then click **Mark as Final**.

6 In the **Microsoft Word** dialog box, click **OK** to confirm that the document will be marked as final.

7 In the **Microsoft Word** message box indicating that the document has been marked as final and saved, click **OK**. Compare your screen with Figure 9.43.

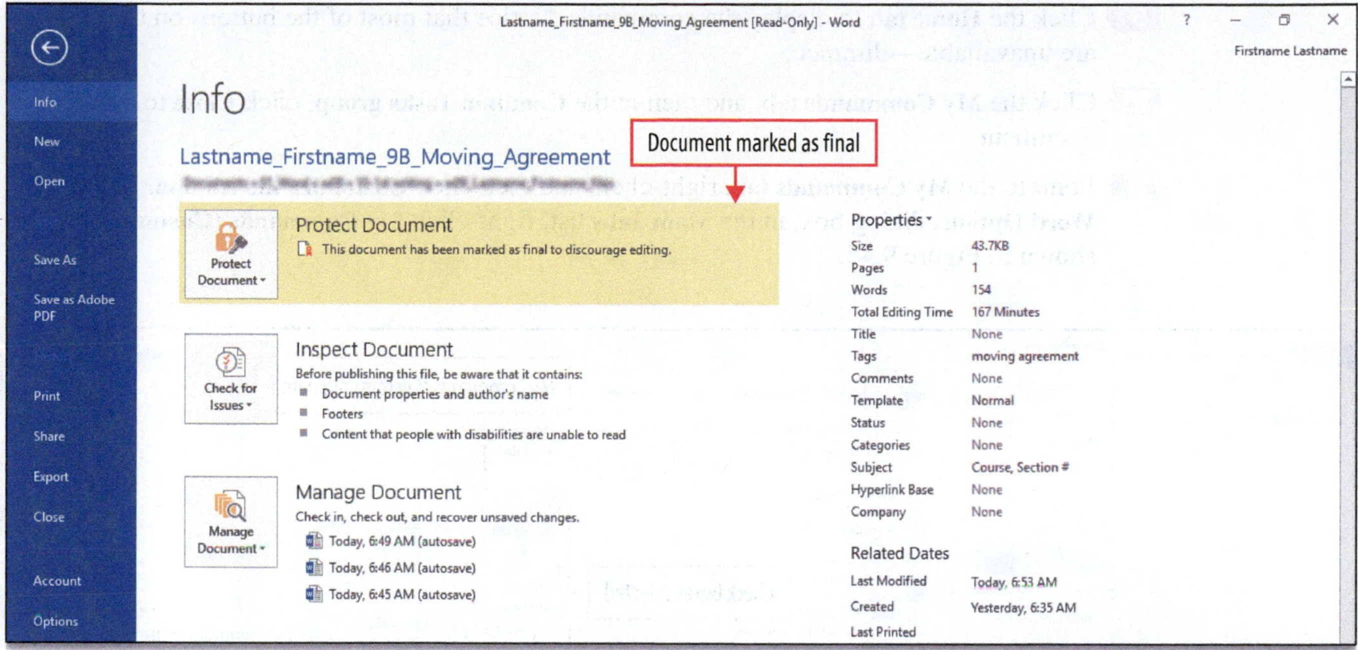

FIGURE 9.43

Word 2016, Windows 10, Microsoft Corporation

8 In the upper left corner, click **Back**, and then compare your screen with Figure 9.44.

The title bar indicates that this is a read-only file. A MARKED AS FINAL banner displays above the document, the commands on the ribbon are hidden, and a Marked as Final icon displays on the status bar. The viewer will be able to read the document but not make any changes.

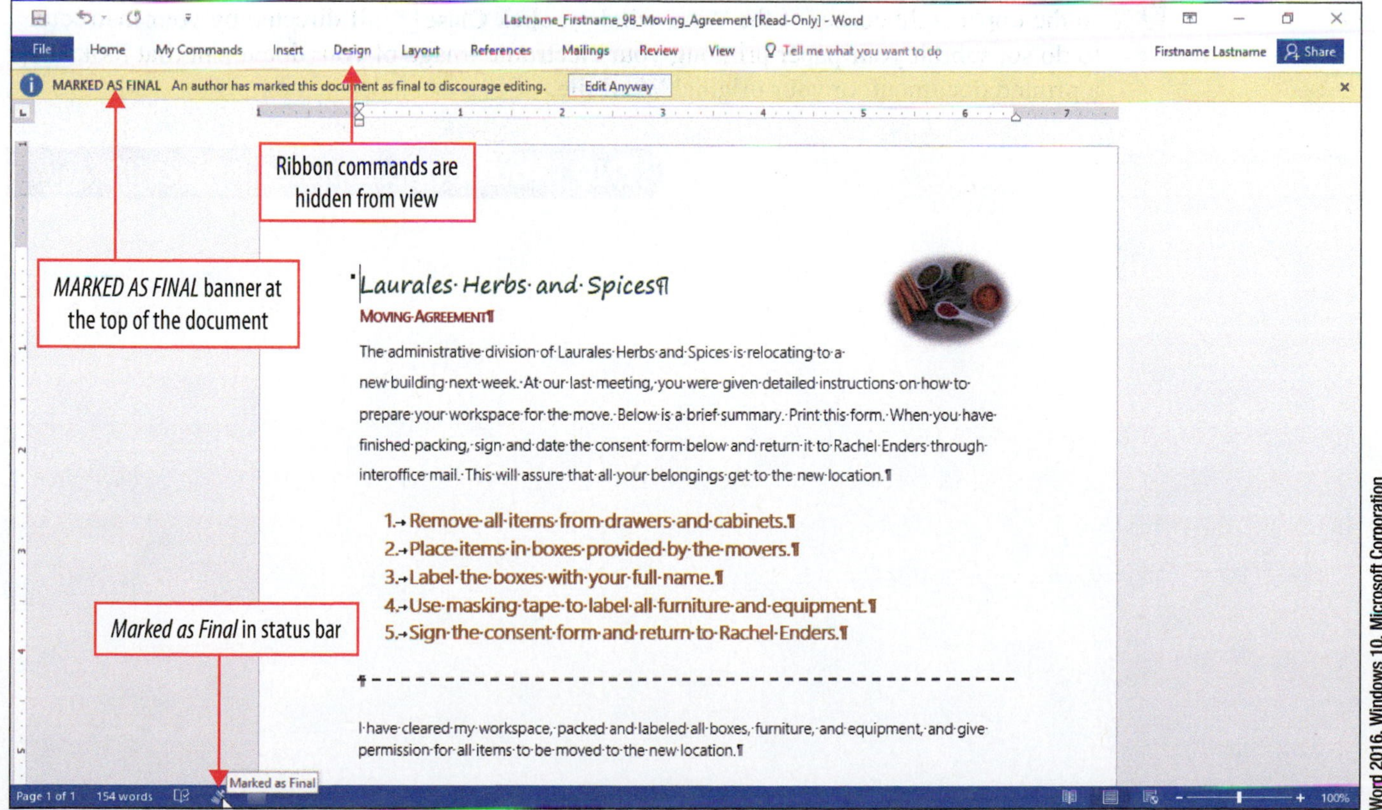

FIGURE 9.44

Word 2016, Windows 10, Microsoft Corporation

9 Click the **Home tab** to display the commands. Notice that most of the buttons on the ribbon are unavailable—dimmed.

10 Click the **My Commands tab**, and then in the **Common Tasks group**, click **Close** to close your document.

11 Point to the **My Commands tab**, right-click, and then click **Customize the Ribbon**. In the **Word Options** dialog box, in the **Main Tabs** list, right-click **My Commands (Custom)** as shown in Figure 9.45.

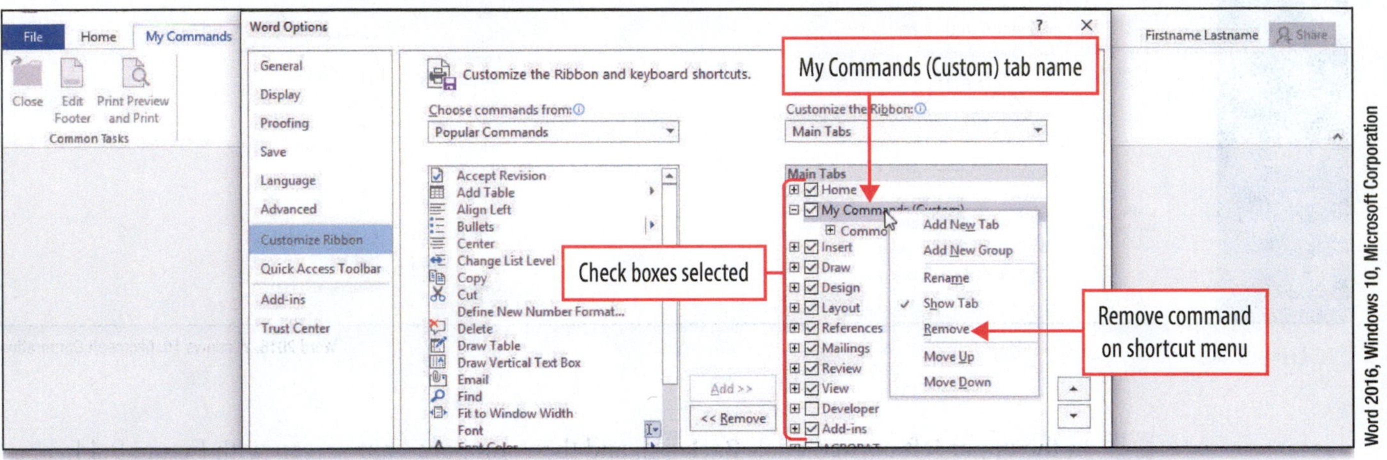

FIGURE 9.45

12 On the shortcut menu, click **Remove**. Click **OK** to close the dialog box, and notice that your custom tab no longer displays on the ribbon.

13 In the upper right corner of the Word window, click **Close** [X]. If directed by your instructor to do so, submit your paper printout, your electronic image of your document that looks like a printed document, or your original Word file.

END | You have completed Project 9B

ALERT! **Optional Activities**

The following two Activities are optional; they are not included in the 9B Grader project. Complete these Activities if they are assigned by your instructor.

Activity 9.23 | Maintaining Backward Compatibility

There may be times when you want a document to be available to persons using versions of Word older than Word 2007. In order to make a document backward compatible, you must save it as a Word 97–2003 document with the file extension .doc.

Some of the features that behave differently and document elements that are not available when editing .doc files—among others—include: text effects are removed, content controls are converted to static content, SmartArt graphics are converted to a single image, building blocks and AutoText entries might lose some information, bibliography and citations are converted to static text.

1. From your student data files, open the file **w09B_Paid_Time_Off_optional**. Click the **File tab**, click **Save As**, click **Browse**, and then navigate to your **Word Chapter 9** folder.
2. At the bottom of the **Save As** dialog box, click the **Save as type arrow**, and then compare your screen with Figure 9.46.

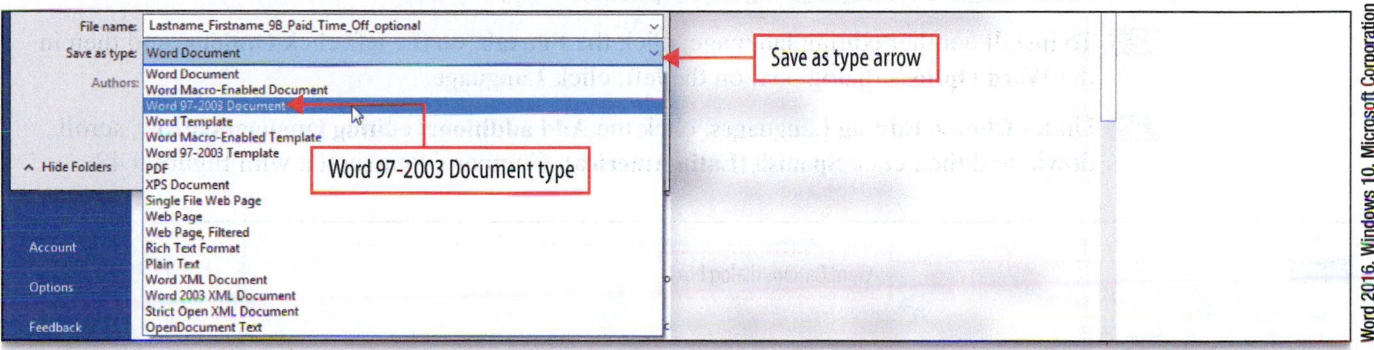

FIGURE 9.46

3. On the list, click **Word 97–2003 Document**. Using your own name, in the **File name** box, type **Lastname_Firstname_9B_Paid_Time_Off_optional** and then click **Save**. Compare your screen with Figure 9.47. Note: If the dialog box does not display, study the figure, and then proceed to the next step.

   The Microsoft Word Compatibility Checker dialog box indicates that some features in the current document are not supported in an older version of Word. The Summary box indicates the elements of the document that may be modified.

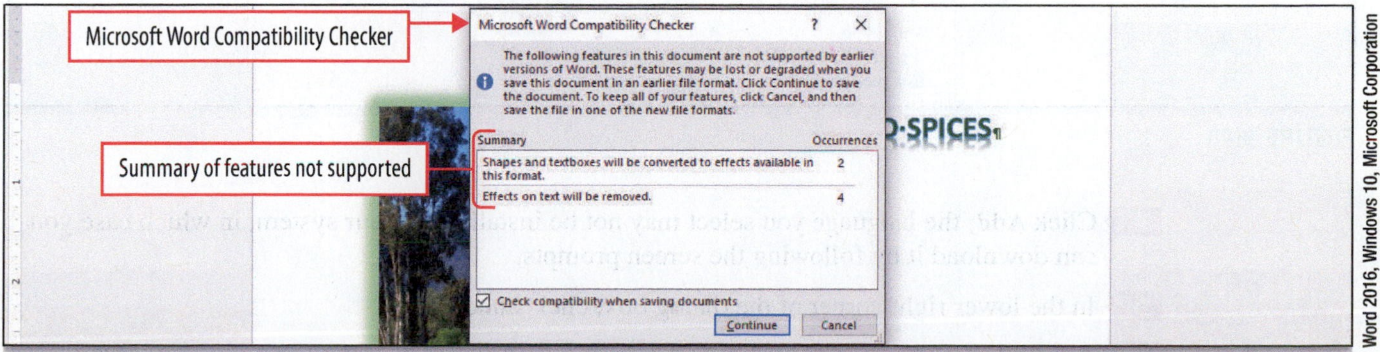

FIGURE 9.47

4 In the **Microsoft Word Compatibility Checker** dialog box, click **Continue**. Notice the Word Art mirroring effect applied to *Laurales Herbs and Spices* no longer displays and that *[Compatibility Mode]* displays in the title bar.

5 In the upper right corner of the Word window, click **Close** [X]. If directed by your instructor to do so, submit your paper printout, your electronic image of your document that looks like a printed document, or your original Word file.

Activity 9.24 | Configure Language Options in Documents

4.3.1 Expert

By default, your installation of Office uses a single language, and the Proofing tools on the Review tab use the default language when you use commands such as Spelling & Grammar.

If your document contains text in multiple languages, you can add other editing languages for use when checking spelling. From the Word Options dialog box, you can change these settings for any document you create in Word.

Additionally, with a Word document displayed, you can display the Language dialog box and specify language for selected text.

1 From your student data files, open the file **w09B_Language_optional**. Click the **File tab**, click **Save As**, click **Browse**, and then navigate to your **Word Chapter 9** folder. In the **Save as type** box, if necessary, change to **Word Document**. Using your own name, save the file as **Lastname_Firstname_9B_Language_optional**

2 To install another editing language, click the **File tab**, on the left click **Options**, and then in the **Word Options** dialog box, on the left, click **Language**.

3 Under **Choose Editing Languages**, click the **Add additional editing languages** arrow, scroll down, and then click **Spanish (Latin America)**. Compare your screen with Figure 9.48.

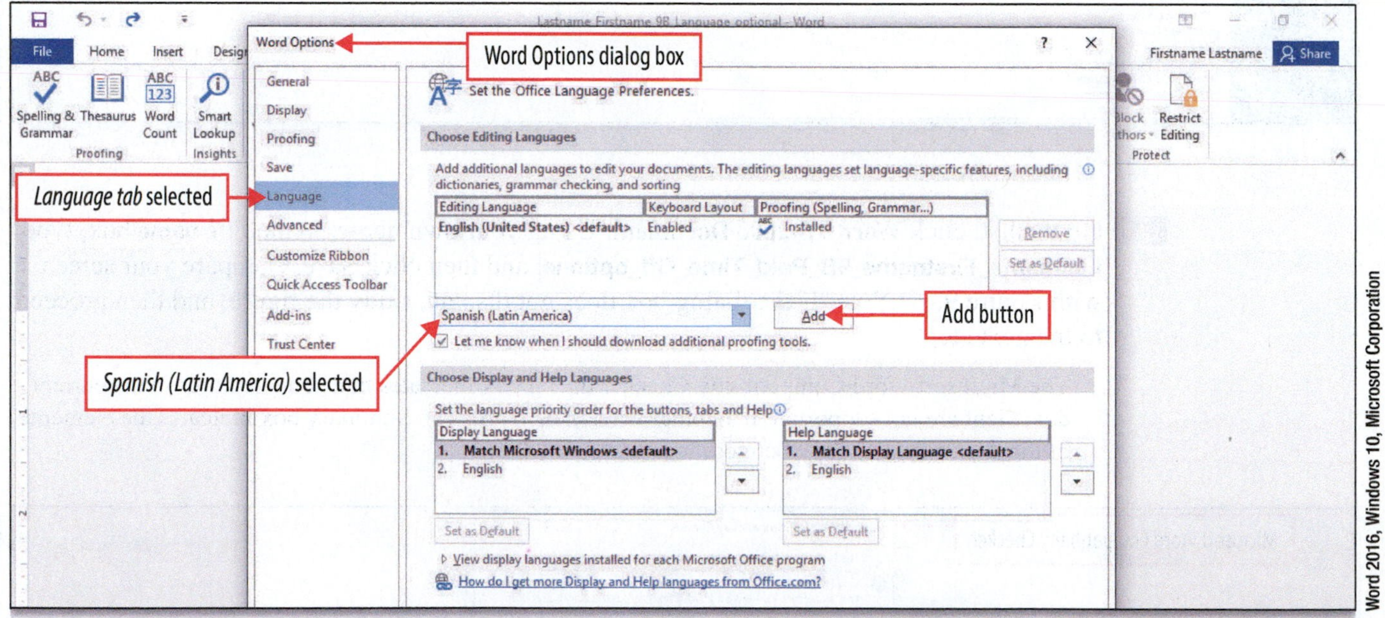

FIGURE 9.48

4 Click **Add**; the language you select may not be installed on your system, in which case you can download it by following the screen prompts.

5 In the lower right corner of the dialog box, click **Cancel**.

6 To check spelling in a document in a different language, select the last paragraph of the document, which is a translation of the paragraph above in Spanish.

7 With the paragraph selected, click the **Review tab**, in the **Language group**, click **Language**, and then click **Set Proofing Language**. Scroll down as necessary, and then click **Spanish (Latin America)**. Click **OK**.

8 On the **Review tab**, in the **Proofing group**, click **Spelling & Grammar**, and then compare your screen with Figure 9.49.

The word *progroma* should be spelled *programa*.

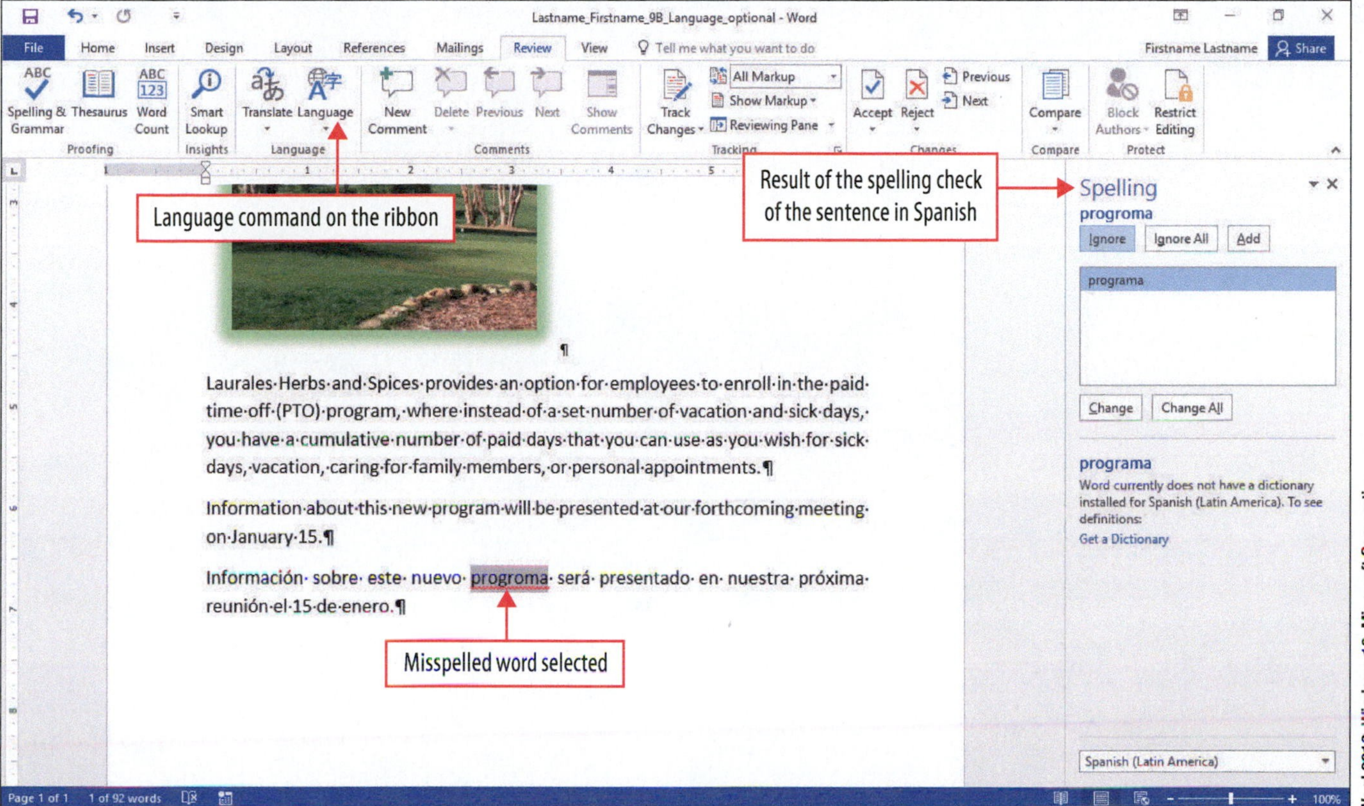

Word 2016, Windows 10, Microsoft Corporation

FIGURE 9.49

9 In the **Spelling pane**, click **Change**. In the message box, click **No**.

10 **Save** your document. In the upper right corner of the Word window, click **Close**. If directed by your instructor to do so, submit your paper printout, your electronic image of your document that looks like a printed document, or your original Word file.

END | You have completed the Optional Activities for Project 9B

GO! To Work

Andrew Rodriguez / Fotolia; FotolEdhar/ Fotolia; apops/ Fotolia; Yuri Arcurs/ Fotolia

9 WORD

MICROSOFT OFFICE SPECIALIST (MOS) SKILLS IN THIS CHAPTER	
PROJECT 9A	**PROJECT 9B**
1.1.7 Expert: Display hidden ribbon tabs	**1.1.3** Expert: Manage document versions
1.2.1 Expert: Restrict editing	**1.2.2** Expert: Mark a document as final
1.2.3 Expert: Protect a document with a password	**4.2.1** Expert: Create custom color sets
3.3.2 Modify field properties	**4.2.2** Expert: Create custom font sets
4.1.4 Insert and configure content controls	**4.2.4** Expert: Create custom style sets
3.1.1 Convert text to tables	**4.3.1** Expert: Configure language options in documents

BUILD YOUR E-PORTFOLIO

An E-Portfolio is a collection of evidence, stored electronically, that showcases what you have accomplished while completing your education. Collecting and then sharing your work products with potential employers reflects your academic and career goals. Your completed documents from the following projects are good examples to show what you have learned: 9G, 9K, and 9L.

GO! FOR JOB SUCCESS

Your instructor may assign this discussion to your class and then ask you to think about, or discuss with your classmates, these questions.

Personal technology has evolved beyond smartphones and now includes wearable devices like watches and fitness bands that enable you to check emails and calendars on your wrist and to track health data such as heart rate. Wearables also provide opportunities for businesses to provide better service and safer workplaces. In a manufacturing environment, smart goggles, badges, and sensors in clothing can detect unsafe conditions or provide real-time information to improve productivity. At a retail store, associates with wearables can access up-to-date inventory data and customer information to provide better service and streamline operations.

Wearable technology also gives employers greater ability to track and monitor employees. In an open office environment, requiring employees to scan a badge every time they enter a cube or conference room is efficient if employees need to be contacted or there is an emergency. Movement and location information of field employees like sales staff or delivery drivers is vital business data. On the other hand, wearables allow employers to also monitor personal data like heart rate, physical activity, and sleep patterns.

FotolEdhar / Fotolia

How could employees with hands-free, wearable devices improve efficiency in a restaurant or enhance care in a hospital?

What are some disadvantages for employees of wearable tracking technology?

Could there be advantages to employees if their stress and fatigue levels were monitored?

END OF CHAPTER

SUMMARY

Adding content controls and protecting the document make it easy for the user to complete a form. By saving the document as a template, the form can be used repeatedly without changing the original file.

Add titles in content controls to clarify the purpose for the user. Add items to Drop-Down Lists and Combo Boxes to provide choices for the user to select. Format static text to improve the form's appearance.

Personalize the ribbon to improve efficiency. In the Word Options dialog box, display the Developer tab, add frequently used commands to existing tabs and groups, or create your own custom tabs and groups.

Add consistency to your documents by creating custom font, color, and style sets. Convert a table to text if it makes the information more readable. Word helps you to recover previous versions of your documents.

GO! LEARN IT ONLINE

Review the concepts, key terms, and MOS skills in this chapter by completing these online challenges, which you can find at **MyITLab**.

Matching and Multiple Choice: Answer matching and multiple choice questions to test what you learned in this chapter.

Lessons on the GO!: Learn how to use all the new apps and features as they are introduced by Microsoft.

MOS Prep Quiz: Answer questions to review the MOS skills that you practiced in this chapter.

9 WORD

PROJECT GUIDE FOR WORD CHAPTER 9

Your instructor will assign Projects from this list to ensure your learning and assess your knowledge.

Project Guide for Word Chapter 9			
Project	**Apply Skills from These Chapter Objectives**	**Project Type**	**Project Location**
9A **MyITLab**	Objectives 1–4 from Project 9A	**9A Instructional Project (Grader Project)** Guided instruction to learn the skills in Project 9A.	In MyITLab and in text
9B **MyITLab**	Objectives 5–8 from Project 9B	**9B Instructional Project (Grader Project)** Guided instruction to learn the skills in Project 9B.	In MyITLab and in text
9C	Objectives 1–4 from Project 9A	**9C Skills Review (Scorecard Grading)** A guided review of the skills from Project 9A.	In text
9D	Objectives 5–8 from Project 9B	**9D Skills Review (Scorecard Grading)** A guided review of the skills from Project 9B.	In text
9E **MyITLab**	Objectives 1–4 from Project 9A	**9E Mastery (Grader Project)** **Mastery and Transfer of Learning** A demonstration of your mastery of the skills in Project 9A with extensive decision making.	In MyITLab and in text
9F **MyITLab**	Objectives 5–8 from Project 9B	**9F Mastery (Grader Project)** **Mastery and Transfer of Learning** A demonstration of your mastery of the skills in Project 9B with extensive decision making.	In MyITLab and in text
9G **MyITLab**	Objectives 1–8 from Projects 9A and 9B	**9G Mastery (Grader Project)** **Mastery and Transfer of Learning** A demonstration of your mastery of the skills in Projects 9A and 9B with extensive decision making.	In MyITLab and in text
9H	Combination of Objectives from Projects 9A and 9B	**9H GO! Fix It (Scorecard Grading)** **Critical Thinking** A demonstration of your mastery of the skills in Projects 9A and 9B by creating a correct result from a document that contains errors you must find.	Instructor Resource Center (IRC) and MyITLab
9I	Combination of Objectives from Projects 9A and 9B	**9I GO! Make It (Scorecard Grading)** **Critical Thinking** A demonstration of your mastery of the skills in Projects 9A and 9B by creating a result from a supplied picture.	IRC and MyITLab
9J	Combination of Objectives from Projects 9A and 9B	**9J GO! Solve It (Rubric Grading)** **Critical Thinking** A demonstration of your mastery of the skills in Projects 9A and 9B, your decision-making skills, and your critical thinking skills. A task-specific rubric helps you self-assess your result.	IRC and MyITLab
9K	Combination of Objectives from Projects 9A and 9B	**9K GO! Solve It (Rubric Grading)** **Critical Thinking** A demonstration of your mastery of the skills in Projects 9A and 9B, your decision-making skills, and your critical thinking skills. A task-specific rubric helps you self-assess your result.	In text
9L	Combination of Objectives from Projects 9A and 9B	**9L GO! Think (Rubric Grading)** **Critical Thinking** A demonstration of your understanding of the Chapter concepts applied in a manner that you would outside of college. An analytic rubric helps you and your instructor grade the quality of your work by comparing it to the work an expert in the discipline would create.	In text
9M	Combination of Objectives from Projects 9A and 9B	**9M GO! Think (Rubric Grading)** **Critical Thinking** A demonstration of your understanding of the Chapter concepts applied in a manner that you would outside of college. An analytic rubric helps you and your instructor grade the quality of your work by comparing it to the work an expert in the discipline would create.	In MyITLab and in text
9N	Combination of Objectives from Projects 9A and 9B	**9N You and GO! (Rubric Grading)** **Critical Thinking** A demonstration of your understanding of the Chapter concepts applied in a manner that you would in a personal situation. An analytic rubric helps you and your instructor grade the quality of your work.	IRC and MyITLab

GLOSSARY

GLOSSARY OF CHAPTER KEY TERMS

AutoRecover option A Word option that automatically saves versions of your file while you are working on it, and also helps to recover unsaved documents.

Check Box content control A content control that allows the user to select, or not select, a specific option.

Check Box form field A legacy control that allows the user to select, or not select, a specific option.

Combo Box content control A content control that allows the user to select an item from a list or enter new text.

Content control A data entry field where the particular type of information is supplied by the user.

Date Picker content control A content control that allows the user to select a date from a calendar.

Design Mode A command that enables the user to edit content controls that are inserted in a document.

Digital certificate (Digital ID) A file that contains information about a person and is used to electronically sign a document.

Digital signature An electronic stamp that is added to a document to verify the document's authenticity.

Drop-Down List content control A content control that allows the user to select a specific item from a list.

Form A structured document that has static text and reserved spaced for information to be entered by the user.

Legacy control A field used in designing a form for persons who possess older versions of Word.

Password A code that is used to gain access to a file.

Plain Text content control A content control that enables the user to enter unformatted text.

Read-only file A file that can be viewed but not changed.

Rich Text content control A content control that enables the user to enter text and apply formatting.

Signature line An element added to a document that specifies who should sign the document.

Static text Descriptive text such as labels or headings.

Style set A group of settings for the Font and Paragraph properties of your document.

Stylus A pen-like device used for writing on an electronic document.

Tablet PC A computer with a monitor that allows you to write on the screen.

Template A predefined structure that contains basic document settings, such as fonts, margins, and available style, and can also store elements such as building blocks and content controls.

Unformatted text Plain text without any special formatting applied.

Apply 9A skills from these Objectives:

1. Create a Customized Form
2. Convert Text to a Table and Insert Content Controls in a Table
3. Modify and Protect a Form
4. Complete a Form

Skills Review Project 9C Meeting Reservation Form

In the following Skills Review, you will add content controls to create a form for reserving space for meetings at Laurales Herbs and Spices headquarters office and then fill in the form. Your completed document will look similar to Figure 9.50.

PROJECT FILES

For Project 9C, you will need the following file:

w09C_Reservation_Form

You will save your documents as:

Lastname_Firstname_9C_Reservation_Form_Completed
Lastname_Firstname_9C_Reservation_Form (you will not submit this file)

PROJECT RESULTS

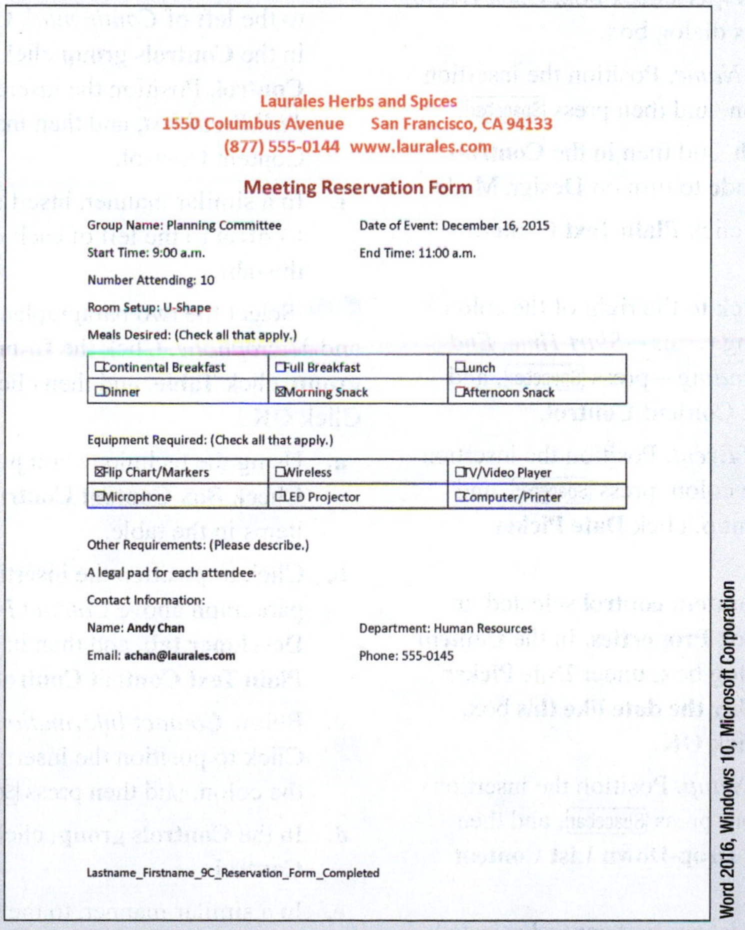

Laurales Herbs and Spices
1550 Columbus Avenue San Francisco, CA 94133
(877) 555-0144 www.laurales.com

Meeting Reservation Form

Group Name: Planning Committee Date of Event: December 16, 2015

Start Time: 9:00 a.m. End Time: 11:00 a.m.

Number Attending: 10

Room Setup: U-Shape

Meals Desired: (Check all that apply.)

☐Continental Breakfast	☐Full Breakfast	☐Lunch
☐Dinner	☒Morning Snack	☐Afternoon Snack

Equipment Required: (Check all that apply.)

☒Flip Chart/Markers	☐Wireless	☐TV/Video Player
☐Microphone	☐LED Projector	☐Computer/Printer

Other Requirements: (Please describe.)

A legal pad for each attendee.

Contact Information:

Name: **Andy Chan** Department: Human Resources

Email: **achan@laurales.com** Phone: 555-0145

Lastname_Firstname_9C_Reservation_Form_Completed

Word 2016, Windows 10, Microsoft Corporation

FIGURE 9.50

(Project 9C Meeting Reservation Form continues on the next page)

Skills Review Project 9C Meeting Reservation Form (continued)

1 Start Word, on the left click **Open Other Documents**, click **Browse**, and then in the **Open** dialog box, navigate to the student data files that accompany this chapter. Open the file **w09C_Reservation_Form**. Click the **File tab**, on the left click **Save As**, click **Browse**, and then in the **Save As** dialog box, navigate to your **Word Chapter 9** folder. Using your own name, save the file as **Lastname_Firstname_9C_Reservation_Form** and if necessary, display the rulers and formatting marks.

- **a.** Click the **File tab**, and then click **Options**. On the left side of the **Word Options** dialog box, click **Customize Ribbon**.
- **b.** In the **Main Tabs** list, locate and then, if necessary, click to select the **Developer** check box. Click **OK** to close the **Word Options** dialog box.

2 Locate the text *Group Name*. Position the insertion point to the right of the colon, and then press Spacebar.

- **a.** Click the **Developer tab**, and then in the **Controls group**, click **Design Mode** to turn on Design Mode.
- **b.** In the **Controls group**, click **Plain Text Content Control.**
- **c.** In a similar manner, click to the right of the colon for each of the following terms—*Start Time*, *End Time*, and *Number Attending*—press Spacebar, and then insert a **Plain Text Content Control**.
- **d.** Locate the text *Date of Event*. Position the insertion point to the right of the colon, press Spacebar, and then in the **Controls group**, click **Date Picker Content Control**.
- **e.** With the **Date Picker content control** selected, in the **Controls group**, click **Properties**. In the **Content Control Properties** dialog box, under **Date Picker Properties**, in the **Display the date like this** box, click the third style. Click **OK**.

3 Locate the text *Room Setup*. Position the insertion point to the right of the colon, press Spacebar, and then in the **Controls group**, click **Drop-Down List Content Control**.

- **a.** With the **Drop-Down List content control** selected, in the **Controls group**, click **Properties**. In the **Content Control Properties** dialog box, under **Drop-Down List Properties**, click **Add**. In the **Add Choice** dialog box, in the **Display Name** box, type **Banquet** Click **OK**.
- **b.** Using the same technique, add the following choices to the **Drop-Down List content control**:

  Classroom

  Hollow Square

  U-Shape
- **c.** Click **OK** to close the dialog box. Select the two paragraphs that begin *Continental* and *Dinner*. Click the **Insert tab**. In the **Tables group**, click **Table**, and then click **Convert Text to Table**. In the **Convert Text to Table** dialog box, click **OK**.
- **d.** In the table, click to position the insertion point to the left of *Continental*. On the **Developer tab**, in the **Controls group** click **Check Box Content Control**. Position the insertion point to the left of *Full Breakfast*, and then insert another Check Box Content Control.
- **e.** In a similar manner, insert a **Check Box Content Control** to the left of each of the remaining items in the table.

4 Select the two paragraphs that begin *Flip Chart* and *Microphone*. Click the **Insert tab**. In the **Tables group**, click **Table**, and then click **Convert Text to Table**. Click **OK**.

- **a.** Using the technique you just practiced, insert a **Check Box Content Control** to the left of all the items in the table.
- **b.** Click to position the insertion point in the blank paragraph above *Contact Information*. Click the **Developer tab**, and then in the **Controls group**, click **Plain Text Content Control**.
- **c.** Below *Contact Information*, locate the text *Name*. Click to position the insertion point to the right of the colon, and then press Spacebar.
- **d.** In the **Controls group**, click **Plain Text Content Control**.
- **e.** In a similar manner, to the right of the colon for each of the following items—*Department*, *Email*, and *Phone*—press Spacebar, and then insert a **Plain Text Content Control**.

(Project 9C Meeting Reservation Form continues on the next page)

Skills Review Project 9C Meeting Reservation Form (continued)

5 To the right of the paragraph that begins *Name*, in the **Plain Text content control**, select the text, and then type **Enter your first and last name.**

a. To the right of the paragraph that begins *Email*, in the **Plain Text content control**, select the text, and then type **Enter your work email address.**

b. To the right of *Name*, click in the **Plain Text content control**. On the **Developer tab**, in the **Controls group**, click **Properties**. In the **Content Control Properties** dialog box, in the **Title** box, type **Name** Select the **Use a style to format text typed into the empty control** check box. Click the **Style arrow**, click **Strong**, and then click **OK**.

c. To the right of *Email*, click in the **Plain Text content control**. On the **Developer tab**, in the **Controls group**, click **Properties**. In the **Content Control Properties** dialog box, in the **Title** box, type **Email Address** Select the **Use a style to format text typed into the empty control** check box. Click the **Style arrow**, click **Strong**, and then click **OK**.

6 Press Ctrl + Home. On the **Developer tab**, in the **Controls group**, click **Design Mode** to turn off Design Mode.

a. On the **Developer tab**, in the **Protect group**, click **Restrict Editing**.

b. In the **Restrict Editing** pane, under **2. Editing restrictions**, select the **Allow only this type of editing in the document** check box. Click the **Allow only this type of editing in the document arrow**, and then click **Filling in forms**.

c. In the **Restrict Editing** pane, under **3. Start enforcement**, click **Yes, Start Enforcing Protection**.

d. In the **Start Enforcing Protection** dialog box, click **OK** without entering a password. **Close** the **Restrict Editing** pane, and then **Save** your document.

7 Click the **File tab**, click **Save As**, click **Browse**, and then in the **Save As** dialog box, navigate to your **Word Chapter 9** folder. In the File name box, using your own name, type **Lastname_Firstname_9C_Reservation_Form_Completed** and then click **Save**.

a. In the content control following *Group Name*, type **Planning Committee** Press Tab, click the **Date Picker content control arrow**, and then click **Today**. Continue filling in the form using the information shown below.

Start Time	**9:00 a.m.**
End Time	**11:00 a.m.**
Number Attending	**10**
Room Setup	U-Shape
Meals Desired	Morning Snack
Equipment Required	Flip Chart/Markers
Other Requirements	**A legal pad for each attendee.**
Name	**Andy Chan**
Department	**Human Resources**
Email	**achan@laurales.com**
Phone	**555-0145**

b. Click the **Developer tab**, and then in the **Protect group**, click **Restrict Editing**. At the bottom of the **Restrict Editing** pane, click **Stop Protection**. **Close** the **Restrict Editing** pane. Press Ctrl + Home, and then insert the file name in the footer.

c. Click the **File tab**, and then click **Show All Properties**. In the **Tags** box, type **meeting reservation, completed** In the **Subject** box, type your course name and section number. If necessary, edit the author name to display your name. On the left, click **Save**.

d. Click the **File tab**, on the left click **Options**. In the **Word Options** dialog box, on the left click **Customize Ribbon**. In the **Main Tabs** list, locate and then click to clear the **Developer** check box. Click **OK**, and notice that the Developer tab no longer displays on the ribbon.

e. **Save** your document. In the upper right corner of the Word window, click **Close** ✕. If directed by your instructor to do so, submit your paper printout, your electronic image of your document that looks like a printed document, or your original Word file.

END | You have completed Project 9C

Apply 9B skills from these Objectives:

5 Create a Custom Ribbon Tab
6 Create Style, Color, and Font Sets
7 Convert a Table to Text
8 Prepare a Document for Review and Distribution

Skills Review Project 9D Privacy Policy

In the following Skills Review, you will finalize a document that explains the privacy policy of Laurales Herbs and Spices. Your completed document will look similar to Figure 9.51.

PROJECT FILES

For Project 9D, you will need the following files:

w09D_Privacy_Policy
w09D_Logo_Photo

You will save your document as:

Lastname_Firstname_9D_Privacy_Policy

PROJECT RESULTS

Laurales Herbs and Spices
Privacy Policy

Laurales Herbs and Spices believes in protecting the privacy of our online visitors. This policy applies only to our website and to emails you may send us; it does not apply to telephone calls you make to us or postal mail you may send.

Information We Collect

- In certain locations on our website we may request that you provide personal information—for example, when filling in order forms or registering for our monthly newsletter.
- We may request your name, email address, mailing address, and telephone number.
- Only information we believe we need to fulfill our obligation to you will be marked *required*.
- You may choose not to provide particular information; however, this may result in not being able to utilize all of our website's services.
- Sign the consent form and return to Rachel Enders.

We may also collect certain non-personal information which cannot be used to identify or contact you. This technical information may include your IP address, the type of browser your system uses, and the websites you visit before and after Laurales Herbs and Spices site.

How Collected Information Is Used

The personal information we gather will usually be in response to a service you are requesting. We will use that information to fulfill your online orders, enter you in a contest, provide information you requested, and compile data you have provided in surveys and polls. We combine the non-personal information we gather to better understand the demographics of our users and determine how our site is being used. This data allows us to refine our website content and improve our product offerings.

If you send us email or fill out an online form, we may use your personal information to contact you with a response to a question or concern. We may also keep information for future data compilation. We do not share your personal information with any non-affiliated third party without your consent. We may, however, disclose the statistical data gathered through non-personal information with our third-party affiliates.

Any questions regarding our Privacy Policy should be directed to privacy@laurales.com.

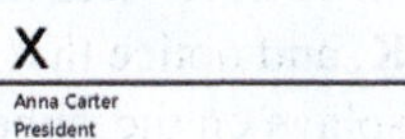

Anna Carter
President

Lastname_Firstname_9D_Privacy_Policy

FIGURE 9.51

(Project 9D Privacy Policy continues on the next page)

Skills Review Project 9D Privacy Policy (continued)

1 Start Word, on the left click **Open Other Documents**, click **Browse**, and then in the **Open** dialog box, navigate to the student data files that accompany this chapter. Open the file **w09D_Privacy_Policy**.

a. Click the **File tab**, on the left click **Save As**, click **Browse**, and then in the **Save As** dialog box, navigate to your **Word Chapter 9** folder. Using your own name, save the file as **Lastname_Firstname_9D_Privacy_Policy**

2 Click the **File tab**, and then on the left click **Options**. In the **Word Options** dialog box, on the left, click **Customize Ribbon**.

a. Below the **Main Tabs** list, with **Home** selected, click **New Tab**. In the list, click **New Tab (Custom)**, and then at the bottom of the list, click **Rename**. In the **Rename** dialog box, in the **Display name** box, type **9D Commands** and then click **OK**.

b. In the list, click **New Group (Custom)**, and then click **Rename**. In the **Rename** dialog box, in the **Display name** box, type **Frequent Tasks** and then click **OK**.

c. With **Frequent Tasks (Custom)** selected, in the upper left portion of the dialog box, click the **Choose commands from arrow**, and then click **All Commands**. Under **All Commands**, scroll as necessary, click **Edit Footer**, and then between the two lists, click **Add**. From the list of **All Commands**, locate and click **Insert Picture**, and then click **Add**. Click **OK** to close the **Word Options** dialog box.

3 On the ribbon, click the **9D Commands tab** that you just created. In the **Frequent Tasks group**, click **Edit Footer**, and then insert the file name in the footer. **Close** the footer area.

a. Select the paragraph **Laurales Herbs and Spices**, and then from the mini toolbar, change the **Font Color** to **Blue, Accent 1**—in the fifth column, the first color.

b. Select the paragraph **Privacy Policy**, and then from the mini toolbar, change the **Font Color** to **Green, Accent 6, Darker 50%**—in the last column, the last color.

c. Press Ctrl + Home. Click the **9D Commands tab**, and then in the **Frequent Tasks group**, click **Pictures**. In the **Insert Picture** dialog box, navigate to the student data files that accompany this chapter, select the picture **w09D_Logo_Photo**, and then click **Insert**.

d. With the picture selected, on the **Picture Tools Format tab**, in the **Size group**, click in the **Shape Height** box, type **1.75** and press Enter.

e. In the **Arrange group**, click **Position**, and then under **With Text Wrapping**, in the first row, click the third wrapping style—**Position in Top Right with Square Text Wrapping**. Click anywhere to deselect the picture.

4 On the **Design tab**, in the **Document Formatting group**, click **Fonts**, and then at the bottom, click **Customize Fonts**.

a. In the **Create New Theme Fonts** dialog box, click the **Heading font arrow**, scroll down the list, and then click **Verdana**.

b. Click the **Body font arrow**, scroll down, and then click **Cambria**. In the **Name** box, name the Font set **Laurales 9D** and click **Save**.

c. Select the paragraph **Laurales Herbs and Spices**, and then on the **Home tab**, in the **Styles group**, click the **Heading 1** style.

5 On the **Design tab**, in the **Document Formatting group**, click **Colors**, and then at the bottom, click **Customize Colors**.

a. In the **Create New Theme Colors** dialog box, click the **Accent 1 arrow**. Click **More Colors**, click the **Standard tab**, and then in the seventh (widest) row, click the next to last color.

b. Click **OK**, and then click then click the **Accent 6 arrow**. Click **More Colors**, click the **Standard tab**, and then in the first row, click the next to last color.

c. Click **OK**, in the **Name** box type **Laurales 9D** and then click **Save**.

6 Click anywhere in the table. On the **Table Tools Layout tab**, in the **Data group**, click **Convert to Text**.

a. In the **Convert to Table To Text** dialog box, click **OK**.

b. With the five paragraphs selected on the **Home tab**, in the **Font group**, change the **Font Color** to **Purple, Accent 1, Darker 50%**—in the fifth column, the last color.

c. In the **Paragraph group**, click **Bullets**.

(Project 9D Privacy Policy continues on the next page)

Skills Review Project 9D Privacy Policy (continued)

7 Press Ctrl + End. On the **Insert tab**, in the **Text group**, click the **Signature Line button arrow**, and then click **Microsoft Office Signature Line**.

a. In the **Signature Setup** dialog box, in the **Suggested signer** box, type **Anna Carter** In the **Suggested signer's title** box, type **President** and then click **OK**.

b. **Save** your document.

8 From **Backstage** view, click **Show All Properties**. In the **Tags** box, type **privacy policy** In the **Subject** box, type your course name and section number. Be sure your name displays as the author.

a. On the left, click **Protect Document**, and then click **Mark as Final**.

b. In the **Microsoft Word** message box, click **OK**. In the second **Microsoft Word** message box, click **OK**.

c. On the left, click **Options**, and then in the **Word Options** dialog box, click **Customize Ribbon**. In the **Main Tabs** list, right-click **9D Commands (Custom)**, and then from the shortcut menu, click **Remove**. Click **OK**, and then **Close** Word.

9 If directed by your instructor to do so, submit your paper printout, your electronic image of your document that looks like a printed document, or your original Word file.

END | You have completed Project 9D

CONTENT-BASED ASSESSMENTS (MASTERY AND TRANSFER OF LEARNING)

Mastering Word Project 9E Ergonomic Study

Apply 9A skills from these Objectives:

1. Create a Customized Form
2. Convert Text to a Table and Insert Content Controls in a Table
3. Modify and Protect a Form
4. Complete a Form

In the following Mastering Word project, you will create a form for the IT Department at Laurales Herbs and Spices. The department plans to survey employees regarding health issues related to their workstations. Your completed document will look similar to Figure 9.52.

PROJECT FILES

For Project 9E, you will need the following file:

w09E_Ergonomic_Study

You will save your document as:

Lastname_Firstname_9E_Ergonomic_Study

PROJECT RESULTS

Laurales Herbs and Spices IT Department

The IT department, in conjunction with the Human Resources department, is conducting an ergonomics study to assess the current status of our equipment as it relates to your workstation and your health and wellbeing. Please send the completed form to technology@laurales.com.

Name: Andy Chan   Date: 12/17/2015

For each job function listed below, indicate the hours per day, on average, that you devote to each task.

Job Function	Hours Per Day
Computer Use	5
Phone Use	Choose an item.
Paperwork/Reading	Choose an item.
Copying/Collating	Choose an item.
Filing/Storing	Choose an item.

Input Devices	Yes	No
1. Does your keyboard have all the features that your job tasks require?	☐	☐
2. Do all of the keys on your keyboard work reliably?	☐	☐
3. Do you regularly use your numeric keypad to enter data?	☐	☐
4. Does your mouse work reliably?	☐	☐
5. Does your mouse provide the features your job requires?	☐	☐

Monitor	Yes	No
1. Is the top of your monitor at or slightly below eye level?	☐	☐
2. Is your monitor located about an arm's reach away?	☐	☐
3. Can your monitor tilt and swivel?	☐	☐
4. Is your monitor easy to read, clear, and free from blurry areas?	☐	☐
5. Is your monitor free from glare?	☐	☐

Special Conditions	Yes	No
1. If you use a wrist rest, is it free from sharp edges and positioned at the same height as your keyboard?	☐	☐
2. If you use a footrest, is it easy to position and adjust in height and angle?	☐	☐
3. If you wear eyeglasses, are the lenses specifically adjusted for computer use?	☐	☐
4. If you wear bifocals, can you view your monitor without backward neck bending?	☐	☐
5. If you share a workstation, is all the equipment adjustable to accommodate you and your job tasks?	☐	☐
6. If you answered NO to Question 5, please indicate the equipment that should be replaced with adjustable equipment. Click or tap here to enter text.		

Lastname_Firstname_9E_Ergonomic_Study

Word 2016, Windows 10, Microsoft Corporation

FIGURE 9.52

(Project 9E Ergonomic Study continues on the next page)

Mastering Word Project 9E Ergonomic Study (continued)

1 Start Word, on the left click **Open Other Documents**, click **Browse**, and then in the **Open** dialog box, navigate to the student data files that accompany this chapter. Open the file **w09E_Ergonomic_Study**. Click the **File tab**, on the left click **Save As**, click **Browse**, and then in the **Save As** dialog box, navigate to your **Word Chapter 9** folder. Using your own name, save the file as **Lastname_Firstname_9E_Ergonomic_Study** and if necessary, display the rulers and formatting marks.

2 From the Word Options dialog box, display the **Developer tab**. Select the first paragraph, change the **Font Size** to **16**, apply **Bold**, and then change the **Font Color** to **Green, Accent 6, Darker 50%**. Center the paragraph.

3 Including the tab marks and the paragraph marks, select the six paragraphs that begin with *Job Function* and end with *Filing/Storing*. Display the **Convert Text to Table** dialog box, be sure the number of columns is **2** and the text is separated at **Tabs**, and then convert the text to a table.

4 Apply the table style **Grid Table 4 – Accent 6** to all four tables.

5 On the **Developer tab**, turn on **Design Mode**. Locate the text *Name*, position the insertion point to the right of the colon, press Spacebar one time, and then insert a **Plain Text Content Control**.

6 Locate the text *Date*, position the insertion point to the right of the colon, press Spacebar one time, and then insert a **Date Picker Content Control**.

7 In the first table, in the second row, click in the second cell, and then insert a **Drop-Down List Content Control**. Display the **Content Control Properties** dialog box, and then display the **Add Choice** dialog box. In the **Display Name** box, type **1** and click **OK** to add the **Value**. In a similar manner, add the numbers **2** through **8** (in numerical order) to the list. Click the **Select Field** button to select the entire control, copy the content control, and then paste it into the remaining empty cells in the first table. Select the second column, and then **Align Center**.

8 In the second table, below **Yes**, position the insertion point in the first empty cell, and then insert a **Check Box Content Control**. Copy the content control, and then paste it into the remaining empty cells in all three tables. For the second, third, and fourth tables, select the second and third columns, and then **Align Center**.

9 In the fourth table, in the last row, click to position the insertion point in the first cell. On the **Table Tools Layout tab**, in the **Rows & Columns group**, click **Insert Below**. With all three cells selected, in the **Merge group** click **Merge Cells**, and then in the **Alignment group**, click **Align Center Left**.

10 On the **Home tab**, in the **Paragraph group**, click **Numbering** to continue numbering with 6. Click in the cell, and then type **If you answered NO to Question 5, please indicate the equipment that should be replaced with adjustable equipment.** Press Enter, press Backspace one time to remove the auto number, and then insert a **Plain Text Content Control**. Turn off **Design Mode**—your document reverts to one page. **Restrict Editing** to only **Filling in forms**. Do not use a password. **Close** the **Restrict Editing** pane.

11 In the content control following **Name**, type **Andy Chan**

12 To the right of **Date**, click the **Date Picker content control arrow**, and then click **Today**. To the right of *Computer Use*, click the **Drop–Down List content control arrow**, and then click **5**.

13 Press Ctrl + Home, and then insert the file name in the footer. Click the **File tab**, and then click **Show All Properties**. In the **Tags** box, type **ergonomic study** In the **Subject** box, type your course name and section number. If necessary, edit the author name to display your name. On the left, click **Save**.

14 Click the **File tab**, on the left click **Options**. In the **Word Options** dialog box, on the left click **Customize Ribbon**. In the **Main Tabs** list, locate and then click to clear the **Developer** check box. Click **OK**, and notice that the Developer tab no longer displays on the ribbon.

15 **Save** your document. In the upper right corner of the Word window, click **Close**. If directed by your instructor to do so, submit your paper printout, your electronic image of your document that looks like a printed document, or your original Word file.

END | You have completed Project 9E

CONTENT-BASED ASSESSMENTS (MASTERY AND TRANSFER OF LEARNING)

9 WORD

Mastering Word Project 9F Staffing Needs

Apply 9B skills from these Objectives:

5 Create a Custom Ribbon Tab
6 Create Style, Color, and Font Sets
7 Convert a Table to Text
8 Prepare a Document for Review and Distribution

In the following Mastering Word project, you will create a memo from George Tillman, Director of Human Resources, explaining staffing needs for next year at Laurales Herbs and Spices. Your completed document will look similar to Figure 9.53.

PROJECT FILES

For Project 9F, you will need the following file:

w09F_Staffing_Needs

You will save your document as:

Lastname_Firstname_9F_Staffing_Needs

PROJECT RESULTS

TO: Anna Carter, President
FROM: George Tillman, Director of Human Resources
DATE: September 8
RE: Next Year's Staffing Needs

Staffing Requirements

In accordance with this year's budget, staffing requirements will remain even with last year. We anticipate a turnover of approximately ten percent based on past years. With no planned changes in product lines or major increases in production requirements, Laurales Herbs and Spices should be able to maintain its high quality merchandise and excellent customer service.

New Positions

Several job descriptions have been changed, and current employees will be invited to apply for those new positions. We believe that current employees will be able to fill the new positions, and we do not anticipate any layoffs based on these changes. We have the resources available to provide new or additional training where necessary. Our staff has always been willing to accept new responsibilities and adapt to change. We anticipate the following new positions:

- Program Development Specialist
- Marketing Campaign Manager
- Product Manager
- Southwest Regional Sales Manager

In accordance with Laurales Herbs and Spices policies and internal guidelines, we will continue to strive for an employee base that is diverse—actively recruiting minorities, veterans, and individuals with physical challenges.

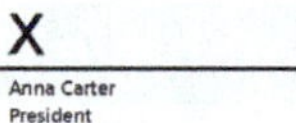

Lastname_Firstname_9F_Staffing_Needs

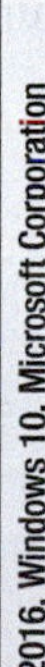

FIGURE 9.53

(Project 9F Staffing Needs continues on the next page)

CONTENT-BASED ASSESSMENTS (MASTERY AND TRANSFER OF LEARNING)

Mastering Word Project 9F Staffing Needs (continued)

1 From the student data files that accompany this chapter, open the file **w09F_Staffing_Needs**, and then using your own name, save the file in your **Word Chapter 9** folder as **Lastname_Firstname_9F_Staffing Needs**

2 Display the **Word Options** dialog box, and then on the left click **Customize Ribbon**. On the right, be sure **Main Tabs** are displayed and that **Home** is selected. Create a **New Tab**, in the **Main Tabs** list select **New Tab (Custom)**, and then **Rename** the tab as **9F Commands** In the list click **New Group (Custom)**, and then **Rename** the group as **Frequent Tasks**

3 On the left, display **All Commands**, and then **Add** the following commands to the **Frequent Tasks group**: **Edit Footer** and **Insert Picture**. Click **OK** to close the **Word Options** dialog box. From the new **9F Commands tab**, add the **File Name** to the footer.

4 Select the paragraphs **Staffing Requirements** and **New Positions**, and then from the mini toolbar, change the **Font Color** to **Blue, Accent 1, Darker 50%**—in the fifth column, the last color.

5 Press Ctrl + Home to move to the top of the document, and then from the **9F Commands tab**, insert the picture **w09F_Logo_Photo** from your student data files. Set the height of the picture to **2"** and then from the **Picture Tools Format tab**, in the **Arrange group**, set the **Position** to **Position in Top Right with Square Text Wrapping**— the third option under **With Text Wrapping**.

6 Create a new font set using **Cambria** as the **Heading font** and **Segoe UI** as the **Body font**. Name the font set **Laurales 9F** Select *Staffing Requirements* and *New Positions*, and then apply the **Heading 1** style.

7 Create a new color set. Change **Accent 1** to the first color in the last row of the **Standard** colors. Change **Accent 4** to the first color in the seventh (widest) row of the **Standard** colors. Name the color set **Laurales 9F**

8 Convert the table to text by separating the text with paragraph marks. Apply **Bullets** to the four new paragraphs.

9 At the end of the document, insert a **Microsoft Office Signature Line** with **Anna Carter** as the Suggested signer and her title **President**

10 Display the document properties. As the **Tags** type **staffing needs** In the **Subject** box, type your course name and section number. Be sure your name displays as the author.

11 Mark the document as final, and then in the **Word Options** dialog box, remove the custom ribbon tab **9F Commands**.

12 If directed by your instructor to do so, submit your paper printout, your electronic image of your document that looks like a printed document, or your original Word file.

END | You have completed Project 9F

CONTENT-BASED ASSESSMENTS (MASTERY AND TRANSFER OF LEARNING)

Mastering Word Project 9G Seminar Evaluation

Apply 9A and 9B skills from these Objectives:

1. Create a Customized Form
2. Convert Text to a Table and Insert Content Controls in a Table
3. Modify and Protect a Form
4. Complete a Form
5. Create a Custom Ribbon Tab
6. Create Style, Color, and Font Sets
7. Convert a Table to Text
8. Prepare a Document for Review and Distribution

In the following Mastering Word project, you will create a custom form that will be used by employees to evaluate training seminars at Laurales Herbs and Spices. Your completed document will look similar to Figure 9.54.

PROJECT FILES

For Project 9G, you will need the following files:

w09G_Seminar_Evaluation
w09G_Logo_Photo

You will save your document as:

Lastname_Firstname_9G_Seminar_Evaluation

PROJECT RESULTS

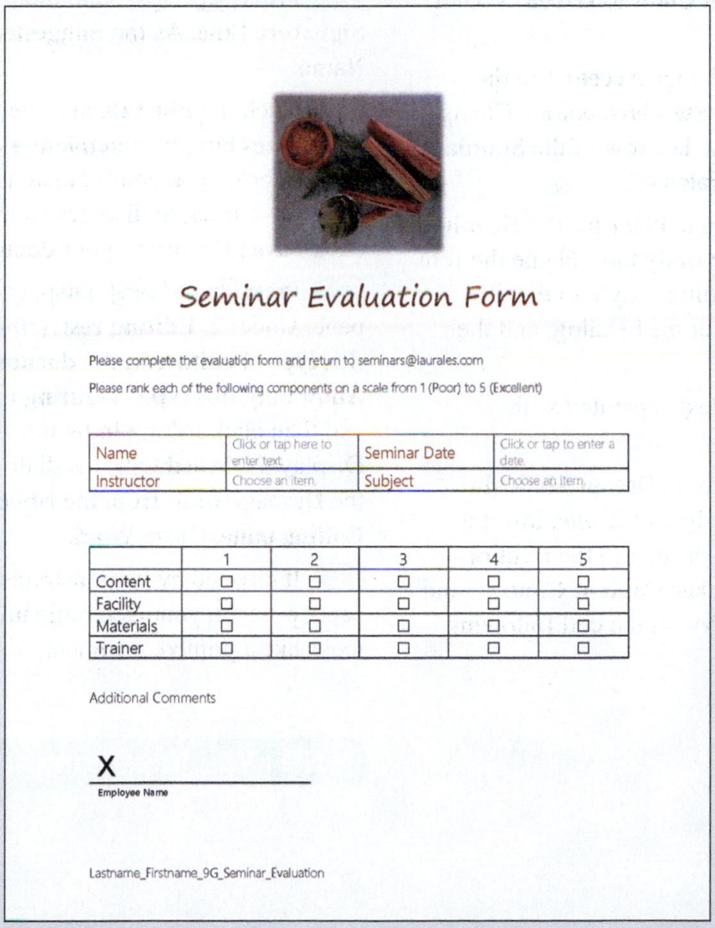

Seminar Evaluation Form

Please complete the evaluation form and return to seminars@laurales.com

Please rank each of the following components on a scale from 1 (Poor) to 5 (Excellent)

Name	Click or tap here to enter text.	Seminar Date	Click or tap to enter a date.
Instructor	Choose an item.	Subject	Choose an item.

	1	2	3	4	5
Content	☐	☐	☐	☐	☐
Facility	☐	☐	☐	☐	☐
Materials	☐	☐	☐	☐	☐
Trainer	☐	☐	☐	☐	☐

Additional Comments

X
Employee Name

Lastname_Firstname_9G_Seminar_Evaluation

Word 2016, Windows 10, Microsoft Corporation

FIGURE 9.54

(Project 9G Seminar Evaluation continues on the next page)

Mastering Word Project 9G Seminar Evaluation (continued)

1 From the student data files that accompany this chapter, open the file **w09G_Seminar_Evaluation**, and then using your own name, save the file in your **Word Chapter 9** folder as **Lastname_Firstname_9G_Seminar_Evaluation** Insert the file name in the footer. If necessary, display rulers and formatting marks. From the **Word Options** dialog box, display the **Developer tab**.

2 Press Ctrl + Home. From your student files, **Insert** the picture **w09G_Logo_Photo**. Change the **Height** to **2"** and then press Ctrl + E to center the picture.

3 Position the insertion point in the empty paragraph immediately below the picture. Type **Seminar Evaluation Form** and then press Enter. Select the paragraph you just typed, and then change the **Font Color** to **Green, Accent 6, Darker 50%**.

4 Create a new color set. Change **Accent 1** to the first color in the last row of the **Standard** colors. Change **Accent 6** to the third color in the last row of the **Standard** colors. Name the color set **Laurales 9G**

5 Create a font set using **Segoe Print** for the **Heading font** and **Segoe UI Light** for the **Body font**. Name the font set **Laurales 9G** Apply the **Heading 1** style to the title *Seminar Evaluation Form*, center the heading, and then change the **Font Size** to **24**.

6 Convert the first table to text separated with paragraph marks.

7 On the **Developer tab**, turn on **Design Mode**. In the first table, in the cell to the right of *Name*, insert a **Plain Text Content Control**. In the cell to the right of *Seminar Date*, insert a **Date Picker Content Control**, and then change the format to **M/d/yy**. In the cell following *Instructor*, insert a **Drop-Down List Content Control**, and then add the following names:

Alvin Barnes
Charles Corbin
Susan Parrish

8 In the last cell of the first table, insert a **Drop-Down List Content Control**, and then add the following topics:

Customer Service
Employee Benefits
Microsoft Office
Safety Issues

9 In the second table, insert a **Check Box Content Control** in each of the empty cells. Turn off **Design Mode**.

10 Press Ctrl + End, and then insert a **Microsoft Office Signature Line**. As the **Suggested signer** type **Employee Name**

11 Click the **File tab**, and then **Show All Properties**. In the **Tags** box, type **seminar evaluation form** In the **Subject** box, type your course name and section number. Be sure your name displays as the author. On the left, click **Save** to return to your document.

12 Press Ctrl + Home. Display the **Restrict Editing** pane. Under **2. Editing restrictions**, select the **Allow only this type of editing in the document** check box. Click the **Allow only this type of editing in the document arrow**, and then click **Filling in forms**. **Save** your document. Display the **Word Options** dialog box, and then remove the **Developer tab** from the ribbon. Close the **Restrict Editing pane**. Close Word.

13 If directed by your instructor to do so, submit your paper printout, your electronic image of your document that looks like a printed document, or your original Word file.

END | You have completed Project 9G

Apply a combination of the 9A and 9B skills.

CONTENT-BASED ASSESSMENTS (CRITICAL THINKING)

GO! Fix It Project 9H Complaint Form **MyITLab**

GO! Make It Project 9I Phone Request **MyITLab**

GO! Solve It Project 9J Accident Report **MyITLab**

GO! Solve It Project 9K Staff Promotion

Build from Scratch

PROJECT FILES

For Project 9K, you will need the following files:

New blank Word document
w09K_Promotion_Data

You will save your document as:

Lastname_Firstname_9K_Staff_Promotion

Anna Carter, President of Laurales Herbs and Spices, needs to fill the position of Executive Assistant. She would like to promote an individual from within the company. She has identified ten candidates; however, she wants the department managers to identify the strengths and weaknesses of the individuals. Create a memorandum from Ms. Carter to department managers, including the current date and an appropriate subject line. In the body of the memo, design a form that includes appropriate content controls to select the name of the individual being evaluated and rate the candidate on a variety of skills using a five-point scale ranging from Poor to Excellent. Information regarding candidates' names and required skills can be found in the student file **w09K_Promotion_Data**. Save the document as a Word template with the file name **Lastname_Firstname_9K_Staff_Promotion** Insert the file name in the footer and add appropriate document properties. Restrict editing to filling in the form. Print your document or submit electronically as directed by your instructor.

Performance Level

Performance Element	Exemplary: You consistently applied the relevant skills	Proficient: You sometimes, but not always, applied the relevant skills	Developing: You rarely or never applied the relevant skills
Insert and format text	All required information is included and the document is formatted as a memo.	Some information is missing or the document is not formatted as a memo.	No specific information is included and the document is not formatted as a memo.
Insert content controls	Appropriate content controls are used and required items are added.	Some content controls are inappropriate or some required items are missing.	No content controls are inserted.
Insert 5-point rating scale	The scale allows for five ratings and displays appropriately with skills and content controls.	The scale does not contain five ratings or does not display appropriately with skills and content controls.	There is no scale.
Save as template and restrict editing	The document is saved as a template and is restricted to filling in forms.	The document is not saved as a template or is not restricted to filling in forms.	The document is not saved as a template and the form is not restricted.

END | You have completed Project 9K

OUTCOMES-BASED ASSESSMENTS (CRITICAL THINKING)

RUBRIC

The following outcomes-based assessments are *open-ended assessments*. That is, there is no specific correct result; your result will depend on your approach to the information provided. Make *Professional Quality* your goal. Use the following scoring rubric to guide you in *how* to approach the problem and then to evaluate *how well* your approach solves the problem.

The *criteria*—Software Mastery, Content, Format and Layout, and Process—represent the knowledge and skills you have gained that you can apply to solving the problem. The *levels of performance*—Professional Quality, Approaching Professional Quality, or Needs Quality Improvements—help you and your instructor evaluate your result.

	Your completed project is of Professional Quality if you:	Your completed project is Approaching Professional Quality if you:	Your completed project Needs Quality Improvements if you:
1-Software Mastery	Choose and apply the most appropriate skills, tools, and features and identify efficient methods to solve the problem.	Choose and apply some appropriate skills, tools, and features, but not in the most efficient manner.	Choose inappropriate skills, tools, or features, or are inefficient in solving the problem.
2-Content	Construct a solution that is clear and well organized, contains content that is accurate, appropriate to the audience and purpose, and is complete. Provide a solution that contains no errors of spelling, grammar, or style.	Construct a solution in which some components are unclear, poorly organized, inconsistent, or incomplete. Misjudge the needs of the audience. Have some errors in spelling, grammar, or style, but the errors do not detract from comprehension.	Construct a solution that is unclear, incomplete, or poorly organized, contains some inaccurate or inappropriate content, and contains many errors of spelling, grammar, or style. Do not solve the problem.
3-Format and Layout	Format and arrange all elements to communicate information and ideas, clarify function, illustrate relationships, and indicate relative importance.	Apply appropriate format and layout features to some elements, but not others. Overuse features, causing minor distraction.	Apply format and layout that does not communicate information or ideas clearly. Do not use format and layout features to clarify function, illustrate relationships, or indicate relative importance. Use available features excessively, causing distraction.
4-Process	Use an organized approach that integrates planning, development, self-assessment, revision, and reflection.	Demonstrate an organized approach in some areas, but not others; or, use an insufficient process of organization throughout.	Do not use an organized approach to solve the problem.

Apply a combination of the 9A and 9B skills.

OUTCOMES-BASED ASSESSMENTS (CRITICAL THINKING)

GO! Think Project 9L Computer Equipment

PROJECT FILES

Build from Scratch

For Project 9L, you will need the following file:

New blank Word document

You will save your documents as:

Lastname_Firstname_9L_Computer_Equipment
Lastname_Firstname_9L_Computer_Request

Every three years, the IT department of Laurales Herbs and Spices updates computer equipment and software for the administrative staff. Employees may choose either a desktop or laptop computer. Other options include, but are not limited to, a choice of printers or a scanner. In conjunction with the new computer rollout, the IT department wants to prioritize training needs by asking employees to select a topic—File Management, Microsoft Office, or Website Development—that would be most helpful to them.

Create a questionnaire that can be sent to the administrative staff. Include appropriate text and content controls for the employee's name, the current date, and types of computer equipment and training. Restrict editing the document to filling in forms. Save the document as a Word template with the file name **Lastname_Firstname_9L_Computer_Equipment** Using the template, create a new document and complete the form, using your name as the employee. Save the document as **Lastname_Firstname_9L_Computer_Request** Add appropriate document properties, and mark the document as final. In your template, stop protection, insert the file name in the footer and add appropriate document properties. Print both documents or submit electronically as directed by your instructor.

END | You have completed Project 9L

Build from Scratch

GO! Think Project 9M Vacation Compensation MyITLab

Build from Scratch

You and GO! Project 9N Cover Page MyITLab

Working with Long Documents

PROJECT 10A

OUTCOMES

Create, navigate, and inspect a master document and subdocuments, and modify footers.

OBJECTIVES

1. Create a Master Document and Subdocuments
2. Manage a Master Document and Subdocuments
3. Navigate and Inspect the Master Document
4. Create and Modify Headers and Footers

PROJECT 10B

OUTCOMES

Work with and format long documents and create an index, table of contents, and table of figures.

OBJECTIVES

5. Create an Index
6. Create a Table of Contents
7. Create a Table of Figures
8. Control the Flow and Formatting of Pages and Text

keller/Fotolia

In This Chapter

When several people work on a document, keeping track of the different versions can be difficult. In this chapter, you will create a master document and subdocuments from a multipage file to allow parts of the document to be edited while maintaining the integrity of the complete document. The navigation features in Word allow you to view and edit the final master document. Additionally, you will create navigational and reference aids for a long document, including a table of contents, a table of figures, and an index. Defining the flow of text on the pages of the document will improve readability.

The projects in this chapter relate to the **City of Tawny Creek**, a growing community located between Los Angeles and San Diego, about 20 miles from the Pacific shore. Just 10 years ago, the population was under 100,000; today it has grown to almost 300,000. Community leaders have always focused on quality of life and economic development in decisions on housing, open space, education, and infrastructure, making the city a model for other communities its size around the United States. The city provides many recreational and cultural opportunities with a large park system and thriving arts community.

PROJECT

10A Autumn Schedule

Project 10A Training
Project 10A Grader

PROJECT ACTIVITIES

In Activities 10.01 through 10.12, you will create a master document with four subdocuments. The finished document will be a description of the autumn activities offered by the City of Tawny Creek. Your completed documents will look similar to Figure 10.1.

Please always review the downloaded Grader instructions before beginning.

PROJECT FILES

If your instructor wants you to submit Project 10A in the MyITLab Grader system, log in to MyITLab, locate Grader Project 10A, and then download the files for this project.

For Project 10A, you will need the following files:
w10A_Autumn_Schedule
w10A_Teens

You will save your files as:
Lastname_Firstname_10A_Autumn_Schedule
Lastname_Firstname_10A_Teens (not shown in Figure)

PROJECT RESULTS

GO! Walk Thru Project 10A

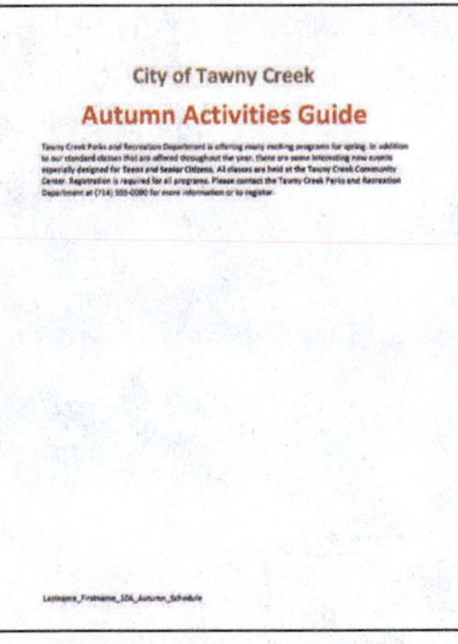

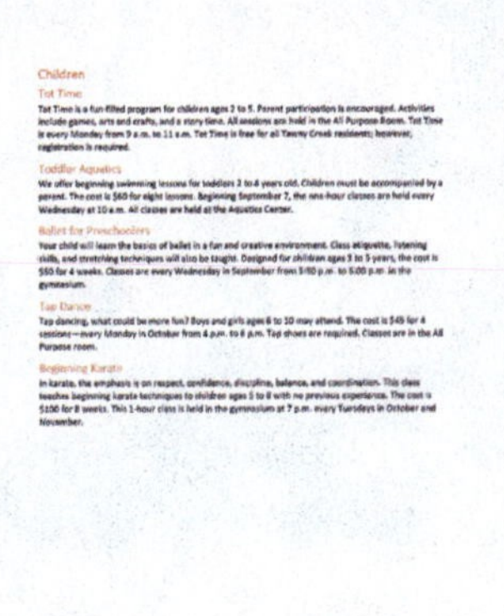

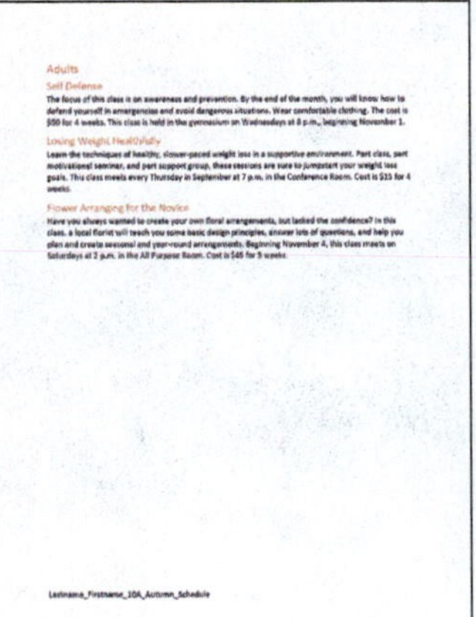

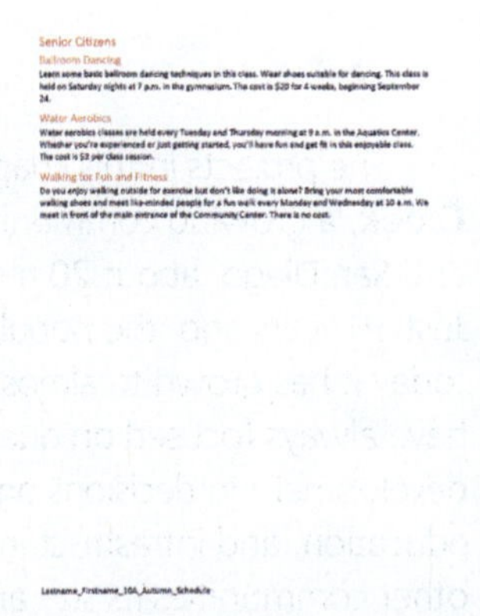

FIGURE 10.1 Project 10A Autumn Schedule

NOTE	If You Are Using a Touchscreen
	Tap an item to click it.
	Press and hold for a few seconds to right-click; release when the information or command displays.
	Touch the screen with two or more fingers and then pinch together to zoom out or stretch your fingers apart to zoom in.
	Slide your finger on the screen to scroll—slide left to scroll right and slide right to scroll left.
	Slide to rearrange—similar to dragging with a mouse.
	Swipe to select—slide an item a short distance with a quick movement to select an item and bring up commands, if any.

Objective 1 Create a Master Document and Subdocuments

GO! Learn How Video W10-1

You can organize a long document into sections—a ***master document*** and ***subdocuments***—to make it easier to work with different parts of the document. A master document is a Word document that serves as a container for the different parts of a document. A subdocument is a section of the document that is linked to the master document. Changes made in the subdocument are reflected in the master document. Using subdocuments enables the individuals collaborating on a project to edit the various sections of the document without altering the entire long document. Each individual can work on a specific section, and then the sections can be integrated into the final document.

Using a master document allows you to maintain consistent formatting and styles across all of the subdocuments even though different people are working on the sections. ***Outline view*** displays the overall organization, or hierarchy, of parts of a document, including headings, subheadings, and subordinate text.

Activity 10.01 | Using the Outlining Feature and Creating a Master Document

1. Start Word. Navigate to your student files, and then locate and open the file **w10A_Autumn_Schedule**. If necessary, display the rulers and formatting marks. Display the **Save As** dialog box, navigate to the location where you are saving your files for this chapter, and create a folder named **Word Chapter 10**

2. Open the **Word Chapter 10** folder. Create a folder named **Project 10A** and then **Save** the document to your **Project 10A** folder as **Lastname_Firstname_10A_Autumn_Schedule**

3. On the **View tab**, in the **Views group**, click **Outline**. If necessary, change the Zoom level to 100%. Compare your screen with Figure 10.2.

   Outline view makes it easy to view the different levels in a document. The paragraphs formatted with the Heading 1 or Heading 2 style are designated as Level 1 or Level 2 headings and display with a gray bullet containing a plus sign—indicating that subordinate levels display below those paragraphs. Level 2 paragraphs are indented. All other paragraphs are indented and display with a smaller gray bullet to indicate ***body text***. Body text paragraphs do not have a heading style applied. Outline view does not display paragraph alignments—in this case, the first two paragraphs do not display as centered.

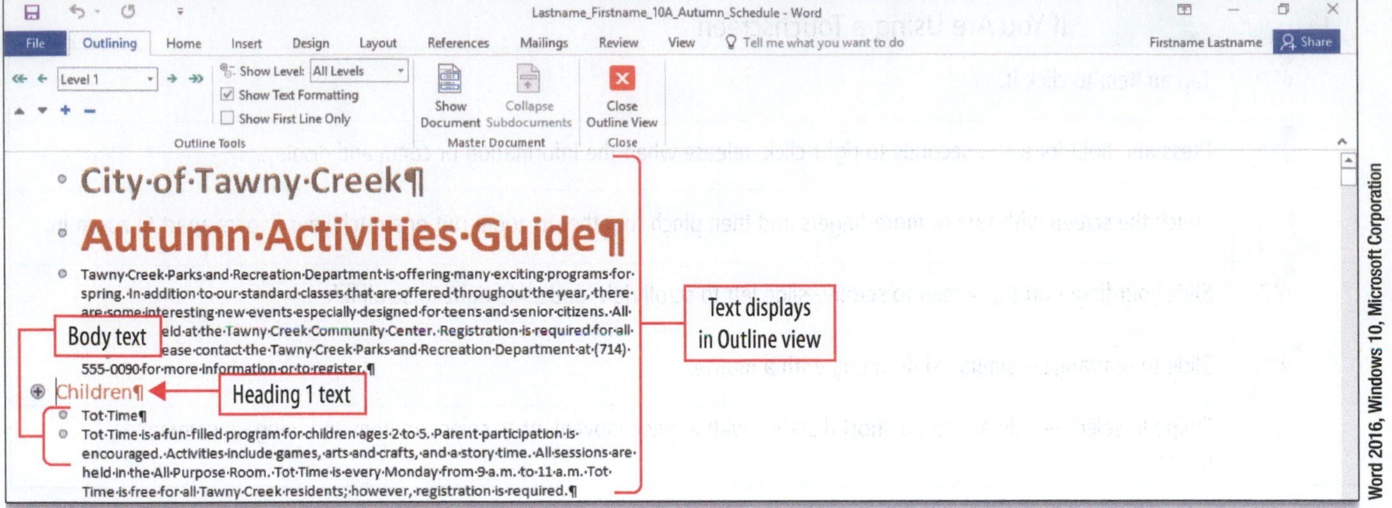

FIGURE 10.2

4 Click to position the insertion point to the left of the paragraph *Children.* Compare your screen with Figure 10.3.

On the Outlining tab, in the Outline Tools group, the Outline Level box displays Level 1. Paragraphs formatted with Heading 1 are the top-level paragraphs in the document.

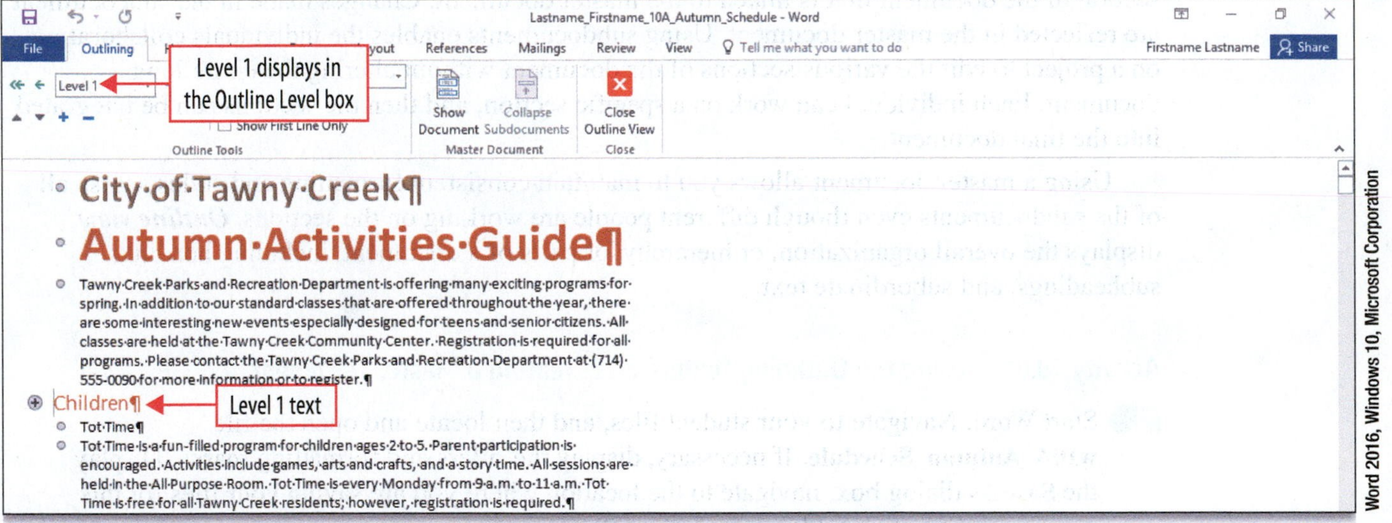

FIGURE 10.3

5 Immediately below the paragraph *Children*, click to position the insertion point to the left of the paragraph *Tot Time*. On the **Outlining tab**, in the **Outline Tools group**, click the **Outline Level arrow** [Body Text], and then compare your screen with Figure 10.4.

You can set up to nine levels for specific paragraphs and you can change a paragraph to Body Text by using Outline view.

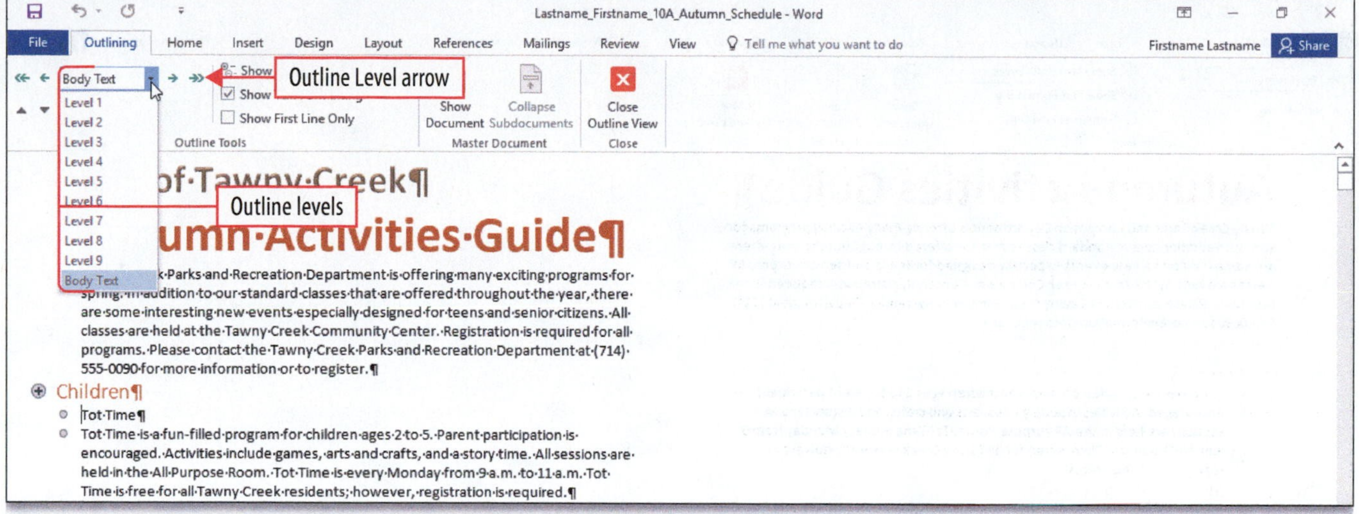

FIGURE 10.4

Word 2016, Windows 10, Microsoft Corporation

6 Click **Level 2**, and then notice that a gray bullet containing a plus sign displays to the left of *Tot Time* and the text formatting is changed.

The *Tot Time* paragraph is assigned a Level 2 heading and the Heading 2 style is applied.

7 Click to position the insertion point in the paragraph *Ballet for Preschoolers*. On the **Outlining tab**, in the **Outline Tools group**, click **Demote** [→].

The Demote button moves a selected paragraph to a lower level. In this case, the paragraph is changed from a Level 1 to a Level 2 and the Heading 2 style is applied.

8 If necessary, scroll down to the view the *Tap Dance* paragraph, and then click to position the insertion point in the paragraph *Tap Dance*. On the **Outlining tab**, in the **Outline Tools group**, click **Promote** [←]. Compare your screen with Figure 10.5.

The Promote button moves a selected paragraph to a higher level. In this case, the paragraph is changed from a Level 3 to a Level 2 and the Heading 2 style is applied. The *Tot Time*, *Toddler Aquatics*, *Ballet for Preschoolers*, *Tap Dance*, and *Beginning Karate* paragraphs all display as Level 2 under the Level 1 *Children* paragraph.

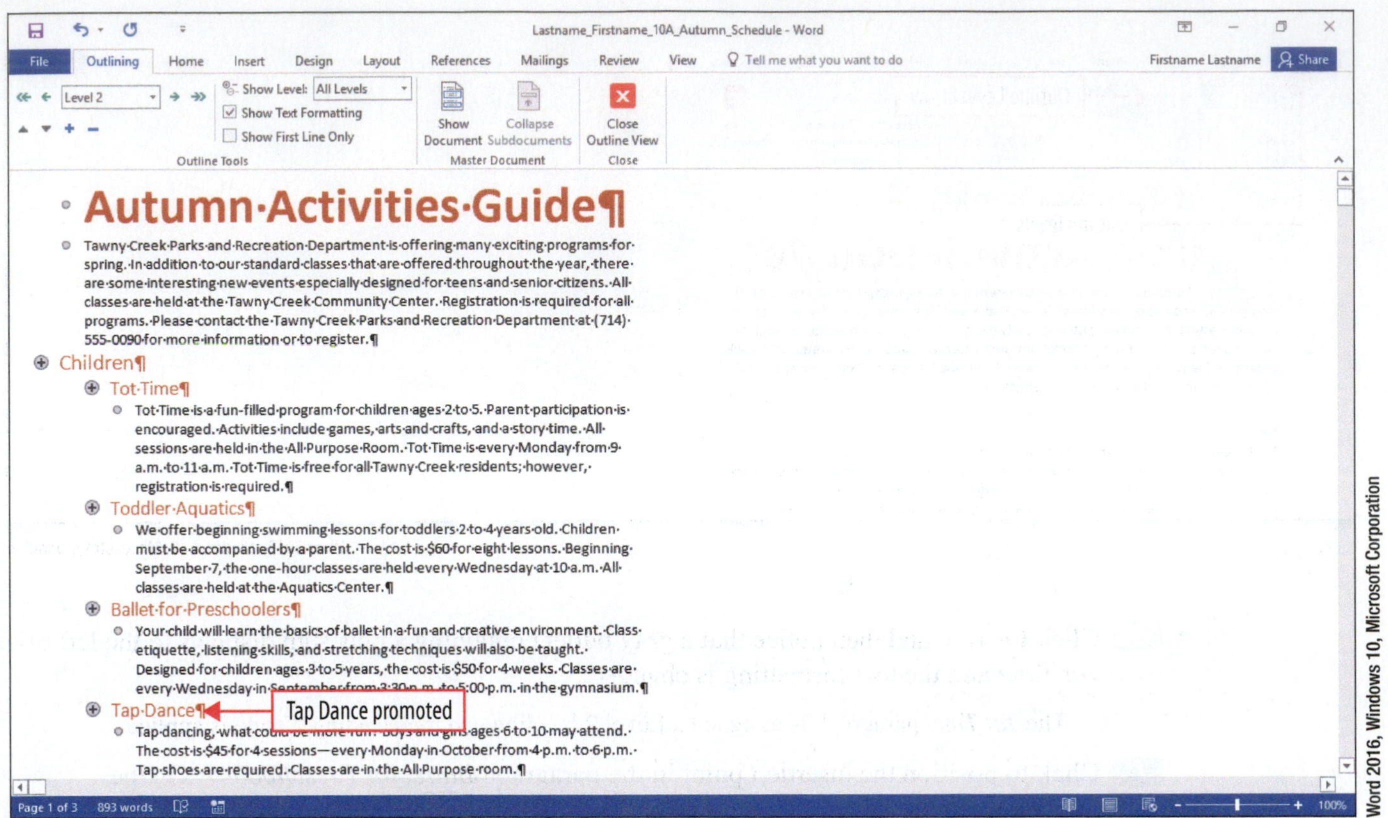

FIGURE 10.5

Word 2016, Windows 10, Microsoft Corporation

9 Press Ctrl + Home, and then click to the left of *Children*. Drag down to select all remaining paragraphs in the document. On the **Outlining tab**, in the **Master Document group**, click **Show Document** to toggle it on, and then click **Create**. Press Ctrl + Home, and then scroll down slightly so that the *Children* paragraph is at the top of the Word window. Compare your screen with Figure 10.6.

The first heading level in the selection determines where each subdocument is created. In this instance, the Level 1 headings of the document are used to create subdocuments. A light gray border displays around each subdocument, and a subdocument icon displays to the left of the first line of each new subdocument.

Continuous section breaks define the beginning and end of each subdocument. Recall that a ***section break*** is a mark that stores the section formatting information, such as the margins, page orientation, headers and footers, and sequence of page numbers. A continuous section break indicates that the section will begin on the same page of the document.

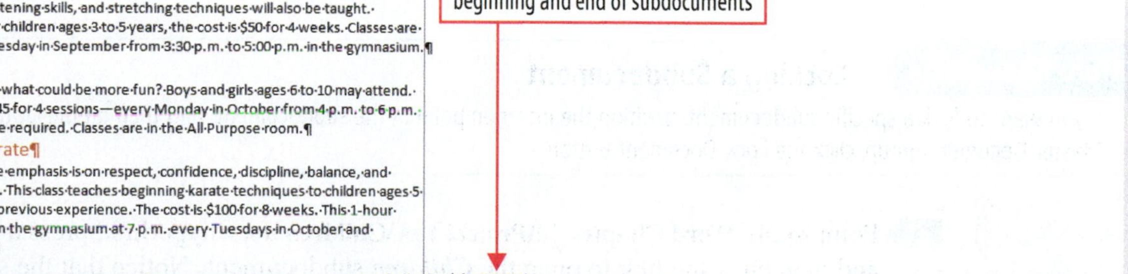

FIGURE 10.6

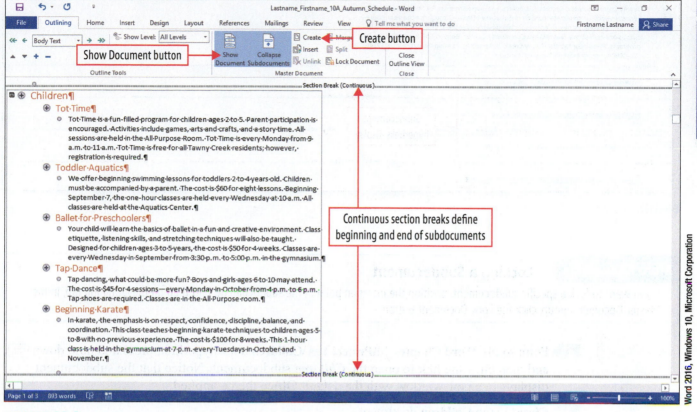

10 **Save** your changes.

Activity 10.02 | Collapsing and Displaying Subdocuments

When a master document is created, the subdocuments display in expanded form—all text in the document is visible. You can collapse one or more subdocuments to hide a portion of the text.

1 On the **Outlining tab**, in the **Master Document group**, click **Collapse Subdocuments**. Compare your screen with Figure 10.7.

The subdocuments are collapsed and display as hyperlinks. Each subdocument is saved as a separate document in the same location as the master document—in this case, your Project 10A folder. The file name of the subdocument is created from the heading text of the subdocument. In this case, the subdocuments are named: *Children*, *Adults*, *Families*, and *Senior Citizens*. The files for a master document and its subdocuments are usually stored in the same folder.

When the master document is collapsed, the Lock icon displays next to the links for all subdocuments. When a subdocument is locked, no one else can make changes to it.

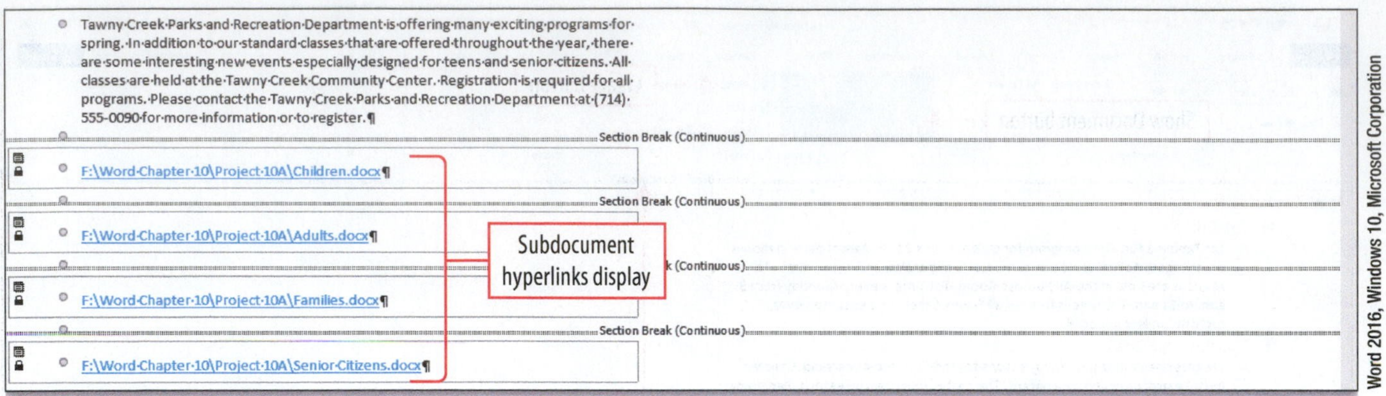

FIGURE 10.7

More Knowledge **Locking a Subdocument**

If you want to lock a specific subdocument, position the insertion point in the subdocument, and then on the Outlining tab, in the Master Document group, click the Lock Document button.

2 Point to the **Word Chapter 10\Project 10A\Children.docx** hyperlink, press and hold down Ctrl, and then click the link to open the *Children* subdocument. Notice that the subdocument displays in a new window with the default Office theme applied.

3 **Close** the **Children** document.

Because you opened the *Children* subdocument by clicking the hyperlink, the color of the hyperlink changes in the master document.

4 **Save** your changes.

Activity 10.03 | Inserting an Existing File as a Subdocument

Any existing document can be inserted as a subdocument in a master document. The subdocuments must be expanded when inserting a new document.

1 On the **Outlining tab**, in the **Master Document group**, click **Expand Subdocuments**. From your student data files, **Open** the file **w10A_Teens**.

The first paragraph is formatted with the Heading 1 style, and the four paragraph headings are formatted with the Heading 2 style.

2 Display the **Save As** dialog box, navigate to your **Project 10A** folder, and then compare your screen with Figure 10.8.

The four subdocuments that were saved when you created the master document display in your Project 10A folder along with your master document.

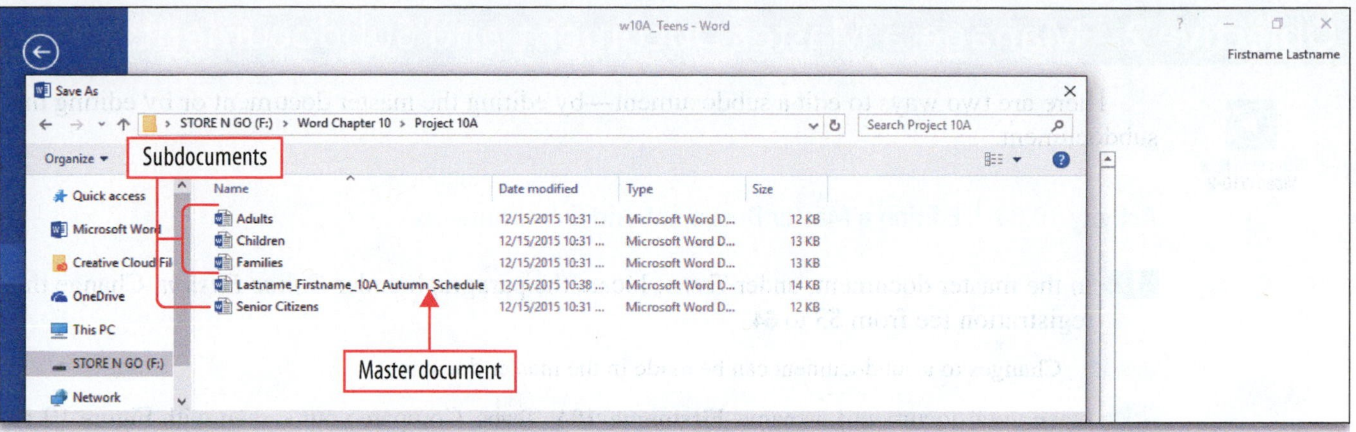

FIGURE 10.8

Word 2016, Windows 10, Microsoft Corporation

3 **Save** the file in your **Project 10A** folder as **Lastname_Firstname_10A_Teens** and then **Close** the *Teens* document.

4 Click in the **Lastname_Firstname_10A_Autumn_Schedule** document to make it active, and then press Ctrl + End. On the **Outlining tab**, in the **Master Document group**, if necessary, click Show Document to toggle it on, and then click **Insert**. In the **Insert Subdocument** dialog box, navigate to your **Project 10A** folder, select **Lastname_Firstname_10A_Teens**, and then click **Open**.

The existing document is inserted as a subdocument. Because Heading 1 and Heading 2 styles were applied in the *Teens* document, the respective levels are maintained in the subdocument.

5 **Save** your changes, and then compare your screen with Figure 10.9.

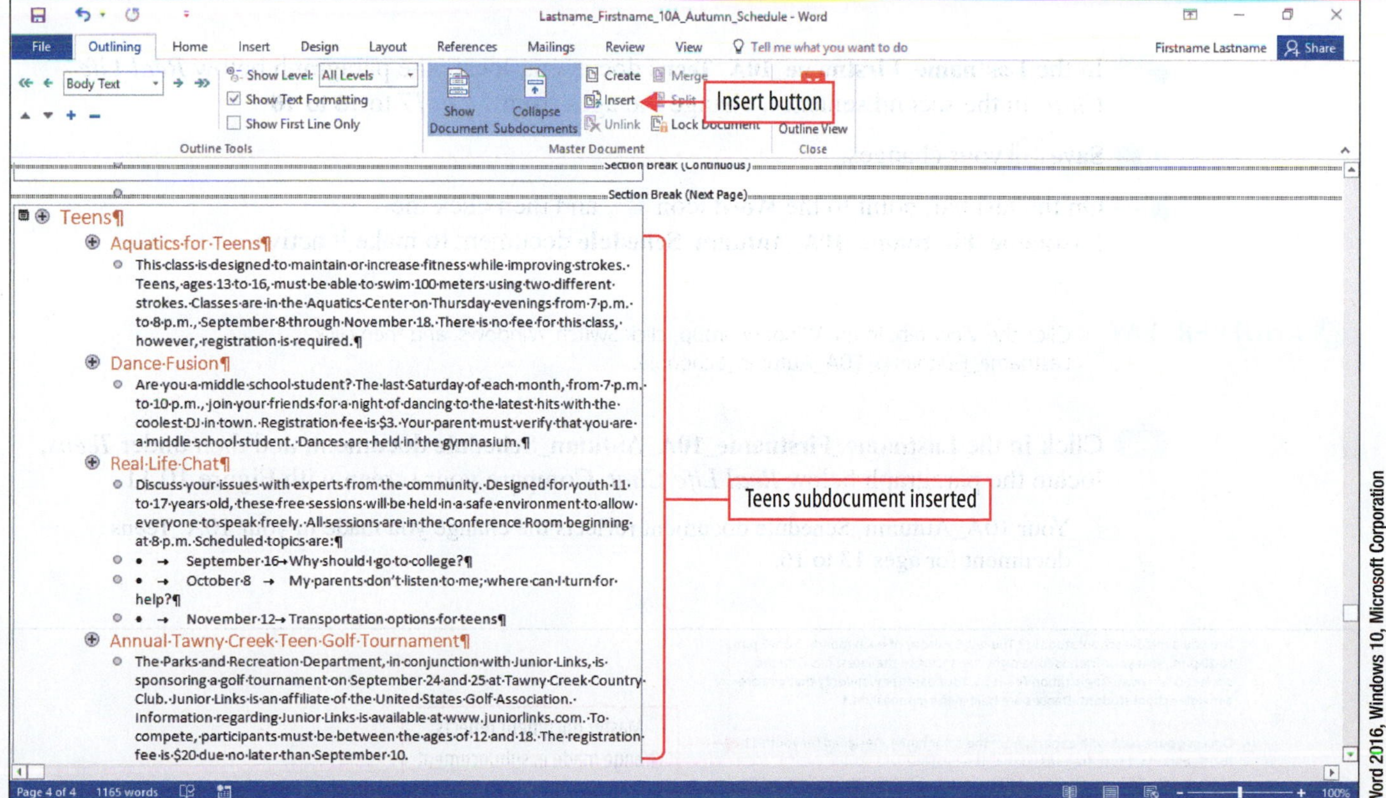

FIGURE 10.9

Word 2016, Windows 10, Microsoft Corporation

Objective 2 Manage a Master Document and Subdocuments

GO! Learn How Video W10-2

There are two ways to edit a subdocument—by editing the master document or by editing the subdocument.

Activity 10.04 | Editing a Master Document and Subdocuments

1. In the master document, under *Teens*, locate the paragraph under *Dance Fusion*. Change the registration fee from *$3* to **$4**

   Changes to a subdocument can be made in the master document.

2. **Open** your document **Lastname_Firstname_10A_Teens**. Compare your screen with Figure 10.10.

   The change that you made to the cost for Dance Fusion displays as $4 in this subdocument. When changes are made to the master document, they are also reflected in the subdocument.

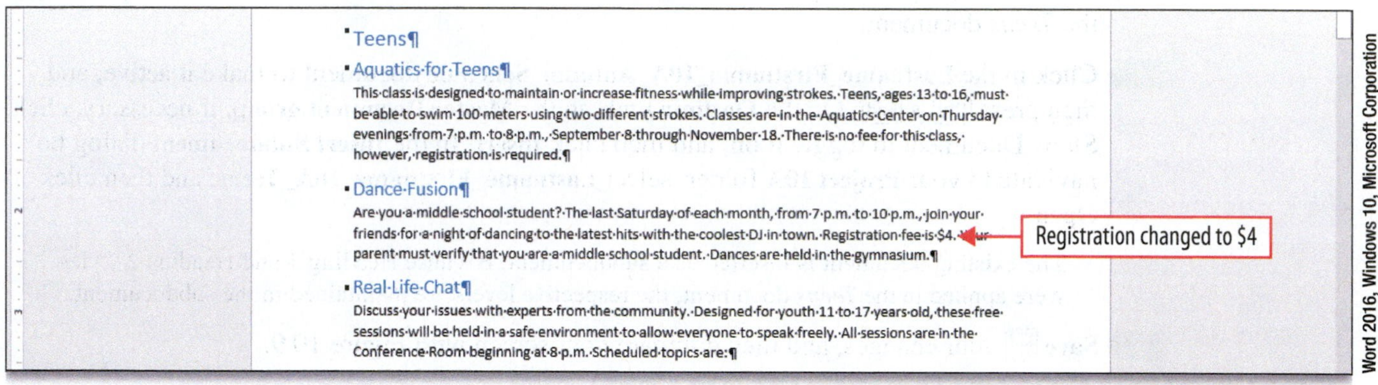

FIGURE 10.10

3. In the **Lastname_Firstname_10A_Teens** document, locate the paragraph below *Real Life Chat*. In the second sentence, change the ages from *11 to 17* to **13 to 16**

4. **Save** your changes.

5. On the taskbar, point to the **Word** icon, and then click the **Lastname_Firstname_10A_Autumn_Schedule** document to make it active.

ANOTHER WAY Click the View tab. In the Window group, click Switch Windows, and then click Lastname_Firstname_10A_Autumn_Schedule.

6. Click in the **Lastname_Firstname_10A_Autumn_Schedule** document, and then under *Teens*, locate the paragraph below *Real Life Chat*. Compare your screen with Figure 10.11.

   Your 10A_Autumn_Schedule document reflects the change you made in your 10A_Teens document for ages 13 to 16.

Are·you·a·middle·school·student?·The·last·Saturday·of·each·month,·from·7·p.m.·to·10·p.m.,·join·your·friends·for·a·night·of·dancing·to·the·latest·hits·with·the·coolest·DJ·in·town.·Registration·fee·is·$4.·Your·parent·must·verify·that·you·are·a·middle·school·student.·Dances·are·held·in·the·gymnasium.¶

Real·Life·Chat¶

Discuss·your·issues·with·experts·from·the·community.·Designed·for·youth·13·to·16·years·old,·these·free·sessions·will·be·held·in·a·safe·environment·to·allow·everyone·to·speak·freely.·All·sessions·are·in·the·Conference·Room·beginning·at·8·p.m.·Scheduled·topics·are:¶

Master document reflects change made in subdocument

FIGURE 10.11

Word 2016, Windows 10, Microsoft Corporation

7 On the taskbar, point to the **Word** icon, and then **Close** the **Lastname_Firstname_10A_Teens** document.

8 If necessary, click in the **Lastname_Firstname_10A_Autumn_Schedule** document to make it active. On the **Outlining tab**, in the **Close group**, click **Close Outline View**. **Save** your changes.

Objective 3 Navigate and Inspect the Master Document

GO! Learn How Video W10-3

After all subdocuments have been edited, it is important to view the master document and, if necessary, make any final revisions. Word provides several features for examining a document—such as browsing the document by pages or locating a specific item. In a long document, these features enable you to navigate quickly to the sections you want to review.

Activity 10.05 | Using the Navigation Pane to View a Document

1 Press Ctrl + Home. Click the **View tab**, and then in the **Show group**, select the **Navigation Pane** check box. Notice that the **Navigation** pane displays to the left of your document. Near the top of the **Navigation** pane, click **Pages**. Compare your screen with Figure 10.12.

The Navigation pane contains three ways to browse your document—by headings, by pages, or by using the results of a search. The Navigation pane displays ***thumbnails***—graphical representations of pages—for all the pages in your document. In this case, the current page—where the insertion point is located—displays and is selected in the Navigation pane.

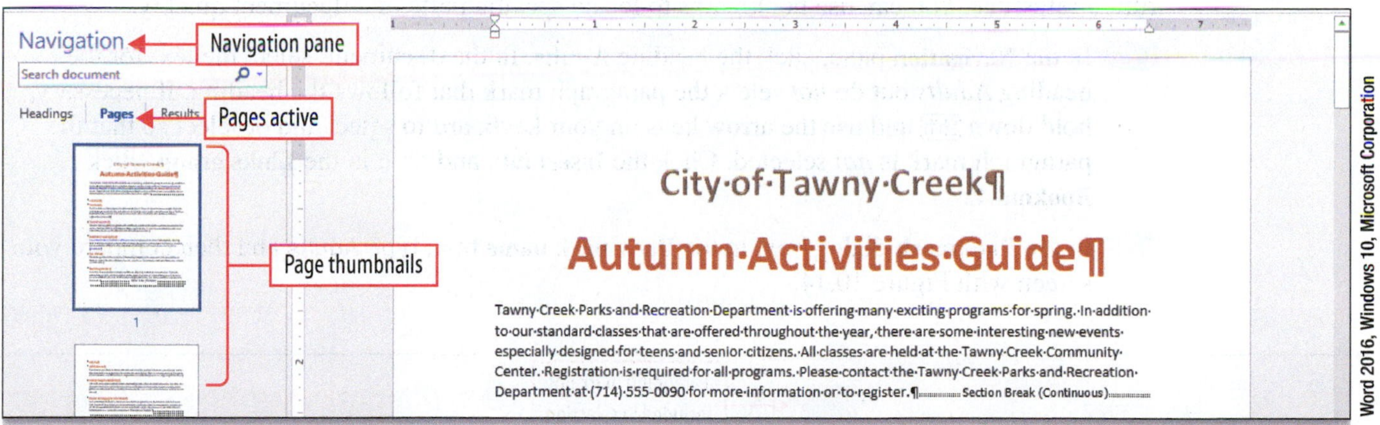

FIGURE 10.12

2 In the **Navigation** pane, click the thumbnail for page **3**. Notice that the top of **Page 3** displays.

3 Near the top of the **Navigation** pane, click **Headings**. Compare your screen with Figure 10.13.

In the Navigation pane, the individual headings in your document display.

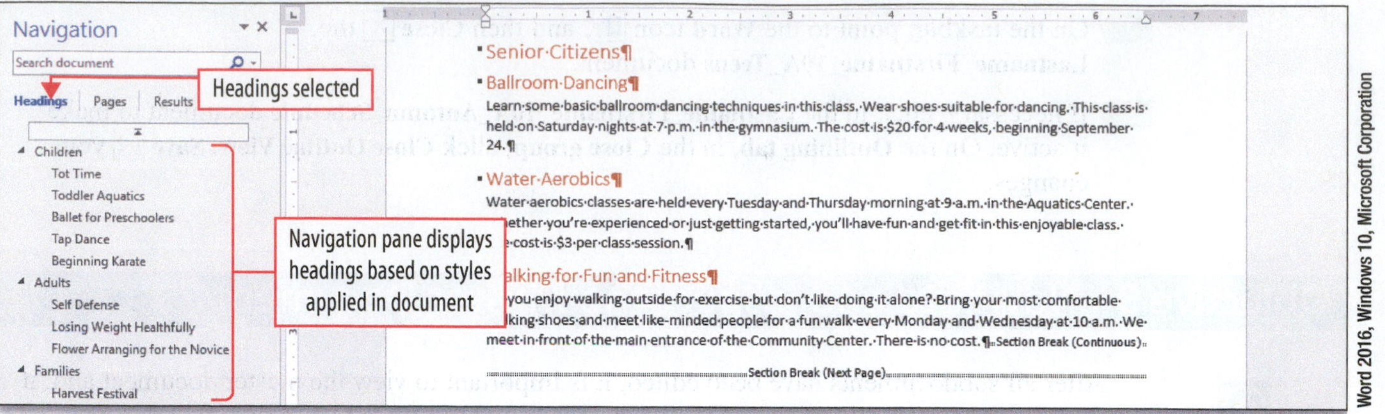

FIGURE 10.13

4 In the **Navigation** pane, under **Children**, click the heading **Beginning Karate**. Notice that the *Beginning Karate* heading displays at the top of your screen. Leave the Navigation pane open for the next activity.

> ***More Knowledge*** **Rearranging the Content in a Document**
>
> You can drag and drop a tab in the Browse Headings list to move a heading or subheading and all related paragraphs to a new location in the document.

Activity 10.06 | Creating Bookmarks

A ***bookmark*** identifies the exact location of text, a table, or other object that you name for future reference. You can use bookmarks to locate specific parts of a document quickly.

1 In the **Navigation** pane, click the heading **Adults**. In the document, select the text for the heading *Adults* but do *not* select the paragraph mark that follows the heading. If necessary, hold down Shift and use the arrow keys on your keyboard to select and deselect so that the paragraph mark is *not* selected. Click the **Insert tab**, and then in the **Links group**, click **Bookmark**.

2 In the **Bookmark** dialog box, in the **Bookmark name** box, type **Adults** and then compare your screen with Figure 10.14.

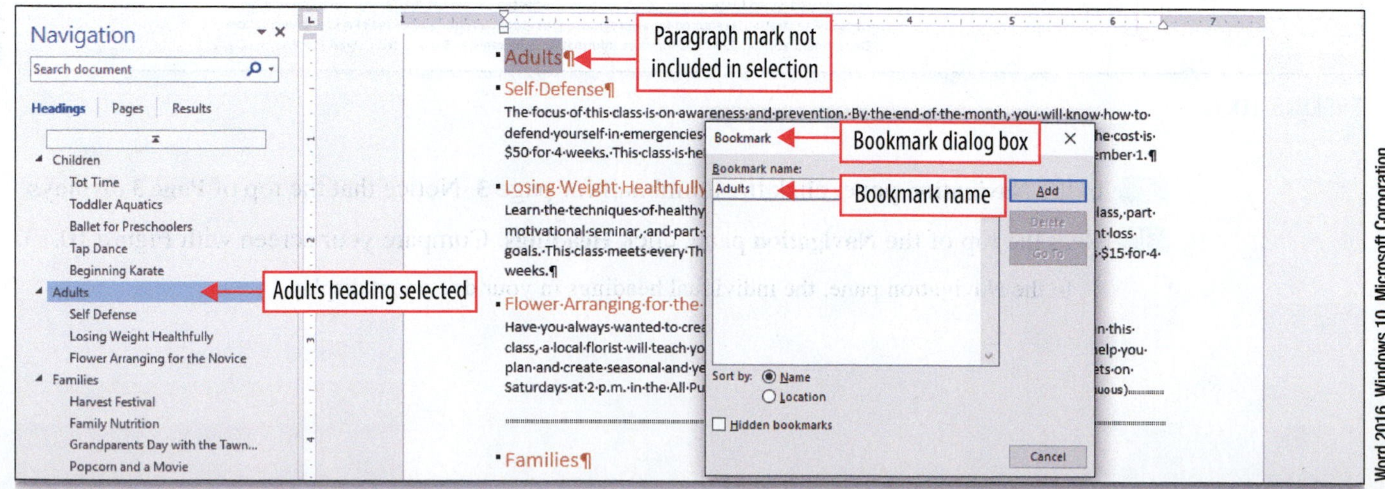

FIGURE 10.14

3 Click **Add**.

4 In the **Navigation** pane, click the heading **Children**. In the document, select the text for the heading **Children** but do *not* select the following paragraph mark. In the **Links group**, click **Bookmark**. In the **Bookmark** dialog box, in the **Bookmark name** box, type **Children** and then click **Add**.

5 Use the same selection technique and then insert bookmarks for the *Families* heading and the *Teens* heading, using the **Bookmark name Families** and **Teens** respectively.

When bookmarks are added to a document, by default they are listed in alphabetical order by name.

6 In the document, select the heading text **Senior Citizens**. In the **Links group**, click **Bookmark**. In the **Bookmark** dialog box, in the **Bookmark name** box, type **Senior_Citizens** and then click **Add**.

Bookmark names cannot include spaces; however, you can insert an underscore between the two words in a bookmark name.

7 Press Ctrl + Home. In the **Navigation** pane, click the **Search document arrow**, and then click **Go To**.

ANOTHER WAY On the Home tab, in the Editing group, click the Find button arrow, and then click Go To.

8 In the **Find and Replace** dialog box, with the **Go To tab** selected, in the **Go to what** box, scroll as necessary and then click **Bookmark**. Click the **Enter bookmark name arrow**, and then compare your screen with Figure 10.15.

All five bookmarks display in alphabetical order.

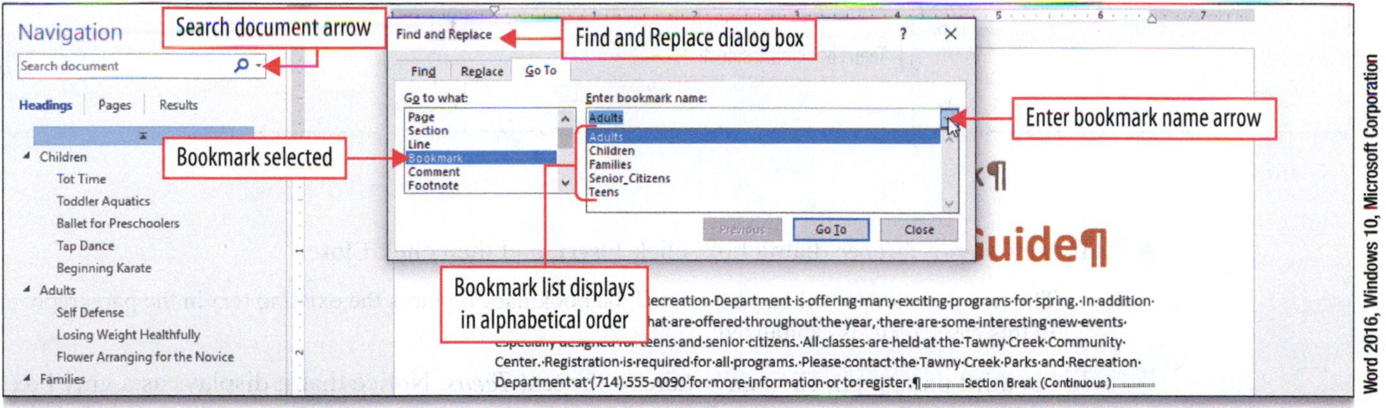

FIGURE 10.15

9 From the list, click **Teens**, and then click **Go To**. **Close** the **Find and Replace** dialog box, and then **Close** the **Navigation** pane.

The section of the document that begins with the bookmark *Teens* displays and the *Teens* heading is selected.

10 **Save** your changes.

More Knowledge **Defining a Bookmark for a Range of Pages**

To define a bookmark for a range of pages—or paragraphs—select the paragraphs you want to include, and then on the Insert tab, in the Links group, click Bookmark. In the Bookmark dialog box, type a name for the bookmark, and then click Add.

Activity 10.07 | Creating Cross-References

A ***cross-reference*** is a text link to an item that displays in another location in the document, such as a heading, a caption of a figure, or a footnote. Cross-references function as internal hyperlinks that enable you to move quickly to specific locations in a document.

1 Press Ctrl + Home. In the paragraph below the document subtitle, in the second sentence, select the text **teens**, being careful not to select any spaces.

When creating a cross-reference, either select text or place the insertion point where you want the cross-reference to display in your document. In this case, you want the cross-reference to display instead of the word *teens*.

2 On the **Insert tab**, in the **Links group**, click **Cross-reference**. In the **Cross-reference** dialog box, click the **Reference type arrow**, and then click **Bookmark**. If necessary, click the Insert reference to arrow to display Bookmark text, and select the Insert as hyperlink check box.

ANOTHER WAY On the References tab, in the Captions group, click Cross-reference.

3 Under **For which bookmark**, click **Teens**, and then compare your screen with Figure 10.16.

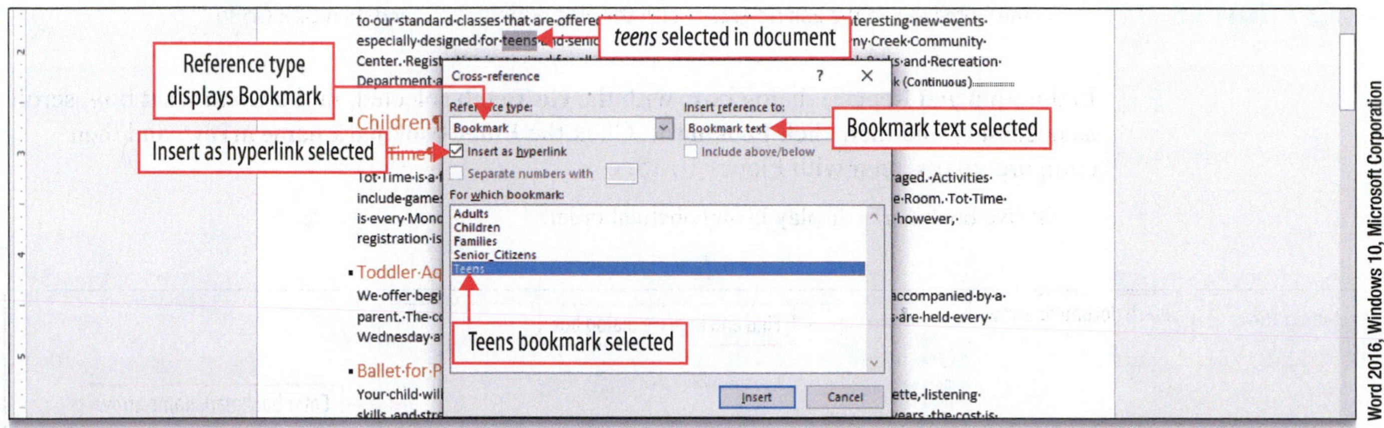

FIGURE 10.16

4 In the **Cross-reference** dialog box, click **Insert**, and then click **Close**.

The text you selected when you created the bookmark replaces the existing text in the paragraph. In this case, *Teens* is capitalized.

5 In the third paragraph, click anywhere in the text *Teens*. Notice that it displays as a gray box representing a field—a cross-reference. Double-click to select the entire field *Teens*. On the mini toolbar, click **Bold** B.

6 In the same sentence, select the text **senior citizens**. On the **Insert tab**, in the **Links group**, click **Cross-reference**.

7 In the **Cross-reference** dialog box, if necessary, click the Reference type arrow, and then click Bookmark. Be sure the **Insert reference to** box displays **Bookmark text**, and the **Insert as hyperlink** check box is selected. Under **For which bookmark**, click **Senior_Citizens**. Click **Insert**, and then click **Close**.

The formatting of the inserted bookmark text matches the rest of the paragraph, except the underscore is replaced with a space.

8 Select the **Senior Citizens** cross-reference text. On the mini toolbar, click **Bold** [B], and then deselect the text.

9 Point to the **Teens** cross-reference. Compare your screen with Figure 10.17.

A ScreenTip displays, indicating how to activate the hyperlink.

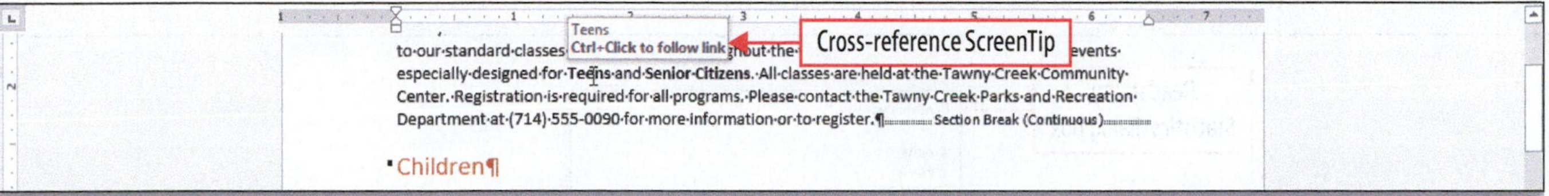

FIGURE 10.17

Word 2016, Windows 10, Microsoft Corporation

10 Hold down [Ctrl], and when the pointer displays, click **Teens**.

The Teens section of the document displays at the bookmark location.

11 Press [Ctrl] + [Home]. **Save** your changes.

Activity 10.08 | Reviewing Word Count and Readability Statistics

The ***word count*** of a document indicates the number of words, paragraphs, pages, and characters in a document. If the document will be distributed to a group of people, you may want to determine the ease of readability based on the average number of syllables per word and words per sentence by viewing the ***readability statistics***. Readability Statistics is a Spelling and Grammar tool that analyzes a document and determines the reading level of the text.

1 On the **Review tab**, in the **Proofing group**, click **Word Count**. Compare your screen with Figure 10.18.

The Word Count dialog box indicates how many words, paragraphs, pages, and characters are contained in the document. In addition, the word count displays on the status bar in Word.

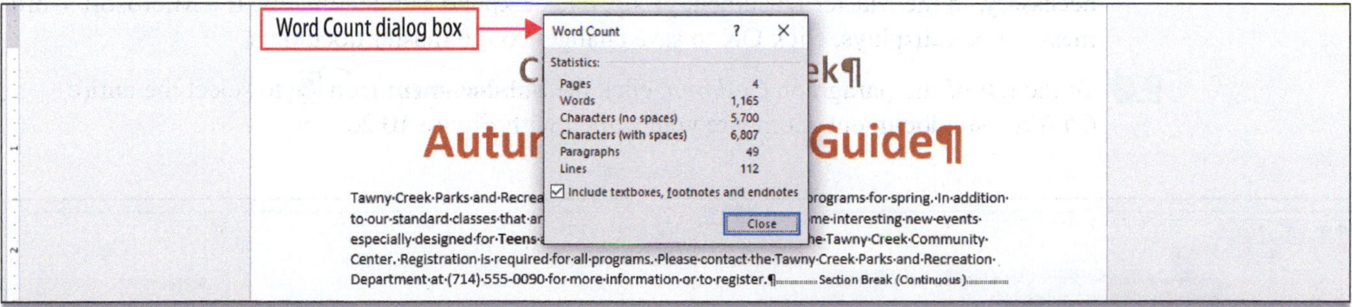

FIGURE 10.18

Word 2016, Windows 10, Microsoft Corporation

2 Click **Close** to close the **Word Count** dialog box.

3 Click the **File tab**, and then click **Options**. In the **Word Options** dialog box, click **Proofing**. Under **When correcting spelling and grammar in Word**, select the **Show readability statistics** check box to turn on the display of readability statistics. Click **OK**.

4 On the **Review tab**, in the **Proofing group**, click **Spelling & Grammar**.

You must complete a spelling and grammar check to review the readability statistics.

5 If the Grammar pane displays, ignore all errors. Compare your screen with Figure 10.19.

In the Readability Statistics dialog box, under Readability, two readability ratings display. The Flesch Reading Ease score is based on a 100-point scale—the higher the score, the easier it is for the reader to understand the document. The Flesch-Kincaid Grade Level score displays the reading level based on U.S. grade levels. For example, 8.0 indicates that the document can be comprehended by a student reading at an eighth grade level.

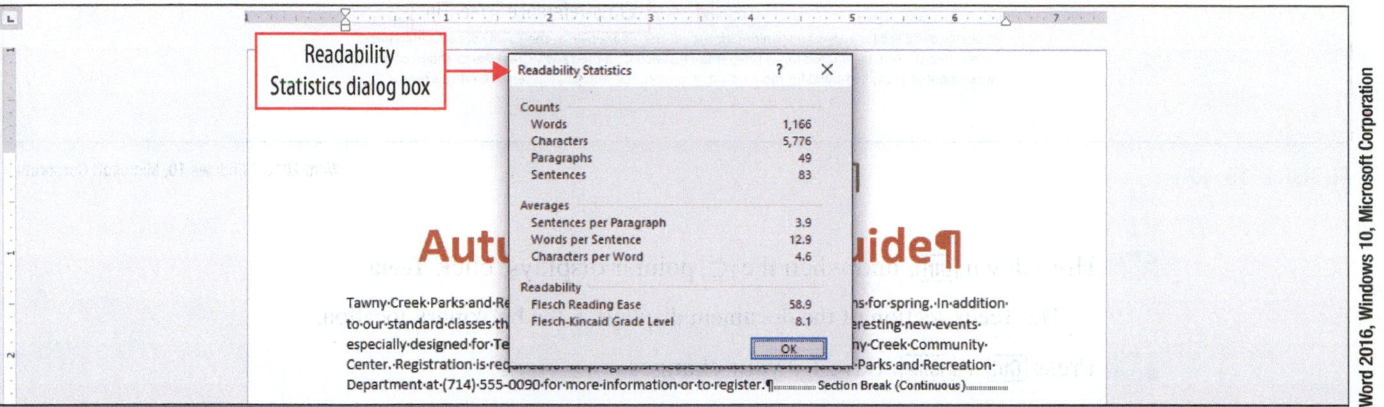

FIGURE 10.19

6 Click **OK** to close the **Readability Statistics** dialog box. Click the **File tab**, and then click **Options**. In the **Word Options** dialog box, click **Proofing**. Under **When correcting spelling and grammar in Word**, clear the **Show readability statistics** check box. Click **OK**.

Activity 10.09 | Finalizing a Master Document

To prepare a master document for distribution, you should remove the links to the subdocuments.

1 If necessary, press Ctrl + Home. On the **View tab**, in the **Views group**, click **Outline**. On the **Outlining tab**, in the **Master Document group**, click **Show Document** to toggle it on. If necessary, in the Master Document group, click Expand Subdocuments. If a Microsoft Word message box displays, click OK to save changes to the master document.

2 To the left of the paragraph *Children*, click the **Subdocument** icon to select the entire *Children* subdocument. Compare your screen with Figure 10.20.

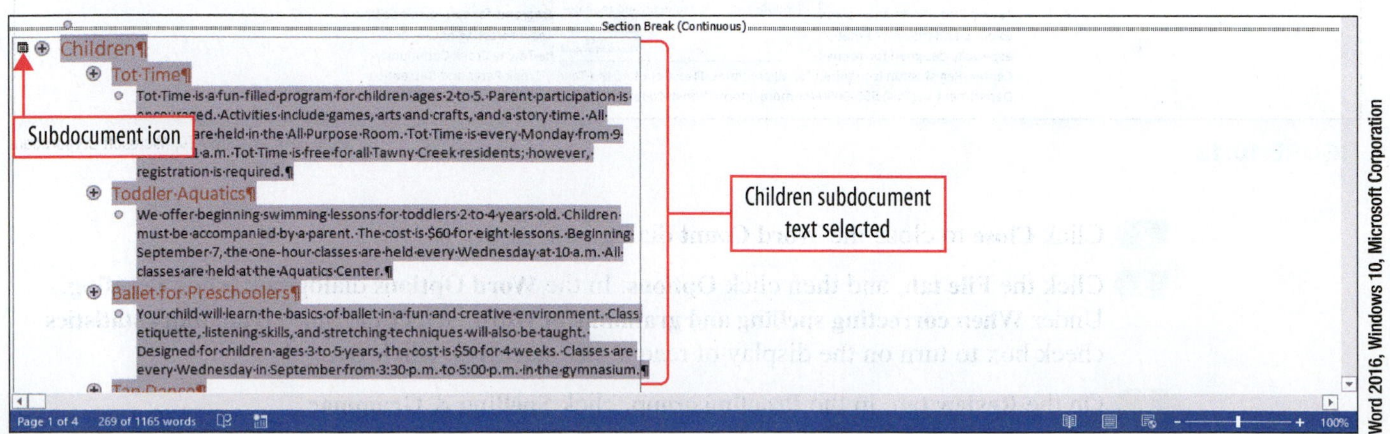

FIGURE 10.20

3 With the *Children* subdocument selected, in the **Master Document group**, click **Unlink**.

The Children paragraph and all subordinate paragraphs are no longer linked to a subdocument. The Subdocument icon and gray border surrounding the text no longer display.

4 Scroll to display the **Adults** heading, and then click the **Subdocument** icon to select the entire *Adults* subdocument. In the **Master Document group**, click **Unlink**.

5 In a similar manner, **Unlink** the subdocuments **Families, Senior Citizens**, and **Teens**.

6 Above the paragraph *Children*, click to position the insertion point to the right of the first bullet for *Section Break (Continuous)*. Compare your screen with Figure 10.21.

Tawny·Creek·Parks·and·Recreation·Department·is·offering·many·exciting·programs·for· spring.·In·addition·to·our·standard·classes·that·are·offered·throughout·the·year,·there· are·some·interesting·new·events·especially·designed·for·**Teens**·and·**Senior·Citizens**.·All· classes·are·held·at·the·Tawny·Creek·Community·Center.·Registration·is·required·for·all· programs.·Please·contact·the·Tawny·Creek·Parks·and·Recreation·Department·at·(714)· 555-0090·fo[...]·register.¶

Insertion point

Section Break (Continuous)

Continuous section break

Children¶

Tot·Time¶

Tot·Time·is·a·fun-filled·program·for·children·ages·2·to·5.·Parent·participation·is· encouraged.·Activities·include·games,·arts·and·crafts,·and·a·story·time.·All· sessions·are·held·in·the·All-Purpose·Room.·Tot·Time·is·every·Monday·from·9· a.m.·to·11·a.m.·Tot·Time·is·free·for·all·Tawny·Creek·residents;·however,·

FIGURE 10.21 Word 2016, Windows 10, Microsoft Corporation

7 Press Delete to remove the **Section Break (Continuous)**. In a similar manner, delete all instances of **Section Break (Continuous)** and **Section Break (Next Page)**.

The section breaks are no longer needed because the subdocuments are no longer defined.

8 On the **Outlining tab**, in the **Close group**, click **Close Outline View**.

9 Press Ctrl + Home, and then **Save** your changes.

More Knowledge **Opening a Master Document**

If you open a master document, the subdocuments are collapsed and display as hyperlinks. To view the entire document, on the View tab, in the Views group, click Outline. On the Outlining tab, click the Expand Subdocuments button.

Objective 4 Create and Modify Headers and Footers

GO! Learn How
Video W10-4

You can display different headers and footers on the first page, odd pages, and even pages in a document by inserting section breaks. Recall that sections are portions of a document that can be formatted differently.

Activity 10.10 | Inserting and Formatting Odd and Even Section Breaks

2.3.3

1 On **Page 1**, position the insertion point to the left of the paragraph *Children*. On the **Layout tab**, in the **Page Setup group**, click **Breaks**, and then under **Section Breaks**, click **Even Page**.

The paragraph *Children* displays at the top of Page 2.

2 Press Ctrl + Home, and then compare your screen with Figure 10.22.

An ***Even Page section break*** is inserted at the end of Page 1. An Even Page section break is a formatting mark that indicates the beginning of a new section on the next even-numbered page.

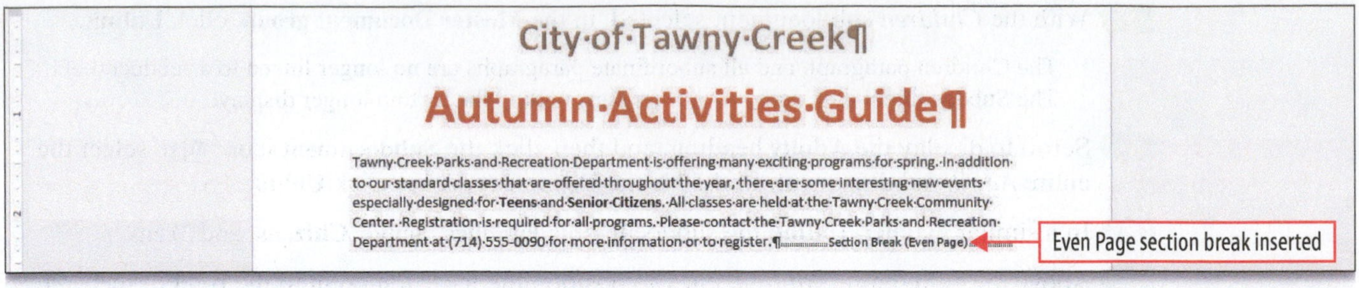

City·of·Tawny·Creek¶

Autumn·Activities·Guide¶

Tawny·Creek·Parks·and·Recreation·Department·is·offering·many·exciting·programs·for·spring.·In·addition·to·our·standard·classes·that·are·offered·throughout·the·year,·there·are·some·interesting·new·events·especially·designed·for·**Teens**·and·**Senior·Citizens**.·All·classes·are·held·at·the·Tawny·Creek·Community·Center.·Registration·is·required·for·all·programs.·Please·contact·the·Tawny·Creek·Parks·and·Recreation·Department·at·(714)·555-0090·for·more·information·or·to·register.¶ Section Break (Even Page)

Even Page section break inserted

FIGURE 10.22

Word 2016, Windows 10, Microsoft Corporation

3 On **Page 2**, under the *Beginning Karate* paragraph, click to position the insertion at the end of the paragraph that begins with *In karate*. On the **Layout tab**, in the **Page Setup group**, click **Breaks**, and then under **Section Breaks**, click **Odd Page**. If a blank paragraph displays at the top of page 3, delete it.

The paragraph *Adults* displays at the top of Page 3. An ***Odd Page section break*** is inserted on Page 2. An Odd Page section break is a formatting mark that indicates the beginning of a new section on the next odd-numbered page.

4 Using the same technique, insert an **Even Page** section break at the end of the paragraph below *Flower Arranging for the Novice* and *Walking for Fun and Fitness*. Insert an **Odd Page** section break at the end of the paragraph below *Popcorn and a Movie*. Scroll through your document and delete any blank paragraphs that display at the top of each page.

5 On **Page 2**, right-click in the footer area, and then click **Edit Footer**. On the **Header & Footer Tools Design tab**, in the **Options group**, select the **Different Odd & Even Pages** check box. Scroll to display the bottom of **Page 2** and the top of **Page 3**. Compare your screen with Figure 10.23.

At the bottom of Page 2, the text *Even Page Footer – Section 2* displays on the footer tab. At the top of Page 3, the text *Odd Page Header – Section 3* displays on the header tab. By inserting section breaks and selecting different formatting options, you can insert different text or objects in the various sections of the document.

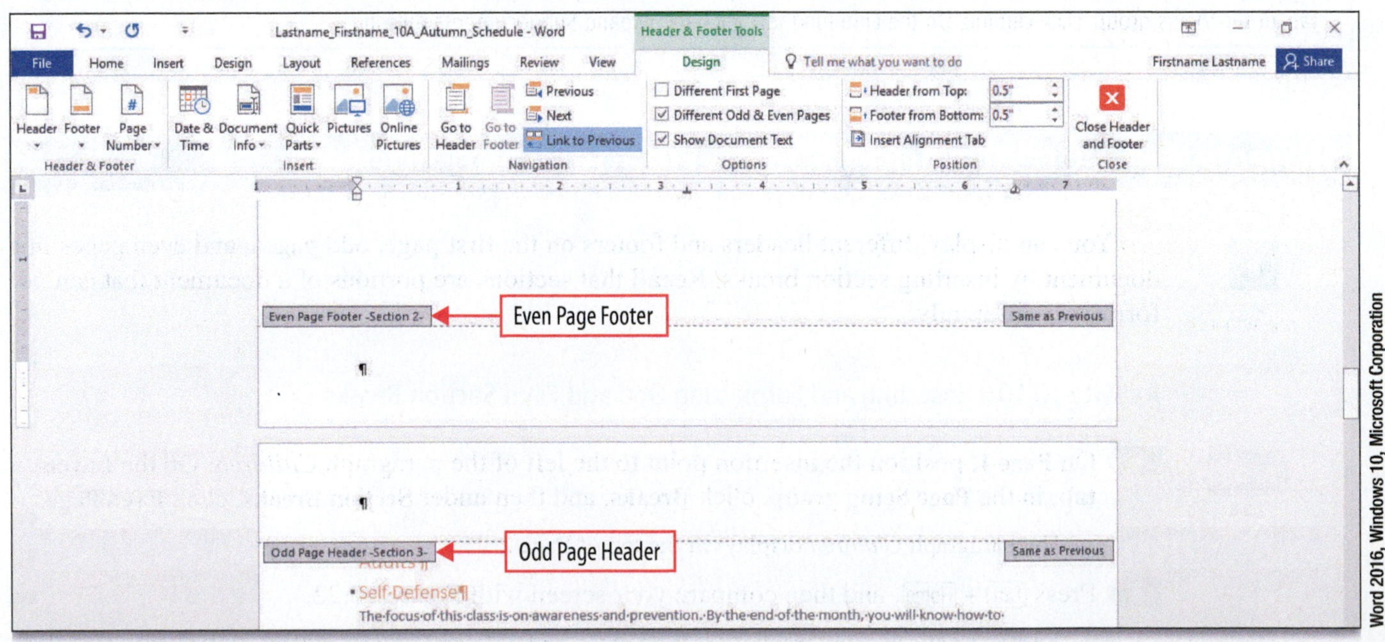

FIGURE 10.23

Word 2016, Windows 10, Microsoft Corporation

6 With the insertion point in the footer **Even Page Footer – Section 2**, press Tab two times, and then type **City of Tawny Creek**

7 On the **Header & Footer Tools Design tab**, in the **Navigation group**, click **Next**. Notice that the insertion point displays in the footer *Odd Page Footer – Section 3*.

8 With the insertion point in the *Odd Page Footer – Section* 3 footer, insert the **File Name**. In the **Navigation group**, click **Next**. Compare your screen with Figure 10.24.

The right-aligned text *City of Tawny Creek* displays. Because this is an even page footer, the file name does not display.

FIGURE 10.24

Word 2016, Windows 10, Microsoft Corporation

9 In the **Navigation group**, click **Previous** three times to display the footer **Odd Page Footer – Section 1**. In the **Close group**, click **Close Header and Footer**. **Save** your changes.

Activity 10.11 | Inserting a Cover Page

4.2.3

A ***cover page*** is the first page of a document that provides introductory information—for example, the title, the author, a brief description, or a date.

1 Press Ctrl + Home. Click the **Insert tab**, and then in the **Pages group**, click **Cover Page** to display the **Cover Page** gallery. Compare your screen with Figure 10.25.

The Cover Page gallery contains predesigned cover page styles.

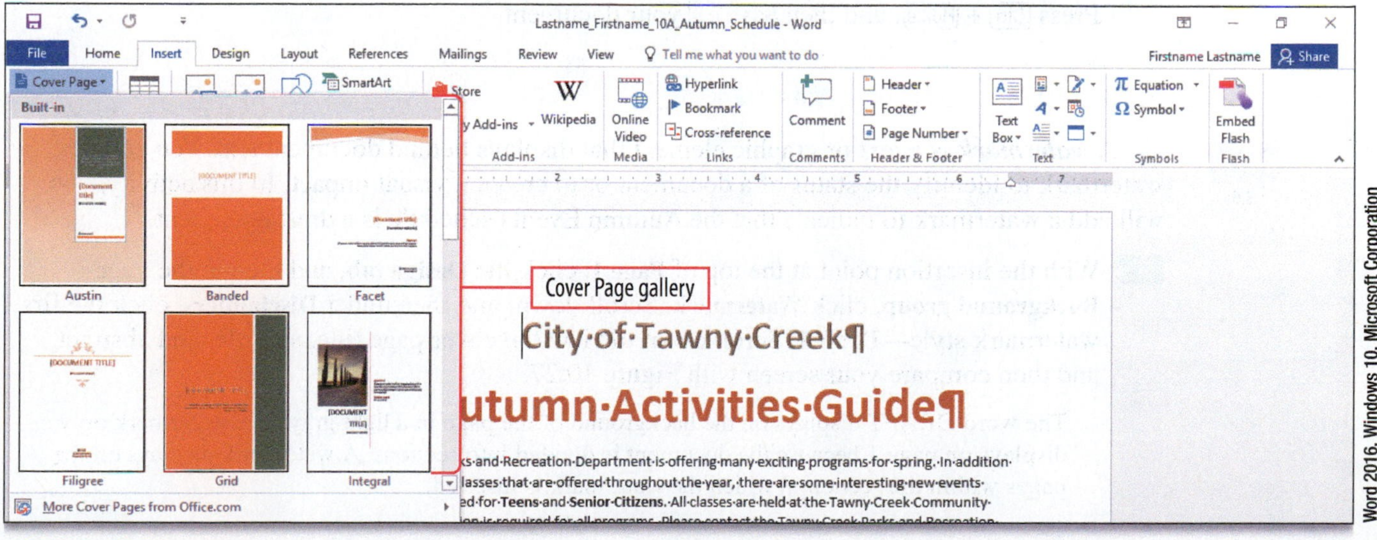

FIGURE 10.25

Word 2016, Windows 10, Microsoft Corporation

2 In the **Cover Page** gallery, in the first row, click the third style—**Facet**.

The cover page, which contains text placeholders, is inserted on a new first page of the document.

3 If necessary, scroll down and then click in the **Document title** placeholder. Type **autumn events** and then below the title, click in the **Document subtitle** placeholder. Type **Tawny Creek** and then click in the **Abstract** placeholder. Type **Draft for autumn activities**

4 Scroll to view the bottom of the page, and then click in the **Email address placeholder** to display the text box enclosing the Author and Email placeholders. Click the text box dashed border, and then press Delete to delete the textbox. Compare your screen with Figure 10.26.

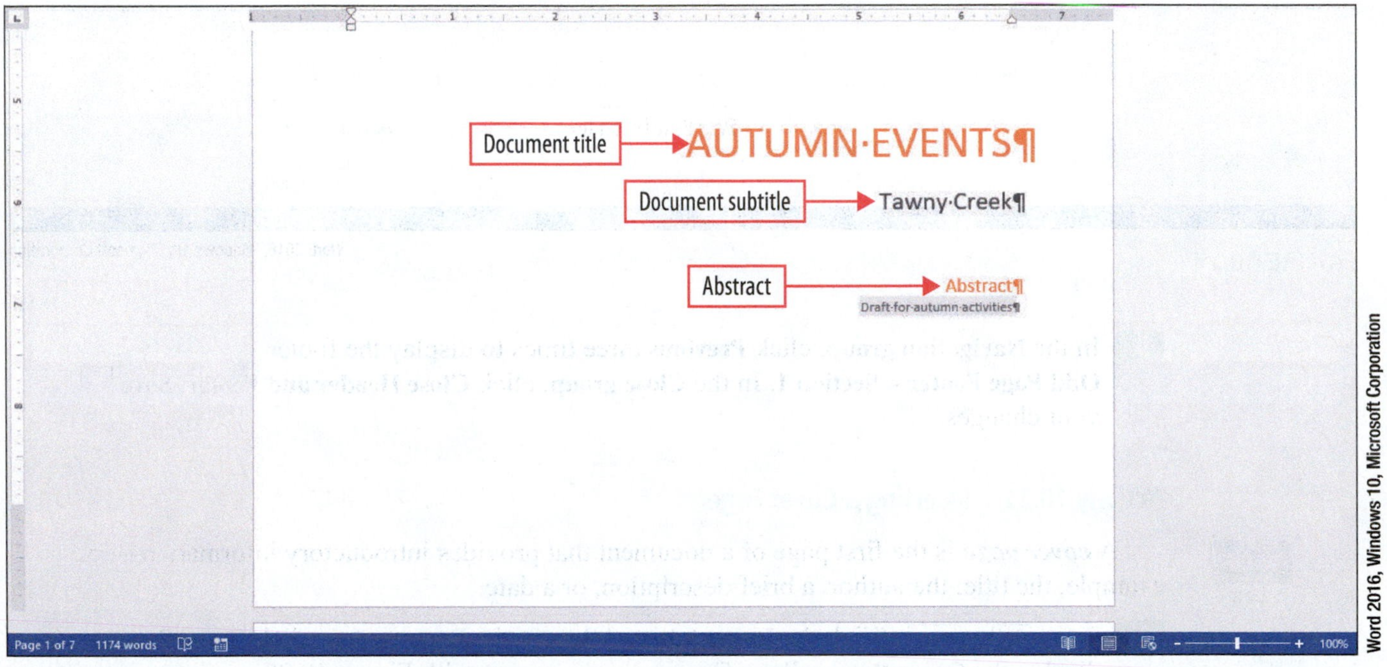

FIGURE 10.26

5 Press Ctrl + Home, and then **Save** your document.

Activity 10.12 | Inserting a Watermark

1.3.6

A ***watermark*** is a text or graphic element that displays behind document text. You add a watermark to identify the status of a document or to create a visual impact. In this activity, you will add a watermark to indicate that the Autumn Events schedule is a draft document.

1 With the insertion point at the top of **Page 1**, click the **Design tab**, and then in the **Page Background group**, click **Watermark**. Scroll down, and then under **Disclaimers**, click the first watermark style—**Draft 1**. Scroll down to view the cover page title, subtitle, and abstract, and then compare your screen with Figure 10.27.

The word DRAFT displays on the background of the page in a light gray. The watermark only displays on page 1 because the document is divided into sections. A watermark displays on the pages within the section in which the watermark is inserted.

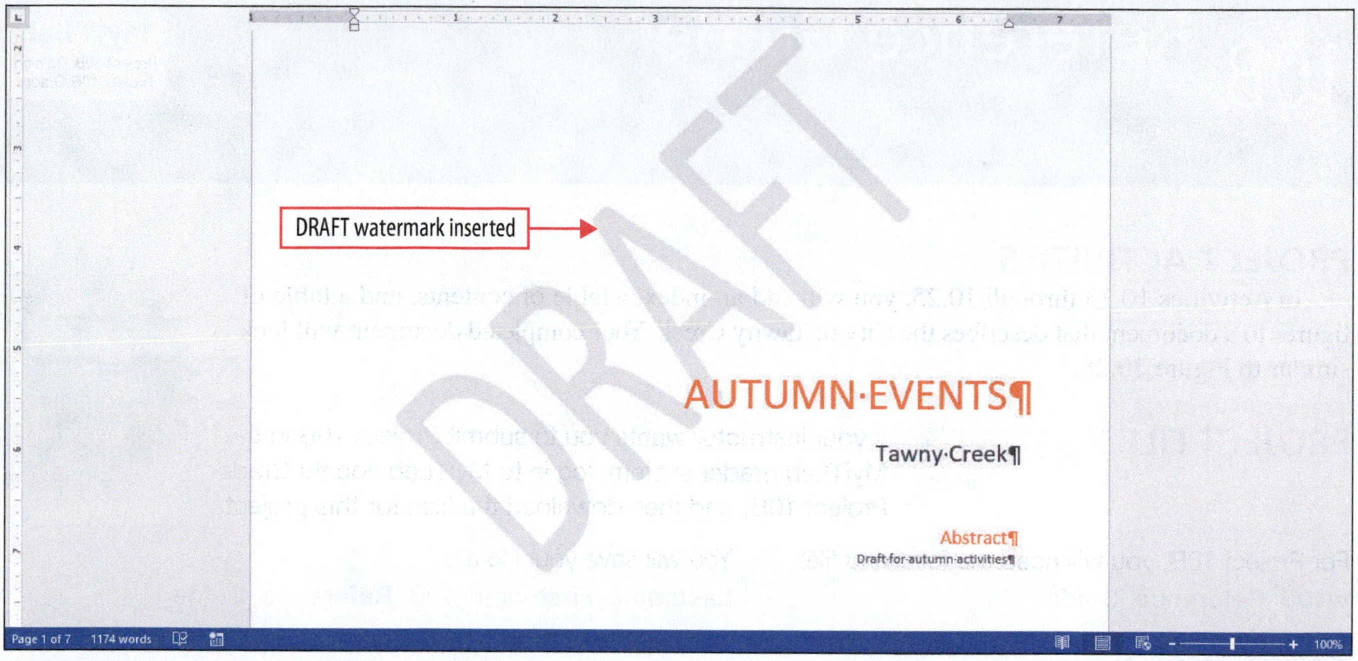

FIGURE 10.27

More Knowledge — Inserting a Picture as a Watermark

To insert a picture as a watermark, on the Design tab, in the Page Background group, click Watermark. In the Watermark gallery, click Custom Watermark. In the Printed Watermark dialog box, select Picture watermark, and then click Select Picture. In the Insert Pictures dialog box, navigate to the location of the image, and then click Insert. Change the Scale and Washout options as desired, and then click OK.

2 Click the **File tab**, and then **Show All Properties**.

The Title and Subtitle placeholders in the cover page are linked to the Title and Subject document properties respectively. The text *autumn events* may display in the Title box and the text *Tawny Creek* may display in the Subject box.

3 In the **Tags** box, type **autumn schedule** and then in the **Subject** box, if necessary, select any existing text, and then type your course name and section number. Edit the author name to display your name. **Save** your document.

4 **Save** and then **Close** your document. If directed by your instructor to do so, submit your paper printout, your electronic image of your document that looks like a printed document, or your original Word file.

END | You have completed Project 10A

PROJECT 10B

Reference Guide

MyITLab

Project 10B Training
Project 10B Grader

PROJECT ACTIVITIES

In Activities 10.13 through 10.25, you will add an index, a table of contents, and a table of figures to a document that describes the City of Tawny Creek. Your completed document will look similar to Figure 10.28.

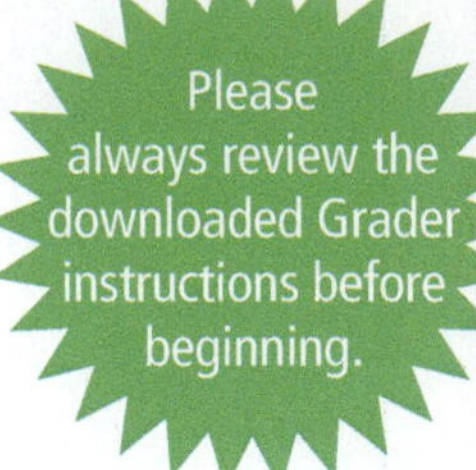
Please
always review the
downloaded Grader
instructions before
beginning.

PROJECT FILES

MyITLab
grader

If your instructor wants you to submit Project 10B in the MyITLab grader system, log in to MyITLab, locate Grader Project 10B, and then download the files for this project.

For Project 10B, you will need the following file:
w10B_Reference_Guide

You will save your file as:
Lastname_Firstname_10B_Reference_Guide

PROJECT RESULTS

GO! Walk Thru Project 10B

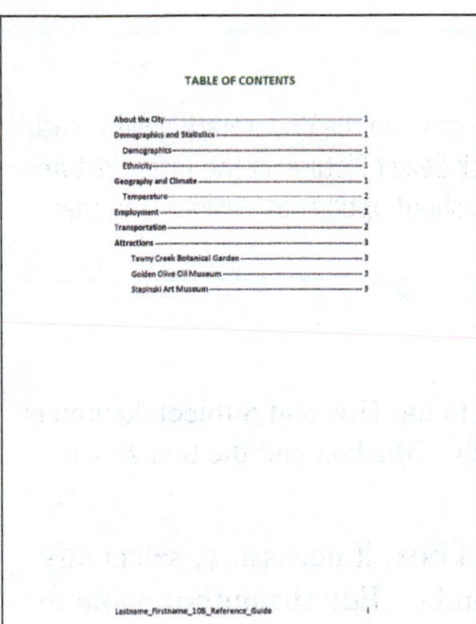

TABLE OF CONTENTS

Lastname_Firstname_10B_Reference_Guide

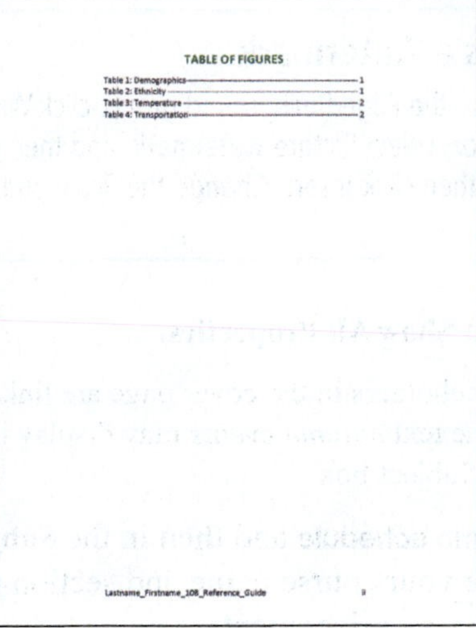

TABLE OF FIGURES

Lastname_Firstname_10B_Reference_Guide

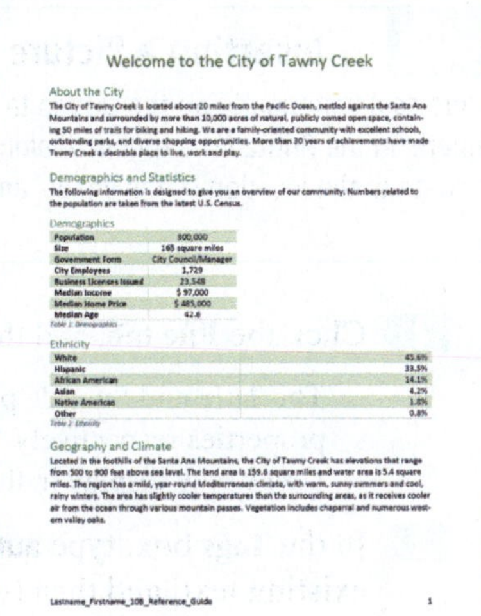

Welcome to the City of Tawny Creek

About the City

Demographics and Statistics

Demographics

Ethnicity

Geography and Climate

Lastname_Firstname_10B_Reference_Guide 1

Word 2016, Windows 10, Microsoft Corporation

FIGURE 10.28 Project 10B Reference Guide

Objective 5 Create an Index

10 WORD

GO! Learn How Video W10-5

An ***index*** is a compilation of topics, names, and terms accompanied by page numbers that displays at the end of a document. Each entry indicates where the ***index entry*** can be found. An index entry is a word or phrase that is listed in the index. To create an entry, you mark the words you want to include in the index as an index entry.

Activity 10.13 | Inserting Page Numbers

1 Start Word. From your student files, open the file **w10B_Reference_Guide**. Save the file in your **Word Chapter 10** folder as **Lastname_Firstname_10B_Reference_Guide** If necessary, display the rulers and formatting marks. **Ignore All** spelling errors.

2 Scroll to the bottom of **Page 1**, right-click in the footer area, and then click **Edit Footer**. Insert the file name in the footer. In the footer area, with the insertion point to the right of the file name, press Tab two times. On the **Header & Footer Tools Design tab**, in the **Header & Footer group**, click **Page Number**, and then point to **Current Position** to display the **Page Number** gallery. Compare your screen with Figure 10.29.

The page numbers in the document are used as a reference in the index. The Page Number gallery provides built-in formats for inserting page number.

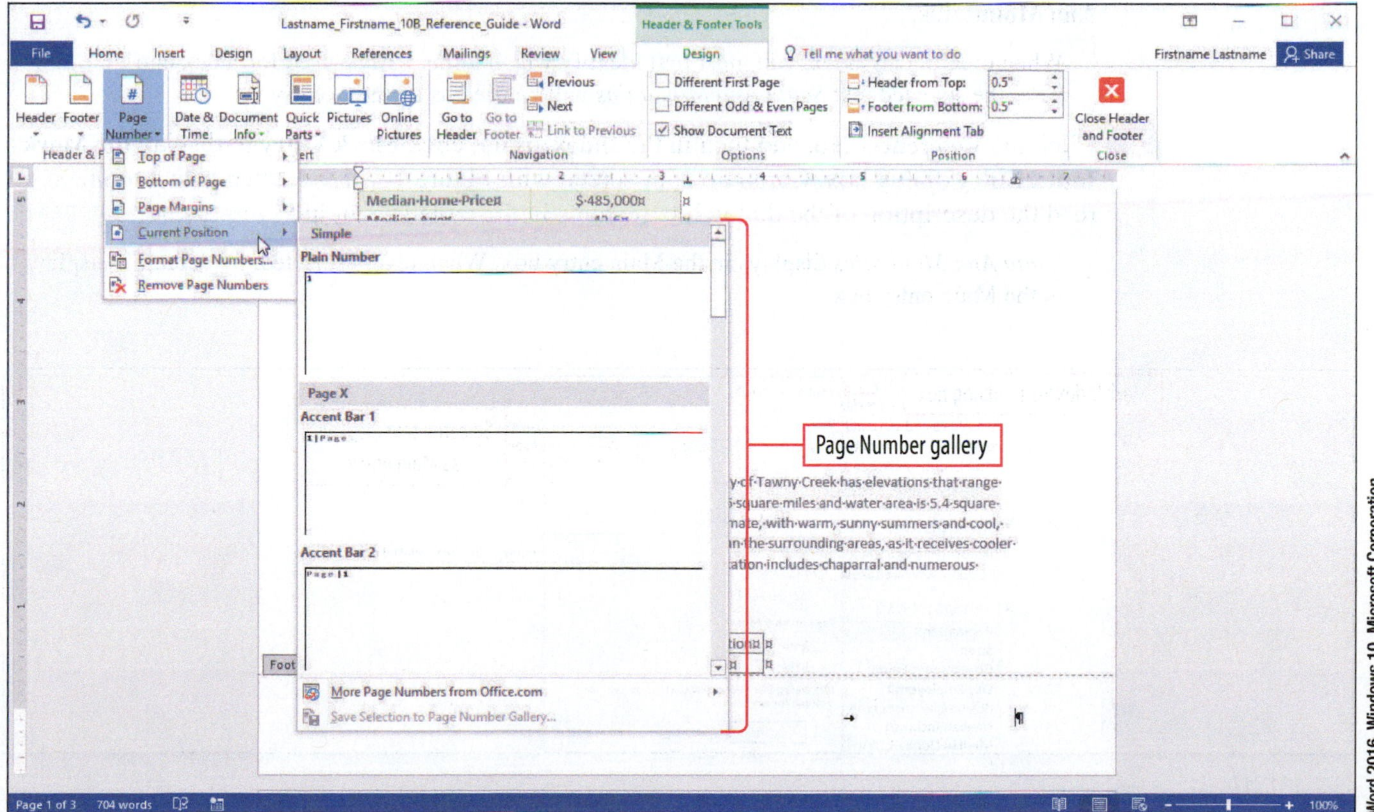

FIGURE 10.29

3 In the **Page Number** gallery, under **Simple**, click the first style—**Plain Number**. Notice that the page number *1* is inserted in the footer at the right margin. In the **Close group**, click **Close Header and Footer**.

4 On **Page 1**, below *Temperature*, click in the first cell of the table. On the **Table Tools Design tab**, in the **Table Styles group**, click **More** under **Grid Tables**, in the fourth row, click the second style—**Grid Table 4 – Accent 1**. Compare your screen with Figure 10.30.

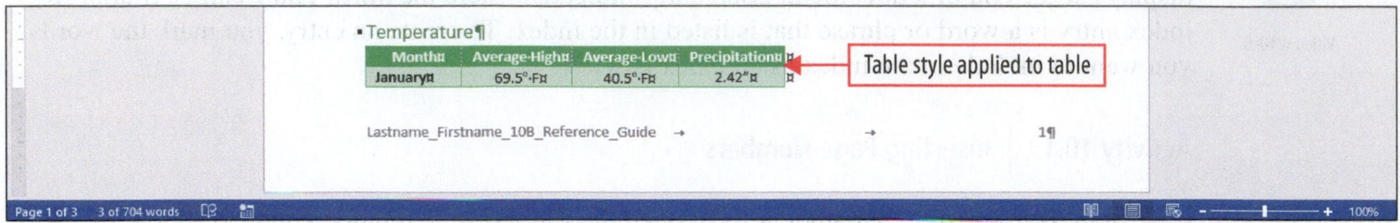

Word 2016, Windows 10, Microsoft Corporation

FIGURE 10.30

5 Scroll to the bottom of **Page 2**, and then apply the same formatting to the table in the *Transportation* section.

6 **Save** your changes.

Activity 10.14 | Marking Index Main Entries

MOS 3.1.1

An index ***main entry*** is a word, phrase, or selected text used to identify the index entry.

1 Press Ctrl + Home. In the paragraph below the heading *About the City*, select the text **Santa Ana Mountains**.

When creating an index, you must first identify which terms will be used for index entries—in this case, the selected text *Santa Ana Mountains* will be used as an index entry.

2 Click the **References tab**, and then in the **Index group**, click **Mark Entry** to display the **Mark Index Entry** dialog box. Compare your screen with Figure 10.31, and then take a moment to read the description of the dialog box features in the table shown in Figure 10.32.

Santa Ana Mountains displays in the Main entry box. When text is selected, by default it displays in the Main entry box.

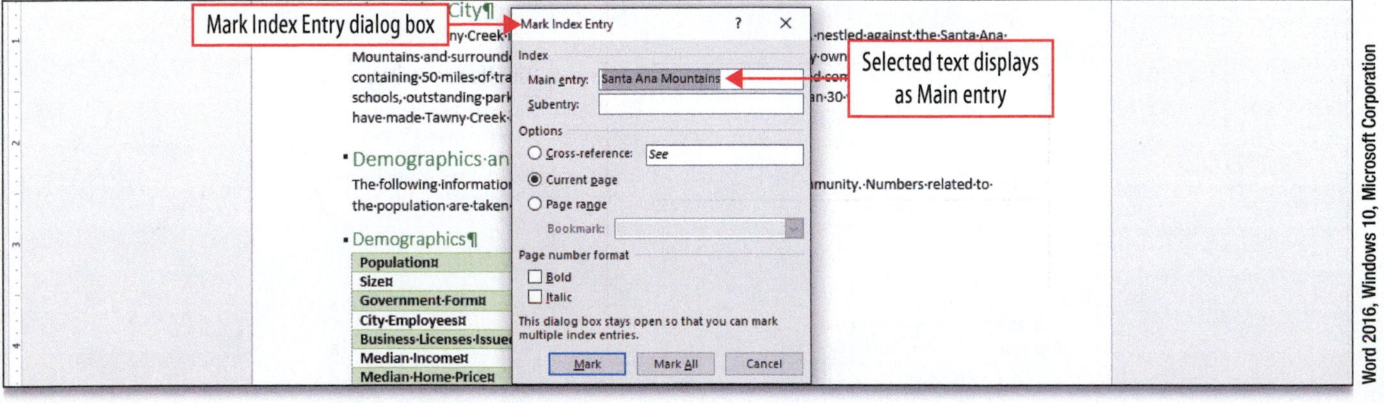

Word 2016, Windows 10, Microsoft Corporation

FIGURE 10.31

MARK INDEX ENTRY DIALOG BOX FEATURES	
FEATURE	**DESCRIPTION**
Main entry	The word, phrases, or selected text that will be used to identify the index entry.
Subentry	A more specific term that refers to the main entry. For example, the index entry *Transportation* could have subentries for *Automobiles*, *Buses*, and *Trains*.
Cross-reference	An entry that refers the reader to another topic that provides more information. For example, the main entry *England* might be listed in the index as *See United Kingdom*.
Current page	The index entry is marked with the current page number.
Page range	The index entry is marked with a range of page numbers.
Page number format	These options control how the page number will display in the index.
Mark	Marks only the selected text.
Mark All	Marks all occurrences of the selected text in the document.

FIGURE 10.32

3 In the **Mark Index Entry** dialog box, click **Mark All**, and then **Close** the **Mark Index Entry** dialog box. Notice that the index entry displays to the right of the selected text. Compare your screen with Figure 10.33.

After you mark text as an index entry, Word inserts an ***index entry field***, to the right of the selected text. An index entry field is code containing the identifier ***XE*** and the term to be used in the index. The code is formatted as ***hidden text***—nonprinting text. Because you clicked the Mark All button, the occurrence of *Santa Ana Mountains* at the bottom of Page 1 is also marked.

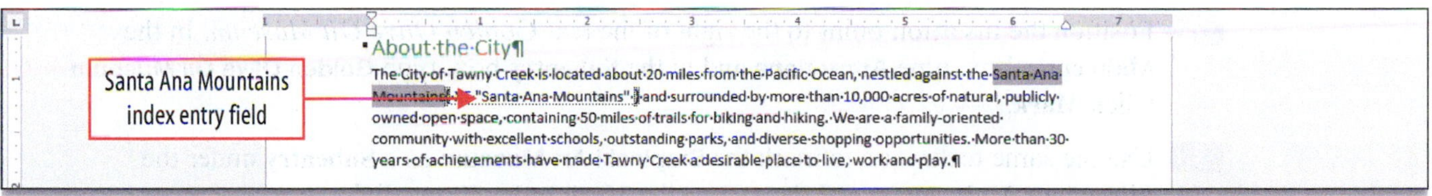

FIGURE 10.33

Word 2016, Windows 10, Microsoft Corporation

4 On **Page 1**, select the heading **Demographics and Statistics**. On the **References tab**, in the **Index group**, click **Mark Entry**. In the **Mark Index Entry** dialog box, with *Demographics and Statistics* displayed in the **Main entry** box, click **Mark**, but do not close the **Mark Index Entry** dialog box.

The text *Demographics and Statistics* is marked as an entry for the index.

5 Click in the document, and then select the paragraph *Geography and Climate*. If necessary, point to the **Mark Index Entry** dialog box title bar to display the pointer, and then drag the **Mark Index Entry** dialog box to the side of your screen. With the paragraph still selected, click in the **Main entry** box, and notice that *Geography and Climate* displays. Click **Mark**.

6 In a similar manner, **Mark** entries for the paragraphs *Employment*, *Transportation*, and *Attractions*. **Save** your document and leave the **Mark Index Entry** dialog box open for the next Activity.

Activity 10.15 | Marking Index Subentries and Using an AutoMark File

An index ***subentry*** is a more specific term that refers to the main entry. In this Activity, you will mark subentries for the Attractions main entry.

1. Below *Attractions*, locate the text *Tawny Creek Botanical Garden*, and then position the insertion point to the right of *Garden*. In the **Mark Index Entry** dialog box, click in the **Main entry** box. Type **Attractions** and then click in the **Subentry** box. Type **Tawny Creek Botanical Garden** and then click **Mark**. Compare your screen with Figure 10.34.

   The text *Tawny Creek Botanical Garden* is added as an index subentry under *Attractions*. The index entry field displays the main entry text, a colon, and the subentry text.

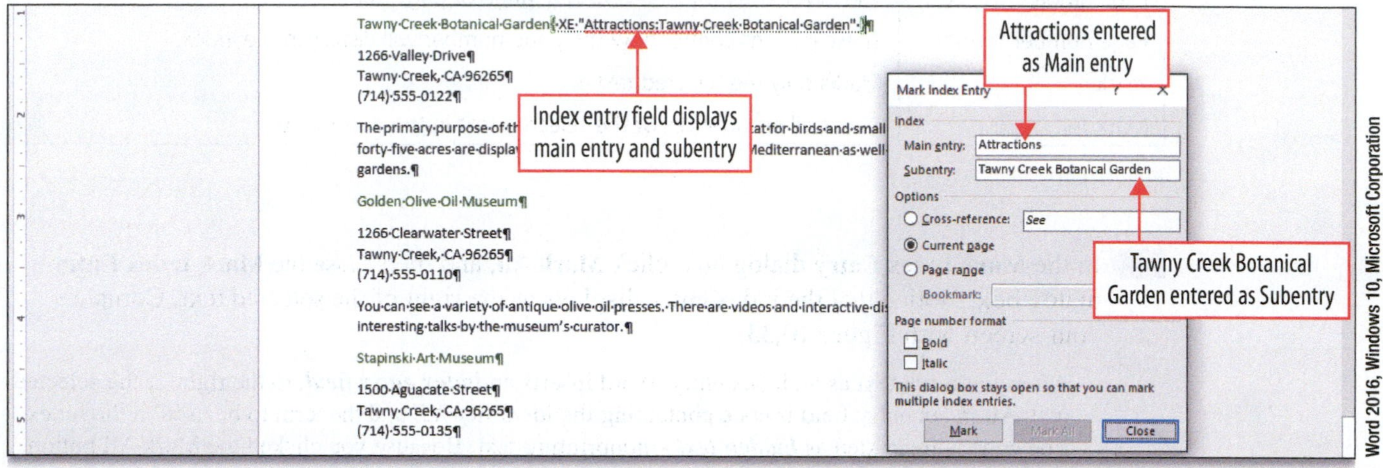

FIGURE 10.34

2. Position the insertion point to the right of the text *Golden Olive Oil Museum*. In the **Main entry** box, type **Attractions** and in the **Subentry** box, type **Golden Olive Oil Museum** Click **Mark**.

3. Use the same technique to mark the **Stapinski Art Museum** as a **Subentry** under the **Attractions Main entry**, and then **Close** the **Mark Index Entry** dialog box.

4. **Save** your changes.

5. In the **Index group**, click **Insert Index**. In the **Index** dialog box, click **AutoMark** to display the **Open Index AutoMark File** dialog box.

   If a document contains words that are frequently used as index entries, the words can be saved as an ***AutoMark file***. An AutoMark file contains a two-column table that is used to mark words that will be used as index entries. The first column lists the terms to be searched for in the document. The second column lists the corresponding entries. In the Open Index AutoMark File dialog box, you can select an AutoMark file to automatically insert index entries in a document.

6. In the **Open Index AutoMark** dialog box, click **Cancel**.

Activity 10.16 | Inserting an Index

3.1.2

After text or phrases have been marked as index entries, the next step is to insert the index. Generally, an index is inserted on a separate page at the end of a document.

1. Press Ctrl + End, and then press Ctrl + Enter to insert a manual page break.

2. With the insertion point at the top of the new page, type **INDEX** and then press Enter two times.

3 Select the *INDEX* paragraph you just typed. On the mini toolbar, change the **Font Size** to **16**, apply **Bold** [B], and then change the **Font Color** [A] to **Green, Accent 1, Darker 50%**—in the fifth column, the last color. Press Ctrl + E to center the text.

4 Position the insertion point in the last paragraph of the document. On the **References tab**, in the **Index group**, click **Insert Index** to display the **Index** dialog box.

5 In the **Index** dialog box, on the **Index tab**, click the **Formats arrow**, and then click **Classic**. Click the **Right align page numbers** check box. Compare your screen with Figure 10.35.

The Index dialog box allows you to select your own options, including predefined index formats, and then preview the selection. You can also create your own index format using a template.

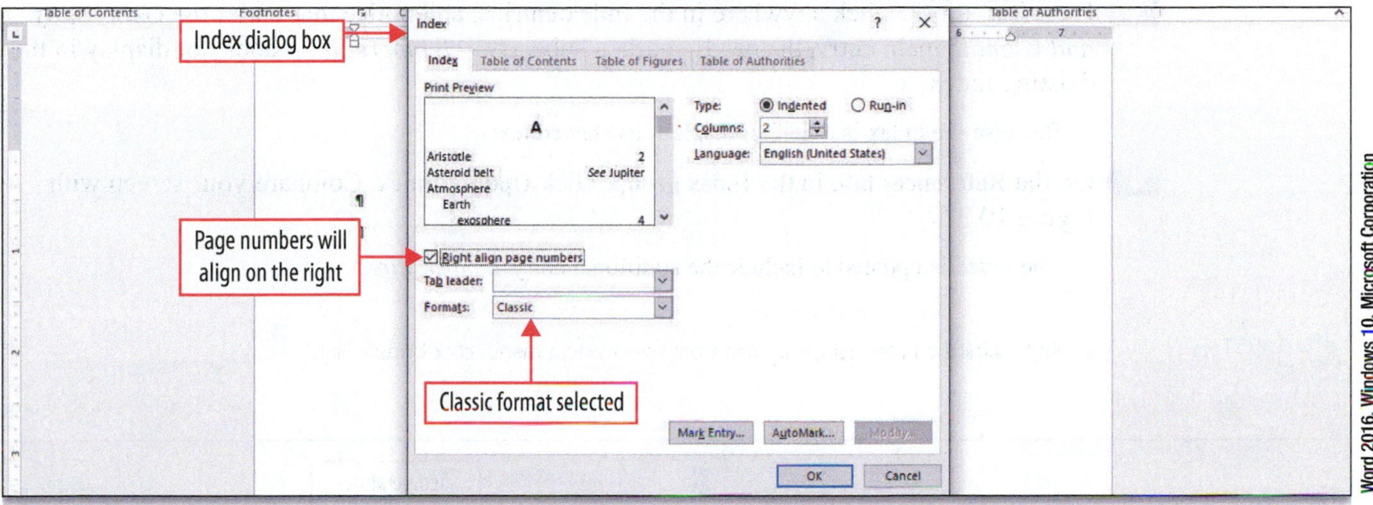

FIGURE 10.35

6 Click **OK**, and then compare your screen with Figure 10.36.

The index is inserted in a two-column format. Word distributes the text evenly between the two columns. The main entries display alphabetically and the marked subentries display under the *Attractions* main entry.

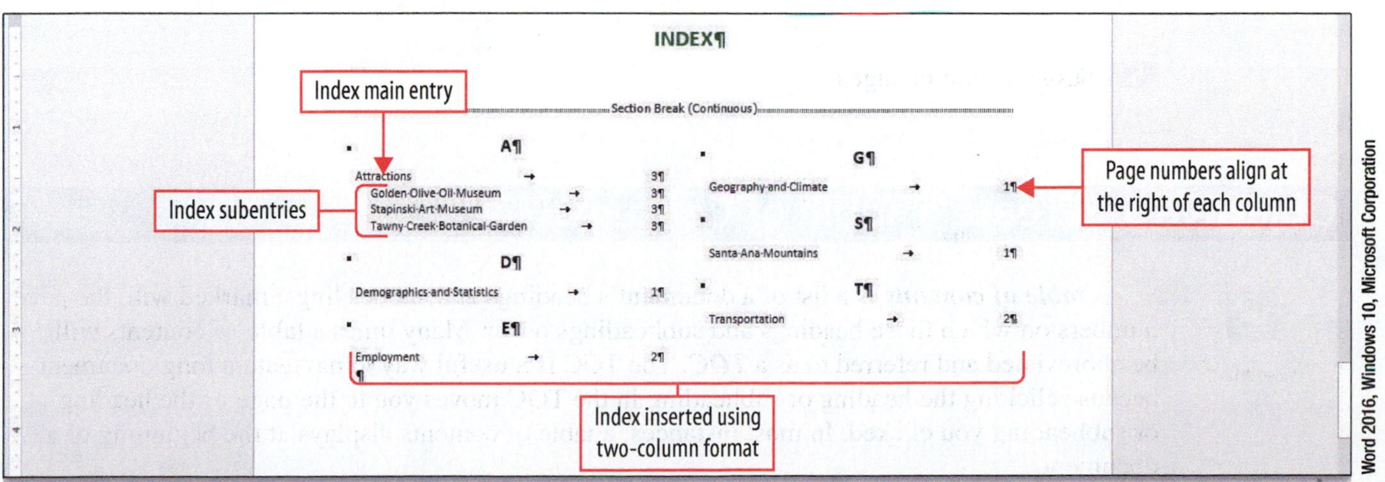

FIGURE 10.36

7 **Save** your changes.

Expert 3.1.3

Activity 10.17 | Updating an Index

After an index has been inserted into a document, the index can be updated if you want to include additional words in the index or if the page numbers in the document change.

1 Scroll to the bottom of **Page 1**, and position the insertion point to the right of *Temperature*.

2 On the **References tab**, in the **Index group**, click **Mark Entry**. In the **Mark Index Entry** dialog box, in the **Main entry** box, type **Geography and Climate** and then click in the **Subentry** box. Type **Temperature** and then click **Mark**. **Close** the **Mark Index Entry** dialog box.

3 Press Ctrl + End. Click anywhere in the index entries, and notice that under the *Geography and Climate* main entry, the newly marked subentry—*Temperature*—does not display in the existing index.

Because the index is a field, it displays as shaded text.

4 On the **References tab**, in the **Index group**, click **Update Index**. Compare your screen with Figure 10.37.

The index is updated to include the additional entry *Temperature*.

ANOTHER WAY Right-click the Index field, and then from the shortcut menu, click Update Field.

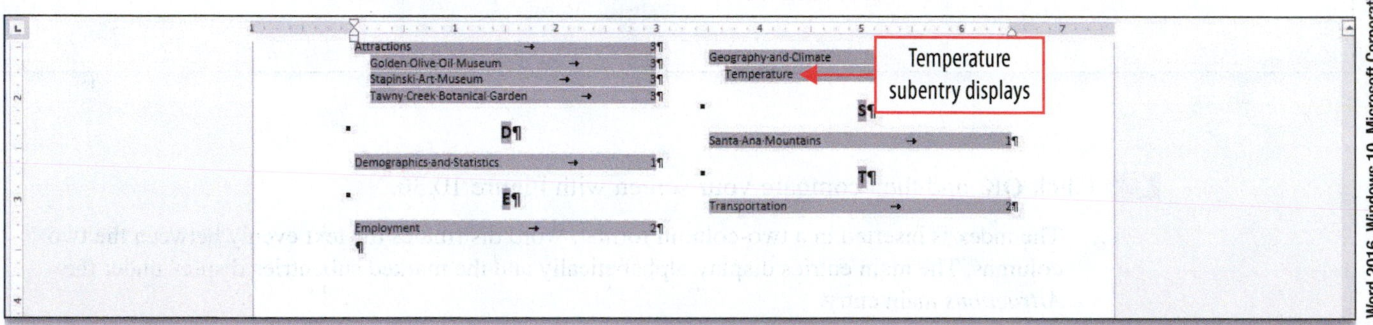

FIGURE 10.37

5 **Save** your changes.

Objective 6 Create a Table of Contents

GO! Learn How Video W10-6

A ***table of contents*** is a list of a document's headings and subheadings, marked with the page numbers on which those headings and subheadings occur. Many times a table of contents will be abbreviated and referred to as a ***TOC***. The TOC is a useful way to navigate a long document because clicking the heading or subheading in the TOC moves you to the page of the heading or subheading you clicked. In most instances, a table of contents displays at the beginning of a document.

Activity 10.18 | Assigning Heading Levels

1 Press Ctrl + Home. At the beginning of **Page 1**, select the second paragraph—*About the City*.

2 On the **References tab**, in the **Table of Contents group**, click **Add Text**. Notice *Level 1* is selected.

The Add Text button is used to identify the entries that will be included in the table of contents. Each entry in the TOC is identified by a heading level—Level 1 being the highest. When text is formatted with a heading style, Word matches the heading style number with the corresponding level number and automatically adds it to the TOC. In this case, Level 1 is selected because the text is formatted with the Heading 1 style. You can change the level for selected text or add unformatted text to the TOC by assigning the appropriate level.

3 On **Page 3**, select the paragraph *Tawny Creek Botanical Garden*. In the **Table of Contents group**, click the **Add Text** button, and then click **Level 3**. In a similar manner, assign **Level 3** to the paragraphs *Golden Olive Oil Museum* and *Stapinski Art Museum*. Compare your screen with Figure 10.38.

Because these paragraphs were not formatted with a Heading style, you must assign a level for the terms to display in the TOC. By selecting *Level 3*, the paragraphs are formatted with the *Heading 3* style.

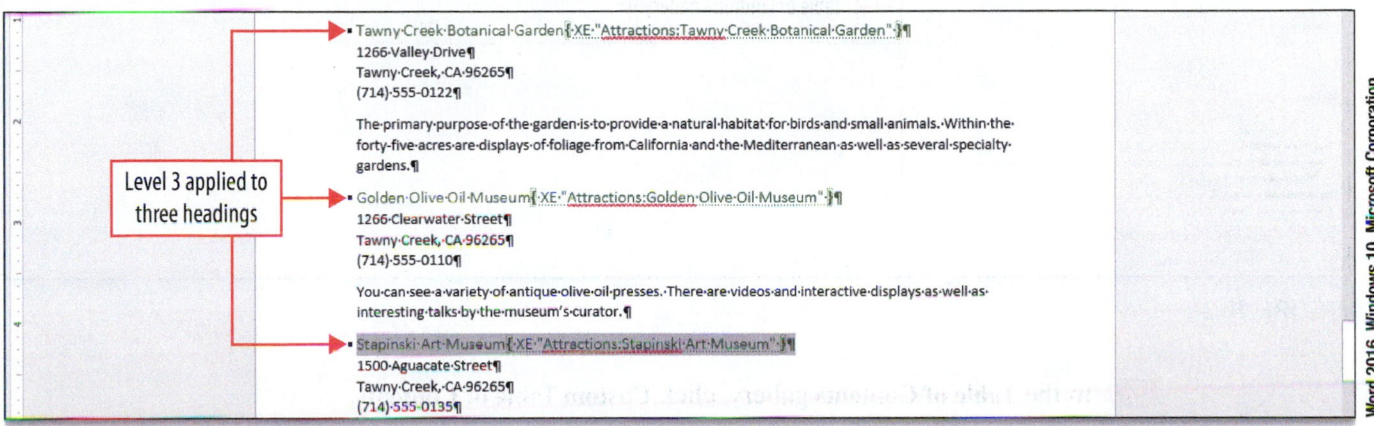

FIGURE 10.38

4 Press Ctrl + Home, and then **Save** your changes.

Activity 10.19 | Creating and Formatting a Table of Contents

4.2.1
Expert 3.2.1

A table of contents can be customized to include formatting. Any formatting added to the TOC will not affect the rest of the document. It is a good idea to format the TOC to make it stand out from the rest of the document.

1 With the insertion point at the beginning of the document, click the **Layout tab**. In the **Page Setup group**, click **Breaks**, and then under **Section Breaks**, click **Next Page**.

A table of contents is typically displayed as a separate, first page of a document.

2 Press Ctrl + Home to move to the beginning of the document. Click the **Home tab**, and then in the **Styles group**, click **Normal**.

3 Type **TABLE OF CONTENTS** and then press Enter two times.

4 Select the paragraph you just typed. On the mini toolbar, change the **Font Size** to **16**, apply **Bold**, and then click **Font Color** to apply the most recently used font color—**Green, Accent 1, Darker 50%**. **Center** the text.

5 On **Page 1**, position the insertion point in the blank paragraph to the left of the section break. Click the **References tab**, and then in the **Table of Contents group**, click **Table of Contents**. Compare your screen with Figure 10.39.

You can insert a built-in table of contents by clicking the style you want, or you can click Custom Table of Contents to create your own TOC style.

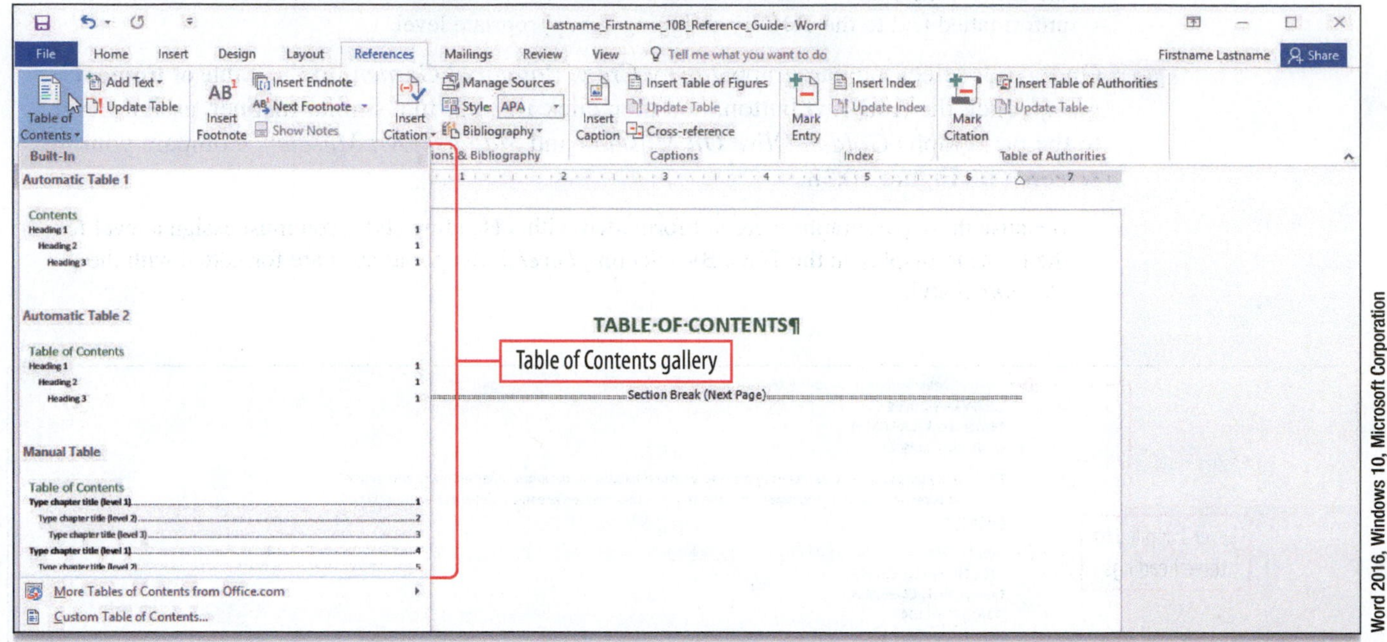

Word 2016, Windows 10, Microsoft Corporation

FIGURE 10.39

6 In the **Table of Contents** gallery, click **Custom Table of Contents**.

7 In the **Table of Contents** dialog box, under **Web Preview**, if necessary, select the Use hyperlinks instead of page numbers check box. Notice that the **Print Preview** box displays the table of contents format with Heading 2 and Heading 3 indented. Compare your screen with Figure 10.40.

A hyperlink will enable a reader of a document to click a page number in the TOC and move to that part of the document. The Show levels box displays *3*—representing the three heading levels assigned to specific text in the document. By using the Formats arrows, you can select a formatting style for the TOC. The Options button allows you to indicate the headings levels that will be used in the TOC. The Modify button allows you to change the formatting of the TOC—for example, fonts, paragraphs, and tabs.

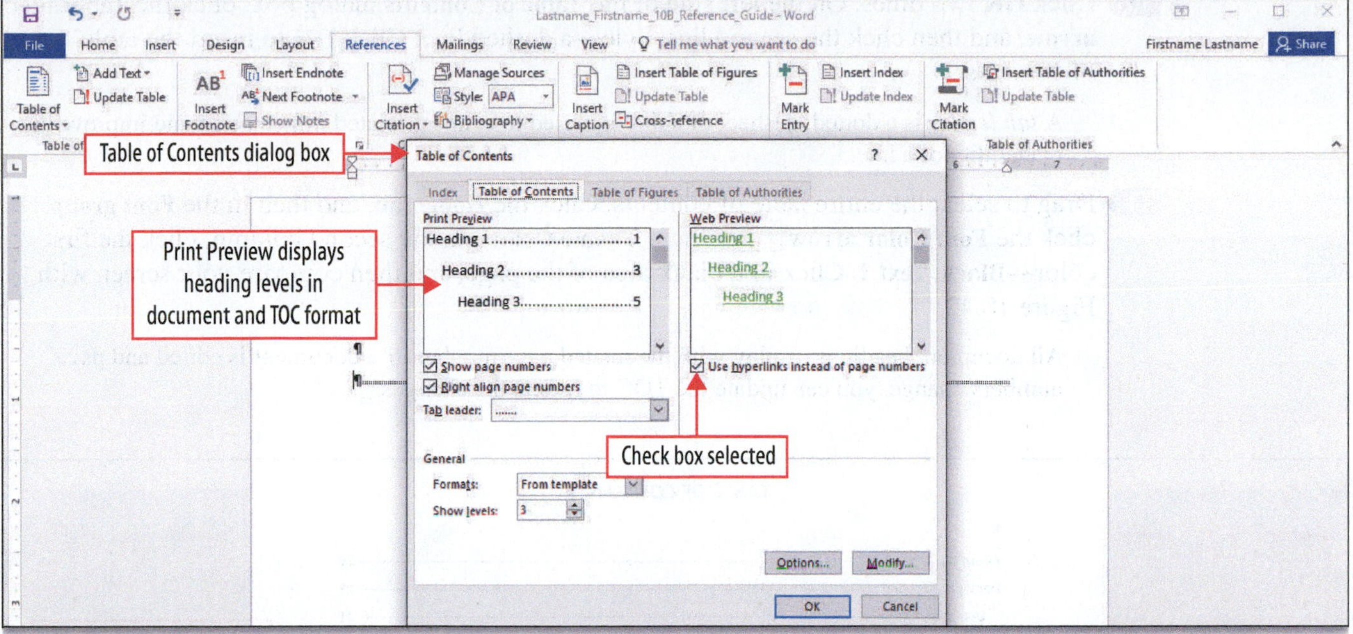

Word 2016, Windows 10, Microsoft Corporation

FIGURE 10.40

8 In the **Table of Contents** dialog box, click **Modify**. In the displayed **Style** dialog box, under **Styles**, if necessary, click to select TOC 1.

Under Preview, the current format for Heading Level 1 displays along with a description of the specific format elements.

9 In the **Style** dialog box, click **Modify**. In the **Modify Style** dialog box, under **Formatting**, click **Bold** [B]. Compare your screen with Figure 10.41.

In the TOC, all text assigned Heading Level 1 will display in bold.

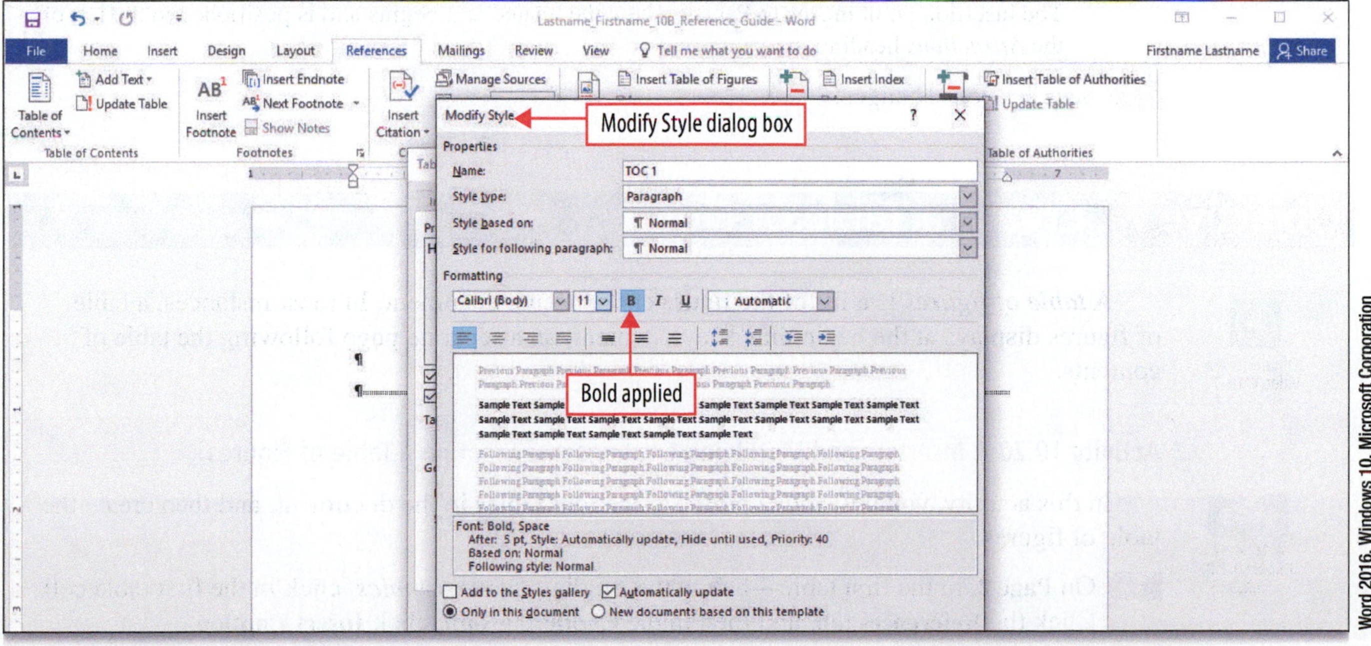

Word 2016, Windows 10, Microsoft Corporation

FIGURE 10.41

10 Click **OK** two times. On the left side of the **Table of Contents** dialog box, click the **Tab leader arrow**, and then click the second line style—a dashed line. Click **OK** to insert the table of contents.

A ***tab leader*** is a dotted, dashed, or solid line used to connect related information and improve the readability of a line.

11 Drag to select the entire table of contents. Click the **Home tab**, and then in the **Font group**, click the **Font Color arrow** [A]. Under **Theme Colors**, in the second column, click the first color—**Black, Text 1**. Click in a blank area of the page, and then compare your screen with Figure 10.42.

All document headings display with the related page number. If a document is edited and page numbers change, you can update the TOC to reflect the changes.

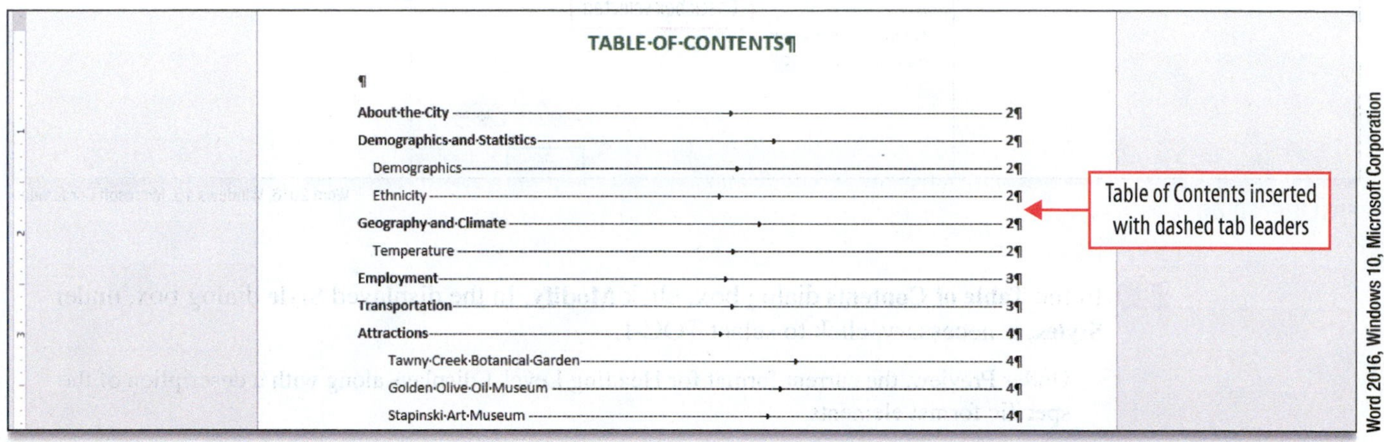

FIGURE 10.42

12 Point to the *Attractions* entry in the table of contents to display the ScreenTip, which indicates the entry is a hyperlink. Press and hold [Ctrl] and click **Attractions**.

The insertion point moves to Page 4 where the related text begins and is positioned to the left of the *Attractions* heading.

13 **Save** [icon] your changes.

Objective 7 Create a Table of Figures

GO! Learn How Video W10-7

A ***table of figures*** is a list of the figure captions in a document. In most instances, a table of figures displays at the beginning of a document, on a separate page following the table of contents.

Activity 10.20 | Inserting and Modifying Captions and Creating a Table of Figures

4.16, 4.17 Expert 3.2.2, 3.2.3

In this activity, you will add captions to the four tables in the document, and then create the table of figures.

1 On **Page 2**, in the first table—below the heading *Demographics*, click in the first table cell. Click the **References tab**, and then in the **Captions group**, click **Insert Caption**.

2 In the **Caption** dialog box, in the **Caption** box, with the insertion point to the right of *Table 1*, type a colon, and then press [Spacebar]. Type **Demographics** and then click the **Position arrow**. Click **Below selected item** and then compare your screen with Figure 10.43.

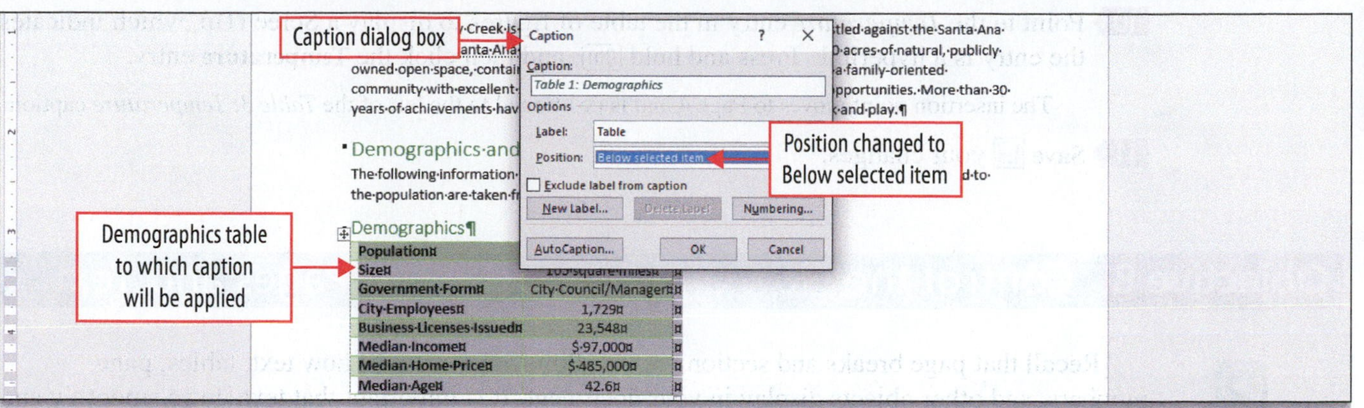

FIGURE 10.43 Word 2016, Windows 10, Microsoft Corporation

3 Click **OK** to display the caption below the table.

Recall that a caption is a title that is added to a Word object and is numbered sequentially.

4 Under **Ethnicity**, click in the first table cell and then insert a caption. In the **Caption** dialog box, under **Caption**, with the insertion point to the right of *Table 2*, type a colon, and then press Spacebar. Type **Ethnicity** and notice that the **Position** box displays *Below selected item*. Click **OK**.

5 In a similar manner, below the third table in the document, insert the caption **Table 3: Temperature** and then, below the fourth table, insert the caption **Table 4: Transportation**

Because the Temperature table is split across two pages, the caption displays at the bottom of the table—on Page 3.

6 Press Ctrl + Home. Click to position the insertion point in the last paragraph of **Page 1**—to the left of the section break. Press Ctrl + Enter to insert a manual page break. Notice that the insertion point moves to the first paragraph on the new, second page.

7 Type **TABLE OF FIGURES** and then press Enter. Press Ctrl + Home and then use **Format Painter** to copy the formatting from the **TABLE OF CONTENTS** text to the **TABLE OF FIGURES** text.

8 Click to position the insertion point in the blank paragraph to the left of the section break. On the **References tab**, in the **Captions group**, click **Insert Table of Figures**. In the **Table of Figures** dialog box, click the **Tab leader arrow**, and then click the second line style—the dashed line.

The Table of Figures dialog box is similar to the Table of Contents dialog box and provides many of the same options.

9 Click **OK** to insert the table of figures. Compare your screen with Figure 10.44.

The captions and their respective page numbers display, separated by the dashed line tab leader.

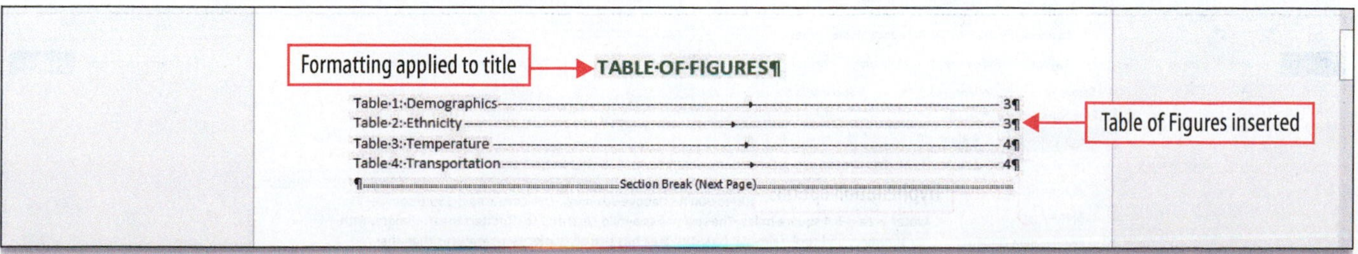

FIGURE 10.44 Word 2016, Windows 10, Microsoft Corporation

10 Point to the *Temperature* entry in the table of figures to display a ScreenTip, which indicates the entry is a hyperlink. Press and hold Ctrl, and then click the **Temperature** entry.

The insertion point moves to Page 4 and is positioned to the left of the *Table 3: Temperature* caption.

11 **Save** your changes.

Objective 8 Control the Flow and Formatting of Pages and Text

GO! Learn How Video W10-8

Recall that page breaks and section breaks allow you to control how text, tables, page numbers, and other objects display in your document. It is important that text flows smoothly and page numbers display properly. The process of arranging and numbering the pages in a document is called ***pagination***.

Activity 10.21 | Hiding White Space and Applying Hyphenation

Expert 2.1.3

In Print Layout view, to maximize your view of the document, you can hide the white spaces at the top and bottom of each page as well as the gray space between the pages. ***Hyphenation*** is a feature that enables control of how words are split between two lines, resulting in a less ragged edge at the right margin.

1 Scroll up to display the bottom of **Page 3** and the top of **Page 4**. Position the mouse pointer between the pages until it changes to the **Double-click to hide white space** pointer, and then double-click. Compare your screen with Figure 10.45.

The white space, including the footer, at the top and bottom of the pages and the gray space between the pages no longer displays. You must be in Print Layout view to use the Hide White Space feature.

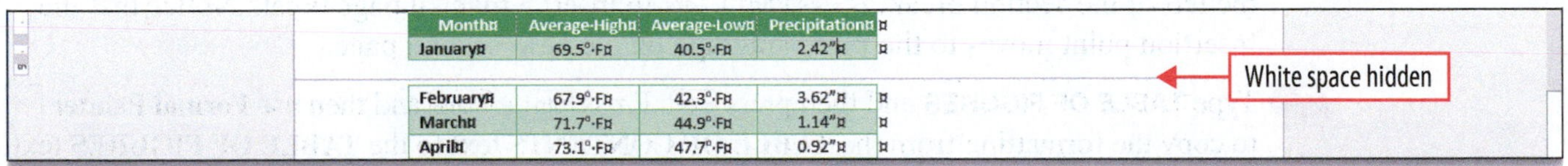

Month	Average High	Average Low	Precipitation
January	69.5° F	40.5° F	2.42"
February	67.9° F	42.3° F	3.62"
March	71.7° F	44.9° F	1.14"
April	73.1° F	47.7° F	0.92"

FIGURE 10.45

Word 2016, Windows 10, Microsoft Corporation

2 Click the **Layout tab**, and then in the **Page Setup group**, click **Hyphenation**. Compare your screen with Figure 10.46.

None is selected because the hyphenation feature is turned off by default. Selecting *Automatic* will cause Word to automatically hyphenate the entire document. If you modify the document, as you work Word will change the hyphenation as necessary. Selecting *Manual* allows you to decide how specific words should be hyphenated. You can select *Hyphenation Options* to modify hyphenation settings for either automatic or manual hyphenation.

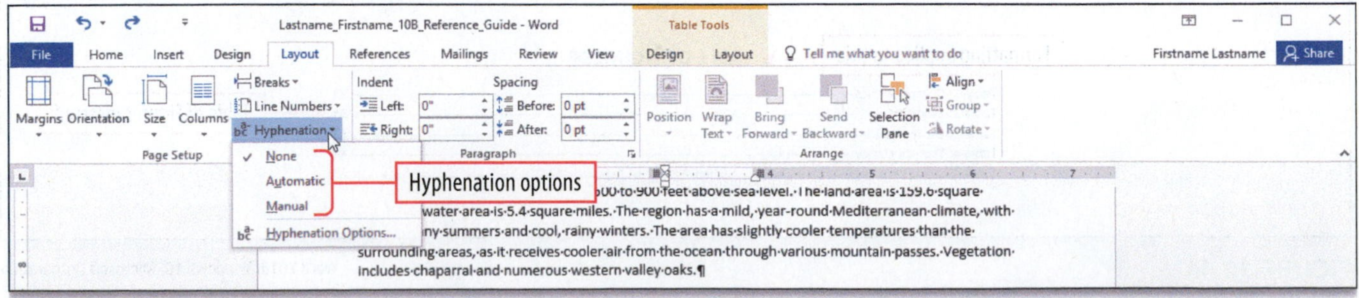

FIGURE 10.46

Word 2016, Windows 10, Microsoft Corporation

3 Click **Hyphenation Options**. In the **Hyphenation** dialog box, select the **Automatically hyphenate document** check box, and then in the **Limit consecutive hyphens to** box, type **2**

If several consecutive lines of text contain words that could be hyphenated, Word applies hyphens on only two consecutive lines.

4 Click **OK** to close the **Hyphenation** dialog box. Click the **Home tab**, and then hide the formatting marks.

To view how hyphenation will be applied in the final document, it is useful to hide the formatting marks for the Mark Entry references.

5 Scroll through the document and notice that on **Page 3**, in the paragraph below the *About the City* heading, in the second line, notice that the word *containing* is hyphenated and in the last paragraph on Page 3, the word *western* is hyphenated.

ALERT! **Different Words Are Hyphenated**

Depending on the width of your screen, word wrapping may cause your text to display differently. The hyphenated word may display on a different line, or the word may display without any hyphenation

6 Scroll to display the bottom of **Page 3** and the top of **Page 4**. Point to the gray border separating the two pages, and then when the **Double-click to show white space** pointer displays, double-click. Notice the white space at the top and bottom of the page and the gray space between the pages display.

7 **Save** your changes.

Activity 10.22 | Setting Paragraph Pagination Options by Keeping Paragraphs Together on a Page

Expert 2.1.5

There are times when it may enhance the readability and appeal of text to keep paragraphs together on the same page. For example, a bulleted list may be separated and displayed on two pages, but you may want to keep the entire list together on a single page.

1 If necessary, scroll the document so that the Temperature table, which is split across Pages 3 and 4, displays.

2 At the bottom of **Page 3**, above the table, drag to select the paragraph *Temperature,* the table, and the *Temperature* caption.

3 On the **Home tab**, in the **Paragraph group**, click the **Dialog Box Launcher** to display the **Paragraph** dialog box.

4 In the **Paragraph** dialog box, click the **Line and Page Breaks tab**, and then under **Pagination**, select the **Keep with next** check box. Compare your screen with Figure 10.47, and then take a moment to study the table in Figure 10.48.

The ***Keep with next*** command causes two elements, such as paragraphs, to display together on the same page. For example, it is good practice to keep a heading together with the paragraph of text that follows it. In this case, Word will keep the entire selection—the paragraph and the table—together on the same page.

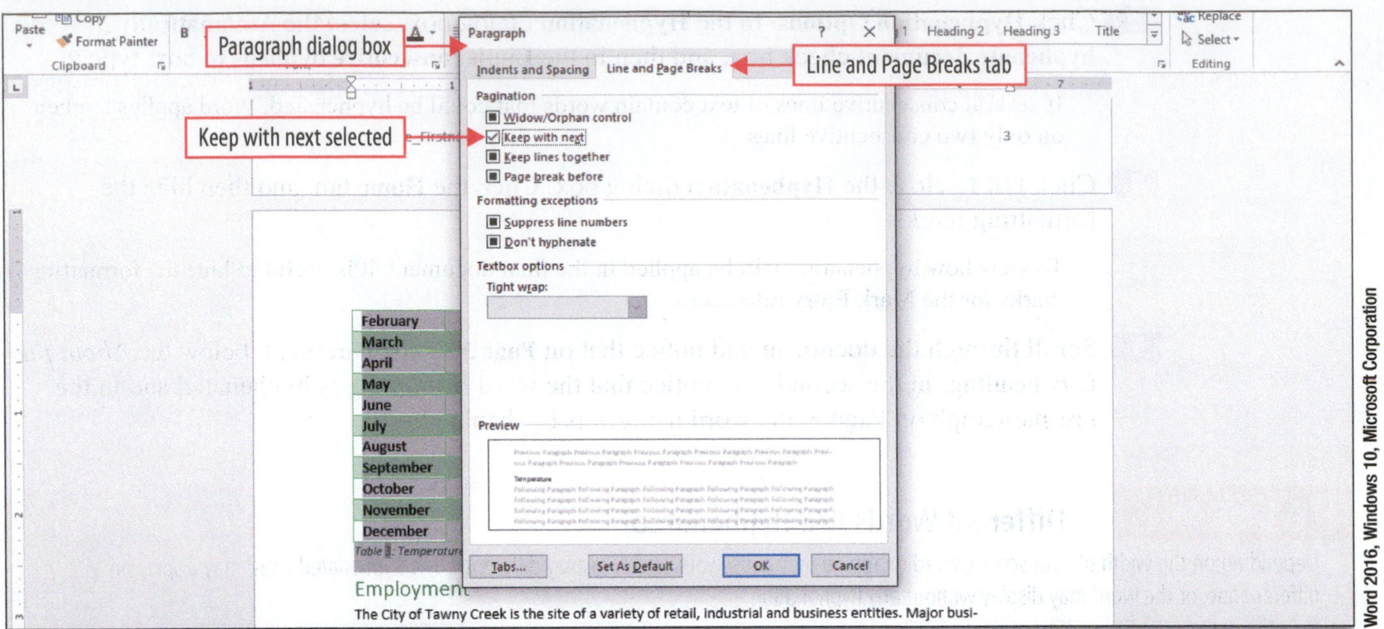

Word 2016, Windows 10, Microsoft Corporation

FIGURE 10.47

PAGINATION COMMANDS	
COMMAND	**DESCRIPTION**
Widow/Orphan control	Prevents a paragraph from splitting to display a single line at the top—widow—or bottom—orphan—of a page.
Keep with next	Causes two elements, such as paragraphs, to display together on the same page. For example, a heading will display on the same page as the paragraph of text that follows it.
Keep lines together	Prevents a page break from occurring within a paragraph.
Page break before	Forces a page break to occur before a paragraph.

FIGURE 10.48

5 Click **OK**. Deselect the text, and notice that the paragraph *Temperature* is at the top of the page, above the table.

The heading paragraph *Temperature* refers to the information in the table. Keeping the paragraph and table together on the same page improves readability.

6 Display formatting marks, and then **Save** your changes.

Because Mark Entry formatting marks are displayed in some paragraphs, the hyphenation of the document changes when formatting marks are displayed.

Activity 10.23 | Changing Page Settings and Splitting the Window, and Formatting Page Numbers

1.4.4

When a document contains section breaks, you can change the page settings—such as orientation or margins—and page numbering formats for different sections. In this activity, you will change the page margins for the TOC and table of figures, modify the page numbering for the document, and then update the TOC, table of figures, and index to reflect the changes you made.

1 Press Ctrl + Home. Click the **Layout tab**. In the **Page Setup group**, click **Margins**, and then click **Wide**.

The left and right margins in Section 1 of the document—Page 1 and Page 2—are changed to 2 inches.

2 Click the **View tab**, and then in the **Window group**, click **Split**.

The ***Split Window*** feature displays a document in two panes so that you can view or work on different parts of the document at the same time.

3 In the top pane, scroll as necessary to display the top of **Page 2**—the paragraph *Table of Figures*—and then click to the left of the word *Table*. In the bottom pane, scroll as necessary to display the top of **Page 3**—the paragraph that begins *Welcome to*—and then click to the left of the word *Welcome*. Compare your screen with Figure 10.49.

Recall that you changed the margins for *Section 1*, which includes the *Table of Figures* page. In the top pane, the horizontal ruler displays left and right margins set to 2 inches. In the bottom pane that displays the beginning of *Section 2*, the horizontal ruler displays the default left and right margin set to 1 inch.

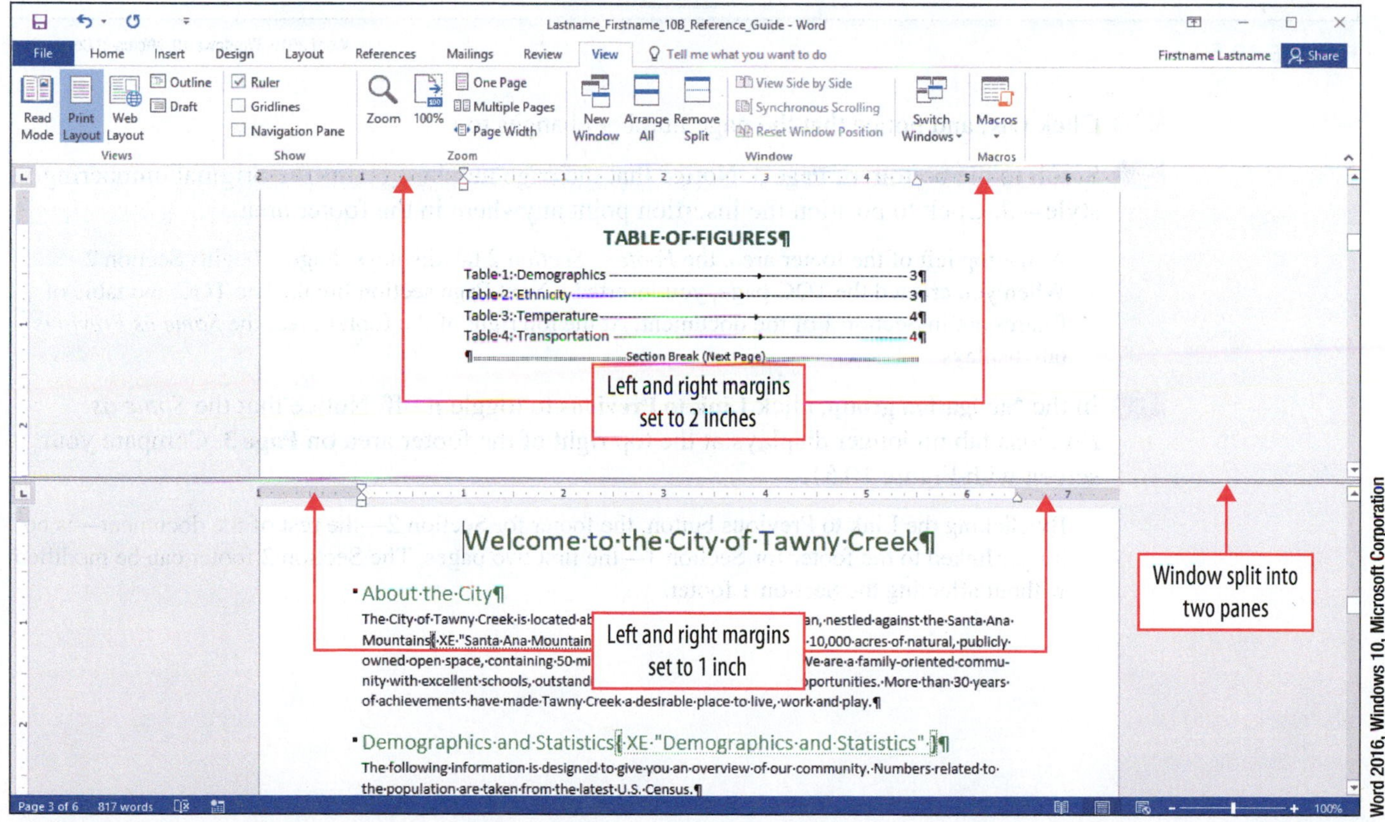

FIGURE 10.49

4 In the **Window group**, click **Remove Split** to return the document to a single full screen. **Save** your document.

Activity 10.24 | Formatting Page Numbers and Updating the Table of Contents, Table of Figures, and Index

4.2.2

Page numbers on the Table of Contents and Table of Figures pages are commonly formatted as roman numerals. In this activity, you will modify the page numbering for the document, and then update the TOC, table of figures, and index to reflect the changes you made.

1. Press Ctrl + Home, and then scroll to the bottom of **Page 1**. Right-click in the footer area, and then click **Edit Footer**.
2. In the footer, select the page number **1**. On the **Header & Footer Tools Design tab**, in the **Header & Footer group**, click **Page Number**, and then click **Format Page Numbers**.

   In the Page Number Format dialog box, you can modify page number styles.

3. In the **Page Number Format** dialog box, click the **Number format arrow**, and then click the fifth numbering style—**i, ii, iii**. Compare your screen with Figure 10.50.

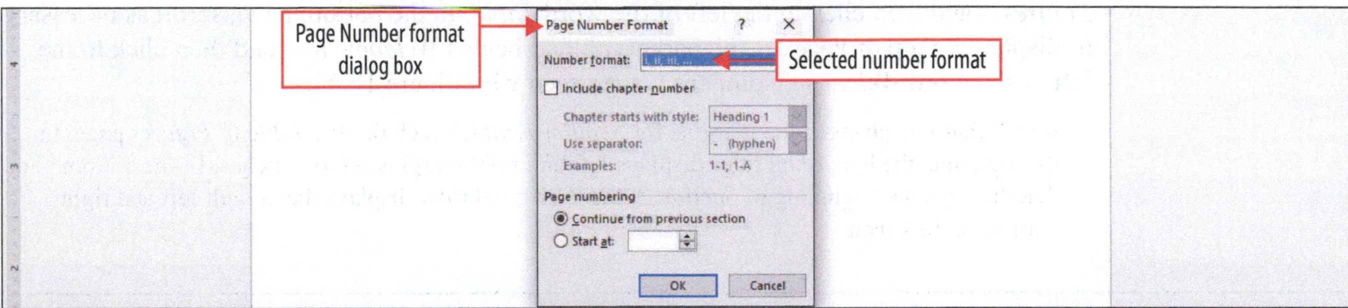

FIGURE 10.50

Word 2016, Windows 10, Microsoft Corporation

4. Click **OK**, and notice that the page number changes to *i*.
5. Scroll to the bottom of **Page 3**. Notice that the page number retains the original numbering style—*3*. Click to position the insertion point anywhere in the footer area.

   At the top left of the footer area, the *Footer - Section 2* tab displays. Page 3 begins Section 2. When you created the TOC page, you inserted a Next Page section break. The TOC and table of figures are in Section 1 of the document. At the top right of the footer area, the *Same as Previous* tab displays.

6. In the **Navigation group**, click **Link to Previous** to toggle it off. Notice that the *Same as Previous* tab no longer displays at the top right of the footer area on **Page 3**. Compare your screen with Figure 10.51.

   By clicking the Link to Previous button, the footer for Section 2—the rest of the document—is no longer linked to the footer for Section 1—the first two pages. The Section 2 footer can be modified without affecting the Section 1 footer.

Word 2016, Windows 10, Microsoft Corporation

FIGURE 10.51

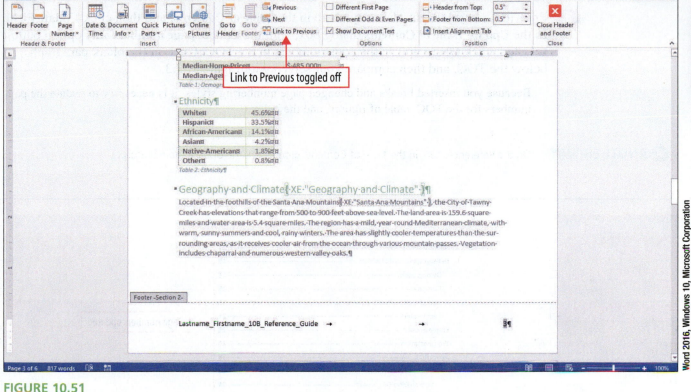

7 In the footer, select the page number **3**, right-click, and then from the shortcut menu, click **Format Page Numbers**. In the **Page Number Format** dialog box, under **Page numbering**, click the **Start at** option button, and then compare your screen with Figure 10.52.

You can use the Start at option to select the first page number that should display in a new section of a document. By default, the number *1* displays in the Start at box.

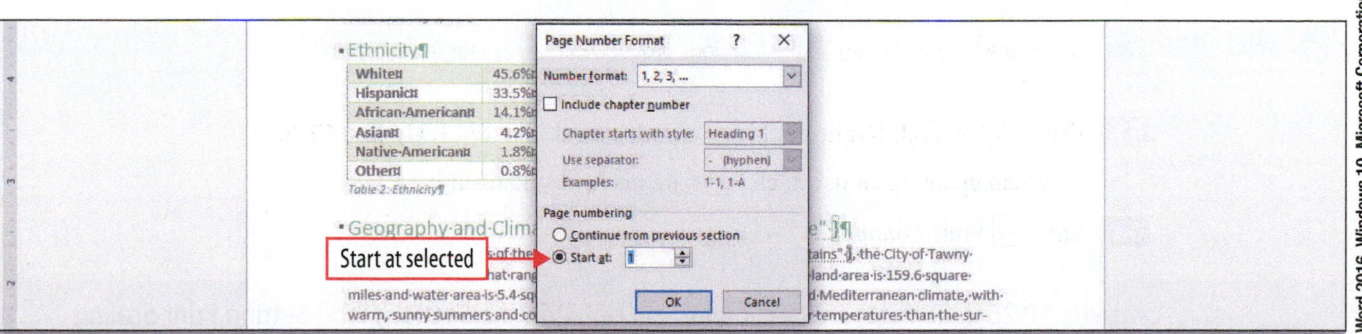

Word 2016, Windows 10, Microsoft Corporation

FIGURE 10.52

8 Click **OK**. Notice that the page number *1* displays in the footer on the third page of the document. In the **Close group**, click **Close Header and Footer**.

9 Press Ctrl + Home. Right-click anywhere in the **Table of Contents**, and then click **Update Field**. In the **Update Table of Contents** dialog box, with the **Update page numbers only** option button selected, click **OK** to update the page numbers in the TOC. Click in the blank paragraph below the TOC, and then compare your screen with Figure 10.53.

Because you inserted breaks and changed page numbering styles, it is necessary to update the page numbers for the TOC, table of figures, and the index.

ANOTHER WAY On the References tab, in the Table of Contents group, click the Update Table button.

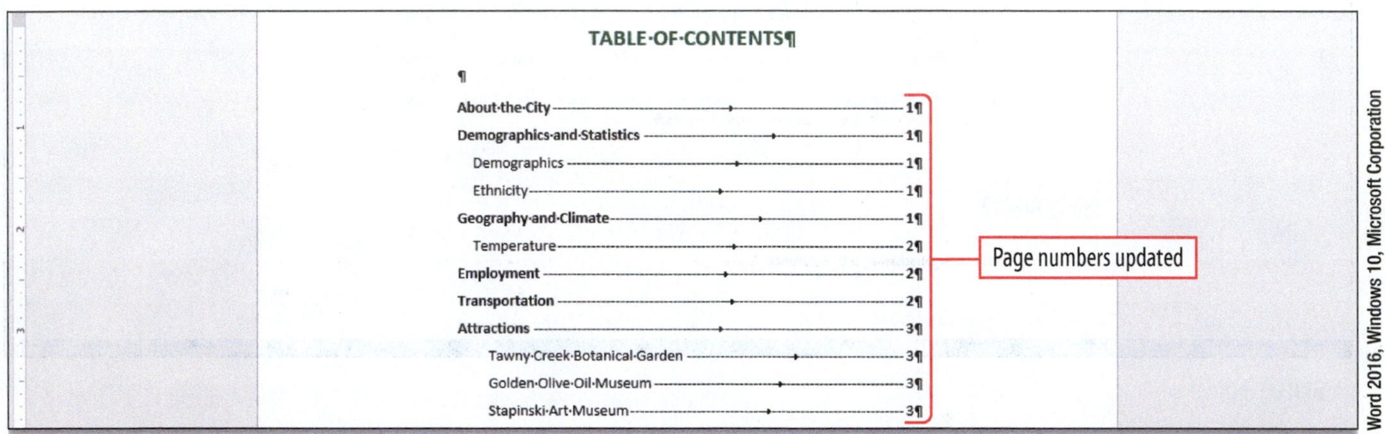

FIGURE 10.53

10 On the second page of the document, right-click in the **Table of Figures**, and then click **Update Field**. In the **Update Table of Figures** dialog box, with the **Update page numbers only** option button selected, click **OK**.

ANOTHER WAY On the References tab, in the Captions group, click the Update Table button.

11 Press Ctrl + End. Right-click in the **index**, and then click **Update Field**.

When updating an index, changes are made automatically.

12 **Save** your changes.

Activity 10.25 | Configuring Documents to Print, Printing Sections, and Setting Print Scaling

1.5.1

You can modify print settings to suit your needs. For example, you may want to print a range of pages or scale the printout for a specific paper size.

1 Press Ctrl + Home. Click the **File tab**, and then at the left of your screen, click **Print**.

2 Under **Settings**, click **Print All Pages**. Compare your screen with Figure 10.54.

A list of *Document* and *Document Info* settings displays. You can print specific pages, selected portions of a document, or information related to the document.

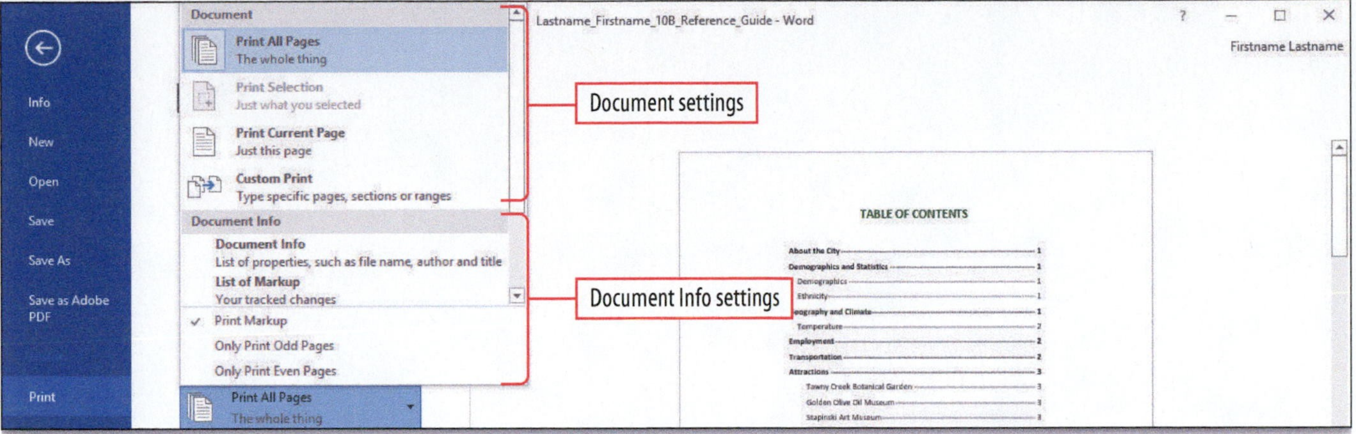

FIGURE 10.54

Word 2016, Windows 10, Microsoft Corporation

3 In the list, scroll as necessary, and then click **Custom Print**. Notice the button immediately below Settings displays *Custom Print* and the insertion point is in the *Pages* box.

4 Immediately below **Custom Print**, point to **Pages**, and take a moment to read the ScreenTip.

The ScreenTip contains information for printing specific pages, a range of pages, or specific sections of a document. For example type *p1s1* to print the first page in section 1.

5 Under **Settings**, click **1 Page Per Sheet**, and then point to **Scale to Paper Size**.

In the main list, you can select the number of pages on which you want to print your document. In the secondary list, you can select the paper size for the printed document.

6 From **Backstage** view, click **Info**, and then **Show All Properties**. In the **Tags** box, type **reference guide** and in the **Subject** box, type your course name and section number. If necessary, edit the author name to display your name.

7 **Save** your changes.

8 Print your document or submit electronically as directed by your instructor. **Close** Word.

END | You have completed Project 10B

GO! To Work

10 WORD

Andrew Rodriguez / Fotolia; FotolEdhar / Fotolia; apops / Fotolia; Yuri Arcurs / Fotolia

Microsoft Office Specialist (MOS) Skills in this Chapter	
PROJECT 10A	**PROJECT 10B**
1.2.3 Create bookmarks	**1.4.4** Split the window
1.3.6 Format page background elements	**1.5.1** Modify print settings
2.3.3 Change page setup options for a section	**4.1.6** Insert figure and table captions
4.2.3 Insert a cover page	**4.1.7** Modify caption properties
	4.2.1 Insert a standard table of contents
	4.2.2 Update a table of contents
	Expert 2.1.3 Set advanced page setup layout options
	Expert 2.1.5 Set paragraph pagination options
	Expert 3.1.1 Mark index entries
	Expert 3.1.2 Create indexes
	Expert 3.1.3 Update indexes
	Expert 3.2.1 Customize a table of contents
	Expert 3.2.2 Insert and modify captions
	Expert 3.2.3 Create and modify a table of figures

BUILD YOUR E-PORTFOLIO

An E-Portfolio is a collection of evidence, stored electronically, that showcases what you have accomplished while completing your education. Collecting and then sharing your work products with potential employers reflects your academic and career goals. Your completed documents from the following projects are good examples to show what you have learned: 10G, 10K, and 10L.

GO! FOR JOB SUCCESS

Discussion: Social Media

Your instructor may assign these questions to your class, and then ask you to think about them or discuss them with your classmates:

You know that you should avoid making social media posts about your employer and never post anything negative about your boss or coworkers. There have been incidents, however, when people lost their jobs over social media posts made on their personal accounts during non-work hours that had nothing to do with their employers. Employers who take this action usually do so in response to an employee post that degrades others or involves illegal activity.

FotolEdhar / Fotolia

Do you think an employer should have the right to fire an employee for making a personal social media post that makes negative comments about coworkers or about the company?

What would you do if you saw a coworker's post that contained negative comments about the company?

What is your employer's or school's policy on social media?

END OF CHAPTER

SUMMARY

When a document is created or edited by several people, one efficient way of assembling or editing the document is to create a master document and subdocuments. Unlink the subdocuments to create a final document.

To navigate to specific locations in a document, use bookmarks, cross-references, and the Navigation pane. Insert section breaks to create different footers on odd and even pages. Include a cover page for interest.

An index indicates where specific text is located in the document. A table of contents helps the reader go directly to specific topics. The reader can use a table of figures to navigate to graphic elements.

Apply hyphenation and pagination options to improve readability. Modify page numbers to differentiate introductory pages—for example, a table of contents—from the main pages of the document.

GO! LEARN IT ONLINE

Review the concepts and key terms in this chapter by completing these online challenges, which you can find at **MyITLab**.

Matching and Multiple Choice: Answer matching and multiple choice questions to test what you learned in this chapter.

Lessons on the GO!: Learn how to use all the new apps and features as they are introduced by Microsoft.

MOS Prep Quiz: Answer questions to review the MOS skills that you practiced in this chapter.

PROJECT GUIDE FOR WORD CHAPTER 10

Your instructor will assign Projects from this list to ensure your learning and assess your knowledge.

PROJECT GUIDE FOR WORD CHAPTER 10			
Project	**Apply Skills from These Chapter Objectives**	**Project Type**	**Project Location**
10A	Objectives 1–4 from Project 10A	**10A Instructional Project (Grader Project)** Guided instruction to learn the skills in Project 10A.	In MyITLab and in text
10B	Objectives 5–8 from Project 10B	**10B Instructional Project (Grader Project)** Guided instruction to learn the skills in Project 10B.	In MyITLab and in text
10C	Objectives 1–4 from Project 10A	**10C Skills Review (Scorecard Grading)** A guided review of the skills from Project 10A.	In text
10D	Objectives 5–8 from Project 10B	**10D Skills Review (Scorecard Grading)** A guided review of the skills from Project 10B.	In text
10E MyITLab	Objectives 1–4 from Project 10A	**10E Mastery (Grader Project)** **Mastery and Transfer of Learning** A demonstration of your mastery of the skills in Project 10A with extensive decision making.	In MyITLab and in text
10F MyITLab	Objectives 5–8 from Project 10B	**10F Mastery (Grader Project)** **Mastery and Transfer of Learning** A demonstration of your mastery of the skills in Project 10B with extensive decision making.	In MyITLab and in text
10G MyITLab	Objectives 1–8 from Project 10A and 10B	**10G Mastery (Grader Project)** **Mastery and Transfer of Learning** A demonstration of your mastery of the skills in Projects 10A and 10B with extensive decision making.	In MyITLab and in text
10H	Combination of Objectives from Projects 10A and 10B	**10H GO! Fix It (Scorecard Grading)** **Critical Thinking** A demonstration of your mastery of the skills in Projects 10A and 10B by creating a correct result from a document that contains errors you must find.	Instructor Resource Center (IRC) and MyITLab
10I	Combination of Objectives from Projects 10A and 10B	**10I GO! Make It (Scorecard Grading)** **Critical Thinking** A demonstration of your mastery of the skills in Projects 10A and 10B by creating a result from a supplied picture.	IRC and MyITLab
10J	Combination of Objectives from Projects 10A and 10B	**10J GO! Solve It (Rubric Grading)** **Critical Thinking** A demonstration of your mastery of the skills in Projects 10A and 10B, your decision-making skills, and your critical thinking skills. A task-specific rubric helps you self-assess your result.	IRC and MyITLab
10K	Combination of Objectives from Projects 10A and 10B	**10K GO! Solve It (Rubric Grading)** **Critical Thinking** A demonstration of your mastery of the skills in Projects 10A and 10B, your decision-making skills, and your critical thinking skills. A task-specific rubric helps you self-assess your result.	In text
10L	Combination of Objectives from Projects 10A and 10B	**10L GO! Think (Rubric Grading)** **Critical Thinking** A demonstration of your understanding of the chapter concepts applied in a manner that you would outside of college. An analytic rubric helps you and your instructor grade the quality of your work by comparing it to the work an expert in the discipline would create.	In text
10M	Combination of Objectives from Projects 10A and 10B	**10M GO! Think (Rubric Grading)** **Critical Thinking** A demonstration of your understanding of the chapter concepts applied in a manner that you would outside of college. An analytic rubric helps you and your instructor grade the quality of your work by comparing it to the work an expert in the discipline would create.	IRC and MyITLab
10N	Combination of Objectives from Projects 10A and 10B	**10N You and GO! (Rubric Grading)** **Critical Thinking** A demonstration of your understanding of the chapter concepts applied in a manner that you would in a personal situation. An analytic rubric helps you and your instructor grade the quality of your work.	IRC and MyITLab

GLOSSARY

GLOSSARY OF CHAPTER KEY TERMS

AutoMark file A Word document that contains a two-column table used to mark words as index entries.

Body text Text that does not have a heading style applied.

Bookmark A link that identifies the exact location of text, a table, or other object.

Continuous section break A mark that defines the beginning and end of each subdocument.

Cover page The first page of a document that provides introductory information.

Cross-reference A text link to an item that appears in another location in the document, such as a heading, a caption, or a footnote.

Even Page section break A formatting mark that indicates the beginning of a new section on the next even-numbered page.

Hidden text Nonprinting text—for example, an index entry field.

Hyphenation A feature that enables control of how words are split between two lines, resulting in a less ragged edge at the right margin.

Index A compilation of topics, names, and terms accompanied by page numbers that displays at the end of a document.

Index entry A word or phrase that is listed in the index.

Index entry field Code, formatted as hidden text and displaying to the right of an index entry, containing the identifier XE and the term to be included in the index.

Keep with next A formatting feature that causes two elements, such as paragraphs, to display together on the same page.

Main entry A word, phrase, or selected text used to identify the index entry.

Master document A Word document that serves as a container for the different parts of a document.

Odd Page section break A formatting mark that indicates the beginning of a new section on the next odd-numbered page.

Outline view A document view that displays the overall organization, or hierarchy, of the document's parts, including headings, subheadings, and subordinate text.

Pagination The process of arranging and numbering the pages in a document.

Readability statistics A Spelling and Grammar tool that analyzes a document and determines the reading level of the text.

Section break A mark that stores the formatting information for a section of a document.

Split Window A Word feature that displays a document in two panes so that you can view or work on different parts of the document at the same time.

Subdocument A section of a document that is linked to the master document.

Subentry A more specific term that refers to the main entry.

Tab leader A dotted, dashed, or solid line used to connect related information and improve the readability of a line.

Table of contents (TOC) A list of a document's headings and subheadings, marked with the page numbers where those headings and subheadings occur.

Table of figures A list of the figure captions in a document.

Thumbnail A graphical representation of a page.

Watermark A text or graphic element that displays behind document text.

Word count A Word feature that indicates the number of words, paragraphs, pages, and characters in a document.

XE Code identifying an index entry.

Apply **10A** skills from these Objectives:

1. Create a Master Document and Subdocuments
2. Manage a Master Document and Subdocuments
3. Navigate and Inspect the Master Document
4. Create and Modify Headers and Footers

Skills Review Project 10C Summer Calendar

In the following Skills Review, you will create a master document and subdocuments for events happening during the summer in the City of Tawny Creek. Your completed document will look similar to Figure 10.55.

PROJECT FILES

For Project 10C, you will need the following files:

w10C_Summer_Calendar

w10C_Shakespeare_Festival

You will save your files as:

Lastname_Firstname_10C_Summer_Calendar

Lastname_Firstname_10C_Shakespeare_Festival (not shown in figure)

PROJECT RESULTS

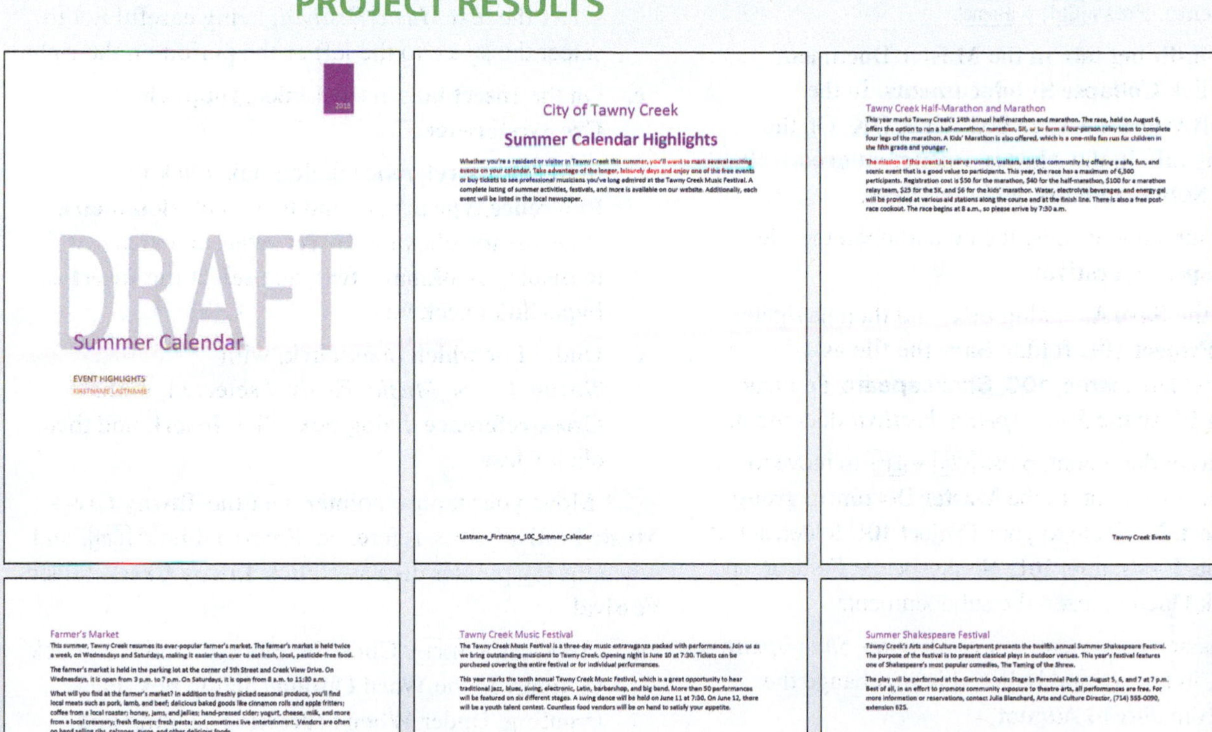

FIGURE 10.55

Word 2016, Windows 10, Microsoft Corporation

(Project 10C Summer Calendar continues on the next page)

Skills Review Project 10C Summer Calendar (continued)

1 Start Word. From your student files, locate and open the file **w10C_Summer_Calendar**. If necessary, display the rulers and formatting marks. Display the **Save As** dialog box, and then open your **Word Chapter 10** folder. Create a folder named **Project 10C** and then save the document in your **Project 10C** folder as **Lastname_Firstname_10C_Summer_Calendar**

- **a.** Click the **View tab**. In the **Views group**, click **Outline** to change to Outline view. Click to position the insertion point to the left of *Tawny Creek Half-Marathon and Marathon*. Drag down to select all remaining paragraphs in the document.
- **b.** On the **Outlining tab**, in the **Master Document group**, click **Show Document** to turn it on, and then click **Create**. Press Ctrl + Home.
- **c.** On the **Outlining tab**, in the **Master Document group**, click **Collapse Subdocuments**. In the **Microsoft Word** message box, click **OK**. On the **Outlining tab**, in the **Master Document group**, click **Expand Subdocuments**, and then **Save**.

2 From your student files, locate and open the file **w10C_Shakespeare_Festival**.

- **a.** Display the **Save As** dialog box, and then navigate to your **Project 10C** folder. **Save** the file as **Lastname_Firstname_10C_Shakespeare_Festival** and then **Close** the *Shakespeare Festival* document.
- **b.** In the master document, press Ctrl + End to move to the end of the document. In the **Master Document group**, click **Insert**. Navigate to your **Project 10C** folder, select **Lastname_Firstname_10C_Shakespeare_Festival**, and then click **Open** to insert the subdocument.
- **c.** In the master document, under *Summer Shakespeare Festival*, in the second bulleted item, change the month from *July* to **August**
- **d.** On the **Outlining tab**, in the **Close group**, click **Close Outline View**. **Save** your changes.

3 Press Ctrl + Home. Click the **View tab**, and then in the **Show group**, select the **Navigation Pane** check box.

- **a.** In the **Navigation** pane, with the **Headings** tab displayed, click the **Tawny Creek Music Festival** heading. In the document, select the text *Tawny Creek Music Festival*, using the Shift and arrow keys as necessary so that the paragraph mark is not selected.
- **b.** Click the **Insert tab**, and then in the **Links group**, click **Bookmark**. In the **Bookmark** dialog box, in the **Bookmark name** box, type **Tawny_Creek_Music_Festival** and then click **Add**. Press Ctrl + Home.

4 In the **Navigation** pane, click the **Search document arrow**, and then click **Go To**. In the **Find and Replace** dialog box, in the **Go to what** box, click **Bookmark**.

- **a.** Below the **Enter bookmark name** box, which displays *Tawny_Creek_Music_Festival*, click **Go To**. **Close** the **Find and Replace** dialog box, and then **Close** the **Navigation** pane.
- **b.** Press Ctrl + Home. In the paragraph that begins *Whether you're a resident*, in the second sentence, select the text *Music Festival*, being careful not to select the space to the left or the period on the right.
- **c.** On the **Insert tab**, in the **Links group**, click **Cross-reference**.
- **d.** In the **Cross-reference** dialog box, click the **Reference type arrow**, and then click **Bookmark**. If necessary, click the **Insert reference to arrow** to display **Bookmark text**, and select the **Insert as hyperlink** check box.
- **e.** Under **For which bookmark**, with *Tawny_Creek_Music_Festival* selected, in the **Cross-reference** dialog box, click **Insert**, and then click **Close**.

5 Move your mouse pointer over the **Tawny Creek Music Festival** cross-reference. Press and hold Ctrl, and when the [pointer] pointer displays, click **Tawny Creek Music Festival**.

- **a.** Press Ctrl + Home. Click the **File tab**, and then click **Options**. In the **Word Options** dialog box, click **Proofing**. Under **When correcting spelling and grammar in Word**, select the **Show readability statistics** check box to turn on the display of readability statistics. Click **OK**.
- **b.** On the **Review tab**, in the **Proofing group**, click **Spelling & Grammar**.
- **c.** Click **OK** to close the **Readability Statistics** dialog box. Click the **File tab**, and then click **Options**. In the **Word Options** dialog box, click **Proofing**. Under **When correcting spelling and grammar in Word**, clear the **Show readability statistics** check box. Click **OK**.

(Project 10C Summer Calendar continues on the next page)

Skills Review Project 10C Summer Calendar (continued)

6 Press Ctrl + Home. On the **View tab**, in the **Views group**, click **Outline**. If the subdocument icons do not display, on the Outlining tab, in the Master Document group, click Show Document.

- **a.** To the left of the paragraph *Tawny Creek Half-Marathon and Marathon*, click the **Subdocument** icon to select the entire subdocument. In the **Master Document group**, click **Unlink**.
- **b.** In a similar manner, **Unlink** the subdocuments *Farmer's Market, Tawny Creek Music Festival*, and *Summer Shakespeare Festival.*
- **c.** Above the paragraph *Tawny Creek Half-Marathon and Marathon*, click to position the insertion point to the right of the first bullet for **Section Break (Continuous)**, and then press Delete.
- **d.** In a similar manner, delete all instances of **Section Break (Continuous)** and **Section Break (Next Page)** that display.
- **e.** On the **Outlining tab**, in the **Close group**, click **Close Outline View**.

7 Position the insertion point at the end of the paragraph under *Summer Calendar Highlights*. Click the **Layout tab**. In the **Page Setup group**, click **Breaks**, and then under **Section Breaks**, click **Even Page**. Under *Farmer's Market*, position the insertion point at the end of the paragraph that begins *What will you find*, and then insert an **Even Page** section break.

- **a.** Insert **Odd Page** section breaks at the end of the paragraphs that begin *The mission of this event* under the Tawny Creek Half Marathon and Marathon heading, and *This year marks* under the Tawny Creek Music Festival heading.
- **b.** Scroll through the document and delete any blank paragraph marks that display at the top of each page.
- **c.** At the bottom of **Page 2**, right-click in the footer area, and then click **Edit Footer**. On the **Header & Footer Tools Design tab**, in the **Options group**, select the **Different Odd & Even Pages** check box.
- **d.** On **Page 2**, click in the **Even Page** footer, press Tab two times, and then type **Tawny Creek Events**
- **e.** On **Page 3**, in the **Odd Page** footer, insert the file name.
- **f.** In the **Close group**, click the **Close Header and Footer** button. **Save** your changes.

8 Press Ctrl + Home. Click the **Insert tab**. In the **Pages group**, click **Cover Page**, and then click the **Ion (Light)** style.

- **a.** Click in the **Document title** placeholder, and then type **Summer Calendar**
- **b.** Click in the **Document Subtitle** placeholder, and then type **Event Highlights**
- **c.** In the upper right corner of the page, Click in the **Year** placeholder, and then type **2018**
- **d.** In the **Author** placeholder, below the subtitle, if necessary, delete the existing text, and then type your first and last names.
- **e.** On the **Design tab**, in the **Page Background group**, click **Watermark**, and then under **Disclaimers**, click **Draft 2**.
- **f.** Click the **File tab**, and then click **Show All Properties**. In the **Author** box, verify that your first and last names display. In the **Tags** box, type **summer calendar** and then in the **Subject** box, type your course name and section number.
- **g.** **Save** and **Close** your document. If directed by your instructor to do so, submit your paper printout, your electronic image of your document that looks like a printed document, or your original Word file.

END | You have completed Project 10C

CHAPTER REVIEW

Apply 10B skills from these Objectives:

5 Create an Index
6 Create a Table of Contents
7 Create a Table of Figures
8 Control the Flow and Formatting of Pages and Text

Skills Review Project 10D Job Descriptions

In the following Skills Review, you will add an index, a table of contents, and a table of figures to the listing of job descriptions for the City of Tawny Creek. Your completed document will look similar to Figure 10.56.

PROJECT FILES

For Project 10D, you will need the following file:
w10D_Job_Descriptions

You will save your file as:
Lastname_Firstname_10D_Job_Descriptions

PROJECT RESULTS

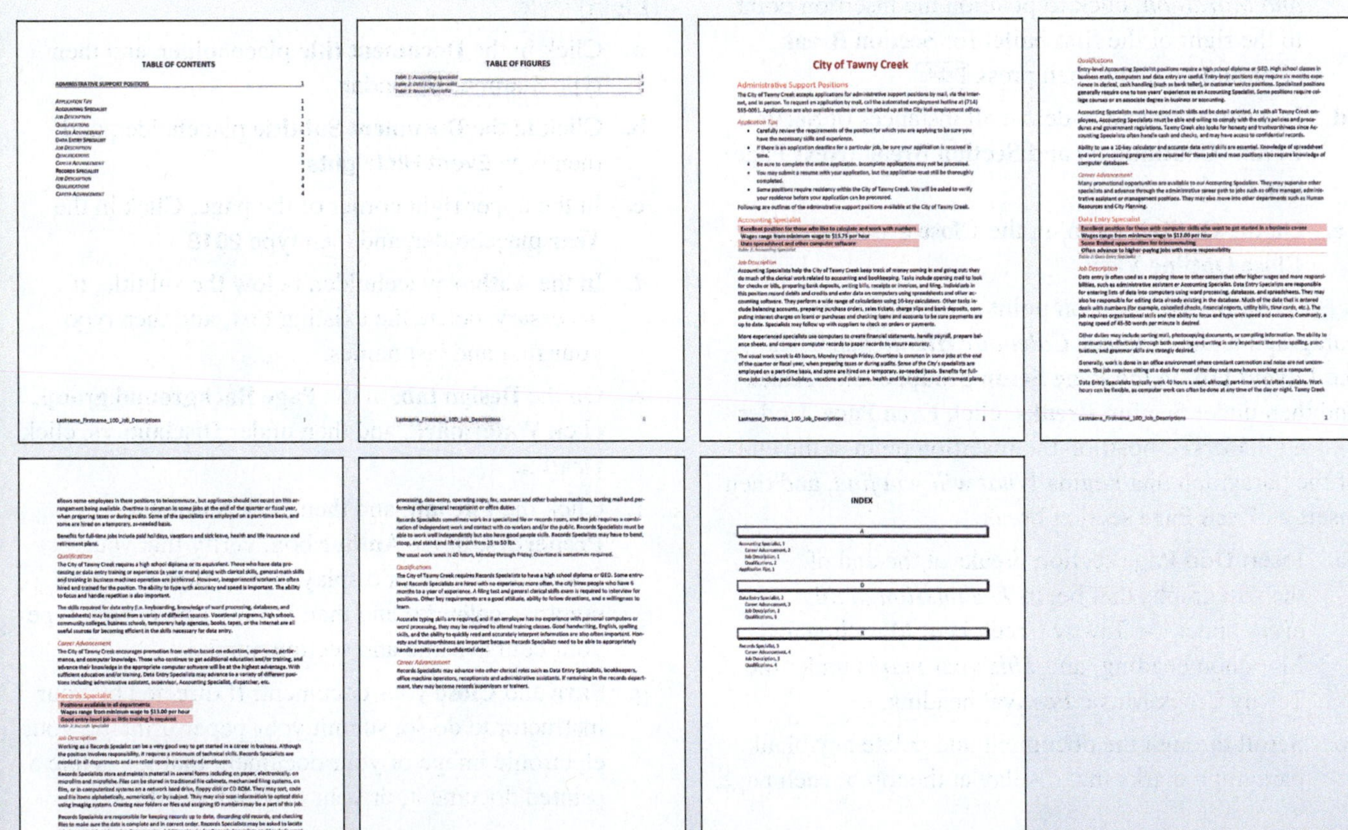

FIGURE 10.56

(Project 10D Job Descriptions continues on the next page)

Skills Review Project 10D Job Descriptions (continued)

1 Start Word. From your student files, open the file **w10D_Job_Descriptions**. **Save** the file in your **Word Chapter 10** folder as **Lastname_Firstname_10D_Job_Descriptions** and if necessary, display the rulers and formatting marks. If any words are flagged as spelling errors, right-click the first occurrence of each, and then click **Ignore All**.

a. Scroll to the bottom of **Page 1**, right-click in the footer area, click **Edit Footer**, and then insert the file name in the footer.

b. With the footer area displayed, be sure the insertion point is to the right of the file name, and then press Tab two times. On the **Header & Footer Tools Design tab**, in the **Header & Footer group**, click **Page Number**, and then point to **Current Position**. In the **Page Number** gallery, under **Simple**, click **Plain Number**. In the **Close group**, click **Close Header and Footer**.

c. Under *Accounting Specialist*, click in the first cell of the table. Click the **Table Tools Design tab**, and then in the **Table Style Options group**, clear the **Header Row** check box. In the **Table Styles group**, click **More**, and then under **Grid Tables**, in the second row, click the fourth style—**Grid Table 2 – Accent 3**.

d. Press Ctrl + Home, and then **Save** your changes.

2 Under *Administrative Support Positions*, select the text **Application Tips**. Click the **References tab**, and then in the **Index group**, click **Mark Entry**. In the **Mark Index Entry** dialog box, click **Mark**.

a. Click in the document, and then select the paragraph *Accounting Specialist*. If necessary, point to the Mark Index Entry dialog box title bar, and then drag the Mark Index Entry dialog box to the side of your screen. With the paragraph selected, click in the **Mark Index Entry** dialog box, and click **Mark**.

b. Without closing the **Mark Index Entry** dialog box, in a similar manner, **Mark** entries for *Data Entry Specialist* and *Records Specialist*.

3 On **Page 1**, position the insertion point to the right of *Job Description*. In the **Mark Index Entry** dialog box, click in the **Main entry** box. Type **Accounting Specialist** and then in the **Subentry** box, type **Job Description** and click **Mark**.

a. On **Page 2**, position the insertion point to the right of *Qualifications*. In the **Main entry** box, type **Accounting Specialist** and in the **Subentry** box, type **Qualifications** and then click **Mark**.

b. On **Page 2**, position the insertion point to the right of *Career Advancement*. Create the **Main entry** box **Accounting Specialist** and the **Subentry Career Advancement**

c. Using the technique you just practiced, under the paragraph heading *Data Entry Specialist*, mark *Job Description*, *Qualifications*, and *Career Advancement* as subentries for the main entry **Data Entry Specialist**

d. In a similar manner, under the paragraph heading *Records Specialist*, mark subentries for *Job Description*, *Qualifications*, and *Career Advancement* as subentries for the main entry **Records Specialist**

e. **Close** the **Mark Index Entry** dialog box and then **Save** your changes.

4 Press Ctrl + End, and then press Ctrl + Enter to insert a manual page break. With the insertion point at the top of the new page, type **INDEX** and then press Enter. Select the text *INDEX*, including the paragraph mark, change the **Font Size** to **16**, apply **Bold**, and **Center** the text.

a. Click in the blank paragraph below the INDEX title. On the **References tab**, in the **Index group**, click **Insert Index** to display the **Index** dialog box.

b. In the **Index** dialog box, on the **Index tab**, click the **Formats arrow**, and then click **Fancy**. On the right side of the **Index** dialog box, click the **Columns spin box down arrow** to **1**. Click **OK**.

c. On **Page 1**, select the first paragraph with italic formatting—*Application Tips*. In the **Table of Contents group**, click **Add Text**, and then click **Level 3**. In a similar manner, assign **Level 3** to the remaining nine italicized paragraph headings. Press Ctrl + Home, and then **Save** your changes.

5 With the insertion point at the beginning of the document, click the **Layout tab**. In the **Page Setup group**, click **Breaks**, and then under **Section Breaks**, click **Next Page**. Press Ctrl + Home to move to the beginning of the document. Click the **Home tab**, and then in the **Styles group**, click **Normal**.

a. Type **TABLE OF CONTENTS** and then press Enter two times. Select the text you just typed, including the

(Project 10D Job Descriptions continues on the next page)

Skills Review Project 10D Job Descriptions (continued)

paragraph mark, change the **Font Size** to **16**, and then apply **Bold** and **Center**.

b. Click to position the insertion point to the left of the section break. Click the **References tab**, and then in the **Table of Contents group**, click **Table of Contents**. In the **Table of Contents** gallery, click **Custom Table of Contents**. In the **Table of Contents** dialog box, if necessary, select the **Use hyperlinks instead of page numbers** check box.

c. Under **General**, click the **Formats arrow**, and then click **Fancy**. Click **OK**, and then **Save** your changes.

6 On **Page 2**, below the heading *Accounting Specialist*, in the first table, click in the first cell. On the **References tab**, in the **Captions group**, click **Insert Caption**.

a. In the **Caption** dialog box, in the **Caption** box, with the insertion point to the right of *Table 1*, type **:** (a colon), press Spacebar, and then type **Accounting Specialist** Click the **Position arrow**, and then click **Below selected item**. Click **OK**.

b. On **Page 3**, click in the first cell of the table. In the **Captions group**, click **Insert Caption**. In the **Caption** dialog box, in the **Caption** box, with the insertion point to the right of *Table 2*, type **:** (a colon), press Spacebar, and then type **Data Entry Specialist** Click **OK**.

c. In a similar manner, insert the caption **Table 3: Records Specialist** below the third table in the document. Click **OK**.

7 Press Ctrl + Home. Click to position the insertion point in the last paragraph of the page—to the left of the section break. Press Ctrl + Enter to insert a manual page break.

a. Type **TABLE OF FIGURES** and then press Enter. Select the text you just typed, change the **Font Size** to **16**, apply **Bold**, and **Center**.

b. Click to position the insertion point in the last paragraph on **Page 2**—to the left of the section break. On the **References tab**, in the **Captions group**, click **Insert Table of Figures**.

c. In the **Table of Figures** dialog box, under **General**, click the **Formats arrow**, and then click **Distinctive**. Click **OK**, and then **Save** your changes.

d. Click the **Layout tab**. In the **Page Setup group**, click **Hyphenation**, and then click **Automatic**.

8 Press Ctrl + Home, and then scroll to the bottom of **Page 1**. Right-click in the footer area, and then click **Edit Footer**. In the footer, select the page number.

a. On the **Header & Footer Tools Design tab**, in the **Header & Footer group**, click **Page Number**, and then click **Format Page Numbers**.

b. In the **Page Number Format** dialog box, click the **Number format arrow**, and then click the fifth numbering style—**i, ii, iii**. Click **OK**.

c. On **Page 3**, in the footer, select the page number **3**. In the **Header & Footer group**, click **Page Number**, and then click **Format Page Numbers**. In the **Page Number Format** dialog box, under **Page numbering**, click the **Start at** option button. With *1* displayed in the **Start at** box, click **OK**. In the **Close group**, click **Close Header and Footer**.

9 Click to position the insertion point in the table of contents, right-click, and then click **Update Field**. In the **Update Table of Contents** dialog box, with the **Update page numbers only** option button selected, click **OK**.

a. On **Page 2**, click to position the insertion point in the table of figures. Right-click, and then click **Update Field**. In the **Update Table of Figures** dialog box, with the **Update page numbers only** option button selected, click **OK**.

b. Press Ctrl + End. Click to position the insertion point in the index, right-click, and then click **Update Field**.

c. Press Ctrl + Home. Click the **File tab**, and then **Show All Properties**. In the **Tags** box, type **job list** and in the **Subject** box, type your course name and section number. If necessary, edit the author name to display your name.

d. **Save** and **Close** your document. If directed by your instructor to do so, submit your paper printout, your electronic image of your document that looks like a printed document, or your original Word file.

END | You have completed Project 10D

Mastering Word Project 10E Council Topics

Apply 10A skills from these Objectives:

1. Create a Master Document and Subdocuments
2. Manage a Master Document and Subdocuments
3. Navigate and Inspect the Master Document
4. Create and Modify Headers and Footers

In the following Mastering Word project, you will create a master document and subdocuments for a document that summarizes topics to be discussed at the February meeting of the Tawny Creek City Council. Your completed documents will look similar to Figure 10.57.

PROJECT FILES

For Project 10E, you will need the following files:

w10E_Council_Topics
w10E_Agenda_Item

You will save your files as:

Lastname_Firstname_10E_Council_Topics
Lastname_Firstname_10E_Agenda_Item (not shown in Figure)

PROJECT RESULTS

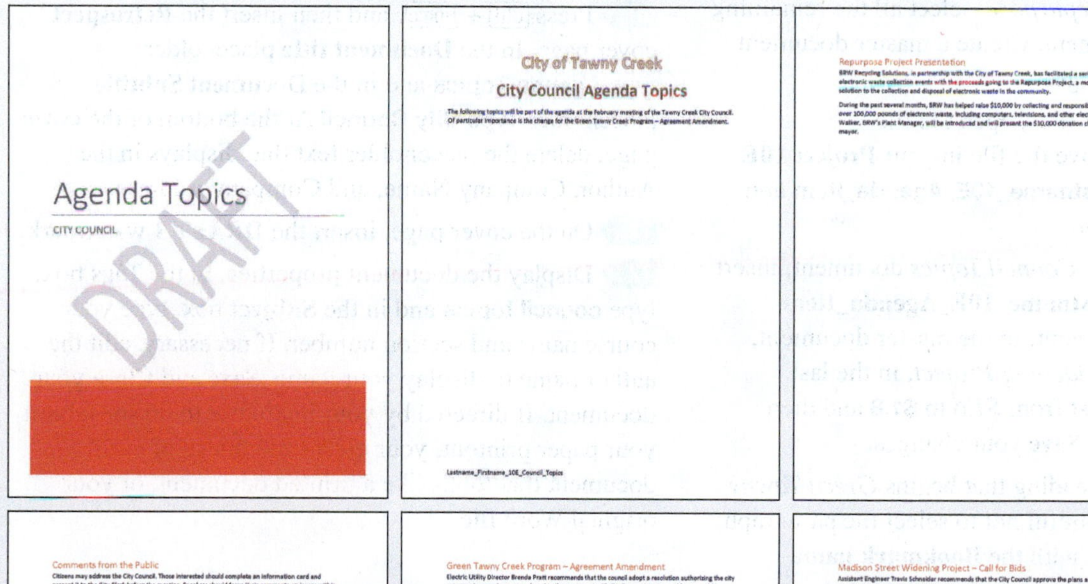

Word 2016, Windows 10, Microsoft Corporation

FIGURE 10.57

(Project 10E Council Topics continues on the next page)

Mastering Word Project 10E Council Topics (continued)

1 Start Word. From your student files, locate and open the file **w10E_Council_Topics**. Navigate to your **Word Chapter 10** folder, and create a folder named **Project 10E** Save the file in your **Project 10E** folder as **Lastname_Firstname_10E_Council_Topics** If necessary, display the rulers and formatting marks.

2 Select the first paragraph of the document, change the **Font Size** to **28**, apply **Center**, and then change the **Text Effects and Typography** to **Gradient Fill - Brown, Accent 4, Outline – Accent 4**. Select the second paragraph, change the **Font Size** to **28**, apply **Bold**, change the **Font Color** to **Brown, Accent 4, Darker 25%**, and then apply **Center**.

3 Apply the **Heading 1** style to the paragraphs that begin *Repurpose, Comments*, and *Green* and then display the document in **Outline** view. Beginning with the paragraph that begins *Repurpose*, select all the remaining paragraphs in the document. Create a master document and then **Save** your changes.

4 From your student files, open the file **w10E_Agenda_Item**. Save the file in your **Project 10E** folder as **Lastname_Firstname_10E_Agenda_Item** and then **Close** the document.

5 At the end of your *Council Topics* document, insert your file **Lastname_Firstname_10E_Agenda_Item** document as a subdocument. In the master document, under *Madison Street Widening Project*, in the last sentence, change the cost from *$1.6* to **$1.8** and then **Close Outline View** and **Save** your changes.

6 Select the entire heading that begins *Green Tawny Creek Program* being careful not to select the paragraph mark. Add a **Bookmark** with the **Bookmark name Agreement_Amendment**

7 In the paragraph below the document subtitle, at the end of the second sentence, select the text **Green Tawny Creek Program**. **Insert** a cross-reference that is linked to the *Agreement_Amendment* bookmark.

8 **Unlink** all of the subdocuments and then delete all of the section breaks in the document. Close Outline view. Insert **Even Page** section breaks at the end of the paragraphs that begin *The following topics* and *Note that all*. Insert **Odd Page** section breaks at the end of the paragraphs that begin *During the past* and *City Renew, Inc*. Delete any blank paragraphs at the top of each page.

9 On **Page 2**, display the footer and select the **Different Odd & Even Pages** check box. On **Page 2**, in the footer, press Tab two times, and then type **Tawny Creek** On **Page 3**, in the footer, insert the file name, and then close the footer.

10 Press Ctrl + Home, and then insert the **Retrospect** cover page. In the **Document title** placeholder, type **Agenda Topics** and in the **Document Subtitle** placeholder, type **City Council** At the bottom of the cover page, delete the placeholder text that displays in the Author, Company Name, and Company Address.

11 On the cover page, insert the **DRAFT 1** watermark.

12 Display the document properties. In the **Tags** box, type **council topics** and in the **Subject** box, type your course name and section number. If necessary, edit the author name to display your name. **Save** and **Close** your document. If directed by your instructor to do so, submit your paper printout, your electronic image of your document that looks like a printed document, or your original Word file.

END | You have completed Project 10E

CONTENT-BASED ASSESSMENTS (MASTERY AND TRANSFER OF LEARNING)

10 WORD

Apply 10B skills from these Objectives:

5 Create an Index
6 Create a Table of Contents
7 Create a Table of Figures
8 Control the Flow and Formatting of Pages and Text

Mastering Word Project 10F Business FAQ

In the following Mastering Word project, you will add an index, a table of contents, and a table of figures to a document containing frequently asked questions and answers related to doing business with the City of Tawny Creek. Your completed document will look similar to Figure 10.58.

PROJECT FILES

For Project 10F, you will need the following file:

w10F_Business_FAQ

You will save your file as:

Lastname_Firstname_10F_Business_FAQ

PROJECT RESULTS

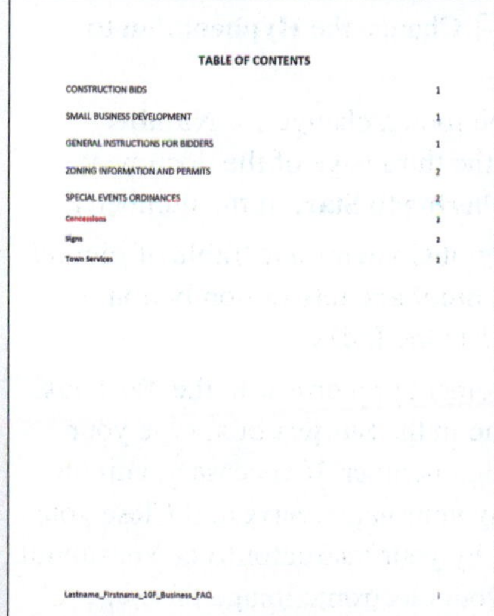

TABLE OF CONTENTS

Lastname_Firstname_10F_Business_FAQ i

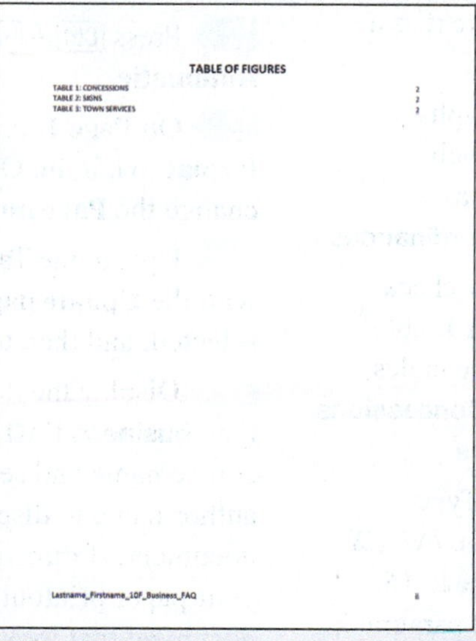

TABLE OF FIGURES

Lastname_Firstname_10F_Business_FAQ ii

Business FAQ

It is the hope of the City of Tawny Creek that this document will answer some of the most frequently asked questions regarding doing business with the city.

Construction Bids

The City of Tawny Creek intends to make information available regarding public improvement projects to all interested parties. Prospective construction projects for the Department of Public Works and Development are advertised regularly in the local newspaper for six business days.

The City of Tawny Creek requires general contractors to be prequalified according to Title 11 Chapter 12 of the City of Tawny Creek ordinances. In some cases, prequalification is not required. All general contractors must be bonded.

Sealed bids are accepted every Friday by 9:00 a.m. at the City Clerk's office. Bids are opened at 9:30 a.m. in the City Council Chambers at the City Hall. Requirements for submitting bids are in the Bidders Requirements document.

Small Business Development

Tawny Creek's Economic Development Department works with various organizations in the city that provide programs assisting small businesses with finances, training, and incentives. City departments also facilitate business development and entrepreneurism.

Many agencies help with these efforts. One is the Small Business Association, which provides assistance to entrepreneurs as they start, run, and grow their businesses. Another is the Tawny Creek Small Business Development Center, which provides training, workshops, and consulting on various areas of interest to small businesses. It also provides business owners with resources from lawyers, accountants, bookkeepers, marketing specialists, and more.

Several basic steps toward developing a small business include the following: evaluate your needs and location, create a business plan, check zoning regulations, determine a business structure, register a name, obtain a business license, get any necessary permits, get employer identification numbers, open a checking account, and recruit and train employees. More resources are available through the Economic Development Department.

General Instructions for Bidders

The City of Tawny Creek requires bidders to use the Purchasing Division bid forms to bid on materials, equipment, and services. Contact the Purchasing Division to request copies of the bid forms. All information on the form must be typed or written in ink. If a mistake is made, start with a new copy.

The bid form must be signed by an authorized individual and affixed with a corporate seal, if signed by a corporation.

A bid bond may be required. If so, it will be stated on the cover sheet. The bid bond must be provided by a corporate surety authorized to do business in the State of California or can be provided in the form of cash, check, or cashier's check payable to the City of Tawny Creek for 10% of the bid.

Lastname_Firstname_10F_Business_FAQ 1

Word 2016, Windows 10, Microsoft Corporation

Securities can be substituted for any monies withheld by the City to ensure contract-related performance. Securities available for investments under this section include those listed in Section 16379 of the Government Code or bank or savings and loan certificates of deposit. The contractor is the beneficiary of any securities substituted for monies withheld and will receive any applicable interest.

Zoning Information and Permits

The Economic Development Department offers services related to development under the City of Tawny Creek Planning Code and General Plan. The Zoning Section provides customer service to answer zoning questions, deal with zoning permit applications, and process environmental review documents. If you are starting a new business or building or renovating a building, the General Plan and the Planning Code should be consulted for guidelines and requirements for your project.

The Tawny Creek Planning Code is Title 18 of the Tawny Creek Municipal Code. It provides regulations and guidelines related to site development, including zoning regulations and environmental review guidelines. A complete copy of the Planning Code and/or the complete Municipal Code can be obtained by contacting the Tawny Creek City Clerk's office.

Special Events Ordinances

Special events are welcome in the City of Tawny Creek. Promoters should register with the Parks and Recreation Department and carefully review all ordinances that pertain to any events conducted in public places within the city limits. Listed below are a few of the regulations.

Concessions

Caterers must be approved by the city.
The promoter must ensure no alcoholic beverages are carried into or out of the event.

Table 1: Concessions

Signs

All signs must be professionally created.
Written permission must be obtained from the city manager prior to placing signs on public property.
Permanent existing signs on public property may not be removed or covered.
Sponsorship and event signs are not allowed on light posts.
Rental cost of directional signs is the responsibility of the applicant.

Table 2: Signs

Town Services

To best serve the safety and welfare of the public, the following services shall be provided by the City of Tawny Creek when deemed necessary.

Police protection, security, and crowd control.
Fire protection and emergency medical services.
Park maintenance.
Street closures.
Traffic and parking control.

Table 3: Town Services

Lastname_Firstname_10F_Business_FAQ 2

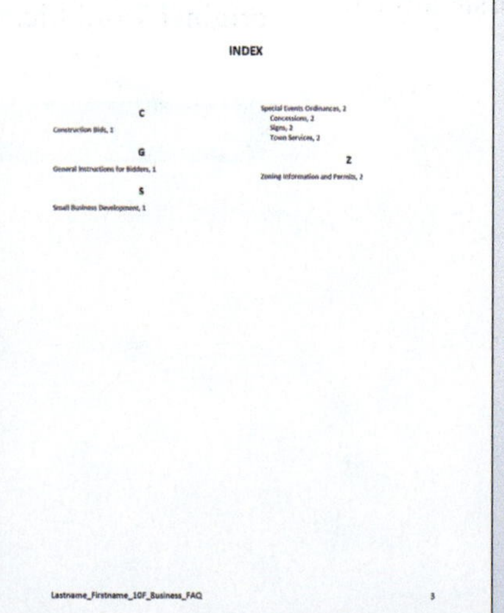

INDEX

Lastname_Firstname_10F_Business_FAQ 3

FIGURE 10.58

(Project 10F Business FAQ continues on the next page)

Mastering Word Project 10F Business FAQ (continued)

1 Start Word. From your student files, open the file **w10F_Business_FAQ.** If necessary, display the rulers and formatting marks. **Save** the file in your **Word Chapter 10** folder as **Lastname_Firstname_10F_Business_FAQ**

2 If necessary, ignore any spelling errors that display. Insert the file name in the footer, and then press Tab two times. Insert a **Plain Number** page number and then close the footer.

3 Select the first paragraph, change the **Font Size** to **22**, apply **Bold**, and then change the **Font Color** to **Orange, Accent 1, Darker 50%**. Apply **Center**.

4 Apply the **Heading 1** style to the paragraph headings that begin *Construction*, *Small Business*, *General Instructions*, *Zoning*, and *Special Events*. For each *Heading 1* paragraph, mark the heading text as a **Main entry** for the index.

5 Apply the **Heading 2** style to the paragraphs *Concessions*, *Signs*, and *Town Services*. For each *Heading 2* paragraph, type the paragraph text as a **Subentry** for the **Main entry** **Special Events Ordinances**

6 For each table, deselect the **Header Row** check box, and then apply the **Grid Table 4 – Accent 1** table style. Apply the following captions to the three tables positioned below the selected item: **Table 1: Concessions** and **Table 2: Signs** and **Table 3: Town Services**

7 At the end of the document, press Enter. Type **INDEX** and then press Enter two times. Select the *INDEX* paragraph you just typed, change the **Font Size** to **16**, apply **Bold**, and then apply **Center**. In the last paragraph of the document, insert an index with the **Classic** format.

8 Press Ctrl + Home, and then insert a **Next Page** section break. Press Ctrl + Home, and then apply the **Normal** style. Type **TABLE OF CONTENTS** and then press Enter two times. Select the text you typed, change the **Font Size** to **16**, apply **Bold**, and then apply **Center**.

9 Click to the left of the section break, and then insert a table of contents with the **Classic** format. **Save** your changes.

10 If necessary, click to position the insertion point to the left of the section break. Press Ctrl + Enter, type **TABLE OF FIGURES** and then press Enter. Select the text you typed, change the **Font Size** to **16**, apply **Bold**, and then apply **Center**.

11 To the left of the section break, insert a table of figures with the **Classic** format. **Save** your changes.

12 Press Ctrl + Home. Change the **Hyphenation** to **Automatic**.

13 On **Page 1**, in the footer, change the **Number format** to **i, ii, iii**. On the third page of the document, change the **Page numbering** to **Start at** the number **1**.

14 Update the Table of Contents and Table of Figures with the **Update page numbers only** option button selected, and then update the Index.

15 Display the document properties. In the **Tags** box, type **business FAQ** and in the **Subject** box, type your course name and section number. If necessary, edit the author name to display your name. **Save** and **Close** your document. If directed by your instructor to do so, submit your paper printout, your electronic image of your document that looks like a printed document, or your original Word file.

END | You have completed Project 10F

CONTENT-BASED ASSESSMENTS (MASTERY AND TRANSFER OF LEARNING)

10 WORD

Mastering Word Project 10G Chamber Programs

Apply 10A and 10B skills from these Objectives:

1 Create a Master Document and Subdocuments
2 Manage a Master Document and Subdocuments
3 Navigate and Inspect the Master Document
4 Create and Modify Headers and Footers
5 Create an Index
6 Create a Table of Contents
7 Create a Table of Figures
8 Control the Flow and Formatting of Pages and Text

In the following Mastering Word project, you will create a master document and subdocuments related to the programs offered by Tawny Creek's Chamber of Commerce. The final document will include an index, a table of contents, and a table of figures. Your completed documents will look similar to Figure 10.59.

PROJECT FILES

For Project 10G, you will need the following files:

w10G_Chamber_Programs
w10G_Ambassadors_Club

You will save your files as:

Lastname_Firstname_10G_Chamber_Programs
Lastname_Firstname_10G_Ambassadors_Club (not shown in Figure)

PROJECT RESULTS

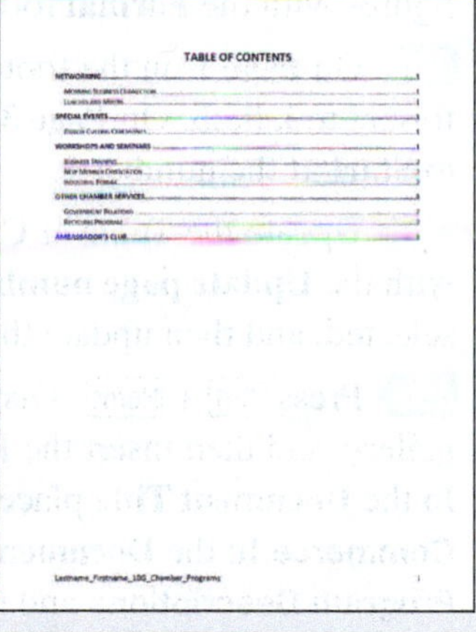

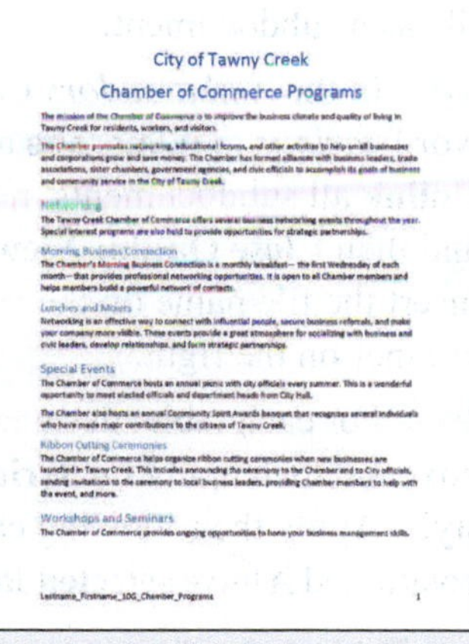

Word 2016, Windows 10, Microsoft Corporation

FIGURE 10.59

(Project 10G Chamber Programs continues on the next page)

CONTENT-BASED ASSESSMENTS (MASTERY AND TRANSFER OF LEARNING)

Mastering Word Project 10G Chamber Programs (continued)

1 Start Word. From your student files, open the file **w10G_Chamber_Programs**. Navigate to your **Word Chapter 10** folder, and then create a folder named **Project 10G Save** the document in your **Project 10G** folder as **Lastname_Firstname_10G_Chamber_Programs**

2 Apply the **Heading 1** style to the paragraphs *Networking*, *Special Events*, *Workshops and Seminars*, and *Other Chamber Services*.

3 Apply the **Heading 2** style to the paragraphs that begin *Morning*, *Lunches*, *Ribbon*, *Business Training*, *New Member*, *Industrial*, *Government*, and *Recycling*.

4 Beginning with the paragraph *Networking*, select all remaining text in the document and then create a master document.

5 From your student files, open the file **w10G_Ambassadors_Club**. **Save** the file in your **Project 10G** folder as **Lastname_Firstname_10G_Ambassadors_Club** and then **Close** the document. At the end of the master document, **Insert** the **Lastname_Firstname_10G_Ambassadors_Club** file as a subdocument.

6 In the *Ambassadors Club* subdocument, change the word *various* to **numerous** and then **Save** your changes. **Unlink** all subdocuments, remove all section breaks, and then **Close Outline View**. On **Page 1**, in the footer, insert the file name on the left and a **Plain Number** page number on the right.

7 For each table, deselect the **Header Row** check box, and then apply the **Grid Table 4 – Accent 1** table style. Apply the following captions to the four tables, positioned **Above selected item**.

Table 1: Appliances
Table 2: Glass and Aluminum
Table 3: Old Tires
Table 4: Scrap Metal

8 If a blank paragraph displays below the *Scrap Metal* table, delete it. Beginning on **Page 1**, for each *Heading 1* paragraph—*Networking*, *Special Events*, *Workshops and Seminars*, *Other Chamber Services*, and *Ambassador's Club*, use the **Mark Entry** dialog box to **Mark** the text as a **Main entry**.

9 Below each *Heading 1* paragraph, mark each *Heading 2* paragraph as a **Subentry** using the appropriate *Heading 1* text for the **Main entry**.

10 At the end of the document, insert a manual page break, type **INDEX** and then press Enter two times. Select the text you typed, change the **Font Size** to **16**, apply **Bold**, and then apply **Center**. In the last paragraph of the document, insert an index with the **Formal** format and the page numbers right aligned.

11 Press Ctrl + Home, and then insert a **Next Page** section break. Press Ctrl + Home, and then apply the **Normal** style. Type **TABLE OF CONTENTS** and then press Enter two times. Select the text you typed, change the **Font Size** to **16**, apply **Bold**, and then apply **Center**. In the last paragraph on the page, insert a table of contents with the **Formal** format. **Save** your changes.

12 On **Page 1**, position the insertion point in the last paragraph of the page—to the left of the section break, and then insert a manual page break. Type **TABLE OF FIGURES** and then press Enter. Select the text you typed, change the **Font Size** to **16**, apply **Bold**, and then apply **Center**. In the last paragraph on the page, insert a table of figures with the **Formal** format. **Save** your changes.

13 On **Page 1**, in the footer, change the page number format to **i, ii, iii**. On **Page 3**, change the **Page numbering** to **Start at** the number **1**.

14 Update the **Table of Contents** and **Table of Figures** with the **Update page numbers only** option button selected, and then update the **Index**.

15 Press Ctrl + Home. Display the **Cover Page** gallery, and then insert the **Retrospect** cover page. In the **Document Title** placeholder, type **Chamber of Commerce** In the **Document Subtitle** placeholder, type **Program Descriptions** and then delete all other text on the page.

16 On the cover page, insert a **DRAFT 1** watermark.

17 Display the document properties. In the **Tags** box, type **chamber programs** and in the **Categories** box, type your course name and section number. If necessary, edit the author name to display your name. **Save** and **Close** your document. If directed by your instructor to do so, submit your paper printout, your electronic image of your document that looks like a printed document, or your original Word file.

END | You have completed Project 10G

Apply a combination of the 10A and 10B skills.

GO! Fix It Project 10H Boards Summary **MyITLab**

GO! Make It Project 10I Internship Program **MyITLab**

GO! Solve It Project 10J Health Department **MyITLab**

GO! Solve It Project 10K Volunteer Program

PROJECT FILES

For Project 10K, you will need the following file:

w10K_Volunteer_Program

You will save your file as:

Lastname_Firstname_10K_Volunteer_Program

Open the file **w10K_Volunteer_Program** and save it to your **Word Chapter 10** folder as **Lastname_Firstname_10K_Volunteer_Program** Insert the file name and page number in the footer. Format the title paragraphs and apply Heading 1 styles to paragraph headings. Format the tables attractively and insert captions. Create a table of contents and table of figures on separate pages. Create an index that displays main headings as well as specific names for departments and organizations. Hyphenate and paginate the document. Modify the page number format for the first two pages. Add appropriate document properties. Print your document or submit electronically as directed by your instructor.

Performance Level

Performance Element	Exemplary: You consistently applied the relevant skills	Proficient: You sometimes, but not always, applied the relevant skills	Developing: You rarely or never applied the relevant skills
Format tables and insert captions	All tables are formatted attractively and appropriate captions are inserted.	At least one table is not formatted or an appropriate caption is not inserted.	No tables are formatted and no captions are inserted.
Create table of contents and table of figures	The table of contents and table of figures are created correctly.	The table of contents or table of figures is not created correctly.	The table of contents and table of figures are not created.
Create index	The index is created and includes appropriate entries.	The index is created but some entries are missing.	The index is not created.
Hyphenate and paginate	The document is hyphenated and paginated appropriately.	The document is not hyphenated or is not paginated appropriately.	The document is not hyphenated and is not paginated appropriately.
Insert and format page numbers	Page numbers are inserted in the footer and formatted correctly.	Page numbers are inserted in the footer but not formatted correctly.	Page numbers are not inserted in the footer.

END | You have completed Project 10K

RUBRIC

The following outcomes-based assessments are *open-ended assessments*. That is, there is no specific correct result; your result will depend on your approach to the information provided. Make *Professional Quality* your goal. Use the following scoring rubric to guide you in *how* to approach the problem and then to evaluate *how well* your approach solves the problem.

The *criteria*—Software Mastery, Content, Format and Layout, and Process—represent the knowledge and skills you have gained that you can apply to solving the problem. The *levels of performance*—Professional Quality, Approaching Professional Quality, or Needs Quality Improvements—help you and your instructor evaluate your result.

	Your completed project is of Professional Quality if you:	Your completed project is Approaching Professional Quality if you:	Your completed project Needs Quality Improvements if you:
1-Software Mastery	Choose and apply the most appropriate skills, tools, and features and identify efficient methods to solve the problem.	Choose and apply some appropriate skills, tools, and features, but not in the most efficient manner.	Choose inappropriate skills, tools, or features, or are inefficient in solving the problem.
2-Content	Construct a solution that is clear and well organized, contains content that is accurate, appropriate to the audience and purpose, and is complete. Provide a solution that contains no errors of spelling, grammar, or style.	Construct a solution in which some components are unclear, poorly organized, inconsistent, or incomplete. Misjudge the needs of the audience. Have some errors in spelling, grammar, or style, but the errors do not detract from comprehension.	Construct a solution that is unclear, incomplete, or poorly organized, contains some inaccurate or inappropriate content, and contains many errors of spelling, grammar, or style. Do not solve the problem.
3-Format and Layout	Format and arrange all elements to communicate information and ideas, clarify function, illustrate relationships, and indicate relative importance.	Apply appropriate format and layout features to some elements, but not others. Overuse features, causing minor distraction.	Apply format and layout that does not communicate information or ideas clearly. Do not use format and layout features to clarify function, illustrate relationships, or indicate relative importance. Use available features excessively, causing distraction.
4-Process	Use an organized approach that integrates planning, development, self-assessment, revision, and reflection.	Demonstrate an organized approach in some areas, but not others; or, use an insufficient process of organization throughout.	Do not use an organized approach to solve the problem.

Apply a combination of the 10A and 10B skills.

GO! Think Project 10L Technology Plan

Build from Scratch

PROJECT FILES

For Project 10L, you will need the following files:

Two new blank Word documents

You will save your files as:

Lastname_Firstname_10L_Technology_Plan
Lastname_Firstname_10L_Maintenance

The City of Tawny Creek is developing a new technology plan. Search online for information related to city or state technology plans. Using the data you find, in your own words, create a report—including headings and subheadings—that explains the steps required to develop a plan. These steps should include the following topics: a vision statement, the goals, a needs assessment, design and purchase, and implementation. Define what each step means; do not enter specific data. Save your file as **Lastname_Firstname_10L_Technology_Plan**

Create a master document with subdocuments for each step. Save a second, new document as **Lastname_Firstname_10L_Maintenance** and then create information defining maintenance. Insert this file as a subdocument in the master document. Unlink the subdocuments. Insert at least one bookmark and related cross-reference. For each document, insert the file name in the footer and add appropriate document properties. Print both documents or submit electronically as directed by your instructor.

END You have completed Project 10L

Build from Scratch

GO! Think Project 10M City Parks — MyITLab

Build from Scratch

You and GO! Project 10N Personal Journal — MyITLab

Embedding and Linking Objects and Using Macros

11

WORD 2016

PROJECT 11A

OUTCOMES

In a Word document, embed and link Microsoft Office objects.

PROJECT 11B

OUTCOMES

In a Word document, create, edit, and run macros.

OBJECTIVES

1. Embed an Excel Chart in a Word Document
2. Embed an Access Table in a Word Document
3. Embed a PowerPoint File in a Word Document
4. Link Objects to a Word Document

OBJECTIVES

5. Create Macros
6. Run Macros
7. Edit a Macro in the Visual Basic Editor

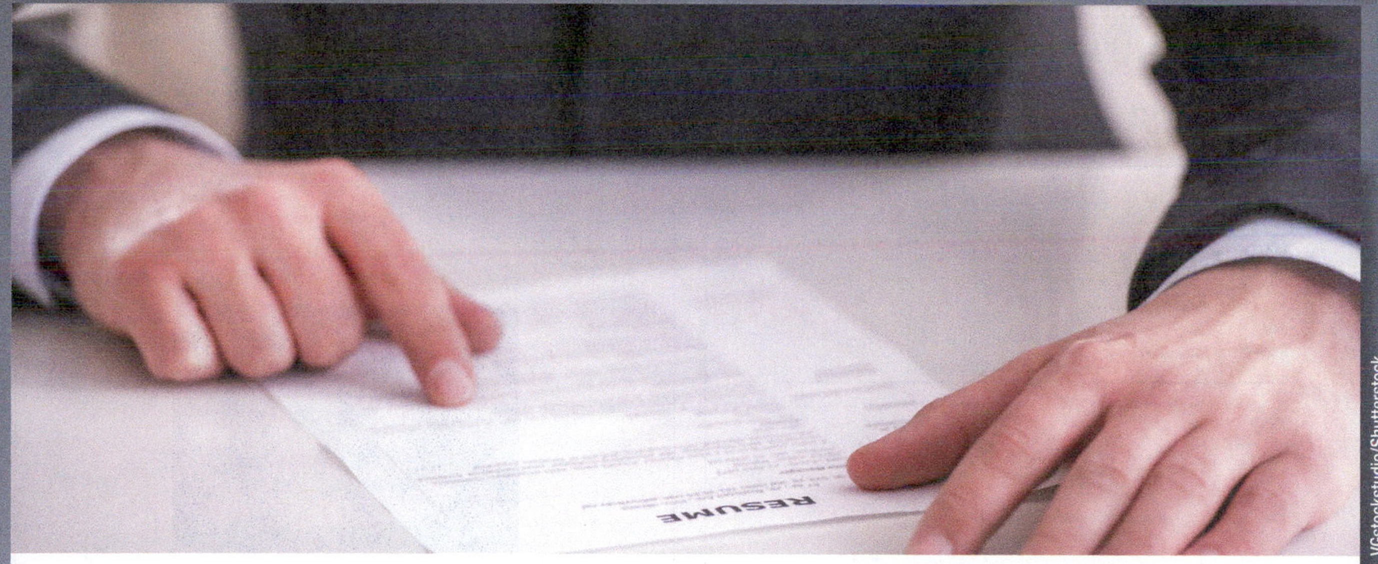

VGstockstudio/Shutterstock

In This Chapter

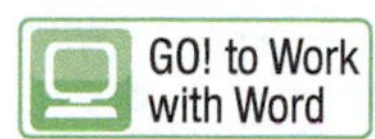

In this chapter, you will add objects to an existing document from files created with other Office applications. Because Microsoft Office is an integrated program suite, you can use the features of other programs within your Word document. In addition to copying and pasting objects and text, you can embed and link data from other Office applications—for example, an Access table, an Excel chart, or a PowerPoint slide. Using Word features and the Visual Basic Editor, you will also create macros. A macro enables you to improve your efficiency by performing a series of tasks in a single action.

The projects in this chapter relate to the **Greater Baltimore Job Fair**. Each year, the organization holds a number of targeted job fairs. In addition, the annual Greater Baltimore Job Fair event draws over two hundred employers in more than forty industries and registers more than eight thousand candidates. Candidate registration is free; employers pay a nominal fee for a booth to display and present at the fair. Candidate resumes and employer postings are managed by a computerized state-of-the-art database system, allowing participants quick and accurate access to job data and candidate qualifications.

Survey Memo

PROJECT ACTIVITIES

In Activities 11.01 through 11.05, you will embed and link objects—Excel charts, an Access table, a PowerPoint presentation, and a Word document—in a memo that discusses a publicity plan for the annual Greater Baltimore Job Fair. Related files are based on survey responses from employers and job seekers. Your completed documents will look similar to Figure 11.1.

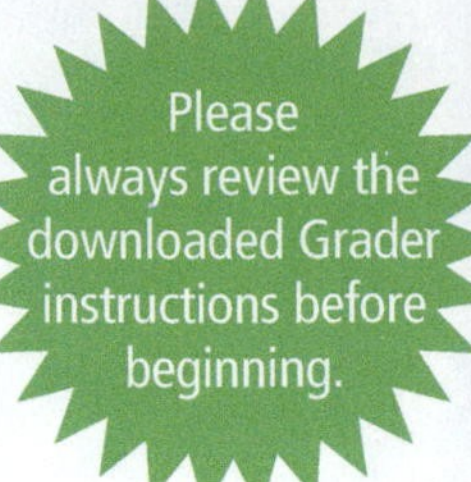

PROJECT FILES

If your instructor wants you to submit Project 11A in the MyITLab Grader system, log into MyITLab, locate Grader Project 11A, and then download the files for this project.

For Project 11A, you will need the following files:

w11A_Fair_Growth (Excel workbook)
w11A_Fair_Participants (Access database)
w11A_Participant_Survey (Word Document)
w11A_Publicity_Strategy (PowerPoint presentation)
w11A_Survey_Memo (Word document)
w11A_Survey_Results (Excel workbook)

You will save your files as:

Lastname_Firstname_11A_Survey_Memo (Word document)
Lastname_Firstname_11A_Survey_Results (Excel workbook)
Lastname_Firstname_11A_Participant_Survey (Word document)

PROJECT RESULTS

GO! Walk Thru Project11A

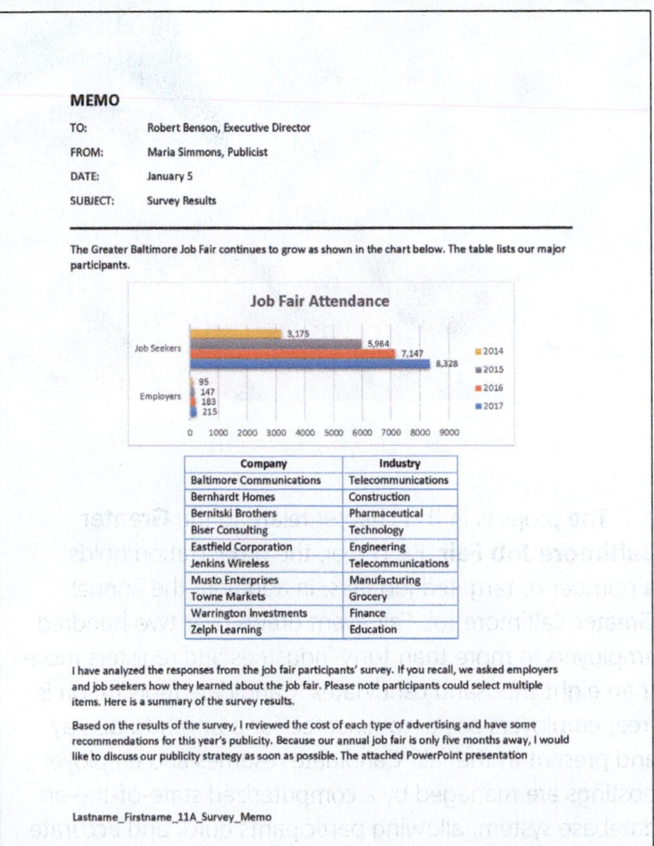

MEMO

TO: Robert Benson, Executive Director

FROM: Maria Simmons, Publicist

DATE: January 5

SUBJECT: Survey Results

The Greater Baltimore Job Fair continues to grow as shown in the chart below. The table lists our major participants.

Company	Industry
Baltimore Communications	Telecommunications
Bernhardt Homes	Construction
Bernitski Brothers	Pharmaceutical
Biser Consulting	Technology
Eastfield Corporation	Engineering
Jenkins Wireless	Telecommunications
Musto Enterprises	Manufacturing
Towne Markets	Grocery
Warrington Investments	Finance
Zelph Learning	Education

I have analyzed the responses from the job fair participants' survey. If you recall, we asked employers and job seekers how they learned about the job fair. Please note participants could select multiple items. Here is a summary of the survey results.

Based on the results of the survey, I reviewed the cost of each type of advertising and have some recommendations for this year's publicity. Because our annual job fair is only five months away, I would like to discuss our publicity strategy as soon as possible. The attached PowerPoint presentation

Lastname_Firstname_11A_Survey_Memo

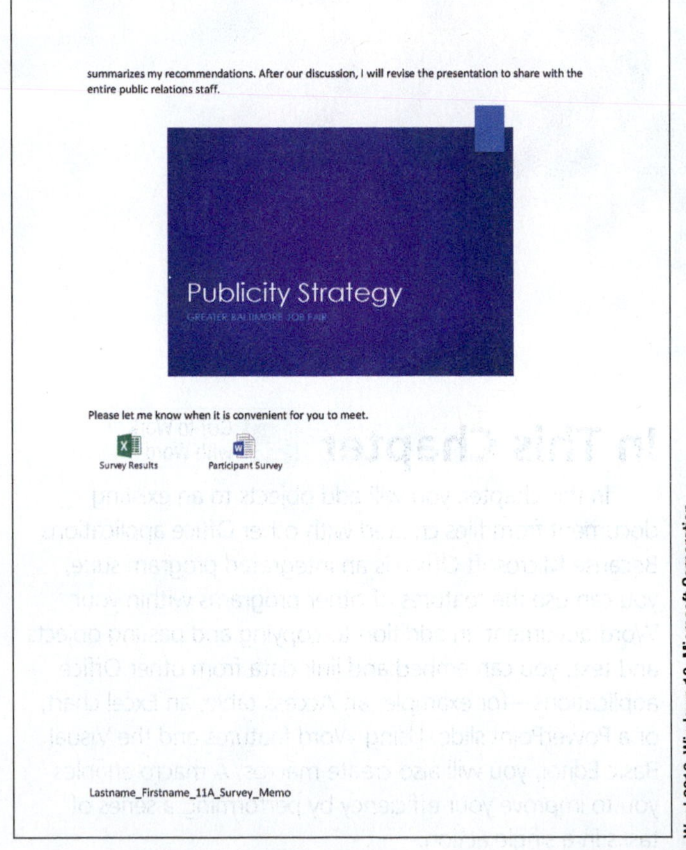

summarizes my recommendations. After our discussion, I will revise the presentation to share with the entire public relations staff.

Please let me know when it is convenient for you to meet.

Lastname_Firstname_11A_Survey_Memo

FIGURE 11.1 Project 11A Survey Memo

Objective 1 Embed an Excel Chart in a Word Document

GO! Learn How Video W11-1

Microsoft Office programs support ***OLE***, which stands for ***Object Linking and Embedding***. OLE is a program-integration technology for sharing information between Office programs. An ***object*** such as a table, chart, file, or other form of information created in one Office program—the ***source file***—can be inserted in a file created with a different Office program—the ***destination file***. ***Embedding*** is the process of inserting information from a source file, using a format that you specify, into a destination file. An ***embedded object*** maintains the structure of the original application but is not connected to the source file.

ALERT! **You Will Need a Computer with Microsoft Access**

You will need a computer with Microsoft Access installed to complete this project.

Activity 11.01 | Using Paste Special to Embed an Excel Chart

When working with numerical data and creating charts, it makes sense to use Excel. Embedding an Excel chart in a Word document enables the reader to review the data in a visual format without viewing an entire spreadsheet.

ALERT! **To submit as an autograded project, log into MyITLab and download the files for this project instead of the student data files.**

1. Start Word, on the left click **Open Other Documents**, click **Browse**, and then in the **Open** dialog box, navigate to the student data files that accompany this chapter. Open the file **w11A_Participant_Survey**.

2. Click the **File tab**, on the left click **Save As**, click **Browse**, and then in the **Save As** dialog box, navigate to the location where you are saving your files for this chapter. Create a new folder named **Word Chapter 11** Using your own name, save the file as **Lastname_Firstname_11A_Participant_Survey**

3. Click **Save** [Save icon], and then in the upper right corner of the Word window, click **Close** [×].

   You will use this Word file later in this Project.

4. Start Excel, on the left click **Open Other Workbooks**, click **Browse**, and then in the **Open** dialog box, navigate to the student data files that accompany this chapter. Open the file **w11A_Survey_Results**.

5. Click the **File tab**, on the left click **Save As**, click **Browse**, and then in the **Save As** dialog box, navigate to your **Word Chapter 11** folder. Using your own name, save the file as **Lastname_Firstname_11A_Survey_Results**

6. Click **Save** [Save icon], and then in the upper right corner of the Excel window, click **Close** [×].

   You will use this Excel file later in this Project.

7. Start Word again, on the left click **Open Other Documents**, click **Browse**, and then in the **Open** dialog box, navigate to the student data files that accompany this chapter. Open the file **w11A_Survey_Memo**.

8. Click the **File tab**, on the left click **Save As**, click **Browse**, and then in the **Save As** dialog box, navigate to your **Word Chapter 11** folder. Using your own name, save the file as **Lastname_Firstname_11A_Survey_Memo** and if necessary, display the rulers and formatting marks.

9. Insert the file name in the footer.

10 On the taskbar, click **File Explorer**, navigate to the student data files that accompany this chapter, and then locate and open the Excel file **w11A_Fair_Growth**. Compare your screen with Figure 11.2.

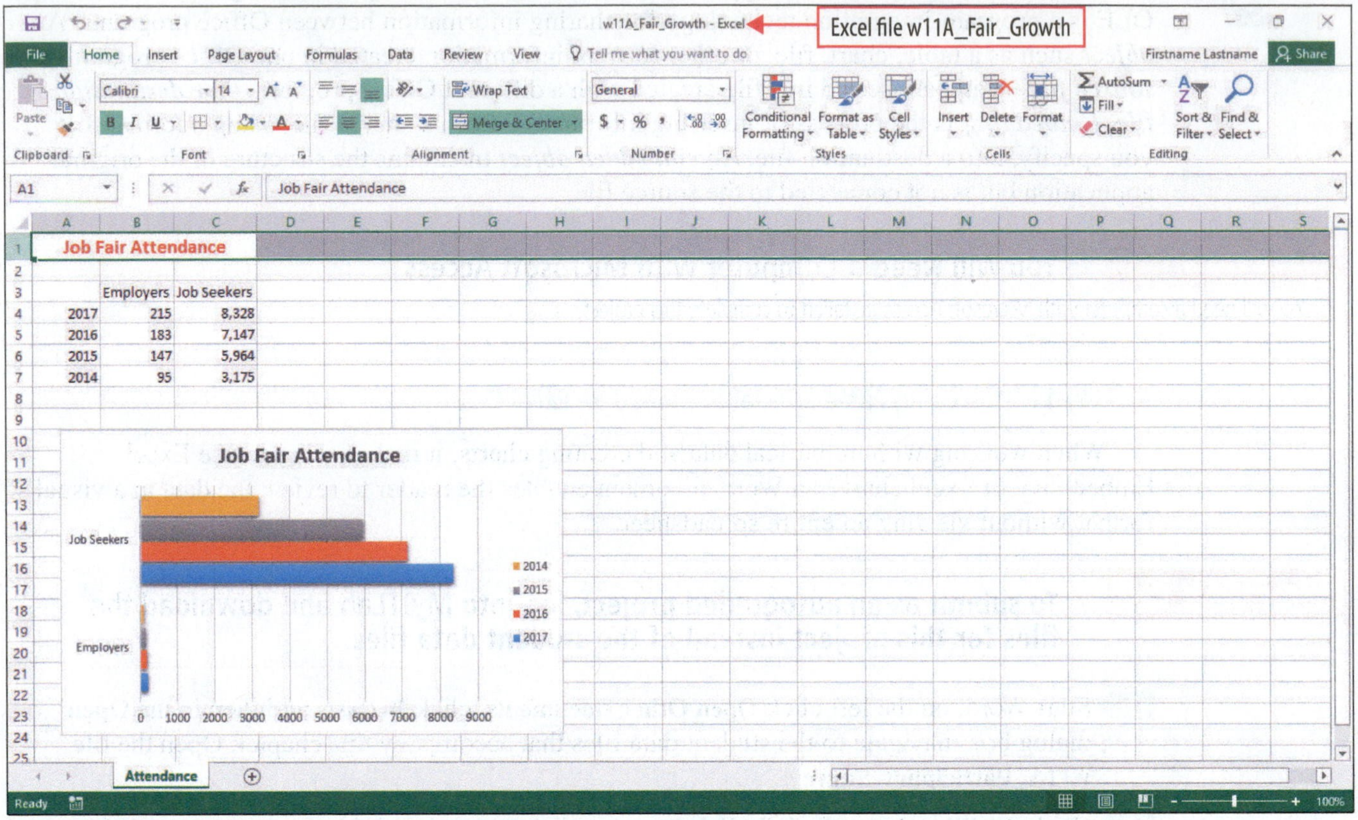

Excel file w11A_Fair_Growth

	A	B	C
1	Job Fair Attendance		
2			
3		Employers	Job Seekers
4	2017	215	8,328
5	2016	183	7,147
6	2015	147	5,964
7	2014	95	3,175

Job Fair Attendance

FIGURE 11.2

11 Click the edge of the chart *Job Fair Attendance* to select the chart, right-click, and then on the shortcut menu, click **Copy** to copy the Excel chart to the Clipboard.

12 On the taskbar, click the **Word** icon to make your *Lastname_Firstname_11A_Survey_Memo* document active. Immediately below the horizontal line, locate the paragraph that begins *The Greater Baltimore*. Click to position the insertion point at the end of the paragraph, and then press Enter one time.

13 On the **Home tab**, in the **Clipboard group**, click the **Paste button arrow** to display the **Paste Options** gallery. Compare your screen with Figure 11.3.

There are different ways to paste an Excel chart into a Word document. The options vary according to the type of object you are pasting in the document.

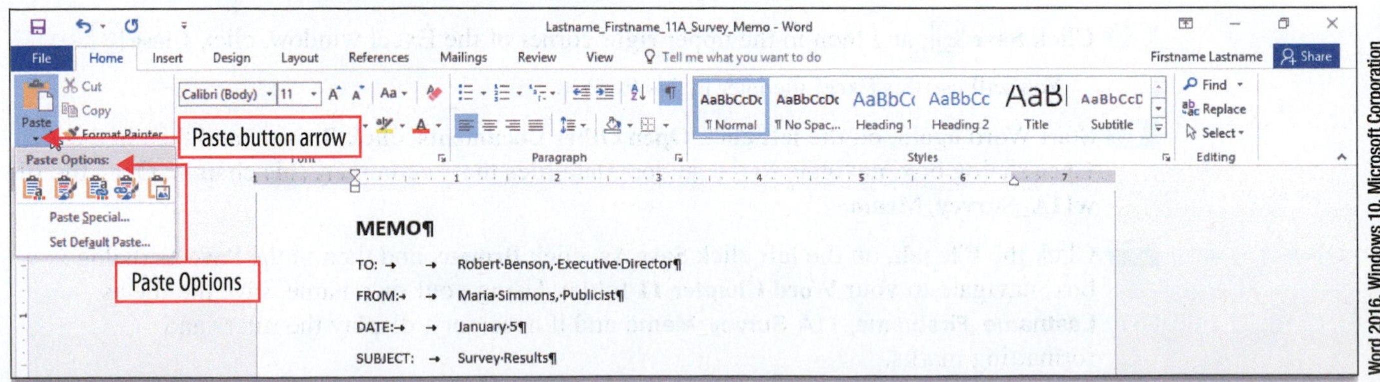

FIGURE 11.3

14 In the **Paste Options** gallery, point to each of the buttons, and then read the **ScreenTip**. Take a moment to study the table shown in Figure 11.4, which describes the various pasting options.

PASTE OPTIONS	
COMMAND NAME	**DESCRIPTION**
Use Destination Theme & Embed Workbook	Pastes the information applying formatting based on the destination file's theme and enables you to edit the object using Word's features without changing the source file.
Keep Source Formatting & Embed Workbook	Pastes the information using the formatting in the source file and enables you to edit the object using Word's features without changing the source file.
Use Destination Theme & Link Data	Pastes the information applying formatting based on the destination file's theme and links the data so that any editing uses the features of—and changes—the source file.
Keep Source Formatting & Link Data	Pastes the information using the formatting of the source file and links the data so that any editing uses the features of—and changes—the source file.
Picture	Pastes the information as a picture object in the document.

FIGURE 11.4

15 In the **Paste Options** gallery, click **Keep Source Formatting & Embed Workbook (K)**.

The Excel chart displays in the Word document.

16 Click in a blank area slightly inside the chart's border. Click **Chart Elements** [+], and then select the **Data Labels** check box. Press Esc. Click again in a blank area of the chart, and then on the ribbon, click the **Chart Tools Format tab**. In the **Size group**, click in the **Shape Height box**, type **2.1** and press Enter.

When you embed an Excel chart using the *Keep Source Formatting & Embed Workbook* paste option, you can use the Chart Tools contextual tabs in Word to edit the chart.

17 With the chart still selected, press Ctrl + E to center the chart horizontally on the page. Click outside the chart to deselect, and then compare your screen with Figure 11.5.

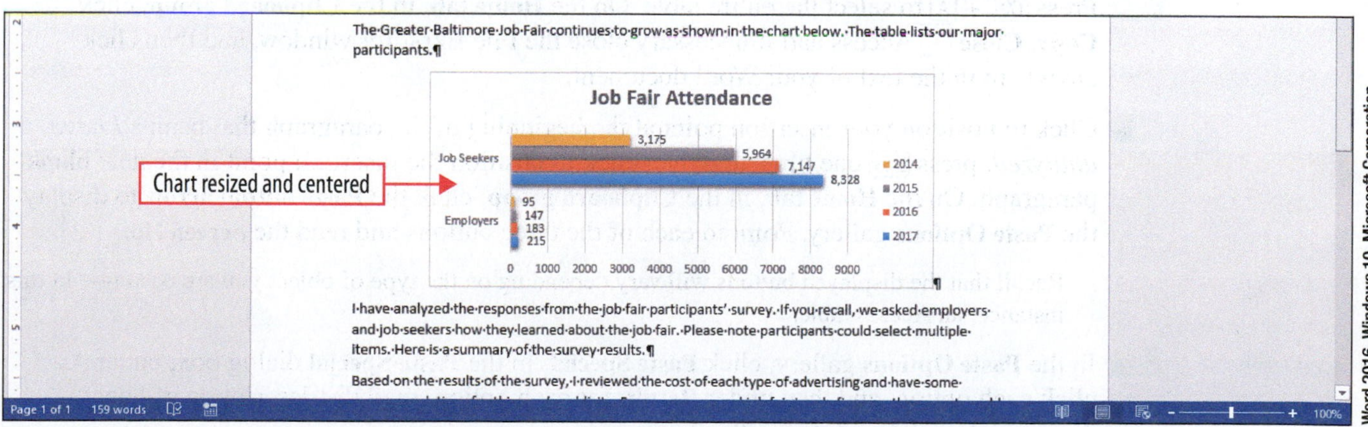

FIGURE 11.5

18 **Save** your document.

19 On the taskbar, click the **Excel** icon to make the *w11A_Fair_Growth* file active.

Because you embedded the chart, the changes you made in your Word document are not reflected in the Excel workbook—the source file.

20 **Close** Excel and do *not* save any changes if prompted to do so.

Objective 2 Embed an Access Table in a Word Document

Recall that Access is a database application. You can copy an Access table, or query, and paste it in a Word document in a tabular format. The embedded table can be modified in Word without opening or changing the Access file.

Activity 11.02 | Using Paste Special to Embed an Access Table

1 On the taskbar, click **File Explorer**, navigate to your student data files, and then locate and open the Access file **w11A_Fair_Participants**. Immediately below the ribbon, if the *Security Warning* banner displays, click Enable Content.

2 On the left side of the Access window, under **Tables**, double-click the table **Major_Participants**. Compare your screen with Figure 11.6.

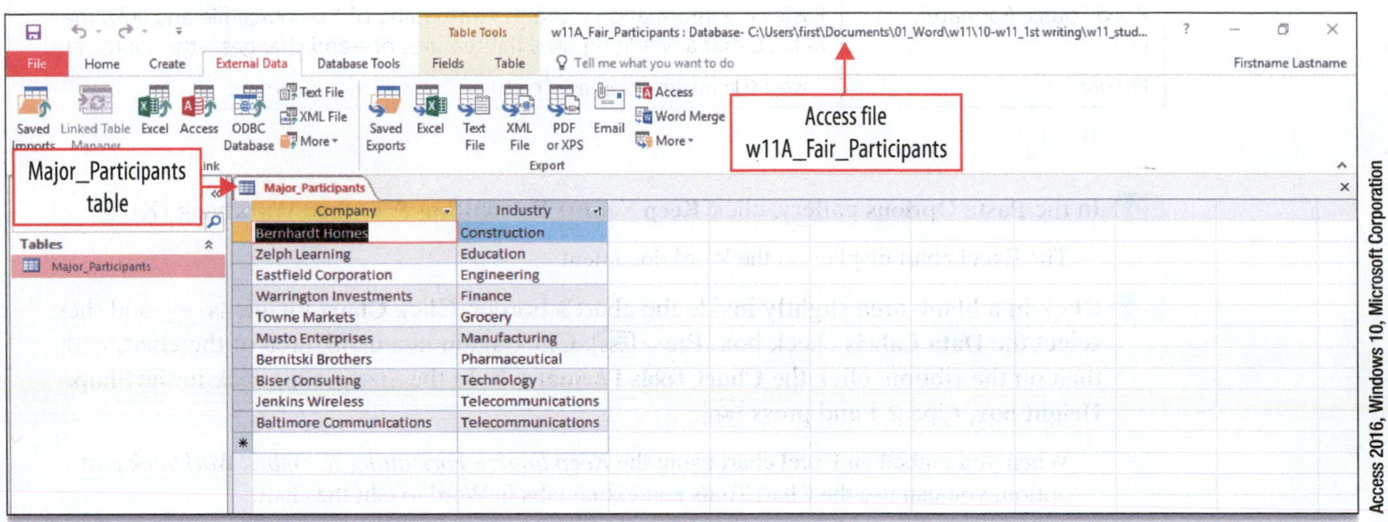

FIGURE 11.6

3 Press Ctrl + A to select the entire table. On the **Home tab**, in the **Clipboard group**, click **Copy**. **Close** Access and if necessary close the File Explorer window, and then click anywhere in the text of your Word document.

4 Click to position your insertion point at the beginning of the paragraph that begins *I have analyzed*, press Enter one time, and then click to position the insertion point in the new blank paragraph. On the **Home tab**, in the **Clipboard group**, click the **Paste button arrow** to display the **Paste Options** gallery. Point to each of the three buttons and read the **ScreenTip**.

Recall that the displayed buttons will vary depending on the type of object you are pasting—in this instance, an Access table.

5 In the **Paste Options** gallery, click **Paste Special**. In the **Paste Special** dialog box, under **As**, click each option, and then under **Result**, for each option, read the description of how the Access data will be pasted in the document.

The Paste Special feature enables you to insert data from the Access table in various formats.

6 In the **Paste Special** dialog box, under **As**, click **Formatted Text (RTF)**. Compare your screen with Figure 11.7.

Selecting the Formatted Text (RTF) option will insert the data in a table format.

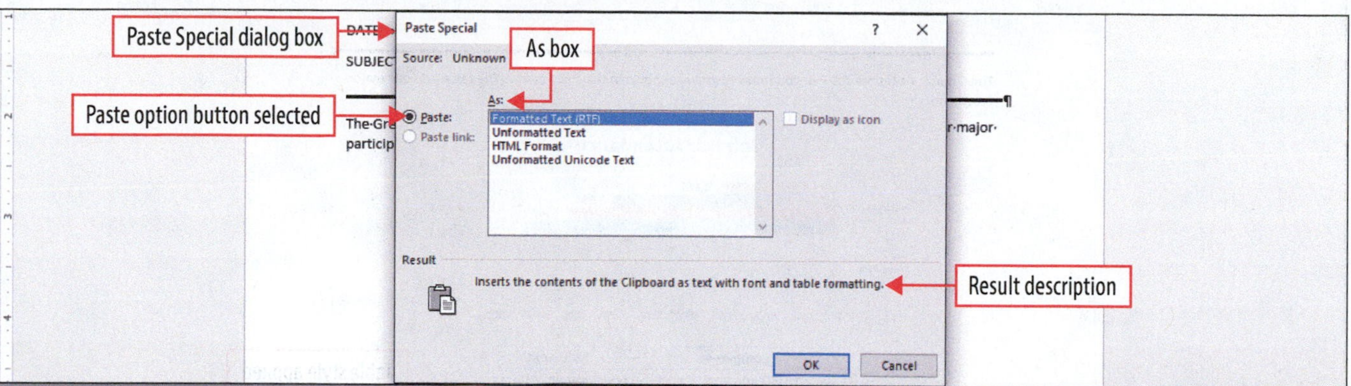

FIGURE 11.7 Word 2016, Windows 10, Microsoft Corporation

7 In the **Paste Special** dialog box, click **OK**.

8 In the table, click in the first cell—*Company*. Click the **Table Tools Design tab**, and then in the **Table Styles group**, click **More** ▾. In the **Table Styles** gallery, scroll as necessary, and then under **List Tables**, in the third row, select the second table style—**List Table 3 – Accent 1**.

The Access table is embedded into the Word document. Because the data was inserted in a tabular format, you can use Table Tools contextual tabs in Word to modify the table.

9 Click the **Table Tools Layout tab**, and then in the **Data group**, click **Sort**. In the **Sort** dialog box, be sure *Company* displays in the **Sort by** box. Under **My list has**, be sure the **Header row** option button is selected, and then click **OK**.

The table is sorted to display company names in ascending order. By embedding the table, you can edit the data in Word without changing the original Access file. Additionally, if changes are made to the Access file, they will not be reflected in the Word document.

10 On the **Table Tools Layout tab**, in the **Table group**, click **Properties**. In the **Table Properties** dialog box, on the **Table tab**, under **Alignment**, click **Center**, and then click **OK**. Deselect the table, and then compare your screen with Figure 11.8.

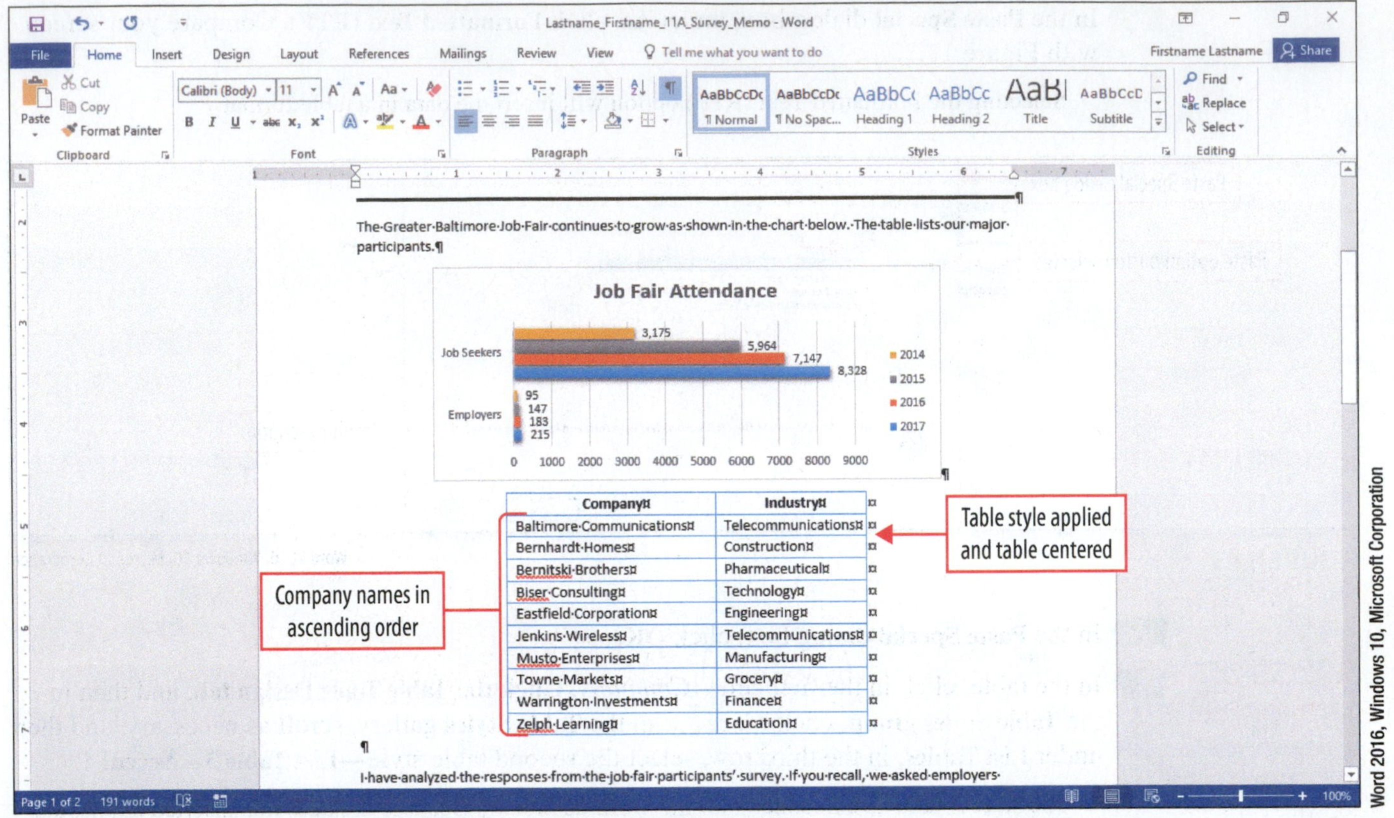

Word 2016, Windows 10, Microsoft Corporation

FIGURE 11.8

11 In the table, right-click any proper names that are flagged as spelling errors, and click **Ignore All** for each. **Save** your document.

Objective 3 Embed a PowerPoint File in a Word Document

GO! Learn How Video W11-3

When you embed a PowerPoint object into your Word file, the information in the Word file will not change if the original PowerPoint is updated. This is useful when you do not want the information in the Word document to change if the PowerPoint file is updated.

Activity 11.03 | Embedding a PowerPoint File

1 On the taskbar, click **File Explorer**, navigate to your student data files that accompany this chapter, and then locate and open the file **w11A_Publicity_Strategy**. Click the **Design tab**, and then compare your screen with Figure 11.9.

PowerPoint is a tool to create slide show presentations. A PowerPoint presentation contains individual slides that may include text, graphic elements, and other objects. This file contains six slides and is formatted with the *Ion Boardroom* theme. You can embed an entire PowerPoint presentation within a Word document.

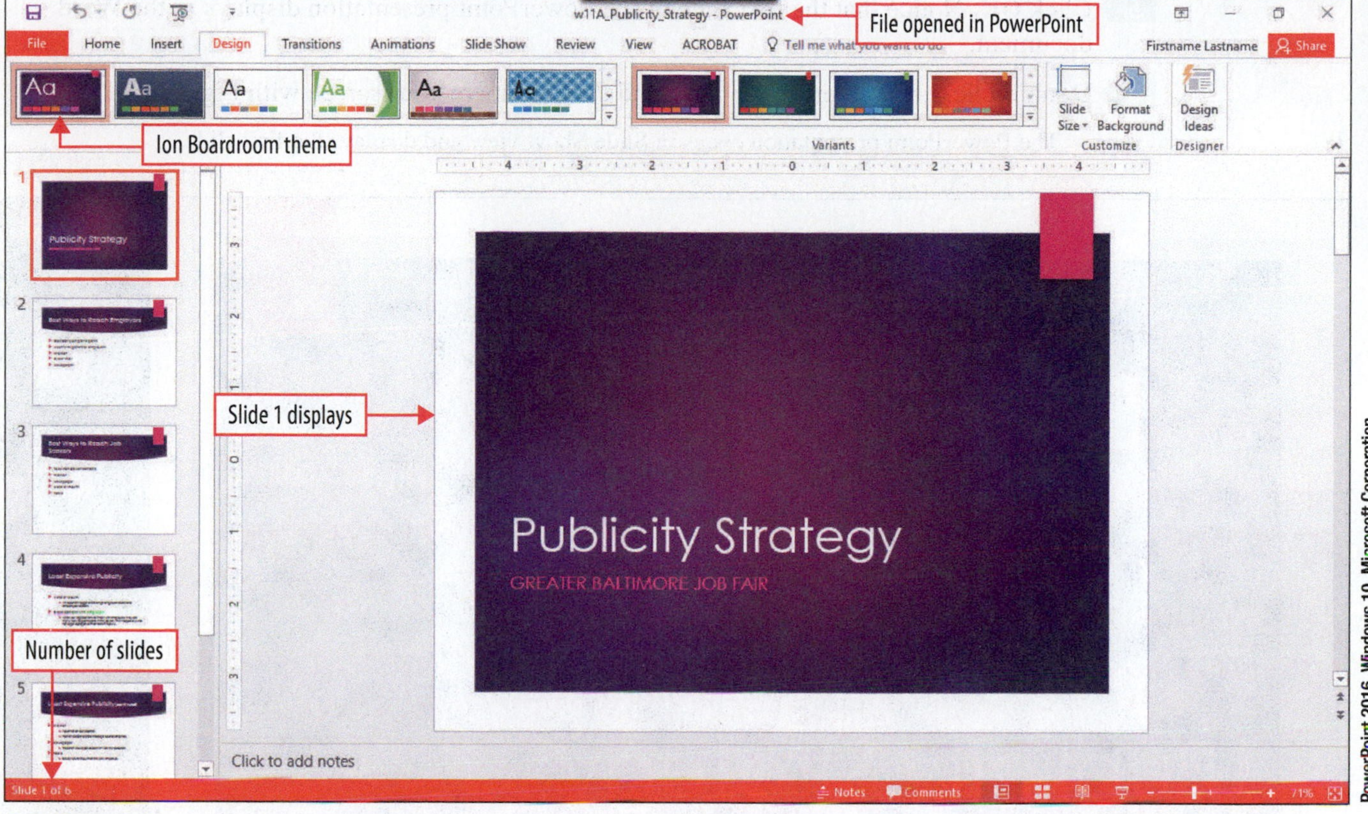

FIGURE 11.9

2 **Close** PowerPoint, and if necessary, close the File Explorer window.

It is good practice to view a file before embedding it to ascertain that the file contains the correct information.

3 In your Word document, locate the paragraph that begins *Based on the results*, and then click to position the insertion point at the end of the paragraph—on **Page 2**. Press Enter one time. Click the **Insert tab**, and then in the **Text group**, click **Object**.

The Object dialog box enables you to choose what type of object to insert in the document. By default, the Create New tab displays—allowing you to create a new object in a variety of formats.

4 In the **Object** dialog box, click the **Create from File tab**. Click **Browse**, navigate to your student data files, click **w11A_Publicity_Strategy**, and then click **Insert**. Compare your screen with Figure 11.10.

Use the Create from File tab when you want to embed an existing object—in this instance, a PowerPoint file. The file name displays in the File name box.

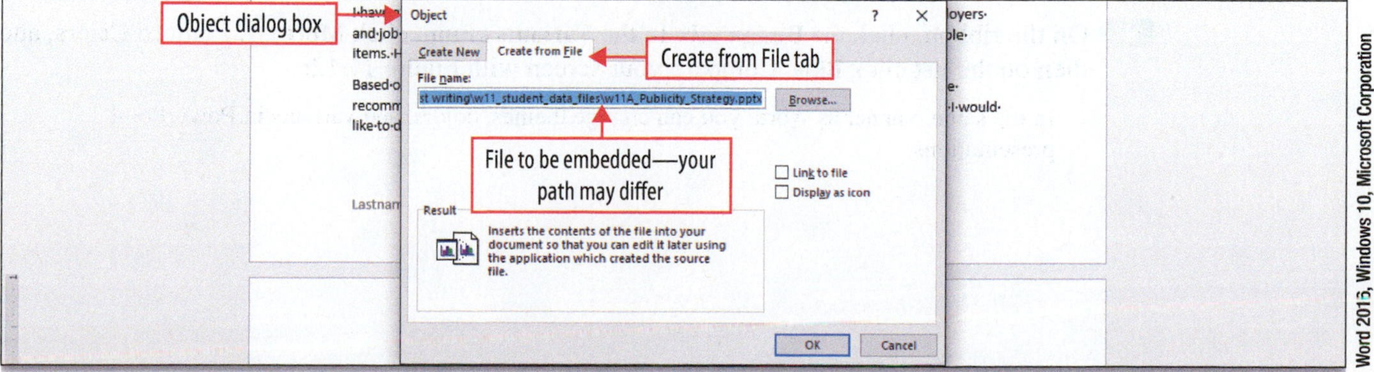

FIGURE 11.10

5 Click **OK**. Notice that the first slide of the PowerPoint presentation displays in the Word document.

6 Double-click the PowerPoint object, and then compare your screen with Figure 11.11.

The PowerPoint presentation opens in Slide Show view and displays the first slide.

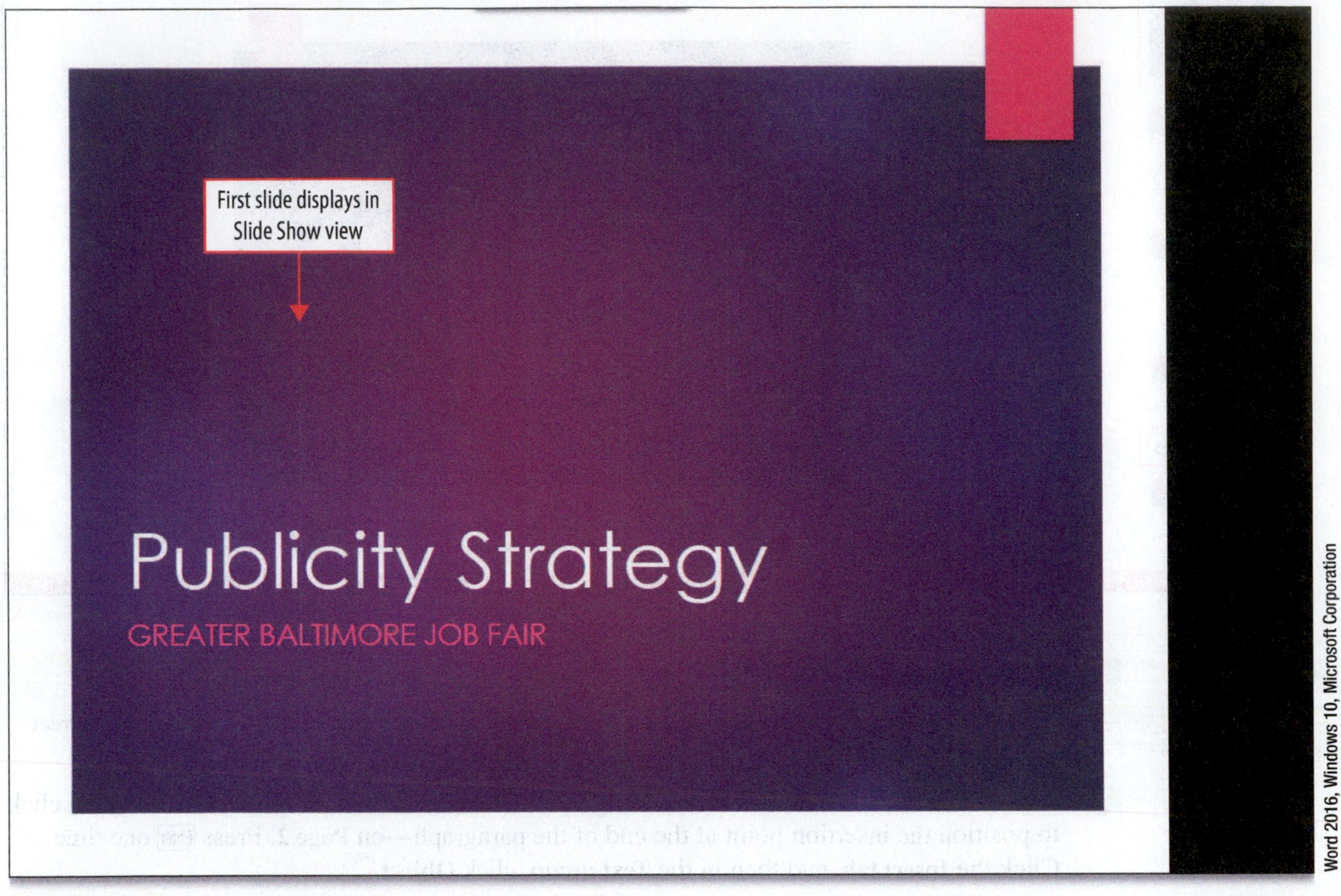

FIGURE 11.11

7 Click the mouse button to advance to the next slide. In the same manner, view the remaining slides in the presentation. Notice that after the last click, you return to the Word document.

8 In the Word document, right-click the PowerPoint object. On the shortcut menu, point to **Presentation Object**, and then click **Edit** to switch to Edit mode.

Although you remain in Word, the ribbon changes to PowerPoint features. You can modify the embedded presentation without changing the original source file.

9 On the ribbon, click the **Design tab**. In the **Variants group**, click **More** . Point to **Colors**, and then on the list click **Blue**. Compare your screen with Figure 11.12.

In the same manner as Word, you can change themes, colors, and variants in PowerPoint presentations.

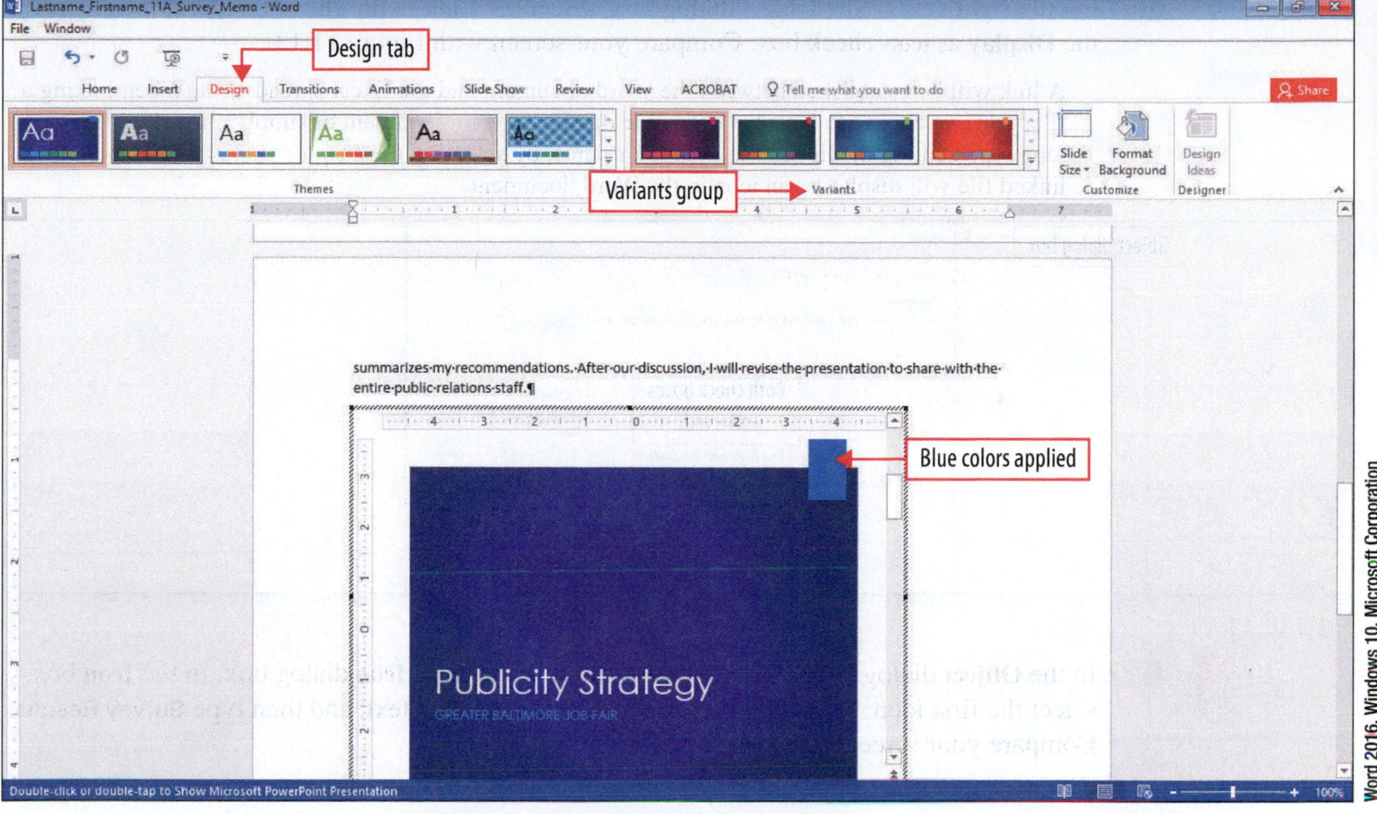

FIGURE 11.12

10 In the Word document, click outside the PowerPoint object to exit Edit mode. Click the slide to select the object, click the **Home tab**, and then in the **Paragraph group**, apply **Center**.

11 Click **Save**.

Objective 4 Link Objects to a Word Document

GO! Learn How Video W11-4

You can modify embedded objects without changing the source files. If you want to make changes to an object in a document and have those changes reflected in the original file, then ***linking*** the object—rather than embedding it—is what you want to do. Linking is the process of inserting information from a source file into a destination file while maintaining a connection between the two.

Activity 11.04 | Linking to an Excel File

1.1.5 Expert

A ***linked object*** is an object that maintains a direct connection to the source file. Linked data is stored in the source file—for example, an Excel workbook; the linked data is not stored in the destination file—in this instance, a Word document.

1 Press Ctrl + End to move to the end of your document, and then press Enter one time.

2 Click the **Insert tab**, and then in the **Text group**, click **Object**. In the **Object** dialog box, click the **Create from File tab**, which enables you to create a link to existing objects.

3 Click **Browse**, navigate to your **Word Chapter 11** folder, and then click the Excel file that you saved earlier with your name, **Lastname_Firstname_11A_Survey_Results**. Click **Insert**.

4 On the right side of the **Object** dialog box, select the **Link to file** check box, and then select the **Display as icon** check box. Compare your screen with Figure 11.13.

A link will be established between the Word document and the Excel spreadsheet. When linking a file, you can choose to have the entire file display in your document or simply choose to display an icon representing the linked file. In this instance, by selecting the *Display as icon* check box, your linked file will display as an icon in the Word document.

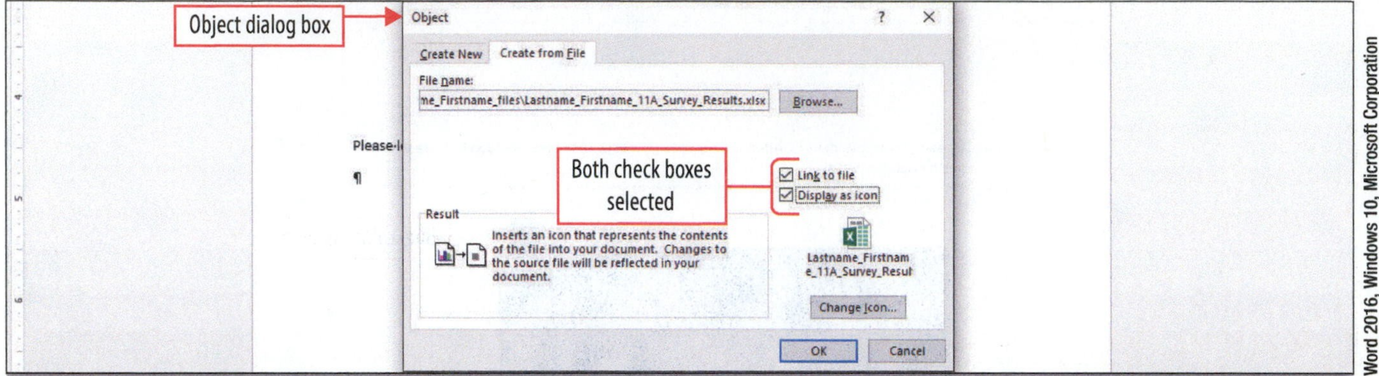

FIGURE 11.13

5 In the **Object** dialog box, click **Change Icon**. In the **Change Icon** dialog box, in the **Icon** box, select the first icon. In the **Caption** box, select the existing text, and then type **Survey Results** Compare your screen with Figure 11.14.

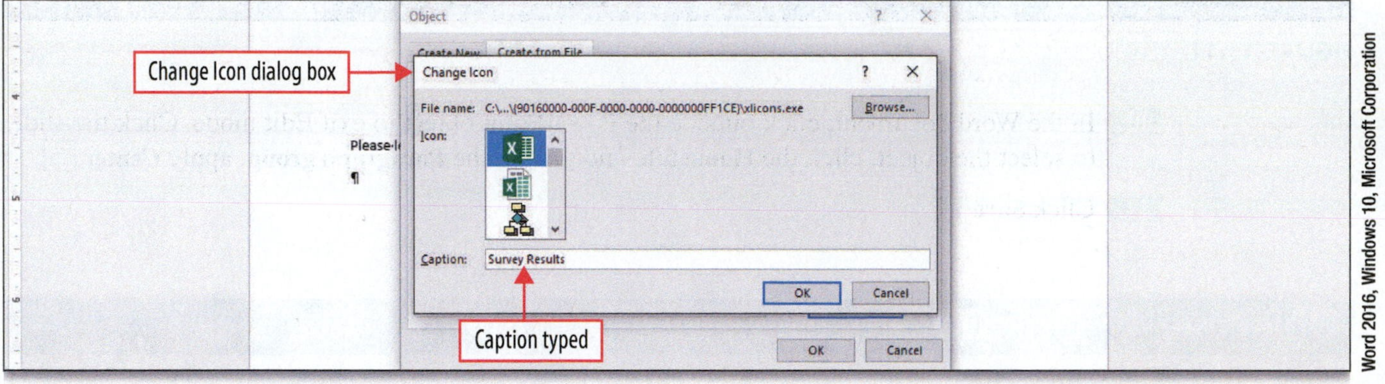

FIGURE 11.14

6 Click **OK** two times, and then compare your screen with Figure 11.15.

An Excel file icon with the modified caption displays in the document. Changing the caption does not change the file name of the linked file.

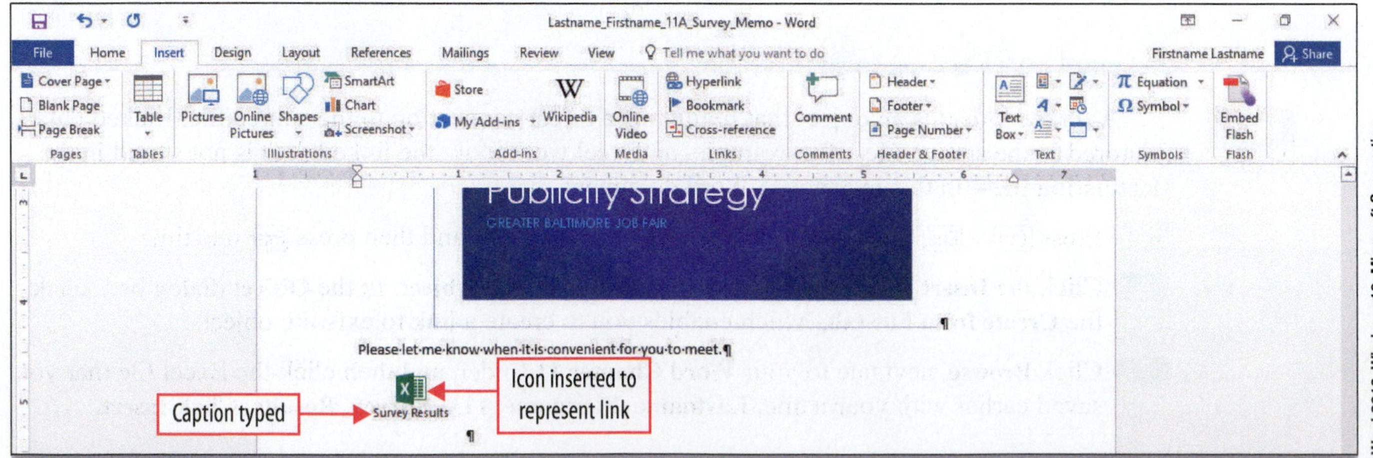

FIGURE 11.15

7 Above *Survey Results,* double-click the icon. If necessary, maximize the Excel window.

Double-clicking the object icon causes the linked object to open in the native application.

ANOTHER WAY Right-click the object icon, from the shortcut menu, point to Linked Worksheet Object, and then click Open Link.

8 Click in cell **B4**—which contains the value *34%*. Type **41** and then press Enter. Notice the chart displays the revised *Job Seekers* value for *Internet*. Compare your screen with Figure 11.16.

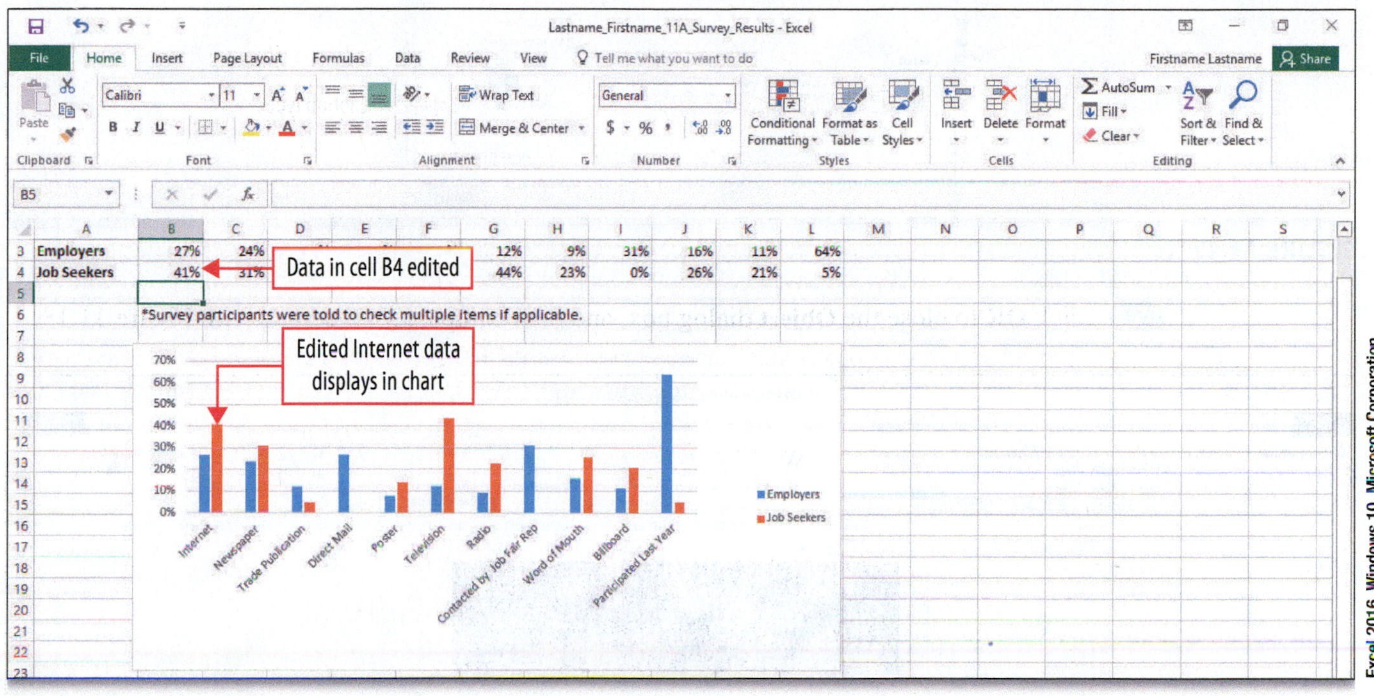

FIGURE 11.16

Excel 2016, Windows 10, Microsoft Corporation

9 **Save** the Excel file, and then **Close** Excel. In your Word document, click **Save**.

NOTE Opening a Document Containing a Linked File

If you close a Word document that contains one or more linked files, when you reopen the document, a Microsoft Word message box will display. The message will prompt you to update the document with data from a linked file. Click Yes to maintain the link and update the information. Additionally, a link will not remain intact if the linked file is moved to a new location.

Activity 11.05 | Linking to Another Word Document

1.1.5 Expert

When linking objects in Word, you are not limited to using different Office application files. You can also link one Word document to another Word document.

1 In your **Lastname_Firstname_11A_Survey_Memo** document, if necessary, click to position the insertion point to the left of the paragraph mark at the end of the document.

2 Press Tab one time.

3 Click the **Insert tab**, and then in the **Text group**, click **Object**. In the **Object** dialog box, click the **Create from File tab**. Click **Browse**, navigate to your **Word Chapter 11** folder, and then click your Word document **Lastname_Firstname_11A_Participant_Survey**. Click **Insert**.

4 On the right side of the **Object** dialog box, select the **Link to file** check box, and then select the **Display as icon** check box. In the **Object** dialog box, click **Change Icon**. In the **Change Icon** dialog box, in the **Caption box**, select the text, and then type **Participant Survey** Click **OK**. Compare your screen with Figure 11.17.

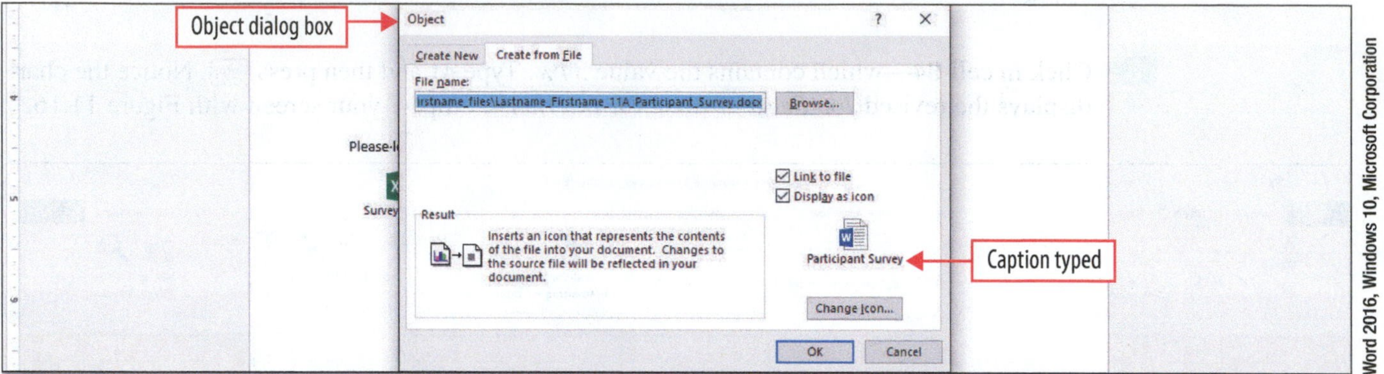

FIGURE 11.17

5 Click **OK** to close the **Object** dialog box, and then compare your screen with Figure 11.18.

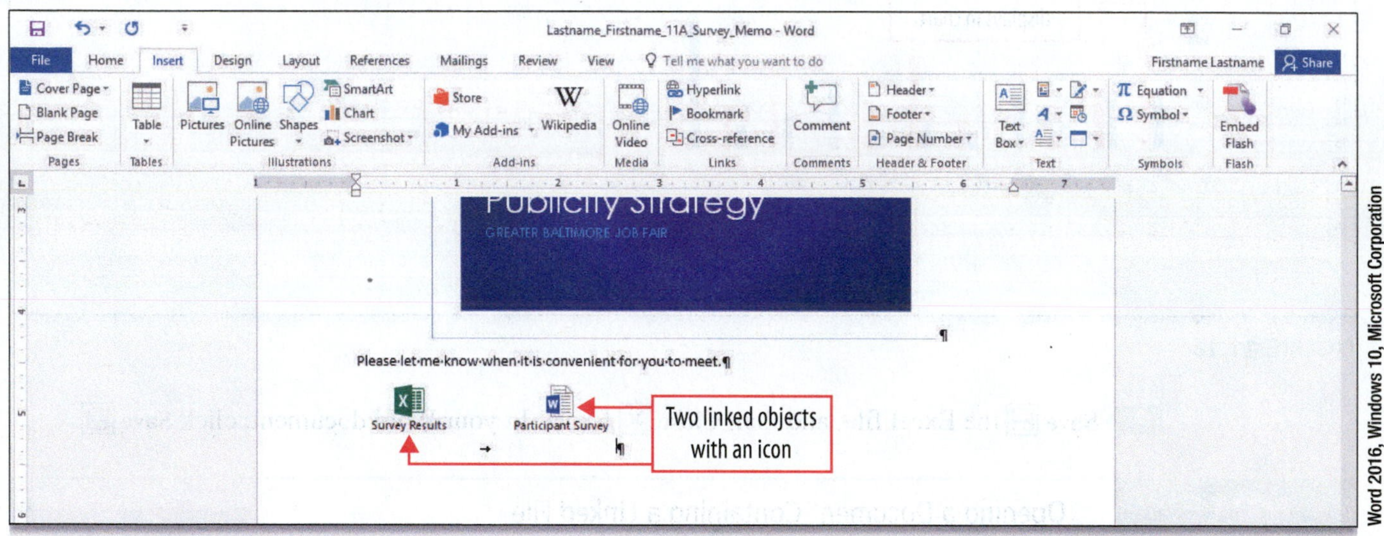

FIGURE 11.18

6 Above *Participant Survey*, double-click the icon, and notice that the linked Word file displays.

When linking an object, it is good practice to verify that the link is working.

7 In your **Lastname_Firstname_11A_Participant_Survey** document, in the first paragraph, select the text **job fair** and then type **Job Fair**

8 **Save** and then **Close** the survey document. In your displayed **Lastname_Firstname_11A_Survey_Memo** document, press Ctrl + Home.

9 Click the **File tab**, and then **Show All Properties**. In the **Tags** box, type **embedded objects** In the **Subject** box, type your course name and section number. If necessary, edit the author name to display your name.

10 On the left, click **Print** to view the Print Preview, and then on the left, click **Save** to save your document and return to the Word window.

11 In the upper right corner of the Word window, click **Close** ☒. If directed by your instructor to do so, for your Lastname_Firstname_11A_Survey_Memo, submit your paper printout, your electronic image of your document that looks like a printed document, or your original Word file. If directed by your instructor, submit your Lastname_Firstname_11A_Survey_Results (Excel file) and your Lastname_Firstname_11A_Participant_Survey (Word document) with this file.

***More* Knowledge** **Editing a Linked File**

You can edit a linked file by directly opening the file and making changes. If the document containing the link is open, right-click the link, and then click Update Link. If the document containing the link is closed, you will be prompted to update the data the next time you open the document.

END | You have completed Project 11A

PROJECT

11B Fair Flyer

PROJECT ACTIVITIES

In Activities 11.06 through 11.14, you will assist Sharon Reynolds, Employer Coordinator for the Greater Baltimore Job Fair, in automating Word tasks by creating macros that will be executed with a single click or a keyboard shortcut. These actions include inserting a specific footer, adding a formatted heading, inserting the current date and time in a header, and adjusting indentation in a bulleted list. Your completed documents will look similar to Figure 11.19.

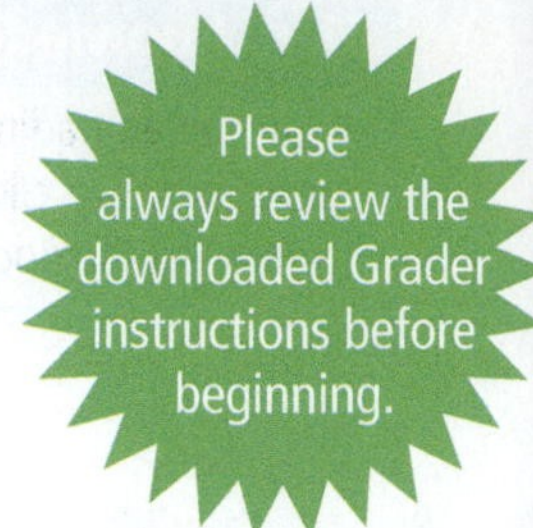

PROJECT FILES

If your instructor wants you to submit Project 11B in the MyITLab grader system, log into MyITLab, locate Grader Project 11B, and then download the files for this project.

For Project 11B, you will need the following files:

w11B_Fair_Flyer (Word document)
w11B_Fair_Memo (Word document)

You will save your files as:

Lastname_Firstname_11B_Fair_Memo
Lastname_Firstname_11B_Fair_Flyer (optional to submit)

PROJECT RESULTS

GO! Walk Thru Project11B

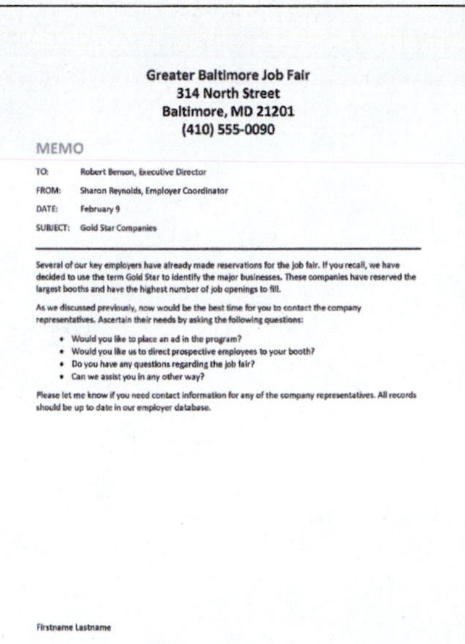

Greater Baltimore Job Fair
314 North Street
Baltimore, MD 21201
(410) 555-0090

MEMO

TO: Robert Benson, Executive Director
FROM: Sharon Reynolds, Employer Coordinator
DATE: February 9
SUBJECT: Gold Star Companies

Several of our key employers have already made reservations for the job fair. If you recall, we have decided to use the term Gold Star to identify the major businesses. These companies have reserved the largest booths and have the highest number of job openings to fill.

As we discussed previously, now would be the best time for you to contact the company representatives. Ascertain their needs by asking the following questions:

- Would you like to place an ad in the program?
- Would you like us to direct prospective employees to your booth?
- Do you have any questions regarding the job fair?
- Can we assist you in any other way?

Please let me know if you need contact information for any of the company representatives. All records should be up to date in our employer database.

Firstname Lastname

```
Sub Footer()
'
' Footer Macro
' Inserts the author's name in the footer
'
    If ActiveWindow.View.SplitSpecial <> wdPaneNone Then
        ActiveWindow.Panes(2).Close
    End If
    If ActiveWindow.ActivePane.View.Type = wdNormalView Or ActiveWindow. _
        ActivePane.View.Type = wdOutlineView Then
        ActiveWindow.ActivePane.View.Type = wdPrintView
    End If
    ActiveWindow.ActivePane.View.SeekView = wdSeekCurrentPageFooter
    Selection.TypeText Text:="Firstname Lastname"
    ActiveWindow.ActivePane.View.SeekView = wdSeekMainDocument
End Sub
Sub Heading()
'
' Heading Macro
' Inserts the name, address, and phone number for the organization
'
    Selection.TypeText Text:="Greater Baltimore Job Fair"
    Selection.TypeParagraph
    Selection.TypeText Text:="314 North Street"
    Selection.TypeParagraph
    Selection.TypeText Text:="Baltimore, MD 21201"
    Selection.TypeParagraph
    Selection.TypeText Text:="(410) 555-0090"
    Selection.HomeKey Unit:=wdStory, Extend:=wdExtend
```

Firstname Lastname

```
    Selection.Style = ActiveDocument.Styles("No Spacing")
    Selection.Font.Size = 18
    Selection.Font.Bold = wdToggle
    Selection.ParagraphFormat.Alignment = wdAlignParagraphCenter
End Sub
```

Firstname Lastname

Word 2016, Windows 10, Microsoft Corporation

FIGURE 11.19 Project 11B Fair Flyer

Objective 5 Create Macros

GO! Learn How Video W11-5

A ***macro*** is set of commands and instructions that you group as a single command to accomplish a task automatically. When using Word, all macros are created in a programming language called ***Visual Basic for Applications,*** or ***VBA***. You can use a macro to save time when performing routine editing and formatting, to combine several repetitive steps into one step, to make an option in a dialog box more accessible, or to automate a complex series of tasks. For example, you could create a macro that performs the steps to produce a customized header, and then you could insert the header into multiple documents without having to re-create the formatting steps for each document.

Activity 11.06 | Saving a Macro-Enabled Document

MOS 1.1.6 Expert

When you create, save, and use macros in a document, you must save the document as a Word Macro-Enabled Template (.dotm) or as a Word Macro-Enabled Document (.docm). Saving a document as either a Word document (.docx) or Word Template (.dotx) will cause any macros to be removed.

ALERT! **To submit as an autograded project, log into MyITLab and download the files for this project.**

1. Start Word. On the left click **Open Other Documents**, click **Browse**, and then in the **Open** dialog box, navigate to the student data files that accompany this chapter. Locate and open **w11B_Fair_Flyer**. Click the **File tab**, on the left click **Save As**, click **Browse**, and then in the **Save As** dialog box, navigate to your **Word Chapter 11** folder.
2. In the lower portion of the dialog box, click the **Save as type arrow**, and then on the list, click **Word Macro-Enabled Document**.
3. In the **File name** box, using your own name, type **Lastname_Firstname_11B_Fair_Flyer** and then compare your screen with Figure 11.20.

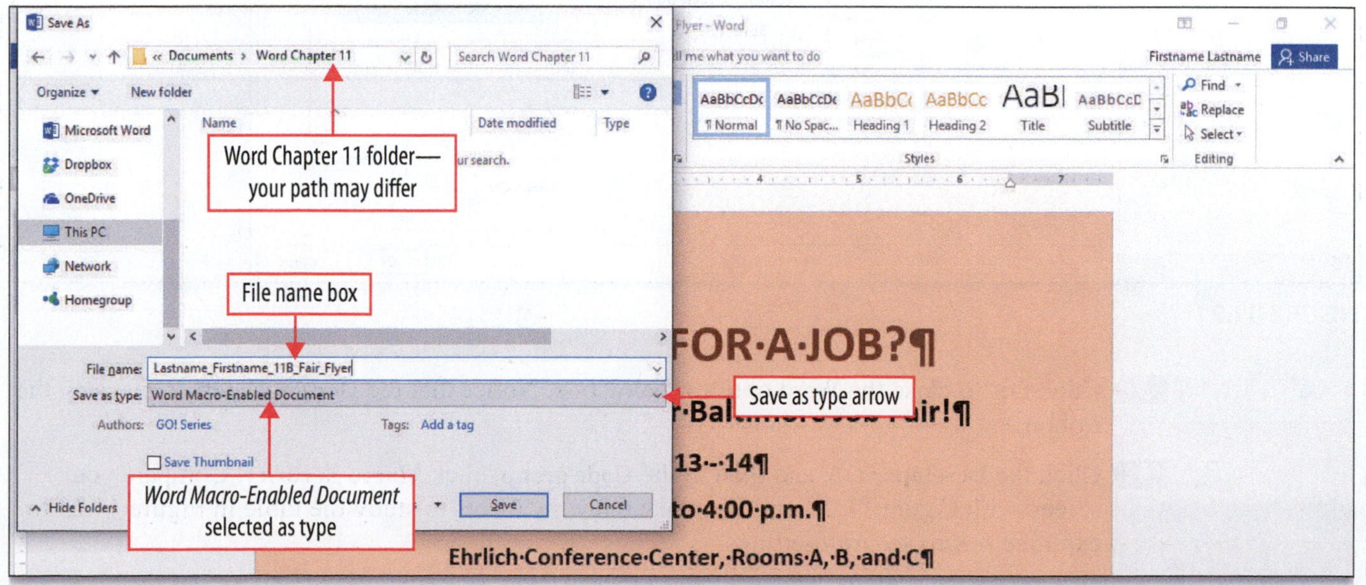

Word 2016, Windows 10, Microsoft Corporation

FIGURE 11.20

4. Click **Save**.

By saving your file as a macro-enabled document, new macros and changes to existing macros are automatically saved.

Activity 11.07 | Changing Macro Security Settings

1.1.6 Expert

When you create your own macros, you can trust the source. However, macros written by others may pose a potential security risk. Because a macro is written in a programming language, files can be erased or damaged by inserting unauthorized code. This unauthorized code is called a ***macro virus***. To protect systems from this type of virus, organizations commonly set their security programs to disable macros automatically or block any email attachment that contains a macro. Because the staff of the Greater Baltimore Job Fair uses macros to automate some of their tasks, you will adjust the security level in Word to allow macros to run.

1 Click the **File tab**, on the left click **Options**, and then in the **Word Options** dialog box, on the left, click **Customize Ribbon**.

Main tabs that display on the ribbon are indicated with a check mark.

2 On the right, in the **Main Tabs** list, locate and then select the **Developer** check box. Compare your screen with Figure 11.21.

The Developer tab extends the capabilities of Word—including commands for inserting content controls and creating macros.

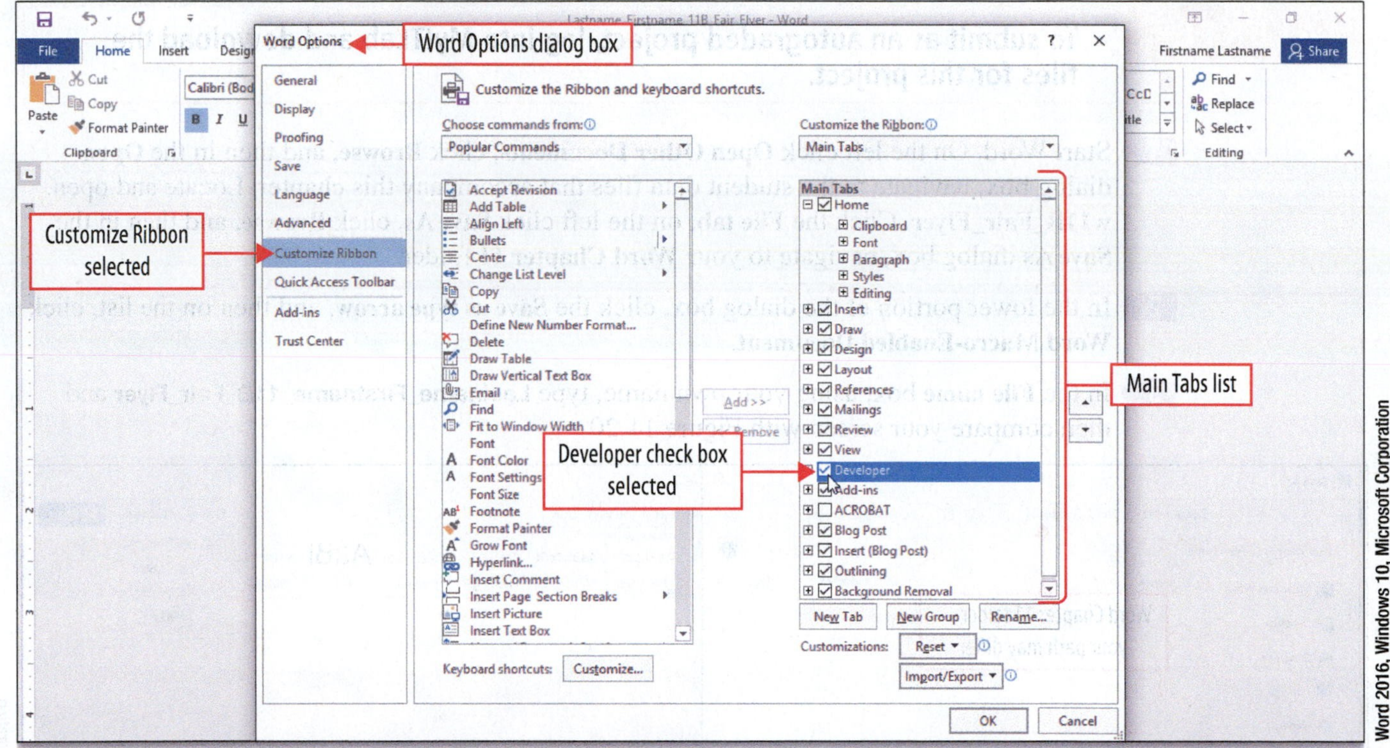

FIGURE 11.21

3 Click **OK** to close the Word options dialog box. Notice that the **Developer tab** displays on the ribbon.

4 Click the **Developer tab**, and then in the **Code group**, click **Macro Security**. Compare your screen with Figure 11.22, and then take a few moments to study the table in Figure 11.23 to examine macro security settings.

Macro Settings display in the Trust Center dialog box. Your selected option may differ.

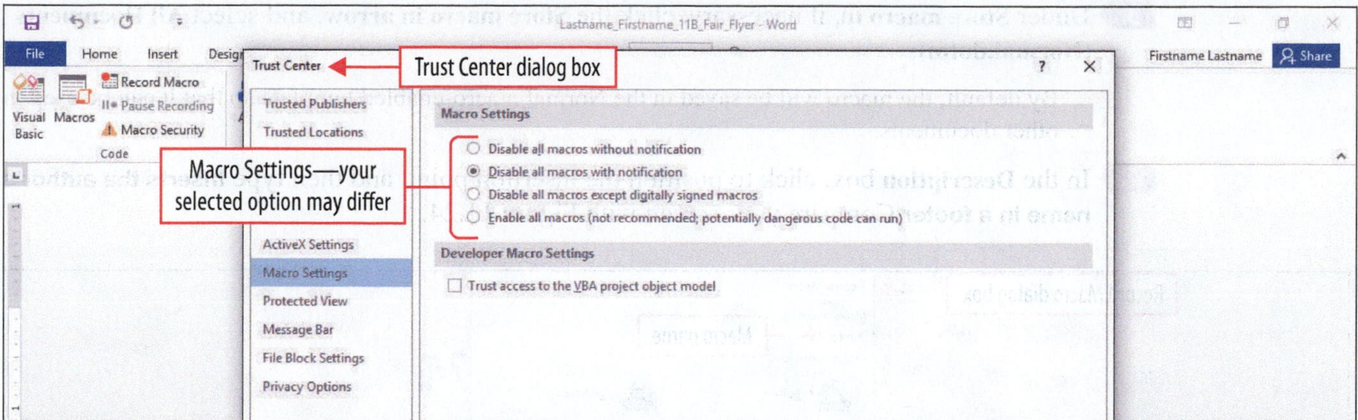

FIGURE 11.22

Word 2016, Windows 10, Microsoft Corporation

MACRO SECURITY SETTINGS	
SETTING	**DESCRIPTION**
Disable all macros without notification	Macros will not run in a document, and no notification message will display.
Disable all macros with notification	Macros will not run in a document, but a notification message will display with an option to run macros.
Disable all macros except digitally signed macros	Macros that have a valid digital signature and have been confirmed by Microsoft will be allowed to run.
Enable all macros	All macros will run. This option is a high security risk.

FIGURE 11.23

5 In the **Trust Center** dialog box, under **Macro Settings**, if necessary, click the **Disable all macros with notification** option button.

By selecting this macro setting, opening a document that has a macro attached causes a security warning to display and gives you the option to disable the macro.

6 Click **OK** to close the **Trust Center** dialog box.

Activity 11.08 | Recording a Keyboard-Activated Macro

4.1.3 Expert

The process of creating a macro while performing specific actions in a document is called ***recording*** a macro. Before you record a macro, the first thing you should do is plan the exact steps you will perform, and it is a good idea to write down those steps. For example, if you want to apply bold formatting and a specific Text Effect style during the recording of a macro, review the steps required to achieve this formatting before you begin recording the macro. Then you can record the macro by completing all of the steps. In this Activity, you will create a macro that will insert the file name in the footer.

1 On the **Developer tab**, in the **Code group**, click **Record Macro**.

2 In the **Record Macro** dialog box, in the **Macro name** box, type **Footer**

Each macro must be given a unique name. It is a good idea to name the macro with a descriptive name to help you recall the function of the macro. If you reuse a name, the new macro will replace the original macro. Macro names cannot contain spaces; however, you can use underscores to improve readability.

3 Under **Store macro in**, if necessary, click the **Store macro in arrow**, and select **All Documents (Normal.dotm)**.

By default, the macro will be saved in the Normal macro-enabled template so that it can be used in other documents.

4 In the **Description** box, click to position the insertion point, and then type **Inserts the author's name in a footer** Compare your screen with Figure 11.24.

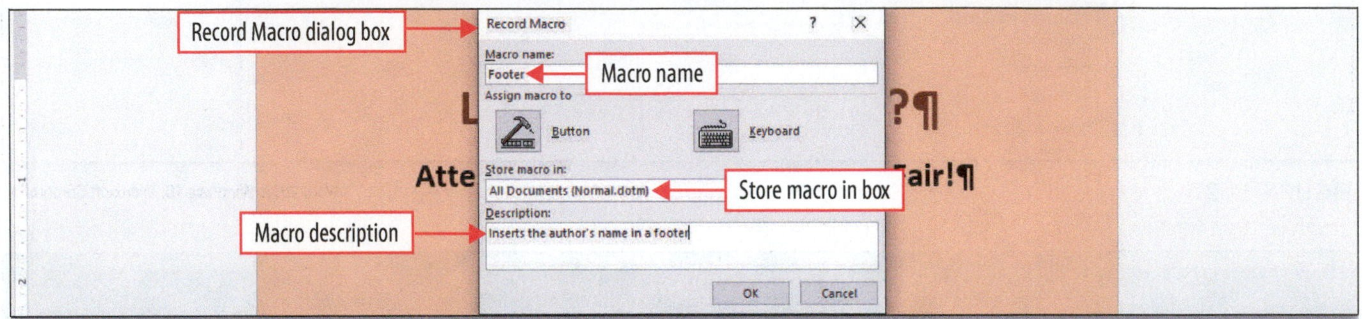

FIGURE 11.24

Word 2016, Windows 10, Microsoft Corporation

5 Under **Assign macro to**, click the **Keyboard** icon.

You can assign a button or a shortcut key to a macro. By clicking the *Keyboard* icon, you can assign a shortcut key that, when pressed, will cause the macro to run, or be executed.

6 In the **Customize Keyboard** dialog box, with the insertion point in the **Press new shortcut key** box, press and hold Alt and Ctrl, and then press B.

Alt+Ctrl+B displays in the *Press new shortcut key* box. If the shortcut key you choose is already in use, you should select another combination so that the original shortcut is not replaced. If the combination of keys is already in use, it will display next to *Currently assigned to.*

7 In the lower left corner of the dialog box, click **Assign**. Compare your screen with Figure 11.25.

Alt+Ctrl+B displays in the Current keys box. This keyboard sequence is assigned to the macro that is selected in the Commands box—your Footer macro. The macro name displays as *Normal. NewMacros.Footer* to indicate that the macro is user-created and stored in the Normal template.

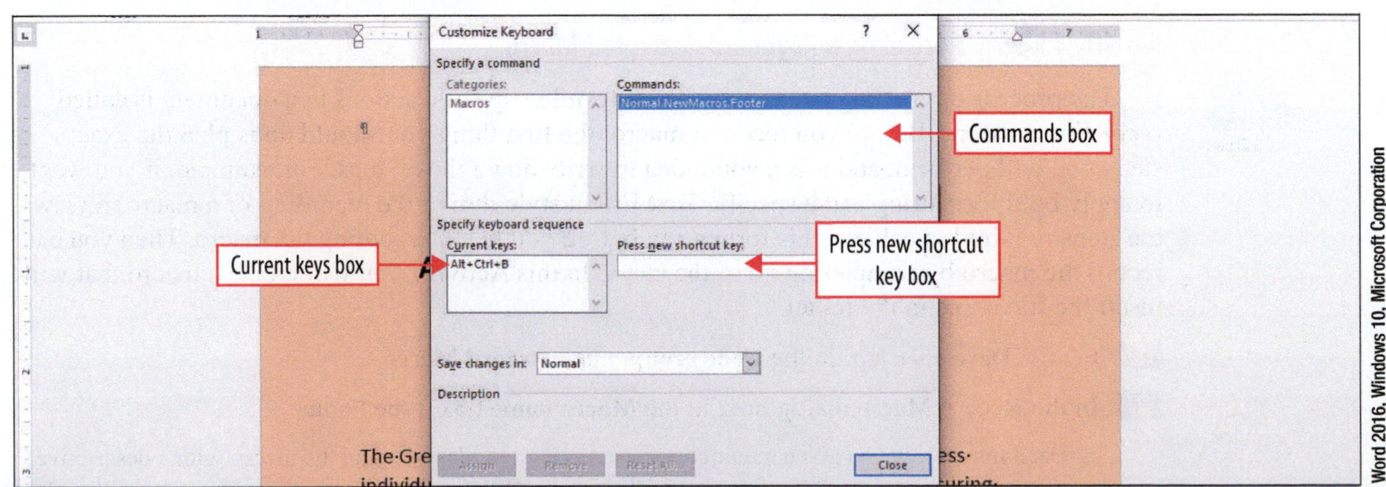

Word 2016, Windows 10, Microsoft Corporation

FIGURE 11.25

8 Near the bottom of the **Customize Keyboard** dialog box, click **Close**. Point anywhere in the document, and notice that the pointer changes. Compare your screen with Figure 11.26.

The pointer indicates that you are now in recording mode. Any actions that you make will be recorded as part of the macro until you turn off the recording of the macro. It is important to take your time as you perform each action so that extra steps are not recorded as part of the macro.

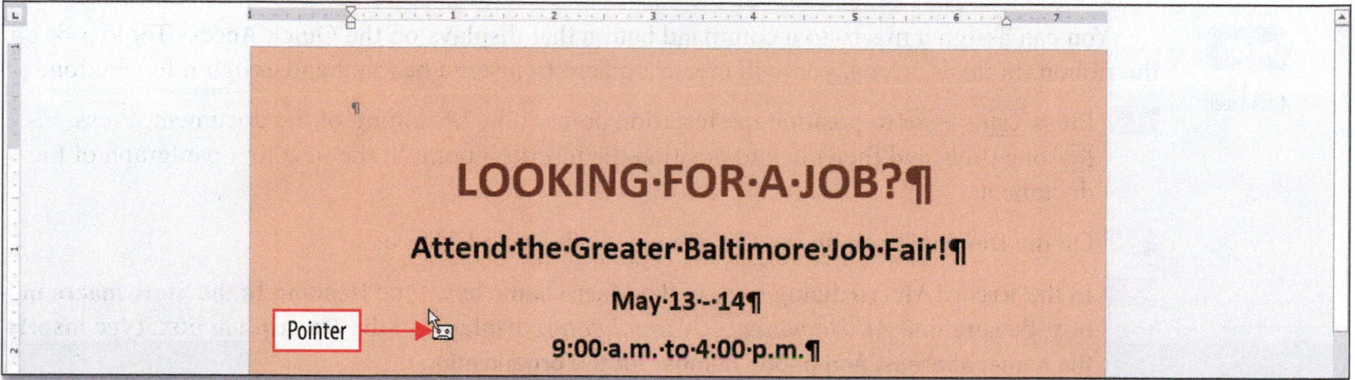

LOOKING·FOR·A·JOB?¶
Attend·the·Greater·Baltimore·Job·Fair!¶
May·13·-·14¶
9:00·a.m.·to·4:00·p.m.¶
Pointer

FIGURE 11.26 Word 2016, Windows 10, Microsoft Corporation

9 Click the **Insert tab**. In the **Header & Footer group**, click **Footer**, and then click **Edit Footer**.

10 With the insertion point in the footer, using your own name, type **Firstname Lastname** and then compare your screen with Figure 11.27.

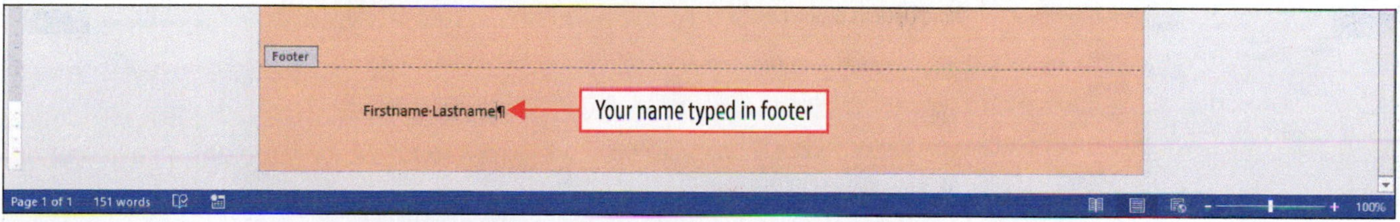

FIGURE 11.27 Word 2016, Windows 10, Microsoft Corporation

11 In the **Close group**, click **Close Header and Footer**.

12 Click the **Developer tab**, and then in the **Code group**, click **Stop Recording**.

All of the actions you performed in Steps 9 through 11 are recorded as part of the *Footer* macro. The same actions can be repeated by pressing Alt + Ctrl + B.

13 To test your macro, press Ctrl + N to display a new blank document. Press and hold Alt + Ctrl, and then press B. Scroll to the bottom of the page to view your name in the footer.

The macro runs—inserting your name in the footer.

ALERT! **What If My Macro Doesn't Work?**

If your macro doesn't work properly, on the Developer tab, in the Code group, click Macros. In the Macros dialog box, click the name of your macro, and then click Delete. Close the dialog box, and then record the macro again.

14 Close the blank document without saving changes, and then **Save** your **Lastname_Firstname_11B_Fair_Flyer** document.

More Knowledge **Pausing While Recording a Macro**

When recording a macro, you can temporarily suspend the recording if you need to perform other actions, and then resume the recording. To pause the recording, in the Code group, click Pause Recording. When you are ready to continue, click Resume Recorder.

Activity 11.09 | Recording a Button-Activated Macro

1.4.3
4.1.3 Expert

You can assign a macro to a command button that displays on the Quick Access Toolbar or on the ribbon. In this Activity, you will create a macro to insert a heading and assign it to a button.

1. Press Ctrl + Home to position the insertion point at the beginning of the document. Press Enter one time, and then click to position the insertion point in the new first paragraph of the document.
2. On the **Developer tab**, in the **Code group**, click **Record Macro**.
3. In the **Record Macro** dialog box, in the **Macro name box**, type **Heading** In the **Store macro in** box, be sure that *All Documents (Normal.dotm)* displays. In the **Description** box, type **Inserts the name, address, and phone number for the organization**
4. Under **Assign macro to**, click the **Button** icon. In the **Word Options** dialog box, in the left pane with **Quick Access Toolbar** selected, in the right pane, under **Choose commands from**, click **Normal.NewMacros.Heading**—the name Word uses for your *Heading* macro.
5. In the middle of the dialog box, click **Add**. Compare your screen with Figure 11.28.

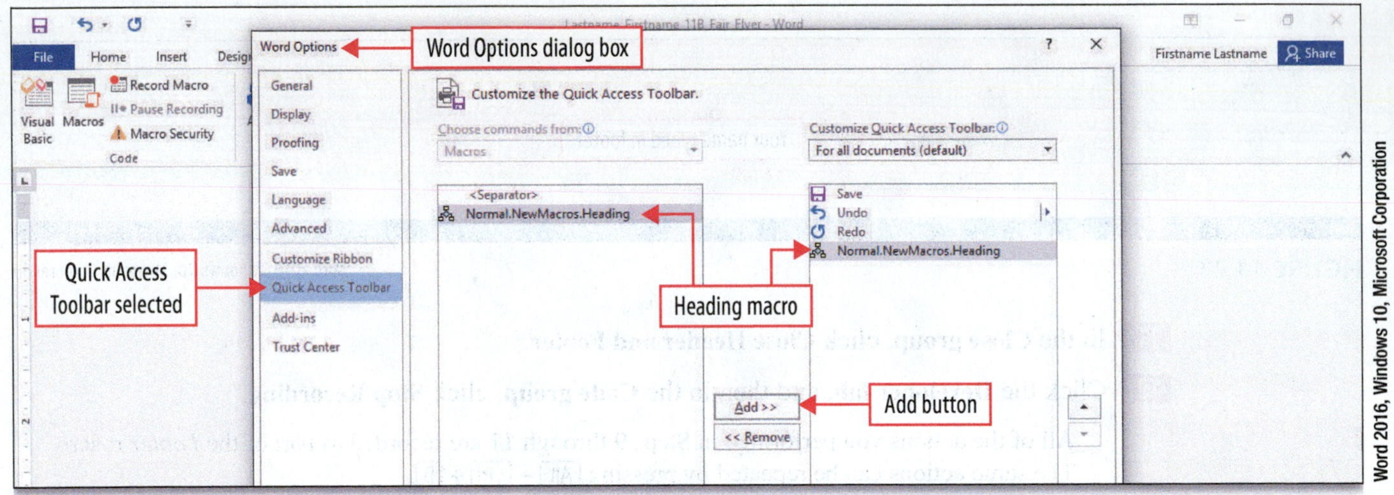

FIGURE 11.28

6. On the right side of the **Word Options** dialog box, click **Normal.NewMacros.Heading**. Below the list of commands, click **Modify**.
7. In the **Modify Button** dialog box, under **Symbol**, in the first row, click the third symbol—a blue circle containing a white i. In the **Display name** box, notice that the macro name displays. Compare your screen with Figure 11.29.

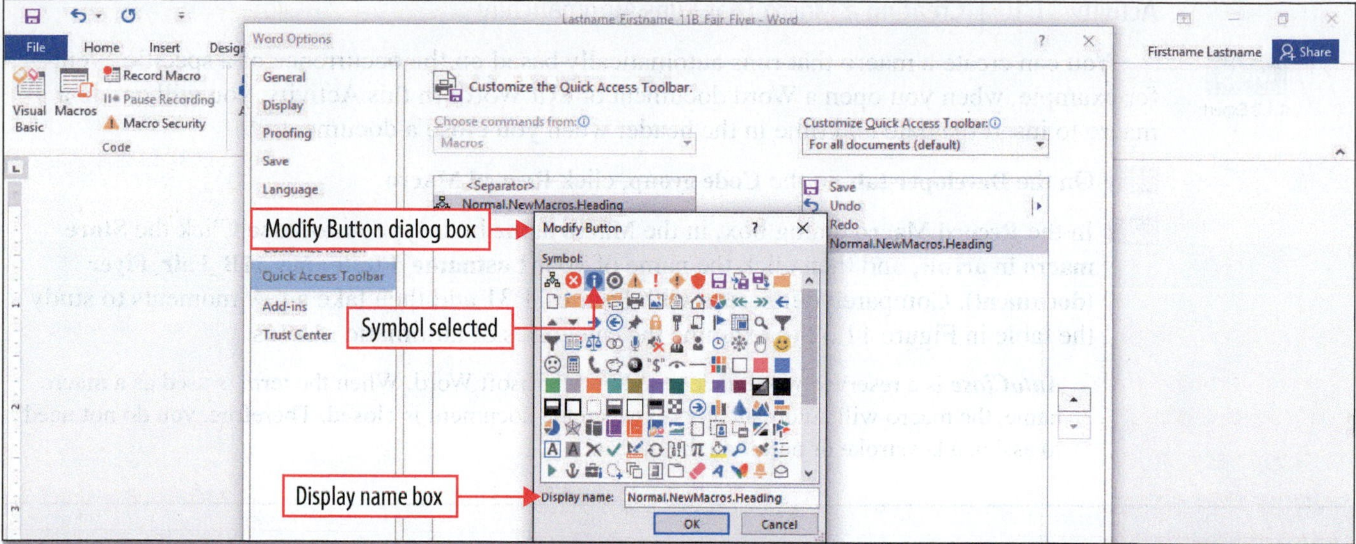

FIGURE 11.29

Word 2016, Windows 10, Microsoft Corporation

8 Click **OK**. In the list of Quick Access Toolbar commands, notice that the selected symbol displays to the left of *Normal.NewMacro.Heading*. Click **OK** to close the Word Options dialog box. Notice that the pointer displays in the document and the *Heading* button displays on the Quick Access Toolbar.

9 Type the following text, pressing Enter after each of the first three lines:

Baltimore Job Fair
314 North Street
Baltimore, MD 21201
(410) 555-0090

10 With the insertion point to the right of the phone number, press Ctrl + Shift + Home to select all four lines.

When you are recording a macro, you must use the keyboard to select text—you cannot drag.

11 With all four lines selected, click the **Home tab**. In the **Styles group**, change the style to **No Spacing**, change the **Font Size** to **18**, apply **Bold** B, and then click **Center**.

12 Click the **Developer tab**, and then in the **Code group**, click **Stop Recording**. Compare your screen with Figure 11.30.

All of the text you typed and formatted is saved as part of the macro.

FIGURE 11.30

Word 2016, Windows 10, Microsoft Corporation

13 Press Ctrl + Home, and then **Save** your document.

Activity 11.10 | Creating a Macro That Runs Automatically

4.1.3 Expert

You can create a macro that runs automatically based on the occurrence of a specific event—for example, when you open a Word document or exit Word. In this Activity, you will create a macro to insert the date and time in the header when you close a document.

1 On the **Developer tab**, in the **Code group**, click **Record Macro**.

2 In the **Record Macro** dialog box, in the **Macro name** box, type **AutoClose** Click the **Store macro in arrow**, and then click the name of your **Lastname_Firstname_11B_Fair_Flyer (document)**. Compare your screen with Figure 11.31 and then take a few moments to study the table in Figure 11.32 to examine the categories of automatic macros.

AutoClose is a reserved word understood by Microsoft Word. When the term is used as a macro name, the macro will automatically run when the document is closed. Therefore, you do not need to assign a keystroke or button to the macro.

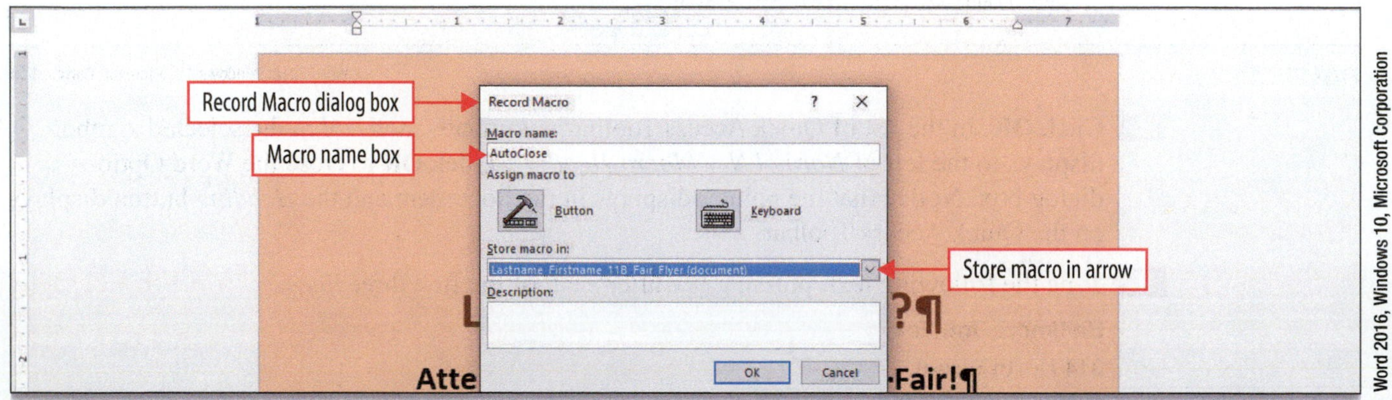

FIGURE 11.31

AUTOMATIC MACROS	
MACRO	**DESCRIPTION**
AutoExec	Runs when Word starts.
AutoOpen	Runs each time a document is opened.
AutoNew	Runs each time a new document is created.
AutoClose	Runs each time a document is closed.
AutoExit	Runs whenever you exit Word.

FIGURE 11.32

ALERT! **Should the Macro Be Saved in the Normal Template?**

Be careful to save this macro in your document rather than in the Normal.dotm template. If you save the macro in the Normal.dotm template on your computer, the macro will run every time *any* document is closed.

3 Click **OK** to start recording mode.

4 Click the **Insert tab**. In the **Header & Footer group**, click **Header**, and then on the list, click **Edit Header**.

5 Press Ctrl + A, and then press Delete.

Any existing text is selected and then deleted. Because this macro will insert the current date and time whenever the document is closed, you want any existing content to be deleted.

6 On the **Header & Footer Design tab**, in the **Insert group**, click **Date & Time**.

7 In the **Date and Time** dialog box, on the list, click the thirteenth format—with the date and time displayed in seconds. Compare your screen with Figure 11.33.

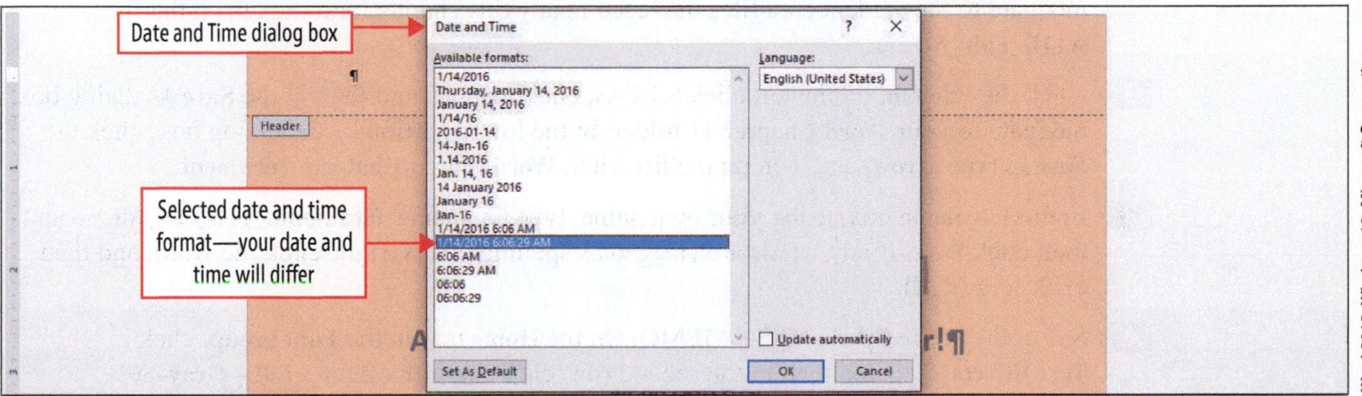

FIGURE 11.33

8 Click **OK** to close the **Date and Time** dialog box. In the **Close group**, click **Close Header and Footer**.

9 Click the **Developer tab**. In the **Code group**, click **Stop Recording**.

10 **Save** your document. Press Ctrl + W to close your document without closing Word. Compare your screen with Figure 11.34.

When you close your document, the *AutoClose* macro runs—inserting the current date and time in the header. Because this change is made while closing the document, a Microsoft Word message box displays prompting you to save your changes.

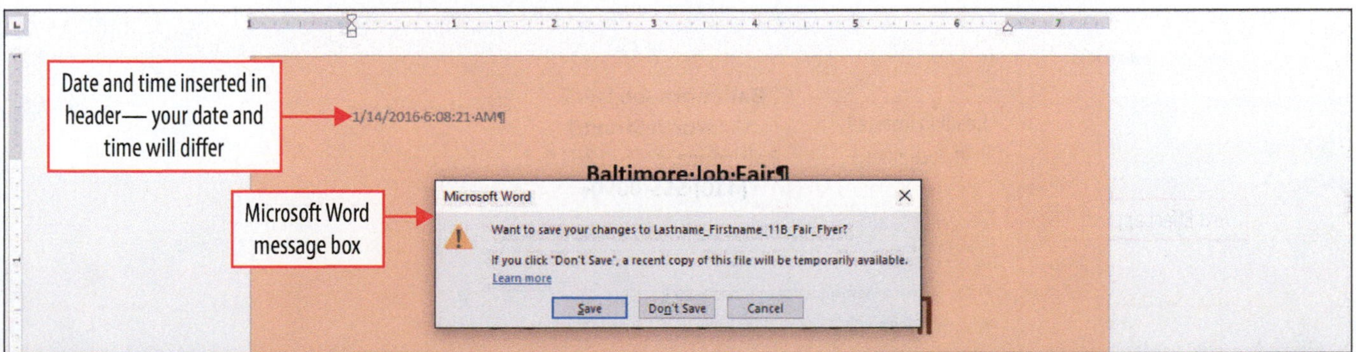

FIGURE 11.34

Word 2016, Windows 10, Microsoft Corporation

11 In the Microsoft Word message box, click **Save** to save your changes and close the document.

12 Hold this file until you complete the remainder of this project.

Objective 6 Run Macros

GO! Learn How Video W11-6

After you record a macro, you can reuse it so that you can work more efficiently.

Activity 11.11 | Running a Macro

1. Click the **File tab**, on the left click **Open**, and then click **Browse**. In the **Open** dialog box, navigate to the student data files that accompany this chapter, and then open the file **w11B_Fair_Memo**.

2. Click the **File tab**, on the left click **Save As**, click **Browse**, and then in the **Save As** dialog box, navigate to your **Word Chapter 11** folder. In the lower portion of the dialog box, click the **Save as type arrow**, and then on the list, click **Word Macro-Enabled Document**.

3. In the **File name** box, using your own name, type **Lastname_Firstname_11B_Fair_Memo** and then click **Save**. If any words are flagged as spelling errors, right-click the word, and then click Ignore All.

4. Select the second paragraph—**MEMO**. On the **Home tab**, in the **Font group**, click **Text Effects**, and then in the second row, click the fifth effect—**Fill – Gray–50%, Accent 3, Sharp Bevel**.

5. Click to position the insertion point in the empty paragraph at the top of the document, and then on the **Quick Access Toolbar**, click the button assigned to your **Heading** macro—the blue circle containing a white i. Click anywhere in the document to cancel the selection, and then compare your screen with Figure 11.35.

   The Heading macro is executed and the heading information is inserted in your document. Recall that although you created the *Heading* macro in your *Lastname_Firstname_11B_Fair_Flyer* document, the macro was saved in the Normal template, allowing it to be available to other documents.

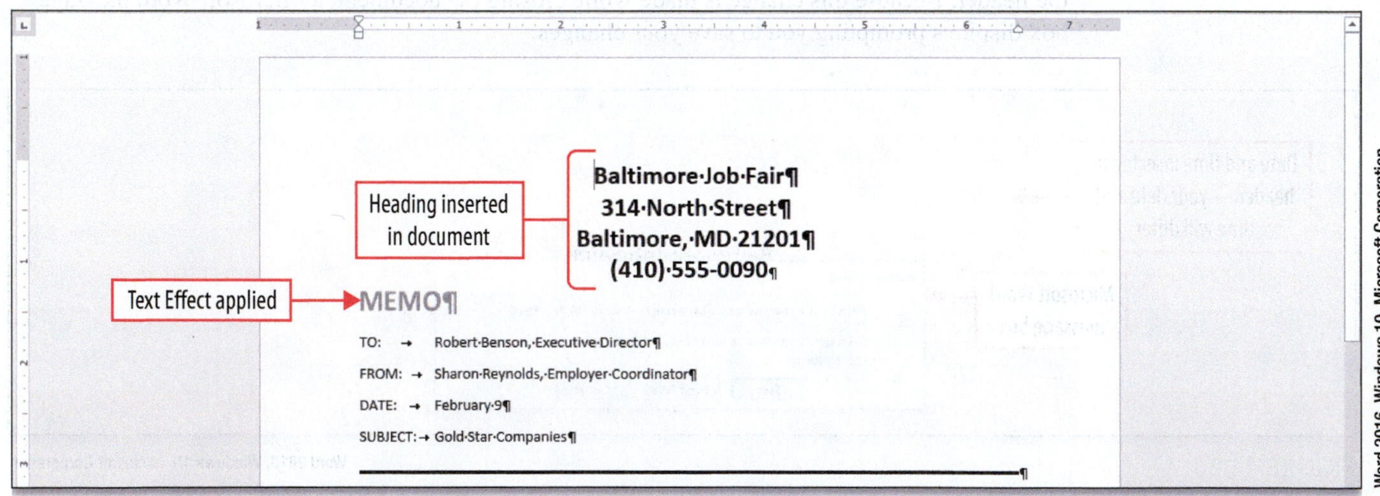

FIGURE 11.35

6. Press and hold Alt + Ctrl, and then press B. If necessary, scroll to the bottom of the page to view the footer.

   The *Footer* macro runs—inserting your name in the footer.

7. Press Ctrl + Home, and then **Save** your document.

Objective 7 Edit a Macro in the Visual Basic Editor

Activity 11.12 | Editing a Macro in the Visual Basic Editor

GO! Learn How Video W11-7

4.1.3

One way to edit macros is by using the ***Visual Basic Editor***. The Visual Basic Editor enables you to view the programming code for existing macros. You can use the Visual Basic Editor either to edit a macro or to create a new macro. The capability of VBA is extensive and can be used to create complex macros.

1. Locate the first paragraph of the document, and notice that it contains the text *Baltimore Job Fair*.

   Recall that the name of the organization is Greater Baltimore Job Fair.

2. Click the **Developer tab**, and then in the **Code group**, click **Macros**. In the **Macros** dialog box, select the **Heading** macro, and then click **Edit**. If necessary, maximize the *Normal – [NewMacros (Code)]* window. Compare your screen with Figure 11.36.

   The Visual Basic Editor displays the code associated with the *Footer* and *Heading* macros. A macro ***procedure***—a block of programming code that performs one or more tasks—begins with the term *Sub* and ends with the term *End Sub*. The name following the word *Sub* indicates the name of the procedure. The description that you typed when you created the *Heading* macro displays as a ***comment***. A comment is a line of text that is used solely for documentation—for example, the name of the individual who wrote the macro or the purpose of the macro. A comment is preceded by a single quotation mark, displays in green text, and is ignored when the macro runs.

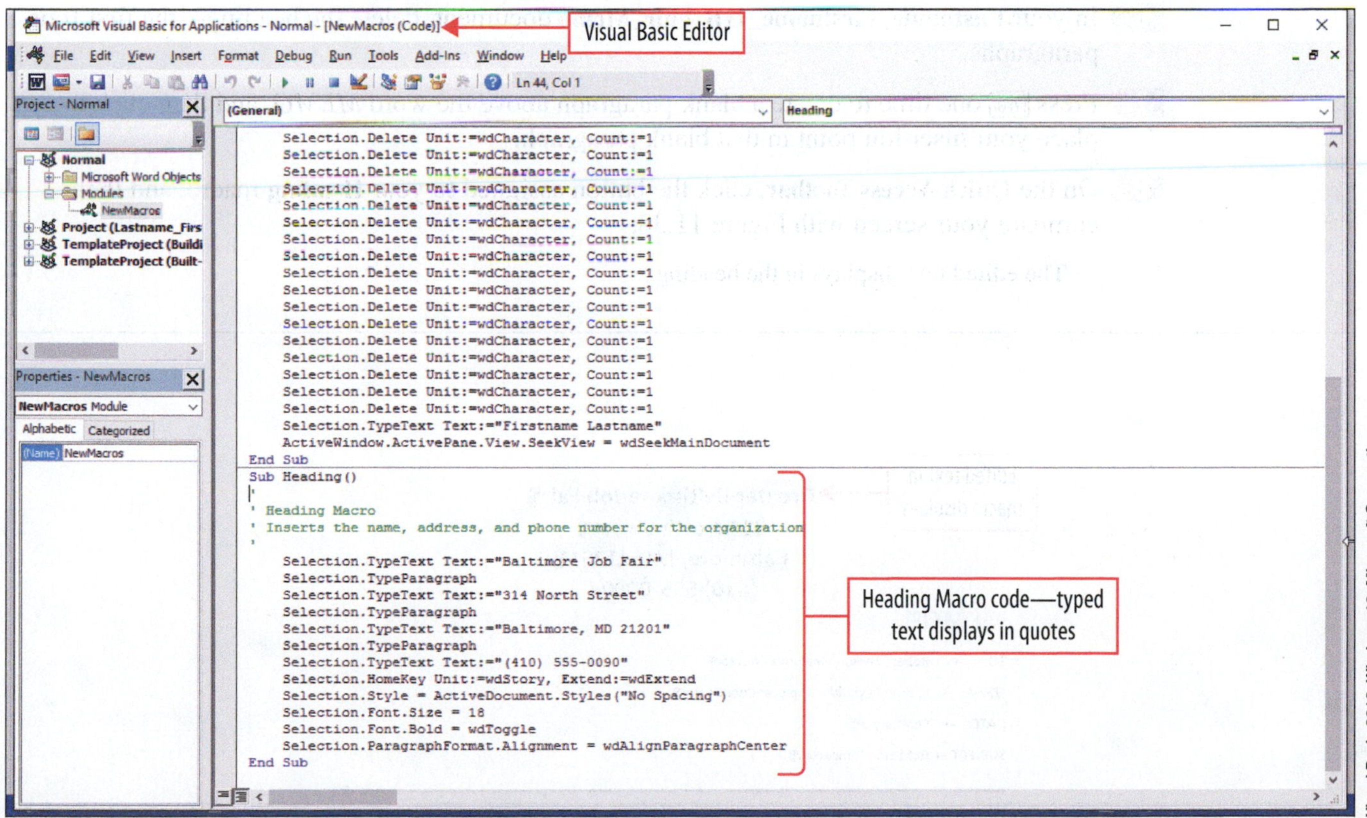

FIGURE 11.36

ALERT! Why Does My Visual Basic Editor Display Differently?

Depending on how the Visual Basic Editor was last used, different panes may be displayed. For purposes of this instruction, the only panes that are required are the Project pane on the left and the Code pane on the right.

3 In the pane on the right, locate the text *Baltimore Job Fair*. Click to position the insertion point to the left of *Baltimore*, type **Greater** and then press Spacebar. Compare your screen with Figure 11.37.

You are editing the macro so that when it runs, the correct name of the organization displays.

```
' Heading Macro
' Inserts the name, address, and phone number for the organization
'
    Selection.TypeText Text:="Greater Baltimore Job Fair"
    Selection.TypeParagraph
    Selection.TypeText Text:="314 North Street"
    Selection.TypeParagraph
    Selection.TypeText Text:="Baltimore, MD 21201"
    Selection.TypeParagraph
    Selection.TypeText Text:="(410) 555-0090"
    Selection.HomeKey Unit:=wdStory, Extend:=wdExtend
    Selection.Style = ActiveDocument.Styles("No Spacing")
    Selection.Font.Size = 18
    Selection.Font.Bold = wdToggle
    Selection.ParagraphFormat.Alignment = wdAlignParagraphCenter
End Sub
```

Edited text

FIGURE 11.37 Visual Basic 2016, Windows 10, Microsoft Corporation

4 Press Ctrl + A to select all of the code in the Visual Basic window. Right-click over the selection, and on the shortcut menu click **Copy**.

5 On the menu bar, click **File**, and then on the list, click **Close and Return to Microsoft Word**.

ANOTHER WAY At the top right of the Visual Basic Editor window, click Close.

6 In your **Lastname_Firstname_11B_Fair_Memo** document, delete the heading—the first four paragraphs.

7 Press Enter one time to create a blank paragraph above the word *MEMO*, and then click to place your insertion point in that blank paragraph.

8 On the **Quick Access Toolbar**, click the button assigned to your **Heading** macro, and then compare your screen with Figure 11.38.

The edited text displays in the heading.

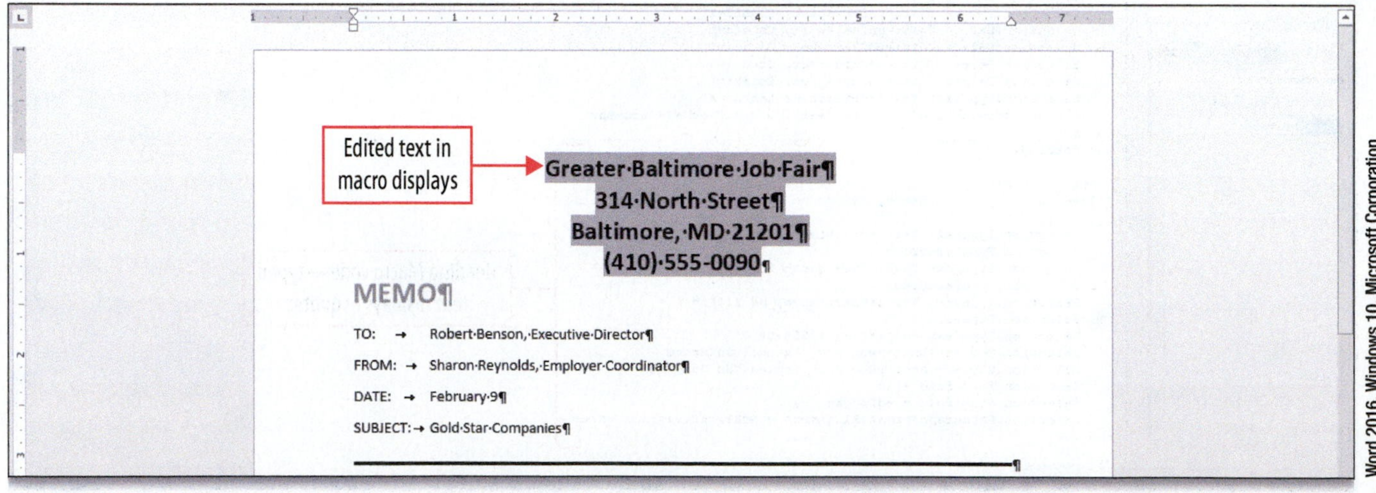

Edited text in macro displays
Greater·Baltimore·Job·Fair¶
314·North·Street¶
Baltimore,·MD·21201¶
(410)·555-0090¶
MEMO¶
TO: → Robert·Benson,·Executive·Director¶
FROM: → Sharon·Reynolds,·Employer·Coordinator¶
DATE: → February·9¶
SUBJECT: → Gold·Star·Companies¶
Word 2016, Windows 10, Microsoft Corporation

FIGURE 11.38

9 Press Ctrl + End to move to the end of the document, and then press Ctrl + Enter to insert a new page. Press Ctrl + V to paste your copied code.

10 **Save** your document.

Activity 11.13 | Using a Built-in Word Macro

Word has many macros that are already built in and available in each document. In this Activity, you will use a macro that allows you to adjust the size of the indents for a bulleted list.

1 On **Page 1**, locate and select the four bulleted paragraphs.

2 On the **Developer tab**, in the **Code group**, click **Macros**. In the **Macros** dialog box, click the **Macros in arrow**, and then click **Word commands**. Under **Macro name**, scroll as necessary, and then on the list, click **AdjustListIndents**. Note: Macro names are in alphabetical order.

A list of available Word commands (macros) displays. The Description area explains what a selected command will do. The ***AdjustListIndents*** built-in macro modifies the indenting of a bulleted or numbered list.

3 In the **Macros** dialog box, click **Run**. In the **Adjust Line Indents** dialog box, click the **Bullet position up spin arrow** to **0.4"**. Click the **Text indent up spin arrow** to **0.6"**. Compare your screen with Figure 11.39.

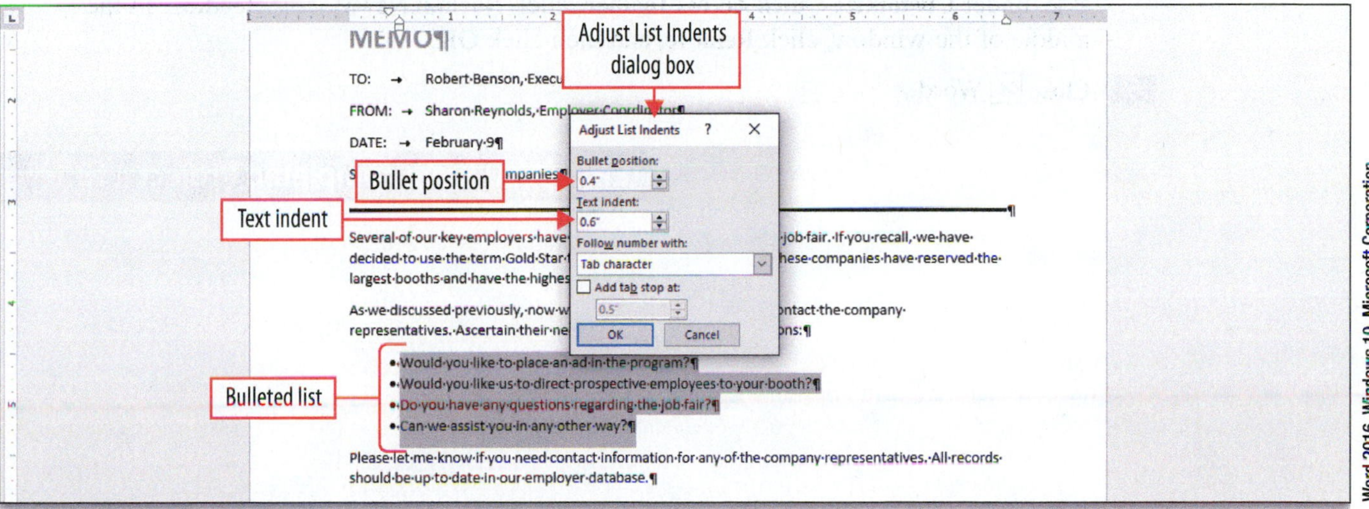

FIGURE 11.39

4 Click **OK**, and notice that the indentation of the bulleted list has changed.

5 Click **Save**. Press Ctrl + Home.

6 Click the **File tab**, and then **Show All Properties**. In the **Tags** box, type **macros** In the **Subject** box, type your course name and section number. If necessary, edit the author name to display your name.

7 On the left, click **Print** to view the Print Preview, and then on the left, click **Close** to close the document but leave Word open. If necessary, click Save.

8 If directed by your instructor to do so, for your Lastname_Firstname_11B_Fair_Memo, submit your paper printout, your electronic image of your document that looks like a printed document, or your original Word file that you created in this project. You do not need to submit your 11B_Fair_Flyer document unless directed to do so by your instructor.

Activity 11.14 | Restoring Default Settings

Because you will not need the macros you created in the Normal template after completing this project, you will delete them and restore the default settings you changed.

1. Click the **Developer tab**, and then in the **Code group**, click **Macros**. In the **Macros** dialog box, at the bottom click the **Macros in arrow**, and then click **All active templates and documents**. Under **Macro name**, click **Footer**, and then click **Delete**. In the **Microsoft Word** dialog box, click **Yes** to confirm the deletion.
2. Using the same technique, delete the **Heading** macro.

   You are not deleting the *AutoClose* macro because it is stored only in this document.
3. Click **Close** to close the **Macros** dialog box.
4. Click the **File tab**, and then click **Options**. In the **Word Options** dialog box, click **Customize Ribbon**. Under **Main Tabs**, clear the **Developer** check box.
5. On the left side of the **Word Options** dialog box, click **Quick Access Toolbar**. On the right side, under **Customize Quick Access Toolbar**, click **Normal.NewMacros.Heading**. In the middle of the window, click **Remove**, and then click **OK**.
6. **Close** ☒ Word.

END | You have completed Project 11B

GO! To Work

Andrew Rodriguez / Fotolia; FotolEdhar / Fotolia; apops / Fotolia; Yuri Arcurs / Fotolia

MICROSOFT OFFICE SPECIALIST (MOS) SKILLS IN THIS CHAPTER	
PROJECT 11A	**PROJECT 11B**
1.1.5 Expert: Link to external document content	**1.4.3** Customize the Quick Access Toolbar **1.1.6** Expert: Enable macros in a document **4.1.3** Expert: Create and modify simple macros

BUILD YOUR E-PORTFOLIO

An E-Portfolio is a collection of evidence, stored electronically, that showcases what you have accomplished while completing your education. Collecting and then sharing your work products with potential employers reflects your academic and career goals. Your completed documents from the following projects are good examples to show what you have learned: 11G, 11K, and 11L.

GO! FOR JOB SUCCESS

Your instructor may assign this discussion to your class and then ask you to think about, or discuss with your classmates, these questions.

Mobile technology, smaller devices, and high-speed Internet connections mean that many business people can work anywhere, any time. Since workers no longer need to be at a desk in an office building every day, some companies are designing new workspaces with a free address system. In a free address environment, employees are not assigned a specific desk, cube, or office. Employees who work in the office can move freely from open, collaborative spaces to private, quiet spaces as their work requires. Most companies implement a free address system to save money on real estate costs. Some have found that at any given time, as much as 50 percent of assigned workspace is empty.

FotolEdhar / Fotolia

What are some reasons that an employee might not use their assigned office space during the course of a day?

In a true free address system, even top executives do not have assigned offices. What are some activities in a CEO's or vice president's day that would be more difficult in this office arrangement?

In addition to high-speed Internet and cell phones, what are some other technologies that would make it easier for a company to adopt a free address office space?

END OF CHAPTER

SUMMARY

You can use the program-integration technology Object Linking & Embedding to link or embed an object that was created in another Office application—such as Access, Excel, or PowerPoint—in a Word document.

Paste Options provide different ways to insert an object in a document. When you edit an embedded object, changes are not reflected in the source file. When a linked object is modified, the source file is changed.

A macro—a set of commands and instructions that can be applied in a single action—helps you work more efficiently. You can use built-in macros or create your own macros by recording actions or typing code.

Visual Basic for Applications, or VBA, is a programming language used to create macros. In the Visual Basic Editor, you can edit the code in an existing macro or type your own procedure to create a new macro.

GO! LEARN IT ONLINE

Review the concepts and key terms in this chapter by completing these online challenges, which you can find at **MyITLab**.

Matching and Multiple Choice: Answer matching and multiple choice questions to test what you learned in this chapter.

Lessons on the GO!: Learn how to use all the new apps and features as they are introduced by Microsoft.

MOS Prep Quiz: Answer questions to review the MOS skills that you practiced in this chapter.

PROJECT GUIDE FOR WORD CHAPTER 11

Your instructor will assign Projects from this list to ensure your learning and assess your knowledge.

PROJECT GUIDE FOR WORD CHAPTER 11			
Project	**Apply Skills from These Chapter Objectives**	**Project Type**	**Project Location**
11A **MyITLab**	Objectives 1–4 from Project 11A	**11A Instructional Project (Grader Project)** Guided instruction to learn the skills in Project 11A.	In MyITLab and in text
11B **MyITLab**	Objectives 5–7 from Project 11B	**11B Instructional Project (Grader Project)** Guided instruction to learn the skills in Project 11B.	In MyITLab and in text
11C	Objectives 1–4 from Project 11A	**11C Skills Review (Scorecard Grading)** A guided review of the skills from Project 11A.	In text
11D	Objectives 5–7 from Project 11B	**11D Skills Review (Scorecard Grading)** A guided review of the skills from Project 11B.	In text
11E **MyITLab**	Objectives 1–4 from Project 11A	**11E Mastery (Grader Project)** **Mastery and Transfer of Learning** A demonstration of your mastery of the skills in Project 11A with extensive decision making.	In MyITLab and in text
11F **MyITLab**	Objectives 5–7 from Project 11B	**11F Mastery (Grader Project)** **Mastery and Transfer of Learning** A demonstration of your mastery of the skills in Project 11B with extensive decision making.	In MyITLab and in text
11G **MyITLab**	Objectives 1–7 from Projects 11A and 11B	**11G Mastery (Grader Project)** **Mastery and Transfer of Learning** A demonstration of your mastery of the skills in Projects 11A and 11B with extensive decision making.	In MyITLab and in text
11H	Combination of Objectives from Projects 11A and 11B	**11H GO! Fix It (Scorecard Grading)** **Critical Thinking** A demonstration of your mastery of the skills in Projects 11A and 11B by creating a correct result from a document that contains errors you must find.	Instructor Resource Center (IRC) and MyITLab
11I	Combination of Objectives from Projects 11A and 11B	**11I GO! Make It (Scorecard Grading)** **Critical Thinking** A demonstration of your mastery of the skills in Projects 11A and 11B by creating a result from a supplied picture.	IRC and MyITLab
11J	Combination of Objectives from Projects 11A and 11B	**11J GO! Solve It (Rubric Grading)** **Critical Thinking** A demonstration of your mastery of the skills in Projects 11A and 11B, your decision-making skills, and your critical thinking skills. A task-specific rubric helps you self-assess your result.	IRC and MyITLab
11K	Combination of Objectives from Projects 11A and 11B	**11K GO! Solve It (Rubric Grading)** **Critical Thinking** A demonstration of your mastery of the skills in Projects 11A and 11B, your decision-making skills, and your critical thinking skills. A task-specific rubric helps you self-assess your result.	In text
11L	Combination of Objectives from Projects 11A and 11B	**11L GO! Think (Rubric Grading)** **Critical Thinking** A demonstration of your understanding of the chapter concepts applied in a manner that you would outside of college. An analytic rubric helps you and your instructor grade the quality of your work by comparing it to the work an expert in the discipline would create.	In text
11M	Combination of Objectives from Projects 11A and 11B	**11M GO! Think (Rubric Grading)** **Critical Thinking** A demonstration of your understanding of the chapter concepts applied in a manner that you would outside of college. An analytic rubric helps you and your instructor grade the quality of your work by comparing it to the work an expert in the discipline would create.	IRC and MyITLab
11N	Combination of Objectives from Projects 11A and 11B	**11N You and GO! (Rubric Grading)** **Critical Thinking** A demonstration of your understanding of the chapter concepts applied in a manner that you would in a personal situation. An analytic rubric helps you and your instructor grade the quality of your work.	IRC and MyITLab

GLOSSARY

GLOSSARY OF CHAPTER KEY TERMS

AdjustListIndents A built-in macro used to modify the indenting of a bulleted or numbered list.

AutoClose A macro that will automatically run when closing a document.

Comment In a macro procedure, a line of text that is used solely for documentation.

Destination file The file where an object is embedded or linked.

Embedded object An object that maintains the structure of the original application but is not connected to the source file.

Embedding The process of inserting an object, such as an Excel chart, into a Word document so that it becomes part of the document.

Linked object An object that maintains a direct connection to the source file.

Linking The process of inserting information from a source file into a destination file, while maintaining a connection between the two files.

Macro A set of commands and instructions that can be grouped as a single command to accomplish a task automatically.

Macro virus A macro that causes files to be erased or damaged by inserting unauthorized code.

Object A table, chart, graphic, file, or other form of information.

Object Linking and Embedding (OLE) A program-integration technology for sharing information between Office programs.

Procedure A block of programming code that performs one or more tasks.

Recording The process of creating a macro while performing specific actions in a document.

Source file The file where an object is created.

Visual Basic Editor An editor that enables you to view and edit existing macro code or create a new macro.

Visual Basic for Applications (VBA) A programming language used to create macros.

CHAPTER REVIEW

Apply 11A skills from these Objectives:

1. Embed an Excel Chart in a Word Document
2. Embed an Access Table in a Word Document
3. Embed a PowerPoint File in a Word Document
4. Link Objects to a Word Document

Skills Review Project 11C Sponsorship Program

In the following project, you will include objects and files from other Office applications in a memo to Robert Benson, Executive Director of the Greater Baltimore Job Fair. The memo and related files explain the corporate sponsorship program. Your completed files will look similar to Figure 11.40.

PROJECT FILES

For Project 11C, you will need the following files:

w11C_Sponsorship_Memo (Word document)
w11C_Sponsors_Chart (Excel workbook)
w11C_Sponsorship_Program (PowerPoint presentation)
w11C_Top_Sponsors (Access database)
w11C_Revenue (Excel workbook)
w11C_Agenda (Word document)

You will save your files as:

Lastname_Firstname_11C_Sponsorship_Memo (Word)
Lastname_Firstname_11C_Revenue (Excel)
Lastname_Firstname_11C_Agenda (Word)

PROJECT RESULTS

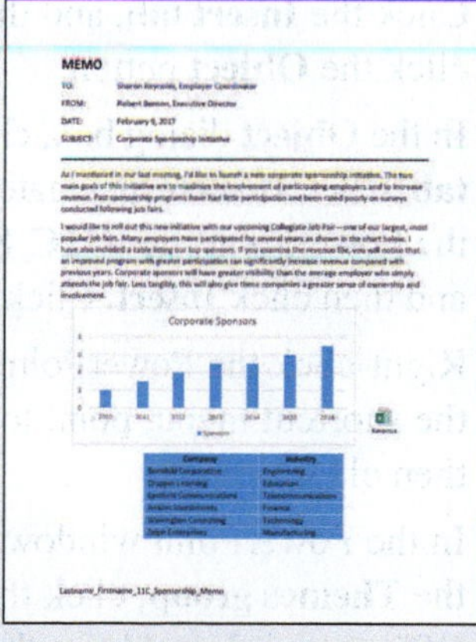

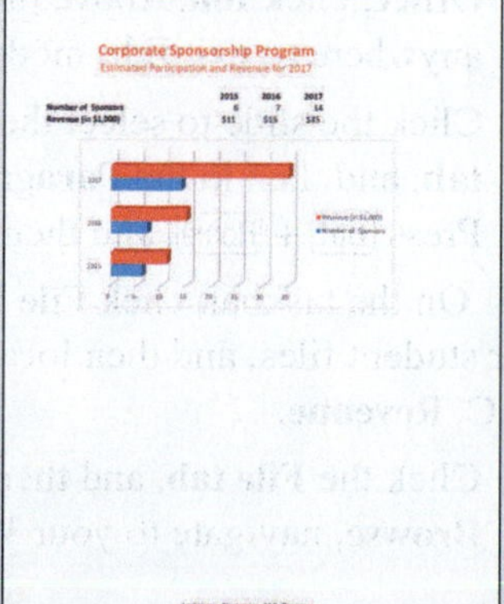

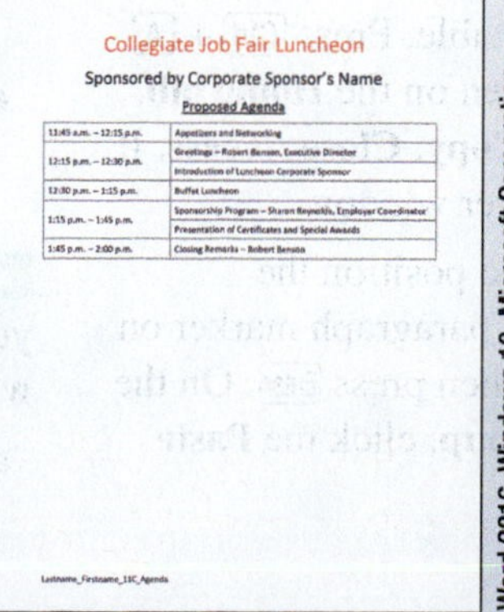

Word 2016, Windows 10, Microsoft Corporation

FIGURE 11.40

(Project 11C Sponsorship Program continues on the next page)

Skills Review Project 11C Sponsorship Program (continued)

1 Start Word. On the left, click **Open Other Documents**, and then from your student files, locate and open the file **w11C_Sponsorship_Memo**. Save it to your **Word Chapter 11** folder as **Lastname_Firstname_11C_Sponsorship_Memo** Insert the file name in the footer.

a. On the taskbar, click **File Explorer**. Navigate to your student files, and then open the Excel file **w11C_Sponsors_Chart**.

b. Right-click a border of the chart, and then click **Copy**. On the taskbar, click the **Word** icon to make the **Lastname_Firstname_11C_Sponsorship_Memo** active. In your Word document, locate the paragraph that begins *I would like*, click to position the insertion point at the end of the paragraph, and then press Enter.

c. On the **Home tab**, in the **Clipboard group**, click the **Paste button arrow**. From the **Paste Options** gallery, click **Keep Source Formatting & Embed Workbook (K)**.

d. Click in a blank area of the chart. Click the **Chart Elements** button, to the right of **Legend**, point to the arrow, and then click **Bottom**.

e. Click the **Format tab**, and then in the **Size group**, click the **Height down spin arrow** to **2.4"**. Click a border of the chart, and then press Ctrl + E.

f. Click outside of the chart to deselect it, click **Save**, and then from the taskbar, **Close** Excel.

2 On the taskbar, click **File Explorer**. Navigate to your student files, locate and then open the Access file **w11C_Top_Sponsors**. If necessary, in the **Security Warning** banner, click **Enable Content**.

a. On the left side of the Access window, under **Tables**, double-click the **Top Sponsors** table. Press Ctrl + A to select the entire table, and then on the **Home tab**, in the **Clipboard group**, click **Copy**. **Close** Access. If necessary, close the File Explorer window.

b. In your Word document, click to position the insertion point to the left of the paragraph marker on the right side of the chart, and then press Enter. On the **Home tab**, in the **Clipboard group**, click the **Paste button arrow**.

c. In the **Paste Options** gallery, click **Paste Special**. In the **Paste Special** dialog box, under **As**, click **Formatted Text (RTF)**, and then click **OK**.

d. Click in the first cell of the table. Click the **Table Tools Design tab**, and then in the **Table Styles group**, click **More**. In the **Table Styles** gallery, under **List Tables**, in the fifth row, select the second table style—**List Table 5 Dark – Accent 1**.

e. Click the **Layout tab**, and then in the **Data group**, click **Sort**. In the **Sort** dialog box, be sure *Company* displays in the **Sort by** box and the **Header row** option button is selected, and then click **OK**.

f. On the **Layout tab**, in the **Table group**, click **Properties**. In the **Table Properties** dialog box, on the **Table tab**, under **Alignment**, click **Center**, and then click **OK**. For each name in the table flagged as a spelling error, right-click, and then click **Ignore All**. **Save** your changes.

3 On **Page 2** of your Word document, click to position the insertion point at the end of the first paragraph, and then press Enter.

a. Click the **Insert tab**, and then in the **Text group**, click the **Object** button.

b. In the **Object** dialog box, click the **Create from File tab**. Click **Browse**, navigate to your student files, click the PowerPoint file **w11C_Sponsorship_Program**, and then click **Insert**. Click **OK**.

c. Right-click the PowerPoint object, and then from the shortcut menu, point to **Presentation Object**, and then click **Edit**.

d. In the PowerPoint window, click the **Design tab**. In the **Themes group**, click the **More** button. Under **Office**, click **Ion**. Above the PowerPoint object, click anywhere to exit Edit mode.

e. Click the slide to select the object. Click the **Home tab**, and then in the **Paragraph group**, click **Center**. Press Ctrl + Home, and then **Save** your changes.

4 On the taskbar, click **File Explorer**. Navigate to your student files, and then locate and open the Excel file **w11C_Revenue**.

a. Click the **File tab**, and then click **Save As**. Click **Browse**, navigate to your **Word Chapter 11** folder,

(Project 11C Sponsorship Program continues on the next page)

Skills Review Project 11C Sponsorship Program (continued)

and then using your own name, save the file as **Lastname_Firstname_11C_Revenue**

b. Click the **Insert tab**, and then in the **Text group**, click **Header & Footer**. On the **Header & Footers Tools Design tab**, in the **Navigation group**, click **Go to Footer**. With the insertion point in the footer box, in the **Header & Footer Elements group**, click **File Name**. Click in a cell above the footer area to deselect the footer. On the **View tab**, in the **Worksheet Views group**, click **Normal**. Press Ctrl + Home.

c. **Save** your changes, and then **Close** Excel. If necessary, close the File Explorer window.

5 Click in your Word document, and then position the insertion point to the right of the chart. Click the **Insert tab**, and then in the **Text group**, click the **Object** button.

a. In the **Object** dialog box, click the **Create from File tab**. Click **Browse**, navigate to your **Word Chapter 11** folder, and then click your **Lastname_Firstname_11C_Revenue** Excel file. Click **Insert**.

b. On the right side of the **Object** dialog box, select the **Link to file** check box, and then select the **Display as icon** check box.

c. In the **Object** dialog box, click the **Change Icon** button, and then in the **Caption** box, delete the existing text, and then type **Revenue** As the icon, click the first icon in the list, and then click **OK** two times.

d. Double-click the icon to open the Excel file. **Maximize** the Excel window.

e. Click in cell **D5**, which contains the value *12*. Type **14** and then press Enter. **Save** your changes, and then **Close** Excel.

f. Press Ctrl + End. **Save** your changes in your Word document.

6 In Word, from your student files, open the file **w11C_Agenda**. Display the **Save As** dialog box, and then using your own name, save the file to your **Word Chapter 11** folder as **Lastname_Firstname_11C_Agenda** Insert the file name in the footer.

a. **Save** your changes. Press Ctrl + W to close your **Lastname_Firstname_11C_Agenda** document but leave Word open.

b. On **Page 2** of your **Lastname_Firstname_11C_Sponsorship_Memo**, click to position the insertion point to the right of the PowerPoint object. On the **Insert tab**, in the **Text group**, click the **Object** button. In the **Object** dialog box, click the **Create from File tab**. Click **Browse**, navigate to your **Word Chapter 11** folder, click **Lastname_Firstname_11C_Agenda**, and then click **Insert**.

c. On the right side of the **Object** dialog box, select the **Link to file** check box, and then select the **Display as icon** check box. Click the **Change Icon** button. In the **Caption** box, delete the existing text, and then type **Agenda** Click **OK** two times.

d. Double-click the **Agenda** icon. In the first paragraph, delete the text *Kick-Off*. **Save** your changes, and then **Close** the document.

e. Press Ctrl + Home. Click the **File tab**, and then **Show All Properties**. In the **Tags** box, type **sponsorship, linked and embedded objects** In the **Subject** box, type your course name and section number. If necessary, edit the author name to display your name. On the left, click **Save**.

7 As directed by your instructor, submit your three files:

Lastname_Firstname_11C_Sponsorship_Memo
Lastname_Firstname_11C_Revenue
Lastname_Firstname_11C_Agenda

Close Word, and then **Close** File Explorer.

END | You have completed Project 11C

CHAPTER REVIEW

Apply **11B** skills from these Objectives:

- 5 Create Macros
- 6 Run Macros
- 7 Edit a Macro in the Visual Basic Editor

Skills Review Project 11D Fair Schedule

In the following project, you will create macros to improve your efficiency in editing a letter and press release that explain the scheduled job fairs conducted by the Greater Baltimore Job Fair. Your completed documents will look similar to Figure 11.41.

PROJECT FILES

For Project 11D, you will need the following files:

w11D_Fair_Schedule
w11D_Press_Release

You will save your files as:

Lastname_Firstname_11D_Fair_Schedule
Lastname_Firstname_11D_Press_Release
Lastname_Firstname_11D_Schedule_Code

PROJECT RESULTS

Greater Baltimore Job Fair
314 North Street
Baltimore, MD 21203

January 4, 2017

Craig Goldsmith
Vice President, Human Resources
Hartnett Industries
526 N. Franklin Road
Baltimore, MD 21201

Dear Mr. Goldsmith,

Thanks for your participation in the 2016 Collegiate Job Fair. We were pleased to have representatives from your company at the fair, and I hope you found many qualified job applicants.

We've recently scheduled our job fairs for 2017. You may not be aware that we offer several other job fairs, including the Greater Baltimore Job Fair and several industry-specific job fairs. Please consider attending as many job fairs as would meet your recruiting needs. Those companies that participate in more than one event per year will receive a ten percent discount on registration fees. I've included a list of the fairs we have scheduled so far for 2017, including dates and contact information for each.

Job Fair	Date	Contact	Phone Number
Greater Baltimore Job Fair	June 8-10	Sharon Reynolds	(410) 555-0094
Collegiate Job Fair	May 19-20	Jude Guernsey	(410) 555-0098
Non-profit Job Fair	March 10-11	Maria Simmons	(410) 555-0094
Health Care Job Fair	March 22	Lance Greenwald	(410) 555-0110
Education Job Fair	April 19	Kaia Blake	(410) 555-0115
Technology Job Fair	September 13	Emilio Santos	(410) 555-0094
Engineering Job Fair	October 4	Jude Guernsey	(410) 555-0098

We look forward to seeing Hartnett Industries at one or more job fairs again this year.

Sincerely,

Sharon Reynolds, Employer Coordinator

Lastname_Firstname_11D_Fair_Schedule

08:33:36

Greater Baltimore Job Fair
314 North Street
Baltimore, MD 21201

FOR IMMEDIATE RELEASE

BALTIMORE, MD, January 4, 2017 – The Greater Baltimore Job Fair has announced that its 2017 job fair schedule is now available. The schedule includes dates for seven upcoming job fairs.

Job Fair	Date
Greater Baltimore Job Fair	June 8-10
Collegiate Job Fair	May 19-20
Non-profit Job Fair	March 10-11
Health Care Job Fair	March 22
Education Job Fair	April 19
Technology Job Fair	September 13
Engineering Job Fair	October 4

In addition to the annual Greater Baltimore Job Fair and the well-known Collegiate Job Fair, several industry-specific job fairs are planned, including health care, education, technology, engineering, and non-profit.

At each job fair, as applicable, organizations will be present to provide information on internships, educational programs, and the military. Job seekers should bring several copies of their resumes.

The Greater Baltimore Job Fair is a non-profit organization that brings together employers and job seekers in the Baltimore and Washington metropolitan areas. Each year the organization holds a number of targeted job fairs, and the annual Greater Baltimore Job Fair draws 200 employers in more than 40 industries and registers more than 8,000 candidates.

Lastname_Firstname_11D_Press_Release

FIGURE 11.41

Word 2016, Windows 10, Microsoft Corporation

(Project 11D Fair Schedule continues on the next page)

Skills Review Project 11D Fair Schedule (continued)

1 Start Word. From your student files, locate and open the file **w11D_Fair_Schedule**. Display the **Save As** dialog box, and then navigate to your **Word Chapter 11** folder. In the lower portion of the dialog box, click the **Save as type arrow**, and then from the list, click **Word Macro-Enabled Document**. In the **File name** box, using your own name, type **Lastname_Firstname_11D_Fair_Schedule** and then click **Save**.

a. Insert the file name in the footer.

b. Click the **File tab**, and then click **Options**. In the **Word Options** dialog box, on the left side, click **Customize Ribbon**.

c. In the **Main Tabs** list, locate and then select the **Developer** check box. Click **OK** to close the **Word Options** dialog box.

d. Click the **Developer tab**, and then in the **Code group**, click **Macro Security**. If necessary, in the Trust Center dialog box, under Macro Settings, select Disable all macros with notification. Click **OK** to close the dialog box. **Save** your document.

2 Press Ctrl + Home. On the **Developer tab**, in the **Code group**, click **Record Macro**.

a. In the **Record Macro** dialog box, in the **Macro name** box, type **Heading** Be sure the **Store macro in** box displays **All Documents (Normal.dotm)**.

b. In the **Description** box, click to position the insertion point, and then type **Inserts the organization's name and address**

c. Under **Assign macro to**, click **Keyboard**. In the **Customize Keyboard** dialog box, with the insertion point in the **Press new shortcut key** box, press and hold Alt + Ctrl, and then press G. Click **Assign**, and then click **Close**.

d. With the insertion point at the beginning of the document, type the following text, pressing Enter after the first two lines:

Greater Baltimore Job Fair
314 North Street
Baltimore, MD 21203

e. With the insertion point to the right of the postal code, press and hold Ctrl + Shift and then press ↑ three times to select all three lines. Click the **Home tab**, change the **Font Size** to **22**, and then apply **Bold** and **Center**. Click the **Developer tab**, and then in the **Code group**, click **Stop Recording**. **Save** your document.

3 In the first cell of the table, click to position the insertion point. On the **Developer tab**, in the **Code group**, click **Record Macro**. In the **Record Macro** dialog box, in the **Macro name** box, type **Table_Style** Be sure the **Store macro in** box displays *All Documents (Normal.dotm)*.

a. Under **Assign macro to**, click the **Button** icon. In the **Word Options** dialog box, in the left pane with **Quick Access Toolbar** selected, in the right pane, under **Choose commands from**, click **Normal.NewMacros.Table_Style**. Click **Add**.

b. On the right side of the **Word Options** dialog box, click to select **Normal.NewMacros.Table_Style**. Below the list of commands, click **Modify**.

c. In the **Modify Button** dialog box, under **Symbol**, in the first row, click the round gray bullseye symbol. Click **OK** two times.

d. With the insertion point in the table, click the **Table Tools Design tab**, and then in the **Table Styles group**, click **More**. In the **Table Styles** gallery, under **Grid Tables**, in the fourth row, click the last style—**Grid Table 4 – Accent 6**.

e. Click the **Table Tools Layout tab**, in the **Cell Size group**, click **AutoFit**, and then click **AutoFit Contents**. In the **Table group**, click **Properties**. In the **Table Properties** dialog box, under **Alignment**, click **Center**, and then click **OK**. Click the **Developer tab**, and then in the **Code group**, click **Stop Recording**. **Save** your document.

4 From your student files, open the file **w11D_Press_Release**. Press F12. In the **Save As** dialog box, navigate to your **Word Chapter 11** folder. In the lower portion of the dialog box, click the **Save as type arrow**, and then from the list, click **Word Macro-Enabled Document**. In the **File name** box, using your own name, type **Lastname_Firstname_11D_Press_Release** and then click **Save**.

(Project 11D Fair Schedule continues on the next page)

Skills Review Project 11D Fair Schedule (continued)

a. Insert the file name in the footer, and then close the footer. Click the **Developer tab**, and then in the **Code group**, click **Record Macro**. In the **Macro name** box, type **AutoClose** Click the **Store macro in arrow**, and then click your **Lastname_Firstname_11D_Press_Release (document)**. Click **OK.**

b. Click the **Insert tab**, in the **Header & Footer group**, click **Header**, and then from the displayed list, click **Edit Header**.

c. Press Ctrl + A, and then press Delete. On the **Header & Footer Tools Design tab**, in the **Insert group**, click **Date & Time**. In the **Date and Time** dialog box, click the last option to display the time, and then click **OK**.

d. On the **Header & Footer Tools Design tab**, in the **Close group**, click **Close Header and Footer**. Click the **Developer tab**, and then in the **Code group**, click **Stop Recording**.

5 In the first cell of the table, click to position the insertion point. On the **Quick Access Toolbar**, click the gray bullseye button to run the *Table_Style* macro and format the table.

a. On the **Developer tab**, in the **Code group**, click **Macros**. In the **Macros** dialog box, select the **Heading** macro, and then click **Edit**.

b. In the **Heading** macro, locate the postal code **21203**. Position the insertion point to the right of *3*, press Backspace, and then type **1**

c. Near the top of the **Visual Basic Editor** window, click **File**, and then click **Close and Return to Microsoft Word**.

d. Press Ctrl + Home, and then press Alt + Ctrl + G to run the *Heading* macro. Deselect the text.

6 Click the **File tab**, and then **Show All Properties**.

a. In the **Tags** box, type **schedule, press release** In the **Subject** box, type your course name and section number. If necessary, edit the author name to display your name. On the left, click **Save**.

b. Display the **Developer tab**, and then in the **Code group**, click **Macros**. In the **Macros** dialog box, delete the Heading macro and then delete the Table_Style macro. Click the **File tab**, and then click **Options**. In the **Word Options** dialog box, click **Quick Access Toolbar**. On the right side of the window, click **Normal.NewMacros.Table_Style**, click **Remove**, and then click **OK**. Display the Word Options dialog box, and deselect the Developer tab. **Close** Word, and then click **Save** to save your documents.

7 Print your two documents or submit electronically as directed by your instructor.

END | You have completed Project 11D

CONTENT-BASED ASSESSMENTS (MASTERY AND TRANSFER OF LEARNING)

MyITLab grader

Mastering Word Project 11E Counseling Program

Apply 11A skills from these Objectives:

1. Embed an Excel Chart in a Word Document
2. Embed an Access Table in a Word Document
3. Embed a PowerPoint File in a Word Document
4. Link Objects to a Word Document

In the following Mastering Word project, you will include objects and files from other Office applications in a memo to Robert Benson, Executive Director of the Greater Baltimore Job Fair. The memo and related files support a proposal to provide career counseling services at job fairs. Your completed documents will look similar to Figure 11.42.

PROJECT FILES

For Project 11E, you will need the following files:

w11E_Counseling_Memo (Word document)
w11E_Counseling_Survey (Excel workbook)
w11E_Scheduled_Fairs (Access database)
w11E_Career_Counseling (PowerPoint presentation)
w11E_Counselors (Excel workbook)
w11E_Jobseeker_Survey (Word document)

You will save your files as:

Lastname_Firstname_11E_Counseling_Memo (Word document)
Lastname_Firstname_11E_Counselors (Excel workbook, linked file)
Lastname_Firstname_11E_Jobseeker_Survey (Word document, linked file)

PROJECT RESULTS

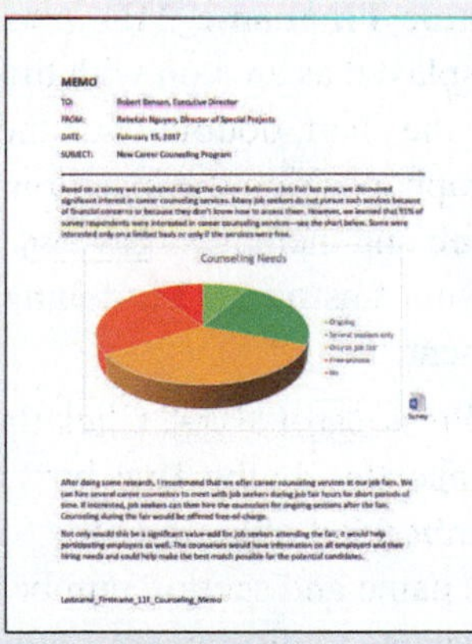

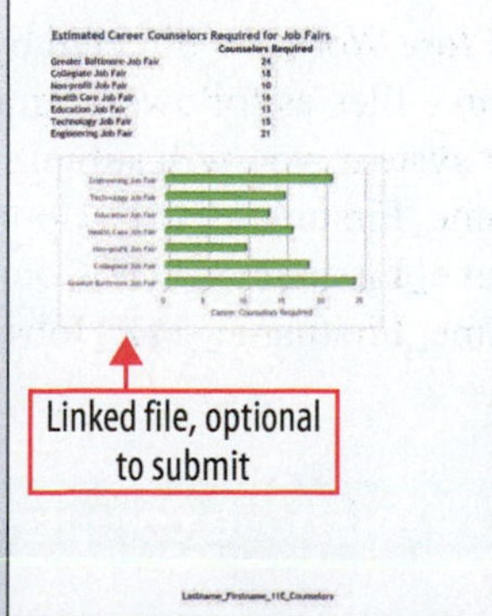

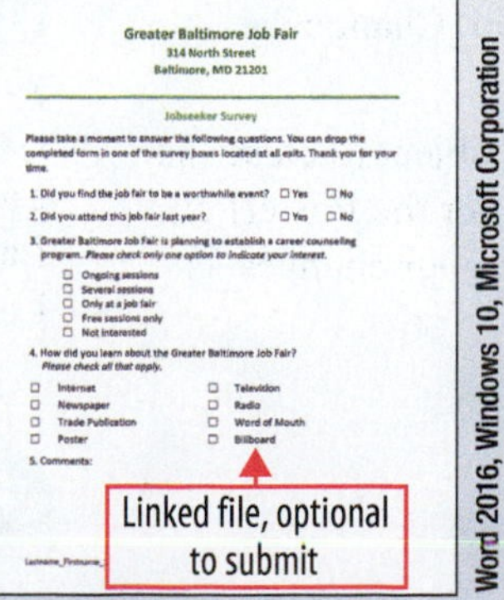

Word 2016, Windows 10, Microsoft Corporation

FIGURE 11.42

(Project 11E Counseling Program continues on the next page)

CONTENT-BASED ASSESSMENTS (MASTERY AND TRANSFER OF LEARNING)

Mastering Word Project 11E Counseling Program (continued)

1 Start Word. Open the file **w11E_Counseling_Memo**, and then save it to your **Word Chapter 11** folder as **Lastname_Firstname_11E_Counseling_Memo** Insert the file name in the footer.

2 From the taskbar, open **File Explorer**, and then from your student files, open the Excel file **w11E_Counseling_Survey**. Select and copy the chart, and then close Excel and close File Explorer. In your Word document, position the insertion point at the end of the paragraph that begins *Based on*, and then press Enter. From the **Paste Options** gallery, click **Keep Source Formatting & Embed Workbook (K)**.

3 **Center** the chart horizontally on the page. If necessary, change the Shape Height of the chart to 3.29 inches. Click **Save**.

4 Open File Explorer, and then open the Access file **w11E_Scheduled_Fairs**. If necessary, click **Enable Content**. Open the **Job Fairs** table, press Ctrl + A to select the entire table, and then **Copy** the table. **Close** Access and close File Explorer. In your Word document, press Ctrl + End, and then press Enter. Paste the table as **Formatted Text (RTF)**.

5 Click to place the insertion point in the table, apply the **List Table 5 Dark – Accent 6** table style—under **List Tables**, in the fifth row, the last style. Display the **Table Properties** dialog box, and then center the table in the document. **Save** your document.

6 In the paragraph below the table, click to position the insertion point, and then press Enter. Display the **Object** dialog box, click the **Create from File tab**, browse to locate the PowerPoint file **w11E_Career_Counseling**, click **Insert**, and then click **OK**. Right-click the PowerPoint object, from the shortcut menu, point to **Presentation Object**, and then click **Edit**. Change the theme to **Facet**.

7 Click outside of the PowerPoint object to close the PowerPoint commands, select and center the PowerPoint object in the document, and then **Save** your changes.

8 Open File Explorer, and then from your student files, open the Excel file **w11E_Counselors. Save** the file in your **Word Chapter 11** folder as **Lastname_Firstname_11E_Counselors** Insert the file name in the footer. **Save** your changes, and then **Close** Excel and close File Explorer.

9 In your Word document, to the right of the PowerPoint object, click to position the insertion point. **Insert** your **Lastname_Firstname_11E_Counselors** file as a linked file displayed as an icon with the modified caption **Counselor Needs** Double-click the inserted icon, click in cell **B5**, and then type **10** Press Enter, **Save** your changes, and then **Close** Excel. **Save** the changes in your Word document.

10 Open File Explorer, and then from your student files, open the Word file **w11E_Jobseeker_Survey**. Save the file in your **Word Chapter 11** folder as **Lastname_Firstname_11E_Jobseeker_Survey** Insert the file name in the footer. **Save** and then close the document.

11 On **Page 1** of your **Lastname_Firstname_11E_Counseling_Memo** document, click to position the insertion point to the right of the chart. Insert your Word file **Lastname_Firstname_11E_Jobseeker_Survey** as a linked file displayed as an icon with the modified caption **Survey** Below the chart, double-click the **Survey** icon. In the first paragraph, position the insertion point to the left of *Fair*, type **Job** and then press Spacebar. Click **Save**, and then close your **Lastname_Firstname_11E_Jobseeker_Survey** document.

12 Press Ctrl + Home. Click the **File tab**, and then **Show All Properties**. In the **Tags** box, type **counseling, linked and embedded objects** In the **Subject** box, type your course name and section number. If necessary, edit the author name to display your name. On the left, click **Save**.

13 **Close** Word. As directed by your instructor, submit your three files as follows (if grading in the MyITLab Grader system, you will submit only the first file):
Lastname_Firstname_11E_Counseling Memo
Lastname_Firstname_11E_Counselors
Lastname_Firstname_11E_Jobseeker_Survey

END | You have completed Project 11E

CONTENT-BASED ASSESSMENTS (MASTERY AND TRANSFER OF LEARNING)

Mastering Word Project 11F Collegiate Fair

Apply 11B skills from these Objectives:

5 Create Macros
6 Run Macros
7 Edit a Macro in the Visual Basic Editor

In the following Mastering Word project, you will create macros to assist you with editing documents that will be sent to employers who are registered for the Collegiate Fair conducted by the Greater Baltimore Job Fair. Your completed documents will look similar to Figure 11.43.

PROJECT FILES

For Project 11F, you will need the following files:

New blank Word document
w11F_Collegiate_Fair

You will save your file as:

Lastname_Firstname_11F_Collegiate_Fair

PROJECT RESULTS

Greater Baltimore Job Fair

Collegiate Job Fair Agenda for Employers
Day 1

Curbside Drop-off Service

- 10:00 a.m. – 1:00 p.m.
- Job fair staff will assist with unloading display materials and direct you to parking facilities.

Booth Setup

- 10:00 a.m. – 1:30 p.m.
- Employers will have access to booths and materials. Job Fair staff will be on hand to assist.

Employer Registration/Check-in

- 10:00 a.m. – 2:00 p.m.
- Company representatives and recruiters will register in the convention center lobby.

Employer Refreshments

- 12:00 p.m. – 5:00 p.m.
- Lunch will be provided from 12:00 p.m. to 2:00 p.m. Afternoon snacks and beverages will also be available.

Job Fair Begins

- 2:00 p.m. – 6:00 p.m.
- Employers and students from area colleges and universities will meet informally at booths to discuss full-time positions and internships.

Employer Presentations

- 4:00 p.m. – 5:00 p.m.
- If desired, representatives of various companies and organizations can make short presentations to interested job seekers in a central area of the job fair's floor. If you are interested, please schedule a time with your job fair contact.

Survey

- Complete at your convenience.
- Your feedback is valuable as we plan future job fairs. Please take a few minutes to complete the survey provided in your folder. Return it to the registration table or any job fair employee.

Project 11F

Greater Baltimore Job Fair

```
Sub Footer()
'
' Footer Macro
' Inserts the project ID in the footer
'
    If ActiveWindow.View.SplitSpecial <> wdPaneNone Then
        ActiveWindow.Panes(2).Close
    End If
    If ActiveWindow.ActivePane.View.Type = wdNormalView Or ActiveWindow. _
        ActivePane.View.Type = wdOutlineView Then
        ActiveWindow.ActivePane.View.Type = wdPrintView
    End If
    ActiveWindow.ActivePane.View.SeekView = wdSeekCurrentPageFooter
    Selection.WholeStory
    Selection.Delete Unit:=wdCharacter, Count:=1
    Selection.TypeText Text:="Project 11F"
    ActiveWindow.ActivePane.View.SeekView = wdSeekMainDocument
End Sub
Sub Header()
'
' Header Macro
'
'
    If ActiveWindow.View.SplitSpecial <> wdPaneNone Then
        ActiveWindow.Panes(2).Close
    End If
    If ActiveWindow.ActivePane.View.Type = wdNormalView Or ActiveWindow. _
        ActivePane.View.Type = wdOutlineView Then
        ActiveWindow.ActivePane.View.Type = wdPrintView
    End If
    ActiveWindow.ActivePane.View.SeekView = wdSeekCurrentPageHeader
    Selection.WholeStory
    Selection.Delete Unit:=wdCharacter, Count:=1
    Selection.TypeText Text:="Greater Baltimore Job Fair"
    ActiveWindow.ActivePane.View.SeekView = wdSeekMainDocument
End Sub
```

Project 11F

FIGURE 11.43

Word 2016, Windows 10, Microsoft Corporation

(Project 11F Collegiate Fair continues on the next page)

CONTENT-BASED ASSESSMENTS (MASTERY AND TRANSFER OF LEARNING)

Mastering Word Project 11F Collegiate Fair (continued)

1 Start Word. Locate and open the file **w11F_Collegiate_Fair**. Save the file in your **Word Chapter 11** folder as a **Word Macro-Enabled Document** with the file name **Lastname_Firstname_11F_Collegiate_Fair** Display the **Developer tab**, and then if necessary, change your **Macro Security** setting to **Disable all macros with notification**.

2 Select the first two paragraphs that form the title and change the **Font Size** to **22**. Display the **Record Macro** dialog box, and then in the **Macro name** box, type **Footer** Be sure the **Store macro in** box displays **All Documents (Normal.dotm)**. In the **Description** box, type **Inserts the project ID in the footer** **Assign** the **shortcut key** Alt + Ctrl + J. Click the **Insert tab**. In the **Header & Footer group**, click **Footer**, and then click **Edit Footer**. Press Ctrl + A, press Delete, and then type **Project 11F** Click **Close Header and Footer**, and then click **Stop Recording**. **Save** your document.

3 Select the heading *Curbside Drop-off Service*, and change the **Font Color** to **Red**. Display the **Record Macro** dialog box, and then in the **Macro name** box, type **Header** Be sure the **Store macro in** box displays **All Documents (Normal.dotm)**. Click the **Button** icon, and then in the **Word Options** dialog box, **Add** the **Normal.NewMacros. Header** to the **Quick Access Toolbar**. Click **Modify**, and then under **Symbol**, in the first row, click the third button—a blue circle containing a white i. Click the **Insert tab**, click **Header**, and then click **Edit Header**. Press Ctrl + A, press Delete, and then type **Greater Baltimore** Click **Close Header and Footer**. Click **Stop Recording**.

4 In the fourth bullet point, in the second sentence, change *fair* to **Fair** Display the **Macros** dialog box, select the **Header** macro, and then click **Edit**. Near the bottom of the *Header* macro code, position the insertion point to the right of *Baltimore*, press Spacebar, and then type **Job Fair** Press Ctrl + A to select all of the text in the Visual Basic window, right-click over the selected text, and click **Copy**. Click **File**, and then click **Close and Return to Microsoft Word**. Press Ctrl + Home. On the **Quick Access Toolbar**, click the **Header** macro button.

5 Press Ctrl + End and then press Ctrl + Enter to insert a new page. Press Backspace one time to turn off the bullets, and then press Ctrl + V to paste the text from the Visual Basic window.

6 Click the **File** tab, and then **Show All Properties**. In the **Tags** box, type **fair agenda, macros** In the **Subject** box, type your course name and section number. If necessary, edit the author name to display your name. On the left click **Close**, and then click **Save**.

7 Display the **Macros** dialog box, click the **Macros in arrow**, and then click **All active templates and documents**. **Delete** the **Header** and **Footer** macros. From **Backstage** view, display the **Word Options** dialog box, click **Quick Access Toolbar**. On the right side of the window, click **Normal.NewMacros.Header**, click **Remove**, and then click **OK**. Redisplay the **Word Options** dialog box, and then remove the Developer tab from the ribbon.

8 Print your 11F_Collegiate_Fair document or submit electronically as directed by your instructor.

END | You have completed Project 11F

Mastering Word Project 11G Catering

Apply 11A and 11B skills from these Objectives:

1. Embed an Excel Chart in a Word Document
2. Embed an Access Table in a Word Document
3. Embed a PowerPoint File in a Word Document
4. Link Objects to a Word Document
5. Create Macros
6. Run Macros
7. Edit a Macro in the Visual Basic Editor

In the following Mastering Word project, you will include objects in a letter to a caterer. The Greater Baltimore Job Fair provides luncheons and snacks to the employers attending the job fairs. You will create macros that will be used to increase your efficiency in creating documents to explain the job fair needs to the caterer. Your completed document will look similar to Figure 11.44.

PROJECT FILES

For Project 11G, you will need the following files:

New blank Word document
w11G_Catering_Letter
w11G_Catering_Needs
w11G_Catering_Budget

You will save your files as:

Lastname_Firstname_11G_Catering_Letter
Lastname_Firstname_11G_Catering_Budget (linked file)

PROJECT RESULTS

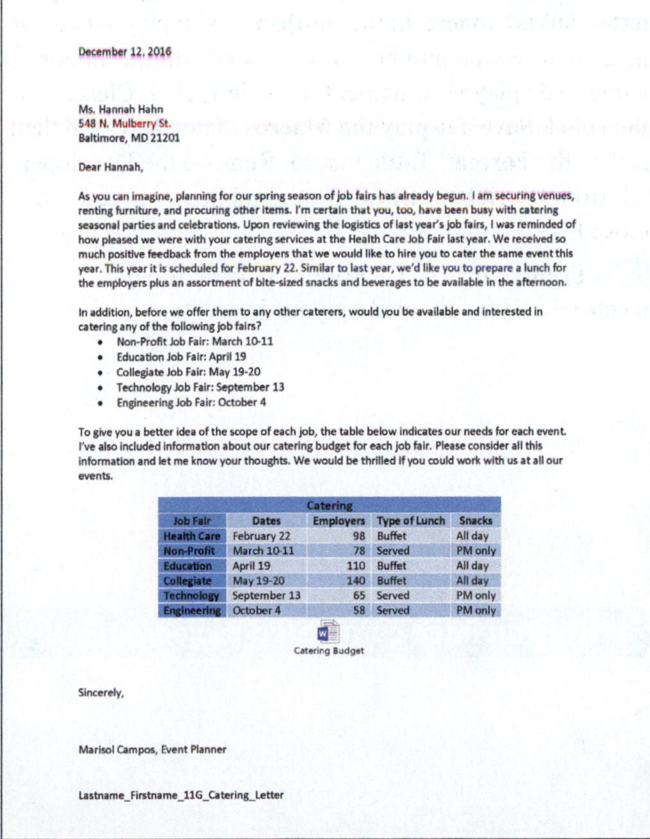

December 12, 2016

Ms. Hannah Hahn
548 N. Mulberry St.
Baltimore, MD 21201

Dear Hannah,

As you can imagine, planning for our spring season of job fairs has already begun. I am securing venues, renting furniture, and procuring other items. I'm certain that you, too, have been busy with catering seasonal parties and celebrations. Upon reviewing the logistics of last year's job fairs, I was reminded of how pleased we were with your catering services at the Health Care Job Fair last year. We received so much positive feedback from the employers that we would like to hire you to cater the same event this year. This year it is scheduled for February 22. Similar to last year, we'd like you to prepare a lunch for the employers plus an assortment of bite-sized snacks and beverages to be available in the afternoon.

In addition, before we offer them to any other caterers, would you be available and interested in catering any of the following job fairs?

- Non-Profit Job Fair: March 10-11
- Education Job Fair: April 19
- Collegiate Job Fair: May 19-20
- Technology Job Fair: September 13
- Engineering Job Fair: October 4

To give you a better idea of the scope of each job, the table below indicates our needs for each event. I've also included information about our catering budget for each job fair. Please consider all this information and let me know your thoughts. We would be thrilled if you could work with us at all our events.

Catering				
Job Fair	Dates	Employers	Type of Lunch	Snacks
Health Care	February 22	98	Buffet	All day
Non-Profit	March 10-11	78	Served	PM only
Education	April 19	110	Buffet	All day
Collegiate	May 19-20	140	Buffet	All day
Technology	September 13	65	Served	PM only
Engineering	October 4	58	Served	PM only

Catering Budget

Sincerely,

Marisol Campos, Event Planner

Lastname_Firstname_11G_Catering_Letter

```
Sub Format_Table()
'
' Format_Table Macro
' Formats the table
'
    Selection.Tables(1).Style = "Grid Table 5 Dark - Accent 1"
    Selection.Tables(1).AutoFitBehavior (wdAutoFitContent)
    Selection.Tables(1).AutoFitBehavior (wdAutoFitContent)
    Selection.Tables(1).Rows.Alignment = wdAlignRowCenter
End Sub
```

Lastname_Firstname_11G_Catering_Letter

FIGURE 11.44 Word 2016, Windows 10, Microsoft Corporation

(Project 11G Catering continues on the next page)

CONTENT-BASED ASSESSMENTS (MASTERY AND TRANSFER OF LEARNING)

Mastering Word Project 11G Catering (continued)

1 Start Word. Open the file **w11G_Catering_Letter**, and then save it to your **Word Chapter 11** folder as a **Word Macro-Enabled Document** with the file name **Lastname_Firstname_11G_Catering_Letter** Insert the file name in the footer.

2 From File Explorer, open the Access file **w11G_Catering_Needs**, and click **Enable Content**. Open and then **Copy** the entire **Catering** table. **Close** Access. In your Word document, position the insertion point at the end of the paragraph that begins *To give you*, and then press Enter two times. Paste the table as **HTML Format**.

3 In the first cell of the table, click to position the insertion point. Display the **Record Macro** dialog box, and then in the **Macro name** box, type **Format_Table** Be sure the **Store macro in** box displays **All Documents (Normal.dotm)**. For the **Description**, type **Formats the table Assign** the **shortcut key** Alt + Ctrl + Q. With the insertion point in the table, click the **Table Tools Design tab**, and then in the **Table Styles group**, click **More**. Under **Grid Tables**, click **Grid Table 5 Dark – Accent 1**—in the fifth row, the second style. Click the **Table Tools Layout tab**, in the **Cell Size group**, click **AutoFit**, and then click **AutoFit Contents**. In the **Table group**, click **Properties**. In the **Table Properties** dialog box, under **Alignment**, click **Center**, and then click **OK**. Click the **Developer tab**, and then in the **Code group**, click **Stop Recording**. **Save** your changes.

4 Open File Explorer, and then from your student files, open the file **w11G_Catering_Budget**. Save the file in your **Word Chapter 11** folder with the file name **Lastname_Firstname_11G_Catering_Budget** Insert the file name in the footer. **Save** your changes, and then **Close** the document.

5 In your **Lastname_Firstname_11G_Catering_Letter**, below the table, position the insertion point in the first blank paragraph. **Insert** your **Lastname_Firstname_11G_Catering_Budget** file as a linked file displayed as an icon with the modified caption **Catering Budget** Select the icon and apply **Center**. Double-click the icon, and then change the **Number Attending** the *Health Care* Job Fair to **100** Press Ctrl + Home. **Save** your changes, and then **Close** your **Lastname_Firstname_11G_Catering_Budget**.

6 On the **Developer tab**, in the **Code group**, click **Visual Basic**. Press Ctrl + A to select all of the code, right-click over the selection, and then click **Copy**. Click **File**, and then click **Close and Return to Microsoft Word**. Press Ctrl + End, press Ctrl + Enter to insert a new page, and then press Ctrl + V to paste the copied code.

7 In your **Lastname_Firstname_11G_Catering_Letter** document, move to the top of the document click the **File tab**, and then **Show All Properties**. In the **Tags** box, type **letter, linked, macro** In the **Subject** box, type your course name and section number. If necessary, edit the author name to display your name. On the left, click **Close**, and then click **Save**. Display the **Macros** dialog box, and then **Delete** the **Format_Table** macro. Remove the Developer tab from the ribbon. **Close** Word, and then if necessary, close File Explorer.

8 Print your 11G_Catering_Letter or submit electronically as directed by your instructor.

END | You have completed Project 11G

Apply a combination of the 11A and 11B skills.

CONTENT-BASED ASSESSMENTS (CRITICAL THINKING)

11 WORD

GO! Fix It — Project 11H Employer Letter — MyITLab

GO! Make It — Project 11I Engineering Fair — MyITLab

GO! Solve It — Project 11J Job Support — MyITLab

GO! Solve It — Project 11K Fair Attendance

PROJECT FILES

For Project 11K, you will need the following files:

New blank Word document
w11K_Attendance_Memo
w11K_Increased_Attendance
w11K_Attendance

You will save your files as:

Lastname_Firstname_11K_Attendance_Memo
Lastname_Firstname_11K_Attendance

Open the Excel file **w11K_Attendance** and save it to your **Word Chapter 11** folder as **Lastname_Firstname_11K_Attendance** Insert the file name in the footer and add appropriate document properties. Open the file **w11K_Attendance_Memo** and save it to your **Word Chapter 11** folder as a macro-enabled document with the file name **Lastname_Firstname_11K_Attendance_Memo** Insert the file name in the footer. Create a macro that inserts the text **Greater Baltimore Job Fair** center-aligned in the header. Assign the macro to the Quick Access Toolbar as a button. Embed the **w11K_Increased_Attendance** PowerPoint file and link the **Lastname_Firstname_11K_Attendance** file as an icon at the appropriate places in the memo. In the Excel file, change the value for *2016 Attendance* to **8,732** Format the document to create a professional appearance. Copy and paste your macro code on a new page at the end of the memo. Add appropriate document properties in both Word documents. Delete the macro you created, and then print both Word documents and the Excel file or submit all three files as directed by your instructor.

(Project 11K Fair Attendance continues on the next page)

GO! Solve It Project 11K Fair Attendance (continued)

Performance Level

Performance Element	Exemplary: You consistently applied the relevant skills	Proficient: You sometimes, but not always, applied the relevant skills	Developing: You rarely or never applied the relevant skills
Create a macro	The macro is created and displays as a button on the Quick Access Toolbar.	The macro is created but does not display as a button on the Quick Access Toolbar.	A macro is not created.
Embed a file	The file is embedded at an appropriate location.	The file is embedded but is at an inappropriate location.	The file is not embedded.
Link and edit a file	The file is linked, displays as an icon, and is edited.	The file is linked but does not display as an icon or is not edited.	The file is not linked.
Format document	Formatting is attractive and appropriate.	Adequate formatting but difficult to read or unattractive.	Either there is no formatting or it is inadequate.
Paste images	Both images are pasted correctly.	Only one image is pasted correctly.	No images are pasted in the document.

END | You have completed Project 11K

OUTCOMES-BASED ASSESSMENTS

RUBRIC

The following outcomes-based assessments are *open-ended assessments*. That is, there is no specific correct result; your result will depend on your approach to the information provided. Make *Professional Quality* your goal. Use the following scoring rubric to guide you in *how* to approach the problem and then to evaluate *how well* your approach solves the problem.

The *criteria*—Software Mastery, Content, Format and Layout, and Process—represent the knowledge and skills you have gained that you can apply to solving the problem. The *levels of performance*—Professional Quality, Approaching Professional Quality, or Needs Quality Improvements—help you and your instructor evaluate your result.

	Your completed project is of Professional Quality if you:	Your completed project is Approaching Professional Quality if you:	Your completed project Needs Quality Improvements if you:
1-Software Mastery	Choose and apply the most appropriate skills, tools, and features and identify efficient methods to solve the problem.	Choose and apply some appropriate skills, tools, and features, but not in the most efficient manner.	Choose inappropriate skills, tools, or features, or are inefficient in solving the problem.
2-Content	Construct a solution that is clear and well organized, contains content that is accurate, appropriate to the audience and purpose, and is complete. Provide a solution that contains no errors of spelling, grammar, or style.	Construct a solution in which some components are unclear, poorly organized, inconsistent, or incomplete. Misjudge the needs of the audience. Have some errors in spelling, grammar, or style, but the errors do not detract from comprehension.	Construct a solution that is unclear, incomplete, or poorly organized, contains some inaccurate or inappropriate content, and contains many errors of spelling, grammar, or style. Do not solve the problem.
3-Format and Layout	Format and arrange all elements to communicate information and ideas, clarify function, illustrate relationships, and indicate relative importance.	Apply appropriate format and layout features to some elements, but not others. Overuse features, causing minor distraction.	Apply format and layout that does not communicate information or ideas clearly. Do not use format and layout features to clarify function, illustrate relationships, or indicate relative importance. Use available features excessively, causing distraction.
4-Process	Use an organized approach that integrates planning, development, self-assessment, revision, and reflection.	Demonstrate an organized approach in some areas, but not others; or, use an insufficient process of organization throughout.	Do not use an organized approach to solve the problem.

Apply a combination of the 11A and 11B skills.

OUTCOMES-BASED ASSESSMENTS (CRITICAL THINKING)

GO! Think Project 11L Health Fair

Build from Scratch

PROJECT FILES

For Project 11L, you will need the following files:

Three new blank Word documents

You will save your files as:

Lastname_Firstname_11L_Health_Flyer
Lastname_Firstname_11L_Health_Letter

The Greater Baltimore Job Fair conducts a healthcare job fair every year. The organization is located at 314 North Street, Baltimore, MD 21201. Search the Internet for the types of job opportunities that are available for healthcare careers. Save a new macro-enabled document as **Lastname_Firstname_11L_Health_Flyer** Create a flyer indicating the types of job recruiters that will be attending the fair. Use fictitious information for the date, time, and location. Create a macro for job fair contact information that will run in all documents. Create an AutoClose macro that will automatically insert the date and time in the header—only in this document. Format the document to create a professional appearance, insert the file name in the footer, and add appropriate document properties. Copy and paste your macro code as the last page of the flyer. Save a second, new macro-enabled document as **Lastname_Firstname_11L_Health_Letter** Create a letter to be sent to the local college—use fictitious information—asking that copies of the flyer be made available to students. Run the job fair's contact information macro in a letterhead and use your own name in the signature line. Insert a link to your flyer, displaying it as an icon. Insert the file name in the footer and add appropriate document properties. Delete the macros you created. Print or submit electronically as directed by your instructor.

END | You have completed Project 11L

Build from Scratch

GO! Think Project 11M Jobseeker Tips MyITLab

Build from Scratch

You and GO! Project 11N Personal Letterhead MyITLab

Integrating Word with PowerPoint and Modifying Document Components

12

WORD 2016

PROJECT 12A

OUTCOMES

Integrate Word with PowerPoint.

OBJECTIVES

1. Integrate Word with PowerPoint
2. Modify a PowerPoint Presentation
3. Create a Table of Authorities

PROJECT 12B

OUTCOMES

Modify the document layout and format graphic and text elements.

OBJECTIVES

4. Modify the Document Layout
5. Format Graphic and Text Elements

txakel/fotolia

In This Chapter

GO! to Work with Word

Microsoft Office 2016 is an integrated application suite. This integration enables you to use each application for its specified purpose and then combine components for a final result. For example, you can create a table in Access and then use that table to perform a mail merge in Word. You can create a table of authorities in a legal document by marking citations. You can customize Word in a variety of ways—for example, change the paper size, apply advanced formatting features to text, and modify graphic and text elements—to create a professional-looking document that meets your exact specifications.

The projects in this chapter relate to **Magical Park Corporation**, which operates 15 regional theme parks across the United States, Mexico, and Canada. Park types include traditional theme parks, water parks, and wildlife adventure parks. This year, the company will launch three of its new "Imagination Parks" where attractions combine fun and the discovery of math and science information, and where teens and adults enjoy the free Friday night concerts. Magical Park Corporation also operates family-friendly resort hotels on many of their properties that include exceptional pools and championship golf courses.

PROJECT 12A Planning Presentation

PROJECT ACTIVITIES

In Activities 12.01 through 12.07, you will prepare an outline in Word and then use the outline to create a PowerPoint presentation. After creating the presentation, you will create handouts in Word that include images of each slide and a place for notes. You will create a PowerPoint presentation and handouts regarding the results of a survey of visitors to the company's animal parks, and you will add a table of authorities to a legal document. Your completed files will look similar to Figure 12.1.

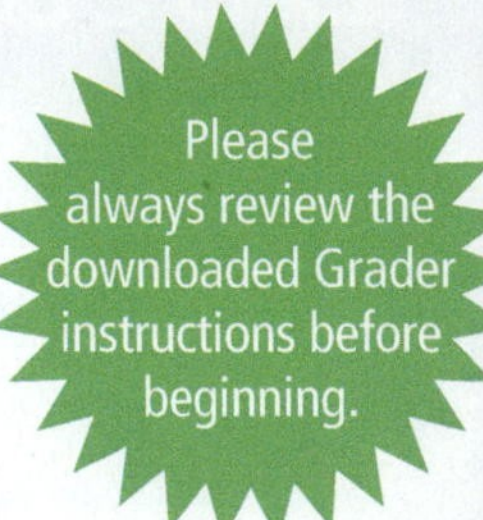

PROJECT FILES

If your instructor wants you to submit Project 12A in the MyITLab Grader system, log into MyITLab, locate Grader Project 12A, and then download the files for the project.

For Project 12A, you will need the following files:

w12A_Planning_Outline
w12A_Park_Brief

You will save your documents as:

Lastname_Firstname_12A_Planning_Outline (not shown)
Lastname_Firstname_12A_Planning_Presentation (not shown)
Lastname_Firstname_12A_Planning_Handout
Lastname_Firstname_12A_Park_Brief

PROJECT RESULTS

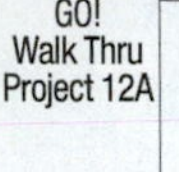

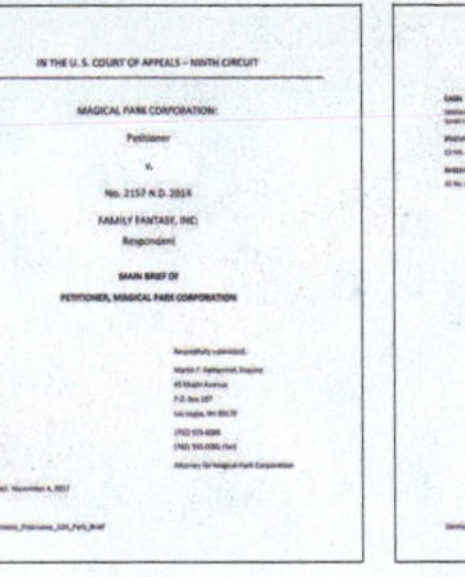

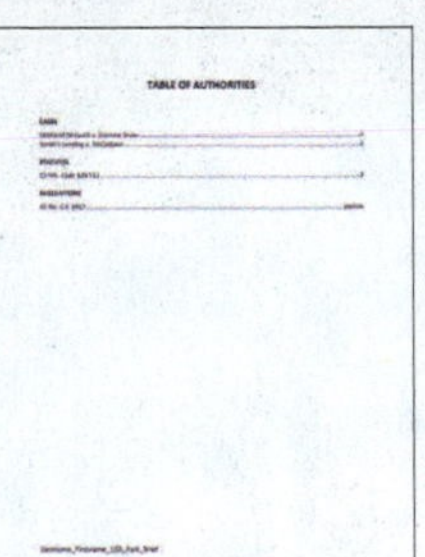

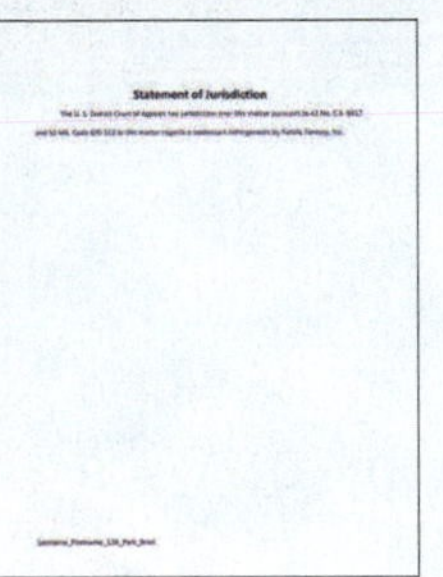

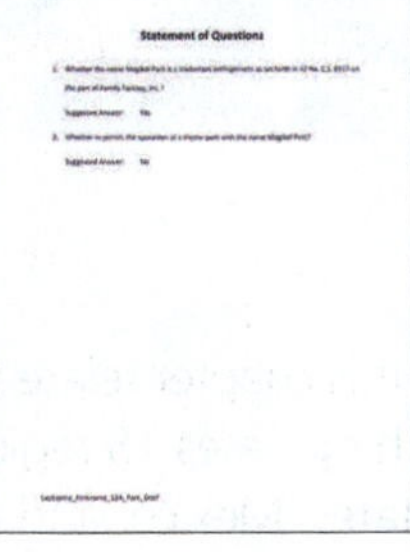

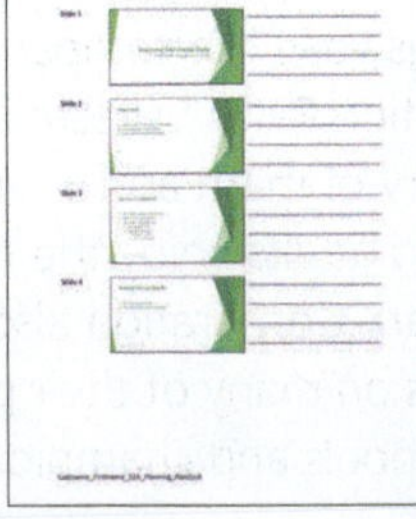

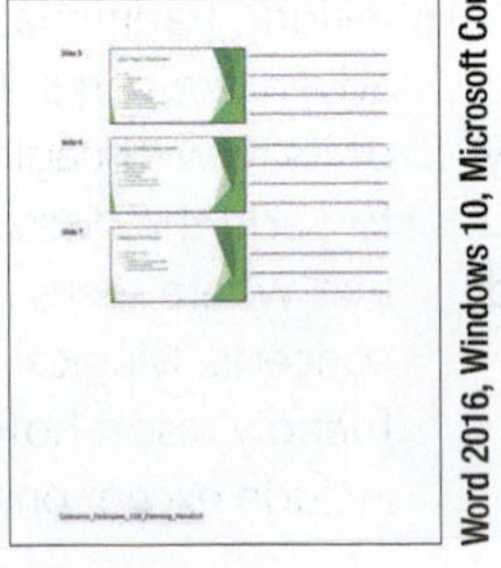

FIGURE 12.1 Project 12A Planning Presentation

Objective 1 Integrate Word with PowerPoint

GO! Learn How Video W12-1

An ***outline*** provides a way to organize the contents of a document in a structured manner. Previously, you used Outline view to create a master document and subdocuments. You can use a Word outline to create slides in PowerPoint. In Outline view, each paragraph is treated as a separate topic, or level, in the outline. Each topic is assigned either an ***outline level*** or is identified as body text. An outline level defines the position of the paragraph in relation to all topics in the document with a corresponding heading style. You can assign up to nine levels in an outline.

Activity 12.01 | Creating an Outline in Outline View

ALERT!

To submit as an autograded project, log into MyITLab and download the files for this Project, and begin with those files instead of w12A_Planning_Outline and w12A_Park_Brief.

In this Activity, you will apply outline levels to existing paragraphs and move paragraphs to create an outline.

1 Start Word. From your student files, open the file **w12A_Planning_Outline**. Navigate to the location where you are saving your files for this chapter, and then create a new folder named **Word Chapter 12** Using your own name, **Save** the document in your **Word Chapter 12** folder as **Lastname_Firstname_12A_Planning_Outline** Insert the file name in the footer and display rulers and formatting marks.

2 Click the **View tab**, and then in the **Views group**, click the **Outline** button.

All paragraphs are preceded by an ***outline symbol***—a small gray circle that identifies heading and body text paragraphs in an outline.

3 In the first paragraph, click the outline symbol to select the paragraph. On the **Outlining tab**, in the **Outline Tools group**, click the **Outline Level arrow** [Body Text], and then click **Level 1**. Compare your screen with Figure 12.2.

The paragraph is designated as Level 1 and is formatted with the Heading 1 style—not visible in Outline view. A ***plus outline symbol*** displays to the left of the paragraph indicating there are subordinate heading or body text paragraphs.

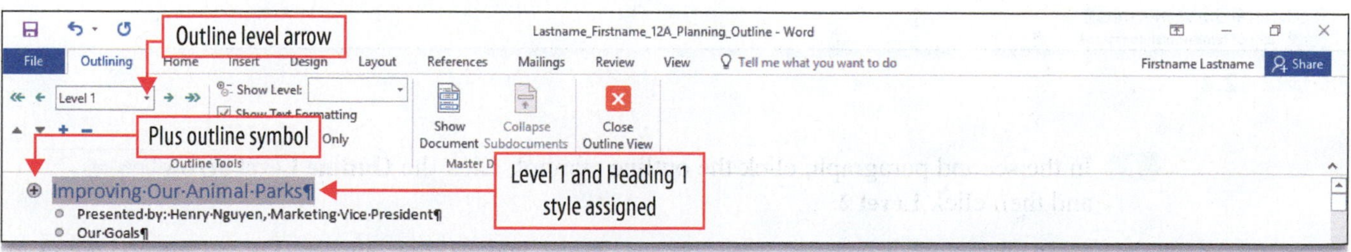

FIGURE 12.2

Word 2016, Windows 10, Microsoft Corporation

4 In the third paragraph, click the outline symbol to select the paragraph. On the **Outlining tab**, in the **Outline Tools group**, click **Promote to Heading 1** [«].

The paragraph is designated as Level 1 and formatted with the Heading 1 style.

5 On the **Outlining tab**, in the **Close group**, click **Close Outline View**. Compare your screen with Figure 12.3.

The paragraphs designated as Level 1 display with the Heading 1 style. In Print Layout view, however, the outline symbols do not display.

ANOTHER WAY Click the Print Layout button on the Status bar.

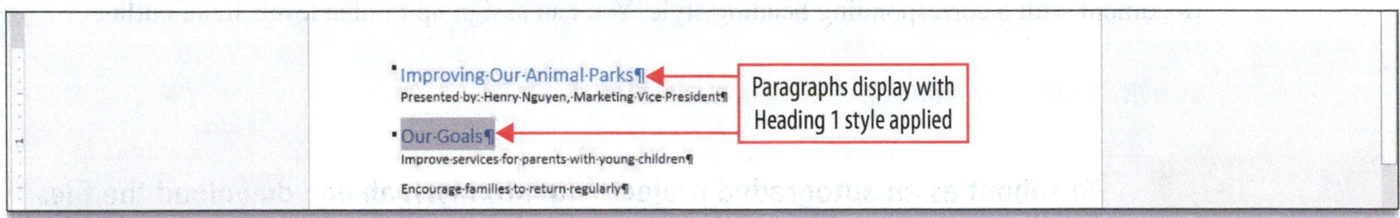

FIGURE 12.3 Word 2016, Windows 10, Microsoft Corporation

6 Click the **View tab**, and then in the **Views group**, click **Outline**. Using the technique you practiced, assign **Level 1** to the paragraphs *Survey Conducted, Most Highly Rated Areas, Areas Needing the Most Improvement, Planning for Change*, and *General Survey Results*. Deselect the text, and then compare your screen with Figure 12.4.

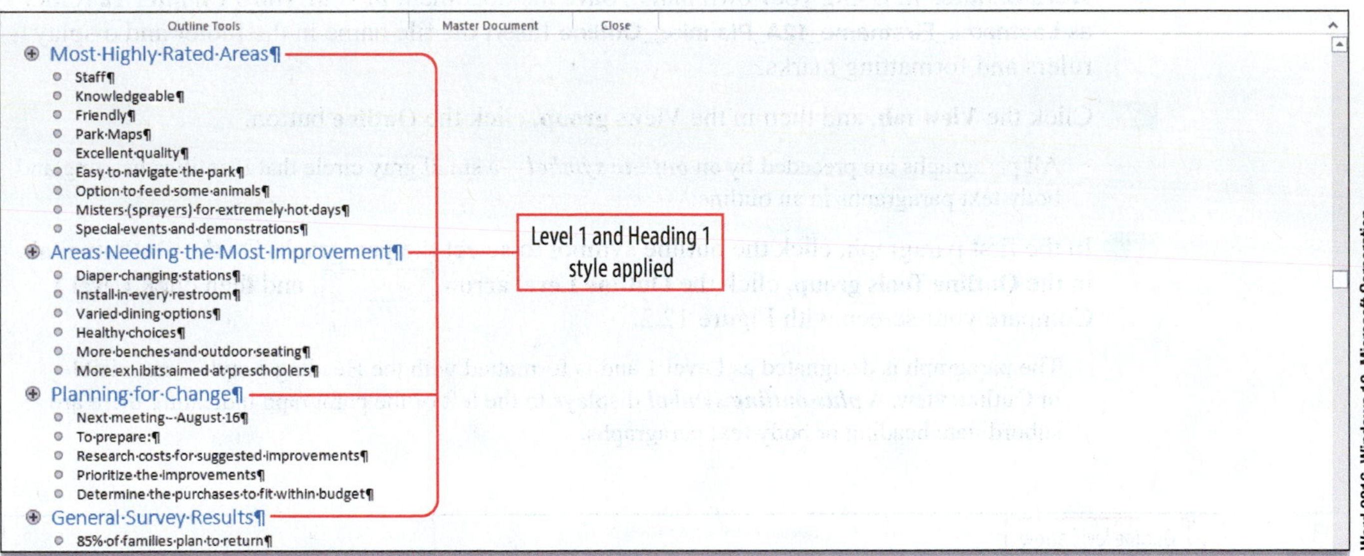

Word 2016, Windows 10, Microsoft Corporation

FIGURE 12.4

7 In the second paragraph, click the outline symbol, click the **Outline Level arrow** [Body Text], and then click **Level 2**.

The paragraph is indented, designated as Level 2, and the Heading 2 style is applied. The ***minus outline symbol*** displays indicating there are no subordinate heading or body text paragraphs. Paragraphs are indented based on the assigned outline level.

8 Below the paragraph *Our Goals*, drag to select all three body text paragraphs. Click the **Outline Level arrow** [Body Text], and then click **Level 2**.

9 In a similar manner, below each of the remaining *Level 1* paragraphs, select the body text paragraphs, and then apply the **Level 2** outline level. Press Ctrl + Home, and then compare your screen with Figure 12.5.

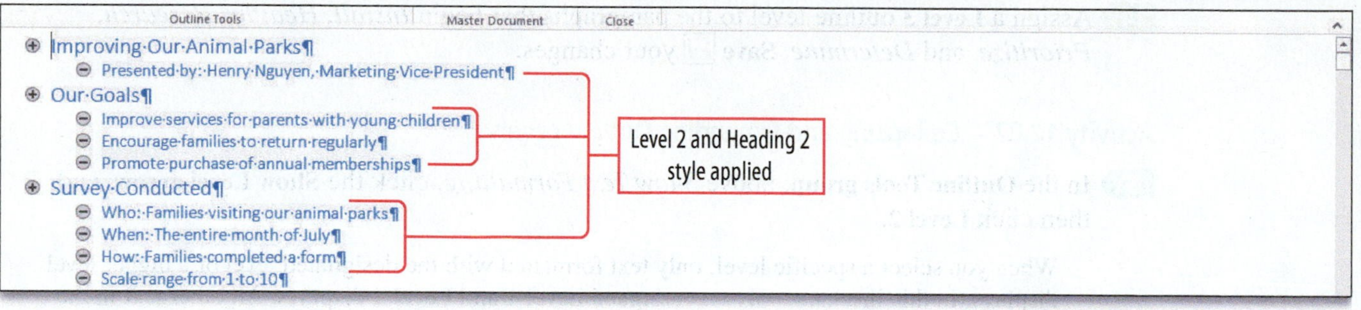

FIGURE 12.5

Word 2016, Windows 10, Microsoft Corporation

10 Below the *Survey Conducted* heading, select the two paragraphs that begin **Scale range** and **Rating scale**. On the **Outlining tab**, in the **Outline Tools group**, click **Demote** [→]. Compare your screen with Figure 12.6.

The Demote button assigns a paragraph to a lower level. In this instance, the paragraphs are assigned a Level 3 outline level and the Heading 3 style is applied.

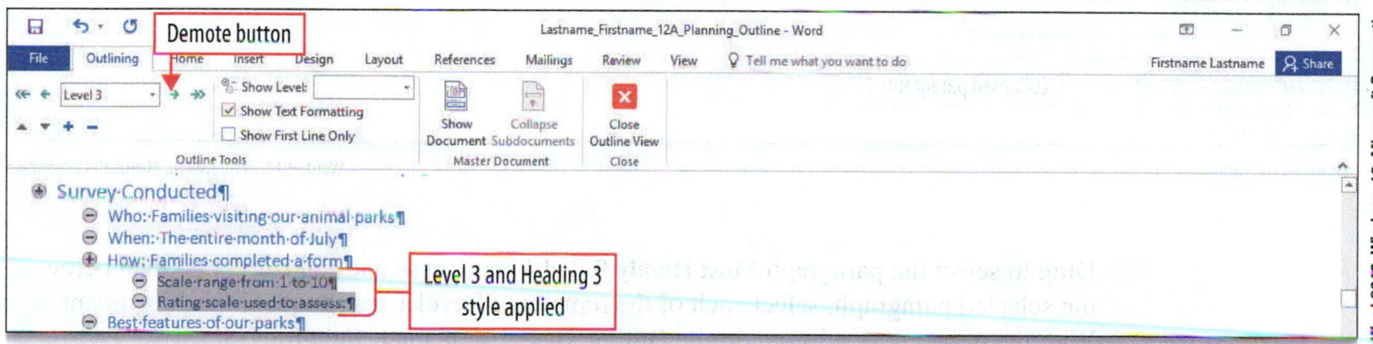

FIGURE 12.6

Word 2016, Windows 10, Microsoft Corporation

11 Below the paragraph that begins *Rating scale*, select the next two paragraphs, and then click **Demote** [→] two times.

The paragraphs are assigned a Level 4 outline level and the Heading 4 style is applied.

12 Below the paragraph *Staff*, select the next five paragraphs, and then click **Demote** [→].

13 Select the paragraph **Park Maps**, and then in the **Outline Tools group**, click **Promote** [←]. Compare your screen with Figure 12.7.

The Promote button assigns a paragraph to a higher level. In this instance, the *Park Maps* paragraph is assigned a Level 2 outline level.

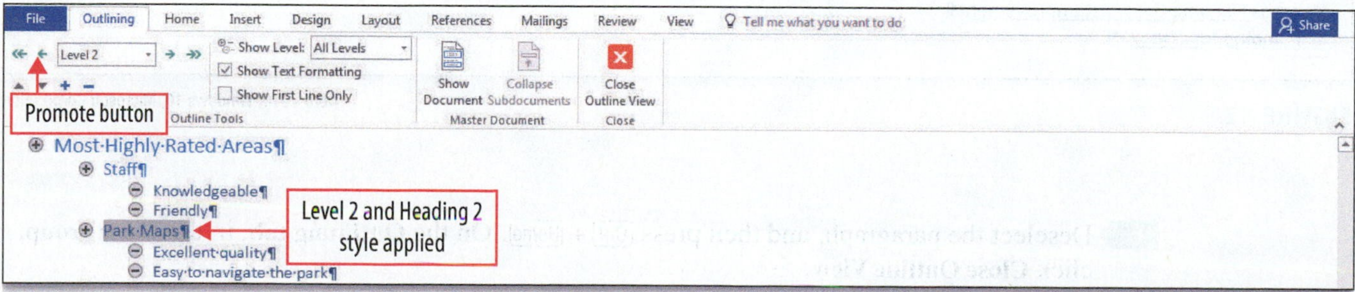

FIGURE 12.7

Word 2016, Windows 10, Microsoft Corporation

14 Assign a **Level 3** outline level to the paragraphs that begin *Install*, *Healthy*, *Research*, *Prioritize*, and *Determine*. **Save** your changes.

Activity 12.02 | Collapsing and Expanding Outline Levels

1 In the **Outline Tools group**, above *Show Text Formatting*, click the **Show Level arrow**, and then click **Level 2**.

When you select a specific level, only text formatted with the designated level or a higher level displays. In this instance, only text assigned Level 1 and Level 2 displays. All other text in the document is hidden.

2 In the **Outline Tools group**, click the **Show Level arrow**, and then click **All Levels** to display the entire document.

3 Locate the paragraph *Survey Conducted*, and then double-click the plus outline symbol to collapse the level. Compare your screen with Figure 12.8.

Collapsing an outline level hides all subordinate heading and body text paragraphs.

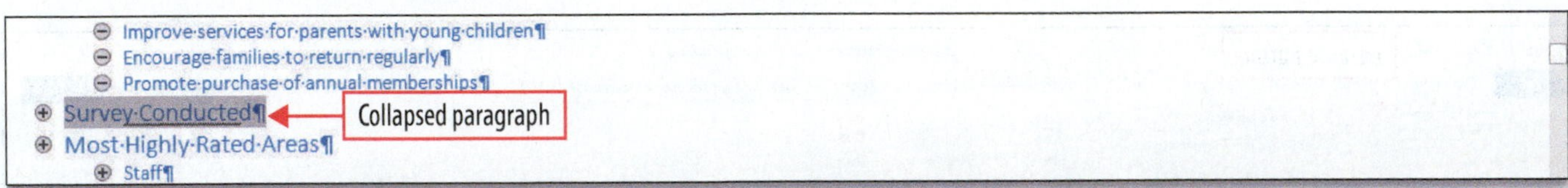

Word 2016, Windows 10, Microsoft Corporation

FIGURE 12.8

4 Drag to select the paragraph **Most Highly Rated Areas**, press and hold Ctrl, and then below the selected paragraph, select each of the remaining Level 1 paragraphs in the document. With the paragraphs selected, in the **Outline Tools group**, click **Collapse** .

5 Select the paragraph **General Survey Results**, and then in the **Outline Tools group**, click **Move Up** three times. Compare your screen with Figure 12.9.

Moving a collapsed level allows you to easily organize the topics in an outline. When you move a collapsed paragraph, all subordinate headings and body text paragraphs are also moved.

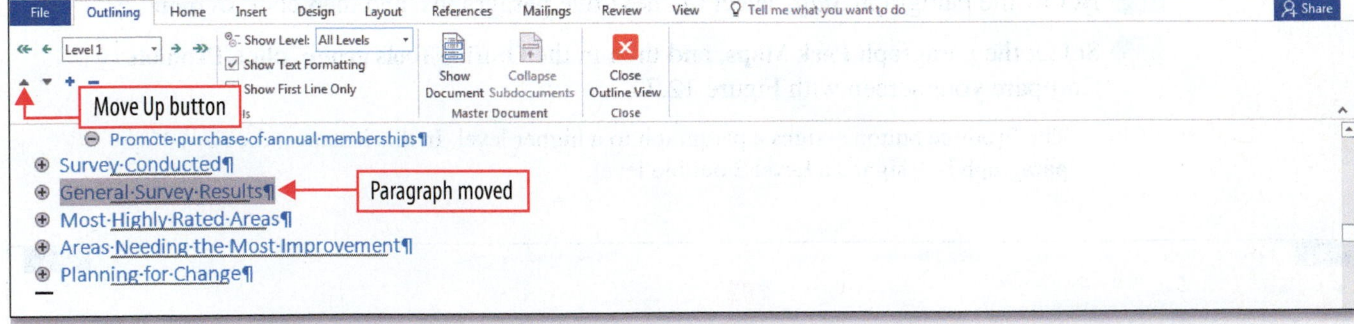

Word 2016, Windows 10, Microsoft Corporation

FIGURE 12.9

6 Deselect the paragraph, and then press Ctrl + Home. On the **Outlining tab**, in the **Close group**, click **Close Outline View**.

Although paragraphs were collapsed in Outline view, all text displays in Print Layout view—the current view.

7 Click the **Design tab**. In the **Document Formatting group**, click **Colors**, and then in the **Theme Colors** gallery, click **Green**. Compare your screen with Figure 12.10.

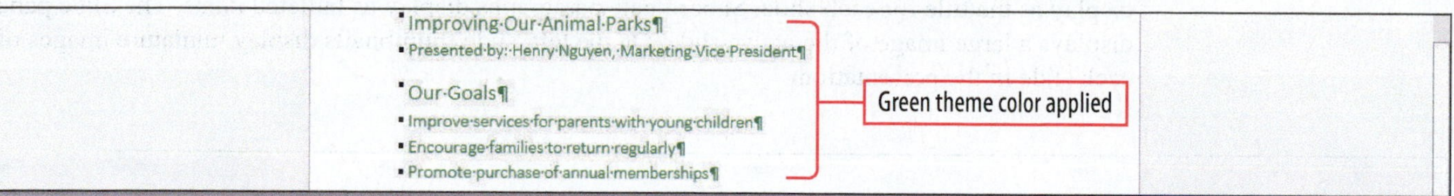

Improving·Our·Animal·Parks¶
Presented·by:·Henry·Nguyen,·Marketing·Vice·President¶
Our·Goals¶
Improve·services·for·parents·with·young·children¶
Encourage·families·to·return·regularly¶
Promote·purchase·of·annual·memberships¶
Green theme color applied

FIGURE 12.10

Word 2016, Windows 10, Microsoft Corporation

8 Click the **File tab**, and then click **Show All Properties**. In the **Tags** box, type **planning presentation, outline** In the **Subject** box, type your course name and section number. If necessary, edit the author name to display your name.

9 **Save** your changes, and then **Close** Word.

Activity 12.03 | Using a Word Outline to Create a PowerPoint Presentation

Because Microsoft Office is an integrated suite of programs, you can open a Word outline in PowerPoint to automatically create slides based on the level in the outline. The outline levels are used to determine the slide titles and bulleted items.

1 Start PowerPoint, and then click **Open Other Presentations**. Click **Browse** to display the **Open** dialog box. Navigate to your **Word Chapter 12** folder. At the bottom of the **Open** dialog box, click the **All PowerPoint Presentations arrow**, and then click **All Outlines**. Notice that your *Lastname_Firstname_12A_Planning_Outline* displays in the file list box. Compare your screen with Figure 12.11.

By default, only existing PowerPoint files display in the Open dialog box. Because your outline is a Word document, it is necessary to change the setting to All Outlines.

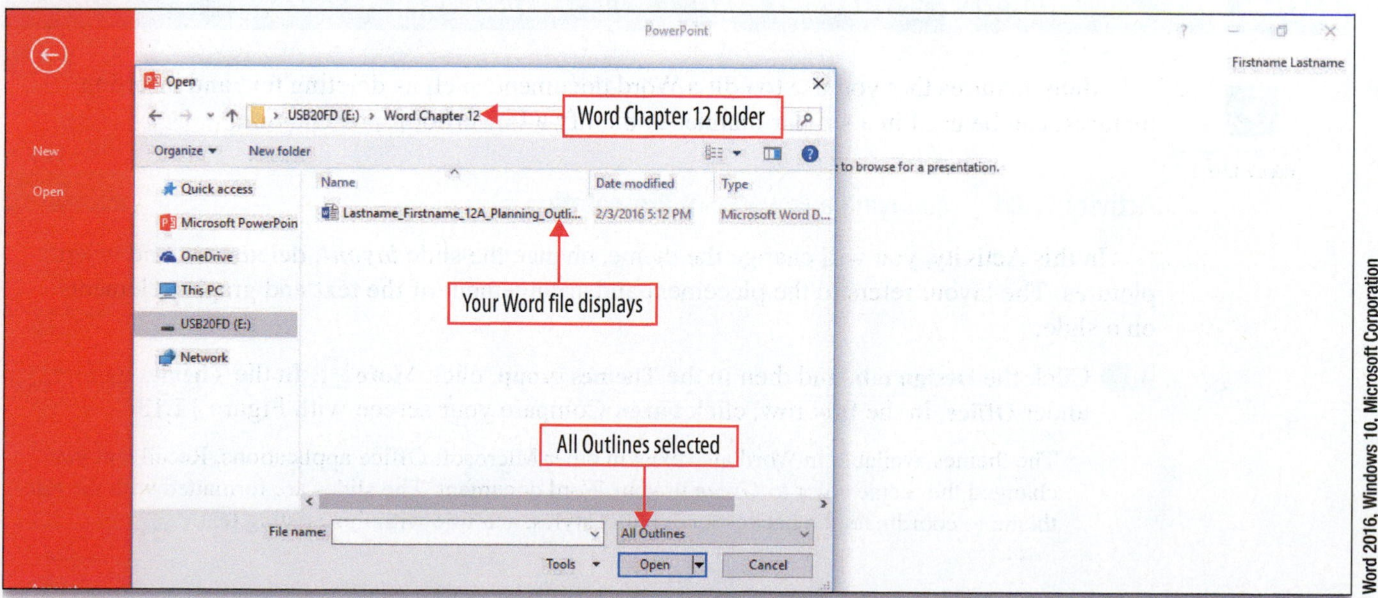

Word 2016, Windows 10, Microsoft Corporation

FIGURE 12.11

2 Click to select **Lastname_Firstname_12A_Planning_Outline**, and then click **Open**. Compare your screen with Figure 12.12.

Seven slides are created based on the outline levels in the outline. Heading 1 style paragraphs display as the title for each slide. Subordinate paragraphs display as bulleted items. The Slide pane displays a large image of the active slide. On the left, slide thumbnails display miniature images of each slide in the presentation.

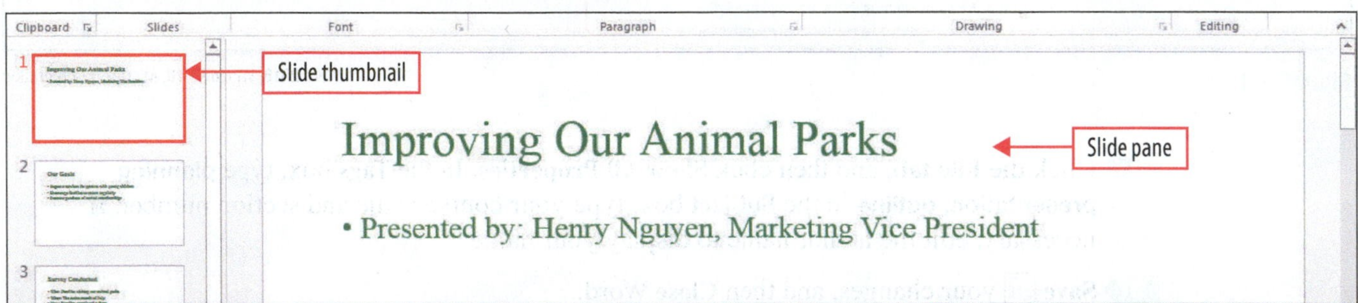

FIGURE 12.12

Powerpoint 2016, Windows 10, Microsoft Corporation

> ***More Knowledge*** **Using Body Text in an Outline**
>
> When you use a Word outline to create slides in PowerPoint, heading styles must be applied to all paragraphs. Body text paragraphs will not display in the slides.

3 On the **File tab**, click **Save As**, and then click **Browse**. In the **Save As** dialog box, navigate to your **Word Chapter 12** folder. Using your own name, **Save** the file as **Lastname_Firstname_12A_Planning_Presentation**

PowerPoint files are saved with the default file extension ***.pptx***.

Objective 2 Modify a PowerPoint Presentation

GO! Learn How Video W12-2

Many features that you use to edit a Word document, such as deleting text and inserting pictures, can be used in a similar manner to modify a PowerPoint presentation.

Activity 12.04 | Modifying a PowerPoint Presentation

In this Activity, you will change the theme, change the slide ***layout***, delete text, and insert pictures. The layout refers to the placement and arrangement of the text and graphic elements on a slide.

1 Click the **Design tab**, and then in the **Themes group**, click **More**. In the **Themes** gallery, under **Office**, in the first row, click **Facet**. Compare your screen with Figure 12.13.

The themes available in Word also exist in other Microsoft Office applications. Recall that you changed the theme color to *Green* in your Word document. The slides are formatted with the *Facet* theme to coordinate the background, bullet styles, and title with the existing text.

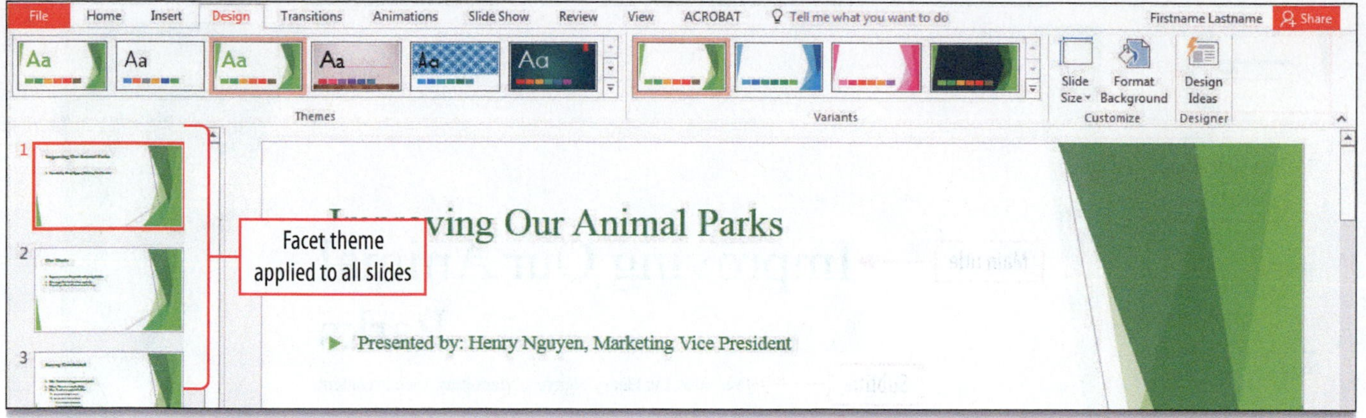

FIGURE 12.13

Powerpoint 2016, Windows 10, Microsoft Corporation

2 Click the **Home tab**, and then in the **Slides group**, click the **Layout arrow** to display the **Slide Layout** gallery. Compare your screen with Figure 12.14.

Fifteen slide arrangements display. By default, when you use a Word outline to create slides in PowerPoint, the Title and Text slide layout is applied to all slides.

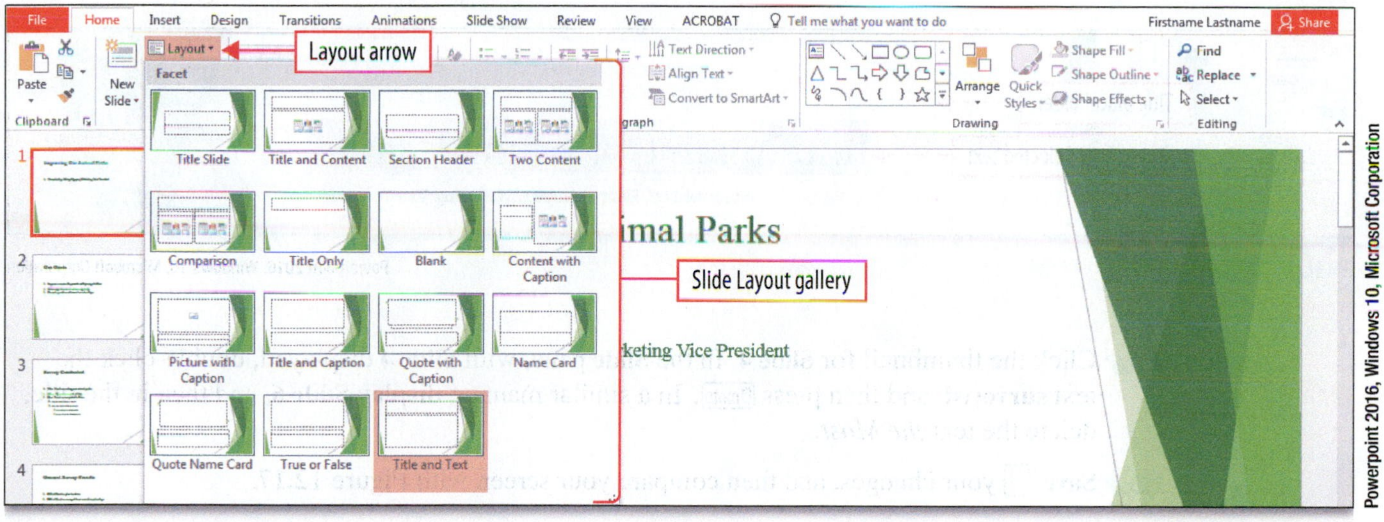

FIGURE 12.14

Powerpoint 2016, Windows 10, Microsoft Corporation

3 With **Slide 1** displayed in the **Slide** pane, in the **Slide Layout** gallery, click the first option—**Title Slide**. Compare your screen with Figure 12.15.

It is good practice to begin each presentation with a title slide. The title slide for the Facet theme displays the main title—the Heading 1 style—near the middle of the slide, and the subtitle—the Heading 2 style—displays below the main title.

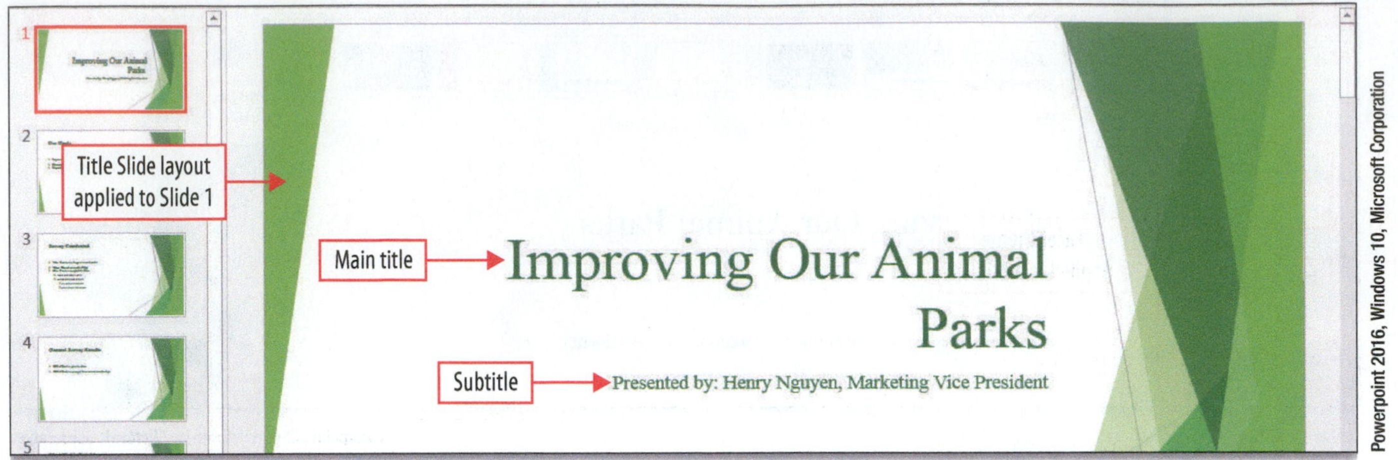

FIGURE 12.15

4 On **Slide 1**, select the text **Improving Our Animal Parks**. On the mini toolbar, change the **Font Size** to **44**. Compare your screen with Figure 12.16.

Content placeholders are used to display all text on slides.

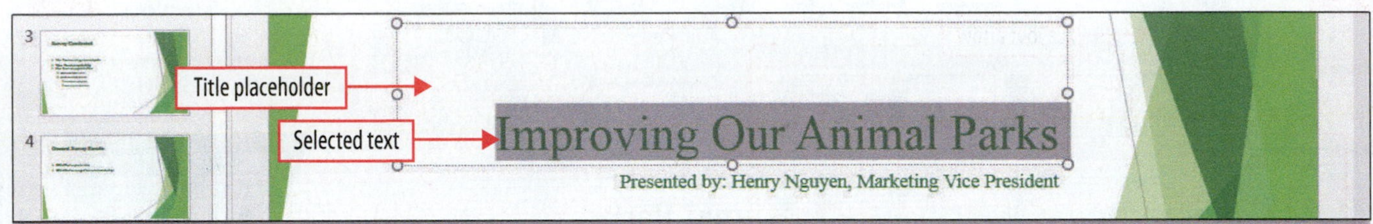

FIGURE 12.16

Powerpoint 2016, Windows 10, Microsoft Corporation

5 Click the thumbnail for **Slide 4**. In the **Slide** pane, with **Slide 4** displayed, double-click the text **surveyed**, and then press Delete. In a similar manner, display **Slide 6**, and then in the title, delete the text *the Most*.

6 **Save** your changes, and then compare your screen with Figure 12.17.

FIGURE 12.17

Powerpoint 2016, Windows 10, Microsoft Corporation

7 Display **Slide 1**. Click the **Insert tab**, and then in the **Text group**, click **Header & Footer**. In the **Header and Footer** dialog box, on the **Slide tab**, select the **Footer** check box. In the **Footer** box, type **Lastname_Firstname_12A_Planning_Presentation**

8 Select the **Don't show on title slide** check box, and then compare your screen with Figure 12.18.

Unlike Word, PowerPoint does not provide the option to insert the file name using the Document Info command. The Header and Footer dialog box allows you to select the slides on which you want the footer to display. In this instance, the footer will display on all slides except the title slide.

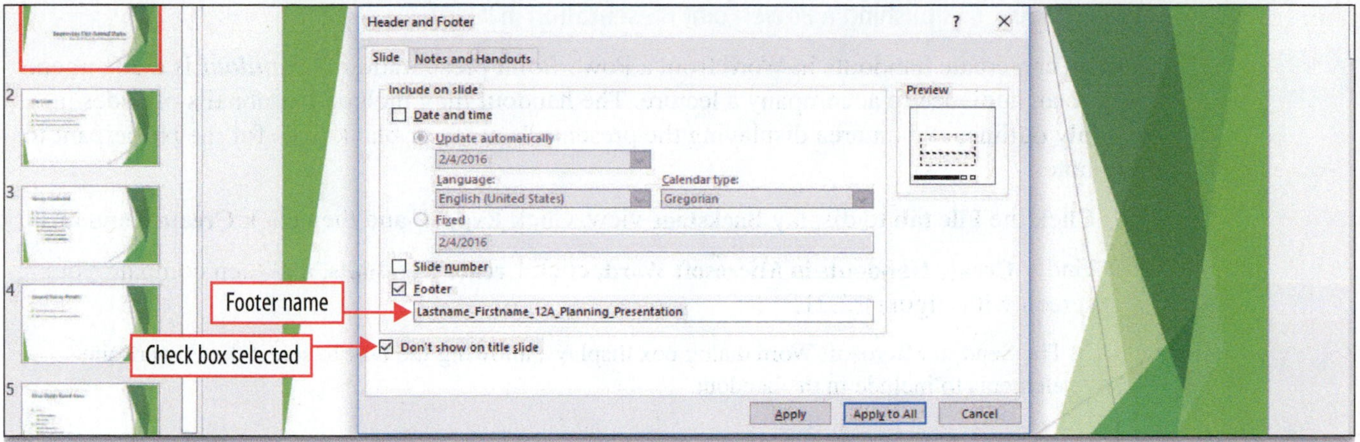

FIGURE 12.18

Powerpoint 2016, Windows 10, Microsoft Corporation

9 Click **Apply to all** and then compare your screen with Figure 12.19.

On Slide 1, the footer does not display.

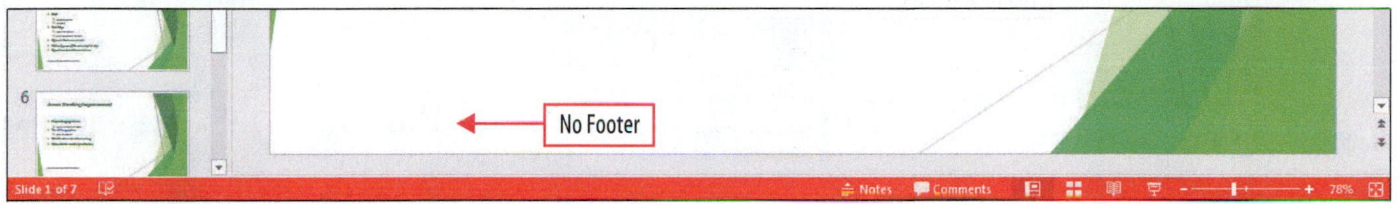

FIGURE 12.19

Powerpoint 2016, Windows 10, Microsoft Corporation

10 Click the thumbnail for **Slide 2**, and notice that the footer displays. Compare your screen with Figure 12.20.

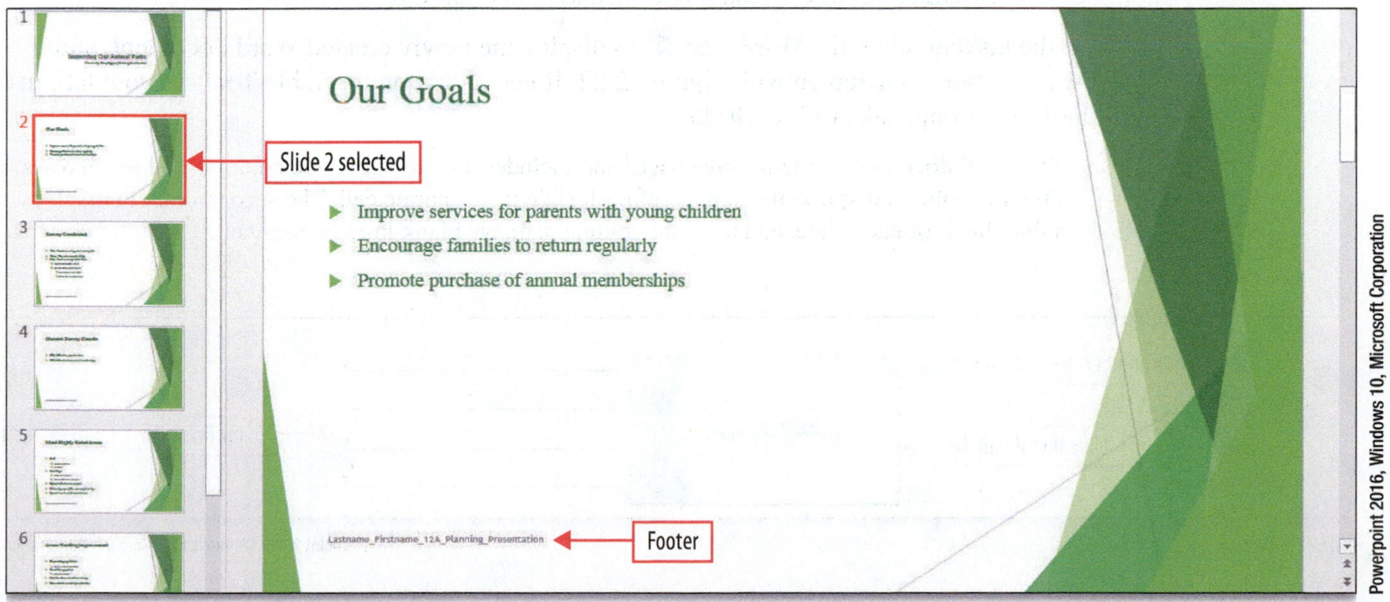

FIGURE 12.20

Powerpoint 2016, Windows 10, Microsoft Corporation

11 Click the thumbnail for **Slide 1**. Click the **File tab**, and then **Show All Properties**. In the **Tags** box, type **presentation, planning** In the **Subject** box, type your course name and section number. If necessary, edit the author name to display your name. **Save** your changes.

Activity 12.05 | Publishing a PowerPoint Presentation in Word

You can create handouts in Word from a PowerPoint presentation. A ***handout*** is a document given to an audience to accompany a lecture. The handout may include thumbnails of slides, a text-only outline, and an area displaying the presenter's notes or blank lines for the participant to enter notes.

1. Click the **File tab** to display **Backstage** view. Click **Export**, and then click **Create Handouts**.
2. Under **Create Handouts in Microsoft Word**, click **Create Handouts**, and then compare your screen with Figure 12.21.

   The Send to Microsoft Word dialog box displays, allowing the user to select the PowerPoint elements to include in the handout.

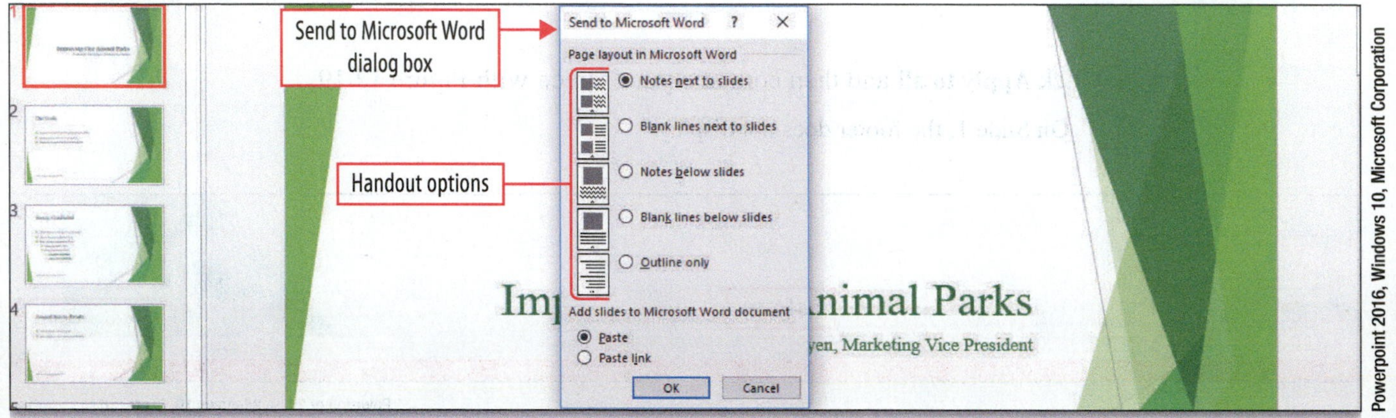

FIGURE 12.21

3. In the **Send to Microsoft Word** dialog box, under **Page layout in Microsoft Word**, click to select the **Blank lines next to slides** option, and then click **OK**.
4. On the taskbar, click the **Word** icon to display the newly created Word document, and then compare your screen with Figure 12.22. If necessary, on the Table Tools Layout tab, in the Table group, select View Gridlines.

   The Word document contains three pages and includes a table with three columns and seven rows. The first column displays the number of each slide in a separate cell. The second column displays a thumbnail of each slide, and the third column displays blank lines in each cell.

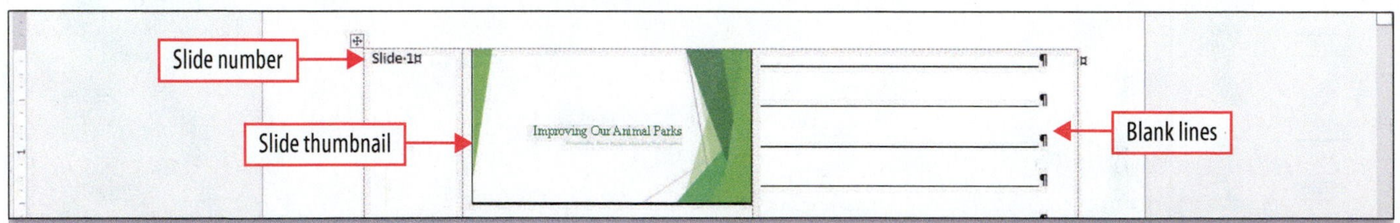

FIGURE 12.22

Powerpoint 2016, Windows 10, Microsoft Corporation

5. Display the **Save As** dialog box. Navigate to your **Word Chapter 12** folder, and then using your own name, **Save** the file as **Lastname_Firstname_12A_Planning_Handout** Insert the file name in the footer.
6. In the first row of the table, in the third cell, select the first three lines, and then press Delete.

7 In a similar manner, in the third column, delete the first three lines from each of the remaining six cells.

8 On **Page 1**, point slightly outside the upper left corner of the table to display the **Table Move Handle** ⊞. With the ✥ pointer displayed, click the **Table Move Handle** ⊞ to select the entire table. Click the **Table Tools Layout tab**, and then in the **Cell Size group**, change the **Height** to **1.8**. Compare your screen with Figure 12.23.

The handout can be modified to suit your purposes. In this instance, you have deleted blank lines and reduced the row height to create a two-page handout.

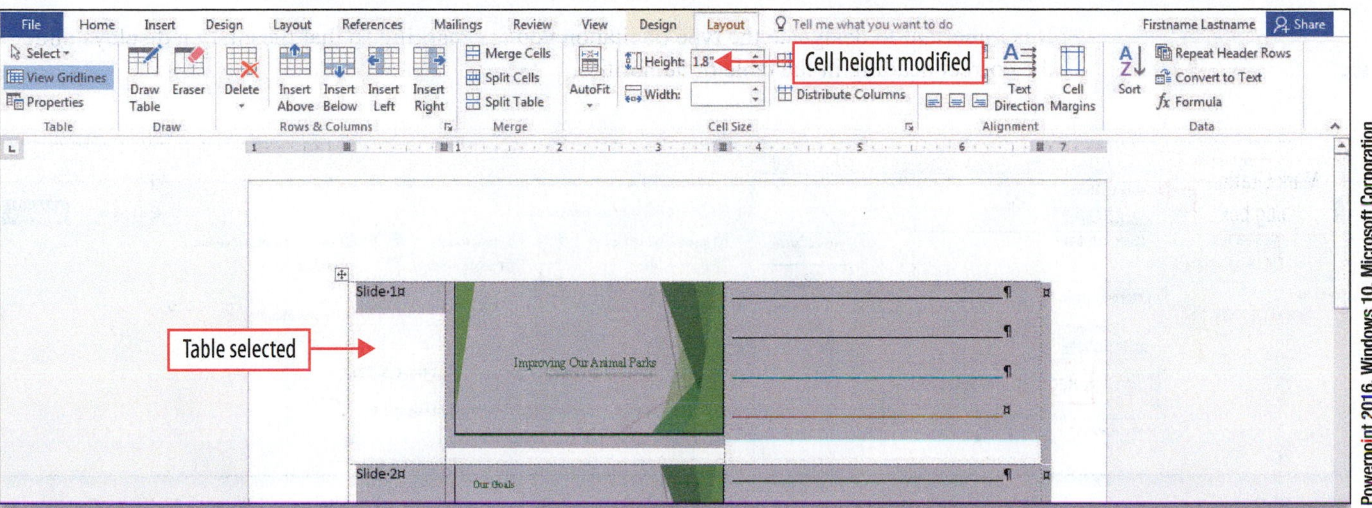

FIGURE 12.23

9 Press Ctrl + Home. Click the **File tab**, and then **Show All Properties**. In the **Tags** box, type **planning presentation, handout** and in the **Subject** box, type your course name and section number. If necessary, edit the author name to display your name. **Save** your changes, and then from **Backstage** view, **Close** the document but leave Word open.

10 On the taskbar, click the **PowerPoint** icon. With your PowerPoint presentation displayed, **Save** your changes, and then **Close** ✕ PowerPoint.

Objective 3 Create a Table of Authorities

GO! Learn How Video W12-3

A ***table of authorities***, which is similar to a table of contents, is a list of all the references in a legal document and the page numbers where the references occur.

Activity 12.06 | Creating a Table of Authorities

In this Activity, you will create a table of authorities based on the ***legal citations*** in the document. A legal citation is a reference to an authoritative document, such as a regulation, a statute, or a case. For purposes of this instruction, you are using a document that is a partial example of a legal brief related to trademark infringement. All citations in the document are fictitious.

1 In Word, from your student files, open the file **w12A_Park_Brief**. **Save** the document in your **Word Chapter 12** folder as **Lastname_Firstname_12A_Park_Brief** Insert the file name in the footer.

2 Scroll to the top of **Page 2**, and then take a moment to read the second paragraph.

The legal citation *42 Ne. C.S. §917* refers to a regulation. The legal citation *52 MS. Code §29.512* references a statute.

3 In the second paragraph, select the text **42 Ne. C.S. §917**. Be careful not to select the spaces before and after the text. Click the **References tab**, and then in the **Table of Authorities group**, click **Mark Citation** to display the **Mark Citation** dialog box.

4 In the **Mark Citation** dialog box, under **Selected text**, notice that your selected text displays. Click the **Category arrow**, and then click **Regulations**. Compare your screen with Figure 12.24.

It is important to designate the type of citation you are marking so that the citation displays under the correct heading in the table of authorities.

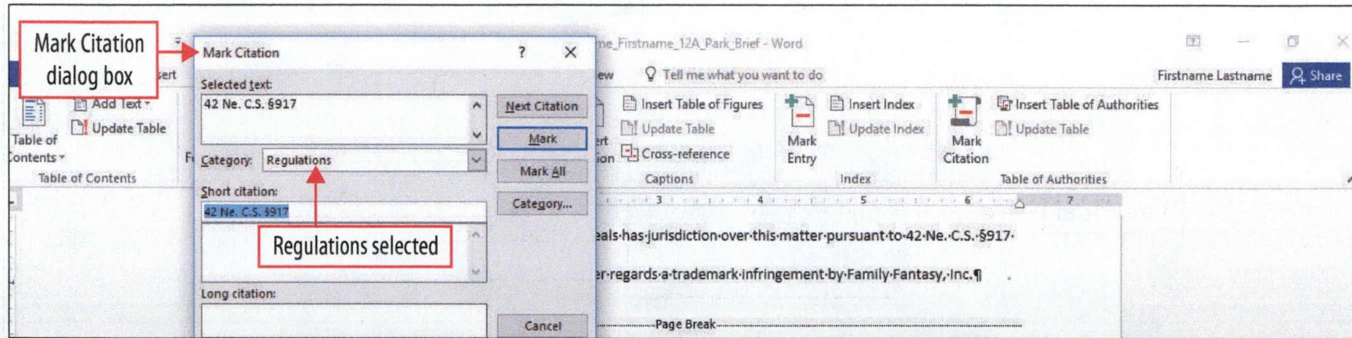

FIGURE 12.24

Powerpoint 2016, Windows 10, Microsoft Corporation

5 Click **Mark All** to mark all occurrences of the citation in the document. Click in the document, and then scroll as necessary to view the marked citation on page 2. Compare your screen with Figure 12.25.

The field related to the marked citation displays to the right of *42 Ne. C.S. §917*. The field is surrounded by braces and begins with the letters *TA*—identifying the code as a table of authorities field.

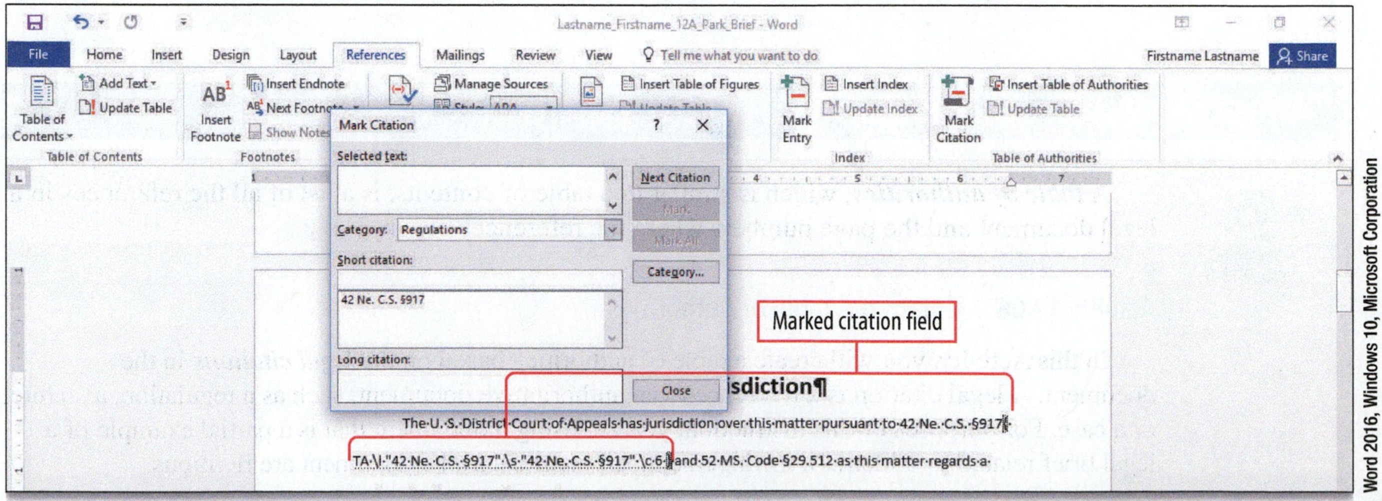

FIGURE 12.25

Word 2016, Windows 10, Microsoft Corporation

6 On **Page 3**, select the text **SkiWorld Network v. Extreme Snow**. Click in the **Mark Citation** dialog box, click the **Category arrow**, and then click **Cases**. Click **Mark**. Click in the document, select the text **Smith's Landing v. McCallister**. Click the **Mark Citation** dialog box, verify **Cases** is selected, and then click **Mark**. **Close** the **Mark Citation** dialog box.

7 At the bottom of **Page 1**, position the insertion point to the right of the date, and then press Ctrl + Enter two times. At the top of **Page 2**, click to position the insertion point to the left of the page break. Type **TABLE OF AUTHORITIES** and then press Enter two times. Select the text you just typed, and then on the mini toolbar, change the **Font Size** to **16** and apply **Bold**. Press Ctrl + E.

8 Click to position the insertion point to the left of the page break. On the **References tab**, in the **Table of Authorities group**, click **Insert Table of Authorities**.

9 In the **Table of Authorities** dialog box, under **Category**, be sure *All* is selected. Select the **Use passim** check box. Click the **Formats arrow**, and then click **Classic**. Compare your screen with Figure 12.26.

You can select a specific type of citation to display in the table of authorities. In this instance, all types of citations will display. The term ***passim*** indicates that a citation occurs on five or more pages in a document. When the *Use passim* check box is selected, the term *passim* displays in a table of authorities instead of multiple page numbers for the citation.

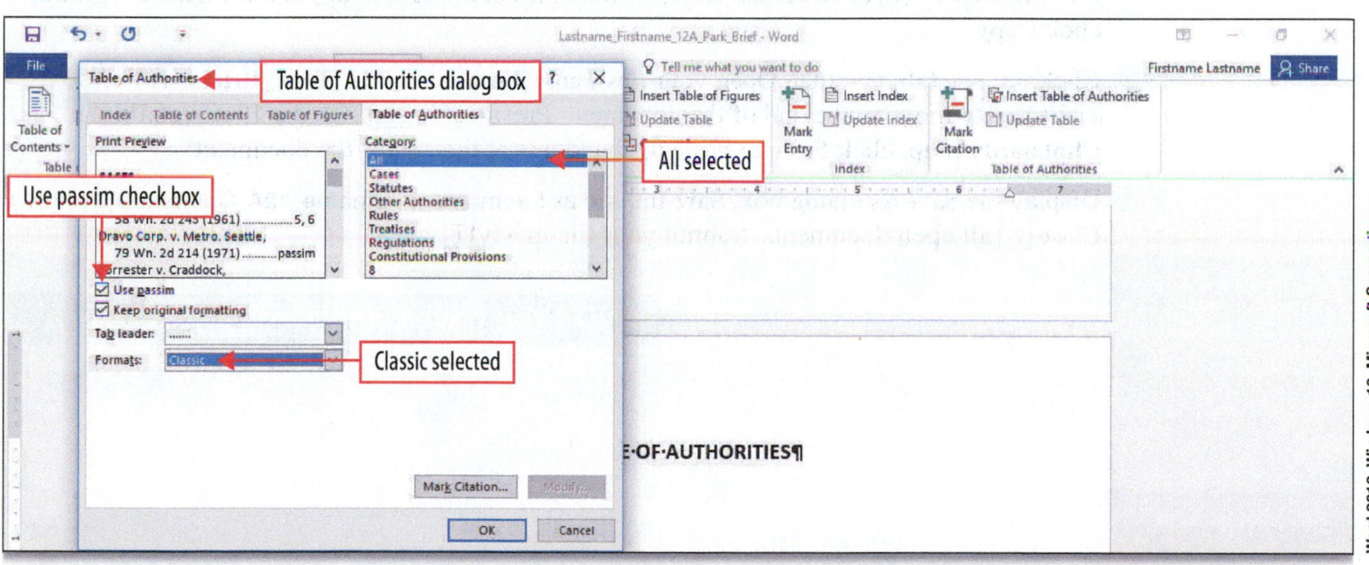

FIGURE 12.26

10 In the **Table of Authorities** dialog box, click **OK**.

The table of authorities displays on page 2 of your document. Based on the type of reference, citations display below the appropriate headings. Because the citation *42 Ne. C.S. §917* occurs on five pages in the document, the term *passim* displays instead of the page numbers.

11 **Save** your changes.

Activity 12.07 | Updating a Table of Authorities

1 Display **Page 3**, and then select the text **52 MS. Code §29.512**. On the **References tab**, in the **Table of Authorities group**, click **Mark Citation**. Click the **Category arrow**, and then click **Statutes**. Click **Mark**, and then click **Close**.

2 Display **Page 2**, select the entire table of authorities—the *Cases* and *Regulations* fields. In the **Table of Authorities group**, click **Insert Table of Authorities**.

3 In the **Table of Authorities** dialog box, under **Category**, click **All**, and then click **OK**. In the Microsoft Word message box, when asked if you want to replace the selected category of the table of authorities, click **No**.

When changes are made in the document—for example, marking a new citation—it is important to update the table of authorities.

4 Press Ctrl + Home. Click the **File tab**, and then **Show All Properties**. In the **Tags** box, type **legal brief, citations** In the **Subject** box, type your course name and section number. If necessary, edit the author name to display your name. **Save** your changes, and then **Close** Word.

5 If directed by your instructor to do so, submit your paper printouts, your electronic images of your documents that look like a printed document, or your original Word files.

ALERT! **If you are submitting your project in MyITLab, complete Steps 6 through 8.**

6 To submit your project in MyITLab, you will combine your legal brief document and your presentation handouts into one file. **Open** your **Lastname_Firstname_12A_Planning_Handout** file. Press Ctrl + A to select the entire document. On the **Home tab**, in the **Clipboard group**, click **Copy**.

7 Click the **File tab**, and then **Open** your **Lastname_Firstname_12A_Park_Brief** file. Press Ctrl + End to move to the end of the document. Press Ctrl + Enter. On the **Home tab**, in the **Clipboard group**, click **Paste** to paste the handouts at the end of the document.

8 Display the **Save As** dialog box. **Save** the file as **Lastname_Firstname_12A_Combined** and then **Close** all open documents. Submit your file in MyITLab.

END | You have completed Project 12A

PROJECT 12B

Park Brochure

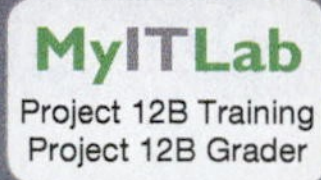

PROJECT ACTIVITIES

In Activities 12.08 through 12.15, you will create a brochure for visitors to the theme parks operated by Magical Park Corporation. To customize the document, you will change the paper size, format text, and edit graphics. Your completed file will look similar to Figure 12.27.

Please always review the downloaded Grader instructions before beginning.

PROJECT FILES

If your instructor wants you to submit Project 12B in the MyITLab Grader system, log into MyITLab, locate Grader Project 12B, and then download the files for the project.

For Project 12B, you will need the following files:

w12B_Park_Brochure
w12B_Wheel
w12B_Coaster
w12B_Comments
w12B_Brochure_Bullet

You will save your document as:

Lastname_Firstname_12B_Park_Brochure

PROJECT RESULTS

GO! Walk Thru Project 12B

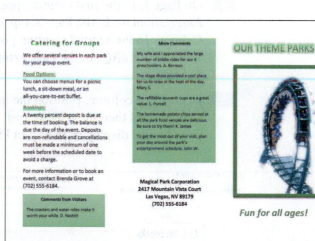

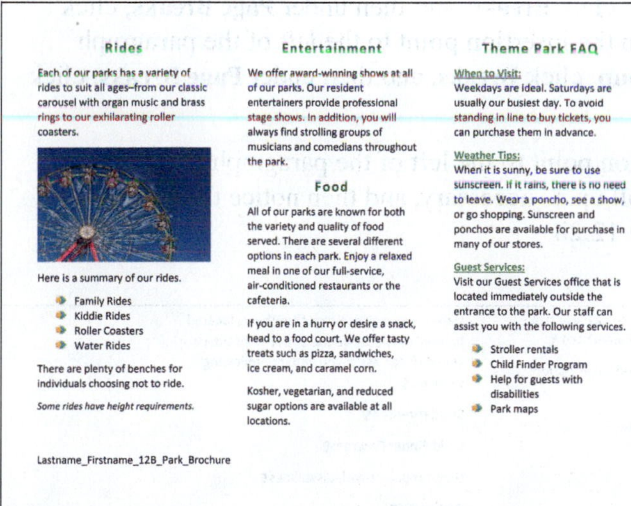

Rides

Each of our parks has a variety of rides to suit all ages–from our classic carousel with organ music and brass rings to our exhilarating roller coasters.

Here is a summary of our rides.

- Family Rides
- Kiddie Rides
- Roller Coasters
- Water Rides

There are plenty of benches for individuals choosing not to ride.

Some rides have height requirements.

Entertainment

We offer award-winning shows at all of our parks. Our resident entertainers provide professional stage shows. In addition, you will always find strolling groups of musicians and comedians throughout the park.

Food

All of our parks are known for both the variety and quality of food served. There are several different options in each park. Enjoy a relaxed meal in one of our full-service, air-conditioned restaurants or the cafeteria.

If you are in a hurry or desire a snack, head to a food court. We offer tasty treats such as pizza, sandwiches, ice cream, and caramel corn.

Kosher, vegetarian, and reduced sugar options are available at all locations.

Theme Park FAQ

When to Visit:
Weekdays are ideal. Saturdays are usually our busiest day. To avoid standing in line to buy tickets, you can purchase them in advance.

Weather Tips:
When it is sunny, be sure to use sunscreen. If it rains, there is no need to leave. Wear a poncho, see a show, or go shopping. Sunscreen and ponchos are available for purchase in many of our stores.

Guest Services:
Visit our Guest Services office that is located immediately outside the entrance to the park. Our staff can assist you with the following services.

- Stroller rentals
- Child Finder Program
- Help for guests with disabilities
- Park maps

Lastname_Firstname_12B_Park_Brochure

Catering for Groups

We offer several venues in each park for your group event.

Food Options:
You can choose menus for a picnic lunch, a sit-down meal, or an all-you-care-to-eat buffet.

Bookings:
A twenty percent deposit is due at the time of booking. The balance is due the day of the event. Deposits are non-refundable and cancellations must be made a minimum of one week before the scheduled date to avoid a charge.

For more information or to book an event, contact Brenda Grove at (702) 555-6184.

Comments from Visitors

The coasters and water rides make it worth your while. D. Nesbitt

Lastname_Firstname_12B_Park_Brochure

More Comments

My wife and I appreciated the large number of kiddie rides for our 4 preschoolers. A. Berman

The stage show provided a cool place for us to relax in the heat of the day. Mary S.

The refillable souvenir cups are a great value. L. Purcell

The homemade potato chips served at all the park food venues are delicious. Be sure to try them! K. James

To get the most out of your visit, plan your day around the park's entertainment schedule. John W.

Magical Park Corporation
2417 Mountain Vista Court
Las Vegas, NV 89179
(702) 555-6184

OUR THEME PARKS

Fun for all ages!

FIGURE 12.27 Project 12B Park Brochure

Objective 4 Modify the Document Layout

GO! Learn How Video W12-4

Word provides many features to format and display text in an attractive manner, such as changing the spacing between characters and controlling the display of phrases where the individual components should not be split between two lines. Additionally, the paper size can be changed to produce the desired result—in this instance, a small brochure.

Activity 12.08 | Changing Paper Size

ALERT! **To submit as an autograded project, log into MyITLab and download the files for this Project, and begin with those files instead w12B_Park_Brochure.**

1.3.1

1. Start Word. From your student data files, open the file **w12B_Park_Brochure**. **Save** the document to your **Word Chapter 12** folder as **Lastname_Firstname_12B_Park_Brochure** Insert the file name in the footer and display rulers and formatting marks. If any words are flagged as spelling errors, click **Ignore All**.
2. Click the **Layout tab**. In the **Page Setup group**, click **Orientation**, and then click **Landscape**.
3. In the **Page Setup group**, click **Margins**, and then click **Narrow**. In the **Page Setup group**, click **Columns**, and then click **Three**.
4. On **Page 1**, in the first column, position the insertion point to the left of the paragraph *Entertainment*. In the **Page Setup group**, click **Breaks**, and then under **Page Breaks**, click **Column**. In the second column, position the insertion point to the left of the paragraph *Theme Park FAQ*. In the **Page Setup group**, click **Breaks**, and then under **Page Breaks**, click **Column**.
5. In the third column, position the insertion point to the left of the paragraph *Catering for Groups*, and then press Ctrl + Enter. Scroll up as necessary, and then notice the column and page breaks display as shown in Figure 12.28.

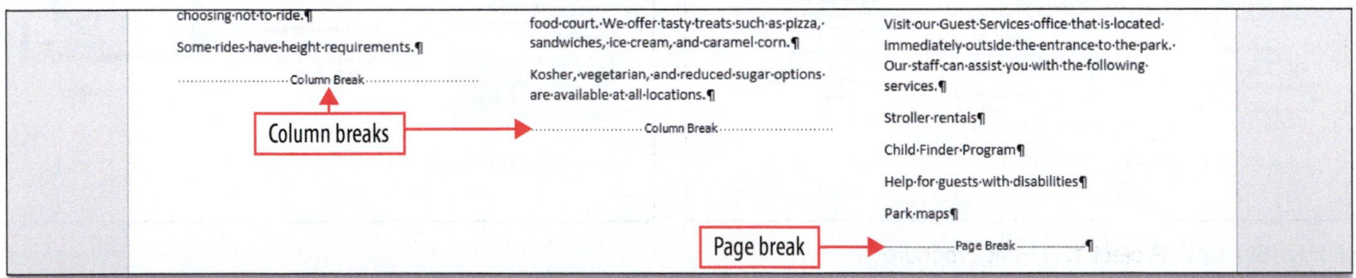

FIGURE 12.28 Word 2016, Windows 10, Microsoft Corporation

6. On **Page 2**, position the insertion point to the left of the paragraph *Magical Park Corporation*. In the **Page Setup group**, click **Breaks**, and then under **Page Breaks**, click **Column**. In the second column, position the insertion point in the last blank paragraph of the document, and then using the technique you practiced, insert a **Column** break.
7. Press Ctrl + Home. In the **Page Setup group**, click **Size**, and then at the bottom of the displayed list, click **More Paper Sizes**.

ANOTHER WAY Click the dialog box launcher to display the Page Setup dialog box, and then click the Paper tab.

8 In the **Page Setup** dialog box, with the **Paper tab** displayed, under **Paper size**, click the **Paper size arrow**, which displays *Letter*, scroll as necessary, and then click **Custom size**. In the **Width** box type **9** and in the **Height** box type **7**. Compare your screen with Figure 12.29.

You can change the paper size to accommodate any type of document. In this instance, the brochure requires a custom paper size.

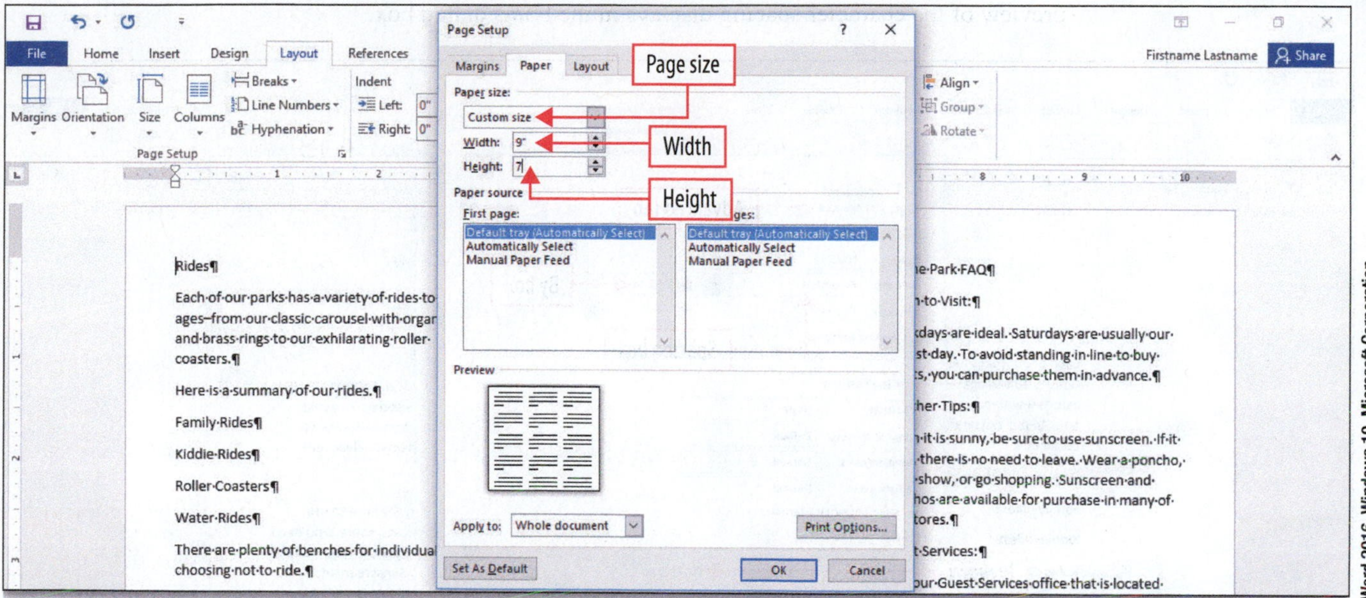

FIGURE 12.29

9 Click **OK** to close the **Page Setup** dialog box.

10 **Save** your changes.

Activity 12.09 | Changing Character Spacing

You will format the text in the brochure by changing font sizes and applying styles. You will also change the ***character spacing*** for selected text to improve the appearance or readability of a document. Character spacing is a Word feature that allows you to change the default spacing constraints between characters. You can manually set spacing options or use ***kerning*** to have Word automatically modify space between characters in selected text. Kerning automatically adjusts the spacing between pairs of characters, with a specified minimum point size, so that words and letters appear equally spaced.

1 In the first column, select the first paragraph—**Rides**. On the mini toolbar, change the **Font Size** to **14**, apply **Bold** [B], click the **Font Color arrow** [A], and then in the last column, click the last color—**Green, Accent 6, Darker 50%**. Press Ctrl + E.

2 With the paragraph *Rides* selected, click the **Home tab**, and then in the **Font group**, click the **dialog box launcher**.

3 In the **Font** dialog box, click the **Advanced tab**. Under **Character Spacing**, click the **Spacing arrow**, and then click **Expanded**. Click the **By spin box up arrow** to **1.2 pt**. Compare your screen with Figure 12.30, and then take a moment to study the character spacing settings in Figure 12.31.

There are several different features that allow you to modify the character spacing. By changing the spacing to Expanded by 1.2 pt, the space between the characters is increased slightly. A preview of the character spacing displays in the Fonts dialog box.

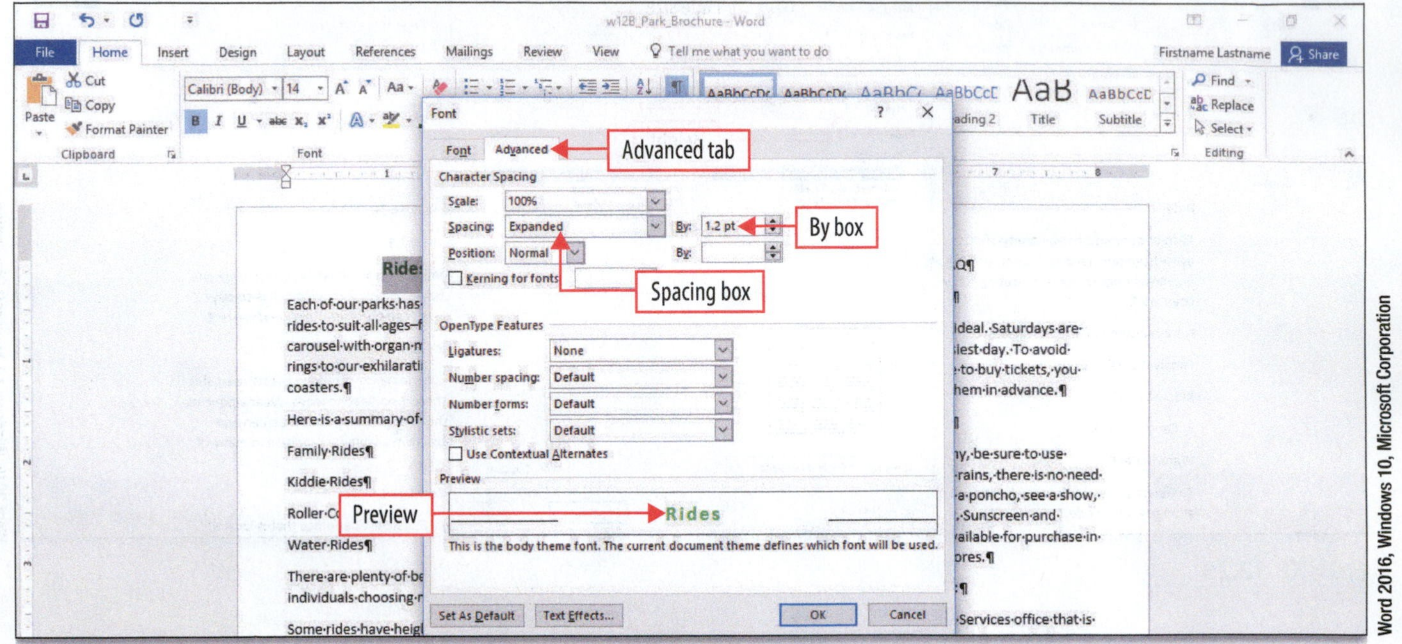

FIGURE 12.30

CHARACTER SPACING SETTINGS	
SETTING	**DESCRIPTION**
Scale	Expands or compresses text horizontally as a percentage of the current size.
Spacing	Expands or compresses spacing between characters by a specified number of points.
Position	Raises or lowers the location of text in relation to the current vertical location.
Kerning for fonts	Automatically adjusts the spacing between pairs of characters, with a specified minimum point size, so that words and letters appear equally spaced.
By	Specifies the number of points that should be used to space characters.

FIGURE 12.31

4 Click **OK** to close the **Font** dialog box. In the **Clipboard group**, double-click **Format Painter** to turn it on. Select each of the following paragraphs to apply the same formatting you applied to *Rides*: **Entertainment**, **Food**, **Theme Park FAQ**, and **Catering for Groups**. In the **Clipboard group**, click **Format Painter** to turn it off. Press Ctrl + Home and then compare your screen with Figure 12.32.

FIGURE 12.32

Word 2016, Windows 10, Microsoft Corporation

5 On **Page 1**, in the first column, select the four paragraphs beginning with **Family Rides** and ending with **Water Rides**. In the **Paragraph group**, click **Bullets** [icon].

6 On **Page 1**, in the third column, select the paragraph **When to Visit**, being sure to include the colon. On the mini toolbar, apply **Bold** [B] and **Underline** [U], click the **Font Color arrow** [A], and then in the last column, click the fifth color—**Green, Accent 6, Darker 25%**. In the **Paragraph group**, click **Line and Paragraph Spacing** [icon], and then click **Remove Space After Paragraph**.

7 In the **Clipboard group**, double-click **Format Painter** [icon], and then apply the formatting you applied to *When to Visit* to the paragraphs *Weather Tips*, *Guest Services*, *Food Options*, and *Bookings*. In the **Clipboard group**, click **Format Painter** [icon] to turn it off.

8 On **Page 1**, at the bottom of the third column, select the four paragraphs beginning with **Stroller rentals** and ending with **Park maps**. In the **Paragraph group**, click **Bullets** [icon]. Click to position the insertion point anywhere in the paragraph *Park maps*. In the **Paragraph group**, click **Line and Paragraph Spacing** [icon], and then click **Remove Space After Paragraph**.

9 At the bottom of **Page 1**, in the first column, select the paragraph that begins **Some rides**. On the mini toolbar, change the **Font Size** to **10**, and then apply **Italic** [I]. Deselect the text, and then compare your screen with Figure 12.33.

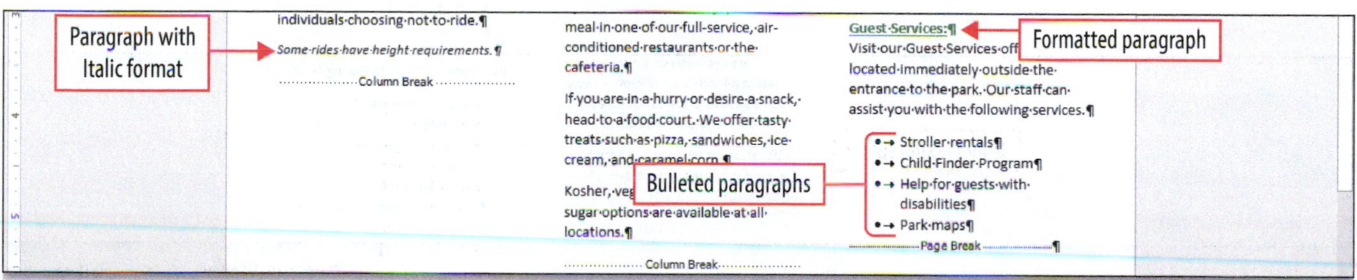

FIGURE 12.33 Word 2016, Windows 10, Microsoft Corporation

10 **Save** [icon] your changes.

Activity 12.10 | Inserting Nonbreaking Hyphens and Nonbreaking Spaces

Recall that word wrap automatically moves text from the right edge of a paragraph to the beginning of the next line as is necessary to fit within the margins. You can insert a ***nonbreaking hyphen*** to prevent a hyphenated word or phrase from being displayed on two lines. Similarly, you can insert a ***nonbreaking space*** to keep two or more words together so that both words will wrap even if only the second word would normally wrap to the next line. For example, inserting nonbreaking spaces in a date will keep the entire date—month, day, and year—on the same line.

1 On **Page 1**, in the second column, in the fourth paragraph, locate the phrase *air-conditioned*. Select the hyphen, and then press Ctrl + Shift + - to insert a nonbreaking hyphen. Notice the entire term *air-conditioned* displays on the same line. Compare your screen with Figure 12.34.

You can improve the readability of a document by inserting a nonbreaking hyphen.

ANOTHER WAY On the Insert tab, in the Symbols group, click Symbol, and then click More Symbols. In the Symbols dialog box, click the Special Characters tab, click Nonbreaking Hyphen, and then click Insert.

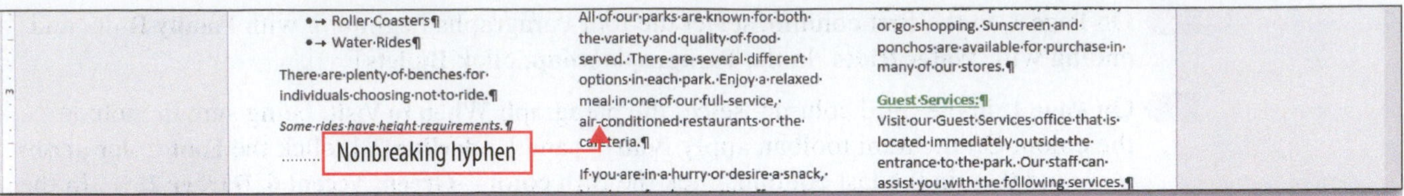

FIGURE 12.34 Word 2016, Windows 10, Microsoft Corporation

2 On **Page 2**, in the first column, in the fourth paragraph, locate the phrase *all-you-care-to-eat*. Select the hyphen between *all* and *you* and then press Ctrl + Shift + -. In a similar manner, insert nonbreaking hyphens to replace each of the remaining three hyphens in the phrase.

If you have a hyphenated term that contains multiple hyphens, it is good practice to replace all hyphens with nonbreaking hyphens. If preceding text or other elements are modified, this will ensure that the text will display on a single line.

3 On **Page 1**, in the second column, in the fifth paragraph, locate the term *ice cream*. Select the space following *ice*, and then press Ctrl + Shift + Spacebar. Compare your screen with Figure 12.35.

The term *ice cream* displays on one line. A small raised circle, the nonbreaking space formatting mark, displays between the two words.

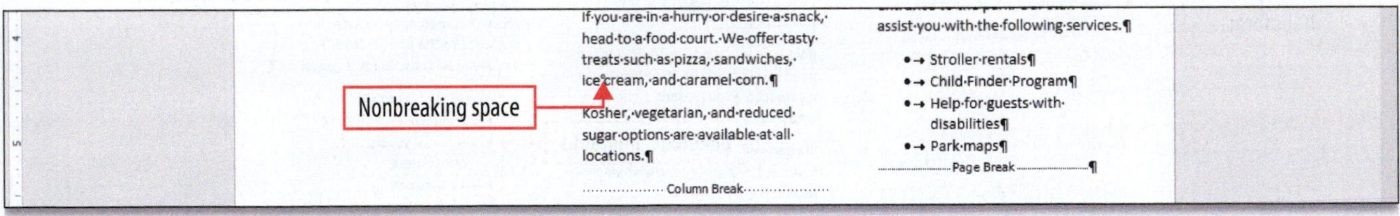

FIGURE 12.35 Word 2016, Windows 10, Microsoft Corporation

4 In the last line of the same paragraph, using the technique you just practiced, replace the space between *caramel* and *corn* with a nonbreaking space.

5 On **Page 2**, in the first column, in the last paragraph, locate the phone number. Using the technique you just practiced, replace the space with a nonbreaking space, and then replace the hyphen with a nonbreaking hyphen. Compare your screen with Figure 12.36.

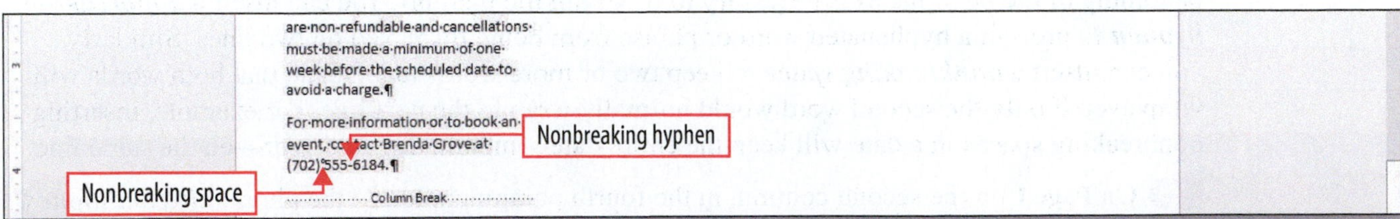

FIGURE 12.36 Word 2016, Windows 10, Microsoft Corporation

6 **Save** your changes.

Objective 5 Format Graphic and Text Elements

GO! Learn How
Video W12-5

Inserting and formatting graphics and text can enhance the appearance of a document. Word provides many features to modify graphic and text elements.

Activity 12.11 | Viewing Document Gridlines

Document gridlines—nonprinting horizontal and vertical lines—assist you in aligning graphics and other elements.

1 On **Page 2**, in the third column, click to position the insertion point in the blank paragraph. Click the **View tab**, and then in the **Show group**, select the **Gridlines** check box. Compare your screen with Figure 12.37.

The gridlines display only within the margins of the document.

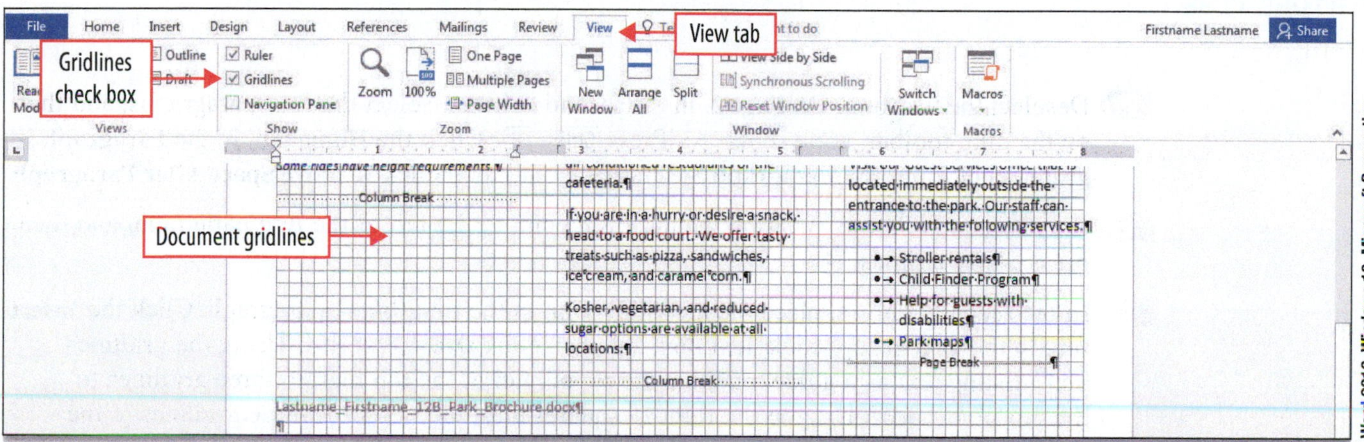

Word 2016, Windows 10, Microsoft Corporation

FIGURE 12.37

Activity 12.12 | Linking Text Boxes

Expert 2.1.4

Recall that text boxes are movable, resizable containers for text or graphics. Word includes a feature to link two or more text boxes. When text boxes are linked, if the first text box cannot hold all of the inserted text, the text will automatically flow into the next, linked text box. In this Activity, you will use gridlines to help position text boxes, link two text boxes, and then insert text from an existing file.

1 On **Page 2**, in the first column, click to position the insertion point at the end of the last paragraph. Click the **Insert tab**. In the **Text group**, click **Text Box**, and then click **Draw Text Box**. Using the gridlines, position the ⊞ pointer at the left margin two gridlines below the last paragraph, drag to the right **18** squares, drag down **7** squares, and then release the mouse button. If necessary, resize the text box so that the right border aligns at approximately 2 inches on the horizontal ruler and the bottom border aligns at approximately 0.75 inch on the lower portion of the vertical ruler. Compare your screen with Figure 12.38.

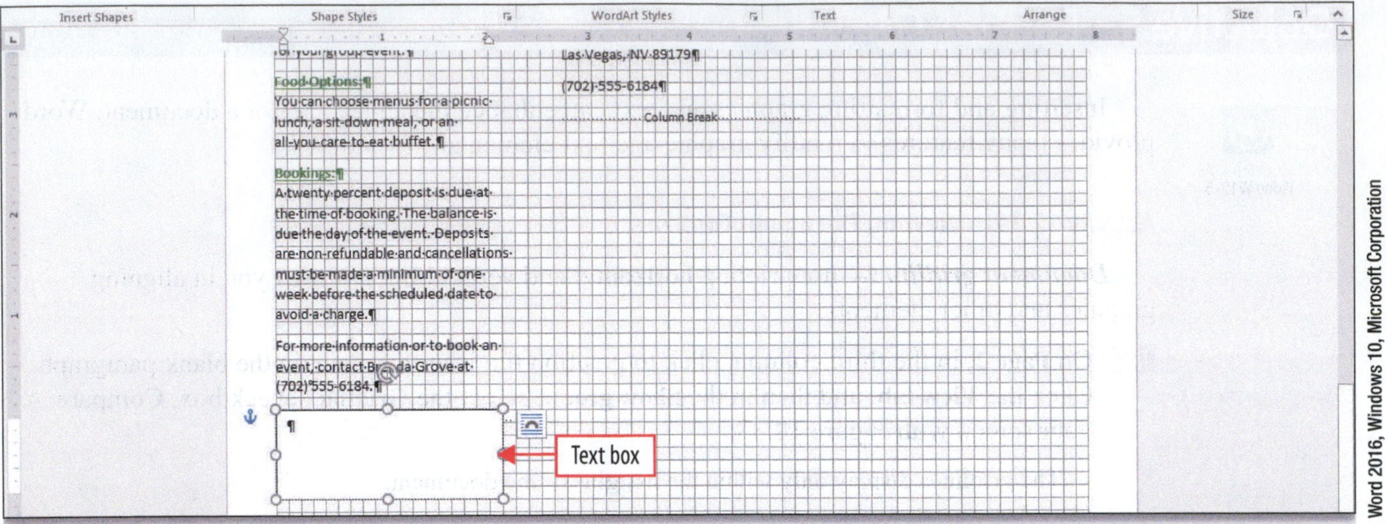

FIGURE 12.38

Word 2016, Windows 10, Microsoft Corporation

2 Deselect the text box. On **Page 2**, in the second column, select the four paragraphs, and then on the mini toolbar, apply **Bold** [B]. Press Ctrl + E. Click the **Home tab**. In the **Paragraph group**, click **Line and Paragraph Spacing** , and then click **Remove Space After Paragraph**.

3 In the second column, position the insertion point to the left of the first paragraph, and then press Enter two times.

4 In the second column, place the insertion point in the first, blank paragraph. Click the **Insert tab**. In the **Text group**, click **Text Box**, and then click **Draw Text Box**. Using the gridlines and existing text as a guide, position the + pointer at the top margin three gridlines to the left of *Magical*. Drag to the right **18** squares until the border is three gridlines to the right of *Corporation*, drag down until the bottom of the text box is aligned with the line below the text *avoid a charge* (in the first column), and then release the mouse button. If necessary, resize the text box so that the right border aligns at approximately 2.25 inches on the horizontal ruler and the bottom border aligns at approximately 3.5 inches on the vertical ruler.

5 With the text box selected, on the **Format tab**, in the **Arrange group**, click **Wrap Text**, and then click **Top and Bottom**. Compare your screen with Figure 12.39.

Top and Bottom text wrapping causes the four paragraphs of text and the two blank paragraphs above them to be moved below the text box.

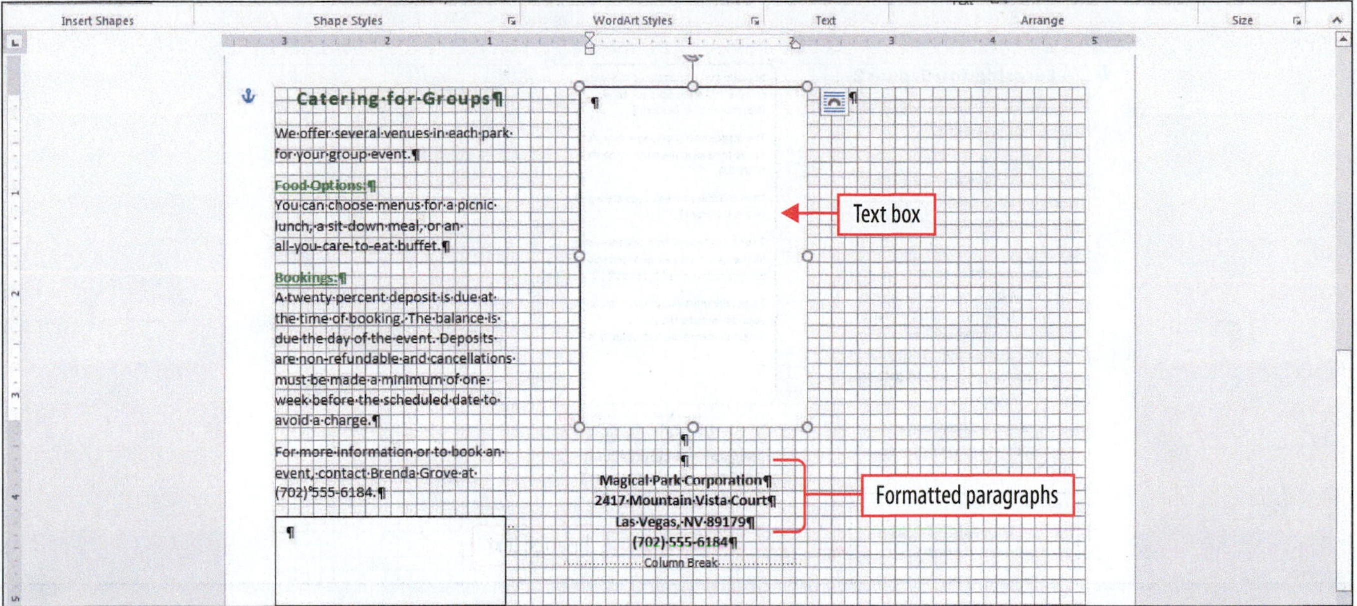

FIGURE 12.39 Word 2016, Windows 10, Microsoft Corporation

6 At the bottom of the first column, click in the text box to select it. On the **Format tab**, in the **Text group**, click **Create Link**.

7 Move the pointer into a blank area of the document, and notice that the pointer displays.

The upright pitcher indicates that the first text box is ready to be linked to another text box.

8 Move your pointer into the text box in the second column, and notice that the pointer displays. Compare your screen with Figure 12.40.

The pouring pitcher indicates that you can link the second text box to the first text box.

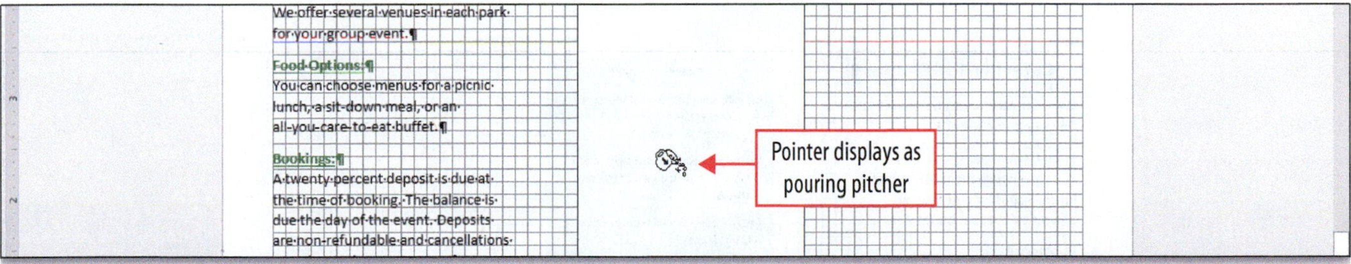

FIGURE 12.40 Word 2016, Windows 10, Microsoft Corporation

9 With the pointer displayed, click in the second text box to create a link.

10 If necessary, click to position the insertion point in the first text box. Click the **Insert tab**. In the **Text group**, click the **Object button arrow**, and then click **Text from File**. Navigate to the student files for this chapter, select the file **w12B_Comments**, and then click **Insert**. Compare your screen with Figure 12.41.

The first two paragraphs of text display in the first text box and the remaining text displays in the second text box.

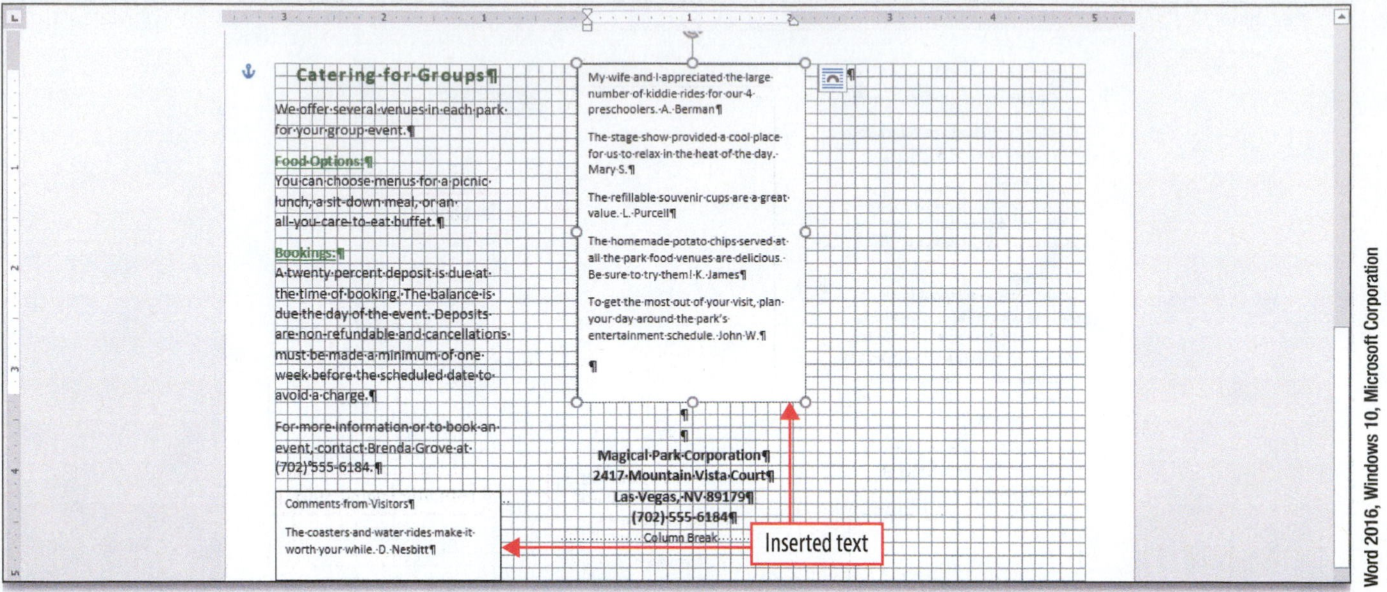

FIGURE 12.41

11 In the first text box, select the first paragraph, and then on the mini toolbar, apply **Bold** [B]. Press Ctrl + E.

12 In the second text box, click to position the insertion point to the left of the first paragraph, then press Enter, press ↑, and then type **More Comments** Select the text you just typed, and then on the mini toolbar, apply **Bold** [B]. Press Ctrl + E.

13 Click the **Format tab**, and then in the **Shape Styles group**, click **More** [▾]. In the **Shape Styles** gallery, in the fourth row, click the last style—**Subtle Effect – Green, Accent 6**. In a similar manner, apply the **Subtle Effect – Green, Accent 6** shape style to the other text box. Compare your screen with Figure 12.42.

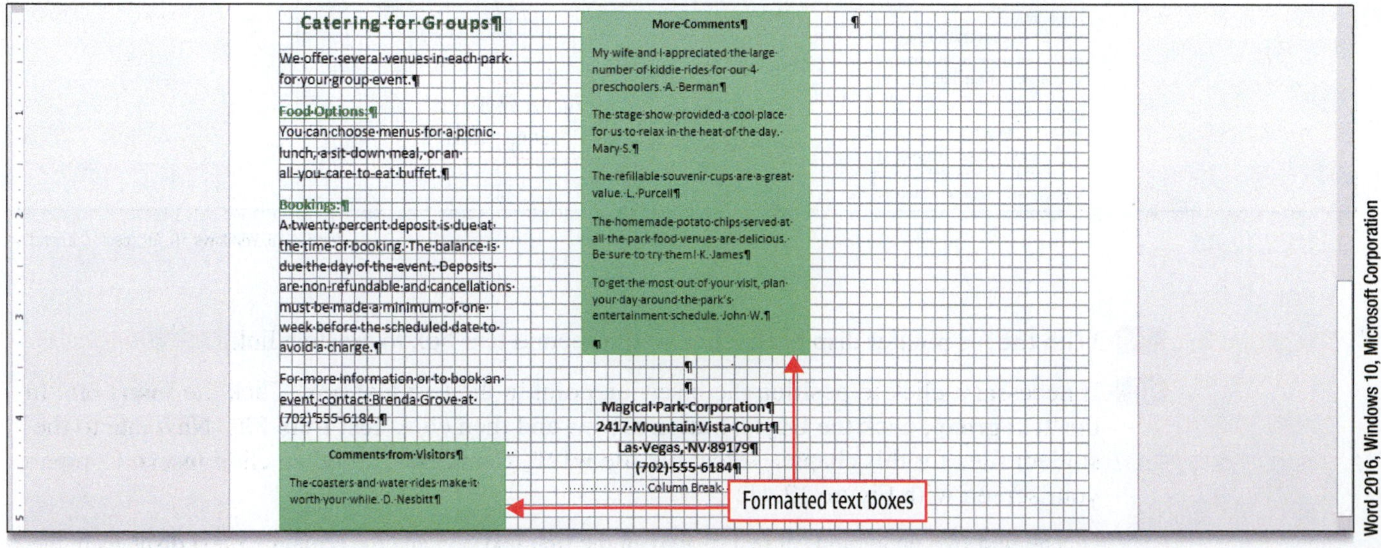

FIGURE 12.42

14 Click the **View tab**, and then in the **Show group**, clear the **Gridlines** check box to hide the gridlines. **Save** your changes.

More Knowledge **Unlinking Text Boxes**

To unlink text boxes, click in the first linked text box, and then on the Format tab, in the Text group, click Break Link.

Activity 12.13 | Modifying Text Effects

You can modify the built-in text effects in Word in a variety of ways—for example, by changing the weight and color of the outline and by altering the type of reflection.

1 On **Page 2**, position the insertion point at the top of the third column, and then type **OUR THEME PARKS**

2 Press Enter two times, and then type **Fun for all ages!** Select the paragraph you just typed, and then on the mini toolbar, change the **Font Size** to **20**, and apply **Italic** I. Press Ctrl + E.

3 Click the **Home tab**, and then in the **Font group**, click **Text Effects and Typography**. In the **Text Effects** gallery, in the first row, click the fifth effect—**Fill – Gold, Accent 4, Soft Bevel**. With the text still selected, click **Text Effects and Typography**, point to **Outline**, and then under **Theme Colors**, in the last column, click the fifth color—**Green, Accent 6, Darker 25%**. In the **Font group**, click the **Font Color button arrow**, and then in the last column, click the fourth color—**Green, Accent 6, Lighter 40%**. Deselect the text, and then compare your screen with Figure 12.43.

The theme allows you to choose a consistent color scheme to create a professional-looking document.

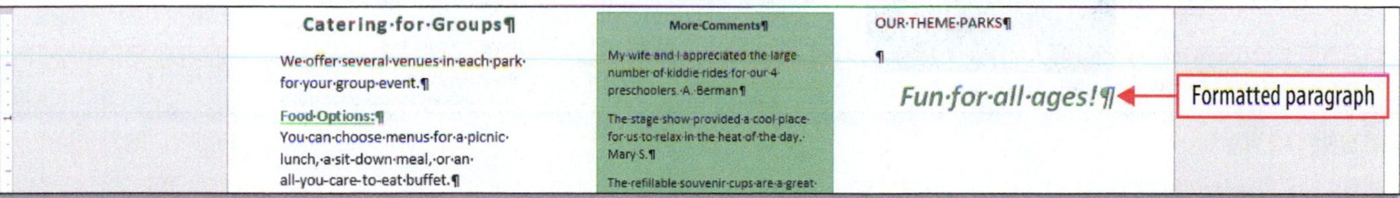

FIGURE 12.43

Word 2016, Windows 10, Microsoft Corporation

4 In the third column, select the first paragraph. On the mini toolbar, change the **Font Size** to **20**, and then apply **Bold** B. Press Ctrl + E.

5 On the **Home tab**, in the **Font group**, click **Text Effects and Typography**, and then in the second row, click the second effect—**Gradient Fill – Blue, Accent 5, Reflection**. Click **Text Effects and Typography**, point to **Glow**, and then under **Glow Variations**, in the third row, click the last option—**Green, 11 pt glow, Accent color 6**.

6 In the **Font group**, change the **Font Color** to **Green, Accent 6, Darker 25%**—in the last column, the fifth color. Deselect the text, and then compare your screen with Figure 12.44.

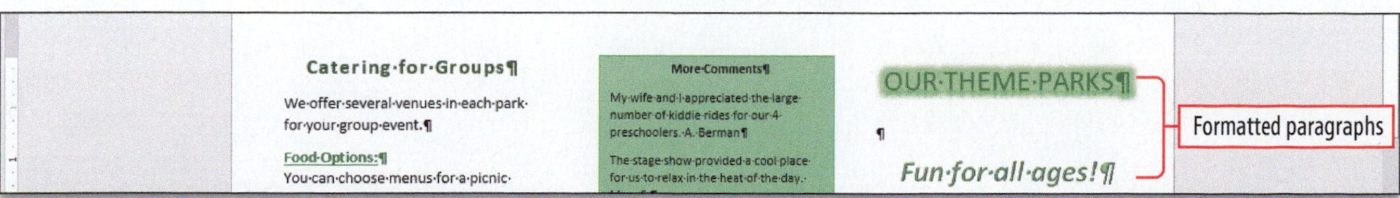

FIGURE 12.44

Word 2016, Windows 10, Microsoft Corporation

7 **Save** your changes.

Activity 12.14 | Applying Artistic Effects to Pictures

You can change the appearance of a picture by applying an ***artistic effect***—a filter that you apply to an image to create a special effect.

1 On **Page 1**, in the first column, position the insertion point at the end of the second paragraph, and then press Enter.

2 Click the **Insert tab**, and then in the **Illustrations group**, click **Pictures**. In the **Insert Picture** dialog box, navigate to your student files, select the file **w12B_Wheel**, and then click **Insert**.

3 On the **Format tab**, in the **Adjust group**, click **Artistic Effects**. Point to several options.

Live preview allows you to see how each option will modify the picture.

4 In the **Artistic Effects** gallery, in the fourth row, click the last option—**Plastic Wrap**. Compare your screen with Figure 12.45.

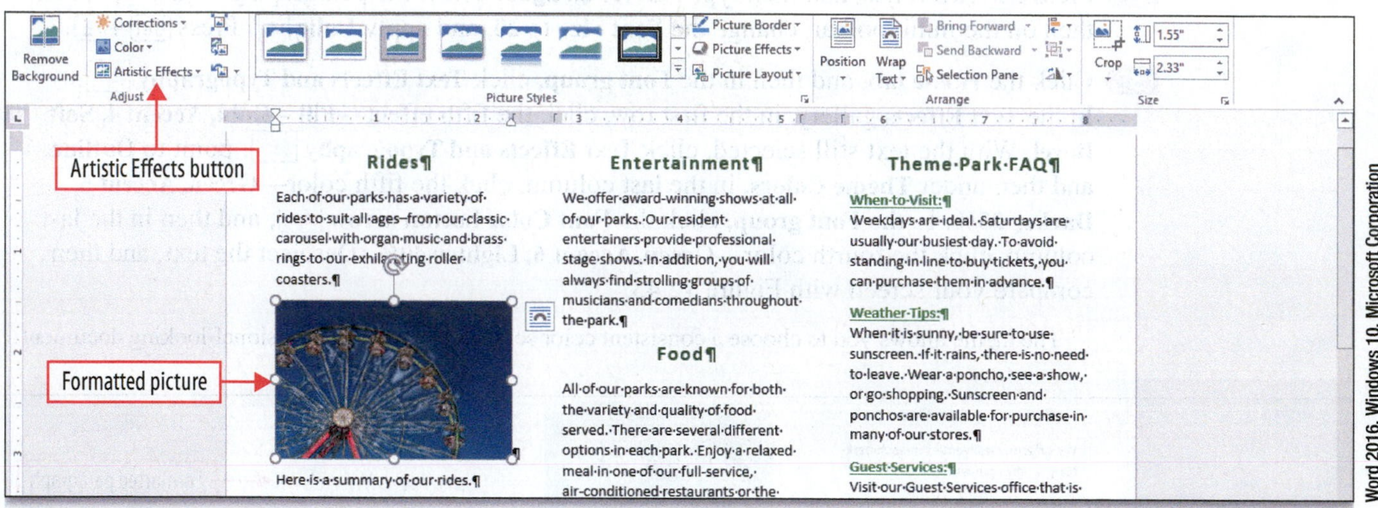

FIGURE 12.45

5 On **Page 2**, in the third column, position the insertion point in the second, blank paragraph, and then press Ctrl + E.

6 Click the **Insert tab**, and then in the **Illustrations group**, click **Pictures**. In the **Insert Picture** dialog box, navigate to your student files, select the file **w12B_Coaster**, and then click **Insert**.

7 In the **Adjust group**, click **Artistic Effects**, and then in the second row, click the fourth option—**Glow Diffused**.

8 On the **Format tab**, in the **Picture Styles group**, click **More**, and then click the first option—**Simple Frame, White**. In the **Picture Styles group**, click the **Picture Border button arrow**, and then in the last column, click the fifth color—**Green, Accent 6, Darker 25%**. Compare your screen with Figure 12.46.

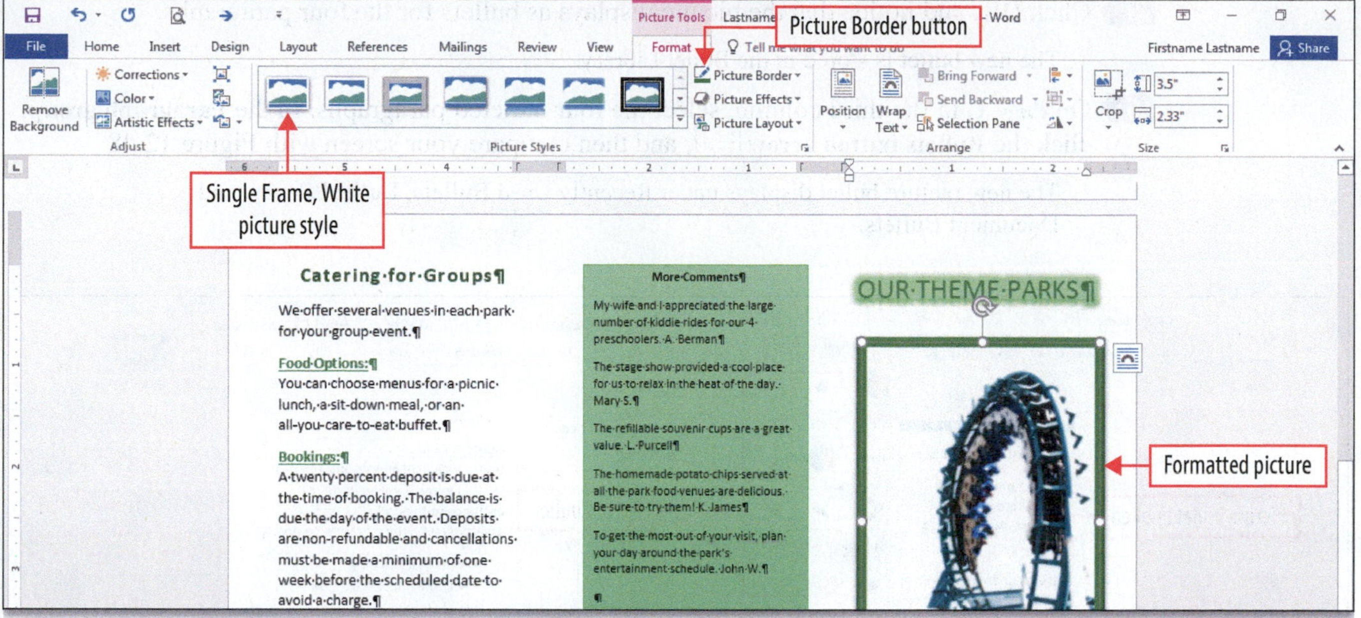

FIGURE 12.46

Word 2016, Windows 10, Microsoft Corporation

9 Save your changes.

Activity 12.15 | Using a Picture as a Bullet

MOS 3.3.3

In this Activity, you will use a picture to replace the bullets in the document.

1 On **Page 1**, in the first column, select the four bulleted paragraphs. Click the **Home tab**, and then in the **Paragraph group**, click the **Bullets button arrow**, and then click **Define New Bullet**.

2 In the **Define New Bullet** dialog box, under **Bullet character**, click **Picture**.

3 In the **Insert Pictures** dialog box, to the right of **From a file**, click **Browse**.

4 In the **Insert Picture** dialog box, navigate to your student files, select the file **w12B_Brochure_Bullet**, and then click **Insert**. Compare your screen with Figure 12.47.

The picture—a combination of yellow, blue, and green arrows—displays as a bullet in the Preview area of the Define New Bullet dialog box.

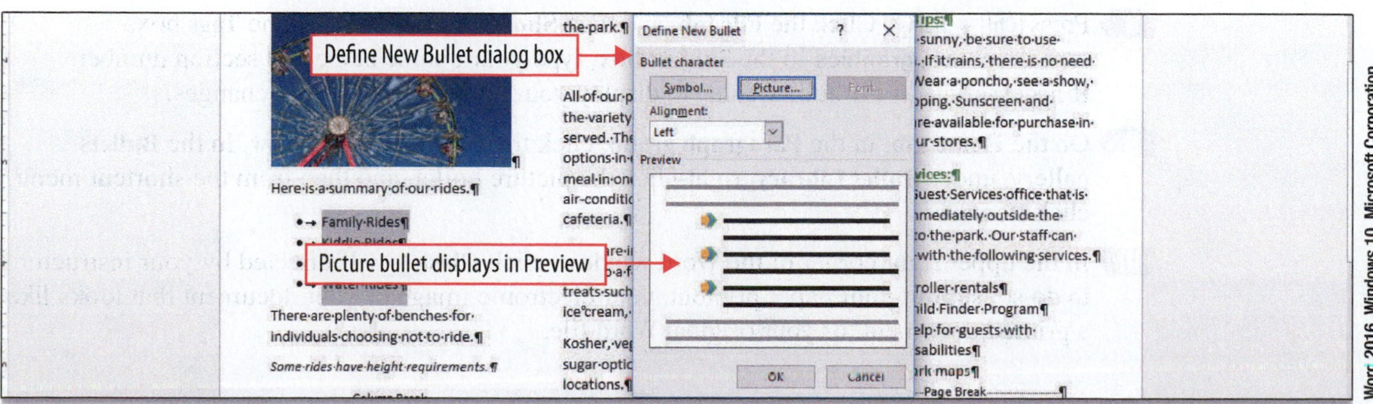

FIGURE 12.47

Word 2016, Windows 10, Microsoft Corporation

5 Click **OK**, and notice that the picture displays as bullets for the four paragraphs.

The new bullet is stored in the Bullet Library.

6 On **Page 1**, in the third column, select the four bulleted paragraphs. In the **Paragraph group**, click the **Bullets button arrow**, and then compare your screen with Figure 12.48.

The new picture bullet displays under Recently Used Bullets, Bullet Library, and Document Bullets.

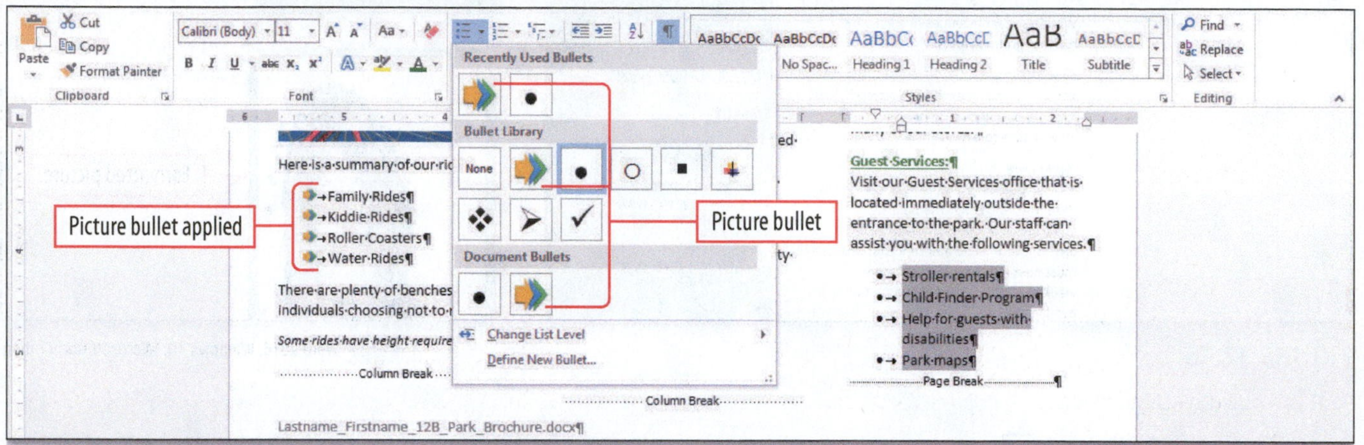

FIGURE 12.48

7 Under **Recently Used Bullets**, click the new picture bullet to apply the bullet to the selected paragraphs. Deselect the paragraphs, and then compare your screen with Figure 12.49.

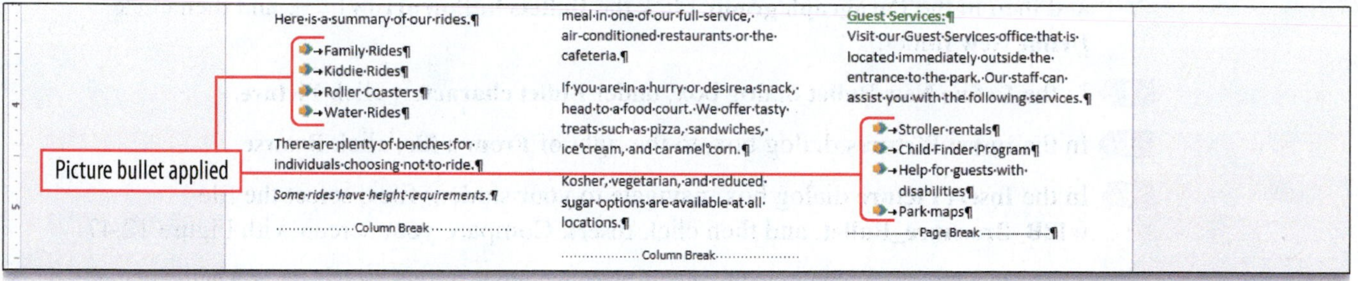

FIGURE 12.49

Word 2016, Windows 10, Microsoft Corporation

8 Press Ctrl + Home. Click the **File tab**, and then **Show All Properties**. In the **Tags** box, type **brochure, graphics** In the **Subject** box, type your course name and section number. If necessary, edit the author name to display your name. **Save** your changes.

9 On the **Home tab**, in the **Paragraph group**, click the **Bullets button arrow**. In the **Bullets** gallery, under **Bullet Library**, right-click the picture bullet, and then from the shortcut menu, click **Remove**.

10 In the upper right corner of the Word window, click **Close**. If directed by your instructor to do so, submit your paper printout, your electronic image of your document that looks like a printed document, or your original Word file.

END | You have completed Project 12B

GO! To Work

Andrew Rodriguez / Fotolia; FotolEdhar / Fotolia; apops / Fotolia; Yuri Arcurs / Fotolia

12 WORD

MICROSOFT OFFICE SPECIALIST (MOS) SKILLS IN THIS CHAPTER
PROJECT 10B
1.3.1 Modify Page Setup **3.3.3** Define a custom bullet character or number format **Expert 2.1.4** Link text boxes

BUILD YOUR E-PORTFOLIO

An E-Portfolio is a collection of evidence, stored electronically, that showcases what you have accomplished while completing your education. Collecting and then sharing your work products with potential employers reflects your academic and career goals. Your completed documents from the following projects are good examples to show what you have learned: 12G, 12K, and 12L.

GO! FOR JOB SUCCESS

Discussion: Cyber Hacking

Your instructor may assign these questions to your class, and then ask you to think about them or discuss them with your classmates:

The U.S. Homeland Security Department describes cyber incidents (hacking) as actions where there is an attempt to gain unauthorized access to a system or its data, unwanted disruption to service, unauthorized use of a system, or change to a system without the owner's permission. As companies store and process more and more data at centralized, offsite "cloud" data centers, the opportunities for criminals to hack data are growing. Cyber security is an important part of every organization's information systems protocols, and many companies now employ a senior executive with the title Chief Information Security Officer.

FotolEdhar / Fotolia

What cyber incidents have you heard of in the news over the last year?

What precautions have you taken with your personal data to prevent a hack?

What would you do if you learned that a company you do business with, such as your bank or college, had been the subject of a cyber incident?

END OF CHAPTER

SUMMARY

You can assign levels to paragraphs to create an outline in Word, and then use the outline to create a PowerPoint presentation. You can publish the presentation in Word as a handout, with an area for notes.

Legal citations are references to documents—for example, statues, regulations, and cases. By marking the citations, you can create a table of authorities that provides a listing of all citations in the document.

Create specialized documents by changing the paper size and the margins. Modify how text displays by changing the character spacing and using nonbreaking hyphens and nonbreaking spaces where appropriate.

Select a theme to maintain a consistent color scheme and create a professional-looking document. You can enhance a document by linking text boxes, applying artistic effects, and using a picture as a bullet.

GO! LEARN IT ONLINE

Review the concepts and key terms in this chapter by completing these online challenges, which you can find at **MyITLab**.

Matching and Multiple Choice: Answer matching and multiple choice questions to test what you learned in this chapter.

Lessons on the GO!: Learn how to use all the new apps and features as they are introduced by Microsoft.

MOS Prep Quiz: Answer questions to review the MOS skills that you practiced in this chapter.

PROJECT GUIDE FOR WORD CHAPTER 12

Your instructor will assign Projects from this list to ensure your learning and assess your knowledge.

Project	Apply Skills from These Chapter Objectives	Project Type	Project Location
12A **MyITLab**	Objectives 1–3 from Project 12A	**12A Instructional Project (Grader Project)** Guided instruction to learn the skills in Project 12A.	In MyITLab and in text
12B **MyITLab**	Objectives 4–5 from Project 12B	**12B Instructional Project (Grader Project)** Guided instruction to learn the skills in Project 12B.	In MyITLab and in text
12C	Objectives 1–3 from Project 12A	**12C Skills Review (Scorecard Grading)** A guided review of the skills from Project 12A.	In text
12D	Objectives 4–5 from Project 12B	**12D Skills Review (Scorecard Grading)** A guided review of the skills from Project 12B.	In text
12E **MyITLab**	Objectives 1–3 from Project 12A	**12E Mastery (Grader Project)** **Mastery and Transfer of Learning** A demonstration of your mastery of the skills in Project 12A with extensive decision making.	In MyITLab and in text
12F **MyITLab**	Objectives 4–5 from Project 12B	**12F Mastery (Grader Project)** **Mastery and Transfer of Learning** A demonstration of your mastery of the skills in Project 12B with extensive decision making.	In MyITLab and in text
12G **MyITLab**	Objectives 1–5 from Project 12A and 12B	**12G Mastery (Grader Project)** **Mastery and Transfer of Learning** A demonstration of your mastery of the skills in Projects 12A and 12B with extensive decision making.	In MyITLab and in text
12H	Combination of Objectives from Projects 12A and 12B	**12H GO! Fix It (Scorecard Grading)** **Critical Thinking** A demonstration of your mastery of the skills in Projects 12A and 12B by creating a correct result from a document that contains errors you must find.	Instructor Resource Center (IRC) and MyITLab
12I	Combination of Objectives from Projects 12A and 12B	**12I GO! Make It (Scorecard Grading)** **Critical Thinking** A demonstration of your mastery of the skills in Projects 12A and 12B by creating a result from a supplied picture.	IRC and MyITLab
12J	Combination of Objectives from Projects 12A and 12B	**12J GO! Solve It (Rubric Grading)** **Critical Thinking** A demonstration of your mastery of the skills in Projects 12A and 12B, your decision-making skills, and your critical thinking skills. A task-specific rubric helps you self-assess your result.	IRC and MyITLab
12K	Combination of Objectives from Projects 12A and 12B	**12K GO! Solve It (Rubric Grading)** **Critical Thinking** A demonstration of your mastery of the skills in Projects 12A and 12B, your decision-making skills, and your critical thinking skills. A task-specific rubric helps you self-assess your result.	In text
12L	Combination of Objectives from Projects 12A and 12B	**12L GO! Think (Rubric Grading)** **Critical Thinking** A demonstration of your understanding of the chapter concepts applied in a manner that you would outside of college. An analytic rubric helps you and your instructor grade the quality of your work by comparing it to the work an expert in the discipline would create.	In text
12M	Combination of Objectives from Projects 12A and 12B	**12M GO! Think (Rubric Grading)** **Critical Thinking** A demonstration of your understanding of the chapter concepts applied in a manner that you would outside of college. An analytic rubric helps you and your instructor grade the quality of your work by comparing it to the work an expert in the discipline would create.	IRC and MyITLab
12N	Combination of Objectives from Projects 12A and 12B	**12N You and GO! (Rubric Grading)** **Critical Thinking** A demonstration of your understanding of the chapter concepts applied in a manner that you would in a personal situation. An analytic rubric helps you and your instructor grade the quality of your work.	IRC and MyITLab
Capstone Project for Word Chapters 1–12	Combination of Objectives from all chapters.	A demonstration of your mastery of the skills in Chapters 1–12 with extensive decision making. **(Grader Project)**	IRC and MyITLab

GLOSSARY

GLOSSARY OF CHAPTER KEY TERMS

Artistic effect A filter that is applied to an image to create a special effect.

Character spacing A Word feature that allows you to change the default spacing constraints between characters.

Document gridlines Nonprinting horizontal and vertical lines used to assist in aligning graphics and other elements in a document.

Handout A document that is given to an audience to accompany a lecture.

Kerning A character spacing option that automatically adjusts the spacing between pairs of characters, with a specified minimum point size, so that words and letters appear equally spaced.

Layout The placement and arrangement of the text and graphic elements on a slide.

Legal citation A reference to an authoritative document, such as a regulation, a statute, or a case.

Minus outline symbol A formatting mark that indicates there are no subordinate heading or body text paragraphs.

Nonbreaking hyphen A formatting mark that prevents a hyphenated word or phrase from being displayed on two lines.

Nonbreaking space A formatting mark that keeps two words together so that both words will wrap even if only the second word would normally wrap to the next line.

Outline A Word feature that allows you to organize the contents of a document in a structured manner.

Outline level A Word feature that defines the position of a paragraph in relation to all topics in a document and is formatted with a corresponding heading style.

Outline symbol A small gray circle that identifies heading and body text paragraphs.

Passim A term that indicates a citation occurs on five or more pages in a document.

Plus outline symbol A formatting mark that indicates there are subordinate heading or body text paragraphs.

.pptx The default file extension for a PowerPoint file.

Table of authorities A list of all references in a legal document and the page numbers where the references occur.

CHAPTER REVIEW

Apply 12A skills from these Objectives:

1. Integrate Word with PowerPoint
2. Modify a PowerPoint Presentation
3. Create a Table of Authorities

Skills Review Project 12C Park Changes

In the following Skills Review, you will create an outline and then use it to create a PowerPoint presentation explaining proposed changes for Magical Park Corporation's water parks for the upcoming season. You will create a handout for management based on the presentation. You will also modify a legal document to include a table of authorities for management review. Your completed files will look similar to Figure 12.50.

PROJECT FILES

For Project 12C, you will need the following files:

w12C_Changes_Outline
w12C_Logo_Brief

You will save your documents as:

Lastname_Firstname_12C_Changes_Outline (not shown)
Lastname_Firstname_12C_Changes_Presentation (not shown)
Lastname_Firstname_12C_Changes_Handout
Lastname_Firstname_12C_Logo_Brief

PROJECT RESULTS

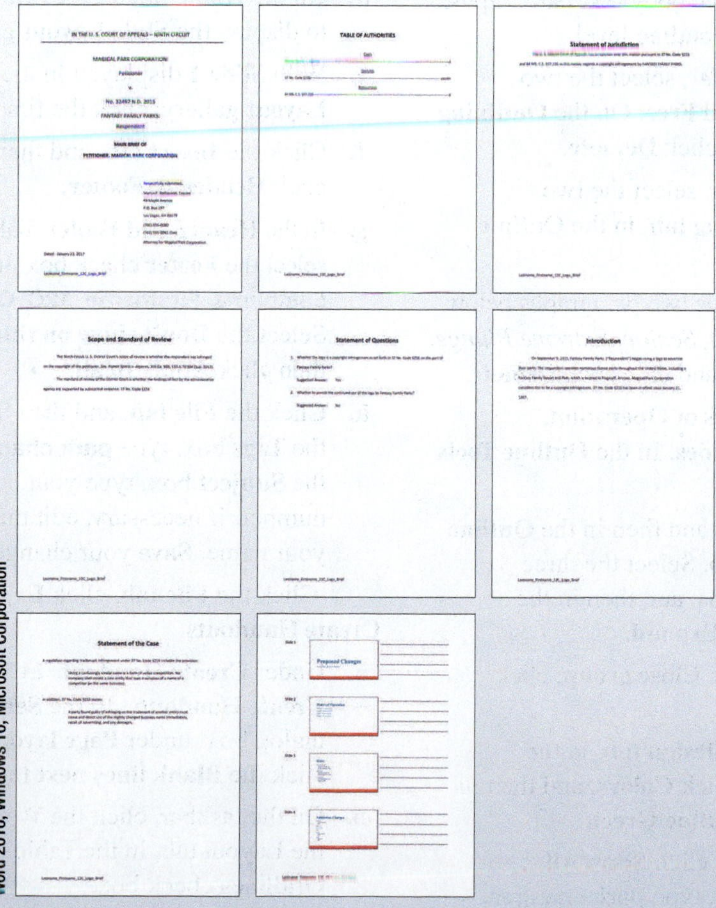

FIGURE 12.50

(Project 12C Park Changes continues on the next page)

Skills Review Project 12C Park Changes (continued)

1 Start Word. From your student files, open the file **w12C_Changes_Outline**. **Save** it to your **Word Chapter 12** folder as **Lastname_Firstname_12C_Changes_Outline** Insert the file name in the footer.

- **a.** On the **View tab**, in the **Views group**, click **Outline**.
- **b.** Select the first paragraph. On the **Outlining tab**, in the **Outline Tools group**, click the **Outline Level arrow**, and then click **Level 1**.
- **c.** For each of the three remaining paragraphs formatted with bold, on the **Outlining tab**, in the **Outline Tools group**, use the **Outline Level arrow** to assign the paragraphs to **Level 1**.
- **d.** Select the second paragraph of the document, click the **Outline Level arrow**, and then click **Level 2**.
- **e.** Below the paragraph *Hours of Operation*, select all four paragraphs, click the **Outline Level arrow**, and then click **Level 2**.
- **f.** In a similar manner, below each of the remaining *Level 1* paragraphs, select the body text paragraphs, and then assign the **Level 2** outline level.

2 Below the paragraph *Toddler*, select the two paragraphs **Age: 3 and under** and **Free**. On the **Outlining tab**, in the **Outline Tools group**, click **Demote**.

- **a.** Below the paragraph *Junior*, select the two paragraphs. On the **Outlining tab**, in the **Outline Tools group**, click **Demote**.
- **b.** In a similar manner, select the two paragraphs below the *Level 2* paragraphs *Adult*, *Senior*, *Extreme Plunge*, *The Vortex*, and *Wave Pool*, and then click **Demote**.
- **c.** Select the paragraphs **Hours of Operation**, **Admission Charges**, and **Rides**. In the **Outline Tools group**, click **Collapse**.
- **d.** Select the paragraph **Rides**, and then in the **Outline Tools group**, click **Move Up**. Select the three collapsed **Level 1** paragraphs, and then in the **Outline Tools group**, click **Expand**.
- **e.** On the **Outlining tab**, in the **Close group**, click **Close Outline View**.

3 Press Ctrl + Home. On the **Design tab**, in the **Document Formatting group**, click **Colors**, and then in the **Theme Colors** gallery, click **Blue Green**.

- **a.** Click the **File tab**, and then click **Show All Properties**. In the **Tags** box, type **park changes, outline** In the **Subject** box, type your course name and section number. If necessary, edit the author name to display your name.
- **b.** **Save** your changes, and then **Close** Word.

4 Start PowerPoint. At the bottom left of the screen, click **Open Other Presentations**, and then click **Browse**.

- **a.** In the **Open** dialog box, navigate to your **Word Chapter 12** folder. At the bottom of the **Open** dialog box, click the **All PowerPoint Presentations arrow**, and then click **All Outlines**. Click to select **Lastname_Firstname_12C_Changes_Outline**, and then click **Open**.
- **b.** Display the **Save As** dialog box, navigate to your **Word Chapter 12** folder, and then using your own name, **Save** the file as **Lastname_Firstname_12C_Changes_Presentation**
- **c.** On the **Design tab**, in the **Themes group**, click **More**. In the **Themes** gallery, click **Retrospect**.
- **d.** On the **Home tab**, in the **Slides group**, click **Layout** to display the **Slide Layout** gallery.
- **e.** With **Slide 1** displayed in the **Slide pane**, in the **Slide Layout** gallery, click the first option—**Title Slide**.
- **f.** Click the **Insert tab**, and then in the **Text group**, click **Header & Footer**.
- **g.** In the **Header and Footer** dialog box, on the **Slide tab**, select the **Footer** check box. In the **Footer** box, type **Lastname_Firstname_12C_Changes_Presentation** Select the **Don't show on title slide** check box, and then click **Apply to all**.
- **h.** Click the **File tab**, and then **Show All Properties**. In the **Tags** box, type **park changes, presentation** In the **Subject** box, type your course name and section number. If necessary, edit the author name to display your name. **Save** your changes.

5 Click the **File tab**, click **Export**, and then click **Create Handouts**.

- **a.** Under **Create Handouts in Microsoft Word**, click **Create Handouts**. In the **Send to Microsoft Word** dialog box, under **Page layout in Microsoft Word**, click the **Blank lines next to slides** option. Click **OK**.
- **b.** On the taskbar, click the **Word** icon. If necessary, on the Layout tab, in the Table group, select the View Gridlines check box.

(Project 12C Park Changes continues on the next page)

Skills Review Project 12C Park Changes (continued)

c. Display the **Save As** dialog box, navigate to your **Word Chapter 12** folder, and then using your own name, **Save** the file as **Lastname_Firstname_12C_Changes_Handout** Insert the file name in the footer.

d. In the first row of the table, in the third cell, select the first three lines, and then press Delete. In a similar manner, in the third column, delete the first three lines from each of the remaining three cells.

e. Point slightly outside the upper left corner of the table to display the **Table Move Handle**. Click the **Table Move Handle** to select the entire table. On the **Layout tab**, in the **Cell Size group**, change the **Shape Height** to **2.2"**.

f. Press Ctrl + Home. Click the **File tab**, and then **Show All Properties**. In the **Tags** box, type **park changes, handout** In the **Subject** box, type your course name and section number. If necessary, edit the author name to display your name. **Save** your changes, and then from **Backstage** view, **Close** the document but leave Word open. On the taskbar, click the **PowerPoint** icon, **Save** your changes, and then **Close** PowerPoint.

6 In Word, from your student files, open the file **w12C_Logo_Brief**. **Save** the file to your **Word Chapter 12** folder as **Lastname_Firstname_12C_Logo_Brief** Insert the file name in the footer.

a. On **Page 2**, in the second paragraph, select the text **37 Ne. Code §216**. Click the **References tab**, and then in the **Table of Authorities group**, click **Mark Citation**. In the **Mark Citation** dialog box, click the **Category arrow**, and then click **Statutes**. Click **Mark All**.

b. Click in the document. On **Page 2**, select the text **64 MS. C.S. §57.226**. In the **Mark Citation** dialog box, click the **Category arrow**, and then click **Regulations**. Click **Mark**. On **Page 3**, select the text **Ramos Sports v. Algieres**. In the **Mark Citation** dialog box, click the **Category arrow**, and then click **Cases**. Click **Mark**, and then **Close** the Mark Citation dialog box.

c. At the bottom of **Page 1**, position the insertion point to the right of the date, and then press Ctrl + Enter two times. On **Page 2**, position the insertion point to the left of the page break, type **TABLE OF AUTHORITIES** and then press Enter two times. Select the text you typed, change the **Font Size** to **16**, and then apply **Bold** and **Center**.

d. Position the insertion point to the left of the page break, and then in the **Table of Authorities group**, click **Insert Table of Authorities**. In the **Table of Authorities** dialog box, under **Category**, click **All**. Click the **Formats arrow**, and then click **Formal**. If necessary, select the **Use passim** check box. Click **OK**.

e. Press Ctrl + Home. Click the **File tab**, and then **Show All Properties**. In the **Tags** box, type **park brief, logo** In the **Subject** box, type your course name and section number. If necessary, edit the author name to display your name. **Save** your changes.

f. In the upper right corner of the Word window, click **Close**. If directed by your instructor to do so, submit your paper printouts, your electronic images of your documents that look like a printed document, or your original Word files.

END | You have completed Project 12C

CHAPTER REVIEW

Skills Review Project 12D Resort Facilities

Apply 12B skills from these Objectives:

4 Modify the Document Layout

5 Format Graphic and Text Elements

In the following Skills Review, you will format a document, insert graphics, and link text boxes to create a brochure containing information about Magical Park Corporation's resorts. Your completed document will look similar to Figure 12.51.

PROJECT FILES

For Project 12D, you will need the following files:

w12D_Resort_Facilities
w12D_Resort_Reviews
w12D_Pools
w12D_Room
w12D_Resort_Bullet

You will save your document as:

Lastname_Firstname_12D_Resort_Facilities

PROJECT RESULTS

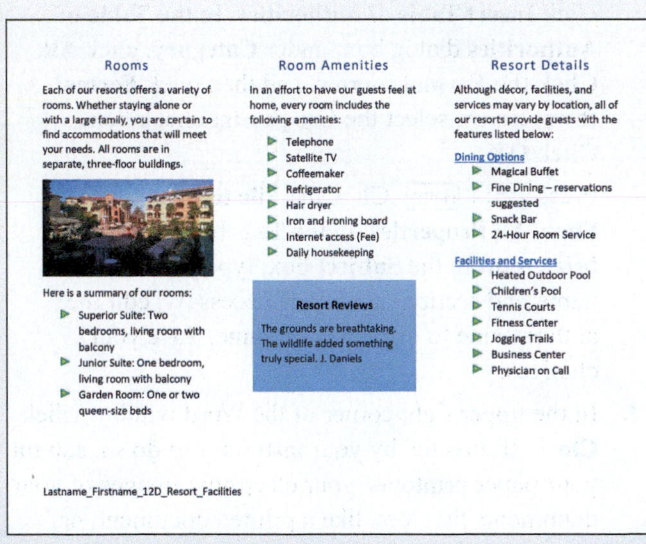

Rooms

Each of our resorts offers a variety of rooms. Whether staying alone or with a large family, you are certain to find accommodations that will meet your needs. All rooms are in separate, three-floor buildings.

Here is a summary of our rooms:

- Superior Suite: Two bedrooms, living room with balcony
- Junior Suite: One bedroom, living room with balcony
- Garden Room: One or two queen-size beds

Room Amenities

In an effort to have our guests feel at home, every room includes the following amenities:

- Telephone
- Satellite TV
- Coffeemaker
- Refrigerator
- Hair dryer
- Iron and ironing board
- Internet access (Fee)
- Daily housekeeping

Resort Reviews

The grounds are breathtaking. The wildlife added something truly special. J. Daniels

Resort Details

Although décor, facilities, and services may vary by location, all of our resorts provide guests with the features listed below:

Dining Options

- Magical Buffet
- Fine Dining – reservations suggested
- Snack Bar
- 24-Hour Room Service

Facilities and Services

- Heated Outdoor Pool
- Children's Pool
- Tennis Courts
- Fitness Center
- Jogging Trails
- Business Center
- Physician on Call

Lastname_Firstname_12D_Resort_Facilities

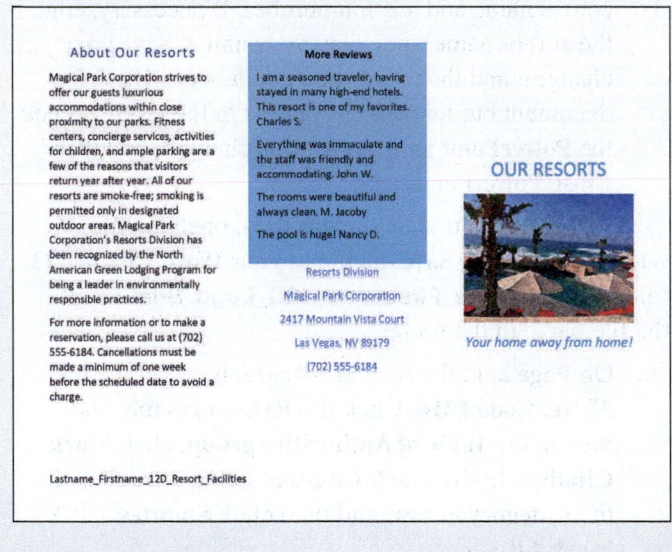

About Our Resorts

Magical Park Corporation strives to offer our guests luxurious accommodations within close proximity to our parks. Fitness centers, concierge services, activities for children, and ample parking are a few of the reasons that visitors return year after year. All of our resorts are smoke-free; smoking is permitted only in designated outdoor areas. Magical Park Corporation's Resorts Division has been recognized by the North American Green Lodging Program for being a leader in environmentally responsible practices.

For more information or to make a reservation, please call us at (702) 555-6184. Cancellations must be made a minimum of one week before the scheduled date to avoid a charge.

More Reviews

I am a seasoned traveler, having stayed in many high-end hotels. This resort is one of my favorites. Charles S.

Everything was immaculate and the staff was friendly and accommodating. John W.

The rooms were beautiful and always clean. M. Jacoby

The pool is huge! Nancy D.

Resorts Division

Magical Park Corporation

2417 Mountain Vista Court

Las Vegas, NV 89179

(702) 555-6184

OUR RESORTS

Your home away from home!

Lastname_Firstname_12D_Resort_Facilities

FIGURE 12.51

(Project 12D Resort Facilities continues on the next page)

Skills Review Project 12D Resort Facilities (continued)

1 Start Word. From your student files, open the file **w12D_Resort_Facilities**. **Save** the document to your **Word Chapter 12** folder as **Lastname_Firstname_12D_Resort_Facilities** Insert the file name in the footer.

a. On the **Layout tab**, in the **Page Setup group**, click **Orientation**, and then click **Landscape**. In the **Page Setup group**, click **Margins**, and then click **Narrow**. In the **Page Setup group**, click **Columns**, and then click **Three**.

b. On **Page 1**, in the first column, position the insertion point to the left of the paragraph *Room Amenities*. In the **Page Setup group**, click **Breaks**, and then under **Page Breaks**, click **Column**. In the second column, position the insertion point to the left of the paragraph *Resort Details*. Using the technique you just practiced, insert a **Column** break.

c. On **Page 2**, position the insertion point to the left of the paragraph *Resorts Division*, and then using the technique you practiced, insert a **Column** break. Press Ctrl + End, and then insert a **Column** break.

d. In the **Page Setup group**, click **Size**, and then at the bottom of the list, click **More Paper Sizes**. In the **Page Setup** dialog box, under **Paper Size**, click the **Paper Size arrow**, scroll down, and then click **Custom size**. Click the **Width spin box down arrow** to **9"**. Click the **Height spin box down arrow** to **7"**. Click **OK**, and then **Save** your changes.

2 In the first column, select the paragraph **Rooms**. On the mini toolbar, change the **Font Size** to **14**, click the **Font Color button arrow**, and then click **Blue, Accent 1, Darker 50%**—in the fifth column, the last color. Press Ctrl + E.

a. With the paragraph still selected, on the **Home tab**, in the **Font group**, click the **dialog box launcher**. In the **Font** dialog box, click the **Advanced tab**. Under **Character Spacing**, click the **Spacing arrow**, and then click **Expanded**. Click the **By spin box up arrow** to **1.2 pt**. Click **OK**.

b. In the **Clipboard group**, double-click **Format Painter**. Select each of the following paragraphs to apply the format: **Room Amenities**, **Resort Details**, and **About Our Resorts**. Click **Format Painter** to turn it off.

c. On **Page 1**, in the first column, select the last three paragraphs, beginning with **Superior Suite**. In the **Paragraph group**, click **Bullets**.

d. On **Page 1**, in the third column, select the paragraph **Dining Options**. On the mini toolbar, apply **Bold** and **Underline**, click the **Font Color button arrow**, and then click **Blue, Accent 1, Darker 25%**—in the fifth column, the fifth color.

e. In the **Paragraph group**, click **Line and Paragraph Spacing**, and then click **Remove Space After Paragraph**. In the **Clipboard group**, click **Format Painter**, and then in the third column, apply the format to the paragraph *Facilities and Services*.

f. In the second column, select the eight paragraphs beginning with **Telephone** and ending with **Daily Housekeeping**, and then in the **Paragraph group**, click **Bullets**. In a similar manner, apply bullets to the four paragraphs below *Dining Options*, and the seven paragraphs below *Facilities and Services*.

g. On **Page 2**, in the first column, in the last paragraph, locate the phone number. Select the space following *(702)*, and then press Ctrl + Shift + Spacebar to insert a nonbreaking space. Select the hyphen following *555*, and then press Ctrl + Shift + - to insert a nonbreaking hyphen. **Save** your changes.

3 Press Ctrl + Home. On the **View tab**, in the **Show group**, select the **Gridlines** check box.

a. On the **Insert tab**, in the **Text group**, click **Text Box**, and then click **Draw Text Box**. On **Page 1**, in the second column, position the ⊞ pointer at the beginning of the column break formatting mark. Drag to the right until you are one gridline past the column break formatting mark, drag down **12** squares, and then release the mouse button. On the **Format tab**, in the **Size group**, click in the **Height** box. type **1.5** and then click in the **Width** box. Type **2.25** and then press Enter.

b. On **Page 2**, in the second column, click to position the insertion point to the left of *Resorts Division*. On the **Insert tab**, in the **Text group**, click **Text Box**, and then click **Draw Text Box**. In the second column, position the ⊞ pointer at the top margin one gridline to the left of the beginning of the paragraph *Resorts*. Drag to the right **18** squares until the border

(Project 12D Resort Facilities continues on the next page)

Skills Review Project 12D Resort Facilities (continued)

is three squares to the right of *Corporation*, and then drag down until the bottom of the text box is aligned with the line below the text *Lodging Program for* (in the first column). Release the mouse button. On the **Format tab**, in the **Size group**, click in the **Height** box. Type **3** and then click in the **Width** box. Type **2.4** and then press Enter.

c. On the **Format tab**, in the **Arrange group**, click **Wrap Text**, and then click **Top and Bottom**. Scroll, if necessary, to display a portion of both text boxes simultaneously. On **Page 1**, in the second column, click the text box to select it. On the **Format tab**, in the **Text group**, click **Create Link**. On **Page 2**, point to the text box, and then click to create a link.

d. If necessary, on Page 1, click to position the insertion point in the text box. On the **Insert tab**, in the **Text group**, click the **Object button arrow**, and then click **Text from File**. From your student files, select the file **w12D_Resort_Reviews**, and then click **Insert**.

e. In the second text box, click to the left of the text *I am*, type **More Reviews** and then press Enter. Select the text you just typed, and on the mini toolbar, apply **Bold**. Press Ctrl + E.

f. With the second text box selected, on the **Format tab**, in the **Shape Styles group**, click **More**. In the **Shape Styles** gallery, in the fourth row, click the second option—**Subtle Effect - Blue, Accent 1**. In a similar manner, apply the shape style to the first text box.

g. On the **View tab**, in the **Show group**, clear the **Gridlines** check box to hide the gridlines. **Save** your changes.

4 On **Page 2**, in the second column, select the five paragraphs below the textbox. On the mini toolbar, apply **Bold**, and then press Ctrl + E. On the **Home tab**, in the **Font group**, click **Text Effects and Typography**, and then in the second row, click the second text effect—**Gradient Fill – Blue, Accent 5, Reflection.**

a. On **Page 2**, position the insertion point at the beginning of the third column. Type **OUR RESORTS** Press Enter two times, and then type **Your home away from home!**

b. Select the paragraph you just typed, and then on the mini toolbar, change the **Font Size** to **14**, apply **Italic**, and press Ctrl + E. On the **Home tab**, in the **Font group**, click **Text Effects and Typography**. In the **Text Effects** gallery, in the first row, click the second effect—**Fill – Blue, Accent 1, Shadow**.

c. Select the first paragraph in the column. On the mini toolbar, change the **Font Size** to **20**, and then apply **Bold** and **Center**. On the **Home tab**, in the **Font group**, click **Text Effects and Typography**, and then in the first row, click the second effect—**Fill – Blue, Accent 1, Shadow**. **Save** your changes.

5 On **Page 1**, in the first column, position the insertion point in the blank paragraph. On the **Insert tab**, in the **Illustrations group**, click **Pictures**. In the **Insert Picture** dialog box, navigate to your student files, select the file **w12D_Room**, and then click **Insert**.

a. On the **Format tab**, in the **Adjust group**, click **Artistic Effects**. In the **Artistic Effects** gallery, in the fourth row, click the second option—**Texturizer**.

b. On **Page 2**, in the third column, click in the blank paragraph. On the **Insert tab**, in the **Illustrations group**, click **Pictures**. In the **Insert Picture** dialog box, navigate to your student files, select the file **w12D_Pools**, and then click **Insert**.

c. On the **Format tab**, in the **Adjust group**, click **Artistic Effects**. In the **Artistic Effects** gallery, in the third row, click the second option—**Watercolor Sponge**.

d. Position the insertion point to the left of the paragraph *Our Resorts*, and then press Enter three times. **Save** your changes.

6 On **Page 1**, in the first column, select the three bulleted paragraphs. On the **Home tab**, in the **Paragraph group**, click the **Bullet button arrow**, and then click **Define New Bullet**.

a. In the **Define New Bullet** dialog box, under **Bullet character**, click **Picture**. In the **Insert Pictures** dialog box, to the right of **From a file**, click **Browse**.

b. In the **Insert Picture** dialog box, navigate to your student files, select **w12D_Resort_Bullet**, and then click **Insert**. Click **OK**.

c. In the second column, select the bulleted list. In the **Paragraph group**, click the **Bullet button arrow**. Under **Recently Used Bullets**, click the *Resort Bullet*. In the same manner, apply the *Resort Bullet*

(Project 12D Resort Facilities continues on the next page)

Skills Review Project 12D Resort Facilities (continued)

to the two bulleted lists in the third column. **Remove** the picture bullet from the Bullet Library.

d. Press Ctrl + Home. Click the **File tab**, and then **Show All Properties**. In the **Tags** box, type **facilities, graphics, reviews** In the **Subject** box, type your course name and section number. If necessary, edit the author name to display your name.

e. **Save** your changes. In the upper right corner of the Word window, click **Close**. If directed by your instructor to do so, submit your paper printout, your electronic image of your document that looks like a printed document, or your original Word file.

END | You have completed Project 12D

MyITLab grader

Apply 12A skills from these Objectives:

1 Integrate Word with PowerPoint
2 Modify a PowerPoint Presentation
3 Create a Table of Authorities

CONTENT-BASED ASSESSMENTS (MASTERY AND TRANSFER OF LEARNING)

Mastering Word Project 12E Summer Employment

In the following Mastering Word project, you will create an outline and then use it to create a PowerPoint presentation that can be shown to individuals interested in summer employment at a Magical Park Corporation theme park. You will create a handout for individuals based on the presentation. You will also modify a legal document for management review. Your completed files will look similar to Figure 12.52.

PROJECT FILES

For Project 12E, you will need the following files:

w12E_Employment_Outline
w12E_Product_Brief

You will save your documents as:

Lastname_Firstname_12E_Employment_Outline (not shown)
Lastname_Firstname_12E_Employment_Presentation (not shown)
Lastname_Firstname_12E_Employment_Handout
Lastname_Firstname_12E_Product_Brief

PROJECT RESULTS

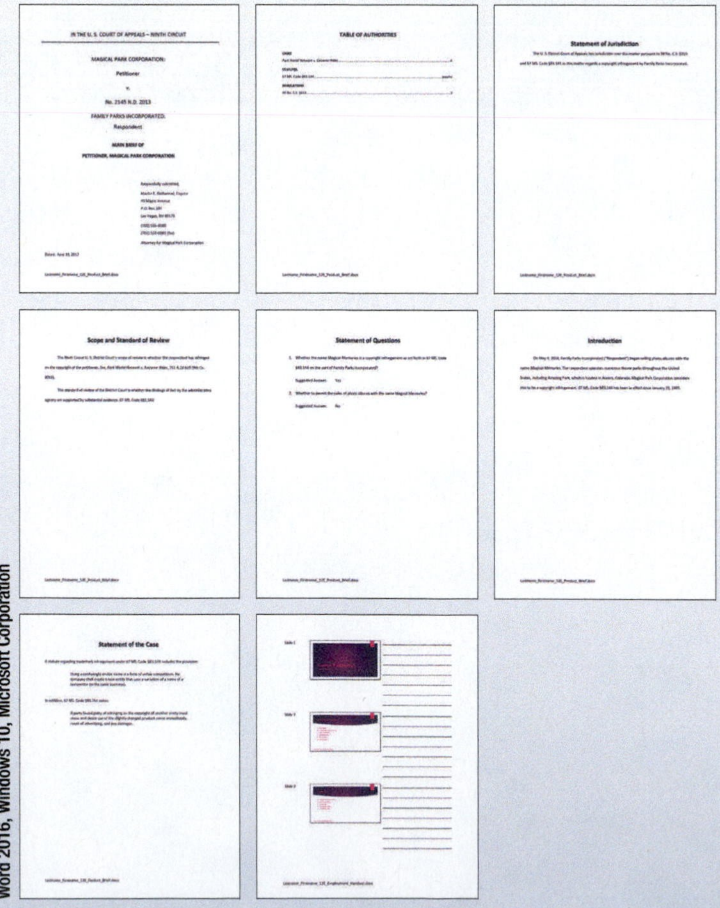

Word 2016, Windows 10, Microsoft Corporation

FIGURE 12.52

(Project 12E Summer Employment continues on the next page)

Mastering Word Project 12E Summer Employment (continued)

1 Start Word. Navigate to your student files, and open the file **w12E_Employment_Outline**. **Save** the document to your **Word Chapter 12** folder as **Lastname_Firstname_12E_Employment_Outline** Insert the file name in the footer.

2 In **Outline** view, assign **Level 1** to all paragraphs formatted with bold, and then assign **Level 2** to all remaining paragraphs. **Collapse** the paragraphs *Benefits* and *Available Positions*. **Move Up** the *Available Positions* paragraph and subtext so that it displays above *Benefits*. **Expand** all *Level 1* paragraphs.

3 In **Print Layout** view, display the **Theme Colors** gallery, and then click **Red Violet**. Press Ctrl + Home. From **Backstage** view, **Show All Properties**. In the **Tags** box, type **employment, outline** In the **Subject** box, type your course name and section number. If necessary, edit the author name to display your name. **Save** your changes, and then **Close** Word.

4 Start PowerPoint. **Open** from your **Word Chapter 12** folder, your Word outline **Lastname_Firstname_12E_Employment_Outline** file. **Save** the PowerPoint file in your **Word Chapter 12** folder as **Lastname_Firstname_12E_Employment_Presentation**

5 Display the **Themes** gallery, and click **Ion Boardroom**. Display the **Layout** gallery, and apply the **Title Slide** layout to **Slide 1**.

6 Insert a footer on the slides but do not show the footer on the title slide. In the **Footer** box, type **Lastname_Firstname_12E_Employment_Presentation** and then **Save** your changes.

7 Display the document properties. In the **Tags** box, type **employment, presentation** and in the **Subject** box, type your course name and section number. If necessary, edit the author name to display your name. **Save** your changes.

8 Send the handouts to Microsoft Word and select the **Blank lines next to slides** option. In Word, **Save** the document in your **Word Chapter 12** folder as **Lastname_Firstname_12E_Employment_Handout**

9 Insert the file name in the footer, and then display the document properties. In the **Tags** box, type **employment, handout** and the **Subject** box, type your course name and section number. If necessary, edit the author name to display your name. **Save** your changes, and then from **Backstage** view, **Close** the document but leave Word open. In PowerPoint, **Save** your changes, and then **Close** PowerPoint.

10 In Word, from your student files, open the file **w12E_Product_Brief**. **Save** the file in your **Word Chapter 12** folder as **Lastname_Firstname_12E_Product_Brief** and then insert the file name in the footer.

11 On **Page 2**, in the second paragraph, select the text **98 Ne. C.S. §213**. Display the **Mark Citation** dialog box, select the category **Regulations**, and then click **Mark**. Select the text **67 MS. Code §83.144**. In the **Mark Citation** dialog box, select the category **Statutes**, and then click **Mark All**. On **Page 3**, select the text **Park World Network v. Extreme Rides**. In the **Mark Citation** dialog box, select the category **Cases**, and then click **Mark**. **Close** the Mark Citation dialog box.

12 At the bottom of **Page 1**, position the insertion point to the right of the date, and then press Ctrl + Enter two times. On **Page 2**, position the insertion point to the left of the page break, type **TABLE OF AUTHORITIES** and then press Enter two times. Select the text you typed, change the **Font Size** to **16**, and then apply **Bold** and **Center**.

13 Position the insertion point to the left of the page break, and then insert a **Table of Authorities** using the **Classic** format. If necessary, select the **Use passim** check box.

14 Display the document properties. In the **Tags** box, type **legal, product, copyright** and in the **Subject** box, type your course name and section number. If necessary, edit the author name to display your name. **Save** your changes.

15 In the upper right corner of the Word window, click **Close**. If directed by your instructor to do so, submit your paper printouts, your electronic images of your documents that look like a printed document, or your original Word files.

(Project 12E Summer Employment continues on the next page)

Mastering Word | Project 12E Summer Employment (continued)

16 **If you are submitting this project in the MyITLab grader system, you will need to combine the two files into one as follows:**

- Open your **Lastname_Firstname_12E_Employment_Handout** document, select the entire document, and then copy the selection.
- Open your **Lastname_Firstname_12E_Product_Brief** document, and then press Ctrl + End. Press Ctrl + Enter, and then paste the selection to the end of the document.
- **Save** your document as **Lastname_Firstname_12E_Combined** and then close all open documents. Submit your file in MyITLab.

END | You have completed Project 12E

Mastering Word Project 12F First Aid

Apply 12B skills from these Objectives:

4 Modify the Document Layout
5 Format Graphic and Text Elements

In the following Mastering Word project, you will format a document, insert graphics, and link text boxes to create a leaflet containing first aid information for Magical Park Corporation's employees. Your completed document will look similar to Figure 12.53.

PROJECT FILES

For Project 12F, you will need the following files:

w12F_First_Aid
w12F_Contact_Information
w12F_Medical
w12F_Medical_Bullet

You will save your document as:

Lastname_Firstname_12F_First_Aid

PROJECT RESULTS

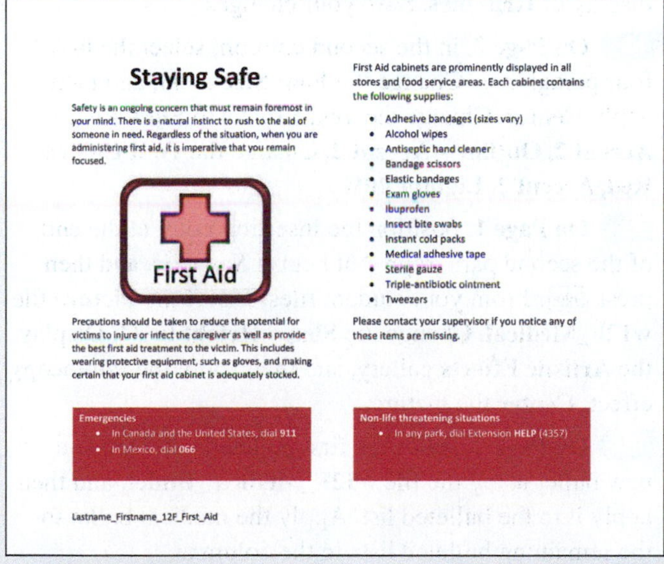

Staying Safe

Safety is an ongoing concern that must remain foremost in your mind. There is a natural instinct to rush to the aid of someone in need. Regardless of the situation, when you are administering first aid, it is imperative that you remain focused.

Precautions should be taken to reduce the potential for victims to injure or infect the caregiver as well as provide the best first aid treatment to the victim. This includes wearing protective equipment, such as gloves, and making certain that your first aid cabinet is adequately stocked.

First Aid cabinets are prominently displayed in all stores and food service areas. Each cabinet contains the following supplies:

- Adhesive bandages (sizes vary)
- Alcohol wipes
- Antiseptic hand cleaner
- Bandage scissors
- Elastic bandages
- Exam gloves
- Ibuprofen
- Insect bite swabs
- Instant cold packs
- Medical adhesive tape
- Sterile gauze
- Triple-antibiotic ointment
- Tweezers

Please contact your supervisor if you notice any of these items are missing.

Emergencies
- In Canada and the United States, dial **911**
- In Mexico, dial **066**

Non-life threatening situations
- In any park, dial Extension **HELP** (4357)

Lastname_Firstname_12F_First_Aid

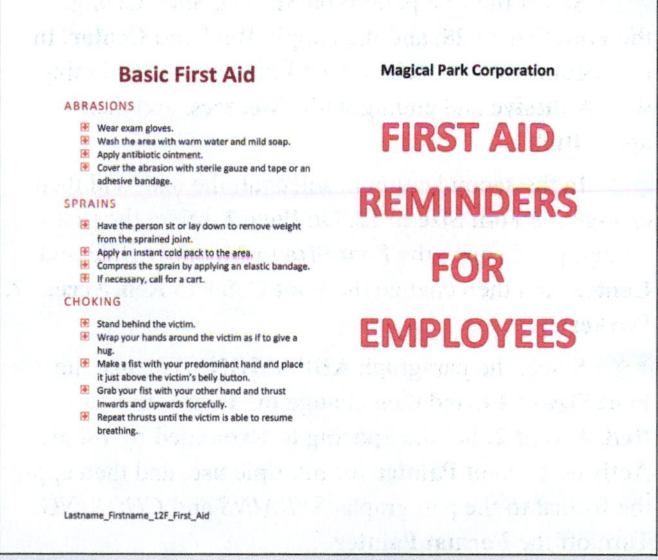

Basic First Aid

ABRASIONS

- Wear exam gloves.
- Wash the area with warm water and mild soap.
- Apply antibiotic ointment.
- Cover the abrasion with sterile gauze and tape or an adhesive bandage.

SPRAINS

- Have the person sit or lay down to remove weight from the sprained joint.
- Apply an instant cold pack to the area.
- Compress the sprain by applying an elastic bandage.
- If necessary, call for a cart.

CHOKING

- Stand behind the victim.
- Wrap your hands around the victim as if to give a hug.
- Make a fist with your predominant hand and place it just above the victim's belly button.
- Grab your fist with your other hand and thrust inwards and upwards forcefully.
- Repeat thrusts until the victim is able to resume breathing.

Magical Park Corporation

FIRST AID REMINDERS FOR EMPLOYEES

Lastname_Firstname_12F_First_Aid

Word 2016, Windows 10, Microsoft Corporation

FIGURE 12.53

(Project 12F First Aid continues on the next page)

Mastering Word Project 12F First Aid (continued)

1 Start Word. From your student files, open the file **w12F_First_Aid**. **Save** the document in your **Word Chapter 12** folder as **Lastname_Firstname_12F_First_Aid** Insert the file name in the footer.

2 On the **Layout tab**, in the **Page Setup group**, change the **Orientation** to **Landscape**, and then change the **Columns** to **Two**. On **Page 1**, in the first column, position the insertion point to the left of the fourth paragraph that begins *First Aid*, and then insert a **Column** break. In the second column, position the insertion point to the left of the paragraph *Basic First Aid*, and then press Ctrl + Enter.

3 On **Page 2**, position the insertion point to the left of *Magical Park Corporation*, and then insert a **Column** break. Display the **Page Setup** dialog box, change the **Paper Size** to **Custom size**, and then change the **Width** to **10"**. **Save** your changes.

4 Select the first paragraph **Staying Safe**. Change the **Font Size** to **28**, and then apply **Bold** and **Center**. In the second column, select the 13 paragraphs beginning with **Adhesive** and ending with **Tweezers**, and then apply **Bullets**.

5 In the second column, select all the text, and then change the **Font Size** to **12**. On **Page 2**, select the first paragraph. Change the **Font Size** to **26**, apply **Bold** and **Center**, and then change the **Font Color** to **Red, Accent 2, Darker 25%**.

6 Select the paragraph **ABRASIONS**. Change the **Font Size** to **14**, and then change the **Font Color** to **Red, Accent 2**. Set the **Spacing** to **Expanded** by **1.4 pt**. Activate **Format Painter** for multiple use, and then apply the format to the paragraphs *SPRAINS* and *CHOKING*. Turn off the **Format Painter**.

7 Select the four paragraphs below *ABRASIONS*, and apply **Bullets**. In a similar manner, apply **Bullets** to the paragraphs below *SPRAINS* and *CHOKING*.

8 On **Page 2**, in the second column, select the first paragraph, change the **Font Size** to **18**, and then apply **Bold** and **Center**.

9 On **Page 1**, in the second paragraph, select the space to the right of *first*, and then insert a nonbreaking space. In a similar manner, in the third paragraph, in the first sentence, select the space to the right of *first*, and then insert a nonbreaking space. **Save** your changes.

10 Display the document **Gridlines**. On **Page 1**, at the bottom of the first column, draw a **Text Box** that begins at the left margin, **4** gridlines below the last paragraph. Drag down **9** squares, and then drag to the right until the border of the text box aligns with the end of the third paragraph mark.

11 In the second column, draw a **Text Box**, beginning **6** gridlines below the left side of the page break, approximately the same size as the first text box. Change the **Shape Width** of both text boxes to **3.63"**.

12 Position the insertion point in the first text box, and then create a link to the second text box. From your student files, insert text from the file **w12F_Contact_Information**.

13 Apply the **Light 1 Outline, Colored Fill - Red, Accent 2** shape style to both text boxes. Turn off the display of **Gridlines**. **Save** your changes.

14 On **Page 2**, in the second column, select the last four paragraphs. Change the **Font Size** to **48**, and then apply **Center**. Change the **Text Effects** to **Fill – Red, Accent 2, Outline – Accent 2**. Change the **Font Color** to **Red, Accent 2, Lighter 40%**.

15 On **Page 1**, position the insertion point at the end of the second paragraph that begins *Safety is*, and then press Enter. From your student files, **Insert** the **Picture** file **w12F_Medical**. Change the **Shape Height** to **2"**. Display the **Artistic Effects** gallery, and then apply the **Photocopy** effect. **Center** the picture.

16 On **Page 2**, select the first bulleted list. Define a new bullet using the file **w12F_Medical_Bullet**, and then apply it to the bulleted list. Apply the medical bullet to the remaining bulleted lists in the column.

17 Display the document properties. In the **Tags** box, type **first aid, leaflet** and in the **Subject** box, type your course name and section number. If necessary, edit the author name to display your name. **Save** your changes. **Remove** the medical bullet from the Bullet Library.

18 In the upper right corner of the Word window, click **Close**. If directed by your instructor to do so, submit your paper printout, your electronic image of your document that looks like a printed document, or your original Word file.

END | You have completed Project 12F

CONTENT-BASED ASSESSMENTS (MASTERY AND TRANSFER OF LEARNING)

12 WORD

Mastering Word Project 12G Imagination Parks

Apply 12A and 12B skills from these Objectives:

1. Integrate Word with PowerPoint
2. Modify a PowerPoint Presentation
3. Create a Table of Authorities
4. Modify the Document Layout
5. Format Graphic and Text Elements

In the following Mastering Word project, you will format an outline and then use it to create a PowerPoint presentation describing features of the new Imagination Parks operated by Magical Park Corporation. You will edit a letter by inserting graphics and modifying text. The company plans to send these files as email attachments to its newsletter subscribers. You will also modify a legal document for management review. Your completed documents will look similar to Figure 12.54.

PROJECT FILES

For Project 12G, you will need the following files:

w12G_Imagination_Outline
w12G_Imagination_Brief
w12G_Park_Letter
w12G_Ride
w12G_Imagination_Bullet

You will save your documents as:

Lastname_Firstname_12G_Imagination_Outline (not shown)
Lastname_Firstname_12G_Imagination_Presentation (not shown)
Lastname_Firstname_12G_Imagination_Handout
Lastname_Firstname_12G_Imagination_Brief
Lastname_Firstname_12G_Park_Letter

PROJECT RESULTS

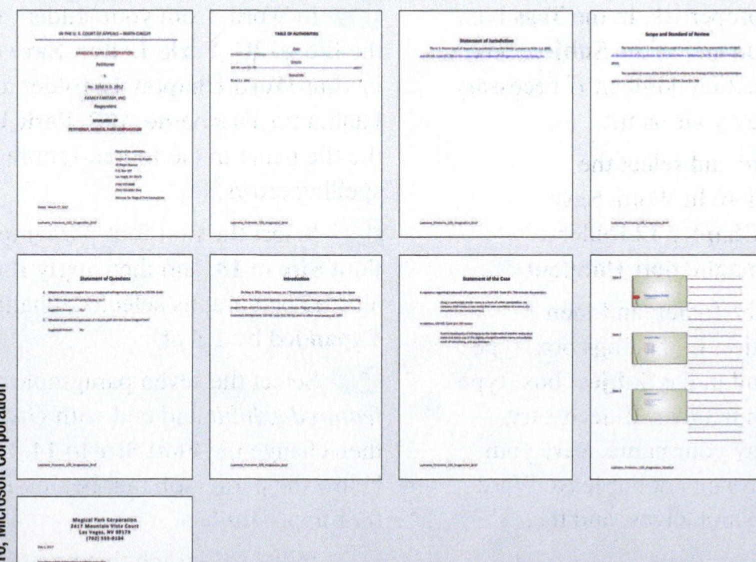

Word 2016, Windows 10, Microsoft Corporation

FIGURE 12.54

(Project 12G Imagination Parks continues on the next page)

Mastering Word Project 12G Imagination Parks (continued)

1 Start Word. Navigate to your student files, and open the file **w12G_Imagination_Outline**. **Save** the document to your **Word Chapter 12** folder as **Lastname_Firstname_12G_Imagination_Outline** Insert the file name in the footer.

2 In **Outline** view, assign **Level 1** to all paragraphs formatted with bold, and then assign **Level 2** to all remaining paragraphs. In **Print Layout** view, display **Backstage** view, and then **Show All Properties**. In the **Tags** box, type **imagination, outline** In the **Subject** box, type your course name and section number. **Save** your changes, and then **Close** Word.

3 Start PowerPoint. Display the **Open** dialog box, change the file type to **All Outlines**, and then from your **Word Chapter 12** folder, open your **Lastname_Firstname_12G_Imagination_Outline** file. **Save** the file in your **Word Chapter 12** folder as **Lastname_Firstname_12G_Imagination_Presentation**

4 Change the theme to **Wisp**. Display the **Layout** gallery, and apply the **Title Slide** layout to **Slide 1**.

5 Display the **Header and Footer** dialog box. Select the **Footer** and **Don't show on title slide** check boxes, and then in the **Footer** box, type **Lastname_Firstname_12G_Imagination_Presentation**

6 Display the document properties. In the **Tags** box, type **imagination, presentation** and in the **Subject** box, type your course name and section number. If necessary, edit the author name to display your name.

7 Create handouts in Word and select the **Blank lines next to slides** option. In Word, **Save** the document in your **Word Chapter 12** folder as **Lastname_Firstname_12G_Imagination_Handout**

8 Insert the file name in the footer, and then display the document properties. In the **Tags** box, type **imagination park, handout** and in the **Subject** box, type your course name and section number. If necessary, edit the author name to display your name. **Save** your changes, and then **Close** the document but leave Word open. In PowerPoint, **Save** your changes, and then **Close** PowerPoint.

9 In Word, from your student files, open the file **w12G_Imagination_Brief**. **Save** the document in your **Word Chapter 12** folder as **Lastname_Firstname_12G_Imagination_Brief** and then insert the file name in the footer.

10 On **Page 2**, in the second paragraph, select the text **92 Ne. C.S. §864**. Mark the citation using the **Regulations** category. Select the text **129 MS. Code §51.789**. Select the category **Statutes**, and then click **Mark All**. On **Page 3**, select the text **Port Santa Maria v. Williamson**. Mark the citation using the **Cases** category, and then **Close** the Mark Citation dialog box.

11 At the bottom of **Page 1**, position the insertion point to the right of the date, and then press Ctrl + Enter two times.

12 On **Page 2**, position the insertion point to the left of the page break, type **TABLE OF AUTHORITIES** and then press Enter two times. Select the text you typed, change the **Font Size** to **16**, and then apply **Bold** and **Center**.

13 Position the insertion point to the left of the page break, and insert a Table of Authorities using the **Formal** format. If necessary, select the **Use passim** check box. Click **OK**.

14 Display the document properties. In the **Tags** box, type **legal, park trademark** and in the **Subject** box, type your course name and section number. If necessary, edit the author name to display your name. **Save** your changes. From **Backstage** view, **Close** the document but leave Word open.

15 In Word, from your student files, open the file **w12G_Park_Letter**. **Save** the document in your **Word Chapter 12** folder as **Lastname_Firstname_12G_Park_Letter** and then insert the file name in the footer. Ignore all words flagged as spelling errors.

16 Select the first four paragraphs. Change the **Font Size** to **18**, and then apply **Bold** and **Center**. With all four paragraphs selected, change the **Spacing** to **Expanded** by **1.5 pt**.

17 Select the seven paragraphs that begin with *The featured exhibit* and end with *Outdoor Laboratory* and then change the **Font Size** to **14**. Select the six paragraphs below the paragraph that begins *The featured exhibit*, and then apply **Bullets**.

18 In the paragraph that begins *Our parks*, locate the phone number, and then change the space to a nonbreaking space, and then change the hyphen to a nonbreaking hyphen. **Save** your changes.

(Project 12G Imagination Parks continues on the next page)

Mastering Word Project 12G Imagination Parks (continued)

19 Position the insertion point to the right of the paragraph that begins *The featured exhibit*. From your student files, **Insert** the **Picture** file **w12G_Ride**. Display the **Artistic Effects** gallery, and then apply the **Glow Edges** effect.

20 Change **Wrap Text** to **Square**, and then change the **Shape Height** to **1.6"**. With the picture selected, display the **Layout** dialog box, and then change the **Horizontal Alignment** to **Right** relative to **Margin** and the **Vertical Absolute position** to **3.7** below the **Margin**.

21 Select the bulleted list. Define a new bullet using the image from your student data files **w12G_Imagination_Bullet**, and then apply it to the bulleted list. Press Ctrl + Home. **Remove** the picture bullet from the Bullet Library.

22 Display the document properties. In the **Tags** box, type **letter, graphics, bullets** and in the **Subject** box, type your course name and section number. If necessary, edit the author name to display your name. **Save** your changes.

23 In the upper right corner of the Word window, click **Close**. If directed by your instructor to do so, submit your paper printouts, your electronic images of your documents that look like a printed document, or your original Word files.

24 **If you are submitting this project in the MyITLab grader system, you will need to combine the three files into one as follows:**

- Open your **Lastname_Firstname_12G_Imagination_Handout** document, select the entire document, and then copy the selection.
- Open your **Lastname_Firstname_12E_Imagination_Brief** document, and then press Ctrl + End. Press Ctrl + Enter, and then paste the selection to the end of the document. Press Ctrl + Enter.
- Open your **Lastname_Firstname_12G_Park_Letter** document, select the entire document, and then copy the selection.
- Display your **Lastname_Firstname_12E_Imagination_Brief** document, and then with the insertion point at the top of the last, blank page, paste the selection.
- **Save** your document as **Lastname_Firstname_12G_Combined** and then close all open documents. Submit your file in MyITLab.

END | You have completed Project 12G

Apply a combination of the 12A and 12B skills.

CONTENT-BASED ASSESSMENTS (CRITICAL THINKING)

GO! Fix It Project 12H Employer Letter MyITLab

GO! Make It Project 12I Engineering Fair MyITLab

GO! Solve It Project 12J Job Support MyITLab

GO! Solve It Project 12K Appreciation Day

PROJECT FILES

For Project 12K, you will need the following files:

w12K_Appreciation_Day
w12K_School_Bullet
w12K_Teacher_Quotes

You will save your document as:

Lastname_Firstname_12K_Appreciation_Day

From your student files, open the file **w12K_Appreciation_Day** and save it to your **Word Chapter 12** folder as **Lastname_Firstname_12K_Appreciation_Day** Change the page orientation to landscape and the paper size to a width of 7 inches and a height of 5 inches. Format the text so that the first five paragraphs display on the first page and the remaining text is on a second page. Format the document attractively and apply character spacing and text effects to the appropriate text. On the second page, create a bulleted list for the five paragraphs describing benefits. Use the file **w12K_School_Bullet** to define and apply a picture bullet to the list. Draw text boxes at the bottom of both pages. Link the text boxes and insert text from the file **w12K_Teacher_Quotes**. Apply a shape style to both text boxes. Insert the file name in the footer and add appropriate document properties. Print your document or submit electronically as directed by your instructor.

(Project 12K Appreciation Day continues on the next page)

GO! Solve It Project 12K Appreciation Day (continued)

Performance Level

Performance Element	Exemplary: You consistently applied the relevant skills	Proficient: You sometimes, but not always, applied the relevant skills	Developing: You rarely or never applied the relevant skills
Change orientation and paper size	Page orientation and paper size are changed correctly.	The page orientation is not changed or the paper size is not changed.	No changes were made to the document layout.
Format text, including character spacing and text effects	Text is formatted attractively and character spacing and text effects are applied.	Text is formatted attractively, but either no character spacing or no text effect is applied.	Text is formatted, but character spacing and text effects are not applied.
Define bullet and apply to list	A bullet is defined and applied to appropriate paragraphs.	A bulleted list is created, but a picture bullet is not defined or applied.	No bulleted list is created.
Insert and link text boxes	Text boxes are inserted appropriately and linked.	Text boxes are inserted, but they do not display appropriately or are not linked.	No text boxes are inserted.
Insert text in text boxes and apply shape style	Text is inserted and a shape style is applied to both text boxes.	Text is not inserted or a shape style is not applied to both text boxes.	No text is inserted and a shape style is not applied.

END | You have completed Project 12K

OUTCOMES-BASED ASSESSMENTS (CRITICAL THINKING)

RUBRIC

The following outcomes-based assessments are *open-ended assessments*. That is, there is no specific correct result; your result will depend on your approach to the information provided. Make *Professional Quality* your goal. Use the following scoring rubric to guide you in *how* to approach the problem and then to evaluate *how well* your approach solves the problem.

The *criteria*—Software Mastery, Content, Format and Layout, and Process—represent the knowledge and skills you have gained that you can apply to solving the problem. The *levels of performance*—Professional Quality, Approaching Professional Quality, or Needs Quality Improvements—help you and your instructor evaluate your result.

	Your completed project is of Professional Quality if you:	Your completed project is Approaching Professional Quality if you:	Your completed project Needs Quality Improvements if you:
1-Software Mastery	Choose and apply the most appropriate skills, tools, and features and identify efficient methods to solve the problem.	Choose and apply some appropriate skills, tools, and features, but not in the most efficient manner.	Choose inappropriate skills, tools, or features, or are inefficient in solving the problem.
2-Content	Construct a solution that is clear and well organized, contains content that is accurate, appropriate to the audience and purpose, and is complete. Provide a solution that contains no errors of spelling, grammar, or style.	Construct a solution in which some components are unclear, poorly organized, inconsistent, or incomplete. Misjudge the needs of the audience. Have some errors in spelling, grammar, or style, but the errors do not detract from comprehension.	Construct a solution that is unclear, incomplete, or poorly organized, contains some inaccurate or inappropriate content, and contains many errors of spelling, grammar, or style. Do not solve the problem.
3-Format and Layout	Format and arrange all elements to communicate information and ideas, clarify function, illustrate relationships, and indicate relative importance.	Apply appropriate format and layout features to some elements, but not others. Overuse features, causing minor distraction.	Apply format and layout that does not communicate information or ideas clearly. Do not use format and layout features to clarify function, illustrate relationships, or indicate relative importance. Use available features excessively, causing distraction.
4-Process	Use an organized approach that integrates planning, development, self-assessment, revision, and reflection.	Demonstrate an organized approach in some areas, but not others; or, use an insufficient process of organization throughout.	Do not use an organized approach to solve the problem.

Apply a combination of the 12A and 12B skills.

GO! Think Project 12L Group Events

PROJECT FILES

For Project 12L, you will need the following file:

New blank Word document

You will save your documents as:

Lastname_Firstname_12L_Group_Outline
Lastname_Firstname_12L_Group_Presentation
Lastname_Firstname_12L_Group_Handout

Magical Park Corporation offers special packages for a variety of groups. Types of groups include schools, family reunions, tour groups, service clubs, youth groups, and businesses. Benefits of a group program include reduced admission, catered meals, priority seating at shows, discounts at all concession stands, free parking, and the services of a park consultant.

Create an outline defining the group program. Save it as **Lastname_Firstname_12L_Group_Outline** Create a PowerPoint presentation from your outline file and apply an appropriate theme. Save the presentation as **Lastname_Firstname_12L_Group_Presentation** Create a one-page handout in Word. Save the document as **Lastname_Firstname_12L_Group_Handout** Insert the file name in the footer and add appropriate document properties to all three files. Print your documents or submit all three files electronically as directed by your instructor.

END | You have completed Project 12L

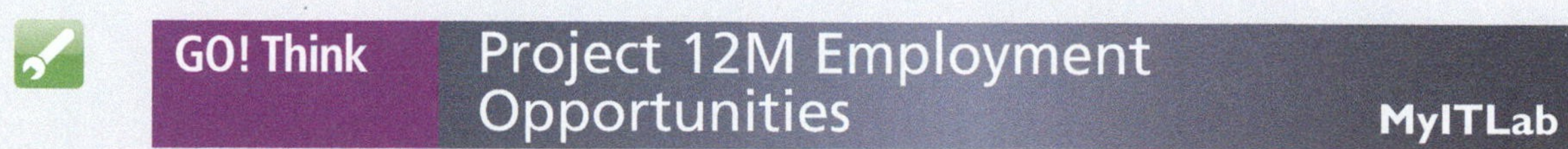

GO! Think Project 12M Employment Opportunities MyITLab

You and GO! Project 12N Personal Highlights MyITLab

Appendix

MICROSOFT OFFICE SPECIALIST WORD 2016			
Obj Number	**Objective text**	**GO! Activity**	**Page Number**
1.0 Create and Manage Documents			
1.1	**Create a document**		
1.1.1	create a blank document	OF 1.01, 1.01	4, 59
1.1.2	create a blank document using a template	2.13	142
1.1.3	open a PDF in Word for editing	3.14	198
1.1.4	insert text from a file or external source	1.02, 2.03	60, 125
1.2	**Navigate through a document**		
1.2.1	search for text	2.17, 7.21, 7.22	148, 457, 458
1.2.2	insert hyperlinks	3.23, 7.05, 7.06, 7.11	213, 435, 437, 443
1.2.3	create bookmarks	OF 1.20, 10.06	43, 604
1.2.4	move to a specific location or object in a document	3.11	194
1.3	**Format a Document**		
1.3.1	modify page setup	1.17, 12.08	80, 722
1.3.2	apply document themes	6.08	381
1.3.3	apply document style sets	2.12	141
1.3.4	insert headers and footers	OF 1.07, 1.15	17, 74
1.3.5	insert page numbers	3.02	182
1.3.6	format page background elements	OF 1.04, 6.08, 7.01, 10.12	9, 381, 429, 612
1.4	**Customize Options and Views for Documents**		
1.4.1	change document views	3.13	196
1.4.2	customize views by using zoom settings	OF 1.14, 3.20	32, 211
1.4.3	customize the Quick Access toolbar	OF 1.11, 11.09	26, 676
1.4.4	split the window	10.23	628
1.4.5	add document properties	1.16	75
1.4.6	show or hide formatting symbols	1.01	59
1.5	**Print and Save Documents**		
1.5.1	modify print settings	10.25	632
1.5.2	save documents in alternative file formats	3.14, 7.08, 7.24	198, 438, 462
1.5.3	print all or part of a document	1.16	75
1.5.4	inspect a document for hidden properties or personal information	OF 1.19	43
1.5.5	inspect a document for accessibility issues	OF 1.19	43
1.5.6	inspect a document for compatibility issues	OF 1.19	43

2.0 Format Text, Paragraphs, and Sections			
2.1	**Insert Text and Paragraphs**		
2.1.1	find and replace text	2.17, 7.21	148, 457
2.1.2	cut, copy and paste text	OF 1.17, 7.15, 7.16	37, 449, 450
2.1.3	replace text by using AutoCorrect	2.15	145
2.1.4	insert special characters	3.25, 7.18	454
2.2	**Format Text and Paragraphs**		
2.2.1	apply font formatting	2.27, 3.24	214
2.2.2	apply formatting by using Format Painter	OF 1.16	35
2.2.3	set line and paragraph spacing and indentation	1.19, 1.20, 1.21, 3.02	82, 84, 182
2.2.4	clear formatting	3.26, 4.07	264
2.2.5	apply a text highlight color to text selections	3.13	196
2.2.6	apply built-in styles to text	OF 1.05, 4.01	11, 255
2.2.7	change text to WordArt	OF 1.18	41
2.3	**Order and Group Text and Paragraphs**		
2.3.1	format text in multiple columns	3.15	202
2.3.2	insert page, section, or column breaks	3.17, 7.18	205, 454
2.3.3	change page setup options for a section	10.10	609
3.0 Create Tables and Lists			
3.1	**Create a Table**		
3.1.1	convert text to tables	5.07, 9.08	321, 544
3.1.2	convert tables to text	9.20	562
3.1.3	create a table by specifying rows and columns	2.01	123
3.1.4	apply table styles	2.19, 5.03	151, 315
3.2	**Modify a Table**		
3.2.1	sort table data	5.06	320
3.2.2	configure cell margins and spacing	5.21	342
3.2.3	merge and split cells	2.07, 5.04	130, 318
3.2.4	resize tables, rows, and columns	2.05, 5.08	128, 322
3.2.5	split tables	5.02	314
3.2.6	configure a repeating row header	online supplemental	
3.3	**Create and Modify a List**		
3.3.1	create a numbered or bulleted list	1.22, 1.23 2.04	87, 88, 127
3.3.2	change bullet characters or number formats for a list level	1.24, 4.10	90, 268
3.3.3	define a custom bullet character or number format	4.10, 12.15	268, 733
3.3.4	increase or decrease list levels	4.11	269

3.3.5	restart or continue list numbering	online supplemental	
3.3.6	set starting number value	online supplemental	
4.0 Create and Manage References			
4.1	**Create and Manage Reference Markers**		
4.1.1	insert footnotes and endnotes	3.03	184
4.1.2	modify footnote and endnote properties	3.04	185
4.1.3	create bibliography citation sources	3.09	192
4.1.4	modify bibliography citation sources	3.06	189
4.1.5	insert citations for bibliographies	3.05	188
4.1.6	insert figure and table captions	10.20, 5.11	624, 328
4.1.7	modify caption properties	10.20, 5.11, 5.13	624, 328, 330
4.2	**Create and Manage Simple References**		
4.2.1	insert a standard table of contents	10.19	621
4.2.2	update a table of contents	10.24	629
4.2.3	insert a cover page	10.11	611
5.0 Insert and Format Graphic Elements			
5.1	**Insert Graphic Elements**		
5.1.1	insert shapes	1.11, 7.04	70, 434
5.1.2	insert pictures	1.04, 5.17	62, 337
5.1.3	insert a screen shot or screen clipping	3.23	
5.1.4	insert text boxes	1.13	72
5.2	**Format Graphic Elements**		
5.2.1	apply artistic effects	1.09	68
5.2.2	apply picture effects	1.08	67
5.2.3	remove picture backgrounds	3.20	211
5.2.4	format objects	1.12, 1.14, 3.19	71, 73, 208
5.2.5	apply a picture style	OF 1.12	27
5.2.6	wrap text around objects	1.05, 3.18, 5.12	63, 206, 329
5.2.7	position objects	1.07, 1.11, 3.18	66, 70, 206
5.2.8	add alternative text to objects for accessibility	OF 1.18, 5.24	41, 345
5.3	**Insert and Format SmartArt Graphics**		
5.3.1	create a SmartArt graphic	1.27	95
5.3.2	format a SmartArt graphic	1.28	96
5.3.3	modify SmartArt graphic content	online supplemental	

MICROSOFT OFFICE EXPERT WORD 2016			
Obj Number	**Objective text**	**GO! Activity**	**Page Number**
1.0 Manage Document Options and Settings			
1.1	**Manage Documents and Templates**		
1.1.1	modify existing templates	online supplemental	
1.1.2	copy custom styles, macros, and building blocks to other documents or templates	5.01	311
1.1.3	manage document versions	7.14, 9.21	447, 563
1.1.4	compare and combine multiple documents	6.2	403
1.1.5	link to external document content	11.04, 11.05	665, 667
1.1.6	enable macros in a document	11.06	671
1.1.7	display hidden ribbon tabs	4.15, 9.01	275, 535
1.1.8	change the application default font	online supplemental	
1.2	**Prepare Documents for Review**		
1.2.1	restrict editing	9.12	548
1.2.2	mark a document as final	9.22	566
1.2.3	protect a document with a password	9.12	548
1.3	**Manage Document Changes**		
1.3.1	track changes	6.15	394
1.3.2	manage tracked changes	6.17, 6.18	398, 399
1.3.3	lock or unlock tracking	6.17	398
1.3.4	add comments	6.13	389
1.3.5	manage comments	6.14	392
2.0 Design Advanced Documents			
2.1	**Perform Advanced Editing and Formatting**		
2.1.1	find and replace text by using wildcards and special characters	7.22	458
2.1.2	find and replace formatting and styles	7.21	457
2.1.3	set advanced page setup layout options	6.11, 10.21	385, 626
2.1.4	link text boxes	12.12	727
2.1.5	set paragraph pagination options	10.22	627
2.1.6	resolve style conflicts by using Paste Options	online supplemental	
2.2	**Create Styles**		
2.2.1	create paragraph and character styles	4.04, 8.01	259, 485
2.2.2	modify existing styles	4.02	227
3.0 Create Advanced References			
3.1	**Create and Manage Indexes**		
3.1.1	mark index entries	10.14	616
3.1.2	create indexes	10.16	618
3.1.3	update indexes	10.17	620

3.2	**Create and Manage References**		
3.2.1	customize a table of contents	10.19	621
3.2.2	insert and modify captions	10.20, 5.11	624, 328
3.2.3	create and modify a table of figures	10.20	624
3.3	**Manage Forms, Fields, and Mail Merge Operations**		
3.3.1	add custom fields	online supplemental	
3.3.2	modify field properties	9.11	547
3.3.3	perform mail merges	8.02, 8.06, 8.07	487, 492, 494
3.3.4	manage recipient lists	8.03, 8.09, 8.10	487, 500, 502
3.3.5	insert merged fields	8.04, 8.12	488, 507
3.3.6	preview merge results	8.05	491
4.0 Create Custom Word Elements			
4.1	**Create and Modify Building Blocks, Macros, and Controls**		
4.1.1	create QuickParts	6.02, 6.04, 6.05	374, 376, 378
4.1.2	manage building blocks	6.03, 6.12	375, 385
4.1.3	create and modify simple macros	11.08, 11.09, 11.10, 11.12	673, 676, 678, 681
4.1.4	insert and configure content controls	9.02, 9.03, 9.04, 9.05, 9.06, 9.09	537, 538, 539, 541, 542, 546
4.2	**Create Custom Style Sets and Templates**		
4.2.1	create custom color sets	6.06, 9.18	379, 559
4.2.2	create custom font sets	6.06, 9.17	379, 557
4.2.3	create custom themes	6.07	380
4.2.4	create custom style sets	9.19	560
4.3	**Prepare a document for Internationalization and Accessibility**		
4.3.1	configure language options in documents	9.24	570
4.3.2	add alt-text to document elements	OF 1.18, 5.24	41, 345
4.3.3	manage multiple options for +Body and +Heading fonts	online supplemental	
4.3.4	utilize global content standards	not in software	

Glossary

AdjustListIndents A built-in macro used to modify the indenting of a bulleted or numbered list.

Address Block A predefined merge field that includes the recipient's name and address.

Alignment The placement of text or objects relative to the left and right margins.

Alignment guide A green vertical or horizontal line that displays when you are moving or sizing an object to assist you with object placement.

All Markup A Track Changes view that displays the document with all revisions and comments visible.

Alternative text Text associated with an image that serves the same purpose and conveys the same essential information as the image.

Alt text Another name for alternative text.

American Psychological Association (APA) One of two commonly used style guides for formatting research papers.

App A self-contained program usually designed for a single purpose and that runs on smartphones and other mobile devices.

Apps for Office A collection of downloadable apps that enable you to create and view information within Office programs, and that combine cloud services and web technologies within the user interface of Office.

Area chart A chart type that shows trends over time.

Artistic effects Formats applied to images that make pictures resemble sketches or paintings.

Ascending The order of text sorted alphabetically from A to Z or numbers sorted from the smallest to the largest.

Author The owner, or creator, of the original document.

AutoClose A macro that will automatically run when closing a document.

AutoCorrect A feature that corrects common typing and spelling errors as you type, for example, changing teh to the.

AutoFit A table feature that automatically adjusts column widths or the width of the entire table.

AutoFit Contents A table feature that resizes the column widths to accommodate the maximum field size.

AutoMark file A Word document that contains a two-column table used to mark words as index entries.

AutoRecover A feature that helps prevent losing unsaved changes by automatically creating a backup version of the current document.

AutoRecover option A Word option that automatically saves versions of your file while you are working on it, and also helps to recover unsaved documents.

Backstage tabs The area along the left side of Backstage view with tabs to display screens with related groups of commands.

Backstage view A centralized space for file management tasks; for example, opening, saving, printing, publishing, or sharing a file. A navigation pane displays along the left side with tabs that group file-related tasks together.

Balloon The outline shape in which a comment or formatting change displays.

Bar chart A chart type that shows a comparison among related data.

Bibliography A list of cited works in a report or research paper; also referred to as Works Cited, Sources, or References, depending upon the report style.

Blog A website that displays dated entries, short for Web log.

Blog post An individual article entered in a blog with a time and date stamp.

Body The text of a letter.

Body text Text that does not have a heading style applied.

Bookmark A command that identifies a word, section, or place in a document so that you can find it quickly without scrolling.

Border Painter A table feature that applies selected formatting to specific borders of a table.

Brightness The relative lightness of a picture.

Building blocks Reusable pieces of content or other document parts—for example, headers, footers, and page number formats—that are stored in galleries.

Building Blocks Organizer A feature that enables you to view—in a single location—all of the available building blocks from all the different galleries.

Bulk mail A large mailing, sorted by postal code, that is eligible for reduced postage rates, available from the United States Postal Service.

Bulleted list A list of items with each item introduced by a symbol such as a small circle or check mark, and which is useful when the items in the list can be displayed in any order.

Bullets Text symbols such as small circles or check marks that precede each item in a bulleted list.

Caption A title that is added to a Word object and numbered sequentially.

Category axis The area of the chart that identifies the categories of data.

Cell The box at the intersection of a row and column in a Word table.

Cell margins The amount of space between a cell's content and the left, right, top, and bottom borders of the cell.

Cell spacing The distance between the individual cells in a table.

Center alignment The alignment of text or objects that is centered horizontally between the left and right margin.

Change Case A formatting command that allows you to quickly change the capitalization of selected text.

Character spacing A Word feature that allows you to change the default spacing constraints between characters.

Character style A style, indicated by the symbol a, that contains formatting characteristics that you apply to text, such as font name, font size, font color, bold emphasis, and so on.

Chart A visual representation of numerical data.

Chart area The entire chart and all its elements.

Chart data range The group of cells with red, purple, and blue shading that is used to create a chart.

Chart Elements A Word feature that displays commands to add, remove, or change chart elements, such as the legend, gridlines, and data labels.

Chart Filters A Word feature that displays commands to define what data points and names display on a chart.

Chart style The overall visual look of a chart in terms of its graphic effects, colors, and backgrounds.

Chart Styles A Word feature that displays commands to apply a style and color scheme to a chart.

Check Accessibility A command that checks the document for content that people with disabilities might find difficult to read.

Check Box content control A content control that allows the user to select, or not select, a specific option.

Check Box form field A legacy control that allows the user to select, or not select, a specific option.

Check Compatibility A command that searches your document for features that may not be supported by older versions of Office.

Citation A note inserted into the text of a research paper that refers the reader to a source in the bibliography.

Clipboard A temporary storage area that holds text or graphics that you select and then cut or copy.

Cloud computing Applications and services that are accessed over the Internet, rather than accessing applications that are installed on your local computer.

Cloud storage Online storage of data so that you can access your data from different places and devices.

Collaborate To work with others as a team in an intellectual endeavor to complete a shared task or to achieve a shared goal.

Column break indicator A dotted line containing the words Column Break that displays at the bottom of the column.

Column chart A chart type that shows a comparison among related data.

Combine A Track Changes feature that enables you to review two different documents containing revisions, both based on an original document.

Combo Box content control A content control that enables the user to select an item from a list or enter new text.

Commands Instructions to a computer program that cause an action to be carried out.

Comment In a macro procedure, a line of text that is used solely for documentation; or, a note that an author or reviewers adds to a document.

Compare A Track Changes feature that enables you to review differences between an original document and the latest version of the document.

Complimentary closing A parting farewell in a business letter.

Compressed file A file that has been reduced in size and thus takes up less storage space and can be transferred to other computers quickly.

Content app An app for Office that integrates web-based features as content within the body of a document.

Content control A data entry field where the particular type of information is supplied by the user.

Context menus Menus that display commands and options relevant to the selected text or object; also called shortcut menus.

Context-sensitive commands Commands that display on a shortcut menu that relate to the object or text that you right-clicked.

Contextual tabs Tabs that are added to the ribbon automatically when a specific object, such as a picture, is selected, and that contain commands relevant to the selected object.

Contiguous Items that are adjacent to one another.

Continuous section break A mark that defines the beginning and end of each subdocument.

Contrast The difference between the darkest and lightest area of a picture.

Copy A command that duplicates a selection and places it on the Clipboard.

Cover letter A document that you send with your resume to provide additional information about your skills and experience.

Cover page The first page of a document that provides introductory information.

Creative Commons A nonprofit organization that enables sharing and use of images and knowledge through free legal tools.

Crop A command that removes unwanted or unnecessary areas of a picture.

Crop handles Handles used to define unwanted areas of a picture.

Crop pointer The pointer used to crop areas of a picture.

Cross-reference A text link to an item that appears in another location in the document, such as a heading, a caption, or a footnote.

Cut A command that removes a selection and places it on the Clipboard.

Database An organized collection of facts about people, events, things, or ideas related to a particular topic or purpose.

Data labels The part of a chart that displays the value represented by each data marker.

Data markers The shapes in a chart representing each of the cells that contain data.

Data points The cells that contain numerical data used in a chart.

Data range border The blue line that surrounds the cells containing numerical data that display in in the chart.

Data series In a chart, related data points represented by a unique color.

Data source A document that contains a list of variable information, such as names and addresses, that is merged with a main document to create customized form letters or labels.

Date & Time A command with which you can automatically insert the current date and time into a document in a variety of formats.

Dateline The first line in a business letter that contains the current date and that is positioned just below the letterhead if a letterhead is used.

Date Picker content control A content control that enables the user to select a date from a calendar.

Default The term that refers to the current selection or setting that is automatically used by a computer program unless you specify otherwise.

Descending The order of text sorted alphabetically from Z to A or numbers sorted from the largest to the smallest.

Deselect The action of canceling the selection of an object or block of text by clicking outside of the selection.

Design Mode A command that enables the user to edit content controls that are inserted in a document.

Desktop app A computer program that is installed on your PC and requires a computer operating system such as Microsoft Windows; also known as a desktop application.

Desktop application A computer program that is installed on your PC and requires a computer operating system such as Microsoft Windows; also known as a desktop app.

Destination file The file where an object is embedded or linked.

Dialog Box Launcher A small icon that displays to the right of some group names on the ribbon and that opens a related dialog box or pane providing additional options and commands related to that group.

Digital certificate (Digital ID) A file that contains information about a person and is used to electronically sign a document.

Digital signature An electronic stamp that is added to a document to verify the document's authenticity.

Direct formatting The process of applying each format separately, for example, bold, then font size, then font color, and so on.

Directory A single list of records using specified fields from a data source.

Distribute Columns A command that adjusts the width of the selected columns so that they are equal.

Distribute Rows A command that causes the height of the selected rows to be equal.

Document gridlines Nonprinting horizontal and vertical lines used to assist in aligning graphics and other elements in a document.

Document properties Details about a file that describe or identify it, including the title, author name, subject, and keywords that identify the document's topic or contents; also known as metadata.

Dot leader A series of dots preceding a tab that guides the eye across the line.

Drag The action of holding down the left mouse button while moving your mouse.

Drag-and-drop A technique by which you can move, by dragging, selected text from one location in a document to another.

Drawing objects Graphic objects, such as shapes, diagrams, lines, or circles.

Drop-Down List content control A content control that allows the user to select a specific item from a list.

Drop cap A large capital letter at the beginning of a paragraph that formats text in a visually distinctive manner.

Dropped The position of a drop cap when it is within the text of the paragraph.

Edit The process of making changes to text or graphics in an Office file.

Ellipsis A set of three dots indicating incompleteness; an ellipsis following a command name indicates that a dialog box will display if you click the command.

Email address link A hyperlink that opens a new message window so that an individual viewing a website can send an email message.

Embed code A code that creates a link to a video, picture, or other type of rich media content.

Embedded object An object that maintains the structure of the original application, but is not connected to the source file.

Embedding The process of inserting an object, such as a chart, into a Word document so that it becomes part of the document.

Em dash A punctuation symbol used to indicate an explanation or emphasis.

Enclosures Additional documents included with a business letter.

Endnote In a research paper, a note placed at the end of a document or chapter.

Enhanced ScreenTip A ScreenTip that displays more descriptive text than a normal ScreenTip.

Even Page section break A formatting mark that indicates the beginning of a new section on the next even-numbered page.

Federal registration symbol The symbol ® that indicates that a patent or trademark is registered with the United States Patent and Trademark Office.

Fields In a mail merge, a category—or column—of data.

Fill The inside color of an object.

Filter A set of criteria applied to fields in a data source to display specific records.

Flip A command that creates a reverse image of a picture or object.

Floating object A graphic that can be moved independently of the surrounding text characters.

Font A set of characters with the same design and shape.

Font styles Formatting emphasis such as bold, italic, and underline.

Footer A reserved area for text or graphics that displays at the bottom of each page in a document.

Footnote In a research paper, a note placed at the bottom of the page.

Form A structured document that has static text and reserved spaced for information to be entered by the user.

Form letter A letter with standardized wording that can be sent to many different people.

Formatting The process of establishing the overall appearance of text, graphics, and pages in an Office file—for example, in a Word document.

Formatting marks Characters that display on the screen, but do not print, indicating where the Enter key, the Spacebar, and the Tab key were pressed; also called nonprinting characters.

Formula A mathematical expression that contains functions, operators, constants, and properties and returns a value to a cell.

Function A predefined formula that performs calculations by using specific values in a particular order.

Gallery An Office feature that displays a list of potential results instead of just the command name.

Gradient fill A fill effect in which one color fades into another.

Graphics Pictures, charts, or drawing objects.

Greeting Line A predefined merge field that includes an introductory word, such as Dear, and the recipient's name.

Gridlines Nonprinting lines that indicate cell borders.

Groups On the Office ribbon, the sets of related commands that you might need for a specific type of task.

Handout A document that is given to an audience to accompany a lecture.

Hanging indent An indent style in which the first line of a paragraph extends to the left of the remaining lines and that is commonly used for bibliographic entries.

Header A reserved area for text or graphics that displays at the top of each page in a document.

Header row The first row of a table containing column titles.

Hidden text Nonprinting text—for example, an index entry field.

Hyperlinks Text, buttons, pictures, or other objects that, when clicked, access other sections of the active document or another file.

Hypertext Markup Language (HTML) The markup language that communicates color and graphics in a format that all computers can understand.

Hyphenation A feature that enables control of how words are split between two lines, resulting in a less ragged edge at the right margin.

Index A compilation of topics, names, and terms accompanied by page numbers that displays at the end of a document.

Index entry A word or phrase that is listed in the index.

Index entry field Code, formatted as hidden text and displaying to the right of an index entry, containing the identifier XE and the term to be included in the index.

Info tab The tab in Backstage view that displays information about the current file.

Ink Revision marks made directly on a document by using a stylus on a Tablet PC.

Inline object An object or graphic inserted in a document that acts like a character in a sentence.

In margin The position of a drop cap when it is in the left margin of a paragraph.

Insertion point A blinking vertical line that indicates where text or graphics will be inserted.

Inside address The name and address of the person receiving the letter; positioned below the date line.

Inspect Document A command that searches your document for hidden data or personal information that you might not want to share publicly.

Interactive media Computer interaction that responds to your actions; for example, by presenting text, graphics, animation, video, audio, or games. Also referred to as rich media.

Justified alignment An arrangement of text in which the text aligns evenly on both the left and right margins.

Keep lines together A formatting feature that prevents a single line from displaying by itself at the bottom of a page or at the top of a page.

Keep with next A formatting feature that causes two elements, such as paragraphs, to display together on the same page.

Keep with next A formatting feature that keeps a heading with its first paragraph of text together on the page.

Kerning A character spacing option that automatically adjusts the spacing between pairs of characters, with a specified minimum point size, so that words and letters appear equally spaced.

Keyboard shortcut A combination of two or more keyboard keys, used to perform a task that would otherwise require a mouse.

KeyTip The letter that displays on a command in the ribbon and that indicates the key you can press to activate the command when keyboard control of the Ribbon is activated.

Keywords Custom file properties in the form of words that you associate with a document to give an indication of the document's content; used to help find and organize files. Also called tags.

Landscape orientation A page orientation in which the paper is wider than it is tall.

Layout The placement and arrangement of the text and graphic elements on a slide.

Layout Options A Word feature that displays commands to control the manner in which text wraps around a chart or other object.

Leader character Characters that form a solid, dotted, or dashed line that fills the space preceding a tab stop.

Left alignment An arrangement of text in which the text aligns at the left margin, leaving the right margin uneven.

Legacy control A field used in designing a form for persons who possess older versions of Word.

Legal citation A reference to an authoritative document, such as a regulation, a statute, or a case.

Legend The part of a chart that identifies the colors assigned to each data series or category.

Letterhead The personal or company information that displays at the top of a letter.

Line break indicator A nonprinting character in the shape of a bent arrow that indicates a manual line break.

Line chart A chart type that shows trends over time.

Line spacing The distance between lines of text in a paragraph.

Linked object An object that maintains a direct connection to the source file.

Linked style A style, indicated by the symbol ¶a, that behaves as either a character style or a paragraph style, depending on what you select.

Linking The process of inserting information from a source file into a destination file, while maintaining a connection between the two files.

List style A style that applies a format to a list.

Live Layout A feature that reflows text as you move or size an object so that you can view the placement of surrounding text.

Live Preview A technology that shows the result of applying an editing or formatting change as you point to possible results—before you actually apply it.

Location Any disk drive, folder, or other place in which you can store files and folders.

Lock Tracking A feature that prevents reviewers from turning off Track Changes and making changes that are not visible in markup.

Macro A set of commands and instructions that can be grouped as a single command to accomplish a task automatically.

Macro virus A macro that causes files to be erased or damaged by inserting unauthorized code.

Mail app An app for Office that displays next to an Outlook item.

Mail merge A feature that joins a main document and a data source to create customized letters or labels.

Main document In a mail merge, the document that contains the text or formatting that remains constant.

Main entry A word, phrase, or selected text used to identify the index entry.

Manual column break An artificial end to a column to balance columns or to provide space for the insertion of other objects.

Manual line break A break that moves text to the right of the insertion point to a new line while keeping the text in the same paragraph.

Manual page break The action of forcing a page to end and placing subsequent text at the top of the next page.

Margins The space between the text and the top, bottom, left, and right edges of the paper.

Markup The formatting Word uses to denote a document's revisions visually.

Markup area The space to the right or left of a document where comments and formatting changes display in balloons.

Master document A Word document that serves as a container for the different parts of a document.

Match Fields A Word feature that maps predefined field names to the field names in a data source.

Memorandum (Memo) A written message sent to someone working in the same organization.

Merge A table feature that combines two or more adjacent cells into one cell so that the text spans across multiple columns or rows.

Merge field In a mail merge, a placeholder that represents specific information in the data source.

Metadata Details about a file that describe or identify it, including the title, author name, subject, and keywords that identify the document's topic or contents; also known as document properties.

Mini toolbar A small toolbar containing frequently used formatting commands that displays as a result of selecting text or objects.

Minus outline symbol A formatting mark that indicates there are no subordinate heading or body text paragraphs.

Modern Language Association (MLA) One of two commonly used style guides for formatting research papers.

MRU Acronym for most recently used, which refers to the state of some commands that retain the characteristic most recently applied; for example, the Font Color button retains the most recently used color until a new color is chosen.

Multilevel list A list in which the items display in a visual hierarchical structure.

Multiple Pages A zoom setting that decreases the magnification to display several pages of a document.

Nameplate The banner on the front page of a newsletter that identifies the publication.

Navigation bar A series of text links across the top or bottom of a webpage that, when clicked, will link to another webpage on the same website.

Nested table A table inserted in a cell of an existing table.

Newsletter A periodical that communicates news and information to a specific group.

No Markup A Track Changes view that displays the document in its final form—with all proposed changes included and comments hidden.

Nonbreaking hyphen A formatting mark that prevents a hyphenated word or phrase from being displayed on two lines.

Nonbreaking space A formatting mark that keeps two words together so that both words will wrap even if only the second word would normally wrap to the next line.

Noncontiguous Items that are not adjacent to one another.

Nonprinting characters Characters that display on the screen, but do not print, indicating where the Enter key, the Spacebar, and the Tab key were pressed; also called formatting marks.

No Paragraph Space Style The built-in paragraph style—available from the Paragraph Spacing command—that inserts no extra space before or after a paragraph and uses line spacing of 1.

Normal The default style in Word for new documents and which includes default styles and customizations that determine the basic look of a document; for example, it includes the Calibri font, 11-pt font size, line spacing at 1.08, and 8-pt spacing after a paragraph.

Normal template The template that serves as a basis for all Word documents.

Note In a research paper, information that expands on the topic, but that does not fit well in the document text.

Numbered list A list that uses consecutive numbers or letters to introduce each item in a list.

Numerical data Numbers that represent facts.

Object A text box, picture, table, or shape that you can select and then move and resize.

Object anchor The symbol that indicates to which paragraph an object is attached.

Object Linking and Embedding (OLE) A program-integration technology for sharing information between Office programs.

Odd Page section break A formatting mark that indicates the beginning of a new section on the next odd-numbered page.

Office 365 A version of Microsoft Office to which you subscribe for an annual fee.

Office Presentation Service A Word feature to present your Word document to others who can watch in a web browser.

Office Store A public marketplace that Microsoft hosts and regulates on Office.com.

One-click Row/Column Insertion A Word table feature with which you can insert a new row or column by pointing to the desired location and then clicking.

OneDrive Microsoft's free cloud storage for anyone with a free Microsoft account.

Open dialog box A dialog box from which you can navigate to, and then open on your screen, an existing file that was created in that same program.

Option button In a dialog box, a round button that enables you to make one choice among two or more options.

Options dialog box A dialog box within each Office application where you can select program settings and other options and preferences.

Organizer A dialog box where you can modify a document by using styles stored in another document or template.

Original A Track Changes view that displays the original, unchanged document with all revisions and comments hidden.

Outline A Word feature that allows you to organize the contents of a document in a structured manner.

Outline level A Word feature that defines the position of a paragraph in relation to all topics in a document and is formatted with a corresponding heading style.

Outline symbol A small gray circle that identifies heading and body text paragraphs.

Outline view A document view that displays the overall organization, or hierarchy, of the document's parts, including headings, subheadings, and subordinate text.

Page break indicator A dotted line with the text Page Break that indicates where a manual page break was inserted.

Page Width A view that zooms the document so that the width of the page matches the width of the window. Find this command on the View tab, in the Zoom group.

Pagination The process of arranging and numbering the pages in a document.

Paragraph style A style, indicated by ¶, that includes everything that a character style contains, plus all aspects of a paragraph's appearance; for example, text alignment, tab stops, line spacing, and borders.

Paragraph symbol The symbol ¶ that represents the end of a paragraph.

Parenthetical references References that include the last name of the author or authors, and the page number in the referenced source.

Passim A term that indicates a citation occurs on five or more pages in a document.

Password A code that is used to gain access to a file.

Paste The action of placing text or objects that have been copied or cut from one location to another location.

Paste Options gallery A gallery of buttons that provides a Live Preview of all the Paste options available in the current context.

PDF The acronym for Portable Document Format, which is a file format that creates an image that preserves the look of your file, but that cannot be easily changed; a popular format for sending documents electronically, because the document will display on most computers.

PDF Reflow The ability to import PDF files into Word so that you can transform a PDF back into a fully editable Word document.

Picture effects Effects that enhance a picture, such as a shadow, glow, reflection, or 3-D rotation.

Picture styles Frames, shapes, shadows, borders, and other special effects that can be added to an image to create an overall visual style for the image.

Pie chart A chart type that shows the proportion of parts to a whole.

Placeholder text Nonprinting text that holds a place in a document where you can type.

Plain Text content control A content control that enables the user to enter unformatted text.

Plus outline symbol A formatting mark that indicates there are subordinate heading or body text paragraphs.

Pointer Any symbol that displays on your screen in response to moving your mouse.

Points A measurement of the size of a font; there are 72 points in an inch.

Portable Document Format A file format that creates an image that preserves the look of your file, but that cannot be easily changed; a popular format for sending documents electronically, because the document will display on most computers; also called a PDF.

Portrait orientation A page orientation in which the paper is taller than it is wide.

.pptx The default file extension for a PowerPoint file.

Print Preview A view of a document as it will appear when you print it.

Procedure A block of programming code that performs one or more tasks.

Protected View A security feature in Office 2016 that protects your computer from malicious files by opening them in a restricted environment until you enable them; you might encounter this feature if you open a file from an e-mail or download files from the Internet.

pt The abbreviation for point; for example, when referring to a font size.

Quick Access Toolbar In an Office program window, the small row of buttons in the upper left corner of the screen from which you can perform frequently used commands.

Quick Parts All of the reusable pieces of content that are available to insert into a document, including building blocks, document properties, and fields.

Quick Tables Tables that are stored as building blocks.

Read Mode A view in Word that optimizes the Word screen for the times when you are reading Word documents on the screen and not creating or editing them.

Read-only A property assigned to a file that prevents the file from being modified or deleted; it indicates that you cannot save any changes to the displayed document unless you first save it with a new name.

Read-only file A file that can be viewed but not changed.

Readability statistics A Spelling and Grammar tool that analyzes a document and determines the reading level of the text.

Recolor A feature that enables you to change all colors in the picture to shades of a single color.

Record All of the categories of data pertaining to one person, place, thing, event, or idea, and which is formatted as a row in a database table.

Recording The process of creating a macro while performing specific actions in a document.

Reveal Formatting A pane that displays the formatted selection and includes a complete description of formats applied.

Reviewer An individual who reviews and marks changes on a document.

Reviewing Pane A separate scrollable window that shows all of the changes and comments that currently display in a document.

Revisions Changes made to a document.

Rich media Computer interaction that responds to your actions; for example, by presenting text, graphics, animation, video, audio, or games. Also referred to as interactive media.

Rich Text content control A content control that enables the user to enter text and apply formatting.

Rich Text Format (RTF) A universal file format, using the .rtf file extension, that can be read by many word processing programs.

Right-click The action of clicking the right mouse button one time.

Right alignment An arrangement of text in which the text aligns at the right margin, leaving the left margin uneven.

Rotation handle A symbol with which you can rotate a graphic to any angle; displays above the top center sizing handle.

Rules Conditional Word fields that allow you to determine how the merge process is completed.

Salutation The greeting line of a letter, such as Dear Sir.

Sans serif font A font design with no lines or extensions on the ends of characters.

Scale A command that resizes a picture to a percentage of its size.

Screen reader Software that enables visually impaired users to read text on a computer screen to understand the content of pictures.

Screenshot An image of an active window on your computer that you can paste into a document.

ScreenTip A small box that that displays useful information when you perform various mouse actions such as pointing to screen elements or dragging.

Section A portion of a document that can be formatted differently from the rest of the document.

Section break A double dotted line that indicates the end of one section and the beginning of another section.

Selecting Highlighting, by dragging with your mouse, areas of text or data or graphics, so that the selection can be edited, formatted, copied, or moved.

Serif font A font design that includes small line extensions on the ends of the letters to guide the eye in reading from left to right.

Shapes Lines, arrows, stars, banners, ovals, rectangles, and other basic shapes with which you can illustrate an idea, a process, or a workflow.

Share button Opens the Share pane from which you can save your file to the cloud—your OneDrive—and then share it with others so you can collaborate.

SharePoint Collaboration software with which people in an organization can set up team sites to share information, manage documents, and publish reports for others to see.

Shortcut menu A menu that displays commands and options relevant to the selected text or object; also called a context menu.

Show Preview A formatting feature that displays a visual representation of each style in the Styles window.

Signature line An element added to a document that specifies who should sign the document.

Simple Markup The default Track Changes view that indicates revisions by vertical red lines in the left margin and displays comment icons in the right margin.

Single spacing The common name for line spacing in which there is no extra space before or after a paragraph and uses line spacing of 1.

Sizing handles Small squares or circles that indicate a picture or object is selected.

Skype A Microsoft product with which you can make voice calls, make video calls, transfer files, or send messages—including instant messages and text messages—over the Internet.

Small caps A font effect that changes lowercase letters to uppercase letters, but with the height of lowercase letters.

Smart Lookup A feature powered by Bing and that enables you to select text, and then have Bing provide search results that are relevant to the surrounding context of the text.

SmartArt A designer-quality visual representation of your information that you can create by choosing from among many different layouts to effectively communicate your message or ideas.

Sorting The action of ordering data, usually in alphabetical or numeric order.

Source file The file where an object is created.

Spin box A small box with an upward- and downward-pointing arrow that lets you move rapidly through a set of values by clicking.

Split A table feature that divides selected cells into multiple cells with a specified number of rows and columns.

Split button A button divided into two parts and in which clicking the main part of the button performs a command and clicking the arrow opens a menu with choices.

Split Table A table feature that divides an existing table into two tables in which the selected row—where the insertion point is located—becomes the first row of the second table.

Split Window A Word feature that displays a document in two panes so that you can view or work on different parts of the document at the same time.

Static text Descriptive text such as labels or headings.

Status bar The area along the lower edge of an Office program window that displays file information on the left and buttons to control how the window looks on the right.

Style A group of formatting commands, such as font, font size, font color, paragraph alignment, and line spacing, that can be applied to selected text with one command.

Style guide A manual that contains standards for the design and writing of documents.

Style Inspector A pane that displays the name of the selected style with formats applied and contains paragraph- and text-level formatting options.

Style set A collection of character and paragraph formatting that is stored and named.

Styles window A pane that displays a list of styles and contains tools to manage styles.

Stylus A pen-like device used for writing on an electronic document.

Subdocument A section of a document that is linked to the master document.

Subentry A more specific term that refers to the main entry.

Subject line The optional line following the inside address in a business letter that states the purpose of the letter.

Suppress A Word feature that hides header and footer information, including the page number, on the first page of a document.

Synchronization The process of updating computer files that are in two or more locations according to specific rules—also called syncing.

Synchronous scrolling The setting that causes two documents to scroll simultaneously.

Syncing The process of updating computer files that are in two or more locations according to specific rules—also called synchronization.

Synonyms Words with the same or similar meaning.

Tab leader A dotted, dashed, or solid line used to connect related information and improve the readability of a line.

Table An arrangement of information organized into rows and columns.

Table of authorities A list of all references in a legal document and the page numbers where the references occur.

Table of contents (TOC) A list of a document's headings and subheadings, marked with the page numbers where those headings and subheadings occur.

Table of figures A list of the figure captions in a document.

Table style A style that includes formatting for the entire table and specific table elements, such as rows and columns.

Tablet PC A computer with a monitor that allows you to write on the screen.

Tab stop A specific location on a line of text, marked on the Word ruler, to which you can move the insertion point by pressing the Tab key, and which is used to align and indent text.

Tabs (ribbon) On the Office ribbon, the name of each task-oriented activity area.

Tags Custom file properties in the form of words that you associate with a document to give an indication of the document's content; used to help find and organize files. Also called keywords.

Task pane app An app for Office that works side-by-side with an Office document by displaying a separate pane on the right side of the window.

Tell Me A search feature for Microsoft Office commands that you activate by typing what you are looking for in the Tell Me box.

Tell me more A prompt within a ScreenTip that opens the Office online Help system with explanations about how to perform the command referenced in the ScreenTip.

Template An existing document that you use as a starting point for a new document; it opens a copy of itself, unnamed, and then you use the structure—and possibly some content, such as headings—as the starting point for new a document.

Text box A movable, resizable container for text or graphics.

Text effects Decorative formats, such as shadowed or mirrored text, text glow, 3-D effects, and colors that make text stand out.

Text link A hyperlink applied to a selected word or phrase.

Text wrapping The manner in which text displays around an object.

Theme A predesigned combination of colors, fonts, and effects that looks good together and is applied to an entire document by a single selection.

Theme template A stored, user-defined set of colors, fonts, and effects that can be shared with other Office programs.

Thesaurus A research tool that provides a list of synonyms.

Thumbnail A graphical representation of a page.

Title bar The bar at the top edge of the program window that indicates the name of the current file and the program name.

Toggle button A button that can be turned on by clicking it once, and then turned off by clicking it again.

Toolbar In a folder window, a row of buttons with which you can perform common tasks, such as changing the view of your files and folders.

Track Changes A feature that makes a record of the changes made to a document.

Triple-click The action of clicking the left mouse button three times in rapid succession.

Trusted Documents A security feature in Office that remembers which files you have already enabled; you might encounter this feature if you open a file from an e-mail or download files from the Internet.

Unformatted text Plain text without any special formatting applied.

Value axis The area of a chart that displays a numerical scale based on the numerical data in a chart.

Variable In an equation, a letter that represents a value.

Vertical change bar A line that displays in the left margin next to each line of text that contains a revision.

View Side by Side A view that displays two open documents, in separate windows, next to each other on the screen.

Visual Basic Editor An editor that enables you to view and edit existing macro code or create a new macro.

Visual Basic for Applications (VBA) A programming language used to create macros.

Watermark A text or graphic element that displays behind document text.

Web browser (Browser) Software that interprets HTML files, formats them into webpages, and then displays them.

Webpage A file coded in HTML that can be viewed on the Internet using a web browser.

Web Page format A file type that saves a Word document as an HTML file, with some elements of the webpage saved in a folder, separate from the webpage itself.

Website A group of related webpages published to a specific location on the Internet.

Wildcard A special character such as * or ? that is used to search for an unknown term.

Windows apps An app that runs on all Windows device families—including PCs, Windows phones, Windows tablets, and the Xbox gaming system.

WordArt An Office feature in Word, Excel, and PowerPoint that enables you to change normal text into decorative stylized text.

Word count A Word feature that indicates the number of words, paragraphs, pages, and characters in a document.

Word Options A collection of settings that you can change to customize Word.

Wordwrap The feature that moves text from the right edge of a paragraph to the beginning of the next line as necessary to fit within the margins.

Works Cited In the MLA style, a list of cited works placed at the end of a research paper or report.

Writer's identification The name and title of the author of a letter, placed near the bottom of the letter under the complimentary closing—also referred to as the writer's signature block.

Writer's signature block The name and title of the author of a letter, placed near the bottom of the letter, under the complimentary closing—also referred to as the writer's identification.

XE Code identifying an index entry.

XML Paper Specification A Microsoft file format that creates an image of your document and that opens in the XPS viewer.

XPS The acronym for XML Paper Specification—a Microsoft file format that creates an image of your document and that opens in the XPS viewer.

Zoom The action of increasing or decreasing the size of the viewing area on the screen.

Index

E

F

J

K

L

S

X

Z